CRAFTING AND EXECUTING STRATEGY

The Quest for Competitive Advantage

Concepts and Cases

CRAFTING AND EXECUTING STRATEGY

The Quest for Competitive Advantage

Concepts and Cases | 22ND EDITION

Arthur A. Thompson
The University of Alabama

Margaret A. Peteraf
Dartmouth College

John E. Gamble
Texas A&M University–Corpus Christi

A.J. Strickland III
The University of Alabama

CRAFTING & EXECUTING STRATEGY: CONCEPTS AND CASES

Published by McGraw-Hill Education, 2 Penn Plaza, New York, NY 10121. Copyright © 2020 by McGraw-Hill Education. All rights reserved. Printed in Singapore. No part of this publication may be reproduced or distributed in any form or by any means, or stored in a database or retrieval system, without the prior written consent of McGraw-Hill Education, including, but not limited to, in any network or other electronic storage or transmission, or broadcast for distance learning.

Some ancillaries, including electronic and print components, may not be available to customers outside the United States.

This book is printed on acid-free paper.

3 4 5 6 7 8 9 MPM 22 21 20

ISBN 978-1-260-56574-4
MHID 1-260-56574-2

mheducation.com/highered

To our families and especially our spouses:
Hasseline, Paul, Heather, and Kitty.

About the Authors

Arthur A. Thompson, Jr., earned his BS and PhD degrees in economics from The University of Tennessee, spent three years on the economics faculty at Virginia Tech, and served on the faculty of The University of Alabama's College of Commerce and Business Administration for 24 years. In 1974 and again in 1982, Dr. Thompson spent semester-long sabbaticals as a visiting scholar at the Harvard Business School.

His areas of specialization are business strategy, competition and market analysis, and the economics of business enterprises. In addition to publishing over 30 articles in some 25 different professional and trade publications, he has authored or co-authored five textbooks and six computer-based simulation exercises. His textbooks and strategy simulations have been used at well over 1,000 college and university campuses worldwide.

Dr. Thompson and his wife of 58 years have two daughters, two grandchildren, and a Yorkshire Terrier.

Margaret A. Peteraf is the Leon E. Williams Professor of Management Emerita at the Tuck School of Business at Dartmouth College. She is an internationally recognized scholar of strategic management, with a long list of publications in top management journals. She has earned myriad honors and prizes for her contributions, including the 1999 Strategic Management Society Best Paper Award recognizing the deep influence of her work on the field of Strategic Management. Professor Peteraf is a fellow of the Strategic Management Society and the Academy of Management. She served previously as a member of the Board of Governors of both the Society and the Academy of Management and as Chair of the Business Policy and Strategy Division of the Academy. She has also served in various editorial roles and on numerous editorial boards, including the *Strategic Management Journal,* the *Academy of Management Review,* and *Organization Science.* She has taught in Executive Education programs in various programs around the world and has won teaching awards at the MBA and Executive level.

Professor Peteraf earned her PhD, MA, and MPhil at Yale University and held previous faculty appointments at Northwestern University's Kellogg Graduate School of Management and at the University of Minnesota's Carlson School of Management.

John E. Gamble is a Professor of Management and Dean of the College of Business at Texas A&M University–Corpus Christi. His teaching and research for more than 20 years has focused on strategic management at the undergraduate and graduate levels. He has conducted courses in strategic management in Germany since 2001, which have been sponsored by the University of Applied Sciences in Worms.

Dr. Gamble's research has been published in various scholarly journals and he is the author or co-author of more than 75 case studies published in an assortment of strategic management and strategic marketing texts. He has done consulting on industry and market analysis for clients in a diverse mix of industries.

Professor Gamble received his PhD, MA, and BS degrees from The University of Alabama and was a faculty member in the Mitchell College of Business at the University of South Alabama before his appointment to the faculty at Texas A&M University–Corpus Christi.

Dr. A. J. (Lonnie) Strickland is the Thomas R. Miller Professor of Strategic Management at the Culverhouse School of Business at The University of Alabama. He is a native of north Georgia, and attended the University of Georgia, where he received a BS degree in math and physics; Georgia Institute of Technology, where he received an MS in industrial management; and Georgia State University, where he received his PhD in business administration.

Lonnie's experience in consulting and executive development is in the strategic management arena, with a concentration in industry and competitive analysis. He has developed strategic planning systems for numerous firms all over the world. He served as Director of Marketing and Strategy at BellSouth, has taken two companies to the New York Stock Exchange, is one of the founders and directors of American Equity Investment Life Holding (AEL), and serves on numerous boards of directors. He is a very popular speaker in the area of strategic management.

Lonnie and his wife, Kitty, have been married for over 49 years. They have two children and two grandchildren. Each summer, Lonnie and his wife live on their private game reserve in South Africa where they enjoy taking their friends on safaris.

Preface

By offering the most engaging, clearly articulated, and conceptually sound text on strategic management, *Crafting and Executing Strategy* has been able to maintain its position as the leading textbook in strategic management for over 30 years. With this latest edition, we build on this strong foundation, maintaining the attributes of the book that have long made it the most teachable text on the market, while updating the content, sharpening its presentation, and providing enlightening new illustrations and examples.

The distinguishing mark of the 22nd edition is its enriched and enlivened presentation of the material in each of the 12 chapters, providing an as up-to-date and engrossing discussion of the core concepts and analytical tools as you will find anywhere. As with each of our new editions, there is an accompanying lineup of exciting new cases that bring the content to life and are sure to provoke interesting classroom discussions, deepening students' understanding of the material in the process.

While this 22nd edition retains the 12-chapter structure of the prior edition, every chapter—indeed every paragraph and every line—has been reexamined, refined, and refreshed. New content has been added to keep the material in line with the latest developments in the theory and practice of strategic management. In other areas, coverage has been trimmed to keep the book at a more manageable size. Scores of new examples have been added, along with 16 new Illustration Capsules, to enrich understanding of the content and to provide students with a ringside view of strategy in action. The result is a text that cuts straight to the chase in terms of what students really need to know and gives instructors a leg up on teaching that material effectively. It remains, as always, solidly mainstream and balanced, mirroring *both* the penetrating insight of academic thought and the pragmatism of real-world strategic management.

A standout feature of this text has always been the tight linkage between the content of the chapters and the cases. The lineup of cases that accompany the 22nd edition is outstanding in this respect—a truly appealing mix of strategically relevant and thoughtfully crafted cases, certain to engage students and sharpen their skills in applying the concepts and tools of strategic analysis. Many involve high-profile companies that the students will immediately recognize and relate to; all are framed around key strategic issues and serve to add depth and context to the topical content of the chapters. We are confident you will be impressed with how well these cases work in the classroom and the amount of student interest they will spark.

For some years now, growing numbers of strategy instructors at business schools worldwide have been transitioning from a purely text-case course structure to a more robust and energizing text-case-simulation course structure. Incorporating a competition-based strategy simulation has the strong appeal of providing class members with *an immediate and engaging opportunity to apply the concepts and analytical tools covered in the chapters and to become personally involved in crafting and executing a strategy for a virtual company that they have been assigned to manage and that competes head-to-head with companies run by other class members.* Two widely used and pedagogically effective online strategy simulations, *The Business Strategy Game* and *GLO-BUS,* are optional companions for this text. Both simulations were created by Arthur Thompson, one of the text authors, and, like the cases, are closely linked to the content of each chapter in the text. The Exercises for Simulation Participants, found at the end of each chapter, provide clear guidance to class members in applying the concepts and analytical tools covered in the chapters to the issues and decisions that they have to wrestle with in managing their simulation company.

To assist instructors in assessing student achievement of program learning objectives, in line with AACSB requirements, the 22nd edition includes a set of Assurance of Learning Exercises at the end of each chapter that link to the specific learning objectives appearing at the beginning of each chapter and highlighted throughout the text. An important instructional feature of the 22nd edition is its more closely *integrated* linkage of selected chapter-end Assurance of Learning Exercises and cases to the publisher's web-based assignment and assessment platform called Connect™. Your students will be able to use the online Connect™ supplement to (1) complete selected Assurance of Learning Exercises appearing at the end of each of the 12 chapters, (2) complete chapter-end quizzes, and (3) enter their answers to a number of the suggested assignment questions for 14 of the 32 cases in this edition. The analysis portion of the Connect™ exercises is automatically graded, thereby enabling you to easily assess the learning that has occurred.

In addition, both of the companion strategy simulations have a built-in Learning Assurance Report that quantifies how well each member of your class performed on nine skills/learning measures *versus tens of thousands of other students worldwide* who completed the simulation in the past 12 months. We believe the chapter-end Assurance of Learning Exercises, the all-new online and automatically graded Connect™ exercises, and the Learning Assurance Report generated at the conclusion of *The Business Strategy Game* and *GLO-BUS* simulations provide you with easy-to-use, empirical measures of student learning in your course. All can be used in conjunction with other instructor-developed or school-developed scoring rubrics and assessment tools to comprehensively evaluate course or program learning outcomes and measure compliance with AACSB accreditation standards.

Taken together, the various components of the 22nd edition package and the supporting set of instructor resources provide you with enormous course design flexibility and a powerful kit of teaching/learning tools. We've done our very best to ensure that the elements constituting the 22nd edition will work well for you in the classroom, help you economize on the time needed to be well prepared for each class, and cause students to conclude that your course is one of the very best they have ever taken—from the standpoint of both enjoyment and learning.

DIFFERENTIATING FEATURES OF THE 22ND EDITION

Eight standout features strongly differentiate this text and the accompanying instructional package from others in the field:

1. *Our integrated coverage of the two most popular perspectives on strategic management—positioning theory and resource-based theory—is unsurpassed by any other leading strategy text.* Principles and concepts from both the positioning perspective and the resource-based perspective are prominently and comprehensively integrated into our coverage of crafting both single-business and multibusiness strategies. By highlighting the relationship between a firm's resources and capabilities to the activities it conducts along its value chain, we show explicitly how these two perspectives relate to one another. Moreover, in Chapters 3 through 8 it is emphasized repeatedly that a company's strategy must be matched *not only* to its external market circumstances *but also* to its internal resources and competitive capabilities.

2. *With this new edition, we provide the clearest, easiest to understand presentation of the value-price-cost framework.* In recent years, this framework has become an essential aid to teaching students how companies create economic value in the course of conducting business. We show how this simple framework informs the concept of the business model as well as the all-important concept of competitive advantage. In Chapter 5, we add further clarity by showing in pictorial fashion how the value-price-cost framework relates to the different sources of competitive advantage that underlie the five generic strategies.

3. *Our coverage of cooperative strategies and the role that interorganizational activity can play in the pursuit of competitive advantage is similarly distinguished.* The topics of the value net, ecosystems, strategic alliances, licensing, joint ventures, and other types of collaborative relationships are featured prominently in a number of chapters and are integrated into other material throughout the text. We show how strategies of this nature can contribute to the success of single-business companies as well as multibusiness enterprises, whether with respect to firms operating in domestic markets or those operating in the international realm.

4. *The attention we give to international strategies, in all their dimensions, make this textbook an indispensable aid to understanding strategy formulation and execution in an increasingly connected, global world.* Our treatment of this topic as one of the most critical elements of the *scope* of a company's activities brings home to students the connection between the topic of international strategy with other topics concerning firm scope, such as multibusiness (or corporate) strategy, outsourcing, insourcing, and vertical integration.

5. *With a standalone chapter devoted to these topics, our coverage of business ethics, corporate social responsibility, and environmental sustainability goes well beyond that offered by any other leading strategy text.* Chapter 9, "Ethics, Corporate Social Responsibility, Environmental Sustainability, and Strategy," fulfills the important functions of (1) alerting students to the role and importance of ethical and socially responsible decision making and (2) addressing the accreditation requirement of the AACSB International that business ethics be visibly and thoroughly embedded in the core curriculum. Moreover, discussions of the roles of values and ethics are integrated into portions of other chapters, beginning with the first chapter, to further reinforce why and how considerations relating to ethics, values, social

responsibility, and sustainability should figure prominently into the managerial task of crafting and executing company strategies.

6. *Long known as an important differentiator of this text, the case collection in the 22nd edition is truly unrivaled* from the standpoints of student appeal, teachability, and suitability for drilling students in the use of the concepts and analytical treatments in Chapters 1 through 12. The 32 cases included in this edition are the very latest, the best, and the most on target that we could find. The ample information about the cases in the Instructor's Manual makes it effortless to select a set of cases each term that will capture the interest of students from start to finish.

7. *The text is now more tightly linked to the publisher's trailblazing web-based assignment and assessment platform called Connect™.* This will enable professors to gauge class members' prowess in accurately completing (a) selected chapter-end exercises, (b) chapter-end quizzes, and (c) the creative author-developed exercises for seven of the cases in this edition.

8. *Two cutting-edge and widely used strategy simulations—The Business Strategy Game and GLO-BUS—are optional companions to the 22nd edition.* These give you an unmatched capability to employ a text-case-simulation model of course delivery.

ORGANIZATION, CONTENT, AND FEATURES OF THE 22ND-EDITION TEXT CHAPTERS

- Chapter 1 serves as a brief, general introduction to the topic of strategy, focusing on the central questions of *"What is strategy?"* and *"Why is it important?"* As such, it serves as the perfect accompaniment for your opening-day lecture on what the course is all about and why it matters. Using the newly added example of Apple, Inc., to drive home the concepts in this chapter, we introduce students to what we mean by "competitive advantage" and the key features of business-level strategy. Describing strategy making as a process, we explain why a company's strategy is partly planned and partly reactive and why a strategy tends to co-evolve with its environment over time. We discuss the importance of ethics in choosing among strategic alternatives and introduce the concept of a business model. We show that a viable business model must provide both an attractive value proposition for the company's customers and a formula for making profits for the company. A key feature of this chapter is a depiction of how the value-price-cost framework can be used to frame this discussion. We show how the mark of a winning strategy is its ability to pass three tests: (1) the *fit test* (for internal and external fit), (2) the *competitive advantage test,* and (3) the *performance test.* And we explain why good company performance depends not only upon a sound strategy but upon solid strategy execution as well.

- Chapter 2 presents a more complete overview of the strategic management process, covering topics ranging from the role of vision, mission, and values to what constitutes good corporate governance. It makes a great assignment for the second day of class and provides a smooth transition into the heart of the course. It introduces students to such core concepts as strategic versus financial objectives, the balanced scorecard, strategic intent, and business-level versus corporate-level strategies. It explains why *all managers are on a company's strategy-making, strategy-executing team* and why a company's strategic plan is a collection of strategies devised by different managers at different levels in the organizational hierarchy. The chapter concludes with a section on the role of the board of directors in the strategy-making, strategy-executing process and examines the conditions that have led to recent high-profile corporate governance failures. The illustration capsule on Volkswagen's emissions scandal brings this section to life.

- The next two chapters introduce students to the two most fundamental perspectives on strategy making: the positioning view, exemplified by Michael Porter's "five forces model of competition"; and the resource-based view. Chapter 3 provides *what has long been the clearest, most straightforward discussion of the five forces framework to be found in any text on strategic management.* It also offers a set of complementary analytical tools for conducting competitor analysis, identifying strategic groups along with the mobility barriers that limit movement among them, and demonstrates the importance of tailoring strategy to fit the circumstances of a company's industry and competitive environment. The chapter includes a discussion of the value net framework, which is useful for conducting analysis of how cooperative as well as competitive moves by various parties contribute to the creation and capture of value in an industry.

- Chapter 4 presents the resource-based view of the firm, showing why resource and capability analysis is such a powerful tool for sizing up a company's competitive assets. It offers a simple framework for identifying a company's resources and capabilities and explains how the VRIN framework can be used to determine whether they can provide the company with a sustainable competitive advantage over its competitors. Other topics covered in this chapter include dynamic capabilities, SWOT analysis, value chain analysis, benchmarking, and competitive strength assessments, thus enabling a solid appraisal of a company's cost position and customer value proposition vis-á-vis its rivals. *An important feature of this chapter is a table showing how key financial and operating ratios are calculated and how to interpret them.* Students will find this table handy in doing the number crunching needed to evaluate whether a company's strategy is delivering good financial performance.

- Chapter 5 sets forth the basic approaches available for competing and winning in the marketplace in terms of the five generic competitive strategies— broad low-cost, broad differentiation, best-cost, focused differentiation, and focused low cost. It demonstrates pictorially the link between generic strategies, the value-price-cost framework, and competitive advantage. The chapter also describes when each of the five approaches works best and what pitfalls to avoid. Additionally, it explains the role of *cost drivers* and *uniqueness drivers* in reducing a company's costs and enhancing its differentiation, respectively.

- Chapter 6 focuses on *other strategic actions* a company can take to complement its competitive approach and maximize the power of its overall strategy. These include a variety of offensive or defensive competitive moves, and their timing, such as blue-ocean strategies and first-mover advantages and disadvantages. It also includes choices concerning the breadth of a company's activities (or its *scope* of operations along an industry's entire value chain), ranging from horizontal mergers and acquisitions, to vertical integration, outsourcing, and strategic alliances. This material serves to segue into the scope issues covered in the next two chapters on international and diversification strategies.

- Chapter 7 takes up the topic of how to compete in international markets. It begins with a discussion of why differing market conditions across countries must necessarily influence a company's strategic choices about how to enter and compete in foreign markets. It presents five major strategic options for expanding a company's geographic scope and competing in foreign markets: export strategies, licensing, franchising, establishing a wholly owned subsidiary via acquisition or "greenfield" venture, and alliance strategies. It includes coverage of topics such as Porter's Diamond of National Competitive Advantage, multi-market competition, and the choice between multidomestic, global, and transnational strategies. This chapter explains the impetus for sharing, transferring, or accessing valuable resources and capabilities across national borders in the quest for competitive advantage, connecting the material to that on the resource-based view from Chapter 4. The chapter concludes with a discussion of the unique characteristics of competing in developing-country markets.

- Chapter 8 concerns strategy making in the multibusiness company, introducing the topic of corporate-level strategy with its special focus on diversification. The first portion of this chapter describes when and why diversification makes good strategic sense, the different means of diversifying a company's business lineup, and the pros and cons of related versus unrelated diversification strategies. The second part of the chapter looks at how to evaluate the attractiveness of a diversified company's business lineup, how to decide whether it has a good diversification strategy, and what strategic options are available for improving a diversified company's future performance. The evaluative technique integrates material concerning both industry analysis and the resource-based view, in that it considers the relative attractiveness of the various industries the company has diversified into, the company's competitive strength in each of its lines of business, and the extent to which its different businesses exhibit both *strategic fit* and *resource fit.*

- Although the topic of ethics and values comes up at various points in this textbook, Chapter 9 brings more direct attention to such issues and may be used as a stand-alone assignment in either the early, middle, or late part of a course. It concerns the themes of ethical standards in business, approaches to ensuring consistent ethical standards for companies with international operations, corporate social responsibility, and environmental sustainability. The contents of this chapter are sure to give students some things to ponder, rouse lively discussion, and help to make students more *ethically aware* and conscious of *why all companies should conduct their business in a socially responsible and sustainable manner.*

- The next three chapters (Chapters 10, 11, and 12) comprise a module on strategy execution that is presented in terms of a 10-step action framework. Chapter 10 provides an overview of this framework and then explores the first three of these tasks: (1) *staffing the organization* with people capable of executing the strategy well, (2) *building the organizational capabilities* needed for successful strategy execution, and (3) *creating an organizational structure* supportive of the strategy execution process.

- Chapter 11 discusses five additional managerial actions that advance the cause of good strategy execution: (1) *allocating resources* to enable the strategy execution process, (2) ensuring that *policies and procedures* facilitate rather than impede strategy execution, (3) using *process management tools* and *best practices* to drive continuous improvement in the performance of value chain activities, (4) installing *information and operating systems* that help company personnel carry out their strategic roles, and (5) using *rewards and incentives* to encourage good strategy execution and the achievement of performance targets.

- Chapter 12 completes the 10-step framework with a consideration of the importance of *creating a healthy* corporate *culture* and *exercising effective leadership* in promoting good strategy execution. The recurring theme throughout the final three chapters is that executing strategy involves deciding on the specific actions, behaviors, and conditions needed for a smooth strategy-supportive operation and then following through to get things done and deliver results. The goal here is to ensure that students understand that the strategy-executing phase is a *make-things-happen and make-them-happen-right* kind of managerial exercise—one that is critical for achieving operating excellence and reaching the goal of strong company performance.

In this latest edition, we have put our utmost effort into ensuring that the 12 chapters are consistent with the latest and best thinking of academics and practitioners in the field of strategic management and provide the topical coverage required for both undergraduate and MBA-level strategy courses. The ultimate test of the text, of course, is the positive pedagogical impact it has in the classroom. If this edition sets a more effective stage for your lectures and does a better job of helping you persuade students that the discipline of strategy merits their rapt attention, then it will have fulfilled its purpose.

THE CASE COLLECTION

The 32-case lineup in this edition is flush with interesting companies and valuable lessons for students in the art and science of crafting and executing strategy. There's a good blend of cases from a length perspective—about two-thirds of the cases are under 15 pages yet offer plenty for students to chew on; seven are medium-length cases; and the remainder are detail-rich cases that call for more sweeping analysis.

At least 25 of the 32 cases involve companies, products, people, or activities that students will have heard of, know about from personal experience, or can easily identify with. The lineup includes at least 20 cases that will deepen student understanding of the special demands of competing in industry environments where product life cycles are short and competitive maneuvering among rivals is quite active. Twenty-three of the cases involve situations in which company resources and competitive capabilities play as large a role in the strategy-making, strategy executing scheme of things as industry and competitive conditions do. Scattered throughout the lineup are 20 cases concerning non-U.S. companies, globally competitive industries, and/or cross-cultural situations. These cases, in conjunction with the globalized content of the text chapters, provide abundant material for linking the study of strategic management tightly to the ongoing globalization of the world economy. You'll also find 10 cases dealing with the strategic problems of family-owned or relatively small entrepreneurial businesses and 20 cases involving public companies and situations where students can do further research on the Internet.

The "Guide to Case Analysis" follows the last case. It contains sections on what a case is, why cases are a standard part of courses in strategy, preparing a case for class discussion, doing a written case analysis, doing an oral presentation, and using financial ratio analysis to assess a company's financial condition. We suggest having students read this guide before the first class discussion of a case.

A number of cases have accompanying YouTube video segments which are listed in Section 3 of the Instructor's Manual and in the Teaching Note for each case.

THE TWO STRATEGY SIMULATION SUPPLEMENTS: *THE BUSINESS STRATEGY GAME* AND *GLO-BUS*

The Business Strategy Game and *GLO-BUS: Developing Winning Competitive Strategies*—two competition-based strategy simulations that are delivered online and that feature automated processing and grading of performance—are being marketed by the publisher as companion supplements for use with the 22nd edition (and other texts in the field).

• *The Business Strategy Game* is the world's most popular strategy simulation, having been used by nearly 3,300 different instructors for courses involving some 900,000 students at 1,235+ university campuses in 76 countries. It features global competition in the athletic footwear industry, a product/market setting familiar to students everywhere and one whose managerial challenges are easily grasped. A freshly updated and much-enhanced version of *The Business Strategy Game* was introduced in August 2018.

• *GLO-BUS,* a newer and somewhat simpler strategy simulation first introduced in 2004 and freshly revamped in 2016 to center on competition in two exciting product categories–wearable miniature action cameras and unmanned camera-equipped drones suitable for multiple commercial purposes, has been used by 1,750+ different instructors for courses involving nearly 300,000 students at 750+ university campuses in 53 countries.

How the Strategy Simulations Work

In both *The Business Strategy Game (BSG)* and *GLO-BUS,* class members are divided into teams of one to five persons and assigned to run a company that competes head-to-head against companies run by other class members. In both simulations, companies compete in a global market arena, selling their products in four geographic regions—Europe-Africa, North America, Asia-Pacific, and Latin America. Each management team is called upon to craft a strategy for their company and make decisions relating to production operations, workforce compensation, pricing and marketing, social responsibility/citizenship, and finance.

Company co-managers are held accountable for their decision making. Each company's performance is scored on the basis of earnings per share, return-on-equity investment, stock price, credit rating, and image rating. Rankings of company performance, along with a wealth of industry and company statistics, are available to company co-managers after each decision round to use in making strategy adjustments and operating decisions for the next competitive round. You can be certain that the market environment, strategic issues, and operating challenges that company co-managers must contend with are *very tightly linked* to what your class members will be reading about in the text chapters. The circumstances that co-managers face in running their simulation company embrace the very concepts, analytical tools, and strategy options they encounter in the text chapters (this is something you can quickly confirm by skimming through some of the Exercises for Simulation Participants that appear at the end of each chapter).

We suggest that you schedule 1 or 2 practice rounds and anywhere from 4 to 10 regular (scored) decision rounds (more rounds are better than fewer rounds). Each decision round represents a year of company operations and will entail roughly two hours of time for company co-managers to complete. In traditional 13-week, semester-long courses, there is merit in scheduling one decision round per week. In courses that run 5 to 10 weeks, it is wise to schedule two decision rounds per week for the last several weeks of the term (sample course schedules are provided for courses of varying length and varying numbers of class meetings).

When the instructor-specified deadline for a decision round arrives, the simulation server automatically accesses the saved decision entries of each company, determines the competitiveness and buyer appeal of each company's product offering relative to the other companies being run by students in your class, and then awards sales and market shares to the competing companies, geographic region by geographic region. The unit sales volumes awarded to each company *are totally governed by*

- How its prices compare against the prices of rival brands.
- How its product quality compares against the quality of rival brands.
- How its product line breadth and selection compare.
- How its advertising effort compares.
- And so on, for a total of 11 competitive factors that determine unit sales and market shares.

The competitiveness and overall buyer appeal of each company's product offering *in comparison to the product offerings of rival companies* is all-decisive—this algorithmic feature is what makes *BSG* and *GLO-BUS* "competition-based" strategy simulations. Once each company's sales and market shares are awarded based on the competitiveness and buyer appeal of its respective overall product offering vis-à-vis those of rival companies, the various company and industry reports detailing the outcomes of the decision round are then generated. Company co-managers can access the results of the decision round 15 to 20 minutes after the decision deadline.

The Compelling Case for Incorporating Use of a Strategy Simulation

There are *three exceptionally important benefits* associated with using a competition-based simulation in strategy courses taken by seniors and MBA students:

- *A three-pronged text-case-simulation course model delivers significantly more teaching-learning power than the traditional text-case model.* Using *both* cases and a strategy simulation to drill students in thinking strategically and applying what they read in the text chapters is a stronger, more effective means of helping them connect theory with practice and develop better business judgment. What cases do that a simulation cannot is give class members broad exposure to a variety of companies and industry situations and insight into the kinds of strategy-related problems managers face. But what a competition-based strategy simulation does far better than case analysis is thrust class members squarely into *an active, hands-on managerial role* where they are totally responsible for assessing market conditions, determining how to respond to the actions of competitors, forging a long-term direction and strategy for their company, and making all kinds of operating decisions. Because they are held fully accountable for their decisions and their company's performance, *co-managers are strongly motivated* to dig deeply into company operations, probe for ways to be more cost-efficient and competitive, and ferret out strategic moves and decisions calculated to boost company performance. *Consequently, incorporating both case assignments and a strategy simulation to develop the skills of class members in thinking strategically and applying the concepts and tools of strategic analysis turns out to be more pedagogically powerful than relying solely on case assignments—there's stronger retention of the lessons learned and better achievement of course learning objectives.*

To provide you with quantitative evidence of the learning that occurs with using *The Business Strategy Game* or *GLO-BUS,* there is a built-in Learning Assurance Report showing how well each class member performs on nine skills/learning measures versus tens of thousands of students worldwide who have completed the simulation in the past 12 months.

• *The competitive nature of a strategy simulation arouses positive energy and steps up the whole tempo of the course by a notch or two.* Nothing sparks class excitement quicker or better than the concerted efforts on the part of class members at each decision round to achieve a high industry ranking and avoid the perilous consequences of being outcompeted by other class members. Students really enjoy taking on the role of a manager, running their own company, crafting strategies, making all kinds of operating decisions, trying to outcompete rival companies, and getting immediate feedback on the resulting company performance. Lots of back-and-forth chatter occurs when the results of the latest simulation round become available and co-managers renew their quest for strategic moves and actions that will strengthen company performance. Co-managers become *emotionally invested* in running their company and figuring out what strategic moves to make to boost their company's performance. Interest levels climb. All this stimulates learning and causes students to see the practical relevance of the subject matter and the benefits of taking your course.

As soon as your students start to say "Wow! Not only is this fun but I am learning a lot," *which they will,* you have won the battle of engaging students in the subject matter and moved the value of taking your course to a much higher plateau in the business school curriculum. This translates into *a livelier, richer learning experience from a student perspective and better instructor-course evaluations.*

• *Use of a fully automated online simulation reduces the time instructors spend on course preparation, course administration, and grading.* Since the simulation exercise involves a 20- to 30-hour workload for student teams (roughly 2 hours per decision round times 10 to 12 rounds, plus optional assignments), simulation adopters often compensate by trimming the number of assigned cases from, say, 10 to 12 to perhaps 4 to 6. This significantly reduces the time instructors spend reading cases, studying teaching notes, and otherwise getting ready to lead class discussion of a case or grade oral team presentations. Course preparation time is further cut because you can use several class days to have students bring their laptops to class or meet in a computer lab to work on upcoming decision rounds or a three-year strategic plan (in lieu of lecturing on a chapter or covering an additional assigned case). Not only does use of a simulation permit assigning fewer cases, but it also permits you to eliminate at least one assignment that entails considerable grading on your part. Grading one less written case or essay exam or other written assignment saves enormous time. With *BSG* and *GLO-BUS,* grading is effortless and takes only minutes; once you enter percentage weights for each assignment in your online grade book, a suggested overall grade is calculated for you. You'll be pleasantly surprised—and quite pleased—at how little time it takes to gear up for and administer *The Business Strategy Game* or *GLO-BUS.*

In sum, incorporating use of a strategy simulation turns out to be *a win–win proposition for both students and instructors.* Moreover, a very convincing argument can be made that a competition-based strategy simulation is *the single most effective teaching/learning tool that instructors can employ to teach the discipline of business and competitive strategy, to make learning more enjoyable, and to promote better achievement of course learning objectives.*

A Bird's-Eye View of *The Business Strategy Game*

The setting for *The Business Strategy Game (BSG)* is the global athletic footwear industry (there can be little doubt in today's world that a globally competitive strategy simulation is *vastly superior* to a simulation with a domestic-only setting). Global market demand for footwear grows at the rate of 7 to 9 percent annually for the first five years and 5 to 7 percent annually for the second five years. However, market growth rates vary by geographic region—North America, Latin America, Europe-Africa, and Asia-Pacific.

Companies begin the simulation producing branded and private-label footwear in two plants, one in North America and one in Asia. They have the option to establish production facilities in Latin America and Europe-Africa. Company co-managers exercise control over production costs on the basis of the styling and quality they opt to manufacture, plant location (wages and incentive compensation vary from region to region), the use of best practices and Six Sigma programs to reduce the production of defective footwear and to boost worker productivity, and compensation practices.

All newly produced footwear is shipped in bulk containers to one of four geographic distribution centers. All sales in a geographic region are made from footwear inventories in that region's distribution center. Costs at the four regional distribution centers are a function of inventory storage costs, packing and shipping fees, import tariffs paid on incoming pairs shipped from foreign plants, and exchange rate impacts. At the start of the simulation, import tariffs average $4 per pair in North America, $6 in Europe-Africa, $8 per pair in Latin America, and $10 in the Asia-Pacific region. Instructors have the option to alter tariffs as the game progresses.

Companies market their brand of athletic footwear to footwear retailers worldwide and to individuals buying online at the company's website. Each company's sales and market share in the branded footwear segments hinge on its competitiveness on 13 factors: attractive pricing, footwear styling and quality, product line breadth, advertising, use of mail-in rebates, appeal of celebrities endorsing a company's brand, success in convincing footwear retailers to carry its brand, number of weeks it takes to fill retailer orders, effectiveness of a company's online sales effort at its website, and brand reputation. Sales of private-label footwear hinge solely on being the low-price bidder.

All told, company co-managers make as many as 57 types of decisions each period that cut across production operations (up to 11 decisions per plant, with a maximum of four plants), the addition of facility space, equipment, and production improvement options (up to 8 decisions per plant), worker compensation and training (up to 6 decisions per plant), shipping and distribution center operations (5 decisions per geographic region), pricing and marketing (up to 9 decisions in four geographic regions), bids to sign celebrities (2 decision entries per bid), financing of company operations (up to 8 decisions), and corporate social responsibility and environmental sustainability (up to 8 decisions). Plus, there are 10 entries for each region pertaining to assumptions about the upcoming-year actions and competitive efforts of rival companies that factor directly into the forecasts of a company's unit sales, revenues, and market share in each of the four geographic regions.

Each time company co-managers make a decision entry, an assortment of on-screen calculations instantly shows the projected effects on unit sales, revenues, market shares, unit costs, profit, earnings per share, ROE, and other operating statistics. The on-screen calculations help team members evaluate the relative merits of one decision entry versus another and put together a promising strategy.

Companies can employ any of the five generic competitive strategy options in selling branded footwear—low-cost leadership, differentiation, best-cost provider, focused low cost, and focused differentiation. They can pursue essentially the same strategy worldwide or craft slightly or very different strategies for the Europe-Africa, Asia-Pacific, Latin America, and North America markets. They can strive for competitive advantage based on more advertising, a wider selection of models, more appealing styling/quality, bigger rebates, and so on.

Any well-conceived, well-executed competitive approach is capable of succeeding, provided it is not overpowered by the strategies of competitors or defeated by the presence of too many copycat strategies that dilute its effectiveness. The challenge for each company's management team is to craft and execute a competitive strategy that produces good performance on five measures: earnings per share, return on equity investment, stock price appreciation, credit rating, and brand image.

All activity for *The Business Strategy Game* takes place at **www.bsg-online.com**.

A Bird's-Eye View of *GLO-BUS*

In *GLO-BUS,* class members run companies that are in a neck-and-neck race for global market leadership in two product categories: (1) wearable video cameras smaller than a teacup that deliver stunning video quality and have powerful photo capture capabilities (comparable to those designed and marketed by global industry leader GoPro and numerous others) and (2) sophisticated camera-equipped copter drones that incorporate a company designed and assembled action-capture camera and that are sold to commercial enterprises for prices in the $850 to 2,000+ range. Global market demand for action cameras grows at the rate of 6 to 8 percent annually for the first five years and 4 to 6 percent annually for the second five years. Global market demand for commercial drones grows briskly at rates averaging 18 percent for the first two years, then gradually slows over 8 years to a rate of 4 to 6 percent.

Companies assemble action cameras and drones of varying designs and performance capabilities at a Taiwan facility and ship finished goods directly to buyers in North America, Asia-Pacific, Europe-Africa, and Latin America. Both products are assembled usually within two weeks of being received and are then shipped to buyers no later than 2 to 3 days after assembly. Companies maintain no finished goods inventories and all parts and components are delivered by suppliers on a just-in-time basis (which eliminates the need to track inventories and simplifies the accounting for plant operations and costs).

Company co-managers determine the quality and performance features of the cameras and drones being assembled. They impact production costs by raising/lowering specifications for parts/components and expenditures for product R&D, adjusting work force compensation, spending more/less on worker training and productivity improvement, lengthening/shortening warranties offered (which affects warranty costs), and how cost-efficiently they manage assembly operations. They have options to manage/control selling and certain other costs as well.

Each decision round, company co-managers make some 50 types of decisions relating to the design and performance of the company's two products (21 decisions, 10 for cameras and 11 for drones), assembly operations and workforce compensation (up to 8 decision entries for each product), pricing and marketing (7 decisions for cameras and 5 for drones), corporate social responsibility and citizenship (up to 6 decisions), and the financing of company operations (up to 8 decisions). In addition, there are 10 entries for cameras and 7 entries for drones involving assumptions about the competitive actions of rivals; these entries help company co-managers to make more accurate forecasts of their company's unit sales (so they have a good idea of how many cameras and drones will need to be assembled each year to fill customer orders). Each time co-managers make a decision entry, an assortment of on-screen calculations instantly shows the projected effects on unit sales, revenues, market shares, total profit, earnings per share, ROE, costs, and other operating outcomes. All of these on-screen calculations help co-managers evaluate the relative merits of one decision entry versus another. Company managers can try out as many different decision combinations as they wish in stitching the separate decision entries into a cohesive whole that is projected to produce good company performance.

Competition in action cameras revolves around 11 factors that determine each company's unit sales/market share:

1. How each company's average wholesale price to retailers compares against the all-company average wholesale prices being charged in each geographic region.

2. How each company's camera performance and quality compares against industry-wide camera performance/quality.

3. How the number of week-long sales promotion campaigns a company has in each region compares against the regional average number of weekly promotions.

4. How the size of each company's discounts off the regular wholesale prices during sales promotion campaigns compares against the regional average promotional discount.

5. How each company's annual advertising expenditures compare against regional average advertising expenditures.

6. How the number of models in each company's camera line compares against the industry-wide average number of models.

7. The number of retailers stocking and merchandising a company's brand in each region.

8. Annual expenditures to support the merchandising efforts of retailers stocking a company's brand in each region.

9. The amount by which a company's expenditures for ongoing improvement and updating of its company's website in a region is above/below the all-company regional average expenditure.

10. How the length of each company's camera warranties compare against the warranty periods of rival companies.

11. How well a company's brand image/reputation compares against the brand images/reputations of rival companies.

Competition among rival makers of commercial copter drones is more narrowly focused on just 9 sales-determining factors:

1. How a company's average retail price for drones at the company's website in each region compares against the all-company regional average website price.

2. How each company's drone performance and quality compares against the all-company average drone performance/quality.

3. How the number of models in each company's drone line compares against the industry-wide average number of models.

4. How each company's annual expenditures to recruit/support third-party online electronics retailers in merchandising its brand of drones in each region compares against the regional average.

5. The amount by which a company's price discount to third-party online retailers is above/below the regional average discounted price.

6. How well a company's expenditures for search engine advertising in a region compares against the regional average.

7. How well a company's expenditures for ongoing improvement and updating of its website in a region compares against the regional average.

8. How the length of each company's drone warranties in a region compares against the regional average warranty period.

9. How well a company's brand image/reputation compares against the brand images/reputations of rival companies.

Each company typically seeks to enhance its performance and build competitive advantage via its own custom-tailored competitive strategy based on more attractive pricing, greater advertising, a wider selection of models, more appealing performance/quality, longer warranties, a better image/reputation, and so on. The greater the differences in the overall competitiveness of the product offerings of rival companies, the bigger the differences in their resulting sales volumes and market shares. Conversely, the smaller the overall competitive differences in the product offerings of rival companies, the smaller the differences in sales volumes and market shares. This algorithmic approach is what makes *GLO-BUS* a "competition-based" strategy simulation and accounts for why *the sales and market share outcomes for each decision round are always unique to the particular strategies and decision combinations employed by the competing companies.*

As with *BSG,* all the various generic competitive strategy options—low-cost leadership, differentiation, best-cost provider, focused low-cost, and focused differentiation—*are viable choices for pursuing competitive advantage and good company performance.* A company can have a strategy aimed at being the clear market leader in either action cameras or drones or both. It can focus its competitive efforts on one or two or three geographic regions or strive to build strong market positions in all four geographic regions. It can pursue essentially the same strategy worldwide or craft customized strategies for the Europe-Africa, Asia-Pacific, Latin America, and North America markets. Just as with *The Business Strategy Game, most any well-conceived, well-executed competitive approach is capable of succeeding, provided it is not overpowered by the strategies of competitors or defeated by the presence of too many copycat strategies that dilute its effectiveness.*

The challenge for each company's management team is to craft and execute a competitive strategy that produces good performance on five measures: earnings per share, return on equity investment, stock price appreciation, credit rating, and brand image.

All activity for *GLO-BUS* occurs at **www.glo-bus.com**.

Special Note: The time required of company co-managers to complete each decision round in *GLO-BUS* is typically about 15 to 30 minutes less than for *The Business Strategy Game* because

(a) there are only 8 market segments (versus 12 in *BSG*),

(b) co-managers have only one assembly site to operate (versus potentially as many as 4 plants in *BSG,* one in each geographic region), and

(c) newly assembled cameras and drones are shipped directly to buyers, eliminating the need to manage finished goods inventories and operate distribution centers.

Administration and Operating Features of the Two Simulations

The Internet delivery and user-friendly designs of both *BSG* and *GLO-BUS* make them incredibly easy to administer, even for first-time users. And the menus and controls are so similar that you can readily switch between the two simulations or use one in your undergraduate class and the other in a graduate class. If you have not yet used either of the two simulations, you may find the following of particular interest:

- Setting up the simulation for your course is done online and takes about 10 to 15 minutes. Once setup is completed, no other administrative actions are required beyond those of moving participants to a different team (should the need arise) and monitoring the progress of the simulation (to whatever extent desired).

- Participant's Guides are delivered electronically to class members at the website—students can read the guide on their monitors or print out a copy, as they prefer.

- There are 2- to 4-minute Video Tutorials scattered throughout the software (including each decision screen and each page of each report) that provide on-demand guidance to class members who may be uncertain about how to proceed.

- Complementing the Video Tutorials are detailed and clearly written Help sections explaining "all there is to know" about (a) each decision entry and the relevant cause-effect relationships, (b) the information on each page of the Industry Reports, and (c) the numbers presented in the Company Reports. *The Video Tutorials and the Help screens allow company co-managers to figure things out for themselves, thereby curbing the need for students to ask the instructor "how things work."*

- Team members running the same company who are logged in simultaneously on different computers at different locations can click a button to enter Collaboration Mode, enabling them to work collaboratively from the same screen in viewing reports and making decision entries, and click a second button to enter Audio Mode, letting them talk to one another.

  - When in "Collaboration Mode," each team member sees the same screen at the same time as all other team members who are logged in and have joined Collaboration Mode. If one team member chooses to view a particular decision screen, that same screen appears on the monitors for all team members in Collaboration Mode.

  - Each team member controls their own color-coded mouse pointer (with their first-name appearing in a color-coded box linked to their mouse pointer) and can make a decision entry or move the mouse to point to particular on-screen items.

  - A decision entry change made by one team member is seen by all, in real time, and all team members can immediately view the on-screen calculations that result from the new decision entry.

  - If one team member wishes to view a report page and clicks on the menu link to the desired report, that same report page will immediately appear for the other team members engaged in collaboration.

  - Use of Audio Mode capability requires that each team member work from a computer with a built-in microphone (if they want to be heard by their team members) and speakers (so they may hear their teammates) or else have a headset with a microphone that they can plug into their desktop or laptop. A headset is recommended for best results, but most laptops now are equipped with a built-in microphone and speakers that will support use of our new voice chat feature.

○ Real-time VoIP audio chat capability among team members who have entered both the Audio Mode and the Collaboration Mode is a tremendous boost in functionality that enables team members to go online simultaneously on computers at different locations and conveniently and effectively collaborate in running their simulation company.

○ In addition, instructors have the capability to join the online session of any company and speak with team members, thus circumventing the need for team members to arrange for and attend a meeting in the instructor's office. Using the standard menu for administering a particular industry, instructors can connect with the company desirous of assistance. Instructors who wish not only to talk but also to enter Collaboration (highly recommended because all attendees are then viewing the same screen) have a red-colored mouse pointer linked to a red box labeled Instructor.

Without a doubt, the Collaboration and Voice-Chat capabilities are hugely valuable for students enrolled in online and distance-learning courses where meeting face-to-face is impractical or time-consuming. Likewise, the instructors of online and distance-learning courses will appreciate having the capability to join the online meetings of particular company teams when their advice or assistance is requested.

- Both simulations are quite suitable for use in distance-learning or online courses (and are currently being used in such courses on numerous campuses).

- Participants and instructors are notified via e-mail when the results are ready (usually about 15 to 20 minutes after the decision round deadline specified by the instructor/game administrator).

- Following each decision round, participants are provided with a complete set of reports—a six-page Industry Report, a Competitive Intelligence report for each geographic region that includes strategic group maps and a set of Company Reports (income statement, balance sheet, cash flow statement, and assorted production, marketing, and cost statistics).

- Two "open-book" multiple-choice tests of 20 questions are built into each simulation. The quizzes, which you can require or not as you see fit, are taken online and automatically graded, with scores reported instantaneously to participants and automatically recorded in the instructor's electronic grade book. Students are automatically provided with three sample questions for each test.

- Both simulations contain a three-year strategic plan option that you can assign. Scores on the plan are automatically recorded in the instructor's online grade book.

- At the end of the simulation, you can have students complete online peer evaluations (again, the scores are automatically recorded in your online grade book).

- Both simulations have a Company Presentation feature that enables each team of company co-managers to easily prepare PowerPoint slides for use in describing their strategy and summarizing their company's performance in a presentation to either the class, the instructor, or an "outside" board of directors.

- *A Learning Assurance Report provides you with hard data concerning how well your students performed vis-à-vis students playing the simulation worldwide over the past 12 months.* The report is based on nine measures of student proficiency, business know-how, and decision-making skill and can also be used in evaluating the extent to which your school's academic curriculum produces the desired degree of student learning insofar as accreditation standards are concerned.

For more details on either simulation, please consult Section 2 of the Instructor's Manual accompanying this text or register as an instructor at the simulation websites (**www.bsg-online.com** and **www.glo-bus.com**) to access even more comprehensive information. You should also consider signing up for one of the webinars that the simulation authors conduct several times each month (sometimes several times weekly) to demonstrate how the software works, walk you through the various features and menu options, and answer any questions. You have an open invitation to call the senior author of this text at (205) 722-9145 to arrange a personal demonstration or talk about how one of the simulations might work in one of your courses. We think you'll be quite impressed with the cutting-edge capabilities that have been programmed into *The Business Strategy Game* and *GLO-BUS,* the simplicity with which both simulations can be administered, and their exceptionally tight connection to the text chapters, core concepts, and standard analytical tools.

RESOURCES AND SUPPORT MATERIALS FOR THE 22ND EDITION

For Students

Key Points Summaries   At the end of each chapter is a synopsis of the core concepts, analytical tools, and other key points discussed in the chapter. These chapter-end synopses, along with the core concept definitions and margin notes scattered throughout each chapter, help students focus on basic strategy principles, digest the messages of each chapter, and prepare for tests.

Two Sets of Chapter-End Exercises   Each chapter concludes with two sets of exercises. The *Assurance of Learning Exercises* are useful for helping students prepare for class discussion and to gauge their understanding of the material. The *Exercises for Simulation Participants* are designed expressly for use in class which incorporate the use of a simulation. These exercises explicitly connect the chapter content to the simulation company the students are running. Even if they are not assigned by the instructor, they can provide helpful practice for students as a study aid.

The Connect™ Management Web-Based Assignment and Assessment Platform   Beginning with the 18th edition, we began taking advantage of the publisher's innovative Connect™ assignment and assessment platform and created several features that simplify the task of assigning and grading three types of exercises for students:

- There are self-scoring chapter tests consisting of 20 to 25 multiple-choice questions that students can take to measure their grasp of the material presented in each of the 12 chapters.
- There are two Interactive Application exercises for each of the 12 chapters that drill students in the use and application of the concepts and tools of strategic analysis.
- The Connect™ platform also includes Interactive Application exercises for 14 of the 32 cases in this edition that require students to work through answers to a select number of the assignment questions for the case. These exercises have multiple components and can include calculating assorted financial ratios to assess a company's financial performance and balance sheet strength, identifying a company's

strategy, doing five-forces and driving-forces analysis, doing a SWOT analysis, and recommending actions to improve company performance. The content of these case exercises is tailored to match the circumstances presented in each case, calling upon students to do whatever strategic thinking and strategic analysis are called for to arrive at pragmatic, analysis-based action recommendations for improving company performance.

All of the analysis portions of the Connect™ exercises are automatically graded, thereby simplifying the task of evaluating each class member's performance and monitoring the learning outcomes. The progress-tracking function built into the Connect™ Management system enables you to

- View scored work immediately and track individual or group performance with assignment and grade reports.
- Access an instant view of student or class performance relative to learning objectives.
- Collect data and generate reports required by many accreditation organizations, such as AACSB International.

LearnSmart and SmartBook™   LearnSmart is an adaptive study tool proven to strengthen memory recall, increase class retention, and boost grades. Students are able to study more efficiently because they are made aware of what they know and don't know. Real-time reports quickly identify the concepts that require more attention from individual students—or the entire class. SmartBook is the first and only adaptive reading experience designed to change the way students read and learn. It creates a personalized reading experience by highlighting the most impactful concepts a student needs to learn at that moment in time. As a student engages with SmartBook, the reading experience continuously adapts by highlighting content based on what the student knows and doesn't know. This ensures that the focus is on the content he or she needs to learn, while simultaneously promoting long-term retention of material. Use SmartBook's real-time reports to quickly identify the concepts that require more attention from individual students—or the entire class. The end result? Students are more engaged with course content, can better prioritize their time, and come to class ready to participate.

For Instructors

Assurance of Learning Aids   Each chapter begins with a set of Learning Objectives, which are tied directly to the material in the text meant to address these objectives with helpful signposts. At the conclusion of each chapter, there is a set of *Assurance of Learning Exercises* that can be used as the basis for class discussion, oral presentation assignments, short written reports, and substitutes for case assignments. Similarly, there is a set of *Exercises for Simulation Participants* that are designed expressly for use by adopters who have incorporated use of a simulation and want to go a step further in tightly and explicitly connecting the chapter content to the simulation company their students are running. The questions in both sets of exercises (along with those Illustration Capsules that qualify as "mini-cases") can be used to round out the rest of a 75-minute class period should your lecture on a chapter last for only 50 minutes.

Instructor Library   The Connect Management Instructor Library is your repository for additional resources to improve student engagement in and out of class. You can select and use any asset that enhances your lecture.

Instructor's Manual   The accompanying IM contains:

- A section on suggestions for organizing and structuring your course.
- Sample syllabi and course outlines.
- A set of lecture notes on each chapter.
- Answers to the chapter-end Assurance of Learning Exercises.
- A test bank for all 12 chapters.
- A comprehensive case teaching note for each of the 32 cases. These teaching notes are filled with suggestions for using the case effectively, have very thorough, analysis-based answers to the suggested assignment questions for the case, and contain an epilogue detailing any important developments since the case was written.

Test Bank   The test bank contains over 900 multiple-choice questions and short-answer/essay questions. It has been tagged with AACSB and Bloom's Taxonomy criteria. All of the test bank questions are also accessible via **TestGen.** TestGen is a complete, state-of-the-art test generator and editing application software that allows instructors to quickly and easily select test items from McGraw Hill's TestGen test-bank content and to organize, edit, and customize the questions and answers to rapidly generate paper tests. Questions can include stylized text, symbols, graphics, and equations that are inserted directly into questions using built-in mathematical templates. TestGen's random generator provides the option to display different text or calculated number values each time questions are used. With both quick-and-simple test creation and flexible and robust editing tools, TestGen is a test generator system for today's educators.

PowerPoint Slides   To facilitate delivery preparation of your lectures and to serve as chapter outlines, you'll have access to approximately 500 colorful and professional-looking slides displaying core concepts, analytical procedures, key points, and all the figures in the text chapters.

CREATE™   is McGraw-Hill's custom-publishing program where you can access full-length readings and cases that accompany *Crafting and Executing Strategy: The Quest for a Competitive Advantage* (**http://create.mheducation.com/thompson**). Through Create™, you will be able to select from 30 readings that go specifically with this text-book. These include cases and readings from Harvard, MIT, and much more! You can assemble your own course and select the chapters, cases, and readings that work best for you. Also, you can choose from several ready-to-go, author-recommended complete course solutions. Among the pre-loaded solutions, you'll find options for undergrad, MBA, accelerated, and other strategy courses.

The Business Strategy Game* and *GLO-BUS Online Simulations   Using one of the two companion simulations is a powerful and constructive way of emotionally connecting students to the subject matter of the course. We know of no more effective way to arouse the competitive energy of students and prepare them for the challenges of real-world business decision making than to have them match strategic wits with classmates in running a company in head-to-head competition for global market leadership.

ACKNOWLEDGMENTS

We heartily acknowledge the contributions of the case researchers whose case-writing efforts appear herein and the companies whose cooperation made the cases possible. To each one goes a very special thank-you. We cannot overstate the importance of timely, carefully researched cases in contributing to a substantive study of strategic management issues and practices.

A great number of colleagues and students at various universities, business acquaintances, and people at McGraw-Hill provided inspiration, encouragement, and counsel during the course of this project. Like all text authors in the strategy field, we are intellectually indebted to the many academics whose research and writing have blazed new trails and advanced the discipline of strategic management. In addition, we'd like to thank the following reviewers who provided seasoned advice and splendid suggestions over the years for improving the chapters:

Robert B. Baden, Edward Desmarais, Stephen F. Hallam, Joy Karriker, Wendell Seaborne, Joan H. Bailar, David Blair, Jane Boyland, William J. Donoher, Stephen A. Drew, Jo Anne Duffy, Alan Ellstrand, Susan Fox-Wolfgramm, Rebecca M. Guidice, Mark Hoelscher, Sean D. Jasso, Xin Liang, Paul Mallette, Dan Marlin, Raza Mir, Mansour Moussavi, James D. Spina, Monica A. Zimmerman, Dennis R. Balch, Jeffrey R. Bruehl, Edith C. Busija, Donald A. Drost, Randall Harris, Mark Lewis Hoelscher, Phyllis Holland, James W. Kroeger, Sal Kukalis, Brian W. Kulik, Paul Mallette, Anthony U. Martinez, Lee Pickler, Sabine Reddy, Thomas D. Schramko, V. Seshan, Charles Strain, Sabine Turnley, S. Stephen Vitucci, Andrew Ward, Sibin Wu, Lynne Patten, Nancy E. Landrum, Jim Goes, Jon Kalinowski, Rodney M. Walter, Judith D. Powell, Seyda Deligonul, David Flanagan, Esmerlda Garbi, Mohsin Habib, Kim Hester, Jeffrey E. McGee, Diana J. Wong, F. William Brown, Anthony F. Chelte, Gregory G. Dess, Alan B. Eisner, John George, Carle M. Hunt, Theresa Marron-Grodsky, Sarah Marsh, Joshua D. Martin, William L. Moore, Donald Neubaum, George M. Puia, Amit Shah, Lois M. Shelton, Mark Weber, Steve Barndt, J. Michael Geringer, Ming-Fang Li, Richard Stackman, Stephen Tallman, Gerardo R. Ungson, James Boulgarides, Betty Diener, Daniel F. Jennings, David Kuhn, Kathryn Martell, Wilbur Mouton, Bobby Vaught, Tuck Bounds, Lee Burk, Ralph Catalanello, William Crittenden, Vince Luchsinger, Stan Mendenhall, John Moore, Will Mulvaney, Sandra Richard, Ralph Roberts, Thomas Turk, Gordon Von Stroh, Fred Zimmerman, S. A. Billion, Charles Byles, Gerald L. Geisler, Rose Knotts, Joseph Rosenstein, James B. Thurman, Ivan Able, W. Harvey Hegarty, Roger Evered, Charles B. Saunders, Rhae M. Swisher, Claude I. Shell, R. Thomas Lenz, Michael C. White, Dennis Callahan, R. Duane Ireland, William E. Burr II, C. W. Millard, Richard Mann, Kurt Christensen, Neil W. Jacobs, Louis W. Fry, D. Robley Wood, George J. Gore, and William R. Soukup.

We owe a debt of gratitude to Professors Catherine A. Maritan, Jeffrey A. Martin, Richard S. Shreve, and Anant K. Sundaram for their helpful comments on various chapters. We'd also like to thank the following students of the Tuck School of Business for their assistance with the revisions: Alen A. Ameni, Dipti Badrinath, Stephanie K. Berger, Courtney D. Bragg, Katie Coster, Jacob Crandall, Robin Daley, Kathleen T. Durante, Shawnda Lee Duvigneaud, Isaac E. Freeman, Vedrana B. Greatorex, Brittany J. Hattingh, Sadé M. Lawrence, Heather Levy, Margaret W. Macauley, Ken Martin, Brian R. McKenzie, Mathew O'Sullivan, Sara Paccamonti, Byron Peyster,

Jeremy Reich, Carry S. Resor, Edward J. Silberman, David Washer, and Lindsey Wilcox. And we'd like to acknowledge the help of Dartmouth students Avantika Agarwal, Charles K. Anumonwo, Maria Hart, Meaghan I. Haugh, Artie Santry, as well as Tuck staff member Doreen Aher.

As always, we value your recommendations and thoughts about the book. Your comments regarding coverage and contents will be taken to heart, and we always are grateful for the time you take to call our attention to printing errors, deficiencies, and other shortcomings. Please e-mail us at **athompso@cba.ua.edu**, **margaret.a.peteraf@tuck.dartmouth.edu**, **john.gamble@tamucc.edu**, or **astrickl@cba.ua.edu**.

Arthur A. Thompson

Margaret A. Peteraf

John E. Gamble

A. J. Strickland

The Business Strategy Game or *GLO-BUS* Simulation Exercises

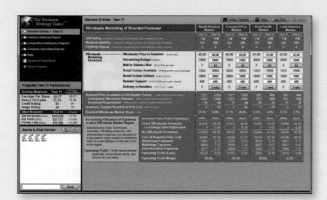 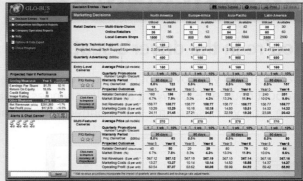

The Business Strategy Game or *GLO-BUS* Simulation Exercises

Either one of these text supplements involves teams of students managing companies in a head-to-head contest for global market leadership. Company co-managers have to make decisions relating to product quality, production, workforce compensation and training, pricing and marketing, and financing of company operations. The challenge is to craft and execute a strategy that is powerful enough to deliver good financial performance despite the competitive efforts of rival companies. Each company competes in North America, Latin America, Europe-Africa, and Asia-Pacific.

CONNECT

Students—study more efficiently, retain more and achieve better outcomes. **Instructors**—focus on what you love—teaching.

SUCCESSFUL SEMESTERS INCLUDE CONNECT

FOR INSTRUCTORS

You're in the driver's seat.

Want to build your own course? No problem. Prefer to use our turnkey, prebuilt course? Easy. Want to make changes throughout the semester? Sure. And you'll save time with Connect's auto-grading too.

65%
Less Time Grading

They'll thank you for it.

Adaptive study resources like SmartBook® help your students be better prepared in less time. You can transform your class time from dull definitions to dynamic debates. Hear from your peers about the benefits of Connect at **www.mheducation.com/highered/connect**

Make it simple, make it affordable.

Connect makes it easy with seamless integration using any of the major Learning Management Systems—Blackboard®, Canvas, and D2L, among others—to let you organize your course in one convenient location. Give your students access to digital materials at a discount with our inclusive access program. Ask your McGraw-Hill representative for more information.

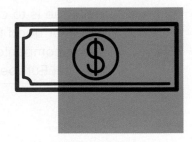

©Hill Street Studios/Tobin Rogers/Blend Images LLC

Solutions for your challenges.

A product isn't a solution. Real solutions are affordable, reliable, and come with training and ongoing support when you need it and how you want it. Our Customer Experience Group can also help you troubleshoot tech problems—although Connect's 99% uptime means you might not need to call them. See for yourself at **status.mheducation.com**

FOR STUDENTS

Effective, efficient studying.

Connect helps you be more productive with your study time and get better grades using tools like SmartBook, which highlights key concepts and creates a personalized study plan. Connect sets you up for success, so you walk into class with confidence and walk out with better grades.

©Shutterstock/wavebreakmedia

> **"I really liked this app—it made it easy to study when you don't have your textbook in front of you."**
>
> - Jordan Cunningham,
> Eastern Washington University

Study anytime, anywhere.

Download the free ReadAnywhere app and access your online eBook when it's convenient, even if you're offline. And since the app automatically syncs with your eBook in Connect, all of your notes are available every time you open it. Find out more at **www.mheducation.com/readanywhere**

No surprises.

The Connect Calendar and Reports tools keep you on track with the work you need to get done and your assignment scores. Life gets busy; Connect tools help you keep learning through it all.

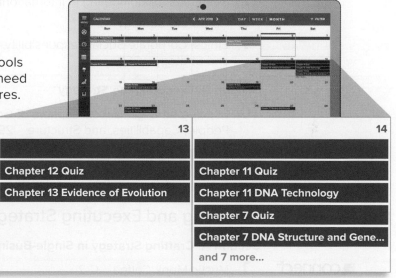

13	14
Chapter 12 Quiz	Chapter 11 Quiz
Chapter 13 Evidence of Evolution	Chapter 11 DNA Technology
	Chapter 7 Quiz
	Chapter 7 DNA Structure and Gene...
	and 7 more...

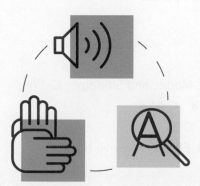

Learning for everyone.

McGraw-Hill works directly with Accessibility Services Departments and faculty to meet the learning needs of all students. Please contact your Accessibility Services office and ask them to email accessibility@mheducation.com, or visit **www.mheducation.com/about/accessibility.html** for more information.

Brief Contents

PART 1 Concepts and Techniques for Crafting and Executing Strategy

Section A: Introduction and Overview

1 What Is Strategy and Why Is It Important?   2

2 Charting a Company's Direction   20

Section B: Core Concepts and Analytical Tools

3 Evaluating a Company's External Environment   48

4 Evaluating a Company's Resources, Capabilities, and Competitiveness   86

Section C: Crafting a Strategy

5 The Five Generic Competitive Strategies   122

6 Strengthening a Company's Competitive Position   152

7 Strategies for Competing in International Markets   182

8 Corporate Strategy   218

9 Ethics, Corporate Social Responsibility, Environmental Sustainability, and Strategy   260

Section D: Executing the Strategy

10 Building an Organization Capable of Good Strategy Execution: People, Capabilities, and Structure   290

11 Managing Internal Operations   322

12 Corporate Culture and Leadership   346

PART 2 Cases in Crafting and Executing Strategy

Section A: Crafting Strategy in Single-Business Companies

connect **1** Mystic Monk Coffee   C-2

connect **2** Airbnb In 2018   C-6

3 Wil's Grill   C-11

connect **4** Costco Wholesale in 2018: Mission, Business Model, and Strategy   C-17

connect **5** Competition in the Craft Beer Industry in 2018   C-41

6 Fixer Upper: Expanding the Magnolia Brand   C-51

connect **7** Under Armour's Turnaround Strategy in 2018: Efforts to Revive North American Sales and Profitability   C-56

8 MoviePass—Are Subscribers Loving It to Death? C-80

9 TOMS Shoes: Expanding Its Successful One For One Business Model C-92

10 Lola's Market: Capturing A New Generation C-101

11 iRobot in 2018: Can the Company Keep the Magic? C-107

12 Chipotle Mexican Grill's Strategy in 2018: Will the New CEO Be Able to Rebuild Customer Trust and Revive Sales Growth? C-120   connect

13 Twitter Inc. in 2018: Too Little Too Late? C-138

14 Netflix's Strategy in 2018: Does the Company Have Sufficient Competitive Strength to Fight Off Aggressive Rivals? C-149   connect

15 Walmart's Expansion into Specialty Online Retailing C-162

16 Amazon.com, Inc.: Driving Disruptive Change in the U.S. Grocery Market C-171

17 Aliexpress: Can It Mount a Global Challenge to Amazon? C-184

18 Tesla Motors in 2018: Will the New Model 3 Save the Company? C-191   connect

19 Mattel Incorporated in 2018: Can Ynon Kreiz Save the Toys? C-216

20 Shearwater Adventures Ltd. C 232

21 TJX Companies: It's Strategy in Off-Price Home Accessories and Apparel Retailing C-240

22 IKEA's International Marketing Strategy in China C-251

Section B: Crafting Strategy in Diversified Companies

23 PepsiCo's Diversification Strategy in 2018: Will the Company's New Businesses Restore its Growth? C-265   connect

24 The Walt Disney Company: Its Diversification Strategy in 2018 C-277   connect

Section C: Implementing and Executing Strategy

25 Robin Hood C-291   connect

26 Dilemma at Devil's Den C-293

27 Nucor Corporation in 2018: Contending with the Challenges of Low-Cost Foreign Imports and Launching Initiatives to Grow Sales and Market Share C-296   connect

28 Vail Resorts, Inc.   C-331

29 Starbucks in 2018: Striving for Operational Excellence and Innovation Agility   C-351

Section D: Strategy, Ethics, and Social Responsibility

30 Concussions in Collegiate and Professional Football: Who Has Responsibility to Protect Players?   C-377

31 Chaos at Uber: The New CEO's Challenge   C-392

32 Profiting from Pain: Business and the U.S. Opioid Epidemic   C-406

Guide to Case Analysis   CA-1

INDEXES

Company   I-1

Name   I-8

Subject   I-13

Contents

PART 1 Concepts and Techniques for
Crafting and Executing Strategy   **1**

Section A: Introduction and Overview

1 What Is Strategy and Why Is It Important?   **2**

WHAT DO WE MEAN BY *STRATEGY*? 4

Strategy Is about Competing Differently   4
Strategy and the Quest for Competitive Advantage   5
Why a Company's Strategy Evolves over Time   8
A Company's Strategy Is Partly Proactive and Partly Reactive   9
Strategy and Ethics: Passing the Test of Moral Scrutiny   9

A COMPANY'S STRATEGY AND ITS BUSINESS MODEL 11

WHAT MAKES A STRATEGY A WINNER? 12

WHY CRAFTING AND EXECUTING STRATEGY ARE IMPORTANT
TASKS 14

Good Strategy + Good Strategy Execution = Good Management   15

THE ROAD AHEAD 15

ILLUSTRATION CAPSULES

1.1   Apple Inc.: Exemplifying a Successful Strategy   7
1.2   Pandora, SiriusXM, and Over-the-Air Broadcast Radio:
Three Contrasting Business Models   13

2 Charting a Company's Direction   **20**

WHAT DOES THE STRATEGY-MAKING, STRATEGY-EXECUTING
PROCESS ENTAIL? 22

STAGE 1: DEVELOPING A STRATEGIC VISION, MISSION STATEMENT,
AND SET OF CORE VALUES 23

Developing a Strategic Vision   23
Communicating the Strategic Vision   24
Expressing the Essence of the Vision in a Slogan   26
Why a Sound, Well-Communicated Strategic Vision Matters   26
Developing a Company Mission Statement   26
Linking the Vision and Mission with Company Values   27

STAGE 2: SETTING OBJECTIVES 30

Setting Stretch Objectives   30
What Kinds of Objectives to Set   30

The Need for a Balanced Approach to Objective Setting   31

Setting Objectives for Every Organizational Level   33

STAGE 3: CRAFTING A STRATEGY 34

Strategy Making Involves Managers at All Organizational Levels   34

A Company's Strategy-Making Hierarchy   35

Uniting the Strategy-Making Hierarchy   38

A Strategic Vision + Mission + Objectives + Strategy = A Strategic Plan   38

STAGE 4: EXECUTING THE STRATEGY 39

STAGE 5: EVALUATING PERFORMANCE AND INITIATING CORRECTIVE ADJUSTMENTS 40

CORPORATE GOVERNANCE: THE ROLE OF THE BOARD OF DIRECTORS IN THE STRATEGY-CRAFTING, STRATEGY-EXECUTING PROCESS 40

ILLUSTRATION CAPSULES

2.1   Examples of Strategic Visions—How Well Do They Measure Up?   25

2.2   TOMS Shoes: A Mission with a Company   29

2.3   Examples of Company Objectives   32

2.4   Corporate Governance Failures at Volkswagen   43

Section B: Core Concepts and Analytical Tools

3 Evaluating a Company's External Environment   48

ANALYZING THE COMPANY'S MACRO-ENVIRONMENT 50

ASSESSING THE COMPANY'S INDUSTRY AND COMPETITIVE ENVIRONMENT 53

THE FIVE FORCES FRAMEWORK 53

Competitive Pressures Created by the Rivalry among Competing Sellers   53

The Choice of Competitive Weapons   57

Competitive Pressures Associated with the Threat of New Entrants   57

Whether Entry Barriers Are High or Low   58

The Expected Reaction of Industry Members in Defending against New Entry   59

Competitive Pressures from the Sellers of Substitute Products   60

Competitive Pressures Stemming from Supplier Bargaining Power   63

Competitive Pressures Stemming from Buyer Bargaining Power and Price Sensitivity   65

Whether Buyers Are More or Less Price Sensitive   67

Is the Collective Strength of the Five Competitive Forces Conducive to Good Profitability?   68

Matching Company Strategy to Competitive Conditions   69

COMPLEMENTORS AND THE VALUE NET 69

INDUSTRY DYNAMICS AND THE FORCES DRIVING CHANGE 70

Identifying the Forces Driving Industry Change   71

Assessing the Impact of the Forces Driving Industry Change   74

Adjusting the Strategy to Prepare for the Impacts of Driving Forces   74

STRATEGIC GROUP ANALYSIS 74

Using Strategic Group Maps to Assess the Market Positions of Key Competitors   74

The Value of Strategic Group Maps   75

COMPETITOR ANALYSIS AND THE SOAR FRAMEWORK 77

Current Strategy   78

Objectives   78

Resources and Capabilities   79

Assumptions   79

KEY SUCCESS FACTORS 79

THE INDUSTRY OUTLOOK FOR PROFITABILITY 80

ILLUSTRATION CAPSULES

3.1 Comparative Market Positions of Selected Companies in the Casual Dining Industry: A Strategic Group Map Example   76

3.2 Business Ethics and Competitive Intelligence   80

4 Evaluating a Company's Resources, Capabilities, and Competitiveness   86

QUESTION 1: HOW WELL IS THE COMPANY'S PRESENT STRATEGY WORKING? 88

QUESTION 2: WHAT ARE THE COMPANY'S STRENGTHS AND WEAKNESSES IN RELATION TO THE MARKET OPPORTUNITIES AND EXTERNAL THREATS? 91

Identifying a Company's Internal Strengths   92

Identifying Company Internal Weaknesses   93

Identifying a Company's Market Opportunities   93

Identifying External Threats   93

What Do the SWOT Listings Reveal?   95

QUESTION 3: WHAT ARE THE COMPANY'S MOST IMPORTANT RESOURCES AND CAPABILITIES, AND WILL THEY GIVE THE COMPANY A LASTING COMPETITIVE ADVANTAGE? 96

Identifying the Company's Resources and Capabilities   96

Types of Company Resources   97

Identifying Capabilities   98

Assessing the Competitive Power of a Company's Resources and Capabilities   99

The Four Tests of a Resource's Competitive Power   99

A Company's Resources and Capabilities Must Be Managed Dynamically   101

The Role of Dynamic Capabilities   101

QUESTION 4: HOW DO VALUE CHAIN ACTIVITIES IMPACT A COMPANY'S COST STRUCTURE AND CUSTOMER VALUE PROPOSITION? 102

The Concept of a Company Value Chain   102

Comparing the Value Chains of Rival Companies   104

A Company's Primary and Secondary Activities Identify the Major Components of Its Internal Cost Structure   104

The Value Chain System   106

Benchmarking: A Tool for Assessing the Costs and Effectiveness of Value Chain Activities   107

Strategic Options for Remedying a Cost or Value Disadvantage   108

Improving Internally Performed Value Chain Activities   108

Improving Supplier-Related Value Chain Activities   110

Improving Value Chain Activities of Distribution Partners   110

Translating Proficient Performance of Value Chain Activities into Competitive Advantage   110

How Value Chain Activities Relate to Resources and Capabilities   111

QUESTION 5: IS THE COMPANY COMPETITIVELY STRONGER OR WEAKER THAN KEY RIVALS? 112

Strategic Implications of Competitive Strength Assessments   114

QUESTION 6: WHAT STRATEGIC ISSUES AND PROBLEMS MERIT FRONT-BURNER MANAGERIAL ATTENTION? 115

ILLUSTRATION CAPSULES

4.1 The Value Chain for Boll & Branch   105

4.2 Benchmarking in the Solar Industry   109

Section C: Crafting a Strategy

5 The Five Generic Competitive Strategies   122

TYPES OF GENERIC COMPETITIVE STRATEGIES 124

BROAD LOW-COST STRATEGIES 125

The Two Major Avenues for Achieving a Cost Advantage   125

Cost-Efficient Management of Value Chain Activities   125

Revamping of the Value Chain System to Lower Costs   128

Examples of Companies That Revamped Their Value Chains to Reduce Costs   128

The Keys to a Successful Broad Low-Cost Strategy   130

When a Low-Cost Strategy Works Best   130

Pitfalls to Avoid in Pursuing a Low-Cost Strategy   131

BROAD DIFFERENTIATION STRATEGIES 132

Managing the Value Chain to Create the Differentiating Attributes   132

Revamping the Value Chain System to Increase Differentiation   134

Delivering Superior Value via a Broad Differentiation Strategy   135

When a Differentiation Strategy Works Best   136

Pitfalls to Avoid in Pursuing a Differentiation Strategy   137

FOCUSED (OR MARKET NICHE) STRATEGIES 138

A Focused Low-Cost Strategy   138

A Focused Differentiation Strategy   140

When a Focused Low-Cost or Focused Differentiation Strategy Is Attractive   140

The Risks of a Focused Low-Cost or Focused Differentiation Strategy   142

BEST-COST (HYBRID) STRATEGIES 142

 When a Best-Cost Strategy Works Best   143

 The Risk of a Best-Cost Strategy   145

THE CONTRASTING FEATURES OF THE GENERIC COMPETITIVE STRATEGIES 145

 Successful Generic Strategies Are Resource-Based   145

 Generic Strategies and the Three Different Approaches to Competitive Advantage   147

ILLUSTRATION CAPSULES

5.1 Vanguard's Path to Becoming the Low-Cost Leader in Investment Management   129

5.2 Clinícas del Azúcar's Focused Low-Cost Strategy   139

5.3 Canada Goose's Focused Differentiation Strategy   141

5.4 Trader Joe's Focused Best-Cost Strategy   144

6 Strengthening a Company's Competitive Position   152

LAUNCHING STRATEGIC OFFENSIVES TO IMPROVE A COMPANY'S MARKET POSITION 154

 Choosing the Basis for Competitive Attack   154

 Choosing Which Rivals to Attack   156

 Blue-Ocean Strategy—a Special Kind of Offensive   156

DEFENSIVE STRATEGIES—PROTECTING MARKET POSITION AND COMPETITIVE ADVANTAGE 157

 Blocking the Avenues Open to Challengers   158

 Signaling Challengers That Retaliation Is Likely   159

TIMING A COMPANY'S STRATEGIC MOVES 159

 The Potential for First-Mover Advantages   159

 The Potential for Late-Mover Advantages or First-Mover Disadvantages   162

 To Be a First Mover or Not   162

STRENGTHENING A COMPANY'S MARKET POSITION VIA ITS SCOPE OF OPERATIONS 163

HORIZONTAL MERGER AND ACQUISITION STRATEGIES 164

 Why Mergers and Acquisitions Sometimes Fail to Produce Anticipated Results   165

VERTICAL INTEGRATION STRATEGIES 167

 The Advantages of a Vertical Integration Strategy   167

  Integrating Backward to Achieve Greater Competitiveness   167

  Integrating Forward to Enhance Competitiveness   168

 The Disadvantages of a Vertical Integration Strategy   169

 Weighing the Pros and Cons of Vertical Integration   170

OUTSOURCING STRATEGIES: NARROWING THE SCOPE OF OPERATIONS 172

 The Risk of Outsourcing Value Chain Activities   173

STRATEGIC ALLIANCES AND PARTNERSHIPS 173

Capturing the Benefits of Strategic Alliances   175

The Drawbacks of Strategic Alliances and
Their Relative Advantages   176

How to Make Strategic Alliances Work   177

ILLUSTRATION CAPSULES

6.1 Bonobos's Blue-Ocean Strategy in the U.S. Men's Fashion Retail Industry   158

6.2 Tinder Swipes Right for First-Mover Success   161

6.3 Walmart's Expansion into E-Commerce via Horizontal Acquisition   166

6.4 Tesla's Vertical Integration Strategy   171

7 Strategies for Competing in International Markets   182

WHY COMPANIES DECIDE TO ENTER FOREIGN MARKETS 184

WHY COMPETING ACROSS NATIONAL BORDERS MAKES STRATEGY MAKING MORE COMPLEX 185

Home-Country Industry Advantages and the Diamond Model   185

Demand Conditions   185

Factor Conditions   186

Related and Supporting Industries   187

Firm Strategy, Structure, and Rivalry   187

Opportunities for Location-Based Advantages   187

The Impact of Government Policies and Economic
Conditions in Host Countries   188

The Risks of Adverse Exchange Rate Shifts   189

Cross-Country Differences in Demographic,
Cultural, and Market Conditions   191

STRATEGIC OPTIONS FOR ENTERING INTERNATIONAL MARKETS 192

Export Strategies   192

Licensing Strategies   193

Franchising Strategies   193

Foreign Subsidiary Strategies   194

Alliance and Joint Venture Strategies   195

The Risks of Strategic Alliances with Foreign Partners   196

INTERNATIONAL STRATEGY: THE THREE MAIN APPROACHES 197

Multidomestic Strategies—a "Think-Local, Act-Local" Approach   198

Global Strategies—a "Think-Global, Act-Global" Approach   199

Transnational Strategies—a "Think-Global, Act-Local" Approach   200

INTERNATIONAL OPERATIONS AND THE QUEST FOR COMPETITIVE ADVANTAGE 202

Using Location to Build Competitive Advantage   203

When to Concentrate Activities in a Few Locations   203

When to Disperse Activities across Many Locations   204

Sharing and Transferring Resources and Capabilities across
Borders to Build Competitive Advantage   204

Benefiting from Cross-Border Coordination   206

CROSS-BORDER STRATEGIC MOVES 206
    Waging a Strategic Offensive   206
    Defending against International Rivals   207
STRATEGIES FOR COMPETING IN THE MARKETS
OF DEVELOPING COUNTRIES 208
    Strategy Options for Competing in Developing-Country Markets   208
DEFENDING AGAINST GLOBAL GIANTS: STRATEGIES FOR
LOCAL COMPANIES IN DEVELOPING COUNTRIES 210

ILLUSTRATION CAPSULES
    7.1 Walgreens Boots Alliance, Inc.: Entering Foreign Markets
         via Alliance Followed by Merger   196
    7.2 Four Seasons Hotels: Local Character, Global Service   202
    7.3 WeChat's Strategy for Defending against International
         Social Media Giants in China   212

8 Corporate Strategy   218

WHAT DOES CRAFTING A DIVERSIFICATION STRATEGY ENTAIL? 220
WHEN TO CONSIDER DIVERSIFYING 220
BUILDING SHAREHOLDER VALUE: THE ULTIMATE
JUSTIFICATION FOR DIVERSIFYING 221
APPROACHES TO DIVERSIFYING THE BUSINESS LINEUP 222
    Diversifying by Acquisition of an Existing Business   222
    Entering a New Line of Business through Internal Development   223
    Using Joint Ventures to Achieve Diversification   223
    Choosing a Mode of Entry   224
        The Question of Critical Resources and Capabilities   224
        The Question of Entry Barriers   224
        The Question of Speed   224
        The Question of Comparative Cost   225
CHOOSING THE DIVERSIFICATION PATH: RELATED
VERSUS UNRELATED BUSINESSES 225
DIVERSIFICATION INTO RELATED BUSINESSES 225
    Identifying Cross-Business Strategic Fit along the Value Chain   228
        Strategic Fit in Supply Chain Activities   229
        Strategic Fit in R&D and Technology Activities   229
        Manufacturing-Related Strategic Fit   229
        Strategic Fit in Sales and Marketing Activities   229
        Distribution-Related Strategic Fit   230
        Strategic Fit in Customer Service Activities   230
    Strategic Fit, Economies of Scope, and Competitive Advantage   230
        From Strategic Fit to Competitive Advantage, Added Profitability, and Gains in Shareholder
        Value   231
DIVERSIFICATION INTO UNRELATED BUSINESSES 233
    Building Shareholder Value via Unrelated Diversification   233
        The Benefits of Astute Corporate Parenting   234
        Judicious Cross-Business Allocation of Financial Resources   235
        Acquiring and Restructuring Undervalued Companies   235

The Path to Greater Shareholder Value through Unrelated
Diversification   236

The Drawbacks of Unrelated Diversification   236

    Demanding Managerial Requirements   236

    Limited Competitive Advantage Potential   237

Misguided Reasons for Pursuing Unrelated Diversification   237

COMBINATION RELATED–UNRELATED DIVERSIFICATION STRATEGIES 238

EVALUATING THE STRATEGY OF A DIVERSIFIED COMPANY 238

Step 1: Evaluating Industry Attractiveness   239

    Calculating Industry-Attractiveness Scores   240

    Interpreting the Industry-Attractiveness Scores   241

Step 2: Evaluating Business Unit Competitive Strength   242

    Calculating Competitive-Strength Scores for Each Business Unit   242

    Interpreting the Competitive-Strength Scores   243

    Using a Nine-Cell Matrix to Simultaneously Portray Industry Attractiveness and Competitive
    Strength   243

Step 3: Determining the Competitive Value of Strategic Fit
in Diversified Companies   246

Step 4: Checking for Good Resource Fit   246

    Financial Resource Fit   247

    Nonfinancial Resource Fit   249

Step 5: Ranking Business Units and Assigning a
Priority for Resource Allocation   250

    Allocating Financial Resources   250

Step 6: Crafting New Strategic Moves to Improve
Overall Corporate Performance   251

    Sticking Closely with the Present Business Lineup   251

    Broadening a Diversified Company's Business Base   251

    Retrenching to a Narrower Diversification Base   253

    Restructuring a Diversified Company's Business Lineup   254

ILLUSTRATION CAPSULES

8.1   The Kraft–Heinz Merger: Pursuing the Benefits of Cross-Business
     Strategic Fit   232

8.2   Restructuring for Better Performance at Hewlett-Packard (HP)   255

9 Ethics, Corporate Social Responsibility, Environmental Sustainability, and Strategy   260

WHAT DO WE MEAN BY *BUSINESS ETHICS? 262*

**WHERE DO ETHICAL STANDARDS COME FROM—ARE THEY
UNIVERSAL OR DEPENDENT ON LOCAL NORMS? 262**

The School of Ethical Universalism   262

The School of Ethical Relativism   263

    The Use of Underage Labor   263

    The Payment of Bribes and Kickbacks   264

    Why Ethical Relativism Is Problematic for Multinational Companies   265

Ethics and Integrative Social Contracts Theory   265

**HOW AND WHY ETHICAL STANDARDS IMPACT THE TASKS
OF CRAFTING AND EXECUTING STRATEGY 266**

DRIVERS OF UNETHICAL BUSINESS STRATEGIES AND BEHAVIOR 267

Faulty Oversight, Enabling the Unscrupulous Pursuit of Personal Gain and Self-Interest   267

Heavy Pressures on Company Managers to Meet Short-Term Performance Targets   269

A Company Culture That Puts Profitability and Business Performance Ahead of Ethical Behavior   270

WHY SHOULD COMPANY STRATEGIES BE ETHICAL? 271

The Moral Case for an Ethical Strategy   271

The Business Case for Ethical Strategies   271

STRATEGY, CORPORATE SOCIAL RESPONSIBILITY, AND ENVIRONMENTAL SUSTAINABILITY 273

The Concepts of Corporate Social Responsibility and Good Corporate Citizenship   274

Corporate Social Responsibility and the Triple Bottom Line   276

What Do We Mean by *Sustainability* and *Sustainable Business Practices?*   279

Crafting Corporate Social Responsibility and Sustainability Strategies   281

The Moral Case for Corporate Social Responsibility and Environmentally Sustainable Business Practices   283

The Business Case for Corporate Social Responsibility and Environmentally Sustainable Business Practices   283

ILLUSTRATION CAPSULES

9.1 Ethical Violations at Uber and their Consequences   268

9.2 How PepsiCo Put Its Ethical Principles into Practice   273

9.3 Warby Parker: Combining Corporate Social Responsibility with Affordable Fashion   277

9.4 Unilever's Focus on Sustainability   282

Section D: Executing the Strategy

10 Building an Organization Capable of Good Strategy Execution: People, Capabilities, and Structure   290

A FRAMEWORK FOR EXECUTING STRATEGY 292

The Principal Components of the Strategy Execution Process   292

What's Covered in Chapters 10, 11, and 12   293

BUILDING AN ORGANIZATION CAPABLE OF GOOD STRATEGY EXECUTION: THREE KEY ACTIONS 294

STAFFING THE ORGANIZATION 296

Putting Together a Strong Management Team   296

Recruiting, Training, and Retaining Capable Employees   297

DEVELOPING AND BUILDING CRITICAL RESOURCES AND CAPABILITIES 299

Three Approaches to Building and Strengthening Capabilities   300

Developing Capabilities Internally   300

Acquiring Capabilities through Mergers and Acquisitions   301

Accessing Capabilities through Collaborative Partnerships   302

The Strategic Role of Employee Training   302

Strategy Execution Capabilities and Competitive Advantage   303

MATCHING ORGANIZATIONAL STRUCTURE TO THE STRATEGY 304

Deciding Which Value Chain Activities to Perform Internally and Which to Outsource   305

Aligning the Firm's Organizational Structure with Its Strategy   307

Making Strategy-Critical Activities the Main Building Blocks of the Organizational Structure   308

Matching Type of Organizational Structure to Strategy Execution Requirements   308

Determining How Much Authority to Delegate   311

Centralized Decision Making: Pros and Cons   312

Decentralized Decision Making: Pros and Cons   313

Capturing Cross-Business Strategic Fit in a Decentralized Structure   314

Providing for Internal Cross-Unit Coordination   314

Facilitating Collaboration with External Partners and Strategic Allies   316

Further Perspectives on Structuring the Work Effort   316

ILLUSTRATION CAPSULES

10.1   Management Development at Deloitte Touche Tohmatsu Limited   298

10.2   Zara's Strategy Execution Capabilities   304

10.3   Which Value Chain Activities Does Apple Outsource and Why?   306

11   Managing Internal Operations   322

ALLOCATING RESOURCES TO THE STRATEGY EXECUTION EFFORT 324

INSTITUTING POLICIES AND PROCEDURES THAT FACILITATE STRATEGY EXECUTION 325

EMPLOYING BUSINESS PROCESS MANAGEMENT TOOLS 327

Promoting Operating Excellence: Three Powerful Business Process Management Tools   327

Business Process Reengineering   327

Total Quality Management Programs   328

Six Sigma Quality Control Programs   329

The Difference between Business Process Reengineering and Continuous-Improvement Programs Like Six Sigma and TQM   331

Capturing the Benefits of Initiatives to Improve Operations   332

INSTALLING INFORMATION AND OPERATING SYSTEMS 333

Instituting Adequate Information Systems, Performance Tracking, and Controls   334

Monitoring Employee Performance   335

USING REWARDS AND INCENTIVES TO PROMOTE BETTER STRATEGY EXECUTION 335

Incentives and Motivational Practices That Facilitate Good Strategy Execution   336

Striking the Right Balance between Rewards and Punishment   337

Linking Rewards to Achieving the Right Outcomes   339

Additional Guidelines for Designing Incentive Compensation Systems   340

ILLUSTRATION CAPSULES

11.1 Charleston Area Medical Center's Six Sigma Program   331

11.2 How Wegmans Rewards and Motivates its Employees   338

11.3 Nucor Corporation: Tying Incentives Directly to Strategy Execution   341

12 Corporate Culture and Leadership   346

INSTILLING A CORPORATE CULTURE CONDUCIVE TO GOOD STRATEGY EXECUTION 348

Identifying the Key Features of a Company's Corporate Culture   350

The Role of Core Values and Ethics   350

Embedding Behavioral Norms in the Organization and Perpetuating the Culture   351

The Role of Stories   352

Forces That Cause a Company's Culture to Evolve   352

The Presence of Company Subcultures   353

Strong versus Weak Cultures   353

Strong-Culture Companies   353

Weak-Culture Companies   354

Why Corporate Cultures Matter to the Strategy Execution Process   355

Healthy Cultures That Aid Good Strategy Execution   356

High-Performance Cultures   356

Adaptive Cultures   356

Unhealthy Cultures That Impede Good Strategy Execution   358

Change-Resistant Cultures   358

Politicized Cultures   358

Insular, Inwardly Focused Cultures   358

Unethical and Greed-Driven Cultures   359

Incompatible, Clashing Subcultures   359

Changing a Problem Culture   359

Making a Compelling Case for Culture Change   360

Substantive Culture-Changing Actions   361

Symbolic Culture-Changing Actions   362

How Long Does It Take to Change a Problem Culture?   362

LEADING THE STRATEGY EXECUTION PROCESS 363

Staying on Top of How Well Things Are Going   364

Mobilizing the Effort for Excellence in Strategy Execution   365

Leading the Process of Making Corrective Adjustments   366

A FINAL WORD ON LEADING THE PROCESS OF CRAFTING AND EXECUTING STRATEGY 367

ILLUSTRATION CAPSULES

12.1 Strong Guiding Principles Drive the High-Performance Culture at Epic   349

12.2 Driving Cultural Change at Goldman Sachs   363

PART 2 Cases in Crafting and Executing Strategy

Section A: Crafting Strategy in Single-Business Companies

connect **1 Mystic Monk Coffee** C-2

David L. Turnipseed, University of South Alabama

connect **2 Airbnb In 2018** C-6

John D. Varlaro, Johnson & Wales University
John E. Gamble, Texas A&M University–Corpus Christi

3 Wil's Grill C-11

Leonard R. Hostetter, Northern Arizona University
Nita Paden, Northern Arizona University

connect **4 Costco Wholesale in 2018: Mission, Business Model, and Strategy** C-17

Arthur A. Thompson Jr., The University of Alabama

connect **5 Competition in the Craft Beer Industry in 2018** C-41

John D. Varlaro, Johnson & Wales University
John E. Gamble, Texas A&M University–Corpus Christi

6 Fixer Upper: Expanding the Magnolia Brand C-51

Rochelle R. Brunson, Baylor University
Marlene M. Reed, Baylor University

connect **7 Under Armour's Turnaround Strategy in 2018: Efforts to Revive North American Sales and Profitability** C-56

Arthur A. Thompson, The University of Alabama

8 MoviePass—Are Subscribers Loving It to Death? C-80

Gretchen Johnson, The University of Alabama
Lou Marino, The University of Alabama
McKenna Marino, The University of Alabama

9 TOMS Shoes: Expanding Its Successful One For One Business Model C-92

Margaret A. Peteraf, Tuck School of Business at Dartmouth
Sean Zhang and Carry S. Resor, Research Assistants, Dartmouth College

10 Lola's Market: Capturing A New Generation C-101

Katherine Gonzalez, MBA Student, Sonoma State University
Sergio Canavati, Sonoma State University
Armand Gilinsky, Sonoma State University

11 iRobot in 2018: Can the Company Keep the Magic? C-107

David L. Turnipseed, University of South Alabama
John E. Gamble, Texas A&M University-Corpus Christi

12 Chipotle Mexican Grill's Strategy in 2018: Will the New CEO Be Able to Rebuild Customer Trust and Revive Sales Growth?   C-120

Arthur A. Thompson, The University of Alabama

13 Twitter Inc. in 2018: Too Little Too Late?   C-138

David L. Turnipseed, University of South Alabama

14 Netflix's Strategy in 2018: Does the Company Have Sufficient Competitive Strength to Fight Off Aggressive Rivals?   C-149

Arthur A. Thompson, The University of Alabama

15 Walmart's Expansion into Specialty Online Retailing   C-162

Rochelle R. Brunson, Baylor University
Marlene M. Reed, Baylor University

16 Amazon.com, Inc.: Driving Disruptive Change in the U.S. Grocery Market   C-171

Syeda Maseeha Qumer, ICFAI Business School, Hyderabad
Debapratim Purkayastha, ICFAI Business School, Hyderabad

17 Aliexpress: Can It Mount a Global Challenge to Amazon?   C-184

A. J. Strickland, The University of Alabama
Muxin Li, Faculty Scholar 2018, The University of Alabama
Joyce L. Meyer, The University of Alabama

18 Tesla Motors in 2018: Will the New Model 3 Save the Company?   C-191

Arthur A. Thompson, The University of Alabama

19 Mattel Incorporated in 2018: Can Ynon Kreiz Save the Toys?   C-216

Randall D. Harris, Texas A&M University—Corpus Christi

20 Shearwater Adventures Ltd.   C-232

A.J. Strickland, The University of Alabama
Ross N. Faires, MBA Student, The University of Alabama

21 TJX Companies: It's Strategy in Off-Price Home Accessories and Apparel Retailing   C-240

David L. Turnipseed, University of South Alabama

22 IKEA's International Marketing Strategy in China   C-251

Debapratim Purkayastha, ICFAI Business School, Hyderabad
Benudhar Sahu, ICFAI Business School, Hyderabad

Section B: Crafting Strategy in Diversified Companies

23 PepsiCo's Diversification Strategy in 2018: Will the Company's New Businesses Restore its Growth?   C-265

John E. Gamble, Texas A&M University–Corpus Christi

connect

24 The Walt Disney Company: Its Diversification Strategy in 2018 C-277

John E. Gamble, Texas A&M University-Corpus Christi

Section C: Implementing and Executing Strategy

connect

25 Robin Hood C-291

Joseph Lampel, Alliance Manchester Business School

26 Dilemma at Devil's Den C-293

Allan R. Cohen, Babson College
Kim Johnson, Babson College

connect

27 Nucor Corporation in 2018: Contending with the Challenges of Low-Cost Foreign Imports and Launching Initiatives to Grow Sales and Market Share C-296

Arthur A. Thompson, The University of Alabama

28 Vail Resorts, Inc. C-331

Herman L. Boschken, San Jose State University

connect

29 Starbucks in 2018: Striving for Operational Excellence and Innovation Agility C-351

Arthur A. Thompson, The University of Alabama

Section D: Strategy, Ethics, and Social Responsibility

30 Concussions in Collegiate and Professional Football: Who Has Responsibility to Protect Players? C-377

David L. Turnipseed, University of South Alabama
A.J. Strickland, The University of Alabama

31 Chaos at Uber: The New CEO's Challenge C-392

Syeda Maseeha Qumer, ICFAI Business School, Hyderabad
Debapratim Purkayastha, ICFAI Business School, Hyderabad

connect

32 Profiting from Pain: Business and the U.S. Opioid Epidemic C-406

Anne T. Lawrence, San Jose State University

Guide to Case Analysis CA-1

INDEXES **Company** I-1
Name I-8
Subject I-13

PART 1

Concepts and Techniques for Crafting and Executing Strategy

chapter 1

What Is Strategy and Why Is It Important?

Learning Objectives

This chapter will help you

LO 1-1 Explain what we mean by a company's *strategy* and why it needs to differ from competitors' strategies.

LO 1-2 Explain the concept of a *sustainable competitive advantage*.

LO 1-3 Identify the five most basic strategic approaches for setting a company apart from its rivals.

LO 1-4 Explain why a company's strategy tends to evolve.

LO 1-5 Identify what constitutes a viable business model.

LO 1-6 Identify the three tests of a winning strategy.

©Roy Scott/Ikon Images/Getty Images

Strategy is about setting yourself apart from the competition.

Michael Porter—*Professor and consultant*

Strategy means making clear-cut choices about how to compete.

Jack Welch—*Former CEO of General Electric*

I believe that people make their own luck by great preparation and good strategy.

Jack Canfield—*Corporate trainer and entrepreneur*

According to *The Economist,* a leading publication on business, economics, and international affairs, "In business, strategy is king. Leadership and hard work are all very well and luck is mighty useful, but it is strategy that makes or breaks a firm."[1] Luck and circumstance can explain why some companies are blessed with initial, short-lived success. But only a well-crafted, well-executed, constantly evolving strategy can explain why an elite set of companies somehow manage to rise to the top and stay there, year after year, pleasing their customers, shareholders, and other stakeholders alike in the process. Companies such as Apple, Disney, Starbucks, Alphabet (parent company of Google), Berkshire Hathaway, General Electric, and Amazon come to mind—but long-lived success is not just the province of U.S. companies. Diverse kinds of companies, both large and small, from many different countries have been able to sustain strong performance records, including Denmark's Lego Group, the United Kingdom's HSBC (in banking), Dubai's Emirates Airlines, Switzerland's Rolex China Mobile (in telecommunications), and India's Tata Steel.

In this opening chapter, we define the concept of strategy and describe its many facets. We introduce you to the concept of competitive advantage and explore the tight linkage between a company's strategy and its quest for competitive advantage. We will also explain why company strategies are partly proactive and partly reactive, why they evolve over time, and the relationship between a company's strategy and its business model. We conclude the chapter with a discussion of what sets a winning strategy apart from others and why that strategy should also pass the test of moral scrutiny. By the end of this chapter, you will have a clear idea of why the tasks of crafting and executing strategy are core management functions and why excellent execution of an excellent strategy is the most reliable recipe for turning a company into a standout performer over the long term.

WHAT DO WE MEAN BY *STRATEGY*?

● ● ● ●

A company's **strategy** is the coordinated set of actions that its managers take in order to outperform the company's competitors and achieve superior profitability. The objective of a well-crafted strategy is not merely temporary competitive success and profits in the short run, but rather the sort of lasting success that can support growth and secure the company's future over the long term. Achieving this entails making a managerial commitment to a coherent array of well-considered choices about how to compete.[2] These include

- *How* to position the company in the marketplace.
- *How* to attract customers.
- *How* to compete against rivals.
- *How* to achieve the company's performance targets.
- *How* to capitalize on opportunities to grow the business.
- *How* to respond to changing economic and market conditions.

● **LO 1-1**

Explain what we mean by a company's *strategy* and why it needs to differ from competitors' strategies.

In most industries, companies have considerable freedom in choosing the *hows* of strategy.[3] Some companies strive to achieve lower costs than rivals, while others aim for product superiority or more personalized customer service dimensions that rivals cannot match. Some companies opt for wide product lines, while others concentrate their energies on a narrow product lineup. Some deliberately confine their operations to local or regional markets; others opt to compete nationally, internationally (several countries), or globally (all or most of the major country markets worldwide). Choices of how best to compete against rivals have to be made in light of the firm's resources and capabilities and in light of the competitive approaches rival companies are employing.

Strategy Is about Competing Differently

Mimicking the strategies of successful industry rivals—with either copycat product offerings or maneuvers to stake out the same market position—rarely works. Rather, every company's strategy needs to have some distinctive element that draws in customers and provides a competitive edge. Strategy, at its essence, is about competing differently—doing what rival firms *don't* do or what rival firms *can't* do.[4] This does not mean that the key elements of a company's strategy have to be 100 percent different, but rather that they must differ in at least *some important respects*. A strategy stands a better chance of succeeding when it is predicated on actions, business approaches, and competitive moves aimed at (1) appealing to buyers in ways that *set a company apart from its rivals* and (2) staking out a market position that is not crowded with strong competitors.

Strategy is about competing differently from rivals—doing what competitors don't do or, even better, doing what they can't do!

A company's strategy provides direction and guidance, in terms of not only what the company *should* do but also what it *should not* do. Knowing what not to do can be as important as knowing what to do, strategically. At best, making the wrong strategic moves will prove a distraction and a waste of company resources. At worst, it can bring about unintended long-term consequences that put the company's very survival at risk.

Figure 1.1 illustrates the broad types of actions and approaches that often characterize a company's strategy in a particular business or industry. For a more concrete example, see Illustration Capsule 1.1 describing the elements of Apple, Inc.'s successful strategy.

FIGURE 1.1   Identifying a Company's Strategy—What to Look For

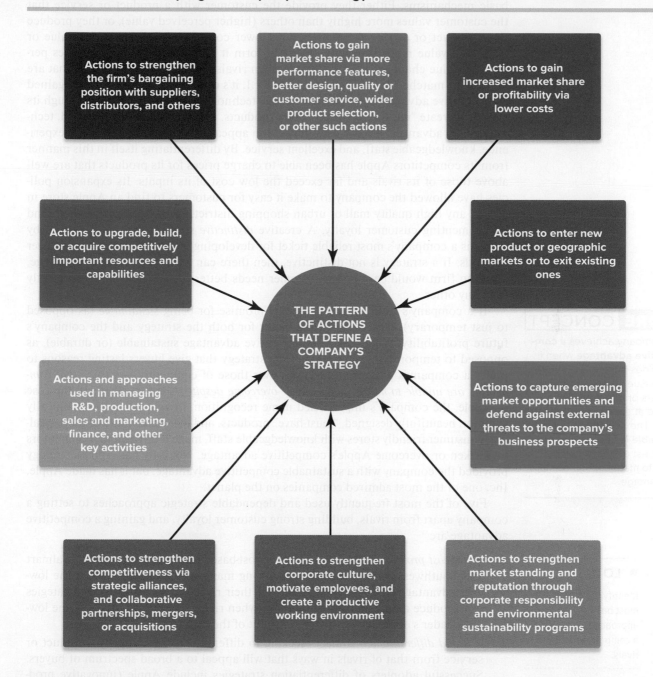

Strategy and the Quest for Competitive Advantage

The heart and soul of any strategy are the actions in the marketplace that managers take to gain a competitive advantage over rivals. A company has a **competitive advantage** whenever it has some type of edge over rivals in attracting buyers and coping with competitive forces. A competitive advantage is essential for realizing greater marketplace success and higher profitability over the long term.

● **LO 1-2**

Explain the concept of a *sustainable competitive advantage.*

There are many routes to competitive advantage, but they all involve one of two basic mechanisms. Either they provide the customer with a product or service that the customer values more highly than others (higher perceived value), or they produce their product or service more efficiently (lower costs). Delivering superior value or delivering value more efficiently—whatever form it takes—nearly always requires performing value chain activities differently than rivals and building capabilities that are not readily matched. In Illustration Capsule 1.1, it's evident that Apple, Inc. has gained a competitive advantage over its rivals in the technological device industry through its efforts to create "must have," exciting new products, that are beautifully designed, technologically advanced, easy to use, and sold in appealing stores that offer a fun experience, knowledgeable staff, and excellent service. By differentiating itself in this manner from its competitors Apple has been able to charge prices for its products that are well above those of its rivals and far exceed the low cost of its inputs. Its expansion policies have allowed the company to make it easy for customers to find an Apple store in almost any high quality mall or urban shopping district, further enhancing the brand and cementing customer loyalty. A creative *distinctive* strategy such as that used by Apple is a company's most reliable ticket for developing a competitive advantage over its rivals. If a strategy is not distinctive, then there can be no competitive advantage, since no firm would be meeting customer needs better or operating more efficiently than any other.

If a company's competitive edge holds promise for being *sustainable* (as opposed to just temporary), then so much the better for both the strategy and the company's future profitability. What makes a competitive advantage **sustainable** (or durable), as opposed to temporary, are elements of the strategy that give buyers lasting reasons to prefer a company's products or services over those of competitors—*reasons that competitors are unable to nullify, duplicate, or overcome despite their best efforts.* In the case of Apple, the company's unparalleled name recognition, its reputation for technically superior, beautifully designed, "must-have" products, and the accessibility of the appealing, consumer-friendly stores with knowledgeable staff, make it difficult for competitors to weaken or overcome Apple's competitive advantage. Not only has Apple's strategy provided the company with a sustainable competitive advantage, but it has made Apple, Inc. one of the most admired companies on the planet.

Five of the most frequently used and dependable strategic approaches to setting a company apart from rivals, building strong customer loyalty, and gaining a competitive advantage are

1. *A low-cost provider strategy*—achieving a cost-based advantage over rivals. Walmart and Southwest Airlines have earned strong market positions because of the low-cost advantages they have achieved over their rivals. Low-cost provider strategies can produce a durable competitive edge when rivals find it hard to match the low-cost leader's approach to driving costs out of the business.

2. *A broad differentiation strategy*—seeking to differentiate the company's product or service from that of rivals in ways that will appeal to a broad spectrum of buyers. Successful adopters of differentiation strategies include Apple (innovative products), Johnson & Johnson in baby products (product reliability), Rolex (luxury and prestige), and BMW (engineering design and performance). One way to sustain this type of competitive advantage is to be sufficiently innovative to thwart the efforts of clever rivals to copy or closely imitate the product offering.

3. *A focused low-cost strategy*—concentrating on a narrow buyer segment (or market niche) and outcompeting rivals by having lower costs and thus being able to serve

LO 1-3

Identify the five most basic strategic approaches for setting a company apart from rivals.

Apple Inc.: Exemplifying a Successful Strategy

Apple Inc. is one of the most profitable companies in the world, with revenues of more than $225 billion. For more than 10 consecutive years, it has ranked number one on Fortune's list of the "World's Most Admired Companies." Given the worldwide popularity of its products and services, along with its reputation for superior technological innovation and design capabilities, this is not surprising. The key elements of Apple's successful strategy include:

- *Designing and developing its own operating systems, hardware, application software, and services.* This allows Apple to bring the best user experience to its customers through products and solutions with innovative design, superior ease-of-use, and seamless integration across platforms. The ability to use services like iCloud across devices incentivizes users to join Apple's technological ecosystem and has been critical to fostering brand loyalty.

- *Continuously investing in research and development (R&D) and frequently introducing products.* Apple has invested heavily in R&D, spending upwards of $11 billion a year, to ensure a continual and timely injection of competitive products, services, and technologies into the marketplace. Its successful products and services include the Mac, iPod, iPhone, iPad, Apple Watch, Apple TV, and Apple Music. It is currently investing in an Apple electric car and Apple solar energy.

- *Strategically locating its stores and staffing them with knowledgeable personnel.* By operating its own Apple stores and positioning them in high-traffic locations, Apple is better equipped to provide its customers with the optimal buying experience. The stores' employees are well versed in the value of the hardware and software integration and demonstrate the unique solutions available on its products. This high-quality sale and after-sale supports allows Apple to continuously attract new and retain existing customers.

- *Expanding Apple's reach domestically and internationally.* Apple operates globally in 500 retail stores across 18 countries. During fiscal year 2017, 63 percent of Apple's revenue came from international sales.

- *Maintaining a quality brand image, supported by premium pricing.* Although the computer industry is incredibly price competitive, Apple has managed to sustain a competitive edge by focusing on its inimitable value proposition and deliberately keeping a price

©Kerstin Meyer/Moment Mobile/Getty Images

premium—thus creating an aura of prestige around its products.

- *Committing to corporate social responsibility and sustainability through supplier relations.* Apple's strict Code of Conduct requires its suppliers to comply with several standards regarding safe working conditions, fair treatment of workers, and environmentally safe manufacturing.

- *Cultivating a diverse workforce rooted in transparency.* Apple believes that diverse teams make innovation possible and is dedicated to incorporating a broad range of perspectives in its workforce. Every year, Apple publishes data showing the representation of women and different race and ethnicity groups across functions.

Note: Developed with Shawnda Lee Duvigneaud
Sources: Apple 10-K, Company website.

niche members at a lower price. Private-label manufacturers of food, health and beauty products, and nutritional supplements use their low-cost advantage to offer supermarket buyers lower prices than those demanded by producers of branded products. IKEA's emphasis on modular furniture, ready for assembly, makes it a focused low-cost player in the furniture market.

4. *A focused differentiation strategy*—concentrating on a narrow buyer segment (or market niche) and outcompeting rivals by offering buyers customized attributes that meet their specialized needs and tastes better than rivals' products. Lululemon, for example, specializes in high-quality yoga clothing and the like, attracting a devoted set of buyers in the process. Tesla Inc, with its electric cars, LinkedIn specializing in the business and employment aspects of social networking, and Goya Foods in Hispanic specialty food products provide some other examples of this strategy.

5. *A best-cost provider strategy*—giving customers more value for the money by satisfying their expectations on key quality features, performance, and/or service attributes while beating their price expectations. This approach is a hybrid strategy that blends elements of low-cost provider and differentiation strategies; the aim is to have lower costs than rivals while simultaneously offering better differentiating attributes. Target is an example of a company that is known for its hip product design (a reputation it built by featuring limited edition lines by designers such as Rodarte, Victoria Beckham, and Jason Wu), as well as a more appealing shopping ambience for discount store shoppers. Its dual focus on low costs as well as differentiation shows how a best-cost provider strategy can offer customers great value for the money.

Winning a *sustainable* competitive edge over rivals with any of the preceding five strategies generally hinges as much on building competitively valuable expertise and capabilities that rivals cannot readily match as it does on having a distinctive product offering. Clever rivals can nearly always copy the attributes of a popular product or service, but for rivals to match the experience, know-how, and specialized capabilities that a company has developed and perfected over a long period of time is substantially harder to do and takes much longer. The success of the Swatch in watches, for example, was driven by impressive design, marketing, and engineering capabilities, while Apple has demonstrated outstanding product innovation capabilities in digital music players, smartphones, and e-readers. Hyundai has become the world's fastest-growing automaker as a result of its advanced manufacturing processes and unparalleled quality control systems. Capabilities such as these have been hard for competitors to imitate or best.

Why a Company's Strategy Evolves over Time

● **LO 1-4**

Explain why a company's strategy tends to evolve.

The appeal of a strategy that yields a sustainable competitive advantage is that it offers the potential for a more enduring edge than a temporary advantage over rivals. But sustainability is a relative term, with some advantages lasting longer than others. And regardless of how sustainable a competitive advantage may appear to be at a given point in time, conditions change. Even a substantial competitive advantage over rivals may crumble in the face of drastic shifts in market conditions or disruptive innovations. Therefore, managers of every company must be willing and ready to modify the strategy in response to changing market conditions, advancing technology, unexpected moves by competitors, shifting buyer needs, emerging market opportunities, and new ideas for improving the strategy. Most of the time, a company's strategy evolves incrementally as management fine-tunes various pieces of the strategy and adjusts the strategy in response to unfolding events.[5] However, on occasion, major strategy shifts are called for, such as when the strategy is clearly failing or when industry conditions change in dramatic ways. Industry environments characterized by high-velocity change require companies to repeatedly adapt their strategies.[6] For example, companies in industries with rapid-fire advances in technology like 3-D printing, shale fracking, and genetic engineering often find it essential to adjust key elements of their strategies several times a year. When the technological change is drastic enough to "disrupt" the entire industry, displacing market leaders and altering market boundaries, companies may find it necessary to "reinvent" entirely their approach to providing value to their customers.

Regardless of whether a company's strategy changes gradually or swiftly, the important point is that the task of crafting strategy is not a one-time event but always a work in progress. Adapting to new conditions and constantly evaluating what is working well enough to continue and what needs to be improved are normal parts of the strategy-making process, resulting in an *evolving strategy.*[7]

A Company's Strategy Is Partly Proactive and Partly Reactive

The evolving nature of a company's strategy means that the typical company strategy is a blend of (1) *proactive,* planned initiatives to improve the company's financial performance and secure a competitive edge and (2) *reactive* responses to unanticipated developments and fresh market conditions. The biggest portion of a company's current strategy flows from previously initiated actions that have proven themselves in the marketplace and newly launched initiatives aimed at edging out rivals and boosting financial performance. This part of management's action plan for running the company is its **deliberate strategy,** consisting of proactive strategy elements that are both planned and realized as planned (while other planned strategy elements may not work out and are abandoned in consequence)—see Figure 1.2.[8]

But managers must always be willing to supplement or modify the proactive strategy elements with as-needed reactions to unanticipated conditions. Inevitably, there will be occasions when market and competitive conditions take an unexpected turn that calls for some kind of strategic reaction. Hence, *a portion of a company's strategy is always developed on the fly,* coming as a response to fresh strategic maneuvers on the part of rival firms, unexpected shifts in customer requirements, fast-changing technological developments, newly appearing market opportunities, a changing political or economic climate, or other unanticipated happenings in the surrounding environment. These adaptive strategy adjustments make up the firm's **emergent strategy.** A company's strategy *in toto* (its **realized strategy**) thus tends to be a *combination* of proactive and reactive elements, with certain strategy elements being *abandoned* because they have become obsolete or ineffective. A company's realized strategy can be observed in the pattern of its actions over time, which is a far better indicator than any of its strategic plans on paper or any public pronouncements about its strategy.

Strategy and Ethics: Passing the Test of Moral Scrutiny

In choosing among strategic alternatives, company managers are well advised to embrace actions that can pass the test of moral scrutiny. Just keeping a company's strategic actions within the bounds of what is legal does not mean the strategy is

---

Changing circumstances and ongoing management efforts to improve the strategy cause a company's strategy to evolve over time—a condition that makes the task of crafting strategy a *work in progress,* not a one-time event.

A company's strategy is shaped partly by management analysis and choice and partly by the necessity of adapting and learning by doing.

CORE CONCEPT

A company's **deliberate strategy** consists of *proactive* strategy elements that are planned; its **emergent strategy** consists of *reactive* strategy elements that emerge as changing conditions warrant.

A strategy cannot be considered ethical just because it involves actions that are legal. To meet the standard of being ethical, a strategy must entail actions and behavior that can pass moral scrutiny in the sense of *not being* deceitful, unfair or harmful to others, disreputable, or unreasonably damaging to the environment.

FIGURE 1.2   A Company's Strategy Is a Blend of Proactive Initiatives and Reactive Adjustments

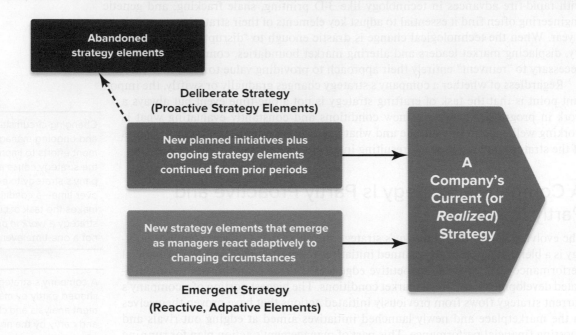

ethical. Ethical and moral standards are not fully governed by what is legal. Rather, they involve issues of "right" versus "wrong" and duty—what one should do. A strategy is ethical only if it does not entail actions that cross the moral line from "can do" to "should not do." For example, a company's strategy *definitely* crosses into the "should not do" zone and cannot pass moral scrutiny if it entails actions and behaviors that are deceitful, unfair or harmful to others, disreputable, or unreasonably damaging to the environment. A company's strategic actions cross over into the "should not do" zone and are likely to be deemed unethical when (1) they reflect badly on the company or (2) they adversely impact the legitimate interests and well-being of shareholders, customers, employees, suppliers, the communities where it operates, and society at large or (3) they provoke public outcries about inappropriate or "irresponsible" actions, behavior, or outcomes.

Admittedly, it is not always easy to categorize a given strategic behavior as ethical or unethical. Many strategic actions fall in a gray zone and can be deemed ethical or unethical depending on how high one sets the bar for what qualifies as ethical behavior. For example, is it ethical for advertisers of alcoholic products to place ads in media having an audience of as much as 50 percent underage viewers? Is it ethical for companies to employ undocumented workers who may have been brought to the United States as children? Is it ethical for Nike, Under Armour, and other makers of athletic wear to pay a university athletic department large sums of money as an "inducement" for the university's athletic teams to use their brand of products? Is it ethical for pharmaceutical manufacturers to charge higher prices for life-saving drugs in some countries than they charge in others? Is it ethical for a company to ignore the damage done to the environment by its operations in a particular country, even though they are in compliance with current environmental regulations in that country?

Senior executives with strong ethical convictions are generally proactive in linking strategic action and ethics; they forbid the pursuit of ethically questionable business opportunities and insist that all aspects of company strategy are in accord with high ethical standards. They make it clear that all company personnel are expected to act with integrity, and they put organizational checks and balances into place to monitor behavior, enforce ethical codes of conduct, and provide guidance to employees regarding any gray areas. Their commitment to ethical business conduct is genuine, not hypocritical lip service.

The reputational and financial damage that unethical strategies and behavior can do is substantial. When a company is put in the public spotlight because certain personnel are alleged to have engaged in misdeeds, unethical behavior, fraudulent accounting, or criminal behavior, its revenues and stock price are usually hammered hard. Many customers and suppliers shy away from doing business with a company that engages in sleazy practices or turns a blind eye to its employees' illegal or unethical behavior. Repulsed by unethical strategies or behavior, wary customers take their business elsewhere and wary suppliers tread carefully. Moreover, employees with character and integrity do not want to work for a company whose strategies are shady or whose executives lack character and integrity. Consequently, solid business reasons exist for companies to shun the use of unethical strategy elements. Besides, immoral or unethical actions are just plain wrong.

A COMPANY'S STRATEGY AND ITS BUSINESS MODEL

At the core of every sound strategy is the company's **business model.** A business model is management's blueprint for delivering a valuable product or service to customers in a manner that will generate revenues sufficient to cover costs and yield an attractive profit.[9] The two elements of a company's business model are (1) its *customer value proposition* and (2) its *profit formula.* The customer value proposition lays out the company's approach to satisfying buyer wants and needs at a price customers will consider a good value. The profit formula describes the company's approach to determining a cost structure that will allow for acceptable profits, given the pricing tied to its customer value proposition. Figure 1.3 illustrates the elements of the business model in terms of what is known as the *value-price-cost framework.*[10] As the framework indicates,

● **LO 1-5**

Identify what constitutes a viable business model.

FIGURE 1.3   The Business Model and the Value-Price-Cost Framework

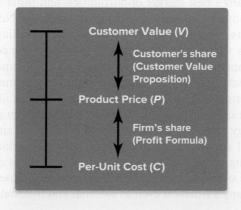

Customer Value (V)

Customer's share
(Customer Value
Proposition)

Product Price (P)

Firm's share
(Profit Formula)

Per-Unit Cost (C)

the customer value proposition can be expressed as $V - P$, which is essentially the customers' perception of how much value they are getting for the money. The profit formula, on a per-unit basis, can be expressed as $P - C$. Plainly, from a customer perspective, the greater the value delivered (V) and the lower the price (P), the more attractive is the company's value proposition. On the other hand, the lower the costs (C), given the customer value proposition ($V - P$), the greater the ability of the business model to be a moneymaker. Thus the profit formula reveals how efficiently a company can meet customer wants and needs and deliver on the value proposition. The nitty-gritty issue surrounding a company's business model is whether it can execute its customer value proposition profitably. Just because company managers have crafted a strategy for competing and running the business does not automatically mean that the strategy will lead to profitability—it may or it may not.

Aircraft engine manufacturer Rolls-Royce employs an innovative "power-by-the-hour" business model that charges airlines leasing fees for engine use, maintenance, and repairs based on actual hours flown. The company retains ownership of the engines and is able to minimize engine maintenance costs through the use of sophisticated sensors that optimize maintenance and repair schedules. Gillette's business model in razor blades involves selling a "master product"—the razor—at an attractively low price and then making money on repeat purchases of razor blades that can be produced cheaply and sold at high profit margins. Printer manufacturers like Hewlett-Packard, Canon, and Epson pursue much the same business model as Gillette—selling printers at a low (virtually break-even) price and making large profit margins on the repeat purchases of ink cartridges and other printer supplies. McDonald's invented the business model for fast food—providing value to customers in the form of economical quick-service meals at clean, convenient locations. Its profit formula involves such elements as standardized cost-efficient store design, stringent specifications for ingredients, detailed operating procedures for each unit, sizable investment in human resources and training, and heavy reliance on advertising and in-store promotions to drive volume. Illustration Capsule 1.2 describes three contrasting business models in radio broadcasting.

WHAT MAKES A STRATEGY A WINNER?

Three tests can be applied to determine whether a strategy is a *winning strategy:*

1. **The Fit Test:** *How well does the strategy fit the company's situation?* To qualify as a winner, a strategy has to be well matched to industry and competitive conditions, a company's best market opportunities, and other pertinent aspects of the business environment in which the company operates. No strategy can work well unless it exhibits good *external fit* with respect to prevailing market conditions. At the same time, a winning strategy must be tailored to the company's resources and competitive capabilities and be supported by a complementary set of functional activities (i.e., activities in the realms of supply chain management, operations, sales and marketing, and so on). That is, it must also exhibit *internal fit* and be compatible with a company's ability to execute the strategy in a competent manner. Unless a strategy exhibits good fit with both the external and internal aspects of a company's overall situation, it is likely to be an underperformer and fall short of producing winning results. Winning strategies also exhibit *dynamic fit* in the sense that they evolve over time in a manner that maintains close and effective alignment with the company's situation even as external and internal conditions change.[11]

Pandora, SiriusXM, and Over-the-Air Broadcast Radio: Three Contrasting Business Models

©Ramin Talaie/Corbis via Getty Images

	Pandora	SiriusXM	Over-the-Air Radio Broadcasters
Customer value proposition	• Through free-of-charge Internet radio service, allowed PC, tablet computer, and smartphone users to create up to 100 personalized music and comedy stations. • Utilized algorithms to generate playlists based on users' predicted music preferences. • Offered programming interrupted by brief, occasional ads; eliminated advertising for Pandora One subscribers.	• For a monthly subscription fee, provided satellite-based music, news, sports, national and regional weather, traffic reports in limited areas, and talk radio programming. • Also offered subscribers streaming Internet channels and the ability to create personalized commercial-free stations for online and mobile listening. • Offered programming interrupted only by brief, occasional ads.	• Provided free-of-charge music, national and local news, local traffic reports, national and local weather, and talk radio programming. • Included frequent programming interruption for ads.
Profit formula	*Revenue generation:* Display, audio, and video ads targeted to different audiences and sold to local and national buyers; subscription revenues generated from an advertising-free option called Pandora One. *Cost structure:* Fixed costs associated with developing software for computers, tablets, and smartphones. Fixed and variable costs related to operating data centers to support streaming network, content royalties, marketing, and support activities.	*Revenue generation:* Monthly subscription fees, sales of satellite radio equipment, and advertising revenues. *Cost structure:* Fixed costs associated with operating a satellite-based music delivery service and streaming Internet service. Fixed and variable costs related to programming and content royalties, marketing, and support activities.	*Revenue generation:* Advertising sales to national and local businesses. *Cost structure:* Fixed costs associated with terrestrial broadcasting operations. Fixed and variable costs related to local news reporting, advertising sales operations, network affiliate fees, programming and content royalties, commercial production activities, and support activities.

(Continued)

Pandora	SiriusXM	Over-the-Air Radio Broadcasters
Profit margin: Profitability dependent on generating sufficient advertising revenues and subscription revenues to cover costs and provide attractive profits.	*Profit margin:* Profitability dependent on attracting a sufficiently large number of subscribers to cover costs and provide attractive profits.	*Profit margin:* Profitability dependent on generating sufficient advertising revenues to cover costs and provide attractive profits.

A **winning strategy** must pass three tests:
1. The fit test
2. The competitive advantage test
3. The performance test

2. **The Competitive Advantage Test:** *Is the strategy helping the company achieve a competitive advantage? Is the competitive advantage likely to be sustainable?* Strategies that fail to achieve a competitive advantage over rivals are unlikely to produce superior performance. And unless the competitive advantage is sustainable, superior performance is unlikely to last for more than a brief period of time. Winning strategies enable a company to achieve a competitive advantage over key rivals that is long-lasting. The bigger and more durable the competitive advantage, the more powerful it is.

3. **The Performance Test:** *Is the strategy producing superior company performance?* The mark of a winning strategy is strong company performance. Two kinds of performance indicators tell the most about the caliber of a company's strategy: (1) competitive strength and market standing and (2) profitability and financial strength. Above-average financial performance or gains in market share, competitive position, or profitability are signs of a winning strategy.

Strategies—either existing or proposed—that come up short on one or more of the preceding tests are plainly less desirable than strategies passing all three tests with flying colors. New initiatives that don't seem to match the company's internal and external situations should be scrapped before they come to fruition, while existing strategies must be scrutinized on a regular basis to ensure they have good fit, offer a competitive advantage, and are contributing to above-average performance or performance improvements. Failure to pass one or more of the three tests should prompt managers to make immediate changes in an existing strategy.

WHY CRAFTING AND EXECUTING STRATEGY ARE IMPORTANT TASKS

● ● ● ●

Crafting and executing strategy are top-priority managerial tasks for two big reasons. First, a clear and reasoned strategy is management's prescription for doing business, its road map to competitive advantage, its game plan for pleasing customers, and its formula for improving performance. High-performing enterprises are nearly always the product of astute, creative, and proactive strategy making. Companies don't get to the top of the industry rankings or stay there with flawed strategies, copycat strategies, or timid attempts to try to do better. Only a handful of companies can boast of hitting home runs in the marketplace due to lucky breaks or the good fortune of having stumbled into the right market at the right time with the right product. Even if this is the case, success will not be lasting unless the companies subsequently craft a strategy that capitalizes on their luck, builds on what is working, and discards the rest. So there can be little argument that the process of crafting a company's strategy matters—and matters a lot.

Second, even the best-conceived strategies will result in performance shortfalls if they are not executed proficiently. The processes of crafting and executing strategies must go hand in hand if a company is to be successful in the long term. The chief executive officer of one successful company put it well when he said

> In the main, our competitors are acquainted with the same fundamental concepts and techniques and approaches that we follow, and they are as free to pursue them as we are. More often than not, the difference between their level of success and ours lies in the relative thoroughness and self-discipline with which we and they develop and execute our strategies for the future.

Good Strategy + Good Strategy Execution = Good Management

Crafting and executing strategy are thus core management tasks. Among all the things managers do, nothing affects a company's ultimate success or failure more fundamentally than how well its management team charts the company's direction, develops competitively effective strategic moves, and pursues what needs to be done internally to produce good day-in, day-out strategy execution and operating excellence. Indeed, *good strategy and good strategy execution are the most telling and trustworthy signs of good management.* The rationale for using the twin standards of good strategy making and good strategy execution to determine whether a company is well managed is therefore compelling: *The better conceived a company's strategy and the more competently it is executed, the more likely the company will be a standout performer in the marketplace.* In stark contrast, a company that lacks clear-cut direction, has a flawed strategy, or can't execute its strategy competently is a company whose financial performance is probably suffering, whose business is at long-term risk, and whose management is sorely lacking.

THE ROAD AHEAD

Throughout the chapters to come and in Part 2 of this text, the spotlight is on the foremost question in running a business enterprise: *What must managers do, and do well, to make a company successful in the marketplace?* The answer that emerges is that doing a good job of managing inherently requires good strategic thinking and good management of the strategy-making, strategy-executing process.

The mission of this book is to provide a solid overview of what every business student and aspiring manager needs to know about crafting and executing strategy. We will explore what good strategic thinking entails, describe the core concepts and tools of strategic analysis, and examine the ins and outs of crafting and executing strategy. The accompanying cases will help build your skills in both diagnosing how well the strategy-making, strategy-executing task is being performed

How well a company performs is directly attributable to the caliber of its strategy and the proficiency with which the strategy is executed.

and prescribing actions for how the strategy in question or its execution can be improved. The strategic management course that you are enrolled in may also include a strategy simulation exercise in which you will run a company in head-to-head competition with companies run by your classmates. Your mastery of the strategic management concepts presented in the following chapters will put you in a strong position to craft a winning strategy for your company and figure out how to execute it in a cost-effective and profitable manner. As you progress through the chapters of the text and the activities assigned during the term, we hope to convince you that first-rate capabilities in crafting and executing strategy are essential to good management.

As you tackle the content and accompanying activities of this book, ponder the following observation by the essayist and poet Ralph Waldo Emerson: "Commerce is a game of skill which many people play, but which few play well." If your efforts help you become a savvy player and better equip you to succeed in business, the time and energy you spend here will indeed prove worthwhile.

KEY POINTS

1. A company's strategy is its game plan to attract customers, outperform its competitors, and achieve superior profitability.

2. The success of a company's strategy depends upon *competing differently* from rivals and gaining a competitive advantage over them.

3. A company achieves a *competitive advantage* when it provides buyers with superior value compared to rival sellers or produces its products or services more efficiently. The advantage is *sustainable* if it persists despite the best efforts of competitors to match or surpass this advantage.

4. A company's strategy typically evolves over time, emerging from a blend of (1) proactive deliberate actions on the part of company managers to improve the strategy and (2) reactive emergent responses to unanticipated developments and fresh market conditions.

5. A company's business model sets forth the logic for how its strategy will create value for customers and at the same time generate revenues sufficient to cover costs and realize a profit. Thus, it contains two crucial elements: (1) the *customer value proposition*—a plan for satisfying customer wants and needs at a price customers will consider good value, and (2) the *profit formula*—a plan for a cost structure that will enable the company to deliver the customer value proposition profitably. These elements are illustrated by the value-price-cost framework.

6. A winning strategy will pass three tests: (1) *fit* (external, internal, and dynamic consistency), (2) *competitive advantage* (durable competitive advantage), and (3) *performance* (outstanding financial and market performance).

7. Ethical strategies must entail actions and behavior that can pass the test of moral scrutiny in the sense of *not being* deceitful, unfair or harmful to others, disreputable, or unreasonably damaging to the environment.

8. Crafting and executing strategy are core management functions. How well a company performs and the degree of market success it enjoys are directly attributable to the caliber of its strategy and the proficiency with which the strategy is executed.

ASSURANCE OF LEARNING EXERCISES

1. Based on your experiences and/or knowledge of Apple's current products and services, does Apple's strategy (as described in Illustration Capsule 1.1) seem to set it apart from rivals? Does the strategy seem to be keyed to a cost-based advantage, differentiating features, serving the unique needs of a niche, or some combination of these? What is there about Apple's strategy that can lead to sustainable competitive advantage?

   LO 1-1, LO 1-2, LO 1-3

2. Elements of eBay's strategy have evolved in meaningful ways since the company's founding in 1995. After reviewing the company's history at **www.ebayinc.com/our-company/our-history/**, and all of the the links at the company's investor relations site (**investors.ebayinc.com/**) prepare a one- to two-page report that discusses how its strategy has evolved. Your report should also assess how well eBay's strategy passes the three tests of a winning strategy.

   LO 1-4, LO 1-6

3. Go to **investor.siriusxm.com** and check whether Sirius XM's recent financial reports indicate that its business model is working. Are its subscription fees increasing or declining? Are its revenue stream advertising and equipment sales growing or declining? Does its cost structure allow for acceptable profit margins?

   LO 1-5

EXERCISE FOR SIMULATION PARTICIPANTS

Three basic questions must be answered by managers of organizations of all sizes as they begin the process of crafting strategy:

- What is our present situation?
- Where do we want to go from here?
- How are we going to get there?

   After you have read the Participant's Guide or Player's Manual for the strategy simulation exercise that you will participate in during this academic term, you and your co-managers should come up with brief one- or two-paragraph answers to these three questions *prior to* entering your first set of decisions. While your answer to the first of the three questions can be developed from your reading of the manual, the second and third questions will require a collaborative discussion among the members of your company's management team about how you intend to manage the company you have been assigned to run.

1. *What is our company's current situation?* A substantive answer to this question should cover the following issues:
   - Is your company in a good, average, or weak competitive position vis-à-vis rival companies?
   - Does your company appear to be in a sound financial condition?
   - Does it appear to have a competitive advantage, and is it likely to be sustainable?
   - What problems does your company have that need to be addressed?

2. *Where do we want to take the company during the time we are in charge?* A complete answer to this question should say something about each of the following:
   - What goals or aspirations do you have for your company?
   - What do you want the company to be known for?

   LO 1-1, LO 1-2, LO 1-3

- What market share would you like your company to have after the first five decision rounds?
- By what amount or percentage would you like to increase total profits of the company by the end of the final decision round?

LO 1-4, LO 1-6
- What kinds of performance outcomes will signal that you and your co-managers are managing the company in a successful manner?

3. *How are we going to get there?* Your answer should cover these issues:

- Which one of the basic strategic and competitive approaches discussed in this chapter do you think makes the most sense to pursue?
- What kind of competitive advantage over rivals will you try to achieve?
- How would you describe the company's business model?

LO 1-4, LO 1-5
- What kind of actions will support these objectives?

ENDNOTES

[1] B. R, "Strategy," *The Economist,* October 19, 2012, www.economist.com/blogs/schumpeter/2012/10/z-business-quotations-1 (accessed January 4, 2014).

[2] Jan Rivkin, "An Alternative Approach to Making Strategic Choices," Harvard Business School case 9-702-433, 2001.

[3] Michael E. Porter, "What Is Strategy?" *Harvard Business Review* 74, no. 6 (November–December 1996), pp. 65–67.

[4] Ibid.

[5] Eric T. Anderson and Duncan Simester, "A Step-by-Step Guide to Smart Business Experiments," *Harvard Business Review* 89, no. 3 (March 2011).

[6] Shona L. Brown and Kathleen M. Eisenhardt, *Competing on the Edge: Strategy as Structured Chaos* (Boston, MA: Harvard Business School Press, 1998).

[7] Cynthia A. Montgomery, "Putting Leadership Back into Strategy," *Harvard Business Review* 86, no. 1 (January 2008).

[8] Henry Mintzberg and J. A. Waters, "Of Strategies, Deliberate and Emergent," *Strategic Management Journal* 6 (1985); Costas Markides, "Strategy as Balance: From 'Either-Or' to 'And,' " *Business Strategy Review* 12, no. 3 (September 2001).

[9] Mark W. Johnson, Clayton M. Christensen, and Henning Kagermann, "Reinventing Your Business Model," *Harvard Business Review* 86, no. 12 (December 2008); Joan Magretta, "Why Business Models Matter," *Harvard Business Review* 80, no. 5 (May 2002).

[10] A. Brandenburger and H. Stuart, "Value-Based Strategy," *Journal of Economics and Management Strategy* 5 (1996), pp. 5–24; D. Hoopes, T. Madsen, and G. Walker, "Guest Editors' Introduction to the Special Issue: Why Is There a Resource-Based View? Toward a Theory of Competitive Heterogeneity," *Strategic Management Journal* 24 (2003), pp. 889–992; M. Peteraf and J. Barney, "Unravelling the Resource-Based Tangle," *Managerial and Decision Economics* 24 (2003), pp. 309–323.

[11] Rivkin, "An Alternative Approach to Making Strategic Choices."

chapter 2

Charting a Company's Direction

Its Vision, Mission, Objectives, and Strategy

Learning Objectives

This chapter will help you

LO 2-1 Explain why it is critical for managers to have a clear strategic vision of where the company needs to head.

LO 2-2 Explain the importance of setting both strategic and financial objectives.

LO 2-3 Explain why the strategic initiatives taken at various organizational levels must be tightly coordinated.

LO 2-4 Identify what a company must do to achieve operating excellence and to execute its strategy proficiently.

LO 2-5 Explain the role and responsibility of a company's board of directors in overseeing the strategic management process.

chapter 2

Charting a Company's Direction

Its Vision, Mission, Objectives, and Strategy

Learning Objectives

This chapter will help you

LO 2-1 Explain why it is critical for managers to have a clear strategic vision of where the company needs to head.

LO 2-2 Explain the importance of setting both strategic and financial objectives.

LO 2-3 Explain why the strategic initiatives taken at various organizational levels must be tightly coordinated.

LO 2-4 Identify what a company must do to achieve operating excellence and to execute its strategy proficiently.

LO 2-5 Explain the role and responsibility of a company's board of directors in overseeing the strategic management process.

©Karen Stolper/Photolibrary/Getty Images

Sound strategy starts with having the right goal.

Michael Porter—*Professor and consultant*

A vision without a strategy remains an illusion.

Lee Bolman—*Author and leadership consultant*

Good business leaders create a vision, articulate the vision, passionately own the vision, and relentlessly drive it to completion.

Jack Welch—*Former CEO of General Electric*

Crafting and executing strategy are the heart and soul of managing a business enterprise. But exactly what is involved in developing a strategy and executing it proficiently? What goes into charting a company's strategic course and long-term direction? Is any analysis required? Does a company need a strategic plan? What are the various components of the strategy-making, strategy-executing process and to what extent are company personnel—aside from senior management—involved in the process?

This chapter presents an overview of the ins and outs of crafting and executing company strategies. The focus is on management's direction-setting responsibilities—charting a strategic course, setting performance targets, and choosing a strategy capable of producing the desired outcomes. There is coverage of why strategy-making is a task for a company's entire management team and which kinds of strategic decisions tend to be made at which levels of management. The chapter concludes with a look at the roles and responsibilities of a company's board of directors and how good corporate governance protects shareholder interests and promotes good management.

WHAT DOES THE STRATEGY-MAKING, STRATEGY-EXECUTING PROCESS ENTAIL?

Crafting and executing a company's strategy is an ongoing process that consists of five interrelated stages:

1. *Developing a strategic vision* that charts the company's long-term direction, a *mission statement* that describes the company's purpose, and a set of *core values* to guide the pursuit of the vision and mission.
2. *Setting objectives* for measuring the company's performance and tracking its progress in moving in the intended long-term direction.
3. *Crafting a strategy* for advancing the company along the path management has charted and achieving its performance objectives.
4. *Executing the chosen strategy* efficiently and effectively.
5. *Monitoring developments, evaluating performance, and initiating corrective adjustments* in the company's vision and mission statement, objectives, strategy, or approach to strategy execution in light of actual experience, changing conditions, new ideas, and new opportunities.

Figure 2.1 displays this five-stage process, which we examine next in some detail. The first three stages of the strategic management process involve making a strategic plan. A **strategic plan** maps out where a company is headed, establishes strategic and financial targets, and outlines the basic business model, competitive moves, and approaches to be used in achieving the desired business results.[1] We explain this more fully at the conclusion of our discussion of stage 3, later in this chapter.

FIGURE 2.1   The Strategy-Making, Strategy-Executing Process

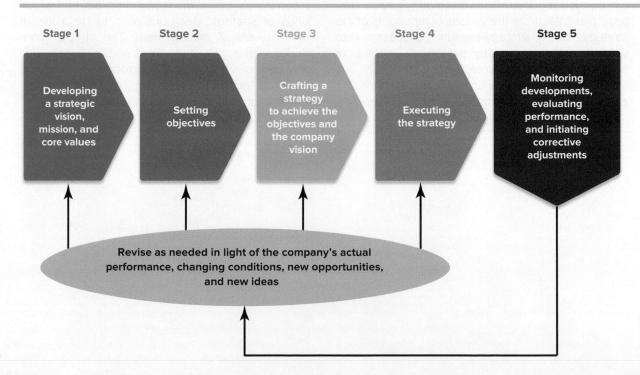

STAGE 1: DEVELOPING A STRATEGIC VISION, MISSION STATEMENT, AND SET OF CORE VALUES

● ● ● ●

Very early in the strategy-making process, a company's senior managers must wrestle with the issue of what directional path the company should take. Can the company's prospects be improved by changing its product offerings, or the markets in which it participates, or the customers it aims to serve? Deciding to commit the company to one path versus another pushes managers to draw some carefully reasoned conclusions about whether the company's present strategic course offers attractive opportunities for growth and profitability or whether changes of one kind or another in the company's strategy and long-term direction are needed.

> ● **LO 2-1**
>
> Explain why it is critical for managers to have a clear strategic vision of where the company needs to head.

Developing a Strategic Vision

Top management's views about the company's long-term direction and what product-market-customer business mix seems optimal for the road ahead constitute a **strategic vision** for the company. A strategic vision delineates management's aspirations for the company's future, providing a panoramic view of "where we are going" and a convincing rationale for why this makes good business sense. A strategic vision thus points an organization in a particular direction, charts a strategic path for it to follow, builds commitment to the future course of action, and molds organizational identity. A clearly articulated strategic vision communicates management's aspirations to stakeholders (customers, employees, stockholders, suppliers, etc.) and helps steer the energies of company personnel in a common direction. The vision of Google's cofounders Larry Page and Sergey Brin "to organize the world's information and make it universally accessible and useful" provides a good example. In serving as the company's guiding light, it has captured the imagination of stakeholders and the public at large, served as the basis for crafting the company's strategic actions, and aided internal efforts to mobilize and direct the company's resources.

> **CORE** CONCEPT
>
> A **strategic vision** describes management's aspirations for the company's future and the course and direction charted to achieve them.

Well-conceived visions are *distinctive* and *specific* to a particular organization; they avoid generic, feel-good statements like "We will become a global leader and the first choice of customers in every market we serve."[2] Likewise, a strategic vision proclaiming management's quest "to be the market leader" or "to be the most innovative" or "to be recognized as the best company in the industry" offers scant guidance about a company's long-term direction or the kind of company that management is striving to build.

A surprising number of the vision statements found on company websites and in annual reports are vague and unrevealing, saying very little about the company's future direction. Some could apply to almost any company in any industry. Many read like a public relations statement—high-sounding words that someone came up with because it is fashionable for companies to have an official vision statement.[3] An example is Hilton Hotel's vision "to fill the earth with light and the warmth of hospitality," which simply borders on the incredulous. The real purpose of a vision statement is to serve as a management tool for giving the organization a sense of direction.

> An effectively communicated vision is a valuable management tool for enlisting the commitment of company personnel to actions that move the company in the intended long-term direction.

For a strategic vision to function as a valuable management tool, it must convey what top executives want the business to look like and provide managers at all organizational levels with a reference point in making strategic decisions and preparing the company for the future. It must say something definitive about how the company's leaders intend to position the company beyond where it is today.

TABLE 2.1   Wording a Vision Statement—the Dos and Don'ts

The Dos	The Don'ts
Be graphic. Paint a clear picture of where the company is headed and the market position(s) the company is striving to stake out.	**Don't be vague or incomplete.** Never skimp on specifics about where the company is headed or how the company intends to prepare for the future.
Be forward-looking and directional. Describe the strategic course that will help the company prepare for the future.	**Don't dwell on the present.** A vision is not about what a company once did or does now; it's about "where we are going."
Keep it focused. Focus on providing managers with guidance in making decisions and allocating resources.	**Don't use overly broad language.** Avoid all-inclusive language that gives the company license to pursue any opportunity.
Have some wiggle room. Language that allows some flexibility allows the directional course to be adjusted as market, customer, and technology circumstances change.	**Don't state the vision in bland or uninspiring terms.** The best vision statements have the power to motivate company personnel and inspire shareholder confidence about the company's future.
Be sure the journey is feasible. The path and direction should be within the realm of what the company can accomplish; over time, a company should be able to demonstrate measurable progress in achieving the vision.	**Don't be generic.** A vision statement that could apply to companies in any of several industries (or to any of several companies in the same industry) is not specific enough to provide any guidance.
Indicate why the directional path makes good business sense. The directional path should be in the long-term interests of stakeholders (especially shareholders, employees, and suppliers).	**Don't rely on superlatives.** Visions that claim the company's strategic course is the "best" or "most successful" usually lack specifics about the path the company is taking to get there.
Make it memorable. A well-stated vision is short, easily communicated, and memorable. Ideally, it should be reducible to a few choice lines or a one-phrase slogan.	**Don't run on and on.** A vision statement that is not concise and to the point will tend to lose its audience.

Sources: John P. Kotter, *Leading Change* (Boston: Harvard Business School Press, 1996); Hugh Davidson, *The Committed Enterprise* (Oxford: Butterworth Heinemann, 2002); Michel Robert, *Strategy Pure and Simple II* (New York: McGraw-Hill, 1992).

Table 2.1 provides some dos and don'ts in composing an effectively worded vision statement. Illustration Capsule 2.1 provides a critique of the strategic visions of several prominent companies.

Communicating the Strategic Vision

A strategic vision offers little value to the organization unless it's effectively communicated down the line to lower-level managers and employees. A vision cannot provide direction for middle managers or inspire and energize employees unless everyone in the company is familiar with it and can observe senior management's commitment to the vision. It is particularly important for executives to provide a compelling rationale for a dramatically *new* strategic vision and company direction. When company

ILLUSTRATION CAPSULE 2.1

Examples of Strategic Visions—How Well Do They Measure Up?

©Philip Arno Photography/Shutterstock

Vision Statement	Effective Elements	Shortcomings
Whole Foods Whole Foods Market is a dynamic leader in the quality food business. We are a mission-driven company that aims to set the standards of excellence for food retailers. We are building a business in which high standards permeate all aspects of our company. Quality is a state of mind at Whole Foods Market. Our motto—Whole Foods, Whole People, Whole Planet—emphasizes that our vision reaches far beyond just being a food retailer. Our success in fulfilling our vision is measured by customer satisfaction, team member happiness and excellence, return on capital investment, improvement in the state of the environment and local and larger community support. Our ability to instill a clear sense of interdependence among our various stakeholders (the people who are interested and benefit from the success of our company) is contingent upon our efforts to communicate more often, more openly, and more compassionately. Better communication equals better understanding and more trust.	• Forward-looking • Graphic • Focused • Makes good business sense	• Long • Not memorable
Keurig Green Mountain Become the world's leading personal beverage systems company.	• Focused • Flexible • Makes good business sense	• Not graphic • Lacks specifics • Not forward-looking
Nike NIKE, Inc. fosters a culture of invention. We create products, services and experiences for today's athlete* while solving problems for the next generation. *If you have a body, you are an athlete.	• Forward-looking • Flexible	• Vague and lacks detail • Not focused • Generic • Not necessarily feasible

Note: Developed with Frances C. Thunder.

Source: Company websites (accessed online February 12, 2016).

personnel don't understand or accept the need for redirecting organizational efforts, they are prone to resist change. Hence, explaining the basis for the new direction, addressing employee concerns head-on, calming fears, lifting spirits, and providing updates and progress reports as events unfold all become part of the task in mobilizing support for the vision and winning commitment to needed actions.

Winning the support of organization members for the vision nearly always requires putting "where we are going and why" in writing, distributing the statement organizationwide, and having top executives personally explain the vision and its rationale to as many people as feasible. Ideally, executives should present their vision for the company in a manner that reaches out and grabs people. An engaging and convincing strategic vision has enormous motivational value—for the same reason that a stonemason is more inspired by the opportunity to build a great cathedral for the ages than a house. Thus, executive ability to paint a convincing and inspiring picture of a company's journey to a future destination is an important element of effective strategic leadership.

Expressing the Essence of the Vision in a Slogan   The task of effectively conveying the vision to company personnel is assisted when management can capture the vision of where to head in a catchy or easily remembered slogan. A number of organizations have summed up their vision in a brief phrase. Instagram's vision is "Capture and share the world's moments," while Charles Schwab's is simply "Helping investors help themselves." Habitat for Humanity's aspirational vision is "A world where everyone has a decent place to live." Even Scotland Yard has a catchy vision, which is to "make London the safest major city in the world." Creating a short slogan to illuminate an organization's direction and using it repeatedly as a reminder of "where we are headed and why" helps rally organization members to maintain their focus and hurdle whatever obstacles lie in the company's path.

Why a Sound, Well-Communicated Strategic Vision Matters   A well-thought-out, forcefully communicated strategic vision pays off in several respects: (1) It crystallizes senior executives' own views about the firm's long-term direction; (2) it reduces the risk of rudderless decision making; (3) it is a tool for winning the support of organization members to help make the vision a reality; (4) it provides a beacon for lower-level managers in setting departmental objectives and crafting departmental strategies that are in sync with the company's overall strategy; and (5) it helps an organization prepare for the future. When top executives are able to demonstrate significant progress in achieving these five benefits, the first step in organizational direction setting has been successfully completed.

> The distinction between a strategic vision and a mission statement is fairly clear-cut: A **strategic vision** portrays a company's aspirations for its *future* ("where we are going"), whereas a company's **mission** describes the scope and purpose of its *present* business ("who we are, what we do, and why we are here").

Developing a Company Mission Statement

The defining characteristic of a strategic vision is what it says about the company's *future strategic course*—"the direction we are headed and the shape of our business in the future." It is aspirational. In contrast, a **mission statement** describes the enterprise's *present business and purpose*—"who we are, what we do, and why we are here." It is purely descriptive. Ideally, a company mission statement (1) identifies the company's products and/or services, (2) specifies the buyer needs that the company seeks to satisfy and the customer groups or markets that it serves, and (3) gives the company its own identity. The mission statements that one finds in company annual reports or posted on company websites are typically quite brief; some do a better job than others of conveying what the enterprise's current business operations and purpose are all about.

Consider, for example, the mission statement of FedEx Corporation, which has long been known for its overnight shipping service, but also for pioneering the package tracking system now in general use:

> The FedEx Corporation offers express and fast delivery transportation services, delivering an estimated 3 million packages daily all around the globe. Its services include overnight courier, ground, heavy freight, document copying, and logistics services.

Note that FedEx's mission statement does a good job of conveying "who we are, what we do, and why we are here," but it provides no sense of "where we are headed." This is as it should be, since a company's vision statement is that which speaks to the future.

Another example of a well-stated mission statement with ample specifics about what the organization does is that of St. Jude Children's Research Hospital: "to advance cures, and means of prevention, for pediatric catastrophic diseases through research and treatment. Consistent with the vision of our founder Danny Thomas, no child is denied treatment based on race, religion or a family's ability to pay." Twitter's mission statement, while short, still captures the essence of what the company is about: "To give everyone the power to create and share ideas and information instantly, without barriers." An example of a not-so-revealing mission statement is that of JetBlue: "To inspire humanity—both in the air and on the ground." It says nothing about the company's activities or business makeup and could apply to many companies in many different industries. A person unfamiliar with JetBlue could not even discern from its mission statement that it is an airline, without reading between the lines. Coca-Cola, which markets more than 500 beverage brands in over 200 countries, also has an uninformative mission statement: "to refresh the world; to inspire moments of optimism and happiness; to create value and make a difference." The usefulness of a mission statement that cannot convey the essence of a company's business activities and purpose is unclear.

All too often, companies couch their mission in terms of making a profit, like Dean Foods with its mission "To maximize long-term stockholder value." This, too, is flawed. Profit is more correctly an *objective* and a *result* of what a company does. Moreover, earning a profit is the obvious intent of every commercial enterprise. Companies such as Gap Inc., Edward Jones, Honda, The Boston Consulting Group, Citigroup, DreamWorks Animation, and Intuit are all striving to earn a profit for shareholders; but plainly the fundamentals of their businesses are substantially different when it comes to "who we are and what we do." It is management's answer to "make a profit doing what and for whom?" that reveals the substance of a company's true mission and business purpose.

> To be well worded, a company mission statement must employ language specific enough to distinguish its business makeup and purpose from those of other enterprises and give the company its own identity.

Linking the Vision and Mission with Company Values

Companies commonly develop a set of values to guide the actions and behavior of company personnel in conducting the company's business and pursuing its strategic vision and mission. By **values** (or **core values**, as they are often called) we mean certain designated beliefs, traits, and behavioral norms that management has determined should guide the pursuit of its vision and mission. Values relate to such things as fair treatment, honor and integrity, ethical behavior, innovativeness, teamwork, a passion for top-notch quality or superior customer service, social responsibility, and community citizenship.

Most companies articulate four to eight core values that company personnel are expected to display and that are supposed to be mirrored in how the company

CORE CONCEPT

A company's **values** are the beliefs, traits, and behavioral norms that company personnel are expected to display in conducting the company's business and pursuing its strategic vision and mission.

conducts its business. Build-A-Bear Workshop, with its cuddly Teddy bears and stuffed animals, credits six core values with creating its highly acclaimed working environment: (1) Reach, (2) Learn, (3) Di-bear-sity (4) Colla-bear-ate, (5) Give, and (6) Cele-bear-ate. Zappos prides itself on its 10 core values, which employees are expected to embody:

1. Deliver WOW Through Service
2. Embrace and Drive Change
3. Create Fun and a Little Weirdness
4. Be Adventurous, Creative, and Open-Minded
5. Pursue Growth and Learning
6. Build Open and Honest Relationships with Communication
7. Build a Positive Team and Family Spirit
8. Do More with Less
9. Be Passionate and Determined
10. Be Humble

Do companies practice what they preach when it comes to their professed values? Sometimes no, sometimes yes—it runs the gamut. At one extreme are companies with window-dressing values; the values are given lip service by top executives but have little discernible impact on either how company personnel behave or how the company operates. Such companies have value statements because they are in vogue and make the company look good. The limitation of these value statements becomes apparent whenever corporate misdeeds come to light. Prime examples include Volkswagen, with its emissions scandal, and Uber, facing multiple allegations of misbehavior and a criminal probe of illegal operations. At the other extreme are companies whose executives are committed to grounding company operations on sound values and principled ways of doing business. Executives at these companies deliberately seek to ingrain the designated core values into the corporate culture—the core values thus become an integral part of the company's DNA and what makes the company tick. At such values-driven companies, executives "walk the talk" and company personnel are held accountable for embodying the stated values in their behavior.

At companies where the stated values are real rather than cosmetic, managers connect values to the pursuit of the strategic vision and mission in one of two ways. In companies with long-standing values that are deeply entrenched in the corporate culture, senior managers are careful to craft a vision, mission, strategy, and set of operating practices that match established values; moreover, they repeatedly emphasize how the value-based behavioral norms contribute to the company's business success. If the company changes to a different vision or strategy, executives make a point of explaining how and why the core values continue to be relevant. Few companies with sincere commitment to established core values ever undertake strategic moves that conflict with ingrained values. In new companies, top management has to consider what values and business conduct should characterize the company and then draft a value statement that is circulated among managers and employees for discussion and possible modification. A final value statement that incorporates the desired behaviors and that connects to the vision and mission is then officially adopted. Some companies combine their vision, mission, and values into a single statement or document, circulate it to all organization members, and in many instances post the vision, mission, and value statement on the company's website. Illustration Capsule 2.2 describes how the success of TOMS Shoes has been largely driven by the nature of its mission, linked to the vision and core values of its founder.

TOMS Shoes: A Mission with a Company

TOMS Shoes was founded in 2006 by Blake Mycoskie after a trip to Argentina where he witnessed many children with no access to shoes in areas of extreme poverty. Mycoskie returned to the United States and founded TOMS Shoes with the purpose of matching every pair of shoes purchased by customers with a new pair of shoes to give to a child in need, a model he called One for One®. In contrast to many companies that begin with a product and then articulate a mission, Mycoskie started with the mission and then built a company around it. Although the company has since expanded their product portfolio, its mission remains essentially the same:

With every product you purchase, TOMS will help a person in need. One for One.®

TOMS's mission is ingrained in their business model. While Mycoskie could have set up a nonprofit organization to address the problem he witnessed, he was certain he didn't want to rely on donors to fund giving to the poor; he wanted to create a business that would fund the giving itself. With the one-for-one model, TOMS built the cost of giving away a pair of shoes into the price of each pair they sold, enabling the company to make a profit while still giving away shoes to the needy.

Much of TOMS's success (and ability to differentiate itself in a competitive marketplace) is attributable to the appeal of its mission and origin story. Mycoskie first got TOMS shoes into a trendy store in LA because he told them the story of why he founded the company, which got picked up by the LA Times and quickly spread. As the company has expanded communication channels, they continue to focus on leading with the story of their mission to ensure that customers know they are doing more than just buying a product.

As TOMS expanded to other products, they stayed true to the one-for-one business model, adapting it to each new product category. In 2011, the company launched TOMS Eyewear, where every purchase of glasses helps restore sight to an individual. They've since launched TOMS Roasting Co. that helps support

©John M. Heller/Getty Images Entertainment

access to safe water with every purchase of coffee, TOMS Bags where purchases fund resources for safe birth, and TOMS High Road Backpack Collection where purchases provide training for bullying prevention.

By ingraining the mission in the company's business model, TOMS has been able to truly live up to Mycoskie's aspiration of a mission with a company, funding giving through a for-profit business. TOMS even ensured that the business model will never change; when Mycoskie sold 50 percent of the company to Bain Capital in 2014, part of the transaction protected the one-for-one business model forever. TOMS is a successful example of a company that proves a commitment to core values can spur both revenue growth and giving back.

Note: Developed with Carry S. Resor

Sources: TOMS Shoes website, accessed February 2018, **http://www.toms.com/about-toms**; Lebowitz, Shana, *Business Insider,* "TOMS Blake Mycoskie Talks Growing a Business While Balancing Profit with Purpose," June 15, 2016, **http://www.businessinsider.com/ toms-blake-mycoskie-talks-growing-a-business-while-balancing-profit-with-purpose-2016-6**; Mycoskie, Blake, *Harvard Business Review,* "The Founder of TOMS on Reimaging the Company's Mission," from January-February 2016 issue, **https://hbr.org/2016/01/ the-founder-of-toms-on-reimagining-the-companys-mission**.

STAGE 2: SETTING OBJECTIVES

CORE CONCEPT

Objectives are an organization's performance targets—the specific results management wants to achieve.

Well-chosen **objectives** are:
- specific
- measurable
- time-limited
- challenging
- achievable

CORE CONCEPT

Stretch objectives set performance targets high enough to *stretch* an organization to perform at its full potential and deliver the best possible results. **Extreme stretch goals** are warranted only under certain conditions.

CORE CONCEPT

Financial objectives communicate management's goals for financial performance. **Strategic objectives** lay out target outcomes concerning a company's market standing, competitive position, and future business prospects.

The managerial purpose of setting **objectives** is to convert the vision and mission into specific performance targets. Objectives reflect management's aspirations for company performance in light of the industry's prevailing economic and competitive conditions and the company's internal capabilities. Well-stated objectives must be *specific,* as well as *quantifiable* or *measurable.* As Bill Hewlett, cofounder of Hewlett-Packard, shrewdly observed, "You cannot manage what you cannot measure. . . . And what gets measured gets done."[4] Concrete, measurable objectives are managerially valuable for three reasons: (1) They focus organizational attention and align actions throughout the organization, (2) they serve as *yardsticks* for tracking a company's performance and progress, and (3) they motivate employees to expend greater effort and perform at a high level. For company objectives to serve their purpose well, they must also meet three other criteria: they must contain a deadline for achievement and they must be challenging, yet achievable.

Setting Stretch Objectives

The experiences of countless companies teach that one of the best ways to promote outstanding company performance is for managers to set performance targets high enough to *stretch an organization to perform at its full potential and deliver the best possible results.* Challenging company personnel to go all out and deliver "stretch" gains in performance pushes an enterprise to be more inventive, to exhibit more urgency in improving both its financial performance and its business position, and to be more intentional and focused in its actions. Employing stretch goals can help create an exciting work environment and attract the best people. In many cases, stretch objectives spur exceptional performance and help build a firewall against contentment with modest gains in organizational performance.

There is a difference, however, between stretch goals that are clearly reachable with enough effort, and those that are well beyond the organization's current capabilities, regardless of the level of effort. Extreme stretch goals, involving radical expectations, fail more often than not. And failure to meet such goals can kill motivation, erode employee confidence, and damage both worker and company performance. CEO Marissa Mayer's inability to return Yahoo to greatness is a case in point.

Extreme stretch goals can work as envisioned under certain circumstances. High profile success stories at companies such as Southwest Airlines, Tesla, 3M, CSX, and General Electric provide evidence. But research suggests that success of this sort depends upon two conditions being met: (1) the company must have ample resources available, and (2) its recent performance must be strong. Under any other circumstances, managers would be well advised not to pursue overly ambitious stretch goals.[5]

What Kinds of Objectives to Set

Two distinct types of performance targets are required: those relating to financial performance and those relating to strategic performance. **Financial objectives** communicate management's goals for financial performance. **Strategic objectives** are goals concerning a company's marketing standing and competitive position. A company's set of financial and strategic objectives should include both near-term and longer-term performance targets. Short-term (quarterly or annual) objectives focus attention on delivering performance improvements in the current period and satisfy shareholder expectations for near-term progress. Longer-term targets (three to five years off) force managers to consider what to do *now* to put the company in position to perform better later. Long-term objectives are critical for achieving optimal long-term performance and stand as a barrier to a nearsighted management philosophy and an undue focus on short-term results. When trade-offs have to be made between achieving long-term objectives and achieving short-term objectives, long-term objectives should take precedence (unless the achievement of one or more short-term performance targets has unique importance). Examples of commonly used financial and strategic objectives are listed in Table 2.2. Illustration Capsule 2.3 provides selected financial and strategic objectives of three prominent companies.

The Need for a Balanced Approach to Objective Setting

The importance of setting and attaining financial objectives is obvious. Without adequate profitability and financial strength, a company's long-term health and ultimate survival are jeopardized. Furthermore, subpar earnings and a weak balance sheet alarm shareholders and creditors and put the jobs of senior executives at risk. In consequence, companies often focus most of their attention on financial outcomes. However, good financial performance, by itself, is not enough. Of equal or greater importance is a company's strategic performance—outcomes that indicate whether a company's market position and competitiveness are deteriorating, holding steady, or improving. *A stronger market standing and greater competitive vitality—especially when accompanied by competitive advantage—is what enables a company to improve its financial performance.*

Moreover, financial performance measures are really *lagging indicators* that reflect the results of past decisions and organizational activities.[6] But a company's past or current financial performance is not a reliable indicator of its future prospects—poor financial performers often turn things around and do better, while good financial

TABLE 2.2   Common Financial and Strategic Objectives

Financial Objectives	Strategic Objectives
• An *x* percent increase in annual revenues	• Winning an *x* percent market share
• Annual increases in after-tax profits *of x* percent	• Achieving lower overall costs than rivals
• Annual increases in earnings per share of *x* percent	• Overtaking key competitors on product performance, quality, or customer service
• Annual dividend increases of *x* percent	• Deriving *x* percent of revenues from the sale of new products introduced within the past five years
• Profit margins of *x* percent	
• An *x* percent return on capital employed (ROCE) or return on shareholders' equity (ROE) investment	• Having broader or deeper technological capabilities than rivals
	• Having a wider product line than rivals
• Increased shareholder value in the form of an upward-trending stock price	• Having a better-known or more powerful brand name than rivals
• Bond and credit ratings of *x*	• Having stronger national or global sales and distribution capabilities than rivals
• Internal cash flows of *x* dollars to fund new capital investment	• Consistently getting new or improved products to market ahead of rivals

Examples of Company Objectives

JETBLUE

Produce above average industry margins by offering a quality product at a competitive price; generate revenues of over $6.6 billion, up 3.4 percent year over year; earn a net income of $759 million, an annual increase of 12.0 percent; further develop fare options, a co-branded credit card, and the Mint franchise; commit to achieving total cost savings of $250 to 300 million by 2020; kickoff multi-year cabin restyling program; convert all core A321 aircraft from 190 to 200 seats; target growth in key cities like Boston, plan to grow 150 flights a day to 200 over the coming years; grow toward becoming the carrier of choice in South Florida; organically grow west coast presence by expanding Mint offering to more transcontinental routes; optimize fare mix to increase overall average fare.

LULULEMON ATHLETICA, INC.

Optimize and strategically grow square footage in North America; explore new concepts such as stores that are tailored to each community; build a robust digital ecosystem with key investments in customer relationship management, analytics, and capabilities to elevate guest experience across all touch points; continue to expand the brand globally through international expansion, open 11 new stores in Asia and Europe, which include the first stores in China, South Korea, and Switzerland—operating a total of 50+ stores across nine countries outside of North America; increase net revenue 14 percent to $2.3 billion in fiscal 2016; increase total comparable sales, which includes comparable store sales and direct to consumer, by 6 percent in fiscal 2016; increase gross profit for fiscal 2016 by 20 percent to $1.2 billion; increase gross profit as a percentage of net revenue, or gross margin, by 51.2 percent; increase income from operations for fiscal 2016 by 14 percent to $421.2 million.

Note: Developed with Kathleen T. Durante

Sources: Information posted on company websites.

©Eric Border Van Dyke/Shutterstock

GENERAL MILLS

Generate low single-digit organic net sales growth and high single-digit growth in earnings per share. Deliver double-digit returns to shareholders over the long term. To drive future growth, focus on Consumer First strategy to gain a deep understanding of consumer needs and respond quickly to give them what they want; more specifically: (1) grow cereal globally with a strong line-up of new products, including new flavors of iconic Cheerios, (2) innovate in fast growing segments of the yogurt category to improve performance and expand the yogurt platform into new cities in China; (3) expand distribution and advertising for high performing brands, such as Häagen-Dazs and Old El Paso; (4) build a more agile organization by streamlining support functions, allowing for more fluid use of resources and idea sharing around the world; enhancing e-commerce know-how to capture more growth in this emerging channel; and investing in strategic revenue management tools to optimize promotions, prices and mix of products to drive sales growth.

performers can fall upon hard times. The best and most reliable *leading indicators* of a company's future financial performance and business prospects are strategic outcomes that indicate whether the company's competitiveness and market position are stronger or weaker. The accomplishment of strategic objectives signals that the company is well positioned to sustain or improve its performance. For instance, if a company is achieving ambitious strategic objectives such that its competitive strength and market position are on the rise, then there's reason to expect that its *future* financial performance will be better than its current or past performance. If a company is losing ground to competitors and its market position is slipping—outcomes that reflect weak strategic performance—then its ability to maintain its present profitability is highly suspect.

Consequently, it is important to use a performance measurement system that strikes a *balance* between financial objectives and strategic objectives.[7] The most widely used framework of this sort is known as the **Balanced Scorecard.**[8] This is a method for linking financial performance objectives to specific strategic objectives that derive from a company's business model. It maps out the key objectives of a company, with performance indicators, along four dimensions:

<table>
<tr><td>

CORE CONCEPT

The **Balanced Scorecard** is a widely used method for combining the use of both strategic and financial objectives, tracking their achievement, and giving management a more complete and balanced view of how well an organization is performing.

</td></tr>
</table>

- Financial: listing financial objectives
- Customer: objectives relating to customers and the market
- Internal process: objectives relating to productivity and quality
- Organizational: objectives concerning human capital, culture, infrastructure, and innovation

Done well, this can provide a company's employees with clear guidelines about how their jobs are linked to the overall objectives of the organization, so they can contribute most productively and collaboratively to the achievement of these goals. The balanced scorecard methodology continues to be ranked as one of the most popular management tools.[9] Over 50 percent of companies in the United States, Europe, and Asia report using a balanced scorecard approach to measuring strategic and financial performance.[10] Organizations that have adopted the balanced scorecard approach include 7-Eleven, Ann Taylor Stores, Allianz Italy, Wells Fargo Bank, Ford Motor Company, Verizon, ExxonMobil, Pfizer, DuPont, Royal Canadian Mounted Police, U.S. Army Medical Command, and over 30 colleges and universities.[11] Despite its popularity, the balanced scorecard is not without limitations. Importantly, it may not capture some of the most important priorities of a particular organization, such as resource acquisition or partnering with other organizations. Further, as with most strategy tools, its value depends on implementation and follow through as much as on substance.

<table>
<tr><td>

CORE CONCEPT

The four dimensions of a **Balanced Scorecard:**
1. Financial
2. Customer
3. Internal Process
4. Organizational (formerly called Growth and Learning)

</td></tr>
</table>

Setting Objectives for Every Organizational Level

Objective setting should not stop with top management's establishing companywide performance targets. Company objectives need to be broken down into performance targets for each of the organization's separate businesses, product lines, functional departments, and individual work units. Employees within various functional areas and operating levels will be guided much better by specific objectives relating directly to their departmental activities than broad organizational-level goals. Objective setting is thus a *top-down process* that must extend to the lowest organizational levels. This means that each organizational unit must take care to set performance targets that support—rather than conflict with or negate—the achievement of companywide strategic and financial objectives.

The ideal situation is a team effort in which each organizational unit strives to produce results that contribute to the achievement of the company's performance targets and strategic vision. Such consistency signals that organizational units know their strategic role and are on board in helping the company move down the chosen strategic path and produce the desired results.

STAGE 3: CRAFTING A STRATEGY

● **LO 2-3**

Explain why the strategic initiatives taken at various organizational levels must be tightly coordinated.

As indicated in Chapter 1, the task of stitching a strategy together entails addressing a series of "hows": *how* to attract and please customers, *how* to compete against rivals, *how* to position the company in the marketplace, *how* to respond to changing market conditions, *how* to capitalize on attractive opportunities to grow the business, and *how* to achieve strategic and financial objectives. Choosing among the alternatives available in a way that coheres into a viable business model requires an understanding of the basic principles of strategic management. Choosing well also depends on an informed understanding of such factors as the nature of the business environment and the various resources available to the company. We will be delving into these issues in subsequent chapters.

But as indicated earlier, not all strategy can be planned deliberately; there is frequently a need for a more adaptive approach. This places a premium on astute entrepreneurship searching for opportunities to do new things or to do existing things in new or better ways.[12] The faster a company's business environment is changing, the more critical it becomes for its managers to be good entrepreneurs in diagnosing the direction and force of the changes underway and in responding with timely adjustments in strategy. Strategy makers have to pay attention to early warnings of future change and be willing to experiment with dare-to-be-different ways to establish a market position in that future. When obstacles appear unexpectedly in a company's path, it is up to management to adapt rapidly and innovatively. *Masterful strategies come from doing things differently from competitors where it counts—out-innovating them, being more efficient, being more imaginative, adapting faster—rather than running with the herd.* Good strategy making is therefore inseparable from good business entrepreneurship. One cannot exist without the other.

Strategy Making Involves Managers at All Organizational Levels

A company's senior executives obviously have lead strategy-making roles and responsibilities. The chief executive officer (CEO), as captain of the ship, carries the mantles of chief direction setter, chief objective setter, chief strategy maker, and chief strategy implementer for the total enterprise. Ultimate responsibility for *leading* the strategy-making, strategy-executing process rests with the CEO. And the CEO is always fully accountable for the results the strategy produces, whether good or bad. In some enterprises, the CEO or owner functions as chief architect of the strategy, personally deciding what the key elements of the company's strategy will be, although he or she may seek the advice of key subordinates and board members. A CEO-centered approach to strategy development is characteristic of small owner-managed companies and some large corporations that were founded by the present CEO or that have a CEO with strong strategic leadership skills. Elon Musk at Tesla Motors and SpaceX, Mark Zuckerberg at Facebook, Jeff Bezos at Amazon, Indra Nooyi at PepsiCo, Jack Ma of Alibaba, Warren Buffett at Berkshire Hathaway, and Marillyn Hewson at Lockheed Martin are examples of high-profile corporate CEOs who have wielded a heavy hand in shaping their company's strategy.

In most corporations, however, strategy is the product of more than just the CEO's handiwork. Typically, other senior executives—business unit heads, the chief financial officer, and vice presidents for production, marketing, and other functional departments—have influential strategy-making roles and help fashion the chief strategy components. Normally, a company's chief financial officer is in charge of devising and implementing an appropriate financial strategy; the production vice president takes the lead in developing the company's production strategy; the marketing vice president orchestrates sales and marketing strategy; a brand manager is in charge of the strategy for a particular brand in the company's product lineup; and so on. Moreover, the strategy-making efforts of top managers are complemented by advice and counsel from the company's board of directors; normally, all major strategic decisions are submitted to the board of directors for review, discussion, perhaps modification, and official approval.

But strategy making is by no means solely a *top* management function, the exclusive province of owner-entrepreneurs, CEOs, high-ranking executives, and board members. The more a company's operations cut across different products, industries, and geographic areas, the more that headquarters executives have little option but to delegate considerable strategy-making authority to down-the-line managers in charge of particular subsidiaries, divisions, product lines, geographic sales offices, distribution centers, and plants. On-the-scene managers who oversee specific operating units can be reliably counted on to have more detailed command of the strategic issues for the particular operating unit under their supervision since they have more intimate knowledge of the prevailing market and competitive conditions, customer requirements and expectations, and all the other relevant aspects affecting the several strategic options available. Managers with day-to-day familiarity of, and authority over, a specific operating unit thus have a big edge over headquarters executives in making wise strategic choices for their unit. The result is that, in most of today's companies, crafting and executing strategy is a *collaborative team effort* in which *every company manager plays a strategy-making role*—ranging from minor to major—for the area he or she heads.

Take, for example, a company like General Electric, a $126 billion global corporation with nearly 300,000 employees, operations in some 170 countries, and businesses that include jet engines, lighting, power generation, electric transmission and distribution equipment, oil and gas equipment, medical imaging and diagnostic equipment, locomotives, security devices, water treatment systems, and financial services. While top-level headquarters executives may well be personally involved in shaping GE's *overall* strategy and fashioning *important* strategic moves, they simply cannot know enough about the situation in every GE organizational unit to direct every strategic move made in GE's worldwide organization. Rather, it takes involvement on the part of GE's whole management team—top executives, business group heads, the heads of specific business units and product categories, and key managers in plants, sales offices, and distribution centers—to craft the thousands of strategic initiatives that end up composing the whole of GE's strategy.

> In most companies, crafting and executing strategy is a *collaborative team effort* in which every manager has a role for the area he or she heads; it is rarely something that only high-level managers do.

> The larger and more diverse the operations of an enterprise, the more points of strategic initiative it has and the more levels of management that have a significant strategy-making role.

A Company's Strategy-Making Hierarchy

In diversified companies like GE, where multiple and sometimes strikingly different businesses have to be managed, crafting a full-fledged strategy involves four distinct types of strategic actions and initiatives. Each of these involves different facets of the company's overall strategy and calls for the participation of different types of managers, as shown in Figure 2.2.

FIGURE 2.2 A Company's Strategy-Making Hierarchy

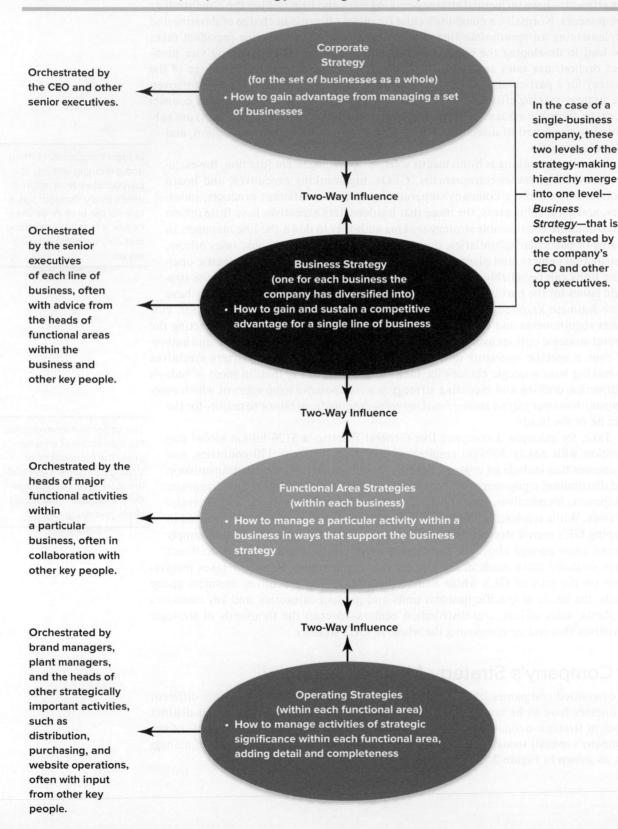

Orchestrated by the CEO and other senior executives.

Corporate Strategy
(for the set of businesses as a whole)
• How to gain advantage from managing a set of businesses

In the case of a single-business company, these two levels of the strategy-making hierarchy merge into one level—*Business Strategy*—that is orchestrated by the company's CEO and other top executives.

Two-Way Influence

Orchestrated by the senior executives of each line of business, often with advice from the heads of functional areas within the business and other key people.

Business Strategy
(one for each business the company has diversified into)
• How to gain and sustain a competitive advantage for a single line of business

Two-Way Influence

Orchestrated by the heads of major functional activities within a particular business, often in collaboration with other key people.

Functional Area Strategies
(within each business)
• How to manage a particular activity within a business in ways that support the business strategy

Two-Way Influence

Orchestrated by brand managers, plant managers, and the heads of other strategically important activities, such as distribution, purchasing, and website operations, often with input from other key people.

Operating Strategies
(within each functional area)
• How to manage activities of strategic significance within each functional area, adding detail and completeness

As shown in Figure 2.2, **corporate strategy** is orchestrated by the CEO and other senior executives and establishes an overall strategy for managing a *set of businesses* in a diversified, multibusiness company. Corporate strategy concerns how to improve the combined performance of the set of businesses the company has diversified into by capturing cross-business synergies and turning them into competitive advantage. It addresses the questions of what businesses to hold or divest, which new markets to enter, and how to best enter new markets (by acquisition, creation of a strategic alliance, or through internal development, for example). Corporate strategy and business diversification are the subjects of Chapter 8, in which they are discussed in detail.

Business strategy is concerned with strengthening the market position, building competitive advantage, and improving the performance of a single line of business. Business strategy is primarily the responsibility of business unit heads, although corporate-level executives may well exert strong influence; in diversified companies it is not unusual for corporate officers to insist that business-level objectives and strategy conform to corporate-level objectives and strategy themes. The business head has at least two other strategy-related roles: (1) seeing that lower-level strategies are well conceived, consistent, and adequately matched to the overall business strategy; and (2) keeping corporate-level officers (and sometimes the board of directors) informed of emerging strategic issues.

Functional-area strategies concern the approaches employed in managing particular functions within a business—like research and development (R&D), production, procurement of inputs, sales and marketing, distribution, customer service, and finance. A company's marketing strategy, for example, represents the managerial game plan for running the sales and marketing part of the business. A company's product development strategy represents the game plan for keeping the company's product lineup in tune with what buyers are looking for.

Functional strategies flesh out the details of a company's business strategy. Lead responsibility for functional strategies within a business is normally delegated to the heads of the respective functions, with the general manager of the business having final approval. Since the different functional-level strategies must be compatible with the overall business strategy and with one another to have beneficial impact, there are times when the general business manager exerts strong influence on the content of the functional strategies.

Operating strategies concern the relatively narrow approaches for managing key operating units (e.g., plants, distribution centers, purchasing centers) and specific operating activities with strategic significance (e.g., quality control, materials purchasing, brand management, Internet sales). A plant manager needs a strategy for accomplishing the plant's objectives, carrying out the plant's part of the company's overall manufacturing game plan, and dealing with any strategy-related problems that exist at the plant. A company's advertising manager needs a strategy for getting maximum audience exposure and sales impact from the ad budget. Operating strategies, while of limited scope, add further detail and completeness to functional strategies and to the overall business strategy. Lead responsibility for operating strategies is usually delegated to frontline managers, subject to the review and approval of higher-ranking managers.

Even though operating strategy is at the bottom of the strategy-making hierarchy, its importance should not be downplayed. A major plant that fails in its strategy to achieve production volume, unit cost, and quality targets can damage the company's reputation for quality products and undercut the achievement of company sales and profit objectives. Frontline managers are thus an important part of an organization's

CORE CONCEPT

Corporate strategy establishes an overall game plan for managing a *set of businesses* in a diversified, multibusiness company. **Business strategy** is primarily concerned with strengthening the company's market position and building competitive advantage in a *single-business company* or in a *single business unit* of a diversified multibusiness corporation.

> A company's strategy is at full power only when its many pieces are united.

strategy-making team. One cannot reliably judge the strategic importance of a given action simply by the strategy level or location within the managerial hierarchy where it is initiated.

In single-business companies, the uppermost level of the strategy-making hierarchy is the business strategy, so a single-business company has three levels of strategy: business strategy, functional-area strategies, and operating strategies. Proprietorships, partnerships, and owner-managed enterprises may have only one or two strategy-making levels since it takes only a few key people to craft and oversee the firm's strategy. The larger and more diverse the operations of an enterprise, the more points of strategic initiative it has and the more levels of management that have a significant strategy-making role.

Uniting the Strategy-Making Hierarchy

The components of a company's strategy up and down the strategy hierarchy should be cohesive and mutually reinforcing, fitting together like a jigsaw puzzle. *Anything less than a unified collection of strategies weakens the overall strategy and is likely to impair company performance.*[13] It is the responsibility of top executives to achieve this unity by clearly communicating the company's vision, mission, objectives, and major strategy components to down-the-line managers and key personnel. Midlevel and frontline managers cannot craft unified strategic moves without first understanding the company's long-term direction and knowing the major components of the corporate and/or business strategies that their strategy-making efforts are supposed to support and enhance. Thus, as a general rule, strategy making must start at the top of the organization, then proceed downward from the corporate level to the business level, and then from the business level to the associated functional and operating levels. Once strategies up and down the hierarchy have been created, lower-level strategies must be scrutinized for consistency with and support of higher-level strategies. Any strategy conflicts must be addressed and resolved, either by modifying the lower-level strategies with conflicting elements or by adapting the higher-level strategy to accommodate what may be more appealing strategy ideas and initiatives bubbling up from below.

A Strategic Vision + Mission + Objectives + Strategy = A Strategic Plan

> **CORE CONCEPT**
>
> A company's **strategic plan** lays out its direction, business model, competitive strategy, and performance targets for some specified period of time.

Developing a strategic vision and mission, setting objectives, and crafting a strategy are basic direction-setting tasks. They map out where a company is headed, delineate its strategic and financial targets, articulate the basic business model, and outline the competitive moves and operating approaches to be used in achieving the desired business results. Together, these elements constitute a **strategic plan** for coping with industry conditions, competing against rivals, meeting objectives, and making progress along the chosen strategic course.[14] Typically, a strategic plan includes a commitment to allocate resources to carrying out the plan and specifies a time period for achieving goals.

In companies that do regular strategy reviews and develop explicit strategic plans, the strategic plan usually ends up as a written document that is circulated to most managers. Near-term performance targets are the part of the strategic plan most often communicated to employees more generally and spelled out explicitly. A number of companies summarize key elements of their strategic plans in the company's annual report to shareholders, in postings on their websites, or in statements provided to the business media; others, perhaps for reasons of competitive sensitivity, make only vague, general statements about their strategic plans.[15] In small, privately owned companies it is rare for strategic plans to exist in written form. Small-company strategic plans tend to reside in the thinking and directives of owner-executives; aspects of the plan are revealed in conversations with company personnel about where to head, what to accomplish, and how to proceed.

STAGE 4: EXECUTING THE STRATEGY

Managing the implementation of a strategy is easily the most demanding and time-consuming part of the strategic management process. Converting strategic plans into actions and results tests a manager's ability to direct organizational change, motivate company personnel, build and strengthen competitive capabilities, create and nurture a strategy-supportive work climate, and meet or beat performance targets. Initiatives to put the strategy in place and execute it proficiently must be launched and managed on many organizational fronts.

> **● LO 2-4**
>
> Identify what a company must do to achieve operating excellence and to execute its strategy proficiently.

Management's action agenda for executing the chosen strategy emerges from assessing what the company will have to do to achieve the financial and strategic performance targets. Each company manager has to think through the answer to the question "What needs to be done in my area to execute my piece of the strategic plan, and what actions should I take to get the process under way?" How much internal change is needed depends on how much of the strategy is new, how far internal practices and competencies deviate from what the strategy requires, and how well the present work culture supports good strategy execution. Depending on the amount of internal change involved, full implementation and proficient execution of the company strategy (or important new pieces thereof) can take several months to several years.

In most situations, managing the strategy execution process includes the following principal aspects:

- Creating a strategy-supporting structure.
- Staffing the organization to obtain needed skills and expertise.
- Developing and strengthening strategy-supporting resources and capabilities.
- Allocating ample resources to the activities critical to strategic success.
- Ensuring that policies and procedures facilitate effective strategy execution.
- Organizing the work effort along the lines of best practice.
- Installing information and operating systems that enable company personnel to perform essential activities.
- Motivating people and tying rewards directly to the achievement of performance objectives.
- Creating a company culture conducive to successful strategy execution.
- Exerting the internal leadership needed to propel implementation forward.

Good strategy execution requires diligent pursuit of operating excellence. It is a job for a company's whole management team. Success hinges on the skills and cooperation of operating managers who can push for needed changes in their organizational units and consistently deliver good results. Management's handling of the strategy implementation process can be considered successful if things go smoothly enough that the company meets or beats its strategic and financial performance targets and shows good progress in achieving management's strategic vision. In Chapters 10, 11, and 12, we discuss the various aspects of the strategy implementation process more fully.

STAGE 5: EVALUATING PERFORMANCE AND INITIATING CORRECTIVE ADJUSTMENTS

The fifth component of the strategy management process—monitoring new external developments, evaluating the company's progress, and making corrective adjustments—is the trigger point for deciding whether to continue or change the company's vision and mission, objectives, strategy, and/or strategy execution methods.[16] As long as the company's strategy continues to pass the three tests of a winning strategy discussed in Chapter 1 (good fit, competitive advantage, strong performance), company executives may decide to stay the course. Simply fine-tuning the strategic plan and continuing with efforts to improve strategy execution are sufficient.

But whenever a company encounters disruptive changes in its environment, questions need to be raised about the appropriateness of its direction and strategy. If a company experiences a downturn in its market position or persistent shortfalls in performance, then company managers are obligated to ferret out the causes—do they relate to poor strategy, poor strategy execution, or both?—and take timely corrective action. A company's direction, objectives, and strategy have to be revisited anytime external or internal conditions warrant.

Likewise, managers are obligated to assess which of the company's operating methods and approaches to strategy execution merit continuation and which need improvement. Proficient strategy execution is always the product of much organizational learning. It is achieved unevenly—coming quickly in some areas and proving troublesome in others. Consequently, top-notch strategy execution entails vigilantly searching for ways to improve and then making corrective adjustments whenever and wherever it is useful to do so.

> A company's vision, mission, objectives, strategy, and approach to strategy execution are never final; reviewing whether and when to make revisions is an ongoing process.

CORPORATE GOVERNANCE: THE ROLE OF THE BOARD OF DIRECTORS IN THE STRATEGY-CRAFTING, STRATEGY-EXECUTING PROCESS

● **LO 2-5**

Explain the role and responsibility of a company's board of directors in overseeing the strategic management process.

Although senior managers have the *lead responsibility* for crafting and executing a company's strategy, it is the duty of a company's board of directors to exercise strong oversight and see that management performs the various tasks involved in each of the five stages of the strategy-making, strategy-executing process in a manner that best serves the interests of shareholders and other stakeholders, including the company's customers, employees, and the communities in which the company operates.[17] A company's board of directors has four important obligations to fulfill:

1. *Oversee the company's financial accounting and financial reporting practices.* While top executives, particularly the company's CEO and CFO (chief financial

officer), are primarily responsible for seeing that the company's financial statements fairly and accurately report the results of the company's operations, board members have a *legal obligation* to warrant the accuracy of the company's financial reports and protect shareholders. It is their job to ensure that generally accepted accounting principles (GAAP) are used properly in preparing the company's financial statements and that proper financial controls are in place to prevent fraud and misuse of funds. Virtually all boards of directors have an audit committee, always composed entirely of *outside directors* (*inside directors* hold management positions in the company and either directly or indirectly report to the CEO). The members of the audit committee have the lead responsibility for overseeing the decisions of the company's financial officers and consulting with both internal and external auditors to ensure accurate financial reporting and adequate financial controls.

2. *Critically appraise the company's direction, strategy, and business approaches.* Board members are also expected to guide management in choosing a strategic direction and to make independent judgments about the validity and wisdom of management's proposed strategic actions. This aspect of their duties takes on heightened importance when the company's strategy is failing or is plagued with faulty execution, and certainly when there is a precipitous collapse in profitability. But under more normal circumstances, many boards have found that meeting agendas become consumed by compliance matters with little time left to discuss matters of strategic importance. The board of directors and management at Philips Electronics hold annual two- to three-day retreats devoted exclusively to evaluating the company's long-term direction and various strategic proposals. The company's exit from the semiconductor business and its increased focus on medical technology and home health care resulted from management-board discussions during such retreats.[18]

3. *Evaluate the caliber of senior executives' strategic leadership skills.* The board is always responsible for determining whether the current CEO is doing a good job of strategic leadership (as a basis for awarding salary increases and bonuses and deciding on retention or removal).[19] Boards must also exercise due diligence in evaluating the strategic leadership skills of other senior executives in line to succeed the CEO. When the incumbent CEO steps down or leaves for a position elsewhere, the board must elect a successor, either going with an insider or deciding that an outsider is needed to perhaps radically change the company's strategic course. Often, the outside directors on a board visit company facilities and talk with company personnel personally to evaluate whether the strategy is on track, how well the strategy is being executed, and how well issues and problems are being addressed by various managers. For example, independent board members at GE visit operating executives at each major business unit once a year to assess the company's talent pool and stay abreast of emerging strategic and operating issues affecting the company's divisions. Home Depot board members visit a store once per quarter to determine the health of the company's operations.[20]

4. *Institute a compensation plan for top executives that rewards them for actions and results that serve stakeholder interests, and most especially those of shareholders.* A basic principle of corporate governance is that the owners of a corporation (the shareholders) delegate operating authority and managerial control to top management in return for compensation. In their role as *agents* of shareholders, top executives have a clear and unequivocal duty to make decisions and operate the company in accord with shareholder interests. (This does not mean disregarding

the interests of other stakeholders—employees, suppliers, the communities in which the company operates, and society at large.) Most boards of directors have a compensation committee, composed entirely of directors from *outside* the company, to develop a salary and incentive compensation plan that rewards senior executives for boosting the company's *long-term* performance on behalf of shareholders. The compensation committee's recommendations are presented to the full board for approval. But during the past 10 years, many boards of directors have done a poor job of ensuring that executive salary increases, bonuses, and stock option awards are tied tightly to performance measures that are truly in the long-term interests of shareholders. Rather, compensation packages at many companies have increasingly rewarded executives for short-term performance improvements—most notably, for achieving quarterly and annual earnings targets and boosting the stock price by specified percentages. This has had the perverse effect of causing company managers to become preoccupied with actions to improve a company's near-term performance, often motivating them to take unwise business risks to boost short-term earnings by amounts sufficient to qualify for multimillion-dollar compensation packages (that many see as obscenely large). The focus on short-term performance has proved damaging to long-term company performance and shareholder interests—witness the huge loss of shareholder wealth that occurred at many financial institutions during the banking crisis of 2008–2009 because of executive risk-taking in subprime loans, credit default swaps, and collateralized mortgage securities. As a consequence, the need to overhaul and reform executive compensation has become a hot topic in both public circles and corporate boardrooms. Illustration Capsule 2.4 discusses how weak governance at Volkswagen contributed to the 2015 emissions cheating scandal, which cost the company billions of dollars and the trust of its stakeholders.

Every corporation should have a strong independent board of directors that (1) is well informed about the company's performance, (2) guides and judges the CEO and other top executives, (3) has the courage to curb management actions the board believes are inappropriate or unduly risky, (4) certifies to shareholders that the CEO is doing what the board expects, (5) provides insight and advice to management, and (6) is intensely involved in debating the pros and cons of key decisions and actions.[21] Boards of directors that lack the backbone to challenge a strong-willed or "imperial" CEO or that rubber-stamp almost anything the CEO recommends without probing inquiry and debate abdicate their fiduciary duty to represent and protect shareholder interests.

In 2015, Volkswagen admitted to installing "defeat devices" on at least 11 million vehicles with diesel engines. These devices enabled the cars to pass emission tests, even though the engines actually emitted pollutants up to 40 times above what is allowed in the United States. Current estimates are that it will cost the company at least €7 billion to cover the cost of repairs and lawsuits. Although management must have been involved in approving the use of cheating devices, the Volkswagen supervisory board has been unwilling to accept any responsibility. Some board members even questioned whether it was the board's responsibility to be aware of such problems, stating "matters of technical expertise were not for us" and "the scandal had nothing, not one iota, to do with the advisory board." Yet governing boards do have a responsibility to be well informed, to provide oversight, and to become involved in key decisions and actions. So what caused this corporate governance failure? Why is this the third time in the past 20 years that Volkswagen has been embroiled in scandal?

The key feature of Volkswagen's board that appears to have led to these issues is a lack of independent directors. However, before explaining this in more detail it is important to understand the German governance model. German corporations operate two-tier governance structures, with a management board, and a separate supervisory board that does not contain any current executives. In addition, German law requires large companies to have at least 50 percent supervisory board representation from workers. This structure is meant to provide more oversight by independent board members and greater involvement by a wider set of stakeholders.

In Volkswagen's case, these objectives have been effectively circumvented. Although Volkswagen's supervisory board does not include any current management, the chairmanship appears to be a revolving door of former senior executives. Ferdinand Piëch, the chair during the scandal, was CEO for 9 years prior to becoming

©Vytautas Kielaitis/Shutterstock

chair in 2002. Martin Winterkorn, the recently ousted CEO, was expected to become supervisory board chair prior to the scandal. The company continues to elevate management to the supervisory board even though they have presided over past scandals. Hans Dieter Poetsch, the newly appointed chair, was part of the management team that did not inform the supervisory board of the EPA investigation for two weeks.

VW also has a unique ownership structure where a single family, Porsche, controls more than 50 percent of voting shares. Piëch, a family member and chair until 2015, forced out CEOs and installed unqualified family members on the board, such as his former nanny and current wife. He also pushed out independent-minded board members, such as Gerhard Cromme, author of Germany's corporate governance code. The company has lost numerous independent directors over the past 10 years, leaving it with only one non-shareholder, non-labor representative. Although Piëch has now been removed, it is unclear that Volkswagen's board has solved the underlying problem. Shareholders have seen billions of dollars wiped away and the Volkswagen brand tarnished. As long as the board continues to lack independent directors, change will likely be slow.

Note: Developed with Jacob M. Crandall.

Sources: "Piëch under Fire," *The Economist,* December 8, 2005; Chris Bryant and Richard Milne, "Boardroom Politics at Heart of VW Scandal," *Financial Times,* October 4, 2015; Andreas Cremer and Jan Schwartz, "Volkswagen Mired in Crisis as Board Members Criticize Piech," Reuters, April 24, 2015; Richard Milne, "Volkswagen: System Failure," *Financial Times,* November 4, 2015.

KEY POINTS

The strategic management process consists of five interrelated and integrated stages:

1. *Developing a strategic vision* of the company's future, a *mission statement* that defines the company's current purpose, and a set of *core values* to guide the pursuit of the vision and mission. This stage of strategy making provides direction for the company, motivates and inspires company personnel, aligns and guides actions throughout the organization, and communicates to stakeholders management's aspirations for the company's future.

2. *Setting objectives* to convert the vision and mission into performance targets that can be used as yardsticks for measuring the company's performance. Objectives need to spell out *how much* of *what kind* of performance *by when.* Two broad types of objectives are required: *financial objectives* and *strategic objectives.* A *balanced scorecard* approach for measuring company performance entails setting both financial objectives and strategic objectives. *Stretch objectives* can spur exceptional performance and help build a firewall against complacency and mediocre performance. Extreme stretch objectives, however, are only warranted in limited circumstances.

3. *Crafting a strategy* to achieve the objectives and move the company along the strategic course that management has charted. Masterful strategies come from doing things differently from competitors where it counts—out-innovating them, being more efficient, being more imaginative, adapting faster—rather than running with the herd. In large diversified companies, the strategy-making hierarchy consists of four levels, each of which involves a corresponding level of management: corporate strategy (multibusiness strategy), business strategy (strategy for individual businesses that compete in a single industry), functional-area strategies within each business (e.g., marketing, R&D, logistics), and operating strategies (for key operating units, such as manufacturing plants). Thus, strategy making is an inclusive collaborative activity involving not only senior company executives but also the heads of major business divisions, functional-area managers, and operating managers on the frontlines.

4. *Executing the chosen strategy* and converting the strategic plan into action. Management's agenda for executing the chosen strategy emerges from assessing what the company will have to do to achieve the targeted financial and strategic performance. Management's handling of the strategy implementation process can be considered successful if things go smoothly enough that the company meets or beats its strategic and financial performance targets and shows good progress in achieving management's strategic vision.

5. *Monitoring developments, evaluating performance, and initiating corrective adjustments* in light of actual experience, changing conditions, new ideas, and new opportunities. This stage of the strategy management process is the trigger point for deciding whether to continue or change the company's vision and mission, objectives, strategy, and/or strategy execution methods.

The sum of a company's strategic vision, mission, objectives, and strategy constitutes a *strategic plan* for coping with industry conditions, outcompeting rivals, meeting objectives, and making progress toward aspirational goals.

Boards of directors have a duty to shareholders as well as other stakeholders to play a vigilant role in overseeing management's handling of a company's strategy-making, strategy-executing process. This entails four important obligations: (1) Ensure that the company issues accurate financial reports and has adequate financial controls; (2) critically appraise the company's direction, strategy, and strategy execution; (3) evaluate the caliber of senior executives' strategic leadership skills; and (4) institute a compensation plan for top executives that rewards them for actions and results that serve stakeholder interests, most especially those of shareholders.

ASSURANCE OF LEARNING EXERCISES

1. Using the information in Table 2.1, critique the adequacy and merit of the following vision statements, listing effective elements and shortcomings. Rank the vision statements from best to worst once you complete your evaluation.

LO 2-1

Vision Statement	Effective Elements	Shortcomings
American Express • We work hard every day to make American Express the world's most respected service brand.		
Hilton Hotels Corporation Our vision is to be the first choice of the world's travelers. Hilton intends to build on the rich heritage and strength of our brands by: • Consistently delighting our customers • Investing in our team members • Delivering innovative products and services • Continuously improving performance • Increasing shareholder value • Creating a culture of pride • Strengthening the loyalty of our constituents		
MasterCard • A world beyond cash.		
BASF We are "The Chemical Company" successfully operating in all major markets. • Our customers view BASF as their partner of choice. • Our innovative products, intelligent solutions and services make us the most competent worldwide supplier in the chemical industry. • We generate a high return on assets. • We strive for sustainable development. • We welcome change as an opportunity. • We, the employees of BASF, together ensure our success.		

Sources: Company websites and annual reports.

LO 2-2   2.   Go to the company investor relations websites for Starbucks (**investor.starbucks.com**), Pfizer (**www.pfizer.com/investors**), and Salesforce (**investor.salesforce.com**) to find examples of strategic and financial objectives. List four objectives for each company, and indicate which of these are strategic and which are financial.

LO 2-3   3.   Boeing has been recognized by Forbes and other business publications as one of the world's best managed companies. The company discusses how its people and organizational units bring to bear the "best of Boeing" to its customers in 150 countries at **www.boeing.com/company**. Prepare a one- to two-page report that explains how the company has become a leader in commercial aviation through tight coordination of strategic initiatives at various organizational levels and functional areas.

LO 2-4   4.   Go to the investor relations website for Walmart (**investors.walmartstores.com**) and review past presentations Walmart has made during various investor conferences by clicking on the Events option in the navigation bar. Prepare a one- to two-page report that outlines what Walmart has said to investors about its approach to strategy execution. Specifically, what has management discussed concerning staffing, resource allocation, policies and procedures, information and operating systems, continuous improvement, rewards and incentives, corporate culture, and internal leadership at the company?

connect   5.   Based on the information provided in Illustration Capsule 2.4, describe the ways in which Volkswagen did not fulfill the requirements of effective corporate governance. In what ways did the board of directors sidestep its obligations to protect shareholder interests? How could Volkswagen better select its board of directors to avoid mistakes such as the emissions scandal in 2015?

LO 2-5

EXERCISE FOR SIMULATION PARTICIPANTS

LO 2-1   1.   Meet with your co-managers and prepare a strategic vision statement for your company. It should be at least one sentence long and no longer than a brief paragraph. When you are finished, check to see if your vision statement meets the conditions for an effectively worded strategic vision set forth in Table 2.1. If not, then revise it accordingly. What would be a good slogan that captures the essence of your strategic vision and that could be used to help communicate the vision to company personnel, shareholders, and other stakeholders?

LO 2-2   2.   What are your company's financial objectives? What are your company's strategic objectives?

LO 2-3   3.   What are the three to four key elements of your company's strategy?

ENDNOTES

[1] Gordon Shaw, Robert Brown, and Philip Bromiley, "Strategic Stories: How 3M Is Rewriting Business Planning," *Harvard Business Review* 76, no. 3 (May–June 1998); David J. Collis and Michael G. Rukstad, "Can You Say What Your Strategy Is?" *Harvard Business Review* 86, no. 4 (April 2008) pp. 82–90.
[2] Hugh Davidson, *The Committed Enterprise: How to Make Vision and Values Work*

(Oxford: Butterworth Heinemann, 2002); W. Chan Kim and Renée Mauborgne, "Charting Your Company's Future," *Harvard Business Review* 80, no. 6 (June 2002), pp. 77–83; James C. Collins and Jerry I. Porras, "Building Your Company's Vision," *Harvard Business Review* 74, no. 5 (September– October 1996), pp. 65–77; Jim Collins and Jerry Porras, *Built to Last: Successful Habits of Visionary Companies* (New

York: HarperCollins, 1994); Michel Robert, *Strategy Pure and Simple II: How Winning Companies Dominate Their Competitors* (New York: McGraw-Hill, 1998).
[3] Davidson, *The Committed Enterprise,* pp. 20 and 54.
[4] As quoted in Charles H. House and Raymond L. Price, "The Return Map: Tracking Product Teams," *Harvard Business Review* 60, no. 1 (January–February 1991), p. 93.

5 Sitkin, S., Miller, C. and See, K., "The Stretch Goal Paradox", *Harvard Business Review,* 95, no. 1 (January–February, 2017, pp. 92–99.

6 Robert S. Kaplan and David P. Norton, *The Strategy-Focused Organization* (Boston: Harvard Business School Press, 2001); Robert S. Kaplan and David P. Norton, *The Balanced Scorecard: Translating Strategy into Action* (Boston: Harvard Business School Press, 1996).

7 Kaplan and Norton, *The Strategy-Focused Organization;* Kaplan and Norton, *The Balanced Scorecard;* Kevin B. Hendricks, Larry Menor, and Christine Wiedman, "The Balanced Scorecard: To Adopt or Not to Adopt," *Ivey Business Journal* 69, no. 2 (November– December 2004), pp. 1–7; Sandy Richardson, "The Key Elements of Balanced Scorecard Success," *Ivey Business Journal* 69, no. 2 (November–December 2004), pp. 7–9.

8 Kaplan and Norton, *The Balanced Scorecard.*

9 Ibid.

10 Ibid.

11 Information posted on the website of the Balanced Scorecard Institute, **balancedscorecard .org** (accessed October, 2015).

12 Henry Mintzberg, Bruce Ahlstrand, and Joseph Lampel, *Strategy Safari: A Guided Tour through the Wilds of Strategic Management* (New York: Free Press, 1998); Bruce Barringer and Allen C. Bluedorn, "The Relationship between Corporate Entrepreneurship and Strategic Management," *Strategic Management Journal* 20 (1999), pp. 421–444; Jeffrey G. Covin and Morgan P. Miles, "Corporate Entrepreneurship and the Pursuit of Competitive Advantage," *Entrepreneurship: Theory and Practice* 23, no. 3 (Spring 1999), pp. 47–63; David A. Garvin and Lynne C. Levesque, "Meeting the Challenge of Corporate Entrepreneurship," *Harvard Business Review* 84, no. 10 (October 2006), pp. 102–112.

13 Joseph L. Bower and Clark G. Gilbert, "How Managers' Everyday Decisions Create or Destroy Your Company's Strategy," *Harvard Business Review* 85, no. 2 (February 2007), pp. 72–79.

14 Gordon Shaw, Robert Brown, and Philip Bromiley, "Strategic Stories: How 3M Is Rewriting Business Planning," *Harvard Business Review* 76, no. 3 (May–June 1998), pp. 41–50.

15 David Collis and Michael Rukstad, "Can You Say What Your Stratgey Is?" *Harvard Business Review,* May 2008, pp. 82–90.

16 Cynthia A. Montgomery, "Putting Leadership Back into Strategy," *Harvard Business Review* 86, no. 1 (January 2008), pp. 54–60.

17 Jay W. Lorsch and Robert C. Clark, "Leading from the Boardroom," *Harvard Business Review* 86, no. 4 (April 2008), pp. 105–111.

18 Ibid.

19 Stephen P. Kaufman, "Evaluating the CEO," *Harvard Business Review* 86, no. 10 (October 2008), pp. 53–57.

20 Ibid.

21 David A. Nadler, "Building Better Boards," *Harvard Business Review* 82, no. 5 (May 2004), pp. 102–105; Cynthia A. Montgomery and Rhonda Kaufman, "The Board's Missing Link," *Harvard Business Review* 81, no. 3 (March 2003), pp. 86–93; John Carver, "What Continues to Be Wrong with Corporate Governance and How to Fix It," *Ivey Business Journal* 68, no. 1 (September–October 2003), pp. 1–5. See also Gordon Donaldson, "A New Tool for Boards: The Strategic Audit," *Harvard Business Review* 73, no. 4 (July–August 1995), pp. 99–107.

chapter 3

Evaluating a Company's External Environment

Learning Objectives

This chapter will help you

LO 3-1 Recognize the factors in a company's broad macro-environment that may have strategic significance.

LO 3-2 Use analytic tools to diagnose the competitive conditions in a company's industry.

LO 3-3 Map the market positions of key groups of industry rivals.

LO 3-4 Determine whether an industry's outlook presents a company with sufficiently attractive opportunities for growth and profitability.

©Imagezoo/Getty Images

No matter what it takes, the goal of *strategy* is to beat the competition.

Kenichi Ohmae—*Consultant and author*

Sometimes by losing a battle you find a new way to win the war.

Donald Trump—*President of the United States and founder of Trump Entertainment Resorts*

Continued innovation is the best way to beat the competition.

Thomas A Edison—*Inventor and Businessman*

In order to chart a company's strategic course wisely, managers must first develop a deep understanding of the company's present situation. Two facets of a company's situation are especially pertinent: (1) its external environment—most notably, the competitive conditions of the industry in which the company operates; and (2) its internal environment—particularly the company's resources and organizational capabilities.

Insightful diagnosis of a company's external and internal environments is a prerequisite for managers to succeed in crafting a strategy that is an excellent *fit* with the company's situation—the first test of a winning strategy. As depicted in Figure 3.1, strategic thinking begins with an appraisal of the company's external and internal environments (as

a basis for deciding on a long-term direction and developing a strategic vision). It then moves toward an evaluation of the most promising alternative strategies and business models, and finally culminates in choosing a specific strategy.

This chapter presents the concepts and analytic tools for zeroing in on those aspects of a company's external environment that should be considered in making strategic choices. Attention centers on the broad environmental context, the specific market arena in which a company operates, the drivers of change, the positions and likely actions of rival companies, and key success factors. In Chapter 4, we explore the methods of evaluating a company's internal circumstances and competitive capabilities.

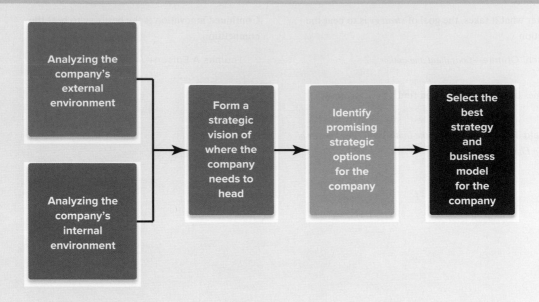

ANALYZING THE COMPANY'S MACRO-ENVIRONMENT

● LO 3-1

Recognize the factors in a company's broad macro-environment that may have strategic significance.

Every company operates in a broad **"macro-environment"** that comprises six principal components: political factors; economic conditions in the firm's general environment (local, country, regional, worldwide); sociocultural forces; technological factors; environmental factors (concerning the natural environment); and legal/regulatory conditions. Each of these components has the potential to affect the firm's more immediate industry and competitive environment, although some are likely to have a more important effect than others (see Figure 3.2). An analysis of the impact of these factors is often referred to as **PESTEL analysis,** an acronym that serves as a reminder of the six components involved (Political, Economic, Sociocultural, Technological, Environmental, Legal/regulatory).

Since macro-economic factors affect different industries in different ways and to different degrees, it is important for managers to determine which of these represent the most *strategically relevant factors* outside the firm's industry boundaries. By *strategically relevant,* we mean important enough to have a bearing on the decisions the company ultimately makes about its long-term direction, objectives, strategy, and business model. The impact of the outer-ring factors depicted in Figure 3.2 on a company's choice of strategy can range from big to small. Those factors that are likely to a bigger impact deserve the closest attention. But even factors that have a low impact on the company's business situation merit a watchful eye since their level of impact may change.

For example, when stringent new federal banking regulations are announced, banks must rapidly adapt their strategies and lending practices to be in compliance. Cigarette producers must adapt to new antismoking ordinances, the decisions of governments

CORE CONCEPT

The **macro-environment** encompasses the broad environmental context in which a company's industry is situated.

FIGURE 3.2 The Components of a Company's Macro-Environment

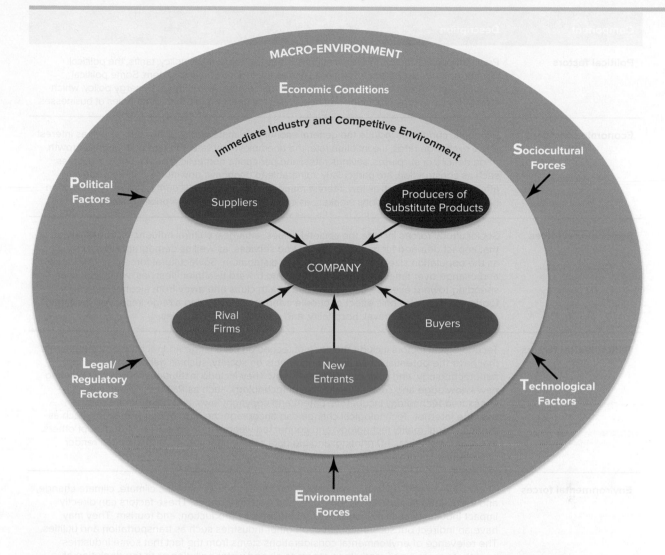

to impose higher cigarette taxes, the growing cultural stigma attached to smoking and newlyemerging e-cigarette technology. The homebuilding industry is affected by such macro-influences as trends in household incomes and buying power, rules and regulations that make it easier or harder for homebuyers to obtain mortgages, changes in mortgage interest rates, shifting preferences of families for renting versus owning a home, and shifts in buyer preferences for homes of various sizes, styles, and price ranges. Companies in the food processing, restaurant, sports, and fitness industries have to pay special attention to changes in lifestyles, eating habits, leisure-time preferences, and attitudes toward nutrition and fitness in fashioning their strategies. Table 3.1 provides a brief description of the components of the macro-environment and some examples of the industries or business situations that they might affect.

As company managers scan the external environment, they must be alert for potentially important outer-ring developments, assess their impact and influence, and adapt the company's direction and strategy as needed. However, the factors in a

CORE CONCEPT

PESTEL analysis can be used to assess the strategic relevance of the six principal components of the macro-environment: **P**olitical, **E**conomic, **S**ocial, **T**echnological, **E**nvironmental, and **L**egal/Regulatory forces.

TABLE 3.1   The Six Components of the Macro-Environment

Component	Description
Political factors	Pertinent political factors include matters such as tax policy, fiscal policy, tariffs, the political climate, and the strength of institutions such as the federal banking system. Some political policies affect certain types of industries more than others. An example is energy policy, which clearly affects energy producers and heavy users of energy more than other types of businesses.
Economic conditions	Economic conditions include the general economic climate and specific factors such as interest rates, exchange rates, the inflation rate, the unemployment rate, the rate of economic growth, trade deficits or surpluses, savings rates, and per-capita domestic product. Some industries, such as construction, are particularly vulnerable to economic downturns but are positively affected by factors such as low interest rates. Others, such as discount retailing, benefit when general economic conditions weaken, as consumers become more price-conscious.
Sociocultural forces	Sociocultural forces include the societal values, attitudes, cultural influences, and lifestyles that impact demand for particular goods and services, as well as demographic factors such as the population size, growth rate, and age distribution. Sociocultural forces vary by locale and change over time. An example is the trend toward healthier lifestyles, which can shift spending toward exercise equipment and health clubs and away from alcohol and snack foods. The demographic effect of people living longer is having a huge impact on the health care, nursing homes, travel, hospitality, and entertainment industries.
Technological factors	Technological factors include the pace of technological change and technical developments that have the potential for wide-ranging effects on society, such as genetic engineering, nanotechnology, and solar energy technology. They include institutions involved in creating new knowledge and controlling the use of technology, such as R&D consortia, university-sponsored technology incubators, patent and copyright laws, and government control over the Internet. Technological change can encourage the birth of new industries, such as drones, virtual reality technology, and connected wearable devices. They can disrupt others, as cloud computing, 3-D printing, and big data solution have done, and they can render other industries obsolete (film cameras, music CDs).
Environmental forces	These include ecological and environmental forces such as weather, climate, climate change, and associated factors like flooding, fire, and water shortages. These factors can directly impact industries such as insurance, farming, energy production, and tourism. They may have an indirect but substantial effect on other industries such as transportation and utilities. The relevance of environmental considerations stems from the fact that some industries contribute more significantly than others to air and water pollution or to the depletion of irreplaceable natural resources, or to inefficient energy/resource usage, or are closely associated with other types of environmentally damaging activities (unsustainable agricultural practices, the creation of waste products that are not recyclable or biodegradable). Growing numbers of companies worldwide, in response to stricter environmental regulations and also to mounting public concerns about the environment, are implementing actions to operate in a more environmentally and ecologically responsible manner.
Legal and regulatory factors	These factors include the regulations and laws with which companies must comply, such as consumer laws, labor laws, antitrust laws, and occupational health and safety regulation. Some factors, such as financial services regulation, are industry-specific. Others affect certain types of industries more than others. For example, minimum wage legislation largely impacts low-wage industries (such as nursing homes and fast food restaurants) that employ substantial numbers of relatively unskilled workers. Companies in coal-mining, meat-packing, and steel-making, where many jobs are hazardous or carry high risk of injury, are much more impacted by occupational safety regulations than are companies in industries such as retailing or software programming.

company's environment having the *greatest* strategy-shaping impact typically pertain to the company's immediate industry and competitive environment. Consequently, it is on a company's industry and competitive environment (depicted in the center of Figure 3.2) that we concentrate the bulk of our attention in this chapter.

ASSESSING THE COMPANY'S INDUSTRY AND COMPETITIVE ENVIRONMENT

Thinking strategically about a company's industry and competitive environment entails using some well-validated concepts and analytic tools. These include the five forces framework, the value net, driving forces, strategic groups, competitor analysis, and key success factors. Proper use of these analytic tools can provide managers with the understanding needed to craft a strategy that fits the company's situation within their industry environment. The remainder of this chapter is devoted to describing how managers can use these tools to inform and improve their strategic choices.

● LO 3-2

Use analytic tools to diagnose the competitive conditions in a company's industry.

THE FIVE FORCES FRAMEWORK

The character and strength of the competitive forces operating in an industry are never the same from one industry to another. The most powerful and widely used tool for diagnosing the principal competitive pressures in a market is the *five forces framework.*[1] This framework, depicted in Figure 3.3, holds that competitive pressures on companies within an industry come from five sources. These include (1) competition from *rival sellers,* (2) competition from *potential new entrants* to the industry, (3) competition from producers of *substitute products,* (4) *supplier* bargaining power, and (5) *customer* bargaining power.

Using the five forces model to determine the nature and strength of competitive pressures in a given industry involves three steps:

- *Step 1:* For each of the five forces, identify the different parties involved, along with the specific factors that bring about competitive pressures.
- *Step 2:* Evaluate how strong the pressures stemming from each of the five forces are (strong, moderate, or weak).
- *Step 3:* Determine whether the five forces, overall, are supportive of high industry profitability.

Competitive Pressures Created by the Rivalry among Competing Sellers

The strongest of the five competitive forces is often the rivalry for buyer patronage among competing sellers of a product or service. The intensity of rivalry among competing sellers within an industry depends on a number of identifiable factors. Figure 3.4 summarizes these factors, identifying those that intensify or weaken rivalry among direct competitors in an industry. A brief explanation of why these factors affect the degree of rivalry is in order:

FIGURE 3.3   The Five Forces Model of Competition: A Key Analytic Tool

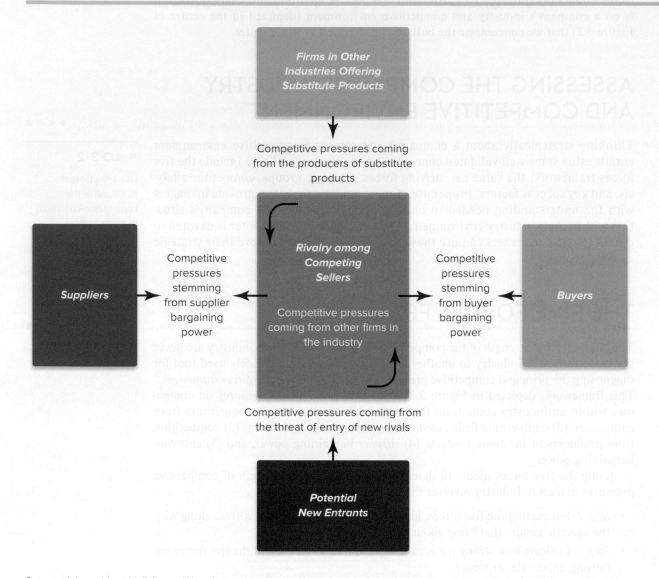

Sources: Adapted from M. E. Porter, "How Competitive Forces Shape Strategy," *Harvard Business Review* 57, no. 2 (1979), pp. 137–145; M. E. Porter, "The Five Competitive Forces That Shape Strategy," *Harvard Business Review* 86, no. 1 (2008), pp. 80–86.

- *Rivalry increases when buyer demand is growing slowly or declining.* Rapidly expanding buyer demand produces enough new business for all industry members to grow without having to draw customers away from rival enterprises. But in markets where buyer demand is slow-growing or shrinking, companies eager to gain more business are likely to engage in aggressive price discounting, sales promotions, and other tactics to increase their sales volumes at the expense of rivals, sometimes to the point of igniting a fierce battle for market share.

- *Rivalry increases as it becomes less costly for buyers to switch brands.* The less costly (or easier) it is for buyers to switch their purchases from one seller to another, the easier it is for sellers to steal customers away from rivals. When the cost of

FIGURE 3.4 Factors Affecting the Strength of Rivalry

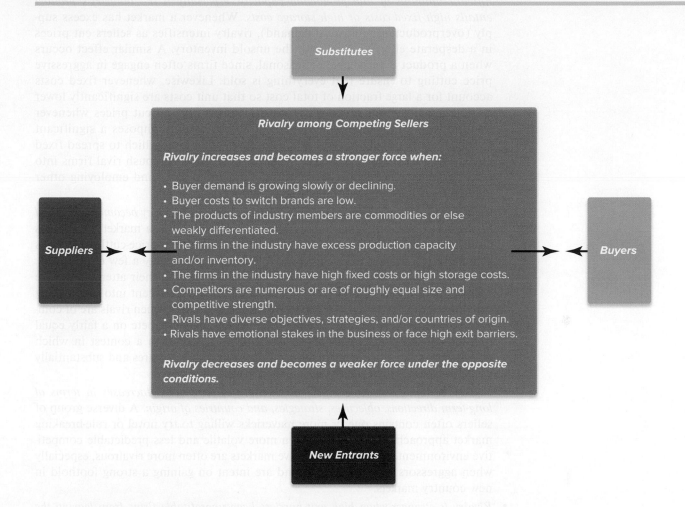

Substitutes

Suppliers

Buyers

Rivalry among Competing Sellers

Rivalry increases and becomes a stronger force when:

- Buyer demand is growing slowly or declining.
- Buyer costs to switch brands are low.
- The products of industry members are commodities or else weakly differentiated.
- The firms in the industry have excess production capacity and/or inventory.
- The firms in the industry have high fixed costs or high storage costs.
- Competitors are numerous or are of roughly equal size and competitive strength.
- Rivals have diverse objectives, strategies, and/or countries of origin.
- Rivals have emotional stakes in the business or face high exit barriers.

Rivalry decreases and becomes a weaker force under the opposite conditions.

New Entrants

switching brands is higher, buyers are less prone to brand switching and sellers have protection from rivalrous moves. Switching costs include not only monetary costs but also the time, inconvenience, and psychological costs involved in switching brands. For example, retailers may not switch to the brands of rival manufacturers because they are hesitant to sever long-standing supplier relationships or incur the additional expense of retraining employees, accessing technical support, or testing the quality and reliability of the new brand. Consumers may not switch brands because they become emotionally attached to a particular brand (e.g. if you identify with the Harley motorcycle brand and lifestyle).

- *Rivalry increases as the products of rival sellers become less strongly differentiated.* When the offerings of rivals are identical or weakly differentiated, buyers have less reason to be brand-loyal—a condition that makes it easier for rivals to convince buyers to switch to their offerings. Moreover, when the products of different sellers are virtually identical, shoppers will choose on the basis of price, which can result in fierce price competition among sellers. On the other hand, strongly differentiated product offerings among rivals breed high brand loyalty on the part of buyers who view the attributes of certain brands as more appealing or better suited to their needs.

- *Rivalry is more intense when industry members have too much inventory or significant amounts of idle production capacity, especially if the industry's product entails high fixed costs or high storage costs.* Whenever a market has excess supply (overproduction relative to demand), rivalry intensifies as sellers cut prices in a desperate effort to cope with the unsold inventory. A similar effect occurs when a product is perishable or seasonal, since firms often engage in aggressive price cutting to ensure that everything is sold. Likewise, whenever fixed costs account for a large fraction of total cost so that unit costs are significantly lower at full capacity, firms come under significant pressure to cut prices whenever they are operating below full capacity. Unused capacity imposes a significant cost-increasing penalty because there are fewer units over which to spread fixed costs. The pressure of high fixed or high storage costs can push rival firms into offering price concessions, special discounts, and rebates and employing other volume-boosting competitive tactics.

- *Rivalry intensifies as the number of competitors increases and they become more equal in size and capability.* When there are many competitors in a market, companies eager to increase their meager market share often engage in price-cutting activities to drive sales, leading to intense rivalry. When there are only a few competitors, companies are more wary of how their rivals may react to their attempts to take market share away from them. Fear of retaliation and a descent into a damaging price war leads to restrained competitive moves. Moreover, when rivals are of comparable size and competitive strength, they can usually compete on a fairly equal footing—an evenly matched contest tends to be fiercer than a contest in which one or more industry members have commanding market shares and substantially greater resources than their much smaller rivals.

- *Rivalry becomes more intense as the diversity of competitors increases in terms of long-term directions, objectives, strategies, and countries of origin.* A diverse group of sellers often contains one or more mavericks willing to try novel or rule-breaking market approaches, thus generating a more volatile and less predictable competitive environment. Globally competitive markets are often more rivalrous, especially when aggressors have lower costs and are intent on gaining a strong foothold in new country markets.

- *Rivalry is stronger when high exit barriers keep unprofitable firms from leaving the industry.* In industries where the assets cannot easily be sold or transferred to other uses, where workers are entitled to job protection, or where owners are committed to remaining in business for personal reasons, failing firms tend to hold on longer than they might otherwise—even when they are bleeding red ink. Deep price discounting typically ensues, in a desperate effort to cover costs and remain in business. This sort of rivalry can destabilize an otherwise attractive industry.

The previous factors, taken as whole, determine whether the rivalry in an industry is relatively strong, moderate, or weak. When rivalry is *strong,* the battle for market share is generally so vigorous that the profit margins of most industry members are squeezed to bare-bones levels. When rivalry is *moderate,* a more normal state, the maneuvering among industry members, while lively and healthy, still allows most industry members to earn acceptable profits. When rivalry is *weak,* most companies in the industry are relatively well satisfied with their sales growth and market shares and rarely undertake offensives to steal customers away from one another. Weak rivalry means that there is no downward pressure on industry profitability due to this particular competitive force.

The Choice of Competitive Weapons

Competitive battles among rival sellers can assume many forms that extend well beyond lively price competition. For example, competitors may resort to such marketing tactics as special sales promotions, heavy advertising, rebates, or low-interest-rate financing to drum up additional sales. Rivals may race one another to differentiate their products by offering better performance features or higher quality or improved customer service or a wider product selection. They may also compete through the rapid introduction of next-generation products, the frequent introduction of new or improved products, and efforts to build stronger dealer networks, establish positions in foreign markets, or otherwise expand distribution capabilities and market presence. Table 3.2 displays the competitive weapons that firms often employ in battling rivals, along with their primary effects with respect to price (P), cost (C), and value (V)—the elements of an effective business model and the value-price-cost framework, discussed in Chapter 1.

Competitive Pressures Associated with the Threat of New Entrants

New entrants into an industry threaten the position of rival firms since they will compete fiercely for market share, add to the number of industry rivals, and add to the industry's production capacity in the process. But even the *threat* of new entry puts added competitive pressure on current industry members and thus functions as an important competitive force. This is because credible threat of entry often prompts industry members to lower their prices and initiate defensive actions in an attempt

TABLE 3.2   Common "Weapons" for Competing with Rivals

Types of Competitive Weapons	Primary Effects
Discounting prices, holding clearance sales	Lowers price (P), increases total sales volume and market share, lowers profits if price cuts are not offset by large increases in sales volume
Offering coupons, advertising items on sale	Increases sales volume and total revenues, lowers price (P), increases unit costs (C), may lower profit margins per unit sold ($P - C$)
Advertising product or service characteristics, using ads to enhance a company's image	Boosts buyer demand, increases product differentiation and perceived value (V), increases total sales volume and market share, but may increase unit costs (C) and lower profit margins per unit sold
Innovating to improve product performance and quality	Increases product differentiation and value (V), boosts buyer demand, boosts total sales volume, likely to increase unit costs (C)
Introducing new or improved features, increasing the number of styles to provide greater product selection	Increases product differentiation and value (V), strengthens buyer demand, boosts total sales volume and market share, likely to increase unit costs (C)
Increasing customization of product or service	Increases product differentiation and value (V), increases buyer switching costs, boosts total sales volume, often increases unit costs (C)
Building a bigger, better dealer network	Broadens access to buyers, boosts total sales volume and market share, may increase unit costs (C)
Improving warranties, offering low-interest financing	Increases product differentiation and value (V), increases unit costs (C), increases buyer switching costs, boosts total sales volume and market share

to deter new entrants. Just how serious the threat of entry is in a particular market depends on (1) whether entry barriers are high or low, and (2) the expected reaction of existing industry members to the entry of newcomers.

Whether Entry Barriers Are High or Low   The strength of the threat of entry is governed to a large degree by the height of the industry's entry barriers. High barriers reduce the threat of potential entry, whereas low barriers enable easier entry. Entry barriers are high under the following conditions:[2]

- *There are sizable economies of scale in production, distribution, advertising, or other activities.* When incumbent companies enjoy cost advantages associated with large-scale operations, outsiders must either enter on a large scale (a costly and perhaps risky move) or accept a cost disadvantage and consequently lower profitability.

- *Incumbents have other hard to replicate cost advantages over new entrants.* Aside from enjoying economies of scale, industry incumbents can have cost advantages that stem from the possession of patents or proprietary technology, exclusive partnerships with the best and cheapest suppliers, favorable locations, and low fixed costs (because they have older facilities that have been mostly depreciated). Learning-based cost savings can also accrue from experience in performing certain activities such as manufacturing or new product development or inventory management. The extent of such savings can be measured with learning/experience curves. The steeper the learning/experience curve, the bigger the cost advantage of the company with the largest *cumulative* production volume. The microprocessor industry provides an excellent example of this:

> *Manufacturing unit costs for microprocessors tend to decline about 20 percent each time cumulative production volume doubles. With a 20 percent experience curve effect, if the first 1 million chips cost $100 each, once production volume reaches 2 million, the unit cost would fall to $80 (80 percent of $100), and by a production volume of 4 million, the unit cost would be $64 (80 percent of $80).*[3]

- *Customers have strong brand preferences and high degrees of loyalty to seller.* The stronger the attachment of buyers to established brands, the harder it is for a newcomer to break into the marketplace. In such cases, a new entrant must have the financial resources to spend enough on advertising and sales promotion to overcome customer loyalties and build its own clientele. Establishing brand recognition and building customer loyalty can be a slow and costly process. In addition, if it is difficult or costly for a customer to switch to a new brand, a new entrant may have to offer a discounted price or otherwise persuade buyers that its brand is worth the switching costs. Such barriers discourage new entry because they act to boost financial requirements and lower expected profit margins for new entrants.

- *Patents and other forms of intellectual property protection are in place.* In a number of industries, entry is prevented due to the existence of intellectual property protection laws that remain in place for a given number of years. Often, companies have a "wall of patents" in place to prevent other companies from entering with a "me too" strategy that replicates a key piece of technology.

- *There are strong "network effects" in customer demand.* In industries where buyers are more attracted to a product when there are many other users of the product, there are said to be "network effects," since demand is higher the larger the network of users. Video game systems are an example because users prefer to have the same systems as their friends so that they can play together on systems they all know and can share games. When incumbents have a large existing base of users, new entrants with otherwise comparable products face a serious disadvantage in attracting buyers.

- *Capital requirements are high.* The larger the total dollar investment needed to enter the market successfully, the more limited the pool of potential entrants. The most obvious capital requirements for new entrants relate to manufacturing facilities and equipment, introductory advertising and sales promotion campaigns, working capital to finance inventories and customer credit, and sufficient cash to cover startup costs.

- *There are difficulties in building a network of distributors/dealers or in securing adequate space on retailers' shelves.* A potential entrant can face numerous distribution-channel challenges. Wholesale distributors may be reluctant to take on a product that lacks buyer recognition. Retailers must be recruited and convinced to give a new brand ample display space and an adequate trial period. When existing sellers have strong, well-functioning distributor–dealer networks, a newcomer has an uphill struggle in squeezing its way into existing distribution channels. Potential entrants sometimes have to "buy" their way into wholesale or retail channels by cutting their prices to provide dealers and distributors with higher markups and profit margins or by giving them big advertising and promotional allowances. As a consequence, a potential entrant's own profits may be squeezed unless and until its product gains enough consumer acceptance that distributors and retailers are willing to carry it.

- *There are restrictive regulatory policies.* Regulated industries like cable TV, telecommunications, electric and gas utilities, radio and television broadcasting, liquor retailing, nuclear power, and railroads entail government-controlled entry. Government agencies can also limit or even bar entry by requiring licenses and permits, such as the medallion required to drive a taxicab in New York City. Government-mandated safety regulations and environmental pollution standards also create entry barriers because they raise entry costs. Recently enacted banking regulations in many countries have made entry particularly difficult for small new bank startups—complying with all the new regulations along with the rigors of competing against existing banks requires very deep pockets.

- *There are restrictive trade policies.* In international markets, host governments commonly limit foreign entry and must approve all foreign investment applications. National governments commonly use tariffs and trade restrictions (antidumping rules, local content requirements, quotas, etc.) to raise entry barriers for foreign firms and protect domestic producers from outside competition.

The Expected Reaction of Industry Members in Defending against New Entry
A second factor affecting the threat of entry relates to the ability and willingness of industry incumbents to launch strong defensive maneuvers to maintain their positions and make it harder for a newcomer to compete successfully and profitably. Entry candidates may have second thoughts about attempting entry if they conclude that existing firms will mount well-funded campaigns to hamper (or even defeat) a newcomer's attempt to gain a market foothold big enough to compete successfully. Such campaigns can include any of the "competitive weapons" listed in Table 3.2, such as ramping up advertising expenditures, offering special price discounts to the very customers a newcomer is seeking to attract, or adding attractive new product features (to match or beat the newcomer's product offering). Such actions can raise a newcomer's cost of entry along with the risk of failing, making the prospect of entry less appealing. The result is that even the expectation on the part of new entrants that industry incumbents will contest a newcomer's entry may

be enough to dissuade entry candidates from going forward. Microsoft can be counted on to fiercely defend the position that Windows enjoys in computer operating systems and that Microsoft Office has in office productivity software. This may well have contributed to Microsoft's ability to continuously dominate this market space.

However, there are occasions when industry incumbents have nothing in their competitive arsenal that is formidable enough to either discourage entry or put obstacles in a newcomer's path that will defeat its strategic efforts to become a viable competitor. In the restaurant industry, for example, existing restaurants in a given geographic market have few actions they can take to discourage a new restaurant from opening or to block it from attracting enough patrons to be profitable. A fierce competitor like Nike was unable to prevent newcomer Under Armour from rapidly growing its sales and market share in sports apparel. Furthermore, there are occasions when industry incumbents can be expected to refrain from taking or initiating any actions specifically aimed at contesting a newcomer's entry. In large industries, entry by small startup enterprises normally poses no immediate or direct competitive threat to industry incumbents and their entry is not likely to provoke defensive actions. For instance, a new online retailer with sales prospects of maybe $5 to $10 million annually can reasonably expect to escape competitive retaliation from much larger online retailers selling similar goods. The less that a newcomer's entry will adversely impact the sales and profitability of industry incumbents, the more reasonable it is for potential entrants to expect industry incumbents to refrain from reacting defensively.

Figure 3.5 summarizes the factors that cause the overall competitive pressure from potential entrants to be strong or weak. An analysis of these factors can help managers determine whether the threat of entry into their industry is high or low, *in general.* But certain kinds of companies—those with sizable financial resources, proven competitive capabilities, and a respected brand name—may be able to hurdle an industry's entry barriers even when they are high.[4] For example, when Honda opted to enter the U.S. lawn-mower market in competition against Toro, Snapper, Craftsman, John Deere, and others, it was easily able to hurdle entry barriers that would have been formidable to other newcomers because it had long-standing expertise in gasoline engines and a reputation for quality and durability in automobiles that gave it instant credibility with homeowners. As a result, Honda had to spend relatively little on inducing dealers to handle the Honda lawn-mower line or attracting customers. Similarly, Samsung's brand reputation in televisions, DVD players, and other electronics products gave it strong credibility in entering the market for smartphones— Samsung's Galaxy smartphones are now a formidable rival of Apple's iPhone.

It is also important to recognize that the barriers to entering an industry can become stronger or weaker over time. For example, once key patents preventing new entry in the market for functional 3-D printers expired, the way was open for new competition to enter this industry. On the other hand, new strategic actions by incumbent firms to increase advertising, strengthen distributor–dealer relations, step up R&D, or improve product quality can erect higher roadblocks to entry.

> Even high entry barriers may not suffice to keep out certain kinds of entrants: those with resources and capabilities that enable them to leap over or bypass the barriers.

> High entry barriers and weak entry threats today do not always translate into high entry barriers and weak entry threats tomorrow.

Competitive Pressures from the Sellers of Substitute Products

Companies in one industry are vulnerable to competitive pressure from the actions of companies in a closely adjoining industry whenever buyers view the products of the two industries as good substitutes. Substitutes do *not* include other brands within your

FIGURE 3.5   Factors Affecting the Threat of Entry

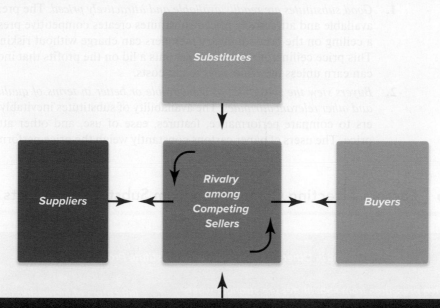

Substitutes

Suppliers

Rivalry among Competing Sellers

Buyers

Competitive Pressures from Potential Entrants

Threat of entry is a stronger force when (1) incumbents are unlikely to make retaliatory moves against new entrants and (2) entry barriers are low. Entry barriers are high (and threat of entry is low) when
• Incumbents have large cost advantages over potential entrants due to
  – High economies of scale
  – Significant experience-based cost advantages or learning curve effects
  – Other cost advantages (e.g., favorable access to inputs, technology, location, or low fixed costs)
• Customers with strong brand preferences and/or loyalty to incumbent sellers
• Patents and other forms of intellectual property protection
• Strong network effects
• High capital requirements
• Limited new access to distribution channels and shelf space
• Restrictive government policies
• Restrictive trade policies

industry; this type of pressure comes from *outside* the industry. Substitute products from outside the industry are those that can perform the same or similar functions for the consumer as products within your industry. For instance, the producers of eyeglasses and contact lenses face competitive pressures from the doctors who do corrective laser surgery. Similarly, the producers of sugar experience competitive pressures from the producers of sugar substitutes (high-fructose corn syrup, agave syrup, and artificial sweeteners). Internet providers of news-related information have put brutal competitive pressure on the publishers of newspapers. The makers of smartphones, by building ever better cameras into their cell phones, have cut deeply into the sales of producers of handheld digital cameras—most smartphone owners now use their phone to take pictures rather than carrying a digital camera for picture-taking purposes.

As depicted in Figure 3.6, three factors determine whether the competitive pressures from substitute products are strong or weak. Competitive pressures are stronger when

1. *Good substitutes are readily available and attractively priced.* The presence of readily available and attractively priced substitutes creates competitive pressure by placing a ceiling on the prices industry members can charge without risking sales erosion. This price ceiling, at the same time, puts a lid on the profits that industry members can earn unless they find ways to cut costs.

2. *Buyers view the substitutes as comparable or better in terms of quality, performance, and other relevant attributes.* The availability of substitutes inevitably invites customers to compare performance, features, ease of use, and other attributes besides price. The users of paper cartons constantly weigh the price-performance trade-offs

FIGURE 3.6   Factors Affecting Competition from Substitute Products

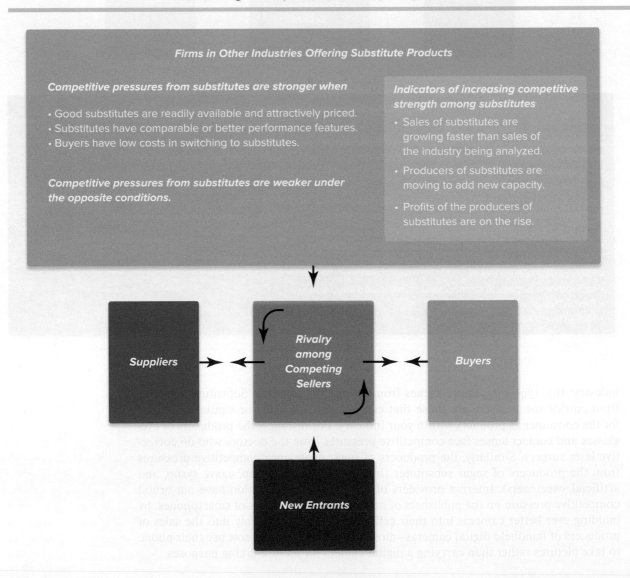

Firms in Other Industries Offering Substitute Products

Competitive pressures from substitutes are stronger when

- Good substitutes are readily available and attractively priced.
- Substitutes have comparable or better performance features.
- Buyers have low costs in switching to substitutes.

Competitive pressures from substitutes are weaker under the opposite conditions.

Indicators of increasing competitive strength among substitutes

- Sales of substitutes are growing faster than sales of the industry being analyzed.
- Producers of substitutes are moving to add new capacity.
- Profits of the producers of substitutes are on the rise.

Suppliers → ← Rivalry among Competing Sellers → ← Buyers

New Entrants

with plastic containers and metal cans, for example. Movie enthusiasts are increasingly weighing whether to go to movie theaters to watch newly released movies or wait until they can watch the same movies streamed to their home TV by Netflix, Amazon Prime, cable providers, and other on-demand sources.

3. *The costs that buyers incur in switching to the substitutes are low.* Low switching costs make it easier for the sellers of attractive substitutes to lure buyers to their offerings; high switching costs deter buyers from purchasing substitute products.

Some signs that the competitive strength of substitute products is increasing include (1) whether the sales of substitutes are growing faster than the sales of the industry being analyzed, (2) whether the producers of substitutes are investing in added capacity, and (3) whether the producers of substitutes are earning progressively higher profits.

But before assessing the competitive pressures coming from substitutes, company managers must identify the substitutes, which is less easy than it sounds since it involves (1) determining where the industry boundaries lie and (2) figuring out which other products or services can address the same basic customer needs as those produced by industry members. Deciding on the industry boundaries is necessary for determining which firms are direct rivals and which produce substitutes. This is a matter of perspective—there are no hard-and-fast rules, other than to say that other brands of the same basic product constitute rival products and not substitutes. Ultimately, it's simply the buyer who decides what can serve as a good substitute.

Competitive Pressures Stemming from Supplier Bargaining Power

Whether the suppliers of industry members represent a weak or strong competitive force depends on the degree to which suppliers have sufficient *bargaining power* to influence the terms and conditions of supply in their favor. Suppliers with strong bargaining power are a source of competitive pressure because of their ability to charge industry members higher prices, pass costs on to them, and limit their opportunities to find better deals. For instance, Microsoft and Intel, both of which supply PC makers with essential components, have been known to use their dominant market status not only to charge PC makers premium prices but also to leverage their power over PC makers in other ways. The bargaining power of these two companies over their customers is so great that both companies have faced antitrust charges on numerous occasions. Prior to a legal agreement ending the practice, Microsoft pressured PC makers to load only Microsoft products on the PCs they shipped. Intel has defended itself against similar antitrust charges, but in filling orders for newly introduced Intel chips, it continues to give top priority to PC makers that use the biggest percentages of Intel chips in their PC models. Being on Intel's list of preferred customers helps a PC maker get an early allocation of Intel's latest chips and thus allows the PC maker to get new models to market ahead of rivals.

Small-scale retailers often must contend with the power of manufacturers whose products enjoy well-known brand names, since consumers expect to find these products on the shelves of the retail stores where they shop. This provides the manufacturer with a degree of pricing power and often the ability to push hard for favorable shelf displays. Supplier bargaining power is also a competitive factor in industries where unions have been able to organize the workforce (which supplies labor). Air pilot unions, for example, have employed their bargaining power to increase pilots' wages and benefits in the air transport industry. The growing clout of the largest healthcare union in the United States has led to better wages and working conditions in nursing homes.

As shown in Figure 3.7, a variety of factors determine the strength of suppliers' bargaining power. Supplier power is stronger when

- *Demand for suppliers' products is high and the products are in short supply.* A surge in the demand for particular items shifts the bargaining power to the suppliers of those products; suppliers of items in short supply have pricing power.
- *Suppliers provide differentiated inputs that enhance the performance of the industry's product.* The more valuable a particular input is in terms of enhancing the performance or quality of the products of industry members, the more bargaining leverage suppliers have. In contrast, the suppliers of commodities are in a weak bargaining position, since industry members have no reason other than price to prefer one supplier over another.
- *It is difficult or costly for industry members to switch their purchases from one supplier to another.* Low switching costs limit supplier bargaining power by enabling industry members to change suppliers if any one supplier attempts to raise prices by more than the costs of switching. Thus, the higher the switching costs of industry members, the stronger the bargaining power of their suppliers.
- *The supplier industry is dominated by a few large companies and it is more concentrated than the industry it sells to.* Suppliers with sizable market shares and strong demand for the items they supply generally have sufficient bargaining power to charge high prices and deny requests from industry members for lower prices or other concessions.

FIGURE 3.7   Factors Affecting the Bargaining Power of Suppliers

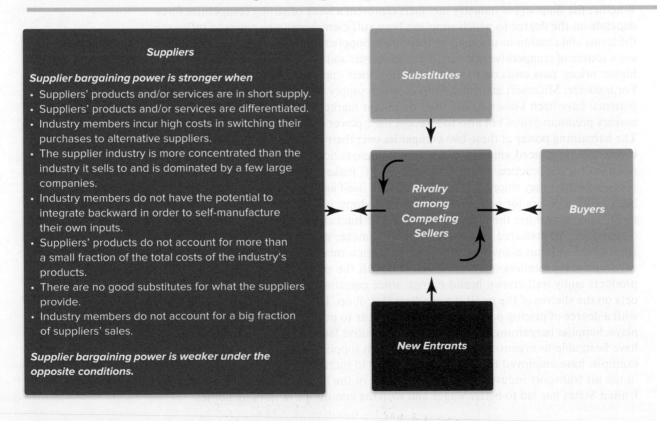

Suppliers

Supplier bargaining power is stronger when
- Suppliers' products and/or services are in short supply.
- Suppliers' products and/or services are differentiated.
- Industry members incur high costs in switching their purchases to alternative suppliers.
- The supplier industry is more concentrated than the industry it sells to and is dominated by a few large companies.
- Industry members do not have the potential to integrate backward in order to self-manufacture their own inputs.
- Suppliers' products do not account for more than a small fraction of the total costs of the industry's products.
- There are no good substitutes for what the suppliers provide.
- Industry members do not account for a big fraction of suppliers' sales.

Supplier bargaining power is weaker under the opposite conditions.

Substitutes

Rivalry among Competing Sellers

Buyers

New Entrants

- *Industry members are incapable of integrating backward to self-manufacture items they have been buying from suppliers.* As a rule, suppliers are safe from the threat of self-manufacture by their customers until the volume of parts a customer needs becomes large enough for the customer to justify backward integration into self-manufacture of the component. When industry members can threaten credibly to self-manufacture suppliers' goods, their bargaining power over suppliers increases proportionately.

- *Suppliers provide an item that accounts for no more than a small fraction of the costs of the industry's product.* The more that the cost of a particular part or component affects the final product's cost, the more that industry members will be sensitive to the actions of suppliers to raise or lower their prices. When an input accounts for only a small proportion of total input costs, buyers will be less sensitive to price increases. Thus, suppliers' power increases when the inputs they provide do *not* make up a large proportion of the cost of the final product.

- *Good substitutes are not available for the suppliers' products.* The lack of readily available substitute inputs increases the bargaining power of suppliers by increasing the dependence of industry members on the suppliers.

- *Industry members are not major customers of suppliers.* As a rule, suppliers have less bargaining leverage when their sales to members of the industry constitute a big percentage of their total sales. In such cases, the well-being of suppliers is closely tied to the well-being of their major customers, and their dependence upon them increases. The bargaining power of suppliers is stronger, then, when they are *not* bargaining with major customers.

In identifying the degree of supplier power in an industry, it is important to recognize that different types of suppliers are likely to have different amounts of bargaining power. Thus, the first step is for managers to identify the different types of suppliers, paying particular attention to those that provide the industry with important inputs. The next step is to assess the bargaining power of each type of supplier separately.

Competitive Pressures Stemming from Buyer Bargaining Power and Price Sensitivity

Whether buyers are able to exert strong competitive pressures on industry members depends on (1) the degree to which buyers have bargaining power and (2) the extent to which buyers are price-sensitive. Buyers with strong bargaining power can limit industry profitability by demanding price concessions, better payment terms, or additional features and services that increase industry members' costs. Buyer price sensitivity limits the profit potential of industry members by restricting the ability of sellers to raise prices without losing revenue due to lost sales.

As with suppliers, the leverage that buyers have in negotiating favorable terms of sale can range from weak to strong. Individual consumers seldom have much bargaining power in negotiating price concessions or other favorable terms with sellers. However, their price sensitivity varies by individual and by the type of product they are buying (whether it's a necessity or a discretionary purchase, for example). Similarly, small businesses usually have weak bargaining power because of the small-size orders they place with sellers. Many relatively small wholesalers and retailers join buying groups to pool their purchasing power and approach manufacturers for better terms than could be gotten individually. Large business buyers, in contrast, can have considerable bargaining power. For example, large retail chains like

Walmart, Best Buy, Staples, and Home Depot typically have considerable bargaining power in purchasing products from manufacturers, not only because they buy in large quantities, but also because of manufacturers' need for access to their broad base of customers. Major supermarket chains like Kroger, Albertsons, Hannaford, and Aldi have sufficient bargaining power to demand promotional allowances and lump-sum payments (called *slotting fees*) from food products manufacturers in return for stocking certain brands or putting them in the best shelf locations. Motor vehicle manufacturers have strong bargaining power in negotiating to buy original-equipment tires from tire makers such as Bridgestone, Goodyear, Michelin, Continental, and Pirelli, partly because they buy in large quantities and partly because consumers are more likely to buy replacement tires that match the tire brand on their vehicle at the time of its purchase. The starting point for the analysis of buyers as a competitive force is to identify the different types of buyers along the value chain—then proceed to analyzing the bargaining power and price sensitivity of each type separately. It is important to recognize that *not all buyers of an industry's product have equal degrees of bargaining power with sellers, and some may be less sensitive than others to price, quality, or service differences.*

Figure 3.8 summarizes the factors determining the strength of buyer power in an industry. The top of this chart lists the factors that increase buyers' bargaining power,

FIGURE 3.8   Factors Affecting the Power of Buyers

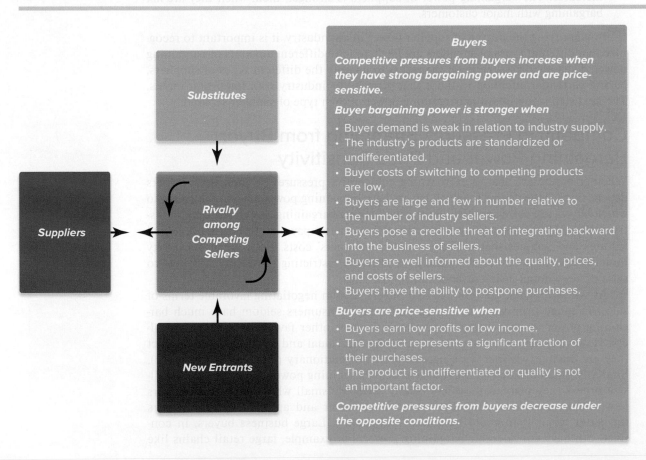

which we discuss next. Note that the first five factors are the mirror image of those determining the bargaining power of suppliers.

Buyer bargaining power is stronger when

- *Buyer demand is weak in relation to the available supply.* Weak or declining demand and the resulting excess supply create a "buyers' market," in which bargain-hunting buyers have leverage in pressing industry members for better deals and special treatment. Conversely, strong or rapidly growing market demand creates a "sellers' market" characterized by tight supplies or shortages—conditions that put buyers in a weak position to wring concessions from industry members.

- *Industry goods are standardized or differentiation is weak.* In such circumstances, buyers make their selections on the basis of price, which increases price competition among vendors.

- *Buyers' costs of switching to competing brands or substitutes are relatively low.* Switching costs put a cap on how much industry producers can raise prices or reduce quality before they will lose the buyer's business.

- *Buyers are large and few in number relative to the number of sellers.* The larger the buyers, the more important their business is to the seller and the more sellers will be willing to grant concessions.

- *Buyers pose a credible threat of integrating backward into the business of sellers.* Beer producers like Anheuser Busch InBev SA/NV (whose brands include Budweiser, Molson Coors, and Heineken) have partially integrated backward into metal-can manufacturing to gain bargaining power in obtaining the balance of their can requirements from otherwise powerful metal-can manufacturers.

- *Buyers are well informed about the product offerings of sellers (product features and quality, prices, buyer reviews) and the cost of production (an indicator of markup).* The more information buyers have, the better bargaining position they are in. The mushrooming availability of product information on the Internet (and its ready access on smartphones) is giving added bargaining power to consumers, since they can use this to find or negotiate better deals. Apps such as ShopSavvy and BuyVia are now making comparison shopping even easier.

- *Buyers have discretion to delay their purchases or perhaps even not make a purchase at all.* Consumers often have the option to delay purchases of durable goods (cars, major appliances), or decline to buy discretionary goods (massages, concert tickets) if they are not happy with the prices offered. Business customers may also be able to defer their purchases of certain items, such as plant equipment or maintenance services. This puts pressure on sellers to provide concessions to buyers so that the sellers can keep their sales numbers from dropping off.

Whether Buyers Are More or Less Price Sensitive Low-income and budget-constrained consumers are almost always price sensitive; bargain-hunting consumers are highly price sensitive by nature. Most consumers grow more price sensitive as the price tag of an item becomes a bigger fraction of their spending budget. Similarly, business buyers besieged by weak sales, intense competition, and other factors squeezing their profit margins are price sensitive. Price sensitivity also grows among businesses as the cost of an item becomes a bigger fraction of their cost structure. Rising prices of frequently purchased items heightens the price sensitivity of all types of buyers. On the other hand, the price sensitivity of all types of buyers decreases the more that the quality of the product matters.

The following factors increase buyer price sensitivity and result in greater competitive pressures on the industry as a result:

- *Buyer price sensitivity increases when buyers are earning low profits or have low income.* Price is a critical factor in the purchase decisions of low-income consumers and companies that are barely scraping by. In such cases, their high price sensitivity limits the ability of sellers to charge high prices.
- *Buyers are more price-sensitive if the product represents a large fraction of their total purchases.* When a purchase eats up a large portion of a buyer's budget or represents a significant part of his or her cost structure, the buyer cares more about price than might otherwise be the case.
- *Buyers are more price-sensitive when the quality of the product is not uppermost in their considerations.* Quality matters little when products are relatively undifferentiated, leading buyers to focus more on price. But when quality affects performance, or can reduce a business buyer's other costs (by saving on labor, materials, etc.), price will matter less.

Is the Collective Strength of the Five Competitive Forces Conducive to Good Profitability?

Assessing whether each of the five competitive forces gives rise to strong, moderate, or weak competitive pressures sets the stage for evaluating whether, overall, the strength of the five forces is conducive to good profitability. Is any of the competitive forces sufficiently powerful to undermine industry profitability? Can companies in this industry reasonably expect to earn decent profits in light of the prevailing competitive forces?

The most extreme case of a "competitively unattractive" industry occurs when all five forces are producing strong competitive pressures: Rivalry among sellers is vigorous, low entry barriers allow new rivals to gain a market foothold, competition from substitutes is intense, and both suppliers and buyers are able to exercise considerable leverage. Strong competitive pressures coming from all five directions drive industry profitability to unacceptably low levels, frequently producing losses for many industry members and forcing some out of business. But an industry can be competitively unattractive without all five competitive forces being strong. In fact, *intense competitive pressures from just one of the five forces may suffice to destroy the conditions for good profitability and prompt some companies to exit the business.*

As a rule, *the strongest competitive forces determine the extent of the competitive pressure on industry profitability.* Thus, in evaluating the strength of the five forces overall and their effect on industry profitability, managers should look to the strongest forces. Having more than one strong force will not worsen the effect on industry profitability, but it does mean that the industry has multiple competitive challenges with which to cope. In that sense, an industry with three to five strong forces is even more "unattractive" as a place to compete. Especially intense competitive conditions due to multiple strong forces seem to be the norm in tire manufacturing, apparel, and commercial airlines, three industries where profit margins have historically been thin.

In contrast, when the overall impact of the five competitive forces is moderate to weak, an industry is "attractive" in the sense that the *average* industry member can reasonably expect to earn good profits and a nice return on investment. The ideal competitive environment for earning superior profits is one in which both suppliers and customers have limited power, there are no good substitutes, high barriers block further entry, and rivalry among present sellers is muted. Weak competition is the best of all possible worlds for also-ran companies because even they can usually eke out a decent profit—if a company can't make a decent profit when competition is weak, then its business outlook is indeed grim.

Matching Company Strategy to Competitive Conditions

Working through the five forces model step by step not only aids strategy makers in assessing whether the intensity of competition allows good profitability but also promotes sound strategic thinking about how to better match company strategy to the specific competitive character of the marketplace. Effectively matching a company's business strategy to prevailing competitive conditions has two aspects:

1. Pursuing avenues that shield the firm from as many of the different competitive pressures as possible.

2. Initiating actions calculated to shift the competitive forces in the company's favor by altering the underlying factors driving the five forces.

But making headway on these two fronts first requires identifying competitive pressures, gauging the relative strength of each of the five competitive forces, and gaining a deep enough understanding of the state of competition in the industry to know which strategy buttons to push.

> A company's strategy is strengthened the more it provides insulation from competitive pressures, shifts the competitive battle in the company's favor, and positions the firm to take advantage of attractive growth opportunities.

COMPLEMENTORS AND THE VALUE NET

Not all interactions among industry participants are necessarily competitive in nature. Some have the potential to be cooperative, as the value net framework demonstrates. Like the five forces framework, the value net includes an analysis of buyers, suppliers, and substitutors (see Figure 3.9). But it differs from the five forces framework in several important ways.

First, the analysis focuses on the interactions of industry participants with a particular company. Thus it places that firm in the center of the framework, as Figure 3.9 shows. Second, the category of "competitors" is defined to include not only the focal firm's direct competitors or industry rivals but also the sellers of substitute products and potential entrants. Third, the value net framework introduces a new category of industry participant that is not found in the five forces framework—that of "complementors." **Complementors** are the producers of complementary products, which are products that enhance the value of the focal firm's products when they are used together. Some examples include snorkels and swim fins or shoes and shoelaces.

The inclusion of complementors draws particular attention to the fact that success in the marketplace need not come at the expense of other industry participants. Interactions among industry participants may be cooperative in nature rather than competitive. In the case of complementors, an increase in sales for them is likely to increase the sales of the focal firm as well. But the value net framework also encourages managers to consider other forms of cooperative interactions and realize that value is created jointly by all industry participants. For example, a company's success in the marketplace depends on establishing a reliable supply chain for its inputs, which implies the need for cooperative relations with its suppliers. Often a firm works

> **CORE CONCEPT**
>
> **Complementors** are the producers of complementary products, which are products that enhance the value of the focal firm's products when they are used together.

FIGURE 3.9   The Value Net

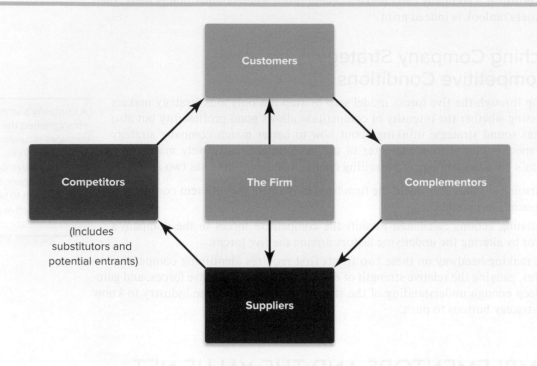

hand in hand with its suppliers to ensure a smoother, more efficient operation for both parties. Newell-Rubbermaid, and Procter & Gamble for example, work cooperatively as suppliers to companies such as Walmart, Target, and Kohl's. Even direct rivals may work cooperatively if they participate in industry trade associations or engage in joint lobbying efforts. Value net analysis can help managers discover the potential to improve their position through cooperative as well as competitive interactions.

INDUSTRY DYNAMICS AND THE FORCES DRIVING CHANGE

While it is critical to understand the nature and intensity of competitive and cooperative forces in an industry, it is equally critical to understand that the intensity of these forces is fluid and subject to change. All industries are affected by new developments and ongoing trends that alter industry conditions, some more speedily than others. The popular hypothesis that industries go through a life cycle of takeoff, rapid growth, maturity, market saturation and slowing growth, followed by stagnation or decline is but one aspect of industry change—many other new developments and emerging trends cause industry change.[5] Any strategies devised by management will therefore play out in a dynamic industry environment, so it's imperative that managers consider the factors driving industry change and how they might affect the industry environment. Moreover, with early notice, managers may be able to influence the direction or scope of environmental change and improve the outlook.

Industry and competitive conditions change because forces are enticing or pressuring certain industry participants (competitors, customers, suppliers, complementors) to alter their actions in important ways. The most powerful of the change agents are called **driving forces** because they have the biggest influences in reshaping the industry landscape and altering competitive conditions. Some driving forces originate in the outer ring of the company's macro-environment (see Figure 3.2), but most originate in the company's more immediate industry and competitive environment.

CORE CONCEPT

Driving forces are the major underlying causes of change in industry and competitive conditions.

Driving-forces analysis has three steps: (1) identifying what the driving forces are; (2) assessing whether the drivers of change are, on the whole, acting to make the industry more or less attractive; and (3) determining what strategy changes are needed to prepare for the impact of the driving forces. All three steps merit further discussion.

Identifying the Forces Driving Industry Change

Many developments can affect an industry powerfully enough to qualify as driving forces. Some drivers of change are unique and specific to a particular industry situation, but most drivers of industry and competitive change fall into one of the following categories:

- *Changes in an industry's long-term growth rate.* Shifts in industry growth up or down have the potential to affect the balance between industry supply and buyer demand, entry and exit, and the character and strength of competition. Whether demand is growing or declining is one of the key factors influencing the intensity of rivalry in an industry, as explained earlier. But the strength of this effect will depend on how changes in the industry growth rate affect entry and exit in the industry. If entry barriers are low, then growth in demand will attract new entrants, increasing the number of industry rivals and changing the competitive landscape.

- *Increasing globalization.* Globalization can be precipitated by such factors as the blossoming of consumer demand in developing countries, the availability of lower-cost foreign inputs, and the reduction of trade barriers, as has occurred recently in many parts of Latin America and Asia. Significant differences in labor costs among countries give manufacturers a strong incentive to locate plants for labor-intensive products in low-wage countries and use these plants to supply market demand across the world. Wages in China, India, Vietnam, Mexico, and Brazil, for example, are much lower than those in the United States, Germany, and Japan. The forces of globalization are sometimes such a strong driver that companies find it highly advantageous, if not necessary, to spread their operating reach into more and more country markets. Globalization is very much a driver of industry change in such industries as energy, mobile phones, steel, social media, public accounting, commercial aircraft, electric power generation equipment, and pharmaceuticals.

- *Emerging new Internet capabilities and applications.* Mushrooming use of high-speed Internet service and Voice-over-Internet-Protocol (VoIP) technology, growing acceptance of online shopping, and the exploding popularity of Internet applications ("apps") have been major drivers of change in industry after industry. The Internet has allowed online discount stock brokers, such as E*TRADE, and TD Ameritrade to mount a strong challenge against full-service firms such as Edward Jones and Merrill Lynch. The newspaper industry has yet to figure out a strategy for surviving the advent of online news.

Massive open online courses (MOOCs) facilitated by organizations such as Coursera, edX, and Udacity are profoundly affecting higher education. The "Internet of things" will feature faster speeds, dazzling applications, and billions of connected gadgets performing an array of functions, thus driving further industry and competitive changes. But Internet-related impacts vary from industry to industry. The challenges are to assess precisely how emerging Internet developments are altering a particular industry's landscape and to factor these impacts into the strategy-making equation.

- *Shifts in who buys the products and how the products are used.* Shifts in buyer demographics and the ways products are used can greatly alter competitive conditions. Longer life expectancies and growing percentages of relatively well-to-do retirees, for example, are driving demand growth in such industries as cosmetic surgery, assisted living residences, and vacation travel. The burgeoning popularity of streaming video has affected broadband providers, wireless phone carriers, and television broadcasters, and created opportunities for such new entertainment businesses as Hulu and Netflix.

- *Technological change and manufacturing process innovation.* Advances in technology can cause disruptive change in an industry by introducing substitutes or can alter the industry landscape by opening up whole new industry frontiers. For instance, revolutionary change in autonomous system technology has put Google, Tesla, Apple, and every major automobile manufacturer into a race to develop viable self-driving vehicles.

- *Product innovation.* An ongoing stream of product innovations tends to alter the pattern of competition in an industry by attracting more first-time buyers, rejuvenating industry growth, and/or increasing product differentiation, with concomitant effects on rivalry, entry threat, and buyer power. Product innovation has been a key driving force in the smartphone industry, which in an ever more connected world is driving change in other industries. Philips Lighting Hue bulbs now allow homeowners to use a smartphone app to remotely turn lights on and off, blink if an intruder is detected, and create a wide range of white and color ambiances. Wearable action-capture cameras and unmanned aerial view drones are rapidly becoming a disruptive force in the digital camera industry by enabling photography shots and videos not feasible with handheld digital cameras.

- *Marketing innovation.* When firms are successful in introducing new ways to market their products, they can spark a burst of buyer interest, widen industry demand, increase product differentiation, and lower unit costs—any or all of which can alter the competitive positions of rival firms and force strategy revisions. Consider, for example, the growing propensity of advertisers to place a bigger percentage of their ads on social media sites like Facebook and Twitter.

- *Entry or exit of major firms.* Entry by a major firm thus often produces a new ball game, not only with new key players but also with new rules for competing. Similarly, exit of a major firm changes the competitive structure by reducing the number of market leaders and increasing the dominance of the leaders who remain.

- *Diffusion of technical know-how across companies and countries.* As knowledge about how to perform a particular activity or execute a particular manufacturing technology spreads, products tend to become more commodity-like. Knowledge diffusion can occur through scientific journals, trade publications, onsite plant tours, word of mouth among suppliers and customers, employee migration, and Internet sources.

- *Changes in cost and efficiency.* Widening or shrinking differences in the costs among key competitors tend to dramatically alter the state of competition. Declining costs of producing tablets have enabled price cuts and spurred tablet sales (especially lower-priced models) by making them more affordable to lower-income households worldwide. Lower cost e-books are cutting into sales of costlier hardcover books as increasing numbers of consumers have laptops, iPads, Kindles, and other brands of tablets.

- *Reductions in uncertainty and business risk.* Many companies are hesitant to enter industries with uncertain futures or high levels of business risk because it is unclear how much time and money it will take to overcome various technological hurdles and achieve acceptable production costs (as is the case in the solar power industry). Over time, however, diminishing risk levels and uncertainty tend to stimulate new entry and capital investments on the part of growth-minded companies seeking new opportunities, thus dramatically altering industry and competitive conditions.

- *Regulatory influences and government policy changes.* Government regulatory actions can often mandate significant changes in industry practices and strategic approaches—as has recently occurred in the world's banking industry. New rules and regulations pertaining to government-sponsored health insurance programs are driving changes in the health care industry. In international markets, host governments can drive competitive changes by opening their domestic markets to foreign participation or closing them to protect domestic companies.

- *Changing societal concerns, attitudes, and lifestyles.* Emerging social issues as well as changing attitudes and lifestyles can be powerful instigators of industry change. Growing concern about the effects of climate change has emerged as a major driver of change in the energy industry. Concerns about the use of chemical additives and the nutritional content of food products have been driving changes in the restaurant and food industries. Shifting societal concerns, attitudes, and lifestyles alter the pattern of competition, favoring those players that respond with products targeted to the new trends and conditions.

> The most important part of driving-forces analysis is to determine whether the collective impact of the driving forces will increase or decrease market demand, make competition more or less intense, and lead to higher or lower industry profitability.

While many forces of change may be at work in a given industry, *no more than three or four* are likely to be true driving forces powerful enough to qualify as the *major determinants* of why and how the industry is changing. Thus, company strategists must resist the temptation to label every change they see as a driving force. Table 3.3 lists the most common driving forces.

TABLE 3.3   The Most Common Drivers of Industry Change

- Changes in the long-term industry growth rate
- Increasing globalization
- Emerging new Internet capabilities and applications
- Shifts in buyer demographics
- Technological change and manufacturing process innovation
- Product and marketing innovation
- Entry or exit of major firms
- Diffusion of technical know-how across companies and countries
- Changes in cost and efficiency
- Reductions in uncertainty and business risk
- Regulatory influences and government policy changes
- Changing societal concerns, attitudes, and lifestyles

Assessing the Impact of the Forces Driving Industry Change

The second step in driving-forces analysis is to determine whether the prevailing change drivers, on the whole, are acting to make the industry environment more or less attractive. Three questions need to be answered:

1. Are the driving forces, on balance, acting to cause demand for the industry's product to increase or decrease?
2. Is the collective impact of the driving forces making competition more or less intense?
3. Will the combined impacts of the driving forces lead to higher or lower industry profitability?

Getting a handle on the collective impact of the driving forces requires looking at the likely effects of each factor separately, since the driving forces may not all be pushing change in the same direction. For example, one driving force may be acting to spur demand for the industry's product while another is working to curtail demand. Whether the net effect on industry demand is up or down hinges on which change driver is the most powerful.

> The real payoff of driving-forces analysis is to help managers understand what strategy changes are needed to prepare for the impacts of the driving forces.

Adjusting the Strategy to Prepare for the Impacts of Driving Forces

The third step in the strategic analysis of industry dynamics—where the real payoff for strategy making comes—is for managers to draw some conclusions about *what strategy adjustments will be needed to deal with the impacts of the driving forces.* But taking the "right" kinds of actions to prepare for the industry and competitive changes being wrought by the driving forces first requires accurate diagnosis of the forces driving industry change and the impacts these forces will have on both the industry environment and the company's business. To the extent that managers are unclear about the drivers of industry change and their impacts, or if their views are off-base, the chances of making astute and timely strategy adjustments are slim. So driving-forces analysis is not something to take lightly; it has practical value and is basic to the task of thinking strategically about where the industry is headed and how to prepare for the changes ahead.

STRATEGIC GROUP ANALYSIS

● ● ● ●

● LO 3-3

Map the market positions of key groups of industry rivals.

Within an industry, companies commonly sell in different price/quality ranges, appeal to different types of buyers, have different geographic coverage, and so on. Some are more attractively positioned than others. Understanding which companies are strongly positioned and which are weakly positioned is an integral part of analyzing an industry's competitive structure. The best technique for revealing the market positions of industry competitors is **strategic group mapping.**

Using Strategic Group Maps to Assess the Market Positions of Key Competitors

A **strategic group** consists of those industry members with similar competitive approaches and positions in the market. Companies in the same strategic group can resemble one another in a variety of ways. They may have comparable product-line breadth, sell in the same price/quality range, employ the same distribution channels, depend on identical technological approaches, compete in much the same geographic areas, or offer buyers essentially the same product attributes or similar services and technical assistance.[6] Evaluating strategy options entails examining what strategic groups exist, identifying the companies within each group, and determining if a competitive "white space" exists where industry competitors are able to create and capture altogether new demand. As part of this process, the number of strategic groups in an industry and their respective market positions can be displayed on a strategic group map.

The procedure for constructing a *strategic group map* is straightforward:

- Identify the competitive characteristics that delineate strategic approaches used in the industry. Typical variables used in creating strategic group maps are price/quality range (high, medium, low), geographic coverage (local, regional, national, global), product-line breadth (wide, narrow), degree of service offered (no frills, limited, full), use of distribution channels (retail, wholesale, Internet, multiple), degree of vertical integration (none, partial, full), and degree of diversification into other industries (none, some, considerable).
- Plot the firms on a two-variable map using pairs of these variables.
- Assign firms occupying about the same map location to the same strategic group.
- Draw circles around each strategic group, making the circles proportional to the size of the group's share of total industry sales revenues.

This produces a two-dimensional diagram like the one for the U.S. casual dining industry in Illustration Capsule 3.1.

Several guidelines need to be observed in creating strategic group maps. First, the two variables selected as axes for the map should *not* be highly correlated; if they are, the circles on the map will fall along a diagonal and reveal nothing more about the relative positions of competitors than would be revealed by comparing the rivals on just one of the variables. For instance, if companies with broad product lines use multiple distribution channels while companies with narrow lines use a single distribution channel, then looking at the differences in distribution-channel approaches adds no new information about positioning.

Second, the variables chosen as axes for the map should reflect important differences among rival approaches—when rivals differ on both variables, the locations of the rivals will be scattered, thus showing how they are positioned differently. Third, the variables used as axes don't have to be either quantitative or continuous; rather, they can be discrete variables, defined in terms of distinct classes and combinations. Fourth, drawing the sizes of the circles on the map proportional to the combined sales of the firms in each strategic group allows the map to reflect the relative sizes of each strategic group. Fifth, if more than two good variables can be used as axes for the map, then it is wise to draw several maps to give different exposures to the competitive positioning relationships present in the industry's structure—there is not necessarily one best map for portraying how competing firms are positioned.

The Value of Strategic Group Maps

Strategic group maps are revealing in several respects. The most important has to do with identifying which industry members are close rivals and which are distant rivals. Firms in the same strategic group are the closest rivals; the next closest rivals

Comparative Market Positions of Selected Companies in the Casual Dining Industry: A Strategic Group Map Example

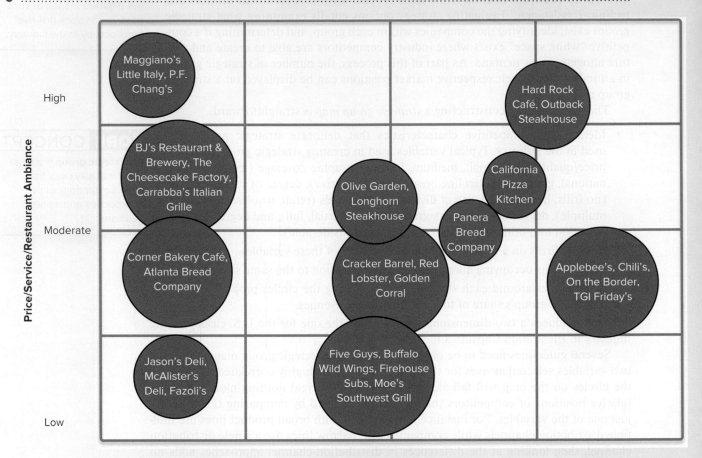

Note: Circles are drawn roughly proportional to the sizes of the chains, based on revenues.

are in the immediately adjacent groups. Often, firms in strategic groups that are far apart on the map hardly compete at all. For instance, Walmart's clientele, merchandise selection, and pricing points are much too different to justify calling Walmart a close competitor of Neiman Marcus or Saks Fifth Avenue. For the same reason, the beers produced by Yuengling are really not in competition with the beers produced by Pabst.

The second thing to be gleaned from strategic group mapping is that *not all positions on the map are equally attractive.*[7] Two reasons account for why some positions can be more attractive than others:

1. *Prevailing competitive pressures from the industry's five forces may cause the profit potential of different strategic groups to vary.* The profit prospects of firms in different strategic groups can vary from good to poor because of differing degrees

of competitive rivalry within strategic groups, differing pressures from potential entrants to each group, differing degrees of exposure to competition from substitute products outside the industry, and differing degrees of supplier or customer bargaining power from group to group. For instance, in the ready-to-eat cereal industry, there are significantly higher entry barriers (capital requirements, brand loyalty, etc.) for the strategic group comprising the large branded-cereal makers than for the group of generic-cereal makers or the group of small natural-cereal producers. Differences among the branded rivals versus the generic cereal makers make rivalry stronger within the generic-cereal strategic group. Among apparel retailers, the competitive battle between Marshall's and TJ MAXX is more intense (with consequently smaller profit margins) than the rivalry among Prada, Burberry, Gucci, Armani, and other high-end fashion retailers.

2. *Industry driving forces may favor some strategic groups and hurt others.* Likewise, industry driving forces can boost the business outlook for some strategic groups and adversely impact the business prospects of others. In the energy industry, producers of renewable energy, such as solar and wind power, are gaining ground over fossil fuel based producers due to improvements in technology and increased concern over climate change. Firms in strategic groups that are being adversely impacted by driving forces may try to shift to a more favorably situated position. If certain firms are known to be trying to change their competitive positions on the map, then attaching arrows to the circles showing the targeted direction helps clarify the picture of competitive maneuvering among rivals.

> Some strategic groups are more favorably positioned than others because they confront weaker competitive forces and/or because they are more favorably impacted by industry driving forces.

Thus, part of strategic group map analysis always entails drawing conclusions about where on the map is the "best" place to be and why. Which companies/strategic groups are destined to prosper because of their positions? Which companies/strategic groups seem destined to struggle? What accounts for why some parts of the map are better than others? Since some strategic groups are more attractive than others, one might ask why less well-positioned firms do not simply migrate to the more attractive position. The answer is that **mobility barriers** restrict movement between groups in the same way that entry barriers prevent easy entry into attractive industries. The most profitable strategic groups may be protected from entry by high mobility barriers.

> **CORE CONCEPT**
>
> **Mobility barriers** restrict firms in one strategic group from entering another more attractive strategic group in the same industry.

COMPETITOR ANALYSIS AND THE SOAR FRAMEWORK

Unless a company pays attention to the strategies and situations of competitors and has some inkling of what moves they will be making, it ends up flying blind into competitive battle. As in sports, scouting the opposition is an essential part of game plan development. Gathering competitive intelligence about the strategic direction and likely moves of key competitors allows a company to prepare defensive countermoves, to craft its own strategic moves with some confidence about what market maneuvers to expect from rivals in response, and to exploit any openings that arise from competitors' missteps. The question is where to look for such information, since rivals rarely reveal their strategic intentions openly. If information is not directly available, what are the best indicators?

> Studying competitors' past behavior and preferences provides a valuable assist in anticipating what moves rivals are likely to make next and outmaneuvering them in the marketplace.

Michael Porter's **SOAR Framework for Competitor Analysis** points to four indicators of a rival's likely strategic moves and countermoves. These include a rival's *Strategy,*

Objectives, Assumptions about itself and the industry, and *Resources and capabilities,* as shown in Figure 3.10. A strategic profile of a competitor that provides good clues to its behavioral proclivities can be constructed by characterizing the rival along these four dimensions. By "behavioral proclivities," we mean what competitive moves a rival is likely to make and how they are likely to react to the competitive moves of your company—its probable actions and reactions. By listing all that you know about a competitor (or a set of competitors) with respect to each of the four elements of the SOAR framework, you are likely to gain some insight about how the rival will behave in the near term. And knowledge of this sort can help you to predict how this will affect you, and how you should position yourself to respond. That is, what should you do to protect yourself or gain advantage now (in advance); and what should you do in response to your rivals next moves?

Current Strategy To succeed in predicting a competitor's next moves, company strategists need to have a good understanding of each rival's current strategy, as an indicator of its pattern of behavior and best strategic options. Questions to consider include: How is the competitor positioned in the market? What is the basis for its competitive advantage (if any)? What kinds of investments is it making (as an indicator of its growth trajectory)?

Objectives An appraisal of a rival's objectives should include not only its financial performance objectives but strategic ones as well (such as those concerning market share). What is even more important is to consider the extent to which the rival is meeting these objectives and whether it is under pressure to improve. Rivals with good financial performance are likely to continue their present strategy with only minor fine-tuning. Poorly performing rivals are virtually certain to make fresh strategic moves.

FIGURE 3.10 The SOAR Framework for Competitor Analysis

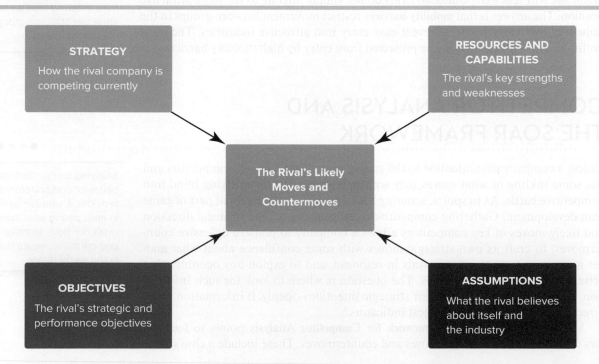

Resources and Capabilities   A rival's strategic moves and countermoves are both enabled and constrained by the set of resources and capabilities the rival has at hand. Thus a rival's resources and capabilities (and efforts to acquire new resources and capabilities) serve as a strong signal of future strategic actions (and reactions to your company's moves). Assessing a rival's resources and capabilities involves sizing up not only its strengths in this respect but its weaknesses as well.

Assumptions   How a rival's top managers think about their strategic situation can have a big impact on how the rival behaves. Banks that believe they are "too big to fail," for example, may take on more risk than is financially prudent. Assessing a rival's assumptions entails considering its assumptions about itself as well as about the industry it participates in.

Information regarding these four analytic components can often be gleaned from company press releases, information posted on the company's website (especially the presentations management has recently made to securities analysts), and such public documents as annual reports and 10-K filings. Many companies also have a competitive intelligence unit that sifts through the available information to construct up-to-date strategic profiles of rivals.[8]

Doing the necessary detective work can be time-consuming, but scouting competitors well enough to anticipate their next moves allows managers to prepare effective countermoves (perhaps even beat a rival to the punch) and to take rivals' probable actions into account in crafting their own best course of action.

KEY SUCCESS FACTORS

An industry's **key success factors (KSFs)** are those competitive factors that most affect industry members' ability to survive and prosper in the marketplace: the particular strategy elements, product attributes, operational approaches, resources, and competitive capabilities that spell the difference between being a strong competitor and a weak competitor—and between profit and loss. KSFs by their very nature are so important to competitive success that *all firms* in the industry must pay close attention to them or risk becoming an industry laggard or failure. To indicate the significance of KSFs another way, how well the elements of a company's strategy measure up against an industry's KSFs determines whether the company can meet the basic criteria for surviving and thriving in the industry. Identifying KSFs, in light of the prevailing and anticipated industry and competitive conditions, is therefore always a top priority in analytic and strategy-making considerations. Company strategists need to understand the industry landscape well enough to separate the factors most important to competitive success from those that are less important.

Key success factors vary from industry to industry, and even from time to time within the same industry, as change drivers and competitive conditions change. But regardless of the circumstances, an industry's key success factors can always be deduced by asking the same three questions:

1. On what basis do buyers of the industry's product choose between the competing brands of sellers? That is, what product attributes and service characteristics are crucial?

2. Given the nature of competitive rivalry prevailing in the marketplace, what resources and competitive capabilities must a company have to be competitively successful?

3. What shortcomings are almost certain to put a company at a significant competitive disadvantage?

Only rarely are there more than five key factors for competitive success. And even among these, two or three usually outrank the others in importance. Managers should therefore bear in mind the purpose of identifying key success factors—to determine which factors are most important to competitive success—and resist the temptation to label a factor that has only minor importance as a KSF.

In the beer industry, for example, although there are many types of buyers (wholesale, retail, end consumer), it is most important to understand the preferences and buying behavior of the beer drinkers. Their purchase decisions are driven by price, taste, convenient access, and marketing. Thus the KSFs include a *strong network of wholesale distributors* (to get the company's brand stocked and favorably displayed in retail outlets, bars, restaurants, and stadiums, where beer is sold) and *clever advertising* (to induce beer drinkers to buy the company's brand and thereby pull beer sales through the established wholesale and retail channels). Because there is a potential for strong buyer power on the part of large distributors and retail chains, competitive success depends on some mechanism to offset that power, of which advertising (to create demand pull) is one. Thus the KSFs also include *superior product differentiation* (as in microbrews) or *superior firm size and branding capabilities* (as in national brands). The KSFs also include *full utilization of brewing capacity* (to keep manufacturing costs low and offset the high costs of advertising, branding, and product differentiation).

Correctly diagnosing an industry's KSFs also raises a company's chances of crafting a sound strategy. The key success factors of an industry point to those things that every firm in the industry needs to attend to in order to retain customers and weather the competition. If the company's strategy cannot deliver on the key success factors of its industry, it is unlikely to earn enough profits to remain a viable business.

THE INDUSTRY OUTLOOK FOR PROFITABILITY

Each of the frameworks presented in this chapter—PESTEL, five forces analysis, driving forces, strategy groups, competitor analysis, and key success factors—provides a useful perspective on an industry's outlook for future profitability. Putting them all together provides an even richer and more nuanced picture. Thus, the final step in evaluating the industry and competitive environment is to use the results of each of the analyses performed to determine whether the industry presents the company with strong prospects for competitive success and attractive profits. The important factors on which to base a conclusion include

- How the company is being impacted by the state of the macro-environment.
- Whether strong competitive forces are squeezing industry profitability to subpar levels.
- Whether the presence of complementors and the possibility of cooperative actions improve the company's prospects.
- Whether industry profitability will be favorably or unfavorably affected by the prevailing driving forces.
- Whether the company occupies a stronger market position than rivals.
- Whether this is likely to change in the course of competitive interactions.
- How well the company's strategy delivers on the industry key success factors.

As a general proposition, *the anticipated industry environment is fundamentally attractive if it presents a company with good opportunity for above-average profitability; the industry outlook is fundamentally unattractive if a company's profit prospects are unappealingly low.*

However, it is a mistake to think of a particular industry as being equally attractive or unattractive to all industry participants and all potential entrants.[9] Attractiveness is relative, not absolute, and conclusions one way or the other have to be drawn from the perspective of a particular company. For instance, a favorably positioned competitor may see ample opportunity to capitalize on the vulnerabilities of weaker rivals even though industry conditions are otherwise somewhat dismal. At the same time, industries attractive to insiders may be unattractive to outsiders because of the difficulty of challenging current market leaders or because they have more attractive opportunities elsewhere.

When a company decides an industry is fundamentally attractive and presents good opportunities, a strong case can be made that it should invest aggressively to capture the opportunities it sees and to improve its long-term competitive position in the business. When a strong competitor concludes an industry is becoming less attractive, it may elect to simply protect its present position, investing cautiously—if at all—and looking for opportunities in other industries. A competitively weak company in an unattractive industry may see its best option as finding a buyer, perhaps a rival, to acquire its business.

● **LO 3-4**

Determine whether an industry's outlook presents a company with sufficiently attractive opportunities for growth and profitability.

The degree to which an industry is attractive or unattractive is not the same for all industry participants and all potential entrants.

KEY POINTS

Thinking strategically about a company's external situation involves probing for answers to the following questions:

1. *What are the strategically relevant factors in the macro-environment, and how do they impact an industry and its members?* Industries differ significantly as to how they are affected by conditions and developments in the broad macro-environment. Using PESTEL analysis to identify which of these factors is strategically relevant is the first step to understanding how a company is situated in its external environment.

2. *What kinds of competitive forces are industry members facing, and how strong is each force?* The strength of competition is a composite of five forces: (1) rivalry within

the industry, (2) the threat of new entry into the market, (3) inroads being made by the sellers of substitutes, (4) supplier bargaining power, and (5) buyer power. All five must be examined force by force, and their collective strength evaluated. One strong force, however, can be sufficient to keep average industry profitability low. Working through the five forces model aids strategy makers in assessing how to insulate the company from the strongest forces, identify attractive arenas for expansion, or alter the competitive conditions so that they offer more favorable prospects for profitability.

3. *What cooperative forces are present in the industry, and how can a company harness them to its advantage?* Interactions among industry participants are not only competitive in nature but cooperative as well. This is particularly the case when complements to the products or services of an industry are important. The Value Net framework assists managers in sizing up the impact of cooperative as well as competitive interactions on their firm.

4. *What factors are driving changes in the industry, and what impact will they have on competitive intensity and industry profitability?* Industry and competitive conditions change because certain forces are acting to create incentives or pressures for change. The first step is to identify the three or four most important drivers of change affecting the industry being analyzed (out of a much longer list of potential drivers). Once an industry's change drivers have been identified, the analytic task becomes one of determining whether they are acting, individually and collectively, to make the industry environment more or less attractive.

5. *What market positions do industry rivals occupy—who is strongly positioned and who is not?* Strategic group mapping is a valuable tool for understanding the similarities, differences, strengths, and weaknesses inherent in the market positions of rival companies. Rivals in the same or nearby strategic groups are close competitors, whereas companies in distant strategic groups usually pose little or no immediate threat. The lesson of strategic group mapping is that some positions on the map are more favorable than others. The profit potential of different strategic groups may not be the same because industry driving forces and competitive forces likely have varying effects on the industry's distinct strategic groups. Moreover, mobility barriers restrict movement between groups in the same way that entry barriers prevent easy entry into attractive industries.

6. *What strategic moves are rivals likely to make next?* Anticipating the actions of rivals can help a company prepare effective countermoves. Using the SOAR Framework for Competitor Analysis is helpful in this regard.

7. *What are the key factors for competitive success?* An industry's key success factors (KSFs) are the particular strategy elements, product attributes, operational approaches, resources, and competitive capabilities that all industry members must have in order to survive and prosper in the industry. For any industry, they can be deduced by answering three basic questions: (1) On what basis do buyers of the industry's product choose between the competing brands of sellers, (2) what resources and competitive capabilities must a company have to be competitively successful, and (3) what shortcomings are almost certain to put a company at a significant competitive disadvantage?

8. *Is the industry outlook conducive to good profitability?* The last step in industry analysis is summing up the results from applying each of the frameworks employed in answering questions 1 to 7: PESTEL, five forces analysis, Value Net, driving forces, strategic group mapping, competitor analysis, and key success factors.

Applying multiple lenses to the question of what the industry outlook looks like offers a more robust and nuanced answer. If the answers from each framework, seen as a whole, reveal that a company's profit prospects in that industry are above-average, then the industry environment is basically attractive *for that company.* What may look like an attractive environment for one company may appear to be unattractive from the perspective of a different company.

Clear, insightful diagnosis of a company's external situation is an essential first step in crafting strategies that are well matched to industry and competitive conditions. To do cutting-edge strategic thinking about the external environment, managers must know what questions to pose and what analytic tools to use in answering these questions. This is why this chapter has concentrated on suggesting the right questions to ask, explaining concepts and analytic approaches, and indicating the kinds of things to look for.

ASSURANCE OF LEARNING EXERCISES

1. Prepare a brief analysis of the organic food industry using the information provided by the Organic Trade Association at **www.ota.com** and the *Organic Report* magazine at **theorganicreport.com.** That is, based on the information provided on these websites, draw a five forces diagram for the organic food industry and briefly discuss the nature and strength of each of the five competitive forces.

connect

LO 3-2

2. Based on the strategic group map in Illustration Capsule 3.1, which casual dining chains are Cracker Barrel's closest competitors? With which strategic group does Panera Bread Company compete the least, according to this map? Why do you think no casual dining chains are positioned in the area above the Olive Garden's group?

connect

LO 3-3

3. The National Restaurant Association publishes an annual industry fact book that can be found at **www.restaurant.org.** Based on information in the latest report, does it appear that macro-environmental factors and the economic characteristics of the industry will present industry participants with attractive opportunities for growth and profitability? Explain.

LO 3-1, LO 3-4

EXERCISE FOR SIMULATION PARTICIPANTS

1. Which of the factors listed in Table 3.1 might have the most strategic relevance for your industry?

LO 3-1, LO 3-2, LO 3-3, LO 3-4

2. Which of the five competitive forces is creating the strongest competitive pressures for your company?

3. What are the "weapons of competition" that rival companies in your industry can use to gain sales and market share? See Table 3.2 to help you identify the various competitive factors.

4. What are the factors affecting the intensity of rivalry in the industry in which your company is competing? Use Figure 3.4 and the accompanying discussion to help you in pinpointing the specific factors most affecting competitive intensity. Would you characterize the rivalry and jockeying for better market position, increased sales, and market share among the companies in your industry as fierce, very strong, strong, moderate, or relatively weak? Why?

5. Are there any driving forces in the industry in which your company is competing? If so, what impact will these driving forces have? Will they cause competition to be more or less intense? Will they act to boost or squeeze profit margins? List at least two actions your company should consider taking in order to combat any negative impacts of the driving forces.

6. Draw a strategic group map showing the market positions of the companies in your industry. Which companies do you believe are in the most attractive position on the map? Which companies are the most weakly positioned? Which companies do you believe are likely to try to move to a different position on the strategic group map?

7. What do you see as the key factors for being a successful competitor in your industry? List at least three.

8. Does your overall assessment of the industry suggest that industry rivals have sufficiently attractive opportunities for growth and profitability? Explain.

ENDNOTES

[1] Michael E. Porter, *Competitive Strategy* (New York: Free Press, 1980); Michael E. Porter, "The Five Competitive Forces That Shape Strategy," *Harvard Business Review* 86, no. 1 (January 2008), pp. 78–93.

[2] J. S. Bain, *Barriers to New Competition* (Cambridge, MA: Harvard University Press, 1956); F. M. Scherer, *Industrial Market Structure and Economic Performance* (Chicago: Rand McNally, 1971).

[3] Ibid.

[4] C. A. Montgomery and S. Hariharan, "Diversified Expansion by Large Established

Firms," *Journal of Economic Behavior & Organization* 15, no. 1 (January 1991).

[5] For a more extended discussion of the problems with the life-cycle hypothesis, see Porter, *Competitive Strategy*, pp. 157–162.

[6] Mary Ellen Gordon and George R. Milne, "Selecting the Dimensions That Define Strategic Groups: A Novel Market-Driven Approach," *Journal of Managerial Issues* 11, no. 2 (Summer 1999), pp. 213–233.

[7] Avi Fiegenbaum and Howard Thomas, "Strategic Groups as Reference Groups: Theory, Modeling and Empirical Examination of

Industry and Competitive Strategy," *Strategic Management Journal* 16 (1995), pp. 461–476; S. Ade Olusoga, Michael P. Mokwa, and Charles H. Noble, "Strategic Groups, Mobility Barriers, and Competitive Advantage," *Journal of Business Research* 33 (1995), pp. 153–164.

[8] Larry Kahaner, *Competitive Intelligence* (New York: Simon & Schuster, 1996).

[9] B. Wernerfelt and C. Montgomery, "What Is an Attractive Industry?" *Management Science* 32, no. 10 (October 1986), pp. 1223–1230.

chapter 4

Evaluating a Company's Resources, Capabilities, and Competitiveness

Learning Objectives

This chapter will help you

LO 4-1 Evaluate how well a company's strategy is working.

LO 4-2 Assess the company's strengths and weaknesses in light of market opportunities and external threats.

LO 4-3 Explain why a company's resources and capabilities are central for gaining a competitive edge over rivals.

LO 4-4 Explain how value-chain activities affect a company's cost structure and customer value proposition.

LO 4-5 Explain how a comprehensive evaluation of a company's competitive situation can assist managers in making critical decisions about their next strategic move.

chapter 4

Evaluating a Company's Resources, Capabilities, and Competitiveness

Learning Objectives

This chapter will help you

LO 4-1 Evaluate how well a company's strategy is working.

LO 4-2 Assess the company's strengths and weaknesses in light of market opportunities and external threats.

LO 4-3 Explain why a company's resources and capabilities are critical for gaining a competitive edge over rivals.

LO 4-4 Explain how value chain activities affect a company's cost structure and customer value proposition.

LO 4-5 Explain how a comprehensive evaluation of a company's competitive situation can assist managers in making critical decisions about their next strategic moves.

©Roy Scott/Ikon Images/Getty Images

Crucial, of course, is having a difference that matters in the industry.

Cynthia Montgomery—*Professor and author*

If you don't have a competitive advantage, don't compete.

Jack Welch—*Former CEO of General Electric*

Organizations succeed in a competitive marketplace over the long run because they can do certain things their customers value better than can their competitors.

Robert Hayes, Gary Pisano, and David Upton—
Professors and consultants

Chapter 3 described how to use the tools of industry and competitor analysis to assess a company's external environment and lay the groundwork for matching a company's strategy to its external situation. This chapter discusses techniques for evaluating a company's internal situation, including its collection of resources and capabilities and the activities it performs along its value chain. Internal analysis enables managers to determine whether their strategy is likely to give the company a significant competitive edge over rival firms. Combined with external analysis, it facilitates an understanding of how to reposition a firm to take advantage of new opportunities and to cope with emerging competitive threats. The analytic spotlight will be trained on six questions:

1. How well is the company's present strategy working?

2. What are the company's most important resources and capabilities, and will they give the

company a lasting competitive advantage over rival companies?

3. What are the company's strengths and weaknesses in relation to the market opportunities and external threats?

4. How do a company's value chain activities impact its cost structure and customer value proposition?

5. Is the company competitively stronger or weaker than key rivals?

6. What strategic issues and problems merit front-burner managerial attention?

In probing for answers to these questions, five analytic tools—resource and capability analysis, SWOT analysis, value chain analysis, benchmarking, and competitive strength assessment—will be used. All five are valuable techniques for revealing a company's competitiveness and for helping company managers match their strategy to the company's particular circumstances.

QUESTION 1: HOW WELL IS THE COMPANY'S PRESENT STRATEGY WORKING?

● ● ● ●

Before evaluating how well a company's present strategy is working, it is best to start with a clear view of what the strategy entails. The first thing to examine is the company's competitive approach. What moves has the company made recently to attract customers and improve its market position—for instance, has it cut prices, improved the design of its product, added new features, stepped up advertising, entered a new geographic market, or merged with a competitor? Is it striving for a competitive advantage based on low costs or a better product offering? Is it concentrating on serving a broad spectrum of customers or a narrow market niche? The company's functional strategies in R&D, production, marketing, finance, human resources, information technology, and so on further characterize company strategy, as do any efforts to establish alliances with other enterprises. Figure 4.1 shows the key components of a single-business company's strategy.

A determination of the effectiveness of this strategy requires a more in-depth type of analysis. The three best indicators of how well a company's strategy is working are (1) whether the company is achieving its stated financial and strategic objectives, (2) whether its financial performance is above the industry average, and (3) whether it is gaining customers and gaining market share. Persistent shortfalls in meeting company performance targets and weak marketplace performance relative to rivals are reliable

FIGURE 4.1 Identifying the Components of a Single-Business Company's Strategy

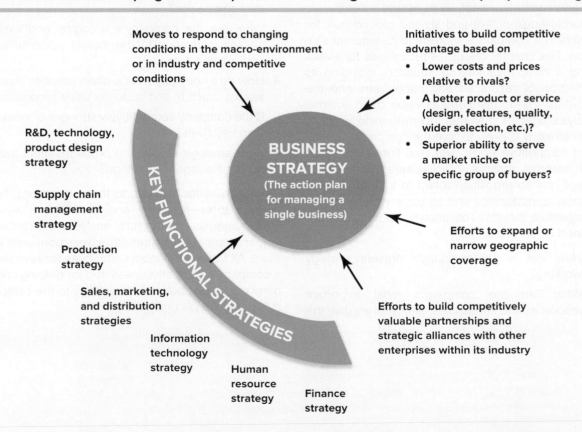

warning signs that the company has a weak strategy, suffers from poor strategy execution, or both. Specific indicators of how well a company's strategy is working include

- Trends in the company's sales and earnings growth.
- Trends in the company's stock price.
- The company's overall financial strength.
- The company's customer retention rate.
- The rate at which new customers are acquired.
- Evidence of improvement in internal processes such as defect rate, order fulfillment, delivery times, days of inventory, and employee productivity.

The stronger a company's current overall performance, the more likely it has a well-conceived, well-executed strategy. The weaker a company's financial performance and market standing, the more its current strategy must be questioned and the more likely the need for radical changes. Table 4.1 provides a compilation of the financial ratios most commonly used to evaluate a company's financial performance and balance sheet strength.

> Sluggish financial performance and second-rate market accomplishments almost always signal weak strategy, weak execution, or both.

TABLE 4.1 Key Financial Ratios: How to Calculate Them and What They Mean

Ratio	How Calculated	What It Shows
Profitability ratios		
1. Gross profit margin	$\dfrac{\text{Sales revenues} - \text{Cost of goods sold}}{\text{Sales revenues}}$	Shows the percentage of revenues available to cover operating expenses and yield a profit.
2. Operating profit margin (or return on sales)	$\dfrac{\text{Sales revenues} - \text{Operating expenses}}{\text{Sales revenues}}$ *or* $\dfrac{\text{Operating income}}{\text{Sales revenues}}$	Shows the profitability of current operations without regard to interest charges and income taxes. Earnings before interest and taxes is known as *EBIT* in financial and business accounting.
3. Net profit margin (or net return on sales)	$\dfrac{\text{Profits after taxes}}{\text{Sales revenues}}$	Shows after-tax profits per dollar of sales.
4. Total return on assets	$\dfrac{\text{Profits after taxes} + \text{Interest}}{\text{Total assets}}$	A measure of the return on total investment in the enterprise. Interest is added to after-tax profits to form the numerator, since total assets are financed by creditors as well as by stockholders.
5. Net return on total assets (ROA)	$\dfrac{\text{Profits after taxes}}{\text{Total assets}}$	A measure of the return earned by stockholders on the firm's total assets.
6. Return on stockholders' equity (ROE)	$\dfrac{\text{Profits after taxes}}{\text{Total stockholders' equity}}$	The return stockholders are earning on their capital investment in the enterprise. A return in the 12% to 15% range is average.
7. Return on invested capital (ROIC)—sometimes referred to as return on capital employed (ROCE)	$\dfrac{\text{Profits after taxes}}{\text{Long-term debt} + \text{Total stockholders' equity}}$	A measure of the return that shareholders are earning on the monetary capital invested in the enterprise. A higher return reflects greater bottom-line effectiveness in the use of long-term capital.

(continued)

TABLE 4.1   *(continued)*

Ratio	How Calculated	What It Shows
Liquidity ratios		
1. Current ratio	$$\frac{\text{Current assets}}{\text{Current liabilities}}$$	Shows a firm's ability to pay current liabilities using assets that can be converted to cash in the near term. Ratio should be higher than 1.0.
2. Working capital	Current assets − Current liabilities	The cash available for a firm's day-to-day operations. Larger amounts mean the company has more internal funds to (1) pay its current liabilities on a timely basis and (2) finance inventory expansion, additional accounts receivable, and a larger base of operations without resorting to borrowing or raising more equity capital.
Leverage ratios		
1. Total debt-to-assets ratio	$$\frac{\text{Total debt}}{\text{Total assets}}$$	Measures the extent to which borrowed funds (both short-term loans and long-term debt) have been used to finance the firm's operations. A low ratio is better—a high fraction indicates overuse of debt and greater risk of bankruptcy.
2. Long-term debt-to-capital ratio	$$\frac{\text{Long-term debt}}{\text{Long-term debt} + \text{Total stockholders' equity}}$$	A measure of creditworthiness and balance sheet strength. It indicates the percentage of capital investment that has been financed by both long-term lenders and stockholders. A ratio below 0.25 is preferable since the lower the ratio, the greater the capacity to borrow additional funds. Debt-to-capital ratios above 0.50 indicate an excessive reliance on long-term borrowing, lower creditworthiness, and weak balance sheet strength.
3. Debt-to-equity ratio	$$\frac{\text{Total debt}}{\text{Total stockholders' equity}}$$	Shows the balance between debt (funds borrowed both short term and long term) and the amount that stockholders have invested in the enterprise. The further the ratio is below 1.0, the greater the firm's ability to borrow additional funds. Ratios above 1.0 put creditors at greater risk, signal weaker balance sheet strength, and often result in lower credit ratings.
4. Long-term debt-to-equity ratio	$$\frac{\text{Long-term debt}}{\text{Total stockholders' equity}}$$	Shows the balance between long-term debt and stockholders' equity in the firm's *long-term* capital structure. Low ratios indicate a greater capacity to borrow additional funds if needed.
5. Times-interest-earned (or coverage) ratio	$$\frac{\text{Operating income}}{\text{Interest expenses}}$$	Measures the ability to pay annual interest charges. Lenders usually insist on a minimum ratio of 2.0, but ratios above 3.0 signal progressively better creditworthiness.
Activity ratios		
1. Days of inventory	$$\frac{\text{Inventory}}{\text{Cost of goods sold} \div 365}$$	Measures inventory management efficiency. Fewer days of inventory are better.

(continued)

TABLE 4.1 *(continued)*

Ratio	How Calculated	What It Shows
2. Inventory turnover	$\dfrac{\text{Cost of goods sold}}{\text{Inventory}}$	Measures the number of inventory turns per year. Higher is better.
3. Average collection period	$\dfrac{\text{Accounts receivable}}{\text{Total sales} \div 365}$ *or* $\dfrac{\text{Accounts receivable}}{\text{Average daily sales}}$	Indicates the average length of time the firm must wait after making a sale to receive cash payment. A shorter collection time is better.

Other important measures of financial performance

1. Dividend yield on common stock	$\dfrac{\text{Annual dividends per share}}{\text{Current market price per share}}$	A measure of the return that shareholders receive in the form of dividends. A "typical" dividend yield is 2% to 3%. The dividend yield for fast-growth companies is often below 1%; the dividend yield for slow-growth companies can run 4% to 5%.
2. Price-to-earnings (P/E) ratio	$\dfrac{\text{Current market price per share}}{\text{Earnings per share}}$	P/E ratios above 20 indicate strong investor confidence in a firm's outlook and earnings growth; firms whose future earnings are at risk or likely to grow slowly typically have ratios below 12.
3. Dividend payout ratio	$\dfrac{\text{Annual dividends per share}}{\text{Earnings per share}}$	Indicates the percentage of after-tax profits paid out as dividends.
4. Internal cash flow	After-tax profits + Depreciation	A rough estimate of the cash a company's business is generating after payment of operating expenses, interest, and taxes. Such amounts can be used for dividend payments or funding capital expenditures.
5. Free cash flow	After-tax profits + Depreciation − Capital expenditures − Dividends	A rough estimate of the cash a company's business is generating after payment of operating expenses, interest, taxes, dividends, and desirable reinvestments in the business. The larger a company's free cash flow, the greater its ability to internally fund new strategic initiatives, repay debt, make new acquisitions, repurchase shares of stock, or increase dividend payments.

QUESTION 2: WHAT ARE THE COMPANY'S STRENGTHS AND WEAKNESSES IN RELATION TO THE MARKET OPPORTUNITIES AND EXTERNAL THREATS?

An examination of the financial and other indicators discussed previously can tell you how well a strategy is working, but they tell you little about the underlying reasons—*why* it's working or not. The simplest and most easily applied tool for gaining some insight into the reasons for the success of a strategy or lack thereof is known as

SWOT analysis. SWOT is an acronym that stands for a company's internal **S**trengths and **W**eaknesses, market **O**pportunities, and external **T**hreats. Another name for SWOT analysis is Situational Analysis. A first-rate SWOT analysis can help explain why a strategy is working well (or not) by taking a good hard look a company's strengths in relation to its weaknesses and in relation to the strengths and weaknesses of competitors. Are the company's strengths great enough to make up for its weaknesses? Has the company's strategy built on these strengths and shielded the company from its weaknesses? Do the company's strengths exceed those of its rivals or have they been overpowered? Similarly, a SWOT analysis can help determine whether a strategy has been effective in fending off external threats and positioning the firm to take advantage of market opportunities.

SWOT analysis has long been one of the most popular and widely used diagnostic tools for strategists. It is used fruitfully by organizations that range in type from large corporations to small businesses, to government agencies to non-profits such as churches and schools. Its popularity stems in part from its ease of use, but also because it can be used not only to evaluate the efficacy of a strategy, but also as the basis for crafting a strategy from the outset that capitalizes on the company's strengths, overcomes its weaknesses, aims squarely at capturing the company's best opportunities, and defends against competitive and macro-environmental threats. Moreover, a SWOT analysis can help a company with a strategy that is working well in the present determine whether the company is in a position to pursue new market opportunities and defend against emerging threats to its future well-being.

Identifying a Company's Internal Strengths

An internal **strength** is something a company is good at doing or an attribute that enhances its competitiveness in the marketplace.

One way to appraise a company's strengths is to ask: What activities does the company perform well? This question directs attention to the company's skill level in performing key pieces of its business—such as supply chain management, R&D, production, distribution, sales and marketing, and customer service. A company's skill or proficiency in performing different facets of its operations can range from the extreme of having minimal ability to perform an activity (perhaps having just struggled to do it the first time) to the other extreme of being able to perform the activity better than any other company in the industry.

When a company's proficiency rises from that of mere ability to perform an activity to the point of being able to perform it consistently well and at acceptable cost, it is said to have a **competence**—a true *capability,* in other words. If a company's competence level in some activity domain is superior to that of its rivals it is known as a **distinctive competence.** A **core competence** is a proficiently performed internal activity that is *central* to a company's strategy and is typically distinctive as well. A core competence is a more competitively valuable strength than a competence because of the activity's key role in the company's strategy and the contribution it makes to the company's market success and profitability. Often, core competencies can be leveraged to create new markets or new product demand, as the engine behind a company's growth. Procter and Gamble has a core competence in brand management, which has led to an ever increasing portfolio of market-leading consumer products, including Charmin, Tide, Crest, Tampax, Olay, Febreze, Luvs, Pampers, and Swiffer. Nike has a core competence in designing and marketing innovative athletic footwear and sports apparel. Kellogg has a core competence in developing, producing, and marketing breakfast cereals.

Identifying Company Internal Weaknesses

An internal **weakness** is something a company lacks or does poorly (in comparison to others) or a condition that puts it at a disadvantage in the marketplace. It can be thought of as a competitive deficiency. A company's internal weaknesses can relate to (1) inferior or unproven skills, expertise, or intellectual capital in competitively important areas of the business, or (2) deficiencies in competitively important physical, organizational, or intangible assets. Nearly all companies have competitive deficiencies of one kind or another. Whether a company's internal weaknesses make it competitively vulnerable depends on how much they matter in the marketplace and whether they are offset by the company's strengths.

Table 4.2 lists many of the things to consider in compiling a company's strengths and weaknesses. Sizing up a company's complement of strengths and deficiencies is akin to constructing a *strategic balance sheet,* where strengths represent *competitive assets* and weaknesses represent *competitive liabilities.* Obviously, the ideal condition is for the company's competitive assets to outweigh its competitive liabilities by an ample margin!

Identifying a Company's Market Opportunities

Market opportunity is a big factor in shaping a company's strategy. Indeed, managers can't properly tailor strategy to the company's situation without first identifying its market opportunities and appraising the growth and profit potential each one holds. Depending on the prevailing circumstances, a company's opportunities can be plentiful or scarce, fleeting or lasting, and can range from wildly attractive to marginally interesting or unsuitable.

Newly emerging and fast-changing markets sometimes present stunningly big or "golden" opportunities, but it is typically hard for managers at one company to peer into "the fog of the future" and spot them far ahead of managers at other companies.[9] But as the fog begins to clear, golden opportunities are nearly always seized rapidly— and the companies that seize them are usually those that have been staying alert with diligent market reconnaissance and preparing themselves to capitalize on shifting market conditions swiftly. Table 4.2 displays a sampling of potential market opportunities.

Identifying External Threats

Often, certain factors in a company's external environment pose *threats* to its profitability and competitive well-being. Threats can stem from such factors as the emergence of cheaper or better technologies, the entry of lower-cost foreign competitors into a company's market stronghold, new regulations that are more burdensome to a company than to its competitors, unfavorable demographic shifts, and political upheaval in a foreign country where the company has facilities.

External threats may pose no more than a moderate degree of adversity (all companies confront some threatening elements in the course of doing business), or they may be imposing enough to make a company's situation look tenuous. On rare occasions, market shocks can give birth to a *sudden-death* threat that throws a

CORE CONCEPT

A **core competence** is an activity that a company performs proficiently and that is also central to its strategy and competitive success.

CORE CONCEPT

A company's **strengths** represent its competitive assets; its **weaknesses** are shortcomings that constitute competitive liabilities.

Simply making lists of a company's strengths, weaknesses, opportunities, and threats is not enough; the payoff from SWOT analysis comes from the conclusions about a company's situation and the implications for strategy improvement that flow from the four lists.

TABLE 4.2   What to Look for in Identifying a Company's Strengths, Weaknesses, Opportunities, and Threats

Strengths and Competitive Assets	Weaknesses and Competitive Deficiencies
• Ample financial resources to grow the business	• No distinctive core competencies
• Strong brand-name image or reputation	• Lack of attention to customer needs
• Distinctive core competencies	• Inferior product quality
• Cost advantages over rivals	• Weak balance sheet, too much debt
• Attractive customer base	• Higher costs than competitors
• Proprietary technology, superior technological skills, important patents	• Too narrow a product line relative to rivals
• Strong bargaining power over suppliers or buyers	• Weak brand image or reputation
• Superior product quality	• Lack of adequate distribution capability
• Wide geographic coverage and/or strong global distribution capability	• Lack of management depth
• Alliances and/or joint ventures that provide access to valuable technology, competencies, and/or attractive geographic markets	• A plague of internal operating problems or obsolete facilities
	• Too much underutilized plant capacity

Market Opportunities	External Threats
• Meet sharply rising buyer demand for the industry's product	• Increased intensity of competition
• Serve additional customer groups or market segments	• Slowdowns in market growth
• Expand into new geographic markets	• Likely entry of potent new competitors
• Expand the company's product line to meet a broader range of customer needs	• Growing bargaining power of customers or suppliers
• Enter new product lines or new businesses	• A shift in buyer needs and tastes away from the industry's product
• Take advantage of falling trade barriers in attractive foreign markets	• Adverse demographic changes that threaten to curtail demand for the industry's product
• Take advantage of an adverse change in the fortunes of rival firms	• Adverse economic conditions that threaten critical suppliers or distributors
• Acquire rival firms or companies with attractive technological expertise or competencies	• Changes in technology—particularly disruptive technology that can undermine the company's distinctive competencies
• Take advantage of emerging technological developments to innovate	• Restrictive foreign trade policies
• Enter into alliances or other cooperative ventures	• Costly new regulatory requirements
	• Tight credit conditions
	• Rising prices on energy or other key inputs

company into an immediate crisis and a battle to survive. Many of the world's major financial institutions were plunged into unprecedented crisis in 2008–2009 by the aftereffects of high-risk mortgage lending, inflated credit ratings on subprime mortgage securities, the collapse of housing prices, and a market flooded with mortgage-related investments (collateralized debt obligations) whose values suddenly evaporated. It is management's job to identify the threats to the company's future prospects and to evaluate what strategic actions can be taken to neutralize or lessen their impact.

What Do the SWOT Listings Reveal?

SWOT analysis involves more than making four lists. In crafting a new strategy, it offers a strong foundation for understanding how to position the company to build on its strengths in seizing new business opportunities and how to mitigate external threats by shoring up its competitive deficiencies. In assessing the effectiveness of an existing strategy, it can be used to glean insights regarding the company's overall business situation (thus the name Situational Analysis); and it can help translate these insights into recommended strategic actions. Figure 4.2 shows the steps involved in gleaning insights from SWOT analysis.

The beauty of SWOT analysis is its simplicity; but this is also its primary limitation. For a deeper and more accurate understanding of a company's situation, more sophisticated tools are required. Chapter 3 introduced you to a set of tools for analyzing a company's external situation. In the rest of this chapter, we look more deeply at a company's internal situation, beginning with the company's resources and capabilities.

FIGURE 4.2 The Steps Involved in SWOT Analysis: Identify the Four Components of SWOT, Draw Conclusions, Translate Implications into Strategic Actions

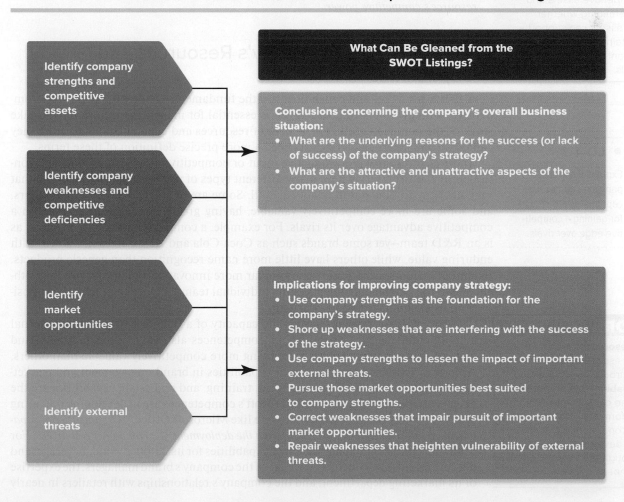

QUESTION 3: WHAT ARE THE COMPANY'S MOST IMPORTANT RESOURCES AND CAPABILITIES, AND WILL THEY GIVE THE COMPANY A LASTING COMPETITIVE ADVANTAGE?

● ● ● ●

CORE CONCEPT

A company's resources and capabilities represent its **competitive assets** and are determinants of its competitiveness and ability to succeed in the marketplace.

An essential element of a company's internal environment is the nature of resources and capabilities. A company's resources and capabilities are its **competitive assets** and determine whether its competitive power in the marketplace will be impressively strong or disappointingly weak. Companies with second-rate competitive assets nearly always are relegated to a trailing position in the industry.

Resource and capability analysis provides managers with a powerful tool for sizing up the company's competitive assets and determining whether they can provide the foundation necessary for competitive success in the marketplace. This is a two-step process. The first step is to identify the company's resources and capabilities. The second step is to examine them more closely to ascertain which are the most competitively important and whether they can support a sustainable competitive advantage over rival firms.[1] This second step involves applying the *four tests of a resource's competitive power*.

Resource and capability analysis is a powerful tool for sizing up a company's competitive assets and determining whether the assets can support a sustainable competitive advantage over market rivals.

Identifying the Company's Resources and Capabilities

A firm's resources and capabilities are the fundamental building blocks of its competitive strategy. In crafting strategy, it is essential for managers to know how to take stock of the company's full complement of resources and capabilities. But before they can do so, managers and strategists need a more precise definition of these terms.

In brief, a **resource** is a productive input or competitive asset that is owned or controlled by the firm. Firms have many different types of resources at their disposal that vary not only in kind but in quality as well. Some are of a higher quality than others, and some are more competitively valuable, having greater potential to give a firm a competitive advantage over its rivals. For example, a company's brand is a resource, as is an R&D team—yet some brands such as Coca-Cola and Xerox are well known, with enduring value, while others have little more name recognition than generic products. In similar fashion, some R&D teams are far more innovative and productive than others due to the outstanding talents of the individual team members, the team's composition, its experience, and its chemistry.

A **capability** (or **competence**) is the capacity of a firm to perform some internal activity competently. Capabilities or competences also vary in form, quality, and competitive importance, with some being more competitively valuable than others. American Express displays superior capabilities in brand management and marketing; Starbucks's employee management, training, and real estate capabilities are the drivers behind its rapid growth; Microsoft's competences are in developing operating systems for computers and user software like Microsoft Office®. *Organizational capabilities are developed and enabled through the deployment of a company's resources.*[2] For example, Nestlé's brand management capabilities for its 2,000 + food, beverage, and pet care brands draw on the knowledge of the company's brand managers, the expertise of its marketing department, and the company's relationships with retailers in nearly

---

● **LO 4-3**

Explain why a company's resources and capabilities are critical for gaining a competitive edge over rivals.

CORE CONCEPT

A **resource** is a competitive asset that is owned or controlled by a company; a **capability** (or **competence**) is the capacity of a firm to perform some internal activity competently. Capabilities are developed and enabled through the deployment of a company's resources.

200 countries. W. L. Gore's product innovation capabilities in its fabrics and medical and industrial product businesses result from the personal initiative, creative talents, and technological expertise of its associates and the company's culture that encourages accountability and creative thinking.

Types of Company Resources   A useful way to identify a company's resources is to look for them within categories, as shown in Table 4.3. Broadly speaking, resources can be divided into two main categories: **tangible** and **intangible** resources. Although *human resources* make up one of the most important parts of a company's resource base, we include them in the intangible category to emphasize the role played by the skills, talents, and knowledge of a company's human resources.

Tangible resources are the most easily identified, since tangible resources are those that can be *touched* or *quantified* readily. Obviously, they include various types of *physical resources* such as manufacturing facilities and mineral resources, but they also include a company's *financial resources, technological resources,* and *organizational resources* such as the company's communication and control systems. Note that technological resources are included among tangible resources, *by convention,* even though some types, such as copyrights and trade secrets, might be more logically categorized as intangible.

Intangible resources are harder to discern, but they are often among the most important of a firm's competitive assets. They include various sorts of *human assets and intellectual capital,* as well as a company's *brands, image, and reputational assets.*

TABLE 4.3   Types of Company Resources

Tangible resources

- *Physical resources:* land and real estate; manufacturing plants, equipment, and/or distribution facilities; the locations of stores, plants, or distribution centers, including the overall pattern of their physical locations; ownership of or access rights to natural resources (such as mineral deposits)
- *Financial resources:* cash and cash equivalents; marketable securities; other financial assets such as a company's credit rating and borrowing capacity
- *Technological assets:* patents, copyrights, production technology, innovation technologies, technological processes
- *Organizational resources:* IT and communication systems (satellites, servers, workstations, etc.); other planning, coordination, and control systems; the company's organizational design and reporting structure

Intangible resources

- *Human assets and intellectual capital:* the education, experience, knowledge, and talent of the workforce, cumulative learning, and tacit knowledge of employees; collective learning embedded in the organization, the intellectual capital and know-how of specialized teams and work groups; the knowledge of key personnel concerning important business functions; managerial talent and leadership skill; the creativity and innovativeness of certain personnel
- *Brands, company image, and reputational assets:* brand names, trademarks, product or company image, buyer loyalty and goodwill; company reputation for quality, service, and reliability; reputation with suppliers and partners for fair dealing
- *Relationships:* alliances, joint ventures, or partnerships that provide access to technologies, specialized know-how, or geographic markets; networks of dealers or distributors; the trust established with various partners
- *Company culture and incentive system:* the norms of behavior, business principles, and ingrained beliefs within the company; the attachment of personnel to the company's ideals; the compensation system and the motivation level of company personnel

While intangible resources have no material existence on their own, they are often embodied in something material. Thus, the skills and knowledge resources of a firm are embodied in its managers and employees; a company's brand name is embodied in the company logo or product labels. Other important kinds of intangible resources include a company's *relationships* with suppliers, buyers, or partners of various sorts, and the *company's culture and incentive system*. A more detailed listing of the various types of tangible and intangible resources is provided in Table 4.3.

Listing a company's resources category by category can prevent managers from inadvertently overlooking some company resources that might be competitively important. At times, it can be difficult to decide exactly how to categorize certain types of resources. For example, resources such as a work group's specialized expertise in developing innovative products can be considered to be technological assets or human assets or intellectual capital and knowledge assets; the work ethic and drive of a company's workforce could be included under the company's human assets or its culture and incentive system. In this regard, it is important to remember that *it is not exactly how a resource is categorized that matters but, rather, that all of the company's different types of resources are included in the inventory.* The real purpose of using categories in identifying a company's resources is *to ensure that none of a company's resources go unnoticed when sizing up the company's competitive assets.*

Identifying Capabilities   Organizational capabilities are more complex entities than resources; indeed, they are built up through the use of resources and draw on some combination of the firm's resources as they are exercised. Virtually all organizational capabilities are *knowledge-based, residing in people and in a company's intellectual capital, or in organizational processes and systems, which embody tacit knowledge.* For example, Amazon's speedy delivery capabilities rely on the knowledge of its fulfillment center managers, its relationship with the United Postal Service, and the experience of its merchandisers to correctly predict inventory flow. Bose's capabilities in auditory system design arise from the talented engineers that form the R&D team as well as the company's strong culture, which celebrates innovation and beautiful design.

Because of their complexity, capabilities are harder to categorize than resources and more challenging to search for as a result. There are, however, two approaches that can make the process of uncovering and identifying a firm's capabilities more systematic. The first method takes the completed listing of a firm's resources as its starting point. Since capabilities are built from resources and utilize resources as they are exercised, a firm's resources can provide a strong set of clues about the types of capabilities the firm is likely to have accumulated. This approach simply involves looking over the firm's resources and considering whether (and to what extent) the firm has built up any related capabilities. So, for example, a fleet of trucks, the latest RFID tracking technology, and a set of large automated distribution centers may be indicative of sophisticated capabilities in logistics and distribution. R&D teams composed of top scientists with expertise in genomics may suggest organizational capabilities in developing new gene therapies or in biotechnology more generally.

The second method of identifying a firm's capabilities takes a functional approach. Many capabilities relate to fairly specific functions; these draw on a limited set of resources and typically involve a single department or organizational unit. Capabilities in injection molding or continuous casting or metal stamping are manufacturing-related; capabilities in direct selling, promotional pricing, or database marketing all connect to the sales and marketing functions; capabilities in basic research, strategic innovation, or new product development link to a company's R&D function. This approach requires managers to survey the various functions a firm performs to find the different capabilities associated with each function.

A problem with this second method is that many of the most important capabilities of firms are inherently *cross-functional.* Cross-functional capabilities draw on a number of different kinds of resources and are multidimensional in nature—they spring from the effective collaboration among people with different types of expertise working in different organizational units. Warby Parker draws from its cross-functional design process to create its popular eyewear. Its design capabilities are not just due to its creative designers, but are the product of their capabilities in market research and engineering as well as their relations with suppliers and manufacturing companies. Cross-functional capabilities and other complex capabilities involving numerous linked and closely integrated competitive assets are sometimes referred to as **resource bundles.**

It is important not to miss identifying a company's resource bundles, since they can be the most competitively important of a firm's competitive assets. Resource bundles can sometimes pass the four tests of a resource's competitive power (described below) even when the individual components of the resource bundle cannot. Although PetSmart's supply chain and marketing capabilities are matched well by rival Petco, the company continues to outperform competitors through its customer service capabilities (including animal grooming and veterinary and day care services). Nike's bundle of styling expertise, marketing research skills, professional endorsements, brand name, and managerial know-how has allowed it to remain number one in the athletic footwear and apparel industry for more than 20 years.

Assessing the Competitive Power of a Company's Resources and Capabilities

To assess a company's competitive power, one must go beyond merely identifying its resources and capabilities to probe its *caliber.*[3] Thus, the second step in resource and capability analysis is designed to ascertain which of a company's resources and capabilities are competitively superior and to what extent they can support a company's quest for a sustainable competitive advantage over market rivals. When a company has competitive assets that are central to its strategy and superior to those of rival firms, they can support a competitive advantage, as defined in Chapter 1. If this advantage proves durable despite the best efforts of competitors to overcome it, then the company is said to have a *sustainable* **competitive advantage.** While it may be difficult for a company to achieve a sustainable competitive advantage, it is an important strategic objective because it imparts a potential for attractive and long-lived profitability.

The Four Tests of a Resource's Competitive Power The competitive power of a resource or capability is measured by how many of four specific tests it can pass.[4] These tests are referred to as the **VRIN tests for sustainable competitive advantage**—*VRIN* is a shorthand reminder standing for *Valuable, Rare, Inimitable,* and *Nonsubstitutable.* The first two tests determine whether a resource or capability can support a competitive advantage. The last two determine whether the competitive advantage can be sustained.

1. *Is the resource or capability competitively* **Valuable?** To be competitively valuable, a resource or capability must be directly relevant to the company's strategy, making the company a more effective competitor. Unless the resource or capability contributes to the effectiveness of the company's strategy, it cannot pass this first

CORE CONCEPT

A **resource bundle** is a linked and closely integrated set of competitive assets centered around one or more cross-functional capabilities.

CORE CONCEPT

Recall that a **competitive advantage** means that you can produce more value (V) for the customer than rivals can, or the same value at lower cost (C). In other words, your **V-C** is *greater than* the V-C of competitors. **V-C** is what we call the *Total Economic Value* produced by a company.

CORE CONCEPT

The **VRIN tests for sustainable competitive advantage** ask whether a resource is valuable, rare, inimitable, and nonsubstitutable.

test. An indicator of its effectiveness is whether the resource enables the company to strengthen its business model by improving its customer value proposition and/or profit formula (see Chapter 1). Google failed in converting its technological resources and software innovation capabilities into success for Google Wallet, which incurred losses of more than $300 million before being abandoned in 2016. While these resources and capabilities have made Google the world's number-one search engine, they proved to be less valuable in the mobile payments industry.

2. *Is the resource or capability **Rare**—is it something rivals lack?* Resources and capabilities that are common among firms and widely available cannot be a source of competitive advantage. All makers of branded cereals have valuable marketing capabilities and brands, since the key success factors in the ready-to-eat cereal industry demand this. They are not rare. However, the brand strength of Oreo cookies is uncommon and has provided Kraft Foods with greater market share as well as the opportunity to benefit from brand extensions such as Golden Oreos, Oreo Thins, and Mega Stuf Oreos. A resource or capability is considered rare if it is held by only a small number of firms in an industry or specific competitive domain. Thus, while general management capabilities are not rare in an absolute sense, they are relatively rare in some of the less developed regions of the world and in some business domains.

3. *Is the resource or capability **Inimitable**—is it hard to copy?* The more difficult and more costly it is for competitors to imitate a company's resource or capability, the more likely that it can also provide a *sustainable* competitive advantage. Resources and capabilities tend to be difficult to copy when they are unique (a fantastic real estate location, patent-protected technology, an unusually talented and motivated labor force), when they must be built over time in ways that are difficult to imitate (a well-known brand name, mastery of a complex process technology, years of cumulative experience and learning), and when they entail financial outlays or large-scale operations that few industry members can undertake (a global network of dealers and distributors). Imitation is also difficult for resources and capabilities that reflect a high level of *social complexity* (company culture, interpersonal relationships among the managers or R&D teams, trust-based relations with customers or suppliers) and *causal ambiguity,* a term that signifies the hard-to-disentangle nature of the complex resources, such as a web of intricate processes enabling new drug discovery. Hard-to-copy resources and capabilities are important competitive assets, contributing to the longevity of a company's market position and offering the potential for sustained profitability.

4. *Is the resource or capability **Nonsubstitutable**—is it invulnerable to the threat of substitution from different types of resources and capabilities?* Even resources that are competitively valuable, rare, and costly to imitate may lose much of their ability to offer competitive advantage if rivals possess equivalent substitute resources. For example, manufacturers relying on automation to gain a cost-based advantage in production activities may find their technology-based advantage nullified by rivals' use of low-wage offshore manufacturing. Resources can contribute to a sustainable competitive advantage only when resource substitutes aren't on the horizon.

The vast majority of companies are not well endowed with standout resources or capabilities, capable of passing all four tests with high marks. Most firms have a mixed bag of resources—one or two quite valuable, some good, many satisfactory to mediocre. Resources and capabilities that are valuable pass the first of the four tests. As key contributors to the effectiveness of the strategy, they are relevant to the firm's competitiveness but are no guarantee of competitive advantage. They may offer no more than competitive parity with competing firms.

Passing both of the first two tests requires more—it requires resources and capabilities that are not only valuable but also rare. This is a much higher hurdle that can be cleared only by resources and capabilities that are *competitively superior*. Resources and capabilities that are competitively superior are the company's true strategic assets. They provide the company with a competitive advantage over its competitors, if only in the short run.

To pass the last two tests, a resource must be able to maintain its competitive superiority in the face of competition. It must be resistant to imitative attempts and efforts by competitors to find equally valuable substitute resources. Assessing the availability of substitutes is the most difficult of all the tests since substitutes are harder to recognize, but the key is to look for resources or capabilities held by other firms or being developed that *can serve the same function* as the company's core resources and capabilities.[5]

Very few firms have resources and capabilities that can pass all four tests, but those that do enjoy a sustainable competitive advantage with far greater profit potential. Costco is a notable example, with strong employee incentive programs and capabilities in supply chain management that have surpassed those of its warehouse club rivals for over 35 years. Lincoln Electric Company, less well known but no less notable in its achievements, has been the world leader in welding products for over 100 years as a result of its unique piecework incentive system for compensating production workers and the unsurpassed worker productivity and product quality that this system has fostered.

A Company's Resources and Capabilities Must Be Managed Dynamically Even companies like Costco and Lincoln Electric cannot afford to rest on their laurels. Rivals that are initially unable to replicate a key resource may develop better and better substitutes over time. Resources and capabilities can depreciate like other assets if they are managed with benign neglect. Disruptive changes in technology, customer preferences, distribution channels, or other competitive factors can also destroy the value of key strategic assets, turning resources and capabilities "from diamonds to rust."[6]

Resources and capabilities must be continually strengthened and nurtured to sustain their competitive power and, at times, may need to be broadened and deepened to allow the company to position itself to pursue emerging market opportunities.[7] Organizational resources and capabilities that grow stale can impair competitiveness unless they are refreshed, modified, or even phased out and replaced in response to ongoing market changes and shifts in company strategy. Management's challenge in managing the firm's resources and capabilities dynamically has two elements: (1) attending to the ongoing modification of existing competitive assets, and (2) casting a watchful eye for opportunities to develop totally new kinds of capabilities.

> A company requires a dynamically evolving portfolio of resources and capabilities to sustain its competitiveness and help drive improvements in its performance.

The Role of Dynamic Capabilities Companies that know the importance of recalibrating and upgrading their most valuable resources and capabilities ensure that these activities are done on a continual basis. By incorporating these activities into their routine managerial functions, they gain the experience necessary to be able to do them consistently well. At that point, their ability to freshen and renew their competitive assets becomes a capability in itself—a **dynamic capability.** A dynamic capability is the ability to modify, deepen, or augment the company's existing resources and capabilities.[8] This includes the capacity to improve existing resources and capabilities incrementally, in the way that Toyota aggressively upgrades the company's capabilities in fuel-efficient hybrid engine technology and constantly fine-tunes its famed Toyota production system. Likewise, management at BMW developed new organizational capabilities in hybrid engine design that allowed the company to launch its highly touted i3 and i8 plug-in hybrids. A dynamic capability

CORE CONCEPT

A **dynamic capability** is an ongoing capacity of a company to modify its existing resources and capabilities or create new ones.

also includes the capacity to add new resources and capabilities to the company's competitive asset portfolio. One way to do this is through alliances and acquisitions. An example is General Motor's partnership with Koren electronics firm LG Corporation, which enabled GM to develop a manufacturing and engineering platform for producing electric vehicles. This enabled GM to beat the likes of Tesla and Nissan to market with the first affordable all-electric car with good driving range—the Chevy Bolt EV.

QUESTION 4: HOW DO VALUE CHAIN ACTIVITIES IMPACT A COMPANY'S COST STRUCTURE AND CUSTOMER VALUE PROPOSITION?

● LO 4-4

Explain how value chain activities can affect a company's cost structure and customer value proposition.

Company managers are often stunned when a competitor cuts its prices to "unbelievably low" levels or when a new market entrant introduces a great new product at a surprisingly low price. While less common, new entrants can also storm the market with a product that ratchets the quality level up so high that customers will abandon competing sellers even if they have to pay more for the new product. This is what seems to have happened with Apple's iPhone 7 and iMac computers.

Regardless of where on the quality spectrum a company competes, it must remain competitive in terms of its customer value proposition in order to stay in the game. Patagonia's value proposition, for example, remains attractive to customers who value quality, wide selection, and corporate environmental responsibility over cheaper outerwear alternatives. Since its inception in 1925, the *New Yorker*'s customer value proposition has withstood the test of time by providing readers with an amalgam of well-crafted, rigorously fact-checked, and topical writing.

The greater the amount of customer value that a company can offer profitably relative to close rivals, the less competitively vulnerable the company becomes.

Recall from our discussion of the Customer Value Proposition in Chapter 1: The value (V) provided to the customer depends on how well a customer's needs are met for the price paid (V-P). How well customer needs are met depends on the perceived quality of a product or service as well as on other, more tangible attributes. The greater the amount of customer value that the company can offer profitably compared to its rivals, the less vulnerable it will be to competitive attack. For managers, the key is to keep close track of how *cost-effectively* the company can deliver value to customers relative to its competitors. If it can deliver the same amount of value with lower expenditures (or more value at the same cost), it will maintain a competitive edge.

The higher a company's costs are above those of close rivals, the more competitively vulnerable the company becomes.

Two analytic tools are particularly useful in determining whether a company's costs and customer value proposition are competitive: value chain analysis and benchmarking.

The Concept of a Company Value Chain

CORE CONCEPT

A company's **value chain** identifies the primary activities and related support activities that create customer value.

Every company's business consists of a collection of activities undertaken in the course of producing, marketing, delivering, and supporting its product or service. All the various activities that a company performs internally combine to form a **value chain**—so called because the underlying intent of a company's activities is ultimately to *create value for buyers*.

As shown in Figure 4.3, a company's value chain consists of two broad categories of activities: the *primary activities* foremost in creating value for customers and the requisite *support activities* that facilitate and enhance the performance of the

FIGURE 4.3   A Representative Company Value Chain

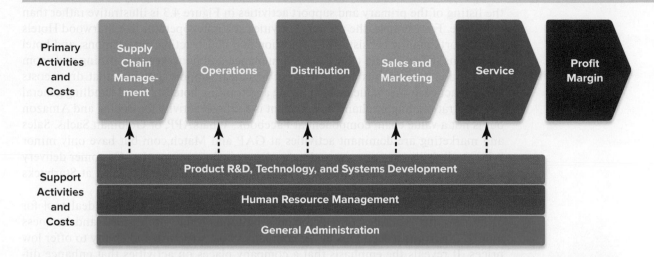

PRIMARY ACTIVITIES

- **Supply Chain Management**—Activities, costs, and assets associated with purchasing fuel, energy, raw materials, parts and components, merchandise, and consumable items from vendors; receiving, storing, and disseminating inputs from suppliers; inspection; and inventory management.

- **Operations**—Activities, costs, and assets associated with converting inputs into final product form (production, assembly, packaging, equipment maintenance, facilities, operations, quality assurance, environmental protection).

- **Distribution**—Activities, costs, and assets dealing with physically distributing the product to buyers (finished goods warehousing, order processing, order picking and packing, shipping, delivery vehicle operations, establishing and maintaining a network of dealers and distributors).

- **Sales and Marketing**—Activities, costs, and assets related to sales force efforts, advertising and promotion, market research and planning, and dealer/distributor support.

- **Service**—Activities, costs, and assets associated with providing assistance to buyers, such as installation, spare parts delivery, maintenance and repair, technical assistance, buyer inquiries, and complaints.

SUPPORT ACTIVITIES

- **Product R&D, Technology, and Systems Development**—Activities, costs, and assets relating to product R&D, process R&D, process design improvement, equipment design, computer software development, telecommunications systems, computer-assisted design and engineering, database capabilities, and development of computerized support systems.

- **Human Resource Management**—Activities, costs, and assets associated with the recruitment, hiring, training, development, and compensation of all types of personnel; labor relations activities; and development of knowledge-based skills and core competencies.

- **General Administration**—Activities, costs, and assets relating to general management, accounting and finance, legal and regulatory affairs, safety and security, management information systems, forming strategic alliances and collaborating with strategic partners, and other "overhead" functions.

Source: Based on the discussion in Michael E. Porter, *Competitive Advantage* (New York: Free Press, 1985), pp. 37–43.

primary activities.[10] The kinds of primary and secondary activities that constitute a company's value chain vary according to the specifics of a company's business; hence, the listing of the primary and support activities in Figure 4.3 is illustrative rather than definitive. For example, the primary activities at a hotel operator like Starwood Hotels and Resorts mainly consist of site selection and construction, reservations, and hotel operations (check-in and check-out, maintenance and housekeeping, dining and room service, and conventions and meetings); principal support activities that drive costs and impact customer value include hiring and training hotel staff and handling general administration. Supply chain management is a crucial activity for Boeing and Amazon but is not a value chain component at Facebook, WhatsAPP, or Goldman Sachs. Sales and marketing are dominant activities at GAP and Match.com but have only minor roles at oil-drilling companies and natural gas pipeline companies. Customer delivery is a crucial activity at Domino's Pizza and Blue Apron but insignificant at Starbucks and Dunkin Donuts.

With its focus on value-creating activities, the value chain is an ideal tool for examining the workings of a company's customer value proposition and business model. It permits a deep look at the company's cost structure and ability to offer low prices. It reveals the emphasis that a company places on activities that enhance differentiation and support higher prices, such as service and marketing. It also includes a profit margin component (P-C), since profits are necessary to compensate the company's owners and investors, who bear risks and provide capital. Tracking the profit margin along with the value-creating activities is critical because unless an enterprise succeeds in delivering customer value profitably (with a sufficient return on invested capital), it can't survive for long. Attention to a company's profit formula in addition to its customer value proposition is the essence of a sound business model, as described in Chapter 1.

Illustration Capsule 4.1 shows representative costs for various value chain activities performed by Boll & Branch, a maker of luxury linens and bedding sold directly to consumers online.

Comparing the Value Chains of Rival Companies   Value chain analysis facilitates a comparison of how rivals, activity by activity, deliver value to customers. Even rivals in the same industry may differ significantly in terms of the activities they perform. For instance, the "operations" component of the value chain for a manufacturer that makes all of its own parts and components and assembles them into a finished product differs from the "operations" of a rival producer that buys the needed parts and components from outside suppliers and performs only assembly operations. How each activity is performed may affect a company's relative cost position as well as its capacity for differentiation. Thus, even a simple comparison of how the activities of rivals' value chains differ can reveal competitive differences.

A Company's Primary and Secondary Activities Identify the Major Components of Its Internal Cost Structure   The combined costs of all the various primary and support activities constituting a company's value chain define its internal cost structure. Further, the cost of each activity contributes to whether the company's overall cost position relative to rivals is favorable or unfavorable. The roles of value chain analysis and benchmarking are to develop the data for comparing a company's costs activity by activity against the costs of key rivals and to learn which internal activities are a source of cost advantage or disadvantage.

The Value Chain for Boll & Branch

©fizkes/Shutterstock

A king-size set of sheets from Boll & Branch is made from 6 meters of fabric, requiring 11 kilograms of raw cotton.

Raw Cotton	$ 28.16	
Spinning/Weaving/Dyeing	12.00	
Cutting/Sewing/Finishing	9.50	
Material Transportation	3.00	
Factory Fee	15.80	
Cost of Goods		**$ 68.46**
Inspection Fees	5.48	
Ocean Freight/Insurance	4.55	
Import Duties	8.22	
Warehouse/Packing	8.50	
Packaging	15.15	
Customer Shipping	14.00	
Promotions/Donations*	30.00	
Total Cost		**$154.38**
Boll & Brand Markup	About 60%	
Boll & Brand Retail Price		**$250.00**
Gross Margin**	**$ 95.62**	

Source: Adapted from Christina Brinkley, "What Goes into the Price of Luxury Sheets?" *The Wall Street Journal,* March 29, 2014, www.wsj.com/articles/SB10001424052702303725404579461953672838672 (accessed February 16, 2016).

> A company's cost-competitiveness depends not only on the costs of internally performed activities (its own value chain) but also on costs in the value chains of its suppliers and distribution-channel allies.

Evaluating a company's cost-competitiveness involves using what accountants call *activity-based costing* to determine the costs of performing each value chain activity.[11] The degree to which a company's total costs should be broken down into costs for specific activities depends on how valuable it is to know the costs of specific activities versus broadly defined activities. At the very least, cost estimates are needed for each broad category of primary and support activities, but cost estimates for more specific activities within each broad category may be needed if a company discovers that it has a cost disadvantage vis-à-vis rivals and wants to pin down the exact source or activity causing the cost disadvantage. However, a company's own *internal costs* may be insufficient to assess whether its product offering and customer value proposition are competitive with those of rivals. Cost and price differences among competing companies can have their origins in activities performed by suppliers or by distribution allies involved in getting the product to the final customers or end users of the product, in which case the company's entire *value chain system* becomes relevant.

The Value Chain System

A company's value chain is embedded in a larger system of activities that includes the value chains of its suppliers and the value chains of whatever wholesale distributors and retailers it utilizes in getting its product or service to end users. This *value chain system* (sometimes called a vertical chain) has implications that extend far beyond the company's costs. It can affect attributes like product quality that enhance differentiation and have importance for the company's customer value proposition, as well as its profitability.[12] Suppliers' value chains are relevant because suppliers perform activities and incur costs in creating and delivering the purchased inputs utilized in a company's own value-creating activities. The costs, performance features, and quality of these inputs influence a company's own costs and product differentiation capabilities. Anything a company can do to help its suppliers drive down the costs of their value chain activities or improve the quality and performance of the items being supplied can enhance its own competitiveness—a powerful reason for working collaboratively with suppliers in managing supply chain activities.[13] For example, automakers have encouraged their automotive parts suppliers to build plants near the auto assembly plants to facilitate just-in-time deliveries, reduce warehousing and shipping costs, and promote close collaboration on parts design and production scheduling.

Similarly, the value chains of a company's distribution-channel partners are relevant because (1) the costs and margins of a company's distributors and retail dealers are part of the price the ultimate consumer pays and (2) the activities that distribution allies perform affect sales volumes and customer satisfaction. For these reasons, companies normally work closely with their distribution allies (who are their direct customers) to perform value chain activities in mutually beneficial ways. For instance, motor vehicle manufacturers have a competitive interest in working closely with their automobile dealers to promote higher sales volumes and better customer satisfaction with dealers' repair and maintenance services. Producers of kitchen cabinets are heavily dependent on the sales and promotional activities of their distributors and building supply retailers and on whether distributors and retailers operate cost-effectively enough to be able to sell at prices that lead to attractive sales volumes.

As a consequence, *accurately assessing a company's competitiveness entails scrutinizing the nature and costs of value chain activities throughout the entire value chain system for delivering its products or services to end-use customers.* A typical value chain system that incorporates the value chains of suppliers and forward-channel allies (if any) is shown in Figure 4.4. As was the case with company value chains, the specific activities constituting

FIGURE 4.4   A Representative Value Chain System

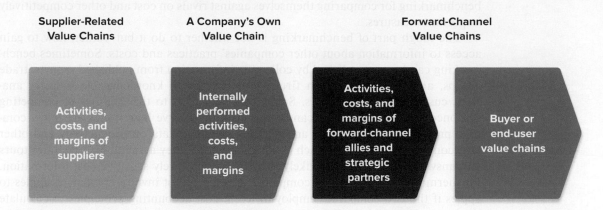

Supplier-Related   A Company's Own   Forward-Channel
Value Chains   Value Chain   Value Chains

Activities, costs, and margins of suppliers

Internally performed activities, costs, and margins

Activities, costs, and margins of forward-channel allies and strategic partners

Buyer or end-user value chains

Source: Based in part on the single-industry value chain displayed in Michael E. Porter, *Competitive Advantage* (New York: Free Press, 1985), p. 35.

value chain systems vary significantly from industry to industry. The primary value chain system activities in the pulp and paper industry (timber farming, logging, pulp mills, and papermaking) differ from the primary value chain system activities in the home appliance industry (parts and components manufacture, assembly, wholesale distribution, retail sales) and yet again from the computer software industry (programming, disk loading, marketing, distribution).

Benchmarking: A Tool for Assessing the Costs and Effectiveness of Value Chain Activities

Benchmarking entails comparing how different companies perform various value chain activities—how materials are purchased, how inventories are managed, how products are assembled, how fast the company can get new products to market, how customer orders are filled and shipped—and then making cross-company comparisons of the costs and effectiveness of these activities.[14] The comparison is often made between companies in the same industry, but benchmarking can also involve comparing how activities are done by companies in other industries. The objectives of benchmarking are simply to identify the best means of performing an activity and to emulate those best practices. It can be used to benchmark the activities of a company's internal value chain or the activities within an entire value chain system.

A **best practice** is a method of performing an activity or business process that consistently delivers superior results compared to other approaches.[15] To qualify as a legitimate best practice, the method must have been employed by at least one enterprise and shown to be *consistently more effective* in lowering costs, improving quality or performance, shortening time requirements, enhancing safety, or achieving some other highly positive operating outcome. Best practices thus identify a path to operating excellence with respect to value chain activities.

Xerox pioneered the use of benchmarking to become more cost-competitive, quickly deciding not to restrict its benchmarking efforts to its office equipment rivals but to extend them to *any company regarded as "world class"* in performing *any activity* relevant to Xerox's business. Other companies quickly picked up on Xerox's approach. Toyota managers got their idea for just-in-time inventory deliveries by studying how U.S. supermarkets replenished their shelves. Southwest Airlines reduced the

CORE CONCEPT

Benchmarking is a potent tool for improving a value chain activities that is based on learning how other companies perform them and borrowing their "best practices."

CORE CONCEPT

A **best practice** is a method of performing an activity that consistently delivers superior results compared to other approaches.

turnaround time of its aircraft at each scheduled stop by studying pit crews on the auto racing circuit. More than 80 percent of Fortune 500 companies reportedly use benchmarking for comparing themselves against rivals on cost and other competitively important measures.

The tough part of benchmarking is not whether to do it but, rather, how to gain access to information about other companies' practices and costs. Sometimes benchmarking can be accomplished by collecting information from published reports, trade groups, and industry research firms or by talking to knowledgeable industry analysts, customers, and suppliers. Sometimes field trips to the facilities of competing or noncompeting companies can be arranged to observe how things are done, compare practices and processes, and perhaps exchange data on productivity and other cost components. However, such companies, even if they agree to host facilities tours and answer questions, are unlikely to share competitively sensitive cost information. Furthermore, comparing two companies' costs may not involve comparing apples to apples if the two companies employ different cost accounting principles to calculate the costs of particular activities.

> Benchmarking the costs of company activities against those of rivals provides hard evidence of whether a company is cost-competitive.

However, a third and fairly reliable source of benchmarking information has emerged. The explosive interest of companies in benchmarking costs and identifying best practices has prompted consulting organizations (e.g., Accenture, A. T. Kearney, Benchnet—The Benchmarking Exchange, and Best Practices, LLC) and several associations (e.g., the QualServe Benchmarking Clearinghouse, and the Strategic Planning Institute's Council on Benchmarking) to gather benchmarking data, distribute information about best practices, and provide comparative cost data without identifying the names of particular companies. Having an independent group gather the information and report it in a manner that disguises the names of individual companies protects competitively sensitive data and lessens the potential for unethical behavior on the part of company personnel in gathering their own data about competitors. Industry associations are another source of data that may be used for benchmarking purposes, as exemplified in the cement industry. Benchmarking data is also provided by some government agencies; data of this sort plays an important role in electricity pricing, for example. Illustration Capsule 4.2 describes benchmarking practices in the solar industry.

Strategic Options for Remedying a Cost or Value Disadvantage

The results of value chain analysis and benchmarking may disclose cost or value disadvantages relative to key rivals. Such information is vital in crafting strategic actions to eliminate any such disadvantages and improve profitability. Information of this nature can also help a company find new avenues for enhancing its competitiveness through lower costs or a more attractive customer value proposition. There are three main areas in a company's total value chain system where company managers can try to improve its efficiency and effectiveness in delivering customer value: (1) a company's own internal activities, (2) suppliers' part of the value chain system, and (3) the forward-channel portion of the value chain system.

Improving Internally Performed Value Chain Activities Managers can pursue any of several strategic approaches to reduce the costs of internally performed value chain activities and improve a company's cost-competitiveness. They can *implement best practices* throughout the company, particularly for high-cost activities. They can

The cost of solar power production is dropping rapidly, leading to lower solar power prices for consumers and an expanding market for solar companies. According to the Solar Energy Industries Association, over 11 gigawatts (GW) of solar serving electric utilities were installed in 2016—enough to supply power for approximately 1.8 million households. Simultaneously, the solar landscape is becoming more competitive. As of 2017, 46 firms had installed a cumulative total of over 45 GW of solar serving electric utilities in the United States.

As competition grows, benchmarking plays an increasingly critical role in assessing a solar company's relative costs and price positioning compared to other firms. This is often measured using the all-in installation and production costs per kilowatt hour generated by a solar asset, called the "Levelized Cost of Energy" (LCOE). Kilowatt hours are the units of electricity that are sold to consumers.

In 2008, SunPower—one of the largest solar firms in the United States—used benchmarking to target a 50 percent decrease in its solar LCOE by 2012. This early benchmarking strategy helped the company to defend against new market entrants offering lower prices. But in the ensuing years, between 2009 and 2014, the overall industry solar LCOE fell by 78 percent, leading the company to conclude that an even more aggressive approach was needed to manage downward pricing pressure. Over the course of 2017, SunPower's quarterly earnings calls highlighted efforts to compete on benchmark prices by simplifying its company structure; divesting from non-core assets; and diversifying beyond the low-cost, large-scale utility solar market and into residential and commercial solar where it could compete more easily on price.

©geniusey/Shutterstock

Continuing to anticipate and adapt to falling solar prices requires reliable industry data on benchmark costs. The National Renewable Energy Laboratory (NREL) Quarterly U.S. Solar Photovoltaic System Cost Benchmark breaks down industry solar costs by inputs, including solar modules, structural hardware, and electrical components, as well as soft costs like labor and land expenses. This enables firms like SunPower to assess how their component costs compare to benchmarks and informs SunPower's outlook for how solar prices will continue to fall over time.

For solar to play a major role in U.S. power generation, costs must keep decreasing. As solar companies race toward lower costs, benchmarking will continue to be a core strategic tool in determining pricing and market positioning.

Note: Developed with Mathew O'Sullivan.

Sources: Solar Power World, "Top 500 Solar Contractors" (2017); SunPower, "The Drivers of the Levelized Cost of Electricity for Utility-Scale Photovoltaics" (2008); Lazard, "Levelized Cost of Energy Analysis, Version 8.0" (2014).

redesign the product and/or some of its components to eliminate high-cost components or facilitate speedier and more economical manufacture or assembly. They can *relocate high-cost activities* (such as manufacturing) to geographic areas where they can be performed more cheaply or *outsource activities* to lower-cost vendors or contractors.

To improve the effectiveness of the company's customer value proposition and enhance differentiation, managers can take several approaches. They can *adopt best practices for quality, marketing, and customer service.* They can *reallocate resources to activities that address buyers' most important purchase criteria,* which will have the biggest impact on the value delivered to the customer. They can *adopt new technologies that spur innovation, improve design, and enhance creativity.* Additional approaches to managing value chain activities to lower costs and/or enhance customer value are discussed in Chapter 5.

Improving Supplier-Related Value Chain Activities   Supplier-related cost disadvantages can be attacked by pressuring suppliers for lower prices, switching to lower-priced substitute inputs, and collaborating closely with suppliers to identify mutual cost-saving opportunities.[16] For example, just-in-time deliveries from suppliers can lower a company's inventory and internal logistics costs and may also allow suppliers to economize on their warehousing, shipping, and production scheduling costs—a win–win outcome for both. In a few instances, companies may find that it is cheaper to integrate backward into the business of high-cost suppliers and make the item in-house instead of buying it from outsiders.

Similarly, a company can enhance its customer value proposition through its supplier relationships. Some approaches include selecting and retaining suppliers that meet higher-quality standards, providing quality-based incentives to suppliers, and integrating suppliers into the design process. Fewer defects in parts from suppliers not only improve quality throughout the value chain system but can lower costs as well since less waste and disruption occur in the production processes.

Improving Value Chain Activities of Distribution Partners   Any of three means can be used to achieve better cost-competitiveness in the forward portion of the industry value chain:

1. Pressure distributors, dealers, and other forward-channel allies to reduce their costs and markups.
2. Collaborate with them to identify win–win opportunities to reduce costs—for example, a chocolate manufacturer learned that by shipping its bulk chocolate in liquid form in tank cars instead of as 10-pound molded bars, it could not only save its candy bar manufacturing customers the costs associated with unpacking and melting but also eliminate its own costs of molding bars and packing them.
3. Change to a more economical distribution strategy, including switching to cheaper distribution channels (selling direct via the Internet) or integrating forward into company-owned retail outlets.

The means to enhancing differentiation through activities at the forward end of the value chain system include (1) engaging in cooperative advertising and promotions with forward allies (dealers, distributors, retailers, etc.), (2) creating exclusive arrangements with downstream sellers or utilizing other mechanisms that increase their incentives to enhance delivered customer value, and (3) creating and enforcing standards for downstream activities and assisting in training channel partners in business practices. Harley-Davidson, for example, enhances the shopping experience and perceptions of buyers by selling through retailers that sell Harley-Davidson motorcycles exclusively and meet Harley-Davidson standards. The bottlers of Pepsi and Coca Cola engage in cooperative promotional activities with large grocery chains such as Kroger, Publix, and Safeway.

Translating Proficient Performance of Value Chain Activities into Competitive Advantage

A company that does a *first-rate job* of managing the activities of its value chain or value chain system *relative to competitors* stands a good chance of profiting from its competitive advantage. A company's value-creating activities can offer a competitive advantage in one of two ways (or both):

1. They can contribute to greater efficiency and lower costs relative to competitors.
2. They can provide a basis for differentiation, so customers are willing to pay relatively more for the company's goods and services.

Achieving a cost-based competitive advantage requires determined management efforts to be cost-efficient in performing value chain activities. Such efforts have to be ongoing and persistent, and they have to involve each and every value chain activity. The goal must be continuous cost reduction, not a one-time or on-again–off-again effort. Companies like Dollar General, Nucor Steel, Irish airline Ryanair, T.J.Maxx, and French discount retailer Carrefour have been highly successful in managing their value chains in a low-cost manner.

Ongoing and persistent efforts are also required for a competitive advantage based on differentiation. Superior reputations and brands are built up slowly over time, through continuous investment and activities that deliver consistent, reinforcing messages. Differentiation based on quality requires vigilant management of activities for quality assurance throughout the value chain. While the basis for differentiation (e.g., status, design, innovation, customer service, reliability, image) may vary widely among companies pursuing a differentiation advantage, companies that succeed do so on the basis of a commitment to coordinated value chain activities aimed purposefully at this objective. Examples include Rolex (status), Braun (design), Room and Board (craftsmanship), Zappos and L.L. Bean (customer service), Salesforce.com and Tesla (innovation), and FedEx (reliability).

How Value Chain Activities Relate to Resources and Capabilities There is a close relationship between the value-creating activities that a company performs and its resources and capabilities. An organizational capability or competence implies a *capacity* for action; in contrast, a value-creating activity *initiates* the action. With respect to resources and capabilities, activities are "where the rubber hits the road." When companies engage in a value-creating activity, they do so by drawing on specific company resources and capabilities that underlie and enable the activity. For example, brand-building activities depend on human resources, such as experienced brand managers (including their knowledge and expertise in this arena), as well as organizational capabilities in advertising and marketing. Cost-cutting activities may derive from organizational capabilities in inventory management, for example, and resources such as inventory tracking systems.

Because of this correspondence between activities and supporting resources and capabilities, value chain analysis can complement resource and capability analysis as another tool for assessing a company's competitive advantage. Resources and capabilities that are *both valuable and rare* provide a company with *what it takes* for competitive advantage. For a company with competitive assets of this sort, the potential is there. When these assets are deployed in the form of a value-creating activity, that potential is realized due to their competitive superiority. Resource analysis is one tool for identifying competitively superior resources and capabilities. But their value and the competitive superiority of that value can be assessed objectively only *after* they are deployed. Value chain analysis and benchmarking provide the type of data needed to make that objective assessment.

There is also a dynamic relationship between a company's activities and its resources and capabilities. Value-creating activities are more than just the embodiment

Performing value chain activities with capabilities that permit the company to either outmatch rivals on differentiation or beat them on costs will give the company a competitive advantage.

of a resource's or capability's potential. They also contribute to the formation and development of capabilities. The road to competitive advantage begins with management efforts to build organizational expertise in performing certain competitively important value chain activities. With consistent practice and continuous investment of company resources, these activities rise to the level of a reliable organizational capability or a competence. To the extent that top management makes the growing capability a cornerstone of the company's strategy, this capability becomes a core competence for the company. Later, with further organizational learning and gains in proficiency, the core competence may evolve into a distinctive competence, giving the company superiority over rivals in performing an important value chain activity. Such superiority, if it gives the company significant competitive clout in the marketplace, can produce an attractive competitive edge over rivals. Whether the resulting competitive advantage is on the cost side or on the differentiation side (or both) will depend on the company's choice of which types of competence-building activities to engage in over this time period.

QUESTION 5: IS THE COMPANY COMPETITIVELY STRONGER OR WEAKER THAN KEY RIVALS?

● LO 4-5

Explain how a comprehensive evaluation of a company's competitive situation can assist managers in making critical decisions about their next strategic moves.

Using resource analysis, value chain analysis, and benchmarking to determine a company's competitiveness on value and cost is necessary but not sufficient. A more comprehensive assessment needs to be made of the company's *overall* competitive strength. The answers to two questions are of particular interest: First, how does the company rank relative to competitors on each of the important factors that determine market success? Second, all things considered, does the company have a *net* competitive advantage or disadvantage versus major competitors?

An easy-to-use method for answering these two questions involves developing quantitative strength ratings for the company and its key competitors on each industry key success factor and each competitively pivotal resource, capability, and value chain activity. Much of the information needed for doing a competitive strength assessment comes from previous analyses. Industry and competitive analyses reveal the key success factors and competitive forces that separate industry winners from losers. Benchmarking data and scouting key competitors provide a basis for judging the competitive strength of rivals on such factors as cost, key product attributes, customer service, image and reputation, financial strength, technological skills, distribution capability, and other factors. Resource and capability analysis reveals which of these are competitively important, given the external situation, and whether the company's competitive advantages are sustainable. SWOT analysis provides a more forward-looking picture of the company's overall situation.

Step 1 in doing a competitive strength assessment is to make a list of the industry's key success factors and other telling measures of competitive strength or weakness (6 to 10 measures usually suffice). Step 2 is to assign weights to each of the measures of competitive strength based on their perceived importance. (The sum of the weights for each measure must add up to 1.) Step 3 is to calculate weighted strength ratings by scoring each competitor on each strength measure (using a 1-to-10 rating scale, where 1 is very weak and 10 is very strong) and multiplying the assigned rating by the assigned weight. Step 4 is to sum the weighted strength ratings on each factor to get an overall measure of competitive strength for each company being rated. Step 5 is to use the overall strength ratings to draw conclusions about the size and extent of the company's net competitive advantage or disadvantage and to take specific note of areas of strength and weakness.

Table 4.4 provides an example of competitive strength assessment in which a hypothetical company (ABC Company) competes against two rivals. In the example, relative cost is the most telling measure of competitive strength, and the other strength measures are of lesser importance. The company with the highest rating on a given measure has an implied competitive edge on that measure, with the size of its edge

TABLE 4.4 A Representative Weighted Competitive Strength Assessment

| Key Success Factor/Strength Measure | Importance Weight | Competitive Strength Assessment (rating scale: 1 = very weak, 10 = very strong) | | | | | |
| | | ABC Co. | | Rival 1 | | Rival 2 | |
		Strength Rating	Weighted Score	Strength Rating	Weighted Score	Strength Rating	Weighted Score
Quality/product performance	0.10	8	0.80	5	0.50	1	0.10
Reputation/image	0.10	8	0.80	7	0.70	1	0.10
Manufacturing capability	0.10	2	0.20	10	1.00	5	0.50
Technological skills	0.05	10	0.50	1	0.05	3	0.15
Dealer network/distribution capability	0.05	9	0.45	4	0.20	5	0.25
New product innovation capability	0.05	9	0.45	4	0.20	5	0.25
Financial resources	0.10	5	0.50	10	1.00	3	0.30
Relative cost position	0.30	5	1.50	10	3.00	1	0.30
Customer service capabilities	0.15	5	0.75	7	1.05	1	0.15
Sum of importance weights	**1.00**						
Overall weighted competitive strength rating			5.95		7.70		2.10

reflected in the difference between its weighted rating and rivals' weighted ratings. For instance, Rival 1's 3.00 weighted strength rating on relative cost signals a considerable cost advantage over ABC Company (with a 1.50 weighted score on relative cost) and an even bigger cost advantage over Rival 2 (with a weighted score of 0.30). The measure-by-measure ratings reveal the competitive areas in which a company is strongest and weakest, and against whom.

The overall competitive strength scores indicate how all the different strength measures add up—whether the company is at a net overall competitive advantage or disadvantage against each rival. The higher a company's *overall weighted strength rating,* the stronger its *overall competitiveness* versus rivals. The bigger the difference between a company's overall weighted rating and the scores of *lower-rated* rivals, the greater is its implied *net competitive advantage.* Thus, Rival 1's overall weighted score of 7.70 indicates a greater net competitive advantage over Rival 2 (with a score of 2.10) than over ABC Company (with a score of 5.95). Conversely, the bigger the difference between a company's overall rating and the scores of *higher-rated* rivals, the greater its implied *net competitive disadvantage.* Rival 2's score of 2.10 gives it a smaller net competitive disadvantage against ABC Company (with an overall score of 5.95) than against Rival 1 (with an overall score of 7.70).

> High-weighted competitive strength ratings signal a strong competitive position and possession of competitive advantage; low ratings signal a weak position and competitive disadvantage.

Strategic Implications of Competitive Strength Assessments

In addition to showing how competitively strong or weak a company is relative to rivals, the strength ratings provide guidelines for designing wise offensive and defensive strategies. For example, if ABC Company wants to go on the offensive to win additional sales and market share, such an offensive probably needs to be aimed directly at winning customers away from Rival 2 (which has a lower overall strength score) rather than Rival 1 (which has a higher overall strength score). Moreover, while ABC has high ratings for technological skills (a 10 rating), dealer network/distribution capability (a 9 rating), new product innovation capability (a 9 rating), quality/product performance (an 8 rating), and reputation/image (an 8 rating), these strength measures have low importance weights—meaning that ABC has strengths in areas that don't translate into much competitive clout in the marketplace. Even so, it outclasses Rival 2 in all five areas, plus it enjoys substantially lower costs than Rival 2 (ABC has a 5 rating on relative cost position versus a 1 rating for Rival 2)—and relative cost position carries the highest importance weight of all the strength measures. ABC also has greater competitive strength than Rival 3 regarding customer service capabilities (which carries the second-highest importance weight). Hence, because ABC's strengths are in the very areas where Rival 2 is weak, ABC is in a good position to attack Rival 2. Indeed, ABC may well be able to persuade a number of Rival 2's customers to switch their purchases over to its product.

> A company's competitive strength scores pinpoint its strengths and weaknesses against rivals and point directly to the kinds of offensive and defensive actions it can use to exploit its competitive strengths and reduce its competitive vulnerabilities.

But ABC should be cautious about cutting price aggressively to win customers away from Rival 2, because Rival 1 could interpret that as an attack by ABC to win away Rival 1's customers as well. And Rival 1 is in far and away the best position to compete on the basis of low price, given its high rating on relative cost in an industry where low costs are competitively important (relative cost carries an importance weight of 0.30). Rival 1's strong relative cost position vis-à-vis both ABC and Rival 2 arms it with the ability to use its lower-cost advantage to thwart any price cutting on

ABC's part. Clearly ABC is vulnerable to any retaliatory price cuts by Rival 1—Rival 1 can easily defeat both ABC and Rival 2 in a price-based battle for sales and market share. If ABC wants to defend against its vulnerability to potential price cutting by Rival 1, then it needs to aim a portion of its strategy at lowering its costs.

The point here is that a competitively astute company should utilize the strength scores in deciding what strategic moves to make. When a company has important competitive strengths in areas where one or more rivals are weak, it makes sense to consider offensive moves to exploit rivals' competitive weaknesses. When a company has important competitive weaknesses in areas where one or more rivals are strong, it makes sense to consider defensive moves to curtail its vulnerability.

QUESTION 6: WHAT STRATEGIC ISSUES AND PROBLEMS MERIT FRONT-BURNER MANAGERIAL ATTENTION?

The final and most important analytic step is to zero in on exactly what strategic issues company managers need to address—and resolve—for the company to be more financially and competitively successful in the years ahead. This step involves drawing on the results of both industry analysis and the evaluations of the company's internal situation. The task here is to get a clear fix on exactly what strategic and competitive challenges confront the company, which of the company's competitive shortcomings need fixing, and what specific problems merit company managers' front-burner attention. *Pinpointing the specific issues that management needs to address sets the agenda for deciding what actions to take next to improve the company's performance and business outlook.*

The "priority list" of issues and problems that have to be wrestled with can include such things as *how* to stave off market challenges from new foreign competitors, *how* to combat the price discounting of rivals, *how* to reduce the company's high costs, *how* to sustain the company's present rate of growth in light of slowing buyer demand, *whether* to correct the company's competitive deficiencies by acquiring a rival company with the missing strengths, *whether* to expand into foreign markets, *whether* to reposition the company and move to a different strategic group, *what to do* about growing buyer interest in substitute products, and *what to do* to combat the aging demographics of the company's customer base. The priority list thus always centers on such concerns as "how to . . . ," "what to do about . . . ," and "whether to . . ." The purpose of the priority list is to identify the specific issues and problems that management needs to address, not to figure out what specific actions to take. Deciding what to do—which strategic actions to take and which strategic moves to make—comes later (when it is time to craft the strategy and choose among the various strategic alternatives).

If the items on the priority list are relatively minor—which suggests that the company's strategy is mostly on track and reasonably well matched to the company's overall situation—company managers seldom need to go much beyond fine-tuning the present strategy. If, however, the problems confronting the company are serious and indicate the present strategy is not well suited for the road ahead, the task of crafting a better strategy needs to be at the top of management's action agenda.

> Compiling a "priority list" of problems creates an agenda of strategic issues that merit prompt managerial attention.

> A good strategy must contain ways to deal with all the strategic issues and obstacles that stand in the way of the company's financial and competitive success in the years ahead.

KEY POINTS

There are six key questions to consider in evaluating a company's ability to compete successfully against market rivals:

1. *How well is the present strategy working?* This involves evaluating the strategy in terms of the company's financial performance and market standing. The stronger a company's current overall performance, the less likely the need for radical strategy changes. The weaker a company's performance, the more its current strategy must be questioned.

2. *What is the company's overall situation, in terms of its internal strengths and weaknesses in relation to its market opportunities and external threats?* The answer to this question comes from performing a SWOT analysis. A company's strengths and competitive assets are strategically relevant because they are the most logical and appealing building blocks for strategy; internal weaknesses are important because they may represent vulnerabilities that need correction. External opportunities and threats come into play because a good strategy necessarily aims at capturing a company's most attractive opportunities and at defending against threats to its well-being.

3. *What are the company's most important resources and capabilities and can they give the company a sustainable advantage?* A company's resources can be identified using the tangible/intangible typology presented in this chapter. Its capabilities can be identified either by starting with its resources to look for related capabilities or looking for them within the company's different functional domains.

   The answer to the second part of the question comes from conducting the four tests of a resource's competitive power—the VRIN tests. If a company has resources and capabilities that are competitively *valuable* and *rare,* the firm will have a competitive advantage over market rivals. If its resources and capabilities are also hard to copy *(inimitable),* with no good substitutes *(nonsubstitutable),* then the firm may be able to sustain this advantage even in the face of active efforts by rivals to overcome it.

4. *Are the company's cost structure and value proposition competitive?* One telling sign of whether a company's situation is strong or precarious is whether its costs are competitive with those of industry rivals. Another sign is how the company compares with rivals in terms of differentiation—how effectively it delivers on its customer value proposition. Value chain analysis and benchmarking are essential tools in determining whether the company is performing particular functions and activities well, whether its costs are in line with those of competitors, whether it is differentiating in ways that really enhance customer value, and whether particular internal activities and business processes need improvement. They complement resource and capability analysis by providing data at the level of individual activities that provide more objective evidence of whether individual resources and capabilities, or bundles of resources and linked activity sets, are competitively superior.

5. *On an overall basis, is the company competitively stronger or weaker than key rivals?* The key appraisals here involve how the company matches up against key rivals on industry key success factors and other chief determinants of competitive success and whether and why the company has a *net* competitive advantage or disadvantage. Quantitative competitive strength assessments, using the method presented in Table 4.4, indicate where a company is competitively strong and weak and provide insight into the company's ability to defend or enhance its market position. As a rule, a company's competitive strategy should be built around its competitive strengths and should aim at shoring up areas where it is competitively vulnerable.

When a company has important competitive strengths in areas where one or more rivals are weak, it makes sense to consider offensive moves to exploit rivals' competitive weaknesses. When a company has important competitive weaknesses in areas where one or more rivals are strong, it makes sense to consider defensive moves to curtail its vulnerability.

6. *What strategic issues and problems merit front-burner managerial attention?* This analytic step zeros in on the strategic issues and problems that stand in the way of the company's success. It involves using the results of industry analysis as well as resource and value chain analysis of the company's competitive situation to identify a "priority list" of issues to be resolved for the company to be financially and competitively successful in the years ahead. Actually deciding on a strategy and what specific actions to take is what comes after developing the list of strategic issues and problems that merit front-burner management attention.

Like good industry analysis, solid analysis of the company's competitive situation vis-à-vis its key rivals is a valuable precondition for good strategy making.

ASSURANCE OF LEARNING EXERCISES

1. Using the financial ratios provided in Table 4.1 and following the financial statement information presented for Urban Outfitters, Inc., calculate the following ratios for Urban Outfitters for both 2016 and 2017:

   a. Gross profit margin

   b. Operating profit margin

   c. Net profit margin

   d. Times-interest-earned (or coverage) ratio

   e. Return on stockholders' equity

   f. Return on assets

   g. Debt-to-equity ratio

   h. Days of inventory

   i. Inventory turnover ratio

   j. Average collection period

   Based on these ratios, did Urban Outfitter's financial performance improve, weaken, or remain about the same from 2016 to 2017?

connect

LO 4-1

Consolidated Income Statements for Urban Outfitters, Inc., 2016–2017 (in thousands, except per share data)

	2016	2017
Net sales (total revenue)	$3,545,794	$3,445,134
Cost of sales	2,301,181	2,243,232
Selling, general, and administrative	906,086	848,323

(continued)

	2016	2017
Operating income	338,527	353,579
Other income (expense)		
Other expenses	(4,587)	(5,449)
Interest income and other, net	4159	1901
Income before income taxes	338,099	350,031
Provision for income taxes	119,979	125,542
Net income	$218,120	$224,489
Basic earnings per share	$ 1.87	$ 1.79
Diluted earnings per share	$ 1.86	$ 1.78

Source: Urban Outfitters, Inc., 2017.

Consolidated Balance Sheets for Urban Outfitters, Inc., 2016–2017 (in thousands, except per share data)

	January 31, 2017	January 31, 2016
Assets		
Current Assets		
Cash and cash equivalents	$ 248,140	$ 248,140
Short-term investments	111,067	61,061
Receivables, net	54,505	75,723
Merchandise inventories	338,590	330,223
Prepaid expenses and other current assets	129,095	102,078
Total current assets	881,397	834,361
Net property and equipment	867,786	863,137
Deferred income taxes and Other assets	153,454	135,803
Total assets	$1,902,637	$1,833,301
Liabilities and Shareholders' Equity		
Current Liabilities		
Accounts payable	$ 119,537	$ 118,035
Accrued salaries and benefits	58,782	41,474
Accrued expenses and Other current liabilities	174,609	169,722
Total current liabilities	352,928	329,231

(continued)

	January 31, 2017	January 31, 2016
Long-term debt	0	150,000
Deferred rent and other liabilities	236,625	216,843
Total liabilities	589,553	696,074
Commitments and Contingencies		
Equity		
Preferred stock $0.001 par value; 10,000,000 shares authorized; no shares issued and outstanding	0	0
Common stock $0.001 par value; 200,000,000 shares authorized; 116,233,781 and 117,321,120 shares issued and outstanding	12	12
Additional paid-in capital	$ 0	$ 0
Retained earnings	1,347,141	1,160,666
Total stockholders' equity	1,313,084	1,137,227
Total Liabilities and Equity	$1,902,637	$1,833,301

Source: Urban Outfitters, Inc., 2017 10-K.

2. Cinnabon, famous for its cinnamon rolls, is an American chain commonly located in high traffic areas, such as airports and malls. They operate more than 1,200 bakeries in more than 48 countries. How many of the four tests of the competitive power of a resource does the store network pass? Using your general knowledge of this industry, perform a SWOT analysis. Explain your answers.   **LO 4-2, LO 4-3**

3. Review the information in Illustration Capsule 4.1 concerning Boll & Branch's average costs of producing and selling a king-size sheet set, and compare this with the representative value chain depicted in Figure 4.3. Then answer the following questions: **LO 4-4**

   a. Which of the company's costs correspond to the primary value chain activities depicted in Figure 4.3?

   b. Which of the company's costs correspond to the support activities described in Figure 4.3?

   c. What value chain activities might be important in securing or maintaining Boll & Branch's competitive advantage? Explain your answer.

4. Using the methodology illustrated in Table 4.3 and your knowledge as an auto-mobile owner, prepare a competitive strength assessment for General Motors and its rivals Ford, Chrysler, Toyota, and Honda. Each of the five automobile manu-facturers should be evaluated on the key success factors and strength measures of cost-competitiveness, product-line breadth, product quality and reliability, financial resources and profitability, and customer service. What does your com-petitive strength assessment disclose about the overall competitiveness of each automobile manufacturer? What factors account most for Toyota's competitive success? Does Toyota have competitive weaknesses that were disclosed by your analysis? Explain.   **LO 4-5**

EXERCISE FOR SIMULATION PARTICIPANTS

LO 4-1   1.   Using the formulas in Table 4.1 and the data in your company's latest financial statements, calculate the following measures of financial performance for your company:

    a. Operating profit margin

    b. Total return on total assets

    c. Current ratio

    d. Working capital

    e. Long-term debt-to-capital ratio

    f. Price-to-earnings ratio

LO 4-1   2.   On the basis of your company's latest financial statements and all the other available data regarding your company's performance that appear in the industry report, list the three measures of financial performance on which your company did best and the three measures on which your company's financial performance was worst.

LO 4-1   3.   What hard evidence can you cite that indicates your company's strategy is working fairly well (or perhaps not working so well, if your company's performance is lagging that of rival companies)?

LO 4-2, LO 4-3   4.   What internal strengths and weaknesses does your company have? What external market opportunities for growth and increased profitability exist for your company? What external threats to your company's future well-being and profitability do you and your co-managers see? What does the preceding SWOT analysis indicate about your company's present situation and future prospects—where on the scale from "exceptionally strong" to "alarmingly weak" does the attractiveness of your company's situation rank?

LO 4-2, LO 4-3   5.   Does your company have any core competencies? If so, what are they?

LO 4-4   6.   What are the key elements of your company's value chain? Refer to Figure 4.3 in developing your answer.

LO 4-5   7.   Using the methodology presented in Table 4.4, do a weighted competitive strength assessment for your company and two other companies that you and your co-managers consider to be very close competitors.

ENDNOTES

[1] Birger Wernerfelt, "A Resource-Based View of the Firm," *Strategic Management Journal* 5, no. 5 (September–October 1984), pp. 171–180; Jay Barney, "Firm Resources and Sustained Competitive Advantage," *Journal of Management* 17, no. 1 (1991), pp. 99–120.
[2] R. Amit and P. Schoemaker, "Strategic Assets and Organizational Rent," *Strategic Management Journal* 14 (1993).
[3] Jay B. Barney, "Looking Inside for Competitive Advantage," *Academy of Management Executive* 9, no. 4 (November 1995), pp. 49–61; Christopher A. Bartlett and Sumantra Ghoshal, "Building Competitive Advantage through People," *MIT Sloan Management Review* 43, no. 2 (Winter 2002),

pp. 34–41; Danny Miller, Russell Eisenstat, and Nathaniel Foote, "Strategy from the Inside Out: Building Capability-Creating Organizations," *California Management Review* 44, no. 3 (Spring 2002), pp. 37–54.
[4] M. Peteraf and J. Barney, "Unraveling the Resource-Based Tangle," *Managerial and Decision Economics* 24, no. 4 (June–July 2003), pp. 309–323.
[5] Margaret A. Peteraf and Mark E. Bergen, "Scanning Dynamic Competitive Landscapes: A Market-Based and Resource-Based Framework," *Strategic Management Journal* 24 (2003), pp. 1027–1042.
[6] C. Montgomery, "Of Diamonds and Rust: A New Look at Resources," in C. Montgomery

(ed.), *Resource-Based and Evolutionary Theories of the Firm* (Boston: Kluwer Academic, 1995), pp. 251–268.
[7] Constance E. Helfat and Margaret A. Peteraf, "The Dynamic Resource-Based View: Capability Lifecycles," *Strategic Management Journal* 24, no. 10 (2003).
[8] D. Teece, G. Pisano, and A. Shuen, "Dynamic Capabilities and Strategic Management," *Strategic Management Journal* 18, no. 7 (1997), pp. 509–533; K. Eisenhardt and J. Martin, "Dynamic Capabilities: What Are They?" *Strategic Management Journal* 21, no. 10–11 (2000), pp. 1105–1121; M. Zollo and S. Winter, "Deliberate Learning and the Evolution of Dynamic Capabilities," *Organization*

Science 13 (2002), pp. 339–351; C. Helfat et al., *Dynamic Capabilities: Understanding Strategic Change in Organizations* (Malden, MA: Blackwell, 2007).

[9] Donald Sull, "Strategy as Active Waiting," *Harvard Business Review* 83, no. 9 (September 2005), pp. 121–126.

[10] Michael Porter in his 1985 best seller *Competitive Advantage* (New York: Free Press).

[11] John K. Shank and Vijay Govindarajan, *Strategic Cost Management* (New York: Free Press, 1993), especially chaps. 2–6, 10, and 11;

Robin Cooper and Robert S. Kaplan, "Measure Costs Right: Make the Right Decisions," *Harvard Business Review* 66, no. 5 (September–October, 1988), pp. 96–103; Joseph A. Ness and Thomas G. Cucuzza, "Tapping the Full Potential of ABC," *Harvard Business Review* 73, no. 4 (July–August 1995), pp. 130–138.

[12] Porter, *Competitive Advantage*, p. 34.

[13] Hau L. Lee, "The Triple-A Supply Chain," *Harvard Business Review* 82, no. 10 (October 2004), pp. 102–112.

[14] Gregory H. Watson, *Strategic Benchmarking: How to Rate Your Company's Performance*

against the World's Best (New York: Wiley, 1993); Robert C. Camp, *Benchmarking: The Search for Industry Best Practices That Lead to Superior Performance* (Milwaukee: ASQC Quality Press, 1989); Dawn Iacobucci and Christie Nordhielm, "Creative Benchmarking," *Harvard Business Review* 78 no. 6 (November–December 2000), pp. 24–25.

[15] **www.businessdictionary.com/definition/ best-practice.html** (accessed December 2, 2009).

[16] Reuben E. Stone, "Leading a Supply Chain Turnaround," *Harvard Business Review* 82, no. 10 (October 2004), pp. 114–121.

chapter 5

The Five Generic Competitive Strategies

Learning Objectives

This chapter will help you

LO 5-1 Distinguish each of the five generic strategies and explain why some of these strategies work better in certain kinds of competitive conditions than in others.

LO 5-2 Identify the major avenues for achieving a competitive advantage based on lower costs.

LO 5-3 Identify the major avenues to a competitive advantage based on differentiating a company's product or service offering from the offerings of rivals.

LO 5-4 Explain the attributes of a best-cost strategy—a hybrid of low-cost and differentiation strategies.

©JDawnInk/DigitalVision Vectors/Getty Images

It's all about strategic positioning and competition.

Michele Hutchins—*Consultant*

Strategic positioning means performing different activities from rivals or performing similar activities in different ways.

Michael E. Porter—*Professor, author, and cofounder of Monitor Consulting*

I learnt the hard way about positioning in business, about catering to the right segments.

Shaffi Mather—*Social entrepreneur*

A company can employ any of several basic approaches to gaining a competitive advantage over rivals, but they all involve *delivering more value* to customers than rivals or *delivering value more efficiently* than rivals (or both). More value for customers can mean a good product at a lower price, a superior product worth paying more for, or a best-value offering that represents an attractive combination of price, features, service, and other appealing attributes. Greater efficiency means delivering a given level of value to customers at a lower cost to the company. But whatever approach to delivering value the company takes, it nearly always requires performing value chain activities differently than rivals and building competitively valuable resources and capabilities that rivals cannot readily match or trump.

This chapter describes the five *generic competitive strategy options*. Each of the five generic strategies represents a distinctly different approach to competing in the marketplace. Which of the five to employ is a company's first and foremost choice in crafting an overall strategy and beginning its quest for competitive advantage.

TYPES OF GENERIC COMPETITIVE STRATEGIES

● ● ● ●

A company's competitive strategy lays out the specific efforts of the company to position itself in the marketplace, please customers, ward off competitive threats, and achieve a particular kind of competitive advantage. The chances are remote that any two companies—even companies in the same industry—will employ competitive strategies that are exactly alike in every detail. However, when one strips away the details to get at the real substance, the two biggest factors that distinguish one competitive strategy from another boil down to (1) whether a company's market target is broad or narrow and (2) whether the company is pursuing a competitive advantage linked to lower costs or differentiation. These two factors give rise to four distinct competitive strategy options, plus one hybrid option, as shown in Figure 5.1 and listed next.[1]

1. *A broad, low-cost strategy*—striving to achieve broad lower overall costs than rivals on comparable products that attract a broad spectrum of buyers, usually by underpricing rivals.

2. *A broad differentiation strategy*—seeking to differentiate the company's product offering from rivals' with attributes that will appeal to a broad spectrum of buyers.

3. *A focused low-cost strategy*—concentrating on the needs and requirements of a narrow buyer segment (or market niche) and striving to meet these needs at lower costs than rivals (thereby being able to serve niche members at a lower price).

4. *A focused differentiation strategy*—concentrating on a narrow buyer segment (or market niche) and offering niche members customized attributes that meet their tastes and requirements better than rivals' products.

FIGURE 5.1   The Five Generic Competitive Strategies

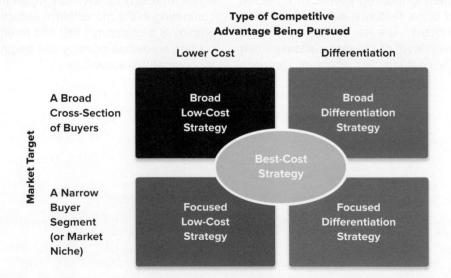

Source: This is an expanded version of a three-strategy classification discussed in Michael E. Porter, *Competitive Strategy* (New York: Free Press, 1980).

5. *A best-cost strategy*—striving to incorporate upscale product attributes at a lower cost than rivals. Being the "best-cost" producer of an upscale, multifeatured product allows a company to *give customers more value for their money* by underpricing rivals whose products have similar upscale, multifeatured attributes. This competitive approach is a *hybrid* strategy that *blends elements of the previous four options* in a unique and often effective way. It may be focused or broad in its appeal.

The remainder of this chapter explores the ins and outs of these five generic competitive strategies and how they differ.

BROAD LOW-COST STRATEGIES

● ● ● ●

● LO 5-2

Identify the major avenues for achieving a competitive advantage based on lower costs.

Striving to achieve lower costs than rivals targeting a broad spectrum of buyers is an especially potent competitive approach in markets with many price-sensitive buyers. A company achieves **low-cost leadership** when it becomes the industry's lowest-cost producer rather than just being one of perhaps several competitors with comparatively low costs. But a low-cost producer's foremost strategic objective is *meaningfully* lower costs than rivals—*not necessarily the absolutely lowest possible cost.* In striving for a cost advantage over rivals, company managers must incorporate features and services that buyers consider essential. A product offering that is too frills-free can be viewed by consumers as offering little value regardless of its pricing.

CORE CONCEPT

The essence of a **broad, low-cost strategy** is to produce goods or services for a broad base of buyers at a lower cost than rivals.

A company has two options for translating a low-cost advantage over rivals into superior profit performance. Option 1 is to use the lower-cost edge to underprice competitors and attract price-sensitive buyers in great enough numbers to increase total profits. Option 2 is to maintain the present price, be content with the present market share, and use the lower-cost edge to raise total profits by earning a higher profit margin on each unit sold.

While many companies are inclined to exploit a low-cost advantage by using option 1 (attacking rivals with lower prices), this strategy can backfire if rivals respond with retaliatory price cuts (in order to protect their customer base and defend against a loss of sales). A rush to cut prices can often trigger a price war that lowers the profits of all price discounters. The bigger the risk that rivals will respond with matching price cuts, the more appealing it becomes to employ the second option for using a low-cost advantage to achieve higher profitability.

The Two Major Avenues for Achieving a Cost Advantage

To achieve a low-cost edge over rivals, a firm's cumulative costs across its overall value chain must be lower than competitors' cumulative costs. There are two major avenues for accomplishing this:[2]

A low-cost advantage over rivals can translate into superior profitability through lower price and higher market share or higher profit margins.

1. Perform value chain activities more cost-effectively than rivals.
2. Revamp the firm's overall value chain to eliminate or bypass some cost-producing activities.

CORE CONCEPT

A **cost driver** is a factor that has a strong influence on a company's costs.

Cost-Efficient Management of Value Chain Activities   For a company to do a more cost-effective job of managing its value chain than rivals, managers must diligently search out cost-saving opportunities in every part of the value chain. No activity can escape cost-saving scrutiny, and all company personnel must be expected to use their talents and ingenuity to come up with innovative and effective ways to keep down costs. Particular attention must be paid to a set of factors known as **cost drivers** that have a strong effect on a company's costs and can be used as levers to lower costs. Figure 5.2 shows the most important cost drivers. Cost-cutting approaches that demonstrate an effective use of the cost drivers include

1. *Capturing all available economies of scale.* Economies of scale stem from an ability to lower unit costs by increasing the scale of operation. Economies of scale may be available at different points along the value chain. Often a large plant is more economical to operate than a small one, particularly if it can be operated round the clock robotically. Economies of scale may be available due to a large warehouse operation on the input side or a large distribution center on the output side. In global industries, selling a mostly standard product worldwide tends to lower unit costs as opposed to making separate products (each at lower scale) for each country market. There are economies of scale in advertising as well. For example, Anheuser-Busch InBev SA/NV could afford to pay the $5 million cost of a 30-second Super Bowl ad in 2018 because the cost could be spread out over the hundreds of millions of units of Budweiser that the company sells.

FIGURE 5.2   Cost Drivers: The Keys to Driving Down Company Costs

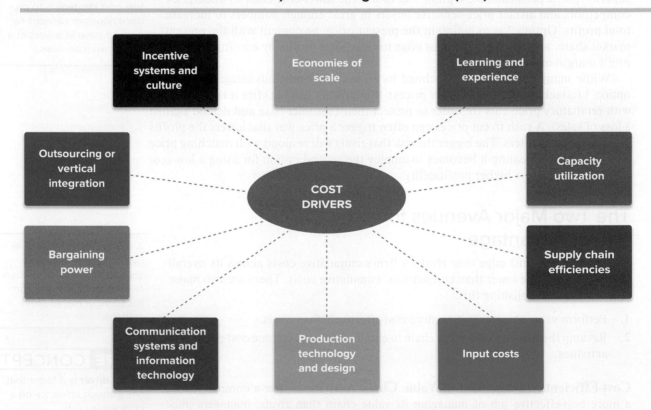

Source: Adapted from Michael E. Porter, *Competitive Advantage: Creating and Sustaining Superior Performance* (New York: Free Press, 1985).

2. *Taking full advantage of experience and learning-curve effects.* The cost of performing an activity can decline over time as the learning and experience of company personnel build. Learning and experience economies can stem from debugging and mastering newly introduced technologies, using the experiences and suggestions of workers to install more efficient plant layouts and assembly procedures, and the added speed and effectiveness that accrues from repeatedly picking sites for and building new plants, distribution centers, or retail outlets.

3. *Operating facilities at full capacity.* Whether a company is able to operate at or near full capacity has a big impact on unit costs when its value chain contains activities associated with substantial fixed costs. Higher rates of capacity utilization allow depreciation and other fixed costs to be spread over a larger unit volume, thereby lowering fixed costs per unit. The more capital-intensive the business and the higher the fixed costs as a percentage of total costs, the greater the unit-cost penalty for operating at less than full capacity.

4. *Improving supply chain efficiency.* Partnering with suppliers to streamline the ordering and purchasing process, to reduce inventory carrying costs via just-in-time inventory practices, to economize on shipping and materials handling, and to ferret out other cost-saving opportunities is a much-used approach to cost reduction. A company with a distinctive competence in cost-efficient supply chain management, such as Colgate-Palmolive or Unilever (leading consumer products companies), can sometimes achieve a sizable cost advantage over less adept rivals.

5. *Substituting lower-cost inputs wherever there is little or no sacrifice in product quality or performance.* If the costs of certain raw materials and parts are "too high," a company can switch to using lower-cost items or maybe even design the high-cost components out of the product altogether.

6. *Using the company's bargaining power vis-à-vis suppliers or others in the value chain system to gain concessions.* Home Depot, for example, has sufficient bargaining clout with suppliers to win price discounts on large-volume purchases.

7. *Using online systems and sophisticated software to achieve operating efficiencies.* For example, sharing data and production schedules with suppliers, coupled with the use of enterprise resource planning (ERP) and manufacturing execution system (MES) software, can reduce parts inventories, trim production times, and lower labor requirements.

8. *Improving process design and employing advanced production technology.* Often production costs can be cut by (1) using design for manufacture (DFM) procedures and computer-assisted design (CAD) techniques that enable more integrated and efficient production methods, (2) investing in highly automated robotic production technology, and (3) shifting to a mass-customization production process. Dell's highly automated PC assembly plant in Austin, Texas, is a prime example of the use of advanced product and process technologies. Many companies are ardent users of total quality management (TQM) systems, business process reengineering, Six Sigma methodology, and other business process management techniques that aim at boosting efficiency and reducing costs.

9. *Being alert to the cost advantages of outsourcing or vertical integration.* Outsourcing the performance of certain value chain activities can be more economical than performing them in-house if outside specialists, by virtue of their expertise and volume, can perform the activities at lower cost. On the other hand, there can be times when integrating into the activities of either suppliers or distribution-channel allies

can lower costs through greater production efficiencies, reduced transaction costs, or a better bargaining position.

10. *Motivating employees through incentives and company culture.* A company's incentive system can encourage not only greater worker productivity but also cost-saving innovations that come from worker suggestions. The culture of a company can also spur worker pride in productivity and continuous improvement. Companies that are well known for their cost-reducing incentive systems and culture include Nucor Steel, which characterizes itself as a company of "20,000 teammates," Southwest Airlines, and DHL Express (rival of FedEx).

Revamping of the Value Chain System to Lower Costs Dramatic cost advantages can often emerge from redesigning the company's value chain system in ways that eliminate costly work steps and entirely bypass certain cost-producing value chain activities. Such value chain revamping can include

- *Selling direct to consumers and bypassing the activities and costs of distributors and dealers.* To circumvent the need for distributors and dealers, a company can create its own direct sales force, which adds the costs of maintaining and supporting a sales force but may be cheaper than using independent distributors and dealers to access buyers. Alternatively, they can conduct sales operations at the company's website, since the costs for website operations and shipping may be substantially cheaper than going through distributor-dealer channels). Costs in the wholesale and retail portions of the value chain frequently represent 35 to 50 percent of the final price consumers pay, so establishing a direct sales force or selling online may offer big cost savings.

- *Streamlining operations by eliminating low-value-added or unnecessary work steps and activities.* At Walmart, some items supplied by manufacturers are delivered directly to retail stores rather than being routed through Walmart's distribution centers and delivered by Walmart trucks. In other instances, Walmart unloads incoming shipments from manufacturers' trucks arriving at its distribution centers and loads them directly onto outgoing Walmart trucks headed to particular stores without ever moving the goods into the distribution center. Many supermarket chains have greatly reduced in-store meat butchering and cutting activities by shifting to meats that are cut and packaged at the meatpacking plant and then delivered to their stores in ready-to-sell form.

- *Reducing materials-handling and shipping costs by having suppliers locate their plants or warehouses close to the company's own facilities.* Having suppliers locate their plants or warehouses close to a company's own plant facilitates just-in-time deliveries of parts and components to the exact workstation where they will be used in assembling the company's product. This not only lowers incoming shipping costs but also curbs or eliminates the company's need to build and operate storerooms for incoming parts and to have plant personnel move the inventories to the workstations as needed for assembly.

Illustration Capsule 5.1 describes the path that Vanguard has followed in achieving its position as the low-cost leader of the investment management industry.

Examples of Companies That Revamped Their Value Chains to Reduce Costs Nucor Corporation, the most profitable steel producer in the United States and one of the largest steel producers worldwide, drastically revamped the value chain process for

Vanguard's Path to Becoming the Low-Cost Leader in Investment Management

Vanguard is now one of the world's largest investment management companies. It became an industry giant by leading the way in low-cost passive index investing. In active trading, an investment manager is compensated for making an educated decision on which stocks to sell and which to buy. This incurs both transactional and management fees. In contrast, passive index portfolios aim to mirror the movements of a major market index like the S&P 500, Dow Jones Industrial Average, or NASDAQ. Passive portfolios incur fewer fees and can be managed with lower operating costs. A measure used to compare operating costs in this industry is known as the expense ratio, which is the percentage of an investment that goes toward expenses. In 2017, Vanguard's expense ratio was less than 18 percent of the industry's average expense ratio. Vanguard was the first to capitalize on what was at the time an underappreciated fact: over long horizons, well-managed index funds, with their lower costs and fees, typically outperform their actively trading competitors.

Vanguard provides low-cost investment options for its clients in several ways. By creating funds that track index(es) over a long horizon, the client does not incur transaction and management fees normally charged in actively managed funds. Possibly more important, Vanguard was created with a unique client-owner structure. When you invest with Vanguard you become an owner of Vanguard. This structure effectively cut out traditional shareholders who seek to share in profits. Under client ownership, any returns in excess of operating costs are returned to the clients/investors.

Vanguard keeps its costs low in several other ways. One notable one is its focus on its employees and organizational structure. The company prides itself on low turnover rates (8 percent) and very flat organizational

©Kristoffer Tripplaar/Alamy Stock Photo

structure. In several instances Vanguard has been able to capitalize on being a fast follower. They launched several product lines after their competitors introduced those products. Being a fast follower allowed them to develop superior products and reach scale more quickly—both further lowering their cost structure.

The low-cost structure has not come at the expense of performance. Vanguard now has 370 funds, over 20 million investors, has surpassed $4.5 trillion in AUM (assets under management), and is growing faster than all its competitors combined. When *Money* published its January 2018 list of recommended investment funds, 42 out of 100 products listed were Vanguard funds.

Vanguard's low-cost strategy has been so successful that industry experts now refer to The Vanguard Effect. This refers to the pressure that this investment management giant has put on competitors to lower their fees in order to compete with Vanguard's low-cost value proposition.

Note: Developed with Vedrana B. Greatorex.

Sources: https://www.nytimes.com/2017/04/14/business/mutfund/vanguard-mutual-index-funds-growth.html; https://investor
.vanguard.com; Sunderam, A., Viceira, L., & Ciechanover, A. (2016) *The Vanguard Group, Inc. in 2015: Celebrating 40.* HBS No. 9-216-026. Boston, MA: Harvard Business School Publishing.

---

manufacturing steel products by using relatively inexpensive electric arc furnaces and continuous casting processes. Using electric arc furnaces to melt recycled scrap steel eliminated many of the steps used by traditional steel mills that made their steel products from iron ore, coke, limestone, and other ingredients using costly coke ovens, basic oxygen blast furnaces, ingot casters, and multiple types of finishing facilities—plus Nucor's value chain system required far fewer employees. As a consequence, Nucor produces steel with a far lower capital investment, a far smaller workforce, and far lower operating costs than traditional steel mills. Nucor's strategy to replace the

> Success in achieving a low-cost edge over rivals comes from out-managing rivals in finding ways to perform value chain activities faster, more accurately, and more cost-effectively.

traditional steelmaking value chain with its simpler, quicker value chain approach has made it one of the world's lowest-cost producers of steel, allowing it to take a huge amount of market share away from traditional steel companies and earn attractive profits. This approach has allowed the company to remain steadily profitable even as a flood of illegally subsidized imports wreaked havoc on the rest of the North American steel market.

Southwest Airlines has achieved considerable cost savings by reconfiguring the traditional value chain of commercial airlines, thereby permitting it to offer travelers lower fares. Its mastery of fast turnarounds at the gates (about 25 minutes versus 45 minutes for rivals) allows its planes to fly more hours per day. This translates into being able to schedule more flights per day with fewer aircraft, allowing Southwest to generate more revenue per plane on average than rivals. Southwest does not offer assigned seating, baggage transfer to connecting airlines, or first-class seating and service, thereby eliminating all the cost-producing activities associated with these features. The company's fast and user-friendly online reservation system facilitates e-ticketing and reduces staffing requirements at telephone reservation centers and airport counters. Its use of automated check-in equipment reduces staffing requirements for terminal check-in. The company's carefully designed point-to-point route system minimizes connections, delays, and total trip time for passengers, allowing about 75 percent of Southwest passengers to fly nonstop to their destinations and at the same time reducing Southwest's costs for flight operations.

The Keys to a Successful Broad Low-Cost Strategy

While broad, low-cost companies are champions of frugality, they seldom hesitate to spend aggressively on resources and capabilities *that promise to drive costs out of the business.* Indeed, having competitive assets of this type and ensuring that they remain competitively superior is essential for achieving competitive advantage as a broad, low-cost leader. Walmart, for example, has been an early adopter of state-of-the-art technology throughout its operations; however, the company *carefully estimates the cost savings of new technologies before it rushes to invest in them.* By continuously investing in complex, cost-saving technologies that are hard for rivals to match, Walmart has sustained its low-cost advantage for over 45 years.

Uber and Lyft, employing a formidable low-cost provider strategy and an innovative business model, have stormed their way into hundreds of locations across the world, totally disrupting and seemingly forever changing competition in the taxi markets where they have a presence. And, most significantly, the ultra-low fares charged by Uber and Lyft have resulted in dramatic increases in the demand for taxi services, particularly those provided by these two low-cost providers. Other companies noted for their successful use of broad low-cost strategies include Spirit Airlines, EasyJet, and Ryanair in airlines; Briggs & Stratton in small gasoline engines; Huawei in networking and telecommunications equipment; Bic in ballpoint pens; Stride Rite in footwear; and Poulan in chain saws.

When a Low-Cost Strategy Works Best

A low-cost strategy becomes increasingly appealing and competitively powerful when

1. *Price competition among rival sellers is vigorous.* Low-cost leaders are in the best position to compete offensively on the basis of price, to gain market share at the expense of rivals, to win the business of price-sensitive buyers, to remain profitable despite strong price competition, and to survive price wars.

2. *The products of rival sellers are essentially identical and readily available from many eager sellers.* Look-alike products and/or overabundant product supply set the stage for lively price competition; in such markets, it is the less efficient, higher-cost companies whose profits get squeezed the most.

3. *It is difficult to achieve product differentiation in ways that have value to buyers.* When the differences between product attributes or brands do not matter much to buyers, buyers are nearly always sensitive to price differences, and industry-leading companies tend to be those with the lowest-priced brands.

4. *Most buyers use the product in the same ways.* With common user requirements, a standardized product can satisfy the needs of buyers, in which case low price, not features or quality, becomes the dominant factor in causing buyers to choose one seller's product over another's.

5. *Buyers incur low costs in switching their purchases from one seller to another.* Low switching costs give buyers the flexibility to shift purchases to lower-priced sellers having equally good products or to attractively priced substitute products. A low-cost leader is well positioned to use low price to induce potential customers to switch to its brand.

Pitfalls to Avoid in Pursuing a Low-Cost Strategy

Perhaps the biggest mistake a low-cost producer can make is getting carried away with overly aggressive price cutting. *Higher unit sales and market shares do not automatically translate into higher profits.* Reducing price results in earning a lower profit margin on each unit sold. Thus reducing price improves profitability *only if* the lower price increases unit sales enough to offset the loss in revenues due to the lower per unit profit margin. A simple numerical example tells the story: Suppose a firm selling 1,000 units at a price of $10, a cost of $9, and a profit margin of $1 opts to cut price 5 percent to $9.50—which reduces the firm's profit margin to $0.50 per unit sold. If unit costs remain at $9, then it takes a 100 percent sales increase to 2,000 units just to offset the narrower profit margin and get back to total profits of $1,000. Hence, whether a price cut will result in higher or lower profitability depends on how big the resulting sales gains will be and how much, if any, unit costs will fall as sales volumes increase.

A second pitfall is *relying on cost reduction approaches that can be easily copied by rivals.* If rivals find it relatively easy or inexpensive to imitate the leader's low-cost methods, then the leader's advantage will be too short-lived to yield a valuable edge in the marketplace.

A third pitfall is *becoming too fixated on cost reduction.* Low costs cannot be pursued so zealously that a firm's offering ends up being too feature-poor to generate buyer appeal. Furthermore, a company driving hard to push down its costs has to guard against ignoring declining buyer sensitivity to price, increased buyer interest in added features or service, or new developments that alter how buyers use the product. Otherwise, it risks losing market ground if buyers start opting for more upscale or feature-rich products.

Even if these mistakes are avoided, a low-cost strategy still entails risk. An innovative rival may discover an even lower-cost value chain approach. Important cost-saving technological breakthroughs may suddenly emerge. And if a low-cost producer has heavy investments in its present means of operating, then it can prove costly to quickly shift to the new value chain approach or a new technology.

> A low-cost producer is in the best position to win the business of price-sensitive buyers, set the floor on market price, and still earn a profit.

> Reducing price does not lead to higher total profits unless the added gains in unit sales are large enough to offset the loss in revenues due to lower margins per unit sold.

> A low-cost producer's product offering must always contain enough attributes to be attractive to prospective buyers—low price, by itself, is not always appealing to buyers.

BROAD DIFFERENTIATION STRATEGIES

● **LO 5-3**

Identify the major avenues to a competitive advantage based on differentiating a company's product or service offering from the offerings of rivals.

CORE CONCEPT

The essence of a **broad differentiation strategy** is to offer unique product attributes that a wide range of buyers find appealing and worth paying more for.

Differentiation strategies are attractive whenever buyers' needs and preferences are too diverse to be fully satisfied by a standardized product offering. Successful product differentiation requires careful study to determine what attributes buyers will find appealing, valuable, and worth paying for.[3] Then the company must incorporate a combination of these desirable features into its product or service that will be different enough to stand apart from the product or service offerings of rivals. A broad differentiation strategy achieves its aim when a wide range of buyers find the company's offering more appealing than that of rivals and worth a somewhat higher price.

Successful differentiation allows a firm to do one or more of the following:

- Command a premium price for its product.
- Increase unit sales (because additional buyers are won over by the differentiating features).
- Gain buyer loyalty to its brand (because buyers are strongly attracted to the differentiating features and bond with the company and its products).

Differentiation enhances profitability whenever a company's product can command a sufficiently higher price or generate sufficiently bigger unit sales *to more than cover the added costs of achieving the differentiation.* Company differentiation strategies fail when buyers don't place much value on the brand's uniqueness and/or when a company's differentiating features are easily matched by its rivals.

Companies can pursue differentiation from many angles: a unique taste (Red Bull, Listerine); multiple features (Microsoft Office, Apple Watch); wide selection and one-stop shopping (Home Depot, Alibaba.com); superior service (Ritz-Carlton, Nordstrom); spare parts availability (John Deere; Morgan Motors); engineering design and performance (Mercedes, BMW); high fashion design (Prada, Gucci); product reliability (Whirlpool, LG, and Bosch in large home appliances); quality manufacture (Michelin); technological leadership (3M Corporation in bonding and coating products); a full range of services (Charles Schwab in stock brokerage); and wide product selection (Campbell's soups).

Managing the Value Chain to Create the Differentiating Attributes

---

CORE CONCEPT

A **value driver** is a factor that can have a strong differentiating effect.

Differentiation is not something hatched in marketing and advertising departments, nor is it limited to the catchalls of quality and service. Differentiation opportunities can exist in activities all along an industry's value chain. The most systematic approach that managers can take, however, involves focusing on the **value drivers,** a set of factors—analogous to cost drivers—that are particularly effective in creating differentiation. Figure 5.3 contains a list of important value drivers. Ways that managers can enhance differentiation based on value drivers include the following:

1. *Create product features and performance attributes that appeal to a wide range of buyers.* The physical and functional features of a product have a big influence on differentiation, including features such as added user safety or enhanced environmental protection. Styling and appearance are big differentiating factors in the apparel and motor vehicle industries. Size and weight matter in binoculars and mobile devices. Most companies employing broad differentiation strategies make a point

FIGURE 5.3   Value Drivers: The Keys to Creating a Differentiation Advantage

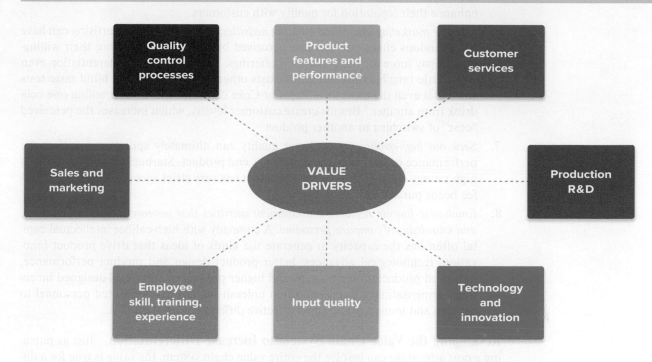

Source: Adapted from Michael E. Porter, *Competitive Advantage: Creating and Sustaining Superior Performance* (New York: Free Press, 1985).

of incorporating innovative and novel features in their product or service offering, especially those that improve performance and functionality.

2. *Improve customer service or add extra services.* Better customer services, in areas such as delivery, returns, and repair, can be as important in creating differentiation as superior product features. Examples include superior technical assistance to buyers, higher-quality maintenance services, more and better product information provided to customers, more and better training materials for end users, better credit terms, quicker order processing, and greater customer convenience.

3. *Invest in production-related R&D activities.* Engaging in production R&D may permit custom-order manufacture at an efficient cost, provide wider product variety and selection through product "versioning," or improve product quality. Many manufacturers have developed flexible manufacturing systems that allow different models and product versions to be made on the same assembly line. Being able to provide buyers with made-to-order products can be a potent differentiating capability.

4. *Strive for innovation and technological advances.* Successful innovation is the route to more frequent first-on-the-market victories and is a powerful differentiator. If the innovation proves hard to replicate, through patent protection or other means, it can provide a company with a first-mover advantage that is sustainable.

5. *Pursue continuous quality improvement.* Quality control processes reduce product defects, prevent premature product failure, extend product life, make it economical to offer longer warranty coverage, improve economy of use, result in more end-user

convenience, or enhance product appearance. Companies whose quality management systems meet certification standards, such as the ISO 9001 standards, can enhance their reputation for quality with customers.

6. *Increase marketing and brand-building activities.* Marketing and advertising can have a tremendous effect on the value perceived by buyers and therefore their willingness to pay more for the company's offerings. They can create differentiation even when little tangible differentiation exists otherwise. For example, blind taste tests show that even the most loyal Pepsi or Coke drinkers have trouble telling one cola drink from another.[4] Brands create customer loyalty, which increases the perceived "cost" of switching to another product.

7. *Seek out high-quality inputs.* Input quality can ultimately spill over to affect the performance or quality of the company's end product. Starbucks, for example, gets high ratings on its coffees partly because it has very strict specifications on the coffee beans purchased from suppliers.

8. *Emphasize human resource management activities that improve the skills, expertise, and knowledge of company personnel.* A company with high-caliber intellectual capital often has the capacity to generate the kinds of ideas that drive product innovation, technological advances, better product design and product performance, improved production techniques, and higher product quality. Well-designed incentive compensation systems can often unleash the efforts of talented personnel to develop and implement new and effective differentiating attributes.

Revamping the Value Chain System to Increase Differentiation   Just as pursuing a cost advantage can involve the entire value chain system, the same is true for a differentiation advantage. Activities performed upstream by suppliers or downstream by distributors and retailers can have a meaningful effect on customers' perceptions of a company's offerings and its value proposition. Approaches to enhancing differentiation through changes in the value chain system include

- *Coordinating with downstream channel allies to enhance customer value.* Coordinating with downstream partners such as distributors, dealers, brokers, and retailers can contribute to differentiation in a variety of ways. Methods that companies use to influence the value chain activities of their channel allies include setting standards for downstream partners to follow, providing them with templates to standardize the selling environment or practices, training channel personnel, or cosponsoring promotions and advertising campaigns. Coordinating with retailers is important for enhancing the buying experience and building a company's image. Coordinating with distributors or shippers can mean quicker delivery to customers, more accurate order filling, and/or lower shipping costs. The Coca-Cola Company considers coordination with its bottler-distributors so important that it has at times taken over a troubled bottler to improve its management and upgrade its plant and equipment before releasing it again.[5]

- *Coordinating with suppliers to better address customer needs.* Collaborating with suppliers can also be a powerful route to a more effective differentiation strategy. Coordinating and collaborating with suppliers can improve many dimensions affecting product features and quality. This is particularly true for companies that engage only in assembly operations, such as Dell in PCs and Ducati in motorcycles. Close coordination with suppliers can also enhance differentiation by speeding up new product development cycles or speeding delivery to end customers. Strong relationships with suppliers can also mean that the company's supply requirements are prioritized when industry supply is insufficient to meet overall demand.

Delivering Superior Value via a Broad Differentiation Strategy

Differentiation strategies depend on meeting customer needs in unique ways or creating new needs through activities such as innovation or persuasive advertising. The objective is to offer customers something that rivals can't—at least in terms of the level of satisfaction. There are four basic routes to achieving this aim:

The first route is to incorporate product attributes and user features that *lower the buyer's overall costs* of using the company's product. This is the least obvious and most overlooked route to a differentiation advantage. It is a differentiating factor since it can help business buyers be more competitive in their markets and more profitable. Producers of materials and components often win orders for their products by reducing a buyer's raw-material waste (providing cut-to-size components), reducing a buyer's inventory requirements (providing just-in-time deliveries), using online systems to reduce a buyer's procurement and order processing costs, and providing free technical support. This route to differentiation can also appeal to individual consumers who are looking to economize on their overall costs of consumption. Making a company's product more economical for a consumer to use can be done by incorporating energy-efficient features (energy-saving appliances and lightbulbs help cut buyers' utility bills; fuel-efficient vehicles cut buyer costs for gasoline) and/or by increasing maintenance intervals and product reliability to lower buyer costs for maintenance and repairs.

A second route is to incorporate *tangible* features that increase customer satisfaction with the product, such as product specifications, functions, and styling. This can be accomplished by including attributes that add functionality; enhance the design; save time for the user; are more reliable; or make the product cleaner, safer, quieter, simpler to use, more portable, more convenient, or longer-lasting than rival brands. Smartphone manufacturers are in a race to introduce next-generation devices capable of being used for more purposes and having simpler menu functionality.

A third route to a differentiation-based competitive advantage is to incorporate *intangible* features that enhance buyer satisfaction in noneconomic ways. Toyota's Prius and GM's Chevy Bolt appeal to environmentally conscious motorists not only because these drivers want to help reduce global carbon dioxide emissions but also because they identify with the image conveyed. Bentley, Ralph Lauren, Louis Vuitton, Burberry, Cartier, and Coach have differentiation-based competitive advantages linked to buyer desires for status, image, prestige, upscale fashion, superior craftsmanship, and the finer things in life. Intangibles that contribute to differentiation can extend beyond product attributes to the reputation of the company and to customer relations or trust.

> Differentiation can be based on *tangible* or *intangible* attributes.

The fourth route is to *signal the value* of the company's product offering to buyers. The value of certain differentiating features is rather easy for buyers to detect, but in some instances buyers may have trouble assessing what their experience with the product will be. Successful differentiators go to great lengths to make buyers knowledgeable about a product's value and employ various signals of value. Typical signals of value include a high price (in instances where high price implies high quality and performance), more appealing or fancier packaging than competing products, ad content that emphasizes a product's standout attributes, the quality of brochures and sales presentations, and the luxuriousness and ambience of a seller's facilities. The nature of a company's facilities are important for high-end retailers and other types of companies whose facilities are frequented by customers); They make potential buyers aware of the professionalism, appearance, and personalities of the seller's employees and/or make potential buyers realize that a company has prestigious customers. Signaling value is particularly important (1) when the nature of differentiation is based on intangible features and is therefore subjective or hard to quantify, (2) when buyers are making a first-time purchase and are unsure what their experience with the product will be, (3) when repurchase is infrequent, and (4) when buyers are unsophisticated.

Regardless of the approach taken, achieving a successful differentiation strategy requires, first, that the company have capabilities in areas such as customer service, marketing, brand management, and technology that can create and support differentiation. That is, the resources, competencies, and value chain activities of the company must be well matched to the requirements of the strategy. For the strategy to result in competitive advantage, the company's competencies must also be sufficiently unique in delivering value to buyers that they help set its product offering apart from those of rivals. They must be competitively superior. There are numerous examples of companies that have differentiated themselves on the basis of distinctive capabilities. Health care facilities like M.D. Anderson, Mayo Clinic, and Cleveland Clinic have specialized expertise and equipment for treating certain diseases that most hospitals and health care providers cannot afford to emulate. When a major news event occurs, many people turn to Fox News and CNN because they have the capabilities to get reporters on the scene quickly, break away from their regular programming (without suffering a loss of advertising revenues associated with regular programming), and devote extensive air time to newsworthy stories.

> Easy-to-copy differentiating features cannot produce sustainable competitive advantage.

The most successful approaches to differentiation are those that are difficult for rivals to duplicate. Indeed, this is the route to a sustainable competitive advantage based on differentiation. While resourceful competitors can, in time, clone almost any tangible product attribute, socially complex intangible attributes such as company reputation, long-standing relationships with buyers, and image are much harder to imitate. Differentiation that creates switching costs that lock in buyers also provides a route to sustainable advantage. For example, if a buyer makes a substantial investment in learning to use one type of system, that buyer is less likely to switch to a competitor's system. (This has kept many users from switching away from Microsoft Office products, despite the fact that there are other applications with superior features.) As a rule, differentiation yields a longer-lasting and more profitable competitive edge when it is based on a well-established brand image, patent-protected product innovation, complex technical superiority, a reputation for superior product quality and reliability, relationship-based customer service, and unique competitive capabilities.

When a Differentiation Strategy Works Best

Differentiation strategies tend to work best in market circumstances where

- *Buyer needs and uses of the product are diverse.* Diverse buyer preferences allow industry rivals to set themselves apart with product attributes that appeal to particular buyers. For instance, the diversity of consumer preferences for menu selection, ambience, pricing, and customer service gives restaurants exceptionally wide latitude in creating a differentiated product offering. Other industries with diverse buyer needs include magazine publishing, automobile manufacturing, footwear, and kitchen appliances.

- *There are many ways to differentiate the product or service that have value to buyers.* Industries in which competitors have opportunities to add features to products and services are well suited to differentiation strategies. For example, hotel chains can differentiate on such features as location, size of room, range of guest services, in-hotel dining, and the quality and luxuriousness of bedding and furnishings. Similarly, cosmetics producers are able to differentiate based on prestige and image, formulations that fight the signs of aging, UV light protection, exclusivity of retail locations, the inclusion of antioxidants and natural ingredients, or prohibitions against animal testing. Basic commodities, such as chemicals, mineral deposits, and agricultural products, provide few opportunities for differentiation.

- *Few rival firms are following a similar differentiation approach.* The best differentiation approaches involve trying to appeal to buyers on the basis of attributes that rivals are not emphasizing. A differentiator encounters less head-to-head rivalry when it goes its own separate way in creating value and does not try to out-differentiate rivals on the very same attributes. When many rivals base their differentiation efforts on the same attributes, the most likely result is weak brand differentiation and "strategy overcrowding"—competitors end up chasing much the same buyers with much the same product offerings.

- *Technological change is fast-paced and competition revolves around rapidly evolving product features.* Rapid product innovation and frequent introductions of next-version products heighten buyer interest and provide space for companies to pursue distinct differentiating paths. In smartphones and wearable Internet devices, drones for hobbyists and commercial use, automobile lane detection sensors, and battery-powered cars, rivals are locked into an ongoing battle to set themselves apart by introducing the best next-generation products. Companies that fail to come up with new and improved products and distinctive performance features quickly lose out in the marketplace.

Pitfalls to Avoid in Pursuing a Differentiation Strategy

Differentiation strategies can fail for any of several reasons. *A differentiation strategy keyed to product or service attributes that are easily and quickly copied is always suspect.* Rapid imitation means that no rival achieves differentiation, since whenever one firm introduces some value-creating aspect that strikes the fancy of buyers, fast-following copycats quickly reestablish parity. This is why a firm must seek out sources of value creation that are time-consuming or burdensome for rivals to match if it hopes to use differentiation to win a sustainable competitive edge.

> Any differentiating feature that works well is a magnet for imitators.

Differentiation strategies can also falter when buyers see little value in the unique attributes of a company's product. Thus, even if a company succeeds in setting its product apart from those of rivals, its strategy can result in disappointing sales and profits if the product does not deliver adequate perceived value to buyers. Anytime many potential buyers look at a company's differentiated product offering with indifference, the company's differentiation strategy is in deep trouble.

The third big pitfall is overspending on efforts to differentiate the company's product offering, thus eroding profitability. Company efforts to achieve differentiation nearly always raise costs—often substantially, since marketing and R&D are expensive undertakings. The key to profitable differentiation is either to keep the unit cost of achieving differentiation below the price premium that the differentiating attributes can command (thus increasing the profit margin per unit sold) or to offset thinner profit margins per unit by selling enough additional units to increase total profits. If a company goes overboard in pursuing costly differentiation, it could be saddled with unacceptably low profits or even losses.

Over-differentiating and overcharging are fatal differentiation strategy mistakes. *A low-cost strategy can defeat a differentiation strategy when buyers are satisfied with a basic product and don't think "extra" attributes are worth a higher price.*

Other common mistakes in crafting a differentiation strategy include

- *Offering only trivial improvements in quality, service, or performance features vis-à-vis rivals' products.* Trivial differences between rivals' product offerings may not be visible or important to buyers. If a company wants to generate the fiercely loyal customer following needed to earn superior profits and open up a differentiation-based competitive advantage over rivals, then its strategy must result in *strong rather than weak product differentiation.* In markets where differentiators do no better than achieve weak product differentiation, customer loyalty is weak, the costs of brand switching are low, and no one company has enough of a differentiation edge to command a price premium over rival brands.

- *Over-differentiating so that product quality, features, or service levels exceed the needs of most buyers.* A dazzling array of features and options not only drives up product price but also runs the risk that many buyers will conclude that a less deluxe and lower-priced brand is a better value since they have little occasion to use the deluxe attributes.

- *Charging too high a price premium.* While buyers may be intrigued by a product's deluxe features, they may nonetheless see it as being overpriced relative to the value delivered by the differentiating attributes. A company must guard against turning off would-be buyers with what is perceived as "price gouging." Normally, the bigger the price premium for the differentiating extras, the harder it is to keep buyers from switching to the lower-priced offerings of competitors.

FOCUSED (OR MARKET NICHE) STRATEGIES

What sets focused strategies apart from broad low-cost and broad differentiation strategies is concentrated attention on a narrow piece of the total market. The target segment, or niche, can be in the form of a geographic segment (such as New England), or a customer segment (such as young urban creatives or "yuccies"), or a product segment (such as a class of models or some version of the overall product type). Community Coffee, the largest family-owned specialty coffee retailer in the United States, has a geographic focus on the state of Louisiana and communities across the Gulf of Mexico. Community holds only a small share of the national coffee market but has recorded sales in excess of $100 million and has won a strong following in the Southeastern United States. Examples of firms that concentrate on a well-defined market niche keyed to a particular product or buyer segment include Zipcar (hourly and daily car rental in urban areas), Airbnb and HomeAway (owner of VRBO) (by-owner lodging rental), Fox News Channel and HGTV (cable TV), Blue Nile (online jewelry), Tesla Motors (electric cars), and CGA, Inc. (a specialist in providing insurance to cover the cost of lucrative hole-in-one prizes at golf tournaments). Microbreweries, local bakeries, bed-and-breakfast inns, and retail boutiques have also scaled their operations to serve narrow or local customer segments.

A Focused Low-Cost Strategy

A focused low-cost strategy aims at securing a competitive advantage by serving buyers in the target market niche at a lower cost (and usually lower price) than those of rival competitors. This strategy has considerable attraction when a firm can lower costs significantly by limiting its customer base to a well-defined buyer segment. The avenues to achieving a cost advantage over rivals also serving the target market niche are the same as those for broad low-cost leadership—use the cost drivers to perform value chain activities more

Though diabetes is a manageable condition, it is the leading cause of death in Mexico. Over 14 million adults (14 percent of all adults) suffer from diabetes, 3.5 million cases remain undiagnosed, and more than 80,000 die due to related complications each year. The key driver behind this public health crisis is limited access to affordable, high-quality care. Approximately 90 percent of the population cannot access diabetes care due to financial and time constraints; private care can cost upwards of $1,000 USD per year (approximately 45 percent of Mexico's population has an annual income less than $2,000 USD) while average wait times alone at public clinics surpass five hours. Clinícas del Azúcar (CDA), however, is quickly scaling a solution that uses a *focused low-cost strategy* to provide affordable and convenient care to low-income patients.

By relentlessly focusing only on the needs of its target population, CDA has reduced the cost of diabetes care by more than 70 percent and clinic visit times by over 80 percent. The key has been the use of proprietary technology and a streamlined care system. First, CDA leverages evidence-based algorithms to diagnose patients for a fraction of the costs of traditional diagnostic tests. Similarly, its mobile outreach significantly reduces the costs of supporting patients in managing their diabetes after leaving CDA facilities. Second, CDA has redesigned the care process to implement a streamlined "patient process flow" that eliminates the need for multiple referrals to other care providers and brings together the necessary professionals and equipment into one facility. Consequently, CDA has become a one-stop shop for diabetes care, providing every aspect of diabetes treatment under one roof.

©Rob Marmion/Shutterstock

The bottom line: CDA's cost structure allows it to keep its prices for diabetes treatment very low, saving patients both time and money. Patients choose from three different care packages, ranging from preventive to comprehensive care, paying an annual fee that runs between approximately $70 and $200 USD. Given this increase in affordability and convenience, CDA estimates that it has saved its patients over $2 million USD in medical costs and will soon increase access to affordable, high-quality care for 10 to 80 percent of the population. These results have attracted investment from major funders including Endeavor, Echoing Green, and the Clinton Global Initiative. As a result, CDA and others expect CDA to grow from 5 clinics serving approximately 5,000 patients to more than 50 clinics serving over 100,000 patients throughout Mexico by 2020.

Note: Developed with David B. Washer.

Sources: www.clinicasdelazucar.com; "Funding Social Enterprises Report," *Echoing Green,* June 2014; Jude Webber, "Mexico Sees Poverty Climb Despite Rise in Incomes," *Financial Times* online, July 2015, www.ft.com/intl/cms/s/3/98460bbc-31e1-11e5-8873-775ba7c2ea3d.html#axzz3zz8grtec; "Javier Lozano," Schwab Foundation for Social Entrepreneurship online, 2016, www.schwabfound.org/content/javier-lozano.

---

efficiently than rivals and search for innovative ways to bypass nonessential value chain activities. The only real difference between a broad low-cost strategy and a focused low-cost strategy is the size of the buyer group to which a company is appealing—the former involves a product offering that appeals to almost all buyer groups and market segments, whereas the latter aims at just meeting the needs of buyers in a narrow market segment.

Budget motel chains, like Motel 6, Sleep Inn, and Super 8, cater to price-conscious travelers who just want to pay for a clean, no-frills place to spend the night. Illustration Capsule 5.2 describes how Clinícas del Azúcar's focus on lowering the costs of diabetes care is allowing it to address a major health issue in Mexico.

Focused low-cost strategies are fairly common. Costco, BJ's, and Sam's Club sell large lots of goods at wholesale prices to small businesses and bargain-hunters. Producers of private-label goods are able to achieve low costs in product development, marketing, distribution, and advertising by concentrating on making generic items imitative of name-brand merchandise and selling directly to retail chains wanting a low-priced store brand. The Perrigo Company Plc has become a leading manufacturer of over-the-counter health care products, with 2017 sales of over $5 billion, by focusing on producing private-label brands for retailers such as Walmart, CVS, Walgreens, Rite Aid, and Safeway.

A Focused Differentiation Strategy

Focused differentiation strategies involve offering superior products or services tailored to the unique preferences and needs of a narrow, well-defined group of buyers. Successful use of a focused differentiation strategy depends on (1) the existence of a buyer segment that is looking for special product or service attributes and (2) a firm's ability to create a product or service offering that stands apart from that of rivals competing in the same target market niche.

Companies like Molton Brown in bath, body, and beauty products, Bugatti in high performance automobiles, and Four Seasons Hotels in lodging employ successful differentiation-based focused strategies targeted at upscale buyers wanting products and services with world-class attributes. Indeed, most markets contain a buyer segment willing to pay a big price premium for the very finest items available, thus opening the strategic window for some competitors to pursue differentiation-based focused strategies aimed at the very top of the market pyramid. Whole Foods Market, which bills itself as "America's Healthiest Grocery Store," has become the largest organic and natural foods supermarket chain in the United States (2017 sales of over $16 billion) by catering to health-conscious consumers who prefer organic, natural, minimally processed, and locally grown foods. Whole Foods prides itself on stocking the highest-quality organic and natural foods it can find; the company defines quality by evaluating the ingredients, freshness, taste, nutritive value, appearance, and safety of the products it carries. Illustration Capsule 5.3 describes how Canada Goose has been gaining attention with a focused differentiation strategy.

When a Focused Low-Cost or Focused Differentiation Strategy Is Attractive

A focused strategy aimed at securing a competitive edge based on either low costs or differentiation becomes increasingly attractive as more of the following conditions are met:

- The target market niche is big enough to be profitable and offers good growth potential.
- Industry leaders have chosen not to compete in the niche—in which case focusers can avoid battling head to head against the industry's biggest and strongest competitors.
- It is costly or difficult for multisegment competitors to meet the specialized needs of niche buyers and at the same time satisfy the expectations of their mainstream customers.
- The industry has many different niches and segments, thereby allowing a focuser to pick the niche best suited to its resources and capabilities. Also, with more niches there is room for focusers to concentrate on different market segments and avoid competing in the same niche for the same customers.
- Few if any rivals are attempting to specialize in the same target segment—a condition that reduces the risk of segment overcrowding.

ILLUSTRATION
CAPSULE 5.3   Canada Goose's Focused Differentiation Strategy

Open up a winter edition of *People* and you will probably see photos of a celebrity sporting a Canada Goose parka. Recognizable by a distinctive red, white, and blue arm patch, the brand's parkas have been spotted on movie stars like Emma Stone and Bradley Cooper, on New York City streets, and on the cover of *Sports Illustrated*. Lately, Canada Goose has become extremely successful thanks to a focused differentiation strategy that enables it to thrive within its niche in the $1.2 trillion fashion industry. By targeting upscale buyers and providing a uniquely functional and stylish jacket, Canada Goose can charge nearly $1,000 per jacket and never need to put its products on sale.

While Canada Goose was founded in 1957, its recent transition to a focused differentiation strategy allowed it to rise to the top of the luxury parka market. In 2001, CEO Dani Reiss took control of the company and made two key decisions. First, he cut private-label and non-outerwear production in order to focus on the branded outerwear portion of Canada Goose's business. Second, Reiss decided to remain in Canada despite many North American competitors moving production to Asia to increase profit margins. Fortunately for him, these two strategy decisions have led directly to the company's current success. While other luxury brands, like Moncler, are priced similarly, no competitor's products fulfill the promise of handling harsh winter weather quite like a Canada Goose "Made in Canada" parka. The Canadian heritage, use of down sourced from rural Canada, real coyote fur (humanely trapped), and promise to provide warmth in sub-25°F

©Galit Rodan/Bloomberg via Getty Images

temperatures have let Canada Goose break away from the pack when it comes to selling parkas. The company's distinctly Canadian product has made it a hit among buyers, which is reflected in the willingness to pay a steep premium for extremely high-quality and warm winter outerwear.

Since Canada Goose's shift to a focused differentiation strategy, the company has seen a boom in revenue and appeal across the globe. Prior to Reiss's strategic decisions in 2001, Canada Goose had annual revenue of about $3 million. Within a decade, the company had experienced over 4,000 percent growth in annual revenue; by the end of 2017, revenues from purchases in more than 50 countries had exceeded $300 million. At this pace, it looks like Canada Goose will remain a hot commodity as long as winter temperatures remain cold.

Note: Developed with Arthur J. Santry.

Sources: Drake Bennett, "How Canada Goose Parkas Migrated South," *Bloomberg Businessweek,* March 13, 2015, www.bloomberg.com; Hollie Shaw, "Canada Goose's Made-in-Canada Marketing Strategy Translates into Success," *Financial Post,* May 18, 2012, www.financialpost.com; "The Economic Impact of the Fashion Industry," *The Economist,* June 13, 2015, www.maloney.house.gov; and company website (accessed February 21, 2016).

The advantages of focusing a company's entire competitive effort on a single market niche are considerable, especially for smaller and medium-sized companies that may lack the breadth and depth of resources to tackle going after a broader customer base with a more complex set of needs. YouTube became a household name by concentrating on short video clips posted online. Papa John's, Little Caesars, and Domino's Pizza have created impressive businesses by focusing on the home delivery segment.

The Risks of a Focused Low-Cost or Focused Differentiation Strategy

Focusing carries several risks. One is the chance that competitors outside the niche will find effective ways to match the focused firm's capabilities in serving the target niche—perhaps by coming up with products or brands specifically designed to appeal to buyers in the target niche or by developing expertise and capabilities that offset the focuser's strengths. In the lodging business, large chains like Marriott and Hilton have launched multibrand strategies that allow them to compete effectively in several lodging segments simultaneously. Hilton has flagship hotels with a full complement of services and amenities that allow it to attract travelers and vacationers going to major resorts; it has Waldorf Astoria, Conrad Hotels & Resorts, Hilton Hotels & Resorts, and DoubleTree hotels that provide deluxe comfort and service to business and leisure travelers; it has Homewood Suites, Embassy Suites, and Home2 Suites designed as a "home away from home" for travelers staying five or more nights; and it has nearly 700 Hilton Garden Inn and 2,100 Hampton by Hilton locations that cater to travelers looking for quality lodging at an "affordable" price. Tru by Hilton is the company's newly introduced brand focused on value-conscious travelers seeking basic accommodations. Hilton has also added Curio Collection, Tapestry Collection, and Canopy by Hilton hotels that offer stylish, distinctive decors and personalized services that appeal to young professionals seeking distinctive lodging alternatives. Multibrand strategies are attractive to large companies such as Hilton precisely because they enable a company to enter a market niche and siphon business away from companies that employ a focus strategy.

A second risk of employing a focused strategy is the potential for the preferences and needs of niche members to shift over time toward the product attributes desired by buyers in the mainstream portion of the market. An erosion of the differences across buyer segments lowers entry barriers into a focuser's market niche and provides an open invitation for rivals in adjacent segments to begin competing for the focuser's customers. A third risk is that the segment may become so attractive that it is soon inundated with competitors, intensifying rivalry and splintering segment profits. And there is always the risk for segment growth to slow to such a small rate that a focuser's prospects for future sales and profit gains become unacceptably dim.

BEST-COST (HYBRID) STRATEGIES

To profitably employ a best-cost strategy, a company *must have the capability to incorporate upscale attributes into its product offering at a lower cost than rivals.* When a company can incorporate more appealing features, good to excellent product performance or quality, or more satisfying customer service into its product offering *at a lower cost than rivals,* then it enjoys "best-cost" status—it is the low-cost provider of a product or service with *upscale attributes.* A best-cost producer can use its low-cost advantage to underprice rivals whose products or services have similarly upscale attributes and still earn attractive profits. As Figure 5.1 indicates, **best-cost strategies** are a hybrid of low-cost and differentiation strategies, incorporating features of both simultaneously. They may address either a broad or narrow (focused) customer base. This permits companies to aim squarely at the sometimes great mass of value-conscious buyers looking for a better product or service at an economical price. Value-conscious buyers frequently shy away from both cheap low-end products and

> **CORE CONCEPT**
>
> **Best-cost strategies** are a *hybrid* of low-cost and differentiation strategies, incorporating features of both simultaneously.

expensive high-end products, but they are quite willing to pay a "fair" price for extra features and functionality they find appealing and useful. The essence of a best-cost strategy is giving customers *more value for the money* by satisfying buyer desires for appealing features and charging a lower price for these attributes compared to rivals with similar-caliber product offerings.[6]

A best cost strategy is different from a low-cost strategy because the additional attractive attributes entail additional costs (which a low-cost producer can avoid by offering buyers a basic product with few frills). Moreover, the two strategies aim at a distinguishably different market target. *The target market for a best-cost producer is value-conscious buyers*—buyers who are looking for appealing extras and functionality at a comparatively low price, regardless of whether they represent a broad or more focused segment of the market. Value-hunting buyers (as distinct from *price-conscious buyers* looking for a basic product at a bargain-basement price) often constitute a very sizable part of the overall market for a product or service. A best cost strategy differs from a differentiation strategy because it entails the ability to produce upscale features at a lower cost than other high-end producers. This implies the ability to profitably offer the buyer more value for the money.

Best cost producers need not offer the highest end products and services (although they may); often the quality levels are simply better than average. Positioning of this sort permits companies to aim squarely at the sometimes great mass of value-conscious buyers looking for a better product or service at an economical price. Value-conscious buyers frequently shy away from both cheap low-end products and expensive high-end products, but they are quite willing to pay a "fair" price for extra features and functionality they find appealing and useful. The essence of a best-cost strategy is the ability to provide *more value for the money* by satisfying buyer desires for better quality while charging a lower price compared to rivals with similar-caliber product offerings.

Toyota has employed a classic best-cost strategy for its Lexus line of motor vehicles. It has designed an array of high-performance characteristics and upscale features into its Lexus models to make them comparable in performance and luxury to Mercedes, BMW, Audi, Jaguar, Cadillac, and Lincoln models. To signal its positioning in the luxury market segment, Toyota established a network of Lexus dealers, separate from Toyota dealers, dedicated to providing exceptional customer service. Most important, though, Toyota has drawn on its considerable know-how in making high-quality vehicles at low cost to produce its high-tech upscale-quality Lexus models at substantially lower costs than other luxury vehicle makers have been able to achieve in producing their models. To capitalize on its lower manufacturing costs, Toyota prices its Lexus models below those of comparable Mercedes, BMW, Audi, and Jaguar models to induce value-conscious luxury car buyers to purchase a Lexus instead. The price differential has typically been quite significant. For example, in 2017 a well-equipped Lexus RX 350 (a midsized SUV) had a sticker price of $54,370, whereas the sticker price of a comparably equipped Mercedes GLE-class SUV was $62,770 and the sticker price of a comparably equipped BMW X5 SUV was $66,670.

When a Best-Cost Strategy Works Best

A best-cost strategy works best in markets where product differentiation is the norm and an attractively large number of value-conscious buyers can be induced to purchase midrange products rather than cheap, basic products or expensive, top-of-the-line products. In markets such as these, a best-cost producer needs to position itself *near the*

LO 5-4

Explain the attributes of a best-cost strategy—a hybrid of low-cost and differentiation strategies.

ILLUSTRATION CAPSULE 5.4   Trader Joe's Focused Best-Cost Strategy

Over the last 50 years, Trader Joe's has built a cult-like following by offering a limited selection of highly popular private-label products at great prices, under the Trader Joe's brand. By pursuing a *focused best-cost* strategy, Trader Joe's has been able to thrive in the notoriously low-margin grocery business. Today, Trader Joe's earns over $1,700 of annual sales per square foot—double that of Whole Foods.

One key to Trader Joe's success, and a major part of its strategy, is its unique approach to product selection. By selling mainly private label goods under its own brand, Trader Joe's keeps its costs low, enabling it to offer lower prices. By being very selective about the particular products that it carries, it has also managed to ensure that its brand is associated with very high quality. The company's policy is to swiftly replace any product that does not prove popular with another more appealing product. This has paid off: when you ask U.S. consumers which grocery store represents quality, Trader Joe's tops the list. On a recent YouGov Brand Index poll, nearly 40 percent of consumers ranked Trader Joe's best for quality—the highest among its competitors. While Trader Joe's offers far fewer stock-keeping units (SKUs) than a typical grocery store—only 4,000 SKUs as compared to 50,000 + in a Kroger or Safeway—the upside for customers is that this also helps to keep costs and prices low. It results in higher inventory turns (a key measure of efficiency in retail), lower inventory costs, and lower rents since stores in any given location can be smaller.

©Ken Wolter/Shutterstock

Trader Joe's also intentionally locates its stores in areas with value-focused customers who appreciate quality. Trader Joe's identifies potential sites for expansion by evaluating demographic information. This enables Trader Joe's to focus on serving young educated singles and couples who may not be able to afford more expensive groceries but prefer organics and ready-to-eat products. Given that it occupies smaller sized retail spaces, Trader Joe's can locate in walkable areas and urban centers, the very same neighborhoods in which its chosen customer base lives. Because of its focused best-cost strategy, it is unlikely that the company's loyal customers will quit lining up to buy its tasty corn salsa or organic cold brew coffee any time soon.

Note: Developed with Stephanie K. Berger.

Sources: Company website; Beth Kowitt, "Inside the Secret World of Trader Joe's," *Fortune* (August 2010); Elain Watson, "Quirky, Cult-life, Aspirational, but Affordable: The Rise and Rise of Trader Joes," Food Navigator USA (April 2014).

middle of the market with either a medium-quality product at a below-average price or a high-quality product at an average or slightly higher price. But as the Lexus example shows, a firm with the capabilities to produce top-of-the-line products more efficiently than its rivals, would also do well to pursue a best cost strategy. Best-cost strategies also work well in recessionary times, when masses of buyers become more value-conscious and are attracted to economically priced products and services with more appealing attributes. However, unless a company has the resources, know-how, and capabilities to incorporate upscale product or service attributes at a lower cost than rivals, adopting a best-cost strategy is ill-advised. Illustration Capsule 5.4 describes how Trader Joe's has applied the principles of a focused best-cost strategy to thrive in the competitive grocery store industry.

The Risk of a Best-Cost Strategy

A company's biggest vulnerability in employing a best-cost strategy is getting squeezed between the strategies of firms using low-cost and high-end differentiation strategies. Low-cost producers may be able to siphon customers away with the appeal of a lower price (despite less appealing product attributes). High-end differentiators may be able to steal customers away with the appeal of better product attributes (even though their products carry a higher price tag). Thus, to be successful, a firm employing a best-cost strategy must achieve significantly lower costs in providing upscale features so that it can outcompete high-end differentiators on the basis of a *significantly* lower price. Likewise, it must offer buyers *significantly* better product attributes to justify a price above what low-cost leaders are charging. In other words, it must offer buyers a more attractive customer value proposition.

THE CONTRASTING FEATURES OF THE GENERIC COMPETITIVE STRATEGIES

Deciding which generic competitive strategy should serve as the framework on which to hang the rest of the company's strategy is not a trivial matter. Each of the five generic competitive strategies *positions* the company differently in its market and competitive environment. Each establishes a *central theme* for how the company will endeavor to outcompete rivals. Each creates some boundaries or guidelines for maneuvering as market circumstances unfold and as ideas for improving the strategy are debated. Each entails differences in terms of product line, production emphasis, marketing emphasis, and means of maintaining the strategy, as shown in Table 5.1.

Thus a choice of which generic strategy to employ spills over to affect many aspects of how the business will be operated and the manner in which value chain activities must be managed. Deciding which generic strategy to employ is perhaps the most important strategic commitment a company makes—it tends to drive the rest of the strategic actions a company decides to undertake.

> A company's competitive strategy should be well matched to its internal situation and predicated on leveraging its collection of competitively valuable resources and capabilities.

Successful Generic Strategies Are Resource-Based

For a company's competitive strategy to succeed in delivering good performance and gain a competitive edge over rivals, it has to be well matched to a company's internal situation and underpinned by an appropriate set of resources, know-how, and competitive capabilities. To succeed in employing a low-cost strategy, a company must have the resources and capabilities to keep its costs below those of its competitors. This means having the expertise to cost-effectively manage value chain activities better than rivals by leveraging the cost drivers more effectively, and/or having the innovative capability to bypass certain value chain activities being performed by rivals. To succeed in a differentiation strategy, a company must have the resources and capabilities to leverage value drivers more effectively than rivals and incorporate attributes into its product offering that a broad range of buyers will find appealing. Successful focus strategies (both low cost and differentiation) require the capability to do an outstanding job of satisfying the needs and expectations of niche buyers. Success in employing a best-cost strategy requires the resources and capabilities to incorporate upscale product or service attributes at a lower cost than rivals. *For all types of generic strategies, success in sustaining the competitive edge depends on having resources and capabilities that rivals have trouble duplicating and for which there are no good substitutes.*

TABLE 5.1 Distinguishing Features of the Five Generic Competitive Strategies

	Broad Low-Cost	Broad Differentiation	Focused Low-Cost	Focused Differentiation	Best-Cost
Strategic target	• A broad cross-section of the market.	• A broad cross-section of the market.	• A narrow market niche where buyer needs and preferences are distinctively different.	• A narrow market niche where buyer needs and preferences are distinctively different.	• A broad or narrow range of value-conscious buyers.
Basis of competitive strategy	• Lower overall costs than competitors.	• Ability to offer buyers something attractively different from competitors' offerings.	• Lower overall cost than rivals in serving niche members.	• Attributes that appeal specifically to niche members.	• Ability to incorporate upscale features and attributes at lower costs than rivals.
Product line	• A good basic product with few frills (acceptable quality and limited selection).	• Many product variations, wide selection; emphasis on differentiating features.	• Features and attributes tailored to the tastes and requirements of niche members.	• Features and attributes tailored to the tastes and requirements of niche members.	• Items with appealing attributes and assorted features; better quality, not necessarily best.
Production emphasis	• A continuous search for cost reduction without sacrificing acceptable quality and essential features.	• Build in whatever differentiating features buyers are willing to pay for; strive for product superiority.	• A continuous search for cost reduction for products that meet basic needs of niche members.	• Small-scale production or custom-made products that match the tastes and requirements of niche members.	• Build in appealing features and better quality at lower cost than rivals.
Marketing emphasis	• Low prices, good value. • Try to make a virtue out of product features that lead to low cost.	• Tout differentiating features. • Charge a premium price to cover the extra costs of differentiating features.	• Communicate attractive features of a budget-priced product offering that fits niche buyers' expectations.	• Communicate how product offering does the best job of meeting niche buyers' expectations.	• Emphasize delivery of best value for the money.
Keys to maintaining the strategy	• Strive to manage costs down, year after year, in every area of the business.	• Stress continuous improvement in products or services and constant innovation to stay ahead of imitative competitors.	• Stay committed to serving the niche at the lowest overall cost; don't blur the firm's image by entering other market segments or adding other products to widen market appeal.	• Stay committed to serving the niche better than rivals; don't blur the firm's image by entering other market segments or adding other products to widen market appeal.	• Stress continuous improvement in products or services and constant innovation, along with continuous efforts to improve efficiency.
Resources and capabilities required	• Capabilities for driving costs out of the value chain system. • *Examples:* large-scale automated plants, an efficiency-oriented culture, bargaining power.	• Capabilities concerning quality, design, intangibles, and innovation. • *Examples:* marketing capabilities, R&D teams, technology.	• Capabilities to lower costs on niche goods. • *Examples:* lower input costs for the specific product desired by the niche, batch production capabilities.	• Capabilities to meet the highly specific needs of niche members. • *Examples:* custom production, close customer relations.	• Capabilities to simultaneously deliver lower cost and higher-quality/differentiated features. • *Examples:* TQM practices, mass customization.

Generic Strategies and the Three Different Approaches to Competitive Advantage

Just as a company's resources and capabilities underlie its choice of generic strategy, its generic strategy determines its approach to gaining a competitive advantage. There are three such approaches. Clearly, low-cost strategies aim for a cost advantage over rivals, differentiation strategies strive to create relatively more perceived value for consumers, while best-cost strategies aim to do better than the average rival on both dimensions. Whether the strategy is broad based or focused makes no difference as to the basic approach employed (see Figure 5.1).

Exactly how this works is best understood with the use of the value-price-cost framework, first introduced in Chapter 1 in the context of different kinds of business models. Figure 5.4 illustrates the three basic approaches to competitive advantage in terms of the value-price-cost framework. The left figure in the diagram represents an average competitor's cost (C) of producing a good, how highly the consumer values it (V), and its price (P). The difference between the good's value to the consumer (V) and its cost (C) is the total economic value (V-C) produced by the average competitor. And as explained in Chapter 4, a company has a competitive advantage over another if its strategy generates *more total economic value*. It is this excess in total economic value over rivals that allows the company to offer consumers a better value proposition or earn larger profits (or both). The dashed yellow lines facilitate a comparison of the average competitor's costs (C) and perceived value (V) with the costs and value produced by each of the three basic types of generic strategies (low cost, differentiation, best cost). In this way, it also facilitates a comparison of the total economic value generated by each of the three representative generic strategies in relation to the average competitor, thereby shedding light on the nature of each strategy's competitive advantage.

FIGURE 5.4   Three Approaches to Competitive Advantage and the Value-Price-Cost Framework

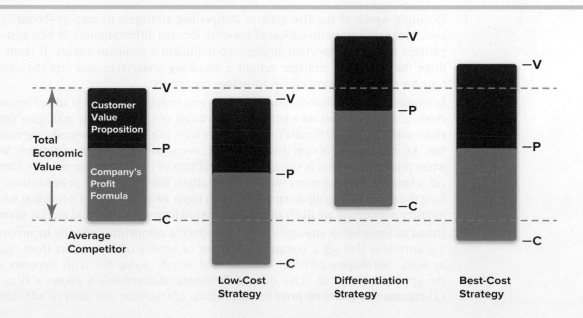

As Figure 5.4 shows, a low-cost generic strategy aims to achieve lower costs than an average competitor, at the sacrifice of some of the perceived value to the consumer. If the decrease in costs is less than the decrease in perceived value, then the total economic value (V-C) for the low-cost leader will be greater than the total economic value produced by its average rival and the low-cost leader will have a competitive advantage. This is clearly the case for the example of a low-cost strategy depicted in Figure 5.4. As is common with low-cost strategies, the example company has chosen to charge a lower price than its average rival. The result is that even with a lower V, the low-cost leader offers the consumer a more attractive (larger) consumer value proposition (depicted in mauve) and finds itself with a better profit formula (depicted in blue).

In contrast, the example of a differentiation strategy shows that costs might well exceed those of the average competitor. But with a successful differentiation strategy, that disadvantage is more than made up for by the rise in the perceived value (V) of the differentiated good, giving the differentiator a clear competitive advantage over the average rival (greater V-C). And while the price charged in this example is a good deal higher in comparison with the average rival's price, this differentiation strategy enables both a larger consumer value proposition (in mauve) as well as greater profits (in blue).

The depiction of a best-cost strategy shows a company pursuing the middle ground of offering neither the most highly valued goods in the market nor the lowest costs. But in comparison with the average rival, it does better on both scores, resulting in more total economic value (V-C) and a substantial competitive advantage. Once again, the example shows both a larger customer value proposition as well as a more attractive profit formula.

The last thing to note is that the generic strategies depicted in Figure 5.4 are examples of *successful* generic strategies. Being successful with a generic strategy depends on much more than positioning. It depends on the competitive context (the company's external situation) and on the company's internal situation, including its complement of resources and capabilities. Importantly, it also depends on how well the strategy is executed—the topic of this text's three concluding chapters.

KEY POINTS

1. Deciding which of the five generic competitive strategies to employ—broad low-cost, broad differentiation, focused low-cost, focused differentiation, or best cost—is perhaps the most important strategic commitment a company makes. It tends to drive the remaining strategic actions a company undertakes and sets the whole tone for pursuing a competitive advantage over rivals.

2. In employing a broad low-cost strategy and trying to achieve a low-cost advantage over rivals, a company must do a better job than rivals of cost-effectively managing value chain activities and/or it must find innovative ways to eliminate cost-producing activities. An effective use of cost drivers is key. Low-cost strategies work particularly well when price competition is strong and the products of rival sellers are virtually identical, when there are not many ways to differentiate, when buyers are price-sensitive or have the power to bargain down prices, when buyer switching costs are low, and when industry newcomers are likely to use a low introductory price to build market share.

3. Broad differentiation strategies seek to produce a competitive edge by incorporating attributes that set a company's product or service offering apart from rivals in ways that buyers consider valuable and worth paying for. This depends on the appropriate use of value drivers. Successful differentiation allows a firm to (1) command a premium price for its product, (2) increase unit sales (if additional

buyers are won over by the differentiating features), and/or (3) gain buyer loyalty to its brand (because some buyers are strongly attracted to the differentiating features and bond with the company and its products). Differentiation strategies work best when buyers have diverse product preferences, when few other rivals are pursuing a similar differentiation approach, and when technological change is fast-paced and competition centers on rapidly evolving product features. A differentiation strategy is doomed when competitors are able to quickly copy the appealing product attributes, when a company's differentiation efforts fail to interest many buyers, and when a company overspends on efforts to differentiate its product offering or tries to overcharge for its differentiating extras.

4. A focused strategy delivers competitive advantage either by achieving lower costs than rivals in serving buyers constituting the target market niche or by developing a specialized ability to offer niche buyers an appealingly differentiated offering that meets their needs better than rival brands do. A focused strategy based on either low cost or differentiation becomes increasingly attractive when the target market niche is big enough to be profitable and offers good growth potential, when it is costly or difficult for multisegment competitors to meet the specialized needs of the target market niche and at the same time satisfy the expectations of their mainstream customers, when there are one or more niches that present a good match for a focuser's resources and capabilities, and when few other rivals are attempting to specialize in the same target segment.

5. Best-cost strategies create competitive advantage on the basis of their capability to incorporate attractive or upscale attributes at a lower cost than rivals. Best-cost strategies can be either broad or focused. A best-cost strategy works best in broad or narrow market segments with value-conscious buyers desirous of purchasing better products and services for less money.

6. In all cases, competitive advantage depends on having competitively superior resources and capabilities that are a good fit for the chosen generic strategy. A sustainable advantage depends on maintaining that competitive superiority with resources, capabilities, and value chain activities that rivals have trouble matching and for which there are no good substitutes.

ASSURANCE OF LEARNING EXERCISES

● ● ● ●

1. Best Buy is the largest consumer electronics retailer in the United States, with fiscal 2017 sales of nearly $40 billion. The company competes aggressively on price with such rivals as Costco, Sam's Club, Walmart, and Target, but it is also known by consumers for its first-rate customer service. Best Buy customers have commented that the retailer's sales staff is exceptionally knowledgeable about the company's products and can direct them to the exact location of difficult-to-find items. Best Buy customers also appreciate that demonstration models of PC monitors, digital media players, and other electronics are fully powered and ready for in-store use. Best Buy's Geek Squad tech support and installation services are additional customer service features that are valued by many customers.

LO 5-1, LO 5-2, LO 5-3, LO 5-4

How would you characterize Best Buy's competitive strategy? Should it be classified as a low-cost strategy? A differentiation strategy? A best-cost strategy? Also, has the company chosen to focus on a narrow piece of the market, or does it appear to pursue a broad market approach? Explain your answer.

■ connect®

LO 5-2

2. Illustration Capsule 5.1 discusses Vanguard's position as the low-cost leader in the investment management industry. Based on information provided in the capsule, explain how Vanguard built its low-cost advantage in the industry and why a low-cost strategy can succeed in the industry.

LO 5-1, LO 5-2,
LO 5-3, LO 5-4

3. USAA is a Fortune 500 insurance and financial services company with 2017 annual sales exceeding $27 billion. The company was founded in 1922 by 25 Army officers who decided to insure each other's vehicles and continues to limit its membership to active-duty and retired military members, officer candidates, and adult children and spouses of military-affiliated USAA members. The company has received countless awards, including being listed among *Fortune*'s World's Most Admired Companies in 2014 through 2018 and 100 Best Companies to Work For in 2010 through 2018. USAA was also ranked as the number-one Bank, Credit Card, and Insurance Company by Forrester Research from 2013 to 2017. You can read more about the company's history and strategy at **www.usaa.com.**

How would you characterize USAA's competitive strategy? Should it be classified as a low-cost strategy? A differentiation strategy? A best-cost strategy? Also, has the company chosen to focus on a narrow piece of the market, or does it appear to pursue a broad market approach? Explain your answer.

■ connect®

LO 5-3

4. Explore Kendra Scott's website at **www.kendrascott.com** and see if you can identify at least three ways in which the company seeks to differentiate itself from rival jewelry firms. Is there reason to believe that Kendra Scott's differentiation strategy has been successful in producing a competitive advantage? Why or why not?

EXERCISE FOR SIMULATION PARTICIPANTS

●●●●

LO 5-1, LO 5-2,
LO 5-3, LO 5-4

1. Which one of the five generic competitive strategies best characterizes your company's strategic approach to competing successfully?

2. Which rival companies appear to be employing a broad low-cost strategy?

3. Which rival companies appear to be employing a broad differentiation strategy?

4. Which rival companies appear to be employing a best-cost strategy?

5. Which rival companies appear to be employing some type of focused strategy?

6. What is your company's action plan to achieve a sustainable competitive advantage over rival companies? List at least three (preferably more than three) specific kinds of decision entries on specific decision screens that your company has made or intends to make to win this kind of competitive edge over rivals.

ENDNOTES

●●●●

[1] Michael E. Porter, *Competitive Strategy: Techniques for Analyzing Industries and Competitors* (New York: Free Press, 1980), chap. 2; Michael E. Porter, "What Is Strategy?" *Harvard Business Review* 74, no. 6 (November–December 1996).
[2] Michael E. Porter, *Competitive Advantage: Creating and Sustaining Superior Performance* (New York: Free Press, 1985).

[3] Richard L. Priem, "A Consumer Perspective on Value Creation," *Academy of Management Review* 32, no. 1 (2007), pp. 219–235.
[4] **jrscience.wcp.muohio.edu/nsfall01/FinalArticles/Final-IsitWorthitBrandsan.html.**
[5] D. Yoffie, "Cola Wars Continue: Coke and Pepsi in 2006," Harvard Business School case 9-706-447.

[6] Peter J. Williamson and Ming Zeng, "Value-for-Money Strategies for Recessionary Times," *Harvard Business Review* 87, no. 3 (March 2009), pp. 66–74.

Strengthening a Company's Competitive Position

Strategic Moves, Timing, and Scope of Operations

Learning Objectives

This chapter will help you

LO 6-1 Identify how and when to deploy offensive or defensive strategic moves.

LO 6-2 Identify when being a first mover, a fast follower, or a late mover is most advantageous.

LO 6-3 Explain the strategic benefits and risks of expanding a company's horizontal scope through mergers and acquisitions.

LO 6-4 Explain the advantages and disadvantages of extending the company's scope of operations via vertical integration.

LO 6-5 Identify the conditions that favor farming out certain value chain activities to outside parties.

LO 6-6 Determine how to capture the benefits and minimize the drawbacks of strategic alliances and partnerships.

Strengthening a Company's Competitive Position

Strategic Moves, Timing, and Scope of Operations

Learning Objectives

This chapter will help you

LO 6-1 Identify how and when to deploy offensive or defensive strategic moves.

LO 6-2 Identify when being a first mover, a fast follower, or a late mover is most advantageous.

LO 6-3 Explain the strategic benefits and risks of expanding a company's horizontal scope through mergers and acquisitions.

LO 6-4 Explain the advantages and disadvantages of extending the company's scope of operations via vertical integration.

LO 6-5 Identify the conditions that favor farming out certain value chain activities to outside parties.

LO 6-6 Determine how to capture the benefits and minimize the drawbacks of strategic alliances and partnerships.

©ImageZoo/Alamy Stock Photo

Whenever you look at any potential merger or acquisition, you look at the potential to create value for your shareholders.

Dilip Shanghvi—*Founder and managing director of Sun Pharmaceuticals*

Alliances have become an integral part of contemporary strategic thinking.

Fortune Magazine

The important thing about outsourcing . . . is that it becomes a very powerful tool to leverage talent, improve productivity, and reduce work cycles.

Azim Premji—*Chairman of Wipro Limited (India's third-largest outsourcer)*

Once a company has settled on which of the five generic competitive strategies to employ, attention turns to what *other strategic actions* it can take to complement its competitive approach and maximize the power of its overall strategy. The first set of decisions concerns whether to undertake offensive or defensive competitive moves, and the timing of such moves. The second set concerns expanding or contracting the breadth of a company's activities (or its *scope* of operations along an industry's entire value chain). All in all, the following measures to strengthen a company's competitive position must be considered:

- Whether to go on the offensive and initiate aggressive strategic moves to improve the company's market position.
- Whether to employ defensive strategies to protect the company's market position.

- When to undertake new strategic initiatives—whether advantage or disadvantage lies in being a first mover, a fast follower, or a late mover.
- Whether to bolster the company's market position by merging with or acquiring another company in the same industry.
- Whether to integrate backward or forward into more stages of the industry value chain system.
- Which value chain activities, if any, should be outsourced.
- Whether to enter into strategic alliances or partnership arrangements with other enterprises.

This chapter presents the pros and cons of each of these strategy-enhancing measures.

LAUNCHING STRATEGIC OFFENSIVES TO IMPROVE A COMPANY'S MARKET POSITION

• • • •

● LO 6-1

Identify how and when to deploy offensive or defensive strategic moves.

No matter which of the five generic competitive strategies a firm employs, there are times when a company should *go on the offensive* to improve its market position and performance. **Strategic offensives** are called for when a company spots opportunities to gain profitable market share at its rivals' expense or when a company has no choice but to try to whittle away at a strong rival's competitive advantage. Companies like Facebook, Amazon, Apple, and Google play hardball, aggressively pursuing competitive advantage and trying to reap the benefits a competitive edge offers—a leading market share, excellent profit margins, and rapid growth.[1] The best offensives tend to incorporate several principles: (1) focusing relentlessly on building competitive advantage and then striving to convert it into a sustainable advantage, (2) applying resources where rivals are least able to defend themselves, (3) employing the element of surprise as opposed to doing what rivals expect and are prepared for, and (4) displaying a capacity for swift and decisive actions to overwhelm rivals.[2]

Sometimes a company's best strategic option is to seize the initiative, go on the attack, and launch a strategic offensive to improve its market position.

Choosing the Basis for Competitive Attack

As a rule, challenging rivals on competitive grounds where they are strong is an uphill struggle.[3] Offensive initiatives that exploit competitor weaknesses stand a better chance of succeeding than do those that challenge competitor strengths, especially if the weaknesses represent important vulnerabilities and weak rivals can be caught by surprise with no ready defense.

The best offensives use a company's most powerful resources and capabilities to attack rivals in the areas where they are competitively weakest.

Strategic offensives should exploit the power of a company's strongest competitive assets—its most valuable resources and capabilities such as a better-known brand name, a more efficient production or distribution system, greater technological capability, or a superior reputation for quality. But a consideration of the company's strengths should not be made without also considering the rival's strengths and weaknesses. A strategic offensive should be based on those areas of strength where the company has its greatest competitive advantage over the targeted rivals.

If a company has especially good customer service capabilities, it can make special sales pitches to the customers of those rivals that provide subpar customer service. Likewise, it may be beneficial to pay special attention to buyer segments that a rival is neglecting or is weakly equipped to serve. The best offensives use a company's most powerful resources and capabilities to attack rivals in the areas where they are weakest.

Ignoring the need to tie a strategic offensive to a company's competitive strengths and what it does best is like going to war with a popgun—the prospects for success are dim. For instance, it is foolish for a company with relatively high costs to employ a price-cutting offensive. Likewise, it is ill-advised to pursue a product innovation offensive without having proven expertise in R&D and new product development.

The principal offensive strategy options include the following:

1. *Offering an equally good or better product at a lower price.* Lower prices can produce market share gains if competitors don't respond with price cuts of their own and if the challenger convinces buyers that its product is just as good or better. However, such a strategy increases total profits only if the gains in additional unit sales are enough to offset the impact of thinner margins per unit sold. Price-cutting offensives should be initiated only by companies that have *first achieved a cost advantage.*[4] British airline EasyJet used this strategy successfully against rivals such as

British Air, Alitalia, and Air France by first cutting costs to the bone and then targeting leisure passengers who care more about low price than in-flight amenities and service.[5] Spirit Airlines is using this strategy in the U.S. airline market.

2. *Leapfrogging competitors by being first to market with next-generation products.* In technology-based industries, the opportune time to overtake an entrenched competitor is when there is a shift to the next generation of the technology. Eero got its whole home Wi-Fi system to market nearly one year before Linksys and Netgear developed competing systems, helping it build a sizable market share and develop a reputation for cutting-edge innovation in Wi-Fi systems.

3. *Pursuing continuous product innovation to draw sales and market share away from less innovative rivals.* Ongoing introductions of new and improved products can put rivals under tremendous competitive pressure, especially when rivals' new product development capabilities are weak. But such offensives can be sustained only if a company can keep its pipeline full with new product offerings that spark buyer enthusiasm.

4. *Pursuing disruptive product innovations to create new markets.* While this strategy can be riskier and more costly than a strategy of continuous innovation, it can be a game changer if successful. Disruptive innovation involves perfecting a new product with a few trial users and then quickly rolling it out to the whole market in an attempt to get many buyers to embrace an altogether new and better value proposition quickly. Examples include online universities, Bumble (dating site where women make the first move), Venmo (digital wallet), Apple Music, CampusBookRentals, and Waymo (Alphabet's self-driving tech company).

5. *Adopting and improving on the good ideas of other companies (rivals or otherwise).* The idea of warehouse-type home improvement centers did not originate with Home Depot cofounders Arthur Blank and Bernie Marcus; they got the "big-box" concept from their former employer, Handy Dan Home Improvement. But they were quick to improve on Handy Dan's business model and take Home Depot to the next plateau in terms of product-line breadth and customer service. Offensive-minded companies are often quick to adopt any good idea (not nailed down by a patent or other legal protection) and build on it to create competitive advantage for themselves.

6. *Using hit-and-run or guerrilla warfare tactics to grab market share from complacent or distracted rivals.* Options for "guerrilla offensives" include occasionally lowballing on price (to win a big order or steal a key account from a rival), surprising rivals with sporadic but intense bursts of promotional activity (offering a discounted trial offer to draw customers away from rival brands), or undertaking special campaigns to attract the customers of rivals plagued with a strike or problems in meeting buyer demand.[6] Guerrilla offensives are particularly well suited to small challengers that have neither the resources nor the market visibility to mount a full-fledged attack on industry leaders.

7. *Launching a preemptive strike to secure an industry's limited resources or capture a rare opportunity.*[7] What makes a move preemptive is its one-of-a-kind nature—whoever strikes first stands to acquire competitive assets that rivals can't readily match. Examples of preemptive moves include (1) securing the best distributors in a particular geographic region or country; (2) obtaining the most favorable site at a new interchange or intersection, in a new shopping mall, and so on; (3) tying up the most reliable, high-quality suppliers via exclusive partnerships, long-term contracts, or acquisition; and (4) moving swiftly to acquire the assets of distressed rivals at bargain prices. To be successful, a preemptive move doesn't have to totally block rivals from following; it merely needs to give a firm a prime position that is not easily circumvented.

How long it takes for an offensive action to yield good results varies with the competitive circumstances.[8] It can be short if buyers respond immediately (as can occur with a dramatic cost-based price cut, an imaginative ad campaign, or a disruptive innovation). Securing a competitive edge can take much longer if winning consumer acceptance of the company's product will take some time or if the firm may need several years to debug a new technology or put a new production capacity in place. But how long it takes for an offensive move to improve a company's market standing—and whether the move will prove successful—depends in part on whether market rivals recognize the threat and begin a counterresponse. Whether rivals will respond depends on whether they are capable of making an effective response and if they believe that a counterattack is worth the expense and the distraction.[9]

Choosing Which Rivals to Attack

Offensive-minded firms need to analyze which of their rivals to challenge as well as how to mount the challenge. The following are the best targets for offensive attacks:[10]

- *Market leaders that are vulnerable.* Offensive attacks make good sense when a company that leads in terms of market share is not a true leader in terms of serving the market well. Signs of leader vulnerability include unhappy buyers, an inferior product line, aging technology or outdated plants and equipment, a preoccupation with diversification into other industries, and financial problems. Caution is well advised in challenging strong market leaders—there's a significant risk of squandering valuable resources in a futile effort or precipitating a fierce and profitless industrywide battle for market share.

- *Runner-up firms with weaknesses in areas where the challenger is strong.* Runner-up firms are an especially attractive target when a challenger's resources and capabilities are well suited to exploiting their weaknesses.

- *Struggling enterprises that are on the verge of going under.* Challenging a hard-pressed rival in ways that further sap its financial strength and competitive position can weaken its resolve and hasten its exit from the market. In this type of situation, it makes sense to attack the rival in the market segments where it makes the most profits, since this will threaten its survival the most.

- *Small local and regional firms with limited capabilities.* Because small firms typically have limited expertise and resources, a challenger with broader and/or deeper capabilities is well positioned to raid their biggest and best customers—particularly those that are growing rapidly, have increasingly sophisticated requirements, and may already be thinking about switching to a supplier with a more full-service capability.

Blue-Ocean Strategy—a Special Kind of Offensive

A **blue-ocean strategy** seeks to gain a dramatic competitive advantage by abandoning efforts to beat out competitors in existing markets and, instead, *inventing a new market segment that allows a company to create and capture altogether new demand.*[11] This strategy views the business universe as consisting of two distinct types of market space. One is where industry boundaries are well defined, the competitive rules of the game are understood, and companies try to outperform rivals by capturing a bigger share of existing demand. In such markets, intense competition constrains a company's prospects for rapid growth and superior profitability since rivals move quickly to either imitate or counter the successes of competitors. The second type of market space is a "blue ocean," where the industry does not really exist yet, is untainted by competition, and offers wide-open opportunity for profitable and rapid growth if a company can create new demand with a new type of product offering. The "blue ocean" represents wide-open opportunity, offering smooth sailing in uncontested waters for the company first to venture out upon it.

A terrific example of such blue-ocean market space is the online auction industry that eBay created and now dominates. Other companies that have created blue-ocean market spaces include NetJets in fractional jet ownership, Drybar in hair blowouts, Tune Hotels in limited service "backpacker" hotels, Uber and Lyft in ride-sharing services, and Cirque du Soleil in live entertainment. Cirque du Soleil "reinvented the circus" by pulling in a whole new group of customers—adults and corporate clients—who not only were noncustomers of traditional circuses (like Ringling Brothers) but also were willing to pay several times more than the price of a conventional circus ticket to have a "sophisticated entertainment experience" featuring stunning visuals and star-quality acrobatic acts. Australian winemaker Casella Wines used a blue ocean strategy to find some uncontested market space for its Yellow Tail brand. By creating a product designed to appeal to wider market—one that also includes beer and spirit drinkers—Yellow Tail was able to unlock substantial new demand, becoming the fastest growing wine brand in U.S. history. Illustration Capsule 6.1 provides another example of a company that has thrived by seeking uncharted blue waters.

Blue-ocean strategies provide a company with a great opportunity in the short run. But they don't guarantee a company's long-term success, which depends more on whether a company can protect the market position it opened up and sustain its early advantage. Gilt Groupe serves as an example of a company that opened up new competitive space in online luxury retailing only to see its blue-ocean waters ultimately turn red. Its competitive success early on prompted an influx of fast followers into the luxury flash-sale industry, including HauteLook, RueLaLa, Lot18, and MyHabit.com. The new rivals not only competed for online customers, who could switch costlessly from site to site (since memberships were free), but also competed for unsold designer inventory. Once valued at over $1 billion, Gilt Groupe was finally sold to Hudson's Bay, the owner of Sak's Fifth Avenue, for just $250 million in 2016.

DEFENSIVE STRATEGIES—PROTECTING MARKET POSITION AND COMPETITIVE ADVANTAGE

In a competitive market, all firms are subject to offensive challenges from rivals. The purposes of defensive strategies are to lower the risk of being attacked, weaken the impact of any attack that occurs, and induce challengers to aim their efforts at other rivals. While defensive strategies usually don't enhance a firm's competitive advantage, they can definitely help fortify the firm's competitive position, protect its most valuable resources and capabilities from imitation, and defend whatever competitive advantage it might have. Defensive strategies can take either of two forms: actions to block challengers or actions to signal the likelihood of strong retaliation.

Bonobos's Blue-Ocean Strategy in the U.S. Men's Fashion Retail Industry

It was not too long ago that young, athletic men struggled to find clothing that adequately fit their athletic frames. It was this issue that led two male Stanford MBA students, in 2007, to create Bonobos, a men's clothing brand that initially focused on selling well-fitting men's pants via the Internet. At the time, this concept occupied relatively blue waters as most other clothing brands and retailers in reasonable price ranges had largely focused on innovating in women's clothing, as opposed to men's. In the years since, Bonobos has expanded its product portfolio to include a full line of men's clothing, while growing its revenue from $4 million in 2009 to over $100 million in 2016.

This success has not gone unnoticed by both established players as well as other entrepreneurs. Numerous startups have jumped on the custom men's clothing bandwagon ranging from the low-cost Combatant Gentlemen, to the many bespoke suit tailors that exist in major cities around the United States. In addition, more mainstream clothing retailers have also identified this new type of male customer, with the CEO of Men's Wearhouse, Doug Ewert, stating that he views custom clothing as a "big growth opportunity." That company recently acquired Joseph Abboud to focus more on millennial customers, and plans to begin offering more types of customized clothing in the future.

In response, Bonobos has focused on a new area of development to move to bluer waters in the brick-and-mortar space. The company's innovation is the Guideshop—a store where you can't actually buy anything to take home. Instead, the Guideshop allows men to have a personalized shopping experience, where they can try on clothing in any size or color, and then have

©NYCStock/Shutterstock

it delivered the next day to their home or office. This model was based on the insight that most men want an efficient shopping experience, with someone to help them identify the right product and proper fit, so that they could order with ease in the future. As Bonobos CEO Andy Dunn stated more simply, the idea was to provide a different experience from existing retail, which had become "a job about keeping clothes folded [rather] than delivering service." Since opening its first Guideshop in 2011, the company has now expanded to 20 Guideshops nationwide and plans to continue this growth moving forward. This strategy has been fueling the company's success, but how long Bonobos has before retail clothing copycats turn these blue waters red remains to be seen.

Note: Developed with Jacob M. Crandall.

Sources: Richard Feloni, "After 8 Years and $128 Million Raised, the Clock Is Ticking for Men's Retailer Bonobos," **BusinessInsider.com**, October 6, 2015; Vikram Alexei Kansara, "Andy Dunn of Bonobos on Building the Armani of the E-commerce Era," **Businessoffashion.com**, July 19, 2013; Hadley Malcolm, "Men's Wearhouse Wants to Suit Up Millennials," *USA Today,* June 8, 2015.

Blocking the Avenues Open to Challengers

> Good defensive strategies can help protect a competitive advantage but rarely are the basis for creating one.

The most frequently employed approach to defending a company's present position involves actions that restrict a challenger's options for initiating a competitive attack. There are any number of obstacles that can be put in the path of would-be challengers. A defender can introduce new features, add new models, or broaden its product line to close off gaps and vacant niches to opportunity-seeking challengers. It can thwart rivals' efforts to attack with a lower price by maintaining its own lineup of economy-priced options. It can discourage buyers from trying competitors' brands by lengthening warranties, making early announcements about impending new products or price changes, offering free training and support services, or providing coupons and sample giveaways to buyers most prone to experiment. It can induce potential buyers to reconsider switching. It can challenge the quality or safety of rivals' products. Finally, a defender can grant volume discounts or better financing terms to dealers and distributors to discourage them from experimenting with other suppliers, or it can convince them to handle its product line *exclusively* and force competitors to use other distribution outlets.

Signaling Challengers That Retaliation Is Likely

The goal of signaling challengers that strong retaliation is likely in the event of an attack is either to dissuade challengers from attacking at all or to divert them to less threatening options. Either goal can be achieved by letting challengers know the battle will cost more than it is worth. Signals to would-be challengers can be given by

> To be an effective defensive strategy signaling needs to be accompanied by a *credible commitment* to follow through.

- Publicly announcing management's commitment to maintaining the firm's present market share.
- Publicly committing the company to a policy of matching competitors' terms or prices.
- Maintaining a war chest of cash and marketable securities.
- Making an occasional strong counterresponse to the moves of weak competitors to enhance the firm's image as a tough defender.

To be an effective defensive strategy, however, signaling needs to be accompanied by a *credible commitment* to follow through.

TIMING A COMPANY'S STRATEGIC MOVES

When to make a strategic move is often as crucial as *what* move to make. Timing is especially important when **first-mover advantages and disadvantages** exist. Under certain conditions, being first to initiate a strategic move can have a high payoff in the form of a competitive advantage that later movers can't dislodge. Moving first is no guarantee of success, however, since first movers also face some significant disadvantages. Indeed, there are circumstances in which it is more advantageous to be a fast follower or even a late mover. Because the timing of strategic moves can be consequential, it is important for company strategists to be aware of the nature of first-mover advantages and disadvantages and the conditions favoring each type of move.[12]

CORE CONCEPT

Because of **first-mover advantages and disadvantages,** competitive advantage can spring from *when* a move is made as well as from what move is made.

The Potential for First-Mover Advantages

Market pioneers and other types of first movers typically bear greater risks and greater development costs than firms that move later. If the market responds well to its initial move, the pioneer will benefit from a monopoly position (by virtue of being first to market) that enables it to recover its investment costs and make an attractive profit. If the firm's pioneering move gives it a competitive advantage that can be sustained even after other firms enter the market space, its first-mover advantage will be greater still. The extent of this type of advantage, however, will depend on whether and how fast follower firms can piggyback on the pioneer's success and either imitate or improve on its move.

● LO 6-2

Identify when being a first mover, a fast follower, or a late mover is most advantageous.

There are six such conditions in which first-mover advantages are most likely to arise:

1. *When pioneering helps build a firm's reputation and creates strong brand loyalty.* Customer loyalty to an early mover's brand can create a tie that binds, limiting the success of later entrants' attempts to poach from the early mover's customer base and steal market share. For example, Open Table's early move as an online restaurant-reservation service built a strong brand that has since fueled its expansion worldwide.

2. *When a first mover's customers will thereafter face significant switching costs.* Switching costs can protect first movers when consumers make large investments in learning how to use a specific company's product or in purchasing complementary products that are also brand-specific. Switching costs can also arise from loyalty programs or long-term contracts that give customers incentives to remain with an initial provider. FreshDirect, for example, offers its grocery-delivery customers bigger savings, the longer they keep their service subscription.

3. *When property rights protections thwart rapid imitation of the initial move.* In certain types of industries, property rights protections in the form of patents, copyrights, and trademarks prevent the ready imitation of an early mover's initial moves. First-mover advantages in pharmaceuticals, for example, are heavily dependent on patent protections, and patent races in this industry are common. In other industries, however, patents provide limited protection and can frequently be circumvented. Property rights protections also vary among nations, since they are dependent on a country's legal institutions and enforcement mechanisms.

4. *When an early lead enables the first mover to reap scale economies or move down the learning curve ahead of rivals.* If significant scale-based advantages are available to an early mover, later entrants (with a smaller market share) will face relatively higher production costs. This disadvantage will make it even harder for later entrants to gain share and overcome the first mover scale advantage. When there is a steep learning curve and when learning can be kept *proprietary,* a first mover can benefit from volume-based cost advantages that grow ever larger as its experience accumulates and its scale of operations increases. This type of first-mover advantage is self-reinforcing and, as such, can preserve a first mover's competitive advantage over long periods of time. Honda's advantage in small multiuse motorcycles has been attributed to such an effect.

5. *When a first mover can set the technical standard for the industry.* In many technology-based industries, the market will converge around a single technical standard. By establishing the industry standard, a first mover can gain a powerful advantage that, like experience-based advantages, builds over time. The lure of such an advantage, however, can result in standard wars among early movers, as each strives to set the industry standard. The key to winning such wars is to enter early on the basis of strong fast-cycle product development capabilities, gain the support of key customers and suppliers, employ penetration pricing, and make allies of the producers of complementary products.

6. *When strong network effects compel increasingly more consumers to choose the first mover's product or service.* As we described in Chapter 3, network effects are at work whenever consumers benefit from having other consumers use the same product or service that they use—a benefit that increases with the number of consumers using the product. An example is FaceTime. The more that people you know have FaceTime on their phones or devices, the more that you are able to have a video conversation with them if you also have FaceTime—a benefit that grows with the number of users in your circle. Network effects can also occur with respect to suppliers. eBay has enjoyed a considerable first mover advantage for years, not just

Tinder Swipes Right for First-Mover Success

Tinder, a simple, swipe-based dating app, entered the market in 2012 with a bang, gaining over a million monthly active users in less than a year. By 2014, Tinder was processing over a billion swipes daily and users were spending an average of an hour and a half on the app each day. (Today, the average user spends about an hour on Facebook, Instagram, Snapchat, and Twitter—combined.)

Tinder's fast start had much to do with the fact that it was easy-to-use, without the time-consuming questionnaires of other dating services, and fun, with a game-like aspect that many called addictive. In addition, Tinder was rolled out on college campuses using viral marketing techniques that helped it to quickly gain acceptance among social circles such as fraternities and sororities, in which "key influencers" boosted its popularity to the point where it reached a critical mass. But its sustained success has had more to do with the fact that it has been able to reap the benefits of a first mover advantage, as the first major entrant into the field of mobile dating.

In the dating service industry, efficacy is wholly dependent on network effects (where users of an app benefit increasingly as the number of users of that same app increases). By focusing first on ensuring high usage among local social domains, Tinder benefited from strong local network effects. As its popularity spread, users increasingly found Tinder to be the most attractive app to use, since so many others were using it—thereby strengthening the network effect advantage, and drawing ever more people to download the Tinder app. With increased volume, Tinder gained other classic first mover advantages, such as enhanced reputational benefits, learning curve efficiencies, and increased interest

©BigTunaOnline/Shutterstock

from investors. By 2018, Tinder had more than 50 million users swiping daily—on average logging in 11 times a day for a total of around 85 minutes.

Tinder's first mover advantage has not kept others from entering the mobile dating market. In fact, Tinder's phenomenal success has led to a surge in new entrants, with many imitating the Tinder's most popular features. Despite this, Tinder's first mover advantage has proven protective in many ways. Tinder's user base far outstrips the user base of rivals. And while other apps have been trying to play catch up, Tinder has been introducing new subscription products and other paid features to turn its market share advantage into a profitability advantage. As it stands, most analysts see Tinder as the mobile dating application with the highest commercial potential. And with a valuation of $3B and the distinction of Apple's *top-grossing* app in August 2017, it seems that Tinder is here to stay.

Note: Developed with Lindsey Wilcox and Charles K. Anumonwo.

Sources: https://www.inc.com/issie-lapowsky/how-tinder-is-winning-the-mobile-dating-wars.html; http://www.adweek.com/digital/mediakix-time-spent-social-media-infographic/; www.pewresearch.org/fact-tank/2016/02/29/5-facts-about-online-dating/; https://www.forbes.com/sites/stevenbertoni/2017/08/31/tinder-hits-3-billion-valuation-after-match-group-converts-options/#653a516f34f9; company website.

because of early brand name recognition but also because of powerful network effects on the supply and demand side. The more suppliers choose to auction their items on eBay, the more attractive it is for others to do so as well, since the greater number of items being auctioned attracts more and more potential buyers, which in turn attracts more and more items being auctioned. Strong network effects are self-reinforcing and may lead to a winner-take-all situation for the first mover.

Illustration Capsule 6.2 describes how Tinder achieved a first-mover advantage in the field of mobile dating.

The Potential for Late-Mover Advantages or First-Mover Disadvantages

In some instances there are advantages *to being an adept follower* rather than a first mover. Late-mover advantages (or *first-mover disadvantages*) arise in four instances:

- When the costs of pioneering are high relative to the benefits accrued and imitative followers can achieve similar benefits with far lower costs. This is often the case when second movers can learn from a pioneer's experience and avoid making the same costly mistakes as the pioneer.

- When an innovator's products are somewhat primitive and do not live up to buyer expectations, thus allowing a follower with better-performing products to win disenchanted buyers away from the leader.

- When rapid market evolution (due to fast-paced changes in either technology or buyer needs) gives second movers the opening to leapfrog a first mover's products with more attractive next-version products.

- When market uncertainties make it difficult to ascertain what will eventually succeed, allowing late movers to wait until these needs are clarified.

- When customer loyalty to the pioneer is low and a first mover's skills, know-how, and actions are easily copied or even surpassed.

- When the first mover must make a risky investment in complementary assets or infrastructure (and these may be enjoyed at low cost or risk by followers).

To Be a First Mover or Not

In weighing the pros and cons of being a first mover versus a fast follower versus a late mover, it matters whether the race to market leadership in a particular industry is a 10-year marathon or a 2-year sprint. In marathons, a slow mover is not unduly penalized—first-mover advantages can be fleeting, and there's ample time for fast followers and sometimes even late movers to catch up.[13] Thus the speed at which the pioneering innovation is likely to catch on matters considerably as companies struggle with whether to pursue an emerging market opportunity aggressively (as a first mover) or cautiously (as a late mover). For instance, it took 5.5 years for worldwide mobile phone use to grow from 10 million to 100 million, and it took close to 10 years for the number of at-home broadband subscribers to grow to 100 million worldwide. The lesson here is that there is a market penetration curve for every emerging opportunity. Typically, the curve has an inflection point at which all the pieces of the business model fall into place, buyer demand explodes, and the market takes off. The inflection point can come early on a fast-rising curve (like the use of e-mail and watching movies streamed over the Internet) or farther up on a slow-rising curve (as with battery-powered motor vehicles, solar and wind power, and textbook rental for college students). Any company that seeks competitive advantage by being a first mover thus needs to ask some hard questions:

- Does market takeoff depend on the development of complementary products or services that currently are not available?

- Is new infrastructure required before buyer demand can surge?

- Will buyers need to learn new skills or adopt new behaviors?

- Will buyers encounter high switching costs in moving to the newly introduced product or service?

- Are there influential competitors in a position to delay or derail the efforts of a first mover?

When the answers to any of these questions are yes, then a company must be careful not to pour too many resources into getting ahead of the market opportunity—the race is likely going to be closer to a 10-year marathon than a 2-year sprint.[14] On the other hand, if the market is a winner-take-all type of market, where powerful first-mover advantages insulate early entrants from competition and prevent later movers from making any headway, then it may be best to move quickly despite the risks.

STRENGTHENING A COMPANY'S MARKET POSITION VIA ITS SCOPE OF OPERATIONS

Apart from considerations of competitive moves and their timing, there is another set of managerial decisions that can affect the strength of a company's market position. These decisions concern the scope of a company's operations—the breadth of its activities and the extent of its market reach. Decisions regarding the **scope of the firm** focus on which activities a firm will perform internally and which it will not.

> **CORE CONCEPT**
>
> The **scope of the firm** refers to the range of activities that the firm performs internally, the breadth of its product and service offerings, the extent of its geographic market presence, and its mix of businesses.

Consider, for example, Ralph Lauren Corporation. In contrast to Rambler's Way, a sustainable clothing company with a small chain of retail stores, Ralph Lauren designs, markets, and distributes fashionable apparel and other merchandise to approximately 13,000 major department stores and specialty retailers throughout the world. In addition, it operates nearly 500 retail stores, more than 270 factory stores, and 10 e-commerce sites. Scope decisions also concern which segments of the market to serve—decisions that can include geographic market segments as well as product and service segments. Almost 40 percent of Ralph Lauren's sales are made outside the United States, and its product line includes apparel, fragrances, home furnishings, eyewear, watches and jewelry, and handbags and other leather goods. The company has also expanded its brand lineup through the acquisitions of Chaps menswear and casual retailer Club Monaco.

Decisions such as these, in essence, determine where the boundaries of a firm lie and the degree to which the operations within those boundaries cohere. They also have much to do with the direction and extent of a business's growth. In this chapter, we discuss different types of decisions regarding the scope of the company in relation to a company's business-level strategy. In the next two chapters, we develop two additional dimensions of a firm's scope; Chapter 7 focuses on international expansion—a matter of extending the company's geographic scope into foreign markets; Chapter 8 takes up the topic of corporate strategy, which concerns diversifying into a mix of different businesses. *Scope issues are at the very heart of corporate-level strategy.*

> **CORE CONCEPT**
>
> **Horizontal scope** is the range of product and service segments that a firm serves within its focal market.

Several dimensions of firm scope have relevance for business-level strategy in terms of their capacity to strengthen a company's position in a given market. These include the firm's **horizontal scope,** which is the range of product and service segments that the firm serves within its product or service market. Mergers and acquisitions involving other market participants provide a means for a company to expand its horizontal scope. Expanding the firm's vertical scope by means of vertical integration can also affect the success of its market strategy. **Vertical scope** is the extent to which the firm engages in the various activities that make up the industry's entire value chain system, from initial activities such as raw-material production all the way to retailing and after-sale service activities. **Outsourcing** decisions concern another dimension of scope since they involve narrowing the firm's boundaries with respect to its participation in value chain activities. We discuss the pros and cons of each of

> **CORE CONCEPT**
>
> **Vertical scope** is the extent to which a firm's internal activities encompass the range of activities that make up an industry's entire value chain system, from raw-material production to final sales and service activities.

these options in the sections that follow. Because **strategic alliances and partnerships** provide an alternative to vertical integration and acquisition strategies and are sometimes used to facilitate outsourcing, we conclude this chapter with a discussion of the benefits and challenges associated with *cooperative arrangements* of this nature.

HORIZONTAL MERGER AND ACQUISITION STRATEGIES

● **LO 6-3**

Explain the strategic benefits and risks of expanding a company's horizontal scope through mergers and acquisitions.

Mergers and acquisitions are much-used strategic options to strengthen a company's market position. A *merger* is the combining of two or more companies into a single corporate entity, with the newly created company often taking on a new name. An *acquisition* is a combination in which one company, the acquirer, purchases and absorbs the operations of another, the acquired. The difference between a merger and an acquisition relates more to the details of ownership, management control, and financial arrangements than to strategy and competitive advantage. The resources and competitive capabilities of the newly created enterprise end up much the same whether the combination is the result of an acquisition or a merger.

Horizontal mergers and acquisitions, which involve combining the operations of firms *within the same product or service market,* provide an effective means for firms to rapidly increase the scale and horizontal scope of their core business. For example, the merger of AMR Corporation (parent of American Airlines) with US Airways has increased the airlines' scale of operations and extended their reach geographically to create the world's largest airline.

Merger and acquisition strategies typically set sights on achieving any of five objectives:[15]

1. *Creating a more cost-efficient operation out of the combined companies.* When a company acquires another company in the same industry, there's usually enough overlap in operations that less efficient plants can be closed or distribution and sales activities partly combined and downsized. Likewise, it is usually feasible to squeeze out cost savings in administrative activities, again by combining and downsizing such administrative activities as finance and accounting, information technology, human resources, and so on. The combined companies may also be able to reduce supply chain costs because of greater bargaining power over common suppliers and closer collaboration with supply chain partners. By helping consolidate the industry and remove excess capacity, such combinations can also reduce industry rivalry and improve industry profitability.

2. *Expanding a company's geographic coverage.* One of the best and quickest ways to expand a company's geographic coverage is to acquire rivals with operations in the desired locations. Since a company's size increases with its geographic scope, another benefit is increased bargaining power with the company's suppliers or buyers. Greater geographic coverage can also contribute to product differentiation by enhancing a company's name recognition and brand awareness. The vacation rental marketplace, HomeAway Inc., relied on an aggressive horizontal acquisition strategy to expand internationally, as well as to extend its reach across the United States. It now offers vacation rentals in 190 countries through its 50 websites in 23 languages. Travel company Expedia has since acquired HomeAway, thus extending its reach horizontally into the vacation rental product category—an objective described in the next point.

3. *Extending the company's business into new product categories.* Many times a company has gaps in its product line that need to be filled in order to offer customers a more effective product bundle or the benefits of one-stop shopping. For example, customers might prefer to acquire a suite of software applications from a single vendor that can offer more integrated solutions to the company's problems. Acquisition can be a quicker and more potent way to broaden a company's product line than going through the exercise of introducing a company's own new product to fill the gap. In 2018, Keurig Green Mountain vastly expanded its range of beverage offerings by acquiring the Dr Pepper Snapple Group in an $18.7 billion deal.

4. *Gaining quick access to new technologies or other resources and capabilities.* Making acquisitions to bolster a company's technological know-how or to expand its skills and capabilities allows a company to bypass a time-consuming and expensive internal effort to build desirable new resources and capabilities. Over the course of its history, Cisco Systems has purchased over 200 companies to give it more technological reach and product breadth, thereby enhancing its standing as the world's largest provider of hardware, software, and services for creating and operating Internet networks.

5. *Leading the convergence of industries whose boundaries are being blurred by changing technologies and new market opportunities.* In fast-cycle industries or industries whose boundaries are changing, companies can use acquisition strategies to hedge their bets about the direction that an industry will take, to increase their capacity to meet changing demands, and to respond flexibly to changing buyer needs and technological demands. News Corporation has prepared for the convergence of media services with the purchase of satellite TV companies to complement its media holdings in TV broadcasting (the Fox network and TV stations in various countries), cable TV (Fox News, Fox Sports, and FX), filmed entertainment (Twentieth Century Fox and Fox studios), newspapers, magazines, and book publishing.

Illustration Capsule 6.3 describes how Walmart employed a horizontal acquisition strategy to expand into the e-commerce domain.

Why Mergers and Acquisitions Sometimes Fail to Produce Anticipated Results

Despite many successes, mergers and acquisitions do not always produce the hoped-for outcomes.[16] Cost savings may prove smaller than expected. Gains in competitive capabilities may take substantially longer to realize or, worse, may never materialize at all. Efforts to mesh the corporate cultures can stall due to formidable resistance from organization members. Key employees at the acquired company can quickly become disenchanted and leave; the morale of company personnel who remain can drop to disturbingly low levels because they disagree with newly instituted changes. Differences in management styles and operating procedures can prove hard to resolve. In addition, the managers appointed to oversee the integration of a newly acquired company can make mistakes in deciding which activities to leave alone and which activities to meld into their own operations and systems.

A number of mergers and acquisitions have been notably unsuccessful. Google's $12.5 billion acquisition of struggling smartphone manufacturer Motorola Mobility in 2012 turned out to be minimally beneficial in helping to "supercharge Google's Android ecosystem" (Google's stated reason for making the acquisition). When Google's attempts to rejuvenate Motorola's smartphone business by spending over $1.3 billion on new

ILLUSTRATION CAPSULE 6.3

Walmart's Expansion into E-Commerce via Horizontal Acquisition

As the boundaries between traditional retailing and online retailing have begun to blur, Walmart has responded by expanding its presence in e-commerce via horizontal acquisition. In 2016, Walmart acquired Jet.com, an innovative U.S. e-commerce start-up that was designed to compete with Amazon. Jet.com rewards customers for ordering multiple items, using a debit card instead of a credit card, or choosing a no-returns option; it passes its cost savings on to customers in the form of lower prices. The low-price approach of Jet.com fit well with Walmart's low-price strategy. In addition, Walmart hoped that the acquisition would help it to accelerate its growth in e-commerce, provide quick access to some valuable e-commerce knowledge and capabilities, increase its breadth of online product offerings, and attract new customer segments.

Walmart, like other brick and mortar retailers, was facing a myriad of issues caused by changing customer expectations. Consumers increasingly valued large assortments of products, a convenient shopping experience, and low prices. Price sensitivity was increasing due to the ease of comparing prices online. As a traditional retailer, Walmart was facing stiff competition from Amazon, the world's largest and fastest growing e-commerce company. Amazon's seemingly endless inventory of goods, excellent customer service, expertise in search engine marketing, and appeal to a wide consumer demographic added pressure on the overall global retail industry.

The acquisition of Jet built on the foundation already in place for Walmart to respond to the external pressure and continue growing as an omni-channel retailer (i.e., bricks and mortar, online, or mobile). After investing heavily in their own online channel, Walmart.com, the company was looking for other ways to attract customers by lowering prices, broadening their product assortment, and offering the simplest, most convenient shopping experience. Jet's breadth of products, access to millennial and higher-income customer segments, and best in-class pricing

©Sundry Photography/Shutterstock

algorithm would accelerate Walmart's progress across all of these priorities.

Jet sells everything from household goods and electronics to beauty products, apparel, and toys from more than 2,400 retailer and brand partners. Jet has also continued to expand its own offerings with private-label groceries, further increasing competition with Amazon's AmazonFresh grocery business. In 2017, Walmart made several other acquisitions of online apparel companies, thereby strengthening Jet's apparel offerings and further expanding Walmart's presence in e-commerce. These include ShoeBuy (a competitor of Amazon-owned Zappos), Bonobos in menswear, Moosejaw in outdoor gear and apparel, and Modcloth in vintage and indie womenswear.

One year later, Jet is averaging 25,000 daily processed orders and is continuing to act as an innovation pilot for Walmart. Over the same period, Walmart's U.S. e-commerce sales had risen, climbing 63 percent in its most recent quarter, and the stock had gained 10 percent over the last year. While Walmart's e-commerce sales still pale in comparison to Amazon, this was significantly better than the broader retail industry and represents a promising start for Walmart, as the retail industry continues to transform.

Note: Developed with Dipti Badrinath.

Sources: http://www.businessinsider.com/jet-walmart-weapon-vs-amazon-2017-9; https://news.walmart.com/2016/08/08/walmart-agrees-to-acquire-jetcom-one-of-the-fastest-growing-e-commerce-companies-in-the-us; https://www.fool.com/investing/2017/10/03/1-year-later-wal-marts-jetcom-acquisition-is-an-un.aspx; https://blog.walmart.com/business/20160919/five-big-reasons-walmart-bought-jetcom.

product R&D and revamping Motorola's product line resulted in disappointing sales and huge operating losses, Google sold Motorola Mobility to China-based PC maker Lenovo for $2.9 billion in 2014 (however, Google retained ownership of Motorola's extensive patent portfolio). The jury is still out on whether Lenovo's acquisition of Motorola will prove to be a moneymaker.

VERTICAL INTEGRATION STRATEGIES

Expanding the firm's vertical scope by means of a vertical integration strategy provides another possible way to strengthen the company's position in its core market. A **vertically integrated firm** is one that participates in multiple stages of an industry's value chain system. Thus, if a manufacturer invests in facilities to produce component parts that it had formerly purchased from suppliers, or if it opens its own chain of retail stores to bypass its former distributors, it is engaging in vertical integration. A good example of a vertically integrated firm is Maple Leaf Foods, a major Canadian producer of fresh and processed meats whose best-selling brands include Maple Leaf and Schneiders. Maple Leaf Foods participates in hog and poultry production, with company-owned hog and poultry farms; it has its own meat-processing and rendering facilities; it packages its products and distributes them from company-owned distribution centers; and it conducts marketing, sales, and customer service activities for its wholesale and retail buyers but does not otherwise participate in the final stage of the meat-processing vertical chain—the retailing stage.

A vertical integration strategy can expand the firm's range of activities *backward* into sources of supply and/or *forward* toward end users. When Tiffany & Co., a manufacturer and retailer of fine jewelry, began sourcing, cutting, and polishing its own diamonds, it integrated backward along the diamond supply chain. Mining giant De Beers Group and Canadian miner Aber Diamond integrated forward when they entered the diamond retailing business.

A firm can pursue vertical integration by starting its own operations in other stages of the vertical activity chain or by acquiring a company already performing the activities it wants to bring in-house. Vertical integration strategies can aim at *full integration* (participating in all stages of the vertical chain) or *partial integration* (building positions in selected stages of the vertical chain). Firms can also engage in *tapered integration* strategies, which involve a mix of in-house and outsourced activity in any given stage of the vertical chain. Oil companies, for instance, supply their refineries with oil from their own wells as well as with oil that they purchase from other producers—they engage in tapered backward integration. Coach, Inc., the maker of Coach handbags and accessories, engages in tapered forward integration since it operates full-price and factory outlet stores but also sells its products through third-party department store outlets.

The Advantages of a Vertical Integration Strategy

Under the right conditions, a vertical integration strategy can add materially to a company's technological capabilities, strengthen the firm's competitive position, and boost its profitability.[17] But it is important to keep in mind that vertical integration has no real payoff strategy-wise or profit-wise unless the extra investment can be justified by compensating improvements in company costs, differentiation, or competitive strength.

Integrating Backward to Achieve Greater Competitiveness It is harder than one might think to generate cost savings or improve profitability by integrating backward

• LO 6-4

Explain the advantages and disadvantages of extending the company's scope of operations via vertical integration.

CORE CONCEPT

A vertically integrated firm is one that performs value chain activities along more than one stage of an industry's value chain system.

into activities such as the manufacture of parts and components (which could otherwise be purchased from suppliers with specialized expertise in making the parts and
components). For **backward integration** to be a cost-saving and profitable strategy, a
company must be able to (1) achieve the same scale economies as outside suppliers
and (2) match or beat suppliers' production efficiency with no drop-off in quality.
Neither outcome is easily achieved. To begin with, a company's in-house requirements are often too small to reach the optimum size for low-cost operation. For
instance, if it takes a minimum production volume of 1 million units to achieve scale
economies and a company's in-house requirements are just 250,000 units, then it
falls far short of being able to match the costs of outside suppliers (which may readily find buyers for 1 million or more units). Furthermore, matching the production
efficiency of suppliers is fraught with problems when suppliers have considerable
production experience, when the technology they employ has elements that are hard
to master, and/or when substantial R&D expertise is required to develop next-version
components or keep pace with advancing technology in components production.

That said, occasions still arise when a company can gain or extend a competitive
advantage by performing a broader range of industry value chain activities internally
rather than having such activities performed by outside suppliers. There are several
ways that backward vertical integration can contribute to a cost-based competitive
advantage. When there are few suppliers and when the item being supplied is a major
component, vertical integration can lower costs by limiting supplier power. Vertical
integration can also lower costs by facilitating the coordination of production flows
and avoiding bottlenecks and delays that disrupt production schedules. Furthermore,
when a company has proprietary know-how that it wants to keep from rivals, then in-
house performance of value-adding activities related to this know-how is beneficial
even if such activities could otherwise be performed by outsiders.

Apple decided to integrate backward into producing its own chips for iPhones,
chiefly because chips are a major cost component, suppliers have bargaining power, and
in-house production would help coordinate design tasks and protect Apple's proprietary
iPhone technology. International Paper Company backward integrates into pulp mills
that it sets up near its paper mills and reaps the benefits of coordinated production flows,
energy savings, and transportation economies. It does this, in part, because outside suppliers are generally unwilling to make a site-specific investment for a buyer.

Backward vertical integration can support a differentiation-based competitive
advantage when performing activities internally contributes to a better-quality product or service offering, improves the caliber of customer service, or in other ways
enhances the performance of the final product. On occasion, integrating into more
stages along the industry value chain system can add to a company's differentiation
capabilities by allowing it to strengthen its core competencies, better master key skills
or strategy-critical technologies, or add features that deliver greater customer value.
Spanish clothing maker Inditex has backward integrated into fabric making, as well
as garment design and manufacture, for its successful Zara brand. By tightly controlling the process and postponing dyeing until later stages, Zara can respond quickly to
changes in fashion trends and supply its customers with the hottest items. Amazon and
Netflix backward integrated by establishing Amazon Studios and Netflix Originals to
produce high-quality original content for their streaming services.

Integrating Forward to Enhance Competitiveness   Like backward integration,
forward integration can enhance competitiveness and contribute to competitive advantage on the cost side as well as the differentiation (or value) side. On the cost side,

forward integration can lower costs by increasing efficiency and reducing or eliminating the bargaining power of companies that had wielded such power further along the value system chain. It can allow manufacturers to gain better access to end users, improve market visibility, and enhance brand name awareness. For example, Harley-Davidson's and Ducati's company-owned retail stores are essentially little museums, filled with iconography, that provide an environment conducive to selling not only motorcycles and gear but also memorabilia, clothing, and other items featuring the brand. Insurance companies and brokerages like Allstate and Edward Jones have the ability to make consumers' interactions with local agents and office personnel a differentiating feature by focusing on building relationships.

In many industries, independent sales agents, wholesalers, and retailers handle competing brands of the same product and have no allegiance to any one company's brand—they tend to push whatever offers the biggest profits. To avoid dependence on distributors and dealers with divided loyalties, Goodyear has integrated forward into company-owned and franchised retail tire stores. Consumer-goods companies like Coach, Under Armour, Pepperidge Farm, Bath & Body Works, Nike, Tommy Hilfiger, and Ann Taylor have integrated forward into retailing and operate their own branded stores in factory outlet malls, enabling them to move overstocked items, slow-selling items, and seconds.

Some producers have opted to integrate forward by selling directly to customers at the company's website. Indochino in custom men's suits, Warby Parker in eyewear, and Everlane in sustainable apparel are examples. Bypassing regular wholesale and retail channels in favor of direct sales and Internet retailing can have appeal if it reinforces the brand and enhances consumer satisfaction or if it lowers distribution costs, produces a relative cost advantage over certain rivals, and results in lower selling prices to end users. In addition, sellers are compelled to include the Internet as a retail channel when a sufficiently large number of buyers in an industry prefer to make purchases online. However, a company that is vigorously pursuing online sales to consumers at the same time that it is also heavily promoting sales to consumers through its network of wholesalers and retailers is *competing directly against its distribution allies.* Such actions constitute *channel conflict* and create a tricky route to negotiate. A company that is actively trying to expand online sales to consumers is signaling a weak strategic commitment to its dealers *and* a willingness to cannibalize dealers' sales and growth potential. The likely result is angry dealers and loss of dealer goodwill. Quite possibly, a company may stand to lose more sales by offending its dealers than it gains from its own online sales effort. Consequently, in industries where the strong support and goodwill of dealer networks is essential, companies may conclude that it is important to avoid channel conflict and that *their websites should be designed to partner with dealers rather than compete against them.*

The Disadvantages of a Vertical Integration Strategy

Vertical integration has some substantial drawbacks beyond the potential for channel conflict.[18] The most serious drawbacks to vertical integration include the following concerns:

- Vertical integration raises a firm's capital investment in the industry, thereby *increasing business risk* (what if industry growth and profitability unexpectedly go sour?).
- Vertically integrated companies are often *slow to adopt technological advances or more efficient production methods* when they are saddled with older technology or facilities. A company that obtains parts and components from outside suppliers can

always shop the market for the newest, best, and cheapest parts, whereas a vertically integrated firm with older plants and technology may choose to continue making suboptimal parts rather than face the high costs of writing off undepreciated assets.

- Vertical integration can result in *less flexibility in accommodating shifting buyer preferences.* It is one thing to eliminate use of a component made by a supplier and another to stop using a component being made in-house (which can mean laying off employees and writing off the associated investment in equipment and facilities). Integrating forward or backward locks a firm into relying on its own in-house activities and sources of supply. Most of the world's automakers, despite their manufacturing expertise, have concluded that purchasing a majority of their parts and components from best-in-class suppliers results in greater design flexibility, higher quality, and lower costs than producing parts or components in-house.

- Vertical integration *may not enable a company to realize economies of scale* if its production levels are below the minimum efficient scale. Small companies in particular are likely to suffer a cost disadvantage by producing in-house.

- Vertical integration poses all kinds of *capacity-matching problems.* In motor vehicle manufacturing, for example, the most efficient scale of operation for making axles is different from the most economic volume for radiators, and different yet again for both engines and transmissions. Building the capacity to produce just the right number of axles, radiators, engines, and transmissions in-house—and doing so at the lowest unit costs for each—poses significant challenges and operating complications.

- Integration forward or backward typically *calls for developing new types of resources and capabilities.* Parts and components manufacturing, assembly operations, wholesale distribution and retailing, and direct sales via the Internet represent different kinds of businesses, operating in different types of industries, with different key success factors. Many manufacturers learn the hard way that company-owned wholesale and retail networks require skills that they lack, fit poorly with what they do best, and detract from their overall profit performance. Similarly, a company that tries to produce many components in-house is likely to find itself very hard-pressed to keep up with technological advances and cutting-edge production practices for each component used in making its product.

In today's world of close working relationships with suppliers and efficient supply chain management systems, relatively few companies can make a strong economic case for integrating backward into the business of suppliers. The best materials and components suppliers stay abreast of advancing technology and best practices and are adept in making good quality items, delivering them on time, and keeping their costs and prices as low as possible.

Weighing the Pros and Cons of Vertical Integration

All in all, therefore, a strategy of vertical integration can have both strengths and weaknesses. The tip of the scales depends on (1) whether vertical integration can enhance the performance of strategy-critical activities in ways that lower cost, build expertise, protect proprietary know-how, or increase differentiation; (2) what impact vertical integration will have on investment costs, flexibility, and response times; (3) what administrative costs will be incurred by coordinating operations across more vertical chain activities; and (4) how difficult it will be for the company to acquire the set of skills and capabilities needed to operate in another stage of the vertical chain. *Vertical integration strategies have merit according to which capabilities and value-adding activities*

Unlike many vehicle manufacturers, Tesla embraces vertical integration from component manufacturing all the way through vehicle sales and servicing. The majority of the company's $11.8 billion in 2017 revenue came from electric vehicle sales and leasing, with the remainder coming from servicing those vehicles and selling residential battery packs and solar energy systems.

At its core an electric vehicle manufacturer, Tesla uses both backward and forward vertical integration to achieve multiple strategic goals. In order to drive innovation in a critical part of its supply chain, Tesla has invested in a "gigafactory" that manufacturers the batteries that are essential for a long-lasting electric vehicle. According to Tesla's former VP of Production, in-house manufacturing of key components and new parts that require frequent updates has enabled the company to learn quickly and launch new versions faster. Moreover, having closer relationships between engineering and manufacturing gives Tesla greater control over product design. Tesla uses forward vertical integration to improve the customer experience by owning the distribution and servicing of the vehicles it builds. Their network of dealerships allows Tesla to sell directly to consumers and handle maintenance needs without relying on third parties that sometimes have competing priorities.

Beyond vertically integrating the manufacture and distribution of their electric vehicles, Tesla uses the strategy to build the ecosystem that is necessary to support further adoption of their vehicles. As many consumers perceive electric cars to have limited range and long charging times that prevent long-distance travel, Tesla is building a network of Supercharger stations to overcome this pain point. By investing in this development themselves, Tesla does not need to wait for another company to deliver the critical infrastructure

©Hadrian/Shutterstock

that drivers demand before they switch from traditional gasoline-powered cars. Similarly, Tesla sells solar power generation and storage products that make it easier for customers to make the switch to transportation powered by sustainable energy.

While Tesla's mission to accelerate the world's transition to sustainable energy has required large investments throughout the value chain, this strategy has not been without challenges. Unlike batteries, seats are of limited strategic importance, yet Tesla decided to manufacture their Model 3 seats in house. While there is no indication that the seats were the source of major production delays in 2017, diverting resources to develop new manufacturing capabilities could have added to the problem. Although Tesla's vertical integration strategy is not without downsides, it has enabled the firm to quickly roll out innovative new products and launch the network that is required for widespread vehicle adoption. Investors have rewarded Tesla for this bold strategy by valuing at almost $51 billion, higher than the other major American automakers.

Note: Developed with Edward J. Silberman.

Sources: Tesla 2017 Annual Report; G. Reichow, "Tesla's Secret Second Floor," *Wired,* October 18,2017, https://www.wired.com/story/teslas-secret-second-floor/; A. Sage, "Tesla's Seat Strategy Goes Against the Grain. . . For Now," *Reuters,* October 26, 2017, https://www.reuters.com/article/us-tesla-seats/teslas-seat-strategy-goes-against-the-grain-for-now-idUSKBN1CV0DS; Yahoo Finance.

truly need to be performed in-house and which can be performed better or cheaper by outsiders. Absent solid benefits, integrating forward or backward is not likely to be an attractive strategy option.

Electric automobile maker Tesla Inc. has made vertical integration a central part of its strategy, as described in Illustration Capsule 6.4.

OUTSOURCING STRATEGIES: NARROWING THE SCOPE OF OPERATIONS

● ● ● ●

● **LO 6-5**

Identify the conditions that favor farming out certain value chain activities to outside parties.

CORE CONCEPT

Outsourcing involves contracting out certain value chain activities that are normally performed in-house to outside vendors.

In contrast to vertical integration strategies, outsourcing strategies narrow the scope of a business's operations, in terms of what activities are performed internally. **Outsourcing** involves contracting out certain value chain activities that are normally performed in-house to outside vendors.[19] Many PC makers, for example, have shifted from assembling units in-house to outsourcing the entire assembly process to manufacturing specialists, which can operate more efficiently due to their greater scale, experience, and bargaining power over components makers. Nearly all name-brand apparel firms have in-house capability to design, market, and distribute their products but they outsource all fabric manufacture and garment-making activities. Starbucks finds purchasing coffee beans from independent growers far more advantageous than having its own coffee-growing operation, with locations scattered across most of the world's coffee-growing regions.

Outsourcing certain value chain activities makes strategic sense whenever

- *An activity can be performed better or more cheaply by outside specialists.* A company should generally *not* perform any value chain activity internally that can be performed more efficiently or effectively by outsiders—the chief exception occurs when a particular activity is strategically crucial and internal control over that activity is deemed essential. Dolce & Gabbana, for example, outsources the manufacture of its brand of sunglasses to Luxottica—a company considered to be the world's best sunglass manufacturing company, known for its Oakley, Oliver Peoples, and Ray-Ban brands. Colgate-Palmolive, for instance, has reduced its information technology operational costs by more than 10 percent annually through an outsourcing agreement with IBM.

- *The activity is not crucial to the firm's ability to achieve sustainable competitive advantage.* Outsourcing of support activities such as maintenance services, data processing, data storage, fringe-benefit management, and website operations has become commonplace. Many smaller companies, for example, find it advantages to outsource HR activities such as benefit administration, training, recruiting, hiring and payroll to specialists, such as XcelHR, Insperity, Paychex, and Aon Hewitt.

- *The outsourcing improves organizational flexibility and speeds time to market.* Outsourcing gives a company the flexibility to switch suppliers in the event that its present supplier falls behind competing suppliers. Moreover, seeking out new suppliers with the needed capabilities already in place is frequently quicker, easier, less risky, and cheaper than hurriedly retooling internal operations to replace obsolete capabilities or trying to install and master new technologies.

- *It reduces the company's risk exposure to changing technology and buyer preferences.* When a company outsources certain parts, components, and services, its suppliers must bear the burden of incorporating state-of-the-art technologies and/or undertaking redesigns and upgrades to accommodate a company's plans to introduce next-generation products. If what a supplier provides falls out of favor with buyers, or is rendered unnecessary by technological change, it is the supplier's business that suffers rather than the company's.

- *It allows a company to concentrate on its core business, leverage its key resources, and do even better what it already does best.* A company is better able to enhance its own capabilities when it concentrates its full resources and energies on performing only those activities. United Colors of Benetton and Sisley, for example, outsource the production of handbags and other leather goods while devoting their energies to the clothing lines for which they are known. Apple outsources production of its iPod, iPhone, and iPad models to Chinese contract manufacturer Foxconn and concentrates in-house on design, marketing, and innovation. Hewlett-Packard and IBM have sold some of their manufacturing plants to outsiders and contracted to repurchase the output instead from the new owners.

The Risk of Outsourcing Value Chain Activities

The biggest danger of outsourcing is that a company will farm out the wrong types of activities and thereby hollow out its own capabilities.[20] For example, in recent years companies eager to reduce operating costs have opted to outsource such strategically important activities as product development, engineering design, and sophisticated manufacturing tasks—the very capabilities that underpin a company's ability to lead sustained product innovation. While these companies have apparently been able to lower their operating costs by outsourcing these functions to outsiders, *their ability to lead the development of innovative new products is weakened because so many of the cutting-edge ideas and technologies for next-generation products come from outsiders.*

> A company must guard against outsourcing activities that hollow out the resources and capabilities that it needs to be a master of its own destiny.

Another risk of outsourcing comes from the lack of direct control. It may be difficult to monitor, control, and coordinate the activities of outside parties via contracts and arm's-length transactions alone. Unanticipated problems may arise that cause delays or cost overruns and become hard to resolve amicably. Moreover, contract-based outsourcing can be problematic because outside parties lack incentives to make investments specific to the needs of the outsourcing company's internal value chain.

Companies like Cisco Systems are alert to these dangers. Cisco guards against loss of control and protects its manufacturing expertise by designing the production methods that its contract manufacturers must use. Cisco keeps the source code for its designs proprietary, thereby controlling the initiation of all improvements and safeguarding its innovations from imitation. Further, Cisco has developed online systems to monitor the factory operations of contract manufacturers around the clock so that it knows immediately when problems arise and can decide whether to get involved.

STRATEGIC ALLIANCES AND PARTNERSHIPS

Strategic alliances and cooperative partnerships provide one way to gain some of the benefits offered by vertical integration, outsourcing, and horizontal mergers and acquisitions while minimizing the associated problems. Companies frequently engage in cooperative strategies as an alternative to vertical integration or horizontal mergers and acquisitions. Increasingly, companies are also employing strategic alliances and partnerships to extend their scope of operations via international expansion and diversification strategies, as we describe in Chapters 7 and 8. Strategic alliances and cooperative arrangements are now a common means of narrowing a company's scope of operations as well, serving as a useful way to manage outsourcing (in lieu of traditional, purely price-oriented contracts).

> **• LO 6-6**
>
> Determine how to capture the benefits and minimize the drawbacks of strategic alliances and partnerships.

For example, oil and gas companies engage in considerable vertical integration—but Shell Oil Company and Pemex (Mexico's state-owned petroleum company) have found that joint ownership of their Deer Park Refinery in Texas lowers their investment costs and risks in comparison to going it alone. The colossal failure of the Daimler–Chrysler merger formed an expensive lesson for Daimler AG about what can go wrong with horizontal mergers and acquisitions; the Renault–Nissan–Mitsubishi Alliance has proved more successful in developing the capabilities for the manufacture of plug-in electric vehicles and introducing the Nissan Leaf.

Many companies employ strategic alliances to manage the problems that might otherwise occur with outsourcing—Cisco's system of alliances guards against loss of control, protects its proprietary manufacturing expertise, and enables the company to monitor closely the assembly operations of its partners while devoting its energy to designing new generations of the switches, routers, and other Internet-related equipment for which it is known.

A **strategic alliance** is a formal agreement between two or more separate companies in which they agree to work collaboratively toward some strategically relevant objective. Typically, they involve shared financial responsibility, joint contribution of resources and capabilities, shared risk, shared control, and mutual dependence. They may be characterized by cooperative marketing, sales, or distribution; joint production; design collaboration; or projects to jointly develop new technologies or products. They can vary in terms of their duration and the extent of the collaboration; some are intended as long-term arrangements, involving an extensive set of cooperative activities, while others are designed to accomplish more limited, short-term objectives.

Collaborative arrangements may entail a contractual agreement, but they commonly stop short of formal ownership ties between the partners (although sometimes an alliance member will secure minority ownership of another member).

A special type of strategic alliance involving ownership ties is the **joint venture.** A joint venture entails forming a *new corporate entity that is jointly owned* by two or more companies that agree to share in the revenues, expenses, and control of the newly formed entity. Since joint ventures involve setting up a mutually owned business, they tend to be more durable but also riskier than other arrangements. In other types of strategic alliances, the collaboration between the partners involves a much less rigid structure in which the partners retain their independence from one another. If a strategic alliance is not working out, a partner can choose to simply walk away or reduce its commitment to collaborating at any time.

An alliance becomes "strategic," as opposed to just a convenient business arrangement, when it serves any of the following purposes:[21]

1. It facilitates achievement of an important business objective (like lowering costs or delivering more value to customers in the form of better quality, added features, and greater durability).
2. It helps build, strengthen, or sustain a core competence or competitive advantage.
3. It helps remedy an important resource deficiency or competitive weakness.
4. It helps defend against a competitive threat, or mitigates a significant risk to a company's business.
5. It increases bargaining power over suppliers or buyers.
6. It helps open up important new market opportunities.
7. It speeds the development of new technologies and/or product innovations.

Strategic cooperation is a much-favored approach in industries where new technological developments are occurring at a furious pace along many different paths and where advances in one technology spill over to affect others (often blurring industry boundaries). Whenever industries are experiencing high-velocity technological advances in many areas simultaneously, firms find it virtually essential to have cooperative relationships with other enterprises to stay on the leading edge of technology, even in their own area of specialization. In industries like these, alliances are all about fast cycles of learning, gaining quick access to the latest round of technological know-how, and developing dynamic capabilities. In bringing together firms with different skills and knowledge bases, alliances open up learning opportunities that help partner firms better leverage their own resources and capabilities.[22]

In 2017, Daimler entered into an agreement with automotive supplier Robert Bosch GmbH to develop self-driving taxis that customers can hail with a smartphone app; the objective is to make this a reality in urban areas by the beginning of the next decade.

Microsoft has been partnering with a variety of companies to advance technology in the healthcare industry. Its 2017 alliance with PAREXEL, a clinical research organization, aims to use their combined capabilities to accelerate drug development and bring new therapies to patients sooner. In 2018, it joined forces with immuno-sequencing company Adaptive Biotechnologies to find ways to detect cancers and other diseases earlier using Microsoft's artificial intelligence capabilities.

> Companies that have formed a host of alliances need to manage their alliances like a portfolio.

Because of the varied benefits of strategic alliances, many large corporations have become involved in 30 to 50 alliances, and a number have formed hundreds of alliances. Hoffmann-La Roche, a multinational healthcare company, has set up Roche Partnering to manage their more than 190 alliances. Companies that have formed a host of alliances need to manage their alliances like a portfolio—terminating those that no longer serve a useful purpose or that have produced meager results, forming promising new alliances, and restructuring existing alliances to correct performance problems and/or redirect the collaborative effort.

> The best alliances are highly selective, focusing on particular value chain activities and on obtaining a specific competitive benefit. They enable a firm to build on its strengths and to learn.

Capturing the Benefits of Strategic Alliances

The extent to which companies benefit from entering into alliances and partnerships seems to be a function of six factors:[23]

1. *Picking a good partner.* A good partner must bring complementary strengths to the relationship. To the extent that alliance members have nonoverlapping strengths, there is greater potential for synergy and less potential for coordination problems and conflict. In addition, a good partner needs to share the company's vision about the overall purpose of the alliance and to have specific goals that either match or complement those of the company. Strong partnerships also depend on good chemistry among key personnel and compatible views about how the alliance should be structured and managed.

2. *Being sensitive to cultural differences.* Cultural differences among companies can make it difficult for their personnel to work together effectively. Cultural differences can be problematic among companies from the same country, but when the partners have different national origins, the problems are often magnified. Unless there is respect among all the parties for cultural differences, including those stemming from different local cultures and local business practices, productive working relationships are unlikely to emerge.

3. *Recognizing that the alliance must benefit both sides.* Information must be shared as well as gained, and the relationship must remain forthright and trustful. If either partner plays games with information or tries to take advantage of the other, the resulting friction can quickly erode the value of further collaboration. Open, trustworthy behavior on both sides is essential for fruitful collaboration.

4. *Ensuring that both parties live up to their commitments.* Both parties have to deliver on their commitments for the alliance to produce the intended benefits. The division of work has to be perceived as fairly apportioned, and the caliber of the benefits received on both sides has to be perceived as adequate.

5. *Structuring the decision-making process so that actions can be taken swiftly when needed.* In many instances, the fast pace of technological and competitive changes dictates an equally fast decision-making process. If the parties get bogged down in discussions or in gaining internal approval from higher-ups, the alliance can turn into an anchor of delay and inaction.

6. *Managing the learning process and then adjusting the alliance agreement over time to fit new circumstances.* One of the keys to long-lasting success is adapting the nature and structure of the alliance to be responsive to shifting market conditions, emerging technologies, and changing customer requirements. Wise allies are quick to recognize the merit of an evolving collaborative arrangement, where adjustments are made to accommodate changing conditions and to overcome whatever problems arise in establishing an effective working relationship.

Most alliances that aim at sharing technology or providing market access turn out to be temporary, lasting only a few years. This is not necessarily an indicator of failure, however. Strategic alliances can be terminated after a few years simply because they have fulfilled their purpose; indeed, many alliances are intended to be of limited duration, set up to accomplish specific short-term objectives. Longer-lasting collaborative arrangements, however, may provide even greater strategic benefits. Alliances are more likely to be long-lasting when (1) they involve collaboration with partners that do not compete directly, such as suppliers or distribution allies; (2) a trusting relationship has been established; and (3) both parties conclude that continued collaboration is in their mutual interest, perhaps because new opportunities for learning are emerging.

The Drawbacks of Strategic Alliances and Their Relative Advantages

While strategic alliances provide a way of obtaining the benefits of vertical integration, mergers and acquisitions, and outsourcing, they also suffer from some of the same drawbacks. Anticipated gains may fail to materialize due to an overly optimistic view of the potential or a poor fit in terms of the combination of resources and capabilities. When outsourcing is conducted via alliances, there is no less risk of becoming dependent on other companies for essential expertise and capabilities—indeed, this may be the Achilles' heel of such alliances. Moreover, there are additional pitfalls to collaborative arrangements. The greatest danger is that a partner will gain access to a company's proprietary knowledge base, technologies, or trade secrets, enabling the partner to match the company's core strengths and costing the company its hard-won competitive advantage. This risk is greatest when the alliance is among industry rivals or when the alliance is for the purpose of collaborative R&D, since this type of partnership requires an extensive exchange of closely held information.

The question for managers is when to engage in a strategic alliance and when to choose an alternative means of meeting their objectives. The answer to this question depends on the relative advantages of each method and the circumstances under which each type of organizational arrangement is favored.

The principal advantages of strategic alliances over vertical integration or horizontal mergers and acquisitions are threefold:

1. They lower investment costs and risks for each partner by facilitating resource pooling and risk sharing. This can be particularly important when investment needs and uncertainty are high, such as when a dominant technology standard has not yet emerged.

2. They are more flexible organizational forms and allow for a more adaptive response to changing conditions. Flexibility is essential when environmental conditions or technologies are changing rapidly. Moreover, strategic alliances under such circumstances may enable the development of each partner's dynamic capabilities.

3. They are more rapidly deployed—a critical factor when speed is of the essence. Speed is of the essence when there is a winner-take-all type of competitive situation, such as the race for a dominant technological design or a race down a steep experience curve, where there is a large first-mover advantage.

The key advantages of using strategic alliances rather than arm's-length transactions to manage outsourcing are (1) the increased ability to exercise control over the partners' activities and (2) a greater willingness for the partners to make relationship-specific investments. Arm's-length transactions discourage such investments since they imply less commitment and do not build trust.

On the other hand, there are circumstances when other organizational mechanisms are preferable to alliances and partnering. Mergers and acquisitions are especially suited for situations in which strategic alliances or partnerships do not go far enough in providing a company with access to needed resources and capabilities. Ownership ties are more permanent than partnership ties, allowing the operations of the merger or acquisition participants to be tightly integrated and creating more in-house control and autonomy. Other organizational mechanisms are also preferable to alliances when there is limited property rights protection for valuable know-how and when companies fear being taken advantage of by opportunistic partners.

While it is important for managers to understand when strategic alliances and partnerships are most likely (and least likely) to prove useful, it is also important to know how to manage them.

How to Make Strategic Alliances Work

A surprisingly large number of alliances never live up to expectations. Even though the number of strategic alliances increases by about 25 percent annually, about 60 to 70 percent of alliances continue to fail each year.[24] The success of an alliance depends on how well the partners work together, their capacity to respond and adapt to changing internal and external conditions, and their willingness to renegotiate the bargain if circumstances so warrant. A successful alliance requires real in-the-trenches collaboration, not merely an arm's-length exchange of ideas. Unless partners place a high value on the contribution each brings to the alliance and the cooperative arrangement results in valuable win–win outcomes, it is doomed to fail.

While the track record for strategic alliances is poor on average, many companies have learned how to manage strategic alliances successfully and routinely defy this average. Samsung Group, which includes Samsung Electronics, successfully manages an ecosystem of over 1,300 partnerships that enable productive activities from global procurement to local marketing to collaborative R&D. Companies that have greater success in managing their strategic alliances and partnerships often credit the following factors:

- *They create a system for managing their alliances.* Companies need to manage their alliances in a systematic fashion, just as they manage other functions. This means setting up a process for managing the different aspects of alliance management from partner selection to alliance termination procedures. To ensure that the system is followed on a routine basis by all company managers, many companies create a set of explicit procedures, process templates, manuals, or the like.

- *They build relationships with their partners and establish trust.* Establishing strong interpersonal relationships is a critical factor in making strategic alliances work since such relationships facilitate opening up channels of communication, coordinating activity, aligning interests, and building trust.

- *They protect themselves from the threat of opportunism by setting up safeguards.* There are a number of means for preventing a company from being taken advantage of by an untrustworthy partner or unwittingly losing control over key assets. Contractual safeguards, including noncompete clauses, can provide other forms of protection.

- *They make commitments to their partners and see that their partners do the same.* When partners make credible commitments to a joint enterprise, they have stronger incentives for making it work and are less likely to "free-ride" on the efforts of other partners. Because of this, equity-based alliances tend to be more successful than nonequity alliances.[25]

- *They make learning a routine part of the management process.* There are always opportunities for learning from a partner, but organizational learning does not take place automatically. Whatever learning occurs cannot add to a company's knowledge base unless the learning is incorporated systematically into the company's routines and practices.

Finally, managers should realize that alliance management is an organizational capability, much like any other. It develops over time, out of effort, experience, and learning. For this reason, it is wise to begin slowly, with simple alliances designed to meet limited, short-term objectives. Short-term partnerships that are successful often become the basis for much more extensive collaborative arrangements. Even when strategic alliances are set up with the hope that they will become long-term engagements, they have a better chance of succeeding if they are phased in so that the partners can learn how they can work together most fruitfully.

KEY POINTS

1. Once a company has settled on which of the five generic competitive strategies to employ, attention turns to how strategic choices regarding (1) competitive actions, (2) timing of those actions, and (3) scope of operations can complement its competitive approach and maximize the power of its overall strategy.

2. Strategic offensives should, as a general rule, be grounded in a company's strategic assets and employ a company's strengths to attack rivals in the competitive areas where they are weakest.

3. Companies have a number of offensive strategy options for improving their market positions: using a cost-based advantage to attack competitors on the basis of price or value, leapfrogging competitors with next-generation technologies, pursuing continuous product innovation, adopting and improving the best ideas of others, using hit-and-run tactics to steal sales away from unsuspecting rivals, and launching preemptive strikes. A blue-ocean type of offensive strategy seeks to gain a dramatic new competitive advantage by inventing a new industry or distinctive market

segment that renders existing competitors largely irrelevant and allows a company to create and capture altogether new demand in the absence of direct competitors.

4. The purposes of defensive strategies are to lower the risk of being attacked, weaken the impact of any attack that occurs, and influence challengers to aim their efforts at other rivals. Defensive strategies to protect a company's position usually take one of two forms: (1) actions to block challengers or (2) actions to signal the likelihood of strong retaliation.

5. The timing of strategic moves also has relevance in the quest for competitive advantage. Company managers are obligated to carefully consider the advantages or disadvantages that attach to being a first mover versus a fast follower versus a late mover.

6. Decisions concerning the scope of a company's operations—which activities a firm will perform internally and which it will not—can also affect the strength of a company's market position. The *scope of the firm* refers to the range of its activities, the breadth of its product and service offerings, the extent of its geographic market presence, and its mix of businesses. Companies can expand their scope horizontally (more broadly within their focal market) or vertically (up or down the industry value chain system that starts with raw-material production and ends with sales and service to the end consumer). Horizontal mergers and acquisitions (combinations of market rivals) provide a means for a company to expand its horizontal scope. Vertical integration expands a firm's vertical scope.

7. Horizontal mergers and acquisitions typically have any of five objectives: lowering costs, expanding geographic coverage, adding product categories, gaining new technologies or other resources and capabilities, and preparing for the convergence of industries.

8. Vertical integration, forward or backward, makes most strategic sense if it strengthens a company's position via either cost reduction or creation of a differentiation-based advantage. Otherwise, the drawbacks of vertical integration (increased investment, greater business risk, increased vulnerability to technological changes, less flexibility in making product changes, and the potential for channel conflict) are likely to outweigh any advantages.

9. Outsourcing involves contracting out pieces of the value chain formerly performed in-house to outside vendors, thereby narrowing the scope of the firm. Outsourcing can enhance a company's competitiveness whenever (1) an activity can be performed better or more cheaply by outside specialists; (2) the activity is not crucial to the firm's ability to achieve sustainable competitive advantage; (3) the outsourcing improves organizational flexibility, speeds decision making, and cuts cycle time; (4) it reduces the company's risk exposure; and (5) it permits a company to concentrate on its core business and focus on what it does best.

10. Strategic alliances and cooperative partnerships provide one way to gain some of the benefits offered by vertical integration, outsourcing, and horizontal mergers and acquisitions while minimizing the associated problems. They serve as an alternative to vertical integration and mergers and acquisitions, and as a supplement to outsourcing, allowing more control relative to outsourcing via arm's-length transactions.

11. Companies that manage their alliances well generally (1) create a system for managing their alliances, (2) build relationships with their partners and establish trust, (3) protect themselves from the threat of opportunism by setting up safeguards, (4) make commitments to their partners and see that their partners do the same, and (5) make learning a routine part of the management process.

ASSURANCE OF LEARNING EXERCISES

connect

LO 6-1, LO 6-2, LO 6-3

1. Live Nation operates music venues, provides management services to music artists, and promotes more than 26,000 live music events annually. The company acquired House of Blues, merged with Ticketmaster and acquired concert and festival promoters in the United States, Australia, and Great Britain. How has the company used horizontal mergers and acquisitions to strengthen its competitive position? Are these moves primarily offensive or defensive? Has either Live Nation or Ticketmaster achieved any type of advantage based on the timing of its strategic moves?

connect

LO 6-4

2. Tesla, Inc. has rapidly become a stand-out among American car companies. Illustration Capsule 6.4 describes how Tesla has made vertical integration a central part of its strategy. What value chain segments has Tesla chosen to enter and perform internally? How has vertical integration and integration of its ecosystem aided the organization in building competitive advantage? Has vertical integration strengthened its market position? Explain why or why not.

LO 6-5

3. Perform an Internet search to identify at least two companies in different industries that have entered into outsourcing agreements with firms with specialized services. In addition, describe what value chain activities the companies have chosen to outsource. Do any of these outsourcing agreements seem likely to threaten any of the companies' competitive capabilities?

LO 6-6

4. Using your university library's business research resources, find two examples of how companies have relied on strategic alliances or joint ventures to substitute for horizontal or vertical integration.

EXERCISE FOR SIMULATION PARTICIPANTS

LO 6-1, LO 6-2

1. Has your company relied more on offensive or defensive strategies to achieve your rank in the industry? What options for being a first mover does your company have? Do any of these first-mover options hold competitive advantage potential?

LO 6-3

2. Does your company have the option to merge with or acquire other companies? If so, which rival companies would you like to acquire or merge with?

LO 6-4

3. Is your company vertically integrated? Explain.

LO 6-5, LO 6-6

4. Is your company able to engage in outsourcing? If so, what do you see as the pros and cons of outsourcing? Are strategic alliances involved? Explain.

ENDNOTES

[1] George Stalk, Jr., and Rob Lachenauer, "Hardball: Five Killer Strategies for Trouncing the Competition," *Harvard Business Review* 82, no. 4 (April 2004); Richard D'Aveni, "The Empire Strikes Back: Counterrevolutionary Strategies for Industry Leaders," *Harvard Business Review* 80, no. 11 (November 2002); David J. Bryce and Jeffrey H. Dyer, "Strategies to Crack Well-Guarded Markets," *Harvard Business Review* 85, no. 5 (May 2007).

[2] George Stalk, "Playing Hardball: Why Strategy Still Matters," *Ivey Business Journal* 69, no.2 (November–December 2004), pp. 1–2; W. J. Ferrier, K. G. Smith, and C. M. Grimm, "The Role of Competitive Action in Market Share Erosion and Industry Dethronement: A Study of Industry Leaders and Challengers," *Academy of Management Journal* 42, no. 4 (August 1999), pp. 372–388.

[3] David B. Yoffie and Mary Kwak, "Mastering Balance: How to Meet and Beat a Stronger Opponent," *California Management Review* 44, no. 2 (Winter 2002), pp. 8–24.
[4] Ian C. MacMillan, Alexander B. van Putten, and Rita Gunther McGrath, "Global Gamesmanship," *Harvard Business Review* 81, no. 5 (May 2003); Ashkay R. Rao, Mark E. Bergen, and Scott Davis, "How to Fight a Price War," *Harvard Business Review* 78, no. 2 (March–April 2000).

[5] D. B. Yoffie and M. A. Cusumano, "Judo Strategy—the Competitive Dynamics of Internet Time," *Harvard Business Review* 77, no. 1 (January–February 1999), pp. 70–81.

[6] Ming-Jer Chen and Donald C. Hambrick, "Speed, Stealth, and Selective Attack: How Small Firms Differ from Large Firms in Competitive Behavior," *Academy of Management Journal* 38, no. 2 (April 1995), pp. 453–482; William E. Rothschild, "Surprise and the Competitive Advantage," *Journal of Business Strategy* 4, no. 3 (Winter 1984), pp. 10–18.

[7] Ian MacMillan, "Preemptive Strategies," *Journal of Business Strategy* 14, no. 2 (Fall 1983), pp. 16–26.

[8] Ian C. MacMillan, "How Long Can You Sustain a Competitive Advantage?" in Liam Fahey (ed.), *The Strategic Planning Management Reader* (Englewood Cliffs, NJ: Prentice Hall, 1989), pp. 23–24.

[9] Kevin P. Coyne and John Horn, "Predicting Your Competitor's Reactions," *Harvard Business Review* 87, no. 4 (April 2009), pp. 90–97.

[10] Philip Kotler, *Marketing Management,* 5th ed. (Englewood Cliffs, NJ: Prentice Hall, 1984).

[11] W. Chan Kim and Renée Mauborgne, "Blue Ocean Strategy," *Harvard Business Review* 82, no. 10 (October 2004), pp. 76–84.

[12] Jeffrey G. Covin, Dennis P. Slevin, and Michael B. Heeley, "Pioneers and Followers: Competitive Tactics, Environment, and Growth," *Journal of Business Venturing* 15, no. 2 (March 1999), pp. 175–210; Christopher A. Bartlett and Sumantra Ghoshal, "Going Global: Lessons from Late-Movers," *Harvard Business Review* 78, no. 2 (March-April 2000), pp. 132–145.

[13] Costas Markides and Paul A. Geroski, "Racing to Be 2nd: Conquering the Industries of the Future," *Business Strategy Review* 15, no. 4 (Winter 2004), pp. 25–31.

[14] Fernando Suarez and Gianvito Lanzolla, "The Half-Truth of First-Mover Advantage," *Harvard Business Review* 83, no. 4 (April 2005), pp. 121–127.

[15] Joseph L. Bower, "Not All M&As Are Alike—and That Matters," *Harvard Business Review* 79, no. 3 (March 2001); O. Chatain and P. Zemsky, "The Horizontal Scope of the Firm: Organizational Tradeoffs vs. Buyer-Supplier Relationships," *Management Science* 53, no. 4 (April 2007), pp. 550–565.

[16] Jeffrey H. Dyer, Prashant Kale, and Harbir Singh, "When to Ally and When to Acquire," *Harvard Business Review* 82, no. 4 (July–August 2004), pp. 109–110.

[17] John Stuckey and David White, "When and When Not to Vertically Integrate," *Sloan Management Review* (Spring 1993), pp. 71–83.

[18] Thomas Osegowitsch and Anoop Madhok, "Vertical Integration Is Dead, or Is It?" *Business Horizons* 46, no. 2 (March–April 2003), pp. 25–35.

[19] Ronan McIvor, "What Is the Right Outsourcing Strategy for Your Process?" *European Management Journal* 26, no. 1 (February 2008), pp. 24–34.

[20] Gary P. Pisano and Willy C. Shih, "Restoring American Competitiveness," *Harvard Business Review* 87, no. 7-8 (July–August 2009), pp. 114–125; Jérôme Barthélemy, "The Seven Deadly Sins of Outsourcing," *Academy of Management Executive* 17, no. 2 (May 2003), pp. 87–100.

[21] Jason Wakeam, "The Five Factors of a Strategic Alliance," *Ivey Business Journal* 68, no. 3 (May–June 2003), pp. 1–4.

[22] A. Inkpen, "Learning, Knowledge Acquisition, and Strategic Alliances," *European Management Journal* 16, no. 2 (April 1998), pp. 223–229.

[23] *Advertising Age,* May 24, 2010, p. 14.

[24] Patricia Anslinger and Justin Jenk, "Creating Successful Alliances," *Journal of Business Strategy* 25, no. 2 (2004), pp. 18–23; Rosabeth Moss Kanter, "Collaborative Advantage: The Art of the Alliance," *Harvard Business Review* 72, no. 4 (July–August 1994), pp. 96-108; Gary Hamel, Yves L. Doz, and C. K. Prahalad, "Collaborate with Your Competitors—and Win," *Harvard Business Review* 67, no. 1 (January–February 1989), pp. 133–139.

[25] Y. G. Pan and D. K. Tse, "The Hierarchical Model of Market Entry Modes," *Journal of International Business Studies* 31, no. 4 (2000), pp. 535–554.

chapter 7

Strategies for Competing in International Markets

Learning Objectives

This chapter will help you

LO 7-1 Identify the primary reasons companies choose to compete in international markets.

LO 7-2 Explain how and why differing market conditions across countries influence a company's strategy choices in international markets.

LO 7-3 Explain the differences among the five primary modes of entry into foreign markets

LO 7-4 Identify the three main strategic approaches for competing internationally.

LO 7-5 Explain how companies are able to use international operations to improve overall competitiveness.

LO 7-6 Identify the unique characteristics of competing in developing-country markets.

©Stephen F. Hayes/Photodisc/Getty Images

Our key words now are globalization, new products and businesses, and speed.

Tsutomu Kanai—*Former chair and president of Hitachi*

You have no choice but to operate in a world shaped by globalization and the information revolution. There are two options: Adapt or die.

Andy Grove—*Former chair and CEO of Intel*

Globalization has created strong networks of markets, infrastructure, people, minds, jobs, and most of all hope. We must build on these networks and partnerships for inclusive global growth.

Arun Jaitley—*Finance Minister of India*

Any company that aspires to industry leadership in the 21st century must think in terms of global, not domestic, market leadership. The world economy is globalizing at an accelerating pace as ambitious, growth-minded companies race to build stronger competitive positions in the markets of more and more countries, as countries previously closed to foreign companies open up their markets, and as information technology shrinks the importance of geographic distance. The forces of globalization are changing the competitive landscape in many industries, offering companies attractive new opportunities and at the same time introducing new competitive threats. Companies in industries where these forces are greatest are therefore under considerable pressure to come up with a strategy for competing successfully in international markets.

This chapter focuses on strategy options for expanding beyond domestic boundaries and competing in the markets of either a few or a great many countries. In the process of exploring these options, we introduce such concepts as the Porter diamond of national competitive advantage; and discuss the specific market circumstances that support the adoption of multidomestic, transnational, and global strategies. The chapter also includes sections on cross-country differences in cultural, demographic, and market conditions; strategy options for entering foreign markets; the importance of locating value chain operations in the most advantageous countries; and the special circumstances of competing in developing markets such as those in China, India, Brazil, Russia, and eastern Europe.

WHY COMPANIES DECIDE TO ENTER FOREIGN MARKETS

• • • •

• LO 7-1

Identify the primary reasons companies choose to compete in international markets.

A company may opt to expand outside its domestic market for any of five major reasons:

1. *To gain access to new customers.* Expanding into foreign markets offers potential for increased revenues, profits, and long-term growth; it becomes an especially attractive option when a company encounters dwindling growth opportunities in its home market. Companies often expand internationally to extend the life cycle of their products, as Honda has done with its classic 50-cc motorcycle, the Honda Cub (which is still selling well in developing markets, more than 50 years after it was first introduced in Japan). A larger target market also offers companies the opportunity to earn a return on large investments more rapidly. This can be particularly important in R&D-intensive industries, where development is fast-paced or competitors imitate innovations rapidly.

2. *To achieve lower costs through economies of scale, experience, and increased purchasing power.* Many companies are driven to sell in more than one country because domestic sales volume alone is not large enough to capture fully economies of scale in product development, manufacturing, or marketing. Similarly, firms expand internationally to increase the rate at which they accumulate experience and move down the learning curve. International expansion can also lower a company's input costs through greater pooled purchasing power. The relatively small size of country markets in Europe and limited domestic volume explains why companies like Michelin, BMW, and Nestlé long ago began selling their products all across Europe and then moved into markets in North America and Latin America.

3. *To gain access to low-cost inputs of production.* Companies in industries based on natural resources (e.g., oil and gas, minerals, rubber, and lumber) often find it necessary to operate in the international arena since raw-material supplies are located in different parts of the world and can be accessed more cost-effectively at the source. Other companies enter foreign markets to access low-cost human resources; this is particularly true of industries in which labor costs make up a high proportion of total production costs.

4. *To further exploit its core competencies.* A company may be able to extend a market-leading position in its domestic market into a position of regional or global market leadership by leveraging its core competencies further. H&M Group is capitalizing on its considerable expertise in fashion retailing to expand its reach internationally. By 2018, it had retail stores operating in 67 countries, along with online presence in 43 of these. Companies can often leverage their resources internationally by replicating a successful business model, using it as a basic blueprint for international operations, as Starbucks and McDonald's have done.[1]

5. *To gain access to resources and capabilities located in foreign markets.* An increasingly important motive for entering foreign markets is to acquire resources and capabilities that may be unavailable in a company's home market. Companies often make acquisitions abroad or enter into cross-border alliances to gain access to capabilities that complement their own or to learn from their partners.[2] In other cases, companies choose to establish operations in other countries to utilize local distribution networks, gain local managerial or marketing expertise, or acquire specialized technical knowledge.

In addition, companies that are the suppliers of other companies often expand internationally when their major customers do so, to meet their customers' needs abroad and retain their position as a key supply chain partner. For example, when motor vehicle companies have opened new plants in foreign locations, big automotive parts suppliers have frequently opened new facilities nearby to permit timely delivery of their parts and components to the plant. Similarly, Newell-Rubbermaid, one of Walmart's biggest suppliers of household products, has followed Walmart into foreign markets.

WHY COMPETING ACROSS NATIONAL BORDERS MAKES STRATEGY MAKING MORE COMPLEX

Crafting a strategy to compete in one or more countries of the world is inherently more complex for five reasons. First, different countries have different home-country advantages in different industries; competing effectively requires an understanding of these differences. Second, there are location-based advantages to conducting particular value chain activities in different parts of the world. Third, different political and economic conditions make the general business climate more favorable in some countries than in others. Fourth, companies face risk due to adverse shifts in currency exchange rates when operating in foreign markets. And fifth, differences in buyer tastes and preferences present a challenge for companies concerning customizing versus standardizing their products and services.

> **LO 7-2**
>
> Explain how and why differing market conditions across countries influence a company's strategy choices in international markets.

Home-Country Industry Advantages and the Diamond Model

Certain countries are known for their strengths in particular industries. For example, Chile has competitive strengths in industries such as copper, fruit, fish products, paper and pulp, chemicals, and wine. Japan is known for competitive strength in consumer electronics, automobiles, semiconductors, steel products, and specialty steel. Where industries are more likely to develop competitive strength depends on a set of factors that describe the nature of each country's business environment and vary from country to country. Because strong industries are made up of strong firms, the strategies of firms that expand internationally are usually grounded in one or more of these factors. The four major factors are summarized in a framework developed by Michael Porter and known as the *Diamond of National Competitive Advantage* (see Figure 7.1).[3]

Demand Conditions   The demand conditions in an industry's home market include the relative size of the market, its growth potential, and the nature of domestic buyers' needs and wants. Differing population sizes, income levels, and other demographic factors give rise to considerable differences in market size and growth rates from country to country. Industry sectors that are larger and more important in their home market tend to attract more resources and grow faster than others. For example, owing to widely differing population demographics and income levels, there is a far bigger market for luxury automobiles in the United States and Germany than in Argentina, India, Mexico, and China. At the same time, in developing markets like India, China, Brazil, and Malaysia, market growth potential is far higher than it is in the more mature economies of Britain, Denmark, Canada, and Japan. The potential for market growth

FIGURE 7.1   The Diamond of National Competitive Advantage

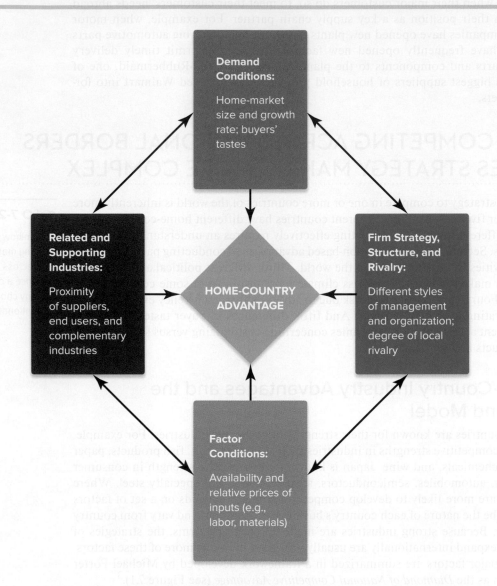

Source: Adapted from Michael E. Porter, "The Competitive Advantage of Nations," *Harvard Business Review,* March–April 1990, pp. 73–93.

in automobiles is explosive in China, where 2017 sales of new vehicles amounted to 28.9 million, surpassing U.S. sales of 17.2 million and making China the world's largest market for the eighth year in a row.[4] Demanding domestic buyers for an industry's products spur greater innovativeness and improvements in quality. Such conditions foster the development of stronger industries, with firms that are capable of translating a home-market advantage into a competitive advantage in the international arena.

Factor Conditions   Factor conditions describe the availability, quality, and cost of raw materials and other inputs (called *factors of production*) that firms in an industry require for producing their products and services. The relevant factors of production vary from industry to industry but can include different types of labor, technical or managerial knowledge, land, financial capital, and natural resources. Elements of a country's infrastructure may be included as well, such as its transportation, communication, and banking systems. For instance, in India there are efficient, well-developed national channels for distributing groceries, personal care items, and other packaged products to the country's 3 million retailers, whereas in China distribution is primarily local and there is a limited national network for distributing most products. Competitively strong industries and firms develop where relevant factor conditions are favorable.

Related and Supporting Industries Robust industries often develop in locales where there is a cluster of related industries, including others within the same value chain system (e.g., suppliers of components and equipment, distributors) and the makers of complementary products or those that are technologically related. The sports car makers Ferrari and Maserati, for example, are located in an area of Italy known as the "engine technological district," which includes other firms involved in racing, such as Ducati Motorcycles, along with hundreds of small suppliers. The advantage to firms that develop as part of a related-industry cluster comes from the close collaboration with key suppliers and the greater knowledge sharing throughout the cluster, resulting in greater efficiency and innovativeness.

Firm Strategy, Structure, and Rivalry Different country environments foster the development of different styles of management, organization, and strategy. For example, strategic alliances are a more common strategy for firms from Asian or Latin American countries, which emphasize trust and cooperation in their organizations, than for firms from North America, where individualism is more influential. In addition, countries vary in terms of the competitive rivalry of their industries. Fierce rivalry in home markets tends to hone domestic firms' competitive capabilities and ready them for competing internationally.

For an industry in a particular country to become competitively strong, all four factors must be favorable for that industry. When they are, the industry is likely to contain firms that are capable of competing successfully in the international arena. Thus the diamond framework can be used to reveal the answers to several questions that are important for competing on an international basis. First, it can help predict *where foreign entrants into an industry are most likely to come from.* This can help managers prepare to cope with new foreign competitors, since the framework also reveals something about the basis of the new rivals' strengths. Second, it can reveal the countries in which foreign rivals are likely to be weakest and thus can help managers decide *which foreign markets to enter first.* And third, because it focuses on the attributes of a country's business environment that allow firms to flourish, it reveals something about the advantages of conducting particular business activities in that country. Thus the diamond framework is an aid to deciding *where to locate different value chain activities most beneficially*—a topic that we address next.

> The Diamond Framework can be used to
> 1. predict from which countries foreign entrants are most likely to come
> 2. decide which foreign markets to enter first
> 3. choose the best country location for different value chain activities

Opportunities for Location-Based Advantages

Increasingly, companies are locating different value chain activities in different parts of the world to exploit location-based advantages that vary from country to country. This is particularly evident with respect to the location of manufacturing activities. Differences in wage rates, worker productivity, energy costs, and the like create sizable variations in manufacturing costs from country to country. By locating its plants in certain countries, firms in some industries can reap major manufacturing cost advantages because of lower input costs (especially labor), relaxed government regulations, the proximity of suppliers and technologically related industries, or unique natural resources. In such cases, the low-cost countries become principal production sites, with most of the output being exported to markets in other parts of the world. Companies that build production facilities in low-cost countries (or that source their products from contract manufacturers in these countries) gain a competitive advantage over rivals with plants in countries where costs are higher. The competitive role of low manufacturing costs is most evident in low-wage countries like China, India, Pakistan, Cambodia, Vietnam, Mexico, Brazil, Guatemala, the Philippines, and several countries in Africa and eastern Europe that have become production havens for manufactured goods with high labor content (especially textiles and apparel). Hourly compensation for manufacturing workers in 2016 averaged about $3.27 in India, $2.06 in the Philippines, $3.60 in China, $3.91 in Mexico, $9.82 in Taiwan, $8.60 in Hungary, $7.98 in Brazil, $10.96 in Portugal, $22.98 in South Korea, $23.67 in New Zealand, $26.46 in Japan, $30.08 in Canada, $39.03 in the United States, $43.18 in Germany, and $60.36 in Switzerland.[5] China emerged as the manufacturing capital of the world in large part because of its low wages—virtually all of the world's major manufacturing companies now have facilities in China.

For other types of value chain activities, input quality or availability are more important considerations. Tiffany & Co. entered the mining industry in Canada to access diamonds that could be certified as "conflict free" and not associated with either the funding of African wars or unethical mining conditions. Many U.S. companies locate call centers in countries such as India and Ireland, where English is spoken and the workforce is well educated. Other companies locate R&D activities in countries where there are prestigious research institutions and well-trained scientists and engineers. Likewise, concerns about short delivery times and low shipping costs make some countries better locations than others for establishing distribution centers.

The Impact of Government Policies and Economic Conditions in Host Countries

Cross-country variations in government policies and economic conditions affect both the opportunities available to a foreign entrant and the risks of operating within the host country. The governments of some countries are eager to attract foreign investments, and thus they go all out to create a business climate that outsiders will view as favorable. Governments eager to spur economic growth, create more jobs, and raise living standards for their citizens usually enact policies aimed at stimulating business innovation and capital investment; Ireland is a good example. They may provide such incentives as reduced taxes, low-cost loans, site location and site development assistance, and government-sponsored training for workers to encourage companies to construct production and distribution facilities. When new business-related issues or developments arise, "pro-business" governments make a practice of seeking advice and counsel from business leaders. When tougher business-related regulations are deemed appropriate, they endeavor to make the transition to more costly and stringent regulations somewhat business-friendly rather than adversarial.

On the other hand, governments sometimes enact policies that, from a business perspective, make locating facilities within a country's borders less attractive. For example, the nature of a company's operations may make it particularly costly to achieve compliance with a country's environmental regulations. Some governments provide subsidies and low-interest loans to domestic companies to enable them to better compete against foreign companies. To discourage foreign imports, governments may enact deliberately burdensome procedures and requirements regarding customs inspection for foreign goods and may impose tariffs or quotas on imports. Additionally, they may specify that a certain percentage of the parts and components used in manufacturing a product be obtained from local suppliers, require prior approval of capital spending projects, limit withdrawal of funds from the country, and require partial ownership of foreign company operations by local companies or investors. There are times when a government may place restrictions on exports to ensure adequate local supplies and regulate the prices of imported and locally produced goods. Such government actions make a country's business climate less attractive and in some cases may be sufficiently onerous as to discourage a company from locating facilities in that country or even selling its products there.

A country's business climate is also a function of the political and economic risks associated with operating within its borders. **Political risks** have to do with the instability of weak governments, growing possibilities that a country's citizenry will revolt against dictatorial government leaders, the likelihood of new onerous legislation or regulations on foreign-owned businesses, and the potential for future elections to produce corrupt or tyrannical government leaders. In industries that a government deems critical to the national welfare, there is sometimes a risk that the government will nationalize the industry and expropriate the assets of foreign companies. In 2012, for example, Argentina nationalized the country's top oil producer, YPF, which was owned by Spanish oil major Repsol. In 2015, they nationalized all of the Argentine railway network, some of which had been in private hands. Other political risks include the loss of investments due to war or political unrest, regulatory changes that create operating uncertainties, security risks due to terrorism, and corruption. **Economic risks** have to do with instability of a country's economy and monetary system—whether inflation rates might skyrocket or whether uncontrolled deficit spending on the part of government or risky bank lending practices could lead to a breakdown of the country's monetary system and prolonged economic distress. In some countries, the threat of piracy and lack of protection for intellectual property are also sources of economic risk. Another is fluctuations in the value of different currencies—a factor that we discuss in more detail next.

CORE CONCEPT

Political risks stem from instability or weakness in national governments and hostility to foreign business. **Economic risks** stem from instability in a country's monetary system, economic and regulatory policies, and the lack of property rights protections.

The Risks of Adverse Exchange Rate Shifts

When companies produce and market their products and services in many different countries, they are subject to the impacts of sometimes favorable and sometimes unfavorable changes in currency exchange rates. The rates of exchange between different currencies can vary by as much as 20 to 40 percent annually, with the changes occurring sometimes gradually and sometimes swiftly. *Sizable shifts in exchange rates pose significant risks for two reasons:*

1. They are hard to predict because of the variety of factors involved and the uncertainties surrounding when and by how much these factors will change.
2. They create uncertainty regarding which countries represent the low-cost manufacturing locations and which rivals have the upper hand in the marketplace.

To illustrate the economic and competitive risks associated with fluctuating exchange rates, consider the case of a U.S. company that has located manufacturing facilities in Brazil (where the currency is *reals*—pronounced "ray-alls") and that exports most of the Brazilian-made goods to markets in the European Union (where the currency is euros). To keep the numbers simple, assume that the exchange rate is 4 Brazilian reals for 1 euro and that the product being made in Brazil has a manufacturing cost of 4 Brazilian reals (or 1 euro). Now suppose that the exchange rate shifts from 4 reals per euro to 5 reals per euro (meaning that the real has declined in value and that the euro is stronger). Making the product in Brazil is now more cost-competitive because a Brazilian good costing 4 reals to produce has fallen to only 0.8 euro at the new exchange rate (4 reals divided by 5 reals per euro = 0.8 euro). This clearly puts the producer of the Brazilian-made good *in a better position to compete* against the European makers of the same good. On the other hand, should the value of the Brazilian real grow stronger in relation to the euro—resulting in an exchange rate of 3 reals to 1 euro—the same Brazilian-made good formerly costing 4 reals (or 1 euro) to produce now has a cost of 1.33 euros (4 reals divided by 3 reals per euro = 1.33 euros), putting the producer of the Brazilian-made good in a weaker competitive position vis-à-vis the European producers. Plainly, the attraction of manufacturing a good in Brazil and selling it in Europe is far greater when the euro is strong (an exchange rate of 1 euro for 5 Brazilian reals) than when the euro is weak and exchanges for only 3 Brazilian reals.

But there is one more piece to the story. When the exchange rate changes from 4 reals per euro to 5 reals per euro, not only is the cost-competitiveness of the Brazilian manufacturer stronger relative to European manufacturers of the same item but the Brazilian-made good that formerly cost 1 euro and now costs only 0.8 euro can also be sold to consumers in the European Union for a lower euro price than before. In other words, the combination of a stronger euro and a weaker real acts to *lower the price of Brazilian-made goods* in all the countries that are members of the European Union, which is likely to *spur sales of the Brazilian-made good in Europe and boost Brazilian exports to Europe.* Conversely, should the exchange rate shift from 4 reals per euro to 3 reals per euro—which makes the Brazilian manufacturer less cost-competitive with European manufacturers of the same item—the Brazilian-made good that formerly cost 1 euro and now costs 1.33 euros will sell for a higher price in euros than before, thus weakening the demand of European consumers for Brazilian-made goods and acting to reduce Brazilian exports to Europe. Brazilian exporters are likely to experience (1) rising demand for their goods in Europe whenever the Brazilian real grows weaker relative to the euro and (2) falling demand for their goods in Europe whenever the real grows stronger relative to the euro. Consequently, from the standpoint of a company with Brazilian manufacturing plants, *a weaker Brazilian real is a favorable exchange rate shift* and *a stronger Brazilian real is an unfavorable exchange rate shift.*

It follows from the previous discussion that shifting exchange rates have a big impact on the ability of domestic manufacturers to compete with foreign rivals. For example, U.S.-based manufacturers locked in a fierce competitive battle with low-cost foreign imports benefit from a *weaker* U.S. dollar. There are several reasons why this is so:

- Declines in the value of the U.S. dollar against foreign currencies raise the U.S. dollar costs of goods manufactured by foreign rivals at plants located in the countries whose currencies have grown stronger relative to the U.S. dollar. A *weaker* dollar acts to reduce or eliminate whatever cost advantage foreign manufacturers may have had over U.S. manufacturers (and helps protect the manufacturing jobs of U.S. workers).

- A *weaker* dollar makes foreign-made goods more expensive in dollar terms to U.S. consumers—this curtails U.S. buyer demand for foreign-made goods, stimulates greater demand on the part of U.S. consumers for U.S.-made goods, and reduces U.S. imports of foreign-made goods.

- A *weaker* U.S. dollar enables the U.S.-made goods to be sold at lower prices to consumers in countries whose currencies have grown stronger relative to the U.S. dollar—such lower prices boost foreign buyer demand for the now relatively cheaper U.S.-made goods, thereby stimulating exports of U.S.-made goods to foreign countries and creating more jobs in U.S.-based manufacturing plants.

- A *weaker* dollar has the effect of increasing the dollar value of profits a company earns in foreign-country markets where the local currency is stronger relative to the dollar. For example, if a U.S.-based manufacturer earns a profit of €10 million on its sales in Europe, those €10 million convert to a larger number of dollars when the dollar grows weaker against the euro.

A weaker U.S. dollar is therefore an economically favorable exchange rate shift for manufacturing plants based in the United States. A decline in the value of the U.S. dollar strengthens the cost-competitiveness of U.S.-based manufacturing plants and boosts buyer demand for U.S.-made goods. When the value of the U.S. dollar is expected to remain weak for some time to come, foreign companies have an incentive to build manufacturing facilities in the United States to make goods for U.S. consumers rather than export the same goods to the United States from foreign plants where production costs in dollar terms have been driven up by the decline in the value of the dollar. Conversely, a *stronger* U.S. dollar is an *unfavorable exchange rate shift* for U.S.-based manufacturing plants because it makes such plants less cost-competitive with foreign plants and weakens foreign demand for U.S.-made goods. A strong dollar also weakens the incentive of foreign companies to locate manufacturing facilities in the United States to make goods for U.S. consumers. The same reasoning applies to companies that have plants in countries in the European Union where euros are the local currency. A weak euro versus other currencies enhances the cost-competitiveness of companies manufacturing goods in Europe vis-à-vis foreign rivals with plants in countries whose currencies have grown stronger relative to the euro; a strong euro versus other currencies weakens the cost-competitiveness of companies with plants in the European Union.

> Fluctuating exchange rates pose significant economic risks to a company's competitiveness in foreign markets. Exporters are disadvantaged when the currency of the country where goods are being manufactured grows stronger relative to the currency of the importing country.

> Domestic companies facing competitive pressure from lower-cost imports benefit when their government's currency grows *weaker* in relation to the currencies of the countries where the lower-cost imports are being made.

Cross-Country Differences in Demographic, Cultural, and Market Conditions

Buyer tastes for a particular product or service sometimes differ substantially from country to country. In France, consumers prefer top-loading washing machines, whereas in most other European countries consumers prefer front-loading machines. People in Hong Kong prefer compact appliances, but in Taiwan large appliances are more popular. Ice cream flavors like matcha, black sesame, and red beans have more appeal to East Asian customers than they have for customers in the United States and in Europe. Sometimes, product designs suitable in one country are inappropriate in another because of differing local standards—for example, in the United States electrical devices run on 110-volt electric systems, but in some European countries the standard is a 240-volt electric system, necessitating the use of different electrical designs and components. Cultural influences can also affect consumer demand for a product. For instance, in South Korea many parents are reluctant to purchase PCs even when they can afford them because of concerns that their children will be distracted from their schoolwork by surfing the Web, playing PC-based video games, and becoming Internet "addicts."[6]

Consequently, companies operating in an international marketplace have to wrestle with *whether and how much to customize their offerings in each country market to match local buyers' tastes and preferences or whether to pursue a strategy of offering a mostly standardized product worldwide.* While making products that are closely matched to local tastes makes them more appealing to local buyers, customizing a company's products country by country may raise production and distribution costs due to the greater variety of designs and components, shorter production runs, and the complications of added inventory handling and distribution logistics. Greater standardization of a global company's product offering, on the other hand, can lead to scale economies and learning-curve effects, thus reducing per-unit production costs and contributing to the achievement of a low-cost advantage. *The tension between the market pressures to localize a company's product offerings country by country and the competitive pressures to lower costs is one of the big strategic issues that participants in foreign markets have to resolve.*

STRATEGIC OPTIONS FOR ENTERING INTERNATIONAL MARKETS

• • • •

● **LO 7-3**

Explain the differences among the five primary modes of entry into foreign markets.

Once a company decides to expand beyond its domestic borders, it must consider the question of how to enter foreign markets. There are five primary *modes of entry* to choose among:

1. Maintain a home-country production base and *export* goods to foreign markets.
2. *License* foreign firms to produce and distribute the company's products abroad.
3. Employ a *franchising* strategy in foreign markets.
4. Establish a *subsidiary* in a foreign market via acquisition or internal development.
5. Rely on *strategic alliances* or joint ventures with foreign companies.

Which mode of entry to employ depends on a variety of factors, including the nature of the firm's strategic objectives, the firm's position in terms of whether it has the full range of resources and capabilities needed to operate abroad, country-specific factors such as trade barriers, and the transaction costs involved (the costs of contracting with a partner and monitoring its compliance with the terms of the contract, for example). The options vary considerably regarding the level of investment required and the associated risks—but higher levels of investment and risk generally provide the firm with the benefits of greater ownership and control.

Export Strategies

Using domestic plants as a production base for exporting goods to foreign markets is an excellent initial strategy for pursuing international sales. It is a conservative way to test the international waters. The amount of capital needed to begin exporting is often minimal; existing production capacity may well be sufficient to make goods for export. With an export-based entry strategy, a manufacturer can limit its involvement in foreign markets by contracting with foreign wholesalers experienced in importing to handle the entire distribution and marketing function in their countries or regions of the world. If it is more advantageous to maintain control over these functions, however, a manufacturer can establish its own distribution and sales organizations in some or all of the target foreign markets. Either way, a home-based production and export strategy helps the firm minimize its direct investments in foreign countries. Such strategies are commonly favored by Chinese, Korean, and Italian companies—products are designed and manufactured at home and then distributed through local channels in the importing countries. The primary functions performed abroad relate chiefly to establishing a network of distributors and perhaps conducting sales promotion and brand-awareness activities.

Whether an export strategy can be pursued successfully over the long run depends on the relative cost-competitiveness of the home-country production base. In some industries, firms gain additional scale economies and learning-curve benefits from centralizing production in plants whose output capability exceeds demand in any one country market; exporting enables a firm to capture such economies. However, an export strategy is vulnerable when (1) manufacturing costs in the home country are substantially higher than in foreign countries where rivals have plants, (2) the costs of shipping the product to distant foreign markets are relatively high, (3) adverse shifts occur in currency exchange rates, and (4) importing countries impose tariffs or erect other trade barriers. Unless an exporter can keep its production and shipping costs competitive with rivals' costs, secure adequate local distribution and marketing support of its products, and effectively hedge against unfavorable changes in currency exchange rates, its success will be limited.

Licensing Strategies

Licensing as an entry strategy makes sense when a firm with valuable technical know-how, an appealing brand, or a unique patented product has neither the internal organizational capability nor the resources to enter foreign markets. Licensing also has the advantage of avoiding the risks of committing resources to country markets that are unfamiliar, politically volatile, economically unstable, or otherwise risky. By licensing the technology, trademark, or production rights to foreign-based firms, a company can generate income from royalties while shifting the costs and risks of entering foreign markets to the licensee. One downside of the licensing alternative is that the partner who bears the risk is also likely to be the biggest beneficiary from any upside gain. Disney learned this lesson when it relied on licensing agreements to open its first foreign theme park, Tokyo Disneyland. When the venture proved wildly successful, it was its licensing partner, the Oriental Land Company, and not Disney who reaped the windfall. Another disadvantage of licensing is the risk of providing valuable technological know-how to foreign companies and thereby losing some degree of control over its use; monitoring licensees and safeguarding the company's proprietary know-how can prove quite difficult in some circumstances. But if the royalty potential is considerable and the companies to which the licenses are being granted are trustworthy and reputable, then licensing can be a very attractive option. Many software and pharmaceutical companies use licensing strategies to participate in foreign markets.

Franchising Strategies

While licensing works well for manufacturers and owners of proprietary technology, franchising is often better suited to the international expansion efforts of service and retailing enterprises. McDonald's, Yum! Brands (the parent of Pizza Hut, KFC, Taco Bell, and WingStreet), the UPS Store, Roto-Rooter, 7-Eleven, and Hilton Hotels have all used franchising to build a presence in foreign markets. Franchising has many of the same advantages as licensing. The franchisee bears most of the costs and risks of establishing foreign locations; a franchisor has to expend only the resources to recruit, train, support, and monitor franchisees. The big problem a franchisor faces is maintaining quality control; foreign franchisees do not always exhibit strong commitment to consistency and standardization, especially when the local culture does not stress the same kinds of quality concerns. A question that can arise is whether to allow foreign franchisees to make modifications in the franchisor's product offering so as to better satisfy the tastes and expectations of local buyers. Should McDonald's give franchisees in each nation some leeway in what products they put on their menus? Should franchised KFC units in China be permitted to substitute spices that appeal to Chinese consumers? Or should the same menu offerings be rigorously and unvaryingly required of all franchisees worldwide?

Foreign Subsidiary Strategies

> **CORE CONCEPT**
>
> A **greenfield venture** (or internal startup) is a subsidiary business that is established by setting up the entire operation from the ground up.

Very often companies electing to compete internationally prefer to have direct control over all aspects of operating in a foreign market. Companies that want to participate in direct performance of all essential value chain activities typically establish a wholly owned subsidiary, either by acquiring a local company or by establishing its own new operating organization from the ground up. A subsidiary business that is established internally from scratch is called an *internal startup* or a **greenfield venture.**

Acquiring a local business is the quicker of the two options; it may be the least risky and most cost-efficient means of hurdling such entry barriers as gaining access to local distribution channels, building supplier relationships, and establishing working relationships with government officials and other key constituencies. Buying an ongoing operation allows the acquirer to move directly to the task of transferring resources and personnel to the newly acquired business, redirecting and integrating the activities of the acquired business into its own operation, putting its own strategy into place, and accelerating efforts to build a strong market position.

One thing an acquisition-minded firm must consider is whether to pay a premium price for a successful local company or to buy a struggling competitor at a bargain price. If the buying firm has little knowledge of the local market but ample capital, it is often better off purchasing a capable, strongly positioned firm. However, when the acquirer sees promising ways to transform a weak firm into a strong one and has the resources and managerial know-how to do so, a struggling company can be the better long-term investment.

Entering a new foreign country via a greenfield venture makes sense when a company already operates in a number of countries, has experience in establishing new subsidiaries and overseeing their operations, and has a sufficiently large pool of resources and capabilities to rapidly equip a new subsidiary with the personnel and what it needs otherwise to compete successfully and profitably. Four more conditions combine to make a greenfield venture strategy appealing:

- When creating an internal startup is cheaper than making an acquisition.
- When adding new production capacity will not adversely impact the supply-demand balance in the local market.
- When a startup subsidiary has the ability to gain good distribution access (perhaps because of the company's recognized brand name).
- When a startup subsidiary will have the size, cost structure, and capabilities to compete head-to-head against local rivals.

Greenfield ventures in foreign markets can also pose problems, just as other entry strategies do. They represent a costly capital investment, subject to a high level of risk. They require numerous other company resources as well, diverting them from other uses. They do not work well in countries without strong, well-functioning markets and institutions that protect the rights of foreign investors and provide other legal protections. Moreover, an important disadvantage of greenfield ventures relative to other means of international expansion is that they are the slowest entry route—particularly if the objective is to achieve a sizable market share. On the other hand, successful greenfield ventures may offer higher returns to compensate for their high risk and slower path.

> Collaborative strategies involving alliances or joint ventures with foreign partners are a popular way for companies to edge their way into the markets of foreign countries.

Alliance and Joint Venture Strategies

Strategic alliances, joint ventures, and other cooperative agreements with foreign companies are a widely used means of entering foreign markets.[7] A company can benefit immensely from a foreign partner's familiarity with local government regulations, its knowledge of the buying habits and product preferences of consumers, its distribution-channel relationships, and so on.[8] Both Japanese and American companies are actively forming alliances with European companies to better compete in the 28-nation European Union (and the five countries that are candidates to become EU members). Many U.S. and European companies are allying with Asian companies in their efforts to enter markets in China, India, Thailand, Indonesia, and other Asian countries.

Another reason for cross-border alliances is to capture economies of scale in production and/or marketing. By joining forces in producing components, assembling models, and marketing their products, companies can realize cost savings not achievable with their own small volumes. A third reason to employ a collaborative strategy is to share distribution facilities and dealer networks, thus mutually strengthening each partner's access to buyers. A fourth benefit of a collaborative strategy is the learning and added expertise that comes from performing joint research, sharing technological know-how, studying one another's manufacturing methods, and understanding how to tailor sales and marketing approaches to fit local cultures and traditions. A fifth benefit is that cross-border allies can direct their competitive energies more toward mutual rivals and less toward one another; teaming up may help them close the gap on leading companies. And, finally, alliances can be a particularly useful way for companies across the world to gain agreement on important technical standards—they have been used to arrive at standards for assorted PC devices, Internet-related technologies, high-definition televisions, and mobile phones.

> Cross-border alliances enable a growth-minded company to widen its geographic coverage and strengthen its competitiveness in foreign markets; at the same time, they offer flexibility and allow a company to retain some degree of autonomy and operating control.

Cross-border alliances are an attractive means of gaining the aforementioned types of benefits (as compared to merging with or acquiring foreign-based companies) because they allow a company to preserve its independence (which is not the case with a merger) and avoid using scarce financial resources to fund acquisitions. Furthermore, an alliance offers the flexibility to readily disengage once its purpose has been served or if the benefits prove elusive, whereas mergers and acquisitions are more permanent arrangements.[9]

Alliances may also be used to pave the way for an intended merger; they offer a way to test the value and viability of a cooperative arrangement with a foreign partner before making a more permanent commitment. Illustration Capsule 7.1 shows how Walgreens pursued this strategy with Alliance Boots in order to facilitate its expansion abroad.

Walgreens Boots Alliance, Inc.: Entering Foreign Markets via Alliance Followed by Merger

Walgreens pharmacy began in 1901 as a single store on the South Side of Chicago and grew to become the largest chain of pharmacy retailers in America. Walgreens was an early pioneer of the "self-service" pharmacy and found success by moving quickly to build a vast domestic network of stores after the Second World War. This growth-focused strategy served Walgreens well up until the beginning of the 21st century, by which time it had nearly saturated the U.S. market. By 2014, 75 percent of Americans lived within five miles of a Walgreens. The company was also facing threats to its core business model. Walgreens relies heavily on pharmacy sales, which generally are paid for by someone other than the patient, usually the government or an insurance company. As the government and insurers started to make a more sustained effort to cut costs, Walgreens's core profit center was at risk. To mitigate these threats, Walgreens looked to enter foreign markets.

Walgreens found an ideal international partner in Alliance Boots. Based in the UK, Alliance Boots had a global footprint with 3,300 stores across 10 countries. A partnership with Alliance Boots had several strategic advantages, allowing Walgreens to gain swift entry into foreign markets as well as complementary assets and expertise. First, it gave Walgreens access to new markets beyond the saturated United States for its retail pharmacies. Second, it provided Walgreens with a new revenue stream in wholesale drugs. Alliance Boots held a vast European distribution network for wholesale drug sales; Walgreens could leverage that network and expertise to build a similar model in the United States. Finally, a merger with Alliance Boots would strengthen Walgreens's existing business by increasing the company's market position and therefore bargaining power

©KarenBleier/AFP/Getty Images

with drug companies. In light of these advantages, Walgreens moved quickly to partner with and later acquire Alliance Boots and merged both companies in 2014 to become Walgreens Boots Alliance. Walgreens Boots Alliance, Inc. is now one of the world's largest drug purchasers, able to negotiate from a strong position with drug companies and other suppliers to realize economies of scale in its current businesses.

The market has thus far responded favorably to the merger. Walgreens Boots Alliance's stock has more than doubled in value since the first news of the partnership in 2012. However, the company is still struggling to integrate and faces new risks such as currency fluctuation in its new combined position. Yet as the pharmaceutical industry continues to consolidate, Walgreens is in an undoubtedly stronger position to continue to grow in the future thanks to its strategic international acquisition.

Note: Developed with Katherine Coster.

Sources: Company 10-K Form, 2015, **investor.walgreensbootsalliance.com/secfiling.cfm?filingID=1140361-15-38791&CIK=1618921;** L. Capron and W. Mitchell, "When to Change a Winning Strategy," *Harvard Business Review,* July 25, 2012, **hbr.org/2012/07/when-to-change-a-winning-strat;** T. Martin and R. Dezember, "Walgreen Spends $6.7 Billion on Alliance Boots Stake," *The Wall Street Journal,* June 20, 2012.

The Risks of Strategic Alliances with Foreign Partners   Alliances and joint ventures with foreign partners have their pitfalls, however. Sometimes a local partner's knowledge and expertise turns out to be less valuable than expected (because its knowledge is rendered obsolete by fast-changing market conditions or because its operating practices are archaic). Cross-border allies typically must overcome language and cultural barriers and figure out how to deal with diverse (or conflicting) operating practices. The transaction costs of working out a mutually agreeable arrangement and monitoring partner compliance with the terms of the arrangement can be high. The communication, trust building, and coordination costs are not trivial in terms of management time.[10] Often, partners soon discover they have conflicting objectives and strategies, deep differences of opinion about how to proceed, or important differences in corporate values and ethical standards. Tensions build, working relationships cool, and the hoped-for benefits never materialize.[11] It is not unusual for there to be little personal chemistry among some of the key people on whom the success or failure of the alliance depends—the rapport such personnel need to work well together may never emerge. And even if allies are able to develop productive personal relationships, they can still have trouble reaching mutually agreeable ways to deal with key issues or launching new initiatives fast enough to stay abreast of rapid advances in technology or shifting market conditions.

One worrisome problem with alliances or joint ventures is that a firm may risk losing some of its competitive advantage if an alliance partner is given full access to its proprietary technological expertise or other competitively valuable capabilities. There is a natural tendency for allies to struggle to collaborate effectively in competitively sensitive areas, thus spawning suspicions on both sides about forthright exchanges of information and expertise. It requires many meetings of many people working in good faith over a period of time to iron out what is to be shared, what is to remain proprietary, and how the cooperative arrangements will work.

Even if the alliance proves to be a win–win proposition for both parties, there is the danger of becoming overly dependent on foreign partners for essential expertise and competitive capabilities. Companies aiming for global market leadership need to develop their own resources and capabilities in order to be masters of their destiny. Frequently, experienced international companies operating in 50 or more countries across the world find less need for entering into cross-border alliances than do companies in the early stages of globalizing their operations.[12] Companies with global operations make it a point to develop senior managers who understand how "the system" works in different countries, plus they can avail themselves of local managerial talent and know-how by simply hiring experienced local managers and thereby detouring the hazards of collaborative alliances with local companies. One of the lessons about cross-border partnerships is that they are more effective in helping a company establish a beachhead of new opportunity in world markets than they are in enabling a company to achieve and sustain global market leadership.

INTERNATIONAL STRATEGY: THE THREE MAIN APPROACHES

Broadly speaking, a firm's **international strategy** is simply its strategy for competing in two or more countries simultaneously. Typically, a company will start to compete internationally by entering one or perhaps a select few foreign markets—selling its products or services in countries where there is a ready market for them. But as it expands further internationally, it will have to confront head-on two conflicting pressures: the demand for responsiveness to local needs versus the prospect of efficiency gains from offering a standardized product globally. Deciding on the competitive approach to best address these competing pressures is perhaps the foremost strategic issue that must be addressed when a company is operating in two or more foreign markets.[13] Figure 7.2 shows a company's three options for resolving this issue: choosing a *multidomestic, global,* or *transnational* strategy.

● LO 7-4

Identify the three main strategic approaches for competing internationally.

CORE CONCEPT

An **international strategy** is a strategy for competing in two or more countries simultaneously.

FIGURE 7.2   Three Approaches for Competing Internationally

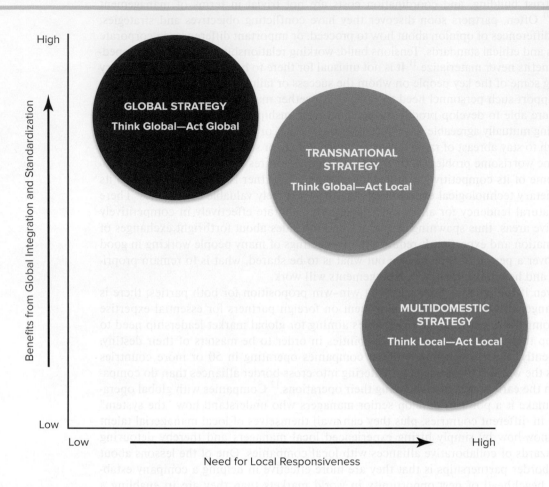

Multidomestic Strategies—a "Think-Local, Act-Local" Approach

A **multidomestic strategy** is one in which a company varies its product offering and competitive approach from country to country in an effort to meet differing buyer needs and to address divergent local-market conditions. It involves having plants produce different product versions for different local markets and adapting marketing and distribution to fit local customs, cultures, regulations, and market requirements. In the food products industry, it is common for companies to vary the ingredients in their products and sell the localized versions under local brand names to cater to country-specific tastes and eating preferences. Government requirements for gasoline additives that help reduce carbon monoxide, smog, and other emissions are almost never the same from country to country. BP utilizes localized strategies in its gasoline and service station business segment because of these cross-country formulation differences and because of customer familiarity with local brand names. For example, the company markets gasoline in the United States under its BP and Arco brands, but markets gasoline in Germany, Belgium, Poland, Hungary, and the Czech Republic under the Aral brand. Castrol, a BP-owned specialist in oil lubricants, produces over 3,000 different formulas of lubricants to meet the requirements of different climates, vehicle types and uses, and equipment applications that characterize different country markets.

In essence, a multidomestic strategy represents a **think-local, act-local** approach to international strategy. A think-local, act-local approach to strategy making is most appropriate when the need for local responsiveness is high due to significant cross-country differences in demographic, cultural, and market conditions and when the potential for efficiency gains from standardization is limited, as depicted in Figure 7.2. A think-local, act-local approach is possible only when decision making is decentralized, giving local managers considerable latitude for crafting and executing strategies for the country markets they are responsible for. Giving local managers decision-making authority allows them to address specific market needs and respond swiftly to local changes in demand. It also enables them to focus their competitive efforts, stake out attractive market positions vis-à-vis local competitors, react to rivals' moves in a timely fashion, and target new opportunities as they emerge.[14]

Despite their obvious benefits, think-local, act-local strategies have three big drawbacks:

1. They hinder transfer of a company's capabilities, knowledge, and other resources across country boundaries, since the company's efforts are not integrated or coordinated across country boundaries. This can make the company less innovative overall.

2. They raise production and distribution costs due to the greater variety of designs and components, shorter production runs for each product version, and complications of added inventory handling and distribution logistics.

3. They are not conducive to building a single, worldwide competitive advantage. When a company's competitive approach and product offering vary from country to country, the nature and size of any resulting competitive edge also tends to vary. At the most, multidomestic strategies are capable of producing a group of local competitive advantages of varying types and degrees of strength.

Global Strategies—a "Think-Global, Act-Global" Approach

A **global strategy** contrasts sharply with a multidomestic strategy in that it takes a standardized, globally integrated approach to producing, packaging, selling, and delivering the company's products and services worldwide. Companies employing a global strategy sell the same products under the same brand names everywhere, utilize much the same distribution channels in all countries, and compete on the basis of the same capabilities and marketing approaches worldwide. Although the company's strategy or product offering may be adapted in minor ways to accommodate specific situations in a few host countries, the company's fundamental competitive approach (low cost, differentiation, best cost, or focused) remains very much intact worldwide and local managers stick close to the global strategy.

A **think-global, act-global** approach prompts company managers to integrate and coordinate the company's strategic moves worldwide and to expand into most, if not all, nations where there is significant buyer demand. It puts considerable strategic emphasis on building a *global* brand name and aggressively pursuing opportunities to transfer ideas, new products, and capabilities from one country to another. Global strategies are characterized by relatively centralized value chain activities, such as production and distribution. While there may be more than one manufacturing plant and distribution center to minimize transportation costs, for example, they tend to be few in number. Achieving the efficiency potential of a global strategy requires that resources and best practices be shared, value chain activities be integrated, and capabilities be transferred from one location to another as they are developed. These objectives are best facilitated through centralized decision making and strong headquarters control.

Because a global strategy cannot accommodate varying local needs, it is an appropriate strategic choice when there are pronounced efficiency benefits from standardization and when buyer needs are relatively homogeneous across countries and regions. A globally standardized and integrated approach is especially beneficial when high volumes significantly lower costs due to economies of scale or added experience (moving the company further down a learning curve). It can also be advantageous if it allows the firm to replicate a successful business model on a global basis efficiently or engage in higher levels of R&D by spreading the fixed costs and risks over a higher-volume output. It is a fitting response to industry conditions marked by global competition.

Consumer electronics companies such as Apple, Nokia, and Motorola Mobility tend to employ global strategies. The development of universal standards in technology is one factor supporting the use of global strategies. So is the rise of global accounting and financial reporting standards. Whenever country-to-country differences are small enough to be accommodated within the framework of a global strategy, a global strategy is preferable because a company can more readily unify its operations and focus on establishing a brand image and reputation that are uniform from country to country. Moreover, with a global strategy a company is better able to focus its full resources on securing a sustainable low-cost or differentiation-based competitive advantage over both domestic rivals and global rivals.

There are, however, several drawbacks to global strategies: (1) They do not enable firms to address local needs as precisely as locally based rivals can; (2) they are less responsive to changes in local market conditions, in the form of either new opportunities or competitive threats; (3) they raise transportation costs and may involve higher tariffs; and (4) they involve higher coordination costs due to the more complex task of managing a globally integrated enterprise.

Transnational Strategies—a "Think-Global, Act-Local" Approach

A **transnational strategy** (sometimes called *glocalization*) incorporates elements of both a globalized and a localized approach to strategy making. This type of middle-ground strategy is called for when there are relatively high needs for local responsiveness as well as appreciable benefits to be realized from standardization, as Figure 7.2 suggests. A transnational strategy encourages a company to use a **think-global, act-local** approach to balance these competing objectives.

Often, companies implement a transnational strategy with mass-customization techniques that enable them to address local preferences in an efficient, semi-standardized manner. McDonald's, KFC, and Starbucks have discovered ways to customize their menu offerings in various countries without compromising costs, product quality, and operating effectiveness. Unilever is responsive to local market needs regarding its consumer products, while realizing global economies of scale in certain functions. Otis Elevator found that a transnational strategy delivers better results than a global strategy when it is competing in countries like China, where local needs are highly differentiated. By switching from its customary single-brand approach to a multibrand strategy aimed at serving different segments of the market, Otis was able to double its market share in China and increased its revenues sixfold over a nine-year period.[15]

As a rule, most companies that operate internationally endeavor to employ as global a strategy as customer needs and market conditions permit. Electronic Arts (EA) has two major design studios—one in Vancouver, British Columbia, and one in Los Angeles—and smaller design studios in locations including San Francisco, Orlando, London, and Tokyo. This dispersion of design studios helps EA design games that are specific to different cultures—for example, the London studio took the lead in designing the popular FIFA Soccer game to suit European tastes and to replicate the stadiums, signage, and team rosters; the U.S. studio took the lead in designing games involving NFL football, NBA basketball, and NASCAR racing.

A transnational strategy is far more conducive than other strategies to transferring and leveraging subsidiary skills and capabilities. But, like other approaches to competing internationally, transnational strategies also have significant drawbacks:

1. They are the most difficult of all international strategies to implement due to the added complexity of varying the elements of the strategy to situational conditions.
2. They place large demands on the organization due to the need to pursue conflicting objectives simultaneously.
3. Implementing the strategy is likely to be a costly and time-consuming enterprise, with an uncertain outcome.

Illustration Capsule 7.2 explains how Four Seasons Hotels has been able to compete successfully on the basis of a transnational strategy.

Table 7.1 provides a summary of the pluses and minuses of the three approaches to competing internationally.

TABLE 7.1 Advantages and Disadvantages of Multidomestic, Global, and Transnational Strategies

	Advantages	Disadvantages
Multidomestic (think local, act local)	• Can meet the specific needs of each market more precisely • Can respond more swiftly to localized changes in demand • Can target reactions to the moves of local rivals • Can respond more quickly to local opportunities and threats	• Hinders resource and capability sharing or cross-market transfers • Has higher production and distribution costs • Is not conducive to a worldwide competitive advantage
Global (think global, act global)	• Has lower costs due to scale and scope economies • Can lead to greater efficiencies due to the ability to transfer best practices across markets • Increases innovation from knowledge sharing and capability transfer • Offers the benefit of a global brand and reputation	• Cannot address local needs precisely • Is less responsive to changes in local market conditions • Involves higher transportation costs and tariffs • Has higher coordination and integration costs
Transnational (think global, act local)	• Offers the benefits of both local responsiveness and global integration • Enables the transfer and sharing of resources and capabilities across borders • Provides the benefits of flexible coordination	• Is more complex and harder to implement • Entails conflicting goals, which may be difficult to reconcile and require trade-offs • Involves more costly and time-consuming implementation

Four Seasons Hotels: Local Character, Global Service

Four Seasons Hotels is a Toronto, Canada–based manager of luxury hotel properties. With more than 100 properties located in many of the world's most popular tourist destinations and business centers, Four Seasons commands a following of many of the world's most discerning travelers. In contrast to its key competitor, Ritz-Carlton, which strives to create one uniform experience globally, Four Seasons Hotels has gained market share by deftly combining local architectural and cultural experiences with globally consistent luxury service.

When moving into a new market, Four Seasons always seeks out a local capital partner. The understanding of local custom and business relationships this financier brings is critical to the process of developing a new Four Seasons hotel. Four Seasons also insists on hiring a local architect and design consultant for each property, as opposed to using architects or designers it's worked with in other locations. While this can be a challenge, particularly in emerging markets, Four Seasons has found it is worth it in the long run to have a truly local team.

The specific layout and programming of each hotel is also unique. For instance, when Four Seasons opened its hotel in Mumbai, India, it prioritized space for large banquet halls to target the Indian wedding market. In India, weddings often draw guests numbering in the thousands. When moving into the Middle East, Four Seasons designed its hotels with separate prayer rooms for men and women. In Bali, where destination weddings are common, the hotel employs a "weather shaman" who, for some guests, provides reassurance that the weather will cooperate for their special day. In all cases, the objective is to provide a truly local experience.

When staffing its hotels, Four Seasons seeks to strike a fine balance between employing locals who have

©Ken Cedeno/Corbis via Getty Images

an innate understanding of the local culture alongside expatriate staff or "culture carriers" who understand the DNA of Four Seasons. It also uses global systems to track customer preferences and employs globally consistent service standards. Four Seasons claims that its guests experience the same high level of service globally but that no two experiences are the same.

While it is much more expensive and time-consuming to design unique architectural and programming experiences, doing so is a strategic trade-off Four Seasons has made to achieve the local experience demanded by its high-level clientele. Likewise, it has recognized that maintaining globally consistent operation processes and service standards is important too. Four Seasons has struck the right balance between thinking globally and acting locally—the marker of a truly transnational strategy. As a result, the company has been rewarded with an international reputation for superior service and a leading market share in the luxury hospitality segment.

Note: Developed with Brian R. McKenzie.

Sources: Four Seasons annual report and corporate website; interview with Scott Woroch, executive vice president of development, Four Seasons Hotels, February 22, 2014.

INTERNATIONAL OPERATIONS AND THE QUEST FOR COMPETITIVE ADVANTAGE

There are three important ways in which a firm can gain competitive advantage (or offset domestic disadvantages) by expanding outside its domestic market. First, it can use location to lower costs or achieve greater product differentiation. Second, it can transfer competitively valuable resources and capabilities from one country to another or share them across international borders to extend its competitive advantages. And third, it can benefit from cross-border coordination opportunities that are not open to domestic-only competitors.

Using Location to Build Competitive Advantage

To use location to build competitive advantage, a company must consider two issues: (1) whether or not to concentrate some of the activities it performs in only a few select countries of those in which they operate and if so (2) in which countries to locate particular activities.

When to Concentrate Activities in a Few Locations   It is advantageous for a company to concentrate its activities in a limited number of locations when

- *The costs of manufacturing or other activities are significantly lower in some geographic locations than in others.* For example, much of the world's athletic footwear is manufactured in Asia (China, Vietnam, and Indonesia) because of low labor costs; much of the production of circuit boards for PCs is located in Taiwan because of both low costs and the high-caliber technical skills of the Taiwanese labor force.

- *Significant scale economies exist in production or distribution.* The presence of significant economies of scale in components production or final assembly means that a company can gain major cost savings from operating a few super-efficient plants as opposed to a host of small plants scattered across the world. Makers of digital cameras and LED TVs located in Japan, South Korea, and Taiwan have used their scale economies to establish a low-cost advantage in this way. Achieving low-cost leadership status often requires a company to have the largest worldwide manufacturing share (as distinct from brand share or market share), with production centralized in one or a few giant plants. Some companies even use such plants to manufacture units sold under the brand names of rivals to further boost production-related scale economies. Likewise, a company may be able to reduce its distribution costs by establishing large-scale distribution centers to serve major geographic regions of the world market (e.g., North America, Latin America, Europe and the Middle East, and the Asia-Pacific region).

- *Sizable learning and experience benefits are associated with performing an activity.* In some industries, learning-curve effects can allow a manufacturer to lower unit costs, boost quality, or master a new technology *more quickly* by concentrating production in a few locations. The key to riding down the learning curve is to concentrate production in a few locations to increase the cumulative volume at a plant (and thus the experience of the plant's workforce) as rapidly as possible.

- *Certain locations have superior resources, allow better coordination of related activities, or offer other valuable advantages.* Companies often locate a research unit or a sophisticated production facility in a particular country to take advantage of its pool of technically trained personnel. Adidas located its first robotic "speedfactory" in Germany to benefit from its superior technological resources and to allow greater oversight from the company's headquarters (which are in Germany). Where just-in-time inventory practices yield big cost savings and/or where an assembly firm has long-term partnering arrangements with its key suppliers, parts manufacturing plants may be clustered around final-assembly plants. A customer service center or sales office may be opened in a particular country to help cultivate strong relationships with pivotal customers located nearby. Airbus established a major assembly site for their commercial aircraft in Alabama since the United States is a major market.

• LO 7-5

Explain how companies are able to use international operations to improve overall competitiveness.

Companies that compete internationally can pursue competitive advantage in world markets by locating their value chain activities in whatever nations prove most advantageous.

When to Disperse Activities across Many Locations   In some instances, dispersing activities across locations is more advantageous than concentrating them. Buyer-related activities—such as distribution, marketing, and after-sale service—usually must take place close to buyers. This makes it necessary to physically locate the capability to perform such activities in every country or region where a firm has major customers. For example, firms that make mining and oil-drilling equipment maintain operations in many locations around the world to support customers' needs for speedy equipment repair and technical assistance. Large public accounting firms have offices in numerous countries to serve the foreign operations of their international corporate clients. Dispersing activities to many locations is also competitively important when high transportation costs, diseconomies of large size, and trade barriers make it too expensive to operate from a central location. Many companies distribute their products from multiple locations to shorten delivery times to customers. In addition, dispersing activities helps hedge against the risks of fluctuating exchange rates, supply interruptions (due to strikes, natural disasters, or transportation delays), and adverse political developments. Such risks are usually greater when activities are concentrated in a single location.

Even though global firms have strong reason to disperse buyer-related activities to many international locations, such activities as materials procurement, parts manufacture, finished-goods assembly, technology research, and new product development can frequently be decoupled from buyer locations and performed wherever advantage lies. Components can be made in Mexico; technology research done in Frankfurt; new products developed and tested in Phoenix; and assembly plants located in Spain, Brazil, Taiwan, or South Carolina, for example. Capital can be raised wherever it is available on the best terms.

Sharing and Transferring Resources and Capabilities across Borders to Build Competitive Advantage

When a company has competitively valuable resources and capabilities, it may be able to leverage them further by expanding internationally. If its resources retain their value in foreign contexts, then entering new foreign markets can extend the company's resource-based competitive advantage over a broader domain. For example, companies like Tiffany, Cartier, and Rolex have utilized their powerful brand names to extend their differentiation-based competitive advantages into markets far beyond their home-country origins. In each of these cases, the luxury brand name represents a valuable competitive asset that can readily be *shared* by all of the company's international stores, enabling them to attract buyers and gain a higher degree of market penetration over a wider geographic area than would otherwise be possible.

Another way for a company to extend its competitive advantage internationally is to *transfer* technological know-how or other important resources and capabilities from its operations in one country to its operations in other countries. For instance, if a company discovers ways to assemble a product faster and more cost-effectively at one plant, then that know-how can be transferred to its assembly plants in other countries. Whirlpool's efforts to link its product R&D and manufacturing operations in North America, Latin America, Europe, and Asia allowed it to accelerate the discovery of innovative appliance features, coordinate the introduction of these features in the appliance products marketed in different countries, and create a cost-efficient worldwide supply chain. Whirlpool's conscious efforts to integrate and coordinate its various operations around the world have helped it achieve operational excellence and speed product innovations to market. Walmart is expanding its international operations with a strategy that involves transferring its considerable resource capabilities in distribution and discount retailing to its retail units in 28 foreign countries.

Cross-border sharing or transferring resources and capabilities provides a cost-effective way for a company to leverage its core competencies more fully and extend its competitive advantages into a wider array of geographic markets. The cost of sharing or transferring already developed resources and capabilities across country borders is low in comparison to the time and considerable expense it takes to create them. Moreover, deploying them abroad spreads the fixed development costs over a greater volume of unit sales, thus contributing to low unit costs and a potential cost-based competitive advantage in recently entered geographic markets. Even if the shared or transferred resources or capabilities have to be adapted to local-market conditions, this can usually be done at low additional cost.

Consider the case of Walt Disney's theme parks as an example. The success of the theme parks in the United States derives in part from core resources such as the Disney brand name and characters like Mickey Mouse that have universal appeal and worldwide recognition. These resources can be freely shared with new theme parks as Disney expands internationally. Disney can also replicate its theme parks in new countries cost-effectively since it has already borne the costs of developing its core resources, park attractions, basic park design, and operating capabilities. The cost of replicating its theme parks abroad is relatively low, even if the parks need to be adapted to a variety of local country conditions. Thus, in establishing Disney parks in Tokyo, Paris, Hong Kong, and Shanghai, Disney has been able to leverage the differentiation advantage conferred by resources such as the Disney name and the park attractions. And by moving into new foreign markets, it has augmented its competitive advantage further through the efficiency gains that come from cross-border resource sharing and low-cost capability transfer and business model replication.

Sharing and transferring resources and capabilities across country borders may also contribute to the development of broader or deeper competencies and capabilities—helping a company achieve *dominating depth* in some competitively valuable area. For example, the reputation for quality that Honda established worldwide began in motorcycles but enabled the company to command a position in both automobiles and outdoor power equipment in multiple-country markets. A one-country customer base is often too small to support the resource buildup needed to achieve such depth; this is particularly true in a developing or protected market, where competitively powerful resources are not required. By deploying capabilities across a larger international domain, a company can gain the experience needed to upgrade them to a higher performance standard. And by facing a more challenging set of international competitors, a company may be spurred to develop a stronger set of competitive capabilities. Moreover, by entering international markets, firms may be able to augment their capability set by learning from international rivals, cooperative partners, or acquisition targets.

However, cross-border resource sharing and transfers of capabilities are not guaranteed recipes for competitive success. For example, whether a resource or capability can confer a competitive advantage abroad depends on the conditions of rivalry in each particular market. If the rivals in a foreign-country market have superior resources and capabilities, then an entering firm may find itself at a competitive disadvantage even if it has a resource-based advantage domestically and can transfer the resources at low cost. In addition, since lifestyles and buying habits differ internationally, resources and capabilities that are valuable in one country may not have value in another. Sometimes a popular or well-regarded brand in one country turns out to have little competitive clout against local brands in other countries.

Benefiting from Cross-Border Coordination

Companies that compete on an international basis have another source of competitive advantage relative to their purely domestic rivals: They are able to benefit from coordinating activities across different countries' domains.[16] For example, an international manufacturer can shift production from a plant in one country to a plant in another to take advantage of exchange rate fluctuations, to cope with components shortages, or to profit from changing wage rates or energy costs. Production schedules can be coordinated worldwide; shipments can be diverted from one distribution center to another if sales rise unexpectedly in one place and fall in another. By coordinating their activities, international companies may also be able to enhance their leverage with host-country governments or respond adaptively to changes in tariffs and quotas. Efficiencies can also be achieved by shifting workloads from where they are unusually heavy to locations where personnel are underutilized.

CROSS-BORDER STRATEGIC MOVES

While international competitors can employ any of the offensive and defensive moves discussed in Chapter 6, there are two types of strategic moves that are particularly suited for companies competing internationally. The first is an offensive move that an international competitor is uniquely positioned to make, due to the fact that it may have a strong or protected market position in more than one country. The second type of move is a type of defensive action involving multiple markets.

Waging a Strategic Offensive

CORE CONCEPT

Cross-market subsidization—supporting competitive offensives in one market with resources and profits diverted from operations in another market—can be a powerful competitive weapon.

One advantage to being an international competitor is the possibility of having more than one significant and possibly protected source of profits. This may provide the company with the financial strength to engage in strategic offensives in selected country markets. The added financial capability afforded by multiple profit sources gives an international competitor the financial strength to wage an offensive campaign against a domestic competitor whose only source of profit is its home market. The international company has the flexibility of lowballing its prices or launching high-cost marketing campaigns in the domestic company's home market and grabbing market share at the domestic company's expense. Razor-thin margins or even losses in these markets can be subsidized with the healthy profits earned in its markets abroad—a practice called **cross-market subsidization.**

The international company can adjust the depth of its price cutting to move in and capture market share quickly, or it can shave prices slightly to make gradual market inroads (perhaps over a decade or more) so as not to threaten domestic firms precipitously and trigger protectionist government actions. If the domestic company retaliates with matching price cuts or increased marketing expenses, it thereby exposes its entire revenue stream and profit base to erosion; its profits can be squeezed substantially and its competitive strength sapped, even if it is the domestic market leader.

When taken to the extreme, cut-rate pricing attacks by international competitors may draw charges of unfair "dumping." A company is said to be *dumping* when it sells its goods in foreign markets at prices that are (1) well below the prices at which it normally sells them in its home market or (2) well below its full costs per unit. Almost all governments can be expected to retaliate against perceived dumping practices by imposing special tariffs on goods being imported from the countries of the guilty companies. Indeed, as the trade among nations has mushroomed over the past 10 years, most governments have joined the World Trade Organization (WTO), which promotes fair trade practices among nations and actively polices dumping. Companies deemed guilty of dumping frequently come under pressure from their own government to cease and desist, especially if the tariffs adversely affect innocent companies based in the same country or if the advent of special tariffs raises the specter of an international trade war.

> A company is said to be *dumping* when it sells its goods in foreign markets at prices that are
> 1. well below the prices at which it normally sells them in its home market or
> 2. well below its full costs per unit.

Defending against International Rivals

Cross-border tactics involving multiple country markets can also be used as a means of defending against the strategic moves of rivals with multiple profitable markets of their own. If a company finds itself under competitive attack by an international rival in one country market, one way to respond is to conduct a counterattack against the rival in one of its key markets in a different country—preferably where the rival is least protected and has the most to lose. This is a possible option when rivals compete against one another in much the same markets around the world and engage in *multimarket competition*.

For companies with at least one major market, having a presence in a rival's key markets can be enough to deter the rival from making aggressive attacks. The reason for this is that the combination of market presence in the rival's key markets and a highly profitable market elsewhere can send a signal to the rival that the company could quickly ramp up production (funded by the profit center) to mount a competitive counterattack if the rival attacks one of the company's key markets.

When international rivals compete against one another in multiple-country markets, this type of deterrence effect can restrain them from taking aggressive action against one another, due to the fear of a retaliatory response that might escalate the battle into a cross-border competitive war. **Mutual restraint** of this sort tends to stabilize the competitive position of multimarket rivals against one another. And while it may prevent each firm from making any major market share gains at the expense of its rival, it also protects against costly competitive battles that would be likely to erode the profitability of both companies without any compensating gain.

> *Multimarket competition* refers to a situation where rivals compete against one another in many of the same markets.

> **CORE CONCEPT**
>
> When the same companies compete against one another in multiple geographic markets, the threat of cross-border counterattacks may be enough to encourage **mutual restraint** among international rivals.

STRATEGIES FOR COMPETING IN THE MARKETS OF DEVELOPING COUNTRIES

● ● ● ●

● **LO 7-6**

Identify the unique characteristics of competing in developing-country markets.

Companies racing for global leadership have to consider competing in developing-economy markets like China, India, Brazil, Indonesia, Thailand, Poland, Mexico, and Russia—countries where the business risks are considerable but where the opportunities for growth are huge, especially as their economies develop and living standards climb toward levels in the industrialized world.[17] In today's world, a company that aspires to international market leadership (or to sustained rapid growth) cannot ignore the market opportunities or the base of technical and managerial talent such countries offer. For example, in 2018 China was the world's second-largest economy (behind the United States), based on the purchasing power of its population of over 1.4 billion people. China's growth in demand for consumer goods has made it the fifth largest market for luxury goods, with sales greater than those in developed markets such as Germany, Spain, and the United Kingdom. Thus, no company that aspires to global market leadership can afford to ignore the strategic importance of establishing competitive market positions in the so-called BRIC countries (Brazil, Russia, India, and China), as well as in other parts of the Asia-Pacific region, Latin America, and eastern Europe.

Tailoring products to fit market conditions in developing countries, however, often involves more than making minor product changes and becoming more familiar with local cultures. McDonald's has had to offer vegetable burgers in parts of Asia and to rethink its prices, which are often high by local standards and affordable only by the well-to-do. Kellogg has struggled to introduce its cereals successfully because consumers in many less developed countries do not eat cereal for breakfast. Single-serving packages of detergents, shampoos, pickles, cough syrup, and cooking oils are very popular in India because they allow buyers to conserve cash by purchasing only what they need immediately. Thus, many companies find that trying to employ a strategy akin to that used in the markets of developed countries is hazardous.[18] Experimenting with some, perhaps many, local twists is usually necessary to find a strategy combination that works.

Strategy Options for Competing in Developing-Country Markets

There are several options for tailoring a company's strategy to fit the sometimes unusual or challenging circumstances presented in developing-country markets:

- *Prepare to compete on the basis of low price.* Consumers in developing markets are often highly focused on price, which can give low-cost local competitors the edge unless a company can find ways to attract buyers with bargain prices as well as better products. For example, in order to enter the market for laundry detergents in India, Unilever had to develop a low-cost detergent (named Wheel), construct new low-cost production facilities, package the detergent in single-use amounts so that it could be sold at a very low unit price, distribute the product to local merchants by handcarts, and craft an economical marketing campaign that included painted signs on buildings and demonstrations near stores. The new brand quickly captured $100 million in sales and by 2014 was the top detergent brand in India-based dollar sales. Unilever replicated the strategy in India with low-priced packets of shampoos and deodorants and in South America with a detergent brand-named Ala.

- *Modify aspects of the company's business model to accommodate the unique local circumstances of developing countries.* For instance, Honeywell had sold industrial products and services for more than 100 years outside the United States and Europe using a foreign subsidiary model that focused international activities on sales only. When Honeywell entered China, it discovered that industrial customers in that country considered how many key jobs foreign companies created in China, in addition to the quality and price of the product or service when making purchasing decisions. Honeywell added about 150 engineers, strategists, and marketers in China to demonstrate its commitment to bolstering the Chinese economy. Honeywell replicated its "East for East" strategy when it entered the market for industrial products and services in India. Within 10 years of Honeywell establishing operations in China and three years of expanding into India, the two emerging markets accounted for 30 percent of the firm's worldwide growth.

- *Try to change the local market to better match the way the company does business elsewhere.* An international company often has enough market clout to drive major changes in the way a local country market operates. When Japan's Suzuki entered India, it triggered a quality revolution among Indian auto parts manufacturers. Local component suppliers teamed up with Suzuki's vendors in Japan and worked with Japanese experts to produce higher-quality products. Over the next two decades, Indian companies became proficient in making top-notch components for vehicles, won more prizes for quality than companies in any country other than Japan, and broke into the global market as suppliers to many automakers in Asia and other parts of the world. Mahindra and Mahindra, one of India's premier automobile manufacturers, has been recognized by a number of organizations for its product quality. Among its most noteworthy awards was its number-one ranking by J.D. Power Asia Pacific for new-vehicle overall quality.

- *Stay away from developing markets where it is impractical or uneconomical to modify the company's business model to accommodate local circumstances.* Home Depot expanded successfully into Mexico, but it has avoided entry into other developing countries because its value proposition of good quality, low prices, and attentive customer service relies on (1) good highways and logistical systems to minimize store inventory costs, (2) employee stock ownership to help motivate store personnel to provide good customer service, and (3) high labor costs for housing construction and home repairs that encourage homeowners to engage in do-it-yourself projects. Relying on these factors in North American markets has worked spectacularly for Home Depot, but the company found that it could not count on these factors in China, from which it withdrew in 2012.

Company experiences in entering developing markets like Brazil, Russia, India, and China indicate that profitability seldom comes quickly or easily. Building a market for the company's products can often turn into a long-term process that involves reeducation of consumers, sizable investments in advertising to alter tastes and buying habits, and upgrades of the local infrastructure (transportation systems, distribution channels, etc.). In such cases, a company must be patient, work within the system to improve the infrastructure, and lay the foundation for generating sizable revenues and profits once conditions are ripe for market takeoff.

> Profitability in developing markets rarely comes quickly or easily—new entrants have to adapt their business models to local conditions, which may not always be possible.

DEFENDING AGAINST GLOBAL GIANTS: STRATEGIES FOR LOCAL COMPANIES IN DEVELOPING COUNTRIES

If opportunity-seeking, resource-rich international companies are looking to enter developing-country markets, what strategy options can local companies use to survive? As it turns out, the prospects for local companies facing global giants are by no means grim. Studies of local companies in developing markets have disclosed five strategies that have proved themselves in defending against globally competitive companies.[19]

1. *Develop business models that exploit shortcomings in local distribution networks or infrastructure.* In many instances, the extensive collection of resources possessed by the global giants is of little help in building a presence in developing markets. The lack of well-established local wholesaler and distributor networks, telecommunication systems, consumer banking, or media necessary for advertising makes it difficult for large internationals to migrate business models proved in developed markets to emerging markets. Emerging markets sometimes favor local companies whose managers are familiar with the local language and culture and are skilled in selecting large numbers of conscientious employees to carry out labor-intensive tasks. Shanda, a Chinese producer of massively multiplayer online role-playing games (MMORPGs), overcame China's lack of an established credit card network by selling prepaid access cards through local merchants. The company's focus on online games also protects it from shortcomings in China's software piracy laws. An India-based electronics company carved out a market niche for itself by developing an all-in-one business machine, designed especially for India's millions of small shopkeepers, that tolerates the country's frequent power outages.

2. *Utilize keen understanding of local customer needs and preferences to create customized products or services.* When developing-country markets are largely made up of customers with strong local needs, a good strategy option is to concentrate on customers who prefer a local touch and to accept the loss of the customers attracted to global brands.[20] A local company may be able to astutely exploit its local orientation—its familiarity with local preferences, its expertise in traditional products, its long-standing customer relationships. A small Middle Eastern cell phone manufacturer competes successfully against industry giants Samsung, Apple, Nokia, and Motorola by selling a model designed especially for Muslims—it is loaded with the Koran, alerts people at prayer times, and is equipped with a compass that points them toward Mecca. Shenzhen-based Tencent has become the leader in instant messaging in China through its unique understanding of Chinese behavior and culture.

3. *Take advantage of aspects of the local workforce with which large international companies may be unfamiliar.* Local companies that lack the technological capabilities of foreign entrants may be able to rely on their better understanding of the local labor force to offset any disadvantage. Focus Media is China's largest outdoor advertising firm and has relied on low-cost labor to update its more than 170,000 LCD displays and billboards in over 90 cities in a low-tech manner, while international companies operating in China use electronically networked screens that

allow messages to be changed remotely. Focus uses an army of employees who ride to each display by bicycle to change advertisements with programming contained on a USB flash drive or DVD. Indian information technology firms such as Infosys Technologies and Satyam Computer Services have been able to keep their personnel costs lower than those of international competitors EDS and Accenture because of their familiarity with local labor markets. While the large internationals have focused recruiting efforts in urban centers like Bangalore and Delhi, driving up engineering and computer science salaries in such cities, local companies have shifted recruiting efforts to second-tier cities that are unfamiliar to foreign firms.

4. *Use acquisition and rapid-growth strategies to better defend against expansion-minded internationals.* With the growth potential of developing markets such as China, Indonesia, and Brazil obvious to the world, local companies must attempt to develop scale and upgrade their competitive capabilities as quickly as possible to defend against the stronger international's arsenal of resources. Most successful companies in developing markets have pursued mergers and acquisitions at a rapid-fire pace to build first a nationwide and then an international presence. Hindalco, India's largest aluminum producer, has followed just such a path to achieve its ambitions for global dominance. By acquiring companies in India first, it gained enough experience and confidence to eventually acquire much larger foreign companies with world-class capabilities.[21] When China began to liberalize its foreign trade policies, Lenovo (the Chinese PC maker) realized that its long-held position of market dominance in China could not withstand the onslaught of new international entrants such as Dell and HP. Its acquisition of IBM's PC business allowed Lenovo to gain rapid access to IBM's globally recognized PC brand, its R&D capability, and its existing distribution in developed countries. This has allowed Lenovo not only to hold its own against the incursion of global giants into its home market but also to expand into new markets around the world.[22]

5. *Transfer company expertise to cross-border markets and initiate actions to contend on an international level.* When a company from a developing country has resources and capabilities suitable for competing in other country markets, launching initiatives to transfer its expertise to foreign markets becomes a viable strategic option. Televisa, Mexico's largest media company, used its expertise in Spanish culture and linguistics to become the world's most prolific producer of Spanish-language soap operas. By continuing to upgrade its capabilities and learn from its experience in foreign markets, a company can sometimes transform itself into one capable of competing on a worldwide basis, as an emerging global giant. Sundaram Fasteners of India began its foray into foreign markets as a supplier of radiator caps to General Motors—an opportunity it pursued when GM first decided to outsource the production of this part. As a participant in GM's supplier network, the company learned about emerging technical standards, built its capabilities, and became one of the first Indian companies to achieve QS 9000 quality certification. With the expertise it gained and its recognition for meeting quality standards, Sundaram was then able to pursue opportunities to supply automotive parts in Japan and Europe.

Illustration Capsule 7.3 discusses the strategy behind the success of WeChat (China's most popular messenger app), in keeping out international social media rivals.

ILLUSTRATION CAPSULE 7.3

WeChat's Strategy for Defending against International Social Media Giants in China

WeChat, a Chinese social media and messenger app similar to Whatsapp, allows users to chat, post photos, shop online, and share information as well as music. It has continued to add new features, such as WeChat Games and WePay, which allow users to send money electronically, much like Venmo. The company now serves more than a billion active users, a testament to the success of its strategy.

WeChat has also had incredible success keeping out international rivals. Due to censorship and regulations in China, Chinese social media companies have an inherent advantage over foreign competitors. However, this is not why WeChat has become an indispensable part of Chinese life.

WeChat has been able to surpass international rivals because by better understanding Chinese customer needs, it can anticipate their desires. WeChat added features that allow users to check traffic cameras during rush hour, purchase tickets to movies, and book doctor appointments all on the app. Booking appointments with doctors is a feature that is wildly popular with the Chinese customer base due to common scheduling difficulties. Essentially, WeChat created its own distribution network for sought after information and goods in busy Chinese cities.

WeChat also has an understanding of local customs that international rivals can't match. In order to promote WePay, WeChat created a Chinese New Year lottery-like promotion in which users could win virtual "red envelopes" on the app. Red envelopes of money are traditionally given on Chinese New Year as presents. WePay was able to grow users from 30 to 100 million in the month

©BigTunaOnline/Shutterstock

following the promotion due to the popularity of the New Year's feature. Today, over 600 million WeChat users actively use WePay. WeChat continues to allow users to send red envelopes and has continued New Years promotions in subsequent years with success. Even Chinese companies have been bested by WeChat. Rival founder of Alibaba, Jack Ma, admitted the promotion put WeChat ahead of his company, saying it was a "pearl harbor attack" on his company. Chinese tech experts noted that the promotion was Ma's nightmare because it pushed WeChat to the forefront of Chinese person-to-person payments.

WeChat's strategy of continually developing new features also keeps the competition at bay. As China's "App for Everything," it now permeates all walks of life in China in a way that will likely continue to keep foreign competitors out.

Note: Developed with Meaghan I. Haugh.

Sources: Guilford, Gwynn. "WeChat's Little Red Envelopes are Brilliant Marketing for Mobile Payments." *Quartz,* January 29, 2014; Pasternack, Alex. "How Social Cash Made WeChat The App For Everything," *Fast Company,* January 3, 2017; "WeChat's World," *The Economist,* August 6, 2016; Stanciu, Tudor. "Why WeChat City Services Is A Game-Changing Move For Smartphone Adoption," *TechCrunch,* April 24, 2015.

KEY POINTS

1. Competing in international markets allows a company to (1) gain access to new customers; (2) achieve lower costs through greater economies of scale, learning, and increased purchasing power; (3) gain access to low-cost inputs of production; (4) further exploit its core competencies; and (5) gain access to resources and capabilities located outside the company's domestic market.

2. Strategy making is more complex for five reasons: (1) Different countries have *home-country advantages* in different industries; (2) there are location-based advantages to performing different value chain activities in different parts of the world; (3) varying political and economic risks make the business climate of some countries more favorable than others; (4) companies face the risk of adverse shifts in exchange rates when operating in foreign countries; and (5) differences in buyer tastes and preferences present a conundrum concerning the trade-off between customizing and standardizing products and services.

3. The strategies of firms that expand internationally are usually grounded in home-country advantages concerning demand conditions; factor conditions; related and supporting industries; and firm strategy, structure, and rivalry, as described by the Diamond of National Competitive Advantage framework.

4. There are five strategic options for entering foreign markets. These include maintaining a home-country production base and *exporting* goods to foreign markets, *licensing* foreign firms to produce and distribute the company's products abroad, employing a *franchising* strategy, establishing a foreign *subsidiary via an acquisition or greenfield venture,* and using *strategic alliances or other collaborative partnerships.*

5. A company must choose among three alternative approaches for competing internationally: (1) a *multidomestic strategy*—a *think-local, act-local* approach to crafting international strategy; (2) a *global strategy*—a *think-global, act-global* approach; and (3) a combination *think-global, act-local* approach, known as a *transnational strategy.* A multidomestic strategy (think local, act local) is appropriate for companies that must vary their product offerings and competitive approaches from country to country in order to accommodate different buyer preferences and market conditions. The global strategy (think global, act global) works best when there are substantial cost benefits to be gained from taking a standardized, globally integrated approach and there is little need for local responsiveness. A transnational strategy (think global, act local) is called for when there is a high need for local responsiveness as well as substantial benefits from taking a globally integrated approach. In this approach, a company strives to employ the same basic competitive strategy in all markets but still customizes its product offering and some aspect of its operations to fit local market circumstances.

6. There are three general ways in which a firm can gain competitive advantage (or offset domestic disadvantages) in international markets. One way involves locating various value chain activities among nations in a manner that lowers costs or achieves greater product differentiation. A second way draws on an international competitor's ability to extend its competitive advantage by cost-effectively sharing, replicating, or transferring its most valuable resources and capabilities across borders. A third looks for benefits from cross-border coordination that are unavailable to domestic-only competitors.

7. Two types of strategic moves are particularly suited for companies competing internationally. The first involves waging strategic offenses in international markets through *cross-subsidization*—a practice of supporting competitive offensives in one

market with resources and profits diverted from operations in another market. The second is a defensive move used to encourage *mutual restraint* among competitors when there is international *multimarket competition* by signaling that each company has the financial capability for mounting a strong counterattack if threatened. For companies with at least one highly profitable or well defended market, having a presence in a rival's key markets can be enough to deter the rival from making aggressive attacks.

8. Companies racing for global leadership have to consider competing in developing markets like the BRIC countries—Brazil, Russia, India, and China—where the business risks are considerable but the opportunities for growth are huge. To succeed in these markets, companies often have to (1) compete on the basis of low price, (2) modify aspects of the company's business model to accommodate local circumstances, and/or (3) try to change the local market to better match the way the company does business elsewhere. Profitability is unlikely to come quickly or easily in developing markets, typically because of the investments needed to alter buying habits and tastes, the increased political and economic risk, and/or the need for infrastructure upgrades. And there may be times when a company should simply stay away from certain developing markets until conditions for entry are better suited to its business model and strategy.

9. Local companies in developing-country markets can seek to compete against large international companies by (1) developing business models that exploit shortcomings in local distribution networks or infrastructure, (2) utilizing a superior understanding of local customer needs and preferences or local relationships, (3) taking advantage of competitively important qualities of the local workforce with which large international companies may be unfamiliar, (4) using acquisition strategies and rapid-growth strategies to better defend against expansion-minded international companies, or (5) transferring company expertise to cross-border markets and initiating actions to compete on an international level.

ASSURANCE OF LEARNING EXERCISES

● ● ● ●

LO 7-1, LO 7-3

1. L'Oréal markets 32 brands of cosmetics, fragrances, and hair care products in 130 countries. The company's international strategy involves manufacturing these products in 42 plants located around the world. L'Oréal's international strategy is discussed in its operations section of the company's website (**www.loreal.com/careers/who-you-can-be/operations**) and in its press releases, annual reports, and presentations. Why has the company chosen to pursue a foreign subsidiary strategy? Are there strategic advantages to global sourcing and production in the cosmetics, fragrances, and hair care products industry relative to an export strategy?

connect

LO 7-1, LO 7-3

2. Alliances, joint ventures, and mergers with foreign companies are widely used as a means of entering foreign markets. Such arrangements have many purposes, including learning about unfamiliar environments, and the opportunity to access the complementary resources and capabilities of a foreign partner. Illustration Capsule 7.1 provides an example of how Walgreens used a strategy of entering foreign markets via alliance, followed by a merger with the same entity. What was this entry strategy designed to achieve, and why would this make sense for a company like Walgreens?

3. Assume you are in charge of developing the strategy for an international company selling products in some 50 different countries around the world. One of the issues you face is whether to employ a multidomestic strategy, a global strategy, or a transnational strategy.

LO 7-2, LO 7-4

   a. If your company's product is mobile phones, which of these strategies do you think it would make better strategic sense to employ? Why?

   b. If your company's product is dry soup mixes and canned soups, would a multidomestic strategy seem to be more advisable than a global strategy or a transnational strategy? Why or why not?

   c. If your company's product is large home appliances such as washing machines, ranges, ovens, and refrigerators, would it seem to make more sense to pursue a multidomestic strategy, a global strategy, or a transnational strategy? Why?

4. Using your university library's business research resources and Internet sources, identify and discuss three key strategies that General Motors is using to compete in China.

LO 7-5, LO 7-6

EXERCISE FOR SIMULATION PARTICIPANTS

The following questions are for simulation participants whose companies operate in an international market arena. If your company competes only in a single country, then skip the questions in this section.

1. To what extent, if any, have you and your co-managers adapted your company's strategy to take shifting exchange rates into account? In other words, have you undertaken any actions to try to minimize the impact of adverse shifts in exchange rates?

LO 7-2

2. To what extent, if any, have you and your co-managers adapted your company's strategy to take geographic differences in import tariffs or import duties into account?

LO 7-2

3. Which one of the following best describes the strategic approach your company is taking in trying to compete successfully on an international basis?

LO 7-4

   • Multidomestic or think-local, act-local approach.

   • Global or think-global, act-global approach.

   • Transnational or think-global, act-local approach.

   Explain your answer and indicate two or three chief elements of your company's strategy for competing in two or more different geographic regions.

ENDNOTES

[1] Sidney G. Winter and Gabriel Szulanski, "Getting It Right the Second Time," *Harvard Business Review* 80, no. 1 (January 2002), pp. 62–69.
[2] P. Dussauge, B. Garrette, and W. Mitchell, "Learning from Competing Partners: Outcomes and Durations of Scale and Link Alliances in Europe, North America and Asia," *Strategic Management Journal* 21, no. 2 (February

2000), pp. 99–126; K. W. Glaister and P. J. Buckley, "Strategic Motives for International Alliance Formation," *Journal of Management Studies* 33, no. 3 (May 1996), pp. 301–332.
[3] Michael E. Porter, "The Competitive Advantage of Nations," *Harvard Business Review,* March–April 1990, pp. 73–93.
[4] Tom Mitchell and Avantika Chilkoti, "China Car Sales Accelerate Away from US and Brazil

in 2013," *Financial Times,* January 9, 2014, www.ft.com/cms/s/0/8c649078-78f8-11e3-b381-00144feabdc0.html#axzz2rpEqjkZO.
[5] U.S. Department of Labor, Bureau of Labor Statistics, "International Comparisons of Hourly Compensation Costs in Manufacturing 2012," August 9, 2013. (The numbers for India and China are estimates.)

[6] Sangwon Yoon, "South Korea Targets Internet Addicts; 2 Million Hooked," *Valley News,* April 25, 2010, p. C2.

[7] Joel Bleeke and David Ernst, "The Way to Win in Cross-Border Alliances," *Harvard Business Review* 69, no. 6 (November–December 1991), pp. 127-133; Gary Hamel, Yves L. Doz, and C. K. Prahalad, "Collaborate with Your Competitors—and Win," *Harvard Business Review* 67, no. 1 (January–February 1989), pp. 134–135.

[8] K. W. Glaister and P. J. Buckley, "Strategic Motives for International Alliance Formation," *Journal of Management Studies* 33, no. 3 (May 1996), pp. 301–332.

[9] Jeffrey H. Dyer, Prashant Kale, and Harbir Singh, "When to Ally and When to Acquire," *Harvard Business Review* 82, no. 7–8 (July–August 2004).

[10] Yves Doz and Gary Hamel, Alliance Advantage: *The Art of Creating Value through Partnering* (Harvard Business School Press, 1998); Rosabeth Moss Kanter, "Collaborative Advantage: The Art of the Alliance," *Harvard Business Review* 72, no. 4 (July–August 1994), pp. 96–108.

[11] Jeremy Main, "Making Global Alliances Work," *Fortune,* December 19, 1990, p. 125.

[12] C. K. Prahalad and Kenneth Lieberthal, "The End of Corporate Imperialism," *Harvard Business Review* 81, no. 8 (August 2003), pp. 109–117.

[13] Pankaj Ghemawat, "Managing Differences: The Central Challenge of Global Strategy," *Harvard Business Review* 85, no. 3 (March 2007).

[14] C. A. Bartlett and S. Ghoshal, *Managing across Borders: The Transnational Solution,* 2nd ed. (Boston: Harvard Business School Press, 1998).

[15] Lynn S. Paine, "The China Rules," *Harvard Business Review* 88, no. 6 (June 2010), pp. 103–108.

[16] C. K. Prahalad and Yves L. Doz, *The Multinational Mission: Balancing Local Demands and Global Vision* (New York: Free Press, 1987).

[17] David J. Arnold and John A. Quelch, "New Strategies in Emerging Markets," *Sloan Management Review* 40, no. 1 (Fall 1998), pp. 7–20.

[18] Tarun Khanna, Krishna G. Palepu, and Jayant Sinha, "Strategies That Fit Emerging Markets," *Harvard Business Review* 83, no. 6 (June 2005), p. 63; Arindam K. Bhattacharya and David C. Michael, "How Local Companies Keep Multinationals at Bay," *Harvard Business Review* 86, no. 3 (March 2008), pp. 94–95.

[19] Tarun Khanna and Krishna G. Palepu, "Emerging Giants: Building World-Class Companies in Developing Countries," *Harvard Business Review* 84, no. 10 (October 2006), pp. 60–69.

[20] Niroj Dawar and Tony Frost, "Competing with Giants: Survival Strategies for Local Companies in Emerging Markets," *Harvard Business Review* 77, no. 1 (January-February 1999), p. 122; Guitz Ger, "Localizing in the Global Village: Local Firms Competing in Global Markets," *California Management Review* 41, no. 4 (Summer 1999), pp. 64–84.

[21] N. Kumar, "How Emerging Giants Are Rewriting the Rules of M&A," *Harvard Business Review,* May 2009, pp. 115–121.

[22] H. Rui and G. Yip, "Foreign Acquisitions by Chinese Firms: A Strategic Intent Perspective," *Journal of World Business* 43 (2008), pp. 213–226.

chapter 8

Corporate Strategy

Diversification and
the Multibusiness Company

Learning Objectives

This chapter will help you

LO 8-1 Explain when and how business diversification can enhance shareholder value.

LO 8-2 Describe how related diversification strategies can produce cross-business strategic fit capable of delivering competitive advantage.

LO 8-3 Identify the merits and risks of unrelated diversification strategies.

LO 8-4 Use the analytic tools for evaluating a company's diversification strategy.

LO 8-5 Explain the four main corporate strategy options a diversified company can employ to improve company performance.

chapter 8

Corporate Strategy
Diversification and the Multibusiness Company

Learning Objectives

This chapter will help you

LO 8-1 Explain when and how business diversification can enhance shareholder value.

LO 8-2 Describe how related diversification strategies can produce cross-business strategic fit capable of delivering competitive advantage.

LO 8-3 Identify the merits and risks of unrelated diversification strategies.

LO 8-4 Use the analytic tools for evaluating a company's diversification strategy.

LO 8-5 Examine the four main corporate strategy options a diversified company can employ to improve company performance.

I suppose my formula might be: dream, diversify, and never miss an angle.

Walt Disney,—*Founder of the Walt Disney Company*

Make winners out of every business in your company. Don't carry losers.

Jack Welch—*Legendary CEO of General Electric*

Fit between a parent and its businesses is a two-edged sword: A good fit can create value; a bad one can destroy it.

Andrew Campbell, Michael Goold, and Marcus Alexander—*Academics, authors, and consultants*

This chapter moves up one level in the strategy-making hierarchy, from strategy-making in a single-business enterprise to strategy making in a diversified, multibusiness enterprise. Because a diversified company is a collection of individual businesses, the strategy-making task is more complicated. In a one-business company, managers have to come up with a plan for competing successfully in only a single industry environment—the result is what Chapter 2 labeled as *business strategy* (or *business-level strategy*). But in a diversified company, the strategy-making challenge involves assessing multiple industry environments and developing a *set of business strategies,* one for each industry arena in which the diversified company operates. And top executives at a diversified company must still go one step further and devise a companywide (or *corporate*) strategy for improving the performance of the company's overall business lineup and for making a rational whole out of its diversified collection of individual businesses.

In the first portion of this chapter, we describe what crafting a diversification strategy entails, when and why diversification makes good strategic sense, the various approaches to diversifying a company's business lineup, and the pros and cons of related versus unrelated diversification strategies. The second part of the chapter looks at how to evaluate the attractiveness of a diversified company's business lineup, how to decide whether it has a good diversification strategy, and the strategic options for improving a diversified company's future performance.

WHAT DOES CRAFTING A DIVERSIFICATION STRATEGY ENTAIL?

The task of crafting a diversified company's overall *corporate strategy* falls squarely in the lap of top-level executives and involves three distinct facets:

1. *Picking new industries to enter and deciding on the means of entry.* Pursuing a diversification strategy requires that management decide which new industries to enter and then, for each new industry, whether to enter by starting a new business from the ground up, by acquiring a company already in the target industry, or by forming a joint venture or strategic alliance with another company. The choice of industries depends upon on the strategic rationale (or justification) for diversifying and the type of diversification being pursued—important issues that we discuss more fully in sections to follow.

2. *Pursuing opportunities to leverage cross-business value chain relationships, where there is strategic fit, into competitive advantage.* The task here is to determine whether there are opportunities to strengthen a diversified company's businesses by such means as transferring competitively valuable resources and capabilities from one business to another, combining the related value chain activities of different businesses to achieve lower costs, sharing resources, such as the use of a powerful and well-respected brand name or an R&D facility, across multiple businesses, and encouraging knowledge sharing and collaborative activity among the businesses.

3. *Initiating actions to boost the combined performance of the corporation's collection of businesses.* Strategic options for improving the corporation's overall performance include (1) sticking closely with the existing business lineup and pursuing opportunities presented by these businesses, (2) broadening the scope of diversification by entering additional industries, (3) retrenching to a narrower scope of diversification by divesting either poorly performing businesses or those that no longer fit into management's long-range plans, and (4) broadly restructuring the entire company by divesting some businesses, acquiring others, and reorganizing, to put a whole new face on the company's business lineup.

The demanding and time-consuming nature of these four tasks explains why corporate executives generally refrain from becoming immersed in the details of crafting and executing business-level strategies. Rather, the normal procedure is to delegate lead responsibility for business strategy to the heads of each business, giving them the latitude to develop strategies suited to the particular industry environment in which their business operates and holding them accountable for producing good financial and strategic results.

WHEN TO CONSIDER DIVERSIFYING

As long as a company has plentiful opportunities for profitable growth in its present industry, there is no urgency to pursue diversification. But growth opportunities are often limited in mature industries and markets where buyer demand is flat or declining. In addition, changing industry conditions—new technologies, inroads being made by substitute products, fast-shifting buyer preferences, or intensifying competition—can undermine a company's ability to deliver ongoing gains in revenues and profits.

Consider, for example, what mobile phone companies and marketers of Voice over Internet Protocol (VoIP) have done to the revenues of long-distance providers such as AT&T, British Telecommunications, and NTT in Japan. Thus, diversifying into new industries always merits strong consideration whenever a single-business company encounters diminishing market opportunities and stagnating sales in its principal business.

The decision to diversify presents wide-ranging possibilities. A company can diversify into closely related businesses or into totally unrelated businesses. It can diversify its present revenue and earnings base to a small or major extent. It can move into one or two large new businesses or a greater number of small ones. It can achieve diversification by acquiring an existing company, starting up a new business from scratch, or forming a joint venture with one or more companies to enter new businesses. In every case, however, the decision to diversify must start with a strong economic justification for doing so.

BUILDING SHAREHOLDER VALUE: THE ULTIMATE JUSTIFICATION FOR DIVERSIFYING

Diversification must do more for a company than simply spread its business risk across various industries. In principle, diversification cannot be considered wise or justifiable unless it results in *added long-term economic value for shareholders*—value that shareholders cannot capture on their own by purchasing stock in companies in different industries or investing in mutual funds to spread their investments across several industries. A move to diversify into a new business stands little chance of building shareholder value without passing the following three **Tests of Corporate Advantage**.[1]

1. *The industry attractiveness test.* The industry to be entered through diversification must be structurally attractive (in terms of the five forces), have resource requirements that match those of the parent company, and offer good prospects for growth, profitability, and return on investment.

2. *The cost of entry test.* The cost of entering the target industry must not be so high as to exceed the potential for good profitability. A catch-22 can prevail here, however. The more attractive an industry's prospects are for growth and good long-term profitability, the more expensive it can be to enter. Entry barriers for startup companies are likely to be high in attractive industries—if barriers were low, a rush of new entrants would soon erode the potential for high profitability. And buying a well-positioned company in an appealing industry often entails a high acquisition cost that makes passing the cost of entry test less likely. Since the owners of a successful and growing company usually demand a price that reflects their business's profit prospects, it's easy for such an acquisition to fail the cost of entry test.

3. *The better-off test.* Diversifying into a new business must offer potential for the company's existing businesses and the new business to perform better together under a single corporate umbrella than they would perform operating as independent, stand-alone businesses—an effect known as **synergy**. For example, let's say that company A diversifies by purchasing company B in another industry. If A and B's consolidated profits in the years to come prove no greater than what each could have earned on its own, then A's diversification won't provide

LO 8-1

Explain when and how business diversification can enhance shareholder value.

CORE CONCEPT

To add shareholder value, a move to diversify into a new business must pass the three **Tests of Corporate Advantage:**
1. The industry attractiveness test
2. The cost of entry test
3. The better-off test

CORE CONCEPT

Creating added value for shareholders via diversification requires building a multibusiness company in which the whole is greater than the sum of its parts; such $1 + 1 = 3$ effects are called **synergy.**

its shareholders with any added value. Company A's shareholders could have achieved the same $1 + 1 = 2$ result by merely purchasing stock in company B. Diversification does not result in added long-term value for shareholders unless it produces a $1 + 1 = 3$ effect, whereby the businesses *perform better together as part of the same firm than they could have performed as independent companies.*

Diversification moves must satisfy all three tests to grow shareholder value over the long term. Diversification moves that can pass only one or two tests are suspect.

APPROACHES TO DIVERSIFYING THE BUSINESS LINEUP

The means of entering new businesses can take any of three forms: acquisition, internal startup, or joint ventures with other companies.

Diversifying by Acquisition of an Existing Business

Acquisition is a popular means of diversifying into another industry. Not only is it quicker than trying to launch a new operation, but it also offers an effective way to hurdle such entry barriers as acquiring technological know-how, establishing supplier relationships, achieving scale economies, building brand awareness, and securing adequate distribution. Acquisitions are also commonly employed to access resources and capabilities that are complementary to those of the acquiring firm and that cannot be developed readily internally. Buying an ongoing operation allows the acquirer to move directly to the task of building a strong market position in the target industry, rather than getting bogged down in trying to develop the knowledge, experience, scale of operation, and market reputation necessary for a startup entrant to become an effective competitor.

However, acquiring an existing business can prove quite expensive. The costs of acquiring another business include not only the acquisition price but also the costs of performing the due diligence to ascertain the worth of the other company, the costs of negotiating the purchase transaction, and the costs of integrating the business into the diversified company's portfolio. If the company to be acquired is a successful company, the acquisition price will include a hefty *premium* over the preacquisition value of the company for the right to control the company. For example, the $1.2 billion that luxury fashion company Michael Kors paid to acquire luxury accessories brand Jimmy Choo included a 36.5 percent premium over Jimmy Choo's share price before being put up for sale. Premiums are paid in order to convince the shareholders and managers of the target company that it is in their financial interests to approve the deal. The average premium paid by U.S. companies over the last 15 years was more often in the 20 to 25 percent range.

While acquisitions offer an enticing means for entering a new business, many fail to deliver on their promise.[2] Realizing the potential gains from an acquisition requires a successful integration of the acquired company into the culture, systems, and structure of the acquiring firm. This can be a costly and time-consuming operation. Acquisitions can also fail to deliver long-term shareholder value if the acquirer overestimates the potential gains and pays a premium in excess of the realized gains. High integration costs and excessive price premiums are two reasons that an acquisition might fail the cost of entry test. Firms with significant experience in making acquisitions are better able to avoid these types of problems.[3]

Entering a New Line of Business through Internal Development

Achieving diversification through *internal development* involves starting a new business subsidiary from scratch. Internal development has become an increasingly important way for companies to diversify and is often referred to as **corporate venturing** or *new venture development*. Although building a new business from the ground up is generally a time-consuming and uncertain process, it avoids the pitfalls associated with entry via acquisition and may allow the firm to realize greater profits in the end. It may offer a viable means of entering a new or emerging industry where there are no good acquisition candidates.

Entering a new business via internal development, however, poses some significant hurdles. An internal new venture not only has to overcome industry entry barriers but also must invest in new production capacity, develop sources of supply, hire and train employees, build channels of distribution, grow a customer base, and so on, unless the new business is quite similar to the company's existing business. The risks associated with internal startups can be substantial, and the likelihood of failure is often high. Moreover, the culture, structures, and organizational systems of some companies may impede innovation and make it difficult for corporate entrepreneurship to flourish.

Generally, internal development of a new business has appeal only when (1) the parent company already has in-house most of the resources and capabilities it needs to piece together a new business and compete effectively; (2) there is ample time to launch the business; (3) the internal cost of entry is lower than the cost of entry via acquisition; (4) adding new production capacity will not adversely impact the supply–demand balance in the industry; and (5) incumbent firms are likely to be slow or ineffective in responding to a new entrant's efforts to crack the market.

Using Joint Ventures to Achieve Diversification

Entering a new business via a joint venture can be useful in at least three types of situations.[4] First, a joint venture is a good vehicle for pursuing an opportunity that is too complex, uneconomical, or risky for one company to pursue alone. Second, joint ventures make sense when the opportunities in a new industry require a broader range of competencies and know-how than a company can marshal on its own. Many of the opportunities in satellite-based telecommunications, biotechnology, and network-based systems that blend hardware, software, and services call for the coordinated development of complementary innovations and the tackling of an intricate web of financial, technical, political, and regulatory factors simultaneously. In such cases, pooling the resources and competencies of two or more companies is a wiser and less risky way to proceed. Third, companies sometimes use joint ventures to diversify into a new industry when the diversification move entails having operations in a foreign country. However, as discussed in Chapters 6 and 7, partnering with another company can have significant drawbacks due to the potential for conflicting objectives, disagreements over how to best operate the venture, culture clashes, and so on. Joint ventures are generally the least durable of the entry options, usually lasting only until the partners decide to go their own ways.

Choosing a Mode of Entry

The choice of how best to enter a new business—whether through internal development, acquisition, or joint venture—depends on the answers to four important questions:

- Does the company have all of the resources and capabilities it requires to enter the business through internal development, or is it lacking some critical resources?
- Are there entry barriers to overcome?
- Is speed an important factor in the firm's chances for successful entry?
- Which is the least costly mode of entry, given the company's objectives?

The Question of Critical Resources and Capabilities If a firm has all the resources it needs to start up a new business or will be able to easily purchase or lease any missing resources, it may choose to enter the business via internal development. However, if missing critical resources cannot be easily purchased or leased, a firm wishing to enter a new business must obtain these missing resources through either acquisition or joint venture. Bank of America acquired Merrill Lynch to obtain critical investment banking resources and capabilities that it lacked. The acquisition of these additional capabilities complemented Bank of America's strengths in corporate banking and opened up new business opportunities for the company. Firms often acquire other companies as a way to enter foreign markets where they lack local marketing knowledge, distribution capabilities, and relationships with local suppliers or customers. McDonald's acquisition of Burghy, Italy's only national hamburger chain, offers an example.[5] If there are no good acquisition opportunities or if the firm wants to avoid the high cost of acquiring and integrating another firm, it may choose to enter via joint venture. This type of entry mode has the added advantage of spreading the risk of entering a new business, an advantage that is particularly attractive when uncertainty is high. De Beers's joint venture with the luxury goods company LVMH provided De Beers not only with the complementary marketing capabilities it needed to enter the diamond retailing business but also with a partner to share the risk.

The Question of Entry Barriers The second question to ask is whether entry barriers would prevent a new entrant from gaining a foothold and succeeding in the industry. If entry barriers are low and the industry is populated by small firms, internal development may be the preferred mode of entry. If entry barriers are high, the company may still be able to enter with ease if it has the requisite resources and capabilities for overcoming high barriers. For example, entry barriers due to reputational advantages may be surmounted by a diversified company with a widely known and trusted corporate name. But if the entry barriers cannot be overcome readily, then the only feasible entry route may be through acquisition of a well-established company. While entry barriers may also be overcome with a strong complementary joint venture, this mode is the more uncertain choice due to the lack of industry experience.

The Question of Speed Speed is another determining factor in deciding how to go about entering a new business. Acquisition is a favored mode of entry when speed is of the essence, as is the case in rapidly changing industries where fast movers can secure long-term positioning advantages. Speed is important in industries where early movers gain experience-based advantages that grow ever larger over time as they move down the learning curve. It is also important in technology-based industries where there is a race to establish an industry standard or leading technological platform. But in other cases it can be better to enter a market after the uncertainties about technology or consumer preferences have been resolved and learn from the missteps of early entrants. In these cases, when it is more advantageous to be a second-mover, joint venture or internal development may be preferred.

The Question of Comparative Cost   The question of which mode of entry is most cost-effective is a critical one, given the need for a diversification strategy to pass the cost of entry test. Acquisition can be a high-cost mode of entry due to the need to pay a premium over the share price of the target company. When the premium is high, the price of the deal will exceed the worth of the acquired company as a stand-alone business by a substantial amount. Whether it is worth it to pay that high a price will depend on how much extra value will be created by the new combination of companies in the form of synergies. Moreover, the true cost of an acquisition must include the **transaction costs** of identifying and evaluating potential targets, negotiating a price, and completing other aspects of deal making. Often, companies pay hefty fees to investment banking firms, lawyers, and others to advise them and assist with the deal-making process. Finally, the true cost must take into account the costs of integrating the acquired company into the parent company's portfolio of businesses.

Joint ventures may provide a way to conserve on such entry costs. But even here, there are organizational coordination costs and transaction costs that must be considered, including settling on the terms of the arrangement. If the partnership doesn't proceed smoothly and is not founded on trust, these costs may be significant.

> **CORE** CONCEPT
>
> **Transaction costs** are the costs of completing a business agreement or deal, over and above the price of the deal. They can include the costs of searching for an attractive target, the costs of evaluating its worth, bargaining costs, and the costs of completing the transaction.

CHOOSING THE DIVERSIFICATION PATH: RELATED VERSUS UNRELATED BUSINESSES

Once a company decides to diversify, it faces the choice of whether to diversify into **related businesses, unrelated businesses,** or some mix of both. Businesses are said to be *related* when their value chains exhibit competitively important cross-business commonalities. By this, we mean that there is a close correspondence between the businesses in terms of *how they perform* key value chain activities and *the resources and capabilities each needs* to perform those activities. The big appeal of related diversification is the opportunity to build shareholder value by leveraging these cross-business commonalities into competitive advantages for the individual businesses, thus allowing the company as a whole to perform better than just the sum of its businesses. Businesses are said to be *unrelated* when the resource requirements and key value chain activities are so dissimilar that no competitively important cross-business commonalities exist.

The next two sections explore the ins and outs of related and unrelated diversification.

> **CORE** CONCEPT
>
> **Related businesses** possess competitively valuable cross-business value chain and resource commonalities; **unrelated businesses** have dissimilar value chains and resource requirements, with no competitively important cross-business commonalities at the value chain level.

DIVERSIFICATION INTO RELATED BUSINESSES

A related diversification strategy involves building the company around businesses where there is good *strategic fit across corresponding value chain activities*. **Strategic fit** exists whenever one or more activities constituting the value chains of different businesses are sufficiently similar to present opportunities for cross-business sharing or

CORE CONCEPT

Strategic fit exists whenever one or more activities constituting the value chains of different businesses are sufficiently similar to present opportunities for cross-business sharing or transferring of the resources and capabilities that enable these activities.

CORE CONCEPT

Related diversification involves sharing or transferring *specialized* resources and capabilities. **Specialized resources and capabilities** have very specific applications and their use is limited to a restricted range of industry and business types, in contrast to **general resources and capabilities**, which can be widely applied and can be deployed across a broad range of industry and business types.

transferring of the resources and capabilities that enable these activities.[6] That is to say, it implies the existence of competitively important cross-business commonalities. Prime examples of such opportunities include

- *Transferring specialized expertise, technological know-how, or other competitively valuable strategic assets from one business's value chain to another's.* Google's ability to transfer software developers and other information technology specialists from other business applications to the development of its Android mobile operating system and Chrome operating system for PCs aided considerably in the success of these new internal ventures.
  - *Sharing costs between businesses by combining their related value chain activities into a single operation.* For instance, it is often feasible to manufacture the products of different businesses in a single plant, use the same warehouses for shipping and distribution, or have a single sales force for the products of different businesses if they are marketed to the same types of customers.
  - *Exploiting the common use of a well-known brand name.* For example, Yamaha's name in motorcycles gave the company instant credibility and recognition in entering the personal-watercraft business, allowing it to achieve a significant market share without spending large sums on advertising to establish a brand identity for the WaveRunner. Likewise, Apple's reputation for producing easy-to-operate computers was a competitive asset that facilitated the company's diversification into digital music players, smartphones, and connected watches.
- *Sharing other resources (besides brands) that support corresponding value chain activities across businesses.* When Disney acquired Marvel Comics, management saw to it that Marvel's iconic characters, such as Spiderman, Iron Man, and the Black Widow, were shared with many of the other Disney businesses, including its theme parks, retail stores, motion picture division, and video game business. (Disney's characters, starting with Mickey Mouse, have always been among the most valuable of its resources.) Automobile companies like Ford share resources such as their relationships with suppliers and dealer networks across their lines of business.
- *Engaging in cross-business collaboration and knowledge sharing to create new competitively valuable resources and capabilities.* Businesses performing closely related value chain activities may seize opportunities to join forces, share knowledge and talents, and collaborate to create altogether new capabilities (such as virtually defect-free assembly methods or increased ability to speed new products to market) that will be mutually beneficial in improving their competitiveness and business performance.

Related diversification is based on value chain matchups with respect to *key* value chain activities—those that play a central role in each business's strategy and that link to its industry's key success factors. Such matchups facilitate the sharing or transfer of the resources and capabilities that enable the performance of these activities and underlie each business's quest for competitive advantage. By facilitating the sharing or transferring of such important competitive assets, related diversification can elevate each business's prospects for competitive success.

The resources and capabilities that are leveraged in related diversification are **specialized resources and capabilities.** By this we mean that they have very *specific* applications; their use is restricted to a limited range of business contexts in which these applications are competitively relevant. Because they are adapted for particular applications, specialized resources and capabilities must be utilized by particular types of businesses operating in specific kinds of industries to have value; they have limited utility outside this designated range of industry and business applications. This is in contrast to **general resources and capabilities** (such as general management capabilities, human resource management capabilities, and general accounting services), which can be applied usefully across a wide range of industry and business types.

L'Oréal is the world's largest beauty products company, with almost $30 billion in revenues and a successful strategy of related diversification built on leveraging a highly specialized set of resources and capabilities. These include 18 dermatologic and cosmetic research centers, R&D capabilities and scientific knowledge concerning skin and hair care, patents and secret formulas for hair and skin care products, and robotic applications developed specifically for testing the safety of hair and skin care products. These resources and capabilities are highly valuable for businesses focused on products for human skin and hair—they are *specialized* to such applications, and, in consequence, they are of little or no value beyond this restricted range of applications. To leverage these resources in a way that maximizes their potential value, L'Oréal has diversified into cosmetics, hair care products, skin care products, and fragrances (but not food, transportation, industrial services, or any application area far from the narrow domain in which its specialized resources are competitively relevant). L'Oréal's businesses are related to one another on the basis of its value-generating specialized resources and capabilities and the cross-business linkages among the value chain activities that they enable.

Corning's most competitively valuable resources and capabilities are specialized to applications concerning fiber optics and specialty glass and ceramics. Over the course of its 165-year history, it has developed an unmatched understanding of fundamental glass science and related technologies in the field of optics. Its capabilities now span a variety of sophisticated technologies and include expertise in domains such as custom glass composition, specialty glass melting and forming, precision optics, high-end transmissive coatings, and optomechanical materials. Corning has leveraged these specialized capabilities into a position of global leadership in five related market segments: display technologies based on glass substrates; environmental technologies using ceramic substrates and filters; optical communications, providing optical fiber, cable and connectivity solutions; life sciences supporting research and drug discovery; and specialty materials employing advanced optics and specialty glass solutions. The market segments into which Corning has diversified are all related by their reliance on Corning's specialized capability set and by the many value chain activities that they have in common as a result.

General Mills has diversified into a closely related set of food businesses on the basis of its capabilities in the realm of "kitchen chemistry" and food production technologies. Its four U.S. retail divisions—meals and baking, cereal, snacks, and yogurt—include brands such as Old El Paso, Cascadian Farm Lucky Charms and General Mills brand cereals, Nature Valley, Annie's Organic, Pillsbury and Betty Crocker, and Yoplait yogurt. Earlier it had diversified into restaurant businesses on the mistaken notion that all food businesses were related. By exiting these businesses in the mid-1990s, the company was able to improve its overall profitability and strengthen its position in its remaining businesses. The lesson from its experience—and a takeaway for the managers of any diversified company—is that *it is not product relatedness that defines a well-crafted related diversification strategy.* Rather, *the businesses must be related in terms of their key value chain activities and the specialized resources and capabilities that enable these activities.*[7] An example is Citizen Watch Company, whose products appear to be different (watches, machine tools, and flat panel displays) but are related in terms of their common reliance on miniaturization know-how and advanced precision technologies.

While companies pursuing related diversification strategies may also have opportunities to share or transfer their *general* resources and capabilities (e.g., information systems; human resource management practices; accounting and tax services; budgeting, planning, and financial reporting systems; expertise in legal and regulatory affairs; and fringe-benefit management systems), *the most competitively valuable opportunities for resource sharing or transfer always come from leveraging their specialized resources and capabilities.* The reason for this is that specialized resources and capabilities drive the key value-creating activities that both connect the businesses (at points along their value chains where there is strategic fit) and link to the key success factors in the markets where they are competitively relevant. Figure 8.1 illustrates the range of opportunities to share and/or transfer specialized resources and capabilities among the value chain activities of related businesses. It is important to recognize that *even though general resources and capabilities may be also shared by multiple business units, such resource sharing alone cannot form the backbone of a strategy keyed to related diversification.*

Identifying Cross-Business Strategic Fit along the Value Chain

Cross-business strategic fit can exist anywhere along the value chain—in R&D and technology activities, in supply chain activities and relationships with suppliers, in manufacturing, in sales and marketing, in distribution activities, or in customer service activities.[8]

FIGURE 8.1   Related Businesses Provide Opportunities to Benefit from Competitively Valuable Strategic Fit

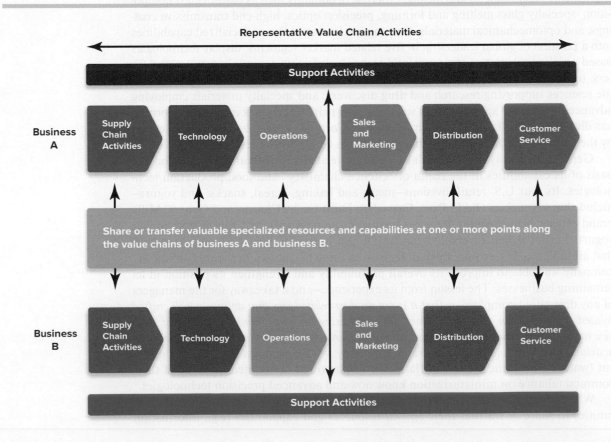

Strategic Fit in Supply Chain Activities   Businesses with strategic fit with respect to their supply chain activities can perform better together because of the potential for transferring skills in procuring materials, sharing resources and capabilities in logistics, collaborating with common supply chain partners, and/or increasing leverage with shippers in securing volume discounts on incoming parts and components. Dell's strategic partnerships with leading suppliers of microprocessors, circuit boards, disk drives, memory chips, flat-panel displays, wireless capabilities, long-life batteries, and other PC-related components have been an important element of the company's strategy to diversify into servers, data storage devices, networking components, plasma TVs, and printers—products that include many components common to PCs and that can be sourced from the same strategic partners that provide Dell with PC components.

Strategic Fit in R&D and Technology Activities   Businesses with strategic fit in R&D or technology development perform better together than apart because of potential cost savings in R&D, shorter times in getting new products to market, and more innovative products or processes. Moreover, technological advances in one business can lead to increased sales for both. Technological innovations have been the driver behind the efforts of cable TV companies to diversify into high-speed Internet access (via the use of cable modems) and, further, to explore providing local and long-distance telephone service to residential and commercial customers either through a single wire or by means of Voice over Internet Protocol (VoIP) technology. These diversification efforts have resulted in companies such as DISH, Network and Comcast (through its XFINITY subsidiary) now offering TV, Internet, and phone bundles.

Manufacturing-Related Strategic Fit   Cross-business strategic fit in manufacturing-related activities can be exploited when a diversifier's expertise in quality control and cost-efficient production methods can be transferred to another business. When Emerson Electric diversified into the chain-saw business, it transferred its expertise in low-cost manufacture to its newly acquired Beaird-Poulan business division. The transfer drove Beaird-Poulan's new strategy—to be the low-cost provider of chain-saw products—and fundamentally changed the way Beaird-Poulan chain saws were designed and manufactured. Another benefit of production-related value chain commonalities is the ability to consolidate production into a smaller number of plants and significantly reduce overall production costs. When snowmobile maker Bombardier diversified into motorcycles, it was able to set up motorcycle assembly lines in the manufacturing facility where it was assembling snowmobiles. When Smucker's acquired Procter & Gamble's Jif peanut butter business, it was able to combine the manufacture of the two brands of peanut butter products while gaining greater leverage with vendors in purchasing its peanut supplies.

Strategic Fit in Sales and Marketing Activities   Various cost-saving opportunities spring from diversifying into businesses with closely related sales and marketing activities. When the products are sold directly to the same customers, sales costs can often be reduced by using a single sales force instead of having two different salespeople call on the same customer. The products of related businesses can be promoted at the same website and included in the same media ads and sales brochures. There may be opportunities to reduce costs by consolidating order processing and billing and by using common promotional tie-ins. When global power toolmaker Black & Decker acquired Vector Products, it was able to use its own global sales force to sell the newly acquired

Vector power inverters, vehicle battery chargers, and rechargeable spotlights because the types of customers that carried its power tools (discounters like Kmart, home centers, and hardware stores) also stocked the types of products produced by Vector.

A second category of benefits arises when different businesses use similar sales and marketing approaches. In such cases, there may be competitively valuable opportunities to transfer selling, merchandising, advertising, and product differentiation skills from one business to another. Procter & Gamble's product lineup includes Pampers diapers, Olay beauty products, Tide laundry detergent, Crest toothpaste, Charmin toilet tissue, Gillette razors and blades, Vicks cough and cold products Oral-B toothbrushes, and Head & Shoulders shampoo. All of these have different competitors and different supply chain and production requirements, but they all move through the same wholesale distribution systems, are sold in common retail settings to the same shoppers, and require the same marketing and merchandising skills.

Distribution-Related Strategic Fit   Businesses with closely related distribution activities can perform better together than apart because of potential cost savings in sharing the same distribution facilities or using many of the same wholesale distributors and retail dealers. When Conair Corporation acquired Allegro Manufacturing's travel bag and travel accessory business, it was able to consolidate its own distribution centers for hair dryers and curling irons with those of Allegro, thereby generating cost savings for both businesses. Likewise, since Conair products and Allegro's neck rests, ear plugs, luggage tags, and toiletry kits were sold by the same types of retailers (discount stores, supermarket chains, and drugstore chains), Conair was able to convince many of the retailers not carrying Allegro products to take on the line.

Strategic Fit in Customer Service Activities   Strategic fit with respect to customer service activities can enable cost savings or differentiation advantages, just as it does along other points of the value chain. For example, cost savings may come from consolidating after-sale service and repair organizations for the products of closely related businesses into a single operation. Likewise, different businesses can often use the same customer service infrastructure. For instance, an electric utility that diversifies into natural gas, water, appliance repair services, and home security services can use the same customer data network, the same call centers and local offices, the same billing and accounting systems, and the same customer service infrastructure to support all of its products and services. Through the transfer of best practices in customer service across a set of related businesses or through the sharing of resources such as proprietary information about customer preferences, a multi-business company can also create a differentiation advantage through higher-quality customer service.

Strategic Fit, Economies of Scope, and Competitive Advantage

Strategic fit in the value chain activities of a diversified corporation's different businesses opens up opportunities for **economies of scope**—a concept distinct from *economies of scale*. Economies of *scale* are cost savings that accrue directly from a larger-sized operation—for example, unit costs may be lower in a large plant than in a small plant. In contrast, economies of scope are cost savings that flow from operating in multiple businesses (a larger *scope* of operation). *They stem directly* *from strategic fit along the value chains of related businesses,* which in turn enables the businesses to share resources or to transfer them from business to business at low cost. Significant scope economies are open only to firms engaged in related diversification, since they are the result of related businesses performing R&D together, transferring managers from one business to another, using common manufacturing or distribution facilities, sharing a common sales force or dealer network, using the same established brand name, and the like. *The greater the cross-business economies associated with resource sharing and transfer, the greater the potential for a related diversification strategy to give the individual businesses of a multibusiness enterprise a cost advantage over rivals.*

From Strategic Fit to Competitive Advantage, Added Profitability, and Gains in Shareholder Value The cost advantage from economies of scope is due to the fact that resource sharing allows a multibusiness firm to spread resource costs across its businesses and to avoid the expense of having to acquire and maintain duplicate sets of resources—one for each business. But related diversified companies can benefit from strategic fit in other ways as well.

Sharing or transferring valuable specialized assets among the company's businesses can help each business perform its value chain activities more proficiently. This translates into competitive advantage for the businesses in one or two basic ways: (1) The businesses can contribute to greater efficiency and lower costs relative to their competitors, and/or (2) they can provide a basis for differentiation so that customers are willing to pay relatively more for the businesses' goods and services. In either or both of these ways, a firm with a well-executed related diversification strategy can boost the chances of its businesses attaining a competitive advantage.

The greater the relatedness among a diversified company's businesses, the bigger a company's window for converting strategic fit into competitive advantage. The strategic and business logic is compelling: Capturing the benefits of strategic fit along the value chains of its related businesses gives a diversified company a clear path to achieving competitive advantage over undiversified competitors and competitors whose own diversification efforts don't offer equivalent strategic-fit benefits.[9] Such competitive advantage potential provides a company with a dependable basis for earning profits and a return on investment that exceeds what the company's businesses could earn as stand-alone enterprises. Converting the competitive advantage potential into greater profitability is what fuels $1 + 1 = 3$ gains in shareholder value—the necessary outcome for satisfying the *better-off test* and proving the business merit of a company's diversification effort.

There are five things to bear in mind here:

> Diversifying into related businesses where competitively valuable strategic-fit benefits can be captured puts a company's businesses in position to perform better financially as part of the company than they could have performed as independent enterprises, thus providing a clear avenue for increasing shareholder value and satisfying the better-off test.

1. Capturing cross-business strategic-fit benefits via a strategy of related diversification builds shareholder value in ways that shareholders cannot undertake by simply owning a portfolio of stocks of companies in different industries.

2. The capture of cross-business strategic-fit benefits is possible only via a strategy of related diversification.

3. The greater the relatedness among a diversified company's businesses, the bigger the company's window for converting strategic fit into competitive advantage for its businesses.

4. The benefits of cross-business strategic fit come from the transferring or sharing of competitively valuable resources and capabilities among the businesses—resources

The Kraft–Heinz Merger: Pursuing the Benefits of Cross-Business Strategic Fit

The $62.6 billion merger between Kraft and Heinz that was finalized in the summer of 2015 created the third largest food and beverage company in North America and the fifth largest in the world. It was a merger predicated on the idea that the strategic fit between these two companies was such that they could create more value as a combined enterprise than they could as two separate companies. As a combined enterprise, Kraft Heinz would be able to exploit its cross-business value chain activities and resource similarities to more efficiently produce, distribute, and sell profitable processed food products.

Kraft and Heinz products share many of the same raw materials (milk, sugar, salt, wheat, etc.), which allows the new company to leverage its increased bargaining power as a larger business to get better deals with suppliers, using strategic fit in supply chain activities to achieve lower input costs and greater inbound efficiencies. Moreover, because both of these brands specialized in prepackaged foods, there is ample manufacturing-related strategic fit in production processes and packaging technologies that allow the new company to trim and streamline manufacturing operations.

Their distribution-related strategic fit will allow for the complete integration of distribution channels and transportation networks, resulting in greater outbound efficiencies and a reduction in travel time for products moving from factories to stores. The Kraft Heinz Company is currently looking to leverage Heinz's global platform to expand Kraft's products internationally. By utilizing Heinz's already highly developed global distribution network and brand familiarity (key specialized resources), Kraft can more easily expand into the global

©Scott Olson/Getty Images

market of prepackaged and processed food. Because these two brands are sold at similar types of retail stores (supermarket chains, wholesale retailers, and local grocery stores), they are now able to claim even more shelf space with the increased bargaining power of the combined company.

Strategic fit in sales and marketing activities will allow the company to develop coordinated and more effective advertising campaigns. Toward this aim, the Kraft Heinz Company is moving to consolidate its marketing capabilities under one marketing firm. Also, by combining R&D teams, the Kraft Heinz Company could come out with innovative products that may appeal more to the growing number of on-the-go and health-conscious buyers in the market. Many of these potential and predicted synergies for the Kraft Heinz Company have yet to be realized, since merger integration activities always take time.

Note: Developed with Maria Hart.

Sources: www.forbes.com/sites/paulmartyn/2015/03/31/heinz-and-kraft-merger-makes-supply-management-sense/; fortune.com/2015/03/25/kraft-mess-how-heinz-deal-helps/; www.nytimes.com/2015/03/26/business/dealbook/kraft-and-heinz-to-merge.html?_r=2; company websites (accessed December 3, 2015).

and capabilities that are *specialized* to certain applications and have value only in specific types of industries and businesses.

5. The benefits of cross-business strategic fit are not automatically realized when a company diversifies into related businesses; *the benefits materialize only after management has successfully pursued internal actions to capture them.*

Illustration Capsule 8.1 describes the merger of Kraft Foods Group, Inc. with the H. J. Heinz Holding Corporation, in pursuit of the strategic-fit benefits of a related diversification strategy.

DIVERSIFICATION INTO UNRELATED BUSINESSES

Achieving cross-business strategic fit is not a motivation for unrelated diversification. Companies that pursue a strategy of unrelated diversification often exhibit a willingness to diversify into *any business in any industry* where senior managers see an opportunity to realize consistently good financial results. Such companies are frequently labeled *conglomerates* because their business interests range broadly across diverse industries. Companies engaged in unrelated diversification nearly always enter new businesses by acquiring an established company rather than by forming a startup subsidiary within their own corporate structures or participating in joint ventures.

With a strategy of unrelated diversification, an acquisition is deemed to have potential if it passes the industry-attractiveness and cost of entry tests and if it has good prospects for attractive financial performance. Thus, with an unrelated diversification strategy, company managers spend much time and effort screening acquisition candidates and evaluating the pros and cons of keeping or divesting existing businesses, using such criteria as

- Whether the business can meet corporate targets for profitability and return on investment.
- Whether the business is in an industry with attractive growth potential.
- Whether the business is big enough to contribute *significantly* to the parent firm's bottom line.

But the key to successful unrelated diversification is to go beyond these considerations and *ensure that the strategy passes the better-off test as well.* This test requires more than just growth in revenues; it requires *growth in profits*—beyond what could be achieved by a mutual fund or a holding company that owns shares of the businesses without adding any value. Unless the combination of businesses is more profitable together under the corporate umbrella than they are apart as independent businesses, *the strategy cannot create economic value for shareholders.* And unless it does so, there is *no real justification for unrelated diversification,* since top executives have a fiduciary responsibility to maximize long-term shareholder value for the company's owners (its shareholders).

A willingness to diversify into any business in any industry is unlikely to result in successful unrelated diversification. The key to success even for unrelated diversification is to create economic value for shareholders.

Building Shareholder Value via Unrelated Diversification

Given the absence of cross-business strategic fit with which to create competitive advantages, building shareholder value via unrelated diversification ultimately hinges on the ability of the parent company to improve its businesses (and make the combination *better off*) via other means. Critical to this endeavor is the role that the parent company plays as a *corporate parent.*[10] To the extent that a company has strong *parenting capabilities*—capabilities that involve nurturing, guiding, grooming, and governing constituent businesses—a corporate parent can propel its businesses forward and help them gain ground over their market rivals. Corporate parents also contribute to the competitiveness of their unrelated businesses by sharing or transferring *general resources and capabilities* across the businesses—competitive assets that have utility in *any type* of industry and that can be leveraged across a wide range of business types as a result. Examples of the kinds of general resources that a corporate parent leverages in unrelated diversification include the corporation's reputation, credit rating, and access to financial markets; governance mechanisms; management training programs;

a corporate ethics program; a central data and communications center; shared administrative resources such as public relations and legal services; and common systems for functions such as budgeting, financial reporting, and quality control.

The Benefits of Astute Corporate Parenting One of the most important ways that corporate parents contribute to the success of their businesses is by offering high-level oversight and guidance.[11] The top executives of a large diversified corporation have among them many years of accumulated experience in a variety of business settings and can often contribute expert problem-solving skills, creative strategy suggestions, and first-rate advice and guidance on how to improve competitiveness and financial performance to the heads of the company's various business subsidiaries. This is especially true in the case of newly acquired, smaller businesses. Particularly astute high-level guidance from corporate executives can help the subsidiaries perform better than they would otherwise be able to do through the efforts of the business unit heads alone. The outstanding leadership of Royal Little, the founder of Textron, was a major reason that the company became an exemplar of the unrelated diversification strategy while he was CEO. Little's bold moves transformed the company from its origins as a small textile manufacturer into a global powerhouse known for its Bell helicopters, Cessna aircraft, and a host of other strong brands in a wide array of industries. Norm Wesley, a former CEO of the conglomerate Fortune Brands, is similarly credited with driving the sharp rise in the company's stock price while he was at the helm. Under his leadership, Fortune Brands became the $7 billion maker of products ranging from spirits (e.g., Jim Beam bourbon and rye, Gilbey's gin and vodka, Courvoisier cognac) to golf products (e.g., Titleist golf balls and clubs, FootJoy golf shoes and apparel, Scotty Cameron putters) to hardware (e.g., Moen faucets, American Lock security devices). (Fortune Brands has since been converted into two separate entities, Beam Inc. and Fortune Brands Home & Security.)

> **CORE CONCEPT**
>
> **Corporate parenting** refers to the role that a diversified corporation plays in nurturing its component businesses through the provision of top management expertise, disciplined control, financial resources, and other types of general resources and capabilities such as long-term planning systems, business development skills, management development processes, and incentive systems.

Corporate parents can also create added value for their businesses by providing them with other types of general resources that lower the operating costs of the individual businesses or that enhance their operating effectiveness. The administrative resources located at a company's corporate headquarters are a prime example. They typically include legal services, accounting expertise and tax services, and other elements of the administrative infrastructure, such as risk management capabilities, information technology resources, and public relations capabilities. Providing individual businesses with general support resources such as these creates value by *lowering companywide overhead costs,* since each business would otherwise have to duplicate the centralized activities.

> An **umbrella brand** is a corporate brand name that can be applied to a wide assortment of business types. As such, it is a type of general resource that can be leveraged in unrelated diversification.

Corporate brands that do not connote any specific type of product are another type of general corporate resource that can be shared among unrelated businesses. General Electric, for example, has successfully applied its GE brand to such unrelated products and businesses as appliances (GE refrigerators, ovens, and washer-dryers), medical products and health care (GE Healthcare), jet engines (GE Aviation), and power and water technologies (GE Power and Water). Corporate brands that are applied in this fashion are sometimes called **umbrella brands.** Utilizing a well-known corporate name (GE) in a diversified company's individual businesses has the potential not only to lower costs (by spreading the fixed cost of developing and maintaining the brand over many businesses) but also to enhance each business's customer value proposition by linking its products to a name that consumers trust. In similar fashion, a corporation's reputation for well-crafted products, for product reliability, or for trustworthiness can lead to greater customer willingness to purchase the products of a wider range of a diversified company's businesses. Incentive systems, financial control systems, and a company's culture are other types of general corporate resources that may prove useful in enhancing the daily operations of a diverse set of businesses. The parenting activities of corporate executives may also include recruiting and hiring talented managers to run individual businesses.

We discuss two other commonly employed ways for corporate parents to add value to their unrelated businesses next.

Judicious Cross-Business Allocation of Financial Resources By reallocating surplus cash flows from some businesses to fund the capital requirements of other businesses—in essence, having the company serve as an *internal capital market*—corporate parents may also be able to create value. Such actions can be particularly important in times when credit is unusually tight (such as in the wake of the worldwide banking crisis that began in 2008) or in economies with less well developed capital markets. Under these conditions, with strong financial resources a corporate parent can add value by shifting funds from business units generating excess cash (more than they need to fund their own operating requirements and new capital investment opportunities) to other, cash-short businesses with appealing growth prospects. A parent company's ability to function as its own internal capital market enhances overall corporate performance and increases shareholder value to the extent that (1) its top managers have better access to information about investment opportunities internal to the firm than do external financiers or (2) it can provide funds that would otherwise be unavailable due to poor financial market conditions.

Acquiring and Restructuring Undervalued Companies Another way for parent companies to add value to unrelated businesses is by acquiring weakly performing companies at a bargain price and then *restructuring* their operations in ways that produce sometimes dramatic increases in profitability. **Restructuring** refers to overhauling and streamlining the operations of a business—combining plants with excess capacity, selling off underutilized assets, reducing unnecessary expenses, revamping its product offerings, consolidating administrative functions to reduce overhead costs, and otherwise improving the operating efficiency and profitability of a company. Restructuring generally involves transferring seasoned managers to the newly acquired business, either to replace the top layers of management or to step in temporarily until the business is returned to profitability or is well on its way to becoming a major market contender.

Restructuring is often undertaken when a diversified company acquires a new business that is performing well below levels that the corporate parent believes are achievable. Diversified companies that have proven *turnaround capabilities* in rejuvenating weakly performing companies can often apply these capabilities in a relatively wide range of unrelated industries. Newell Brands (whose diverse product line includes Rubbermaid food storage, Sharpie pens, Graco strollers and car seats, Goody hair accessories, Calphalon cookware, and Yankee Candle—all businesses with different value chain activities) developed such a strong set of turnaround capabilities that the company was said to "Newellize" the businesses it acquired.

Successful unrelated diversification strategies based on restructuring require the parent company to have considerable expertise in identifying underperforming target companies and in negotiating attractive acquisition prices so that each acquisition passes the cost of entry test. The capabilities in this regard of Lord James Hanson and Lord Gordon White, who headed up the storied British conglomerate Hanson Trust, played a large part in Hanson Trust's impressive record of profitability.

CORE CONCEPT

Restructuring refers to overhauling and streamlining the activities of a business—combining plants with excess capacity, selling off underutilized assets, reducing unnecessary expenses, and otherwise improving the productivity and profitability of a company.

The Path to Greater Shareholder Value through Unrelated Diversification

For a strategy of unrelated diversification to produce companywide financial results above and beyond what the businesses could generate operating as standalone entities, corporate executives must do three things to pass the three Tests of Corporate Advantage:

1. Diversify into industries where the businesses can produce consistently good earnings and returns on investment (to satisfy the industry-attractiveness test).
2. Negotiate favorable acquisition prices (to satisfy the cost of entry test).
3. Do a superior job of corporate parenting via high-level managerial oversight and resource sharing, financial resource allocation and portfolio management, and/or the restructuring of underperforming businesses (to satisfy the better-off test).

> **CORE CONCEPT**
>
> A diversified company has a **parenting advantage** when it is more able than other companies to boost the combined performance of its individual businesses through high-level guidance, general oversight, and other corporate-level contributions.

The best corporate parents understand the nature and value of the kinds of resources at their command and know how to leverage them effectively across their businesses. Those that are able to create more value in their businesses than other diversified companies have what is called a **parenting advantage.** When a corporation has a parenting advantage, its top executives have the best chance of being able to craft and execute an unrelated diversification strategy that can satisfy all three Tests of Corporate Advantage and truly enhance long-term economic shareholder value.

The Drawbacks of Unrelated Diversification

Unrelated diversification strategies have two important negatives that undercut the pluses: very demanding managerial requirements and limited competitive advantage potential.

Demanding Managerial Requirements   Successfully managing a set of fundamentally different businesses operating in fundamentally different industry and competitive environments is a challenging and exceptionally difficult proposition.[12] Consider, for example, that corporations like General Electric, ITT, Mitsubishi, and Bharti Enterprises have dozens of business subsidiaries making hundreds and sometimes thousands of products. While headquarters executives can glean information about an industry from third-party sources, ask lots of questions when making occasional visits to the operations of the different businesses, and do their best to learn about the company's different businesses, they still remain heavily dependent on briefings from business unit heads and on "managing by the numbers"—that is, keeping a close track on the financial and operating results of each subsidiary. Managing by the numbers works well enough when business conditions are normal and the heads of the various business units are capable of consistently meeting their numbers. But problems arise if things start to go awry in a business and corporate management has to get deeply involved in the problems of a business it does not know much about. Because every business tends to encounter rough sledding at some juncture, unrelated diversification is thus a somewhat risky strategy from a managerial perspective.[13] Just one or two unforeseen problems or big strategic mistakes—which are much more likely without close corporate oversight—can cause a precipitous drop in corporate earnings and crash the parent company's stock price.

Hence, competently overseeing a set of widely diverse businesses can turn out to be much harder than it sounds. In practice, comparatively few companies have proved that they have top-management capabilities that are up to the task. There are far more companies whose corporate executives have failed at delivering consistently good financial results with an unrelated diversification strategy than there are companies with corporate executives who have been successful.[14] Unless a company truly has a parenting advantage, the odds are that the result of unrelated diversification will be $1 + 1 = 2$ or even less.

Limited Competitive Advantage Potential   The second big negative is that *unrelated diversification offers only a limited potential for competitive advantage beyond what each individual business can generate on its own.* Unlike a related diversification strategy, unrelated diversification provides no cross-business strategic-fit benefits that allow each business to perform its key value chain activities in a more efficient and effective manner. A cash-rich corporate parent pursuing unrelated diversification can provide its subsidiaries with much-needed capital, may achieve economies of scope in activities relying on general corporate resources, may extend an umbrella brand and may even offer some managerial know-how to help resolve problems in particular business units, but otherwise it has little to add in the way of enhancing the competitive strength of its individual business units. In comparison to the highly specialized resources that facilitate related diversification, the general resources that support unrelated diversification tend to be relatively low value, for the simple reason that they are more common. Unless they are of exceptionally high quality (such as GE's world-renowned general management capabilities and umbrella brand or Newell Rubbermaid's turnaround capabilities), resources and capabilities that are general in nature are less likely to provide a significant source of competitive advantage for the businesses of diversified companies. Without the competitive advantage potential of strategic fit in competitively important value chain activities, consolidated performance of an unrelated group of businesses may not be very much more than the sum of what the individual business units could achieve if they were independent, in most circumstances.

> Relying solely on leveraging general resources and the expertise of corporate executives to wisely manage a set of unrelated businesses is a much weaker foundation for enhancing shareholder value than is a strategy of related diversification.

Misguided Reasons for Pursuing Unrelated Diversification

Companies sometimes pursue unrelated diversification for reasons that are entirely misguided. These include the following:

- *Risk reduction.* Spreading the company's investments over a set of diverse industries to spread risk cannot create long-term shareholder value since the company's shareholders can more flexibly (and more efficiently) reduce their exposure to risk by investing in a diversified portfolio of stocks and bonds.
- *Growth.* While unrelated diversification may enable a company to achieve rapid or continuous growth, firms that pursue growth for growth's sake are unlikely to maximize shareholder value. Only *profitable growth*—the kind that comes from creating added value for shareholders—can justify a strategy of unrelated diversification.
- *Stabilization.* Managers sometimes pursue broad diversification in the hope that market downtrends in some of the company's businesses will be partially offset by cyclical upswings in its other businesses, thus producing somewhat less earnings volatility. In actual practice, however, there's no convincing evidence that the consolidated profits of firms with unrelated diversification strategies are more stable or less subject to reversal in periods of recession and economic stress than the profits of firms with related diversification strategies.

- *Managerial motives.* Unrelated diversification can provide benefits to managers such as higher compensation (which tends to increase with firm size and degree of diversification) and reduced their unemployment risk. Pursuing diversification for these reasons will likely reduce shareholder value and violate managers' fiduciary responsibilities.

> Only profitable growth—the kind that comes from creating added value for shareholders—can justify a strategy of unrelated diversification.

Because unrelated diversification strategies *at their best* have only a limited potential for creating long-term economic value for shareholders, it is essential that managers not compound this problem by taking a misguided approach toward unrelated diversification, in pursuit of objectives that are more likely to destroy shareholder value than create it.

COMBINATION RELATED–UNRELATED DIVERSIFICATION STRATEGIES

There's nothing to preclude a company from diversifying into both related and unrelated businesses. Indeed, in actual practice the business makeup of diversified companies varies considerably. Some diversified companies are really *dominant-business enterprises*—one major "core" business accounts for 50 to 80 percent of total revenues and a collection of small related or unrelated businesses accounts for the remainder. Some diversified companies are *narrowly diversified* around a few (two to five) related or unrelated businesses. Others are *broadly diversified* around a wide-ranging collection of related businesses, unrelated businesses, or a mixture of both. A number of multibusiness enterprises have diversified into unrelated areas but have a collection of related businesses within each area—thus giving them a business portfolio consisting of *several unrelated groups of related businesses.* There's ample room for companies to customize their diversification strategies to incorporate elements of both related and unrelated diversification, as may suit their own competitive asset profile and strategic vision. *Combination related-unrelated diversification strategies have particular appeal for companies with a mix of valuable competitive assets, covering the spectrum from general to specialized resources and capabilities.*

Figure 8.2 shows the range of alternatives for companies pursuing diversification.

EVALUATING THE STRATEGY OF A DIVERSIFIED COMPANY

> ● **LO 8-4**
>
> Use the analytic tools for evaluating a company's diversification strategy.

Strategic analysis of diversified companies builds on the concepts and methods used for single-business companies. But there are some additional aspects to consider and a couple of new analytic tools to master. The procedure for evaluating the pluses and minuses of a diversified company's strategy and deciding what actions to take to improve the company's performance involves six steps:

1. Assessing the attractiveness of the industries the company has diversified into, both individually and as a group.

2. Assessing the competitive strength of the company's business units and drawing a nine-cell matrix to simultaneously portray industry attractiveness and business unit competitive strength.

FIGURE 8.2   Three Strategy Options for Pursuing Diversification

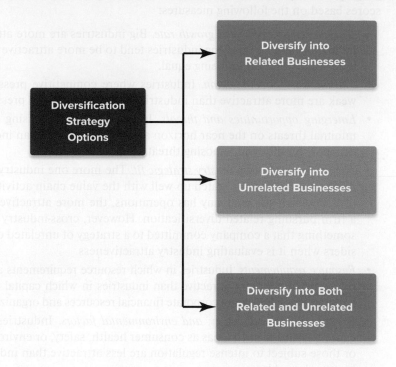

3. Evaluating the extent of cross-business strategic fit along the value chains of the company's various business units.
4. Checking whether the firm's resources fit the requirements of its present business lineup.
5. Ranking the performance prospects of the businesses from best to worst and determining what the corporate parent's priorities should be in allocating resources to its various businesses.
6. Crafting new strategic moves to improve overall corporate performance.

The core concepts and analytic techniques underlying each of these steps merit further discussion.

Step 1: Evaluating Industry Attractiveness

A principal consideration in evaluating the caliber of a diversified company's strategy is the attractiveness of the industries in which it has business operations. Several questions arise:

1. Does each industry the company has diversified into represent a good market for the company to be in—does it pass the industry-attractiveness test?
2. Which of the company's industries are most attractive, and which are least attractive?
3. How appealing is the whole group of industries in which the company has invested?

The more attractive the industries (both individually and as a group) that a diversified company is in, the better its prospects for good long-term performance.

Calculating Industry-Attractiveness Scores   A simple and reliable analytic tool for gauging industry attractiveness involves calculating quantitative industry-attractiveness scores based on the following measures:

- *Market size and projected growth rate.* Big industries are more attractive than small industries, and fast-growing industries tend to be more attractive than slow-growing industries, other things being equal.
- *The intensity of competition.* Industries where competitive pressures are relatively weak are more attractive than industries where competitive pressures are strong.
- *Emerging opportunities and threats.* Industries with promising opportunities and minimal threats on the near horizon are more attractive than industries with modest opportunities and imposing threats.
- *The presence of cross-industry strategic fit.* The more one industry's value chain and resource requirements match up well with the value chain activities of other industries in which the company has operations, the more attractive the industry is to a firm pursuing related diversification. However, cross-industry strategic fit is not something that a company committed to a strategy of unrelated diversification considers when it is evaluating industry attractiveness.
- *Resource requirements.* Industries in which resource requirements are within the company's reach are more attractive than industries in which capital and other resource requirements could strain corporate financial resources and organizational capabilities.
- *Social, political, regulatory, and environmental factors.* Industries that have significant problems in such areas as consumer health, safety, or environmental pollution or those subject to intense regulation are less attractive than industries that do not have such problems.
- *Industry profitability.* Industries with healthy profit margins and high rates of return on investment are generally more attractive than industries with historically low or unstable profits.

Each attractiveness measure is then assigned a weight reflecting its relative importance in determining an industry's attractiveness, since not all attractiveness measures are equally important. The intensity of competition in an industry should nearly always carry a high weight (say, 0.20 to 0.30). Strategic-fit considerations should be assigned a high weight in the case of companies with related diversification strategies; but for companies with an unrelated diversification strategy, strategic fit with other industries may be dropped from the list of attractiveness measures altogether. The importance weights must add up to 1.

Finally, each industry is rated on each of the chosen industry-attractiveness measures, using a rating scale of 1 to 10 (where a *high* rating signifies *high* attractiveness, and a *low* rating signifies *low* attractiveness). *Keep in mind here that the more intensely competitive an industry is, the lower the attractiveness rating for that industry.* Likewise, the more the resource requirements associated with being in a particular industry are beyond the parent company's reach, the lower the attractiveness rating. On the other hand, the presence of good cross-industry strategic fit should be given a very high attractiveness rating, since there is good potential for competitive advantage and added shareholder value. Weighted attractiveness scores are then calculated by multiplying the industry's rating on each measure by the corresponding weight. For example, a rating of 8 times a weight of 0.25 gives a weighted attractiveness score of 2. The sum of the weighted scores for all the attractiveness measures provides an overall industry-attractiveness score. This procedure is illustrated in Table 8.1.

TABLE 8.1 Calculating Weighted Industry-Attractiveness Scores

Industry-Attractiveness Measure	Importance Weight	Industry A		Industry B		Industry C	
		Attractiveness Rating*	Weighted Score	Attractiveness Rating*	Weighted Score	Attractiveness Rating*	Weighted Score
Market size and projected growth rate	0.10	8	0.80	3	0.30	5	0.50
Intensity of competition	0.25	8	2.00	2	0.50	5	1.25
Emerging opportunities and threats	0.10	6	0.60	5	0.50	4	0.40
Cross-industry strategic fit	0.30	8	2.40	2	0.60	3	0.90
Resource requirements	0.10	5	0.50	5	0.50	4	0.40
Social, political, regulatory, and environmental factors	0.05	8	0.40	3	0.15	7	1.05
Industry profitability	0.10	5	0.50	4	0.40	6	0.60
Sum of importance weights	1.00						
Weighted overall industry-attractiveness scores			7.20		2.95		5.10

*Rating scale: 1 = very unattractive to company; 10 = very attractive to company.

Interpreting the Industry-Attractiveness Scores Industries with a score much below 5 probably do not pass the attractiveness test. If a company's industry-attractiveness scores are all above 5, it is probably fair to conclude that the group of industries the company operates in is attractive as a whole. But the group of industries takes on a decidedly lower degree of attractiveness as the number of industries with scores below 5 increases, especially if industries with low scores account for a sizable fraction of the company's revenues.

For a diversified company to be a strong performer, a substantial portion of its revenues and profits must come from business units with relatively high attractiveness scores. It is particularly important that a diversified company's principal businesses be in industries with a good outlook for growth and above-average profitability. Having a big fraction of the company's revenues and profits come from industries with slow growth, low profitability, intense competition, or other troubling conditions tends to drag overall company performance down. Business units in the least attractive industries are potential candidates for divestiture, unless they are positioned strongly enough to overcome the unattractive aspects of their industry environments or they are a strategically important component of the company's business makeup.

Step 2: Evaluating Business Unit Competitive Strength

The second step in evaluating a diversified company is to appraise the competitive strength of each business unit in its respective industry. Doing an appraisal of each business unit's strength and competitive position in its industry not only reveals its chances for success in its industry but also provides a basis for ranking the units from competitively strongest to competitively weakest and sizing up the competitive strength of all the business units as a group.

Calculating Competitive-Strength Scores for Each Business Unit   Quantitative measures of each business unit's competitive strength can be calculated using a procedure similar to that for measuring industry attractiveness. The following factors are used in quantifying the competitive strengths of a diversified company's business subsidiaries:

- *Relative market share.* A business unit's *relative market share* is defined as the ratio of its market share to the market share held by the largest rival firm in the industry, with market share measured in unit volume, not dollars. For instance, if business A has a market-leading share of 40 percent and its largest rival has 30 percent, A's relative market share is 1.33. (Note that only business units that are market share leaders in their respective industries can have relative market shares greater than 1.) If business B has a 15 percent market share and B's largest rival has 30 percent, B's relative market share is 0.5. *The further below 1 a business unit's relative market share is, the weaker its competitive strength and market position vis-à-vis rivals.*

- *Costs relative to competitors' costs.* Business units that have low costs relative to those of key competitors tend to be more strongly positioned in their industries than business units struggling to maintain cost parity with major rivals. The only time a business unit's competitive strength may not be undermined by having higher costs than rivals is when it has incurred the higher costs to strongly differentiate its product offering and its customers are willing to pay premium prices for the differentiating features.

- *Ability to match or beat rivals on key product attributes.* A company's competitiveness depends in part on being able to satisfy buyer expectations with regard to features, product performance, reliability, service, and other important attributes.

- *Brand image and reputation.* A widely known and respected brand name is a valuable competitive asset in most industries.

- *Other competitively valuable resources and capabilities.* Valuable resources and capabilities, including those accessed through collaborative partnerships, enhance a company's ability to compete successfully and perhaps contend for industry leadership.

- *Ability to benefit from strategic fit with other business units.* Strategic fit with other businesses within the company enhances a business unit's competitive strength and may provide a competitive edge.
- *Ability to exercise bargaining leverage with key suppliers or customers.* Having bargaining leverage signals competitive strength and can be a source of competitive advantage.
- *Profitability relative to competitors.* Above-average profitability on a consistent basis is a signal of competitive advantage, whereas consistently below-average profitability usually denotes competitive disadvantage.

After settling on a set of competitive-strength measures that are well matched to the circumstances of the various business units, the company needs to assign weights indicating each measure's importance. As in the assignment of weights to industry-attractiveness measures, the importance weights must add up to 1. Each business unit is then rated on each of the chosen strength measures, using a rating scale of 1 to 10 (where a *high* rating signifies competitive *strength,* and a *low* rating signifies competitive *weakness*). In the event that the available information is too limited to confidently assign a rating value to a business unit on a particular strength measure, it is usually best to use a score of 5—this avoids biasing the overall score either up or down. Weighted strength ratings are calculated by multiplying the business unit's rating on each strength measure by the assigned weight. For example, a strength score of 6 times a weight of 0.15 gives a weighted strength rating of 0.90. The sum of the weighted ratings across all the strength measures provides a quantitative measure of a business unit's overall competitive strength. Table 8.2 provides sample calculations of competitive-strength ratings for three businesses.

Interpreting the Competitive-Strength Scores

Business units with competitive-strength ratings above 6.7 (on a scale of 1 to 10) are strong market contenders in their industries. Businesses with ratings in the 3.3-to-6.7 range have moderate competitive strength vis-à-vis rivals. Businesses with ratings below 3.3 have a competitively weak standing in the marketplace. If a diversified company's business units all have competitive-strength scores above 5, it is fair to conclude that its business units are all fairly strong market contenders in their respective industries. But as the number of business units with scores below 5 increases, there's reason to question whether the company can perform well with so many businesses in relatively weak competitive positions. This concern takes on even more importance when business units with low scores account for a sizable fraction of the company's revenues.

Using a Nine-Cell Matrix to Simultaneously Portray Industry Attractiveness and Competitive Strength

The industry-attractiveness and business-strength scores can be used to portray the strategic positions of each business in a diversified company. Industry attractiveness is plotted on the vertical axis and competitive strength on the horizontal axis. A nine-cell grid emerges from dividing the vertical axis into three regions (high, medium, and low attractiveness) and the horizontal axis into three regions (strong, average, and weak competitive strength). As shown in Figure 8.3, scores of 6.7 or greater on a rating scale of 1 to 10 denote high industry attractiveness, scores of 3.3 to 6.7 denote medium attractiveness, and scores below 3.3 signal low attractiveness. Likewise, high competitive strength is defined as scores greater than 6.7, average strength as scores of 3.3 to 6.7, and low strength as scores below 3.3. *Each business unit*

TABLE 8.2   Calculating Weighted Competitive-Strength Scores for a Diversified Company's Business Units

Competitive-Strength Measures	Importance Weight	Competitive-Strength Assessments					
		Business A in Industry A		Business B in Industry B		Business C in Industry C	
		Strength Rating*	Weighted Score	Strength Rating*	Weighted Score	Strength Rating*	Weighted Score
Relative market share	0.15	10	1.50	2	0.30	6	0.90
Costs relative to competitors' costs	0.20	7	1.40	4	0.80	5	1.00
Ability to match or beat rivals on key product attributes	0.05	9	0.45	5	0.25	8	0.40
Ability to benefit from strategic fit with sister businesses	0.20	8	1.60	4	0.80	8	0.80
Bargaining leverage with suppliers/customers	0.05	9	0.45	2	0.10	6	0.30
Brand image and reputation	0.10	9	0.90	4	0.40	7	0.70
Other valuable resources/ capabilities	0.15	7	1.05	2	0.30	5	0.75
Profitability relative to competitors	0.10	5	0.50	2	0.20	4	0.40
Sum of importance weights	1.00						
Weighted overall competitive strength scores			7.85		3.15		5.25

Rating scale: 1 = very weak; 10 = very strong.

is plotted on the nine-cell matrix according to its overall attractiveness score and strength score, and then it is shown as a "bubble." The size of each bubble is scaled to the percentage of revenues the business generates relative to total corporate revenues. The bubbles in Figure 8.3 were located on the grid using the three industry-attractiveness scores from Table 8.1 and the strength scores for the three business units in Table 8.2.

The locations of the business units on the attractiveness–strength matrix provide valuable guidance in deploying corporate resources. Businesses positioned in the three cells in the upper left portion of the attractiveness–strength matrix (like business A) have both favorable industry attractiveness and competitive strength.

Next in priority come businesses positioned in the three diagonal cells stretching from the lower left to the upper right (like business C). Such businesses usually merit intermediate priority in the parent's resource allocation ranking. However, some

FIGURE 8.3 A Nine-Cell Industry-Attractiveness–Competitive-Strength Matrix

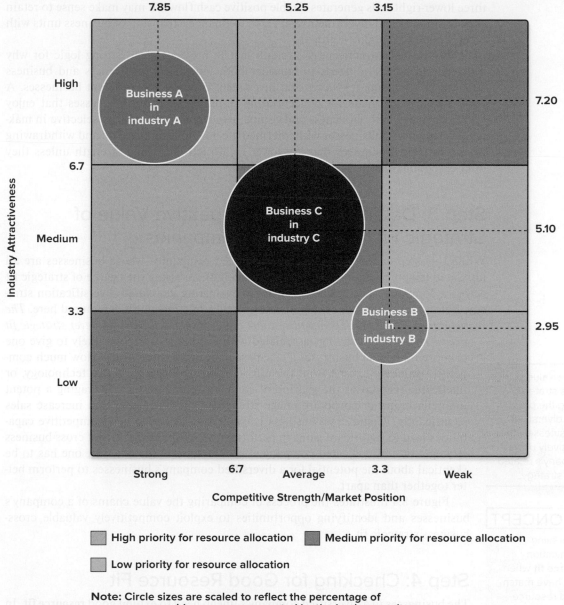

High priority for resource allocation   Medium priority for resource allocation

Low priority for resource allocation

Note: Circle sizes are scaled to reflect the percentage of companywide revenues generated by the business unit.

businesses in the medium-priority diagonal cells may have brighter or dimmer prospects than others. For example, a small business in the upper right cell of the matrix, despite being in a highly attractive industry, may occupy too weak a competitive position in its industry to justify the investment and resources needed to turn it into a strong market contender.

Businesses in the three cells in the lower right corner of the matrix (like business B) have comparatively low industry attractiveness and minimal competitive strength, making them weak performers with little potential for improvement. At best, they have the lowest claim on corporate resources and may be good candidates for being divested (sold to other companies). However, there are occasions when a business located in the three lower-right cells generates sizable positive cash flows. It may make sense to retain such businesses and divert their cash flows to finance expansion of business units with greater potential for profit growth.

The nine-cell attractiveness–strength matrix provides clear, strong logic for why a diversified company needs to consider both industry attractiveness and business strength in allocating resources and investment capital to its different businesses. A good case can be made for concentrating resources in those businesses that enjoy higher degrees of attractiveness and competitive strength, being very selective in making investments in businesses with intermediate positions on the grid, and withdrawing resources from businesses that are lower in attractiveness and strength unless they offer exceptional profit or cash flow potential.

Step 3: Determining the Competitive Value of Strategic Fit in Diversified Companies

While this step can be bypassed for diversified companies whose businesses are all unrelated (since, by design, strategic fit is lacking), assessing the degree of strategic fit across a company's businesses is central to evaluating its related diversification strategy. But more than just checking for the presence of strategic fit is required here. *The real question is how much competitive value can be generated from whatever strategic fit exists.* Are the cost savings associated with economies of scope likely to give one or more individual businesses a cost-based advantage over rivals? How much competitive value will come from the cross-business transfer of skills, technology, or intellectual capital or the sharing of competitive assets? Can leveraging a potent umbrella brand or corporate image strengthen the businesses and increase sales significantly? Could cross-business collaboration to create new competitive capabilities lead to significant gains in performance? Without significant cross-business strategic fit and dedicated company efforts to capture the benefits, one has to be skeptical about the potential for a diversified company's businesses to perform better together than apart.

Figure 8.4 illustrates the process of comparing the value chains of a company's businesses and identifying opportunities to exploit competitively valuable cross-business strategic fit.

> The greater the value of cross-business strategic fit in enhancing the performance of a diversified company's businesses, the more competitively powerful is the company's related diversification strategy.

Step 4: Checking for Good Resource Fit

The businesses in a diversified company's lineup need to exhibit good **resource fit.** In firms with a related diversification strategy, good resource fit exists *when the firm's businesses have well-matched specialized resource requirements at points along their value chains* that are critical for the businesses' market success. Matching resource requirements are important in related diversification because they facilitate resource sharing and low-cost resource transfer. In companies pursuing unrelated diversification, resource fit exists when the company has solid *parenting capabilities or resources of a general nature that it can share or transfer to its component businesses.* Firms pursuing related diversification and firms with combination related–unrelated diversification strategies can also benefit from leveraging corporate parenting capabilities

> **CORE CONCEPT**
>
> A company pursuing related diversification exhibits **resource fit** when its businesses have matching specialized resource requirements along their value chains; a company pursuing unrelated diversification has resource fit when the parent company has adequate corporate resources (parenting and general resources) to support its businesses' needs and add value.

and other general resources. Another dimension of resource fit that concerns all types of multibusiness firms is whether they have resources sufficient to support their group of businesses without being spread too thin.

Financial Resource Fit   The most important dimension of financial resource fit concerns whether a diversified company can generate the internal cash flows sufficient to fund the capital requirements of its businesses, pay its dividends, meet its debt obligations, and otherwise remain financially healthy. (Financial resources, including the firm's ability to borrow or otherwise raise funds, are a type of general resource.) While additional capital can usually be raised in financial markets, it is important for a diversified firm to have a healthy **internal capital market** that can support the financial requirements of its business lineup. The greater the extent to which a diversified company is able to fund investment in its businesses through internally generated cash flows rather than from equity issues or borrowing, the more powerful its financial resource fit and the less dependent the firm is on external financial resources. This can provide a competitive advantage over single business rivals when credit market conditions are tight, as they have been in the United States and abroad in recent years.

> **CORE** CONCEPT
>
> A strong **internal capital market** allows a diversified company to add value by shifting capital from business units generating free cash flow to those needing additional capital to expand and realize their growth potential.

FIGURE 8.4   Identifying the Competitive Advantage Potential of Cross-Business Strategic Fit

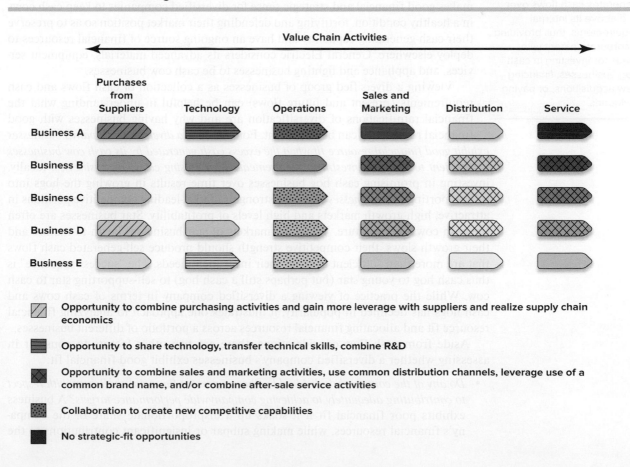

Value Chain Activities

	Purchases from Suppliers	Technology	Operations	Sales and Marketing	Distribution	Service
Business A						
Business B						
Business C						
Business D						
Business E						

Opportunity to combine purchasing activities and gain more leverage with suppliers and realize supply chain economics

Opportunity to share technology, transfer technical skills, combine R&D

Opportunity to combine sales and marketing activities, use common distribution channels, leverage use of a common brand name, and/or combine after-sale service activities

Collaboration to create new competitive capabilities

No strategic-fit opportunities

A **portfolio approach** to ensuring financial fit among a firm's businesses is based on the fact that different businesses have different cash flow and investment characteristics. For example, business units in rapidly growing industries are often **cash hogs**—so labeled because the cash flows they are able to generate from internal operations aren't big enough to fund their operations and capital requirements for growth. To keep pace with rising buyer demand, rapid-growth businesses frequently need sizable annual capital investments—for new facilities and equipment, for new product development or technology improvements, and for additional working capital to support inventory expansion and a larger base of operations. Because a cash hog's financial resources must be provided by the corporate parent, corporate managers have to decide whether it makes good financial and strategic sense to keep pouring new money into a cash hog business.

In contrast, business units with leading market positions in mature industries may be **cash cows** in the sense that they generate substantial cash surpluses over what is needed to adequately fund their operations. Market leaders in slow-growth industries often generate sizable positive cash flows *over and above what is needed for growth and reinvestment* because their industry-leading positions tend to generate attractive earnings and because the slow-growth nature of their industry often entails relatively modest annual investment requirements. Cash cows, although not attractive from a growth standpoint, are valuable businesses from a financial resource perspective. The surplus cash flows they generate can be used to pay corporate dividends, finance acquisitions, and provide funds for investing in the company's promising cash hogs. It makes good financial and strategic sense for diversified companies to keep cash cows in a healthy condition, fortifying and defending their market position so as to preserve their cash-generating capability and have an ongoing source of financial resources to deploy elsewhere. General Electric considers its advanced materials, equipment services, and appliance and lighting businesses to be cash cow businesses.

Viewing a diversified group of businesses as a collection of cash flows and cash requirements (present and future flows) can be helpful in understanding what the financial ramifications of diversification are and why having businesses with good financial resource fit can be important. For instance, *a diversified company's businesses exhibit good financial resource fit when the excess cash generated by its cash cow businesses is sufficient to fund the investment requirements of promising cash hog businesses.* Ideally, investing in promising cash hog businesses over time results in growing the hogs into self-supporting *star businesses* that have strong or market-leading competitive positions in attractive, high-growth markets and high levels of profitability. Star businesses are often the cash cows of the future. When the markets of star businesses begin to mature and their growth slows, their competitive strength should produce self-generated cash flows that are more than sufficient to cover their investment needs. The "success sequence" is thus cash hog to young star (but perhaps still a cash hog) to self-supporting star to cash cow. While the practice of viewing a diversified company in terms of cash cows and cash hogs has declined in popularity, it illustrates one approach to analyzing financial resource fit and allocating financial resources across a portfolio of different businesses.

Aside from cash flow considerations, there are two other factors to consider in assessing whether a diversified company's businesses exhibit good financial fit:

• *Do any of the company's individual businesses present financial challenges with respect to contributing adequately to achieving companywide performance targets?* A business exhibits poor financial fit if it soaks up a disproportionate share of the company's financial resources, while making subpar or insignificant contributions to the bottom line. Too many underperforming businesses reduce the company's overall performance and ultimately limit growth in shareholder value.

- *Does the corporation have adequate financial strength to fund its different businesses and maintain a healthy credit rating?* A diversified company's strategy fails the resource-fit test when the resource needs of its portfolio unduly stretch the company's financial health and threaten to impair its credit rating. Many of the world's largest banks, including Royal Bank of Scotland, Citigroup, and HSBC, recently found themselves so undercapitalized and financially overextended that they were forced to sell off some of their business assets to meet regulatory requirements and restore public confidence in their solvency.

Nonfinancial Resource Fit Just as a diversified company must have adequate financial resources to support its various individual businesses, it must also have a big enough and deep enough pool of managerial, administrative, and other parenting capabilities to support all of its different businesses. The following two questions help reveal whether a diversified company has sufficient nonfinancial resources:

- *Does the parent company have (or can it develop) the specific resources and capabilities needed to be successful in each of its businesses?* Sometimes the resources a company has accumulated in its core business prove to be a poor match with the competitive capabilities needed to succeed in the businesses into which it has diversified. For instance, BTR, a multibusiness company in Great Britain, discovered that the company's resources and managerial skills were quite well suited for parenting its industrial manufacturing businesses but not for parenting its distribution businesses (National Tyre Services and Texas-based Summers Group). As a result, BTR decided to divest its distribution businesses and focus exclusively on diversifying around small industrial manufacturing. For companies pursuing related diversification strategies, a mismatch between the company's competitive assets and the key success factors of an industry can be serious enough to warrant divesting businesses in that industry or not acquiring a new business. In contrast, when a company's resources and capabilities are a good match with the key success factors of industries it is not presently in, it makes sense to take a hard look at acquiring companies in these industries and expanding the company's business lineup.

- *Are the parent company's resources being stretched too thinly by the resource requirements of one or more of its businesses?* A diversified company must guard against overtaxing its resources and capabilities, a condition that can arise when (1) it goes on an acquisition spree and management is called on to assimilate and oversee many new businesses very quickly or (2) it lacks sufficient resource depth to do a creditable job of transferring skills and competencies from one of its businesses to another. The broader the diversification, the greater the concern about whether corporate executives are overburdened by the demands of competently parenting so many different businesses. Plus, the more a company's diversification strategy is tied to transferring know-how or technologies from existing businesses to newly acquired businesses, the more time and money that has to be put into developing a deep-enough resource pool to supply these businesses with the resources and capabilities they need to be successful.[15] Otherwise, its resource pool ends up being spread too thinly across many businesses, and the opportunity for achieving $1 + 1 = 3$ outcomes slips through the cracks.

Step 5: Ranking Business Units and Assigning a Priority for Resource Allocation

Once a diversified company's strategy has been evaluated from the perspective of industry attractiveness, competitive strength, strategic fit, and resource fit, the next step is to use this information to rank the performance prospects of the businesses from best to worst. Such ranking helps top-level executives assign each business a priority for resource support and capital investment.

The locations of the different businesses in the nine-cell industry-attractiveness–competitive-strength matrix provide a solid basis for identifying high-opportunity businesses and low-opportunity businesses. Normally, competitively strong businesses in attractive industries have significantly better performance prospects than competitively weak businesses in unattractive industries. Also, the revenue and earnings outlook for businesses in fast-growing industries is normally better than for businesses in slow-growing industries. As a rule, *business subsidiaries with the brightest profit and growth prospects, attractive positions in the nine-cell matrix, and solid strategic and resource fit should receive top priority for allocation of corporate resources.* However, in ranking the prospects of the different businesses from best to worst, it is usually wise to also take into account each business's past performance in regard to sales growth, profit growth, contribution to company earnings, return on capital invested in the business, and cash flow from operations. While past performance is not always a reliable predictor of future performance, it does signal whether a business is already performing well or has problems to overcome.

Allocating Financial Resources   Figure 8.5 shows the chief strategic and financial options for allocating a diversified company's financial resources. Divesting businesses

FIGURE 8.5   The Chief Strategic and Financial Options for Allocating a Diversified Company's Financial Resources

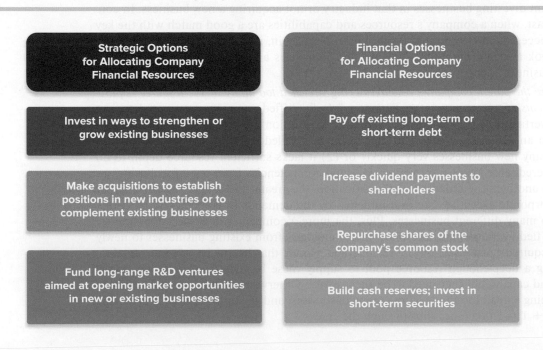

Strategic Options for Allocating Company Financial Resources

- Invest in ways to strengthen or grow existing businesses
- Make acquisitions to establish positions in new industries or to complement existing businesses
- Fund long-range R&D ventures aimed at opening market opportunities in new or existing businesses

Financial Options for Allocating Company Financial Resources

- Pay off existing long-term or short-term debt
- Increase dividend payments to shareholders
- Repurchase shares of the company's common stock
- Build cash reserves; invest in short-term securities

with the weakest future prospects and businesses that lack adequate strategic fit and/ or resource fit is one of the best ways of generating additional funds for redeployment to businesses with better opportunities and better strategic and resource fit. Free cash flows from cash cow businesses also add to the pool of funds that can be usefully redeployed. *Ideally,* a diversified company will have sufficient financial resources to strengthen or grow its existing businesses, make any new acquisitions that are desirable, fund other promising business opportunities, pay off existing debt, and periodically increase dividend payments to shareholders and/or repurchase shares of stock. But, as a practical matter, a company's financial resources are limited. Thus, to make the best use of the available funds, top executives must steer resources to those businesses with the best prospects and either divest or allocate minimal resources to businesses with marginal prospects—this is why ranking the performance prospects of the various businesses from best to worst is so crucial. *Strategic* uses of corporate financial resources should usually take precedence over strictly financial considerations (see Figure 8.5) unless there is a compelling reason to strengthen the firm's balance sheet or better reward shareholders.

Step 6: Crafting New Strategic Moves to Improve Overall Corporate Performance

• LO 8-5

Examine the four main corporate strategy options a diversified company can employ to improve company performance.

The conclusions flowing from the five preceding analytic steps set the agenda for crafting strategic moves to improve a diversified company's overall performance. The strategic options boil down to four broad categories of actions (see Figure 8.6):

1. Sticking closely with the existing business lineup and pursuing the opportunities these businesses present.
2. Broadening the company's business scope by making new acquisitions in new industries.
3. Divesting certain businesses and retrenching to a narrower base of business operations.
4. Restructuring the company's business lineup and putting a whole new face on the company's business makeup.

Sticking Closely with the Present Business Lineup   The option of sticking with the current business lineup makes sense when the company's existing businesses offer attractive growth opportunities and can be counted on to create economic value for shareholders. As long as the company's set of existing businesses have good prospects and are in alignment with the company's diversification strategy, then major changes in the company's business mix are unnecessary. Corporate executives can concentrate their attention on getting the best performance from each of the businesses, steering corporate resources into the areas of greatest potential and profitability. The specifics of "what to do" to wring better performance from the present business lineup have to be dictated by each business's circumstances and the preceding analysis of the corporate parent's diversification strategy.

Broadening a Diversified Company's Business Base   Diversified companies sometimes find it desirable to build positions in new industries, whether related or unrelated. Several motivating factors are in play. One is sluggish growth that makes the potential revenue and profit boost of a newly acquired business look attractive. A second is the potential for transferring resources and capabilities to other related or complementary businesses.

FIGURE 8.6   A Company's Four Main Strategic Alternatives after It Diversifies

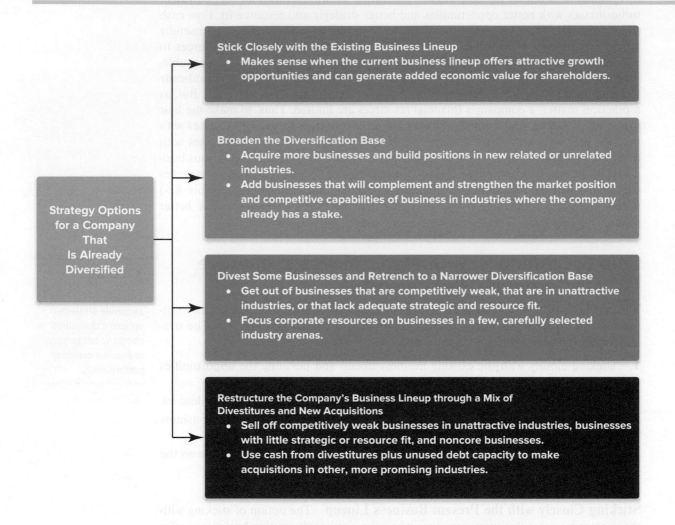

Stick Closely with the Existing Business Lineup
- Makes sense when the current business lineup offers attractive growth opportunities and can generate added economic value for shareholders.

Broaden the Diversification Base
- Acquire more businesses and build positions in new related or unrelated industries.
- Add businesses that will complement and strengthen the market position and competitive capabilities of business in industries where the company already has a stake.

Strategy Options for a Company That Is Already Diversified

Divest Some Businesses and Retrench to a Narrower Diversification Base
- Get out of businesses that are competitively weak, that are in unattractive industries, or that lack adequate strategic and resource fit.
- Focus corporate resources on businesses in a few, carefully selected industry arenas.

Restructure the Company's Business Lineup through a Mix of Divestitures and New Acquisitions
- Sell off competitively weak businesses in unattractive industries, businesses with little strategic or resource fit, and noncore businesses.
- Use cash from divestitures plus unused debt capacity to make acquisitions in other, more promising industries.

A third is rapidly changing conditions in one or more of a company's core businesses, brought on by technological, legislative, or demographic changes. For instance, the passage of legislation in the United States allowing banks, insurance companies, and stock brokerages to enter each other's businesses spurred a raft of acquisitions and mergers to create full-service financial enterprises capable of meeting the multiple financial needs of customers. A fourth, and very important, motivating factor for adding new businesses is to complement and strengthen the market position and competitive capabilities of one or more of the company's present businesses. Procter & Gamble's acquisition of Gillette strengthened and extended P&G's reach into personal care and household products—Gillette's businesses included Oral-B toothbrushes, Gillette razors and razor blades, Duracell batteries, Braun shavers, small appliances (coffeemakers, mixers, hair dryers, and electric toothbrushes), and toiletries. Johnson & Johnson has used acquisitions to diversify far beyond its well-known Band-Aid and baby care businesses and become a major player in pharmaceuticals, medical devices, and medical diagnostics.

Another important avenue for expanding the scope of a diversified company is to grow by extending the operations of existing businesses into additional country markets, as discussed in Chapter 7. Expanding a company's geographic scope may offer an exceptional competitive advantage potential by facilitating the full capture of economies of scale and learning- and experience-curve effects. In some businesses, the volume of sales needed to realize full economies of scale and/or benefit fully from experience-curve effects exceeds the volume that can be achieved by operating within the boundaries of just one or several country markets, especially small ones.

Retrenching to a Narrower Diversification Base A number of diversified firms have had difficulty managing a diverse group of businesses and have elected to exit some of them. Selling a business outright to another company is far and away the most frequently used option for divesting a business. In 2017, Samsung Electronics sold its printing business to HP, Inc. in order better focus on its core smartphone, television, and memory chip businesses. But sometimes a business selected for divestiture has ample resources and capabilities to compete successfully on its own. In such cases, a corporate parent may elect to *spin off* the unwanted business as a financially and managerially independent company, either by selling shares to the public via an initial public offering or by distributing shares in the new company to shareholders of the corporate parent. eBay spun off PayPal in 2015 at a valuation of $45 billion—a value 30 times more than what eBay paid for the company in a 2002 acquisition. In 2018, pesticide maker FMC Corp. spun off its lithium business to boost profitability by focusing on its core business.

Retrenching to a narrower diversification base is usually undertaken when top management concludes that its diversification has ranged too far afield and that the company can improve long-term performance by concentrating on a smaller number of businesses. But there are other important reasons for divesting one or more of a company's present businesses. Sometimes divesting a business has to be considered because market conditions in a once-attractive industry have badly deteriorated. A business can become a prime candidate for divestiture because it lacks adequate strategic or resource fit, because it is a cash hog with questionable long-term potential, or because remedying its competitive weaknesses is too expensive relative to the likely gains in profitability. Sometimes a company acquires businesses that, down the road, just do not work out as expected even though management has tried its best. Subpar performance by some business units is bound to occur, thereby raising questions of whether to divest them or keep them and attempt a turnaround. Other business units, despite adequate financial performance, may not mesh as well with the rest of the firm as was originally thought. For instance, PepsiCo divested its group of fast-food restaurant businesses (Kentucky Fried Chicken, Pizza Hut, and Taco Bell) to focus on its core soft-drink and snack-food businesses, where their specialized resources and capabilities could add more value.

On occasion, a diversification move that seems sensible from a strategic-fit standpoint turns out to be a poor *cultural fit*.[16] When several pharmaceutical companies diversified into cosmetics and perfume, they discovered their personnel had little respect for the "frivolous" nature of such products compared to the far nobler task of developing miracle drugs to cure the ill. The absence of shared values and cultural compatibility between the medical research and chemical-compounding expertise of the pharmaceutical companies and the fashion and marketing orientation of the cosmetics business was the undoing of what otherwise was diversification into businesses

A **spin-off** is an independent company created when a corporate parent divests a business either by selling shares to the public via an initial public offering or by distributing shares in the new company to shareholders of the corporate parent.

CORE CONCEPT

with technology-sharing potential, product development fit, and some overlap in distribution channels.

A useful guide to determine whether or when to divest a business subsidiary is to ask, "If we were not in this business today, would we want to get into it now?" When the answer is no or probably not, divestiture should be considered. Another signal that a business should be divested occurs when it is worth more to another company than to the present parent; in such cases, shareholders would be well served if the company sells the business and collects a premium price from the buyer for whom the business is a valuable fit.

Restructuring a Diversified Company's Business Lineup Restructuring a diversified company on a companywide basis *(corporate restructuring)* involves divesting some businesses and/or acquiring others, so as to put a whole new face on the company's business lineup.[17] Performing radical surgery on a company's business lineup is appealing when its financial performance is being squeezed or eroded by

- A serious mismatch between the company's resources and capabilities and the type of diversification that it has pursued.
- Too many businesses in slow-growth, declining, low-margin, or otherwise unattractive industries.
- Too many competitively weak businesses.
- The emergence of new technologies that threaten the survival of one or more important businesses.
- Ongoing declines in the market shares of one or more major business units that are falling prey to more market-savvy competitors.
- An excessive debt burden with interest costs that eat deeply into profitability.
- Ill-chosen acquisitions that haven't lived up to expectations.

On occasion, corporate restructuring can be prompted by special circumstances—such as when a firm has a unique opportunity to make an acquisition so big and important that it has to sell several existing business units to finance the new acquisition or when a company needs to sell off some businesses in order to raise the cash for entering a potentially big industry with wave-of-the-future technologies or products. As businesses are divested, corporate restructuring generally involves aligning the remaining business units into groups with the best strategic fit and then redeploying the cash flows from the divested businesses to either pay down debt or make new acquisitions to strengthen the parent company's business position in the industries it has chosen to emphasize.

Over the past decade, corporate restructuring has become a popular strategy at many diversified companies, especially those that had diversified broadly into many different industries and lines of business. VF Corporation, maker of North Face and other popular "lifestyle" apparel brands, has used a restructuring strategy to provide its shareholders with returns that are more than five times greater than shareholder returns for competing apparel makers. Since its acquisition and turnaround of North Face in 2000, VF has spent nearly $5 billion to acquire 19 additional businesses, including about $2 billion in 2011 for Timberland. New apparel brands acquired by VF Corporation include Rock & Republic jeans, Vans skateboard shoes, Nautica, John Varvatos, Reef surf wear, and Eagle Creek luggage. By 2017, VF Corporation had become a $12 billion powerhouse—one of the largest and most profitable apparel

Restructuring for Better Performance at Hewlett-Packard (HP)

Since its misguided acquisition of PC maker Compaq (under former CEO Carly Fiorina), Hewlett-Packard has been struggling. In the past few years, it has faced declining demand, rapid technological change, and fierce new competitors, such as Google and Apple, in its core markets. To address these problems, CEO Meg Whitman announced a restructuring of the company that was approved by the company's board of directors in October 2015. In addition to trimming operations, the plan was to split the company into two independent entities: HP Inc. and HP Enterprise. The former would primarily house the company's legacy PC and printer businesses, while the latter would retain the company's technology infrastructure, services, and cloud computing businesses.

©Sergiy Palamarchuk/Shutterstock

A variety of benefits were anticipated as a result of this fundamental reshaping of the company. First, the split would enable the faster-growing enterprise business to pursue opportunities that are less relevant to the concerns of its more staid sister business. As several have observed, "it is hard to be good at both consumer and enterprise computing," which suggests an absence of strategic fit along the value chains of the two newly separated businesses. Second, in creating smaller, more nimble entities, the new companies would be better positioned to respond to competitive moves and anticipate the evolving needs of customers. This is primarily because management teams would be responsible for a smaller, more focused set of products, which would leave them better equipped to innovate in the fast-moving world of technology. Third, the more streamlined organizations would better align incentives for managers, since they would be more likely to see their individual efforts hit the bottom line under a more focused operation.

By cutting back operations to match areas of declining demand and moving some operations overseas, the company anticipated a reduction in costs of more than $2 billion. But despite having made significant progress toward being a smaller, more nimble company, significant challenges in returning to profitability still remain.

Note: Developed with Ken Martin, CFA.

Sources: CNBC Online, "Former HP Chair: Spinoff Not a Defensive Play," October 6, 2015, www.cnbc.com/2014/10/06/hairman-spin-off-not-a-defensive-play.html; S. Mukherjee and E. Chan, Reuters Online, "Hewlett-Packard to Split into Two Public Companies, Lay Off 5,000," October 6, 2015, www.reuters.com/article/us-hp-restructuring-idUSKCN0HV0U720141006; J. Vanian, *Fortune* Online, "How Hewlett-Packard Plans to Split in Two," July 1, 2015, fortune.com/2015/07/01/hewlett-packard-filing-split/; company website (accessed March 3, 2016).

and footwear companies in the world. It was listed as number 230 on Fortune's 2017 list of the 500 largest U.S. companies. Sears Holding (with its Sears and KMart stores) has been engaged in an ongoing restructuring effort in a more desperate attempt to turn around the struggling company. By simplifying their organizational structure and streamlining operations, they were able to reduce costs by $1.25 billion on an annualized basis.

Illustration Capsule 8.2 discusses how HP Inc. has been restructuring its operations to address internal problems and improve its profitability.

KEY POINTS

1. The purpose of diversification is to build shareholder value. Diversification builds shareholder value only when a diversified group of businesses can perform better under the auspices of a single corporate parent than they would as independent, standalone businesses. The goal is to achieve not just a $1 + 1 = 2$ result but rather to realize important $1 + 1 = 3$ performance benefits—an effect known as *synergy*. For a move to diversify into a new business to have a reasonable prospect of adding shareholder value, it must be capable of passing the three Tests of Corporate Advantage: the industry attractiveness test, the cost-of-entry test, and the better-off test.

2. Entry into new businesses can take any of three forms: acquisition, internal startup, or joint venture. The choice of which is best depends on the firm's resources and capabilities, the industry's entry barriers, the importance of speed, and relative costs.

3. There are two fundamental approaches to diversification—into related businesses and into unrelated businesses. The rationale for *related* diversification is to benefit from *strategic fit:* diversify into businesses with commonalities across their respective value chains, and then capitalize on the strategic fit by sharing or transferring the resources and capabilities across matching value chain activities to gain competitive advantages.

4. *Unrelated* diversification strategies surrender the competitive advantage potential of strategic fit at the value chain level in return for the potential that can be realized from superior corporate parenting or the sharing and transfer of general resources and capabilities. An outstanding corporate parent can benefit its businesses through (1) providing high-level oversight and making available other corporate resources, (2) allocating financial resources across the business portfolio (under certain circumstances), and (3) restructuring underperforming acquisitions.

5. Related diversification provides a stronger foundation for creating shareholder value than does unrelated diversification, since the *specialized resources and capabilities* that are leveraged in related diversification tend to be more valuable competitive assets than the *general resources and capabilities* underlying unrelated diversification, which in most cases are relatively common and easier to imitate.

6. Analyzing how good a company's diversification strategy is consists of a six-step process:

   Step 1: *Evaluate the long-term attractiveness of the industries into which the firm has diversified.* Determining industry attractiveness involves developing a list of industry-attractiveness measures, each of which might have a different importance weight.

   Step 2: *Evaluate the relative competitive strength of each of the company's business units.* The purpose of rating the competitive strength of each business is to gain a clear understanding of which businesses are strong contenders in their industries, which are weak contenders, and what the underlying reasons are for their strength or weakness. The conclusions about industry attractiveness can be joined with the conclusions about competitive strength by drawing a nine-cell industry-attractiveness–competitive-strength matrix that helps identify the prospects of each business and the level of priority each business should be given in allocating corporate resources and investment capital.

   Step 3: *Check for the competitive value of cross-business strategic fit.* A business is more attractive strategically when it has value chain relationships with the other business units that offer the potential to (1) combine operations to realize economies of scope, (2) transfer technology, skills, know-how, or other resource capabilities from one business to another, (3) leverage the use of a trusted brand name or other resources that enhance differentiation, (4) share other competitively valuable resources among the company's businesses, and (5) build new resources and competitive capabilities via cross-business collaboration. Cross-business strategic fit represents a significant avenue for producing competitive advantage beyond what any one business can achieve on its own.

Step 4: *Check whether the firm's resources fit the resource requirements of its present business lineup.* In firms with a related diversification strategy, resource fit exists when the firm's businesses have matching resource requirements at points along their value chains that are critical for the businesses' market success. In companies pursuing unrelated diversification, resource fit exists when the company has solid parenting capabilities or resources of a general nature that it can share or transfer to its component businesses. When there is financial resource fit among the businesses of any type of diversified company, the company can generate internal cash flows sufficient to fund the capital requirements of its businesses, pay its dividends, meet its debt obligations, and otherwise remain financially healthy.

Step 5: *Rank the performance prospects of the businesses from best to worst, and determine what the corporate parent's priority should be in allocating resources to its various businesses.* The most important considerations in judging business unit performance are sales growth, profit growth, contribution to company earnings, and the return on capital invested in the business. Normally, strong business units in attractive industries should head the list for corporate resource support.

Step 6: *Craft new strategic moves to improve overall corporate performance.* This step draws on the results of the preceding steps as the basis for selecting one of four different strategic paths for improving a diversified company's performance: (1) Stick closely with the existing business lineup and pursue opportunities presented by these businesses, (2) broaden the scope of diversification by entering additional industries, (3) retrench to a narrower scope of diversification by divesting poorly performing businesses, or (4) broadly restructure the business lineup with multiple divestitures and/or acquisitions.

ASSURANCE OF LEARNING EXERCISES

1. See if you can identify the value chain relationships that make the businesses of the following companies related in competitively relevant ways. In particular, you should consider whether there are cross-business opportunities for (1) transferring skills and technology, (2) combining related value chain activities to achieve economies of scope, and/or (3) leveraging the use of a well-respected brand name or other resources that enhance differentiation.

Bloomin' Brands
- Outback Steakhouse
- Carrabba's Italian Grill
- Bonefish Grill (market-fresh fine seafood)
- Fleming's Prime Steakhouse & Wine Bar

L'Oréal
- Maybelline, Lancôme, Helena Rubinstein, essie, Kiehl's and Shu Uemura cosmetics
- L'Oréal and Soft Sheen/Carson hair care products

connect

LO 8-1, LO 8-2,
LO 8-3, LO 8-4

- Redken, Matrix, L'Oréal Professional, and Kerastase Paris professional hair care and skin care products
- Ralph Lauren and Giorgio Armani fragrances
- Biotherm skin care products
- La Roche–Posay and Vichy Laboratories dermo-cosmetics

Johnson & Johnson

- Baby products (powder, shampoo, oil, lotion)
- Band-Aids and other first-aid products
- Women's health and personal care products (Stayfree, Carefree, Sure & Natural)
- Neutrogena, and Aveeno skin care products
- Nonprescription drugs (Tylenol, Motrin, Pepcid AC, Mylanta, Monistat)
- Prescription drugs
- Prosthetic and other medical devices
- Surgical and hospital products
- Acuvue contact lenses

LO 8-1, LO 8-2, LO 8-3, LO 8-4

2. Peruse the business group listings for 3M Company shown as follows and listed at its website. How would you characterize the company's corporate strategy—related diversification, unrelated diversification, or a combination related–unrelated diversification strategy? Explain your answer.

- Consumer products—for the home and office including Post-it® and Scotch®
- Electronics and Energy—technology solutions for customers in electronics and energy markets
- Health Care—products for health care professionals
- Industrial—abrasives, adhesives, specialty materials and filtration systems
- Safety and Graphics—safety and security products; graphic solutions

connect

LO 8-1, LO 8-2, LO 8-3, LO 8-4, LO 8-5

3. ITT is a technology-oriented engineering and manufacturing company with the following business divisions and products:

- Industrial Process Division—industrial pumps, valves, and monitoring and control systems; aftermarket services for the chemical, oil and gas, mining, pulp and paper, power, and biopharmaceutical markets
- Motion Technologies Division—durable brake pads, shock absorbers, and damping technologies for the automotive and rail markets
- Interconnect Solutions—connectors and fittings for the production of automobiles, aircraft, railcars and locomotives, oil field equipment, medical equipment, and industrial equipment
- Control Technologies—energy absorption and vibration dampening equipment, transducers and regulators, and motion controls used in the production of robotics, medical equipment, automobiles, subsea equipment, industrial equipment, aircraft, and military vehicles

Based on the previous listing, would you say that ITT's business lineup reflects a strategy of related diversification, unrelated diversification, or a combination of related and unrelated diversification? What benefits are generated from any strategic fit existing between ITT's businesses? Also, what types of companies should ITT consider acquiring that might improve shareholder value? Justify your answer.

EXERCISE FOR SIMULATION PARTICIPANTS

1. In the event that your company has the opportunity to diversify into other products or businesses of your choosing, would you opt to pursue related diversification, unrelated diversification, or a combination of both? Explain why.   **LO 8-1, LO 8-2, LO 8-3**

2. What specific resources and capabilities does your company possess that would make diversifying into related businesses attractive? Indicate what kinds of strategic-fit benefits could be captured by transferring these resources and competitive capabilities to newly acquired related businesses.   **LO 8-1, LO 8-2**

3. If your company opted to pursue a strategy of related diversification, what industries or product categories could it diversify into that would allow it to achieve economies of scope? Name at least two or three such industries or product categories, and indicate the specific kinds of cost savings that might accrue from entry into each.   **LO 8-1, LO 8-2**

4. If your company opted to pursue a strategy of unrelated diversification, what industries or product categories could it diversify into that would allow it to capitalize on using its present brand name and corporate image to good advantage in the newly entered businesses or product categories? Name at least two or three such industries or product categories, and indicate the *specific benefits* that might be captured by transferring your company's umbrella brand name to each.   **LO 8-1, LO 8-3**

ENDNOTES

[1] Michael E. Porter, "From Competitive Advantage to Corporate Strategy," *Harvard Business Review* 45, no. 3 (May–June 1987), pp. 46–49.

[2] A. Shleifer and R. Vishny, "Takeovers in the 60s and the 80s—Evidence and Implications," *Strategic Management Journal* 12 (Winter 1991), pp. 51–59; T. Brush, "Predicted Change in Operational Synergy and Post-Acquisition Performance of Acquired Businesses," *Strategic Management Journal* 17, no. 1 (1996), pp. 1–24; J. P. Walsh, "Top Management Turnover Following Mergers and Acquisitions," *Strategic Management Journal* 9, no. 2 (1988), pp. 173–183; A. Cannella and D. Hambrick, "Effects of Executive Departures on the Performance of Acquired Firms," *Strategic Management Journal* 14 (Summer 1993), pp. 137–152; R. Roll, "The Hubris Hypothesis of Corporate Takeovers," *Journal of Business* 59, no. 2 (1986), pp. 197–216; P. Haspeslagh and D. Jemison, *Managing Acquisitions* (New York: Free Press, 1991).

[3] M.L.A. Hayward, "When Do Firms Learn from Their Acquisition Experience? Evidence from 1990–1995," *Strategic Management Journal* 23, no. 1 (2002), pp. 21–29; G. Ahuja and R. Katila, "Technological Acquisitions and the Innovation Performance of Acquiring Firms: A Longitudinal Study," *Strategic Management Journal* 22, no. 3 (2001), pp. 197–220; H. Barkema and F. Vermeulen, "International Expansion through Start-Up or Acquisition: A Learning Perspective," *Academy of Management Journal* 41, no. 1 (1998), pp. 7–26.

[4] Yves L. Doz and Gary Hamel, *Alliance Advantage: The Art of Creating Value through Partnering* (Boston: Harvard Business School Press, 1998), chaps. 1 and 2.

[5] J. Glover, "The Guardian," March 23, 1996, www.mcspotlight.org/media/press/guardpizza_23mar96.html.

[6] Michael E. Porter, *Competitive Advantage* (New York: Free Press, 1985), pp. 318–319, 337–353; Porter, "From Competitive Advantage to Corporate Strategy," pp. 53–57; Constantinos C. Markides and Peter J. Williamson, "Corporate Diversification and Organization Structure: A Resource-Based View," *Academy of Management Journal* 39, no. 2 (April 1996), pp. 340–367.

[7] David J. Collis and Cynthia A. Montgomery, "Creating Corporate Advantage," *Harvard Business Review* 76, no. 3 (May–June 1998), pp. 72–80; Markides and Williamson, "Corporate Diversification and Organization Structure."

[8] Jeanne M. Liedtka, "Collaboration across Lines of Business for Competitive Advantage," *Academy of Management Executive* 10, no. 2 (May 1996), pp. 20–34.

[9] Kathleen M. Eisenhardt and D. Charles Galunic, "Coevolving: At Last, a Way to Make Synergies Work," *Harvard Business Review* 78, no. 1 (January–February 2000), pp. 91–101; Constantinos C. Markides and Peter J. Williamson, "Related Diversification, Core Competences and Corporate Performance," *Strategic Management Journal* 15 (Summer 1994), pp. 149–165.

[10] A. Campbell, M. Goold, and M. Alexander, "Corporate Strategy: The Quest for Parenting Advantage," *Harvard Business Review* 73, no. 2 (March–April 1995), pp. 120–132.

[11] Cynthia A. Montgomery and B. Wernerfelt, "Diversification, Ricardian Rents, and Tobin-Q," *RAND Journal of Economics* 19, no. 4 (1988), pp. 623–632.

[12] Patricia L. Anslinger and Thomas E. Copeland, "Growth through Acquisitions: A Fresh Look," *Harvard Business Review* 74, no. 1 (January–February 1996), pp. 126–135.

[13] M. Lubatkin and S. Chatterjee, "Extending Modern Portfolio Theory," *Academy of Management Journal* 37, no.1 (February 1994), pp. 109–136.

[14] Lawrence G. Franko, "The Death of Diversification? The Focusing of the World's Industrial Firms, 1980–2000," *Business Horizons* 47, no. 4 (July–August 2004), pp. 41–50.

[15] David J. Collis and Cynthia A. Montgomery, "Competing on Resources: Strategy in the 90s," *Harvard Business Review* 73, no. 4 (July–August 1995), pp. 118–128.

[16] Peter F. Drucker, *Management: Tasks, Responsibilities, Practices* (New York: Harper & Row, 1974), p. 709.

[17] Lee Dranikoff, Tim Koller, and Anton Schneider, "Divestiture: Strategy's Missing Link," *Harvard Business Review* 80, no. 5 (May 2002), pp. 74–83.

A well-run business must have high and consistent standards of ethics.

Richard Branson—*Founder of Virgin Atlantic Airlines and Virgin Group*

When sustainability is viewed as being a matter of survival for your business, I believe you can create massive change.

Cameron Sinclair—*Head of social innovation at Airbnb*

Clearly, in capitalistic or market economies, a company has a responsibility to make a profit and grow the business. Managers of public companies have a fiduciary duty to operate the enterprise in a manner that creates value for the company's shareholders—a legal obligation. Just as clearly, a company and its personnel are duty-bound to obey the law otherwise and comply with governmental regulations. But does a company also have a duty to go beyond legal requirements and hold all company personnel responsible for conforming to high ethical standards? Does it have an obligation to contribute to the betterment of society, independent of the needs and preferences of the customers it serves? Should a company display a social conscience by devoting a portion of its resources to bettering society? Should its strategic initiatives be screened for possible negative effects on future generations of the world's population?

This chapter focuses on whether a company, in the course of trying to craft and execute a strategy that delivers value to both customers and shareholders, also has a duty to (1) act in an ethical manner; (2) be a committed corporate citizen and allocate some of its resources to improving the well-being of employees, the communities in which it operates, and society as a whole; and (3) adopt business practices that conserve natural resources, protect the interests of future generations, and preserve the well-being of the planet.

WHAT DO WE MEAN BY *BUSINESS ETHICS?*

Ethics concerns principles of right or wrong conduct. **Business ethics** is the application of ethical principles and standards to the actions and decisions of business organizations and the conduct of their personnel.[1] *Ethical principles in business are not materially different from ethical principles in general.* Why? Because business actions have to be judged in the context of society's standards of right and wrong, not with respect to a special set of ethical standards applicable only to business situations. If dishonesty is considered unethical and immoral, then dishonest behavior in business—whether it relates to customers, suppliers, employees, shareholders, competitors, or government—qualifies as equally unethical and immoral. If being ethical entails not deliberately harming others, then businesses are ethically obliged to recall a defective or unsafe product swiftly, regardless of the cost. If society deems bribery unethical, then it is unethical for company personnel to make payoffs to government officials to win government contracts or bestow favors to customers to win or retain their business. In short, ethical behavior in business situations requires adhering to generally accepted norms about right or wrong conduct. As a consequence, company managers have an obligation—indeed, a duty—to observe ethical norms when crafting and executing strategy.

● **LO 9-1**

Explain how the ethical standards in business are no different from the ethical norms of the larger society in which a company operates.

WHERE DO ETHICAL STANDARDS COME FROM—ARE THEY UNIVERSAL OR DEPENDENT ON LOCAL NORMS?

Notions of right and wrong, fair and unfair, moral and immoral are present in all societies and cultures. But there are three distinct schools of thought about the extent to which ethical standards travel across cultures and whether multinational companies can apply the same set of ethical standards in any and all locations where they operate.

The School of Ethical Universalism

According to the school of **ethical universalism,** the most fundamental conceptions of right and wrong are *universal* and transcend culture, society, and religion.[2] For instance, being truthful (not lying and not being deliberately deceitful) strikes a chord of what's right in the peoples of all nations. Likewise, demonstrating integrity of character, not cheating or harming people, and treating others with decency are concepts that resonate with people of virtually all cultures and religions.

Common moral agreement about right and wrong actions and behaviors across multiple cultures and countries gives rise to universal ethical standards that apply to members of all societies, all companies, and all businesspeople. These universal ethical principles set forth the traits and behaviors that are considered virtuous and that a good person is supposed to believe in and to display. Thus, adherents of the school of ethical universalism maintain that it is entirely appropriate to expect all members of society (including all personnel of all companies worldwide) to conform to these universal ethical standards.[3] For example, people in most societies would concur that it is unethical for companies to knowingly expose workers to toxic chemicals and hazardous materials or to sell products known to be unsafe or harmful to the users.

The strength of ethical universalism is that it draws on the collective views of multiple societies and cultures to put some clear boundaries on what constitutes ethical and unethical business behavior, regardless of the country or culture in which a company's personnel are conducting activities. This means that with respect to basic moral standards that do not vary significantly according to local cultural beliefs, traditions, or religious convictions, a multinational company can develop a code of ethics that it applies more or less evenly across its worldwide operations. It can avoid the slippery slope that comes from having different ethical standards for different company personnel depending on where in the world they are working.

The School of Ethical Relativism

While undoubtedly there are some universal moral prescriptions (like being truthful and trustworthy), there are also observable variations from one society to another as to what constitutes ethical or unethical behavior. Indeed, differing religious beliefs, social customs, traditions, core values, and behavioral norms frequently give rise to different standards about what is fair or unfair, moral or immoral, and ethically right or wrong. For instance, European and American managers often establish standards of business conduct that protect human rights such as freedom of movement and residence, freedom of speech and political opinion, and the right to privacy. In China, where societal commitment to basic human rights is weak, human rights considerations play a small role in determining what is ethically right or wrong in conducting business activities. In Japan, managers believe that showing respect for the collective good of society is a more important ethical consideration. In Muslim countries, managers typically apply ethical standards compatible with the teachings of Muhammad. Consequently, the school of **ethical relativism** holds that a "one-size-fits-all" template for judging the ethical appropriateness of business actions and the behaviors of company personnel is totally inappropriate. Rather, the underlying thesis of ethical relativism is that whether certain actions or behaviors are ethically right or wrong depends on the ethical norms of the country or culture in which they take place. For businesses, this implies that when there are cross-country or cross-cultural differences in ethical standards, it is appropriate for *local ethical standards to take precedence over what the ethical standards may be in a company's home market.*[4] In a world of ethical relativism, there are few absolutes when it comes to business ethics, and thus few ethical absolutes for consistently judging the ethical correctness of a company's conduct in various countries and markets.

This need to contour local ethical standards to fit local customs, local notions of fair and proper individual treatment, and local business practices gives rise to multiple sets of ethical standards. It also poses some challenging ethical dilemmas. Consider the following two examples.

The Use of Underage Labor   In industrialized nations, the use of underage workers is considered taboo. Social activists are adamant that child labor is unethical and that companies should neither employ children under the age of 18 as full-time employees nor source any products from foreign suppliers that employ underage workers. Many countries have passed legislation forbidding the use of underage labor or, at a minimum, regulating the employment of people under the age of 18. However, in Eretria, Uzbekistan, Myanmar, Somalia, Zimbabwe, Afghanistan, Sudan, North Korea, Yemen, and more than 50 other countries, it is customary to view children as potential, even necessary, workers. In other countries, like China, India, Russia, and Brazil, child labor laws are often poorly enforced.[5] As of 2016, the International Labor Organization estimated that there were about 152 million child laborers age 5 to 17 and that some 73 million of them were engaged in hazardous work.[6]

While exposing children to hazardous work and long work hours is unquestionably deplorable, the fact remains that poverty-stricken families in many poor countries cannot subsist without the work efforts of young family members; sending their children to school instead of having them work is not a realistic option. If such children are not permitted to work (especially those in the 12-to-17 age group)—due to pressures imposed by activist groups in industrialized nations—they may be forced to go out on the streets begging or to seek work in parts of the "underground" economy such as drug trafficking and prostitution.[7] So, if all businesses in countries where employing underage workers is common succumb to the pressures to stop employing underage labor, then have they served the best interests of the underage workers, their families, and society in general? In recognition of this issue, organizations opposing child labor are targeting certain forms of child labor such as enslaved child labor and hazardous work. IKEA is an example of a company that has worked hard to prevent any form of child labor by its suppliers. Its practices go well beyond standards and safeguards to include measures designed to address the underlying social problems of the communities in which their suppliers operate.

The Payment of Bribes and Kickbacks   A particularly thorny area facing multinational companies is the degree of cross-country variability in paying bribes.[8] In many countries in eastern Europe, Africa, Latin America, and Asia, it is customary to pay bribes to government officials in order to win a government contract, obtain a license or permit, or facilitate an administrative ruling.[9] In some developing nations, it is difficult for any company, foreign or domestic, to move goods through customs without paying off low-level officials. Senior managers in China and Russia often use their power to obtain kickbacks when they purchase materials or other products for their companies.[10] Likewise, in many countries it is normal to make payments to prospective customers in order to win or retain their business. Some people stretch to justify the payment of bribes and kickbacks on grounds that bribing government officials to get goods through customs or giving kickbacks to customers to retain their business or win new orders is simply a payment for services rendered, in the same way that people tip for service at restaurants.[11] But while this is a clever rationalization, it rests on moral quicksand.

Companies that forbid the payment of bribes and kickbacks in their codes of ethical conduct and that are serious about enforcing this prohibition face a particularly vexing problem in countries where bribery and kickback payments are an entrenched local custom. Complying with the company's code of ethical conduct in these countries is very often tantamount to losing business to competitors that have no such scruples—an outcome that penalizes ethical companies and ethical company personnel (who may suffer lost sales commissions or bonuses). On the other hand, the payment of bribes or kickbacks not only undercuts the company's code of ethics but also risks breaking the law. The Foreign Corrupt Practices Act (FCPA) prohibits U.S. companies from paying bribes to government officials, political parties, political candidates, or others in all countries where they do business. The Organization for Economic Cooperation and Development (OECD) has antibribery standards that criminalize the bribery of foreign public officials in international business transactions—all 35 OECD member countries and 7 nonmember countries have adopted these standards.

Despite laws forbidding bribery to secure sales and contracts, the practice persists. As of January 2017, 443 individuals and 158 entities were sanctioned under criminal proceedings for foreign bribery by the OECD. At least 125 of the sanctioned individuals were sentenced to prison. In 2017, in the midst of a national opioid drug crisis, the executive chairman of Insys Therapeutics was arrested for bribing doctors to overprescribe the company's opioid products. In the same year, oil services giant Halliburton agreed to pay $29.2 million to settle charges brought against it by the Security and Exchange Commission's Foreign Corrupt Practices Act Enforcement Division; one of their executives had to pay a $75,000 penalty. The global snack company Cadbury Limited/Mondelez International had to pay a $13 million penalty for violations that included illicit payments to get approvals for a new chocolate factory in India. Other well-known companies caught up in recent bribery cases include JPMorgan; pharmaceutical companies GlaxoSmithKline, Novartis, and AstraZeneca; casino company Las Vegas Sands; and aircraft manufacturer Embraer.

Why Ethical Relativism Is Problematic for Multinational Companies   Relying on the principle of ethical relativism to determine what is right or wrong poses major problems for multinational companies trying to decide which ethical standards to enforce companywide. It is a slippery slope indeed to resolve conflicting ethical standards for operating in different countries without any kind of higher-order moral compass. Consider, for example, the ethical inconsistency of a multinational company that, in the name of ethical relativism, declares it impermissible to engage in kickbacks unless such payments are customary and generally overlooked by legal authorities. It is likewise problematic for a multinational company to declare it ethically acceptable to use underage labor at its plants in those countries where child labor is allowed but ethically inappropriate to employ underage labor at its plants elsewhere. If a country's culture is accepting of environmental degradation or practices that expose workers to dangerous conditions (toxic chemicals or bodily harm), should a multinational company lower its ethical bar in that country but rule the very same actions to be ethically wrong in other countries?

Business leaders who rely on the principle of ethical relativism to justify conflicting ethical standards for operating in different countries have little moral basis for establishing or enforcing ethical standards companywide. Rather, when a company's ethical standards vary from country to country, the clear message being sent to employees is that the company has no ethical standards or convictions of its own and prefers to let its standards of ethical right and wrong be governed by the customs and practices of the countries in which it operates. Applying multiple sets of ethical standards without some kind of higher-order moral compass is scarcely a basis for holding company personnel to high standards of ethical behavior. And it can lead to prosecutions of both companies and individuals alike when there are conflicting sets of laws.

> Codes of conduct based on ethical relativism can be *ethically problematic* for multinational companies by creating a maze of conflicting ethical standards.

Ethics and Integrative Social Contracts Theory

Integrative social contracts theory provides a middle position between the opposing views of ethical universalism and ethical relativism.[12] According to this theory, the ethical standards a company should try to uphold are governed by both (1) a limited number of universal ethical principles that are widely recognized as putting legitimate ethical boundaries on behaviors in *all* situations and (2) the circumstances of local cultures, traditions, and values that further prescribe what constitutes ethically permissible behavior. The universal ethical principles are based on the collective views of multiple cultures and societies and combine to form a "social contract" that all individuals, groups, organizations, and businesses in all situations have a duty to observe. *Within the boundaries of this social contract,* local cultures or groups can specify what *other* actions may or may not be ethically permissible. While this

> **CORE** CONCEPT
>
> According to **integrated social contracts theory**, universal ethical principles based on the collective views of multiple societies form a "social contract" that all individuals and organizations have a duty to observe in all situations. *Within the boundaries of this social contract,* local cultures or groups can specify what *additional* actions may or may not be ethically permissible.

system leaves some "moral free space" for the people in a particular country (or local culture, or profession, or even a company) to make specific interpretations of what other actions may or may not be permissible, *universal ethical norms always take precedence.* Thus, local ethical standards can be *more* stringent than the universal ethical standards but *never less so.* For example, both the legal and medical professions have standards regarding what kinds of advertising are ethically permissible that extend beyond the universal norm that advertising not be false or misleading.

The strength of integrated social contracts theory is that it accommodates the best parts of ethical universalism and ethical relativism. Moreover, integrative social contracts theory offers managers in multinational companies clear guidance in resolving cross-country ethical differences: Those parts of the company's code of ethics that involve universal ethical norms must be enforced worldwide, but within these boundaries there is room for ethical diversity and the opportunity for host-country cultures to exert *some* influence over the moral and ethical standards of business units operating in that country.

A good example of the application of integrative social contracts theory to business involves the payment of bribes and kickbacks. Yes, bribes and kickbacks are common in some countries. But the fact that bribery flourishes in a country does not mean it is an authentic or legitimate ethical norm. Virtually all of the world's major religions (e.g., Buddhism, Christianity, Confucianism, Hinduism, Islam, Judaism, Sikhism, and Taoism) and all moral schools of thought condemn bribery and corruption. Therefore, a multinational company might reasonably conclude that there is a universal ethical principle to be observed here—one of refusing to condone bribery and kickbacks on the part of company personnel no matter what the local custom is and no matter what the sales consequences are.

> According to integrated social contracts theory, adherence to universal or "first-order" ethical norms should always take precedence over local or "second-order" norms.

> In instances involving *universally applicable* ethical norms (like paying bribes), there can be *no compromise* on what is ethically permissible and what is not.

HOW AND WHY ETHICAL STANDARDS IMPACT THE TASKS OF CRAFTING AND EXECUTING STRATEGY

Many companies have acknowledged their ethical obligations in official codes of ethical conduct. In the United States, for example, the Sarbanes-Oxley Act, passed in 2002, requires that companies whose stock is publicly traded have a code of ethics or else explain in writing to the SEC why they do not. But the senior executives of ethically principled companies understand that there's a big difference between having a code of ethics because it is mandated and having ethical standards that truly provide guidance for a company's strategy and business conduct.[13] They know that *the litmus test of whether a company's code of ethics is cosmetic is the extent to which it is embraced in crafting strategy and in operating the business day to day.* Executives committed to high standards make a point of considering three sets of questions whenever a new strategic initiative or policy or operating practice is under review:

- Is what we are proposing to do fully compliant with our code of ethical conduct? Are there any areas of ambiguity that may be of concern?
- Is there any aspect of the strategy (or policy or operating practice) that gives the appearance of being ethically questionable?
- Is there anything in the proposed action that customers, employees, suppliers, stockholders, competitors, community activists, regulators, or the media might consider ethically objectionable?

Unless questions of this nature are posed—either in open discussion or by force of habit in the minds of company managers—there's a risk that strategic initiatives and/or the way daily operations are conducted will become disconnected from the company's code of ethics. If a company's executives believe strongly in living up to the company's ethical standards, they will unhesitatingly reject strategic initiatives and operating approaches that don't measure up. However, in companies with a cosmetic approach to ethics, any linkage of the professed standards to its strategy and operating practices stems mainly from a desire to avoid the risk of embarrassment and possible disciplinary action for approving actions that are later deemed unethical and perhaps illegal.

While most company managers are careful to ensure that a company's strategy is within the bounds of what is *legal*, evidence indicates they are not always so careful to ensure that all elements of their strategies and operating activities are within the bounds of what is considered *ethical*. In recent years, there have been revelations of ethical misconduct on the part of managers at such companies as Samsung, Kobe Steel, credit rating firm Equifax, United Airlines, several leading investment banking firms, and a host of mortgage lenders. Sexual harassment allegations plagued many companies in 2017, including film company Weinstein Company LLC and entertainment giant 21st Century Fox. The consequences of crafting strategies that cannot pass the test of moral scrutiny are manifested in sizable fines, devastating public relations hits, sharp drops in stock prices that cost shareholders billions of dollars, criminal indictments, and convictions of company executives. The fallout from all these scandals has resulted in heightened management attention to legal and ethical considerations in crafting strategy.

• LO 9-2

Explain what drives unethical business strategies and behavior.

DRIVERS OF UNETHICAL BUSINESS STRATEGIES AND BEHAVIOR

Apart from the "business of business is business, not ethics" kind of thinking apparent in recent high-profile business scandals, three other main drivers of unethical business behavior also stand out:[14]

- Faulty oversight, enabling the unscrupulous pursuit of personal gain and self-interest.
- Heavy pressures on company managers to meet or beat short-term performance targets.
- A company culture that puts profitability and business performance ahead of ethical behavior.

Faulty Oversight, Enabling the Unscrupulous Pursuit of Personal Gain and Self-Interest   People who are obsessed with wealth accumulation, power, status, and their own self-interest often push aside ethical principles in their quest for personal gain. Driven by greed and ambition, they exhibit few qualms in skirting the rules or doing whatever is necessary to achieve their goals. A general disregard for business ethics can prompt all kinds of unethical strategic maneuvers and behaviors at companies. The numerous scandals that have tarnished the reputation of ridesharing company Uber and forced the resignation of its CEO is a case in point, as described in Illustration Capsule 9.1.

Responsible corporate governance and oversight by the company's corporate board is necessary to guard against self-dealing and the manipulation of information to

ILLUSTRATION
CAPSULE 9.1   Ethical Violations at Uber and their Consequences

The peer-to-peer ridesharing company Uber has been credited with transforming the transportation industry, upending the taxi market, and changing the way consumers travel from place to place. But its lack of attention to ethics has resulted in numerous scandals, a tarnished reputation, a loss of market share to rival companies, and the ouster of its co-founder Travis Kalanick from his position as the company's CEO. The ethical lapses for which Uber has been criticized include the following:

- **Sexual harassment and a toxic workplace culture.** In June 2017, Uber fired over 20 employees as a result of an investigation that uncovered widespread sexual harassment that had been going on for years at the company. Female employees who had reported incidents of sexual harassment were subjected to retaliation by their managers, and reports of the incidents to senior executives resulted in inaction.

- **Price gouging during crises.** During emergencies situations such as Hurricane Sandy and the 2017 London Bridge attack, Uber added high surcharges to the cost of their services. This drew much censure, particularly since its competitors offered free or reduced cost rides during those same times.

- **Data breaches and violations of user privacy.** Since 2014, the names, email addresses, and license information of over 700,000 drivers and the personal information of over 65 million users have been disclosed as a result of data breaches. Moreover, in 2016 the company paid a hacker $100,000 in ransom to prevent the dissemination of personal driver and user data that had been breached, but it failed to publicly disclose the situation for over six months.

- **Inadequate attention to consumer safety.** Substandard vetting practices at Uber came to light after one of its drivers was arrested as the primary suspect in a mass shooting in Kalamazoo, Michigan, and after a series of reports alleging sexual assault and misconduct by its drivers. Uber's concern for safety was further questioned

©TY Lim/Shutterstock

when a pedestrian was tragically struck and killed by one of its self-driving vehicles in 2018.

- **Unfair competitive practices.** When nascent competitor Gett launched in New York City, Uber employees ordered and cancelled hundreds of rides to waste driver's time and then offered the drivers cash to drop Gett and join Uber. Uber has been accused of employing similar practices against Lyft.

The ethical violations at Uber have not been without economic consequence. They contributed to a significant market share loss to Lyft, Uber's closest competitor in the United States. In January 2017, when Uber was thought to have gouged its prices during protests against legislation banning immigrants from specific countries, its market share dropped 5 percentage points in a week. While Uber's ethical dilemmas are not the sole contributor to Lyft's increase in market share and expansion rate, the negative perceptions of Uber's brand from its unethical actions has afforded its competitors significant opportunities for brand and market share growth. And without a real change in Uber's culture and corporate governance practices, there is a strong likelihood that ethical scandals involving Uber will continue to surface.

Note: Developed with Alen A. Amini.

Sources: https://www.recode.net/2017/8/31/16227670/uber-lyft-market-share-deleteuber-decline-users; https://www.inc.com/associated-press/lyft-thrives-while-rival-uber-tries-to-stabilize-regain-control-2017.html; https://www.entrepreneur.com/article/300789.

disguise such actions by a company's managers. **Self-dealing** occurs when managers take advantage of their position to further their own private interests rather than those of the firm. As discussed in Chapter 2, the duty of the corporate board (and its compensation and audit committees in particular) is to guard against such actions. A strong, independent board is necessary to have proper oversight of the company's financial practices and to hold top managers accountable for their actions.

> ### CORE CONCEPT
> **Self-dealing** occurs when managers take advantage of their position to further their own private interests rather than those of the firm.

A particularly egregious example of the lack of proper oversight is the scandal over mortgage lending and banking practices that resulted in a crisis for the U.S. residential real estate market and heartrending consequences for many home buyers. This scandal stemmed from consciously unethical strategies at many banks and mortgage companies to boost the fees they earned on home mortgages by deliberately lowering lending standards to approve so-called subprime loans for home buyers whose incomes were insufficient to make their monthly mortgage payments. Once these lenders earned their fees on these loans, they repackaged the loans to hide their true nature and auctioned them off to unsuspecting investors, who later suffered huge losses when the high-risk borrowers began to default on their loan payments. (Government authorities later forced some of the firms that auctioned off these packaged loans to repurchase them at the auction price and bear the losses themselves.) A lawsuit by the attorneys general of 49 states charging widespread and systematic fraud ultimately resulted in a $26 billion settlement by the five largest U.S. banks (Bank of America, Citigroup, JPMorgan Chase, Wells Fargo, and Ally Financial). Included in the settlement were new rules designed to increase oversight and reform policies and practices among the mortgage companies. The settlement includes what are believed to be a set of robust monitoring and enforcement mechanisms that should help prevent such abuses in the future.[15]

Heavy Pressures on Company Managers to Meet Short-Term Performance Targets   When key personnel find themselves scrambling to meet the quarterly and annual sales and profit expectations of investors and financial analysts, they often feel enormous pressure to *do whatever it takes* to protect their reputation for delivering good results. Executives at high-performing companies know that investors will see the slightest sign of a slowdown in earnings growth as a red flag and drive down the company's stock price. In addition, slowing growth or declining profits could lead to a downgrade of the company's credit rating if it has used lots of debt to finance its growth. The pressure to "never miss a quarter"—to not upset the expectations of analysts, investors, and creditors—prompts nearsighted managers to engage in short-term maneuvers to make the numbers, regardless of whether these moves are really in the best long-term interests of the company. Sometimes the pressure induces company personnel to continue to stretch the rules until the limits of ethical conduct are overlooked.[16] Once ethical boundaries are crossed in efforts to "meet or beat their numbers," the threshold for making more extreme ethical compromises becomes lower.

To meet its demanding profit target, Wells Fargo put such pressure on its employees to hit sales quotas that many employees responded by fraudulently opening customer accounts. In 2017, after the practices came to light, the bank was forced to return $2.6 million to customers and pay $186 million in fines to the government. Wells Fargo's reputation took a big hit, its stock price plummeted, and its CEO lost his job.

Company executives often feel pressured to hit financial performance targets because their compensation depends heavily on the company's performance. Over the last two decades, it has become fashionable for boards of directors to grant lavish bonuses, stock option awards, and other compensation benefits to executives for meeting specified performance targets. So outlandishly large were these rewards that executives had strong personal incentives to bend the rules and engage in behaviors that allowed the targets to be met. Much of the accounting manipulation at the root of recent corporate scandals has entailed situations in which executives benefited enormously from misleading accounting or other shady activities that allowed them to hit the numbers and receive incentive awards ranging from $10 million to more than $1 billion for hedge fund managers.

The fundamental problem with **short-termism**—the tendency for managers to focus excessive attention on short-term performance objectives—is that it doesn't create value for customers or improve the firm's competitiveness in the marketplace; that is, it sacrifices the activities that are the most reliable drivers of higher profits and added shareholder value in the long run. Cutting ethical corners in the name of profits carries exceptionally high risk for shareholders—the steep stock price decline and tarnished brand image that accompany the discovery of scurrilous behavior leave shareholders with a company worth much less than before—and the rebuilding task can be arduous, taking both considerable time and resources.

A Company Culture That Puts Profitability and Business Performance Ahead of Ethical Behavior   When a company's culture spawns an ethically corrupt or amoral work climate, people have a company-approved license to ignore "what's right" and engage in any behavior or strategy they think they can get away with. Such cultural norms as "Everyone else does it" and "It is okay to bend the rules to get the job done" permeate the work environment. At such companies, ethically immoral people are certain to play down observance of ethical strategic actions and business conduct. Moreover, cultural pressures to utilize unethical means if circumstances become challenging can prompt otherwise honorable people to behave unethically. A perfect example of a company culture gone awry on ethics is Enron, a now-defunct but infamous company found guilty of one of the most sprawling business frauds in U.S. history.[17]

Enron's leaders pressured company personnel to be innovative and aggressive in figuring out how to grow current earnings—*regardless of the methods.* Enron's annual "rank and yank" performance evaluation process, in which the lowest-ranking 15 to 20 percent of employees were let go, made it abundantly clear that bottom-line results were what mattered most. The name of the game at Enron became devising clever ways to boost revenues and earnings, even if this sometimes meant operating outside established policies (and legal limits). In fact, outside-the-lines behavior was celebrated if it generated profitable new business.

A high-performance–high-rewards climate came to pervade the Enron culture, as the best workers (determined by who produced the best bottom-line results) received impressively large incentives and bonuses. On Car Day at Enron, an array of luxury sports cars arrived for presentation to the most successful employees. Understandably, employees wanted to be seen as part of Enron's star team and partake in the benefits granted to Enron's best and brightest employees. The high monetary rewards, the ambitious and hard-driving people whom the company hired and promoted, and the competitive, results-oriented culture combined to give Enron a reputation not only for trampling competitors but also for internal ruthlessness. The company's win-at-all-costs mindset nurtured a culture that gradually and then more rapidly fostered the erosion of ethical standards, eventually making a mockery of the company's stated values of integrity and respect. When it became evident that Enron was a house of cards propped up by deceitful accounting and myriad unsavory practices, the company imploded in a matter of weeks—one of the biggest bankruptcies of all time, costing investors $64 billion in losses.

In contrast, when high ethical principles are deeply ingrained in the corporate culture of a company, culture can function as a powerful mechanism for communicating ethical behavioral norms and gaining employee buy-in to the company's moral standards, business principles, and corporate values. In such cases, the ethical principles embraced in the company's code of ethics and/or in its statement of corporate values are seen as integral to the company's identity, self-image, and ways of operating. The message that ethics matters—and matters a lot—resounds loudly and clearly throughout the organization and in its strategy and decisions.

WHY SHOULD COMPANY STRATEGIES BE ETHICAL?

There are two reasons why a company's strategy should be ethical: (1) because a strategy that is unethical is morally wrong and reflects badly on the character of the company and its personnel, and (2) because an ethical strategy can be good business and serve the self-interest of shareholders.

The Moral Case for an Ethical Strategy

Managers do not dispassionately assess what strategic course to steer—how strongly committed they are to observing ethical principles and standards definitely comes into play in making strategic choices. Ethical strategy making is generally the product of managers who are of strong moral character (i.e., who are trustworthy, have integrity, and truly care about conducting the company's business honorably). Managers with high ethical principles are usually advocates of a corporate code of ethics and strong ethics compliance, and they are genuinely committed to upholding corporate values and ethical business principles. They demonstrate their commitment by displaying the company's stated values and living up to its business principles and ethical standards. They understand the difference between merely adopting value statements and codes of ethics and ensuring that they are followed strictly in a company's actual strategy and business conduct. As a consequence, ethically strong managers consciously opt for strategic actions that can pass the strictest moral scrutiny—they display no tolerance for strategies with ethically controversial components.

● **LO 9-3**

Identify the costs of business ethics failures.

The Business Case for Ethical Strategies

In addition to the moral reasons for adopting ethical strategies, there may be solid business reasons. Pursuing unethical strategies and tolerating unethical conduct not only damages a company's reputation but also may result in a wide-ranging set of other costly consequences. Figure 9.1 shows the kinds of costs a company can incur when unethical behavior on its part is discovered, the wrongdoings of company personnel are headlined in the media, and it is forced to make amends for its behavior. The more egregious are a company's ethical violations, the higher the costs and the bigger the damage to its reputation (and to the reputations of the company personnel involved). In high-profile instances, the costs of ethical misconduct can easily run into the hundreds of millions and even billions of dollars, especially if they provoke widespread public outrage and many people were harmed. The penalties levied on executives caught in wrongdoing can skyrocket as well, as the 150-year prison term sentence of infamous financier and Ponzi scheme perpetrator Bernie Madoff illustrates.

The fallout of a company's ethical misconduct goes well beyond the costs of making amends for the misdeeds. Customers shun companies caught up in highly publicized

FIGURE 9.1　The Costs Companies Incur When Ethical Wrongdoing Is Discovered

Visible Costs	Internal Administrative Costs	Intangible or Less Visible Costs
• Government fines and penalties • Civil penalties arising from class-action lawsuits and other litigation aimed at punishing the company for its offense and the harm done to others • The costs to shareholders in the form of a lower stock price (and possibly lower dividends)	• Legal and investigative costs incurred by the company • The costs of providing remedial education and ethics training to company personnel • The costs of taking corrective actions • Administrative costs associated with ensuring future compliance	• Customer defections • Loss of reputation • Lost employee morale and higher degrees of employee cynicism • Higher employee turnover • Higher recruiting costs and difficulty in attracting talented employees • Adverse effects on employee productivity • The costs of complying with often harsher government regulations

Source: Adapted from Terry Thomas, John R. Schermerhorn, and John W. Dienhart, "Strategic Leadership of Ethical Behavior," *Academy of Management Executive* 18, no. 2 (May 2004), p. 58.

ethical scandals. Rehabilitating a company's shattered reputation is time-consuming and costly. Companies with tarnished reputations have difficulty in recruiting and retaining talented employees. Most ethically upstanding people are repulsed by a work environment where unethical behavior is condoned; they don't want to get entrapped in a compromising situation, nor do they want their personal reputations tarnished by the actions of an unsavory employer. Creditors are unnerved by the unethical actions of a borrower because of the potential business fallout and subsequent higher risk of default on loans.

> Shareholders suffer major damage when a company's unethical behavior is discovered. Making amends for unethical business conduct is costly, and it takes years to rehabilitate a tarnished company reputation.

All told, a company's unethical behavior can do considerable damage to shareholders in the form of lost revenues, higher costs, lower profits, lower stock prices, and a diminished business reputation. To a significant degree, therefore, ethical strategies and ethical conduct are *good business.* Most companies understand the value of operating in a manner that wins the approval of suppliers, employees, investors, and society at large. Most businesspeople recognize the risks and adverse fallout attached to the discovery of unethical behavior. Hence, companies have an incentive to employ strategies that can pass the test of being ethical. Even if a company's managers are not personally committed to high ethical standards, they have good reason to operate within ethical bounds, if only to (1) avoid the risk of embarrassment, scandal, disciplinary action, fines, and possible jail time for unethical conduct on their part; and (2) escape being held accountable for lax enforcement of ethical standards and unethical behavior by personnel under their supervision. Illustration Capsule 9.2 discusses PepsiCo's commitment to high ethical standards and their approach to putting their ethical principles into practice.

ILLUSTRATION
CAPSULE 9.2   How PepsiCo Put Its Ethical Principles into Practice

PepsiCo is one of the world's leading food and beverage companies with over $65 billion in net revenue, coming from iconic brands such as Lays and Ruffles potato chips, Quaker Oatmeal, Tropicana juice, Mountain Dew, and Diet Pepsi. The company is also known for its dedication to ethical business practices, having ranked consistently as among the World's Most Ethical Companies by business ethics think tank *Ethicsphere* ever since the award program was initiated. PepsiCo's Global Code of Conduct plays a pivotal role in ensuring that PepsiCo's employees, managers, and directors around the world are complying with the company's high ethical standards. It provides specific guidance concerning how to make decisions, how to treat others, and how to conduct business globally, organized around four key operating principles: (1) respect in the workplace, (2) integrity in the marketplace, (3) ethics in business activities, and (4) responsibility to shareholders. Essentially, the Code of Conduct lays out a set of behavioral norms that has come to define the company's culture.

Even with a strong ethical culture, implementing a code of conduct across a global organization of over 250,000 employees is challenging. To assist, PepsiCo set up a Global Compliance & Ethics Department with primary responsibility for promoting, monitoring, and enforcing the code. Employees at all levels are required to participate in annual Code of Conduct training, through online courses as well as in-person, manager-led workshops. Compliance training also takes place in a more targeted fashion, based on role and geography, concerning such issues as bribery. Other types of communications throughout the year, such as internal newsletter articles and messaging from the leadership, reinforce the annual training.

©monticello/Shutterstock

Employees are encouraged to seek guidance when faced with an ethical dilemma. They are also encouraged to raise concerns and are obligated to report any Code violations. A variety of channels have been set up for them to do this, including a hotline operated by an independent third party. All reports of suspected violations are reviewed in accordance with company policies designed to foster consistency of the investigative process and corrective actions (which may include termination of employment). PepsiCo has also established an annual peer-nominated Ethical Leadership Award designed to recognize instances of exceptional ethical conduct by employees.

The leadership at PepsiCo believes that their commitment to ethical principles has helped the company in attracting and retaining the best people. Indeed, PepsiCo has been listed as among the Top Attractors of talent globally. In addition, the company has regularly been listed as among the World's Most Respected Companies (Barron) and the World's Most Admired Companies (Fortune).

Sources: Company website; **https://ethisphere.com/pepsico-performance-purpose/**.

STRATEGY, CORPORATE SOCIAL RESPONSIBILITY, AND ENVIRONMENTAL SUSTAINABILITY

The idea that businesses have an obligation to foster social betterment, a much-debated topic over the past 50 years, took root in the 19th century when progressive companies in the aftermath of the industrial revolution began to provide workers with housing and other amenities. The notion that corporate executives should balance the interests of all stakeholders—shareholders, employees, customers, suppliers, the communities in

● LO 9-4

Explain the concepts of corporate social responsibility and environmental sustainability and how companies balance these duties with economic responsibilities to shareholders.

CORE CONCEPT

Corporate social responsibility (CSR) refers to a company's *duty* to operate in an honorable manner, provide good working conditions for employees, encourage workforce diversity, be a good steward of the environment, and actively work to better the quality of life in the local communities where it operates and in society at large.

which they operate, and society at large—began to blossom in the 1960s. Some years later, a group of chief executives of America's 200 largest corporations, calling themselves the Business Roundtable, came out in strong support of the concept of **corporate social responsibility (CSR):**

> Balancing the shareholder's expectations of maximum return against other priorities is one of the fundamental problems confronting corporate management. The shareholder must receive a good return but the legitimate concerns of other constituencies (customers, employees, communities, suppliers and society at large) also must have the appropriate attention. . . . [Leading managers] believe that by giving enlightened consideration to balancing the legitimate claims of all its constituents, a corporation will best serve the interest of its shareholders.

Today, corporate social responsibility is a concept that resonates in western Europe, the United States, Canada, and such developing nations as Brazil and India.

The Concepts of Corporate Social Responsibility and Good Corporate Citizenship

The essence of socially responsible business behavior is that a company should balance strategic actions to benefit shareholders against the *duty* to be a good corporate citizen. The underlying thesis is that company managers should display a *social conscience* in operating the business and specifically take into account how management decisions and company actions affect the well-being of employees, local communities, the environment, and society at large.[18] Acting in a socially responsible manner thus encompasses more than just participating in community service projects and donating money to charities and other worthy causes. Demonstrating social responsibility also entails undertaking actions that earn trust and respect from all stakeholders—operating in an honorable and ethical manner, striving to make the company a great place to work, demonstrating genuine respect for the environment, and trying to make a difference in bettering society. As depicted in Figure 9.2, corporate responsibility programs commonly include the following elements:

- *Striving to employ an ethical strategy and observe ethical principles in operating the business.* A sincere commitment to observing ethical principles is a necessary component of a CSR strategy simply because unethical conduct is incompatible with the concept of good corporate citizenship and socially responsible business behavior.

- *Making charitable contributions, supporting community service endeavors, engaging in broader philanthropic initiatives, and reaching out to make a difference in the lives of the disadvantaged.* Some companies fulfill their philanthropic obligations by spreading their efforts over a multitude of charitable and community activities—for instance, Cisco, LinkedIn, IBM, and Google support a broad variety of community, art, and social welfare programs. Others prefer to focus their energies more narrowly. McDonald's concentrates on sponsoring the Ronald McDonald House program (which provides a home away from home for the families of seriously ill children receiving treatment at nearby hospitals). Genentech and many pharmaceutical companies run prescription assistance programs to provide expensive medications at little or no cost to needy patients. Companies frequently reinforce their philanthropic efforts by encouraging employees to support charitable causes and participate in community affairs, often through programs that match employee contributions.

- *Taking actions to protect the environment and, in particular, to minimize or eliminate any adverse impact on the environment stemming from the company's own business activities.*

FIGURE 9.2   The Five Components of a Corporate Social Responsibility Strategy

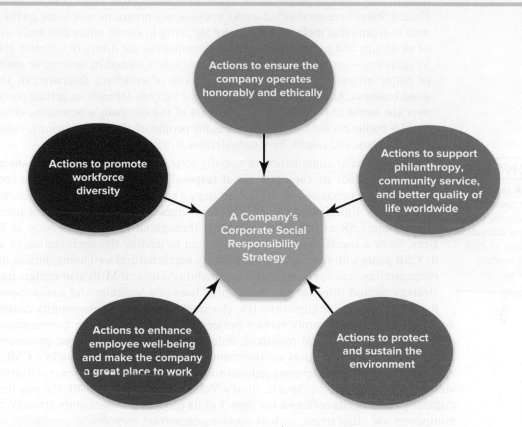

Source: Adapted from material in Ronald Paul Hill, Debra Stephens, and Iain Smith, "Corporate Social Responsibility: An Examination of Individual Firm Behavior," *Business and Society Review* 108, no. 3 (September 2003), p. 348.

Corporate social responsibility as it applies to environmental protection entails actively striving to be a good steward of the environment. This means using the best available science and technology to reduce environmentally harmful aspects of the company's operations *below the levels required by prevailing environmental regulations*. It also means putting time and money into improving the environment in ways that extend beyond a company's own industry boundaries—such as participating in recycling projects, adopting energy conservation practices, and supporting efforts to clean up local water supplies. Häagen-Dazs, a maker of all-natural ice creams, started a social media campaign to raise awareness about the dangers associated with the decreasing honeybee population; it donates a portion of its profits to research on this issue. The Walt Disney Company has created strict environmental targets for themselves and created the "Green Standard" to inspire employees to reduce their environmental impact.

- *Creating a work environment that enhances the quality of life for employees.* Numerous companies exert extra effort to enhance the quality of life for their employees at work and at home. This can include onsite day care, flexible work schedules, workplace exercise facilities, special leaves for employees to care for sick family members, work-at-home opportunities, career development programs and education opportunities, showcase plants and offices, special safety programs, and the like.

• *Building a diverse workforce with respect to gender, race, national origin, and other aspects that different people bring to the workplace.* Most large companies in the United States have established workforce diversity programs, and some go the extra mile to ensure that their workplaces are attractive to ethnic minorities and inclusive of all groups and perspectives. At some companies, the diversity initiative extends to suppliers—sourcing items from small businesses owned by women or members of ethnic minorities, for example. The pursuit of workforce diversity can also be good business. At Coca-Cola, where strategic success depends on getting people all over the world to become loyal consumers of the company's beverages, efforts to build a public persona of inclusiveness for people of all races, religions, nationalities, interests, and talents have considerable strategic value.

The particular combination of socially responsible endeavors a company elects to pursue defines its **corporate social responsibility (CSR) strategy.** The specific components emphasized in a CSR strategy vary from company to company and are typically linked to a company's core values. Few companies have managed to integrate CSR as fully and seamlessly throughout their organization as Burt's Bees; there a special committee is dedicated to leading the organization to attain its CSR goals with respect to three primary areas: natural well-being, humanitarian responsibility, and environmental sustainability. General Mills also centers its CSR strategy around three themes: nourishing lives (via healthier and easier-to-prepare foods), nourishing communities (via charitable donations to community causes and volunteerism for community service projects), and nourishing the environment (via efforts to conserve natural resources, reduce energy and water usage, promote recycling, and otherwise support environmental sustainability).[19] Starbucks's CSR strategy includes four main elements (ethical sourcing, community service, environmental stewardship, and farmer support), all of which have touch points with the way that the company procures its coffee—a key aspect of its product differentiation strategy. Some companies use other terms, such as *corporate citizenship, corporate responsibility,* or *sustainable responsible business (SRB)* to characterize their CSR initiatives. Illustration Capsule 9.3 describes Warby Parker's approach to corporate social responsibility—an approach that ensures that social responsibility is reflected in all of the company's actions and endeavors.

Although there is wide variation in how companies devise and implement a CSR strategy, communities of companies concerned with corporate social responsibility (such as CSR Europe) have emerged to help companies share best CSR practices. Moreover, a number of reporting standards have been developed, including ISO 26000—a new internationally recognized standard for social responsibility set by the International Standards Organization (ISO).[20] Companies that exhibit a strong commitment to corporate social responsibility are often recognized by being included on lists such as *Corporate Responsibility* magazine's "100 Best Corporate Citizens" or *Corporate Knights* magazine's "Global 100 Most Sustainable Corporations."

Corporate Social Responsibility and the Triple Bottom Line   CSR initiatives undertaken by companies are frequently directed at improving the company's *triple bottom line (TBL)*—a reference to three types of performance metrics: *economic, social,* and *environmental.* The goal is for a company to succeed simultaneously in all three dimensions, as illustrated in Figure 9.3.[21] The three dimensions of performance are often referred to in terms of the "three pillars" of "people, planet, and profit." The term *people* refers to the various social initiatives that make up CSR strategies, such as corporate giving, community involvement, and company efforts to improve the lives of its internal

Warby Parker: Combining Corporate Social Responsibility with Affordable Fashion

Since its founding in 2010, Warby Parker has succeeded in selling over one million pairs of high-fashion glasses at a discounted price of $95—roughly 80 percent below the average $500 price tag on a comparable pair of eyeglasses from another producer. With more than 45 stores in the United States, the company has built a brand recognized universally as one of the strongest in the world; it consistently posts a net promoter score (a measure of how likely someone would be to recommend the product) of close to 90—higher than companies like Zappos and Apple.

Under its Buy a Pair, Give a Pair program, nearly four million pairs of glasses have been distributed to needy people around the world. Warby Parker also supports partners, like Vision Spring, enabling them to provide basic eye exams and teach community members how to manufacture and sell glasses at very low prices to amplify beneficial effects in their communities. To date, VisionSpring alone has trained nearly 20,000 people across 35 countries with average impacts of 20 percent increase in income and 35 percent increase in productivity.

Efforts to be a responsible company expand beyond Warby Parker's international partnerships. The company voluntarily evaluates itself against benchmarks in the fields of "environment," "workers," "customers," "community," and "governance," demonstrating a nearly unparalleled dedication to outcomes outside of profit. The company is widely seen as an employer of choice and regularly attracts top talent for all roles across the organization. It holds to an extremely high environmental standard, running an entirely carbon neutral operation.

©Pat Greenhouse/The Boston Globe via Getty Images

While socially impactful actions matter at Warby Parker, the company is mindful of the critical role of its suppliers as well. Both founders spent countless hours coordinating partnerships with dedicated suppliers to ensure quality, invested deeply in building a lean manufacturing operation to minimize cost, and sought to build an organization that would keep buyers happy. The net effect is a very economically healthy company—they post around $3,000 in sales per square foot, second only to Apple stores—with financial stability to pursue responsibilities outside of customer satisfaction.

The strong fundamentals put in place by the firm's founders blend responsibility into its DNA and attach each piece of commercial success to positive outcomes in the world. The company was recently recognized as number one on *Fast Company*'s "Most Innovative Companies" list and continues to build loyal followers—both of its products and its CSR efforts—as it expands.

Note: Developed with Jeremy P. Reich.

Sources: Warby Parker and "B Corp" websites; Max Chafkin, "Warby Parker Sees the Future of Retail," *Fast Company,* February 17, 2015 (accessed February 22, 2016); Jenni Avins, "Warby Parker Proves Customers Don't Have to Care about Your Social Mission," *Quartz,* December 29, 2014 (accessed February 14, 2016).

and external stakeholders. *Planet* refers to a firm's ecological impact and environmental practices. The term *profit* has a broader meaning with respect to the triple bottom line than it does otherwise. It encompasses not only the profit a firm earns for its shareholders but also the economic impact that the company has on society more generally, in terms of the overall value that it creates and the overall costs that it imposes on society. For example, Procter & Gamble's Swiffer cleaning system, one of the company's best-selling products, not only offers an earth-friendly design but also outperforms less ecologically friendly alternatives in terms of its broader economic impact: It reduces

FIGURE 9.3   The Triple Bottom Line: Excelling on Three Measures of Company Performance

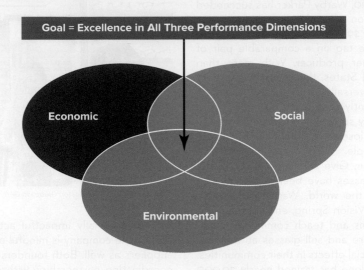

Source: Developed with help from Amy E. Florentino.

demands on municipal water sources, saves electricity that would be needed to heat mop water, and doesn't add to the amount of detergent making its way into waterways and waste treatment facilities. Nike sees itself as bringing people, planet, and profits into balance by producing innovative new products in a more sustainable way, recognizing that sustainability is key to its future profitability. TOMS shoes, which donates a pair of shoes to a child in need in over 50 different countries for every pair purchased, has also built its strategy around maintaining a well-balanced triple bottom line.

Many companies now make a point of citing the beneficial outcomes of their CSR strategies in press releases and issue special reports for consumers and investors to review. Southwest Airlines makes reporting an important part of its commitment to corporate responsibility; the company posts its annual Southwest Airlines One Report on its website that describes its initiatives and accomplishments with respect to each of the three pillars of triple bottom line performance—people, planet, profit. Triple-bottom-line reporting is emerging as an increasingly important way for companies to make the results of their CSR strategies apparent to stakeholders and for stakeholders to hold companies accountable for their impact on society. The use of standard reporting frameworks and metrics, such as those developed by the Global Reporting Initiative, promotes greater transparency and facilitates benchmarking CSR efforts across firms and industries.

Investment firms have created mutual funds consisting of companies that are excelling on the basis of the triple bottom line in order to attract funds from environmentally and socially aware investors. The Dow Jones Sustainability World Index is made up of the top 10 percent of the 2,500 companies listed in the Dow Jones World Index in terms of economic performance, environmental performance, and social performance. Companies are evaluated in these three performance areas, using indicators such as corporate governance, climate change mitigation, and labor practices. Table 9.1 shows a sampling of the companies selected for the Dow Jones Sustainability World Index in 2013.

TABLE 9.1   A Selection of Companies Recognized for Their Triple-Bottom-Line Performance in 2013

Name	Market Sector	Country
Peugeot SA	Automobiles & Components	France
Westpac Banking Group	Banks	Australia
CNH Industrial NV	Capital Goods	Great Britain
SGS SA	Commercial & Professional Services	Switzerland
LG Electronics Inc.	Consumer Durables & Apparel	South Korea
Intercontintenal Hotels Group	Consumer Services	Great Britain
UBS Group AB	Diversified Financials	Switzerland
Thai Oil PCL	Energy	Thailand
METRO AG	Food & Staples Retailing	Germany
Coca-Cola HBC AG	Food, Beverage & Tobacco	Switzerland
Abbott Laboratories	Health Care Equipment & Services	United States
Henkel AG & Co. KGaA	Household & Personal Products	Germany
Allianz SE	Insurance	Germany
Grupo Argos SA	Materials	Colombia
Pearson PLC	Media	Great Britain
Roche Holding AG	Pharmaceuticals, Biotechnology & Life Sciences	Switzerland
Mirvac Group	Real Estate	Australia
Industria de Diseno Textil SA	Retailing	Spain
Advanced Semiconductor Engineering Inc.	Semiconductors & Semiconductor Equipment	Taiwan
Amadeus IT Group SA	Software & Services	Spain
Konica Minolta Inc.	Technology Hardware & Equipment	Japan
Koninklijke KPN NV	Telecommunication Services	Netherlands
Royal Mail PLC	Transportation	Great Britain
Red Electric Corp SA	Utilities	Spain

Source: Adapted from RobecoSAM AG, www.sustainability-indices.com/review/industry-group-leaders-2017.jsp (accessed March 4, 2018).

What Do We Mean by *Sustainability* and *Sustainable Business Practices?*

The term *sustainability* is used in a variety of ways. In many firms, it is synonymous with corporate social responsibility; it is seen by some as a term that is gradually replacing *CSR* in the business lexicon. Indeed, sustainability reporting and TBL reporting are often one and the same, as illustrated by the Dow Jones Sustainability World Index, which tracks the same three types of performance measures that constitute the triple bottom line.

More often, however, the term takes on a more focused meaning, concerned with the relationship of a company to its *environment* and its use of *natural resources,* including land, water, air, plants, animals, minerals, fossil fuels, and biodiversity. It is widely recognized that the world's natural resources are finite and are being consumed and degraded at rates that threaten their capacity for renewal. Since corporations are the biggest users of natural resources, managing and maintaining these resources is critical for the long-term economic interests of corporations.

For some companies, this issue has direct and obvious implications for the continued viability of their business model and strategy. Pacific Gas and Electric has begun measuring the full carbon footprint of its supply chain to become not only a "greener" company but a more efficient energy producer.[22] Beverage companies such as Coca-Cola and PepsiCo are having to rethink their business models because of the prospect of future worldwide water shortages. For other companies, the connection is less direct, but all companies are part of a business ecosystem whose economic health depends on the availability of natural resources. In response, most major companies have begun to change *how* they do business, emphasizing the use of **sustainable business practices,** defined as those capable of meeting the needs of the present without compromising the ability to meet the needs of the future. Many have also begun to incorporate a consideration of environmental sustainability into their strategy-making activities.

Environmental sustainability strategies entail deliberate and concerted actions to operate businesses in a manner that protects natural resources and ecological support systems, guards against outcomes that will ultimately endanger the planet, and is therefore sustainable for centuries.[23] One aspect of environmental sustainability is keeping use of the Earth's natural resources within levels that can be replenished via the use of sustainable business practices. In the case of some resources (like crude oil, freshwater, and edible fish from the oceans), scientists say that use levels either are already unsustainable or will be soon, given the world's growing population and propensity to consume additional resources as incomes and living standards rise. Another aspect of sustainability concerns containing the adverse effects of greenhouse gases and other forms of air pollution to reduce their impact on undesirable climate and atmospheric changes. Other aspects of sustainability include greater reliance on sustainable energy sources; greater use of recyclable materials; the use of sustainable methods of growing foods (to reduce topsoil depletion and the use of pesticides, herbicides, fertilizers, and other chemicals that may be harmful to human health or ecological systems); habitat protection; environmentally sound waste management practices; and increased attempts to decouple environmental degradation and economic growth (according to scientists, economic growth has historically been accompanied by declines in the well-being of the environment).

Unilever, a diversified producer of processed foods, personal care, and home cleaning products, is among the many committed corporations pursuing sustainable business practices. The company tracks 11 sustainable agricultural indicators in its processed-foods business and has launched a variety of programs to improve the environmental performance of its suppliers. Examples of such programs include special low-rate financing for tomato suppliers choosing to switch to water-conserving irrigation systems and training programs in India that have allowed contract cucumber growers to reduce pesticide use by 90 percent while improving yields by 78 percent. Unilever has

CORE CONCEPT

Sustainable business practices are those that meet the needs of the present without compromising the ability to meet the needs of the future.

CORE CONCEPT

A company's **environmental sustainability strategy** consists of its deliberate actions to protect the environment, provide for the longevity of natural resources, maintain ecological support systems for future generations, and guard against ultimate endangerment of the planet.

also reengineered many internal processes to improve the company's overall performance on sustainability measures. For example, the company has reduced water usage in the production of their products by 37 percent since 2008 through the implementation of sustainability initiatives. Unilever has also redesigned packaging for many of its products to conserve natural resources and reduce the volume of consumer waste. The company's Suave shampoo bottles were reshaped to save almost 150 tons of plastic resin per year, which is the equivalent of 15 million fewer empty bottles making it to landfills annually. As the producer of Lipton Tea, Unilever is the world's largest purchaser of tea leaves; the company committed to sourcing all of its tea from Rainforest Alliance Certified farms, due to its comprehensive triple-bottom-line approach toward sustainable farm management. Illustration Capsule 9.4 sheds more light on Unilever's focus on sustainability.

Crafting Corporate Social Responsibility and Sustainability Strategies

While CSR and environmental sustainability strategies take many forms, those that both provide valuable social benefits *and* fulfill customer needs in a superior fashion may also contribute to a company's competitive advantage.[24] For example, while carbon emissions may be a generic social concern for financial institutions such as Wells Fargo, Ford's sustainability strategy for reducing carbon emissions has produced both competitive advantage and environmental benefits. Its Ford Fusion hybrid is among the least polluting automobiles on the road and ranks first among hybrid cars in terms of fuel economy and cabin size. It has gained the attention and loyalty of fuel-conscious buyers and given Ford a new green image. Keurig Green Mountain is committed to caring for the environment while also improving the livelihoods in coffee-growing communities. Their focus is on three primary solutions: (1) helping farmer improve their farming techniques; (2) addressing local water scarcity and planning for climate change; and (3) strengthening farmers' organizations. Its consumers are aware of these efforts and purchase Green Mountain coffee, in part, to encourage such practices.

CSR strategies and environmental sustainability strategies are more likely to contribute to a company's competitive advantage if they are linked to a company's competitively important resources and capabilities or value chain activities. Thus, it is common for companies engaged in natural resource extraction, electric power production, forestry and paper products manufacture, motor vehicles production, and chemical production to place more emphasis on addressing environmental concerns than, say, software and electronics firms or apparel manufacturers. Companies whose business success is heavily dependent on maintaining high employee morale or attracting and retaining the best and brightest employees are somewhat more prone to stress the well-being of their employees and foster a positive, high-energy workplace environment that elicits the dedication and enthusiastic commitment of employees, thus putting real meaning behind the claim "Our people are our greatest asset." EY, the third largest global accounting firm, has been on Fortune's list of 100 Best Companies to Work for every year for the last 20 years. It has long been known for respecting differences, fostering individuality, and promoting inclusiveness so that its more than 245,000 employees in over 150 countries can feel valued, engaged, and empowered in developing creative ways to serve the firm's clients.

At Whole Foods Market, a $16 billion supermarket chain specializing in organic and natural foods, its environmental sustainability strategy is evident in almost every

> CSR strategies and environmental sustainability strategies that both provide valuable social benefits *and* fulfill customer needs in a superior fashion can lead to competitive advantage. Corporate social agendas that address only social issues may help boost a company's reputation for corporate citizenship but are unlikely to improve its competitive strength in the marketplace.

With over 53.7 billion euros in revenue in 2017, Unilever is one of the world's largest companies. The global consumer goods giant has products that are used by over 2 billion people on any given day. It manufactures iconic global brands like Dove, Axe, Hellman's, Heartbrand, and many others. What it is also known for, however, is its commitment to sustainability, leading GlobeScan's Global Sustainability Survey for sustainable companies with a score 2.5 times higher than its closest competitor.

Unilever implemented its sustainability plan in as transparent and explicit way as possible, evidenced by the Unilever Sustainable Living Plan (USLP). The USLP was released in 2010 by CEO Paul Polman, stating that the company's goal was to double the size of the business while halving its environmental footprint by 2020. Importantly, the USLP has remained a guiding force for the company, which dedicates significant resources and time to pursuing its sustainability goals. The plan is updated each year with targets and goals, as well as an annual progress report.

According to Polman, Unilever's focus on sustainability isn't just charity, but is really an act of self-interest. The company's most recent annual report states "growth and sustainability are not in conflict. In fact, in our experience, sustainability drives growth." Polman insists that this is the modern-day way to maximize profits, and that doing so is simply rational business thinking.

To help implement this plan, Unilever has instituted a corporate accountability plan. Each year, Unilever benchmarks its progress against three leading indices: the UN Global Compact, the Global Reporting Initiative's Index, and the UN Millennium Development Goals. In its annual

©McGraw-Hill Education/David A. Tietz, photographer

sustainability report, the company details its progress toward its many sustainability goals. By 2018, Unilever had helped more than 601 million people to improve their health and hygiene habits and had enabled over 716,000 small farmers to improve their agricultural practices and/or their incomes.

Unilever has also created new business practices to reach even more ambitious targets. Unilever set up a central corporate team dedicated to spreading best sustainability practices from one factory or business unit to the rest of the company, a major change from the siloed manner in which the company previously operated. Moreover, the company set up a "small actions, big differences" fund to invest in innovative ideas that help the company achieve its sustainability goal. To reduce emissions from the overall footprint of its products and extend its sustainability efforts to its entire supply chain, it has worked with its suppliers to source sustainable agricultural products, improving from 14 percent sustainable in 2010 to 56 percent in 2017.

Note: Developed with Byron G. Peyster.

Sources: www.globescan.com/component/edocman/?view=document&id=179&Itemid=591; www.fastcocreate.com/3051498/behind-the-brand/why-unilever-is-betting-big-on-sustainability; www.economist.com/news/business/21611103-second-time-its-120-year-history—unilever-trying-redefine-what-it-means-be; *company website (accessed March 13, 2016).*

segment of its company value chain and is a big part of its differentiation strategy. The company's procurement policies encourage stores to purchase fresh fruits and vegetables from local farmers and screen processed-food items for more than 400 common ingredients that the company considers unhealthy or environmentally unsound. Spoiled food items are sent to regional composting centers rather than landfills, and all cleaning products used in its stores are biodegradable. The company also has created the Animal Compassion Foundation to develop natural and humane ways of raising farm animals and has converted all of its vehicles to run on biofuels.

Not all companies choose to link their corporate environmental or social agendas to their value chain, their business model, or their industry. For example, the Clorox Company Foundation supports programs that serve youth, focusing its giving on non-profit civic organizations, schools, and colleges. However, unless a company's social responsibility initiatives become part of the way it operates its business every day, the initiatives are unlikely to catch fire and be fully effective. As an executive at Royal Dutch/Shell put it, corporate social responsibility "is not a cosmetic; it must be rooted in our values. It must make a difference to the way we do business."[25] The same is true for environmental sustainability initiatives.

The Moral Case for Corporate Social Responsibility and Environmentally Sustainable Business Practices

The moral case for why businesses should act in a manner that benefits all of the company's stakeholders—not just shareholders—boils down to "It's the right thing to do." Ordinary decency, civic-mindedness, and contributions to society's well-being should be expected of any business.[26] In today's social and political climate, most business leaders can be expected to acknowledge that socially responsible actions are important and that businesses have a duty to be good corporate citizens. But there is a complementary school of thought that business operates on the basis of an implied social contract with the members of society. According to this contract, society grants a business the right to conduct its business affairs and agrees not to unreasonably restrain its pursuit of a fair profit for the goods or services it sells. In return for this "license to operate," a business is obligated to act as a responsible citizen, do its fair share to promote the general welfare, and avoid doing any harm. Such a view clearly puts a moral burden on a company to operate honorably, provide good working conditions to employees, be a good environmental steward, and display good corporate citizenship.

> Every action a company takes can be interpreted as a statement of what it stands for.

The Business Case for Corporate Social Responsibility and Environmentally Sustainable Business Practices

Whatever the moral arguments for socially responsible business behavior and environmentally sustainable business practices, there are definitely good business reasons why companies should be public-spirited and devote time and resources to social responsibility initiatives, environmental sustainability, and good corporate citizenship:

- *Such actions can lead to increased buyer patronage.* A strong visible social responsibility or environmental sustainability strategy gives a company an edge in appealing to consumers who prefer to do business with companies that are good corporate citizens. Ben & Jerry's, Whole Foods Market, Stonyfield Farm, TOMS, Keurig Green Mountain, and Patagonia have definitely expanded their customer bases because of their visible and well-publicized activities as socially conscious companies. More and more companies are also recognizing the cash register payoff of social responsibility strategies that reach out to people of all cultures and demographics (women, retirees, and ethnic groups).

- *A strong commitment to socially responsible behavior reduces the risk of reputation-damaging incidents.* Companies that place little importance on operating in a

The higher the public profile of a company or its brand, the greater the scrutiny of its activities and the higher the potential for it to become a target for pressure group action.

socially responsible manner are more prone to scandal and embarrassment. Consumer, environmental, and human rights activist groups are quick to criticize businesses whose behavior they consider to be out of line, and they are adept at getting their message into the media and onto the Internet. Pressure groups can generate widespread adverse publicity, promote boycotts, and influence like-minded or sympathetic buyers to avoid an offender's products.

Research has shown that product boycott announcements are associated with a decline in a company's stock price.[27] When a major oil company suffered damage to its reputation on environmental and social grounds, the CEO repeatedly said that the most negative impact the company suffered—and the one that made him fear for the future of the company—was that bright young graduates were no longer attracted to working for the company. For many years, Nike received stinging criticism for not policing sweatshop conditions in the Asian factories that produced Nike footwear, a situation that caused Nike cofounder and chair Phil Knight to observe that "Nike has become synonymous with slave wages, forced overtime, and arbitrary abuse."[28] In response, Nike began an extensive effort to monitor conditions in the 800 factories of the contract manufacturers that produced Nike shoes. As Knight said, "Good shoes come from good factories and good factories have good labor relations." Nonetheless, Nike has continually been plagued by complaints from human rights activists that its monitoring procedures are flawed and that it is not doing enough to correct the plight of factory workers. As this suggests, a damaged reputation is not easily repaired.

- *Socially responsible actions and sustainable business practices can lower costs and enhance employee recruiting and workforce retention.* Companies with deservedly good reputations for social responsibility and sustainable business practices are better able to attract and retain employees, compared to companies with tarnished reputations. Some employees just feel better about working for a company committed to improving society. This can contribute to lower turnover and better worker productivity. Other direct and indirect economic benefits include lower costs for staff recruitment and training. For example, Starbucks is said to enjoy much lower rates of employee turnover because of its full-benefits package for both full-time and part-time employees, management efforts to make Starbucks a great place to work, and the company's socially responsible practices. Sustainable business practices are often concomitant with greater operational efficiencies. For example, when a U.S. manufacturer of recycled paper, taking eco-efficiency to heart, discovered how to increase its fiber recovery rate, it saved the equivalent of 20,000 tons of waste paper—a factor that helped the company become the industry's lowest-cost producer. By helping two-thirds of its employees to stop smoking and by investing in a number of wellness programs for employees, Johnson & Johnson saved $250 million on its health care costs over a 10-year period.[29]

- *Opportunities for revenue enhancement may also come from CSR and environmental sustainability strategies.* The drive for sustainability and social responsibility can spur innovative efforts that in turn lead to new products and opportunities for revenue enhancement. Electric cars such as the Chevy Bolt and the Nissan Leaf are one example. In many cases, the revenue opportunities are tied to a company's core products. PepsiCo and Coca-Cola, for example, have expanded into the juice business to offer a healthier alternative to their carbonated beverages. General Electric has created a profitable new business in wind turbines. In other cases, revenue enhancement opportunities come from innovative ways to reduce waste and use the by-products of a company's production. Tyson Foods now produces jet fuel for B-52 bombers from the vast amount of animal waste resulting from its meat product business. Staples has become one of the largest nonutility corporate producers of renewable energy in the United States due to its installation of solar power panels in all of its outlets (and the sale of what it does not consume in renewable energy credit markets).

- *Well-conceived CSR strategies and sustainable business practices are in the best long-term interest of shareholders.* When CSR and sustainability strategies increase buyer patronage, offer revenue-enhancing opportunities, lower costs, increase productivity, and reduce the risk of reputation-damaging incidents, they contribute to the economic value created by a company and improve its profitability. A two-year study of leading companies found that improving environmental compliance and developing environmentally friendly products can enhance earnings per share, profitability, and the likelihood of winning contracts. The stock prices of companies that rate high on social and environmental performance criteria have been found to perform 35 to 45 percent better than the average of the 2,500 companies that constitute the Dow Jones Global Index.[30] A review of 135 studies indicated there is a positive, but small, correlation between good corporate behavior and good financial performance; only 2 percent of the studies showed that dedicating corporate resources to social responsibility harmed the interests of shareholders.[31] Furthermore, socially responsible business behavior helps avoid or preempt legal and regulatory actions that could prove costly and otherwise burdensome. In some cases, it is possible to craft corporate social responsibility strategies that contribute to competitive advantage and, at the same time, deliver greater value to society. For instance, Walmart, by working with its suppliers to reduce the use of packaging materials and revamping the routes of its delivery trucks to cut out 100 million miles of travel, saved $200 million in costs (which enhanced its cost-competitiveness vis-à-vis rivals) and lowered carbon emissions.[32] Thus, a social responsibility strategy that packs some punch and is more than rhetorical flourish can produce outcomes that are in the best interest of shareholders.

In sum, companies that take social responsibility and environmental sustainability seriously can improve their business reputations and operational efficiency while also reducing their risk exposure and encouraging loyalty and innovation. Overall, companies that take special pains to protect the environment (beyond what is required by law), are active in community affairs, and are generous supporters of charitable causes and projects that benefit society are more likely to be seen as good investments and as good companies to work for or do business with. Shareholders are likely to view the business case for social responsibility as a strong one, particularly when it results in the creation of more customer value, greater productivity, lower operating costs, and lower business risk—all of which should increase firm profitability and enhance shareholder value even as the company's actions address broader stakeholder interests.

Companies are, of course, sometimes rewarded for bad behavior—a company that is able to shift environmental and other social costs associated with its activities onto society as a whole can reap large short-term profits. The major cigarette producers for many years were able to earn greatly inflated profits by shifting the health-related costs of smoking onto others and escaping any

> Socially responsible strategies that create value for customers and lower costs can improve company profits and shareholder value at the same time that they address other stakeholder interests.

> There's little hard evidence indicating shareholders are disadvantaged in any meaningful way by a company's actions to be socially responsible.

responsibility for the harm their products caused to consumers and the general public. Only recently have they been facing the prospect of having to pay high punitive damages for their actions. Unfortunately, the cigarette makers are not alone in trying to evade paying for the social harms of their operations for as long as they can. Calling a halt to such actions usually hinges on (1) the effectiveness of activist social groups in publicizing the adverse consequences of a company's social irresponsibility and marshaling public opinion for something to be done, (2) the enactment of legislation or regulations to correct the inequity, and (3) decisions on the part of socially conscious buyers to take their business elsewhere.

KEY POINTS

1. Ethics concerns standards of right and wrong. Business ethics concerns the application of ethical principles to the actions and decisions of business organizations and the conduct of their personnel. Ethical principles in business are not materially different from ethical principles in general.

2. There are three schools of thought about ethical standards for companies with international operations:
   - According to the *school of ethical universalism,* common understandings across multiple cultures and countries about what constitutes right and wrong behaviors give rise to universal ethical standards that apply to members of all societies, all companies, and all businesspeople.
   - According to the *school of ethical relativism,* different societal cultures and customs have divergent values and standards of right and wrong. Thus, what is ethical or unethical must be judged in the light of local customs and social mores and can vary from one culture or nation to another.
   - According to the *integrated social contracts theory,* universal ethical principles based on the collective views of multiple cultures and societies combine to form a "social contract" that all individuals in all situations have a duty to observe. Within the boundaries of this social contract, local cultures or groups can specify what additional actions are not ethically permissible. However, universal norms always take precedence over local ethical norms.

3. Apart from the "business of business is business, not ethics" kind of thinking, three other factors contribute to unethical business behavior: (1) faulty oversight that enables the unscrupulous pursuit of personal gain, (2) heavy pressures on company managers to meet or beat short-term earnings targets, and (3) a company culture that puts profitability and good business performance ahead of ethical behavior. In contrast, culture can function as a powerful mechanism for promoting ethical business conduct when high ethical principles are deeply ingrained in the corporate culture of a company.

4. Business ethics failures can result in three types of costs: (1) visible costs, such as fines, penalties, and lower stock prices; (2) internal administrative costs, such as legal costs and costs of taking corrective action; and (3) intangible costs or less visible costs, such as customer defections and damage to the company's reputation.

5. The term *corporate social responsibility* concerns a company's *duty* to operate in an honorable manner, provide good working conditions for employees, encourage workforce diversity, be a good steward of the environment, and support philanthropic endeavors in local communities where it operates and in society at large.

The particular combination of socially responsible endeavors a company elects to pursue defines its corporate social responsibility (CSR) strategy.

6. The triple bottom line refers to company performance in three realms: economic, social, and environmental, often referred to as profit, people, and planet. Increasingly, companies are reporting their performance with respect to all three performance dimensions.

7. *Sustainability* is a term that is used in various ways, but most often it concerns a firm's relationship to the environment and its use of natural resources. Sustainable business practices are those capable of meeting the needs of the present without compromising the world's ability to meet future needs. A company's environmental sustainability strategy consists of its deliberate actions to protect the environment, provide for the longevity of natural resources, maintain ecological support systems for future generations, and guard against ultimate endangerment of the planet.

8. CSR strategies and environmental sustainability strategies that both provide valuable social benefits *and* fulfill customer needs in a superior fashion can lead to competitive advantage.

9. The moral case for corporate social responsibility and environmental sustainability boils down to a simple concept: It's the right thing to do. There are also solid reasons why CSR and environmental sustainability strategies may be good business—they can be conducive to greater buyer patronage, reduce the risk of reputation-damaging incidents, provide opportunities for revenue enhancement, and lower costs. Well-crafted CSR and environmental sustainability strategies are in the best long-term interest of shareholders, for the reasons just mentioned and because they can avoid or preempt costly legal or regulatory actions.

ASSURANCE OF LEARNING EXERCISES

1. Widely known as an ethical company, Dell recently committed itself to becoming a more environmentally sustainable business. After reviewing the About Dell section of its website (**www.dell.com/learn/us/en/uscorp1/about-dell**), prepare a list of 10 specific policies and programs that help the company achieve its vision of driving social and environmental change while still remaining innovative and profitable.

LO 9-1, LO 9-4

2. Prepare a one- to two-page analysis of a recent ethics scandal using your university library's resources. Your report should (1) discuss the conditions that gave rise to unethical business strategies and behavior and (2) provide an overview of the costs to the company resulting from the company's business ethics failure.

LO 9-2, LO 9-3

3. Based on information provided in Illustration Capsule 9.3, explain how Warby Parker's CSR strategy has contributed to its success in the marketplace. How are the company's various stakeholder groups affected by its commitment to social responsibility? How would you evaluate its triple-bottom-line performance?

connect

LO 9-4

4. The British outdoor clothing company, Páramo, was a Guardian Sustainable Business Award winner in 2016. (Guardian stopped giving the award afterward.) The company's fabric technology and use of chemicals is discussed at **https://www.theguardian.com/sustainable-business/2016/may/27/outdoor-clothing-paramo-toxic-pfc-greenpeace-fabric-technology**. Describe how Páramo's business practices allowed it to become recognized for its bold moves. How do these initiatives help build competitive advantage?

connect

LO 9-4

EXERCISE FOR SIMULATION PARTICIPANTS

LO 9-1

1. Is your company's strategy ethical? Why or why not? Is there anything that your company has done or is now doing that could legitimately be considered "shady" by your competitors?

LO 9-4

2. In what ways, if any, is your company exercising corporate social responsibility? What are the elements of your company's CSR strategy? Are there any changes to this strategy that you would suggest?

LO 9-3, LO 9-4

3. If some shareholders complained that you and your co-managers have been spending too little or too much on corporate social responsibility, what would you tell them?

LO 9-4

4. Is your company striving to conduct its business in an environmentally sustainable manner? What specific *additional* actions could your company take that would make an even greater contribution to environmental sustainability?

LO 9-4

5. In what ways is your company's environmental sustainability strategy in the best long-term interest of shareholders? Does it contribute to your company's competitive advantage or profitability?

ENDNOTES

[1] James E. Post, Anne T. Lawrence, and James Weber, *Business and Society: Corporate Strategy, Public Policy, Ethics,* 10th ed. (New York: McGraw-Hill, 2002).

[2] Mark S. Schwartz, "Universal Moral Values for Corporate Codes of Ethics," *Journal of Business Ethics* 59, no. 1 (June 2005), pp. 27–44.

[3] Mark S. Schwartz, "A Code of Ethics for Corporate Codes of Ethics," *Journal of Business Ethics* 41, no. 1–2 (November–December 2002), pp. 27–43.

[4] T. L. Beauchamp and N. E. Bowie, *Ethical Theory and Business* (Upper Saddle River, NJ: Prentice-Hall, 2001).

[5] www.cnn.com/2013/10/15/world/child-labor-index-2014/ (accessed February 6, 2014).

[6] U.S. Department of Labor, "The Department of Labor's 2013 Findings on the Worst Forms of Child Labor," www.dol.gov/ilab/programs/ocft/PDF/2012OCFTreport.pdf.

[7] W. M. Greenfield, "In the Name of Corporate Social Responsibility," *Business Horizons* 47, no. 1 (January–February 2004), p. 22.

[8] Rajib Sanyal, "Determinants of Bribery in International Business: The Cultural and Economic Factors," *Journal of Business Ethics* 59, no. 1 (June 2005), pp. 139–145.

[9] Transparency International, *Global Corruption Report,* www.globalcorruptionreport.org.

[10] Roger Chen and Chia-Pei Chen, "Chinese Professional Managers and the Issue of Ethical Behavior," *Ivey Business Journal* 69, no. 5 (May–June 2005), p. 1.

[11] Antonio Argandoa, "Corruption and Companies: The Use of Facilitating Payments," *Journal of Business Ethics* 60, no. 3 (September 2005), pp. 251–264.

[12] Thomas Donaldson and Thomas W. Dunfee, "Towards a Unified Conception of Business Ethics: Integrative Social Contracts Theory," *Academy of Management Review* 19, no. 2 (April 1994), pp. 252–284; Andrew Spicer, Thomas W. Dunfee, and Wendy J. Bailey, "Does National Context Matter in Ethical Decision Making? An Empirical Test of Integrative Social Contracts Theory," *Academy of Management Journal* 47, no. 4 (August 2004), p. 610.

[13] Lynn Paine, Rohit Deshpandé, Joshua D. Margolis, and Kim Eric Bettcher, "Up to Code: Does Your Company's Conduct Meet World-Class Standards?" *Harvard Business Review* 83, no. 12 (December 2005), pp. 122–133.

[14] John F. Veiga, Timothy D. Golden, and Kathleen Dechant, "Why Managers Bend Company Rules," *Academy of Management Executive* 18, no. 2 (May 2004).

[15] Lorin Berlin and Emily Peck, "National Mortgage Settlement: States, Big Banks Reach $25 Billion Deal," *Huff Post Business,* February 9, 2012, www.huffingtonpost.com/2012/02/09/-national-mortgage-settlement_n_1265292.html (accessed February 15, 2012).

[16] Ronald R. Sims and Johannes Brinkmann, "Enron Ethics (Or: Culture Matters More than Codes)," *Journal of Business Ethics* 45, no. 3 (July 2003), pp. 244–246.

[17] Kurt Eichenwald, *Conspiracy of Fools: A True Story* (New York: Broadway Books, 2005).

[18] Timothy M. Devinney, "Is the Socially Responsible Corporation a Myth? The Good, the Bad, and the Ugly of Corporate Social Responsibility," *Academy of Management Perspectives* 23, no. 2 (May 2009), pp. 44–56.

[19] Information posted at www.generalmills.com (accessed March 13, 2013).

[20] Adrian Henriques, "ISO 26000: A New Standard for Human Rights?" *Institute for Human Rights and Business,* March 23, 2010, www.institutehrb.org/blogs/guest/iso_26000_a_new_standard_for_human_rights.html?gclid=CJih7NjN2aICFVs65QodrVOdyQ (accessed July 7, 2010).

[21] Gerald I. J. M. Zetsloot and Marcel N. A. van Marrewijk, "From Quality to Sustainability," *Journal of Business Ethics* 55 (2004), pp. 79–82.

[22] Tilde Herrera, "PG&E Claims Industry First with Supply Chain Footprint Project," *GreenBiz.com,* June 30, 2010, www.greenbiz.com/news/2010/06/30/-pge—claims-industry-first-supply-chain-carbon-footprint-project.

[23] J. G. Speth, *The Bridge at the End of the World: Capitalism, the Environment, and Crossing from Crisis to Sustainability* (New Haven, CT: Yale University Press, 2008).

[24] Michael E. Porter and Mark R. Kramer, "Strategy & Society: The Link between Competitive Advantage and Corporate Social Responsibility," *Harvard Business Review* 84, no. 12 (December 2006), pp. 78–92.

[25] N. Craig Smith, "Corporate Responsibility: Whether and How," *California Management Review* 45, no. 4 (Summer 2003), p. 63.

[26] Jeb Brugmann and C. K. Prahalad, "Cocreating Business's New Social Compact," *Harvard Business Review* 85, no. 2 (February 2007), pp. 80–90.

[27] Wallace N. Davidson, Abuzar El-Jelly, and Dan L. Worrell, "Influencing Managers to Change Unpopular Corporate Behavior through Boycotts and Divestitures: A Stock Market Test," *Business and Society* 34, no. 2 (1995), pp. 171–196.

[28] Tom McCawley, "Racing to Improve Its Reputation: Nike Has Fought to Shed Its Image as an Exploiter of Third-World Labor Yet It Is Still a Target of Activists," *Financial Times,* December 2000, p. 14.

[29] Michael E. Porter and Mark Kramer, "Creating Shared Value," *Harvard Business Review* 89, no. 1–2 (January–February 2011).

[30] James C. Collins and Jerry I. Porras, *Built to Last: Successful Habits of Visionary Companies,* 3rd ed. (London: HarperBusiness, 2002).

[31] Joshua D. Margolis and Hillary A. Elfenbein, "Doing Well by Doing Good: Don't Count on It," *Harvard Business Review* 86, no. 1 (January 2008), pp. 19–20; Lee E. Preston, Douglas P. O'Bannon, Ronald M. Roman, Sefa Hayibor, and Bradley R. Agle, "The Relationship between Social and Financial Performance: Repainting a Portrait," *Business and Society* 38, no. 1 (March 1999), pp. 109–125.

[32] Leonard L. Berry, Ann M. Mirobito, and William B. Baun, "What's the Hard Return on Employee Wellness Programs?" *Harvard Business Review* 88, no. 12 (December 2010), p. 105.

references, Social and Financial Performance,"
Propelling it Forward," *Business and Society*
42, no. 1 (March 1998): no. 1 (2003): 296.
Decoena L. Ilin, Vy, Ann M. Molines, and
Spitania J. Baus, "Why Hay Have Corpo...
2008, pp. 79; 20; 24; E. Preston Shapiro,
U. Dunton, Ronald M. Borjas, Self Interac...
and Emilio, P. Agnello, *The Relationship, The*
p. 708
Works U. Cabian and Jerry I. Porro, Cult D...
Tost and assists a book of function Companies
and a function Hem philosophy, 2003,
Remain D. Matplus and Julley A. Efficient
Deing Walfan being good; Doing About of...
Provost Benames Review 84, nol. (January
Tom Mr Dunron, "Racing to Improve its
Reputation once His Revolt to Shed its image
as an Explained of, Think World I about That it
will a Target of A, Implicit Tanotrus Threaten
December 2006, p. 14.
Michael F. Rosse' and Block Kramer,
Ongoing Shared van ip,"Improvil Business
Revw, r 50, ro, 1–2 Ganuar, wel ebruary,
2011)

Building an Organization Capable of Good Strategy Execution

People, Capabilities, and Structure

Learning Objectives

This chapter will help you

LO 10-1 Identify what managers must do to execute strategy successfully.

LO 10-2 Explain why hiring, training, and retaining the right people constitute a key component of the strategy execution process.

LO 10-3 Recognize that good strategy execution requires continuously building and upgrading the organization's resources and capabilities.

LO 10-4 Identify and establish a strategy-supportive organizational structure and organize the work effort.

LO 10-5 Explain the pros and cons of centralized and decentralized decision making in implementing the chosen strategy.

©Gregory Baldwin/Ikon Images/Getty Images

Without strategy, execution is aimless; Without execution, strategy is useless.

> Morris Chang—*Founder, CEO, and Chairman of TSMC*
> *(Taiwan Semiconductor Manufacturing Company)*

I try to motivate people and align our individual incentives with organizational incentives. And then let people do their best.

> John D. Liu—*CEO, Essex Equity Management*

People are not your most important asset. The right people are.

> Jim Collins—*Professor and author*

Once managers have decided on a strategy, the emphasis turns to converting it into actions and good results. Putting the strategy into place and getting the organization to execute it well call for different sets of managerial skills rather than crafting strategy. Whereas crafting strategy is largely an analysis-driven activity focused on market conditions and the company's resources and capabilities, executing strategy is primarily operations-driven, revolving around the management of people, resources, business processes, and organizational structure. Successful strategy execution depends on doing a good job of working with and through others; building and strengthening competitive capabilities; creating an appropriate organizational structure; allocating resources; instituting strategy-supportive policies, processes, and systems; and instilling a discipline of getting things done. Executing strategy is an action-oriented task that tests a manager's ability to direct organizational change, achieve improvements in day-to-day operations, create and nurture a culture that supports good strategy execution, and meet or beat performance targets.

Experienced managers are well aware that it is much easier to develop a sound strategic plan than it is to execute the plan and achieve targeted outcomes. A study of 400 CEOs in the United States, Europe, and Asia found that executional excellence was the number-one challenge facing their companies.[1] According to one executive, "It's been rather easy for us to decide where we wanted to go. The hard part is to get the organization to act on the new priorities."[2] It takes adept managerial leadership to convincingly communicate the reasons for a new strategy and overcome pockets of doubt, secure the commitment of key personnel, build consensus for how to implement the strategy, and move forward to get all the pieces into place and deliver results. *Just because senior managers announce a new strategy doesn't mean that organization members will embrace it and move forward enthusiastically to implement it.* Company personnel must understand—in their heads and hearts—why a new strategic direction is necessary and where the new strategy is taking them.[3] Instituting change is, of course, easier when the problems with the old strategy have become obvious and/or the company has spiraled into a financial crisis.

But the challenge of successfully implementing new strategic initiatives goes well beyond managerial adeptness in overcoming resistance to change. What really make executing strategy a tougher, more time-consuming management challenge than crafting strategy are the wide array of managerial activities that must be attended to, the many ways to put new strategic initiatives in place and keep things moving, and the number of bedeviling issues that always crop up and have to be resolved. It takes first-rate "managerial smarts" to zero in on what exactly needs to be done and how to get good results in a timely manner. Excellent people-management skills and perseverance are needed to get a variety of initiatives underway and to integrate the efforts of many different work groups into a smoothly functioning whole. Depending on how much consensus building and organizational change is involved, the process of implementing strategy changes can take several months to several years. And executing the strategy with *real proficiency* takes even longer.

Like crafting strategy, *executing strategy is a job for a company's whole management team—not just a few senior managers.* While the chief executive officer and the heads of major units (business divisions, functional departments, and key operating units) are ultimately responsible for seeing that strategy is executed successfully, the process typically affects every part of the firm—all value chain activities and all work groups. Top-level managers must rely on the active support of middle and lower managers to institute whatever new operating practices are needed in the various operating units to achieve proficient strategy execution. Middle and lower-level managers must ensure that frontline employees perform strategy-critical value chain activities proficiently enough to allow companywide performance targets to be met. Consequently, *all company personnel are actively involved in the strategy execution process in one way or another.*

A FRAMEWORK FOR EXECUTING STRATEGY

CORE CONCEPT

Good strategy execution requires a *team effort.* All managers have strategy-executing responsibility in their areas of authority, and all employees are active participants in the strategy execution process.

The managerial approach to executing a strategy always has to be customized to fit the particulars of a company's situation. Making minor changes in an existing strategy differs from implementing radical strategy changes. The techniques for successfully executing a low-cost leader strategy are different from those for executing a high-end differentiation strategy. Implementing a new strategy for a struggling company in the midst of a financial crisis is a different job from improving strategy execution in a company that is doing relatively well. Moreover, some managers are more adept than others at using particular approaches to achieving certain kinds of organizational changes. Hence, there's no definitive managerial recipe for successful strategy execution that cuts across all company situations and strategies or that works for all managers. Rather, the specific actions required to execute a strategy—the "to-do list" that constitutes management's action agenda—always represent management's judgment about how best to proceed in light of prevailing circumstances.

LO 10-1

Identify what managers must do to execute strategy successfully.

The Principal Components of the Strategy Execution Process

Despite the need to tailor a company's strategy-executing approaches to the situation at hand, certain managerial bases must be covered no matter what the circumstances. These include 10 basic managerial tasks (see Figure 10.1):

1. Staffing the organization with managers and employees capable of executing the strategy well.
2. Developing the resources and organizational capabilities required for successful strategy execution.
3. Creating a strategy-supportive organizational structure.

4. Allocating sufficient resources (budgetary and otherwise) to the strategy execution effort.

5. Instituting policies and procedures that facilitate strategy execution.

6. Adopting business management processes that drive continuous improvement in strategy execution activities.

7. Installing information and operating systems that support strategy implementation activities.

8. Tying rewards directly to the achievement of performance objectives.

9. Fostering a corporate culture that promotes good strategy execution.

10. Exercising the leadership needed to propel implementation forward.

How well managers perform these 10 tasks has a decisive impact on whether the outcome of the strategy execution effort is a spectacular success, a colossal failure, or something in between.

In devising an action agenda for executing strategy, managers should start by conducting *a probing assessment of what the organization must do differently to carry out the strategy successfully.* Each manager needs to ask the question "What needs to be done in my area of responsibility to implement our part of the company's strategy, and what should I do to get these things accomplished in a timely fashion?" It is then incumbent on every manager to determine *precisely how to make the necessary internal changes.* Strong managers have a knack for diagnosing what their organizations need to do to execute the chosen strategy well and figuring out how to get these things done efficiently. They are masters in promoting results-oriented behaviors on the part of company personnel and following through on making the right things happen to achieve the target outcomes.[4]

When strategies fail, it is often because of poor execution. Strategy execution is therefore a critical managerial endeavor. The two best signs of good strategy execution are whether a company is meeting its performance targets and whether it is performing value chain activities in a manner that is conducive to companywide operating excellence. In big organizations with geographically scattered operating units, senior executives' action agenda mostly involves communicating the case for change, building consensus for how to proceed, installing strong managers to move the process forward in key organizational units, directing resources to the right places, establishing deadlines and measures of progress, rewarding those who achieve implementation milestones, and personally leading the strategic change process. Thus, the bigger the organization, the more that successful strategy execution depends on the cooperation and implementation skills of operating managers who can promote needed changes at the lowest organizational levels and deliver results. In small organizations, top managers can deal directly with frontline managers and employees, personally orchestrating the action steps and implementation sequence, observing firsthand how implementation is progressing, and deciding how hard and how fast to push the process along. Whether the organization is large or small and whether strategy implementation involves sweeping or minor changes, effective leadership requires a keen grasp of what to do and how to do it in light of the organization's circumstances. Then it remains for company personnel in strategy-critical areas to step up to the plate and produce the desired results.

> When strategies fail, it is often because of poor execution. Strategy execution is therefore a critical managerial endeavor.

> The two best signs of good strategy execution are whether a company is meeting or beating its performance targets and whether it is performing value chain activities in a manner that is conducive to companywide operating excellence.

What's Covered in Chapters 10, 11, and 12   In the remainder of this chapter and in the next two chapters, we discuss what is involved in performing the 10 key managerial tasks that shape the process of executing strategy. This chapter explores the first three of these tasks (highlighted in blue in Figure 10.1): (1) staffing the organization with people

FIGURE 10.1   The 10 Basic Tasks of the Strategy Execution Process

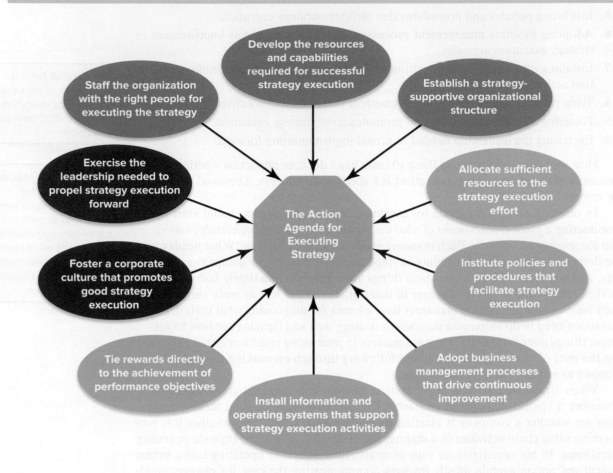

capable of executing the strategy well, (2) developing the resources and organizational capabilities needed for successful strategy execution, and (3) creating an organizational structure supportive of the strategy execution process. Chapter 11 concerns the tasks of allocating resources (budgetary and otherwise), instituting strategy-facilitating policies and procedures, employing business process management tools installing operating and information systems, and tying rewards to the achievement of good results (highlighted in green in Figure 10.1). Chapter 12 deals with the two remaining tasks: instilling a corporate culture conducive to good strategy execution, and exercising the leadership needed to drive the execution process forward (highlighted in purple).

BUILDING AN ORGANIZATION CAPABLE OF GOOD STRATEGY EXECUTION: THREE KEY ACTIONS

Proficient strategy execution depends foremost on having in place an organization capable of the tasks demanded of it. Building an execution-capable organization is thus always a top priority. As shown in Figure 10.2, three types of organization-building actions are paramount:

1. *Staffing the organization*—putting together a strong management team, and recruiting and retaining employees with the needed experience, technical skills, and intellectual capital.

2. *Acquiring, developing, and strengthening the resources and capabilities required for good strategy execution*—accumulating the required resources, developing proficiencies in performing strategy-critical value chain activities, and updating the company's capabilities to match changing market conditions and customer expectations.

3. *Structuring the organization and work effort*—organizing value chain activities and business processes, establishing lines of authority and reporting relationships, and deciding how much decision-making authority to delegate to lower-level managers and frontline employees.

Implementing a strategy depends critically on ensuring that strategy-supportive resources and capabilities are in place, ready to be deployed. These include the skills, talents, experience, and knowledge of the company's human resources (managerial and otherwise)—see Figure 10.2. Proficient strategy execution depends heavily on

FIGURE 10.2   Building an Organization Capable of Proficient Strategy Execution: Three Key Actions

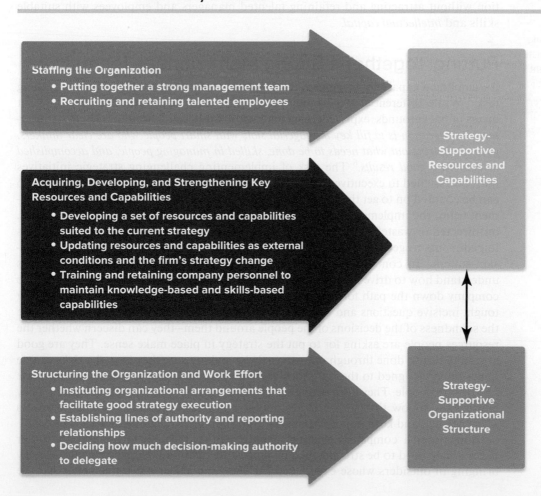

competent personnel of all types, but because of the many managerial tasks involved and the role of leadership in strategy execution, assembling a strong management team is especially important.

If the strategy being implemented is a new strategy, the company may need to add to its resource and capability mix in other respects as well. But renewing, upgrading, and revising the organization's resources and capabilities is a part of the strategy execution process even if the strategy is fundamentally the same, since strategic assets depreciate and conditions are always changing. Thus, augmenting and strengthening the firm's core competencies and seeing that they are suited to the current strategy are also top priorities.

Structuring the organization and work effort is another critical aspect of building an organization capable of good strategy execution. An organization structure that is well matched to the strategy can help facilitate its implementation; one that is not well suited can lead to higher bureaucratic costs and communication or coordination breakdowns.

STAFFING THE ORGANIZATION

● **LO 10-2**

Explain why hiring, training, and retaining the right people constitute a key component of the strategy execution process.

No company can hope to perform the activities required for successful strategy execution without attracting and retaining talented managers and employees with suitable skills and *intellectual capital.*

Putting Together a Strong Management Team

Assembling a capable management team is a cornerstone of the organization-building task.[5] While different strategies and company circumstances often call for different mixes of backgrounds, experiences, management styles, and know-how, *the most important consideration is to fill key managerial slots with smart people who are clear thinkers, good at figuring out what needs to be done, skilled in managing people, and accomplished in delivering good results.*[6] The task of implementing challenging strategic initiatives must be assigned to executives who have the skills and talents to handle them and who can be counted on to get the job done well. Without a capable, results-oriented management team, the implementation process is likely to be hampered by missed deadlines, misdirected or wasteful efforts, and managerial ineptness. Weak executives are serious impediments to getting optimal results—the caliber of work done under their supervision suffers.[7] In contrast, managers with strong strategy implementation capabilities understand how to drive organizational change, and know how to motivate and lead the company down the path for first-rate strategy execution. They have a talent for asking tough, incisive questions and know enough about the details of the business to ensure the soundness of the decisions of the people around them—they can discern whether the resources people are asking for to put the strategy in place make sense. They are good at getting things done through others, partly by making sure they have the right people under them, assigned to the right jobs and partly because they know how to motivate and inspire people. They have strong social skills and high emotional intelligence. They consistently follow through on issues, monitor progress carefully, make adjustments when needed, and keep important details from slipping through the cracks.

Sometimes a company's existing management team is up to the task. At other times it may need to be strengthened by promoting qualified people from within or by bringing in outsiders whose experiences, talents, and leadership styles better suit the situation. In turnaround and rapid-growth situations, and in instances when company managers lack the requisite know-how, filling key management slots from the outside is a standard organization-building approach. In all situations, it is important to identify and replace managers who are incapable, for whatever reason, of making the required changes in a timely and cost-effective manner. For a management team to be truly effective at strategy execution, it must be composed of managers who recognize that organizational changes are needed and who are both capable and ready to get on with the process.

> Putting together a talented management team with the right mix of experiences, skills, and abilities to get things done is one of the first steps to take in launching the strategy-executing process.

The overriding aim in building a management team should be to assemble a *critical mass* of talented managers who can function as agents of change and spearhead excellent strategy execution. Every manager's success is enhanced (or limited) by the quality of his or her managerial colleagues and the degree to which they freely exchange ideas, debate ways to make operating improvements, and join forces to tackle issues and solve problems. When a first-rate manager enjoys the help and support of other first-rate managers, it's possible to create a managerial whole that is greater than the sum of individual efforts—talented managers who work well together as a team can produce organizational results that are dramatically better than what one or two star managers acting individually can achieve.[8]

Illustration Capsule 10.1 describes Deloitte's highly effective approach to developing employee talent and a top-caliber management team.

Recruiting, Training, and Retaining Capable Employees

Assembling a capable management team is not enough. Staffing the organization with the right kinds of people must extend to all kinds of company personnel for value chain activities to be performed competently. *The quality of an organization's people is always an essential ingredient of successful strategy execution.* Companies like Mercedes-Benz, Alphabet, SAS, Boston Consulting Group, Edward Jones, Quicken Loans, Genentech, Intuit, Salesforce.com, and Goldman Sachs make a concerted effort to recruit the best and brightest people they can find and then retain them with excellent compensation packages, opportunities for rapid advancement and professional growth, and interesting assignments. Having a pool of "A players" with strong skill sets and lots of brainpower is essential to their business.

> In many industries, adding to a company's talent base and building intellectual capital are more important to good strategy execution than are additional investments in capital projects.

Facebook makes a point of hiring the very brightest and most talented programmers it can find and motivating them with both good monetary incentives and the challenge of working on cutting-edge technology projects. McKinsey & Company, one of the world's premier management consulting firms, recruits only cream-of-the-crop MBAs at the nation's top-10 business schools; such talent is essential to McKinsey's strategy of performing high-level consulting for the world's top corporations. The leading global accounting firms screen candidates not only on the basis of their accounting expertise but also on whether they possess the people skills needed to relate well with clients and colleagues. Zappos goes to considerable lengths to hire people who can have fun and be fun on the job; it has done away with traditional job postings and instead asks prospective hires to join a social network, called Zappos Insiders, where they will interact with current employees and have opportunities to demonstrate their passion for joining the company. Zappos is so selective about finding people who fit their culture that only about 1.5 percent of the people who apply are offered jobs.

Management Development at Deloitte Touche Tohmatsu Limited

©Ken Wolter/Shutterstock

Hiring, retaining, and cultivating talent are critical activities at Deloitte, the world's largest professional services firm. By offering robust learning and development programs, Deloitte has been able to create a strong talent pipeline to the firm's partnership. Deloitte's emphasis on learning and development, across all stages of the employee life cycle, has led to recognitions such as being ranked number-one on *Chief Executives*'s list of "Best Private Companies for Leaders" and being listed among *Fortune*'s "100 Best Companies to Work For." The following programs contribute to Deloitte's successful execution of its talent strategy:

- *Clear path to partnership.* During the initial recruiting phase and then throughout an employee's tenure at the firm, Deloitte lays out a clear career path. The path indicates the expected timeline for promotion to each of the firm's hierarchy levels, along with the competencies and experience required. Deloitte's transparency on career

paths, coupled with its in-depth performance management process, helps employees clearly understand their performance. This serves as a motivational tool for top performers, often leading to career acceleration.

- *Formal training programs.* Like other leading organizations, Deloitte has a program to ensure that recent college graduates are equipped with the necessary training and tools for succeeding on the job. Yet Deloitte's commitment to formal training is evident at all levels within the organization. Each time an employee is promoted, he or she attends "milestone" school, a weeklong simulation that replicates true business situations employees would face as they transition to new stages of career development. In addition, Deloitte institutes mandatory training hours for all of its employees to ensure that individuals continue to further their professional development.

- *Special programs for high performers.* Deloitte also offers fellowships and programs to help employees acquire new skills and enhance their leadership development. For example, the Global Fellows program helps top performers work with senior leaders in the organization to focus on the realities of delivering client service across borders. Deloitte has also established the Emerging Leaders Development program, which utilizes skill building, 360-degree feedback, and one-on-one executive coaching to help top-performing managers and senior managers prepare for partnership.

- *Sponsorship, not mentorship.* To train the next generation of leaders, Deloitte has implemented formal mentorship programs to provide leadership development support. Deloitte, however, uses the term *sponsorship* to describe this initiative. A sponsor is tasked with taking a vested interest in an individual and advocating on his or her behalf. Sponsors help rising leaders navigate the firm, develop new competencies, expand their network, and hone the skills needed to accelerate their career.

Note: Developed with Heather Levy.

Sources: Company websites; www.accountingweb.com/article/leadership-development-community-service-integral-deloitte-university/220845 (accessed February 2014).

In high-tech companies, the challenge is to staff work groups with gifted, imaginative, and energetic people who can bring life to new ideas quickly and inject into the organization what one Dell executive calls "hum."[9] The saying "People are our most important asset" may seem trite, but it fits high-technology companies precisely. Besides checking closely for functional and technical skills, Dell tests applicants for their tolerance of ambiguity and change, their capacity to work in teams, and their ability to learn on the fly. Companies like Zappos, Amazon.com, Google, and Cisco Systems have broken new ground in recruiting, hiring, cultivating, developing, and retaining talented employees—almost all of whom are in their 20s and 30s. Cisco goes after the top 10 percent, raiding other companies and endeavoring to retain key people at the companies it acquires. Cisco executives believe that a cadre of star engineers, programmers, managers, salespeople, and support personnel is the backbone of the company's efforts to execute its strategy and remain the world's leading provider of Internet infrastructure products and technology.

> The best companies make a point of recruiting and retaining talented employees—the objective is to make the company's entire workforce (managers and rank-and-file employees) a genuine competitive asset.

In recognition of the importance of a talented and energetic workforce, companies have instituted a number of practices aimed at staffing jobs with the best people they can find:

1. Spending considerable effort on screening and evaluating job applicants—selecting only those with suitable skill sets, energy, initiative, judgment, aptitude for learning, and personality traits that mesh well with the company's work environment and culture.

2. Providing employees with training programs that continue throughout their careers.

3. Offering promising employees challenging, interesting, and skill-stretching assignments.

4. Rotating people through jobs that span functional and geographic boundaries. Providing people with opportunities to gain experience in a variety of international settings is increasingly considered an essential part of career development in multinational companies.

5. Making the work environment stimulating and engaging so that employees will consider the company a great place to work.

6. Encouraging employees to challenge existing ways of doing things, to be creative in proposing better ways of operating, and to push their ideas for new products or businesses. Progressive companies work hard at creating an environment in which employees are made to feel that their views and suggestions count.

7. Striving to retain talented, high-performing employees via promotions, salary increases, performance bonuses, stock options and equity ownership, benefit packages including health insurance and retirement packages, and other perks, such as flexible work hours and onsite day care.

8. Coaching average performers to improve their skills and capabilities, while weeding out underperformers.

DEVELOPING AND BUILDING CRITICAL RESOURCES AND CAPABILITIES

High among the organization-building priorities in the strategy execution process is the need to build and strengthen the company's portfolio of resources and capabilities with which to perform strategy-critical value chain activities. As explained in Chapter 4, a company's chances of gaining a sustainable advantage over its market rivals depends on the caliber of its resource portfolio. In the course of crafting strategy, managers may well have well have identified the strategy-critical resources and capabilities it needs. But getting the strategy execution process underway requires acquiring or developing these resources and capabilities, putting them into place, upgrading them as needed, and then modifying them as market conditions evolve.

● ● ● ●

● LO 10-3

Recognize that good strategy execution requires continuously building and upgrading the organization's resources and capabilities.

If the strategy being implemented has important new elements, company managers may have to acquire new resources, significantly broaden or deepen certain capabilities, or even add entirely new competencies in order to put the strategic initiatives in place and execute them proficiently. But even when a company's strategy has not changed materially, good strategy execution still involves continually upgrading the firm's resources and capabilities to keep them in top form and perform value chain activities ever more proficiently.

Three Approaches to Building and Strengthening Capabilities

Building new capabilities is a multistage process that occurs over a period of months and years. It is not something that is accomplished overnight.

Building the right kinds of capabilities and keeping them finely honed is a time-consuming, managerially challenging exercise. While some assistance can be gotten from discovering how best-in-industry or best-in-world companies perform a particular activity, trying to replicate and then improve on the capabilities of others is easier said than done—for the same reasons that one is unlikely to ever become a world-class halfpipe snowboarder just by studying legendary Olympic gold medalist Shaun White.

With deliberate effort, well-orchestrated organizational actions, and continued practice, however, it is possible for a firm to become proficient at capability building despite the difficulty. Indeed, by making capability-building activities a *routine* part of their strategy execution endeavors, some firms are able to develop *dynamic capabilities* that assist them in managing resource and capability change, as discussed in Chapter 4. The most common approaches to capability building include (1) developing and strengthening capabilities internally, (2) acquiring capabilities through mergers and acquisitions, and (3) developing new capabilities via collaborative partnerships.

Developing Capabilities Internally   Internal efforts to create or upgrade capabilities is an evolutionary process that entails a series of deliberate and well-orchestrated steps as organizations search for solutions to their problems. The process is a complex one, since capabilities are the product of *bundles of skills and know-how that are integrated into organizational routines* and *deployed within activity systems* through the combined efforts of teams that are often cross-functional in nature, spanning a variety of departments and locations. For instance, the capability of speeding new products to market involves the *collaborative efforts* of personnel in R&D, engineering and design, purchasing, production, marketing, and distribution. Similarly, the capability to provide superior customer service is a team effort among people in customer call centers (where orders are taken and inquiries are answered), shipping and delivery, billing and accounts receivable, and after-sale support. The process of building a capability begins when managers set an objective of developing a particular capability and organize activity around that objective.[10]

A company's capabilities must be continually refreshed to remain aligned with changing customer expectations, altered competitive conditions, and new strategic initiatives.

Because the process is incremental, the first step is to develop the *ability* to do something, however imperfectly or inefficiently. This entails selecting people with the requisite skills and experience, enabling them to upgrade their abilities as needed, and then molding the efforts of individuals into a joint effort to create an organizational ability. At this stage, progress can be fitful since it depends on experimenting, actively searching for alternative solutions, and learning through trial and error.[11]

As experience grows and company personnel learn how to perform the activities consistently well and at an acceptable cost, the ability *evolves* into a tried-and-true competence. Getting to this point requires a *continual investment* of resources and *systematic efforts* to improve processes and solve problems creatively as they arise. Improvements in the functioning of a capability come from task repetition and the resulting *learning by doing* of individuals and teams. But the process can be accelerated by making learning a more deliberate endeavor and providing the incentives that will motivate company personnel to achieve the desired ends.[12] This can be critical to successful strategy execution when market conditions are changing rapidly.

It is generally much easier and less time-consuming to update and remodel a company's existing capabilities as external conditions and company strategy change than it is to create them from scratch. Maintaining capabilities in top form may simply require exercising them continually and fine-tuning them as necessary. Similarly, augmenting a capability may require less effort if it involves the recombination of well-established company capabilities and draws on existing company resources. For example, Williams-Sonoma first developed the capability to expand sales beyond its brick-and-mortar location in 1970, when it launched a catalog that was sent to customers throughout the United States. The company extended its mail-order business with the acquisitions of Hold Everything, a garden products catalog, and Pottery Barn, and entered online retailing in 2000 when it launched e-commerce sites for Pottery Barn and Williams-Sonoma. The ongoing renewal of these capabilities has allowed Williams-Sonoma to generate revenues of more than $5 billion in 2017 and become one of the largest online retailers in the United States. Toyota, en route to overtaking General Motors as the global leader in motor vehicles, aggressively upgraded its capabilities in fuel-efficient hybrid engine technology and constantly fine-tuned its famed Toyota Production System to enhance its already proficient capabilities in manufacturing top-quality vehicles at relatively low costs.

Managerial actions to develop competitive capabilities generally take one of two forms: either strengthening the company's base of skills, knowledge, and experience or coordinating and integrating the efforts of the various work groups and departments. Actions of the first sort can be undertaken at all managerial levels, but actions of the second sort are best orchestrated by senior managers who not only appreciate the strategy-executing significance of strong capabilities but also have the clout to enforce the necessary cooperation and coordination among individuals, groups, and departments.[13]

Acquiring Capabilities through Mergers and Acquisitions   Sometimes the best way for a company to upgrade its portfolio of capabilities is by acquiring (or merging with) another company with attractive resources and capabilities.[14] An acquisition aimed at building a stronger portfolio of resources and capabilities can be every bit as valuable as an acquisition aimed at adding new products or services to the company's lineup of offerings. The advantage of this mode of acquiring new capabilities is primarily one of speed, since developing new capabilities internally can, at best, take many years of effort and, at worst, come to naught. Capabilities-motivated acquisitions are essential (1) when the company does not have the ability to create the needed capability internally (perhaps because it is too far afield from its existing capabilities) and (2) when industry conditions, technology, or competitors are moving at such a rapid clip that time is of the essence.

At the same time, acquiring capabilities in this way is not without difficulty. Capabilities involve tacit knowledge and complex routines that cannot be transferred readily from one organizational unit to another. This may limit the extent to which the new capability can be utilized. For example, Facebook acquired Oculus VR, a company that makes virtual reality headsets, to add capabilities that might enhance the social media experience. Transferring and integrating these capabilities to other parts of the Facebook organization prove easier said than done, however, as many technology acquisitions fail to yield the hoped-for benefits. Integrating the capabilities of two companies is particularly problematic when there are underlying incompatibilities in their supporting systems or processes. Moreover, since internal fit is important, there is always the risk that under new management the acquired capabilities may not be as productive as they had been. In a worst-case scenario, the acquisition process may end up damaging or destroying the very capabilities that were the object of the acquisition in the first place.

Accessing Capabilities through Collaborative Partnerships   A third way of obtaining valuable resources and capabilities is to form collaborative partnerships with suppliers, competitors, or other companies having the cutting-edge expertise. There are three basic ways to pursue this course of action:

1. *Outsource the function in which the company's capabilities are deficient to a key supplier or another provider.* Whether this is a wise move depends on whether developing the capabilities internally are key to the company's long-term success. But if this is not the case, then outsourcing may be a good choice especially for firms that are too small and resource-constrained to execute all the parts of their strategy internally.

2. *Collaborate with a firm that has complementary resources and capabilities in a joint venture, strategic alliance, or other type of partnership established for the purpose of achieving a shared strategic objective.* This requires launching initiatives to identify the most attractive potential partners and to establish collaborative working relationships. Since the success of the venture will depend on how well the partners work together, potential partners should be selected as much for their management style, culture, and goals as for their resources and capabilities. In the past 15 years, close collaboration with suppliers to achieve mutually beneficial outcomes has become a common approach to building supply chain capabilities.

3. *Engage in a collaborative partnership for the purpose of learning how the partner does things, internalizing its methods and thereby acquiring its capabilities.* This may be a viable method when each partner has something to learn from the other and can achieve an outcome *beneficial to both partners.* For example, firms sometimes enter into collaborative marketing arrangements whereby each partner is granted access to the other's dealer network for the purpose of expanding sales in geographic areas where the firms lack dealers. But if the intended gains are only one-sided, the arrangement more likely involves an abuse of trust. In consequence, it not only puts the cooperative venture at risk but also encourages the firm's partner to treat the firm similarly or refuse further dealings with the firm.

The Strategic Role of Employee Training

Training and retraining are important when a company shifts to a strategy requiring different skills, competitive capabilities, and operating methods. Training is also strategically important in organizational efforts to build skill-based competencies. And it is a key activity in businesses where technical know-how is changing so rapidly that a company loses its ability to compete unless its employees have cutting-edge knowledge and expertise. Successful strategy implementation requires that the training function is both adequately funded and effective. If better execution of the chosen strategy calls for new skills, deeper technological capability, or the building and deploying of new capabilities, training efforts need to be placed near the top of the action agenda.

The strategic importance of training has not gone unnoticed. Over 4,000 companies around the world have established internal "universities" to lead the training effort, facilitate continuous organizational learning, and upgrade their company's knowledge resources. General Electric has long been known for the excellence of its management training program at Crotonville, outside of New York City. McDonald's maintains a 130,000-square-foot training facility that they call Hamburger University.

Many companies conduct orientation sessions for new employees, fund an assortment of competence-building training programs, and reimburse employees for tuition and other expenses associated with obtaining additional college education, attending professional development courses, and earning professional certification of one kind or another. A number of companies offer online training courses that are available to employees around the clock. Increasingly, companies are expecting employees at all levels are expected to take an active role in their own professional development and assume responsibility for keeping their skills up to date and in sync with the company's needs.

Strategy Execution Capabilities and Competitive Advantage

As firms get better at executing their strategies, they develop capabilities in the domain of strategy execution much as they build other organizational capabilities. Superior strategy execution capabilities allow companies to get the most from their other organizational resources and competitive capabilities. In this way they contribute to the success of a firm's business model. But excellence in strategy execution can also be a more direct source of competitive advantage, since more efficient and effective strategy execution can lower costs and permit firms to deliver more value to customers. Superior strategy execution capabilities may also enable a company to react more quickly to market changes and beat other firms to the market with new products and services. This can allow a company to profit from a period of uncontested market dominance. See Illustration Capsule 10.2 for an example of Zara's route to competitive advantage.

Because strategy execution capabilities are socially complex capabilities that develop with experience over long periods of time, they are hard to imitate. And there is no substitute for good strategy execution. (Recall the tests of resource advantage from Chapter 4.) As such, they may be as important a source of sustained competitive advantage as the core competencies that drive a firm's strategy. Indeed, they may be a far more important avenue for securing a competitive edge over rivals in situations where it is relatively easy for rivals to copy promising strategies. In such cases, the only way for firms to achieve lasting competitive advantage is to *out-execute* their competitors.

> Superior strategy execution capabilities are the only source of sustainable competitive advantage when strategies are easy for rivals to copy.

ILLUSTRATION CAPSULE 10.2 Zara's Strategy Execution Capabilities

©lentamart/Shutterstock

Zara, a major division of Inditex Group, is a leading "fast fashion" retailer. As soon as designs are seen in high-end fashion houses such as Prada, Zara's design team sets to work altering the clothing designs so that it can produce high fashion at mass-retailing prices. Zara's strategy is clever, but by no means unique. The company's competitive advantage is in strategy execution. Every step of Zara's value chain execution is geared toward putting fashionable clothes in stores quickly, realizing high turnover, and strategically driving traffic.

The first key lever is a quick production process. Zara's design team uses inspiration from high fashion and nearly real-time feedback from stores to create up-to-the-minute pieces. Manufacturing largely occurs in factories close to headquarters in Spain, northern Africa, and Turkey, all areas considered to have a high cost of labor. Placing the factories strategically close allows for more flexibility and greater responsiveness to market needs, thereby outweighing the additional labor costs. The entire production process, from design to arrival at stores, takes only two weeks, while other retailers take six months. Whereas traditional retailers commit up to 80 percent of their lines by the start of the season, Zara commits only 50 to 60 percent, meaning that up to half of the merchandise to hit stores is designed and manufactured during the season. Zara purposefully manufactures in small lot sizes to avoid discounting later on and also to encourage impulse shopping, as a particular item could be gone in a few days. From start to finish, Zara has engineered its production process to maximize turnover and turnaround time, creating a true advantage in this step of strategy execution.

Zara also excels at driving traffic to stores. First, the small lot sizes and frequent shipments (up to twice a week per store) drive customers to visit often and purchase quickly. Zara shoppers average 17 visits per year, versus 4 to 5 for The Gap. On average, items stay in a Zara store only 11 days. Second, Zara spends no money on advertising, but it occupies some of the most expensive retail space in town, always near the high-fashion houses it imitates. Proximity reinforces the high-fashion association, while the busy street drives significant foot traffic. Overall, Zara has managed to create competitive advantage in every level of strategy execution by tightly aligning design, production, advertising, and real estate with the overall strategy of fast fashion: extremely fast and extremely flexible.

Note: Developed with Sara Paccamonti.

Sources: Suzy Hansen, "How Zara Grew into the World's Largest Fashion Retailer," *The New York Times,* November 9, 2012, www.nytimes.com/2012/11/11/magazine/how-zara-grew-into-the-worlds-largest-fashion-retailer.html?pagewanted=all (accessed February 5, 2014); Seth Stevenson, "Polka Dots Are In? Polka Dots It Is!" *Slate,* June 21, 2012, www.slate.com/articles/arts/operations/2012/06/zara_s_fast_fashion_how_the_company_gets_new_styles_to_stores_so_quickly.html (accessed February 5, 2014).

MATCHING ORGANIZATIONAL STRUCTURE TO THE STRATEGY

• • • •

While there are few hard-and-fast rules for organizing the work effort to support good strategy execution, there is one: A firm's organizational structure should be *matched* to the particular requirements of implementing the firm's strategy. Every company's strategy is grounded in its own set of organizational capabilities and value chain activities. Moreover, every firm's organizational chart is partly a product of its particular situation, reflecting prior organizational patterns, varying internal circumstances, and executive judgments about how to best structure reporting relationships. Thus, the determinants of the fine details of each firm's organizational structure are unique. But some considerations in organizing the work effort are common to all companies. These are summarized in Figure 10.3 and discussed in the following sections.

● **LO 10-4**

Identify and establish a strategy-supportive organizational structure and organize the work effort.

Deciding Which Value Chain Activities to Perform Internally and Which to Outsource

Aside from the fact that an outsider, because of its expertise and specialized know-how, may be able to perform certain value chain activities better or cheaper than a company can perform them internally (as discussed in Chapter 6), outsourcing can also sometimes contribute to better strategy execution. Outsourcing the performance of selected activities to outside vendors enables a company to heighten its strategic focus and *concentrate its full energies on performing those value chain activities that are at the core of its strategy, where it can create unique value.* For example, 83 percent of the top 10 pharmaceutical companies outsource tactical roles such as clinical data management and trial monitoring; they are much less likely to outsource more strategic functions, such as new product planning. Broadcom, (now part of semiconductor maker Avago Technologies) outsources the manufacture of its chips, thus freeing company personnel to focus their full energies on R&D, new chip design, and marketing. Nike concentrates on design, marketing, and distribution to retailers, while outsourcing virtually all production of its shoes and sporting apparel. Interestingly,

A company's organizational structure should be matched to the particular requirements of implementing the firm's strategy.

FIGURE 10.3   Structuring the Work Effort to Promote Successful Strategy Execution

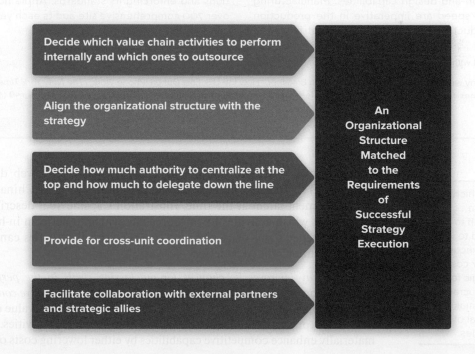

ILLUSTRATION CAPSULE 10.3 — Which Value Chain Activities Does Apple Outsource and Why?

©Qilai Shen/In Pictures Ltd./Corbis via Getty Images

Innovation and design are core competencies for Apple and the drivers behind the creation of winning products such as the iPod, iPhone, and iPad. In consequence, all activities directly related to new product development and product design are performed internally. For example, Apple's Industrial Design Group is responsible for creating the look and feel of all Apple products—from the MacBook Air to the iPhone, and beyond to future products.

Producing a continuing stream of great new products and product versions is key to the success of Apple's strategy. But executing this strategy takes more than innovation and design capabilities. Manufacturing flexibility and speed are imperative in the production of Apple products to ensure that the latest ideas are reflected in the products and that the company meets the high demand for its products—especially around launch.

For these capabilities, Apple turns to outsourcing, as do the majority of its competitors in the consumer electronics space. Apple outsources the manufacturing of products like its iPhone to Asia, where contract manufacturing organizations (CMOs) create value through their vast scale, high flexibility, and low cost. Perhaps no company better epitomizes the Asian CMO value proposition than Foxconn, a company that assembles not only for Apple but for Hewlett-Packard, Motorola, Amazon.com, and Samsung as well. Foxconn's scale is incredible, with 1.3 million people on its payroll as of 2017. Such scale offers companies a significant degree of flexibility, as Foxconn has the ability to hire 3,000 employees on practically a moment's notice. Apple, more so than its competitors, is able to capture CMO value creation by leveraging its immense sales volume and strong cash position to receive preferred treatment. While outsourcing has allowed Apple to reap the benefits of lower cost and more flexible manufacturing, the lack of direct control has proven to be a challenge. Working conditions at Foxconn were so bad at one point that Foxconn installed suicide prevention nets below its windows. Apple responded by tightening its supplier standards and increasing its efforts at monitoring conditions and enforcing its standards. Apple now conducts over 700 comprehensive site audits each year to ensure compliance.

Note: Developed with Margaret W. Macauley.

Sources: Company website; Charles Duhigg and Keith Bradsher, "How the U.S. Lost Out on iPhone Work," *The New York Times,* January 21, 2012, **www.nytimes.com/2012/01/22/business/apple-america-and-a-squeezed-middle-class.html?pagewanted=all&_r=0** (accessed March 5, 2012).

Wisely choosing which activities to perform internally and which to outsource can lead to several strategy-executing advantages—lower costs, heightened strategic focus, less internal bureaucracy, speedier decision making, and a better arsenal of organizational capabilities.

e-commerce powerhouse Alibaba got its start by outsourcing web development (a key function) to a U.S. firm; but this was due to the fact that China lacked sufficient development talent at the time. Illustration Capsule 10.3 describes Apple's decisions about which activities to outsource and which to perform in-house.

Such heightened focus on performing strategy-critical activities can yield three important execution-related benefits:

- *The company improves its chances for outclassing rivals in the performance of strategy-critical activities and turning a competence into a distinctive competence.* At the very least, the heightened focus on performing a select few value chain activities should promote more effective performance of those activities. This could materially enhance competitive capabilities by either lowering costs or improving product or service quality. Businesses that get a lot of inquiries from customers or that have to provide 24/7 technical support to users of their products around the world often find that it is considerably less expensive to outsource these functions to specialists (often located in foreign countries where skilled personnel are readily available and worker compensation costs are much lower) than to operate their own call centers. Many businesses also outsource IT functions such as desktop support, disaster recovery, help desk, and data center operations, which often results in cost savings due to the economies of scale available to service providers.

- *The streamlining of internal operations that flows from outsourcing often acts to decrease internal bureaucracies, flatten the organizational structure, speed internal decision making, and shorten the time it takes to respond to changing market conditions.* In consumer electronics, where advancing technology drives new product innovation, organizing the work effort in a manner that expedites getting next-generation products to market ahead of rivals is a critical competitive capability. The world's motor vehicle manufacturers have found that they can shorten the cycle time for new models by outsourcing the production of many parts and components to independent suppliers. They then work closely with the suppliers to swiftly incorporate new technology and to better integrate individual parts and components to form engine cooling systems, transmission systems, electrical systems, and so on.

- *Partnerships with outside vendors can add to a company's arsenal of capabilities and contribute to better strategy execution.* Outsourcing activities to vendors with first-rate capabilities can enable a firm to concentrate on strengthening its own complementary capabilities internally; the result will be a more powerful package of organizational capabilities that the firm can draw upon to deliver more value to customers and attain competitive success. Soft-drink and beer manufacturers cultivate their relationships with their bottlers and distributors to strengthen access to local markets and build loyalty, support, and commitment for corporate marketing programs, without which their own sales and growth would be weakened. Similarly, fast-food enterprises like Wendy's and Burger King find it essential to work hand in hand with franchisees on outlet cleanliness, consistency of product quality, in-store ambience, courtesy and friendliness of store personnel, and other aspects of store operations. Unless franchisees continuously deliver sufficient customer satisfaction to attract repeat business, a fast-food chain's reputation, sales, and competitive standing will quickly suffer. Companies like Boeing, Dell, and Apple have learned that their central R&D groups cannot begin to match the innovative capabilities of a well-managed network of supply chain partners.

However, as emphasized in Chapter 6, a company must guard against going overboard on outsourcing and becoming overly dependent on outside suppliers. A company cannot be the master of its own destiny unless it maintains expertise and resource depth in performing those value chain activities that underpin its long-term competitive success.[15]

Aligning the Firm's Organizational Structure with Its Strategy

The design of the firm's **organizational structure** is a critical aspect of the strategy execution process. The organizational structure comprises the formal and informal arrangement of tasks, responsibilities, and lines of authority and communication by which the firm is administered.[16] It specifies the linkages among parts of the

CORE CONCEPT

A firm's **organizational structure** comprises the formal and informal arrangement of tasks, responsibilities, lines of authority, and reporting relationships by which the firm is administered.

organization, the reporting relationships, the direction of information flows, and the decision-making processes. It is a key factor in strategy implementation since it exerts a strong influence on how well managers can coordinate and control the complex set of activities involved.[17]

A well-designed organizational structure is one in which the various parts (e.g., decision-making rights, communication patterns) are aligned with one another and also matched to the requirements of the strategy. With the right structure in place, managers can orchestrate the various aspects of the implementation process with an even hand and a light touch. Without a supportive structure, strategy execution is more likely to become bogged down by administrative confusion, political maneuvering, and bureaucratic waste.

Good organizational design may even contribute to the firm's ability to create value for customers and realize a profit. By enabling lower bureaucratic costs and facilitating operational efficiency, it can lower a firm's operating costs. By facilitating the coordination of activities within the firm, it can improve the capability-building process, leading to greater differentiation and/or lower costs. Moreover, by improving the speed with which information is communicated and activities are coordinated, it can enable the firm to beat rivals to the market and profit from a period of unrivaled advantage.

Making Strategy-Critical Activities the Main Building Blocks of the Organizational Structure   In any business, some activities in the value chain are always more critical to successful strategy execution than others. For instance, ski apparel companies like Sport Obermeyer, Arc'teryx, and Spyder must be good at styling and design, low-cost manufacturing, distribution (convincing an attractively large number of dealers to stock and promote the company's brand), and marketing and advertising (building a brand image that generates buzz among ski enthusiasts). For brokerage firms like Charles Schwab Corporation and TD Ameritrade, the strategy-critical activities are fast access to information, accurate order execution, efficient record keeping and transaction processing, and full-featured customer service. With respect to such core value chain activities, it is important for management to build its organizational structure around proficient performance of these activities, making them the centerpieces or main building blocks in the enterprise's organizational structure.

The rationale is compelling: If activities crucial to strategic success are to have the resources, decision-making influence, and organizational impact they need, they must be centerpieces in the enterprise's organizational scheme. Making them the focus of structuring efforts will also facilitate their coordination and promote good internal fit—an essential attribute of a winning strategy, as summarized in Chapter 1 and elaborated in Chapter 4. To the extent that implementing a new strategy entails new or altered key activities or capabilities, different organizational arrangements may be required.

Matching Type of Organizational Structure to Strategy Execution Requirements   Organizational structures can be classified into a limited number of standard types. Which type makes the most sense for a given firm depends largely on the firm's size and business makeup, but not so much on the specifics of its strategy. As firms grow and their needs for structure evolve, their structural form is likely to evolve from one type to another. The four basic types are the *simple structure,* the *functional structure,* the *multidivisional structure,* and the *matrix structure,* as described next.

1. Simple Structure A **simple structure** is one in which a central executive (often the owner-manager) handles all major decisions and oversees the operations of the organization with the help of a small staff.[18] Simple structures are also known as *line-and-staff structures,* since a central administrative staff supervises line employees who conduct the operations of the firm, or *flat structures,* since there are few levels of hierarchy. The simple structure is characterized by limited task specialization; few rules; informal relationships; minimal use of training, planning, and liaison devices; and a lack of sophisticated support systems. It has all the advantages of simplicity, including low administrative costs, ease of coordination, flexibility, quick decision making, adaptability, and responsiveness to change. Its informality and lack of rules may foster creativity and heightened individual responsibility.

Simple organizational structures are typically employed by small firms and entrepreneurial startups. The simple structure is the most common type of organizational structure since small firms are the most prevalent type of business. As an organization grows, however, this structural form becomes inadequate to the demands that come with size and complexity. In response, growing firms tend to alter their organizational structure from a simple structure to a *functional structure.*

2. Functional Structure A **functional structure** is one that is organized along functional lines, where a function represents a major component of the firm's value chain, such as R&D, engineering and design, manufacturing, sales and marketing, logistics, and customer service. Each functional unit is supervised by functional line managers who report to the chief executive officer and a corporate staff. This arrangement allows functional managers to focus on their area of responsibility, leaving it to the CEO and headquarters to provide direction and ensure that the activities of the functional managers are coordinated and integrated. Functional structures are also known as *departmental structures,* since the functional units are commonly called departments, and *unitary structures* or *U-forms,* since a single unit is responsible for each function.

In large organizations, functional structures lighten the load on top management, in comparison to simple structures, and enable more efficient use of managerial resources. Their primary advantage, however, is greater *task specialization,* which promotes learning, enables the realization of scale economies, and offers productivity advantages not otherwise available. Their chief disadvantage is that the departmental boundaries can inhibit the flow of information and limit the opportunities for cross-functional cooperation and coordination.

It is generally agreed that a functional structure is the best organizational arrangement when a company is in just one particular business (irrespective of which of the five generic competitive strategies it opts to pursue). For instance, a technical instruments manufacturer may be organized around research and development, engineering, supply chain management, assembly, quality control, marketing, and technical services. A discount retailer, such as Dollar General or Family Dollar, may organize around such functional units as purchasing, warehousing, distribution logistics, store operations, advertising, merchandising and promotion, and customer service. Functional structures can also be appropriate for firms with high-volume production, products that are closely related, and a limited degree of vertical integration. For example, General Motors now manages all of its brands (Cadillac, GMC, Chevrolet, Buick, etc.) under a common functional structure designed to promote technical transfer and capture economies of scale.

As firms continue to grow, they often become more diversified and complex, placing a greater burden on top management. At some point, the centralized control that

---

CORE CONCEPT

A **simple structure** consists of a central executive (often the owner-manager) who handles all major decisions and oversees all operations with the help of a small staff. Simple structures are also called *line-and-staff structures* or *flat structures.*

CORE CONCEPT

A **functional structure** is organized into functional departments, with departmental managers who report to the CEO and small corporate staff. Functional structures are also called *departmental structures* and *unitary structures* or *U-forms.*

The primary advantage of a functional structure is greater task specialization, which promotes learning, enables the realization of scale economies, and offers productivity advantages not otherwise available.

characterizes the functional structure becomes a liability, and the advantages of functional specialization begin to break down. To resolve these problems and address a growing need for coordination across functions, firms generally turn to the *multidivisional structure*.

3. Multidivisional Structure A **multidivisional structure** is a decentralized structure consisting of a set of operating divisions organized along market, customer, product, or geographic lines, along with a central corporate headquarters, which monitors divisional activities, allocates resources, performs assorted support functions, and exercises overall control. Since each division is essentially a business (often called a *single business unit* or *SBU),* the divisions typically operate as independent profit centers (i.e., with profit and loss responsibility) and are organized internally along functional lines. Division managers oversee day-to-day operations and the development of business-level strategy, while corporate executives attend to overall performance and corporate strategy, the elements of which were described in Chapter 8. Multidivisional structures are also called *divisional structures* or *M-forms,* in contrast with U-form (functional) structures.

Multidivisional structures are common among companies pursuing some form of diversification strategy or international strategy, with operations in a number of businesses or countries. When the strategy is one of unrelated diversification, as in a conglomerate, the divisions generally represent businesses in separate industries. When the strategy is based on related diversification, the divisions may be organized according to industries, customer groups, product lines, geographic regions, or technologies. In this arrangement, the decision about where to draw the divisional lines depends foremost on the nature of the relatedness and the strategy-critical building blocks, in terms of which businesses have key value chain activities in common. For example, a company selling closely related products to business customers as well as two types of end consumers—online buyers and in-store buyers—may organize its divisions according to customer groups since the value chains involved in serving the three groups differ. Another company may organize by product line due to commonalities in product development and production within each product line. Multidivisional structures are also common among vertically integrated firms. There the major building blocks are often divisional units performing one or more of the major processing steps along the value chain (e.g., raw-material production, components manufacture, assembly, wholesale distribution, retail store operations).

Multidivisional structures offer significant advantages over functional structures in terms of facilitating the management of a complex and diverse set of operations.[19] Putting business-level strategy in the hands of division managers while leaving corporate strategy to top executives reduces the potential for information overload and improves the quality of decision making in each domain. This also minimizes the costs of coordinating division-wide activities while enhancing top management's ability to control a diverse and complex operation. Moreover, multidivisional structures can help align individual incentives with the goals of the corporation and spur productivity by encouraging competition for resources among the different divisions.

But a multidivisional structure can also present some problems to a company pursuing related diversification, because having independent business units—each running its own business in its own way—inhibits cross-business collaboration and the capture of cross-business synergies, which are critical for the success of a related diversification strategy, as Chapter 8 explains. To solve this type of problem, firms turn to more complex structures, such as the matrix structure.

4. Matrix Structure   A **matrix structure** is a combination structure in which the organization is organized along two or more dimensions at once (e.g., business, geographic area, value chain function) for the purpose of enhancing cross-unit communication, collaboration, and coordination. In essence, it overlays one type of structure onto another type. Matrix structures are managed through multiple reporting relationships, so a middle manager may report to several bosses. For instance, in a matrix structure based on product line, region, and function, a sales manager for plastic containers in Georgia might report to the manager of the plastics division, the head of the southeast sales region, and the head of marketing.

Matrix organizational structures have evolved from the complex, over-formalized structures that were popular in the late 20th century but often produced inefficient, unwieldy bureaucracies. The modern incarnation of the matrix structure is generally a more flexible arrangement, with a single primary reporting relationship that can be overlaid with a *temporary* secondary reporting relationship as need arises. For example, a software company that is organized into functional departments (software design, quality control, customer relations) may assign employees from those departments to different projects on a temporary basis, so an employee reports to a project manager as well as to his or her primary boss (the functional department head) for the duration of a project.

Matrix structures are also called *composite structures* or *combination structures.* They are often used for project-based, process-based, or team-based management. Such approaches are common in businesses involving projects of limited duration, such as consulting, architecture, and engineering services. The type of close cross-unit collaboration that a flexible matrix structure supports is also needed to build competitive capabilities in strategically important activities, such as speeding new products to market, that involve employees scattered across several organizational units.[20] Capabilities-based matrix structures that combine process departments (like new product development) with more traditional functional departments provide a solution.

An advantage of matrix structures is that they facilitate the sharing of plant and equipment, specialized knowledge, and other key resources. Thus, they lower costs by enabling the realization of economies of scope. They also have the advantage of flexibility in form and may allow for better oversight since supervision is provided from more than one perspective. A disadvantage is that they add another layer of management, thereby increasing bureaucratic costs and possibly decreasing response time to new situations.[21] In addition, there is a potential for confusion among employees due to dual reporting relationships and divided loyalties. While there is some controversy over the utility of matrix structures, the modern approach to matrix structures does much to minimize their disadvantages.[22]

Determining How Much Authority to Delegate

Under any organizational structure, there is room for considerable variation in how much authority top-level executives retain and how much is delegated to down-the-line managers and employees. In executing strategy and conducting daily operations, companies must decide how much authority to delegate to the managers of each organizational unit—especially the heads of divisions, functional departments, plants, and other operating units—and how much decision-making latitude to give individual employees in performing their jobs. The two extremes are to *centralize decision making* at the top or to *decentralize decision making* by giving managers and employees at all levels considerable decision-making latitude in their areas of responsibility. As shown in Table 10.1, the two approaches are based on sharply different underlying principles and beliefs, with each having its pros and cons.

> **CORE CONCEPT**
>
> A **matrix structure** is a combination structure that overlays one type of structure onto another type, with multiple reporting relationships. It is used to foster cross-unit collaboration. Matrix structures are also called *composite structures* or *combination structures.*

> **LO 10-5**
>
> Explain the pros and cons of centralized and decentralized decision making in implementing the chosen strategy.

TABLE 10.1   Advantages and Disadvantages of Centralized versus Decentralized Decision Making

Centralized Organizational Structures	Decentralized Organizational Structures
Basic tenets	**Basic tenets**
• Decisions on most matters of importance should be in the hands of top-level managers who have the experience, expertise, and judgment to decide what is the best course of action.	• Decision-making authority should be put in the hands of the people closest to, and most familiar with, the situation.
• Lower-level personnel have neither the knowledge, time, nor inclination to properly manage the tasks they are performing.	• Those with decision-making authority should be trained to exercise good judgment.
• Strong control from the top is a more effective means for coordinating company actions.	• A company that draws on the combined intellectual capital of all its employees can outperform a command-and-control company.
Chief advantages	**Chief advantages**
• Fixes accountability through tight control from the top.	• Encourages company employees to exercise initiative and act responsibly.
• Eliminates potential for conflicting goals and actions on the part of lower-level managers.	• Promotes greater motivation and involvement in the business on the part of more company personnel.
• Facilitates quick decision making and strong leadership under crisis situations.	• Spurs new ideas and creative thinking.
	• Allows for fast response to market change.
	• Entails fewer layers of management.
Primary disadvantages	**Primary disadvantages**
• Lengthens response times by those closest to the market conditions because they must seek approval for their actions.	• May result in higher-level managers being unaware of actions taken by empowered personnel under their supervision.
• Does not encourage responsibility among lower-level managers and rank-and-file employees.	• Can lead to inconsistent or conflicting approaches by different managers and employees.
• Discourages lower-level managers and rank-and-file employees from exercising any initiative.	• Can impair cross-unit collaboration.

Centralized Decision Making: Pros and Cons   In a highly centralized organizational structure, *top executives retain authority for most strategic and operating decisions* and keep a tight rein on business unit heads, department heads, and the managers of key operating units. Comparatively little discretionary authority is granted to frontline supervisors and rank-and-file employees. The command-and-control paradigm of centralized decision making is based on the underlying assumptions that frontline personnel have neither the time nor the inclination to direct and properly control the work they are performing and that they lack the knowledge and judgment to make wise decisions about how best to do it—hence the need for prescribed policies and procedures for a wide range of activities, close supervision, and tight control by top executives. The thesis underlying centralized structures is that strict enforcement of detailed procedures backed by rigorous managerial oversight is the most reliable way to keep the daily execution of strategy on track.

One advantage of a centralized structure, with tight control by the manager in charge, is that it is easy to know who is accountable when things do not go well. This structure can also reduce the potential for conflicting decisions and actions among lower-level managers who may have differing perspectives and ideas about how to tackle certain tasks or resolve particular issues. For example, a manager in charge of an engineering department may be more interested in pursuing a new technology than is a marketing manager who doubts that customers will value the technology as highly. Another advantage of a command-and-control structure is that it can facilitate strong leadership from the top in a crisis situation that affects the organization as a whole and can enable a more uniform and swift response.

But there are some serious disadvantages as well. Hierarchical command-and-control structures do not encourage responsibility and initiative on the part of lower-level managers and employees. They can make a large organization with a complex structure sluggish in responding to changing market conditions because of the time it takes for the review-and-approval process to run up all the layers of the management bureaucracy. Furthermore, to work well, centralized decision making requires top-level managers to gather and process whatever information is relevant to the decision. When the relevant knowledge resides at lower organizational levels (or is technical, detailed, or hard to express in words), it is difficult and time-consuming to get all the facts in front of a high-level executive located far from the scene of the action—full understanding of the situation cannot be readily copied from one mind to another. Hence, centralized decision making is often impractical—the larger the company and the more scattered its operations, the more that decision-making authority must be delegated to managers closer to the scene of the action.

Decentralized Decision Making: Pros and Cons   In a highly decentralized organization, *decision-making authority is pushed down to the lowest organizational level capable of making timely, informed, competent decisions.* The objective is to put adequate decision-making authority in the hands of the people closest to and most familiar with the situation and train them to weigh all the factors and exercise good judgment. At Starbucks, for example, employees are encouraged to exercise initiative in promoting customer satisfaction—there's the oft-repeated story of a store employee who, when the computerized cash register system went offline, offered free coffee to waiting customers, thereby avoiding customer displeasure and damage to Starbucks's reputation.[23]

> The ultimate goal of decentralized decision making is to put authority in the hands of those persons closest to and most knowledgeable about the situation.

The case for empowering down-the-line managers and employees to make decisions related to daily operations and strategy execution is based on the belief that a company that draws on the combined intellectual capital of all its employees can outperform a command-and-control company.[24] The challenge in a decentralized system is maintaining adequate control. With decentralized decision making, top management maintains control by placing limits on the authority granted to company personnel, installing companywide strategic control systems, holding people accountable for their decisions, instituting compensation incentives that reward people for doing their jobs well, and creating a corporate culture where there's strong peer pressure on individuals to act responsibly.[25]

Decentralized organizational structures have much to recommend them. Delegating authority to subordinate managers and rank-and-file employees encourages them to take responsibility and exercise initiative. It shortens organizational response times to market changes and spurs new ideas, creative thinking, innovation, and greater involvement on the part of all company personnel. At TJX Companies Inc., parent company of T.J.Maxx, Marshalls, and five other fashion and home decor retail store chains, buyers are encouraged to be intelligent risk takers in deciding what items to purchase for TJX stores—there's the story of a buyer for a seasonal product category who cut her own budget to have dollars allocated to other categories where sales were expected to be stronger. In worker-empowered structures, jobs can be defined more broadly, several tasks can be integrated into a single job, and people can direct their own work. Fewer managers are needed because deciding how to do things becomes part of each person's or team's job. Further, today's online communication systems and smartphones make it easy and relatively inexpensive for people at all organizational levels to have direct access to data, other employees, managers, suppliers, and customers. They can access information quickly (via the Internet or company network), readily check with superiors or whomever else as needed, and take responsible action. Typically, there are genuine gains in morale and productivity when people are provided with the tools and information they need to operate in a self-directed way.

But decentralization also has some disadvantages. Top managers lose an element of control over what goes on and may thus be unaware of actions being taken by personnel under their supervision. Such lack of control can be problematic in the event that empowered employees make decisions that conflict with those of others or that serve their unit's interests at the expense of other parts of the company. Moreover, because decentralization gives organizational units the authority to act independently, there is risk of too little collaboration and coordination between different units.

Many companies have concluded that the advantages of decentralization outweigh the disadvantages. Over the past several decades, there's been a decided shift from centralized, hierarchical structures to flatter, more decentralized structures that stress employee empowerment. This shift reflects a strong and growing consensus that authoritarian, hierarchical organizational structures are not well suited to implementing and executing strategies in an era when extensive information and instant communication are the norm and when a big fraction of the organization's most valuable assets consists of intellectual capital that resides in its employees' capabilities.

> Efforts to decentralize decision making and give company personnel some leeway in conducting operations must be tempered with the need to maintain adequate control and cross-unit coordination.

Capturing Cross-Business Strategic Fit in a Decentralized Structure

Diversified companies striving to capture the benefits of synergy between separate businesses must beware of giving business unit heads full rein to operate independently. Cross-business strategic fit typically must be captured either by enforcing close cross-business collaboration or by centralizing the performance of functions requiring close coordination at the corporate level.[26] For example, if businesses with overlapping process and product technologies have their own independent R&D departments—each pursuing its own priorities, projects, and strategic agendas—it's hard for the corporate parent to prevent duplication of effort, capture either economies of scale or economies of scope, or encourage more collaborative R&D efforts. Where cross-business strategic fit with respect to R&D is important, one solution is to centralize the R&D function and have a coordinated corporate R&D effort that serves the interests of both the individual businesses and the company as a whole. Likewise, centralizing the related activities of separate businesses makes sense when there are opportunities to share a common sales force, use common distribution channels, rely on a common field service organization, use common e-commerce systems, and so on. Another structural solution to realizing the benefits of strategic fit is to create business groups consisting of those business units with common strategic-fit opportunities

Providing for Internal Cross-Unit Coordination

Close cross-unit collaboration is usually needed to build capabilities in such strategically important activities as speeding new products to market and providing superior customer service. This is because these activities involve collaboration among the efforts of company personnel who work in different departments or organizational units (and perhaps the employees of outside strategic partners or specialty vendors). For example, being first-to-market with new products involves coordinating the efforts of personnel in R&D (to develop a stream of new products with appealing attributes), design and engineering (to prepare a cost-efficient design and set of specifications), purchasing (to obtain the needed parts and components), manufacturing (to carry out all the production activities), and sales and marketing (to secure orders, arrange for introductory advertising and the distribution of product information, and get the products on retailers' shelves). Achieving the simple strategic objective of filling customer orders accurately and promptly involves personnel from sales (to win the order); finance (to check credit terms or approve special financing); production (to produce the goods and replenish warehouse inventories as needed); and warehousing and shipping (to verify whether the items are in stock, pick the order from the warehouse, package it for shipping, and choose the best carrier to deliver the goods).

To achieve tight coordination when pieces of execution-critical tasks are performed in multiple organizational units, company executives typically emphasize the necessity of cross-unit teamwork and cooperation and the importance of frequent back-and-forth communication among key people in the various related organizational units to resolve problems, avoid delays, and keep things moving along. The executives supervising the units performing parts of the execution-critical task typically make it clear that the relevant department heads and key personnel are all *expected to work closely together and coordinate their actions.* There are meetings to discuss schedules and set deadlines, often ending with the verbal commitments of everyone involved to stick close to the agreed-upon schedule, coordinate their activities, and meet the established deadlines. Gaining such commitments is almost always imperative, along with ensuring that everyone lives up to their commitments.

Normally, the supervising executives follow up, check on progress, and, in many cases, visit the different units to personally determine how well things are going and solicit the views of numerous people about what problems exist and what they think should be done to resolve them. They seldom hesitate to intervene to make corrective adjustments and to reiterate their expectations of teamwork, close communication, effective collaboration, and cooperation to resolve issues, avoid delays, and achieve the needed degree of cross-unit coordination. Such executive interventions, together with added executive pressure on the managers of units where close collaboration and coordinated action is lacking, may suffice. If it does, then all is well and good. But if such efforts fail, execution suffers and it becomes the responsibility of executives to determine the causes and take corrective action.

In many instances, the chief cause of ineffective cross-unit coordination in building capabilities rests with departmental-level managers and other key operating personnel who, for assorted reasons, don't or won't spend the time and effort needed to partner with other organizational units in the capability-building process. But it also has to be recognized that top-executive urging that departmental managers and their staff *voluntarily* place high priority on coordinating their respective activities *poses significant challenges* in achieving effective cross-unit coordination. This is especially true in decentralized organizational structures where department heads are delegated a high degree of decision-making authority in running their respective units and, thus, have a natural tendency to place a lower priority on cooperating closely with other organizational units than on ensuring that the activities under their direct supervision are done well. The weakness of heavily depending on the largely voluntary efforts of personnel for the development of critical cross-unit capabilities has prompted many companies to supplement such efforts by forming cross-functional committees, project management teams, and centralized project management offices to forge better cross-unit working relationships and improve coordination across multiple organizational units. While these arrangements have proved helpful in a number of organizations, more effective solutions involve creating incentive compensation systems where the payouts are tied to effective group performance of cross-unit tasks.

> Getting managers of execution-critical activities to live up to their commitments to coordinate closely with sister organizational unit is a *key* factor in achieving good internal cross-unit coordination.

Facilitating Collaboration with External Partners and Strategic Allies

Organizational mechanisms—whether formal or informal—are also required to ensure effective working relationships with each major outside constituency involved in strategy execution. Strategic alliances, outsourcing arrangements, joint ventures, and cooperative partnerships can contribute little of value without active management of the relationship. Unless top management sees that constructive organizational bridge building with external partners occurs and that productive working relationships emerge, the potential value of cooperative relationships is lost and the company's power to execute its strategy is weakened. For example, if close working relationships with suppliers are crucial, then supply chain management must enter into considerations of how to create an effective organizational structure. If distributor, dealer, or franchisee relationships are important, then someone must be assigned the task of nurturing the relationships with such forward-channel allies.

Building organizational bridges with external partners and strategic allies can be accomplished by appointing "relationship managers" with responsibility for making particular strategic partnerships generate the intended benefits. Relationship managers have many roles and functions: getting the right people together, promoting good rapport, facilitating the flow of information, nurturing interpersonal communication and cooperation, and ensuring effective coordination.[27] Multiple cross-organization ties have to be established and kept open to ensure proper communication and coordination. There has to be enough information sharing to make the relationship work and periodic frank discussions of conflicts, trouble spots, and changing situations.

> **CORE** CONCEPT
>
> A **network structure** is a configuration composed of a number of independent organizations engaged in some common undertaking, with one firm typically taking on a more central role.

Organizing and managing a network structure provides a mechanism for encouraging more effective collaboration and cooperation among external partners. A **network structure** is the arrangement linking a number of independent organizations involved in some common undertaking. A well-managed network structure typically includes one firm in a more central role, with the responsibility of ensuring that the right partners are included and the activities across the network are coordinated. The high-end Italian motorcycle company Ducati operates in this manner, assembling its motorcycles from parts obtained from a handpicked integrated network of parts suppliers.

Further Perspectives on Structuring the Work Effort

All organizational designs have their strategy-related strengths and weaknesses. To do a good job of matching structure to strategy, strategy implementers first have to pick a basic organizational design and modify it as needed to fit the company's particular business lineup. They must then (1) supplement the design with appropriate coordinating mechanisms (cross-functional task forces, special project teams, self-contained work teams, etc.) and (2) institute whatever networking and communications arrangements are necessary to support effective execution of the firm's strategy. Some companies may avoid setting up "ideal" organizational arrangements because they do not want to disturb existing reporting relationships or because they need to accommodate other situational idiosyncrasies, yet they must still work toward the goal of building a competitively capable organization.

What can be said unequivocally is that building a capable organization entails a process of consciously knitting together the efforts of individuals and groups. Organizational capabilities emerge from establishing and nurturing cooperative working relationships among people and groups to perform activities in a more efficient, value-creating fashion. While an appropriate organizational structure can facilitate this, organization building is a task in which senior management must be deeply involved. Indeed, effectively managing both internal organizational processes and external collaboration to create and develop competitively valuable organizational capabilities remains a top challenge for senior executives in today's companies.

KEY POINTS

1. Executing strategy is an action-oriented, operations-driven activity revolving around the management of people, business processes, and organizational structure. In devising an action agenda for executing strategy, managers should start by conducting a probing assessment of what the organization must do to carry out the strategy successfully. They should then consider precisely *how* to go about this.

2. Good strategy execution requires a *team effort*. All managers have strategy-executing responsibility in their areas of authority, and all employees are active participants in the strategy execution process.

3. Ten managerial tasks are part of every company effort to execute strategy: (1) staffing the organization with the right people, (2) developing and augmenting the necessary resources and organizational capabilities, (3) creating a supportive organizational structure, (4) allocating sufficient resources (budgetary and otherwise), (5) instituting supportive policies and procedures, (6) adopting processes for continuous improvement, (7) installing systems that enable proficient company operations, (8) tying incentives to the achievement of desired targets, (9) instilling the right corporate culture, and (10) exercising the leadership needed to propel strategy execution forward.

4. The two best signs of good strategy execution are that a company is meeting or beating its performance targets and is performing value chain activities in a manner that is conducive to companywide operating excellence. *Shortfalls in performance signal weak strategy, weak execution, or both.*

5. Building an organization capable of good strategy execution entails three types of actions: (1) *staffing the organization*—assembling a talented management team and recruiting and retaining employees with the needed experience, technical skills, and intellectual capital; (2) *acquiring, developing, and strengthening strategy-supportive resources and capabilities*—accumulating the required resources, developing proficiencies in performing strategy-critical value chain activities, and updating the company's capabilities to match changing market conditions and customer expectations; and (3) *structuring the organization and work effort*—instituting organizational arrangements that facilitate good strategy execution, deciding how much decision-making authority to delegate, facilitating cross-unit coordination, and managing external relationships.

6. Building competitive capabilities is a time-consuming, managerially challenging exercise that can be approached in three ways: (1) developing capabilities internally, (2) acquiring capabilities through mergers and acquisitions, and (3) accessing capabilities via collaborative partnerships.

7. In building capabilities internally, the first step is to develop the *ability* to do something, through experimenting, actively searching for alternative solutions, and learning by trial and error. As experience grows and company personnel learn how to perform the activities consistently well and at an acceptable cost, the ability evolves into a tried-and-true capability. The process can be accelerated by making learning a more deliberate endeavor and providing the incentives that will motivate company personnel to achieve the desired ends.

8. As firms get better at executing their strategies, they develop capabilities in the domain of strategy execution. Superior strategy execution capabilities allow companies to get the most from their resources and capabilities. But excellence in strategy execution can also be a more direct source of competitive advantage, since more efficient and effective strategy execution can lower costs and permit firms to deliver more value to customers. Because they are socially complex capabilities, superior strategy execution capabilities are hard to imitate and have no good substitutes. As such, they can be an important source of *sustainable* competitive advantage. Anytime rivals can readily duplicate successful strategies, making it impossible to *out-strategize* rivals, the chief way to achieve lasting competitive advantage is to *out-execute* them.

9. Structuring the organization and organizing the work effort in a strategy-supportive fashion has five aspects: (1) deciding which value chain activities to perform internally and which ones to outsource, (2) aligning the firm's organizational structure with its strategy, (3) deciding how much authority to centralize at the top and how much to delegate to down-the-line managers and employees, (4) providing for the internal cross-unit coordination needed to build and strengthen capabilities; and (5) facilitating the necessary collaboration and coordination with external partners and strategic allies.

10. To align the firm's organizational structure with its strategy, it is important to make strategy-critical activities the main building blocks. There are four basic types of organizational structures: the simple structure, the functional structure, the multidivisional structure, and the matrix structure. Which is most appropriate depends on the firm's size, complexity, and strategy.

ASSURANCE OF LEARNING EXERCISES

connect

LO 10-1

1. The heart of Zara's strategy in the apparel industry is to outcompete rivals by putting fashionable clothes in stores quickly and maximizing the frequency of customer visits. Illustration Capsule 10.2 discusses the capabilities that the company has developed in the execution of its strategy. How do its capabilities lead to a quick production process and new apparel introductions? How do these capabilities encourage customers to visit its stores every few weeks? Does the execution of the company's site selection capability also contribute to its competitive advantage? Explain.

connect

LO 10-2

2. Search online to read about Jeff Bezos's management of his new executives. Specifically, explore **Amazon.com's** "S-Team" meetings (**management.fortune.cnn.com/2012/11/16/jeff-bezos-amazon/**). Why does Bezos begin meetings of

senior executives with 30 minutes of silent reading? How does this focus the group? Why does Bezos insist new ideas must be written and presented in memo form? How does this reflect the founder's insistence on clear, concise, and innovative thinking in his company? And does this exercise work as a de facto crash course for new Amazon executives? Explain why this small but crucial management strategy reflects Bezos's overriding goal of cohesive and clear idea presentation.

3. Review Facebook's Careers page (**www.Facebook.com/careers/**). The page emphasizes Facebook's core values and explains how potential employees could fit that mold. Bold and decisive thinking and a commitment to transparency and social connectivity drive the page and the company as a whole. Then research Facebook's internal management training programs, called "employee boot camps," using a search engine like Google or Bing. How do these programs integrate the traits and stated goals on the Careers page into specific and tangible construction of employee capabilities? Boot camps are open to all Facebook employees, not just engineers. How does this internal training prepare Facebook employees of all types to "move fast and break things"?   **LO 10-2, 10-3**

4. Review Valve Corporation's company handbook online: **www.valvesoftware.com/ company/Valve_Handbook_LowRes.pdf.** Specifically, focus on Valve's corporate structure. Valve has hundreds of employees but no managers or bosses at all. Valve's gaming success hinges on innovative and completely original experiences like Portal and Half-Life. Does it seem that Valve's corporate structure uniquely promotes this type of gaming innovation? Why or why not? How would you characterize Valve's organizational structure? Is it completely unique, or could it be characterized as a multidivisional, matrix, or functional structure? Explain your answer.   **LO 10-4**

5. Johnson & Johnson, a multinational health care company responsible for manufacturing medical, pharmaceutical, and consumer goods, has been a leader in promoting a decentralized management structure. Perform an Internet search to gain some background information on the company's products, value chain activities, and leadership. How does Johnson & Johnson exemplify (or not exemplify) a decentralized management strategy? Describe the advantages and disadvantages of a decentralized system of management in the case of Johnson & Johnson. Why was it established in the first place? Has it been an effective means of decision making for the company?   **LO 10-5**

EXERCISE FOR SIMULATION PARTICIPANTS

1. How would you describe the organization of your company's top-management team? Is some decision making decentralized and delegated to individual managers? If so, explain how the decentralization works. Or are decisions made more by consensus, with all co-managers having input? What do you see as the advantages and disadvantages of the decision-making approach your company is employing?   **LO 10-5**

2. What specific actions have you and your co-managers taken to develop core competencies or competitive capabilities that can contribute to good strategy execution and potential competitive advantage? If no actions have been taken, explain your rationale for doing nothing.   **LO 10-3**

3. What value chain activities are most crucial to good execution of your company's strategy? Does your company have the ability to outsource any value chain activities? If so, have you and your co-managers opted to engage in outsourcing? Why or why not?   **LO 10-1**

ENDNOTES

[1] Donald Sull, Rebecca Homkes, and Charles Sull, "Why Strategy Execution Unravels—and What to Do About It," *Harvard Business Review* 93, no. 3 (March 2015), p. 60.

[2] Steven W. Floyd and Bill Wooldridge, "Managing Strategic Consensus: The Foundation of Effective Implementation," *Academy of Management Executive* 6, no. 4 (November 1992), p. 27.

[3] Jack Welch with Suzy Welch, *Winning* (New York: HarperBusiness, 2005).

[4] Larry Bossidy and Ram Charan, *Execution: The Discipline of Getting Things Done* (New York: Crown Business, 2002).

[5] Christopher A. Bartlett and Sumantra Ghoshal, "Building Competitive Advantage through People," *MIT Sloan Management Review* 43, no. 2 (Winter 2002), pp. 34–41.

[6] Justin Menkes, "Hiring for Smarts," *Harvard Business Review* 83, no. 11 (November 2005), pp. 100–109; Justin Menkes, *Executive Intelligence* (New York: HarperCollins, 2005).

[7] Menkes, *Executive Intelligence,* pp. 68, 76.

[8] Jim Collins, *Good to Great* (New York: HarperBusiness, 2001).

[9] John Byrne, "The Search for the Young and Gifted," *Businessweek,* October 4, 1999, p. 108.

[10] C. Helfat and M. Peteraf, "The Dynamic Resource-Based View: Capability Lifecycles," *Strategic Management Journal* 24, no. 10 (October 2003), pp. 997–1010.

[11] G. Dosi, R. Nelson, and S. Winter (eds.), *The Nature and Dynamics of Organizational Capabilities* (Oxford, England: Oxford University Press, 2001).

[12] S. Winter, "The Satisficing Principle in Capability Learning," *Strategic Management Journal* 21, no. 10–11 (October–November 2000), pp. 981–996; M. Zollo and S. Winter, "Deliberate Learning and the Evolution of

Dynamic Capabilities," *Organization Science* 13, no. 3 (May–June 2002), pp. 339–351.

[13] Robert H. Hayes, Gary P. Pisano, and David M. Upton, *Strategic Operations: Competing through Capabilities* (New York: Free Press, 1996); Jonas Ridderstrale, "Cashing In on Corporate Competencies," *Business Strategy Review* 14, no. 1 (Spring 2003), pp. 27–38; Danny Miller, Russell Eisenstat, and Nathaniel Foote, "Strategy from the Inside Out: Building Capability-Creating Organizations," *California Management Review* 44, no. 3 (Spring 2002), pp. 37–55.

[14] S. Karim and W. Mitchell, "Path-Dependent and Path-Breaking Change: Reconfiguring Business Resources Following Acquisitions in the US Medical Sector, 1978–1995," *Strategic Management Journal* 21, no. 10–11 (October–November 2000), pp. 1061–1082; L. Capron, P. Dussauge, and W. Mitchell, "Resource Redeployment Following Horizontal Acquisitions in Europe and North America, 1988–1992," *Strategic Management Journal* 19, no. 7 (July 1998), pp. 631–662.

[15] Gary P. Pisano and Willy C. Shih, "Restoring American Competitiveness," *Harvard Business Review* 87, no. 7–8 (July–August 2009), pp. 114–125.

[16] A. Chandler, *Strategy and Structure* (Cambridge, MA: MIT Press, 1962).

[17] E. Olsen, S. Slater, and G. Hult, "The Importance of Structure and Process to Strategy Implementation," *Business Horizons* 48, no. 1 (2005), pp. 47–54; H. Barkema, J. Baum, and E. Mannix, "Management Challenges in a New Time," *Academy of Management Journal* 45, no. 5 (October 2002), pp. 916–930.

[18] H. Mintzberg, *The Structuring of Organizations* (Englewood Cliffs, NJ: Prentice Hall, 1979); C. Levicki, *The Interactive Strategy*

Workout, 2nd ed. (London: Prentice Hall, 1999).

[19] O. Williamson, *Market and Hierarchies* (New York: Free Press, 1975); R. M. Burton and B. Obel, "A Computer Simulation Test of the M-Form Hypothesis," *Administrative Science Quarterly* 25 (1980), pp. 457–476.

[20] J. Baum and S. Wally, "Strategic Decision Speed and Firm Performance," *Strategic Management Journal* 24 (2003), pp. 1107–1129.

[21] C. Bartlett and S. Ghoshal, "Matrix Management: Not a Structure, a Frame of Mind," *Harvard Business Review,* July–August 1990, pp. 138–145.

[22] M. Goold and A. Campbell, "Structured Networks: Towards the Well Designed Matrix," *Long Range Planning* 36, no. 5 (2003), pp. 427–439.

[23] Iain Somerville and John Edward Mroz, "New Competencies for a New World," in Frances Hesselbein, Marshall Goldsmith, and Richard Beckard (eds.), *The Organization of the Future* (San Francisco: Jossey-Bass, 1997), p. 70.

[24] Stanley E. Fawcett, Gary K. Rhoads, and Phillip Burnah, "People as the Bridge to Competitiveness: Benchmarking the 'ABCs' of an Empowered Workforce," *Benchmarking: An International Journal* 11, no. 4 (2004), pp. 346–360.

[25] Robert Simons, "Control in an Age of Empowerment," *Harvard Business Review* 73 (March–April 1995), pp. 80–88.

[26] Jeanne M. Liedtka, "Collaboration across Lines of Business for Competitive Advantage," *Academy of Management Executive* 10, no. 2 (May 1996), pp. 20–34.

[27] Rosabeth Moss Kanter, "Collaborative Advantage: The Art of the Alliance," *Harvard Business Review* 72, no. 4 (July–August 1994), pp. 96–108.

Managing Internal Operations

Actions That Promote Good Strategy Execution

Learning Objectives

This chapter will help you

LO 11-1 Explain why resource allocation should always be based on strategic priorities.

LO 11-2 Explain how well-designed policies and procedures can facilitate good strategy execution.

LO 11-3 Explain how process management tools drive continuous improvement in the performance of value chain activities.

LO 11-4 Describe the role of information systems and operating systems in enabling company personnel to carry out their strategic roles proficiently.

LO 11-5 Explain how and why the use of well-designed incentives can be management's single most powerful tool for promoting adept strategy execution.

chapter 11

Managing Internal Operations
Actions That Promote Good Strategy Execution

Learning Objectives

This chapter will help you

LO 11-1 Explain why resource allocation should always be based on strategic priorities.

LO 11-2 Explain how well-designed policies and procedures can facilitate good strategy execution.

LO 11-3 Explain how process management tools drive continuous improvement in the performance of value chain activities.

LO 11-4 Describe the role of information systems and operating systems in enabling company personnel to carry out their strategic roles proficiently.

LO 11-5 Explain how and why the use of well-designed incentives can be management's single most powerful tool for promoting adept strategy execution.

©Roy Scott/Ikon Images/Getty Images

Processes underpin business capabilities, and capabilities underpin strategy execution.

Pearl Zhu

I don't pay good wages because I have a lot of money; I have a lot of money because I pay good wages.

Robert Bosch—*Founder of engineering company Robert Bosch GmbH*

Apple is a very disciplined company, and we have great processes. But that's not what it's about. Process makes you more efficient.

Steve Jobs—*Cofounder of Apple, Inc.*

In Chapter 10, we emphasized that proficient strategy execution begins with three types of managerial actions: staffing the organization with the right people; acquiring, developing, and strengthening the firm's resources and capabilities; and structuring the organization in a manner supportive of the strategy execution effort.

In this chapter, we discuss five additional managerial actions that advance the cause of good strategy execution:

- Allocating ample resources to execution-critical value chain activities.

- Instituting policies and procedures that facilitate good strategy execution.
- Employing process management tools to drive continuous improvement in how value chain activities are performed.
- Installing information and operating systems that enable company personnel to carry out their strategic roles proficiently.
- Using rewards and incentives to promote better strategy execution and the achievement of strategic and financial targets.

ALLOCATING RESOURCES TO THE STRATEGY EXECUTION EFFORT

● ● ● ●

● **LO 11-1**

Explain why resource allocation should always be based on strategic priorities.

A company's strategic priorities must drive how capital allocations are made and the size of each unit's operating budgets.

Early in the strategy implementation process, managers must determine what resources (in terms of funding, people, and so on) will be required and how they should be distributed across the company's various organizational units. This includes carefully screening requests for more people and new facilities and equipment, approving those that will contribute to the strategy execution effort, and turning down those that don't. Should internal cash flows prove insufficient to fund the planned strategic initiatives, then management must raise additional funds through borrowing or selling additional shares of stock to investors.

A company's ability to marshal the resources needed to support new strategic initiatives has a major impact on the strategy execution process. Too little funding and an insufficiency of other types of resources slow progress and impede the efforts of organizational units to execute their pieces of the strategic plan competently. Too much funding of particular organizational units and value chain activities wastes organizational resources and reduces financial performance. Both of these scenarios argue for managers to become deeply involved in reviewing budget proposals and directing the proper kinds and amounts of resources to strategy-critical organizational units.

A change in strategy nearly always calls for budget reallocations and resource shifting. Previously important units with a lesser role in the new strategy may need downsizing. Units that now have a bigger strategic role may need more people, new equipment, additional facilities, and above-average increases in their operating budgets. Implementing new strategy initiatives requires managers to take an active and sometimes forceful role in shifting resources, not only to better support activities now having a higher priority but also to capture opportunities to operate more cost-effectively. This requires putting enough resources behind new strategic initiatives to fuel their success and making the tough decisions to kill projects and activities that are no longer justified.

Google's strong support of R&D activities helped it grow to a $527 billion giant in just 18 years. In 2013, however, Google decided to kill its 20 percent time policy, which allowed its staff to work on side projects of their choice one day a week. While this side project program gave rise to many innovations, such as Gmail and AdSense (a big contributor to Google's revenues), it also meant that fewer resources were available for projects that were deemed closer to the core of Google's mission. In the years since Google killed the 20 percent policy, the company has consistently topped *Fortune, Forbes,* and *Fast Company* magazines' "most innovative companies" lists for ideas such as Google Glass, self-driving automobiles, and Chromebooks.

Visible actions to reallocate operating funds and move people into new organizational units signal a determined commitment to strategic change. Such actions can catalyze the implementation process and give it credibility. Microsoft has made a practice of regularly shifting hundreds of programmers to new high-priority programming initiatives within a matter of weeks or even days. Fast-moving developments in many markets are prompting companies to abandon traditional annual budgeting and resource allocation cycles in favor of resource allocation processes supportive of more rapid adjustments in strategy. In response to rapid technological change in the communications industry, AT&T has prioritized investments and acquisitions that have allowed it to offer its enterprise customers faster, more flexible networks and provide innovative new customer services, such as its Sponsored Data plan.

Merely fine-tuning the execution of a company's existing strategy seldom requires big shifts of resources from one area to another. In contrast, new strategic initiatives generally require not only big shifts in resources but a larger allocation of resources to the effort as well. However, there are times when strategy changes or new execution initiatives need to be made without adding to total company expenses. In such circumstances, managers have to work their way through the existing budget line by line and activity by activity, looking for ways to trim costs and shift resources to activities that are higher-priority in the strategy execution effort. In the event that a company needs to make significant cost cuts during the course of launching new strategic initiatives, managers must be especially creative in finding ways to do more with less. Indeed, it is common for strategy changes and the drive for good strategy execution to be aimed at achieving considerably higher levels of operating efficiency and, at the same time, making sure the most important value chain activities are performed as effectively as possible.

INSTITUTING POLICIES AND PROCEDURES THAT FACILITATE STRATEGY EXECUTION

A company's policies and procedures can either support or hinder good strategy execution. Anytime a company moves to put new strategy elements in place or improve its strategy execution capabilities, some changes in work practices are usually needed. Managers are thus well advised to carefully consider whether existing policies and procedures fully support such changes and to revise or discard those that do not.

As shown in Figure 11.1, well-conceived policies and operating procedures facilitate strategy execution in three ways:

> **LO 11-2**
>
> Explain how well-designed policies and procedures can facilitate good strategy execution.

> A company's policies and procedures provide a set of well-honed routines for running the company and executing the strategy.

1. *By providing top-down guidance regarding how things need to be done.* Policies and procedures provide company personnel with a set of guidelines for how to perform organizational activities, conduct various aspects of operations, solve problems as they arise, and accomplish particular tasks. In essence, they represent a store of organizational or managerial knowledge about efficient and effective ways of doing things—a set of well-honed *routines* for running the company. They clarify uncertainty about how to proceed in executing strategy and align the actions and behavior of company personnel with the requirements for good strategy execution. Moreover, they place limits on ineffective independent action. When they are well matched with the requirements of the strategy implementation plan, they channel the efforts of individuals along a path that supports the plan. When existing ways of doing things pose a barrier to strategy execution initiatives, actions and behaviors have to be changed. Under these conditions, the managerial role is to establish and enforce new policies and operating practices that are more conducive to executing the strategy appropriately. Policies are a particularly useful way to counteract tendencies for some people to resist change. People generally refrain from violating company policy or going against recommended practices and procedures without gaining clearance or having strong justification.

2. *By helping ensure consistency in how execution-critical activities are performed.* Policies and procedures serve to standardize the way that activities are performed. This can be important for ensuring the quality and reliability of the strategy execution process. It helps align and coordinate the strategy execution efforts of individuals and groups throughout the organization—a feature that is particularly beneficial

FIGURE 11.1   How Policies and Procedures Facilitate Good Strategy Execution

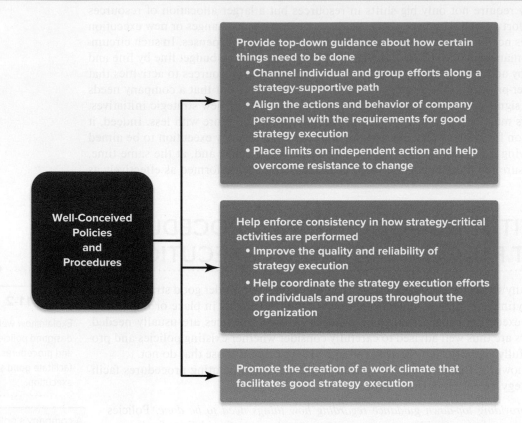

Well-Conceived Policies and Procedures

Provide top-down guidance about how certain things need to be done
- Channel individual and group efforts along a strategy-supportive path
- Align the actions and behavior of company personnel with the requirements for good strategy execution
- Place limits on independent action and help overcome resistance to change

Help enforce consistency in how strategy-critical activities are performed
- Improve the quality and reliability of strategy execution
- Help coordinate the strategy execution efforts of individuals and groups throughout the organization

Promote the creation of a work climate that facilitates good strategy execution

when there are geographically scattered operating units. For example, eliminating significant differences in the operating practices of different plants, sales regions, or customer service centers or in the individual outlets in a chain operation helps a company deliver consistent product quality and service to customers. Good strategy execution nearly always entails an ability to replicate product quality and the caliber of customer service at every location where the company does business—anything less blurs the company's image and lowers customer satisfaction.

3. *By promoting the creation of a work climate that facilitates good strategy execution.* A company's policies and procedures help set the tone of a company's work climate and contribute to a common understanding of "how we do things around here." Because abandoning old policies and procedures in favor of new ones invariably alters the internal work climate, managers can use the policy-changing process as a powerful lever for changing the corporate culture in ways that better support new strategic initiatives. The trick here, obviously, is to come up with new policies or procedures that catch the immediate attention of company personnel and prompt them to quickly shift their actions and behaviors in the desired ways.

To ensure consistency in product quality and service behavior patterns, McDonald's policy manual spells out detailed procedures that personnel in each McDonald's unit are expected to observe. For example, "Cooks must turn, never flip, hamburgers. If they haven't been purchased, Big Macs must be discarded in 10 minutes after being cooked and French fries in 7 minutes. Cashiers must make eye contact with and smile at every customer." Retail chain stores and other organizational chains (e.g., hotels, hospitals, child care centers) similarly rely on detailed policies and procedures to ensure consistency in their operations and reliable service to their customers. Video game developer Valve Corporation prides itself on a lack of rigid policies and procedures; its 37-page handbook for new employees details how things get done in such an environment—an ironic tribute to the fact that all types of companies need policies.

One of the big policy-making issues concerns what activities need to be strictly prescribed and what activities ought to allow room for independent action on the part of personnel. Few companies need thick policy manuals to prescribe exactly how daily operations are to be conducted. Too much policy can be as obstructive as wrong policy and as confusing as no policy. There is wisdom in a middle approach: *Prescribe enough policies to give organization members clear direction and to place reasonable boundaries on their actions; then empower them to act within these boundaries in pursuit of company goals.* Allowing company personnel to act with some degree of freedom is especially appropriate when individual creativity and initiative are more essential to good strategy execution than are standardization and strict conformity. Instituting policies that facilitate strategy execution can therefore mean policies more policies, fewer policies, or different policies. It can mean policies that require things be done according to a precisely defined standard or policies that give employees substantial leeway to do activities the way they think best.

> There is wisdom in a middle-ground approach: Prescribe enough policies to give organization members clear direction and to place reasonable boundaries on their actions; then empower them to act within these boundaries in pursuit of company goals.

EMPLOYING BUSINESS PROCESS MANAGEMENT TOOLS

Company managers can significantly advance the cause of competent strategy execution by using business process management tools to drive continuous improvement in how internal operations are conducted. Process management tools are used to model, control, measure, and optimize a variety of organizational activities that may span departments, functions, value chain systems, employees, customers, suppliers, and other partners in support of company goals. They also provide corrective feedback, allowing managers to change and improve company operations in an ongoing manner.

● **LO 11-3**

Explain how process management tools drive continuous improvement in the performance of value chain activities.

Promoting Operating Excellence: Three Powerful Business Process Management Tools

Three of the most powerful management tools for promoting operating excellence and better strategy execution are business process reengineering, total quality management (TQM) programs, and Six Sigma quality control programs. Each of these merits discussion since many companies around the world use these tools to help execute strategies tied to cost reduction, defect-free manufacture, superior product quality, superior customer service, and total customer satisfaction.

Business Process Reengineering   Companies searching for ways to improve their operations have sometimes discovered that the execution of strategy-critical activities is hampered by a disconnected organizational arrangement whereby pieces of an activity are performed in several different functional departments, with no one manager or group being accountable for optimal performance of the entire activity. This can easily occur in such inherently cross-functional activities as customer service (which can involve personnel in order filling, warehousing and shipping, invoicing, accounts receivable, after-sale repair, and technical support), particularly for companies with a functional organizational structure.

> **CORE CONCEPT**
>
> **Business process reengineering** involves radically redesigning and streamlining how an activity is performed, with the intent of achieving quantum improvements in performance.

To address the suboptimal performance problems that can arise from this type of situation, a company can *reengineer the work effort,* pulling the pieces of an activity out of different departments and creating a cross-functional work group or single department (often called a *process department*) to take charge of the whole process. The use of cross-functional teams has been popularized by the practice of **business process reengineering,** which involves radically redesigning and streamlining the workflow (typically enabled by cutting-edge use of online technology and information systems), with the goal of achieving quantum gains in performance of the activity.[1]

The reengineering of value chain activities has been undertaken at many companies in many industries all over the world, with excellent results being achieved at some firms.[2] Hallmark reengineered its process for developing new greeting cards, creating teams of mixed-occupation personnel (artists, writers, lithographers, merchandisers, and administrators) to work on a single holiday or greeting card theme. The reengineered process speeded development times for new lines of greeting cards by up to 24 months, reduced costs, and increased customer satisfaction.[3] In the order-processing section of General Electric's circuit breaker division, elapsed time from order receipt to delivery was cut from three weeks to three days by consolidating six production units into one, reducing a variety of former inventory and handling steps, automating the design system to replace a human custom-design process, and cutting the organizational layers between managers and workers from three to one. Productivity rose 20 percent in one year, and unit manufacturing costs dropped 30 percent. In the health care industry, business process reengineering is being used to lower health care costs and improve patient outcomes in a variety of ways. South Africa is attempting to reengineer its primary health care system, which is in need of significant reform. Similar initiatives are ongoing in India. In the United States, exemplary health care providers, such Mayo Clinic, are using reengineering tools on a continuous basis to achieve outcomes such as fewer hospitalizations, improved patient–physician interactions, and the delivery of lower cost health care.

While business process reengineering has been criticized as an excuse for downsizing, it has nonetheless proved itself a useful tool for streamlining a company's work effort and moving closer to operational excellence. It has also inspired more technologically based approaches to integrating and streamlining business processes, such as *enterprise resource planning,* a software-based system implemented with the help of consulting companies such as SAP (the leading provider of business software).

Total Quality Management Programs

> **CORE CONCEPT**
>
> **Total quality management (TQM)** entails creating a total quality culture, involving managers and employees at all levels, bent on continuously improving the performance of every value chain activity.

Total quality management (TQM) is a management approach that emphasizes continuous improvement in all phases of operations, 100 percent accuracy in performing tasks, involvement and empowerment of employees at all levels, team-based work design, benchmarking, and total customer satisfaction.[4] While TQM concentrates on producing quality goods and fully satisfying customer expectations, it achieves its biggest successes when it is extended to employee efforts in *all departments*—human resources, billing, accounting, and information systems—that may lack pressing, customer-driven incentives to improve. It involves reforming the corporate culture and shifting to a continuous-improvement business philosophy that permeates every facet of the organization.[5] TQM aims at instilling enthusiasm and commitment to doing things right from the top to the bottom of the organization. Management's job is to kindle an organizationwide search for ways to improve that involves all company personnel exercising initiative and using their ingenuity. TQM doctrine preaches that there's no such thing as "good enough" and that everyone has a responsibility to participate in continuous improvement. TQM is thus a race without a finish. Success comes from making little steps forward each day, a process that the Japanese call *kaizen.*

TQM takes a fairly long time to show significant results—very little benefit emerges within the first six months. The long-term payoff of TQM, if it comes, depends heavily on management's success in implanting a culture within which the TQM philosophy and practices can thrive. But it is a management tool that has attracted numerous users and advocates over several decades, and it can deliver good results when used properly.

Six Sigma Quality Control Programs   **Six Sigma programs** offer another way to drive continuous improvement in quality and strategy execution. This approach entails the use of advanced statistical methods to identify and remove the causes of defects (errors) and undesirable variability in performing an activity or business process. When performance of an activity or process reaches "Six Sigma quality," there are *no more than 3.4 defects per million iterations* (equal to 99.9997 percent accuracy).[6]

There are two important types of Six Sigma programs. The Six Sigma process of define, measure, analyze, improve, and control (DMAIC, pronounced "de-may-ic") is an improvement system for existing processes falling below specification and needing incremental improvement. The Six Sigma process of define, measure, analyze, design, and verify (DMADV, pronounced "de-mad-vee") is used to develop *new* processes or products at Six Sigma quality levels. DMADV is sometimes referred to as Design for Six Sigma, or DFSS. Both Six Sigma programs are overseen by personnel who have completed Six Sigma "master black belt" training, and they are executed by personnel who have earned Six Sigma "green belts" and Six Sigma "black belts." According to the Six Sigma Academy, personnel with black belts can save companies approximately $230,000 per project and can complete four to six projects a year.[7]

The statistical thinking underlying Six Sigma is based on the following three principles: (1) All work is a process, (2) all processes have variability, and (3) all processes create data that explain variability.[8] Six Sigma's DMAIC process is a particularly good vehicle for improving performance when there are *wide variations* in how well an activity is performed. For instance, airlines striving to improve the on-time performance of their flights have more to gain from actions to curtail the number of flights that are late by more than 30 minutes than from actions to reduce the number of flights that are late by less than 5 minutes. Six Sigma quality control programs are of particular interest for large companies, which are better able to shoulder the cost of the large investment required in employee training, organizational infrastructure, and consulting services. For example, to realize a cost savings of $4.4 billion from rolling out its Six Sigma program, GE had to invest $1.6 billion and suffer losses from the program during its first year.[9]

Since the programs were first introduced, thousands of companies and nonprofit organizations around the world have used Six Sigma to promote operating excellence. For companies at the forefront of this movement, such as Motorola, General Electric (GE), Ford, and Honeywell (Allied Signal), the cost savings as a percentage of revenue varied from 1.2 to 4.5 percent, according to data analysis conducted by iSixSigma (an organization that provides free articles, tools, and resources

CORE CONCEPT

Six Sigma programs utilize advanced statistical methods to improve quality by reducing defects and variability in the performance of business processes.

concerning Six Sigma). More recently, there has been a resurgence of interest in Six Sigma practices, with companies such as Siemens, Coca-Cola, Ocean Spray, GEICO, and Merrill Lynch turning to Six Sigma as a vehicle to improve their bottom lines. In the first five years of its adoption, Six Sigma at Bank of America helped the bank reap about $2 billion in revenue gains and cost savings; the bank holds an annual "Best of Six Sigma Expo" to celebrate the teams and the projects with the greatest contribution to the company's bottom line. GE, one of the most successful companies implementing Six Sigma training and pursuing Six Sigma perfection across the company's entire operations, estimated benefits of some $10 billion during the first five years of implementation—its Lighting division, for example, cut invoice defects and disputes by 98 percent.[10]

Six Sigma has also been used to improve processes in health care. Froedtert Hospital in Milwaukee, Wisconsin, used Six Sigma to improve the accuracy of administering the proper drug doses to patients. DMAIC analysis of the three-stage process by which prescriptions were written by doctors, filled by the hospital pharmacy, and then administered to patients by nurses revealed that most mistakes came from misreading the doctors' handwriting. The hospital implemented a program requiring doctors to enter the prescription on the hospital's computers, which slashed the number of errors dramatically. In recent years, Pfizer embarked on 85 Six Sigma projects to streamline its R&D process and lower the cost of delivering medicines to patients in its pharmaceutical sciences division.

Illustration Capsule 11.1 describes Charleston Area Medical Center's use of Six Sigma as a health care provider coping with the current challenges facing this industry.

Despite its potential benefits, Six Sigma is not without its problems. There is evidence, for example, that Six Sigma techniques can stifle innovation and creativity. The essence of Six Sigma is to reduce variability in processes, but creative processes, by nature, include quite a bit of variability. In many instances, breakthrough innovations occur only after thousands of ideas have been abandoned and promising ideas have gone through multiple iterations and extensive prototyping. Alphabet Executive Chairman of the Board Eric Schmidt has declared that applying Six Sigma measurement and control principles to creative activities at Google would choke off innovation altogether.[11]

A blended approach to Six Sigma implementation that is gaining in popularity pursues incremental improvements in operating efficiency, while R&D and other processes that allow the company to develop new ways of offering value to customers are given freer rein. Managers of these **ambidextrous organizations** are adept at employing continuous improvement in operating processes but allowing R&D to operate under a set of rules that allows for exploration and the development of breakthrough innovations. However, the two distinctly different approaches to managing employees must be carried out by tightly integrated senior managers to ensure that the separate and diversely oriented units operate with a common purpose. Ciba Vision, now part of eye care multinational Alcon, dramatically reduced operating expenses through the use of continuous-improvement programs, while simultaneously and harmoniously developing a new series of contact lens products that have allowed its revenues to increase by 300 percent over a 10-year period.[12] An enterprise that systematically and wisely applies Six Sigma methods to its value chain, activity by activity, can make major strides in improving the proficiency with which its strategy is executed without sacrificing innovation. As is the case with TQM, obtaining managerial commitment, establishing a quality culture, and fully involving employees are all of critical importance to the successful implementation of Six Sigma quality programs.[13]

©ERproductions Ltd/Blend Images LLC

Established in 1972, Charleston Area Medical Center (CAMC) is West Virginia's largest health care provider in terms of beds, admissions, and revenues. In 2000, CAMC implemented a Six Sigma program to examine quality problems and standardize care processes. Performance improvement was important to CAMC's management for a variety of strategic reasons, including competitive positioning and cost control.

The United States has been evolving toward a pay-for-performance structure, which rewards hospitals for providing quality care. CAMC has utilized its Six Sigma program to take advantage of these changes in the health care environment. For example, to improve its performance in acute myocardial infarction (AMI), CAMC applied a Six Sigma DMAIC (define-measure-analyze-improve-control) approach. Nursing staff members were educated on AMI care processes, performance targets were posted in nursing units, and adherence to the eight Hospital Quality Alliance (HQA) indicators of quality care for AMI patients was tracked. As a result of the program, CAMC improved its compliance with HQA-recommended treatment for AMI from 50 to 95 percent. Harvard researchers identified CAMC as one of the top-performing hospitals reporting comparable data.

Controlling cost has also been an important aspect of CAMC's performance improvement initiatives due to local regulations. West Virginia is one of two states where medical services rates are set by state regulators. This forces CAMC to limit expenditures because the hospital cannot raise prices. CAMC first applied Six Sigma in an effort to control costs by managing the supply chain more effectively. The effort created a one-time $150,000 savings by working with vendors to remove outdated inventory. As a result of continuous improvement, CAMC managed to achieve supply chain management savings of $12 million in just four years.

Since CAMC introduced Six Sigma, over 100 quality improvement projects have been initiated. A key to CAMC's success has been instilling a continuous improvement mindset into the organization's culture. Dale Wood, chief quality officer at CAMC, stated. "If you have people at the top who completely support and want these changes to occur, you can still fall flat on your face. . . . You need a group of networkers who can carry change across an organization." Due to CAMC's performance improvement culture, the hospital ranks high nationally in ratings for quality of care and patient safety, as reported on the Centers for Medicare and Medicaid Services (CMS) website.

Note: Developed with Robin A. Daley.

Sources: CAMC website; Martha Hostetter, "Case Study: Improving Performance at Charleston Area Medical Center," *The Commonwealth Fund,* November–December 2007, **www.commonwealthfund.org/publications/newsletters/quality-matters/2007/november-december/ case-study-improving-performance-at-charleston-area-medical-center** (accessed January 2016); J. C. Simmons, "Using Six Sigma to Make a Difference in Health Care Quality," *The Quality Letter,* April 2002.

The Difference between Business Process Reengineering and Continuous-Improvement Programs Like Six Sigma and TQM Whereas business process reengineering aims at *quantum gains* on the order of 30 to 50 percent or more, total quality programs like TQM and Six Sigma stress *ongoing incremental progress,* striving for inch-by-inch gains again and again in a never-ending stream. The two approaches to improved performance of value chain activities and operating excellence are not mutually exclusive; it makes sense to use them in tandem. Reengineering can be used first to produce a good basic design that yields

> Business process reengineering aims at one-time quantum improvement, while continuous-improvement programs like TQM and Six Sigma aim at ongoing incremental improvements.

quick, dramatic improvements in performing a business process. TQM or Six Sigma programs can then be used as a follow-on to reengineering and/or best-practice implementation to deliver incremental improvements over a longer period of time.

Capturing the Benefits of Initiatives to Improve Operations

The biggest beneficiaries of process improvement initiatives, reengineering, TQM, and Six Sigma are companies that view such programs not as ends in themselves but as tools for implementing company strategy more effectively. The least rewarding payoffs occur when company managers seize on the programs as novel ideas that might be worth a try. In most such instances, they result in strategy-blind efforts to simply manage better.

There's an important lesson here. Business process management tools all need to be linked to a company's strategic priorities to contribute effectively to improving the strategy's execution. Only strategy can point to which value chain activities matter and what performance targets make the most sense. Without a strategic framework, managers lack the context in which to fix things that really matter to business unit performance and competitive success.

To get the most from initiatives to execute strategy more proficiently, managers must have a clear idea of what specific outcomes really matter. Is it high on-time delivery, lower overall costs, fewer customer complaints, shorter cycle times, a higher percentage of revenues coming from recently introduced products, or something else? Benchmarking best-in-industry and best-in-world performance of targeted value chain activities provides a realistic basis for setting internal performance milestones and longer-range targets. Once initiatives to improve operations are linked to the company's strategic priorities, then comes the managerial task of building a total quality culture that is genuinely committed to achieving the performance outcomes that strategic success requires.[14]

Managers can take the following action steps to realize full value from TQM, reengineering, or Six Sigma initiatives and promote a culture of operating excellence:[15]

1. Demonstrating visible, unequivocal, and unyielding commitment to total quality and continuous improvement, including specifying measurable objectives for increasing quality and making continual progress.

2. Nudging people toward quality-supportive behaviors by
   a. Screening job applicants rigorously and hiring only those with attitudes and aptitudes that are right for quality-based performance.
   b. Providing quality training for employees.
   c. Using teams and team-building exercises to reinforce and nurture individual effort. (The creation of a quality culture is facilitated when teams become more cross-functional, multitask-oriented, and increasingly self-managed.)
   d. Recognizing and rewarding individual and team efforts to improve quality regularly and systematically.
   e. Stressing prevention (doing it right the first time), not correction (instituting ways to undo or overcome mistakes).

3. Empowering employees so that authority for delivering great service or improving products is in the hands of those who do the job rather than their managers: *improving quality has to be seen as part of everyone's job.*

4. Using online systems to provide all relevant parties with the latest best practices, thereby speeding the diffusion and adoption of best practices throughout the organization. Online systems can also allow company personnel to exchange data and opinions about how to upgrade the prevailing best-in-company practices.

5. Emphasizing that performance can and must be improved, because competitors are not resting on their laurels and customers are always looking for something better.

In sum, initiatives to improve operations, like business process reengineering, TQM, and Six Sigma techniques all need to be seen and used as part of a bigger-picture effort to execute strategy proficiently. Used properly, all of these tools are capable of improving the proficiency with which an organization performs its value chain activities. Not only do improvements from such initiatives add up over time and strengthen organizational capabilities, but they also help build a culture of operating excellence. All this lays the groundwork for gaining a competitive advantage.[16] While it is relatively easy for rivals to also implement process management tools, it is much more difficult and time-consuming for them to instill a deeply ingrained culture of operating excellence (as occurs when such techniques are religiously employed and top management exhibits lasting commitment to operational excellence throughout the organization).

> The purpose of using business process management tools, such as business process reengineering, TQM, and Six Sigma programs is to improve the performance of strategy-critical activities and thereby enhance strategy execution.

INSTALLING INFORMATION AND OPERATING SYSTEMS

Company strategies can't be executed well without a number of internal systems for business operations. American Airlines, Delta, Ryanair, Lufthansa, and other successful airlines cannot hope to provide passenger-pleasing service without a user-friendly online reservation system, an accurate and speedy baggage-handling system, and a strict aircraft maintenance program that minimizes problems requiring at-the-gate service that delays departures. FedEx has internal communication systems that allow it to coordinate its over 100,000 vehicles in handling a daily average of 12.1 million shipments to more than 220 countries and territories. Its leading-edge flight operations systems allow a single controller to direct as many as 200 of FedEx's 659 aircraft simultaneously, overriding their flight plans should weather problems or other special circumstances arise. FedEx also has created a series of e-business tools for customers that allow them to ship and track packages online, create address books, review shipping history, generate custom reports, simplify customer billing, reduce internal warehousing and inventory management costs, purchase goods and services from suppliers, and respond to their own quickly changing customer demands. All of FedEx's systems support the company's strategy of providing businesses and individuals with a broad array of package delivery services and enhancing its competitiveness against United Parcel Service, DHL, and the U.S. Postal Service.

Amazon.com ships customer orders from a global network of some 707 technologically sophisticated order fulfillment and distribution centers. Using complex picking algorithms, computers initiate the order-picking process by sending signals to workers' wireless receivers, telling them which items to pick off the shelves in which order. Computers also generate data on mix-boxed items, chute backup times, line speed, worker productivity, and shipping weights on orders. Systems are upgraded regularly, and productivity improvements are aggressively pursued. Amazon has been experimenting with drone delivery in order to lower costs and speed package delivery; more

> • **LO 11-4**
>
> Describe the role of information systems and operating systems in enabling company personnel to carry out their strategic roles proficiently.

recently it has begun marketing a pilot project called "Seller Flex" as part of its effort to develop its own delivery service.

Otis Elevator, the world's largest manufacturer of elevators, with more than 2.6 million elevators and escalators installed worldwide, has a 24/7 remote electronic monitoring system that can detect when an elevator or escalator installed on a customer's site has any of 325 problems. If the monitoring system detects a problem, it analyzes and diagnoses the cause and location, then makes the service call to an Otis mechanic at the nearest location, and helps the mechanic (who is equipped with a web-enabled cell phone) identify the component causing the problem. The company's maintenance system helps keep outage times under three hours—the elevators are often back in service before people even realize there was a problem. All trouble-call data are relayed to design and manufacturing personnel, allowing them to quickly alter design specifications or manufacturing procedures when needed to correct recurring problems. All customers have online access to performance data on each of their Otis elevators and escalators.

Well-conceived state-of-the-art operating systems not only enable better strategy execution but also strengthen organizational capabilities—enough at times to provide a competitive edge over rivals. For example, a company with a differentiation strategy based on superior quality has added capability if it has systems for training personnel in quality techniques, tracking product quality at each production step, and ensuring that all goods shipped meet quality standards. If these quality control systems are better than those employed by rivals, they provide the company with a competitive advantage. Similarly, a company striving to be a low-cost provider is competitively stronger if it has an unrivaled benchmarking system that identifies opportunities to implement best-in-the-world practices and drive costs out of the business faster than rivals. Fast-growing companies get an important assist from having capabilities in place to recruit and train new employees in large numbers and from investing in infrastructure that gives them the capability to handle rapid growth as it occurs, rather than having to scramble to catch up to customer demand.

Instituting Adequate Information Systems, Performance Tracking, and Controls

Accurate and timely information about daily operations is essential if managers are to gauge how well the strategy execution process is proceeding. Companies everywhere are capitalizing on today's technology to install real-time data-generating capability. Most retail companies now have automated online systems that generate daily sales reports for each store and maintain up-to-the-minute inventory and sales records on each item. Manufacturing plants typically generate daily production reports and track labor productivity on every shift. Transportation companies have elaborate information systems to provide real-time arrival information for buses and trains that is automatically sent to digital message signs and platform audio address systems.

Siemens Healthcare, one of the largest suppliers to the health care industry, uses a cloud-based business activity monitoring (BAM) system to continuously monitor and improve the company's processes across more than 190 countries. Customer satisfaction is one of Siemens's most important business objectives, so the reliability of its order management and services is crucial. Caesars Entertainment, owner of casinos and hotels, uses a sophisticated customer relationship database that records detailed information about its customers' gambling habits. When a member of Caesars's Total Rewards program calls to make a reservation, the representative can review previous spending, including average bet size, to offer an upgrade or complimentary stay at

Caesars Palace or one of the company's other properties. At Uber, the popular ride-sharing service, there are systems for locating vehicles near a customer and real-time demand monitoring to price fares during high-demand periods.

Information systems need to cover five broad areas: (1) customer data, (2) operations data, (3) employee data, (4) supplier and/or strategic partner data, and (5) financial performance data. All key strategic performance indicators must be tracked and reported in real time whenever possible. Real-time information systems permit company managers to stay on top of implementation initiatives and daily operations and to intervene if things seem to be drifting off course. Tracking key performance indicators, gathering information from operating personnel, quickly identifying and diagnosing problems, and taking corrective actions are all integral pieces of the process of managing strategy execution and overseeing operations.

Statistical information gives managers a feel for the numbers, briefings and meetings provide a feel for the latest developments and emerging issues, and personal contacts add a feel for the people dimension. All are good barometers of how well things are going and what operating aspects need management attention. Managers must identify problem areas and deviations from plans before they can take action to get the organization back on course by either improving the approaches to strategy execution or fine-tuning the strategy. Jeff Bezos, Amazon.com's CEO, is an ardent proponent of managing by the numbers. As he puts it, "Math-based decisions always trump opinion and judgment. The trouble with most corporations is that they make judgment-based decisions when data-based decisions could be made."[17]

> Having state-of-the-art operating systems, information systems, and real-time data is integral to superior strategy execution and operating excellence.

Monitoring Employee Performance Information systems also provide managers with a means for monitoring the performance of empowered workers to see that they are acting within the specified limits.[18] Leaving empowered employees to their own devices in meeting performance standards without appropriate checks and balances can expose an organization to excessive risk.[19] Instances abound of employees' decisions or behavior going awry, sometimes costing a company huge sums or producing lawsuits and reputation-damaging publicity.

Scrutinizing daily and weekly operating statistics is one of the ways in which managers can monitor the results that flow from the actions of subordinates without resorting to constant over-the-shoulder supervision; if the operating results look good, then it is reasonable to assume that empowerment is working. But close monitoring of operating performance is only one of the control tools at management's disposal. Another valuable lever of control in companies that rely on empowered employees, especially in those that use self-managed work groups or other such teams, is peer-based control. Because peer evaluation is such a powerful control device, companies organized into teams can remove some layers of the management hierarchy and rely on strong peer pressure to keep team members operating between the white lines. This is especially true when a company has the information systems capability to monitor team performance daily or in real time.

USING REWARDS AND INCENTIVES TO PROMOTE BETTER STRATEGY EXECUTION

It is essential that company personnel be enthusiastically committed to executing strategy successfully and achieving performance targets. Enlisting such commitment typically requires use of an assortment of motivational techniques and rewards.

Indeed, *an effectively designed incentive and reward structure is the single most powerful tool management has for mobilizing employee commitment to successful strategy execution.* But incentives and rewards do more than just strengthen the resolve of company personnel to succeed—they also focus employees' attention on the accomplishment of specific strategy execution objectives. Not only do they spur the efforts of individuals to achieve those aims, but they also help coordinate the activities of individuals throughout the organization by aligning their personal motives with the goals of the organization. In this manner, reward systems serve as an indirect type of control mechanism that conserves on the more costly control mechanism of supervisory oversight.

To win employees' sustained, energetic commitment to the strategy execution process, management must be resourceful in designing and using motivational incentives—*both monetary and nonmonetary.* The more a manager understands what motivates subordinates and the more he or she relies on motivational incentives as a tool for achieving the targeted strategic and financial results, the greater will be employees' commitment to good day-in, day-out strategy execution and the achievement of performance targets.[20]

Incentives and Motivational Practices That Facilitate Good Strategy Execution

Financial incentives generally head the list of motivating tools for gaining wholehearted employee commitment to good strategy execution and focusing attention on strategic priorities. Generous financial rewards always catch employees' attention and produce *high-powered incentives* for individuals to exert their best efforts. A company's package of monetary rewards typically includes some combination of base-pay increases, performance bonuses, profit-sharing plans, stock awards, company contributions to employee 401(k) or retirement plans, and piecework incentives (in the case of production workers). But most successful companies and managers also make extensive use of nonmonetary incentives. Some of the most important nonmonetary approaches companies can use to enhance employee motivation include the following:[21]

- *Providing attractive perks and fringe benefits.* The various options include coverage of health insurance premiums, wellness programs, college tuition reimbursement, generous paid vacation time, onsite child care, onsite fitness centers and massage services, opportunities for getaways at company-owned recreational facilities, personal concierge services, subsidized cafeterias and free lunches, casual dress every day, personal travel services, paid sabbaticals, maternity and paternity leaves, paid leaves to care for ill family members, telecommuting, compressed workweeks (four 10-hour days instead of five 8-hour days), flextime (variable work schedules that accommodate individual needs), college scholarships for children, and relocation services.

- *Giving awards and public recognition to high performers and showcasing company successes.* Many companies hold award ceremonies to honor top-performing individuals, teams, and organizational units and to celebrate important company milestones and achievements. Others make a special point of recognizing the outstanding accomplishments of individuals, teams, and organizational units at informal company gatherings or in the company newsletter. Such actions foster a positive *esprit de corps* within the organization and may also act to spur healthy competition among units and teams within the company.

- *Relying on promotion from within whenever possible.* This practice helps bind workers to their employer, and employers to their workers. Moreover, it provides strong incentives for good performance. Promoting from within also helps ensure that people in positions of responsibility have knowledge specific to the business, technology, and operations they are managing.

- *Inviting and acting on ideas and suggestions from employees.* Many companies find that their best ideas for nuts-and-bolts operating improvements come from the suggestions of employees. Moreover, research indicates that giving decision-making power to down-the-line employees increases their motivation and satisfaction as well as their productivity. The use of self-managed teams has much the same effect.

- *Creating a work atmosphere in which there is genuine caring and mutual respect among workers and between management and employees.* A "family" work environment where people are on a first-name basis and there is strong camaraderie promotes teamwork and cross-unit collaboration.

- *Stating the strategic vision in inspirational terms that make employees feel they are a part of something worthwhile in a larger social sense.* There's strong motivating power associated with giving people a chance to be part of something exciting and personally satisfying. Jobs with a noble purpose tend to inspire employees to give their all. As described in Chapter 9, this not only increases productivity but reduces turnover and lowers costs for staff recruitment and training as well.

- *Sharing information with employees about financial performance, strategy, operational measures, market conditions, and competitors' actions.* Broad disclosure and prompt communication send the message that managers trust their workers and regard them as valued partners in the enterprise. Keeping employees in the dark denies them information useful to performing their jobs, prevents them from being intellectually engaged, saps their motivation, and detracts from performance.

- *Providing an appealing working environment.* An appealing workplace environment can have decidedly positive effects on employee morale and productivity. Providing a comfortable work environment, designed with ergonomics in mind, is particularly important when workers are expected to spend long hours at work. But some companies go beyond the mundane to design exceptionally attractive work settings. The workspaces and surrounding parklands of Apple's new multibillion dollar campus headquarters were designed to inspire Apple's people, foster innovative collaboration, while also benefiting the environment. Employees have access to a 100,000 square foot fitness center, two miles of walking and running paths, an orchard, meadow, and pond as well as community bicycles, electric golf carts, and commuter shuttles for getting around. Facebook and defense contractor Oshkosh Corporation also have dramatic headquarters projects underway.

For a specific example of the motivational tactics employed by one of the best companies to work for in America, see Illustration Capsule 11.2 on the supermarket chain, Wegmans.

Striking the Right Balance between Rewards and Punishment

While most approaches to motivation, compensation, and people management accentuate the positive, companies also make it clear that lackadaisical or indifferent effort and subpar performance can result in negative consequences. At General Electric,

How Wegmans Rewards and Motivates its Employees

©tarheel1776/Shutterstock

Companies use a variety of tools and strategies designed to motivate employees and engender superior strategy execution. In this respect, Wegmans Food Markets, Inc. serves as an exemplar. With approximately 48,000 employees spread across 96 stores across the Northeast and Mid-Atlantic, Wegmans stands out as an organization that delivers above average results in an industry known for its low margins, low wages, and challenging employee relationships. Guided by a philosophy of *employees first,* Wegmans employs an array of programs that enables the company to attract and retain the best people.

Since the creation of its broad benefits program for full-time employees in the 1950s, Wegmans has had a strong benefits philosophy. Today, flexible or compressed schedules are common, and policies extend to same-sex partners. Regarding financial compensation, wages are above average for the grocery retail industry, which also has an added benefit of keeping its workforce nonunionized.

In addition to the traditional elements of compensation and benefits, Wegmans invests considerably in the training and education of its employees. Known for its strength in employee development, upwards of $50 million annually is spent on employee learning. Since 1984, the company has awarded nearly $110 million in tuition assistance, and over $50 million in scholarships.

Another crucial aspect of employee motivation is feeling heard. Employees see their ideas put into action through a series of programs designed to capture and implement their ideas. Wegmans deploys a series of programs, including open-door days, team huddles, focus groups, and two-way Q&As with senior management.

With the recognition that employees are critical to delivering a great customer experience, Wegmans directs a considerable amount of resources to its biggest asset, its people. Its suite of programs and benefits, along with a policy of filling at least half of its open opportunities internally, lead to one of the lowest turnover rates in its industry. They have also resulted in Wegmans placing among the top five firms on Fortune's list of *The 100 Best Companies to Work For,* year after year.

Note: Developed with Sadé M. Lawrence.

Sources: Company website; Boyle, M., *The Wegmans Way,* January 24, 2005, http://archive.fortune.com/magazines/fortune/fortune_archive/2005/01/24/8234048/index.htm; "Great Place to Work," *Wegmans Food Markets, Inc. - Great Place to Work Reviews,* February 14, 2018, http://reviews.greatplacetowork.com/wegmans-food-markets-inc.

McKinsey & Company, several global public accounting firms, and other companies that look for and expect top-notch individual performance, there's an "up-or-out" policy—managers and professionals whose performance is not good enough to warrant promotion are first denied bonuses and stock awards and eventually weeded out. At most companies, senior executives and key personnel in underperforming units are pressured to raise performance to acceptable levels and keep it there or risk being replaced.

As a general rule, it is unwise to take off the pressure for good performance or play down the adverse consequences of shortfalls in performance. There is scant evidence that a no-pressure, no-adverse-consequences work environment leads to superior strategy execution or operating excellence. As the CEO of a major bank put it, "There's a deliberate policy here to create a level of anxiety. Winners usually play like they're one touchdown behind."[22] A number of companies deliberately give employees heavy work-loads and tight deadlines to test their mettle—personnel are pushed hard to achieve "stretch" objectives and are expected to put in long hours (nights and weekends if need be). High-performing organizations nearly always have a cadre of ambitious people who relish the opportunity to climb the ladder of success, love a challenge, thrive in a performance-oriented environment, and find some competition and pressure useful to satisfy their own drives for personal recognition, accomplishment, and self-satisfaction.

However, if an organization's motivational approaches and reward structure induce too much stress, internal competitiveness, job insecurity, and fear of unpleasant consequences, the impact on workforce morale and strategy execution can be counter-productive. Evidence shows that managerial initiatives to improve strategy execution should incorporate more positive than negative motivational elements because when cooperation is positively enlisted and rewarded, rather than coerced by orders and threats (implicit or explicit), people tend to respond with more enthusiasm, dedication, creativity, and initiative.[23]

Linking Rewards to Achieving the Right Outcomes

To create a strategy-supportive system of rewards and incentives, a company must reward people for accomplishing results, not for just dutifully performing assigned tasks. Showing up for work and performing assignments do not, by themselves, guarantee results. To make the work environment results-oriented, managers need to focus jobholders' attention and energy on what to *achieve* as opposed to what to *do*.[24] Employee productivity among employees at Best Buy's corporate headquarters rose by 35 percent after the company began to focus on the results of each employee's work rather than on employees' willingness to come to work early and stay late.

Ideally, every organizational unit, every manager, every team or work group, and every employee should be held accountable for achieving outcomes that contribute to good strategy execution and business performance. If the company's strategy is to be a low-cost leader, the incentive system must reward actions and achievements that result in lower costs. If the company has a differentiation strategy focused on delivering superior quality and service, the incentive system must reward such outcomes as Six Sigma defect rates, infrequent customer complaints, speedy order processing and delivery, and high levels of customer satisfaction. If a company's growth is predicated on a strategy of new product innovation, incentives should be tied to such metrics as the percentages of revenues and profits coming from newly introduced products.

Incentives must be based on accomplishing results, not on dutifully performing assigned tasks.

Incentive compensation for top executives is typically tied to such financial measures as revenue and earnings growth, stock price performance, return on investment, and creditworthiness or to strategic measures such as market share growth. However, incentives for department heads, teams, and individual workers tend to be tied to performance outcomes more closely related to their specific area of responsibility. For instance, in manufacturing, it makes sense to tie incentive compensation to such outcomes as unit manufacturing costs, on-time production and shipping, defect rates, the number and extent of work stoppages due to equipment breakdowns, and so on. In sales and marketing, incentives tend to be based on achieving dollar sales or unit volume targets, market share, sales penetration of each target customer group, the fate of newly introduced products, the frequency of customer complaints, the number of new accounts acquired, and measures of customer satisfaction. Which performance measures to base incentive compensation on depends on the situation—the priority placed on various financial and strategic objectives, the requirements for strategic and competitive success, and the specific results needed to keep strategy execution on track.

Illustration Capsule 11.3 provides a vivid example of how one company has designed incentives linked directly to outcomes reflecting good execution.

The first principle in designing an effective incentive compensation system is to tie rewards to performance outcomes directly linked to good strategy execution and the achievement of financial and strategic objectives.

Additional Guidelines for Designing Incentive Compensation Systems

It is not enough to link incentives to the right kinds of results—performance outcomes that signal that the company's strategy and its execution are on track. For a company's reward system to truly motivate organization members, inspire their best efforts, and sustain high levels of productivity, it is also important to observe the following additional guidelines in designing and administering the reward system:

- *Make the performance payoff a major, not minor, piece of the total compensation package.* Performance bonuses must be at least 10 to 12 percent of base salary to have much impact. Incentives that amount to 20 percent or more of total compensation are big attention-getters, likely to really drive individual or team efforts. Incentives amounting to less than 5 percent of total compensation have a comparatively weak motivational impact. Moreover, the payoff for high-performing individuals and teams must be meaningfully greater than the payoff for average performers, and the payoff for average performers meaningfully bigger than that for below-average performers.

- *Have incentives that extend to all managers and all workers, not just top management.* It is a gross miscalculation to expect that lower-level managers and employees will work their hardest to hit performance targets if only senior executives qualify for lucrative rewards.

- *Administer the reward system with scrupulous objectivity and fairness.* If performance standards are set unrealistically high or if individual and group performance evaluations are not accurate and well documented, dissatisfaction with the system will overcome any positive benefits.

- *Ensure that the performance targets set for each individual or team involve outcomes that the individual or team can personally affect.* The role of incentives is to enhance individual commitment and channel behavior in beneficial directions. This role is not well served when the performance measures by which company personnel are judged are outside their arena of influence.

- *Keep the time between achieving the performance target and receiving the reward as short as possible.* Nucor, a leading producer of steel products, has achieved high labor productivity by paying its workers weekly bonuses based on prior-week production levels. Annual bonus payouts work best for higher-level managers and for situations where the outcome target relates to overall company profitability.

- *Avoid rewarding effort rather than results.* While it is tempting to reward people who have tried hard, gone the extra mile, and yet fallen short of achieving performance targets because of circumstances beyond their control, it is ill advised to do so. The problem with making exceptions for unknowable, uncontrollable, or unforeseeable circumstances is that once "good excuses" start to creep into justifying rewards for subpar results, the door opens to all kinds of reasons why actual performance has failed to match targeted performance. A "no excuses" standard is more evenhanded, easier to administer, and more conducive to creating a results-oriented work climate.

ILLUSTRATION CAPSULE 11.3   Nucor Corporation: Tying Incentives Directly to Strategy Execution

The strategy at Nucor Corporation, the largest steel producers in the United States, is to be *the* low-cost producer of steel products. Because labor costs are a significant fraction of total cost in the steel business, successful implementation of Nucor's low-cost leadership strategy entails achieving lower labor costs per ton of steel than competitors' costs. Nucor management uses an incentive system to promote high worker productivity and drive labor costs per ton below those of rivals. Each plant's workforce is organized into production teams (each assigned to perform particular functions), and weekly production targets are established for each team. Base-pay scales are set at levels comparable to wages for similar manufacturing jobs in the local areas where Nucor has plants, but workers can earn a 1 percent bonus for each 1 percent that their output exceeds target levels. If a production team exceeds its weekly production target by 10 percent, team members receive a 10 percent bonus in their next paycheck; if a team exceeds its quota by 20 percent, team members earn a 20 percent bonus. Bonuses, paid every two weeks, are based on the prior two weeks' actual production levels measured against the targets.

Nucor's piece-rate incentive plan has produced impressive results. The production teams put forth exceptional effort; it is not uncommon for most teams to beat their weekly production targets by 20 to 50 percent. When added to employees' base pay, the bonuses earned by Nucor workers make Nucor's workforce among the highest paid in the U.S. steel industry. From a management perspective, the incentive system has resulted in Nucor having labor productivity levels 10 to 20 percent above the average of the unionized workforces at several of its largest rivals, which in turn has given Nucor a significant labor cost advantage over most rivals.

©Glow Images

After years of record-setting profits, Nucor struggled in the economic downturn of 2008–2010, along with the manufacturers and builders who buy its steel. But while bonuses dwindled, Nucor showed remarkable loyalty to its production workers, avoiding layoffs by having employees get ahead on maintenance, perform work formerly done by contractors, and search for cost savings. Morale at the company remained high, and Nucor's CEO at the time, Daniel DiMicco, was inducted into *Industry-Week* magazine's Manufacturing Hall of Fame because of his no-layoff policies. As industry growth resumed, Nucor was in the position of having a well-trained workforce, more committed than ever to achieving the kind of productivity for which Nucor is justifiably famous. DiMicco had good reason to expect Nucor to be "first out of the box" following the crisis, and although he has since stepped aside, the company's culture of making its employees think like owners has not changed.

Sources: Company website (accessed March 2012); N. Byrnes, "Pain, but No Layoffs at Nucor," *BusinessWeek,* March 26, 2009; J. McGregor, "Nucor's CEO Is Stepping Aside, but Its Culture Likely Won't," *The Washington Post* Online, November 20, 2012 (accessed April 3, 2014).

For an organization's incentive system to work well, the details of the reward structure must be communicated and explained. Everybody needs to understand how his or her incentive compensation is calculated and how individual and group performance targets contribute to organizational performance targets. The pressure to achieve the targeted financial and strategic performance objectives and continuously improve on strategy execution should be unrelenting. People at all levels must be held accountable for carrying out their assigned parts of the strategic

> The unwavering standard for judging whether individuals, teams, and organizational units have done a good job must be whether they meet or beat performance targets that reflect good strategy execution.

plan, and they must understand that their rewards are based on the caliber of results achieved. But with the pressure to perform should come meaningful rewards. Without an attractive payoff, the system breaks down, and managers are left with the less workable options of issuing orders, trying to enforce compliance, and depending on the goodwill of employees.

KEY POINTS

1. Implementing a new or different strategy calls for managers to identify the resource requirements of each new strategic initiative and then consider whether the current pattern of resource allocation and the budgets of the various subunits are suitable.

2. Company policies and procedures facilitate strategy execution when they are designed to fit the strategy and its objectives. Anytime a company alters its strategy, managers should review existing policies and operating procedures and replace those that are out of sync. Well-conceived policies and procedures aid the task of strategy execution by (1) providing top-down guidance to company personnel regarding how things need to be done and what the limits are on independent actions; (2) enforcing consistency in the performance of strategy-critical activities, thereby improving the quality of the strategy execution effort and coordinating the efforts of company personnel, however widely dispersed; and (3) promoting the creation of a work climate conducive to good strategy execution.

3. Competent strategy execution entails visible unyielding managerial commitment to continuous improvement. Business process management tools, such as reengineering, total quality management (TQM), and Six Sigma programs are important process management tools for promoting better strategy execution.

4. Company strategies can't be implemented or executed well without well-conceived internal systems to support daily operations. Real-time information systems and control systems further aid the cause of good strategy execution. In some cases, state-of-the-art operating and information systems strengthen a company's strategy execution capabilities enough to provide a competitive edge over rivals.

5. Strategy-supportive motivational practices and reward systems are powerful management tools for gaining employee commitment and focusing their attention on the strategy execution goals. The key to creating a reward system that promotes good strategy execution is to make measures of good business performance and good strategy execution the *dominating basis* for designing incentives, evaluating individual and group efforts, and handing out rewards. While financial rewards provide high-powered incentives, nonmonetary incentives are also important. For an incentive compensation system to work well, (1) the performance payoff should be a major percentage of the compensation package, (2) the use of incentives should extend to all managers and workers, (3) the system should be administered with objectivity and fairness, (4) each individual's performance targets should involve outcomes the person can personally affect, (5) rewards should promptly follow the achievement of performance targets, and (6) rewards should be given for results and not just effort.

ASSURANCE OF LEARNING EXERCISES

1. Implementing a new or different strategy calls for new resource allocations. Using your university's library resources search for recent articles that discuss how a company has revised its pattern of resource allocation and divisional budgets to support new strategic initiatives.

LO 11-1

2. Netflix avoids the use of formal policies and procedures to better empower its employees to maximize innovation and productivity. The company goes to great lengths to hire, reward, and tolerate only what it considers mature, "A" player employees. How does the company's selection process affect its ability to operate without formal travel and expense policies, a fixed number of vacation days for employees, or a formal employee performance evaluation system?

LO 11-2

3. Illustration Capsule 11.1 discusses Charleston Area Medical Center's use of Six Sigma practices. List three tangible benefits provided by the program. Explain why a commitment to quality control is particularly important in the hospital industry. How can the use of a Six Sigma program help medical providers survive and thrive in the current industry climate?

connect

LO 11-3

4. Read some of the recent Six Sigma articles posted at **www.isixsigma.com**. Prepare a one-page report to your instructor detailing how Six Sigma is being used in two companies and what benefits the companies are reaping as a result. Further, discuss two to three criticisms of, or potential difficulties with, Six Sigma implementation.

LO 11-3

5. Company strategies can't be executed well without a number of support systems to carry on business operations. Using your university's library resources, search for recent articles that discuss how a company has used real-time information systems and control systems to aid the cause of good strategy execution.

LO 11-4

6. Illustration Capsule 11.2 provides a description of the motivational practices employed by Wegmans Food Markets, a supermarket chain that is routinely listed as among the top five companies to work for in the United States. Discuss how rewards and practices at Wegman's aid in the company's strategy execution efforts.

connect

LO 11-5

EXERCISE FOR SIMULATION PARTICIPANTS

1. Have you and your co-managers allocated ample resources to strategy-critical areas? If so, explain how these investments have contributed to good strategy execution and improved company performance.

LO 11-1

2. What actions, if any, is your company taking to pursue continuous improvement in how it performs certain value chain activities?

LO 11-2, LO 11-3, LO 11-4

3. Are benchmarking data available in the simulation exercise in which you are participating? If so, do you and your co-managers regularly study the benchmarking data to see how well your company is doing? Do you consider the benchmarking information provided to be valuable? Why or why not? Cite three recent instances in which your examination of the benchmarking statistics has caused you and your co-managers to take corrective actions to improve operations and boost company performance.

LO 11-3

4. What hard evidence can you cite that indicates your company's management team is doing a *better* or *worse* job of achieving operating excellence and executing strategy than are the management teams at rival companies?

LO 11-3

LO 11-2, LO 11-3, LO 11-4

5. Are you and your co-managers consciously trying to achieve operating excellence? Explain how you are doing this and how you will track the progress you are making.

LO 11-5

6. Does your company have opportunities to use incentive compensation techniques? If so, explain your company's approach to incentive compensation. Is there any hard evidence you can cite that indicates your company's use of incentive compensation techniques has worked? For example, have your company's compensation incentives actually increased productivity? Can you cite evidence indicating that the productivity gains have resulted in lower labor costs? If the productivity gains have *not* translated into lower labor costs, is it fair to say that your company's use of incentive compensation is a failure?

ENDNOTES

[1] M. Hammer and J. Champy, *Reengineering the Corporation: A Manifesto for Business Revolution* (New York: HarperCollins, 1993).

[2] James Brian Quinn, *Intelligent Enterprise* (New York: Free Press, 1992); Ann Majchrzak and Qianwei Wang, "Breaking the Functional Mind-Set in Process Organizations," *Harvard Business Review* 74, no. 5 (September–October 1996), pp. 93–99; Stephen L. Walston, Lawton R. Burns, and John R. Kimberly, "Does Reengineering Really Work? An Examination of the Context and Outcomes of Hospital Reengineering Initiatives," *Health Services Research* 34, no. 6 (February 2000), pp. 1363–1388; Allessio Ascari, Melinda Rock, and Soumitra Dutta, "Reengineering and Organizational Change: Lessons from a Comparative Analysis of Company Experiences," *European Management Journal* 13, no. 1 (March 1995), pp. 1–13; Ronald J. Burke, "Process Reengineering: Who Embraces It and Why?" *The TQM Magazine* 16, no. 2 (2004), pp. 114–119.

[3] www.answers.com (accessed July 8, 2009); "Reengineering: Beyond the Buzzword," *Businessweek*, May 24, 1993, www.businessweek.com (accessed July 8, 2009).

[4] M. Walton, *The Deming Management Method* (New York: Pedigree, 1986); J. Juran, *Juran on Quality by Design* (New York: Free Press, 1992); Philip Crosby, *Quality Is Free: The Act of Making Quality Certain* (New York: McGraw-Hill, 1979); S. George, *The Baldrige Quality System* (New York: Wiley, 1992); Mark J. Zbaracki, "The Rhetoric and Reality of Total Quality Management," *Administrative Science Quarterly* 43, no. 3 (September 1998), pp. 602–636.

[5] Robert T. Amsden, Thomas W. Ferratt, and Davida M. Amsden, "TQM: Core Paradigm Changes," *Business Horizons* 39, no. 6 (November–December 1996), pp. 6–14.

[6] Peter S. Pande and Larry Holpp, *What Is Six Sigma?* (New York: McGraw-Hill, 2002); Jiju Antony, "Some Pros and Cons of Six Sigma: An Academic Perspective," *TQM Magazine* 16, no. 4 (2004), pp. 303–306; Peter S. Pande, Robert P. Neuman, and Roland R. Cavanagh, *The Six Sigma Way: How GE, Motorola and Other Top*

Companies Are Honing Their Performance (New York: McGraw-Hill, 2000); Joseph Gordon and M. Joseph Gordon, Jr., *Six Sigma Quality for Business and Manufacture* (New York: Elsevier, 2002); Godecke Wessel and Peter Burcher, "Six Sigma for Small and Medium-Sized Enterprises," *TQM Magazine* 16, no. 4 (2004), pp. 264–272.

[7] www.isixsigma.com (accessed November 4, 2002); www.villanovau.com/certificate-programs/six-sigma-training.aspx (accessed February 16, 2012).

[8] Kennedy Smith, "Six Sigma for the Service Sector," *Quality Digest Magazine,* May 2003; www.qualitydigest.com (accessed September 28, 2003).

[9] www.isixsigma.com/implementation/-financial-analysis/six-sigma-costs-and-savings/ (accessed February 23, 2012).

[10] Pande, Neuman, and Cavanagh, *The Six Sigma Way,* pp. 5–6.

[11] "A Dark Art No More," *The Economist* 385, no. 8550 (October 13, 2007), p. 10; Brian Hindo, "At 3M, a Struggle between Efficiency and Creativity," *Businessweek,* June 11, 2007, pp. 8–16.

[12] Charles A. O'Reilly and Michael L. Tushman, "The Ambidextrous Organization," *Harvard Business Review* 82, no. 4 (April 2004), pp. 74–81.

[13] Terry Nels Lee, Stanley E. Fawcett, and Jason Briscoe, "Benchmarking the Challenge to Quality Program Implementation," *Benchmarking: An International Journal* 9, no. 4 (2002), pp. 374–387.

[14] Milan Ambroé, "Total Quality System as a Product of the Empowered Corporate Culture," *TQM Magazine* 16, no. 2 (2004), pp. 93–104; Nick A. Dayton, "The Demise of Total Quality Management," *TQM Magazine* 15, no. 6 (2003), pp. 391–396.

[15] Judy D. Olian and Sara L. Rynes, "Making Total Quality Work: Aligning Organizational Processes, Performance Measures, and Stakeholders," *Human Resource Management* 30, no. 3 (Fall 1991), pp. 310–311; Paul S. Goodman and Eric D. Darr, "Exchanging Best Practices Information through Computer-Aided Systems," *Academy of Management Executive* 10, no. 2 (May 1996), p. 7.

[16] Thomas C. Powell, "Total Quality Management as Competitive Advantage," *Strategic Management Journal* 16 (1995), pp. 15–37; Richard M. Hodgetts, "Quality Lessons from America's Baldrige Winners," *Business Horizons* 37, no. 4 (July–August 1994), pp. 74–79; Richard Reed, David J. Lemak, and Joseph C. Montgomery, "Beyond Process: TQM Content and Firm Performance," *Academy of Management Review* 21, no. 1 (January 1996), pp. 173–202.

[17] Fred Vogelstein, "Winning the Amazon Way," *Fortune* 147, no. 10 (May 26, 2003), pp. 60–69.

[18] Robert Simons, "Control in an Age of Empowerment," *Harvard Business Review* 73 (March–April 1995), pp. 80–88.

[19] David C. Band and Gerald Scanlan, "Strategic Control through Core Competencies," *Long Range Planning* 28, no. 2 (April 1995), pp. 102–114.

[20] Stanley E. Fawcett, Gary K. Rhoads, and Phillip Burnah, "People as the Bridge to Competitiveness: Benchmarking the 'ABCs' of an Empowered Workforce," *Benchmarking: An International Journal* 11, no. 4 (2004), pp. 346–360.

[21] Jeffrey Pfeffer and John F. Veiga, "Putting People First for Organizational Success," *Academy of Management Executive* 13, no. 2 (May 1999), pp. 37–45; Linda K. Stroh and Paula M. Caliguiri, "Increasing Global Competitiveness through Effective People Management," *Journal of World Business* 33, no. 1 (Spring 1998), pp. 1–16; articles in *Fortune* on the 100 best companies to work for (various issues).

[22] As quoted in John P. Kotter and James L. Heskett, *Corporate Culture and Performance* (New York: Free Press, 1992), p. 91.

[23] Clayton M. Christensen, Matt Marx, and Howard Stevenson, "The Tools of Cooperation and Change," *Harvard Business Review* 84, no. 10 (October 2006), pp. 73–80.

[24] Steven Kerr, "On the Folly of Rewarding A While Hoping for B," *Academy of Management Executive* 9, no. 1 (February 1995), pp. 7–14; Doran Twer, "Linking Pay to Business Objectives," *Journal of Business Strategy* 15, no. 4 (July–August 1994), pp. 15–18.

chapter 12

Corporate Culture and Leadership

Keys to Good Strategy Execution

Learning Objectives

This chapter will help you

LO 12-1 Identify the key features of a company's corporate culture and the role of a company's core values and ethical standards in building corporate culture.

LO 12-2 Explain how and why a company's culture can aid the drive for proficient strategy execution.

LO 12-3 Identify the kinds of actions management can take to change a problem corporate culture.

LO 12-4 Explain what constitutes effective managerial leadership in achieving superior strategy execution.

chapter **12**

Corporate Culture and Leadership

Keys to Good Strategy Execution

Learning Objectives

This chapter will help you

LO 12-1 Identify the key features of a company's corporate culture and the role of a company's core values and ethical standards in building corporate culture.

LO 12-2 Explain how and why a company's culture can aid the drive for proficient strategy execution.

LO 12-3 Identify the kinds of actions management can take to change a problem corporate culture.

LO 12-4 Explain what constitutes effective managerial leadership in achieving superior strategy execution.

©Ilyaf/iStock/Getty Images

I came to see, in my time at IBM, that culture isn't just one aspect of the game, it is the game.

Louis Gerstner—*Former Chairman and CEO of IBM*

As we look ahead into the next century, leaders will be those who empower others.

Bill Gates—*Cofounder and former CEO and chair of Microsoft*

A genuine leader is not a searcher for consensus but a molder of consensus.

Martin Luther King, Jr.—*Civil Rights Leader*

In the previous two chapters, we examined eight of the managerial tasks that drive good strategy execution: staffing the organization, acquiring the needed resources and capabilities, designing the organizational structure, allocating resources, establishing policies and procedures, employing process management tools, installing operating systems, and providing the right incentives. In this chapter, we explore the two remaining managerial tasks that contribute to good strategy execution: creating a supportive corporate culture and leading the strategy execution process.

INSTILLING A CORPORATE CULTURE CONDUCIVE TO GOOD STRATEGY EXECUTION

● **LO 12-1**

Identify the key features of a company's corporate culture and the role of a company's core values and ethical standards in building corporate culture.

Every company has its own unique **corporate culture**—the shared values, ingrained attitudes, and company traditions that determine norms of behavior, accepted work practices, and styles of operating.[1] The character of a company's culture is a product of the core values and beliefs that executives espouse, the standards of what is ethically acceptable and what is not, the "chemistry" and the "personality" that permeate the work environment, the company's traditions, and the stories that get told over and over to illustrate and reinforce the company's values, business practices, and traditions. In a very real sense, the culture is the company's automatic, self-replicating "operating system" that defines "how we do things around here."[2]

It can be thought of as the company's psyche or *organizational DNA*.[3] A company's culture is important because it influences the organization's actions and approaches to conducting business. As such, it plays an important role in strategy execution and may have an appreciable effect on business performance as well.

Corporate cultures vary widely. For instance, the bedrock of Walmart's culture is zealous pursuit of low costs and frugal operating practices, a strong work ethic, ritualistic headquarters meetings to exchange ideas and review problems, and company executives' commitment to visiting stores, listening to customers, and soliciting suggestions from employees. The culture at Apple is customer-centered, secretive, and highly protective of company-developed technology. Apple employees share a common goal of making the best products for the consumer; the aim is to make the customer feel delight, surprise, and connection to each Apple device. The company expects creative thinking and inspired solutions from everyone—as the company puts it, "We're perfectionists. Idealists. Inventors. Forever tinkering with products and processes, always on the lookout for better." According to a former employee, "Apple is one of those companies where people work on an almost religious level of commitment." To spur innovation and creativity, the company fosters extensive collaboration and cross-pollination among different work groups. But it does so in a manner that demands secrecy—employees are expected not to reveal anything relevant about what new project they are working on, not to employees outside their immediate work group and especially not to family members or other outsiders; it is common for different employees working on the same project to be assigned different project code names. The different pieces of a new product launch often come together like a puzzle at the last minute.[4] W. L. Gore & Associates, best known for GORE-TEX, credits its unique culture for allowing the company to pursue multiple end-market applications simultaneously, enabling rapid growth from a niche business into a diversified multinational company. The company's culture is team-based and designed to foster personal initiative, with no traditional organizational charts, no chains of command, no predetermined channels of communication. The culture encourages multidiscipline teams to organize around opportunities, and in the process, leaders emerge. At Nordstrom, the corporate culture is centered on delivering exceptional service to customers, where the company's motto is "Respond to unreasonable customer requests," and each out-of-the-ordinary request is seen as an opportunity for a "heroic" act by an employee that can further the company's reputation for unparalleled customer service. Nordstrom makes a point of promoting employees noted for their heroic acts and dedication to outstanding service.

Illustration Capsule 12.1 describes the corporate culture of another exemplary company—Epic Systems, well known by health care providers.

Strong Guiding Principles Drive the High-Performance Culture at Epic

©Kamon_Wongnon/Shutterstock

Epic Systems Corporation creates software to support record keeping for mid- to large-sized health care organizations, such as hospitals and managed care organizations. Founded in 1979 by CEO Judith Faulkner, the company claims that its software is "quick to implement, easy to use and highly interoperable through industry standards." Widely recognized for superior products and high levels of customer satisfaction, Epic won the Best Overall Software Suite award for the sixth consecutive year—a ranking determined by health care professionals and compiled by KLAS, a provider of company performance reviews. Part of this success has been attributed to Epic's strong corporate culture—one based on the slogan "Do good, have fun, make money." By remaining true to its 10 commandments and principles, its homegrown version of core values, Epic has nurtured a work climate where employees are on the same page and all have an overarching standard to guide their actions.

Epic's 10 Commandments:

1. Do not go public.
2. Do not be acquired.
3. Software must work.
4. Expectations = reality.
5. Keep commitments.
6. Focus on competency. Do not tolerate mediocrity.
7. Have standards. Be fair to all.
8. Have courage. What you put up with is what you stand for.
9. Teach philosophy and culture.
10. Be frugal. Do not take on debt for operations.

Epic's Principles:

1. Make our products a joy to use.
2. Have fun with customers.
3. Design in collaboration with users.
4. Make it easy for users to do the right thing.
5. Improve the patient's health and healthcare experience.
6. Generalize to benefit more.
7. Follow processes. Find root causes. Fix processes.
8. Dissent when you disagree; once decided, support.
9. Do what is difficult for us if it makes things easier for our users.
10. Escalate problems at the start, not when all hell breaks loose.

Epic fosters this high-performance culture from the get-go. It targets top-tier universities to hire entry level talent, focusing on skills rather than personality. A rigorous training and orientation program indoctrinates each new employee. In 2002, Faulkner claimed that someone coming straight from college could become an "Epic person" in three years, whereas it takes six years for someone coming from another company. This culture positively affects Epic's strategy execution because employees are focused on the most important actions, there is peer pressure to contribute to Epic's success, and employees are genuinely excited to be involved. Epic's faith in its ability to acculturate new team members and stick true to its core values has allowed it to sustain its status as a premier provider of health care IT systems.

Note: Developed with Margo Cox.

Sources: Company website; communications with an Epic insider; "Epic Takes Back 'Best in KLAS' title," *Healthcare IT News,* January 29, 2015, www.healthcareitnews.com/news/epic-takes-back-best-klas; "Epic Systems' Headquarters Reflect Its Creativity, Growth," *Boston Globe,* July 28, 2015, www.bostonglobe.com/business/2015/07/28/epic-systems-success-like-its-headquarters-blend-creativity-and-diligence/LpdQ5m0DDS4UVilCVooRUJ/story.html (accessed December 5, 2015).

Identifying the Key Features of a Company's Corporate Culture

A company's corporate culture is mirrored in the character or "personality" of its work environment—the features that describe how the company goes about its business and the workplace behaviors that are held in high esteem. Some of these features are readily apparent, and others operate quite subtly. The chief things to look for include:

- The values, business principles, and ethical standards that management preaches and *practices*—these are the key to a company's culture, but actions speak much louder than words here.
- The company's approach to people management and the official policies, procedures, and operating practices that provide guidelines for the behavior of company personnel.
- The atmosphere and spirit that pervades the work climate—whether the workplace is competitive or cooperative, innovative or resistant to change, collegial or politicized, all business or fun-loving, and the like.
- How managers and employees interact and relate to one another—whether people tend to work independently or collaboratively, whether communications among employees are free-flowing or infrequent, whether people are called by their first names, whether co-workers spend little or lots of time together outside the workplace, and so on.
- The strength of peer pressure to do things in particular ways and conform to expected norms.
- The actions and behaviors that management explicitly encourages and rewards and those that are frowned upon.
- The company's revered traditions and oft-repeated stories about "heroic acts" and "how we do things around here."
- The manner in which the company deals with external stakeholders—whether it treats suppliers as business partners or prefers hard-nosed, arm's-length business arrangements and whether its commitment to corporate citizenship and environmental sustainability is strong and genuine.

The values, beliefs, and practices that undergird a company's culture can come from anywhere in the organizational hierarchy. Typically, key elements of the culture originate with a founder or certain strong leaders who articulated them as a set of business principles, company policies, operating approaches, and ways of dealing with employees, customers, vendors, shareholders, and local communities where the company has operations. They also stem from exemplary actions on the part of company personnel and evolving consensus about "how we ought to do things around here."[5] Over time, these cultural underpinnings take root, come to be accepted by company managers and employees alike, and become ingrained in the way the company conducts its business.

> A company's culture is grounded in and shaped by its core values and ethical standards.

> A company's value statement and code of ethics communicate expectations of how employees should conduct themselves in the workplace.

The Role of Core Values and Ethics   The foundation of a company's corporate culture nearly always resides in its dedication to certain core values and the bar it sets for ethical behavior. The culture-shaping significance of core values and ethical behaviors accounts for why so many companies have developed a formal value statement and a code of ethics. Many executives want the work climate at their companies to mirror certain values and ethical standards, partly because of personal

FIGURE 12.1 The Two Culture-Building Roles of a Company's Core Values and Ethical Standards

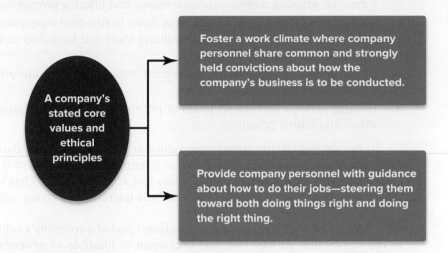

A company's stated core values and ethical principles

Foster a work climate where company personnel share common and strongly held convictions about how the company's business is to be conducted.

Provide company personnel with guidance about how to do their jobs—steering them toward both doing things right and doing the right thing.

convictions but mainly because they are convinced that adherence to such principles will promote better strategy execution, make the company a better performer, and positively impact its reputation.[6] Not incidentally, strongly ingrained values and ethical standards reduce the likelihood of lapses in ethical behavior that mar a company's public image and put its financial performance and market standing at risk.

As depicted in Figure 12.1, a company's stated core values and ethical principles have two roles in the culture-building process. First, a company that works hard at putting its core values and ethical principles into practice fosters a work climate in which company personnel share strongly held convictions about how the company's business is to be conducted. Second, the stated values and ethical principles provide company personnel with guidance about the manner in which they are to do their jobs—which behaviors and ways of doing things are approved (and expected) and which are out-of-bounds. These value-based and ethics-based cultural norms serve as yardsticks for gauging the appropriateness of particular actions, decisions, and behaviors, thus helping steer company personnel toward both doing things right and doing the right thing.

Embedding Behavioral Norms in the Organization and Perpetuating the Culture

Once values and ethical standards have been formally adopted, they must be institutionalized in the company's policies and practices and embedded in the conduct of company personnel. This can be advanced in a number of different ways.[7] Tradition-steeped companies with a rich folklore rely heavily on word-of-mouth indoctrination and the power of tradition to instill values and enforce ethical conduct. But most companies employ a variety of techniques, drawing on some or all of the following:

1. Screening applicants and hiring those who will mesh well with the culture.

2. Incorporating discussions of the company's culture and behavioral norms into orientation programs for new employees and training courses for managers and employees.

3. Having senior executives frequently reiterate the importance and role of company values and ethical principles at company events and in internal communications to employees.

4. Expecting managers at all levels to be cultural role models and exhibit the advocated cultural norms in their own behavior.

5. Making the display of cultural norms a factor in evaluating each person's job performance, granting compensation increases, and offering promotions.

6. Stressing that line managers all the way down to first-level supervisors give ongoing attention to explaining the desired cultural traits and behaviors in their areas and clarifying why they are important.

7. Encouraging company personnel to exert strong peer pressure on co-workers to conform to expected cultural norms.

8. Holding periodic ceremonies to honor people who excel in displaying the company values and ethical principles.

To deeply ingrain the stated core values and high ethical standards, companies must turn them into *strictly enforced cultural norms.* They must make it unequivocally clear that living up to the company's values and ethical standards has to be "a way of life" at the company and that there will be little toleration for errant behavior.

The Role of Stories   Frequently, a significant part of a company's culture is captured in the stories that get told over and over again to illustrate to newcomers the importance of certain values and the depth of commitment that various company personnel have displayed. One of the folktales at Zappos, known for its outstanding customer service, is about a customer who ordered shoes for her ill mother from Zappos, hoping the shoes would remedy her mother's foot pain and numbness. When the shoes didn't work, the mother called the company to ask how to return them and explain why she was returning them. Two days later, she received a large bouquet of flowers from the company, along with well wishes and a customer upgrade giving her free expedited service on all future orders. Specialty food market Trader Joe's is similarly known for its culture of going beyond the call of duty for its customers. When a World War II veteran was snowed in without any food for meals, his daughter called several supermarkets to see if they offered grocery delivery. Although Trader Joe's technically doesn't offer delivery, it graciously helped the veteran, even recommending items for his low-sodium diet. When the store delivered the groceries, the veteran wasn't charged for either the groceries or the delivery. Stories of employees at Ritz Carlton going the extra mile for customers both showcase and reinforce its customer-centric culture. Recently, a family arrived at a Ritz-Carlton only to find that the specialized eggs and milk they had brought along for their son had spoiled. (The child suffered from food allergies.) When the products could not be found locally, the hotel's staff had the products flown in from Singapore, approximately 1,050 miles away!

Forces That Cause a Company's Culture to Evolve   Despite the role of time-honored stories and long-standing traditions in perpetuating a company's culture, cultures are far from static—just like strategy and organizational structure, they evolve. New challenges in the marketplace, revolutionary technologies, and shifting internal conditions—especially an internal crisis, a change in company direction, or top-executive turnover—tend to breed new ways of doing things and, in turn, drive cultural evolution. An incoming CEO who decides to shake up the existing business and take it in new directions often triggers a cultural shift, perhaps one of major proportions. Likewise, diversification into new businesses, expansion into foreign countries, rapid growth that brings an influx of new employees, and the merger with or acquisition of another company can all precipitate significant cultural change.

The Presence of Company Subcultures Although it is common to speak about corporate culture in the singular, it is not unusual for companies to have multiple cultures (or subcultures). Values, beliefs, and practices within a company sometimes vary significantly by department, geographic location, division, or business unit. Subcultures can exist because a company has recently acquired other companies. Global and multinational companies tend to be at least partly multicultural because cross-country organization units have different operating histories and work climates, as well as members who speak different languages, have grown up under different social customs and traditions, and have different sets of values and beliefs. The problem with subcultures is that they can clash, or at least not mesh well, particularly if they embrace conflicting business philosophies or operating approaches, if key executives employ different approaches to people management, or if important differences between a company's culture and those of recently acquired companies have not yet been ironed out. On a number of occasions, companies have decided to pass on acquiring particular companies because of culture conflicts they believed would be hard to resolve.

Nonetheless, the existence of subcultures does not preclude important areas of commonality and compatibility. Company managements are quite alert to the importance of cultural compatibility in making acquisitions and the need to integrate the cultures of newly acquired companies. Indeed, cultural due diligence is often as important as financial due diligence in deciding whether to go forward on an acquisition or merger. Also, in today's globalizing world, multinational companies are learning how to make strategy-critical cultural traits travel across country boundaries and create a workably uniform culture worldwide. AES, a sustainable energy company with 10,000 employees and operations on four continents, has found that people in most countries readily embrace the five core values that underlie its culture—putting safety first, acting with integrity, remaining nimble, having fun through work, and striving for excellence. Moreover, AES tries to define and practice its cultural values the same way in all of its locations while still being sensitive to differences that exist among various peoples and groups around the world. Top managers at AES have expressed the view that people across the globe are more similar than different and that the company's culture is as meaningful in Brazil, Vietnam, or Kazakhstan as in the United States.

Strong versus Weak Cultures

Company cultures vary widely in strength and influence. Some are strongly embedded and have a big influence on a company's operating practices and the behavior of company personnel. Others are weakly ingrained and have little effect on behaviors and how company activities are conducted.

Strong-Culture Companies The hallmark of a **strong-culture company** is the dominating presence of certain deeply rooted values, business principles, and behavioral norms that "regulate" the conduct of company personnel and determine the climate of the workplace.[8] In strong-culture companies, senior managers make a point of explaining and reiterating why these values, principles, norms, and operating approaches need to govern how the company conducts its business and how they ultimately lead to better business performance. Furthermore, they make a conscious effort to display these values, principles, and behavioral norms in their own actions—*they walk the talk.* An unequivocal expectation that company personnel will

> **CORE CONCEPT**
>
> In a **strong-culture company,** deeply rooted values and norms of behavior are widely shared and regulate the conduct of the company's business.

act and behave in accordance with the adopted values and ways of doing business leads to two important outcomes: (1) Over time, the professed values come to be widely shared by rank-and-file employees—people who dislike the culture tend to leave—and (2) individuals encounter strong peer pressure from co-workers to observe the culturally approved norms and behaviors. Hence, a strongly implanted corporate culture ends up having a powerful influence on behavior because so many company personnel are accepting of the company's culturally approved traditions and because this acceptance is reinforced by both management expectations and co-worker peer pressure to conform to cultural norms.

Strong cultures emerge only after a period of deliberate and rather intensive culture building that generally takes years (sometimes decades). Two factors contribute to the development of strong cultures: (1) a founder or strong leader who established core values, principles, and practices that are viewed as having contributed to the success of the company; and (2) a sincere, long-standing company commitment to operating the business according to these established traditions and values. Continuity of leadership, low workforce turnover, geographic concentration, and considerable organizational success all contribute to the emergence and sustainability of a strong culture.[9]

In strong-culture companies, values and behavioral norms are so ingrained that they can endure leadership changes at the top—although their strength can erode over time if new CEOs cease to nurture them or move aggressively to institute cultural adjustments. The cultural norms in a strong-culture company typically do not change much as strategy evolves, either because the culture constrains the choice of new strategies or because the dominant traits of the culture are somewhat strategy-neutral and compatible with evolving versions of the company's strategy. As a consequence, *strongly implanted cultures provide a huge assist in executing strategy* because company managers can use the traditions, beliefs, values, common bonds, or behavioral norms as levers to mobilize commitment to executing the chosen strategy.

Weak-Culture Companies   In direct contrast to strong-culture companies, weak-culture companies lack widely shared and strongly held values, principles, and behavioral norms. As a result, they also lack cultural mechanisms for aligning, constraining, and regulating the actions, decisions, and behaviors of company personnel. In the absence of any long-standing top management commitment to particular values, beliefs, operating practices, and behavioral norms, individuals encounter little pressure to do things in particular ways. Such a dearth of companywide cultural influences and revered traditions produces a work climate where there is no strong employee allegiance to what the company stands for or to operating the business in well-defined ways. While individual employees may well have some bonds of identification with and loyalty toward their department, their colleagues, their union, or their immediate boss, there's neither passion about the company nor emotional commitment to what it is trying to accomplish—a condition that often results in many employees' viewing their company as just a place to work and their job as just a way to make a living.

As a consequence, *weak cultures provide little or no assistance in executing strategy* because there are no traditions, beliefs, values, common bonds, or behavioral norms that management can use as levers to mobilize commitment to executing the chosen strategy. Without a work climate that channels organizational energy in the direction of good strategy execution, managers are left with the options of either using compensation incentives and other motivational devices to mobilize employee commitment, supervising and monitoring employee actions more closely, or trying to establish cultural roots that will in time start to nurture the strategy execution process.

Why Corporate Cultures Matter to the Strategy Execution Process

Even if a company has a strong culture, the culture and work climate may or may not be compatible with what is needed for effective implementation of the chosen strategy. When a company's present culture promotes attitudes, behaviors, and ways of doing things that are *in sync with the chosen strategy and conducive to first-rate strategy execution,* the culture functions as a valuable ally in the strategy execution process. For example, a corporate culture characterized by frugality and thrift prompts employee actions to identify cost-saving opportunities—the very behavior needed for successful execution of a low-cost leadership strategy. A culture that celebrates taking initiative, exhibiting creativity, taking risks, and embracing change is conducive to successful execution of product innovation and technological leadership strategies.[10]

● **LO 12-2**

Explain how and why a company's culture can aid the drive for proficient strategy execution.

A culture that is grounded in actions, behaviors, and work practices that are conducive to good strategy implementation supports the strategy execution effort in three ways:

1. *A culture that is well matched to the chosen strategy and the requirements of the strategy execution effort focuses the attention of employees on what is most important to this effort.* Moreover, it directs their behavior and serves as a guide to their decision making. In this manner, it can align the efforts and decisions of employees throughout the firm and minimize the need for direct supervision.

2. *Culture-induced peer pressure further induces company personnel to do things in a manner that aids the cause of good strategy execution.* The stronger the culture (the more widely shared and deeply held the values), the more effective peer pressure is in shaping and supporting the strategy execution effort. Research has shown that strong group norms can shape employee behavior even more powerfully than can financial incentives.

3. *A company culture that is consistent with the requirements for good strategy execution can energize employees, deepen their commitment to execute the strategy flawlessly, and enhance worker productivity in the process.* When a company's culture is grounded in many of the needed strategy-executing behaviors, employees feel genuinely better about their jobs, the company they work for, and the merits of what the company is trying to accomplish. Greater employee buy-in for what the company is trying to accomplish boosts motivation and marshals organizational energy behind the drive for good strategy execution. An energized workforce enhances the chances of achieving execution-critical performance targets and good strategy execution.

In sharp contrast, when a culture is in conflict with the chosen strategy or what is required to execute the company's strategy well, the culture becomes a stumbling block.[11] Some of the very behaviors needed to execute the strategy successfully run contrary to the attitudes, behaviors, and operating practices embedded in the prevailing culture. Such a clash poses a real dilemma for company personnel. Should they be loyal to the culture and company traditions (to which they are likely to be emotionally attached) and thus resist or be indifferent to actions that will promote better strategy execution—a choice that will certainly weaken the drive for good strategy execution? Alternatively, should they go along with management's strategy execution effort and engage in actions that run counter to the culture—a choice that will likely impair morale and lead to a less-than-enthusiastic commitment to good strategy execution? Neither choice leads to desirable outcomes. Culture-bred resistance to the

A strong culture that encourages actions, behaviors, and work practices that are in sync with the chosen strategy is a valuable ally in the strategy execution process.

actions and behaviors needed for good strategy execution, particularly if strong and widespread, poses a formidable hurdle that must be cleared for a strategy's execution to be successful.

The consequences of having—or not having—an execution-supportive corporate culture says something important about the task of managing the strategy execution process: *Closely aligning corporate culture with the requirements for proficient strategy execution merits the full attention of senior executives.* The culture-building objective is to create a work climate and style of operating that mobilize the energy of company personnel squarely behind efforts to execute strategy competently. The more deeply management can embed execution-supportive ways of doing things, the more management can rely on the culture to automatically steer company personnel toward behaviors and work practices that aid good strategy execution and veer from doing things that impede it. Moreover, culturally astute managers understand that nourishing the right cultural environment not only adds power to their push for proficient strategy execution but also promotes strong employee identification with, and commitment to, the company's vision, performance targets, and strategy.

> It is in management's best interest to dedicate considerable effort to establishing a corporate culture that encourages behaviors and work practices conducive to good strategy execution.

Healthy Cultures That Aid Good Strategy Execution

A strong culture, provided it fits the chosen strategy and embraces execution-supportive attitudes, behaviors, and work practices, is definitely a healthy culture. Two other types of cultures exist that tend to be healthy and largely supportive of good strategy execution: high-performance cultures and adaptive cultures.

High-Performance Cultures   Some companies have so-called high-performance cultures where the standout traits are a "can-do" spirit, pride in doing things right, no-excuses accountability, and a pervasive results-oriented work climate in which people go all out to meet or beat stretch objectives.[12] In high-performance cultures, there's a strong sense of involvement on the part of company personnel and emphasis on individual initiative and effort. Performance expectations are clearly delineated for the company as a whole, for each organizational unit, and for each individual. Issues and problems are promptly addressed; there's a razor-sharp focus on what needs to be done. The clear and unyielding expectation is that all company personnel, from senior executives to frontline employees, will display high-performance behaviors and a passion for making the company successful. Such a culture—permeated by a spirit of achievement and constructive pressure to achieve good results—is a valuable contributor to good strategy execution and operating excellence.[13]

The challenge in creating a high-performance culture is to inspire high loyalty and dedication on the part of employees, such that they are energized to put forth their very best efforts. Managers have to take pains to reinforce constructive behavior, reward top performers, and purge habits and behaviors that stand in the way of high productivity and good results. They must work at knowing the strengths and weaknesses of their subordinates to better match talent with task and enable people to make meaningful contributions by doing what they do best. They have to stress learning from mistakes and must put an unrelenting emphasis on moving forward and making good progress—in effect, there has to be a disciplined, performance-focused approach to managing the organization.

Adaptive Cultures   The hallmark of adaptive corporate cultures is willingness on the part of organization members to accept change and take on the challenge of introducing and executing new strategies. Company personnel share a feeling of confidence that the organization can deal with whatever threats and opportunities arise; they are receptive to risk taking, experimentation, innovation, and changing strategies and practices. The work climate is supportive of managers and employees who propose or initiate useful change. Internal entrepreneurship (often called *intrapreneurship*) on the part of individuals and groups is encouraged and rewarded. Senior executives seek out, support, and promote individuals who exercise initiative, spot opportunities for improvement, and display the skills to implement them. Managers openly evaluate ideas and suggestions, fund initiatives to develop new or better products, and take prudent risks to pursue emerging market opportunities. As in high-performance cultures, the company exhibits a proactive approach to identifying issues, evaluating the implications and options, and moving ahead quickly with workable solutions. Strategies and traditional operating practices are modified as needed to adjust to, or take advantage of, changes in the business environment.

> As a company's strategy evolves, an adaptive culture is a definite ally in the strategy-implementing, strategy-executing process as compared to cultures that are resistant to change.

But why is change so willingly embraced in an adaptive culture? Why are organization members not fearful of how change will affect them? Why does an adaptive culture not break down from the force of ongoing changes in strategy, operating practices, and behavioral norms? The answers lie in two distinctive and dominant traits of an adaptive culture: (1) Changes in operating practices and behaviors must *not* compromise core values and long-standing business principles (since they are at the root of the culture), and (2) changes that are instituted must satisfy the legitimate interests of key constituencies—customers, employees, shareholders, suppliers, and the communities where the company operates. In other words, what sustains an adaptive culture is that organization members perceive the changes that management is trying to institute as *legitimate,* in keeping with the core values, and in the overall best interests of stakeholders.[14] Not surprisingly, company personnel are usually more receptive to change when their employment security is not threatened and when they view new duties or job assignments as part of the process of adapting to new conditions. Should workforce downsizing be necessary, it is important that layoffs be handled humanely and employee departures be made as painless as possible.

Technology companies, software companies, and Internet-based companies are good illustrations of organizations with adaptive cultures. Such companies thrive on change—driving it, leading it, and capitalizing on it. Companies like Amazon, Google, Apple, Facebook, Adobe, Groupon, Intel, and Yelp cultivate the capability to act and react rapidly. They are avid practitioners of entrepreneurship and innovation, with a demonstrated willingness to take bold risks to create altogether new products, new businesses, and new industries. To create and nurture a culture that can adapt rapidly to shifting business conditions, they make a point of staffing their organizations with people who are flexible, who rise to the challenge of change, and who have an aptitude for adapting well to new circumstances. Wayfair, the largest online retailer of home furnishings in the United States, attributes its rapid growth to an entrepreneurial and collaborative culture that encourages employee innovation. They hire individuals who are willing to solve problems creatively and develop new initiatives, and empower them to take measured risks.

In fast-changing business environments, a corporate culture that is receptive to altering organizational practices and behaviors is a virtual necessity. However, adaptive cultures work to the advantage of all companies, not just those in rapid-change environments. Every company operates in a market and business climate that is changing to one degree or another and that, in turn, requires internal operating responses and new behaviors on the part of organization members.

Unhealthy Cultures That Impede Good Strategy Execution

The distinctive characteristic of an unhealthy corporate culture is the presence of counterproductive cultural traits that adversely impact the work climate and company performance. Five particularly unhealthy cultural traits are hostility to change, heavily politicized decision making, insular thinking, unethical and greed-driven behaviors, and the presence of incompatible, clashing subcultures.

Change-Resistant Cultures   Change-resistant cultures—where fear of change and skepticism about the importance of new developments are the norm—place a premium on not making mistakes, prompting managers to lean toward safe, conservative options intended to maintain the status quo, protect their power base, and guard their immediate interests. When such companies encounter business environments with accelerating change, going slow on altering traditional ways of doing things can be a serious liability. Under these conditions, change-resistant cultures encourage a number of unhealthy behaviors—avoiding risks, not capitalizing on emerging opportunities, taking a lax approach to both product innovation and continuous improvement in performing value chain activities, and responding more slowly than is warranted to market change. In change-resistant cultures, word quickly gets around that proposals to do things differently face an uphill battle and that people who champion them may be seen as something of a nuisance or a troublemaker. Executives who don't value managers or employees with initiative and new ideas put a damper on product innovation, experimentation, and efforts to improve.

Hostility to change is most often found in companies with stodgy bureaucracies that have enjoyed considerable market success in years past and that are wedded to the "We have done it this way for years" syndrome. General Motors, IBM, Sears, and Eastman Kodak are classic examples of companies whose change-resistant bureaucracies have damaged their market standings and financial performance; clinging to what made them successful, they were reluctant to alter operating practices and modify their business approaches when signals of market change first sounded. As strategies of gradual change won out over bold innovation, all four lost market share to rivals that quickly moved to institute changes more in tune with evolving market conditions and buyer preferences. While IBM and GM have made strides in building a culture needed for market success, Sears and Kodak are still struggling to recoup lost ground.

Politicized Cultures   What makes a politicized internal environment so unhealthy is that political infighting consumes a great deal of organizational energy, often with the result that what's best for the company takes a backseat to political maneuvering. In companies where internal politics pervades the work climate, empire-building managers pursue their own agendas and operate the work units under their supervision as autonomous "fiefdoms." The positions they take on issues are usually aimed at protecting or expanding their own turf. Collaboration with other organizational units is viewed with suspicion, and cross-unit cooperation occurs grudgingly. The support or opposition of politically influential executives and/or coalitions among departments with vested interests in a particular outcome tends to shape what actions the company takes. All this political maneuvering takes away from efforts to execute strategy with real proficiency and frustrates company personnel who are less political and more inclined to do what is in the company's best interests.

Insular, Inwardly Focused Cultures   Sometimes a company reigns as an industry leader or enjoys great market success for so long that its personnel start to believe they have all the answers or can develop them on their own. There is a strong tendency to neglect what customers are saying and how their needs and expectations are changing.

Such confidence in the correctness of how the company does things and an unflinching belief in its competitive superiority breed arrogance, prompting company personnel to discount the merits of what outsiders are doing and to see little payoff from studying best-in-class performers. Insular thinking, internally driven solutions, and a must-be-invented-here mindset come to permeate the corporate culture. An inwardly focused corporate culture gives rise to managerial inbreeding and a failure to recruit people who can offer fresh thinking and outside perspectives. The big risk of insular cultural thinking is that the company can underestimate the capabilities of rival companies while overestimating its own—all of which diminishes a company's competitiveness over time.

Unethical and Greed-Driven Cultures   Companies that have little regard for ethical standards or are run by executives driven by greed and ego gratification are scandals waiting to happen. Executives exude the negatives of arrogance, ego, greed, and an "ends-justify-the-means" mentality in pursuing overambitious revenue and profitability targets.[15] Senior managers wink at unethical behavior and may cross over the line to unethical (and sometimes criminal) behavior themselves. They are prone to adopt accounting principles that make financial performance look better than it really is. Legions of companies have fallen prey to unethical behavior and greed, most notably Turing Pharmaceuticals, Enron, Three Ocean Shipping, BP, AIG, Countrywide Financial, and JPMorgan Chase, with executives being indicted and/or convicted of criminal behavior.

Incompatible, Clashing Subcultures   Company subcultures are unhealthy when they embrace conflicting business philosophies, support inconsistent approaches to strategy execution, and encourage incompatible methods of people management. Clashing subcultures can prevent a company from coordinating its efforts to craft and execute strategy and can distract company personnel from the business of business. Internal jockeying among the subcultures for cultural dominance impedes teamwork among the company's various organizational units and blocks the emergence of a collaborative approach to strategy execution. Such a lack of consensus about how to proceed is likely to result in fragmented or inconsistent approaches to implementing new strategic initiatives and in limited success in executing the company's overall strategy.

Changing a Problem Culture

When a strong culture is unhealthy or otherwise out of sync with the actions and behaviors needed to execute the strategy successfully, the culture must be changed as rapidly as can be managed. This means eliminating any unhealthy or dysfunctional cultural traits as fast as possible and aggressively striving to ingrain new behaviors and work practices that will enable first-rate strategy execution. The more entrenched the unhealthy or mismatched aspects of a company culture, the more likely the culture will impede strategy execution and the greater the need for change.

● **LO 12-3**

Identify the kinds of actions management can take to change a problem corporate culture.

Changing a problem culture is among the toughest management tasks because of the heavy anchor of ingrained behaviors and attitudes. It is natural for company personnel to cling to familiar practices and to be wary of change, if not hostile to new approaches concerning how things are to be done. Consequently, it takes concerted management action over a period of time to root out unwanted behaviors and replace an unsupportive culture with more effective ways of doing things. *The single most visible factor that distinguishes successful culture-change efforts from failed attempts is competent leadership at the top.* Great power is needed to force major cultural change and overcome the stubborn resistance of entrenched cultures—and great power is possessed only by the most senior executives, especially the CEO. However, while top management must lead the change effort, the tasks of marshaling support for a new culture and

FIGURE 12.2   Changing a Problem Culture

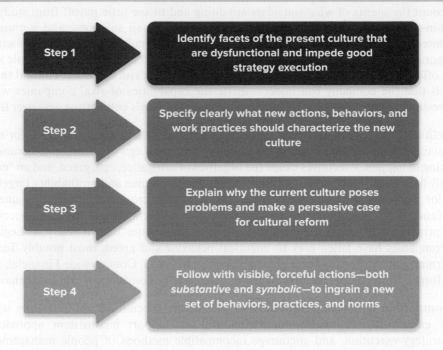

Step 1 — Identify facets of the present culture that are dysfunctional and impede good strategy execution

Step 2 — Specify clearly what new actions, behaviors, and work practices should characterize the new culture

Step 3 — Explain why the current culture poses problems and make a persuasive case for cultural reform

Step 4 — Follow with visible, forceful actions—both *substantive* and *symbolic*—to ingrain a new set of behaviors, practices, and norms

instilling the desired cultural behaviors must involve a company's whole management team. Middle managers and frontline supervisors play a key role in implementing the new work practices and operating approaches, helping win rank-and-file acceptance of and support for changes, and instilling the desired behavioral norms.

As shown in Figure 12.2, the first step in fixing a problem culture is for top management to identify those facets of the present culture that are dysfunctional and pose obstacles to executing strategic initiatives. Second, managers must clearly define the desired new behaviors and features of the culture they want to create. Third, they must convince company personnel of why the present culture poses problems and why and how new behaviors and operating approaches will improve company performance—the case for cultural reform has to be persuasive. Finally, and most important, all the talk about remodeling the present culture must be followed swiftly by visible, forceful actions to promote the desired new behaviors and work practices—actions that company personnel will interpret as a determined top-management commitment to bringing about a different work climate and new ways of operating. The actions to implant the new culture must be both substantive and symbolic.

Making a Compelling Case for Culture Change   The way for management to begin a major remodeling of the corporate culture is by selling company personnel on the need for new-style behaviors and work practices. This means making a compelling case for why the culture-remodeling efforts are in the organization's best interests and why company personnel should wholeheartedly join the effort to do things somewhat differently. This can be done by

• Explaining why and how certain behaviors and work practices in the current culture pose obstacles to good strategy execution.

- Explaining how new behaviors and work practices will be more advantageous and produce better results. Effective culture-change leaders are good at telling stories to describe the new values and desired behaviors and connect them to everyday practices.
- Citing reasons why the current strategy has to be modified, if the need for cultural change is due to a change in strategy. This includes explaining why the new strategic initiatives will bolster the company's competitiveness and performance and how a change in culture can help in executing the new strategy.

It is essential for the CEO and other top executives to talk personally to personnel all across the company about the reasons for modifying work practices and culture-related behaviors. For the culture-change effort to be successful, frontline supervisors and employee opinion leaders must be won over to the cause, which means convincing them of the merits of *practicing* and *enforcing* cultural norms at every level of the organization, from the highest to the lowest. Arguments for new ways of doing things and new work practices tend to be embraced more readily if employees understand how they will benefit company stakeholders (particularly customers, employees, and shareholders). Until a large majority of employees accept the need for a new culture and agree that different work practices and behaviors are called for, there's more work to be done in selling company personnel on the whys and wherefores of culture change. Building widespread organizational support requires taking every opportunity to repeat the message of why the new work practices, operating approaches, and behaviors are good for company stakeholders and essential for the company's future success.

Substantive Culture-Changing Actions   No culture-change effort can get very far when leaders merely talk about the need for different actions, behaviors, and work practices. Company executives must give the culture-change effort some teeth by initiating *a series of actions* that company personnel will see as unmistakably indicative of the seriousness of management's commitment to cultural change. The strongest signs that management is truly committed to instilling a new culture include

- Replacing key executives who are resisting or obstructing needed cultural changes.
- Promoting individuals who have stepped forward to spearhead the shift to a different culture and who can serve as role models for the desired cultural behavior.
- Appointing outsiders with the desired cultural attributes to high-profile positions—bringing in new-breed managers sends an unambiguous message that a new era is dawning.
- Screening all candidates for new positions carefully, hiring only those who appear to fit in with the new culture.
- Mandating that all company personnel attend culture-training programs to better understand the new culture-related actions and behaviors that are expected.
- Designing compensation incentives that boost the pay of teams and individuals who display the desired cultural behaviors. Company personnel are much more inclined to exhibit the desired kinds of actions and behaviors when it is in their financial best interest to do so.
- Letting word leak out that generous pay raises have been awarded to individuals who have stepped out front, led the adoption of the desired work practices, displayed the new-style behaviors, and achieved pace-setting results.
- Revising policies and procedures in ways that will help drive cultural change.

Executives must launch enough companywide culture-change actions at the outset to leave no room for doubt that management is dead serious about changing the present culture and that a cultural transformation is inevitable. Management's commitment to cultural change in the company must be made credible. The series of actions initiated by top management must command attention, get the change process off to a fast start, and be followed by unrelenting efforts to firmly establish the new work practices, desired behaviors, and style of operating as "standard."

> The most important symbolic cultural-changing action that top executives can take is to *lead by example*.

Symbolic Culture-Changing Actions   There's also an important place for symbolic managerial actions to alter a problem culture and tighten the strategy–culture fit. The most important symbolic actions are those that top executives take to *lead by example*. For instance, if the organization's strategy involves a drive to become the industry's low-cost producer, senior managers must display frugality in their own actions and decisions. Examples include inexpensive decorations in the executive suite, conservative expense accounts and entertainment allowances, a lean staff in the corporate office, scrutiny of budget requests, few executive perks, and so on. At Walmart, all the executive offices are simply decorated; executives are habitually frugal in their own actions, and they are zealous in their efforts to control costs and promote greater efficiency. At Nucor, one of the world's low-cost producers of steel products, executives fly coach class and use taxis at airports rather than limousines. Top executives must be alert to the fact that company personnel will be watching their behavior to see if their actions match their rhetoric. Hence, they need to make sure their current decisions and actions will be construed as consistent with the new cultural values and norms.[16]

Another category of symbolic actions includes holding ceremonial events to single out and honor people whose actions and performance exemplify what is called for in the new culture. Such events also provide an opportunity to celebrate each culture-change success. Executives sensitive to their role in promoting strategy–culture fit make a habit of appearing at ceremonial functions to praise individuals and groups that exemplify the desired behaviors. They show up at employee training programs to stress strategic priorities, values, ethical principles, and cultural norms. Every group gathering is seen as an opportunity to repeat and ingrain values, praise good deeds, expound on the merits of the new culture, and cite instances of how the new work practices and operating approaches have produced good results. Ceremonial events can also be used to drive home the commitment to changing culture. The late Steve Jobs, visionary co-founder of Apple, once countered resistance to change by dramatizing the death of "the old" with a coffin.

The use of symbols in culture building is widespread. Numerous businesses have employee-of-the-month awards. The military has a long-standing custom of awarding ribbons and medals for exemplary actions. Mary Kay Cosmetics awards an array of prizes ceremoniously to its beauty consultants for reaching various sales plateaus, including the iconic pink Cadillac.

How Long Does It Take to Change a Problem Culture?
Planting the seeds of a new culture and helping the culture grow strong roots require a determined, sustained effort by the chief executive and other senior managers. Changing a problem culture is never a short-term exercise; it takes time for a new culture to emerge and take root. And it takes even longer for a new culture to become deeply embedded. The bigger the organization and the greater the cultural shift needed to produce an execution-supportive fit, the longer it takes. In large companies, fixing a problem culture and instilling a new set of attitudes and behaviors can take two to five years. In fact, it is usually tougher to reform an entrenched problematic culture than it is to instill a strategy-supportive culture from scratch in a brand-new organization.

Illustration Capsule 12.2 discusses the approaches used at Goldman Sachs to change a culture that was impeding its efforts to recruit the best young talent.

Goldman Sachs was long considered one of the best financial services companies to work for, due to its prestige, high salaries, bonuses, and perks. Yet by 2014, Goldman was beginning to have trouble recruiting the best and brightest MBAs at top business schools. Part of this was due to the banking crisis of 2008–2009 and the scandals that continued to plague the industry year after year, tarnishing the industry's reputation. But another reason was a change in the values and aspirations of the younger generation that made banking culture far less appealing than that of consulting, technology, and start-up companies. Newly minted MBAs were no longer as willing to accept the grueling hours and unpredictable schedules that were the norm in investment banking. They wanted to derive meaning and purpose from their work and prized work/life balance over monetary gain. The tech industry was known for fun, youth-oriented, and collaborative working environments, while the excitement and promise of entrepreneurial ventures offered much appeal. Goldman found itself competing with Amazon, Google, Microsoft, and Facebook as well as with start-ups for the best young talent—and losing out.

Goldman's problem was compounded by the fact that its culture was regarded as stuffy and stodgy—qualities not likely to appeal to the young, particularly when contrasted with the hip cultures of tech and start-up companies. Further, it had always been slow-moving in terms of implementing organizational change. Recognizing the problem, the leadership at Goldman attempted to pivot sharply, asking its executives to think of Goldman as a tech company, complete with the associated values. The Chief Learning Office at Goldman Sachs was put in charge of the effort to transform its culture and began

©Michael Nagle/Bloomberg via Getty Images

taking deliberate steps to enact changes. Buy-in was sought from the full C-suite—the leadership team at the very top of the firm. To foster a more familial atmosphere at work, the company began with small steps, such as setting up sports leagues and encouraging regular team happy hours. More significantly, they instituted more employee-friendly work schedules and policies, more accommodating of work-life balance. They liberalized their parental leave policies, provided greater flexibility in work schedules, and enacted protections for interns and junior bankers designed to limit their working hours. They also overhauled their performance review and promotion systems as well as their recruiting practices and policies regarding diversity. Although cultural change never comes swiftly, by 2017 results were apparent even to outside observers. That year, the career website Vault.com named Goldman Sachs as the best banking firm to work for, noting that when it came to workplace policies, Goldman led the industry.

Sources: http://www.goldmansachs.com/careers/blog/posts/goldman-sachs-vault-2017.html; http://sps.columbia.edu/news/how-goldman-sachs-drives-culture-change-in-the-financial-industry.

LEADING THE STRATEGY EXECUTION PROCESS

For an enterprise to execute its strategy in truly proficient fashion, top executives must take the lead in the strategy implementation process and personally drive the pace of progress. They have to be out in the field, seeing for themselves how well operations are going, gathering information firsthand, and gauging the progress being made. Proficient strategy execution requires company managers to be diligent and adept in spotting problems, learning what obstacles lay in the path of good execution, and then clearing the way for progress—the goal must be to produce better

• LO 12-4

Explain what constitutes effective managerial leadership in achieving superior strategy execution.

results speedily and productively. There must be constructive, but unrelenting, pressure on organizational units to (1) demonstrate excellence in all dimensions of strategy execution and (2) do so on a consistent basis—ultimately, that's what will enable a well-crafted strategy to achieve the desired performance results.

The specifics of how to implement a strategy and deliver the intended results must start with understanding the requirements for good strategy execution. Afterward comes a diagnosis of the organization's preparedness to execute the strategic initiatives and decisions on how to move forward and achieve the targeted results.[17] In general, leading the drive for good strategy execution and operating excellence calls for three actions on the part of the managers in charge:

- Staying on top of what is happening and closely monitoring progress.
- Putting constructive pressure on the organization to execute the strategy well and achieve operating excellence.
- Initiating corrective actions to improve strategy execution and achieve the targeted performance results.

Staying on Top of How Well Things Are Going

To stay on top of how well the strategy execution process is going, senior executives have to tap into information from a wide range of sources. In addition to communicating regularly with key subordinates and reviewing the latest operating results, watching the competitive reactions of rival firms, and visiting with key customers and suppliers to get their perspectives, they usually visit various company facilities and talk with many different company personnel at many different organizational levels—a technique often labeled **management by walking around (MBWA).** Most managers attach great importance to spending time with people at company facilities, asking questions, listening to their opinions and concerns, and gathering firsthand information about how well aspects of the strategy execution process are going. Facilities tours and face-to-face contacts with operating-level employees give executives a good grasp of what progress is being made, what problems are being encountered, and whether additional resources or different approaches may be needed. Just as important, MBWA provides opportunities to give encouragement, lift spirits, focus attention on key priorities, and create some excitement—all of which generate positive energy and help boost strategy execution efforts.

Jeff Bezos, Amazon's CEO, is noted for his practice of MBWA, firing off a battery of questions when he tours facilities, and insisting that Amazon managers spend time in the trenches with their people to prevent getting disconnected from the reality of what's happening. Walmart executives have had a long-standing practice of spending two to three days every week visiting Walmart's stores and talking with store managers and employees. Sam Walton, Walmart's founder, insisted, "The key is to get out into the store and listen to what the associates have to say." Jack Welch, the highly effective former CEO of General Electric, not only made it a priority to personally visit GE operations and talk with major customers but also routinely spent time exchanging information and ideas with GE managers from all over the world who were attending classes at the company's leadership development center near GE's headquarters.

Many manufacturing executives make a point of strolling the factory floor to talk with workers and meeting regularly with union officials. Some managers operate out of open cubicles in big spaces filled with open cubicles for other personnel so that they can interact easily and frequently with co-workers. Managers at some companies host weekly get-togethers (often on Friday afternoons) to create a regular opportunity for information to flow freely between down-the-line employees and executives.

Mobilizing the Effort for Excellence in Strategy Execution

Part of the leadership task in mobilizing organizational energy behind the drive for good strategy execution entails nurturing a results-oriented work climate, where performance standards are high and a spirit of achievement is pervasive. Successfully leading the effort is typically characterized by such leadership actions and managerial practices as

- *Treating employees as valued partners.* Some companies symbolize the value of individual employees and the importance of their contributions by referring to them as cast members (Disney), crew members (McDonald's), job owners (Graniterock), partners (Starbucks), or associates (Walmart, LensCrafters, W. L. Gore, Edward Jones, Publix Supermarkets, and Marriott International). Very often, there is a strong company commitment to training each employee thoroughly, offering attractive compensation and benefits, emphasizing promotion from within and promising career opportunities, providing a high degree of job security, and otherwise making employees feel well treated and valued.

- *Fostering an esprit de corps that energizes organization members.* The task here is to skillfully use people-management practices calculated to build morale, foster pride in working for the company, promote teamwork and collaborative group effort, win the emotional commitment of individuals and organizational units to what the company is trying to accomplish, and inspire company personnel to do their best in achieving good results.[18]

- *Using empowerment to help create a fully engaged workforce.* Top executives—and, to some degree, the enterprise's entire management team—must seek to engage the full organization in the strategy execution effort. A fully engaged workforce, where individuals bring their best to work every day, is necessary to produce great results.[19] So is having a group of dedicated managers committed to making a difference in their organization. The two best things top-level executives can do to create a fully engaged organization are (1) delegate authority to middle and lower-level managers to get the strategy execution process moving and (2) empower rank-and-file employees to act on their own initiative. Operating excellence requires that everybody contribute ideas, exercise initiative and creativity in performing his or her work, and have a desire to do things in the best possible manner.

- *Nurturing a results-oriented work climate and clearly communicating an expectation that company personnel are to give their best in achieving performance targets.* Managers must make it abundantly clear that they expect all company personnel to put forth every effort to meet performance targets. But executives cannot expect directives to "try harder" to produce the desired outcomes in the absence of a results-oriented work climate. Nor can they expect innovative improvements in operations if they do no more than exhort people to "be creative." Rather, they must foster a strong culture with high performance standards and where innovative ideas and experimentation with new ways of doing things can blossom and thrive.

- *Using the tools of benchmarking, best practices, business process reengineering, TQM, and Six Sigma to focus attention on continuous improvement.* These are proven approaches to getting better operating results and facilitating better strategy execution.

- *Using the full range of motivational techniques and compensation incentives to inspire company personnel and reward high performance.* Individuals and groups should be strongly encouraged to brainstorm, let their imaginations fly in all directions, and come up with proposals for improving the way that things are done. This means giving company personnel enough autonomy to stand out, excel, and contribute. And it means that the rewards for successful champions of new ideas and operating improvements should be large and visible. It is particularly important that people who champion an unsuccessful idea are not punished or sidelined but, rather, encouraged to try again. Finding great ideas requires taking risks and recognizing that many ideas won't pan out.

- *Celebrating individual, group, and company successes.* Top management should miss no opportunity to express respect for individual employees and appreciation of extraordinary individual and group effort.[20] Companies like Google, Mary Kay, Tupperware, and McDonald's actively seek out reasons and opportunities to give pins, ribbons, buttons, badges, and medals for good showings by average performers—the idea being to express appreciation and give a motivational boost to people who stand out in doing ordinary jobs. At Kimpton Hotels and Restaurants, employees who create special moments for guests are rewarded with "Kimpton Moment" tokens that can be redeemed for paid days off, gift certificates to restaurants, flat-screen TVs, and other prizes. Cisco Systems and 3M Corporation make a point of ceremoniously honoring individuals who believe so strongly in their ideas that they take it on themselves to hurdle the bureaucracy, maneuver their projects through the system, and turn them into improved services, new products, or even new businesses.

While leadership efforts to instill a results-oriented, high-performance culture usually accentuate the positive, negative consequences for poor performance must be in play as well. Managers whose units consistently perform poorly must be replaced. Low-performing employees must be weeded out or at least employed in ways better suited to their aptitudes. Average performers should be candidly counseled that they have limited career potential unless they show more progress in the form of additional effort, better skills, and improved ability to execute the strategy well and deliver good results.

Leading the Process of Making Corrective Adjustments

There comes a time at every company when managers have to fine-tune or overhaul the approaches to strategy execution since no action plan for executing strategy can foresee all the problems that will arise. Clearly, when a company's strategy execution effort is not delivering good results, it is the leader's responsibility to step forward and initiate corrective actions, although sometimes it must be recognized that unsatisfactory performance may be due as much or more to flawed strategy as to weak strategy execution.[21]

Success in making corrective adjustments hinges on (1) a thorough analysis of the situation, (2) the exercise of good business judgment in deciding what actions to take, and (3) good implementation of the corrective actions that are initiated. Successful managers are skilled in getting an organization back on track rather quickly. They (and their staffs) are good at discerning what adjustments to make and in bringing them to a successful conclusion. Managers who struggle to show measurable progress in implementing corrective actions in a timely fashion are candidates for being replaced.

The *process* of making corrective adjustments in strategy execution varies according to the situation. In a crisis, taking remedial action quickly is of the essence. But it still takes time to review the situation, examine the available data, identify and evaluate options (crunching whatever numbers may be appropriate to determine which options are likely to generate the best outcomes), and decide what to do. When the situation allows managers to proceed more deliberately in deciding when to make changes and what changes to make, most managers seem to prefer a process of incrementally solidifying commitment to a particular course of action.[22] The process that managers go through in deciding on corrective adjustments is essentially the same for both proactive and reactive changes: They sense needs, gather information, broaden and deepen their understanding of the situation, develop options and explore their pros and cons, put forth action proposals, strive for a consensus, and finally formally adopt an agreed-on course of action. The time frame for deciding what corrective changes to initiate can be a few hours, a few days, a few weeks, or even a few months if the situation is particularly complicated.

The challenges of making the right corrective adjustments and leading a successful strategy execution effort are, without question, substantial.[23] There's no generic, by-the-books procedure to follow. Because each instance of executing strategy occurs under different organizational circumstances, the managerial agenda for executing strategy always needs to be situation-specific. But the job is definitely doable. Although there is no prescriptive answer to the question of exactly what to do, any of several courses of action may produce good results. As we said at the beginning of Chapter 10, executing strategy is an action-oriented task that challenges a manager's ability to lead and direct organizational change, create or reinvent business processes, manage and motivate people, and achieve performance targets. If you now better understand what the challenges are, what tasks are involved, what tools can be used to aid the managerial process of executing strategy, and why the action agenda for implementing and executing strategy sweeps across so many aspects of managerial work, then the discussions in Chapters 10, 11, and 12 have been a success.

A FINAL WORD ON LEADING THE PROCESS OF CRAFTING AND EXECUTING STRATEGY

In practice, it is hard to separate leading the process of executing strategy from leading the other pieces of the strategy process. As we emphasized in Chapter 2, the job of crafting and executing strategy consists of five interrelated and linked stages, with much looping and recycling to fine-tune and adjust the strategic vision, objectives, strategy, and implementation approaches to fit one another and to fit changing circumstances. The process is continuous, and the conceptually separate acts of crafting and executing strategy blur together in real-world situations. *The best tests of good strategic leadership are whether the company has a good strategy (given its internal and external situation), whether the strategy is being competently executed, and whether the enterprise is meeting or beating its performance targets.* If these three conditions exist, then there is every reason to conclude that the company has good strategic leadership and is a well-managed enterprise.

KEY POINTS

1. Corporate culture is the character of a company's internal work climate—the shared values, ingrained attitudes, core beliefs and company traditions that determine norms of behavior, accepted work practices, and styles of operating. A company's culture is important because it influences the organization's actions, its approaches to conducting business, and ultimately its performance in the marketplace. It can be thought of as the company's organizational DNA.

2. The key features of a company's culture include the company's values and ethical standards, its approach to people management, its work atmosphere and company spirit, how its personnel interact, the strength of peer pressure to conform to norms, the behaviors awarded through incentives (both financial and symbolic), the traditions and oft-repeated "myths," and its manner of dealing with stakeholders.

3. A company's culture is grounded in and shaped by its core values and ethical standards. Core values and ethical principles serve two roles in the culture-building process: (1) They foster a work climate in which employees share common and strongly held convictions about how company business is to be conducted, and (2) they provide company personnel with guidance about the manner in which they are to do their jobs—which behaviors and ways of doing things are approved (and expected) and which are out-of-bounds. They serve as yardsticks for gauging the appropriateness of particular actions, decisions, and behaviors.

4. Company cultures vary widely in strength and influence. Some cultures are *strong* and have a big impact on a company's practices and behavioral norms. Others are *weak* and have comparatively little influence on company operations.

5. Strong company cultures can have either positive or negative effects on strategy execution. When they are in sync with the chosen strategy and well matched to the behavioral requirements of the company's strategy implementation plan, they can be a powerful aid to strategy execution. A culture that is grounded in the types of actions and behaviors that are conducive to good strategy execution assists the effort in three ways:

   • By focusing employee attention on the actions that are most important in the strategy execution effort.

   • By inducing peer pressure for employees to contribute to the success of the strategy execution effort.

   • By energizing employees, deepening their commitment to the strategy execution effort, and increasing the productivity of their efforts

   It is thus in management's best interest to dedicate considerable effort to establishing a strongly implanted corporate culture that encourages behaviors and work practices conducive to good strategy execution.

6. Strong corporate cultures that are conducive to good strategy execution are healthy cultures. So are high-performance cultures and adaptive cultures. The latter are particularly important in dynamic environments. Strong cultures can also be unhealthy. The five types of unhealthy cultures are those that are (1) change-resistant, (2) heavily politicized, (3) insular and inwardly focused, (4) ethically unprincipled and infused with greed, and (5) composed of incompatible, clashing subcultures. All five impede good strategy execution.

7. Changing a company's culture, especially a strong one with traits that don't fit a new strategy's requirements, is a tough and often time-consuming challenge. Changing a culture requires competent leadership at the top. It requires making a compelling case for cultural change and employing both symbolic actions and substantive actions that unmistakably indicate serious and credible commitment on the part of top management. The more that culture-driven actions and behaviors fit what's needed for good strategy execution, the less managers must depend on policies, rules, procedures, and supervision to enforce what people should and should not do.

8. Leading the drive for good strategy execution and operating excellence calls for three actions on the part of the manager in charge:

   • Staying on top of what is happening and closely monitoring progress. This is often accomplished through management by walking around (MBWA).

   • Mobilizing the effort for excellence in strategy execution by putting constructive pressure on the organization to execute the strategy well.

   • Initiating corrective actions to improve strategy execution and achieve the targeted performance results.

ASSURANCE OF LEARNING EXERCISES

1. Salesforce.com earned the top spot on Fortune's list of the Best Companies to Work for in 2018, having been on the list for over 10 years. Use your university library's resources to see what their company culture and values might have to do with this. What are the key features of its culture? Do features of Salesforce.com's culture influence the company's ethical practices? If so, how?

   connect LO 12-1

2. Based on what you learned about Salesforce.com from answering the previous question, how do you think the company's culture affects its ability to execute strategy and operate with excellence?

   LO 12-2

3. Illustration Capsule 12.1 discusses Epic's strategy-supportive corporate culture. What are the standout features of Epic's corporate culture? How does Epic's culture contribute to its winning best-in-class awards year after year? How does the company's culture make Epic a good place to work?

   connect LO 12-1, LO 12-2

4. If you were an executive at a company that had a pervasive yet problematic culture, what steps would you take to change it? Using Google Scholar or your university library's access to EBSCO, LexisNexis, or other databases, search for recent articles in business publications on "culture change." What role did the executives play in the culture change? How does this differ from what you would have done to change the culture?

   LO 12-3

5. Leading the strategy execution process involves staying on top of the situation and monitoring progress, putting constructive pressure on the organization to achieve operating excellence, and initiating corrective actions to improve the execution effort. Using your university library's resources discuss a recent example of how a company's managers have demonstrated the kind of effective internal leadership needed for superior strategy execution.

   LO 12-4

EXERCISE FOR SIMULATION PARTICIPANTS

LO 12-1, LO 12-2   1.   If you were making a speech to company personnel, what would you tell employees about the kind of corporate culture you would like to have at your company? What specific cultural traits would you like your company to exhibit? Explain.

LO 12-2   2.   What core values would you want to ingrain in your company's culture? Why?

LO 12-3, LO 12-4   3.   Following each decision round, do you and your co-managers make corrective adjustments in either your company's strategy or the way the strategy is being executed? List at least three such adjustments you made in the most recent decision round. What hard evidence (in the form of results relating to your company's performance in the most recent year) can you cite that indicates that the various corrective adjustments you made either succeeded at improving or failed to improve your company's performance?

LO 12-4   4.   What would happen to your company's performance if you and your co-managers stick with the status quo and fail to make any corrective adjustments after each decision round?

ENDNOTES

[1] Jennifer A. Chatham and Sandra E. Cha, "Leading by Leveraging Culture," *California Management Review* 45, no. 4 (Summer 2003), pp. 20–34; Edgar Shein, *Organizational Culture and Leadership: A Dynamic View* (San Francisco, CA: Jossey-Bass, 1992).
[2] T. E. Deal and A. A. Kennedy, *Corporate Cultures: The Rites and Rituals of Corporate Life* (Harmondsworth, UK: Penguin, 1982).
[3] Joanne Reid and Victoria Hubbell, "Creating a Performance Culture," *Ivey Business Journal* 69, no. 4 (March–April 2005), p. 1.
[4] Ibid.
[5] John P. Kotter and James L. Heskett, *Corporate Culture and Performance* (New York: Free Press, 1992), p. 7. See also Robert Goffee and Gareth Jones, *The Character of a Corporation* (New York: HarperCollins, 1998).
[6] Joseph L. Badaracco, *Defining Moments: When Managers Must Choose between Right and Wrong* (Boston: Harvard Business School Press, 1997); Joe Badaracco and Allen P. Webb, "Business Ethics: A View from the Trenches," *California Management Review* 37, no. 2 (Winter 1995), pp. 8–28; Patrick E. Murphy, "Corporate Ethics Statements: Current Status and Future Prospects," *Journal of Business Ethics* 14 (1995), pp. 727–740; Lynn Sharp Paine, "Managing for Organizational Integrity," *Harvard Business Review* 72, no. 2 (March–April 1994), pp. 106–117.
[7] Emily F. Carasco and Jang B. Singh, "The Content and Focus of the Codes of Ethics of the World's Largest Transnational Corporations," *Business and Society Review* 108, no. 1 (January 2003), pp. 71–94; Patrick E. Murphy, "Corporate Ethics Statements: Current Status and Future Prospects," *Journal of Business Ethics* 14 (1995), pp. 727–740; John Humble, David Jackson, and Alan Thomson, "The Strategic Power of Corporate Values," *Long Range Planning* 27, no. 6 (December 1994), pp.

28–42; Mark S. Schwartz, "A Code of Ethics for Corporate Codes of Ethics," *Journal of Business Ethics* 41, no. 1–2 (November–December 2002), pp. 27-43.
[8] Terrence E. Deal and Allen A. Kennedy, *Corporate Cultures* (Reading, MA: Addison-Wesley, 1982); Terrence E. Deal and Allen A. Kennedy, *The New Corporate Cultures: Revitalizing the Workplace after Downsizing, Mergers, and Reengineering* (Cambridge, MA: Perseus, 1999).
[9] Vijay Sathe, *Culture and Related Corporate Realities* (Homewood, IL: Irwin, 1985).
[10] Avan R. Jassawalla and Hemant C. Sashittal, "Cultures That Support Product-Innovation Processes," *Academy of Management Executive* 16, no. 3 (August 2002), pp. 42–54.
[11] Kotter and Heskett, *Corporate Culture and Performance*, p. 5.
[12] Reid and Hubbell, "Creating a Performance Culture," pp. 1–5.
[13] Jay B. Barney and Delwyn N. Clark, *Resource-Based Theory: Creating and Sustaining Competitive Advantage* (New York: Oxford University Press, 2007), chap. 4.
[14] Rosabeth Moss Kanter, "Transforming Giants," *Harvard Business Review* 86, no. 1 (January 2008), pp. 43–52.
[15] Kurt Eichenwald, *Conspiracy of Fools: A True Story* (New York: Broadway Books, 2005).
[16] Judy D. Olian and Sara L. Rynes, "Making Total Quality Work: Aligning Organizational Processes, Performance Measures, and Stakeholders," *Human Resource Management* 30, no. 3 (Fall 1991), p. 324.
[17] Larry Bossidy and Ram Charan, *Confronting Reality: Doing What Matters to Get Things Right* (New York: Crown Business, 2004); Larry Bossidy and Ram Charan, *Execution: The Discipline of Getting Things Done* (New York: Crown Business, 2002); John P. Kotter, "Leading Change: Why Transformation Efforts Fail," *Harvard Business Review* 73,

no. 2 (March–April 1995), pp. 59–67; Thomas M. Hout and John C. Carter, "Getting It Done: New Roles for Senior Executives," *Harvard Business Review* 73, no. 6 (November–December 1995), pp. 133–145; Sumantra Ghoshal and Christopher A. Bartlett, "Changing the Role of Top Management: Beyond Structure to Processes," *Harvard Business Review* 73, no. 1 (January–February 1995), pp. 86–96.
[18] For a more in-depth discussion of the leader's role in creating a results-oriented culture that nurtures success, see Benjamin Schneider, Sarah K. Gunnarson, and Kathryn Niles-Jolly, "Creating the Climate and Culture of Success," *Organizational Dynamics,* Summer 1994, pp. 17–29.
[19] Michael T. Kanazawa and Robert H. Miles, *Big Ideas to Big Results* (Upper Saddle River, NJ: FT Press, 2008).
[20] Jeffrey Pfeffer, "Producing Sustainable Competitive Advantage through the Effective Management of People," *Academy of Management Executive* 9, no.1 (February 1995), pp. 55–69.
[21] Cynthia A. Montgomery, "Putting Leadership Back into Strategy," *Harvard Business Review* 86, no. 1 (January 2008), pp. 54–60.
[22] James Brian Quinn, *Strategies for Change: Logical Incrementalism* (Homewood, IL: Irwin, 1980).
[23] Daniel Goleman, "What Makes a Leader," *Harvard Business Review* 76, no. 6 (November–December 1998), pp. 92–102; Ronald A. Heifetz and Donald L. Laurie, "The Work of Leadership," *Harvard Business Review* 75, no. 1 (January–February 1997), pp. 124–134; Charles M. Farkas and Suzy Wetlaufer, "The Ways Chief Executive Officers Lead," *Harvard Business Review* 74, no. 3 (May–June 1996), pp. 110–122; Michael E. Porter, Jay W. Lorsch, and Nitin Nohria, "Seven Surprises for New CEOs," *Harvard Business Review* 82, no. 10 (October 2004), pp. 62–72.

PART 2

Cases in Crafting and
Executing Strategy

Mystic Monk Coffee

David L. Turnipseed

University of South Alabama

As Father Daniel Mary, the prior of the Carmelite Order of monks in Clark, Wyoming, walked to chapel to preside over Mass, he noticed the sun glistening across the four-inch snowfall from the previous evening. Snow in June was not unheard of in Wyoming, but the late snowfall and the bright glow of the rising sun made him consider the opposing forces accompanying change and how he might best prepare his monastery to achieve his vision of creating a new Mount Carmel in the Rocky Mountains. His vision of transforming the small brotherhood of 13 monks living in a small home used as makeshift rectory into a 500-acre monastery that would include accommodations for 30 monks, a Gothic church, a convent for Carmelite nuns, a retreat center for lay visitors, and a hermitage presented a formidable challenge. However, as a former high school football player, boxer, bull rider, and man of great faith, Father Prior Daniel Mary was unaccustomed to shrinking from a challenge.

Father Prior had identified a nearby ranch for sale that met the requirements of his vision perfectly, but its current listing price of $8.9 million presented a financial obstacle to creating a place of prayer, worship, and solitude in the Rockies. The Carmelites had received a $250,000 donation that could be used toward the purchase, and the monastery had earned nearly $75,000 during the first year of its Mystic Monk coffee-roasting operations, but more money would be needed. The coffee roaster used to produce packaged coffee sold to Catholic consumers at the Mystic Monk Coffee website was reaching its capacity, but a larger roaster could be purchased for $35,000. Also, local Cody, Wyoming, business owners had begun a foundation for those wishing to donate to the monks' cause. Father Prior Daniel Mary did not have a great deal of experience in business matters but considered to what extent the monastery could rely on its Mystic Monk Coffee operations to fund the purchase of the ranch. If Mystic Monk Coffee was capable of making the vision a reality, what were the next steps in turning the coffee into land?

THE CARMELITE MONKS OF WYOMING

Carmelites are a religious order of the Catholic Church that was formed by men who traveled to the Holy Land as pilgrims and crusaders and had chosen to remain near Jerusalem to seek God. The men established their hermitage at Mount Carmel because of its beauty, seclusion, and biblical importance as the site where Elijah stood against King Ahab and the false prophets of Jezebel to prove Jehovah to be the one true God. The Carmelites led a life of solitude, silence, and prayer at Mount Carmel before eventually returning to Europe and becoming a recognized order of the Catholic Church. The size of the Carmelite Order varied widely throughout the centuries with its peak in the 1600s and stood at approximately 2,200 friars living on all inhabited continents at the beginning of the 21st century.

The Wyoming Carmelite monastery was founded by Father Daniel Mary, who lived as a Carmelite hermit in Minnesota before moving to Clark, Wyoming, to establish the new monastery. The Wyoming Carmelites were a cloistered order and were allowed to leave the monastery only by permission of the bishop for medical needs or the death of a family member. The Wyoming monastery's abbey bore little resemblance to the great stone cathedrals and monasteries of Europe and was confined to a rectory that had once been a four-bedroom ranch-style home and an adjoining 42 acres of land that had been donated to the monastery.

There were 13 monks dedicated to a life of prayer and worship in the Wyoming Carmelite monastery. Since the founding of the monastery six years ago, there had been more than 500 inquiries from young men considering becoming a Wyoming Carmelite. Father Prior Daniel Mary wished to eventually have 30 monks who would join the brotherhood at ages 19 to 30 and live out their lives in the monastery. However, the selection criteria for acceptance into the monastery were rigorous, with the monks making certain that applicants understood the reality of the vows of obedience, chastity, and poverty and the sacrifices associated with living a cloistered religious life.

The Daily Activities of a Carmelite Monk

The Carmelite monks' day began at 4:10 a.m., when they arose and went to chapel for worship wearing traditional brown habits and handmade sandals. At about 6:00 a.m., the monks rested and contemplated in silence for one hour before Father Prior began morning Mass. After Mass, the monks went about their manual labors. In performing their labors, each brother had a special set of skills that enabled the monastery to independently maintain its operations. Brother Joseph Marie was an excellent mechanic, Brother Paul was a carpenter, Brother Peter Joseph (Brother Cook) worked in the kitchen, and five-foot, four-inch Brother Simon Mary (Little Monk) was the secretary to Father Daniel Mary. Brother Elias, affectionately known as Brother Java, was Mystic Monk Coffee's master roaster, although he was not a coffee drinker.

Each monk worked up to six hours per day; however, the monks' primary focus was spiritual, with eight hours of each day spent in prayer. At 11:40 a.m., the monks stopped work and went to Chapel. Afterward they had lunch, cleaned the dishes, and went back to work. At 3:00 p.m., the hour that Jesus was believed to have died on the cross, work stopped

again for prayer and worship. The monks then returned to work until the bell was rung for Vespers (evening prayer). After Vespers, the monks had an hour of silent contemplation, an evening meal, and more prayers before bedtime.

The New Mount Carmel

Soon after arriving in Wyoming, Father Daniel Mary had formed the vision of acquiring a large parcel of land—a new Mount Carmel—and building a monastery with accommodations for 30 monks, a retreat center for lay visitors, a Gothic church, a convent for Carmelite nuns, and a hermitage. In a letter to supporters posted on the monastery's website, Father Daniel Mary succinctly stated his vision: "We beg your prayers, your friendship and your support that this vision, our vision may come to be that Mount Carmel may be refounded in Wyoming's Rockies for the glory of God."

The brothers located a 496-acre ranch for sale that would satisfy all of the requirements to create a new Mount Carmel. The Irma Lake Ranch was located about 21 miles outside Cody, Wyoming, and included a remodeled 17,800-square-foot residence, a 1,700-square-foot caretaker house, a 2,950-square-foot guesthouse, a hunting cabin, a dairy and horse barn, and forested land. The ranch was at the end of a seven-mile-long private gravel road and was bordered on one side by the private Hoodoo Ranch (100,000 acres) and on the other by the Shoshone National Park (2.4 million acres). Although the asking price was $8.9 million, the monks believed they would be able to acquire the property through donations and the profits generated by the monastery's Mystic Monk Coffee operations. The $250,000 donation they had received from an individual wishing to support the Carmelites could be applied toward whatever purpose the monks chose. Additionally, a group of Cody business owners had formed the New Mount Carmel Foundation to help the monks raise funds.

OVERVIEW OF THE COFFEE INDUSTRY

About 150 million consumers in the United States drank coffee, with 89 percent of U.S. coffee drinkers brewing their own coffee at home rather than purchasing ready-to-drink coffee at coffee shops and restaurants such as Starbucks, Dunkin' Donuts, or

McDonald's. Packaged coffee for home brewing was easy to find in any grocery store and typically carried a retail price of $4 to $6 for a 12-ounce package. About 30 million coffee drinkers in the United States preferred premium-quality specialty coffees that sold for $7 to $10 per 12-ounce package. Specialty coffees were made from high-quality Arabica beans instead of the mix of low-quality Arabica beans and bitter, less flavorful Robusta beans that makers of value brands used. The wholesale price of Robusta coffee beans averaged $1.15 per pound, while mild Columbian Arabica wholesale prices averaged $1.43 per pound.

Prior to the 1990s, the market for premium-quality specialty coffees barely existed in the United States, but Howard Schultz's vision for Starbucks of bringing the Italian espresso bar experience to America helped specialty coffees become a large and thriving segment of the industry. The company's pursuit of its mission, "To inspire and nurture the human spirit—one person, one cup, and one neighborhood at a time," had allowed Starbucks to become an iconic brand in most parts of the world. The company's success had given rise to a number of competing specialty coffee shops and premium brands of packaged specialty coffee, including Seattle's Best, Millstone, Green Mountain Coffee Roasters, and First Colony Coffee and Tea. Some producers such as First Colony had difficulty gaining shelf space in supermarkets and concentrated on private-label roasting and packaging for fine department stores and other retailers wishing to have a proprietary brand of coffee.

Specialty coffees sold under premium brands might have been made from shade-grown or organically grown coffee beans, or have been purchased from a grower belonging to a World Fair Trade Organization (WFTO) cooperative. WFTO cooperative growers were paid above-market prices to better support the cost of operating their farms—for example, WFTO-certified organic wholesale prices averaged $1.55 per pound. Many consumers who purchased specialty coffees were willing to pay a higher price for organic, shade-grown, or fair trade coffee because of their personal health or social concerns—organic coffees were grown without the use of synthetic fertilizers or pesticides, shade-grown coffee plants were allowed to grow beneath the canopies of larger indigenous trees, and fair trade pricing made it easier for farmers in developing countries to pay workers a living wage. The specialty coffee segment of the retail coffee industry had grown dramatically in the United States, with retail sales increasing from $8.3 billion to $13.5 billion during the last seven years. The retail sales of organic coffee accounted for about $1 billion of industry sales and had grown at an annual rate of 32 percent for each of the last seven years.

MYSTIC MONK COFFEE

Mystic Monk Coffee was produced using high-quality fair trade Arabica and fair trade/organic Arabica beans. The monks produced whole-bean and ground caffeinated and decaffeinated varieties in dark, medium, and light roasts and in different flavors. The most popular Mystic Monk flavors were Mystical Chants of Carmel, Cowboy Blend, Royal Rum Pecan, and Mystic Monk Blend. With the exception of sample bags, which carried a retail price of $2.99, all varieties of Mystic Monk Coffee were sold via the monastery's website (**www.mysticmonkcoffee.com**) in 12-ounce bags at a price of $9.95. All purchases from the website were delivered by United Parcel Service (UPS) or the U.S. Postal Service. Frequent customers were given the option of joining a "coffee club," which offered monthly delivery of one to six bags of preselected coffee. Purchases of three or more bags qualified for free shipping. The Mystic Monk Coffee website also featured T-shirts, gift cards, CDs featuring the monastery's Gregorian chants, and coffee mugs.

Mystic Monk Coffee's target market was the segment of the U.S. Catholic population who drank coffee and wished to support the monastery's mission. More than 69 million Americans were members of the Catholic Church—making it four times larger than the second-largest Christian denomination in the United States. An appeal to Catholics to "use their Catholic coffee dollar for Christ and his Catholic church" was published on the Mystic Monk Coffee website.

Mystic Monk Coffee–Roasting Operations

After the morning religious services and breakfast, Brother Java roasted the green coffee beans delivered each week from a coffee broker in Seattle, Washington. The monks paid the Seattle broker the prevailing wholesale price per pound, which fluctuated daily with global supply and demand. The capacity of Mystic Monk Coffee's roaster limited production to 540 pounds per day; production was also limited by time devoted to prayer, silent meditation, and worship. Demand for Mystic Monk Coffee had not yet exceeded the roaster's capacity, but the monastery planned to purchase a larger, 130-pound-per-hour roaster when demand further approached the current roaster's capacity. The monks had received a quote of $35,000 for the new larger roaster.

Marketing and Website Operations

Mystic Monk Coffee was promoted primarily by word of mouth among loyal customers in Catholic parishes across the United States. The majority of Mystic Monk's sales were made through its website, but on occasion telephone orders were placed with the monks' secretary, who worked outside the cloistered part of the monastery. Mystic Monk also offered secular website operators commissions on its sales through its Mystic Monk Coffee Affiliate Program, which placed banner ads and text ads on participating websites. Affiliate sites earned an 18 percent commission on sales made to customers who were directed to the Mystic Monk site from their site. The affiliate program's Share A Sale participation level allowed affiliates to refer new affiliates to Mystic Monk and earn 56 percent of the new affiliate's commission. The monks had also just recently expanded Mystic Monk's business model to include wholesale sales to churches and local coffee shops.

Mystic Monk's Financial Performance

At the conclusion of Mystic Monk Coffee's first year in operation, its sales of coffee and coffee accessories averaged about $56,500 per month. Its cost of sales averaged about 30 percent of revenues, inbound shipping costs accounted for 19 percent of revenues, and broker fees were 3 percent of revenues—for a total cost of goods sold of 52 percent. Operating expenses such as utilities, supplies, telephone, and website maintenance averaged 37 percent of revenues. Thus, Mystic Monk's net profit margin averaged 11 percent of revenues.

REALIZING THE VISION

During a welcome period of solitude before his evening meal, Father Prior Daniel Mary again contemplated the purchase of the Irma Lake Ranch. He realized that his vision of purchasing the ranch would require careful planning and execution. For the Wyoming Carmelites, coffee sales were a means of support from the outside world that might provide the financial resources to purchase the land. Father Prior understood that the cloistered monastic environment offered unique challenges to operating a business enterprise, but it also provided opportunities that were not available to secular businesses. He resolved to develop an execution plan that would enable Mystic Monk Coffee to minimize the effect of its cloistered monastic constraints, maximize the potential of monastic opportunities, and realize his vision of buying the Irma Lake Ranch.

Airbnb In 2018

John D. Varlaro
Johnson & Wales University

John E. Gamble
Texas A&M University–Corpus Christi

Airbnb was founded in 2008 when Brian Chesky and a friend decided to rent their apartment to guests for a local convention. To accommodate the guests, they used air mattresses and referred to it as the "Air Bed & Breakfast." It was that weekend when the idea—and the potential viability—of a peer-to-peer room-sharing business model was born. By 2018, Airbnb had seen immense growth and success in its 10-year existence. The room-sharing company had expanded to over 190 countries with more than 4 million listed properties, and had an estimated valuation of $31 billion. Airbnb seemed poised to revolutionize the hotel and tourism industry through its business model that allowed hosts to offer spare rooms or entire homes to potential guests, in a peer-reviewed digital marketplace.

This business model's success was leveraging what had become known as the sharing economy. Yet, with its growth and usage of a new business model, Airbnb was now faced with resistance, as city officials, owners and operators of hotels, motels, and bed and breakfasts were all crying foul. While these traditional brick-and-mortar establishments were subject to regulations and taxation, Airbnb hosts were able to circumvent and avoid such liabilities due to participation in Airbnb's digital marketplace. In other instances, Airbnb hosts had encountered legal issues due to city and state ordinances governing hotels and apartment leases. Stories of guests who would not leave and hosts needing to evict them because city regulations deemed the guests apartment leasees were beginning to make headlines.

As local city and government officials across the United States, and in countries like Japan, debated regulations concerning Airbnb, Brian Chesky needed to manage this new business model, which had led to phenomenal success within a new, sharing economy.

OVERVIEW OF ACCOMODATION MARKET

Hotels, motels, and bed and breakfasts competed within the larger, tourist accommodation market. All businesses operating within this sector offered lodging, but were differentiated by their amenities. Hotels and motels were defined as larger facilities accommodating guests in single or multiple rooms. Motels specifically offered smaller rooms with direct parking lot access from the unit and amenities such as laundry facilities to travelers who were using their own transportation. Motels might also be located closer to roadways, providing guests quicker and more convenient access to highways. It was also not uncommon for motel guests to segment a longer road trip as they commuted to a vacation destination, thereby potentially staying at several motels during their travel. Hotels, however, invested heavily in additional amenities as they competed for all segments of travelers. Amenities, including on-premise spa facilities and fine dining, were often offered by the hotel. Further, properties offering spectacular views, bolstering a hotel as the vacation destination, may contribute to significant operating costs. In total, wages, property, and utilities, as well as purchases such as food, accounted for 59 percent of the industry's total costs—see Exhibit 1.

EXHIBIT 1   Hotel, Motel, and Bed & Breakfast Industry Costs as Percentage of Revenue, 2017

Costs	Hotels/ Motels	Bed & Breakfasts
Wages	24%	19%
Purchases	27%	21%
Depreciation	10%	9%
Marketing	2%	2%
Rent and Utilities	8%	11%
Other	13%	22%

Source: www.ibisworld.com.

EXHIBIT 2   Major Market Segments for Hotels/Motels & Bed & Breakfast/Hostels Sectors, 2017

Market Segment	B&Bs*	Hotels**
Recreation	80%	70%
Business	12%	18%
Other, including meetings	8%	12%
Total	100%	100%

*The bed & breakfast market was primarily domestic.
**Includes both domestic and international travelers. Approximately 20% was associated with international travelers.

Source: www.ibisworld.com.

Bed and breakfasts, however, were much smaller, usually where owner-operators offered a couple of rooms within their own home to accommodate guests. The environment of the bed and breakfast—one of a cozy, home-like ambience—was what the guest desired when booking a room. Contrasted with the hotel or motel, a bed and breakfast offered a more personalized, yet quieter atmosphere. Further, many bed and breakfast establishments were in rural areas where the investment to establish a larger hotel may have been cost prohibitive, yet the location itself could be an attraction to tourists. In these areas individuals invested in a home and property, possibly with a historical background, to offer a bed and breakfast with great allure and ambience for the guests' experiences. Thus, the bed and breakfast competed through offering an ambience associated with a more rural, slower pace through which travelers connected with their hosts and the surrounding community. A comparison of the primary market segments of bed and breakfasts and hotels in 2017 is presented in Exhibit 2.

While differing in size and target consumer, all hotels, motels, and bed and breakfasts were subject to city, state, and federal regulations. These regulations covered areas such as the physical property and food safety, access for persons with disabilities, and even alcohol distribution. Owners and operators were subject to paying fees for different licenses to operate. Due to operating as a business, these properties and the associated revenues were also subject to state and federal taxation.

In addition to regulations, the need to construct physical locations prevented hotels and motels from expanding quickly, especially in new international markets. Larger chains tended to expand by purchasing preexisting physical locations, or through mergers and acquisitions, such as Marriott International Inc.'s acquisition of Starwood Hotels and Resorts Worldwide in 2016.

A BUSINESS MODEL FOR THE SHARING ECONOMY

Startup companies have been functioning in a space commonly referred to as the "sharing economy" for several years. According to Chesky, the previous model for the economy was based on ownership.[1] Thus, operating a business first necessitated ownership of the assets required to do business. Any spare capacity the business faced—either within production or service—was a direct result of the purchase of hard assets in the daily activity of conducting business.

Airbnb and other similar companies, however, operated through offering a technological platform, where individuals with spare capacity could offer their services. By leveraging the ubiquitous usage of smartphones and the continual decrease in technology costs, these companies provided a platform for individuals to instantly share a number of resources. Thus, a homeowner with a spare room could offer it for rent. Or, the car owner with spare time could offer [his or her] services a couple of nights a week as a taxi service. The individual simply signed up through the platform and began to offer the service or resource. The company then charged a small transaction fee as the service between both users was facilitated.

Within its business model, Airbnb received a percentage of what the host received for the room. For Airbnb, its revenues were decoupled from the considerable operating expenses of traditional lodging establishments and provided it with significantly smaller operating costs than hotels, motels, and bed and breakfasts. Rather than expenses related to owning and operating real estate properties, Airbnb's expenses were that of a technology company. Airbnb's business model, therefore, was based on the revenue-cost-margin structure of an online marketplace, rather than a lodging establishment. With an estimated 11 percent fee per room stay, it was reported that Airbnb achieved profitability for a first time in 2016.[2] Airbnb's revenues were estimated to increase from approximately $6 million in 2010 to a projected $1.2 billion in 2017—see Exhibit 3. However, it was announced in an annual investors' meeting that the company had recorded nearly $3 billion in revenue and earned over $90 million in profit in 2017.[3]

A CHANGE IN THE CONSUMER EXPERIENCE AND RATE

Airbnb, however, was not just leveraging technology. It was also leveraging the change in how the current consumer interacted with businesses. In conjunction with

this change seemed to be how the consumer had deemphasized ownership. Instead of focusing on ownership, consumers seemed to prefer sharing or renting. Other startup companies have been targeting these segments through subscription-based services and on-demand help. From luxury watches to clothing, experiencing—and not owning—assets seemed to be on the rise. Citing a more experiential-based economy, Chesky believed Airbnb guests desired a community and a closer relationship with the host—and there seemed to be support for this assertion.[4] A recent Goldman Sachs study showed that once someone used Airbnb, their preference for a traditional accommodation was greatly reduced.[5] The appeal of the company's value proposition with customers had allowed it to readily raise capital to support its growth, including an $850 million cash infusion in 2016 that raised its estimated valuation to $30 billion. A comparison of Airbnb's 2018 estimated market capitalization of $31 billion to the world's largest hoteliers is presented in Exhibit 4.

EXHIBIT 4   Market Capitalization Comparison, 2018 (in billions)

Competitor	Market Capitalization
Marriot International Inc.	$49
Airbnb	$31
Hilton Worldwide Holdings.	$25
Intercontinental Hotels Group	$11

Source: Yahoo Finance (accessed April 2018); "Airbnb Announces It Won't Go Public in 2018," *Business Insider,* http://www.businessinsider.com/airbnb-announces-it-wont-go-public-in-2018-2018-2 (accessed April 20, 2018).

EXHIBIT 3   Airbnb Estimated Revenue and Bookings Growth, 2010–2017 (in millions)

	2010	2011	2012	2013	2014	2015	2016	2017
Estimated Revenue	$6	$44	$132	$264	$436	$675	$945	$1,229
Estimated Bookings Growth	273%	666%	200%	100%	65%	55%	40%	30%

Source: Ali Rafat, "Airbnb's Revenues Will Cross Half Billion Mark in 2015," *Analysts Estimate,* March 25, 2015, skift.com/2015/03/25/airbnbs-revenues-will-cross-half-billion-mark-in-2015-analysts-estimate/.

Recognizing this shift in consumer preference, traditional brick-and-mortar operators were responding. Hilton was considering offering a hostel-like option to travelers.[6] Other entrepreneurs were constructing urban properties to specifically leverage Airbnb's platform and offer rooms only to Airbnb users, such as in Japan[7] where rent and hotel costs were extremely high.

To govern the community of hosts and guests, Airbnb had instituted a rating system. Popularized by companies such as Amazon, eBay, and Yelp, peer-to-peer ratings helped police quality. Both guests and hosts rated each other in Airbnb. This approach incentivized hosts to provide quality service, while encouraging guests to leave a property as they found it. Further, the peer-to-peer rating system greatly minimized the otherwise significant task and expense of Airbnb employees assessing and rating each individual participant within Airbnb's platform.

NOT PLAYING BY THE SAME RULES

Local and global businesses criticized Airbnb for what they claimed were unfair business practices and lobbied lawmakers to force the company to comply with lodging regulations. These concerns illuminated how due to its business model, Airbnb and its users seemed to not need to abide by these same regulations. This could have been concerning on many levels. For the guest, regulations exist for protection from unsafe accommodations. Fire codes and occupation limits all exist to prevent injury and death. Laws also exist to prevent discrimination, as traditional brick-and-mortar accommodations are barred from not providing lodging to guests based on race and other protected classes. But, there seemed to be evidence that Airbnb guests had faced such discrimination from hosts.[8]

Hosts might also expose themselves to legal and financial problems from accommodating guests. There had been stories of hosts needing to evict guests who would not leave, and due to local ordinances the guests were actually protected as apartment leasees. Other stories highlighted rooms and homes being damaged by huge parties given by Airbnb guests. Hosts might also be exposed to liability issues in the instance of an injury or even a death of a guest.

Finally, there were accusations of businesses using Airbnb's marketplace to own and operate accommodations without obtaining the proper licenses. These locations appeared to be individuals on the surface, but were actually businesses. And, because of Airbnb's platform, these pseudo-businesses could operate and generate revenue without meeting regulations or claiming revenues for taxation.

Airbnb continued to respond to some of these issues. A report was written and released by Airbnb in 2015 detailing both discrimination on its platform and how it would be mitigated. Airbnb also settled its lawsuit with San Francisco in early 2017. The city was demanding Airbnb enforce a city regulation requiring host registration, or incur significant fines. As part of the settlement, Airbnb agreed to offer more information on its hosts within the city.[9] And in 2018, Airbnb began partnering with local municipalities to help collect taxes automatically for rentals within their jurisdictions, helping to potentially recoup millions in lost tax revenue.[10][11]

"WE WISH TO BE REGULATED, THIS WOULD LEGITIMIZE US"

Recognizing that countries and local municipalities were responding to the local business owner and their constituents' concerns, Chesky and Airbnb have focused on mobilizing and advocating for consumers and business owners who utilize the app. Airbnb's website provided support for guests and hosts who wished to advocate for the site. A focal point of the advocacy emphasized how those particularly hit hard at the height of the recession relied on Airbnb to establish a revenue stream, and prevent the inevitable foreclosure and bankruptcy.

Yet, traditional brick-and-mortar establishments subject to taxation and regulations have continued to put pressure on government officials to level the playing field. "We wish to be regulated; this would legitimize us," Chesky remarked to Noah in the same interview on *The Daily Show*.[12] Proceeding forward and possibly preparing for a future public offering, Chesky would need to manage how the progressive business model—while fit for the new, global sharing economy—may not fit older, local regulations.

ENDNOTES

[1] Interview with Airbnb founder and CEO Brian Chesky, *The Daily Show with Trevor Noah, Comedy Central,* February 24, 2016.

[2] B. Stone and O. Zaleski, "Airbnb Enters the Land of Profitability," *Bloomberg,* January 26, 2017, https://www.bloomberg.com/news/articles/2017-01-26/airbnb-enters-the-land-of-profitability (accessed June 20, 2017).

[3] O. Zaleski, "Inside Airbnb's Battle to Stay Private," *Bloomberg.Com,* February 6, 2018, https://www.bloomberg.com/news/articles/2018-02-06/inside-airbnb-s-battle-to-stay-private (accessed April 20, 2018).

[4] Interview with Airbnb founder and CEO Brian Chesky, *The Daily Show with Trevor Noah,* Comedy Central, February 24, 2016.

[5] J. Verhage, "Goldman Sachs: More and More People Who Use Airbnb Don't Want to Go Back to Hotels," *Bloomberg,* February 26, 2016, www.bloomberg.com/news/articles/2016-02-16/goldman-sachs-more-and-more-people-who-use-airbnb-don-t-want-to-go-back-to-hotels.

[6] D. Fahmy, "Millennials Spending Power Has Hilton Weighing a 'Hostel-Like' Brand," March 8, 2016, *Bloomberg Businessweek,* www.bloomberg.com/businessweek.

[7] Y. Nakamura and M. Takahashi, "Airbnb Faces Major Threat in Japan, Its Fastest-Growing Market," *Bloomberg,* February 18, 2016, www.bloomberg.com/news/articles/2016-02-18/fastest-growing-airbnb-market-under-threat-as-japan-cracks-down.

[8] R. Greenfield, "Study Finds Racial Discrimination by Airbnb Hosts," *Bloomberg,* December 10, 2015, www.bloomberg.com/news/articles/2015-12-10/study-finds-racial-discrimination-by-airbnb-hosts.

[9] K. Benner, "Airbnb Adopts Rules to Fight Discrimination by Its Hosts," *New York Times,* (September 8, 2016) http://www.nytimes.com/2016/09/09/technology/airbnb-anti-discrimination-rules.html (accessed June 20, 2017).

[10] S. Cameron, "New TN Agreement Ensures $13M in Airbnb Rental Taxes Collected," *wjhl.com,* April 20, 2018, http://www.wjhl.com/local/new-tn-agreement-ensures-13m-in-airbnb-rental-taxes-collected/1131192392 (accessed April 20, 2018).

[11] "Duluth, Airbnb Make Deal on Lodging Tax Collection," *TwinCitiesPioneerPress,* April 19, 2018, https://www.twincities.com/2018/04/19/duluth-airbnb-make-deal-on-lodging-tax-collection/ (accessed April 20, 2018).

[12] Interview with Airbnb founder and CEO Brian Chesky, *The Daily Show with Trevor Noah,* Comedy Central, February 24, 2016.

Wil's Grill

Leonard R. Hostetter
Northern Arizona University

Nita Paden
Northern Arizona University

In January 2017, John Christ needed to make some decisions about his business, Wil's Grill. Not long ago, his dad had said, "Son, passion has gotten you here; not the money." Now, John needed to focus on "the money"—but which path should he take? He could expand his "street food" business, add a catering business, or do something else. John, who loved to make customers happy by serving them great healthy local food, recognized that he also needed to do so profitably.

BACKGROUND

John grew up on a ranch in Cave Creek, AZ, a small community northeast of Phoenix Arizona. His parents had food service and restaurant experience, and cooking and entertaining were an integral part of spending time with them. "By age 10," John recalled, "I could cook."

As a teenager, John bussed tables at a restaurant where his dad Wil worked. He also spent many mornings with his dad at a clay-bird sport shooting range near Cave Creek. When done, they needed to go elsewhere for lunch, since the range did not offer food or beverages. So, father and son worked out an agreement with the range owner to open a small food booth on-site, which they named "Wil's Grill." On a single grill they cooked burgers, fries, and served beverages. Wil taught his son the nuts and bolts of running the business: obtaining necessary permits and licenses, ordering food and supplies, shopping, transportation, inventorying, cooking, cleaning and most importantly, "treating customers as friends." Hospitality-driven service was a core value.

To celebrate his high school graduation in December 2009, John went on a 30-day backpacking excursion with the National Outdoor Leadership School in Wyoming, where he later recalled, "I honed my leadership skills there and this would serve me well in managing my future business."

In August 2010 Wil closed Wil's Grill when John enrolled at Northern Arizona University (NAU), in Flagstaff, about 120 miles north of Phoenix. At that time NAU enrolled about 23,000 students. John majored in Environmental Studies and also took classes in other areas, driven by "my inquisitive nature to learn as much as I could about the world around me." At the NAU School of Hotel and Restaurant Management John learned about the "clean food" movement—characterized by locally produced, organic foods and sustainable practices.[1] Clean food was healthy for both the planet and for people through production of efficient amounts of food, provision of leftovers to local shelters, and minimization of waste via biodegradable products and recycling practices.

Copyright ©2017 by the Case Research Journal and by Leonard R. Hostetter, Jr. and Nita Paden. This case study was prepared as the basis for classroom discussion rather than to illustrate either effective or ineffective handling of an administrative situation. The authors wish to thank John Lawrence, Brent Beal, Gina Grandy, Janis Gogan, Kathryn Savage, Lance Rohs, Joseph Anderson and the anonymous CRJ reviewers for their helpful suggestions on how to make this a more effective case. An earlier version of the case was presented at the 2016 Annual Meeting of the North American Case Research Association in Las Vegas, NV, United States.

Reprinted by permission from the Case Research Journal, copyright 2017 by the North American Case Research Association and Leonard R. Hostetter and Nita Paden.

WIL'S GRILL FLAGSTAFF

On a visit to Costa Rica in 2013, John and another NAU student, Karl Shilhanek, observed a vibrant "street food" community.[2] The "chicken lady," "kabob guy," and many other vendors served tasty, locally sourced and ready-to-eat fresh foods to local residents on the street, in the market, at a fair or other public place. Vendors sold "street food" from a portable stall, cart or food truck. John and Karl were inspired to start their own business, and the flames of Wil's Grill were reignited when they founded their own Wil's Grill in Flagstaff, AZ in January 2014.

The young men worked hard to get Wil's Grill off the ground. They wrote a business plan, secured the required permits and licenses, and set up as a general partnership. The two partners each invested $500 to get the business off the ground, and John's parents provided a $2,000 low-interest loan to help them purchase grilling equipment.

"We earned our stripes in the first year," John recalled. "We were hands-on with every aspect of the business." Karl focused on business strategy, marketing, and social media. He created a website that included their "clean food" menu, a mobile app, and a social media presence (on Facebook). John focused on operations and food preparation. He established relationships with five local food sources—including John's parents' Happy Mountain Farms. John believed his relationship with farms and producers "allowed me to have a unique understanding of the local supply chain."

Wil's Grill was highly portable, and targeted two main markets: (1) NAU students who were tired of chain-based fast food and wanted good, reasonably priced, late night food, and (2) community events, where organizers and customers wanted reasonably priced, clean, high-quality street food (in contrast, many street food vendors served manufacturer prepared and processed food). Operations included procuring food, preparing main courses and sides, transporting food to venues, and hiring temporary labor for serving and clean-up. Wil's Grill leased excess kitchen space in non-competing Flagstaff restaurants and bars, for prepping or cooking some food. Once the food was prepared in these locations it was served on tables with warming trays. For outdoor events, an event management company assigned Wil's Grill and other vendors to specific locations for specific hours. Most food (e.g., burgers, vegetables) was prepared on site, in view of customers.

Within four months John and Karl were able to pay off the $2,000 loan; since then, they had taken no further loans. The business was not profitable and they did not pay themselves a salary. John and Karl both worked second jobs to cover basic living expenses in 2014 and 2015, and their parents paid their college tuition. John lived a simple lifestyle with minimal financial obligations. They did not invest in a brick-and-mortar operation. Their "office" was as portable as the business.

In May 2014, Karl decided to relocate to Bellingham, WA, to be closer to his family. The breakup was amicable. John reestablished Wil's Grill as a sole proprietorship. Without his partner, at first John relied on "gut instinct" to run his business. Summer 2014 was tough, especially interviewing and hiring people. John felt this "was challenging. I didn't know what I was looking for." To hire temporary employees for street events he posted ads and networked with local bar owners. In June John hired what he referred to as "my first permanent part-time employee, Cody McCrae, a Hotel and Restaurant Management student." Cody had also "grown up in the kitchen." On his first day John gave him some instructions and left for another commitment. Working alone, Cody prepared sliders and coleslaw and proved himself. John placed a lot of trust in Cody, his first assistant manager. Cody flexed his hours and worked as business levels demanded.

Preparation and cooking was fast paced, whether in a leased kitchen or on the grill at an event. There were many 18- to 20-hour work days. John believed that he treated his temporary employees fairly, and therefore they were customer focused and wanted to work for him again. John also learned that he needed to define routines and flowchart responsibilities for some job positions, and to calculate staffing based on the estimated number of plates/day to be served.

STREET FOOD EVENTS

Street events involved lots of guess work, since both weather and attendance were unpredictable. John told a friend, "It's like rolling the dice to try and guess what food people will want." During the Flagstaff Pro Rodeo, Wil's Grill served 425 plates of barbecue per day, whereas for most events, 200 to 300 plates a day was typical. During the Rodeo, one employee quit. John recalled: "Lines formed quickly; everyone came to the booth around lunch time, hungry. We performed well–though there's always room for improvement." Getting food out quickly was most important, and food quality was more important than presentation or quantity.

Customers enjoyed watching food preparation, including the employee chatter. Pricing was customized for each event client (Exhibit 1 includes sample menus), so event revenue varied. A 200 to 300 plate day could gross $2,000 to $3,000, enough to sustain operations. Ongoing grill maintenance and food purchases were the main operating costs. Other expenses included liability insurance, permitting,

licensing, and payroll. John lived modestly, paid bills in cash, and avoided debt. He used his personal pick-up truck to transport food, and budgeted for fixed costs, irrespective of ebbs and flows of revenue. He estimated that profit margins averaged 18 percent to 25 percent–good for the street food business. Exhibit 2 shows that revenues for 2014 through 2016 totaled $129,000.

John had "learned on the fly"; he worked hard and wasn't discouraged by challenges. Feelings he experienced when customers told him how much they enjoyed his street food and his passion for clean food outweighed any discouragement. Street food was fun and fast-paced. John loved it.

EXHIBIT 1   Wil's Grill Sample Menu Items

Individual Serving Pricing			
Marinated Chicken & Veggie Kabob	$ 5.00	Pork & Brisket Sandwich	$12.00*
Grass-fed Hamburgers	$10.00	Grilled Chicken Legs	$ 5.00
Beer Brat with Sauerkraut	$ 8.00*	Loaded French Fries	$ 6.00*
Mac & Cheese, Cole Slaw, Beans	$ 3.00*	Gatorade	$ 2.00
Bottled Water	$ 1.00		

Source: John Christ – Owner, Wil's Grill (July 2017) – *Sample Street Food Menu.*

*Price varied based upon the vendor fee charged by event management.

Note: John targeted a minimum avg. ticket order of $10.00 and a 25%–35% food cost.

Example – BBQ Lunch Garden Party for 30 people			
Buffet Service *Sample Catering Menu*	**Quantity**	**Unit Price**	**Line Total**
Appetizer – Garden Fresh Bruschetta	1 tray	$120/tray	$ 120.00
Salad – Mixed Field Greens	30 cnt	3.50/cnt	$ 105.00
Entrée – Slow Smoked Brisket	8 lbs	22.99/lb	$ 183.92
Entrée – Slow Smoked Turkey	8 lbs	22.99/lb	$ 183.92
Side – Buttermilk Cornbread	3 trays	4.99/dzn	$ 37.50
Side – Mama's Tater Salad	7.5 lbs	9.99/lb	$ 74.93
Side – Cowboy Beans	7.5 lbs	7.50/lb	$ 56.25
BBQ Sauce	0.75 gal	20.00/gal	$ 15.00
Beverage – Unsweetened Tea	1.5 gal	5.50/gal	$ 8.25
Beverage – Fresh Squeezed Lemonade	1.5 gal	10.00/gal	$ 15.00
Services – On-site Buffet	1 hour	125.00/hr	$ 125.00
		Sub-Total	$ 924.77
		Tax at 10.95%	$ 101.26
		Grand Total	$1,026.33

Source: John Christ – Owner, Wil's Grill (April 2017).

Notes: Menus available on Wil's Grill website.
     Clean food discussed on website and menu boards at events.

EXHIBIT 2   Profit and Loss Statement (2014–2016)

Ordinary Income/Expense ($US) – Accrual Basis January through December				
	2016	**2015**	**2014**	**Comments**
Income				
Food Sales	$86,921	$24,568	$18,000	
				2014: 8 special public events & seasonal weekend street service; 2015: 15 special public events; 2016: 40 special public events
Total Income	86,921	24,568	18,000	
Cost of Goods Sold				
Food Purchases	32,401	12,533		Goal: = 30% of Food Sales thru purchasing efficiencies and sourcing cooperative
Direct Labor Payroll (Cody paid $3,613 (2015) and $6,470 (2016))	10,675	4,937		2015: Cody (450 hrs) & sub-contract labor 2016: Cody (650 hrs) & sub-contract labor
Business Licenses/ Permits/Insurance	4,005	1,434		Per event basis
Total COGS	47,081	18,904	6,000	
Gross Profit	39,840	5,664	12,000	
Operating Expense (Fixed)				
Advertising & Promotion	2,131	1,105		
Automobile Expenses	4,700	369		Fuel and maintenance
Bank Service Charges	210	287		
Computer and Internet Expenses	1,000	228		
Office Supplies	53	283		
Professional Fees	2,300	2,043		Client meetings, Legal, Acct, R&D
Propane	555	286		
Reimbursement	109			
Rent Expense	1,500	1,412		Leased kitchen space
Repairs and Maintenance	92			
Restaurant Supplies	549	1,454		
Supplies	1,239	382		
Uniforms	73			
Utilities	255			
Total Operating Expense	14,766	7,849	15,000	2014 Operating Expense not itemized
Net Ordinary Income	25,074	(2,185)		
Other Income/Expense				
Ask My Accountant	1,604	33		
Total Other Expense	1,604	33	—	
Net Operating Income	$23,470	$ (2,218)	$ (3,000)	John paid himself a salary from Net Income after reinvesting back in business (2016)

Source: John Christ – Owner, Wil's Grill (July 2017).

THE WIL'S GRILL MARKET

By 2015 Wil's Grill primarily served Flagstaff, along with Prescott and Sedona to the south, Williams to the west and most of Northern Arizona (with a combined population of about 275,000 people).[3] Winter weather limited the number of street food events in Flagstaff, given its 7,000-foot elevation. Sedona,

Prescott, and the Verde Valley (all within 100 miles of Flagstaff), at lower elevations, were warmer. Collectively, each of these communities held almost 50 events that featured street food. For special events John sometimes traveled as far as Phoenix or Page (both within 150 miles of Flagstaff); he included fuel costs in his pricing. Phoenix was the 12th largest metropolitan area in the United States with a population of 4.57 million people and a vibrant street food scene.[4] Wil's Grill had received excellent reviews from local writers, food critics and customers, and was featured in the July 2015 issue of *Flagstaff Business News.* More food trucks were also appearing on the scene, and some new entrants served healthier fare. John's promotional marketing budget for 2016 was $2,100, although he believed he should spend $5,000.

As for catering, large competitors included Big Foot BBQ and Satchmo's (local barbeque restaurants that also offered catering), as well as Main Street Catering and Thorneger's Catering. Some competitors had been in business for 20 years or more, and were well-established in the local catering market. Wil's Grill had the strongest focus on clean food, and John received referrals from caterers for specialties Wil's Grill was known for—smoked meats and barbeque.

Various studies conducted in the United States indicated a growing interest in "clean food" and this was beginning to influence some customers' food and beverage purchase decisions. Consideration for healthy choices had reportedly increased from 61 percent in 2012 to 71 percent in 2014, and in 2015 67 percent of respondents had given thought to environmental sustainability, 72 percent had given consideration to how food was produced or farmed, and 26 percent regularly purchased locally sourced items.[5] John believed that the demographics and psychographics of people in Northern Arizona aligned well with the national clean food movement.

THE CATERING MARKET SEGMENT

In fall 2015, John coordinated with NAU marketing research students on an exploratory survey to learn more about customer perceptions of the Wil's Grill brand, food offerings, the clean food movement, and the catering market segment. He realized that with just 79 respondents, the survey results were directional at best.[6] The survey indicated that 56 percent of respondents were willing to spend at least $11/person on a catered event, of which 24 percent were willing to spend about $16/person and 78 percent were willing to spend an additional $1 to $6/person for clean food; 72 percent of respondents had never heard of Wil's Grill. Regarding the decision to use a caterer, barbeque beef and pork, Mexican, Italian, Asian, and vegetarian were the most desired catered event food options. A caterer's reputation, customer reviews, service, food selection and price were critical factors in selecting a caterer, and 63 percent indicated that locally sourced food would influence their decision.

To keep current on trends and opportunities, John was a voracious reader of food trade journals. One article stated that "farm to fork has been a trend emerging in weddings."[7] Catered events could have margins of up to 40 percent. Catering customers were typically older, more affluent, and included both individuals and businesses. The business model was somewhat more predictable than street food vending, with a predetermined number of guests, food type, pricing, and event specifics. Catering opportunities were available year-round in the Northern Arizona market.

Catering could be labor intensive. John estimated that a buffet-styled catered event required one staff member for every 30 guests, and a "plated, waited, and served" event would need up to twice as many staff members. New job descriptions and training would need to be developed. John expected that he would need to expand his menu and improve the food presentation, based on what clients wanted. Customers also often asked caterers to provide décor, entertainment, etc.

John would need to invest in new kitchen equipment, logistics, and a cargo trailer to store, maintain, and transport food. The required investment would increase if John planned to cater multiple events simultaneously. John realized he'd need to get out of his comfort zone and assume debt to expand into the catering segment. He would have to figure out a way to secure financing.

John estimated his annual catering marketing expenses would be $7,500. He believed he would realize synergies with his existing street food segment marketing investment, but a catering client base would need to be developed. John saw his brand as "Wil's Grill and not Wil's Barbeque, offering a wide assortment and variety of foods and flavors off the grill. We can be so much more than barbeque." In street food, John focused on smoked meats and barbeque because it was easily prepared and sold at a reasonable price. Wil's Grill stood for street food among those who were aware of the brand. His motto "Have grill will travel" reflected that he traveled to various street food events. He had never copyrighted this motto, but he had trademarked the Wil's Grill name.

John developed high-level ballpark estimates for future cash flows and investment associated with the options under consideration for growing the business (see Exhibit 3). He strongly believed that the Wil's Grill brand was defined by "our reputation among those we've served, and those who have heard about us. Our reputation is one of sincerity, transparency, consistency, and quality."

John needed to make a strategic decision: how to move forward with Wil's Grill and his livelihood.

EXHIBIT 3   Estimated Investment Levels and Future Revenue Projections (rounded)

2016 Actual Revenue	Est. Investment	2017 Total/YOY Rev.	2018 Total/YOY Rev.	2019 Total/YOY Rev.
(A) Expand Street Food: $87,000	$9,000	$122,000/$35,000	$162,000/$40,000	$212,000/$50,000
(B) Add Catering and Maintain Street Food: $87,000	$25,000	$147,000/$60,000	$217,000/$70,000	$307,000/$90,000

Source: John Christ – Owner, Wil's Grill (July 2017).

John's research assumed:

- 20%–25% (A) & 40%–45% (B) profit before taxes
- discount rate range 5%-18%
- 20% YOY "normal" growth rate for street food revenue (2016–2019)
- +2% YOY inflation rate; +3% YOY contingency expense
- $3,500 revenue per catering event (2017)
- 5% YOY higher operating expenses for (B) vs. (A)
- 2017 COGS 50% (A) and 52% (B) of Total Income bef. inflation/contingency
- "Est. Investment" primarily kitchen equipment

ENDNOTES

[1] Feine, Suzy, *Green, The New Color of Love,* CaterSource, May 1, 2009, http://www.catersource.com/green-catering/green-new-color-love.
[2] "What Is Street Food?", *The Street Food Institute,* n.d., http://www.streetfoodinstitute.org/what-is-street-food/.
[3] Arizona Cities by Population, United States Census Bureau/American Fact Finder, May 2015, https://www.arizona-demographics.com/cities_by_population.

[4] Theobald, B., Census: Phoenix area population grew rapidly, March 26, 2015, http://www.azcentral.com/story/news/arizona/politics/2015/03/26/census-phoenix-area-population-grew-rapidly/70507534/.
[5] *International Food Information Council Federation – Food and Health Survey 2015,* http://ljournal.ru/wp-content/uploads/2017/03/a-2017-023.pdf.
[6] Survey Monkey September 2015 – *Wil's Grill* Case Author and MKT 439 Marketing

Research Students; 79 respondents to a 20-question survey.
[7] Jacobs, A. S., Relaxed Luxury: New Farm-to-Fab Wedding Inspiration, March 29, 2016, http://www.instyle.com/news/relaxed-luxury-new-farm-fab-wedding-inspiration.

Costco Wholesale in 2018: Mission, Business Model, and Strategy

Arthur A. Thompson Jr.,
The University of Alabama

Six years after turning the leadership of Costco Wholesale over to then-president, Craig Jelinek, Jim Sinegal, Costco's co-founder and chief executive officer (CEO) from 1983 until year-end 2011, had ample reason to be pleased with the company's ongoing revenue growth and competitive standing as one of the world's biggest and best consumer goods merchandisers. Sinegal had been the driving force behind Costco's 35-year evolution from a startup entrepreneurial venture into the third largest retailer in the United States, the seventh largest retailer in the world, and the undisputed leader of the discount warehouse and wholesale club segment of the North American retailing industry. Since January 2012, when Craig Jelinek took the reins as Costco Wholesale's president and CEO, the company had prospered, growing from annual revenues of $89 billion and 598 membership warehouses at year-end fiscal 2011 to annual revenues of $126.2 billion and 741 membership warehouses at year-end fiscal 2017. Costco's growth continued in the first nine months of fiscal 2018; 9-month revenues were $95.0 billion, up 12.0 percent over the first 9 months of fiscal 2017, and the company had opened four additional warehouses. As of June 2018, Costco ranked as the second largest retailer in both the United States and the world (behind Walmart).

COMPANY BACKGROUND

The membership warehouse concept was pioneered by discount merchandising sage Sol Price, who opened the first Price Club in a converted airplane hangar on Morena Boulevard in San Diego in 1976. Price Club lost $750,000 in its first year of operation, but by 1979 it had two stores, 900 employees, 200,000 members, and a $1 million profit. Years earlier, Sol Price had experimented with discount retailing at a San Diego store called Fed-Mart. Jim Sinegal got his start in retailing at the age of 18, loading mattresses for $1.25 an hour at Fed-Mart while attending San Diego Community College. When Sol Price sold Fed-Mart, Sinegal left with Price to help him start the San Diego Price Club store; within a few years, Sol Price's Price Club emerged as the unchallenged leader in member warehouse retailing, with stores operating primarily on the West Coast.

Although Price originally conceived Price Club as a place where small local businesses could obtain needed merchandise at economical prices, he soon concluded that his fledgling operation could achieve far greater sales volumes and gain buying clout with suppliers by also granting membership to individuals—a conclusion that launched the deep-discount warehouse club industry on a steep growth curve.

When Sinegal was 26, Sol Price made him the manager of the original San Diego store, which had become unprofitable. Price saw that Sinegal had a special knack for discount retailing and for spotting what a store was doing wrong (usually either not being in the right merchandise categories or not selling items at the right price points)—the very things that Sol Price was good at and that were at the root of Price Club's growing success in the marketplace. Sinegal soon got the San Diego store back into the black. Over the next several years, Sinegal continued to build his prowess and talents for discount merchandising. He mirrored Sol Price's attention to detail and absorbed all the nuances and subtleties of his mentor's style of operating—constantly improving store operations, keeping operating costs and overhead low, stocking items that moved quickly, and charging ultra-low prices that kept customers coming back to shop. Realizing that he had mastered the tricks of running a successful membership warehouse business from Sol Price, Sinegal decided to leave Price Club and form his own warehouse club operation.

Sinegal and Seattle entrepreneur Jeff Brotman founded Costco, and the first Costco store began operations in Seattle in 1983—the same year that Walmart launched its warehouse membership format, Sam's Club. By the end of 1984, there were nine Costco stores in five states serving over 200,000 members. In December 1985, Costco became a public company, selling shares to the public and raising additional capital for expansion. Costco became the first ever U.S. company to reach $1 billion in sales in less than six years. In October 1993, Costco merged with Price Club. Jim Sinegal became CEO of the merged company, presiding over 206 PriceCostco locations, with total annual sales of $16 billion. Jeff Brotman, who had functioned as Costco's chairman since the company's founding, became vice chairman of PriceCostco in 1993 and was elevated to chairman of the company's board of directors in December 1994, a position he held until his unexpected death in 2017.

In January 1997, after the spin-off of most of its non-warehouse assets to Price Enterprises Inc., PriceCostco changed its name to Costco Companies Inc. When the company reincorporated from Delaware to Washington in August 1999, the name was changed to Costco Wholesale Corporation. The company's headquarters was in Issaquah, Washington, not far from Seattle.

Jim Sinegal's Leadership Style

Sinegal was far from the stereotypical CEO. He dressed casually and unpretentiously, often going to the office or touring Costco stores wearing an open-collared cotton shirt that came from a Costco bargain rack and sporting a standard employee name tag that said, simply, "Jim." His informal dress and unimposing appearance made it easy for Costco shoppers to mistake him for a store clerk. He answered his own phone, once telling ABC News reporters, "If a customer's calling and they have a gripe, don't you think they kind of enjoy the fact that I picked up the phone and talked to them?"[1]

Sinegal spent considerable time touring Costco stores, using the company plane to fly from location to location and sometimes visiting 8 to 10 stores daily (the record for a single day was 12). Treated like a celebrity when he appeared at a store (the news "Jim's in the store" spread quickly), Sinegal made a point of greeting store employees. He observed, "The employees know that I want to say hello to them, because I like them. We have said from the very beginning: 'We're going to be a company that's on a first-name basis with everyone.'"[2] Employees genuinely seemed to like Sinegal. He talked quietly, in a commonsensical manner that suggested what he was saying was no big deal.[3] He came across as kind yet stern, but he was prone to display irritation when he disagreed sharply with what people were saying to him.

In touring a Costco store with the local store manager, Sinegal was very much the person-in-charge. He functioned as producer, director, and knowledgeable critic. He cut to the chase quickly, exhibiting intense attention to detail and pricing, wandering through store aisles firing a barrage of questions at store managers about sales volumes and stock levels of particular items, critiquing merchandising displays or the position of certain products in the stores, commenting on any aspect of store operations that caught his eye, and asking managers to do further research and get back to him with more information whenever he found their answers to his questions less than satisfying. Sinegal had tremendous merchandising savvy, demanded much of store managers and employees, and definitely set the tone for how the company operated its discounted retailing business. Knowledgeable observers regarded Jim Sinegal's merchandising expertise as being on a par with Walmart's legendary founder, Sam Walton.

In September 2011, at the age of 75, Jim Sinegal informed Costco's Board of Directors of his intention to step down as CEO of the company effective January 2012. The Board elected Craig Jelinek, President and Chief Operating Officer since February 2010, to succeed Sinegal and hold the titles of both President and CEO. Jelinek was a highly experienced retail executive with 37 years in the industry, 28 of them at Costco, where he started as one of the Company's first warehouse managers in 1984. He had served in every major role related to Costco's business operations and merchandising activities during his tenure. When he stepped down as CEO, Sinegal retained his position on the company's Board of Directors and, at the age of 79, was re-elected to another three-year term on Costco's board in December 2015; he retired from Costco's Board at the end of his term in January 2018.

COSTCO WHOLESALE IN 2018

In June 2018, Costco was operating 750 membership warehouses, including 520 in the United States and Puerto Rico, 98 in Canada, 38 in Mexico, 28 in the United Kingdom, 26 in Japan, 14 in South Korea, 13 in Taiwan, 9 in Australia, 2 in Spain, 1 in France, and 1 in Iceland. Costco also sold merchandise to members at websites in the United States, Canada, the United Kingdom, Mexico, South Korea, and Taiwan. Over 90 million cardholders were entitled to shop at Costco as of January 2018; in fiscal year 2017, membership fees generated over $2.85 billion in revenues for the company. Headed into 2018, on average, traffic at Costco's warehouse locations averaged 3 million members per day. Annual sales per store averaged about $170 million ($3.3 million per week) in 2017, over 70 percent higher than the $99.2 million per year and $1.9 million per week averages for Sam's Club, Costco's chief competitor. In 2014, 165 of Costco's warehouses generated sales exceeding $200 million annually, up from 56 in 2010; and 60 warehouses had sales exceeding $250 million, including two that had more than $400 million in sales.[4] In 2018, Costco was the only national retailer in the history of the United States that could boast of average annual revenue in excess of $170 million *per location.*

Exhibit 1 contains a financial and operating summary for Costco for fiscal years 2000, 2005, and from 2014 through 2017.

EXHIBIT 1 Selected Financial and Operating Data for Costco Wholesale Corp., Fiscal Years 2000, 2005, and 2014–2017 ($ in millions, except for per share data)

Selected Income Statement Data	Fiscal years ending on Sunday closest to August 31					
	2017	2016	2015	2014	2005	2000
Net sales	$126,172	$116,073	$113,666	$110,212	$51,862	$31,621
Membership fees	2,853	2,646	2,533	2,428	1,073	544
Total revenue	129,025	118,719	116,199	112,640	52,935	32,164
Operating expenses						
Merchandise costs	111,882	102,901	101,065	98,458	46,347	28,322
Selling, general and administrative	12,950	12,068	11,445	10,899	5,044	2,755
Preopening expenses	82	78	65	63	53	42
Provision for impaired assets and store closing costs	———	———	———	———	16	7
Total operating expenses	124,914	115,047	112,575	109,420	51,460	31,126
Operating income	4,111	3,672	3,624	3,220	1,474	1,037
Other income (expense)						
Interest expense	(134)	(133)	(124)	(113)	(34)	(39)
Interest income and other, net	62	80	104	90	109	54
Income before income taxes	4,039	3,619	3,604	3,197	1,549	1,052
Provision for income taxes	1,325	1,243	1,195	1,109	486	421
Net income	$ 2,714	$ 2,350	$ 2,377	$ 2,058	$ 1,063	$ 631
Diluted net income per share	$ 6.08	$5.33	$5.37	$4.65	$2.18	$ 1.35
Dividends per share (not including special dividend of $7.00 in 2017 and $5.00 in 2015)	$ 1.90	$1.70	$1.51	$1.33	0.43	0.00
Millions of shares used in per share calculations	440.9	441.3	442.7	442.5	492.0	475.7

(Continued)

	2017	2016	2015	2014	2005	2000
Balance Sheet Data						
Cash and cash equivalents	$ 4,546	$ 3,379	$ 4,801	$ 5,738	$ 2,063	$　525
Merchandise inventories	9,834	8,969	8,908	8,456	4,015	2,490
Current assets	17,317	15,218	16,779	17,588	8,238	3,470
Current liabilities	17,485	15,575	16,539	14,412	6,761	3,404
Net property and equipment	18,161	17,043	15,401	14,830	7,790	4,834
Total assets	36,347	33,163	33,017	33,024	16,514	8,634
Long-term debt	6.573	4,061	4,852	5,093	711	790
Stockholders' equity	10,778	12,079	10,617	12,515	8,881	4,240
Cash Flow Data						
Net cash provided by operating activities	$ 6,726	$ 3,292	$ 4,285	$3,984	$ 1,773	$ 1,070
Warehouse Operations						
Warehouses in operation at beginning of year[a]	715	686	663	634	417	292
New warehouses opened (including relocations)	28	33	26	30	21	25
Existing warehouses closed (including relocations)	(2)	(4)	(3)	(1)	(5)	(4)
Warehouses at end of year	741	715	686	663	433	313
Net sales per warehouse open at year-end (in millions)	$　170	$　162	$　166	$　166	$　120	$　101
Average annual growth at warehouses open more than a year (excluding the impact of changing gasoline prices and foreign exchange rates)	4%	4%	7%	6%	7%	11%
Members at year-end						
Businesses, including add-on members (000s)	10,800	10,800	10,600	10,400	5,000	4,200
Gold Star members (000s)	38,600	36,800	34,000	31,600	16,200	10,500
Total paid members	49,400	47,600	44,600	42,000	21,200	14,700
Household cardholders that both business and Gold Star members were automatically entitled to receive	42,600	42,600	40,200	34,400	n.a.	n.a.
Total cardholders	90,300	86,700	81,300	76,400	———	———

[a] At the beginning of Costco's 2011 fiscal year, the operations of 32 warehouses in Mexico that were part of a 50 percent-owned joint venture were consolidated and reported as part of Costco's total operations.

Note: Some totals may not add due to rounding and to not including some line items of minor significance in the company's statement of income.

Sources: Company 10-K reports for fiscal years 2000, 2005, 2015, 2016, and 2017.

COSTCO'S MISSION, BUSINESS MODEL, AND STRATEGY

Costco's stated mission in the membership warehouse business was: "To continually provide our members with quality goods and services at the lowest possible prices."[5] However, in a "Letter to Shareholders" in the company's 2011 Annual Report, Costco's three top executives—Jeff Brotman, Jim Sinegal, and Craig Jelinek—provided a more expansive view of Costco's mission, stating:

> The company will continue to pursue its mission of bringing the highest quality goods and services to market at the lowest possible prices while providing excellent customer service and adhering to a strict code of ethics that includes taking care of our employees and members, respecting our suppliers, rewarding our shareholders, and seeking to be responsible corporate citizens and environmental stewards in our operations around the world."[6]

In the company's 2017 Annual Report, Craig Jelinek elaborated on how environmental sustainability fit into Costco's mission:

> Sustainability to us is remaining a profitable business while doing the right thing. We are committed to lessening our environmental impact, decreasing our carbon footprint, sourcing our products responsibly, and working with our suppliers, manufacturers, and farmers to preserve natural resources. This will remain at the forefront of our business practices. [7]

The centerpiece of Costco's business model was a powerful value proposition that featured a combination of (1) ultra-low prices on a limited selection of nationally branded and Costco's private-label Kirkland Signature products in a wide range of merchandise categories, (2) very good to excellent product quality, and (3) intriguing product selection that included both everyday items and ongoing special purchases from a big variety of merchandise suppliers that turned shopping at Costco into a money-saving treasure hunt. Ever since the company's founding, Costco management had strived diligently to ensure that shopping at Costco delivered enough value to keep existing members returning frequently to a nearby warehouse and spur membership growth every year, thereby generating high sales volumes and rapid inventory turnover at each warehouse and creating opportunities to open new warehouses.

Big sales volumes and rapid inventory turnover—when combined with the low operating costs achieved by volume purchasing, efficient distribution, and reduced handling of merchandise in no-frills, self-service warehouse facilities—enabled Costco to operate profitably at significantly lower gross margins than traditional wholesalers, mass merchandisers, supermarkets, and supercenters. Membership fees were a critical element of Costco's business model because they provided sufficient supplemental revenues to boost the company's overall profitability to acceptable levels. Indeed, Costco's revenues from membership fees typically exceeded 100 percent of the company's net income, meaning that the rest of Costco's worldwide business operated on a slightly below breakeven basis (see Exhibit 1)—which translated into Costco's prices being exceptionally competitive when compared to the prices that Costco members paid when shopping elsewhere.

Another important business model element was that Costco's high sales volume and rapid inventory turnover generally allowed it to sell and receive cash for inventory before it had to pay many of its merchandise vendors, even when vendor payments were made in time to take advantage of early payment discounts. Thus, Costco was able to finance a big percentage of its merchandise inventory through the payment terms provided by vendors rather than by having to maintain sizable working capital (defined as current assets minus current liabilities) to enable timely payment of suppliers.

Costco's Strategy

The key elements of Costco's strategy were ultra-low prices, a limited selection of nationally branded and top-quality Kirkland Signature products covering diverse merchandise categories, a "treasure hunt" shopping environment that stemmed from a constantly-changing inventory of about 900 "while-they-last specials," strong emphasis on low operating costs, and ongoing expansion of its geographic network of store locations.

Pricing   Costco's philosophy was to keep customers coming in to shop by wowing them with low prices and thereby generating big sales volumes. Examples of Costco's 2015 sales volumes that contributed to low prices in particular product categories included 156,000 carats of diamonds, meat sales of $6.4 billion, seafood sales of $1.3 billion, television sales of $1.8 billion, fresh produce sales of $5.8 billion (sourced from 44 countries), 83 million rotisserie chickens, 7.9 million tires, 41 million prescriptions, 6 million pairs of glasses, and 128 million hot dog/soda pop combinations. Costco was the world's largest seller of fine wines ($965 million out of total 2015 wine sales of $1.7 billion).

For many years, a key element of Costco's pricing strategy had been to cap its markup on brand-name merchandise at 14 percent (compared to 25 percent and higher markups for other discounters and most supermarkets and 50 percent and higher markups for department stores). Markups on Costco's private-label Kirkland Signature items were a maximum of 15 percent, but the sometimes fractionally higher markups still resulted in Kirkland Signature items being priced about 20 percent below comparable name-brand items. Except for Walmart, Costco's prices for fresh foods and grocery items ranged 20 to 30 percent below of the leading supermarket chains. Aside from being lower-priced, Costco's Kirkland Signature products—which included vitamins, juice, bottled water, coffee, spices, olive oil, canned salmon and tuna, nuts, laundry detergent, baby products, dog food, luggage, cookware, trash bags, batteries, wines and spirits, paper towels and toilet paper, and clothing—were designed to be of *equal or better* quality than national brands.

As a result of its low markups, Costco's prices were just fractionally above breakeven levels, producing net sales revenues (not counting membership fees) that exceeded all operating expenses (merchandise costs + selling, general and administrative expenses + preopening expenses and store relocation expenses) by only $1.0 billion to $1. 2 billion in fiscal years 2017, 2016, and 2015 and by just $400 million to $800 million dollars in fiscal years 2014, 2005 and 2005. As can be verified from Exhibit 1, Costco's revenues from membership fees accounted for 69 to 75 percent of the company's operating profits in fiscal years 2014 to 2017 and exceeded the company's net income after taxes in every fiscal year shown in Exhibit 1 except for fiscal year 2000—chiefly because of the company's ultra-low pricing strategy and practice of capping the margins on branded goods at 14 percent and private-label goods at 15 percent.

Jim Sinegal explained the company's approach to pricing:

> We always look to see how much of a gulf we can create between ourselves and the competition. So that the competitors eventually say, "These guys are crazy. We'll

compete somewhere else." Some years ago, we were selling a hot brand of jeans for $29.99. They were $50 in a department store. We got a great deal on them and could have sold them for a higher price but we went down to $29.99. Why? We knew it would create a riot.[8]

At another time, he said:

> We're very good merchants, and we offer value. The traditional retailer will say: "I'm selling this for $10. I wonder whether we can get $10.50 or $11." We say: "We're selling this for $9. How do we get it down to $8?" We understand that our members don't come and shop with us because of the window displays or the Santa Claus or the piano player. They come and shop with us because we offer great values.[9]

Indeed, Costco's markups and prices were so fractionally above the level needed to cover company-wide operating costs and interest expenses that Wall Street analysts had criticized Costco management for going all out to please customers at the expense of increasing profits for shareholders. One retailing analyst said, "They could probably get more money for a lot of the items they sell."[10] During his tenure as CEO, Sinegal had never been impressed with Wall Street calls for Costco to abandon its ultra-low pricing strategy, commenting: "Those people are in the business of making money between now and next Tuesday. We're trying to build an organization that's going to be here 50 years from now."[11] He went on to explain why Costco's approach to pricing would remain unaltered during his tenure:

> When I started, Sears, Roebuck was the Costco of the country, but they allowed someone else to come in under them. We don't want to be one of the casualties. We don't want to turn around and say, "We got so fancy we've raised our prices, and all of a sudden a new competitor comes in and beats our prices."[12]

Product Selection Whereas typical supermarkets stocked about 40,000 items and a Walmart Supercenter or a SuperTarget might have 125,000 to 150,000 items for shoppers to choose from, Costco's merchandising strategy was to provide members with a selection of approximately 3,800 active items that could be priced at bargain levels and thus provide members with significant cost savings. Of these, about 75 percent were quality brand-name products and 25 percent carried the company's private-label Kirkland Signature brand. The Kirkland Signature label appeared on everything from men's dress shirts to laundry detergent, pet food to toilet paper, canned foods to cookware, olive oil to beer, automotive products to health and beauty aids. According to Craig Jelinek, "The working rule followed by Costco buyers is that all Kirkland Signature products must be equal to or better than the national brands, and must offer a savings to our members." Management believed that there were opportunities to increase the number of Kirkland Signature selections and gradually build sales penetration of Kirkland-branded items to at least 30 percent of total sales—in 2017 Kirkland-brand sales exceeded 27 percent of total sales. Costco executives in charge of sourcing Kirkland Signature products constantly looked for ways to make all Kirkland Signature items better than their brand name counterparts and even more attractively priced. Costco members were very much aware that one of the great perks of shopping at Costco was the opportunity to buy top quality Kirkland Signature products at prices substantially lower than name brand products.

Costco's product range covered a broad spectrum—rotisserie chicken, all types of fresh meats, seafood, fresh and canned fruits and vegetables, paper products, cereals, coffee, dairy products, cheeses, frozen foods, flat-screen televisions, iPods, digital cameras, fresh flowers, fine wines, caskets, baby strollers, toys and games, musical instruments, ceiling fans, vacuum cleaners, books, apparel, cleaning supplies, DVDs, light bulbs, batteries, cookware, electric toothbrushes, vitamins, and washers and dryers—but the selection in each product category was deliberately limited to fast-selling models, sizes, and colors. Many consumable products like detergents, canned goods, office supplies, and soft drinks were sold only in big-container, case, carton, or multiple-pack quantities. In a few instances, the selection within a product category was restricted to a single offering. For example, Costco stocked only a 325-count bottle of Advil—a size many shoppers might find too large for their needs. Sinegal explained the reasoning behind limited selections:

> If you had 10 customers come in to buy Advil, how many are not going to buy any because you just have one size? Maybe one or two. We refer to that as the intelligent loss of sales. We are prepared to give up that one customer. But if we had four or five sizes of Advil, as most grocery stores do, it would make our business more difficult to manage. Our business can only succeed if we are efficient. You can't go on selling at these margins if you are not.[13]

In the last several years, organics had become a fast-growing category in both the fresh produce section and the grocery items section, and Costco buyers were devoting increased attention to growing the selection of organic items. In the fresh meats category, Costco was pursuing increased vertical integration, constructing a meat plant in Illinois and a poultry plant in Nebraska. The approximate percentage of net sales accounted for by each major category of items stocked by Costco is shown in Exhibit 2.

Costco had opened ancillary departments within or next to most Costco warehouses to give reasons

EXHIBIT 2   Costco's Sales by Major Product Category, 2005–2017

	2017	2016	2010	2005
Food (fresh produce, meats and fish, bakery and deli products, and dry and institutionally packaged foods)	35%	36%	33%	30%
Sundries (candy, snack foods, tobacco, alcoholic and nonalcoholic beverages, and cleaning and institutional supplies)	20%	21%	23%	25%
Hardlines (major appliances, electronics, health and beauty aids, hardware, office supplies, garden and patio, sporting goods, furniture, cameras, and automotive supplies)	16%	16%	18%	20%
Softlines (including apparel, domestics, jewelry, housewares, books, movie DVDs, video games and music, home furnishings, and small appliances)	12%	12%	10%	12%
Ancillary and Other (gasoline, pharmacy, food court, optical, one-hour photo, hearing aids, and travel)	17%	16%	16%	13%

Source: Company 10-K reports, 2005, 2011, 2016, and 2017.

to shop at Costco more frequently and make Costco more of a one-stop shopping destination. Some locations had more ancillary offerings than others:

	2015	2010	2007
Warehouses having stores with			
Food Court	680	534	482
One-Hour Photo Centers	656	530	480
Optical Dispensing Centers	662	523	472
Pharmacies	606	480	429
Gas Stations	472	343	279
Hearing Aid Centers	581	357	237

Note: The company did not report the number of ancillary offerings for its warehouses at year-end 2016 and 2017, but the company did increase the number of gas stations to 508 in 2016 and to 536 in 2017. Costco did not sell gasoline at its warehouses in France and South Korea.

Source: Company 10-K reports, 2007, 2011, 2015, and 2017.

Costco's pharmacies were highly regarded by members because of the low prices. The company's practice of selling gasoline at discounted prices at those store locations where there was sufficient space to install gas pumps had boosted the frequency with which nearby members shopped at Costco and made in-store purchases (only members were eligible to buy gasoline at Costco's stations). Almost all new Costco locations in the United States and Canada were opening with gas stations; globally, gas stations were being added at locations where local regulations and space permitted.

Treasure-Hunt Merchandising   While Costco's product line consisted of approximately 3,800 active items, some 20 to 25 percent of its product offerings were constantly changing. Costco's merchandise buyers were continuously making one-time purchases of items that would appeal to the company's clientele and likely to sell out quickly. A sizable number of these featured specials were high-end or luxury-brand products that carried big price tags; examples included $1,000 to $4,500 big-screen Ultra HD LCD and LED TVs, $800 espresso machines, expensive jewelry and diamond rings (priced from $10,000 to $200,000+), Omega watches, Waterford Crystal, exotic cheeses, Coach bags, cashmere sports coats, $1,500 digital pianos, $800 treadmills, $2,500 memory foam

mattresses, and Dom Perignon champagne. Many of the featured specials came and went quickly, sometimes in several days or a week—like Italian-made Hathaway shirts priced at $29.99 and $800 leather sectional sofas. The strategy was to entice shoppers to spend more than they might by offering irresistible deals on big-ticket items or name-brand specials and, further, to keep the mix of featured and treasure-hunt items constantly changing so that bargain-hunting shoppers would go to Costco more frequently rather than only for periodic "stock up" trips.

Costco members quickly learned that they needed to go ahead and buy treasure-hunt specials that interested them because the items would very likely not be available on their next shopping trip. In many cases, Costco did not obtain its upscale treasure hunt items directly from high-end manufacturers like Calvin Klein or Waterford (who were unlikely to want their merchandise marketed at deep discounts at places like Costco); rather, Costco buyers searched for opportunities to source such items legally on the gray market from other wholesalers or distressed retailers looking to get rid of excess or slow-selling inventory.

Management believed that these practices kept its marketing expenses low relative to those at typical retailers, discounters, and supermarkets.

Low-Cost Emphasis   Keeping operating costs at a bare minimum was a major element of Costco's strategy and a key to its low pricing. As Jim Sinegal explained:

> Costco is able to offer lower prices and better values by eliminating virtually all the frills and costs historically associated with conventional wholesalers and retailers, including salespeople, fancy buildings, delivery, billing, and accounts receivable. We run a tight operation with extremely low overhead which enables us to pass on dramatic savings to our members.[14]

While Costco management made a point of locating warehouses on high-traffic routes in or near upscale suburbs that were easily accessible by small businesses and residents with above-average incomes, it avoided prime real estate sites in order to contain land costs.

Because shoppers were attracted principally by Costco's low prices and merchandise selection, most warehouses were of a metal pre-engineered design, with concrete floors and minimal interior décor. Floor plans were designed for economy and efficiency in use of selling space, the handling of merchandise, and the control of inventory. Merchandise was often stored on racks above the sales floor and/or displayed on pallets containing large quantities of each item, thereby reducing labor required for handling and stocking. In-store signage was done mostly on laser printers; there were no shopping bags at the checkout counter—merchandise was put directly into the shopping cart or sometimes loaded into empty boxes. Costco warehouses ranged in size from 73,000 to 205,000 square feet; the average size was about 145,000 square feet. Newer units were usually in the 150,000- to 205,000-square-foot range, but the world's largest Costco warehouse was a 235,000 square-foot store in Salt Lake City that opened in 2015. Images of Costco's warehouses are shown in Exhibit 3.

Warehouses generally operated on a 7-day, 70-hour week, typically being open between 10:00 a.m. and 8:30 p.m. weekdays, with earlier closing hours on the weekend; the gasoline operations outside many stores usually had extended hours. The shorter hours of operation as compared to those of traditional retailers, discount retailers, and supermarkets resulted in lower labor costs relative to the volume of sales. By strictly controlling the entrances and exits of its warehouses and using a membership format, Costco had inventory losses (shrinkage) well below those of typical retail operations.

Growth Strategy   Costco's growth strategy was to increase sales at existing stores by 5 percent or more annually and to open additional warehouses, both domestically and internationally. Average annual growth at stores open at least a year was 10 percent

in fiscal 2011, 6 percent in both fiscal 2013 and 2014, 7 percent in fiscal 2015, and 4 percent in 2016 and 2017 (see Exhibit 1).

Costco had been aggressive in opening new warehouses and entering new geographic areas. As of December 2000, the Company operated a chain of 349 warehouses in 32 states (251 locations), 9 Canadian provinces (59 locations), the United Kingdom (11 locations, through an 80 percent-owned subsidiary), South Korea (four locations), Taiwan (three locations, through a 55 percent-owned subsidiary) and Japan (two locations), as well as 19 warehouses in Mexico through a 50 percent joint venture partner. Ten years later, in December 2010, Costco was operating 585 warehouses in 42 states (425 locations), 9 Canadian provinces (80 locations), Mexico (32 locations), the United Kingdom (22 locations), Japan (9 locations), South Korea (7 locations), Taiwan (6 locations), and Australia (1 location). Since then, Costco had opened an additional 165 warehouses and entered 2 more states and 3 additional countries. In 2017, Costco opened 28 new warehouses, including its first ones in Iceland and France. Costco expected to open 20 to 25 new warehouses and relocate up to six warehouses in fiscal year 2018 beginning September 4, 2017.

Exhibit 4 shows a breakdown of Costco's geographic operations for fiscal years 2005, 2010, 2015, 2016, and 2017.

Marketing and Advertising

Costco's low prices and its reputation for making shopping at Costco something of a treasure-hunt

EXHIBIT 3   Images of Costco's Warehouses

©Casiohabib/Shutterstock

©a katz/Shutterstock

EXHIBIT 4   Selected Geographic Operating Data, Costco Wholesale Corporation, Fiscal Years 2005–2017 ($ in millions)

	United States Operations	Canadian Operations	Other International Operations	Total
Year Ended September 3, 2017				
Total revenue (including membership fees)	$93,889	$18,775	$16,361	$129,025
Operating income	2,644	841	626	4,111
Capital expenditures	1,714	277	511	2,502
Number of warehouses (as of December 31, 2017)	518	98	130	746
Year Ended August 30, 2016				
Total revenue (including membership fees)	$86,579	$17,028	$15,112	$118,719
Operating income	2,326	778	568	3,672
Capital expenditures	1,823	299	527	2,649
Number of warehouses	501	91	123	715
Year Ended August 29, 2015				
Total revenue (including membership fees)	$84,451	$17,341	$14,507	$116,199
Operating income	2,308	771	545	3,624
Capital expenditures	1,574	148	671	2,393
Number of warehouses	487	90	120	697
Year Ended August 29, 2010				
Total revenue (including membership fees)	$59,624	$12,501	$ 6,271	$ 77,946
Operating income	1,310	547	220	2,077
Capital expenditures	804	162	89	1,055
Number of warehouses	416	79	45	540
Year Ended August 28, 2005				
Total revenue (including membership fees)	$43,064	$ 6,732	$ 3,155	$ 52,952
Operating income	1,168	242	65	1,474
Capital expenditures	734	140	122	995
Number of warehouses	338	65	30	433

Note: The dollar numbers shown for the "Other International" categories represent only Costco's ownership share, since all foreign operations were joint ventures (although Costco was the majority owner of these ventures). Countries with warehouses in the Other International category as of year-end 2017 included Mexico (37), United Kingdom (28), Japan (26), South Korea (13), Taiwan (13), Australia (9), Puerto Rico (2), Spain (2), Iceland (1), and France (1); Costco's two warehouses in Puerto Rico were included in the United States Operations category. The warehouses operated by Costco Mexico in which Costco was a 50 percent joint venture partner were not included in the data for "Other International" until Fiscal Year 2011.

Source: Company 10-K reports, 2017, 2016, 2015, 2010, and 2007.

made it unnecessary to engage in extensive advertising or sales campaigns. Marketing and promotional activities were generally limited to monthly coupon mailers to members, weekly e-mails to members from Costco.com, occasional direct mail to prospective new members, and regular direct marketing programs (such as *The Costco Connection,* a magazine published for members), in-store product sampling, and special campaigns for new warehouse openings.

For new warehouse openings, marketing teams personally contacted businesses in the area that were potential wholesale members; these contacts were supplemented with direct mailings during the period immediately prior to opening. Potential Gold Star (individual) members were contacted by direct mail or by promotions at local employee associations and businesses with large numbers of employees. After a membership base was established in an area, most new memberships came from word of mouth (existing members telling friends and acquaintances about their shopping experiences at Costco), follow-up messages distributed through regular payroll or other organizational communications to employee groups, and ongoing direct solicitations to prospective business and Gold Star members.

Website Sales

Costco operated websites in the United States, Canada, Mexico, the United Kingdom, Taiwan, and South Korea—both to enable members to shop for many in-store products online and to provide members with a means of obtaining a much wider variety of value-priced products and services that were not practical to stock at the company's warehouses. Craig Jelinek was committed to a website strategy that provided exceptional service and value to Costco members who wanted to shop online. In recent years, online merchandise offerings had expanded significantly, and the company was continuously exploring opportunities to deliver added value to members via a broader array of online offerings. Examples of value-priced items that members could buy online included sofas, beds, mattresses, entertainment centers and TV lift cabinets, outdoor furniture, office furniture, kitchen appliances, billiard tables, and hot tubs. Members could also use the company's websites for such services as digital photo processing, prescription fulfillment, travel, the Costco auto program (for purchasing selected new vehicles with discount prices through participating dealerships), and other membership services. In 2015, Costco sold 465,000 vehicles through its 3,000 dealer partners; the big attraction to members of buying a new or used vehicle through Costco's auto program was being able to skip the hassle of bargaining with the dealer over price and, instead, paying an attractively low price pre-arranged by Costco. At Costco's online photo center, customers could upload images and pick up the prints at their local warehouse in little over an hour. Website sales accounted for 4 percent of Costco's total net sales in fiscal 2017 and 2016, versus 3 percent in 2015 and 2014.

In 2017, Costco made improvements in website functionality, search capability, checkout, and delivery times. New offerings were added at Costco Travel, and the company introduced hotel-only booking reservations. Costco Travel's rental car rates were consistently some of the lowest in the marketplace and in 2017 car rentals became available to members in Canada and the United Kingdom. Additionally, the annual 2 percent reward for Executive members was extended to apply to Costco Travel purchases in the United States and Canada. Lastly, the company launched Costco Grocery, a two-day delivery on dry grocery items, and a same-day delivery offering both fresh and dry grocery items through partnering with Instacart.

Supply Chain and Distribution

Costco bought the majority of its merchandise directly from manufacturers, routing it either directly to its warehouse stores or to one of the company's cross-docking depots that served as distribution points for nearby stores and for shipping orders to members making online purchases. In early 2018, Costco had 24 cross-docking depots with a combined space of approximately 11 million square feet in the United States, Canada, and various other international locations. Depots received container-based shipments from manufacturers, transferred the goods to pallets, and then shipped full-pallet quantities of several types to goods to individual warehouses via rail or semi-trailer trucks, generally in less than 24 hours. This maximized freight volume and handling efficiencies. Depots were also used to ship bulky merchandise to members that had been ordered online; members typically picked up online orders that would fit in their vehicles at nearby warehouses.

When merchandise arrived at a warehouse, forklifts moved the full pallets straight to the sales floor and onto racks and shelves (without the need for multiple employees to touch the individual packages/cartons on the pallets)—the first time most items were physically touched at a warehouse was when shoppers reached onto the shelf/rack to pick it out of a carton and put it into their shopping cart. Very little incoming merchandise was stored in locations off the sales floor in order to minimize receiving and handling costs.

Costco had direct buying relationships with many producers of national brand-name merchandise and with manufacturers that supplied its Kirkland Signature products. Costco's merchandise buyers were always alert for opportunities to add products of top quality manufacturers and vendors on a one-time or ongoing basis. No one manufacturer supplied a significant percentage of the merchandise that Costco stocked. Costco had not experienced difficulty in obtaining sufficient quantities of merchandise, and management believed that if one or more of its current sources of supply became unavailable, the company could switch its purchases to alternative manufacturers without experiencing a substantial disruption of its business.

Costco's Membership Base and Member Demographics

Costco attracted the most affluent customers in discount retailing—the average annual income of Costco members was approximately $100,000 (in 2015 Costco management believed the 8.6 million subscribers to the company's monthly *Costco Connection* magazine had an average annual income of $156,000).[15] Many members were affluent urbanites, living in nice neighborhoods not far from Costco warehouses. One loyal Executive member, a criminal defense lawyer, said, "I think I spend over $20,000 to $25,000 a year buying all my products here from food to clothing—except my suits. I have to buy them at the Armani stores."[16] Another Costco loyalist said, "This is the best place in the world. It's like going to church on Sunday. You can't get anything better than this. This is a religious experience."[17]

Costco had two primary types of memberships: Business and Gold Star (individual). Business memberships were limited to businesses, but included individuals with a business license, retail sales license, or other evidence of business existence. A business membership also included a free household card (a significant number of business members shopped at Costco for their personal needs). Business members also had the ability to purchase "add-on" membership cards for up to six partners or associates in the business. Costco's current annual fee for Business and Gold Star memberships was $60 in the United States and Canada and varied by country in its Other International operations. Individuals in the United States and Canada who did not qualify for business membership could purchase a Gold Star membership, which included a household card for another family member (additional add-on cards could not be purchased by Gold Star members). All types of members (including household card members) could shop at any Costco warehouse.

Business, Business add-on, and Gold Star members in the United States and Canada could upgrade to Executive membership for an additional $60 (an annual membership fee of $120); upgrade fees to Executive memberships elsewhere varied by country. The primary appeal of upgrading to Executive membership was eligibility for a 2 percent annual reward (rebate) on qualified pre-tax purchases. Reward certificates were issued annually and could be used toward purchases of most merchandise at the front-end registers of Costco warehouses—rebate awards could not be used to purchase alcohol and tobacco products, gasoline, postage stamps, and food court items. The 2 percent rebate for Executive members was capped at $1,000 for any 12-month period in the United States and Canada (equivalent to annual qualified pre-tax purchases of $50,000); the maximum rebate varied in other countries. Executive members also were eligible for savings and benefits on various business and consumer services offered by Costco, including merchant credit card processing, small-business loans, auto and home insurance, long-distance telephone service, check printing, and real estate and mortgage services; these services were mostly offered by third-party providers and varied by state—Executive members did not receive 2 percent rebate credit on purchases of these ancillary services. In fiscal 2017, Executive members represented 38 percent of Costco's cardholders (including add-ons, but not holders of household cards) and accounted for approximately two-thirds of total company sales. Costco's member renewal rate was 90 percent in the United States and Canada, and 87 percent on a worldwide basis in 2017. Recent trends in membership are shown at the bottom of Exhibit 1.

In general, with variations by country, Costco members could pay for their purchases with certain debit and credit cards, co-branded Costco credit cards, cash, or checks; in the United States and Puerto Rico, members could use a co-branded Citi/Costco Visa Anywhere credit card for purchases at Costco and elsewhere, Costco Cash cards, and all Visa cards. Since the June 2016 launch of Citi/Costco Visa® Anywhere Card, 1.8 million new member accounts (approximately 2.4 million new credit cards) were opened. The enhanced cash-back Visa Anywhere rewards included earning 4 percent on gas; 3 percent on restaurant, hotel, and eligible travel; 2 percent at Costco and Costco.com; and 1 percent on all other purchases, exceeding the company's previous co-branded credit card offering with American

Express. Executive Members using the new Visa Anywhere card continued to earn a 2 percent rebate on qualified purchases.

Costco accepted merchandise returns when members were dissatisfied with their purchases. Losses associated with dishonored checks were minimal because any member whose check had been dishonored was prevented from paying by check or cashing a check at the point of sale until restitution was made. The membership format facilitated strictly controlling the entrances and exits of warehouses, resulting in limited inventory losses of less than two-tenths of 1 percent of net sales—well below those of typical discount retail operations.

Warehouse Management

Costco warehouse managers were delegated considerable authority over store operations. In effect, warehouse managers functioned as entrepreneurs running their own retail operation. They were responsible for coming up with new ideas about what items would sell in their stores, effectively merchandising the ever-changing lineup of treasure-hunt products, and orchestrating in-store product locations and displays to maximize sales and quick turnover. In experimenting with what items to stock and what in-store merchandising techniques to employ, warehouse managers had to know the clientele who patronized their locations—for instance, big-ticket diamonds sold well at some warehouses but not at others. Costco's best managers kept their finger on the pulse of the members who shopped their warehouse location to stay in sync with what would sell well, and they had a flair for creating a certain element of excitement, hum, and buzz in their warehouses. Such managers spurred above-average sales volumes—sales at Costco's top-volume warehouses ran about $4 million to $7 million a week, with sales exceeding $1 million on many days. Successful managers also thrived on the rat race of running a high-traffic store and solving the inevitable crises of the moment.

Compensation and Workforce Practices

As of September 2017, Costco had 133,000 full-time employees and 98,000 part-time employees. Approximately 15,600 hourly employees at locations in California, Maryland, New Jersey, and New York, as well as at one warehouse in Virginia, were represented by the International Brotherhood of Teamsters. All remaining employees were non-union.

Starting wages for entry-level jobs for new Costco employees were raised to $13.00 to $13.50 in March 2016; hourly pay scales for warehouse jobs ranged from $13 to $24, depending on the type of job. The highest paid full-time warehouse employees could earn about $22.50 per hour after 4 years; compensation for a Costco pharmacist reportedly ranged from $45 to over $60 per hour.[18] In 2016, Costco's chief financial officer told *The Seattle Times,* "About 60 to 65 percent of Costco's employees make top-scale wages, which are in the $23 range." [19]

Salaried Costco employees earned anywhere from $30,000 to $125,000 annually.[20] For example, salaries for merchandise and department managers reportedly were in the $65,000 to $80,000 range; salaries for supervisors ranged from $45,000 to $75,000; salaries for database, computer systems, and software applications developers/analysts/project managers were in the $85,000 to $125,000 range; and salaries for general managers of warehouses ranged from $90,000 to $145,000. Employees enjoyed the full spectrum of benefits. Salaried employees were eligible for benefits on the first of the second month after the date of hire. Full-time hourly employees were eligible for benefits on the first day of the second month after completing 250 eligible paid hours; part-time hourly employees became benefit-eligible on the first day of the second month after completing 450 eligible paid hours. The benefit package included the following:

- Health care plans for full-time and part-time employees that included coverage for mental illness, substance abuse, and professional counseling for assorted personal and family issues.

- A choice of a core dental plan or a premium dental plan.

- A pharmacy plan that entailed (1) co-payments of $3 for generic drugs and $10 to $50 for brand-name prescriptions filled at a Costco warehouse or online pharmacy and (2) co-payments of $15 to $50 for generic or brand-name prescriptions filled at all other pharmacies.

- A vision program that paid up to $60 for a refraction eye exam (the amount charged at Costco's Optical Centers) and had $175 annual allowances for the purchase of glasses and contact lenses at Costco Optical Centers. Employees located more than 25 miles from a Costco Optical Center could visit any provider of choice for annual eye exams and could purchase eyeglasses from any in-network source and submit claim forms for reimbursement.

- A hearing aid benefit of up to $1,750 every four years (available only to employees and their eligible dependents enrolled in a Costco medical plan, and the hearing aids had to be supplied at a Costco Hearing Aid Center).

- A 401(k) plan open to all employees who had completed 90 days of employment. Costco matched hourly employee contributions by 50 cents on the dollar for the first $1,000 annually (the maximum company match was $500 per year). The company's union employees on the West Coast qualified for matching contributions of 50 cents on the dollar up to a maximum company match of $250 a year. In addition to the matching contribution, Costco also normally made a discretionary contribution to the accounts of eligible employees based on the number of years of service with the company (or in the case of union employees based on the straight-time hours worked). For other than union employees, this discretionary contribution was a percentage of the employee's compensation that ranged from a low of 3 percent (for employees with 1 to 3 years of service) to a high of 9 percent (for employees with 25 or more years of service). Company contributions to employee 410(k) plans were $436 million in fiscal 2014, $454 million in fiscal 2015, $489 million in 2016, and $543 million in 2017.

- A dependent care reimbursement plan in which Costco employees whose families qualified could pay for day care for children under 13 or adult day care with pretax dollars and realize savings of anywhere from $750 to $2,000 per year.

- Long-term and short-term disability coverage.

- Generous life insurance and accidental death and dismemberment coverage, with benefits based on years of service and whether the employee worked full-time or part-time. Employees could elect to purchase supplemental coverage for themselves, their spouses, or their children.

- An employee stock purchase plan allowing all employees to buy Costco stock via payroll deduction so as to avoid commissions and fees.

Although Costco's longstanding practice of paying good wages and good benefits was contrary to conventional wisdom in discount retailing, co-founder and former CEO Jim Sinegal, who originated the practice, firmly believed that having a well-compensated workforce was very important to executing Costco's strategy successfully. He said, "Imagine that you have 120,000 loyal ambassadors out there who are constantly saying good things about Costco. It has to be a significant advantage for you. . . . Paying good wages and keeping your people working with you is very good business."[21] When a reporter asked him about why Costco treated its workers so well compared to other retailers (particularly Walmart, which paid lower wages and had a skimpier benefits package), Sinegal replied: "Why shouldn't employees have the right to good wages and good careers. . . . It absolutely makes good business sense. Most people agree that we're the lowest-cost producer. Yet we pay the highest wages. So it must mean we get better productivity. Its axiomatic in our business—you get what you pay for."[22]

Good wages and benefits were said to be why employee turnover at Costco typically ran under 6 to 7 percent after the first year of employment. Some Costco employees had been with the company since its founding in 1983. Many others had started working part-time at Costco while in high school or college and opted to make a career at the company. One Costco employee told an ABC *20/20* reporter, "It's a good place to work; they take good care of us."[23] A Costco vice president and head baker said working for Costco was a family affair: "My whole family works for Costco, my husband does, my daughter does, my new son-in-law does."[24] Another employee, a receiving clerk who made about $40,000 a year, said, "I want to retire here. I love it here."[25] An employee with over two years of service could not be fired without the approval of a senior company officer.

Selecting People for Open Positions Costco's top management wanted employees to feel that they could have a long career at Costco. It was company policy to fill the vast majority of its higher-level openings by promotions from within; at one recent point, the percentage ran close to 98 percent, which meant that the majority of Costco's management team members (including warehouse, merchandise, administrative, membership, front end, and receiving managers) had come up through the ranks. Many of the company's vice presidents had started in entry-level jobs. According to Jim Sinegal, "We have guys who started pushing shopping carts out on the parking lot for us who are now vice presidents of our company."[26] Costco made a point of recruiting at local universities; Sinegal explained why: "These people are smarter than the average person, hardworking, and they haven't made a career choice."[27] On another occasion, he said, "If someone came to us and said he just got a master's in business at Harvard, we would say fine, would you like to start pushing carts?"[28] Those employees who demonstrated smarts and strong people management skills moved up through the ranks.

But without an aptitude for the details of discount retailing, even up-and-coming employees stood no chance of being promoted to a position of warehouse manager. Top Costco executives who oversaw warehouse operations insisted that candidates for warehouse managers be top-flight merchandisers with a gift for the details of making items fly off the shelves. Based on his experience as CEO, Sinegal said, "People who have a feel for it just start to get it. Others, you look at them and it's like staring at a blank canvas. I'm not trying to be unduly harsh, but that's the way it works."[29] Most newly appointed warehouse managers at Costco came from the ranks of assistant warehouse managers who had a track record of being shrewd merchandisers and tuned into what new or different products might sell well given the clientele that patronized their particular warehouse. Just having the requisite skills in people management, crisis management, and cost-effective warehouse operations was not enough.

Executive Compensation Executives at Costco did not earn the outlandish salaries that had become customary over the past decade at most large corporations. In Jim Sinegal's last two years as Costco's CEO, he received a salary of $350,000 and a bonus of $190,400 in fiscal 2010 and a salary of $350,000 and a bonus of $198,400 in fiscal 2011. Co-founder and Chairman Jeff Brotman's compensation in 2010 and 2011 was the same as Sinegal's. Craig Jelinek's salary as President and CEO in fiscal 2017 was $713,462, and he received a bonus of $192,800; Richard Galanti's salary as Executive Vice-President and Chief Financial Officer in fiscal 2017 was $745,000, and he received a bonus of $77,120. Other Costco executive officers received salaries in the $685,000 range and bonuses of $77,000 to $82,490 in fiscal 2017.

Asked why executive compensation at Costco was only a fraction of the amounts typically paid to top-level executives at other corporations with revenues and operating scale comparable to Costco's, Sinegal replied: "I figured that if I was making something like 12 times more than the typical person working on the floor, that that was a fair salary."[30] To another reporter, he said: "Listen, I'm one of the founders of this business. I've been very well rewarded. I don't require a salary that's 100 times more than the people who work on the sales floor."[31] During his tenure as CEO, Sinegal's employment contract was only a page long and provided that he could be terminated for cause.

However, while executive salaries and bonuses were modest in comparison with those at other companies Costco's size, Costco did close the gap via an equity compensation program that featured awarding restricted stock units (RSUs) to executives based on defined performance criteria. The philosophy at Costco was that equity compensation should be the largest component of compensation for all executive officers and be tied directly to achievement of pre-tax income targets. In fiscal 2017, the Compensation Committee of the Board of Directors granted RSUs to Craig Jelinek worth about $5.53 million on the date of the grant, but subject to time-vesting restrictions. The company's other four top executives were granted RSUs worth about $2.9 million on the date of the grant, but also subject to various restrictions. In December 2017, Jim Sinegal was deemed to be the beneficial owner of 1.3 million shares of Costco stock, and Craig Jelinek the beneficial owner of 312,687 shares. All directors and officers as a group (21 persons) were the beneficial owners of almost 2.57 million shares in December 2017.

Costco's Business Philosophy, Values, and Code of Ethics

Jim Sinegal, who was the son of a steelworker, had ingrained five simple and down-to-earth business principles into Costco's corporate culture and the manner in which the company operated. The following are excerpts of these principles and operating approaches:

1. **Obey the law**—The law is irrefutable! Absent a moral imperative to challenge a law, we must conduct our business in total compliance with the laws of every community where we do business. We pledge to:

- Comply with all laws and other legal requirements.
- Respect all public officials and their positions.
- Comply with safety and security standards for all products sold.
- Exceed ecological standards required in every community where we do business.
- Comply with all applicable wage and hour laws.
- Comply with all applicable antitrust laws.
- Conduct business in and with foreign countries in a manner that is legal and proper under United States and foreign laws.
- Not offer, give, ask for, or receive any form of bribe or kickback to or from any person or pay to expedite government action or otherwise act in violation of the Foreign Corrupt Practices Act or the laws of other countries.
- Promote fair, accurate, timely, and understandable disclosure in reports filed with the Securities and Exchange Commission and in other public communications by the Company.

2. **Take care of our members**—Costco membership is open to business owners, as well as individuals. Our members are our reason for being—the key to our success. If we don't keep our members happy, little else that we do will make a difference. There are plenty of shopping alternatives for our members, and if they fail to show up, we cannot survive. Our members have extended a trust to Costco by virtue of paying a fee to shop with us. We will succeed only if we do not violate the trust they have extended to us, and that trust extends to every area of our business. We pledge to:

- Provide top-quality products at the best prices in the market.
- Provide high-quality, safe, and wholesome food products by requiring that both vendors and employees be in compliance with the highest food safety standards in the industry.
- Provide our members with a 100 percent satisfaction guaranteed warranty on every product and service we sell, including their membership fee.
- Assure our members that every product we sell is authentic in make and in representation of performance.
- Make our shopping environment a pleasant experience by making our members feel welcome as our guests.

- Provide products to our members that will be ecologically sensitive.
- Provide our members with the best customer service in the retail industry.
- Give back to our communities through employee volunteerism and employee and corporate contributions to United Way and Children's Hospitals.

3. **Take care of our employees**—Our employees are our most important asset. We believe we have the very best employees in the warehouse club industry, and we are committed to providing them with rewarding challenges and ample opportunities for personal and career growth. We pledge to provide our employees with:

- Competitive wages.
- Great benefits.
- A safe and healthy work environment.
- Challenging and fun work.
- Career opportunities.
- An atmosphere free from harassment or discrimination.
- An Open-Door Policy that allows access to ascending levels of management to resolve issues.
- Opportunities to give back to their communities through volunteerism and fundraising.

4. **Respect our suppliers**—Our suppliers are our partners in business and for us to prosper as a company, they must prosper with us. To that end, we strive to:

- Treat all suppliers and their representatives as we would expect to be treated if visiting their places of business.
- Honor all commitments.
- Protect all suppliers' property assigned to Costco as though it were our own.
- Not accept gratuities of any kind from a supplier.
- If in doubt as to what course of action to take on a business matter that is open to varying ethical interpretations, TAKE THE HIGH ROAD AND DO WHAT IS RIGHT.

If we do these four things throughout our organization, then we will achieve our ultimate goal, which is to:

5. **Reward our shareholders**—As a company with stock that is traded publicly on the NASDAQ stock exchange, our shareholders are our business

partners. We can only be successful so long as we are providing them with a good return on the money they invest in our company. . . . We pledge to operate our company in such a way that our present and future stockholders, as well as our employees, will be rewarded for our efforts.[32]

Environmental Sustainability

In recent years, Costco management had undertaken a series of initiatives to invest in various environmental and energy saving systems. The stated objective was to ensure that the company's carbon footprint grew at a slower rate than the company's sales growth. Costco's metal warehouse design, which included use of recycled steel, was consistent with the requirements of the Silver Level LEED Standard—the certification standards of the organization Leadership in Energy and Environmental Design (LEED) were nationally accepted as a benchmark green building design and construction. Costco's recently-developed non-metal designs for warehouses had resulted in the ability to meet Gold Level LEED Standards.

All new facilities were being designed and constructed to be more energy efficient; this included using LED lighting and energy efficient mechanical systems for heating, cooling, and refrigeration in both new and existing facilities. In 2016, Costco began retrofitting existing facilities with LED lighting; as of year-end 2017, 364 retrofits had been completed, resulting in a total estimated energy savings of 110.5 million kilowatt-hours per year. Going into 2018, Costco had rooftop solar photovoltaic systems in operation at 100 of its warehouses; some warehouses used solar power to light their parking lots. In fiscal 2017, Costco began installing fuel cells as an alternate source of electricity as part of its ongoing effort to reduce the cost of energy at its facilities.

Another energy-saving initiative had been to install Internet-based energy management systems at all Costco warehouses in North America and at some international locations, giving Costco the ability to regulate energy usage on an hourly basis. These, along with installation of LED lighting and warehouse skylights, had reduced the lighting loads on Costco's sales floors by over 50 percent since 2001.

In September 2017, 154 warehouses were participating in the company's water efficiency program, with savings ranging from 20 percent to 25 percent;

additional warehouses were scheduled to participate in 2018 and beyond. Irrigation systems at warehouse sites used smart technologies and subsurface irrigation to improve water use efficiency. Site designs for warehouses aimed at managing stormwater runoff. Some locations had their own wastewater treatment systems. Recycled asphalt was being used for paving most warehouse parking lots. Other initiatives included working with suppliers to make greater use of sales-floor-ready packaging, changing container shapes from round to square (to enable more units to be stacked on a single pallet on warehouse sales floors and to conserve on trucking freight costs), making greater use of recycled plastic packaging, reusing cardboard packaging (empty store cartons were given to members to carry their purchases home), and expanding the use of non-chemical water treatment systems used in warehouse cooling towers to reduce the amount of chemicals going into sewer systems. In addition, a bigger portion of the trash that warehouses generated each week, much of which was formerly sent to landfills, was being recycled into usable products or diverted to facilities that used waste as fuel for generating electricity.

Costco was committed to sourcing all of the seafood it sold from responsible and environmentally sustainable sources that were certified by the Marine Stewardship Council; in no instances did Costco sell seafood species that were classified as environmentally endangered and it monitored the aquaculture practices of its suppliers that farmed seafood. The company had long been committed to enhancing the welfare and proper handling of all animals used in food products sold at Costco. According to the company's official statement on animal welfare, "This is not only the right thing to do, it is an important moral and ethical obligation we owe to our members, suppliers, and most of all to the animals we depend on for products that are sold at Costco."[33] As part of the company's commitment, Costco had established an animal welfare audit program that utilized recognized audit standards and programs conducted by trained, certified auditors and that reviewed animal welfare both on the farm and at slaughter.

Costco had been an active member of the Environmental Protection Agency's Energy Star and Climate Protection Partnerships since 2002 and was a major retailer of Energy Star qualified compact florescent lamp (CFL) bulbs and LED light bulbs.

COMPETITION

According to IBISWorld, the Warehouse Clubs and Supercenters industry—defined as companies that provided a range of general merchandise including food and beverages, furniture and appliances, health and wellness products, apparel and accessories, fuel and ancillary services—had total 2017 sales of approximately $457 billion in the United State alone. There were three main wholesale club competitors—Costco Wholesale, Sam's Club, and BJ's Wholesale Club. In early 2018, these three rivals had about 1,460 warehouse locations across the United States and Canada; most every major metropolitan area had one, if not several, warehouse clubs. The combined 2017 sales of Costco, Sam's Club, and BJ's Wholesale in the United States and Canada was $198 billion. Costco had close to a 64 percent share of warehouse club sales across the United States and Canada, with Sam's Club (a division of Walmart) having a 29 percent share and BJ's Wholesale Club and several small warehouse club competitors close to a 7 percent share. The warehouse club channel was projected to grow about 4 percent annually from 2017 through 2022.[34]

Competition among the warehouse clubs was based on such factors as price, merchandise quality and selection, location, and member service. However, warehouse clubs also competed with a wide range of other types of retailers, including retail discounters like Walmart and Dollar General, supermarkets, general merchandise chains, specialty chains, gasoline stations, and Internet retailers. Not only did Walmart, the world's largest retailer, compete directly with Costco via its Sam's Club subsidiary, but its Walmart Supercenters sold many of the same types of merchandise at attractively low prices as well. Target, Kohl's, Kroger, and Amazon.com had emerged as significant retail competitors in certain general merchandise categories. Low-cost operators selling a single category or narrow range of merchandise—such as Trader Joe's, Lowe's, Home Depot, Office Depot, Staples, Best Buy, PetSmart, and Barnes & Noble—had significant market shares in their respective product categories. Notwithstanding the competition from other retailers and discounters, the low prices and merchandise selection found at Costco, Sam's Club, and BJ's Wholesale were attractive to small business owners, individual households (particularly bargain-hunters and those with large families), churches and nonprofit organizations, caterers, and small restaurants. The internationally located warehouses faced similar types of competitors.

Brief profiles of Costco's two primary competitors in North America are presented in the following sections.

Sam's Club

The first Sam's Club opened in 1984, and Walmart management in the ensuing years proceeded to grow the warehouse membership club concept into a significant business and major Walmart division. The concept of the Sam's Club format was to sell merchandise at very low profit margins, resulting in low prices to members. The mission of Sam's Club was "to make savings simple for members by providing them with exciting, quality merchandise and a superior shopping experience, all at a great value."[35]

In early 2018, Sam's Club operated 597 locations in 44 states and Puerto Rico, many of which were adjacent to Walmart Supercenters, and about 100 Sam's Club locations in Mexico, Brazil, and China. (Financial and operating data for the Sam's Club locations in Mexico, Brazil, and China were not separately available because Walmart grouped its reporting of all store operations in 27 countries outside the United States into a segment called Walmart International that did not break out the international operations of Sam's Club.) In fiscal year 2018 (ending January 31, 2018), the Sam's Club locations in the United States and Puerto Rico and operations at **www.samsclub.com** had record revenues of $59.2 billion (including membership fees), making it the eighth largest retailer in the United States.

Sam's Clubs generally ranged between 94,000 and 168,000 square feet, with the average at the end of fiscal 2018 being 134,100 square feet; several newer locations were as large as 190,000 square feet. All Sam's Club warehouses had concrete floors, sparse décor, and goods displayed on pallets, simple wooden shelves, or racks in the case of apparel. In 2009 and 2010, Sam's Club began a long-term warehouse remodeling program for its older locations. During fiscal 2018, management closed 67 underperforming Sam's Club locations.

Exhibit 5 provides financial and operating highlights for selected years from 2016 to 2018.

Merchandise Offerings Sam's Club warehouses stocked about 4,000 items, a big fraction of which were standard and a small fraction of which represented special buys and one-time offerings. The treasure-hunt

EXHIBIT 5 Selected Financial and Operating Data for Sam's Club, Fiscal Years 2001, 2010–2018

Sam's Club	Fiscal Years Ending January 31				
	2018	2017	2016	2010	2001
Net sales in the United States and Puerto Rico, including membership fees[a] (millions of $)	$59,216	$57,365	$56,828	$47,806	$26,798
Operating income in the United States (millions of $)	982	1,671	1,820	1,515	942
Assets in the United States and Puerto Rico (millions of $)	13,418	14,125	13,998	12,073	3,843
Number of U.S. and Puerto Rico locations at year-end	597	660	655	605	475
Average sales per year-end U.S. and Puerto Rican location, including membership fees (in millions of $)	$ 99.2	$ 86.9	$ 86.8	$ 79.0	$ 56.4
Sales growth at existing U.S. and Puerto Rico warehouses open more than 12 months:					
Including gasoline sales	2.8%	0.5%	(3.2)%	−1.4%	n.a.
Not including gasoline sales	1.8%	1.8%	1.4%	0.7%	n.a.
Average warehouse size in the United States and Puerto Rico (square feet)	134,100	133,900	133,700	133,000	122,100

[a] The sales figure includes membership fees and is only for warehouses in the United States and Puerto Rico. For financial reporting purposes, Walmart consolidates the operations of all foreign-based stores into a single "international" segment figure. Thus, separate financial information for only the foreign-based Sam's Club locations in Mexico, China, and Brazil is not separately available.

Source: Walmart's 10-K reports and annual reports, fiscal years 2018, 2016, 2010, and 2001.

items at Sam's Club tended to be less upscale and less expensive than those at Costco. The merchandise selection included brand-name merchandise in a variety of categories and a selection of private-label items sold under the "Member's Mark," "Daily Chef," and "Sam's Club" brands. Most club locations had fresh-foods departments that included bakery, meat, produce, floral products, and a Sam's Café. A significant number of clubs had a one-hour photo processing department, a pharmacy that filled prescriptions, hearing aid and optical departments, tire and battery

centers, and self-service gasoline pumps. Sam's Club guaranteed it would beat any price for branded prescriptions. Members could shop for a wider assortment of merchandise (about 59,000 items) and services online at www.samsclub.com. Samsclub.com had an average of 20.4 million unique visitors per month and provided members the option of pick-up at local Sam's Club locations or direct-to-home delivery.

The percentage composition of sales (including ecommerce sales) across major merchandise categories was:

	Fiscal year ending January 31		
	2018	2017	2016
Grocery and consumables (dairy, meat, bakery, deli, produce, dry, chilled or frozen packaged foods, alcoholic and nonalcoholic beverages, floral, snack foods, candy, other grocery items, health and beauty aids, paper goods, laundry and home care, baby care, pet supplies, and other consumable items)	58%	59%	59%

(Continued)

	Fiscal year ending January 31		
	2018	2017	2016
Fuel and other categories (gasoline, tobacco, tools and power equipment, and tire and battery centers)	21%	20%	20%
Technology, office and entertainment (electronics, wireless, software, video games, movies, books, music, toys, office supplies, office furniture, photo processing, and gift cards)	6%	6%	7%
Home and apparel (home improvement, outdoor living, grills, gardening, furniture, apparel, jewelry, housewares, toys, seasonal items, mattresses, and small appliances)	9%	9%	9%
Health and wellness (pharmacy, hearing and optical services, and over-the-counter drugs)	6%	6%	5%

Source: Walmart's Fiscal Year 2016 10-K Report.

Membership and Hours of Operation   The annual fee for Sam's Club members was $45 for a Club membership card, with a spouse card available at no additional cost. Club members could purchase up to 8 "add-on" memberships for an additional $40 each. Alternatively, members could purchase a "Plus" membership for $100, and up to 16 "add-on" memberships for $40 each. Plus members were eligible for free shipping on ecommerce orders and for Cash Rewards, a benefit that provided a cashback of $10 for each $500 in qualifying pre-tax Sam's Club purchases up to an annual maximum cash reward of $500. Cash-back rewards could be used for purchases, membership fees, or redeemed for cash. About 600,000 members shopped at Sam's Club weekly. Income from membership fees was a significant percentage of the operating income earned by Sam's Club.

Regular hours of operations were Monday through Friday from 10:00 a.m. to 8:30 p.m., Saturday from 9:00 a.m. to 8:30 p.m., and Sunday from 10:00 a.m. to 6:00 p.m.; all Plus cardholders had the ability to shop before the regular operating hours Monday through Saturday, starting at 7 a.m. All club members could use a variety of payment methods, including Visa credit and debit cards, American Express cards, and a co-branded Sam's Club "Cash-Back" Mastercard. The pharmacy and optical departments accepted payments for products and services through members' health benefit plans.

Distribution   Approximately 68 percent of the non-fuel merchandise at Sam's Club was shipped from some 22 distribution facilities dedicated to Sam's Club operations that were strategically located across the continental United States, and in the case of perishable items, from nearby Walmart grocery distribution centers; the balance was shipped by suppliers direct to Sam's Club locations. Of these 22 distribution facilities, 6 were owned or leased and operated by Sam's Club, 13 were owned and operated by third parties, and 3 were leased and operated by third parties. Like Costco, Sam's Club distribution centers employed cross-docking techniques whereby incoming shipments were transferred immediately to outgoing trailers destined for Sam's Club locations; shipments typically spent less than 24 hours at a cross-docking facility and in some instances were there only an hour. A combination of company-owned trucks and independent trucking companies were used to transport merchandise from distribution centers to club locations.

Employment   In 2017, Sam's Club employed about 100,000 people across all aspects of its operations in the United States. While the people who worked at Sam's Club warehouses were in all stages of life, a sizable fraction had accepted job offers because they had minimal skill levels and were looking for their first job, or needed only a part-time job, or were wanting to start a second career. More than 60 percent of managers of Sam's Club warehouses had begun their careers at Sam's Club as hourly warehouse employees and had moved up through the ranks to their present positions.

BJ's Wholesale Club

BJ's Wholesale Club introduced the member warehouse concept to the northeastern United States in the mid-1980s and, as of June 2018, operated 215 warehouses in 16 eastern states extending from Maine to Florida. BJ's warehouse clubs ranged in size from 63,000 square feet to 150,000 square feet; newer clubs were typically about 85,000 square feet. In its core New England market region, BJ's had about three times the number of locations compared to its next largest warehouse club competitor. Approximately 85 percent of BJ's warehouse clubs had at least one Costco or Sam's Club warehouse operating in their trading areas (within a distance of 10 miles or less). Six distribution centers served BJ's existing locations and had the capacity to support up to 100 additional clubs along the East Coast of the United States. BJ's targeted households with an average annual income of approximately $75,000.

In late June 2011, BJ's Wholesale agreed to a buyout offer from two private equity firms and shortly thereafter became a privately held company. However, in May 2018, the private company (recently renamed BJ's Wholesale Club Holdings) announced its intent to become a public company again and filed the necessary registration for an initial public offering of common stock with the Securities and Exchange Commission. Management said the new company was planning to open 15 to 20 new clubs in each of the next five years. Exhibit 6 shows selected financial and operating data for BJ's Wholesale Club Holdings, Inc. for the three most recent fiscal years.

Product Offerings and Merchandising   Like Costco and Sam's Club, BJ's Wholesale sold high-quality, brand-name merchandise at prices that were significantly lower than the prices found at supermarkets, discount retail chains, department stores, drugstores, and specialty retail stores like Best Buy. Its merchandise lineup of about 7,200 items included consumer electronics, prerecorded media, small appliances, tires, jewelry, health and beauty aids, household products, computer software, books, greeting cards, apparel, furniture, toys, seasonal items, frozen foods, fresh meat and dairy products, beverages, dry grocery items, fresh produce, flowers, canned goods, and household products. About 70 percent of BJ's product line could be found in supermarkets. Sales of the company's two private-label brands, Wellsley Farms® and Berkley Jensen®, accounted for sales of over $2 billion, more than 16 percent of total net sales. BJ's prices of a representative basket of 100 items were consistently about 25 percent below comparable brand name products

sold by its four leading supermarket competitors. Members could purchase additional products at the company's website, **www.bjs.com**.

BJ's warehouses had a number of specialty services that were designed to enable members to complete more of their shopping at BJ's and to encourage more frequent trips to the clubs. Like Costco and Sam's Club, BJ's sold gasoline at a discounted price as a means of displaying a low-price image to prospective members and providing added value to existing members; in 2018, there were gas station operations at 134 BJ's locations. Other specialty services included full-service optical and hearing centers (more than 150 locations), food courts, a check printing service, vacation and travel packages, DirecTV packages, members-only Geico auto insurance deals, garden and storage shed installations, members-only Verizon deals, patios and sunrooms, a propane tank filling service, an automobile buying program, a car rental service, tire services, and electronics and jewelry protection plans. Most of these services were provided by outside operators in space leased from BJ's. In early 2007, BJ's abandoned prescription filling and closed all of its 46 in-club pharmacies.

Membership   BJ's Wholesale Club had more than 5 million paid memberships and a total of 10 million cardholders that generated $259 million annually in May 2018. In its fiscal year ending February 2018, the company had net sales of $12.5 billion, operating income of $220.3 million, and net income of $50.3 million (see Exhibit 6). In 2018, individuals could become Inner Circle members for a fee of $55 per year that included a second card for a household member; cards for up to three other family members and friends could be added to an Inner Circle member's account for an additional $30 per card. Individuals and businesses could upgrade to BJ's Perks/Rewards card for $110; Perks/Reward members received a free second card for a household member and could add up to three additional members for $30 each. BJ's Perks Rewards members earn 2 percent cash back on in-club and online purchases; cash awards were issued in $20 increments and could be used for in-store purchases; awards expired 6 months from the date issued. BJ's online access could be purchased for $10 per year, which provided the benefits of member pricing for online purchases. Members could apply for a BJ's Perks Plus® credit card (MasterCard) that had no annual credit card fee and earned 3 percent cash back on in-club and online

EXHIBIT 6   Selected Financial and Operating Data, BJ's Wholesale Club Holdings, Inc, Fiscal Years 2016–2018

	Fiscal Years Ended		
	January 30 2016	January 28 2017	February 3 2018
Selected Income Statement Data (in millions, except per share data)			
Net sales	$12,220.2	$12,095.3	$12,496.0
Membership fees	247.3	255.2	258.6
Total revenues	12,467.5	12,350.5	12,754.6
Cost of sales	10,476.5	10,223.0	10,513.5
Selling, general and administrative expenses	1,797.8	1,908.8	2,017.8
Preopening expenses	6.5	2.7	3.0
Operating income	186.8	216.0	220.3
Interest expense, net	150.1	143.4	196.7
Provision for income taxes	12.0	28.0	(28.4)
Net income	$ 24.1	$ 44.2	$ 50.3
Balance Sheet and Cash Flow Data (in millions)			
Cash and cash equivalents			$ 34.9
Merchandise inventories			1,019.1
Property and equipment, net			758.8
Net working capital			51.8
Total assets			2,021
Total debt			2,748.1
Total stockholders' deficit			(1,029.9)
Cash flow from operations	159.4	297.4	210.1
Free cash flow	46.9	182.7	72.6
Capital expenditures	112.3	114.8	137.5
Selected Operating Data			
Clubs open at end of year	213	214	2150
Sales growth at existing clubs open more than 12 months	(4.2%)	(2.6%)	0.8%
Sales growth at existing clubs open more than 12 months, excluding gasoline sales	(0.5%)	(2.3%)	(0.9%)
Average sales per club location, including online sales	$ 57.4	$ 56.5	$ 58.1
Membership renewal rate	84%	85%	86%

Source: Company Form S-1 Registration Statement, May 17, 2018.

purchases made with the credit card, 10 cents off per gallon at BJ's gas stations when using the card to pay for fuel purchases, and 1 percent cash back on all non-BJ's purchases everywhere else MasterCard was accepted. If members upgraded to a BJ's Perks Elite® card, they earned 5 percent cash back on in-club and online purchases made with the card, 10 cents off per gallon at BJ's gas stations when paying with the card,

and 1 percent cash back on all non-BJ's purchases everywhere MasterCard was accepted. Fuel purchases made with these credit cards were not eligible for further cash back rewards; moreover, supplement members had to upgrade to primary membership to be eligible for a BJ's Plus or Elite credit card. BJ's accepted MasterCard, Visa, Discover, and American Express cards at all locations; members could also pay for purchases by cash, check, or magnetically encoded Electronic Benefit Transfer cards (issued by state welfare departments). Manufacturer's coupons were accepted for merchandise purchased at the register in any Club where the product was sold. BJ's accepted returns of most merchandise within 30 days after purchase.

Marketing and Promotion   BJ's increased customer awareness of its clubs primarily through direct mail, public relations efforts, marketing programs for newly opened clubs, and a publication called *BJ's Journal,* which was mailed to members throughout the year.

Warehouse Club Operations   BJ's warehouses were located in both freestanding locations and shopping centers. Construction and site development costs for a full-sized owned BJ's club were in the $6 million to $10 million range; land acquisition costs ranged from $3 million to $10 million but could be significantly higher in some locations. Each warehouse generally had an investment of $3 to $4 million for fixtures and equipment. Pre-opening expenses at a new club ran $1.0 to $2.0 million. Including space for parking, a typical full-sized BJ's club required 13 to 14 acres of land; smaller clubs typically required about 8 acres. Prior to being acquired in 2011, BJ's had financed all of its club expansions, as well as all other capital expenditures, with internally generated funds.

Merchandise purchased from manufacturers was routed either to a BJ's cross-docking facility or directly to clubs. Personnel at the cross-docking facilities broke down truckload quantity shipments from manufacturers and reallocated goods for shipment to individual clubs, generally within 24 hours. BJ's worked closely with manufacturers to minimize the amount of handling required once merchandise is received at a club. Merchandise was generally displayed on pallets containing large quantities of each item, thereby reducing labor required for handling, stocking, and restocking. Backup merchandise was generally stored in steel racks above the sales floor. Most merchandise was pre-marked by the manufacturer so it did not require ticketing at the club. Full-sized clubs had approximately $4 million in inventory. Management was able to limit inventory

shrinkage to a small fraction of 1 percent of net sales by strictly controlling the exits of clubs, generally limiting customers to members, and using state-of-the-art electronic article surveillance technology.

Growth Strategies   BJ's Wholesale Club Holdings had developed a four-pronged approach to growing the business when BJ's once again became a public company:

1. Grow the member base.
2. Relentlessly focus on the consumer to drive sales.
3. Expand the company's footprint of warehouse club locations.
4. Continue to enhance profitability.

Top management believed the company had five competitive strengths:

1. The ability to provide a differentiated shopping experience based on (1) prices that were 25 percent lower on a representative basket of manufacturer-branded groceries compared to traditional supermarket competitors, (2) a wider product selection then Costco and Sam's Club, including 950 fresh food selections in selectively smaller package sizes, (3) a continually refreshed assortment of on-trend general merchandise, and (4) competitively priced gasoline and a variety of ancillary services.
2. A well-positioned store footprint in some of the most attractive geographic markets in the United States, coupled with experience in locating and operating a wide range of warehouse sizes. This allowed for a more flexible real estate expansion strategy that could be customized for infill or adjacent markets.
3. A large and loyal membership base that liked to shop at BJ's warehouses. The 16-state trade area in which BJ's warehouses were located included 9 million households with $7 billion of annual warehouse club spend.
4. Attractive strong free cash flow across economic cycles, owing to the company's membership model, low operating cost structure, and disciplined capital spending.
5. An experienced management team with a proven track record.

ENDNOTES

[1] As quoted in Alan B. Goldberg and Bill Ritter, "Costco CEO Finds Pro-Worker Means Profitability," an ABC News original report on *20/20,* August 2, 2006, http://abcnews. go.com/2020/Business/story?id=1362779 (accessed November 15, 2006).

[2] Ibid.

[3] As described in Nina Shapiro, "Company for the People," *Seattle Weekly,* December 15, 2004, www.seattleweekly.com (accessed November 14, 2006).

[4] Investopedia, "How Much Does a Costco Store Sell Each Year?" June 19, 2015, http://www.investopedia.com/stock-analysis/061915/how-much-does-costco-store-sell-each-year-cost.aspx#ixzz3zF8H31dL accessed February 4, 2016.

[5] See, for example, Costco's "Code of Ethics," posted in the investor relations section of Costco's website under a link entitled "Corporate Governance and Citizenship," (accessed on February 4, 2016).

[6] Costco Wholesale, 2011 Annual Report for the year ended August 28, 2011, p. 5.

[7] Costco Wholesale, 2017 Annual Report for the year ended September 3, 2017, p. 3.

[8] As quoted in ibid., pp. 128–29.

[9] Steven Greenhouse, "How Costco Became the Anti-Wal-Mart," *The New York Times,* July 17, 2005, www.wakeupwalmart.com/news (accessed November 28, 2006).

[10] As quoted in Greenhouse, "How Costco Became the Anti-Wal-Mart," *The New York Times,* July 17, 2005, www.wakeupwalmart.com/news (accessed November 28, 2006).

[11] As quoted in Shapiro, "Company for the People," *Seattle Weekly,* December 15, 2004, www.seattleweekly.com (accessed November 14, 2006).

[12] As quoted in Greenhouse, "How Costco Became the Anti-Wal-Mart," *The New York Times,* July 17, 2005, www.wakeupwalmart.com/news (accessed November 28, 2006).

[13] Boyle, "Why Costco Is So Damn Addictive," *Fortune,* October 30, 2006, p. 132.

[14] Costco's 2005 Annual Report.

[15] Jeremy Bowman, "Who Is Costco's Favorite Customer?" *The Motley Fool,* June 17, 2016, www.fool.com (accessed June 5, 2017); J. Max Robins, "Costco's Surprisingly Large-Circulation Magazine," *MediaPost,* March 6, 2015, www.mediapost.com (accessed June 5, 2017).

[16] As quoted in Goldberg and Ritter, "Costco CEO Finds Pro-Worker Means Profitability," an ABC News original report on *20/20,* August 2, 2006, http://abcnews.go.com/2020/Business/story?id=1362779 (accessed November 15, 2006).

[17] Ibid.

[18] Information posted at www.glassdoor.com (accessed January 29,2018).

[19] Susan Shain, "Costco's New Starting Pay Is So Good, You Might Want to Apply," The Penny Hoarder, Taylor Media, March 10, 2016, www.the penny hoarder.com (accessed January 28, 2018).

[20] Based on information posted at www.glass-door.com (accessed February 28, 2012).

[21] Ibid.

[22] Nina Shapiro, "Company for the People," *Seattle Weekly,* December 15, 2004, www.seattleweekly.com (accessed November 14, 2006).

[23] As quoted in Goldberg and Ritter, "Costco CEO Finds Pro-Worker Means Profitability," an ABC News original report on *20/20,* August 2, 2006, http://abcnews.go.com/2020/Business/story?id=1362779 (accessed November 15, 2006).

[24] Ibid.

[25] As quoted in Greenhouse, "How Costco Became the Anti-Wal-Mart," *The New York Times,* July 17, 2005, www.wakeupwalmart.com/news (accessed November 28, 2006).

[26] As quoted in Goldberg and Ritter, "Costco CEO Finds Pro-Worker Means Profitability," an ABC News original report on *20/20,* August 2, 2006, http://abcnews.go.com/2020/Business/story?id=1362779 (accessed November 15, 2006).

[27] Boyle, "Why Costco Is So Damn Addictive," *Fortune,* October 30, 2006, p. 132.

[28] As quoted in Shapiro, "Company for the People," *Seattle Weekly,* December 15, 2004, www.seattleweekly.com (accessed November 14, 2006).

[29] Ibid.

[30] As quoted in Goldberg and Ritter, "Costco CEO Finds Pro-Worker Means Profitability," an ABC News original report on *20/20,* August 2, 2006, http://abcnews.go.com/2020/Business/story?id=1362779 (accessed November 15, 2006).

[31] As quoted in Shapiro, "Company for the People," *Seattle Weekly,* December 15, 2004, www.seattleweekly.com (accessed November 14, 2006).

[32] Costco Code of Ethics, posted in the investor relations section of Costco's website, (accessed February 8, 2016).

[33] "Mission Statement on Animal Welfare," posted at www.costco.com in the Investor Relations section, (accessed February 8, 2016).

[34] According to the Warehouse Club Intelligence Center, as stated on page 5 of the prospectus for BJ's Wholesale Club Holdings initial public offering of common stock.

[35] Walmart 2010 Annual Report, p. 8.

CASE 5

Competition in the Craft Beer Industry in 2018

connect

John D. Varlaro
Johnson & Wales University

John E. Gamble
Texas A&M University–Corpus Christi

Locally produced or regional craft beers caused a seismic shift in the U.S. beer industry during the early 2010s with the gains of the small, regional newcomers coming at the expense of such well-known brands as Budweiser, Miller, Coors, and Bud Light. Craft breweries, which by definition sold fewer than 6 million barrels (bbls) per year, expanded rapidly with the deregulation of intrastate alcohol distribution and retail laws and a change in consumer preferences toward unique and high-quality beers. The growing popularity of craft beers led to an approximate 5 percent sales volume increase in craft beer in 2017.[1]

Yet, the overall beer industry had remained flat in 2017 with total beer sales dropping by 1.2 percent in the United States.[2] The craft beer industry, too, had begun to show signs of a slowdown going into 2018. While volume sales had increased by 5 percent in 2017 and annual growth had averaged 13.6 percent from 2012 to 2017, projections had slowed dramatically to 1.3 percent from 2017 to 2022.[3] Yet there did not seem to be a slowdown in the number of new craft brewers entering the market. Industry competition was increasing as grain price fluctuations affected cost structures and growing consolidation within the beer industry—led most notably by AB InBev's acquisition of several craft breweries, Grupo Modelo, and its acquisition of SABMiller—and created a battle for market share. While the market for specialty beer was expected to gradually plateau by 2020, it appeared that the slowing growth had arrived by 2017. Nevertheless, craft breweries and microbreweries were expected to expand in number and in terms of market share as consumers sought out new pale ales, stouts, wheat beers, pilsners, and lagers with regional or local flairs.

THE BEER MARKET

The total economic impact of the beer market was estimated to be 2.0 percent of total U.S. GDP in 2016 when variables such as jobs within beer production, sales and distribution were included.[4] Total revenue for the craft beer industry was estimated at $6 billion.[5] Exhibit 1 presents annual per production statistics for the United States between 2006 and 2017.

Although U.S. production had declined since 2008, consumption was increasing elsewhere in the world, resulting in a forecasted global market of over $700 billion in sales by 2022.[6] Global growth seemed to be fueled by the introduction of differing styles of beer to regions where consumers had not previously had access and the expansion of demographics not normally known for consuming beer. Thus, exported beer to both developed and developing regions helped drive future growth. As an example, China recently saw a number of domestic craft breweries producing beer as well as experimenting with locally and regionally known flavors, enticing the domestic palette with flavors such as green tea.

The Brewers Association, a trade association for brewers, suppliers and others within the industry, designated a brewery as a craft brewer when output was less than 6 million barrels annually and the ownership was more than 75 percentindependent of another non-craft beer producer or entity. The rapid increase in popularity for local beers led to the number of U.S. brewers to reach over 6,000

EXHIBIT 1   Barrels of Beer Produced in the United States, 2006–2017 (millions of barrels)

Year	Barrels produced (in millions)*
2006	198
2007	200
2008	200
2009	197
2010	195
2011	193
2012	196
2013	192
2014	193
2015	191
2016	190
2017	186

*Rounded to the nearest million.

Source: Alcohol and Tobacco Tax and Trade Bureau website

in 2017—nearly triple the number in 2012. Of these breweries, 99 percent were identified as craft breweries with distribution ranging from local to national. While large global breweries occupied the top positions among the largest U.S. breweries, three craft breweries were ranked among the top-10 largest U.S. brewers in 2017—see Exhibit 2. Exhibit 3 shows the production volume of the 10 largest beer producers worldwide from 2014 to 2016. The number of craft breweries in each U.S. state in 2015 and 2017 are presented in Exhibit 4.

THE BEER PRODUCTION PROCESS

The beer production process involves the fermentation of grains. The cereal grain barley is the most common grain used in the production of beer. Before fermentation, however, barley must be malted and milled. Malting allows the barley to germinate and produce the sugars that would be fermented by the yeast, yielding the sweetness of beer. By soaking the barley in water, the barley germinates, or grows, as it would when planted in the ground. This process is halted through the introduction of hot air and drying after germination began.

EXHIBIT 2   Top 10 U.S. Breweries in 2017

Rank	Brewery
1	Anheuser-Busch, Inc
2	MillerCoors
3	Constellation
4	Heineken
5	Pabst Brewing Company
6	D.G. Yuengling and Son, Inc
7	North American Breweries
8	Diageo
9	Boston Beer Company
10	Sierra Nevada Brewing Company

Source: Brewers Association.

After malting, the barley is milled to break open the husk while also cracking the inner seed that has begun to germinate. Once milled, the barley is mashed, or added to hot water. The addition of the hot water produces sugar from the grain. This mixture is then filtered, resulting in the wort. The wort is then boiled,

EXHIBIT 3   Top 10 Global Beer Producers by Volume, 2014–2016 (millions of barrels)*

Rank	Producer	2014	2015	2016
1	Ab InBev**	351	353	435
2	Heineken	180	186	195
3	Carlsberg	110	107	102
4	CR Snow***	N/A	N/A	100
5	Molson Coors Brewing Company	54	54	82
6	Tsingtao (Group)	78	72	67
7	Asahi	26	24	60
8	Beijing Yanjing	45	41	38
9	Castel BGI	26	26	26
10	Kirin	36	35	24

* Originally reported as hectoliters. Computed using 1 hL = .852 barrel for comparison; to nearest million bbl.

** Now includes SABMiller; previous volumes for SABMiller in years 2014 and 2015 prior to acquisition were 249 and 353, respectively, ranking it as second for both years.

*** Was not in top 10 for 2014 and 2015.

N/A: Not available.

Source: AB InBev 20-F SEC Document, 2015, 2016, 2017.

EXHIBIT 4 Number of Craft Brewers by State, 2015 and 2017

State	2015	2017
Alabama	24	34
Alaska	27	36
Arizona	78	96
Arkansas	26	35
California	518	764
Colorado	284	348
Connecticut	35	60
Delaware	15	21
Florida	151	243
Georgia	45	69
Hawaii	13	18
Idaho	50	54
Illinois	157	200
Indiana	115	137
Iowa	58	76
Kansas	26	36
Kentucky	24	52
Louisiana	20	33
Maine	59	99
Maryland	60	73
Massachusetts	84	129
Michigan	205	330
Minnesota	105	158
Mississippi	8	12
Missouri	71	91
Montana	49	75
Nebraska	33	49
Nevada	34	40
New Hampshire	44	58
New Jersey	51	90
New Mexico	45	67
New York	208	329
North Carolina	161	257
North Dakota	9	12
Ohio	143	225
Oklahoma	14	27
Oregon	228	266
Pennsylvania	178	282
Rhode Island	14	17
South Carolina	36	61
South Dakota	14	16
Tennessee	52	82

State	2015	2017
Texas	189	251
Utah	22	30
Vermont	44	55
Virginia	124	190
Washington	305	369
West Virginia	12	23
Wisconsin	121	160
Wyoming	23	24

Source: Brewers Association.

which sterilizes the beer. It is at this stage that hops are added. The taste and aroma of beer depend on the variety of hops and when the hops were added.

After boiling, the wort is cooled and then poured into the fermentor where yeast is added. The sugar created in the previous stages is broken down by the yeast through fermentation. The different styles of beer depend on the type of yeast used, typically either an ale or lager yeast. The time for this process could take a couple of weeks to a couple of months. After fermentation, the yeast is removed. The process is completed after carbon dioxide is added and the product is packaged.

Beer is a varied and differentiated product, with over 70 styles in 15 categories. Each style is dependent on a number of variables. These variables are controlled by the brewer through the process, and could include the origin of raw materials, approach to fermentation, and yeast used. For example, Guinness referenced on its website how barley purchased by the brewer was not only grown locally, but was also toasted specifically after malting, lending to its characteristic taste and color. As another example of differentiation through raw materials, wheat beers, such as German-style *hefeweizen,* are brewed with a minimum of 50 percent wheat instead of barley grain.

DEVELOPMENT OF MICROBREWERIES AND ECONOMICS OF SCALE

Although learning the art of brewing takes time, beer production lends itself to scalability and variety. For example, an amateur; or home brewer; could brew beer for home consumption. There had been a significant increase in the interest in home brewing, with over 1 million people pursuing the hobby in 2016.[7] It was also not uncommon for a home brewer to venture into entrepreneurship and begin brewing for commercial sales. However, beer production was highly labor intensive with much of the work done by hand. A certain level of production volume was necessary to achieve breakeven and make the microbrewery a successful commercial operation.

A small nanobrewery may brew a variety of flavor experiences and compete in niche markets, while the macrobrewery may focus on economies of scale and mass produce one style of beer. Both may attract consumers across segments and were attributed to the easily scalable yet highly variable process of brewing beer. In contrast, a global producer such as AB InBev could produce beer for millions of consumers worldwide with factory-automated processes.

LEGAL ENVIRONMENT OF BREWERIES

As beer was an alcoholic beverage, the industry was subject to much regulation. Further, these regulations could vary by state and municipality. One such regulation was regarding sales and distribution.

Distribution could be distinguished through direct sales (or self-distribution), and two-tier and three-tier systems. Regulations permitting direct sales allow the brewery to sell directly to the consumer. Growlers, bottle sales as well as tap rooms were all forms of direct, or retail, sales. There were usually requirements concerning direct sales, including limitations on volume sold to the consumer.

Even where self-distribution was legal, the legal volumes could be very small and limited. Very few brewers were exempt from distributing through wholesalers, referred to as a three-tier distribution system. And often to be operationally viable, brewers need access to this distribution system to generate revenue. In a three-tier system, the brewery must first sell to a wholesaler—the liquor or beer distributer. This distributor then sells to the retailer, who then ultimately sells to the consumer.

This distribution structure, however, had ramifications for the consumer, as much of what was available at retail outlets and restaurants were impacted by the distributor. This was further impacted by whether a brewery bottles or cans its beer or distributes through kegs. While restaurants and bars could carry kegs, retail shelves at a local liquor store needed to have cans and bottles, as a relatively small number of consumers could accommodate kegs for home use. Thus, there may only be a few liquor stores or restaurants where a consumer may find a locally-brewed beer. In states that do not allow self-distribution or on-premise sales, distribution and exposure to consumers could represent a barrier for breweries, especially those that were small or new.

The Alcohol and Tobacco Tax and Trade Bureau (TTB) was the main federal agency for regulating this industry. As another example of regulations, breweries, were required to have labels for beers approved by the federal government, ensuring they meet advertising guidelines. In some instances, the TTB may need to approve the formula used for brewing the specific beer prior to the label receiving approval. Given the approval process, and the growth of craft breweries, the length of time this takes could reach several months. For a small, microbrewery first starting, the delay in sales could potentially impact cash flow.

Employment law was another area impacting breweries. The Affordable Care Act (ACA) and changes to the Fair Labor Standards Act (FLSA) greatly affected labor cost in the industry. Where the ACA mandated health care coverage by employers, the FLSA changed overtime rules for employees previously classified as exempt or salaried. Finally, many states and municipalities passed or were considering passing, increases to minimum wage. These changes in regulations could lead to significant increases in business costs, potentially impacting a brewery's ability to remain viable or competitive.

Lawsuits might also impact breweries' operations. Trademark infringement lawsuits regarding brewery and beer names were common. Further, food-related lawsuits could occur. In 2017, there were potential lawsuits against breweries distributing in California that did not meet the May 2016 requirement of providing an additional sign warning against pregnancy and BPA (Bisphenyl-A) consumption. BPA was commonly found in both cans and bottle caps, and thus breweries were potentially legally exposed, exemplifying the potential legal exposure to any brewery.

SUPPLIERS TO BREWERIES

The main suppliers to the industry were those who supply grain and hops. Growers might sell direct to breweries or distribute through wholesalers. Brewers who wish to produce a grain-specific beer would be required to procure the specific grain. Further, recipes might call for a variety of grains, including rye, wheat, and corn. As previously mentioned, the definition of craft was changed not only to include a higher threshold for annual production, but it also changed to not exclude producers who used other grains, such as corn, in their production. Finally, origin-specific beers, such as German- or Belgian-styles might also require specific grains.

The more specialized the grain or hop, the more difficult it was to obtain. Those breweries, then, competing based on specialized brewing would be required to identify such suppliers. Conversely, larger, global producers of single-style beers were able to utilize economies of scale and demand lower prices from suppliers. Organically-grown grains and hops suppliers would also fall into this category of providing specialized ingredients, and specialty brewers tend to use such ingredients.

Exhibit 5 illustrates the amount of grain products used between 2010 and 2014 in the United States by breweries.

It was estimated that hops acreage within the United States grew almost 80 percent from 2012 to 2017,[8] which seems to follow the growing demand due to the increased number of breweries. Hops were primarily grown in the Pacific Northwest states of Idaho, Washington, and Oregon. Washington's

EXHIBIT 5 Total Grain Usage in the Production of Beer, 2010–2014 (in millions of pounds)

Grain Type*	2010	2011	2012	2013	2014
Corn	701	629	681	593	574
Rice	714	749	717	724	604
Barley	88	128	136	158	169
Wheat	22	24	26	30	33
Malt	4,147	4,028	4,117	3,916	3,689

*Includes products derived from the type of grain for brewing process.

Source: Alcohol and Tobacco Tax and Trade Bureau (TTB) website. Due to a request from the brewing industry to simplify reporting, the TTB stopped requiring producers to report grain usage in production in 2015.

Yakima Valley was probably one of the more recognizable geographic-growing regions. There were numerous varieties of hops, however, and each contributes a different aroma and flavor profile. Hop growers have also trademarked names and varieties of hops. Further, as with grains, some beer-styles require specific hops. Farmlands that were formerly known for hops have started to see a rejuvenation of this crop, such as in New England. In other areas, farmers were introducing hops as a new, cash crop. Some hops farms were also dual purpose, combining the growing operations with brewing, thus serving as both a supplier of hops to breweries while also producing their own beer for retail. Recent news reports, however, were citing current and future shortages of hops due to the increased number of breweries. Rising temperatures in Europe led to a diminished yield in 2015, further impacting hops supplies. For breweries using recipes that require these specific hops, shortages could be detrimental to production. In some instances, larger beer producers had vertically integrated into hops farming to protect their supply.

Suppliers to the industry also include manufacturers and distributors of brewing equipment, such as fermentation tanks and refrigeration equipment. Purification equipment and testing tools were also necessary, given the brewing process and the need to ensure purity and safety of the product.

Depending on distribution and the distribution channel, breweries might need bottling or canning equipment. Thus, breweries might invest heavily in automated bottling capabilities to expand capacity. Recently, however, there had been shortages in the 16-ounce size of aluminum cans.

HOW BREWERIES COMPETE: INNOVATION AND QUALITY VERSUS PRICE

The consumer might seek out a specific beer or brewery's name or purchase the lower-priced globally known brand. For some, beer drinking might also be seasonal, as tastes change with the seasons. Lighter beers were consumed in hotter months, while heavier beers were consumed in the colder months. Consumers might associate beer styles with the time of year or season. Oktoberfest and German-style beers were associated with fall, following the German-traditional celebration of Oktoberfest. Finally, any one consumer might enjoy several styles, or choose to be brewery or brand loyal.

The brewing process and the multiple varieties and styles of beer allow for breweries to compete across the strategy spectrum—low price and high volume, or higher price and low volume. Industry competitors, then, might target both price-point and differentiation. The home brewer, who decided to invest several thousand dollars in a small space to produce very small quantities of their beer and start a nanobrewery, might utilize a niche competitive strategy. The consumer might patronize the brewery on location or seek it out on tap at a restaurant given the quality and the style of beer brewed. If allowed by law, the brewery might offer tastings or sell onsite to visitors. Further, the nanobrewer was free to explore and experiment with unusual flavors. To drive awareness, the brewer might enter competitions, attend beer festivals, or host tastings and "tap takeovers" at local restaurants. If successful, the brewer might invest in larger facilities and equipment to increase capacity with growing demand.

The larger, more established craft brewers, especially those considered regional breweries, might compete through marketing and distribution, while offering a higher value compared to the mass production of macrobreweries. However, the consumer might at times be sensitive to and desire the craft beer experience through smaller breweries—so much so that even craft breweries who by definition were craft might draw the ire of the consumer due to its size and scope. Boston Beer Company was one such company. Even though James Koch had started it as a microbrewery, pioneering the craft beer movement in the 1980s, some craft beer consumers do not view it as authentically craft.

Larger, macrobreweries mass produced and competed using economies of scale and established distribution systems. Thus, low cost preserves margins as lower price points drive volume sales. Many of these brands were sold en masse at sporting and entertainment venues, as well as larger restaurant chains, driving volume sales.

Companies like AB InBev possessed brands within the portfolio that were sold under the perception of craft beer, in what Boston Beer Company deems the better beer category—beer with a higher price point, but also of higher quality. For example, Blue Moon, a Belgian-style wheat ale, was produced by MillerCoors. Blue Moon's market share had increased significantly since 2006 following the rise in craft beer popularity, competing against Boston Beer Company's Sam Adams in this better beer segment. AB InBev had also acquired larger better-known craft breweries, including Goose Island, in 2011. With a product portfolio that included both low-price and premium craft beer brands, macrobreweries were competing across the spectrum and putting pressure on breweries within the better and craft beer segments—segments demanding a higher price point due to production.

However, a lawsuit claimed the marketing of Blue Moon was misleading and its marketing obscured the ownership structure. Although the case was dismissed, it further illustrated consumer sentiment regarding what was perceived as craft beer. It also illustrated the power of marketing and how a macrobrewery might position a brand within these segments.

CONSOLIDATIONS AND ACQUISITIONS

In 2015 AB InBev offered to purchase SABMiller for $108 billion, which was approved by the European Union in May 2016 and finalized in 2016. To allow for the acquisition, many of SABMiller's brands were required to be divested. Asahi Group Holdings Ltd. purchased the European brands Peroni and Grolsch from SABMiller. Molson Coors purchased SABMiller's 58 percent ownership in MillCoors LLC—originally a joint venture between Molson Coors and SABMiller. This transaction provided Molson Coors 100 percent ownership of MillerCoors. It should be noted that AB InBev and MillerCoors represented over 80 percent of the beer produced in the United States for domestic consumption.

Purchases of craft breweries by larger companies had also increased during the 2010s. AB InBev had purchased around 10 craft breweries since 2011, including Goose Island, Blue Point and Devil's Backbone Brewing. MillerCoors—whose brands already included Killian's Irish Red, Leinenkugel's, and Foster's—acquired Saint Archer Brewing Company. Ballast Point Brewing & Spirits was acquired by Constellations Brands. Finally, Heineken NV purchased a stake in Lagunitas Brewing Company. It would seem that craft beer and breweries had not only obtained the attention of the consumer, but also the larger multinational breweries and corporations.

PROFILES OF BEER PRODUCERS

Anheuser-Busch InBev

As the world's largest producer by volume, AB InBev had 200,000 employees globally. The product portfolio included the production, marketing, and distribution of over 500 beers, malt beverages, as well as soft drinks in more than 150 countries. These brands included Budweiser, Stella Artois, Leffe, and Hoegaarden.

AB InBev managed its product portfolio through three tiers. Global brands, such as Budweiser, Stella Artois, and Corona, were distributed throughout the world. International brands (Beck's, Hoegaarden, Leffe) were found in multiple countries. Local champions (i.e., local brands) represented regional or domestic brands acquired by AB InBev, such as Goose Island in the United States and Cass in South Korea. While some of the local brands were found in different countries, it was due to geographic proximity and the potential to grow the brand larger.

AB InBev reported its 2017 revenues grew in all its Latin America regions, Europe, Africa, and Asia, but declined slightly in the United States and Canada.[9] Its strength in brand recognition and focused marketing drove its global brands of Budweiser, Stella Artois, and Corona to experience almost 10 percent revenue growth. AB InBev had focused on growing brands outside of their respective home markets in 2017. Due to this investment, Budweiser, Stella Artois, and Corona experienced almost 17 percent revenue growth outside of their home markets.

AB InBev invested heavily in sponsorships to bolster marketing and brand recognition globally. Budweiser planned to sponsor the 2018 and 2022 FIFA World Cups™, as it had sponsored the 2014 competition. Globally, the Budweiser brand experienced revenue growth of 4.1 percent, driven by 11 percent growth with sales outside of the United States in 2017. Bud Light was the official sponsor of the National Football League through 2022.

AB InBev had also actively acquired other brands and breweries since the 1990s, including Labatt in 1995, Beck's in 2002, Anheuser-Bush in 2008, and Grupo Modelo in 2013. All of these acquisitions proceeded the SABMiller purchase. These acquisitions provided AB InBev greater market share and penetration through combining marketing and operations to all brands. The reacquisition of the Oriental Brewery in 2014 was a good example of the potential synergies garnered. Cass was the leading beer in Korea and was produced by Oriental Brewery; however, while Cass represented the local brand for AB InBev in Korea, Hoegaarden was distributed in Korea, along with the global brands of Budweiser, Corona, and Stella Artois.

A summary of AB InBev's financial performance from 2014 to 2017 is presented in Exhibit 6.

Boston Beer Company

Boston Beer Company was the second largest craft brewer by volume in the United States[10] and reported sales of less than 4 million barrels in 2017. The company's 2017 sales volume declined by 6 percent from 2016, which was preceded by a decrease of over 5 percent from 2015 to 2016. Accordingly, it dropped

EXHIBIT 6 Financial Summary for AB InBev, 2014–2017 (in millions of $)

	2017	2016	2015	2014
Revenue	$ 56,444	$ 45,517	$ 43,604	$ 47,063
Cost of sales	(21,386)	(17,803)	(17,137)	(18,756)
Gross Profit	35,058	27,715	26,467	28,307
Selling, general and administrative expenses	(18,099)	(15,171)	(13,732)	(10,285)
Other operating income/expenses	854	732	1,032	1,386
Non-recurring items	(662)	(394)	136	(197)
Profit from operations (EBIT)	17,152	12,882	13,904	15,111
Depreciation, amortization and impairment	4,276	3,479	3,153	3,354
EBITDA	$ 21,429	$ 16,361	$ 17,057	$ 18,465

Source: AB InBev Annual Reports, 2015, 2016, 2017.

from the fifth largest overall brewer in the United States in 2015 to ninth in 2017—see Exhibit 2. The company history states the recipe for Sam Adams was actually company founder Jim Koch's great-great-grandfather's recipe. The story of Boston Beer Company and Jim Koch's success was referenced at times as the beginning of the craft beer movement, often citing how Koch originally sold his beer to bars with the beer and pitching on the spot.

This beginning seemed to underpin much of Boston Beer Company's strategy as it competed in the higher value and higher price point category it refers to as the *better beer segment.* Focusing on quality and taste, Boston Beer Company marketed Samuel Adams Boston Lager as the original beer Koch first discovered. The company also produced several Sam Adams seasonal beers, such as Sam Adams Summer Ale and Sam Adams Octoberfest. Other seasonal Sam Adams beers have limited release in seasonal variety packs, including Samuel Adams Harvest Pumpkin and Samuel Adams Holiday Porter. In addition, there was also a Samuel Adams Brewmaster's Collection, a much smaller, limited release set of beers at much higher points, including the Small Batch Collection and Barrel Room Collection. Utopia—its highest priced beer—was branded as highly experimental and under very limited release.

In the spirit of craft beer and innovation, several years ago Boston Beer Company launched a craft brew incubator as a subsidiary, which had led to the successful development and sales of beers under the Traveler Beer Company brand. The incubator, Alchemy and Science, also built Concrete Beach Brewery and Coney Island Brewery. Alchemy and Science contributed 7 percent of the total net sales in 2015 and 4 percent of net sales in 2016.

Boston Beer Company offered three non-beer brands. The Twisted Tea brand was launched in 2001 and the Angry Orchard was originated in 2011. Truly Spiked & Sparkling was a 5 percent alcohol sparkling water launched in 2016. These other brands and products compete in the flavored malt beverage and the hard cider categories, respectively.

A summary of Boston Brewing Company's financial performance from 2014 to 2017 is presented in Exhibit 7.

Craft Brew Alliance

Craft Brew Alliance was ranked ninth for overall brewing by volume in 2017.[11] Founded in 2008, it resulted from the mergers between Redhook Brewery, Widmer Brothers Brewing, and Kona Brewing Company. Each with substantial history, the decision to merge was to help assist with growth and meeting demand. The Craft Brew Alliance also included Omission Brewery, Resignation Brewery, and Square Mile Cider Company. In addition to these brands, Craft Brew Alliance operated five brewpubs. In total, there were 820 people employed at Craft Brew Alliance, producing just over 1 million barrels in 2016.

EXHIBIT 7   Financial Summary for Boston Brewing Company, 2014–2017 (in thousands of $)

	2017	2016	2015	2014
Revenue	$921,736	$968,994	$1,024,040	$966,478
Excise taxes*	(58,744)	(62,548)	(64,106)	(63,471)
Cost of goods sold	(413,091)	(446,776)	(458,317)	(437,996)
Gross Profit	449,901	459,670	501,617	465,011
Advertising, promotional and selling expenses	258,649	244,213	273,629	250,696
General and administrative expenses	73,126	78,033	71,556	65,971
Impairment of assets	2,451	(235)	258	1,777
Operating Income	115,675	137,659	156,174	146,567
Other expense, net	467	(538)	(1,164)	(973)
Provision for income taxes	17,093	49,772	56,596	54,851
Net Income	$ 99,049	$ 87,349	$ 98,414	$ 90,743

Source: Boston Beer Company Annual Report, 2017.

Craft Brew Alliance utilized automated brewing equipment and distributed nationally through the Anheuser-Busch wholesaler network alliance, leveraging many of the logistics and thus cost advantages associated. Yet, it remained independent, leveraging both its craft brewery brands and the cost advantage associated with larger distribution networks. It was the only independent craft brewer to achieve this relationship and sought to leverage the partnership to distribute its products in international markets, leading to the beginning of Kona's global distribution.

Craft Brew Alliance engaged in contract brewing—a practice where spare capacity in production was utilized to produce beer under contract for sale under a different label or brand. In addition, it had partnerships with retailers like Costco and Buffalo Wild Wings, garnering further consumer exposure as well as sales.

A summary of Craft Brew Alliance's financial performance from 2014 to 2017 is presented in Exhibit 8.

STRATEGIC ISSUES CONFRONTING CRAFT BREWERIES IN 2018

The vast majority of the craft breweries might produce only enough beer for the local population in their area. Many of these breweries started the same way as the larger breweries—home brewers or hobbyists decided to start to brew and sell their own beer. Many obtained startup capital through their own savings or solicited investments from friends and family.

Given their entrepreneurial beginnings, these microbreweries and even smaller nanobreweries were usually located in industrial spaces. They were solely operated by the brewer-turned-entrepreneur, or a small staff of two or three. This staff would help with brewing and production, as well as potentially brewery tours and visits—probably the most common marketing and consumer relations tactic utilized by smaller breweries. While almost all breweries offered tours and tastings, these became ever more critical to the smaller brewery with limited capital for marketing and advertising. If onsite sales were available, the brewer could sell growlers to visitors.

Social media websites also offered significant exposure for free and had become a foundational element of brewery marketing. These websites helped the brewery reach the craft beer consumer, who tended to seek out and follow new and upcoming breweries. There were also mobile phone applications specific to the craft beer industry that could help a startup gain exposure. Participating in craft beer festivals, where local and regional breweries were able to offer samples to attendees, was another opportunity to gain exposure.

Some small microbreweries did not have enough employees for bottling and labeling and had been known to solicit volunteers through social media. To gain exposure and boost sales, the brewery might host events at local restaurants, such as tap-takeovers, where several of its beers are featured on draft. If

EXHIBIT 8   Financial Summary for Craft Brew Alliance, 2014–2017 (in thousands of $)

	2017	2016	2015	2014
Revenue	$207,456	$202,507	$204,168	$200,022
Cost of sales	(142,198)	(142,908)	(141,972)	(141,312)
Gross Profit	65,258	59,599	62,196	58,710
Selling, general and administrative expenses	60,463	59,224	57,932	53,000
Operating Income	4,796	375	4,264	5,710
Income before provision for income taxes	4,041	(306)	3,718	5,099
Provision for income taxes	(5,482)	14	1,500	2,022
Net Income	$ 9,523	$ (320)	$ 2,218	$ 3,077

Source: Craft Brew Alliance Annual Reports, 2015 and 2016, and March 7, 2018 Press Release, "Craft Brew Alliance Reports Record Performance in 2017 and Expects Continued Improvements in 2018," **http://phx.corporate-ir.net/phoenix.zhtml?c=95666&p=irol-newsArticle&ID=2336844**

enough consumers were engaged, local restaurants were enticed to purchase more beer from the distributor of the brewery. However, any number of variables—raw material shortages, tight retail competition, price-sensitive consumers—could dramatically impact future viability.

The number of beers available to the consumer throughout all segments and price points had continued to steadily climb since the mid-2000s. While the overall beer industry had seemed to plateau, the significant growth appeared to be in the craft beer, or better beer segments. Further, larger macrobreweries and regional craft breweries were seizing the opportunity to acquire other breweries as a method

of obtaining distribution and branding synergies, while also mitigating the amount of direct competition. Complicating the competitive landscape were increasing availability and price fluctuations of raw materials. These sporadic shortages might impact the industry's growth and affect the production stability of breweries, especially those smaller operations that did not have capacity to purchase in bulk or outbid larger competitors.

Overall, the growth in the consumers' desire for craft beer was likely to continue to attract more entrants, while encouraging larger breweries to seek additional acquisitions of successful craft beer brands.

ENDNOTES

[1] IBISWorld Industry Report 0D4302 Craft Beer Production in the U.S., December 2017.
[2] Brewers Association, National Beer Sales and Production Data, https://www.brewers-association.org/statistics/national-beer-sales-production-data/ (accessedMay 19, 2018).
[3] IBISWorld Industry Report 0D4302 Craft Beer Production in the U.S., December 2017.
[4] "Beer Serves America: A Study of the U.S. Beer Industry's Economic Contribution in 2016," The Beer Institute and The National Beer Wholesalers Association, May 2017,

http://beerservesamerica.org/ (accessed June 18, 2017).
[5] IBISWorld Industry Report 0D4302 Craft Beer Production in the U.S., December 2017.
[6] Research, Z. M. "Global Beer Market Predicted to Reach by $750.00 Billion in 2022," March 2, 2018, http://globenewswire.com/news-release/2018/03/02/1414335/0/en/Global-Beer-Market-Predicted-to-Reach-by-750-00-Billion-in-2022.html.
[7] American Homebrewers Association, Homebrewing Stats, https://www.homebrewersassociation.org/membership/

homebrewing-stats/ (accessed December 17, 2017).
[8] Hop Growers of America 2017 Statistical Report, https://www.usahops.org/img/blog_pdf/105.pdf (accessed May 19, 2017).
[9] Anheuser-Busch InBev 2017 Annual Report.
[10] "Brewers Association Releases 2017 Top 50 Brewing Companies By Sales Volume," March 14, 2018, https://www.brewersassociation.org/press-releases/brewers-association-releases-2017-top-50-brewing-companies-by-sales-volume/.
[11] Ibid.

Fixer Upper: Expanding the Magnolia Brand

Rochelle R. Brunson
Baylor University

Marlene M. Reed
Baylor University

I n the spring of 2018, Home and Garden Television (HGTV) aired the *Fixer Upper* season finale closing five years on the network during which the series had become increasingly more popular. Not only had the program drawn attention to the other properties of Chip and Joanna Gaines, the stars of the show, but a spotlight had also been focused on the site of the show—Waco, Texas. With the end of *Fixer Upper,* people wondered what would happen to the various Magnolia businesses, as well as the host city whose prominence had grown along with the popularity of not only the *Fixer Upper* show, but also the Gaines family.

BACKGROUND ON CHIP AND JOANNA GAINES

Both Chip and Joanna Gaines graduated from Baylor University, but they graduated three years apart and had not met until after they had left Baylor. Chip received a degree in marketing and started a few small businesses. He had hoped to play professional baseball until he was cut from the Baylor baseball team after his sophomore year. Joanna majored in communications and planned on becoming a broadcast journalist. Joanna's father owned an automobile shop—Jerry Stevens' Firestone—in Waco, Texas, and it was there that the couple met. Chip had come into the store and noticed a picture of Joanna and immediately decided that was the girl he wanted to marry. Later when he brought his car in to have the brakes fixed, he met Joanna and later asked her out on a date. That was in 2001, and in 2003 after many dates, the couple got married. For the next few years, the couple began to establish a real estate business for

themselves, invested in other ventures, and become the parents of five children. A timeline of Gaines' real estate investments is presented in Exhibit 1.

House Flipping

When Joanna married Chip, she decided to join him in his latest entrepreneurial venture of "flipping houses." This was the practice of buying a home as inexpensively as possible, renovating it, and then attempting to sell the house at the highest possible margin. Then the

EXHIBIT 1 Timeline of the Gaines' Properties

Date	Initiation of Property
2003	House flipping
	Magnolia Market
2013	Pilot of *Fixer Upper*
2015	Silos opened
	(Magnolia Market at the Silos)
	Magnolia House
2016	The Magnolia Journal
2017	Hearth & Home for Target
	Hillcrest House
2018	*Fixer Upper ends*
	Fixer Upper: Behind the Design
	Magnolia Warehouse Shop (opens periodically for warehouse sales)
	Magnolia Table

entrepreneur normally takes the profits from the first home and invests in another home to start the process all over again. With the first home they flipped, the couple found they had much to learn about the practice. Joanna said of the experience,

> "We painted over the wallpaper, left the popcorn ceilings intact, and spent most of our bathroom renovation budget on double shower heads."[1]

Magnolia Market

Soon after flipping their first house, the Gaines borrowed $5,000 and opened their first retail store named Magnolia Market in 2003.[2] They privately called the operation the "Little Shop on Bosque." It was in this store that Joanna suggests she developed her design style and skills, grew as a business owner, and gained confidence in the store and herself. However, after their first two children were born, Chip and Joanna decided to close the store and concentrate on their Magnolia Homes real estate company. The store was reopened later for a couple of years and then began to be used in March 2018 as a type of "outlet" for the Magnolia Market at the Silos. The shop featured last chance items and slightly damaged products at a discount. It was renamed the Magnolia Warehouse Shop and opened periodically for warehouse sales.[3]

Pilot of *Fixer Upper*

The show's pilot aired on April 23, 2013, on HGTV. The full season began on April 2, 2014. After five years of filming, the final season premiered on November 21, 2017. The thesis of the show was to showcase the work that Chip and Joanna Gaines had been doing in Waco, Texas, helping their clients to purchase and remodel homes. Normally, the buyers had an overall budget of under $200,000 with at least $30,000 to be invested in renovations. Viewers were often surprised to find that some of the homes selected for renovation sold for as little as $35,000. The Gaines were paid a fee by the television production company plus an undisclosed fee by the people for whom the renovations had been performed. Exhibit 2 presents a summary of estimated revenues from *Fixer Upper* and the Gaines' net worth. The program was immediately popular, and the Season 4 finale attracted more than five million viewers. This made it the second most watched cable broadcast in the second quarter of 2017 only behind *The Walking Dead.*

Silos Opened

After the television program *Fixer Upper* began to take off, the Gaines spent most of 2015 renovating and preparing to open their new Magnolia Market in two rusting silos near downtown Waco (see Exhibits 3 and 4). In order to avoid painting the massive silos, the couple had to get permission from the City of Waco to let them remain as they were—adding to the historic nature of the site. In addition to the silos, there was a 20,000 square foot barn that now houses a marketplace full of decorating accessories. The market covers 2.5 acres and provides a large outside play area for children and a space for food trucks to park and deliver food to the store's patrons.

EXHIBIT 2   Estimated Revenues From *Fixer Upper* and Gaines' Net Worth

Revenues from *Fixer Upper*
$30,000 per episode for first 4 years × 14 episodes = $420,000 each season
4 first seasons = × 4 seasons
Total = $1,680,000
Plus the last season = 540,000
Total for 5 seasons = $2,220,000

Not included in these revenues are undisclosed fees from families helped with renovations.

The Magnolia Brand was estimated to be worth more than $5 million in 2018.[11]

The net worth each of Chip and Joanna Gaines was estimated at $9 million in 2018.[12]

Sources: Here's How Much Chip and Joanna Gaines are Really Making for the Last Season of Fixer Upper. https://www.cheatsheet.com/money-career/heres-much-chip-joanna-gaines-really-making-last-season-fixer-upper.html/?a=viewall; Celebrity Net Worth. https://www.celebritynetworth.com/chip-and-joanna-gaines/.

EXHIBIT 3   The Silos

©Magnolia Market

At the far end of the property, Joanna established the Magnolia Seed & Supply store complete with flower beds filled with seasonal herbs and flowers.

In 2016, not long after the silos became operational, Chip and Joanna secured a small building on the corner of their property that had previously housed a floral shop and converted it into the Silos Baking Co. The shop serves a variety of cupcakes and breads whose names are associated with *Fixer Upper* such as "The Silo's Cookie" and the "Shiplap" cupcake as well as the classic cinnamon roll and the "Prize Pig" biscuit.

The Magnolia Journal

Building on the success of the Magnolia brand, Chip and Joanna launched the Magnolia Journal as a

EXHIBIT 4   Outside of Magnolia Market

©Magnolia Market

quarterly lifestyle publication in 2016. Joanna said of the magazine:

> My goal in creating this magazine was to connect with readers from all walks of life, to share content so valuable and so meaningful that you hold on to each issue and return to them again and again.[4]

The journal contains Joanna's personal reflections and design tips with a focus on entertaining and seasonal celebrations. Exhibit 5 presents a review of the brand footprint, which describes the typical journal reader.

Hearth & Hand with Magnolia

On November 5 of 2017, Target released an exclusive home brand line of home goods in collaboration with Magnolia. The Hearth & Hand collection includes 300 items that range from home décor to gifts. Most of the items are priced under $30. Gaines said of the collaboration:

> Just as we've never created an exclusive line of product for a retailer before, Target has never done anything like this before either. Let me try to give you a visual; it's like a little shop inside of Target. Jo keeps calling the look "modern farmhouse," whatever that means. All I know is she's so excited about this collection that she wants to register for our wedding all over again.[5]

Fixer Upper Concludes

In fall 2017, Chip and Joanna announced to the public that their *Fixer Upper* television program would be coming to an end in the spring of 2018 (end of Season 5). The couple said they had mixed emotions about the closure, but that the taping schedule was beginning to wear upon them. Initially, they had

EXHIBIT 5   Magnolia Journal Typical Reader

Median income	$92,540
Home ownership	81%
Married	83%
Millenials	36%
Parents	44%
Median age	50

Source: www.meredith.com/brand/themagnoliajournal/.

anticipated that they would be filming about eight hours a day, but they soon found that was not to be. They discovered that to put together a season of programs, they had to film 11 months out of the year. They decided to spend more time with their family and have time to welcome a new baby to the family in the summer of 2018. However, a source told *Vanity Fair* magazine that Chip and Joanna clashed with HGTV executives over not being able to showcase their furniture line on the show.[6] The *New York Post* reported that Chip and Joanna were unhappy with their contract because it was so restrictive. The source reported in the *Post* suggested that their present contract would have prevented them from taking advantage of some lucrative deals.[7]

Fixer Upper: Behind the Design

The Gaines' brand would not be separated from television for long. On April 10, 2018, Joanna launched a *Fixer Upper* spinoff series entitled "Behind the Design." In this series, Joanna plans to share details on her design strategies, decorating, and staging a home. The program will cover all the elements that go into home makeovers. The format of the program took the viewer through the designs in the original *Fixer Upper* series room-by-room offering design secrets, insights, recommendations, and tips.

Magnolia Table

In February 2016, a Waco landmark, the Elite Café, was closed due to lack of profitability. The café had been opened 97 years earlier at a busy traffic circle in Waco and had served as a meeting place for local customers as well as tourists traveling between Dallas and Austin. One of the favorite stories about the restaurant concerned a young soldier stationed at nearby Fort Hood name Elvis Presley who had eaten at the Elite. The café had also become a favorite gathering place for Baylor University football fans in the fall of the year.

After the closing of the Elite, the Gaines acquired the 8,356 square foot facility, renovated it and opened it under the name "Magnolia Table" in early 2018. Some history buffs in the city complained that the name "Elite" should have been retained since the café's history had been so intertwined with that of the town. However, Chip and Joanna Gaines realized that the success of the renovated restaurant depended upon the Magnolia brand.

The Elite Café is a big part of Waco's history, and we wanted to honor that legacy, so we really, really struggled with whether to keep the original name or not. We knew that changing it could be an unpopular decision here in town, and we nearly kept it for that reason alone. But as we considered all that we hoped for this place—what we wanted this new iteration of the old restaurant to be—we quickly realized that the new hope and old name were diametrically opposed. After much deliberation, we decided to name the café Magnolia Table. We chose this new name because we wanted our restaurant to be a clear representation of a place where *all* were welcome.[8]

Shortly after the opening of Magnolia Table, customers had already resigned themselves to waiting in line for 30 minutes to get their name on the list for a table and then another hour-and-a-half to finally get seated. However, because of the friendly greetings and accommodations of the staff who invited waiting customers to have a seat in a pavilion outside where they could purchase hot or cold beverages as well as some pastries, customers appeared to take the wait in stride. Some have even waited as long as two and-a-half hours to be seated with no complaints. Magnolia Table is only open from 6am until 3pm Monday through Saturday. They do have a Take Away area and gift store.

Magnolia Stay

During the taping of the *Fixer Upper* show, Chip and Joanna Gaines were able to secure a property in McGregor, Texas, 20 minutes outside of Waco known as the "Magnolia House." The renovation was featured on the show and it was available to reserve with a two night minimum at $695/night (sleeps 8 people). They also purchased "Hillcrest Estate" in Waco, Texas, which was built in 1903 and renovated this home that can be reserved as well with a two night minimum at $995/night (sleeps 12 people). These two properties at Magnolia Stay are another part of the Magnolia/Gaines properties (businesses).[9]

THE EFFECT ON WACO

Rarely had a business have the kind of impact on a city that *Fixer Upper* and its brand extensions have had on Waco, Texas. The impact on the city of Waco was a realization of the company's mission to "Do good work that matters." Chip commented on the selection of the city for their television program:

> People typically reacted to the news of my being from Waco with sympathy or disdain. After the Branch Davidian incident, the name of our town even became part of popular culture. Considering Waco's reputation and small size, it was hard to convince HGTV to believe that basing our show solely in Waco, Texas, would be a recipe for success. . . . The network tried to talk us into doing just the first few homes in Waco and then branching out into neighboring cities like Austin or Dallas. . . . After some discussion, the network understood that if they wanted us, a show based in Waco, Texas, had to be enough for them.[10]

The Waco Convention Center and Visitors' Bureau reported that the Magnolia Market at the Silos attracts a minimum of 30,000 visitors a week to the city. Parking had become a major challenge near the Silos, and some organizations are charging up to $10 a car for a favorable place to park. The Convention Center predicted that the Silos attraction could potentially draw 1.6 million visitors annually with roughly 50 percent of those visitors from outside of Texas. Local hotels and restaurants have been the recipients of increased traffic since the opening of the Silos; however, some locals have complained about the increased traffic, which makes it harder to maneuver downtown Waco. In March 2015, properties in Waco on **Realtor.com** were reported to be viewed at four times the national average. There had been speculation about whether the Silos would be able to maintain its popularity after the demise of the popular television program *Fixer Upper*.

FUTURE OF THE MAGNOLIA BRAND

By 2018, the Magnolia brand had been leveraged into such undertakings as a real estate company, television program, bed and breakfast, retail store, magazine, and restaurant. Magnolia now had 200 employees at Magnolia Table and approximately 800 employees companywide. The sky seemed to be the limit for the company and the city in which it was located. However, skeptics speculated about how sustainable the brand would be in the future with its primary driver—*Fixer Upper*—now canceled.

ENDNOTES

[1] Joanna Gaines, Instagram.

[2] Ibid.

[3] Magnolia. **https://twitter.com/magnolia/ status/975453791188340736/**.

[4] Joanna Gaines. Our Story. **https://magnolia. com/about/**.

[5] ChipGaines, **https://magnolia.com/journal/**.

[6] *New York Post.* **https://pagesix. com/2017/10/09/the-real-reason-chip-and- joanna-gaines-quit-hgtv/**.

[7] Ibid.

[8] *Vanity Fair.* **https://www.vanityfair.com/ hollywood/2017/11/fixer-upper-hgtv- chip-joanna-gaines-new-show/**. As quoted

in *Capital Gaines: Smart Things I Learned Doing Stupid Stuff,* Chip Gaines, Harper Collins Publishers, 2017, pp. 150–151.

[9] **https://magnolia.com/stay**.

[10] As quoted in Gaines, 2017, p. 109

Under Armour's Turnaround Strategy in 2018: Efforts to Revive North American Sales and Profitability

connect

Arthur A. Thompson

The University of Alabama

Founded in 1996 by former University of Maryland football player Kevin Plank, Under Armour was the originator of sports apparel made with performance-enhancing fabrics—gear engineered to wick moisture from the body, regulate body temperature, and enhance comfort regardless of weather conditions and activity levels. It started with a simple plan to make a T-shirt that provided compression and wicked perspiration off the wearer's skin, thereby avoiding the discomfort of sweat-absorbed apparel.

Plank formed KP Sports as a subchapter S corporation in Maryland in 1996 and commenced selling a performance fabric T-shirt to athletes and sports teams. He worked the phone and, with a trunk full of shirts in the back of his car, visited schools and training camps in person to show his products. Plank's sales successes were soon good enough that he convinced Kip Fulks, who played lacrosse at Maryland, to become a partner in his enterprise. Operations were conducted on a shoestring budget out of the basement of Plank's grandmother's house in Georgetown, a Washington, D.C. suburb. In 1998, the company's sales revenues and growth prospects were sufficient to secure a $250,000 small-business loan, enabling the company to move operations to a facility in Baltimore. Ryan Wood, one of Plank's acquaintances from high school, joined the company in 1999 and became a partner.

KP Sports' sales grew briskly as it expanded its product line to include high-tech undergarments tailored for athletes in different sports and for cold as well as hot temperatures, plus jerseys, team uniforms, socks, and other accessories. Increasingly, the company was able to secure deals not just to provide gear for a particular team but for most or all of a school's sports teams. However, the company's partners came to recognize the merits of tapping the retail market for high-performance apparel and began making sales calls on sports apparel retailers. In 2000, Scott Plank, Kevin's older brother, joined the company in 2000 as Vice President of Finance and certain other operational and strategic responsibilities. When Galyan's, a large retail chain since acquired by Dick's Sporting Goods, signed on to carry KP Sports' expanding line of performance apparel for men, women, and youth in 2000, sales to other sports apparel retailers began to explode. By the end of 2000, the company's products were available in some 500 retail locations.

Prompted by growing operational complexity, increased financial requirements, and plans for further geographic expansion, KP Sports revoked its "S" corporation status and became a "C" corporation on January 1, 2002. The company opened a Canadian sales office in 2003 and began selling its products in the United Kingdom in 2005. At year-end 2005, about 90 percent of the company's revenues came from sales to some 6,000 retail stores in the United States and 2,000 stores in Canada, Japan, and the United Kingdom. In addition, sales were being made to high profile athletes and teams, most notably in the National Football League, Major League Baseball, the National Hockey League, and some 400 men's and women's sports team s at NCAA Division 1-A colleges and universities.

In late 2005, KP Sports changed its name to Under Armour and became a public company with an initial public offering of common stock that generated net proceeds of nearly $115 million. Under Armour immediately began pursuing a long-term strategy to grow its product line, establish a market presence in a growing number of countries across the world, and build public awareness of the Under Armour brand and its interlocking "U" and "A" logo.

Under Armour quickly earned a reputation as an up-and-coming company in the sports apparel business, achieving sales of $1 billion in 2010 and $3 billion in 2014. Starting in the second-quarter of 2010 and continuing through the third-quarter of 2016, Under Armour cemented its status as a growth company by achieving revenue growth of 20 + percent for 26 consecutive quarters (see Exhibit 1). In announcing the company's 2016 third-quarter financial results,

Chairman and chief executive officer (CEO) Kevin Plank said:

> Over the past 20 years, we have established ourselves as a premium global brand with a track record of strong financial results. Looking back over the past nine months, it has never been more evident that we are at a pivotal moment in time, where the investments we are making today will fuel our growth and drive our industry leadership position for years to come. As a growth company with an expanding global footprint and businesses like footwear and women's each approaching a billion dollars this year, we have never been more focused on the long-term success of our Brand.[1]

But despite Plank's optimism about Under Armour's future prospects, management announced a reduced sales and earnings outlook for the fourth quarter of 2016 and weakening demand for Under Armour products in North America. The company's sales growth in North America during the first nine months of 2016 dropped from 25.7 percent in Q1 to 21.5 percent in Q2 to 15.6 percent in Q3. The prices of Under Armour's Class A shares (trading under the symbol UAA) and Class C shares (trading under the symbol UA) dropped nearly 30 percent in the next three trading days, not only because of the weak outlook, but also because of investor concerns about reports of a slowdown in retail sales of sports apparel products in the United States.

EXHIBIT 1   Growth in Under Armour's Quarterly Revenues, 2010–2017 (in millions)

	Quarter 1 (Jan.–March)		Quarter 2 (April–June)		Quarter 3 (July–Sept.)		Quarter 4 (Oct.–Dec.)	
	Revenues	Percent Change from Prior Year's Quarter 1	Revenues	Percent Change from Prior Year's Quarter 2	Revenues	Percent Change from Prior Year's Quarter 3	Revenues	Percent Change from Prior Year's Quarter 4
2010	$ 229.4	14.7%	$ 204.8	24.4%	$ 328.6	21.9%	$ 301.2	35.5%
2011	312.7	36.3%	291.3	42.3%	465.5	41.7%	403.1	33.9%
2012	384.4	23.0%	369.5	26.8%	575.2	23.6%	505.9	25.5%
2013	471.6	22.7%	454.5	23.0%	723.1	25.7%	682.8	35.0%
2014	641.6	36.0%	609.7	34.1%	937.9	29.7%	895.2	31.1%
2015	804.9	25.5%	783.6	28.5%	1,204.1	28.4%	1,170.7	30.8%
2016	1,047.8	30.2%	1,000.8	27.7%	1,471.6	22.4%	1,305.3	11.5%
2017	1,117.3	(2.9)%	1,088.2	8.7%	1,405.6	(4.5)%	1,365.4	4.6%

Source: Company 10-K reports, 2017, 2016, 2015, 2013, 2012, and 2010.

A SUDDEN COLLAPSE IN UNDER ARMOUR'S FINANCIAL PERFORMANCE AND GROWTH PROSPECTS

Under Armour's report of its 2016 fourth quarter and full-year results in January 2017 rang alarm bells. Total fourth-quarter revenues rose 11.7 percent; revenues in North America were up only 5.9 percent; income from operations dropped 6.1 percent companywide and 15.0 percent in North America. To make matters worse, the company's outlook for full-year 2017 was gloomy—expected revenue growth of 11 to 12 percent (the lowest annual growth rate since the company became a "C" corporation in 2002) and a decline in operating income to approximately $320 million, partly because of "strategic investments in the company's fastest growing businesses."[2] Nonetheless, Kevin Plank believed the company's resources and capabilities would enable it to cope with the challenges ahead:

> We are incredibly proud that in 2016, we once again posted record revenue and earnings; however, numerous challenges and disruptions in North American retail tempered our fourth quarter results. The strength of our Brand, an unparalleled connection with our consumers, and the continuation of investments in our fastest growing businesses—footwear, international and direct-to-consumer—give us great confidence in our ability to navigate the current retail environment, execute against our long-term growth strategy, and create value to our shareholders.[3]

In the days following the full-year 2016 earnings release and the 2017 outlook presented by management, the prices of the company's Class A shares and Class C shares—which were already trading about 30 percent below their highs earlier in 2016—dropped another 28 percent.

2017 Turned Out to Be a Terrible Year for Under Armour
Overall, Under Armour's performance in 2017 turned out to be worse than management's earlier expectations. In its core North American market, Under Armour found itself on the defensive throughout 2017. A year after growing North American sales from almost $1.0 billion in 2012 to $4.0 billion in 2016 (a compound growth rate of 41.4 percent), Under Armour's 2017 sales in North America dropped $200 million (5.1 percent) to $3.8 billion. Total revenues worldwide

were up a meager 3.1 percent—from $4.83 billion to $4.98 billion, after growing at a compound rate of 27.3 percent from 2012 to 2016. Operating income dropped from $417.5 million in 2016 to $27.8 million in 2017. Net income fell from a record high of $257.0 million to a net loss of $48.3 million. The prices of the company's Class A shares and Class C shares which began 2017 trading at $29.34 and $25.49, respectively, closed at $14.43 and $13.32 on the last trading day of December 2017. These declines in Under Armour's stock prices were all the more disheartening to the company's shareholders because the value of stocks listed on the NYSE and Nasdaq stock exchanges had climbed by more than $7 trillion in the 16 months since the 2016 presidential election.

The big drops in Under Armour's operating income and the net loss of $48.3 million were partially due to management's announcement in August 2017 that it would pursue a $140 to $150 million restructuring plan to address operating inefficiencies, transition to a product category management structure, and reengineer the company's go-to-market process (product innovation and design, vendor relationships, delivery times of seasonal products, inventory management, profit margin control, and speed of response to shifting consumer preferences and market conditions); in addition, the plan called for a global workforce reduction of about 300 people, inventory reductions and write-downs, and charges for asset impairments, facility and lease terminations, and contract terminations. These restructuring efforts resulted in $39 million in cash-related charges and $90 million in non-cash related charges against full-year 2017 results.

But the stock price declines were also a reflection of investor concerns about whether the Under Armour brand was in trouble in North America—the experiences of other troubled brands had demonstrated it was extremely difficult to rebuild a brand once it had fallen out of favor with the public. Investors had also been unnerved weeks earlier when analysts at 24/7 Wall St. had ranked Kevin Plank as No. 4 on its list of "20 Worst CEOs in America 2017."[4] Plank had been under the microscope since a controversial split of the company's stock in April 2016 into Class A (vote-entitled), Class B, and Class C (no voting power) shares, where Kevin Plank was granted Class B shares equal to his Class A shareholdings; each Class B share owned by Plank entitled him to 10 votes for every Class A share he owned. Since he owned about 15.8 percent of the Class A shares (as of April 2017), his super-vote Class B shares gave him about 65 percent of the total shareholder voting power on every shareholder vote taken.

Since the stock split, Plank had sold some of his Class C shares to fund the creation of Plank Industries, a privately-held investment company with ownership interests in commercial real estate, hospitality, food and beverage, venture capital, and thoroughbred horse racing. Plank's critics had claimed the new venture was absorbing too much of his time. Plank's time in dealing with UA's operating issues and sales slowdown had also been constrained by his involvement in helping spearhead a 25-year, $5.5 billion project (being partially financed with bonds issued by the City of Baltimore's Baltimore Development Corp.) to develop waterfront property in South Baltimore into a mini-city called Port Covington that would create thousands of jobs and drive demand for office buildings, houses, shops and restaurants. Plank Industries' Sycamore Development Co. was the lead private developer of the Port Covington project. So far, Sycamore had completed a number of properties in the project, including a $24 million renovation of a former Sam's Club into a 170,000 square-foot facility for Under Armour, tentatively named Building 37 (Plank's number on his University of Maryland football jersey was 37). Building 37 was on acreage Under Armour had purchased for $70.3 million in 2014 and was being leased by Sycamore to Under Armour for $1.1 million annually. Building 37 was the first phase of Under Armour's plan to create a 50-acre global headquarters campus that would include a new headquarters building on the site of Building 37, additional Under Armour facilities and manufacturing space, a man-made lake, and a small stadium—a layout designed to house as many as 10,000 Under Armour employees (UA employed approximately 2,100 people in Baltimore in early 2018, some 600 of which were housed in Building 37).

To compensate for the time he was spending on outside interests, Plank engineered the appointment of Patrik Frisk, formerly CEO of the ALDO Group, a global footwear and accessories company, as President and Chief Operating Officer (COO) of Under Armour in June 2017. Frisk had 30 years of experience in the apparel, footwear, and retail industry, holding top management positions with responsibility for such brands as The North Face®, Timberland®, JanSport®, lucy®, and SmartWool®. As president and COO, Frisk was assigned responsibility for Under Armour's go-to-market strategy and the successful

execution of its long-term growth plan. Kevin Plank titles were Chairman of the Board and CEO.

In 2008, Plank voluntarily reduced his salary from $500,000 to $26,000, which was his approximate salary when he founded Under Armour. As UA's largest stockholder, Plank believed he should be compensated for his services based primarily on the company's annual incentive plan tied to the company's performance and on annual performance-based equity awards. Plank's $26,000 salary remained in place in 2018.

How Under Armour's 2017 Sales Performance in North America Compared Against Its Two Biggest Rivals Under Armour's 5.1 percent decline in 2017 sales in the North American market compared unfavorably with long-time industry leader Nike, whose sales of $15.2 billion in North America during December 1, 2016 through November 30, 2017 were essentially unchanged from the $15.1 billion in sales Nike reported for December 1, 2015 through November 30, 2016.[5] But the real threat to Under Armour's competitive standing in the North American market going into 2018 came from Germany-based The adidas Group—the industry's second-ranking company in terms of global revenues in sports apparel, athletic footwear, and sports equipment and accessories. Two years earlier, Under Armour had overtaken adidas (pronounced ah-di-dah) to become the second largest seller of sports apparel, active wear, and athletic footwear in North America.[6] However, top executives at adidas launched an unusually strong series of strategic initiatives at the beginning of 2017 to increase its share of the sports apparel, active wear, and athletic footwear market in North America from an estimated 10 percent to around 15 to 20 percent. The results were impressive considering stagnant market demand for sports apparel and products in North America—sales of adidas-branded products in North America grew by a resounding 34 percent in the first nine months of 2017.

Under Armour's Outlook for 2018 In February 2018, top executives at Under Armour did not foresee a quick turnaround. Their 2018 outlook for North American revenues was a mid-single-digit decline, although international sales were expected to grow 25 percent. Gross margins were expected to improve 50 basis points to 45.5 percent, but only because of lower planned promotional activity, anticipated savings in product costs, favorable shifts in sales to distribution channels with better margins, and favorable changes in foreign currency. Operating income was projected to be $20 million to $30 million (versus $28.7 million in 2017). Management explained the projections of operating income were low because, after additional review, a decision had been made to pursue a second restructuring plan in 2018 to further optimize operations. This plan entailed:

- Up to $105 million in cash-related charges, consisting of up to $55 million in facility and lease terminations and up to $50 million in contract termination and other restructuring charges; and
- Up to $25 million in non-cash charges, comprised of up to $10 million of inventory related charges and up to $15 million of asset-related impairments.

Management said it expected the 2017 and 2018 restructuring efforts to produce a minimum of $75 million in savings annually in 2019 and beyond.

The two restructuring programs were partly necessitated by 2015 management efforts to begin scaling the company's infrastructure to accommodate expected sales of $7.5 billion in 2018. When it became apparent to top executives that Under Armour would not achieve that level of sales until several years later, then scaling back internal operations, budgets, and workforce sizes accordingly was necessary to transform Under Armour into a leaner, more cost-efficient operation.

Exhibit 2 shows selected financial statement data for Under Armour for 2014 through 2017.

EXHIBIT 2   Selected Financial Data for Under Armour, Inc., 2014–2017 (in millions)

Selected Income Statement Data	2017	2016	2015	2014
Net revenues	$4,976.6	$4,825.3	$3,963.3	$3,084.4
Cost of goods sold	2,737.8	2,584.7	2,057.8	1,152.2
Gross profit	2,238.7	2,240.6	1,905.5	1,512.2
Selling, general and administrative expenses	2,086.8	1823.1	1,497.0	1,158.3
Restructuring and impairment charges	124.0	—	—	—
Income from operations	27.8	417.5	408.5	354.0
Interest expense, net	(34.5)	(26.4)	(14.6)	(5.3)
Other expense, net	(3.6)	(2.8)	(7.2)	(6.4)
Income (loss) before income taxes	(10.3)	388.3	386.7	342.2
Provision for income taxes	38.0	131.3	154.1	134.2
Net income (loss)	$ (48.3)	$ 257.0	$ 232.6	$ 208.0

Selected Balance Sheet Data				
Cash and cash equivalents	$ 312.5	$ 250.5	$ 129.9	$ 593.2
Working capital*	1,277.3	1,279.3	1,020.0	1,127.8
Inventories at year-end	1,158.5	917.5	783.0	536.7
Total assets	4,006.4	3,644.3	2,866.0	2,092.4
Long-term debt, including current maturities	792.0	817.4	666.1	281.5
Total stockholders' equity	2,018.6	2,030.9	1,668.2	1,350.3

Selected Cash Flow Data				
Net cash provided by operating activities	$ 234.1	$ 364.4	($ 14.5)	$ 219.0

*Working capital is defined as current assets minus current liabilities.

Note: Some totals may not add up due to rounding.

Source: Company 10-K reports for 2017 and 2016.

UNDER ARMOUR'S STRATEGY IN 2018

Until 2018, Under Armour's mission was "to make all athletes better through passion, design, and the relentless pursuit of innovation." A reworded mission—"Under Armour Makes You Better"—was publicly announced in early 2018. Kevin Plank said the new wording was meant to better convey that "in every way we connect, through the products we create, the experience we deliver and the inspiration we provide, we simply make you better."[7]

The company's principal business activities in 2018 were the development, marketing, and distribution of branded performance apparel, footwear, and related sports accessories for men, women, and youth. The brand's moisture-wicking apparel products were engineered in many designs and styles for wear in nearly every climate to provide a performance alternative to traditional products. Under Armour sports apparel was worn by athletes at all levels, from youth to professional, and by consumers with active lifestyles. Sales of these products were made through two primary channels—wholesale sales to retailers and direct-to-consumer sales (sales at the company's websites in various geographic regions and at its rapidly growing number of company-owned brick-and-mortar Brand Houses and factory outlet stores). In the company's earlier years, revenue growth was achieved primarily by growing wholesale sales to retailers of sports apparel, athletic footwear, and sports equipment and accessories. More recently, however, sales at the company's websites and company-owned retail stores had become the company's biggest growth engine in North America. Starting in 2010, Under Armour had steadily mounted greater efforts to increase its global footprint and increase its wholesale and online sales outside North America, most especially in countries in Europe, the Middle East, and Africa (EMEA), the Asia-Pacific, and Latin America.

In 2013, Under Armour acquired MapMyFitness, a provider of website services and mobile apps to fitness-minded consumers across the world; Under Armour used this acquisition, along with several follow-on acquisitions in 2014 and 2015, to create what it termed a "connected fitness" business offering digital fitness subscriptions and licenses, mobile apps, and other fitness-tracking and nutritional-tracking solutions to athletes and fitness-conscious individuals across the world. Kevin Plank expected the company's connected fitness strategic initiative to become a major revenue driver in the years to come.

In 2018, Under Armour divided its sales into five product categories and also reported its sales and operating income by geographic segment. These are displayed in Exhibit 3 for the years 2014 through 2017.

Growth Strategy

Under Armour's growth strategy in 2018 was centered on six strategic initiatives:

- Continuing to broaden the company's product offerings to men, women, and youth for wear in a widening variety of sports and recreational activities and to increase their appeal to buyers. Special emphasis was being placed on expanding Under Armour's line of women's products to better capitalize on the growth opportunities in the women's segment.
- Increasing its sales and market share in the athletic footwear segment.
- Securing additional distribution of Under Armour products in the retail marketplace by (1) opening greater numbers of Under Armour Brand House stores and factory outlets and (2) capitalizing on growing consumer preferences to shop online. UA management had recently concluded the company's profit opportunities were often better selling its products direct to consumers at retail prices than they were selling to retail stores at wholesale prices sufficiently low to be competitive with the wholesale prices being offered by Nike and adidas.
- Growing Under Armour's global footprint by expanding its sales in foreign countries and becoming an ever-stronger global competitor in the world market for sports apparel, athletic footwear, and related sports products.
- Growing global awareness of the Under Armour brand name and strengthening the connection between consumers and Under Armour branded products worldwide.
- Growing the company's connected fitness business and making it profitable.

Most pressing, of course, was the strategic urgency to revive the company's sales growth, particularly in North America, and return the company to attractive profitability.

EXHIBIT 3   Under Armour's Revenues and Operating Income, by Product Category and Geographic Region, 2014–2017

A. Net revenues by product category (in millions of $)

	2017		2016		2015		2014	
	Dollars	Percent	Dollars	Percent	Dollars	Percent	Dollars	Percent
Apparel	$3,287.1	66.1%	$3,229.1	66.9%	$2,801.1	70.7%	$ 853.5	80.2%
Footwear	1,037.8	20.9	1,010.7	20.9	677.7	17.1	127.2	12.0
Accessories	445.8	9.0	406.6	8.4	346.9	8.8	43.9	4.1
Total net sales	4,770.8	95.9%	4,646.4	96.3%	3,825.7	96.6%	$1,024.6	96.3%
License revenues	116.6	2.3	99.8	2.1	84.2	2.1	39.4	3.7
Connected fitness	89.2	1.8	80.4	1.7	53.4	1.3	19.2	—
Total net revenues	$4,976.6	100.0%	$4,825.3	100.0%	$3,963.3	100.0%	$1,063.9	100.0%

B. Net revenues by geographic region (in millions of $)

	2017	2016	2015	2014
North America	$3,802.4	$4,005.3	$3,455.8	$2,796.4
EMEA*	470.0	330.6	203.1	134.1
Asia-Pacific	433.6	268.6	144.9	70.4
Latin America	181.3	141.8	106.2	41.9
Connected fitness	89.2	80.4	53.4	19.2
Total net revenues	$4,976.6	$4,825.3	$3,963.3	$3,084.4

C. Operating income (loss) by geographic region (in millions of $)

	2017	2016	2015	2014
North America	$ 20.2	$408.4	$461.0	$372.3
EMEA*	18.0	11.4	3.1	(11.8)
Asia-Pacific	82.0	68.3	36.4	21.9
Latin America	(37.1)	(33.9)	(30.6)	(15.4)
Connected fitness	(55.3)	(36.8)	(61.3)	(13.1)
Total operating income	$ 27.8	$417.5	$408.5	$354.0

*Europe–Middle East–Africa

Source: Company 10-K reports, 2017 and 2016.

Product Line Strategy

For a number of years, expanding the company's product offerings and marketing them at multiple price points had been a key element of Under Armour's strategy. The goal for each new item added to the line-up of offerings was to provide consumers with a product that was a *superior* alternative to the traditional products of rivals—striving to always introduce a superior product would, management believed, help foster and nourish a culture of innovation among all company personnel. According to Kevin Plank, "we focus on creating products you don't know you need yet, but once you have them, you won't remember how you lived without them."[8]

Apparel The company designed and merchandised three lines of apparel gear intended to regulate body temperature and enhance comfort, mobility, and performance regardless of weather conditions: HEATGEAR® for hot weather conditions; COLDGEAR® for cold weather conditions; and ALLSEASONGEAR® for temperature conditions between the extremes.

HeatGear. HeatGear was designed to be worn in warm to hot temperatures under equipment or as a single layer. The company's first compression T-shirt was the original HeatGear product and was still one of the company's signature styles in 2015. In sharp contrast to a sweat soaked cotton T-shirt that could weigh two to three pounds, HeatGear was engineered with a microfiber blend featuring what Under Armour termed a "Moisture Transport System" that ensured the body would stay cool, dry, and light. HeatGear was offered in a variety of tops and bottoms in a broad array of colors and styles for wear in the gym or outside in warm weather.

ColdGear. Under Armour high performance fabrics were appealing to people participating in cold-weather sports and vigorous recreational activities like snow skiing who needed both warmth and moisture-wicking protection from becoming overheated. ColdGear was designed to wick moisture from the body while circulating body heat from hotspots to maintain core body temperature. All ColdGear apparel provided dryness and warmth in a single light layer that could be worn beneath a jersey, uniform, protective gear or ski-vest, or other cold weather outerwear. ColdGear products generally were sold at higher price points than other Under Armour gear lines.

AllSeasonGear. AllSeasonGear was designed to be worn in temperatures between the extremes of hot and cold and used technical fabrics to keep the wearer cool and dry in warmer temperatures while preventing a chill in cooler temperatures.

Each of the three apparel lines contained three fit types: compression (tight fit), fitted (athletic fit), and loose (relaxed). In 2016, Under Armour introduced apparel items containing MicroThread, a fabric technology that used elastomeric (stretchable) thread to create a cool moisture-wicking microclimate, prevented clinging and chafing, allowed garments to dry 30 percent faster and be 70 percent more breathable than similar Lycra construction, and were so lightweight as to "feel like nothing." It also began using a newly developed insulation called Reactor in selected ColdGear items and introduced a new apparel collection with an exclusive CoolSwitch coating on the inside of the fabric that pulled heat away from the skin, allowing the wearer to feel cooler and perform longer.

Footwear Under Armour began marketing athletic footwear for men, women, and youth in 2006 and had expanded its footwear line every year since. Its 2018 offerings included footwear models specifically designed for performance training, running, footwear, basketball, golf, and outdoor wear, plus football, baseball, lacrosse, softball, and soccer cleats. Under Armour's footwear models were light, breathable, and built with performance attributes specific to their intended use. Over the past 5 years, a stream of innovative technologies had been incorporated in the ongoing generations of footwear models/styles to improve stabilization, cushioning, moisture management, comfort, directional control, and performance.

New footwear collections for men, women, and youth were introduced annually, sometimes seasonally. Most new models and styles incorporated fresh technological features of one kind or another. Since 2012, Under Armour had more than tripled the number of footwear styles/models priced above $100 per pair. Its best-selling offerings were in the basketball and running shoe categories.

To capitalize on a recently signed long-term endorsement contract with pro basketball superstar Stephen Curry, Under Armour began marketing a Stephen Curry Signature line of basketball shoes in 2014; the so-called Curry One models had a price point of $120. This was followed by a Curry Two collection in 2015 at a price point of $130, a Curry 2.5 collection at a price point of $135 during the NBA playoffs in May and June 2016, a Curry Three collection in Fall 2016, a Curry 4 collection at a price point of $130 in Fall 2017, and a Curry 5 collection at a price point of $130 at the start of the NBA playoffs in May 2018.

After signing pro golfer Jordan Spieth to a 10-year endorsement contract in early 2015—Spieth had a spectacular year on the Professional Golf Association (PGA) tour in 2015 and was named 2015 PGA Tour Player of the Year—Under Armour promptly sought to leverage the signing by introducing an all-new 2016 golf shoe collection in April 2016. The collection had 3 styles, ranging in price from $160 to $220. A new Spieth One Signature collection was introduced in early 2017 with much the same price points, followed by a Spieth Two collection in early 2018, which was accompanied by a Spieth Tour™ golf glove.

Under Armour debuted its first "smart shoe" (called the SpeedForm Gemini 2 Record Equipped) at a price point of $150 in 2016; smart shoe models were equipped with the capability to connect automatically to UA's connected fitness website and record certain activities in the wearer's fitness tracking account.

In 2018, using freshly-developed connected fitness technologies and several other innovations, Under Armour debuted a new, multi-featured HOVR™ running shoe, which Kevin Plank hailed as a new product that hit what the company called "the trifecta–style, performance, and fit." HOVR models were priced from $100 to $140; all models used compression mesh and a special molded foam that provided a "zero gravity feel," gave the runner return energy with each step to reduce impact, and claimed to deliver "unmatched comfort." The higher-priced "Connected" HOVR models had built-in Under Armour Record Sensor™ technology that could be paired with a mobile phone and used to track, analyze, and store most every known running metric, enabling runners to know what they needed to do to get better. Plank believed the HOVR was "a home run" and a reflection of the company's growing capabilities to churn out innovative products.

Accessories   Under Armour's accessory line in 2018 included gloves, socks, hats and headwear, backpacks and bags, eyewear, protective gear, and equipment. All of these accessories featured performance advantages and functionality similar to other Under Armour products. For instance, the company's baseball batting, football, golf, and running gloves included HEATGEAR® and COLDGEAR® technologies and were designed with advanced fabrics to provide various high-performance attributes that differentiated Under Armour gloves from those of rival brands.

Connected Fitness   In December 2013, Under Armour acquired MapMyFitness, which served one of the largest fitness communities in the world at its website and offered a diverse suite of websites and mobile applications under its flagship brands, MapMyRun and MapMyRide. Utilizing GPS and other advanced technologies, MapMyFitness provided users with the ability to map, record, and share their workouts. Under Armour acquired European fitness app Endomondo and food-logging app MyFitnessPal in 2015, enabling UA to create a multifaceted connected fitness dashboard that used four independently functioning apps (MapMyFitness, MyFitnessPal, Endomondo, and UA Record™) to enable subscribers to log workouts, runs, and foods eaten, and to use a digital dashboard to review measures relating to their sleep, fitness, activity, and nutrition. Next, UA introduced a Connected Fitness System called Under Armour HealthBox™ that consisted of a multifunctional wristband (that measured sleep, resting heart rate, steps taken, and workout intensity), heart rate strap, and a smart scale (that tracked bodyweight, body fat percentage, and progress toward a weight goal); the wristband was water resistant, could be worn 24/7, and had Bluetooth connectivity with UA Record.

By April 2016, Under Armour had over 160 million users of its various Connected Fitness offerings, with new user registrations growing at the rate of 100,000 per day.[9] Kevin Plank was so enthusiastic about the long-term potential of Under Armour's Connected Fitness business that he had boosted the company's team of engineers and software developers from 20 to over 350 during 2014 and 2015. In 2016, Under Armour organized all of its digital and fitness technologies and products into a new business division called Connected Fitness, under the leadership of a senior vice president of digital revenue.

While Connected Fitness sales grew rapidly, the business lost millions of dollars annually–see Exhibits 3B and 3C. As part of the 2017 restructuring program, Under Armour merged its core connect fitness digital products, digital engineering, and digital media under the direction of a chief technology officer; this management arrangement evolved further in early 2018 with the appointment of a new senior vice president, digital product, who reported to the chief technology officer and had responsibility for leading the strategy for all digital product development in collaboration with executive management, product category heads, marketing, and creative/design. In Under Armour's February 2018 earnings announcement, the Connected Fitness business reported its first-ever positive operating income (almost $800,000) for the fourth quarter of 2017.

Licensing Under Armour had licensing agreements with a number of firms to produce and market Under Armour apparel, accessories, and equipment. Under Armour product, marketing, and sales teams were actively involved in all steps of the design process for licensed products in order to maintain brand standards and consistency. During 2017, licensees sold UA-branded collegiate, National Football League and Major League Baseball apparel and accessories, baby and kids' apparel, team uniforms, socks, water bottles, eyewear, and other hard goods equipment. Under Armour pre-approved all products manufactured and sold by licensees, and UA's quality assurance personnel were assigned the task of ensuring that licensed products met the same quality and compliance standards as the products Under Armour sold directly.

Marketing, Promotion, and Brand Management Strategies

Under Armour had an in-house marketing and promotions department that designed and produced most of its advertising campaigns to drive consumer demand for its products and build awareness of Under Armour as a leading performance athletic brand. The company's total marketing expenses were $565.1 million in 2017, $477.5 million in 2016, $417.8 million in 2015, and $333.0 million in 2014. These totals included the costs of sponsoring events and various sports teams, the costs of athlete endorsements, and ads placed in a variety of television, print, radio, and social media outlets. All were included as part of selling, general, and administrative expenses shown in Exhibit 1.

Sports Marketing Under Armour's sports marketing and promotion strategy began with promoting the sales and use of its products to high-performing athletes and teams on the high school, collegiate, and professional levels. This strategy was executed by entering into outfitting agreements with a variety of collegiate and professional sports teams, sponsoring an assortment of collegiate and professional sports events, entering into endorsement agreements with individual athletes, and selling Under Armour products directly to team equipment managers and to individual athletes. As a result, UA products were seen on the playing field (typically with the Under Armour logo prominently displayed), giving them exposure to various consumer audiences attending live sports events or watching these events on

television and through other media (pictures and videos accessed via the Internet and social media, magazines, and print). Management believed such exposure helped the company establish the on-field authenticity of the Under Armour brand with consumers. In addition, UA hosted combines, camps, and clinics for athletes in many sports at regional sites across the United States and was the title sponsor of a collection of high school All-America Games that created significant on-field and media exposure of its products and brand.

Going into 2018, Under Armour was the official outfitter of men's and women's athletic teams at such collegiate institutions as Notre Dame, UCLA, Boston College, Northwestern, Texas Tech, Maryland, South Carolina, the U.S. Naval Academy, Wisconsin, Indiana, Missouri, California, Utah, and Auburn. All told, it was the official outfitter of close to 100 men's and women's collegiate athletic teams, growing numbers of high school athletic teams, and it supplied sideline apparel and fan gear for many collegiate teams as well. Under Armour had been the official supplier of competition suits, uniforms, and training resources for a number of U.S. teams in the 2014 Winter Olympics, 2016 Summer Olympics, and 2018 Winter Olympics.

Under Armour was equally active in negotiating agreements to supply products to high profile professional athletes and professional sports teams, most notably in the National Football League (NFL), Major League Baseball (MLB), the National Hockey League (NHL), and the National Basketball Association (NBA). Under Armour had been an official supplier of football cleats to all NFL teams since 2006, the official supplier of gloves to NFL teams beginning in 2011, and a supplier of training apparel for athletes attending NFL tryout camps beginning in 2012. In 2011 Under Armour became the official supplier of performance footwear to all MLB teams; after signing a 10-year deal with MLB in 2016, Under Armour was scheduled in 2020 to become the official supplier of on-field uniforms, performance apparel, and connected fitness accessories to all 30 MLB clubs on an exclusive basis; and, together with its manufacturing partner, sell a broad range of MLB licensed merchandise. Starting with the 2011/2012 season, UA was granted rights by the NBA to show ads and promotional displays of players who were official endorsers of Under Armour products in their NBA game uniforms wearing UA-branded basketball footwear.

Internationally, Under Armour sponsored and sold its products to several Canadian, European, and Latin American soccer and rugby teams to help drive brand awareness in various countries and regions across the world. In Canada, it was an official supplier of performance apparel to Rugby Canada and Hockey Canada, had advertising rights at many locations in the Air Canada Center during the NHL Toronto Maple Leafs' home games, and was the official supplier of performance products to the Maple Leafs. In Europe, Under Armour was the official supplier of performance apparel to two professional soccer teams and the Welsh Rugby Union. In 2014 and 2015, Under Armour became the official match-day and training wear supplier for the Colo-Colo soccer club in Chile, the Cruz Azul soccer team in Mexico, and the São Paulo soccer team in Brazil.

In addition to sponsoring teams and events, Under Armour's brand-building strategy in the United States was to secure the endorsement of individual athletes. One facet of this strategy was to sign endorsement contracts with newly emerging sports stars—examples included Jacksonville Jaguars running back Leonard Fournette, Milwaukee Bucks point guard Brandon Jennings, Charlotte Bobcats point guard Kemba Walker, 2012 National League (baseball) Most Valuable Player Buster Posey, 2012 National League Rookie of the Year Bryce Harper, tennis phenom Sloane Stephens, WBC super-welterweight boxing champion Camelo Alvarez, and PGA golfer Jordan Spieth. But the company's endorsement roster also included established stars: NFL football players Tom Brady, Julio Jones, and Anquan Boldin; Golden State Warriors point guard Stephen Curry; professional baseball players Ryan Zimmerman, Jose Reyes, and Clayton Kershaw; tennis star Andy Murray; U.S. Women's National Soccer Team players Heather Mitts and Lauren Cheney; U.S. Olympic and professional volleyball player Nicole Branagh; and U.S. Olympic swimmer Michael Phelps. In 2015, Under Armour negotiated 10-year extensions of its endorsement contracts with Stephen Curry and Jordan Spieth; both deals included grants of stock in the company. Recently, Under Armour had signed celebrities outside the sports world to multi-year contracts, including ballerina soloist Misty Copeland and fashion model Giselle Bündchen; wrestler, actor, and producer Dwayne "The Rock" Johnson; and rapper A$AP Rocky (Rakim Mayers). Copeland was featured in one of Under Armour's largest

advertising campaigns for women's apparel offerings. Johnson was playing an integral role in promoting UA's connected fitness, apparel, footwear, and accessory products. Mayers was expected to have his own line of premium clothing in a forthcoming Under Armour Sportswear collection. In addition to signing endorsement agreements with prominent sports figures and celebrities in the United States, Under Armour had become increasingly active in using endorsement agreements with well-known athletes to help build public awareness of the Under Armour brand in those foreign countries where it was striving to build a strong market presence. Headed into 2018, Under Armour had signed endorsement agreements with several hundred international athletes in a wide variety of sports.

Under Armour's strategy of signing high-profile sports figures to endorsement contracts, sponsoring a variety of sports events, and supplying products to sports teams emblazoned with the company's logo had long been used by Nike and The adidas Group. Both rivals had far larger rosters of sports figure endorsements than Under Armour and supplied their products to more collegiate and professional sports teams than Under Armour.

Nonetheless, Under Armour's aggressive entry into the market for securing such endorsement agreements had spawned intense competition among the three rivals to win the endorsement of athletes and teams with high profiles and high perceived public appeal had caused the costs of winning such agreements to spiral upward. In 2014, Under Armour reportedly offered between $265 million and $285 million to entice NBA star Kevin Durant, who plays for the Golden State Warriors, away from Nike; Nike matched the offer and Durant elected to stay with Nike.[10] In 2015, adidas bested Nike in a bidding war to sign Houston Rockets star and runner-up NBA most valuable player James Harden to a 13-year endorsement deal, when Nike opted not to match adidas' offer of $200 million. The deal with Harden was said to be a move by adidas to reclaim its number two spot in sports apparel sales in North America behind Nike, months after being surpassed by Under Armour.[11] In 2016, it took $150 million—$10 million per year—for Under Armour to secure a 10-year deal with UCLA to outfit all of UCLA's men's and women's athletic teams.

Under Armour spent approximately $150.4 million in 2017 for athlete and superstar endorsements, various team and league sponsorships, athletic events, and other marketing commitments, compared to about $176.1 million in 2016, $126.5 million in 2015, $90.1 million in 2014, $53.0 million in 2012, and $29.4 million in 2010.[12] The company was contractually obligated to spend a minimum of $261.2 million for endorsements, sponsorships, events, and other marketing commitments from 2018 to 2020.[13] Under Armour did not know precisely what its future endorsement and sponsorship costs would be because its contractual agreements with most athletes were subject to certain performance-based variables and because it was actively engaged in efforts to sign additional endorsement contracts and sponsor additional sports teams and athletic events.

Retail Marketing and Product Presentation The primary thrust of Under Armour's retail marketing strategy was to increase the floor space *exclusively* dedicated to Under Armour products in the stores of its major retail accounts. The key initiative here was to design and fund Under Armour "concept shops"—including flooring, lighting, walls, fixtures and product displays, and images—within the stores of its major retail customers. This shop-in-shop approach was seen as an effective way to gain the placement of Under Armour products in prime floor space and create a more engaging and sales-producing way for consumers to shop for Under Armour products.

In stores that did not have Under Armour concept shops, Under Armour worked with retailers to establish sales-enhancing placement of its products. In "big-box" sporting goods stores, it was important to be sure that Under Armour's growing variety of products gained visibility in all of the various departments (hunting apparel in the hunting goods department, footwear and socks in the footwear department, and so on). Except for the retail stores with Under Armour concept shops, company personnel worked with retailers to employ in-store fixtures, life-size mannequins, and displays that highlighted the UA logo and conveyed a performance-oriented, athletic look. The merchandising strategy was not only to enhance the visibility of Under Armour products and drive sales but also grow consumer awareness that Under Armour products delivered performance-enhancing advantages.

Media and Promotion Under Armour advertised in a variety of national digital, broadcast, and print media outlets, as well as social and mobile media.

Its advertising campaigns were of varying lengths and formats and frequently included prominent athletes and personalities. Advertising and promotional campaigns in 2015-2017 featured Michael Phelps, Stephen Curry, Jordan Spieth, Tom Brady, Lindsey Vonn, Misty Copeland, and Dwayne Johnson.

Distribution Strategy

Under Armour products were available in roughly 17,000 retail store locations worldwide in 2018. In many foreign countries, Under Armour relied on independent marketing and sales agents, instead of its own marketing staff, to recruit retail accounts and solicit orders from retailers for UA merchandise. Under Armour also sold its products directly to consumers through its own Brand House stores, factory outlet stores, and various geographic websites.

Wholesale Distribution In 2018, Under Armour had an estimated 11,000 points of distribution in North America. The company's biggest retail account was Dick's Sporting Goods, which in 2017 accounted for 10 percent of the company's net revenues. Until its bankruptcy and subsequent store liquidation in 2016, The Sports Authority had been UA's second largest retail account; the loss of this account was a principal factor in Under Armour's struggle to grow wholesale sales to retailers in North America. Other important retail accounts included Academy Sports and Outdoors, Hibbett Sporting Goods, Modell's Sporting Goods, Bass Pro Shops, Cabela's, Footlocker, The Army and Air Force Exchange Service, and such well-known department store chains as Macy's, Nordstrom, Belk, Dillard's, and Kohl's. In Canada, the company's important retail accounts included Sport Chek and Hudson's Bay. Roughly 75 percent of all sales made to retailers were to large-format national and regional retail chains. The remaining 25 percent of wholesale sales were to lesser-sized outdoor and specialty retailers, institutional athletic departments, leagues, teams, and fitness specialists. Independent and specialty retailers were serviced by a combination of in-house sales personnel and third-party commissioned manufacturer's representatives.

Direct-to-Consumer Sales In 2017, 30 percent of Under Armour's net revenues were generated through direct-to-consumer sales, versus 23 percent in 2010 and 6 percent in 2005; the direct-to-consumer channel included sales of discounted merchandise at

Under Armour's factory outlet stores and full-price sales at Under Armour Brand Houses, and various country websites. The factory outlet stores gave Under Armour added brand exposure and helped familiarize consumers with Under Armour's product lineup while also functioning as an important channel for selling discontinued, out-of-season, and/or overstocked products at discount prices without undermining the prices of Under Armour merchandise being sold at retail stores, Brand Houses, and company websites. Going into 2018, Under Armour had 162 stores in factory outlet malls in North America; these stores attracted close to 75 million shoppers in 2017.

During the past several years, Under Armour had begun opening company-owned Brand House stores in high-traffic retail locations in the United States to showcase its branded apparel and sell its products direct-to-consumers at retail prices. At year-end 2017, the company was operating 19 Under Armour Brand House stores in North America. Plans called for having close to 200 Brand House locations in North America by year-end 2018.[14] However, part of Under Armour's 2017 restructuring plan reportedly included closing 33 factory outlet stores and 23 Brand House locations that had not met sales expectations; these closings were responsible for many of the lease terminations disclosed in the restructuring effort.[15]

UA management's e-commerce strategy called for sales at **www.underarmour.com** (and 26 other in-country websites as of 2016) to be one of the company's principal vehicles for sales growth in upcoming years. To help spur e-commerce sales, the company was enhancing its efforts to drive traffic to its websites, improve its online merchandising techniques and storytelling about the many different Under Armour products sold on its sites, and use promotions to attract online buyers. From time-to-time, its websites offered free limited-time shipping on specified items. Recently, to better compete with Amazon, the company had begun offering free 4 to 6 business day shipping on orders over $60 and free 3 business day shipping on orders over $150. Free shipping on returns within 60 days was standard.

Product Licensing   In 2017, 2.3 percent of the company's net revenues ($116.6 million) came from licensing arrangements to manufacture and distribute Under Armour branded products. Under Armour pre-approved all products manufactured and sold by its licensees, and the company's quality assurance team strived to ensure that licensed products met the same quality and compliance standards as company-sold products. Under Armour had relationships with several licensees for team uniforms, eyewear, and custom-molded mouth guards, as well as the distribution of Under Armour products to college bookstores and golf pro shops.

Distribution outside North America   Under Armour's first strategic move to gain international distribution occurred in 2002 when it established a relationship with a Japanese licensee, Dome Corporation, to be the exclusive distributor of Under Armour products in Japan. The relationship evolved, with Under Armour making a minority equity investment in Dome Corporation in 2011 and Dome gaining distribution rights for South Korea. Dome sold Under Armour branded apparel, footwear, and accessories to professional sports teams, large sporting goods retailers, and several thousand independent retailers of sports apparel in Japan and South Korea. Under Armour worked closely with Dome to develop variations of Under Armour products to better accommodate the different sports interests and preferences of Japanese and Korean consumers.

A European headquarters was opened in 2006 in Amsterdam, The Netherlands, to conduct and oversee sales, marketing, and logistics activities across Europe. The strategy was to first sell Under Armour products directly to teams and athletes and then leverage visibility in the sports segment to access broader audiences of potential consumers. By 2011, Under Armour had succeeded in selling products to Premier League Football clubs and multiple running, golf, and cricket clubs in the United Kingdom; soccer teams in France, Germany, Greece, Ireland, Italy, Spain, and Sweden; as well as First Division Rugby clubs in France, Ireland, Italy, and the United Kingdom. Sales to European retailers quickly followed on the heels of gains being made in the sports team segment. By year-end 2012, Under Armour had 4,000 retail customers in Austria, France, Germany, Ireland, and the United Kingdom and was generating revenues from sales to independent distributors who resold Under Armour products to retailers in Italy, Greece, Scandinavia, and Spain. In 2014-2017, sales continued to expand at a rapid clip in countries in Europe, the Middle East, and Africa; sales in EMEA countries surpassed $1 billion in 2017 (see Exhibit 3B). However, operating profits in this region were small (see Exhibit 3C). Adidas strongly defended its industry-leading position with European retailers, and Under Armour frequently found itself embroiled in hotly contested price-cutting battles with adidas and Nike to win orders from retailers in many EMEA locations.

In 2010 and 2011, Under Armour began selling its products in parts of Latin America and Asia. In Latin America, Under Armour sold directly to retailers in some countries and in other countries sold its products to independent distributors who then were responsible for securing sales to retailers. In 2014, Under Armour launched efforts to make Under Armour products available in over 70 of Brazil's premium points of sale and e-commerce hubs; expanded sales efforts were also initiated in Chile and Mexico.

In 2011, Under Armour opened a retail showroom in Shanghai, China—the first of a series of steps to begin the long-term process of introducing Chinese athletes and consumers to the Under Armour brand, showcase Under Armour products, and learn about Chinese consumers. Additional retail locations in Shanghai and Beijing soon followed (some operated by local partners). By April 2014, there were five company-owned and franchised retail locations in mainland China that merchandised Under Armour products; additionally, the Under Armour brand had been recently introduced in Hong Kong through a partnership with leading retail chain GigaSports.

Under Armour began selling its branded apparel, footwear, and accessories to independent distributors in Australia, New Zealand, and Taiwan in 2014; these distributors were responsible for securing retail accounts to merchandise Under Armour products to consumers. The distribution of Under Armour products to retail accounts across Asia was handled by a third-party logistics provider based in Hong Kong.

In 2013, Under Armour organized its international activities into four geographic regions—North America (the United States and Canada), Latin America, Asia-Pacific, and Europe/Middle East/ Africa (EMEA). In his Letter to Shareholders in the company's 2013 Annual Report, Kevin Plank said, "We are committed to being a global brand with global stories to tell, and we are on our way." Sales of Under Armour products in EMEA, the Asia-Pacific, and Latin America accounted for 21.8 of Under Armour's total net revenues in 2017, up from 11.5 percent in 2015, and 8.7 percent in 2014 (see

Exhibit 3B). Under Armour saw growth in foreign sales as the company's biggest market opportunity in upcoming years, chiefly because of the sheer number of people residing outside the United States who could be attracted to patronize the Under Armour brand. In 2017 Nike generated about 53 percent of its revenues outside North America, and adidas got about 70 percent of its sales outside its home market of Western Europe and 80 percent outside of North America—these big international sales percentages for Nike and adidas were a big reason why Under Armour executives were confident that growing UA's international sales represented an enormous market opportunity for the company, despite the stiff competition it could expect from its two bigger global rivals.

One of Under Armour's chief initiatives to build international awareness of the Under Armour brand and rapidly grow its sales internationally was to open growing numbers of stores in popular factory outlet malls and to locate Brand Houses in visible, high-traffic locations in major cities. So far, the company had opened 57 factory outlet stores and 57 Brand House stores in international locations as of year-end 2017, versus 37 factory outlet stores and 35 Brand Houses at year-end 2016. Current long-range plans called for perhaps as many as 800 such stores in 40+ countries outside North America sometime in the 2020 to 2025 period.

Product Design and Development

Top executives believed that product innovation—as concerns both technical design and aesthetic design—was the key to driving Under Armour's sales growth and building a stronger brand name.

UA products were manufactured with technically advanced specialty fabrics produced by third parties. The company's product development team collaborated closely with fabric suppliers to ensure that the fabrics and materials used in UA's products had the desired performance and fit attributes. Under Armour regularly upgraded its products as next-generation fabrics with better performance characteristics became available and as the needs of athletes changed. Product development efforts also aimed at broadening the company's product offerings in both new and existing product categories and market segments. An effort was made to design products with "visible technology," utilizing color, texture, and fabrication that would enhance customers' perception and understanding of the use and benefits of Under Armour products.

Under Armour's product development team had significant prior industry experience at leading fabric and other raw material suppliers and branded athletic apparel and footwear companies throughout the world. The team worked closely with Under Armour's sports marketing and sales teams as well as professional and collegiate athletes to identify product trends and determine market needs. Collaboration among the company's product development, sales, and sports marketing team had proved important in identifying the opportunity and market for four recently launched product lines and fabric technologies:

- CHARGED COTTON™ products, which were made from natural cotton but performed like the products made from technically advanced synthetic fabrics, drying faster and wicking moisture away from the body.
- STORM Fleece products, which had a unique, water-resistant finish that repelled water without stifling airflow.
- Products with a COLDBLACK® technology fabric that repelled heat from the sun and kept the wearer cooler outside.
- ColdGear® Infrared, a ceramic print technology applied to the inside of garments that provided wearers with lightweight warmth.

Sourcing, Manufacturing, and Quality Assurance

Many of the high-tech specialty fabrics and other raw materials used in UA products were developed by third parties and sourced from a limited number of preapproved specialty fabric manufacturers; no fabrics were manufactured in-house. Under Armour executives believed outsourcing fabric production enabled the company to seek out and utilize whichever fabric suppliers were able to produce the latest and best performance-oriented fabrics to Under Armour's specifications, while also freeing more time for UA's product development staff to concentrate on upgrading the performance, styling, and overall appeal of existing products and expanding the company's overall lineup of product offerings.

In 2017, approximately 53 percent of the fabric used in UA products came from five suppliers, with primary locations in Malaysia, Taiwan, and Mexico. Because a big fraction of the materials used in UA products were petroleum-based synthetics, fabric costs were subject to crude oil price fluctuations. The cotton fabrics used in the CHARGED COTTON™ products were also subject to price fluctuations and varying availability based on cotton harvests.

In 2017, substantially all UA products were made by 39 primary contract manufacturers, operating in 17 countries; 10 manufacturers produced approximately 57 percent of UA's products. Approximately 61 percent of UA's apparel and accessories products were manufactured in China, Jordan, Vietnam, and Malaysia. Under Armour's footwear products were made by seven primary contract manufacturers operating primarily in Vietnam, China, and Indonesia. All contract manufacturers making Under Armour apparel products purchased the fabrics they needed from the 5 fabric suppliers preapproved by Under Armour. All of the makers of UA products were evaluated for quality systems, social compliance, and financial strength by Under Armour's quality assurance team, prior to being selected and also on an ongoing basis. The company strived to qualify multiple manufacturers for particular product types and fabrications and to seek out contractors that could perform multiple manufacturing stages, such as procuring raw materials and providing finished products, which helped UA control its cost of goods sold. All contract manufacturers were required to adhere to a code of conduct regarding quality of manufacturing, working conditions, and other social concerns. However, the company had no long-term agreements requiring it to continue to use the services of any manufacturer, and no manufacturer was obligated to make products for UA on a long-term basis. UA had subsidiaries strategically located near its manufacturing partners to support its manufacturing, quality assurance, and sourcing efforts for its products.

Under Armour had a 17,000 square-foot Special Make-Up Shop located at one of its distribution facilities in Maryland where it had the capability to make and ship customized apparel products on tight deadlines for high-profile athletes and teams. While these apparel products represented a tiny fraction of Under Armour's revenues, management believed the facility helped provide superior service to select customers.

Inventory Management

Under Armour based the amount of inventory it needed to have on hand for each item in its product line on existing orders, anticipated sales, and the need to rapidly deliver orders to customers. Its inventory strategy was focused on (1) having sufficient inventory to fill incoming orders promptly and (2) putting strong systems and procedures in place to improve the efficiency with which it managed its inventories of individual products and total inventory. The amounts of seasonal products it ordered from manufacturers were based on current bookings, the need to ship seasonal items at the start of the shipping window in order to maximize the floor space productivity of retail customers, the need to adequately stock its Factory House and Brand House stores, and the need to fill customer orders. Excess inventories of particular products were either shipped to its Factory House stores or earmarked for sale to third-party liquidators.

However, the growing number of individual items in UA's product line and uncertainties surrounding upcoming consumer demand for individual items made it difficult to accurately forecast how many units to order from manufacturers and what the appropriate stocking requirements were for many items. New inventory management practices were instituted in 2012 to better cope with stocking requirements for individual items and avoid excessive inventory buildups. Year-end inventories of $1.16 billion in 2017 equated to 154.6 days of inventory and inventory turnover of 2.36 turns per year. UA's description of its restructuring plans signaled that inventory reduction initiatives were included.

COMPETITION

The $250 billion global market for sports apparel, athletic footwear, and related accessories was fragmented among some 25 brand-name competitors with diverse product lines and varying geographic coverage and numerous small competitors with specialized-use apparel lines that usually operated within a single country or geographic region. Industry participants included athletic and leisure shoe companies, athletic and leisure apparel companies, sports equipment companies, and large companies having diversified lines of athletic and leisure shoes, apparel, and equipment. The global market for athletic footwear was projected to reach $114.8 billion by 2022, growing at a CAGR of 2.1 percent during the period 2016 to 2022.[16] The global market for athletic and fitness apparel was forecast to grow about 4.3 percent annually from 2015 to 2020 and reach about $185 billion by 2020.[17] Exhibit 4 shows a representative sample of the best-known companies and brands in selected segments of the sports apparel, athletic footwear, and sports equipment industry.

In 2017 and 2018, consumers across the world shopped for the industry's products digitally (online) or physically in stores. And they shopped either for a favorite brand or for multi-brand. The trend was for more consumers to shop digitally and for a brand deemed to be the best or their favorite. Multi-brand shoppers typically wanted to explore and compare the options, either through a dot.com experience or in stores where could view the products firsthand, get advice or personalized assistance, and/or get the product immediately.

As Exhibit 4 indicates, the sporting goods industry consisted of many distinct product categories and market segments. Because the product mixes of different companies varied considerably, it was common for the product offerings of industry participants to be extensive in some segments, moderate in others, and limited to nonexistent in still others. Consequently, the leading competitors and the intensity of competition varied significantly from market segment to market segment. Nonetheless, competition tended to be intense in most every segment with substantial sales volume and typically revolved around performance and reliability, the breadth of product selection, new product development, price, brand name strength and identity through marketing and promotion, the ability of companies to convince retailers to stock and effectively merchandise their brands, and the capabilities of the various industry participants to sell directly to consumers through their own retail/factory outlet stores and/or at their company websites. It was common for the leading companies selling athletic footwear, sports uniforms, and sports equipment to actively sponsor sporting events and clinics and to contract with prominent and influential athletes, coaches, professional sports teams, colleges, and sports leagues to endorse their brands and use their products.

Nike was the clear global market leader in the sporting goods industry, with a global market share in athletic footwear of about 25 percent and a sports apparel

EXHIBIT 4   Major Competitors and Brands in Selected Segments of the Sports Apparel, Athletic Footwear, and Accessory Industry, 2018

Performance Apparel for Sports (baseball, football, basketball, softball, volleyball, hockey, lacrosse, soccer, track & field, and other action sports)	Performance-Driven Athletic Footwear	Training/Fitness Clothing
• Nike • Under Armour • Adidas • Eastbay • Russell	• Nike • Adidas • New Balance • Reebok • Saucony • Puma • Rockport • Converse • Ryka • Asics • Li Ning	• Nike • Under Armour • Adidas • Puma • Fila • Lululemon athletica • Champion • Asics • Eastbay • SUGOI • Li Ning

Performance Activewear and Sports-Inspired Lifestyle Apparel	Performance Skiwear	Performance Golf Apparel
• Polo Ralph Lauren • Lacoste • Izod • Cutter & Buck • Timberland • Columbia • Puma • Li Ning • Many others	• Salomon • North Face • Descente • Columbia • Patagonia • Marmot • Helly Hansen • Bogner • Spyder • Many others	• Footjoy • Nike • Adidas • Under Armour • Polo Golf • Ashworth • Cutter & Buck • Greg Norman • Puma • Many others

share of 5 percent. The adidas Group, with businesses that produced athletic footwear, sports uniforms, fitness apparel, sportswear, and a variety of sports equipment and marketed them across the world, was the second largest global competitor. These two major competitors of Under Armour are profiled as follows.

Nike, Inc.

Incorporated in 1968, Nike was the dominant global leader in the design, development, and worldwide marketing and selling of footwear, sports apparel, sports equipment, and accessory products. Nike was a truly global brand, with a broader and deeper portfolio of products, models, and styles than any other industry participant. The company had 2017 global sales of $34.4 billion and net income of $4.2 billion in fiscal year ending May 31, 2017. Nike was the world's largest seller of footwear with sales of $21 billion; it held the number 1 market share in all markets and in all categories of athletic footwear (its running shoe

business alone had sales of $5.3 billion). Nike's footwear line included some 1,500 models/styles. Nike was also the world's largest sports apparel brand, with 2017 sales of $9.5 billion. Sales of Nike products to women reached $7 billion in 2017.

Nike's strategy in 2017 and 2018 was driven by three core beliefs. One was that the growing popularity of sports and active lifestyles reflected a desire to lead healthier lives. As a result, companies like Nike were becoming more relevant for more moments in people's lives because of their growing participation in calorie-burning, wellness, and fitness activities and because active lifestyles stimulated greater interest in sports-related activities and sports events. Moreover, streaming of sports events and social media were changing the ways people consumed sports content. The NBA, for example, had over 1.3 billion social media followers across the league, teams, and player pages. The growth of watching streamed events on mobile phones was exploding. Second, in a connected, mobile-led world, consumers had become infinitely better informed and, thus, more powerful because of the information they could access in seconds and the options this opened up—"powered consumers" were prone to consult their phones (or conduct Internet searches on other devices) for price comparisons and availability before deciding where to shop or what to purchase online. Third, the world was operating at faster speeds and the numbers of powered consumers was about to explode. Nike's CEO expected over 2 billion digitally connected people in markets in China, India, and Latin America would join the middle class by 2030. In North America, Nike estimated that its primary consumer base was 50 million people, but that if population trends in China continued at the expected rate, Nike's projected consumer base in China would be more than 500 million people by 2030.

For years, the heart and soul of Nike's strategy had been creating innovative products and powerful storytelling that produced an emotional connection with consumers and caused them to gravitate to purchase Nike products. But at the same time Nike executives understood that brand strength had to be earned every day by satisfying consumer needs and meeting, if not exceeding, their expectations. Exhibit 5 shows Nike's worldwide retail and distribution network at the end of fiscal 2017.

In October 2017, Nike CEO Mark Parker provided a brief overview of the company's "Triple Double" strategy that had three components: 2X Innovation, 2X Speed, and 2X Direct:

> In 2X Innovation, we will lead with more distinct platforms, moving from seeding to scaling a lot faster. We'll . . . give consumers better choices to match their preferences. And we'll set a new expectation for style, creating a new aesthetic to wear in all moments of their lives. To the consumer, there is no trade-off between sport and style. We know that more than half of the athletic footwear and apparel is bought for non-sport activities, and we have even more room to grow in this market.
>
> In 2X Speed, we're investing in digital end to end to serve this insatiable consumer demand for new and fresh products. To use a sports analogy, you can't run an up-tempo offense if only half your plays are designed for speed. So we're building new capabilities and analytics to deliver personalized products in real time, and we're engaging with more partners companywide to move faster against our goals. In our supply chain, we've joined forces with leading robotics and automation companies, and we're serving millions of athletes and sports fans faster through manufacturing bases that are closer to our North American consumer. 2X Speed is really all about delivering the right product in the moment, 100 percent of the time.
>
> We never ever take the strength of our brand and premium product for granted. They are indeed our most valuable assets. With 2X Direct [to Consumer], we want as many Nike touch points as possible to live up to those expectations, and that's why we are investing heavily in our own channel and leading with digital. And with our strategic partners, we'll move resources away from undifferentiated retail and toward environments where we can better control with distinct consumer experiences.[18]

Principal Products   Nike's 1,500 athletic footwear models and styles were designed primarily for specific athletic use, although many were worn for casual or leisure purposes. Running, training, basketball, soccer, sport-inspired casual shoes, and kids' shoes were the company's top-selling footwear categories. It also marketed footwear designed for baseball, football, golf, lacrosse, cricket, outdoor activities,

EXHIBIT 5   Nike's Worldwide Retail and Distribution Network, 2017

United States	Foreign Countries
• ~15,000 retail accounts	• ~15,000 retail accounts
• 209 Nike factory outlet stores	• 642 Nike factory outlet stores
• 34 Nike and NIKETOWN stores	• 71 Nike and NIKETOWN stores
• 112 Converse retail and factory outlet stores	• 45 Converse retail and factory outlet stores
• 29 Hurley stores	• —
• 8 Distribution centers	• 45 Distribution centers
• Company website (www.nike.com)	• Independent distributors and licensees in over 190 countries
	• 40 + www.nike.com websites

tennis, volleyball, walking, and wrestling. The company designed and marketed Nike-branded sports apparel and accessories for most all of these same sports categories, as well as sports-inspired lifestyle apparel, athletic bags, and accessory items. Footwear, apparel, and accessories were often marketed in "collections" of similar design or for specific purposes. It also marketed apparel with licensed college and professional team and league logos. Nike-brand offerings in sports equipment included bags, socks, sport balls, eyewear, timepieces, electronic devices, bats, gloves, protective equipment, and golf clubs. Nike was also the owner of the Converse brand of athletic footwear and the Hurley brand of swimwear, assorted other apparel items, and surfing gear.

Exhibit 6 shows a breakdown of Nike's sales of footwear, apparel, and equipment by geographic region for fiscal years 2015 to 2017.

Marketing, Promotions, and Endorsements Nike responded to trends and shifts in consumer preferences by (1) adjusting the mix of existing product offerings, (2) developing new products, styles, and categories, and (3) striving to influence sports and fitness preferences through aggressive marketing, promotional activities, sponsorships, and athlete endorsements. Nike spent $3.34 billion in fiscal 2017 (as compared to $2.75 billion in 2013 for) what it termed "demand creation expense" that included the costs of advertising, promotional activities, and endorsement contracts. Well over 500 professional, collegiate, club, and Olympic sports teams in football, basketball, baseball, ice hockey, soccer, rugby, speed skating, tennis, swimming, and other sports wore Nike uniforms with the Nike swoosh prominently visible. There were over 1,000 prominent professional athletes with Nike endorsement contracts in 2011-2017, including former basketball great Michael Jordan, NFL player Drew Brees, NBA players LeBron James, Kobe Bryant, Kevin Durant, and Dwayne Wade; professional golfers Tiger Woods and Michelle Wie; soccer player Cristiano Ronaldo; and professional tennis players Venus and Serena Williams, Roger Federer, and Rafael Nadal. When Tiger Woods turned pro, Nike signed him to a 5-year $100 million endorsement contract and made him the centerpiece of its campaign to make Nike a factor in the golf equipment and golf apparel marketplace. Nike's long-standing endorsement relationship with Michael Jordan led to the introduction of the highly popular line of Air Jordan footwear and, more recently, to the launch of the Jordan brand of athletic shoes, clothing, and gear. In 2003 LeBron James signed an endorsement deal with Nike worth

EXHIBIT 6   Nike's Sales of Nike Brand Footwear, Apparel, and Equipment, by Geographic Region and by Wholesale and Direct-to-Customer, Fiscal Years 2015–2017

Sales Revenues and Earnings (in millions)	Fiscal Years Ending May 31		
	2017	2016	2015
North America			
Revenues—Nike Brand footwear	$ 9,684	$ 9,299	$ 8,506
Nike Brand apparel	4,866	4,746	4,410
Nike Brand equipment	646	719	824
Total Nike Brand revenues	$15,216	$14,764	$13,740
Sales to Wholesale Customers	10,756	10,674	10,243
Sales Direct to Consumer	4,460	4,090	3,497
Earnings before interest and taxes	$ 3,875	$ 3,763	$ 3,645
Profit margin	25.6%	25.5%	26.5%

Sales Revenues and Earnings (in millions)	Fiscal Years Ending May 31		
	2017	**2016**	**2015**
Western Europe			
Revenues—Nike Brand footwear	$ 4,068	$ 3,985	$ 3,876
Nike Brand apparel	1,868	1,628	1,552
Nike Brand equipment	275	271	277
Total Nike Brand revenues	$ 6,211	$ 5,884	$ 5,705
Sales to Wholesale Customers	4,443	4,429	4,451
Sales Direct to Consumer	1,768	1,455	1,254
Earnings before interest and taxes	$ 1,203	$ 1,434	$ 1,275
Profit margin	19.4%	24.4%	22.4%
Greater China			
Revenues—Nike Brand footwear	$ 2,920	$ 2,599	$ 2,016
Nike Brand apparel	1,188	1,055	925
Nike Brand equipment	129	131	126
Total Nike Brand revenues	$ 4,237	$ 3,785	$ 3,067
Sales to Wholesale Customers	2,774	2,623	2,234
Sales Direct to Consumer	1,463	1,162	833
Earnings before interest and taxes	$ 1,507	$ 1,372	$ 993
Profit margin	35.6%	36.2%	32.4%
Other Regions			
Revenues—Nike Brand footwear	$ 4,409	$ 3,988	$ 3,920
Nike Brand apparel	1,712	1,638	1,750
Nike Brand equipment	375	375	404
Total Nike Brand revenues	$ 6,496	$ 6,001	$ 6,074
Sales to Wholesale Customers	5,105	4,851	5,024
Sales Direct to Consumer	1,391	1,150	1,050
Earnings before interest and taxes	$ 1,284	$ 1,355	$ 1,167
Profit margin	19.8%	22.6%	19.2%
All Regions			
Revenues—Nike Brand footwear	$21,081	$19,871	$18,318
Nike Brand apparel	9,654	9,067	8,637
Nike Brand equipment	1,425	1,496	1,631
Total Nike Brand revenues	$32,160	$30,434	$28,586
Sales to Wholesale Customers	23,078	22,577	21,952
Sales Direct to Consumer	9,082	7,857	6,634
Earnings before interest and taxes	$ 7,869	$ 7,924	$ 7,080
Profit margin	24.5%	26.0%	24.8%
Converse			
Revenues	$ 2,042	$ 1,955	$ 1,982
Earnings before interest and taxes	$ 477	$ 487	$ 517
Profit margin	23.4%	24.9%	26.1%

Note: The revenue and earnings figures for all geographic regions include the effects of currency exchange fluctuations. The Nike Brand revenues for equipment include the Hurley brand, and the Nike Brand revenues for footwear include the Jordan brand. The earnings before interest and taxes figures associated with Total Nike Brand Revenues include those for the Hurley and Jordan brands.

Source: Nike's 10-K Report for Fiscal Year 2017, pp. 26–37.

$90 million over 7 years, and in 2015 he signed a lifetime deal with Nike. Because soccer was such a popular sport globally, Nike had more endorsement contracts with soccer athletes than with athletes in any other sport; track and field athletes had the second largest number of endorsement contracts.

Resources and Capabilities Nike had an incredibly deep pool of valuable resources and capabilities that enhanced its competitive power in the marketplace and helped spur product innovation, shorten speed-to-market, enable customers to use digital tools to customize the colors and styling of growing numbers of Nike products, and thereby drive strong brand attachment and sales growth. Examples of these included the following:

- The company's Nike APP and the SNKRS app were in more than 20 countries across North America and Europe, plus China and Japan, countries that drove close to 90 percent of Nike's growth. These apps provided easy access to Nike products and were becoming a popular way for customers to shop Nike products and make online purchases. The Nike App was the number one mono-brand retail app in the United States. Nike's apps and growing digital product ecosystem were key components of the company's 2X Speed strategy to operate faster and get innovative products in the hands of consumers faster.

- The creation and ongoing enhancement of the NikePlus membership program which in 2017 connected 100 million consumers to Nike—NikePlus members who used the company's mobile apps spent more than three times as much time on nike.com as other site visitors. Starting in 2018, NikePlus members were entitled to "reserved-for-you service" that used machine learning-powered algorithms to set aside products in a member's size that the algorithms predicted members would like. Members could also use a "reserved-by-you" service to gain guaranteed access to products they wanted; this newly developed capability was deemed especially valuable to members wanting a recently-introduced product in high demand. In 2018, Nike began accelerating invitations to NikePlus members to personalized events and experiences and extending benefits and offers from NikePlus partners like Apple Music, Headspace, and Class Pass. Special Nike Unlock offers were sent to members once a month. Nike

expected that NikePlus membership would triple over the next five years. Nike executives anticipated that converting consumers into NikePlus members would heighten their relationship to and connection with Nike.

- The establishment of an Advanced Product Creation Center charged with keeping the pipeline flowing with product innovations, new digital products, and manufacturing innovations to make 2X Speed a reality. Nike was aggressively investing in 3D modeling and other related technology to quickly create prototypes of new products; with traditional technology, it often took four-to-six months go from new idea-to-design-to-product prototype. So far, Nike had been able to go from design, to prototyping, to manufacturing, to delivery in less than 6 months, as compared to 9 to 12 months. Nike's goal was to improve its rapid prototyping capabilities to the point where 100 percent of new product innovations could be rapid-prototyped at the Advanced Product Creation Center in Portland, Oregon. Employee athletes, athletes engaged under sports marketing contracts, and other athletes wear-tested and evaluated products during the development and prototyping process.

- A relaunch of all 40+ nike.com websites in late 2017 that featured a new design with better visual appeal and functionality, more storytelling, eye-catching product displays, and better product descriptions—all aimed at generating more visitor traffic, longer shopping times, increased online sales, and achieving 2X Direct.

- Implementing robot-assisted manufacturing capabilities and other recently-developed manufacturing innovations (such as oscillating knives, laser cutting and trimming, phylon mold transfer, and computerized stitching) on a broad scale. In one instance, the use of advanced robotics and digitization techniques was generating a continuous, automated flow of the upper portion of a footwear model with 30 percent fewer steps, 50 percent less labor, and less waste in just 30 seconds per shoe—a total of 1,200 automated robots had been installed to perform an assortment of activities at various manufacturing facilities in 2017. In another instance, Nike had made manufacturing breakthroughs in producing the bottoms of its footwear (the midsoles and outsoles) using innovative techniques capable of delivering a pair of midsoles and outsoles, on average, in 2.5 minutes, compared to more than 50 minutes with previously-used techniques. This new process used 75 percent less energy, entailed 50 percent less tooling cost, and enabled a 60 percent reduction in labor.

- Revamped supply chain practices that had shortened the lead times from manufacturing to market availability from 60 days to 10 days in one instance and from 6 to 9 months to 3 months in other instances.

- Creating a digital technology called Nike iD, whereby customers could go to Nike iD, design their own customized version of a product (say a pair of Free Run Flyknit shoes), view a prototype in an hour or so, have the shoes knitted to order, and get them delivered in 10 days or less.[19]

All of Nike's competitively valuable resources and capabilities were being dynamically managed; enhancements were made as fast as ways to improve could be developed and instituted and new capabilities were being added in an effort (1) to provide customers with a better "Nike Experience" and (2) to respond faster to ongoing changes in consumer preferences and expectations. Collaborative efforts were underway in Nike's organizational units to transfer new or enhanced resources and capabilities to all seven of the company's product categories and also extend them to all of geographic regions and countries where Nike had a market presence. The goal was to mobilize Nike's resources and capabilities to produce an enduring competitive advantage over rivals and give customers the best possible experience in purchasing and using Nike products.

Manufacturing   In fiscal year 2017, Nike sourced its athletic footwear from 127 factories in 15 countries. About 94 percent of Nike's footwear was produced by independent contract manufacturers in Vietnam, China, and Indonesia but the company had manufacturing agreements with independent factories in Argentina, Brazil, India, and Mexico to manufacture footwear for sale primarily within those countries. Nike-branded apparel was manufactured outside of the United States by 363 independent contract manufacturers located in 39 countries; most of the apparel production occurred in China, Vietnam, Thailand, Indonesia, Sri Lanka, Malaysia, and Cambodia.

The adidas Group

The mission of The adidas Group was to be the best sports company in the world. Headquartered in Germany, its businesses and brands in 2017 consisted of:

- Adidas—a designer and marketer of active sportswear, uniforms, footwear, and sports products in football, basketball, soccer, running, training, outdoor, and 6 other categories (89.2 percent of Group sales in 2017). The mission at adidas was to be the best sports brand in the world.

- Reebok—a well-known global provider of athletic footwear for multiple uses, sports and fitness apparel, and accessories (8.7 percent of Group sales in 2017). The mission at Reebok was to be the best fitness brand in the world.

- Other businesses (2.1% of Group sales in 2017).

Exhibit 7 shows the company's financial highlights for 2015 to 2017. The company had recently divested five businesses—TaylorMade Golf, Adams Golf, Ashworth brand sports apparel, CCR Hockey, and Rockport brand shoes—to focus all of its resources on achieving faster and more profitable sales growth in both its adidas and Reebok businesses.

The company sold products in virtually every country of the world. In 2017, its extensive product offerings were marketed through thousands of third-party retailers (sporting goods chains, department stores, independent sporting goods retailer buying groups, and lifestyle retailing chains—with a combined total of 150,000 locations worldwide, and Internet retailers), 2,588 company-owned retail stores, 13,000 franchised adidas and Reebok branded stores with varying formats, and company websites (**www.adidas.com** and **www.reebok.com**) in 40 countries.

Like Under Armour and Nike, both adidas and Reebok were actively engaged in sponsoring major sporting events, teams, and leagues and in using athlete endorsements to promote their products. Recent high-profile sponsorships and promotional partnerships included numerous professional soccer and rugby teams, sports teams at the University of Miami, Arizona State University, and Texas A&M University; FIFA World Cup events; the Summer and Winter Olympics; the Boston Marathon and London Marathon; and official outfitters of items for assorted professional sports leagues (NBA, NHL, NFL, and MLB) and teams. High-profile athletes that were under contract to endorse adidas and Reebok products included NBA players James Harden and Damian Lillard; soccer players David Beckham and Lionel Messi; NFL players Aaron Rodgers, C.J. Spiller, Robert Griffin III, Demarco

EXHIBIT 7   Financial Highlights for The adidas Group, 2015–2017 (in millions of €)

	2017	2016	2015
Income Statement Data			
Net sales	€21,218	€18,483	€16,915
Gross profit	10,703	9,100	8,168
Gross profit margin	50.4%	49.2%	48.3%
Operating profit	2,070	1,582	1,094
Operating profit margin	9.8%	8.6%	6.5%
Net income	1,173	1,017	668
Net profit margin	5.5%	5.5%	4.0%
Balance Sheet Data			
Inventories	€ 3,692	€ 3,763	€ 3,113
Working capital	4,033	3,468	2,133
Net sales by brand			
adidas	€18,993	€16,334	€13,939
Reebok	1,843	1,770	1,731
Net sales by product			
Footwear	€12,427	€10,132	€ 8,360
Apparel	7,747	7,352	6,970
Equipment*	1,044	999	1,585
Net sales by region			
Western Europe	€ 5,883	€ 4,275	€ 4,539
North America	4,275	3,412	2,753
Greater China	3,789	3,010	2,469
Latin America	1,907	1,731	1,783
Japan	1,056	1,007	776
Middle East, Africa, and other Asian Markets	2,907	2,685	2,388
Russia and Commonwealth of Independent States	660	679	739

* In 2017, the company completed the previously announced divestitures of its TaylorMade Golf, Adams Golf, Ashworth, and CCM Hockey businesses; the divestures of TaylorMade Golf, Adams Golf, and the CCM Hockey businesses accounted for the decline in Equipment sales from 2015 levels. In 2016, the company completed its divestiture of its Rockport brand shoe business.

Source: Company annual reports, 2017 and 2015.

Murray, Landon Collins, and Von Miller; and MLB players Chase Utley, brothers B.J. and Justin Upton, Carlos Correa, Josh Harrison, and Chris Bryant. It had also signed non-sports celebrities Kanye West and Pharrell. In 2003, soccer star David Beckham, who had been wearing adidas products since the age of 12, signed a $160 million lifetime endorsement deal with adidas that called for an immediate payment of $80 million and subsequent payments said to be worth an average of $2 million annually for the next 40 years.[20] Adidas was anxious to sign Beckham to a lifetime deal not only to prevent Nike from trying to sign him but also because soccer was considered

the world's most lucrative sport and adidas management believed that Beckham's endorsement of adidas products resulted in more sales than all of the company's other athlete endorsements combined. Companywide expenditures for advertising, event sponsorships, athlete endorsements, public relations, and other marketing activities were €2.14 billion in 2017, €1.89 billion in 2016, €1.89 billion in 2015, and €1.55 billion in 2014.

In 2015-2017, adidaslaunched a number of initiatives to become more America-centric and regain its #2 market position lost to Under Armour in 2015. This included a campaign to sign up to 250

National Football League players and 250 Major League Baseball players over the next three years. It had secured 1,100 new retail accounts that involved prominent displays of freshly styled adidas products and newly introduced running shoes with high-tech features. The adidas brand regained its #2 position in the United States in 2017.

Research and development activities commanded considerable emphasis at The adidas Group. Management had long stressed the critical importance of innovation in improving the performance characteristics of its products. New apparel and footwear collections featuring new fabrics, colors, and the latest fashion were introduced on an ongoing basis to heighten consumer interest, as well as to provide performance enhancements—indeed, in 2017, 79 percent of sales at adidas came from products launched in 2017; at Reebok, 69 percent of sales came from products launched in 2017. About 1,060 people were employed in research and development (R&D) activities; in addition, the company drew upon the services of well-regarded researchers at universities in Canada, the United States, England, and Germany. R&D expenditures in 2017 were €187 million, versus €149 million in 2016, €139 million in 2015, and €126 million in 2014.

Over 95 percent of production was outsourced to about 300 independent contract manufacturers located in China and other Asian countries (79 percent), Europe (9 percent), the Americas (11 percent), and Africa (1 percent). The Group operated 10 relatively small production and assembly sites of its own in Germany (1), Sweden (1), Finland (1), the United States (4), and Canada (3). Close to 97 percent of the Group's production of footwear was performed in Asia; annual volume sourced from footwear suppliers had ranged from a low of 256 million pairs to a high of 403 million pairs during 2013-2017. During the same time frame, apparel production ranged from 292 million to 404 million units and the production of hardware products ranged from 94 million to 110 million units. In all three categories, the largest production volumes occurred in 2017.

The company was stepping up its investments in company-owned, robot-intensive micro-factories to speed certain products to key geographic markets in Europe and the United States much faster and to also lower production costs and boost gross profit margins. At the same time, the company had begun reengineering its existing supply chain and production processes to enable the company to respond quicker to shifts in buyer preferences, be able to reorder seasonal products and sell them to buyers within the season, and to reduce the time it took to get freshly designed products manufactured and into the marketplace.

Executives at The adidas Group expected that the Group's global sales would increase by 10 percent in 2018; management also wanted to achieve a 2018 operating margin of 10.3 to 10.5 percent, and grow 2018 net income to a level between €1.62 billion and €1.68 billion (about 40 percent higher than 2017—see Exhibit 7).

ENDNOTES

[1] Company press release, October 25, 2016.

[2] Company press release, January 31, 2017.

[3] Company press release, January 31, 2017.

[4] Douglas A. McIntyre and Jon C. Ogg, "20 Worst CEOs in America 2017," December 26, 2017, https//247wallst.com (accessed February 22, 2017).

[5] Nike's fiscal year runs from June 1 to May 31, so Nike's reported sales from December 1, 2016 through November 30, 2017 (its last two quarters of fiscal 2017 and first two quarters of fiscal 2018) represent a reasonable approximation of its sales in North America and its sales globally during the months of 2017.

[6] Sara Germano, "Under Armour Overtakes Adidas in the U.S. Sportswear Market," *Wall Street Journal*, January 8, 2015, www.wsj.com (accessed April 19, 2016).

[7] Transcript of Quarter 4 2017 Earnings Conference Call, February 13, 2018.

[8] Under Armour's Q4 2015 Earnings Call Transcript, January 26, 2016,

www.seekingalpha.com (accessed on March 30, 2016).

[9] "Under Armour Kevin A. Plank on Q1 2016 Results—Earnings Call Transcript," April 21, 2016, www.seekingalpha.com (accessed April 21, 2016).

[10] Dennis Green, "Kevin Durant: 'No one wants to play in Under Armour' shoes," *Business Insider*, August 30, 2017, www.businessinsider.com (accessed February 22, 2018).

[11] Nate Scott, "James Harden signs 13-year, $200 million deal with adidas after Nike opts not to match," *USA Today*, August 13, 2015, www.usatoday.com (accessed February 21, 2018).

[12] Company 10-K Reports, 2014, 2015, 2016, and 2017.

[13] Company 10-K report for 2017.

[14] According to information in the company's slide presentation for Investors Day 2015, September 16, 2015.

[15] The store closing numbers were part of a Reuters report authored by Gayathree

Ganesan under the title "Under Armour Loses Money and Launches a Restructuring Plan," August 1, 2017, www.businessinsider.com (accessed February 23, 2018).

[16] According to Allied Market Research, "Athletic Footwear Market—Report" published June 2016, www.alliedmarketresearch.com.

[17] Allied Market Research, "Sports Apparel Market—Report," published October 2015, www.alliedmarketresearch.com.

[18] Transcript of "Nike Investor Day 2017," October 25, 2017, posted in the Investor Relations section of www.nike.com (accessed February 24, 2018).

[19] Transcript of presentations by Nike's top executives at "Nike Investor Day 2017," October 25, 2017, posted in the Investor Relations section of www.nike.com (accessed February 24, 2018).

[20] Steve Seepersaud, "5 of the Biggest Athlete Endorsement Deals," www.askmen.com (accessed February 5, 2012).

MoviePass—Are Subscribers Loving It to Death?

Gretchen Johnson
The University of Alabama

Lou Marino
The University of Alabama

McKenna Marino
The University of Alabama

In 2011, Stacy Spikes and Hamet Watt launched MoviePass to combat the steady decline in ticket sales experienced by movie theaters in the United States as ticket sales fell from a high of 1.58 billion tickets in 2002 to 1.28 billion in 2011. The pair noticed that Americans were willing to pay for subscriptions for home movie rentals through Netflix and for entertainment through cable TV, and they believed they could drive patrons to theaters through a subscription-based movie ticket service. The traditional movie ticket model was based on a transaction between theaters and customers. Each time a customer wanted to see a movie, they purchased a ticket for a specific time and location they wanted to attend. However, Spikes and Watt introduced a service that allowed customers to pay a flat monthly fee, originally set at $30 per month and fallen to as low as $7.95 per month by 2018, that allows customers to see one 2D movie a day (no 3D or IMAX movies are allowed), and to choose between a variety of theaters.

Even in the early days the company met with skepticism and resistance from investors and established theater industry players. Many questioned how the company could make money when, in many markets, ticket prices were already over $10. While Spikes and Watt positioned themselves as an ally for movie theaters that made a much higher percentage of their revenue from sales of soft drinks, popcorn, candy, and other food at their concession stands, some major theater chains saw the company as a rival trying to capture a portion of the industry's already

declining revenues. Despite the fact that MoviePass estimated that subscribers went to the movies more often and increased their concession purchases by 120 percent, several theater chains refused to work with the company.

In 2016 Mitch Lowe, an executive with previous experience at Redbox and Netflix, joined the company and began to experiment with the company's offerings. Under Lowe, the company experimented with pricing and offering various levels of service ranging from $15 a month plan for two movies a month in small markets to an unlimited plan for $50. In early August 2017 the company had approximately 20,000 subscribers. On August 15, 2017, the company announced it was going to an aggressive $9.95 subscription price and that an agreement had been made for Helios and Matheson Analytics, Inc., to acquire 53.71 percent of MoviePass for $28.5 million. The plan was for Helios and Matheson to monetize the data generated by MoviePass's subscriber platform. By October 24, when the deal with Helios and Matheson Analytics, Inc. closed, MoviePass's subscriber base had grown to over 600,000.

By June 1, 2018, MoviePass had grown to over three million subscribers with projections of five million by the end of the year. The company under Helios and Matheson became the fastest growing subscription company in the history of the internet, reaching one million subscribers in only four months, beating Spotify (which took five months) and Netflix (which took 39 months) to reach one million subscribers.[1] The company's subscription numbers were bolstered by aggressive marketing and a very strong 96 percent customer retention rate. Despite this growth in subscribers, the company had not yet achieved profitability leading to questions about their future viability. MoviePass and their parent company Helios and Matheson were actively building additional revenue streams to support operations including negotiations with smaller theaters to split profits on ticket and concession sales, the acquisition of Moviefone by Helios and Matheson to generate advertising revenue, and the launch of a movie distribution company—MoviePass Ventures—that would allow them to distribute independently.

The question remaining was whether or not they would be able to achieve profitability before cash runs out. One analyst conjectured that perhaps MoviePass fans loved the service too much. It was estimated that while the average American saw approximately 4.5 movies a year, the average MoviePass subscriber doubled this. Some of the earliest MoviePass subscribers tended to be among the 11 percent of the U.S. population who were categorized as heavy moviegoers seeing more than 18 movies a year and accounting for approximately 50 percent of the movie tickets sold in a given year. Indeed, some MoviePass power users saw as many as 24 movies a month (prior to restrictions being put into place limiting users to being able to see a movie only once) with one subscriber boasting he saw a movie 40 days in a row to celebrate his 40th birthday.

As of June 2018, it was clear that MoviePass subscribers loved paying a $9.95 monthly fee to attend an unlimited number of movies at most any theater, or for a $7.95 monthly fee to attend up to three movies a month, but were they loving the company's subscription service to death? During the first five months of 2018, with MoviePass subscribers using their pass to attend as many as double the anticipated number of movies, the agreed-upon fees MoviePass had to pay theaters for each movie a MoviePass subscriber attended greatly exceeded its income from monthly subscriptions. Confronted with estimated monthly cash flow deficits approaching $22 million and having rapidly burned through the cash raised from earlier rounds of financing, MoviePass's parent, Helios and Matheson, was scrambling to raise additional long-term capital—chiefly by issuing additional shares of stock. These new stock issues, however, had greatly diluted the price per share and triggered widespread concern whether the company could survive. The closing price of Helios and Matheson's common stock on June 22, 2018, was $0.32 per share, down from $20.40 in October 2017.

From the outset, Lowe and the MoviePass management team had counted on being able to attract a much bigger percentage of casual movie-goers who would likely attend only one to two movies per month and thus override the money-losing effects of early subscribers whose frequent movie attendance generated ticket fee payments to theaters that greatly surpassed their monthly subscription fees. MoviePass's parent company, Helios and Matheson, had also concluded that efforts to sustain the company's business model needed to include the development of new revenue streams that would have synergy with the company's growing subscriber base. One such possibility included internally producing its own movies and inducing subscribers to attend these movies—its first movie, *American Animals,* was scheduled to begin running in theaters in June 2018. The benefits of subscribers attending movies that were wholly or partially funded and produced by MoviePass included paying significantly lower ticket fees to theaters showing these movies and also receiving a share of the ticket price (typically, movie producers received a 60 percent share of the ticket price). There was no question that MoviePass's innovative business model had the potential to disrupt the movie theater industry, but a number of analysts believed that unless MoviePass could rather quickly transform its business model into something that was more sustainable, it could not survive long enough to profit from its game-changing innovation.

COMPANY BACKGROUND

Launch of the MoviePass Concept, 2011 to 2012

MoviePass "was originally conceived as being exclusively for avid movie fans who attend the cinema multiple times a month" and used a voucher system that allowed subscribers to print tickets at home and redeem them at the theater for movie tickets.[2] With their idea, Spikes and Watt planned to launch a beta in June 2011; however, they did not secure agreements with their key partners, the theaters, on their initial list in the San Francisco area prior to launching the beta. Once theaters heard about the scheduled launch, they indicated that they did not wish to participate. One of these theaters, AMC, would go on to become one of MoviePass's largest critics. Resistance from the theaters caused the company to shut down the night before the launch and go on a "temporary hiatus" until August 2011 when they partnered with Hollywood Movie Money to leverage its existing theater network and voucher system.[3]

During this soft launch with Movie Money, MoviePass offered its services to a select few on an invitation-only member list with thousands waiting for a public launch. With this small list of subscribers, MoviePass found that "64 percent started going to the movies more often, and not having to pay for a ticket (in the traditional sense) meant they were dropping about 123 percent more on concessions."[4] This success encouraged the entrepreneurs, and MoviePass was launched nationwide in October 2012 with reduced membership fees and an app instead of a printed voucher system.

Initial Struggles

"MoviePass . . . struggled to gain traction in its early years because of pricing [$50 a month] and pushback from exhibitors, who worried that a subscription service would undermine per-ticket pricing."[5] Despite changes made after the "temporary hiatus," the company continued to face challenges because of their small number of subscribers. On top of this, a subscriber's location determined how much their monthly fee would be leading customers in larger cities to complain because of their higher fee.

During this time, the conflict between MoviePass and AMC began to develop beyond comments prior to the first scheduled launch. Once available nationwide, AMC issued a statement that they had "no affiliation with MoviePass and had no discussions with the company about participation" in the service.[6] In 2016, Mitch Lowe, a former executive at Netflix and Redbox, became CEO and began to experiment with different subscription levels. Even with his ideas and new pricing, MoviePass was facing struggles from potential partners and customers, and the outlook for the company looked bleak until August of 2017.

Success and Growth

Helios and Matheson purchased a majority stake in MoviePass in October 2017 with a plan to collect data on subscribers and monetize this data through the use of analytics-based marketing. With the announcement of the investment in August 2017, MoviePass dropped its subscription fee to $9.95 and the number of subscribers skyrocketed. Helios and Matheson's stock price soared to $32.90, a 52-week high. As a response to the growing popularity of MoviePass, large theater chains, namely AMC, took notice and began issuing statements about their relationship, or lack thereof, with MoviePass. Resistance from AMC was significant as they controlled approximately 29.4 percent of the industry market share in the United States in 2016 in terms of revenues, followed by Regal with 18.5 percent, and Cinemark with 13.6 percent. In terms of number of screens in 2016 in the United States, AMC controlled 28 percent (11,247 screens), Regal controlled 18.2 percent (7,315), and Cinemark 14.8 percent (5,957).

However, smaller independent movie theater chains, which tended to have 5 to 20 theaters per chain, began to consider partnering with MoviePass to drive up concession sales. One such theater chain, Studio Movie Grill, credits their investment with MoviePass for increased attendance, especially on week nights. "I know it's getting a bad rap in some circles, but we love MoviePass," said Brian Schultz, Studio Movie Grill's chief executive. "Some people aren't sure they want to pay $10 to $12 to see a movie like 'Lady Bird.' MoviePass takes out that hurdle."[7] With locations in nine states, this chain offers a potentially large subscription base.

Another small chain that MoviePass partnered with is Flix Brewhouse: "On April 6th [2018], MoviePass announced a partnership with Flix Brewhouse, the nation's only cinema circuit that pairs full service in-theater dining with an award-winning craft brewery at every location."[8] With this type of venue, both MoviePass and Flix Brewhouse have the potential to make large profits off concession sales when customers use the ticket subscription.

BUSINESS OPERATIONS

"Purchasing" a Ticket

The initial business model for MoviePass had subscribers print out ticket vouchers at home and bring them to theaters to redeem them for a printed theater ticket. This process worked for the initial launch in 2011 and nationwide launch in 2012, but customers soon began to complain about forgetting vouchers at home. Under the new business model, "people who sign up receive a membership card that functions like a debit card. When members want to see a movie (no more than one a day) they use a MoviePass smartphone app to check in at the theater. The app instantly transfers the price of a ticket to the membership card. Members in turn use the card to pay for entry."[9]

With this change, MoviePass also eliminated the potential rejection of vouchers by theaters because the debit cards issued are MasterCard debit cards. Unless a theater rejects all MasterCard customers, they must accept payment from a MoviePass MasterCard. This has led to continued strained relations with some theaters, like AMC who threatened to take legal action after the change in the redemption process.

Developments and Changes

MoviePass's growth took off with the Helios and Matheson Analytics purchase of a controlling stake in the company bringing new revenue streams for MoviePass. Helios and Matheson advertised itself as a "Big Data company that helps global enterprises make informed decisions by providing insights into social phenomena;"[10] the company's consulting services served customers in the financial, healthcare, retail, education, and government sectors. The company had recently merged with Zone Technologies, Inc., which was described as a leader in predictive analytics. The intention was to bring Helios and Matheson's Big Data and analytic competencies to MoviePass's data to unlock significant revenue streams.

These synergies were not reflected in the company's 2017 annual report, which reported a net loss of $145 million (see Exhibit 1). Despite the losses, Farnsworth was committed to continue to fund MoviePass through Helios and Matheson. In March, Helios and Matheson forgave $55.5 million in cash advances given to MoviePass in January and February 2018, in exchange for increasing its stake in Movie Pass to 81.2 percent. By June 2018, Helios and Matheson had advanced another $35 million in exchange for additional equity that took their stake in MoviePass to over 91 percent (see Exhibit 2).

To help bolster MoviePass's advertising revenue Helios and Matheson acquired Moviefone

from Verizon in early April 2018, reportedly paying Verizon $23 million for the movie-ticket site. Canaccord Genuity analyst Austin Moldow said, "We believe this deal gives MoviePass the opportunity to convert a large number of users into subscribers and provides a platform for enhanced studio marketing and user engagement,"[11] in relation to MoviePass acquiring Moviefone.

The 2017 financial statements for Helios and Matheson, parent company of MoviePass are shown in Exhibits 1, 2, and 3. The company's consolidated income statement for the first quarter of 2018 is shown in Exhibit 4; this exhibit is particularly important because it signals the extent of the company's rapidly deteriorating financial position.

COMPETITION AND CHALLENGES

Pushback from Major Theaters

When theaters first heard about MoviePass, their pushback was so strong that the company had to postpone its initial launch. The tension has seen little reduction since this first encounter, but AMC and MoviePass did try a premium joint subscription plan for a year before returning to their initial relationship. Despite the option for both parties to benefit from a partnership, both sides have made gestures indicating this is not likely in the near future.

"By August of this year [2017], when MoviePass introduced a cut-rate, subscription-based plan—go to the movies 365 times a year for $9.95 a month—Mr. Lowe had been declared an enemy of the state. 'Not welcome here,' AMC Entertainment . . . said in an indignant August news release that threatened legal action."[12] Even before this change in MoviePass's business model, the two companies shared conflict over splitting profits from concessions: "we appreciate their business," Adam Aron, AMC's chief executive, said on a conference call with analysts last month. But Mr. Aron added, "AMC has absolutely no intention—I repeat, no intention—of sharing any—I repeat, any—of our admissions revenue or our concessions revenue."[13]

As MoviePass began to gain momentum, executives "celebrated the milestone [one million subscribers] by cheekily posing for photos at an AMC theater in Times Square."[14] While smaller theaters have

EXHIBIT 1   Helios and Matheson Analytics, Inc. Consolidated Statements of Operations and Comprehensive Loss, 2016–2017

	Year Ended December 31,	
	2017	**2016**
Revenues:		
Consulting	$ 4,512,300	$ 6,759,700
Subscription	5,929,267	–
Total revenues	10,441,567	6,759,700
Cost of revenue	20,538,709	4,860,927
Gross (loss)/profit	(10,097,142)	1,898,773
Operating expenses:		
Selling, general & administrative	35,698,134	3,602,267
Research and development	2,012,548	133,462
Loss on impairment of Zone goodwill and intangible assets	6,256,983	–
Depreciation & amortization	1,951,977	259,379
Total operating expenses	45,919,642	3,995,108
Loss from operations	(56,016,784)	(2,096,335)
Other income/(expense):		
Change in fair market value – derivative liabilities	28,303,612	(192,339)
Change in fair market value – warrant liabilities	(20,409,937)	85,090
Loss on extinguishment of debt	(4,346,885)	–
Interest expense	(98,478,473)	(5,210,413)
Interest income	177,157	18,261
Total other expense	(94,754,526)	(5,299,401)
Loss before income taxes	(150,771,310)	(7,395,736)
Income tax (expense)/benefit	(53,532)	14,665
Net loss	(150,824,842)	(7,381,071)
Net loss attributable to the non-controlling interest	4,850,308	–
Net loss attributable to Helios and Matheson Analytics Inc	(145,974,534)	(7,381,071)
Other comprehensive income - foreign currency adjustment	3,011	13,721
Comprehensive loss	$(145,971,523)	$ (7,367,350)
Net loss per share attributable to common stockholders Basic and Diluted	$(17.46)	$(2.74)
Weighted average shares	8,361,094	2,691,448

Source: Company 10-K Report, 2017.

begun to partner with MoviePass, it appears that larger chains, specifically AMC, are unlikely to join. Despite the potential benefit for both companies and customers, it will take time to repair damage done by both sides in this heated disagreement.

Competitors

In terms of movie subscription services, MoviePass only had two major competitors when it reached its three million member mark in June 2018. The first

was an internal venture launched by Cinemark theaters and the second was Sinemia.

Cinemark Movie Club   In December 2017, Cinemark Theaters, one of the largest movie theater chains in the United States, launched a proprietary movie subscription service that could only be used in Cinemark theaters. For $8.99 per month members received one 2D movie ticket a month, 20 percent off of concessions, and waived online fees for services such as reserved seating. Members could purchase up to two

EXHIBIT 2   Helios and Matheson Analytics, Inc., Consolidated Balance Sheets, 2016–2017

	December 31, 2017	December 31, 2016
ASSETS		
Current assets:		
Cash and cash equivalents	$ 24,949,393	$ 2,747,240
Accounts receivable - less allowance for doubtful accounts of $72,335 and $428,719 at December 31, 2017 and December 31, 2016, respectively	27,470,219	410,106
Unbilled receivables	–	45,207
Prepaid expenses and other current assets	3,557,811	597,171
Total current assets	55,977,423	3,799,724
Property and equipment, net	234,035	45,212
Intangible assets, net	28,536,782	6,004,691
Goodwill	79,137,177	4,599,969
Deposits and other assets	147,171	59,189
Total assets	$164,032,588	$14,508,785
LIABILITIES AND STOCKHOLDERS' EQUITY		
Current liabilities:		
Accounts payable and accrued expenses	$ 13,144,003	$ 1,331,118
Deferred revenue	54,425,630	–
Liabilities to be settled in stock	21,320,705	–
Convertible notes payable, net of debt discount of $2,444,368 and $2,200,575, respectively	2,061,072	31,425
Warrant liability	67,288,800	230,663
Derivative liability	4,834,462	977,129
Total current liabilities	163,074,672	2,570,335
Convertible notes payable, net of current portion and debt discount of $1,392,514 and $0, respectively	1,550,555	–
Total liabilities	164,625,227	2,570,335
COMMITMENTS AND CONTINGENCIES		
Stockholders' (deficit) equity:		
Preferred stock, $0.01 par value; 2,000,000 shares authorized; no shares issued and outstanding as of December 31, 2017 and December 31, 2016	–	–
Common stock, $0.01 par value; 100,000,000 shares authorized; 23,981,253 issued and outstanding as of December 31, 2017; 4,874,839 issued and outstanding as of December 31, 2016	239,813	48,748
Additional paid-in capital	150,356,757	55,258,111
Accumulated other comprehensive loss - foreign currency translation	(103,980)	(106,991)
Accumulated deficit	(189,495,185)	(43,261,418)
Total Helios stockholders' (deficit) equity	(39,002,595)	11,938,450
Non-controlling interest	38,409,956	–
Total stockholders' (deficit) equity	(592,639)	11,938,450
Total liabilities and stockholders' equity	$164,032,588	$14,508,785

Source: Company 10-K Report, 2017.

EXHIBIT 3   Helios and Matheson Analytics, Inc., Consolidated Statement of Cash Flows, 2016–2017

	For the Year Ended December 31,	
	2017	2016
CASH FLOWS FROM OPERATING ACTIVITIES:		
Net loss	$(150,824,842)	$ 7,381,071)
Adjustments to reconcile net loss to net cash provided by (used in) operating activities:		
Depreciation and amortization	1,951,977	259,379
Accretion of debt discount	56,444,825	4,000,500
Change in fair market value – warrant liabilities	20,409,937	–
Change in fair market value – derivative liabilities	(28,303,612)	107,249
Loss on extinguishment of debt	4,346,885	–
Provision for doubtful accounts	72,336	386,516
Non-cash interest expense	37,136,900	–
Shares issued in exchange for services	23,946,227	–
Loss on impairment of goodwill and intangibles	6,256,983	–
Change in operating assets and liabilities:		
Accounts receivable	(17,463,058)	589,533
Unbilled receivables	45,207	250,266
Prepaid expenses and other current assets	116,818	(379,581)
Accounts payable and accrued expenses	1,138,970	(1,112)
Deferred revenue	17,425,739	–
Deposits and other assets	(79,982)	34,008
Net cash used in operating activities	(27,378,690)	(2,134,313)
CASH FLOWS FROM INVESTING ACTIVITIES:		
Sale of property and equipment	1,928	867
Pre-acquisition loan to Zone Technologies, Inc.	–	(1,291,208)
Purchases of equipment	(186,162)	(11,064)
Patent acquisition	(196,353)	–
Payments for acquisition of businesses net of cash acquired	(25,192,246)	170,760
Net cash used in investing activities	(25,572,833)	(1,130,645)
CASH FLOWS PROVIDED BY FINANCING ACTIVITIES:		
Proceeds from notes payable	40,320,000	5,100,000
Proceeds from public offering, net	55,333,523	–
Note repayments	(21,480,000)	–
Exercise of warrants	977,142	–
Net cash provided by financing activities	75,150,665	5,100,000
Net change in cash	22,199,142	1,835,042
Effect of foreign currency exchange rate changes on cash and cash equivalents	3,011	13,721
Cash, beginning of period	2,747,240	898,477
Cash, end of period	$ 24,949,393	$ 2,747,240

		For the Year Ended December 31,	
		2017	2016
SUPPLEMENTAL DISCLOSURE OF CASH AND NON-CASH TRANSACTIONS:			
Cash paid for income taxes		$ 37,931	$ 4,379
Cash paid during the period for interest		$ 4,849,587	$ –
Change in carrying value of convertible common stock equity		$ 259,233	$ –
Conversion of convertible notes and interest to shares of common stock		$(16,837,895)	$ 4,015,358
Debt discount on convertible notes		$ –	$11,101,075
Increase in debt for new original issue discount		$ 51,067,455	$ –
Derivative ceases to exist - reclassified to paid in capital		$ 14,009,686	$ 3,999,457
Embedded derivative – conversion feature and warrants		$ –	$ 6,391,364

Source: Company 10-K Report, 2017.

add-on tickets to share with family and friends for each transaction for $8.99, and unused ticket credits could be rolled over as long as the membership stayed active. Members could pay an upcharge to see movies in 3D and IMAX formats.

Sinemia   Sinemia is a Turkish firm founded in 2015 by Rifat Oguz that offered a movie subscription service that touted allowing members to see any movie, in any theater, at any showtime. In its home country of Turkey, Sinemia offered a subscription plan for 19 lira a month or approximately $5 and had about 350,000 users of its mobile app. Sinemia launched in the United States in January of 2018 and was a leader in the movie subscription industry in Canada, the UK, Turkey, and Australia. Sinemia planned to expand to Hong Kong, Singapore, South Africa, and India. The company planned to aggressively target MoviePass customers arguing that MoviePass's unlimited plan was unnecessary as the average movie patron in the United States only saw four movies per year. Sinemia planned to offer an enhanced movie subscription service that saved frequent moviegoers money while not forcing them to sacrifice their moviegoing experience. Sinemia had experienced steady growth after entering the United States in May 2018 and reveled in growing more than 50 percent each month since its U.S. launch. Initial projections were that Sinemia would reach 1.3 million U.S. subscribers and over $330 million in revenues within three years, but early growth seemed to indicate that these projections were overly conservative.

Sinemia's business model was similar to that of MoviePass; Sinemia relied on a combination of the Sinemia app and a prepaid debit card. Similar to MoviePass, Sinemia paid full price to theaters for ticket purchases. The company reported that 85 percent of its revenue came from subscriptions, with the remaining 15 percent coming from advertising deals with restaurants and movie studios that were featured on the app. Elements of their business model were so similar that MoviePass launched legal action claiming that Sinemia was illegally infringing on MoviePass's electronic payment technology and that it had infringed on its copyrights by mimicking key features.

However, unlike MoviePass, Sinemia offered a variety of plans ranging from $4.99 a month that allowed users to see one standard movie per month, to a $14.99 a month premium plan that allowed users to see three movies per month, including 3D and IMAX movies. Subscribers were not limited to a single viewing of a movie as they were with MoviePass, and Sinemia also offered a two-person plan named Sinemia for Two that allowed the cardholder to take an additional person with them to the movies; the additional person did not have to be the same person each time. Sinemia also allowed users to purchase their tickets in advance through services such as Fandango, so users did not have to be physically at the theater to buy a ticket.

CUSTOMER RELATIONS

MoviePass largely used a limited call center and social media accounts on Facebook and Twitter (@MoviePass_CS) to interact with its customers.

EXHIBIT 4   Helios and Matheson Analytics, Inc.

HELIOS AND MATHESON ANALYTICS INC. CONDENSED CONSOLIDATED STATEMENTS OF OPERATIONS AND COMPREHENSIVE INCOME/(LOSS) (UNAUDITED)		
	Three Months Ended March 31,	
	2018	**2017**
Revenues:		
Consulting	$ 839,503	$ 1,358,062
Subscription	47,162,447	–
Marketing and promotional services	1,440,910	–
Total revenues	49,442,860	1,358,062
Cost of revenue	135,968,976	1,105,485
Gross (loss) profit	(86,526,116)	252,577
Operating expenses:		
Selling, general & administrative	19,709,831	4,180,172
Research and development	224,771	–
Depreciation and amortization	1,271,275	430,925
Total operating expenses	21,205,877	4,611,097
Loss from operations	(107,731,993)	(4,358,520)
Other income/(expense):		
Change in fair market value – derivative liabilities	8,597,378	867,468
Change in fair market value – warrant liabilities	93,608,200	114,863
Gain on extinguishment of debt	15,007,699	–
Interest expense	(35,534,899)	(3,108,832)
Interest income	15,341	17,950
Total other income/(expense)	81,693,719	(2,108,551)
Loss before income taxes	(26,038,274)	(6,467,071)
Provision for income taxes	7,951	30,484
Net loss	(26,046,225)	(6,497,555)
Net loss attributable to the noncontrolling interest	31,222,100	–
Net income/(loss) attributable to Helios and Matheson Analytics Inc.	$ 5,175,875	$ (6,497,555)
Other comprehensive (loss)/income – foreign currency adjustment	(7,150)	823
Comprehensive income/(loss)	$ 5,168,725	$ (6,496,732)
Basic income (loss) per share:		
Net income (loss) per share attributable to common stockholders – basic	$0.15	$(1.17)
Weighted average shares – basic	34,850,281	5,530,083
Diluted income (loss) per share:		
Net income (loss) per share attributable to common stockholders – diluted	$0.09	$(1.17)
Weighted average shares – diluted	36,602,367	5,530,083

Source: Company 10-Q Report for the first three months of 2018, filed May 15, 2018.

This strategy proved an effective way to communicate with customers during normal operations, especially when the company was in its early growth stages. For example, in 2015, MoviePass subscribers Irina Gonzalez, Gene Deems, and Dauren had praised the company's customer service.

As MoviePass has grown, handling all its customers and their concerns has proved problematic for the company. Many of these customers have taken to social media to state their concerns leaving a lasting scar for the company; these customers often feel that their complaints disappear into a black hole, never to be dealt with.

MoviePass was quick to respond to the public complaints about its customer service and implemented a number of changes. For example, when it lowered its subscription price in August 2017, the company's nine employees were quickly overwhelmed, and the company was slow to send out cards. Lowe admitted to underestimating demand, and the company quickly expanded its staffing to 35 employees. Following challenges faced in spring 2018, MoviePass hired a new head of customer experience, and, subsequently, some of the problems seemed to be slowly diminishing.[15]

Even with these changes, other developments in subscriptions had pushed some customers away.

For example, in the spring of 2018, MoviePass believed it was facing significant fraudulent activity on some accounts. This activity included individuals sharing a card, despite the rules clearly stating each person was required to have their own membership, subscribers reserving one movie on the app and buying another ticket at the box office (only one screening of a movie was allowed), users checking in for a 2D movie ticket but then paying an upcharge for a 3D, IMAX or Real D ticket, using MoviePass to purchase gift cards from theaters, and using the card to buy concession. In response to this, MoviePass terminated a small percentage of users' accounts. This served to give the company the reputation for heavy-handed administration of its rules and caused customers to fear getting banned. Additionally, some of the banned customers protested their innocence and blamed inadequate documentation of the rules and poor operating procedures on the part of MoviePass. In some cases, the customers' accounts were reactivated.

Another challenge reported on the Facebook page and Twitter feed were regular problems with the software. Customers reported that the app would have inaccurate showtimes or would list a 2D movie as a 3D movie, thus not allowing the movie to be seen. Other customers reported challenges with using the photo verification system that MoviePass began to require in spring 2018 to fight ticket fraud. To prove customers had purchased the tickets that matched the ones they reserved on the app, some customers had to upload a photo of their tickets before they could reserve another movie; sometimes the app generated errors that prevented customers from doing so. Customers would also face significant frustration when the app would crash, and they were not able to reserve movies. Stated company policy was that customers could get preapproval to see a movie if the app was down by direct messaging the company via Twitter. However, when the app crashed as it did on June 14, 2018, the number of messages quickly overwhelmed MoviePass's response capabilities and a number of subscribers used Twitter to express their frustrations. Other subscribers reported problems with getting a refund from MoviePass for movies that had been seen when the app was unavailable.

Finally, customers expressed frustration with what was perceived as MoviePass's regular experimentation with pricing strategies and inaccurate order processing. Throughout its history, MoviePass had experimented with a number of pricing plans including a $50 a month unlimited plan to as low as $6.95 a month for its one movie a day plan. At times the company also offered various plans with costs that varied depending on how many moves the subscriber wanted to see. For example, in 2016 customers could choose between one, two, three, or unlimited movies per month, and the prices for the two-movie plan varied depending on whether the customer lived in a small market with comparatively low ticket prices (subscription price of $15 per month) or a larger market where ticket prices were higher (subscription price of $21 per month).

While the company offered their unlimited plan for prices ranging from $6.95 a month to $9.95 a month depending on whether the company was offering a special promotion, through the fall of 2017 and spring of 2018 they experimented with prices again in April 2018. In April 2018, the company discontinued the one movie a day plan and offered a joint promotion with iHeartRadio that featured four 2D movies a month for three months and three months of iHeartRadio's All Access on-demand music. Customer reaction was swift and overwhelmingly negative forcing the company to go back to its one movie a day plan. However, analysts predicted that MoviePass would continue to experiment with pricing and value-added bundling with other partners to find a way to drive subscription prices up. In June 2018, MoviePass was running a special promotion plan of $7.95 per month for up to three movies per month.

The Future Path to Profitability

In June 2018, even as MoviePass exceeded three million subscribers, Helios and Matheson's stock price fell to record lows of less than 40 cents a share. Investor confidence was deeply shaken as the company's cash flow deficits ballooned past $20 million per month. Even an assurance by the company's CEO that it had secured a $300 million line of credit to sustain operations did little to calm the concerns of some analysts and investors.

In an interview with Yahoo Finance published in April 2018, Mitch Lowe, MoviePass CEO, laid out MoviePass's plan to reach profitability by both driving down costs and increasing revenues. The long-term goal was to reach a breakeven point on the MoviePass subscriptions and to realize profit through revenues related to marketing and data.[16]

Lowe expected four key factors to evolve that would help drive down subscription related costs:

1. MoviePass subscribers would eventually start seeing fewer movies. Lowe predicted that while MoviePass subscribers were very enthusiastic and saw a number of movies each month, by the fourth or fifth month the novelty wore off, and MoviePass subscribers would see fewer movies each, thus reducing cost.

2. While initial MoviePass subscribers tended to be heavy users, more occasional moviegoers, who don't go to the moves often, would join MoviePass. This would significantly reduce the average number of movies seen by MoviePass members.

3. MoviePass planned to market to users who were in locations where movie tickets cost less, perhaps $7 or $8 in Omaha or Kansas versus $15 in New York or Los Angeles. When MoviePass first started, 55 percent of subscribers were from large cities where tickets tend to be more expensive. By April 2018, only 30 percent of subscribers were from those areas, a trend Lowe predicted would continue.

4. The company planned to leverage its market strength to negotiate discounts with theater chains of up to 20 percent per ticket. According to Helios and Matheson's CEO, Ted Farnsworth, MoviePass controls, on average across all movies, approximately 6.1 percent of the U.S. box office, and as much as 10 to 25 percent of box office sales for movies promoted through the app.[17] Given this power, Lowe believes it is reasonable for the company to receive discounts similar to Costco, where customers can purchase tickets to AMC, Regal, and Cinemark Theaters for 20 to 25 percent off of retail price.

The company also planned to increase revenues by marketing films for studios, selling advertising on its app for movies and restaurants near movie theaters, and taking a percentage of the concession sales in a theater. In over 1,000 independent theaters, MoviePass has been able to leverage its considerable power to negotiate a $3 commission on each ticket sale, 25 percent commission on concession sales, or sometimes both.[18] In total, Lowe believed the company could earn as much as $6 per subscriber through these initiatives.

In addition to the original plan, MoviePass has begun to branch out into other parts of the movie industry. In April 2018, MoviePass, through a new subsidiary named MoviePass Ventures, invested in two movies—*American Animals* and *Gotti*—with mixed success. *American Animals* received positive reviews but only opened in a limited number of theaters earning just over $500,000 in two weeks. *Gotti,* on the other hand, was called "a dismal mess" by the *New York Times* and "the worst mob movie of all time" by the *New York Post.* It was unclear if MoviePass had the competencies to make this type of investment consistently pay off.

Headed into summer 2018, analysts were generally pessimistic on the future of MoviePass and its parent Helios and Matheson. Many argued that the numbers simply didn't add up and that the company would burn through its reserves before it could achieve profitability. Further, AMC, the largest theater chain in the United States, announced it would launch its own subscription plan in summer 2018 called AMC Stubs A-List. This plan would cost $20 and would allow subscribers to see three movies a week, including Real 3D and IMAX movies. Perhaps the most concerning factor for investors occurred in April 2018, when the company acknowledged in its prospectus that it did not have sufficient accounting resources to ensure adequate internal control over financial reporting mechanisms due to significant and complex transactions such as MoviePass's acquisition.[19]

Despite these challenges Lowe believe the company would not only break even and achieve five million subscribers by the end of 2018, but that the company would eventually become a major competitor with Netflix, Hulu, and Amazon over a fight for leisure time. Lowe predicted that his company could disrupt the "Netflix and chill" trend toward cocooning and encourage customers to reengage with the moviegoing experience. To further extend the reach of the company, MoviePass planned to roll out family plans during the summer of 2018, and it was planning to offer a new bring-a-friend option that allowed users to purchase a ticket for a friend at a little below retail price; and it would allow subscribers to pay an additional fee to see 3D and IMAX movies. However,

MoviePass also planned to introduce surge pricing for subscribers who were on the monthly plan, which would force them to pay a $2 surcharge to see popular movies and movies on opening weekends or at high demand times such as nights and weekends. Subscribers who had annual plans would not be forced to pay the surge pricing.

There was no question that MoviePass had the support of some customers who loved the service and were willing to voluntarily limit the number of movies they saw to help the struggling company. When these same customers discovered that MoviePass had invested in *Gotti,* they encouraged members of the MoviePass Fans Facebook page to see the movie despite its unfavorable reviews to support the company. With this ardent customer support, the debate raged on as to whether MoviePass was doomed to failure with a fatally flawed business model, or, as Lowe argued, it was an industry disruptor, and rumors of the company's death had been greatly exaggerated.

ENDNOTES

[1] O'Falt, Chris, "MoviePass Boom: 500,000 New Subscribers join in less than 30 Days," Indiewire, January 9, 2018, http://www.indiewire.com/2018/01/moviepass-1-5-million-subscribers-1201915498/.

[2] Lang, Brent, "The Great Disruptor: MoviePass Upends the Movie Business, but Can It Survive?" https://variety.com/2018/film/features/moviepass-movie-business-studios-amc-1202754312/

[3] Long, Christian, "A Brief History of MoviePass and Its Feud with AMC," https://uproxx.com/entertainment/moviepass-amc-history/ January 30, 2018.

[4] Ibid.

[5] Barnes, Brooks, "MoviePass Adds a Million Subscribers, Even if Theatres Aren't Sold on It," December 27, 2017, https://www.nytimes.com/2017/12/27/business/media/moviepass-theaters-tickets.html.

[6] Long, Christian, "A Brief History of MoviePass and Its Feud with AMC," January 30, 2018, https://uproxx.com/entertainment/moviepass-amc-history/.

[7] Barnes, Brooks, "MoviePass Adds a Million Subscribers, Even if Theatres Aren't Sold on It," December 27, 2017, https://www.nytimes.com/2017/12/27/business/media/moviepass-theaters-tickets.html.

[8] Schneider, George, "Missed A Hot IPO? Subscriptions Soar Towards 5 Million At This Startup," April 14, 2018, https://seekingalpha.com/article/4162329-missed-hot-ipo-subscriptions-soar-towards-5-million-startup?lift_email_rec=false.

[9] Barnes, Brooks, "MoviePass Adds a Million Subscribers, Even if Theatres Aren't Sold on It," December 27, 2017, https://www.nytimes.com/2017/12/27/business/media/moviepass-theaters-tickets.html.

[10] Helios and Matheson, "Who We Are," 2018, https://www.hmny.com/who-we-are/.

[11] Schneider, George, "Missed A Hot IPO? Subscriptions Soar Towards 5 Million At This Startup," April 14, 2018, https://seekingalpha.com/article/4162329-missed-hot-ipo-subscriptions-soar-towards-5-million-startup?lift_email_rec=false.

[12] Barnes, Brooks, "MoviePass Adds a Million Subscribers, Even if Theatres Aren't Sold on It," December 27, 2017, https://www.nytimes.com/2017/12/27/business/media/moviepass-theaters-tickets.html.

[13] Ibid.

[14] Ibid.

[15] Lang, Brent, "The Great Disruptor: MoviePass Upends the Movie Business, But Can It Survive?" https://variety.com/2018/film/features/moviepass-movie-business-studios-amc-1202754312/.

[16] Pogue, David, "MoviePass CEO on How the Company Will Finally Break Even," Yahoo

Finance, April 12, 2018, https://finance.yahoo.com/news/moviepass-ceo-company-will-finally-break-even-185917883.html.

[17] Guerrasio, J. and McAlone, N., "There Are Red Flags All Over MoviePass' Financial Statements That Should Scare Investors," *Business Insider,* April 20, 2018, http://www.businessinsider.com/moviepass-owner-financial-statement-should-scare-investors-2018-4.

[18] Duprey, R., "Growing Pains? Or Does MoviePass Have a Serious Problem?" The Motley Fool, March 14, 2018, https://www.fool.com/investing/2018/03/14/growing-pains-or-does-moviepass-have-a-serious-pro.aspx.

[19] Guerrasio, J. and McAlone, N. There are red flags all over MoviePass' financial statements that should scare investors," *BusinessInsider*, April. 20, 2018, http://www.businessinsider.com/moviepass-owner-financial-statement-should-scare-investors-2018-4?r=UK&IR=T.

TOMS Shoes: Expanding Its Successful One For One Business Model

Margaret A. Peteraf
Tuck School of Business at Dartmouth

Sean Zhang and Carry S. Resor
Research Assistants, Dartmouth College

While traveling in Argentina in 2006, Blake Mycoskie witnessed the hardships that children without shoes experienced and became committed to making a difference. Rather than focusing on charity work, Mycoskie sought to build an organization capable of sustainable, repeated giving, where children would be guaranteed shoes throughout their childhood. He established Shoes for a Better Tomorrow, better known as TOMS, as a for-profit company based on the premise of the "One for One" Pledge. For every pair of shoes TOMS sold, TOMS would donate a pair to a child in need. By mid-2018, TOMS had given away over 75 million pairs of shoes in over 70 different countries.[1]

As a relatively new and privately-held company, TOMS experienced consistent and rapid growth despite the global recession that began in 2009. By 2015, TOMS had matured into an organization with nearly 500 employees and almost $400 million in revenues. TOMS shoes could be found in several major retail stores such as Nordstrom, Bloomingdale's, and Urban Outfitters. In addition to providing shoes for underprivileged children, TOMS also expanded its mission to include restoring vision to those with curable sight-related illnesses by developing a new line of eyewear products. They began selling other products to help provide clean water and safe birth services where the needs existed. For an overview of how quickly TOMS expanded in its first seven years of business, see Exhibit 1.

COMPANY BACKGROUND

While attending Southern Methodist University, Blake Mycoskie founded the first of his six start-ups, a laundry service company that encompassed seven colleges and staffed over 40 employees.[2] Four start-ups and a short stint on *The Amazing Race* later, Mycoskie found himself vacationing in Argentina where he not only learned about the Alpargata shoe originally used by local peasants in the 14th century, but also witnessed the extreme poverty in rural Argentina.

Determined to make a difference, Mycoskie believed that providing shoes could more directly impact the children in these rural communities than delivering medicine or food. Aside from protecting children's feet from infections, parasites, and diseases,

EXHIBIT 1   TOMS' Growth Since 2006

	2016	2015	2014	2013	2012	2011	2010	2009	2008	2007	2006
Total Employees	750	580	550	400	320	250	72	46	33	19	4
Thousands of Pairs of Shoes Sold	60,000*	25,000	10,000	7,250	2,700	1,300	1,000	230	110	50	10

*Estimated based on shoes donated.

Source: PrivCo, Private Company Financial Report, "TOM's Shoes, Inc.," April 22, 2018

shoes were often required for a complete school uniform. In addition, research had shown that shoes were found to significantly increase children's self-confidence, help them develop into more active community members, and lead them to stay in school. Thus, by ensuring access to shoes, Mycoskie could effectively increase children's access to education and foster community activism, raising the overall standard of living for people living in poor Argentinian rural areas.

Dedicated to his mission, Mycoskie purchased 250 pairs of Alpargatas and returned home to Los Angeles, where he subsequently founded TOMS Shoes. He built the company on the promise of "One for One," donating a pair of shoes for every pair sold. With an initial investment of $300,000, Mycoskie's business concept of social entrepreneurship was simple: sell both the shoe and the story behind it. Building on a simple slogan that effectively communicated his goal, Mycoskie championed his personal experiences passionately and established deep and lasting relationships with customers.

Operating from his apartment with three interns he found on Craigslist, Mycoskie quickly sold out his initial inventory and expanded considerably, selling 10,000 pairs of shoes by the end of his first year. With family and friends, Mycoskie ventured back to Argentina, where they hand-delivered 10,000 pairs of shoes to children in need. Because he followed through on his mission statement, Mycoskie was able to subsequently attract investors to support his unique business model and expand his venture significantly.

When TOMS was initially founded, TOMS operated as the for-profit financial arm while a separate entity entitled "Friends of TOMS" focused on charity work and giving. After 2011, operations at Friends of TOMS were absorbed into TOMS' own operations as TOMS itself matured. In Friends of TOMS' latest accessible 2011 501(c)(3) filing, assets were reported at less than $130,000.[3] Moreover, as of May 2013, the Friends of TOMS website was discontinued while TOMS also ceased advertising its partnership with Friends of TOMS in marketing campaigns and on its corporate website. The developments suggested that Friends of TOMS became a defunct entity as TOMS incorporated all of its operations under the overarching TOMS brand.

INDUSTRY BACKGROUND

Even though Mycoskie's vision for his company was a unique one, vying for a position in global footwear manufacturing was a risky and difficult venture. The industry was both stable and mature—one in which large and small companies competed on the basis of price, quality, and service. Competitive pressures came from foreign as well as domestic companies and new entrants needed to fight for access to downstream retailers.

Further, the cost of supplies was forecasted to increase between 2017 and 2022. Materials and wages constituted almost 80 percent of industry costs—clearly a sizable concern for competitors. Supply purchases included leather, rubber, plastic compounds, foam, nylon, canvas, laces, etc. While the price of leather rose steadily each year, the price of natural and synthetic rubber was also expected to rise over the next five years. In addition, wages as a share of revenue were expected to increase at a rate of 5.5 percent over a five-year period, from 17.1 percent in 2017 to an estimated 17.8 percent in 2022.[4]

In order to thrive in the footwear manufacturing industry, firms needed to differentiate their products in a meaningful way. Selling good quality products at a reasonable price was rarely enough; they needed to target a niche market that desired a certain image. Product innovation and advertising campaigns therefore became the most successful competitive weapons. For example, Clarks adopted a sophisticated design, appealing to a wealthier, more mature customer base. Nike, adidas, and Skechers developed athletic footwear and aggressively marketed their brands to reflect that image. Achieving economies of scale, increasing technical efficiency, and developing a cost-effective distribution system were also essential elements for success.

Despite the presence of established incumbents, global footwear manufacturing was an attractive industry to potential entrants based on the prediction of increased demand and therefore sales revenue. Moreover, the industry offered incumbents one of the highest profit margins in the fashion industry. But because competitors were likely to open new locations and expand their brands in order to discourage competition, new companies' only option was to attempt to undercut them on cost. Acquiring capital equipment and machinery to manufacture footwear on a large scale was expensive. Moreover, potential entrants also needed to launch costly large-scale marketing campaigns to promote brand awareness. Thus, successful incumbents were traditionally able to maintain an overwhelming portion of the market.

Building the TOMS Brand

Due to its humble beginnings, TOMS struggled to gain a foothold in the footwear industry. While companies like Nike had utilized high-profile athletes like Michael Jordan and Tiger Woods to establish brand recognition, TOMS had relatively limited financial resources and tried to appeal to a more socially conscious consumer. Luckily, potential buyers enjoyed a rise in disposable income over time as the economy recovered from the recession. As a result, demand for high-quality footwear increased for affluent shoppers, accompanied by a desire to act (and be *seen* acting) charitably and responsibly.

While walking through the airport one day, Mycoskie encountered a girl wearing TOMS shoes. Mycoskie recounts:

> I asked her about her shoes, and she went on to tell me this amazing story about TOMS and the model that it uses and my personal story. I realized the importance of having a story today is what really separates companies. People don't just wear our shoes, they tell our story. That's one of my favorite lessons that I learned early on.

Moving forward, TOMS focused more on selling the story behind the shoe rather than product features or celebrity endorsements. Moreover, rather than relying primarily on mainstream advertising, TOMS emphasized a grassroots approach using social media and word-of-mouth. With over 4 million Facebook "Likes" and over 2 million Twitter "Followers" in 2018, TOMS' social media presence eclipsed that of its much larger rivals, Sketchers and Clarks. Based on 2018 data, TOMS had fewer "Followers" and fewer "Likes" than both Nike and adidas. However, TOMS had more "Followers" and "Likes" per dollar of revenue. So when taking company size into account, TOMS also had a greater media presence than the industry's leading competitors (see Exhibit 2 for more information).

TOMS' success with social media advertising can be attributed to the story crafted and championed by Mycoskie. Industry incumbents generally dedicated a substantial portion of revenue and effort to advertising since they were simply selling a product. TOMS, on the other hand, used its mission to ask customers to buy into a *cause,* limiting their need to devote resources to brand-building. TOMS lets their charitable work and social media presence generate interest for them organically. This strategy also increased the likelihood that consumers would place repeat purchases and share the story behind their purchases with family and friends. TOMS' customers took pride in supporting a grassroots cause instead of a luxury footwear supplier and encouraged others to share in the rewarding act.

A BUSINESS MODEL DEDICATED TO SOCIALLY RESPONSIBLE BEHAVIOR

Traditionally, the content of advertisements for many large apparel companies focused on the attractive aspects of the featured products. TOMS' advertising, on the other hand, showcased its charitable contributions and the story of its founder Blake Mycoskie. While the CEOs of Nike, adidas, and Clarks rarely appeared in

EXHIBIT 2 TOMS' Use of Social Media Compared to Selected Footwear Competitors

	2016 Revenue (Mil. of $)	Facebook "Likes"	"Likes" per Mil. of $ in revenue	Twitter "Followers"	"Followers" per mil. of $ in revenue
TOMS	$ 416	4,117,118	9,897	2,113,698	5,081
Clarks	2,330	2,293,975	985	48,424	21
Skechers	3,560	4,830,560	1,357	45,740	13
adidas	18,480	33,713,131	1,824	3,426,554	185
Nike	32,460	30,725,299	947	7,449,306	229

Source: Author data from Facebook and Twitter May 2, 2018; revenue numbers obtained from MarketWatch and Statista.

their companies' advertisements, TOMS ran as many ads with its founder as it did without him, emphasizing the inseparability of the TOMS product from Mycoskie's story. In all of his appearances, Mycoskie was dressed in casual and friendly attire so that customers could easily relate to Blake and his mission. This advertising method conveyed a small-company feel and encouraged consumers to connect personally with the TOMS brand. It also worked to increase buyer patronage through differentiating the TOMS product from others. Consumers were convinced that every time they purchased a pair of TOMS, they became instruments of the company's charitable work.

As a result (although statistical measures of repeating-buying and total product satisfaction among TOMS' customers were not publicly available), the volume of repeat purchases and buyer enthusiasm likely fueled TOMS' success in a critical way. One reviewer commented, "This is my third pair of TOMS and I absolutely love them!... I can't wait to buy more!"[5] Another wrote, "Just got my 25th pair! Love the color! They. . .are my all-time favorite shoe for comfort, looks & durability. AND they are for a great cause!! Gotta go pick out my next pair.. . ."[6]

Virtually all consumer reports on TOMS shoes shared similar themes. Though not cheap, TOMS footwear was priced lower than rivals' products, and customers overwhelmingly agreed that the value was worth the cost. Reviewers described TOMS as comfortable, true to size, lightweight, and versatile ("go with everything"). The shoes had "cute shapes and patterns" and were made of canvas and rubber that molded to customers' feet with wear. Because TOMS products were appealing and trendy yet also basic and comfortable, they were immune to changing fashion trends and consistently attracted a variety of consumers. (see Exhibit 3).

In addition to offering a high quality product that people valued, TOMS was able to establish a positive repertoire with its customers through efficient distribution. Maintaining an online shop helped TOMS save money on retail locations but also allowed it to serve a wide geographic range. Further, the company negotiated with well-known retailers like Nordstrom and Neiman Marcus to assist in distribution. Through thoughtful planning and structured coordination, TOMS limited operation costs and provided prompt service for its customers.

EXHIBIT 3   Representative Advertisement for TOMS Shoes Company

©John M. Heller/Getty Images

Giving Partners

As it continued to grow, TOMS sought to improve its operational efficiency by teaming up with "Giving Partners," nonprofit organizations that helped to distribute the shoes that TOMS donated. By teaming up with Giving Partners, TOMS streamlined its charity operations by shifting many of its distributional responsibilities to organizations that were often larger, more resourceful, and able to distribute TOMS shoes more efficiently. Moreover, these organizations possessed more familiarity and experience dealing with the communities that TOMS was interested in helping and could therefore better allocate shoes that suited the needs of children in the area. Giving Partners also provided feedback to help TOMS improve upon its giving and distributional efforts.

Each Giving Partner also magnified the impact of TOMS' shoes by bundling their distribution with other charity work that the organization specialized in. For example, Partners in Health, a nonprofit organization that spent almost $100 million in 2012 on providing healthcare for the poor (more than TOMS' total revenue that year), dispersed thousands of shoes to schoolchildren in Rwanda and Malawi while also screening them for malnutrition. Cooperative giving further strengthened the TOMS brand by association with well-known and highly regarded Giving Partners. Complementary services expanded the scope of TOMS' mission, enhanced the impact that each pair of TOMS had on a child's life, and increased the number of goodwill and business opportunities available to TOMS.

In order to ensure quality of service and adherence to its fundamental mission, TOMS maintained five criteria for Giving Partners:

- Repeat Giving: Giving partners must be able to work with the same communities in multi-year commitments, regularly providing shoes to the same children as they grow.
- High Impact: Shoes must aid Giving Partners with their existing goals in the areas of health and education, providing children with opportunities they would not have otherwise.
- Considerate of Local Economy: Providing shoes cannot have negative socioeconomic effects on the communities where shoes are given.
- Large Volume Shipments: Giving Partners must be able to accept large shipments of giving pairs.
- Health/Education Focused: Giving Partners must only give shoes in conjunction with health and education efforts.[7]

As of 2016, TOMS had built relationships with over 100 Giving Partners, including Save the Children, U.S. Fund for UNICEF, and IMA World Health. In order to remain accountable to their mission in these joint ventures, TOMS also performed unannounced audit reports that ensured shoes were distributed according to the One for One model.

Building a Relationship with Giving Partners

Having Giving Partners offered TOMS the valuable opportunity to shift some of its philanthropic costs onto other parties. However, TOMS also proactively maintained strong relationships with their Giving Partners. Kelly Gibson, the program director of National Relief Charities (NRC), a Giving Partner and nonprofit organization dedicated to improving the lives of Native Americans, highlighted the respect with which TOMS treated its Giving Partners:

> TOMS treats their Giving Partners (like us) and the recipients of their giveaway shoes (the Native kids in this case) like customers. We had a terrific service experience with TOMS. They were meticulous about getting our shoe order just right. They also insist that the children who receive shoes have a customer-type experience at distributions.

From customizing Giving Partners' orders to helping pick up the tab for transportation and distribution, TOMS treated its Giving Partners as valuable customers and generated a sense of goodwill that extended beyond its immediate One for One mission. By ensuring that their Giving Partners and recipients of shoes were treated respectfully, TOMS developed a unique ability to sustain business relationships that other for-profit organizations more concerned with the financial bottom line did not.

MAINTAINING A DEDICATION TO CORPORATE SOCIAL RESPONSIBILITY

Although TOMS manufactured its products in Argentina, China, and Ethiopia (countries which have all been cited as areas with a high degree of child and forced labor by the Bureau of International Labor Affairs), regular third-party factory audits and a Supplier Code of Conduct helped to ensure compliance with fair labor standards.[8] Audits were conducted on both an announced and unannounced basis while the Supplier Code of Conduct was publicly posted in the local language of every work site. The Supplier Code of Conduct enforced standards such as minimum work age, requirement of voluntary employment, non-discrimination, maximum work week hours, and right to unionize. It also protected workers from physical, sexual, verbal, or psychological harassment in accordance with a country's legally mandated standards. Workers were encouraged to report violations directly to TOMS, and suppliers found in violation of TOMS' Supplier Code of Conduct faced termination.

In addition to ensuring that suppliers met TOMS' ethical standards, TOMS also emphasized its own dedication to ethical behavior in a number of ways. TOMS was a member of the American Apparel and Footwear Association (AAFA) and was registered with the Fair Labor Association (FLA). Internally, TOMS educated its own employees on human trafficking and slavery prevention and partnered with several organizations dedicated to raising awareness about such issues, including Hand of Hope.[9]

Giving Trips

Aside from material shoe contributions, TOMS also held a series of "Giving Trips" that supported the broader notion of community service. Giving Trips were first-hand opportunities for employees of TOMS and selected TOMS customers to partake in the delivery of TOMS shoes. These trips increased the transparency of TOMS' philanthropic efforts, further engaging customers and employees. They generated greater social awareness as well, since participants on these trips often became more engaged in local community service efforts at home.

From a business standpoint, Giving Trips also represented a marketing success. First, a large number of participants were customers and journalists unassociated with TOMS who circulated their stories online through social media upon their return. Second, TOMS was able to motivate participants and candidates to become more involved in their mission by increasing public awareness. In 2013, instead of internally selecting customers to participate on the Giving Trips, TOMS opted to hold an open voting process that encouraged candidates to reach out to their known contacts and ask them to vote for their inclusion. This contest drew thousands of contestants and likely hundreds of thousands of voters, although the final vote tallies were not publicly released.

Environmental Sustainability

Dedicated to minimizing its environmental impact, TOMS pursued a number of sustainable practices that included offering vegan shoes, incorporating recycled bottles into its products, and printing with soy ink. TOMS also used a blend of organic canvas and post-consumer, recycled plastics to create shoes that were both comfortable and durable. By utilizing natural hemp and organic cotton, TOMS eliminated pesticide and insecticide use that adversely affected the environment.

In addition, TOMS supported several environmental organizations like Surfers Against Sewage, a movement that raised awareness about excess sewage discharge in the UK. Formally, TOMS was a member of the Textile Exchange, an organization dedicated to textile sustainability and protecting the environment. The company also participated actively in the AAFA's Environmental Responsibility Committee.

Creating the TOMS Workforce

When asked what makes a great employee, Mycoskie blogged,

> As TOMS has grown, we've continued to look for these same traits in the interns and employees that we hire. Are you passionate? Can you creatively solve problems? Can you be resourceful without resources? Do you have the compassion to serve others? You can teach a new hire just about any skill . . . but you absolutely cannot inspire creativity and passion in someone that doesn't have it.[10]

The company's emphasis on creativity and passion was part of the reason why TOMS relied so heavily on interns and new hires rather than experienced workers. By hiring younger, more inexperienced employees, TOMS was able to be more cost-effective in terms of personnel. The company could also recruit young and energetic individuals who were more likely to think innovatively and out of the box. These employees were placed in specialized teams under the leadership of strong, experienced managerial talent. This human intellectual capital generated a competitive advantage for the TOMS brand.

Together with these passionate individuals, Mycoskie strove to create a family-like work atmosphere where openness and collaboration were celebrated. With his cubicle located in one of the most highly-trafficked areas of the office (right next to customer service), Mycoskie made a point to interact with his employees on a daily basis, in all-staff meetings, and through weekly personal e-mails while traveling. Regarding his e-mails, Mycoskie reflected,

I'm a very open person, so I really tell the staff what I'm struggling with and what I'm happy about. I tell them what I think the future of TOMS is. I want them to understand what I'm thinking. It's like I'm writing to a best friend.[11]

This notion of "family" was further solidified through company dinners, ski trips, and book clubs where TOMS employees were encouraged to socialize in informal settings. These casual opportunities to interact with colleagues created a "balanced" work atmosphere where employees celebrated not only their own successes, but the successes of their co-workers

Diversity and inclusion were also emphasized at TOMS. For example, cultural traditions like the Chinese Lunar New Year were celebrated publicly on the TOMS' company blog. Moreover, as TOMS began expanding and distributing globally, the company increasingly sought to recruit a more diverse workforce by hiring multilingual individuals who were familiar with TOMS' diverse customer base and could communicate with their giving communities.[12]

The emphasis that Mycoskie placed on each individual employee was one of the key reasons why employees at TOMS often felt "lucky" to be part of the movement.[13] Coupled with the fact that TOMS employees knew their efforts fostered social justice, these "Agents of Change," as they referred to themselves, were generally quite satisfied with their work, making TOMS Forbes's 4th Most Inspiring Company in 2014. Overall, the culture allowed TOMS to recruit and retain high-quality employees invested in achieving its social mission.

FINANCIAL SUCCESS AT TOMS

With a Compound Annual Growth Rate (CAGR) of 4.8 percent from 2010 to 2014, global footwear manufacturing developed into an industry worth over $289.7 billion.[14] While TOMS remained a privately held company with limited financial data, the estimated growth rate of TOMS' revenue was astounding. In the seven years after his company's inception, Mycoskie was able to turn his initial $300,000 investment into a company with over $200 million in yearly revenues. As Exhibit 4 shows, the average growth rate of TOMS on a yearly basis was 145 percent, even excluding its first major spike of 457 percent. During the same period, Nike experienced a growth rate of roughly 8.5 percent, with a *decline* in revenues from 2009 to 2010.

The fact that TOMS was able to experience consistent growth despite financial turmoil post-2008 illustrates the strength of the One for One Movement to survive times of recession. Mycoskie attributed his success during the recession to two factors: (1) As consumers became more conscious of their spending during recessions, products like TOMS that gave to others actually became *more* appealing (according to Mycoskie); (2) The giving model that TOMS employed is not "priced in." Rather than commit a percentage of profits or revenues to charity, Mycoskie noted that TOMS simply gave away a pair for every pair it sold. This way, socially-conscious consumers knew exactly where their money was going without having to worry that TOMS would cut-back on its charity efforts in order to turn a profit.[15]

EXHIBIT 4   Revenue Comparison for TOMS Shoes and the Footwear Industry, 2006–2016

	2016	2015	2014	2013	2012	2011	2010	2009	2008	2007	2006
TOMS (in Mils. of $s)											
Revenue	$416	$390	$370.9	$285	$101.8	$46.9	$25.1	$8.4	$3.1	$1.2	$0.2
Growth (%)	6.7%	5.1%	30.1%	180%	117%	86.9%	199%	171%	158.3%	500%	
Industry (in Bil. of $s)											
Revenue	$239.8	$229.4	$230.6	$221.0	$210.2	$208.1	$179.6	$162.4	$159.3	$145.8	
Growth (%)	4.5%	−0.5%	4.3%	5.1%	1.0%	15.9%	10.6%	1.9%	9.3%	0.0%	

Source: PrivCo and "Global Footwear Manufacturing," *IBISWorld,* April 18, 2016. http://clients1.ibisworld.com/reports/gl/industry/currentperformance.aspx?entid=500.

Production at TOMS

Although TOMS manufactured shoes in Argentina, Ethiopia, and China, only shoes made in China were brought to the retail market. Shoes made in Argentina and Ethiopia were strictly used for donation purposes. TOMS retailed its basic Alpargata shoes in the $50 price range, even though the cost of producing each pair was estimated at around $9.[16] Estimates for the costs of producing TOMS' more expensive lines of shoes were unknown, but they retailed for upwards of $150.

In comparison, manufacturing the average pair of Nike shoes in Indonesia cost around $20, and they were priced at around $70.[17] Factoring in the giving aspect, TOMS seemed to have a slightly smaller mark-up than companies like Nike, yet it still maintained considerable profit margins. More detailed information on trends in TOMS' production costs and practices is limited due to the private nature of the company.

The Future

Because demand and revenues were predicted to increase in the global footwear manufacturing industry, incumbents like TOMS needed to find ways to defend their position in the market. One method was to continue to differentiate products based on quality, image, or price. Another strategy was to focus on R&D and craft new brands and product lines that appealed to different audiences. It was also recommended that companies investigate how to mitigate the threat posed by an increase in supply costs.

In an effort to broaden its mission and product offerings, TOMS began to expand both its consumer base and charitable-giving product lines. For its customers, TOMS started offering stylish wedges, ballet flats, and even wedding apparel in an effort to reach more customers and satisfy the special needs of current ones. For the children it sought to help, TOMS expanded past its basic black canvas shoe offerings to winter boots in order to help keep children's feet dry and warm during the winter months in cold climate countries.

On another front, TOMS entered the eyewear market in hopes of restoring vision to the 285 million blind or visually-impaired individuals around the world. For every pair of TOMS glasses sold, TOMS restored vision to one individual either through donating prescription glasses or offering medical treatment for those suffering from cataracts and eye infections. TOMS began by focusing its vision-related efforts in Nepal but as of 2018 TOMS had teamed up with 14 Giving Partners to help restore sight to over 500,000 individuals in 13 countries.

Through TOMS' additional product launches of coffee and bags, the company has been able to expand giving efforts to the global issues of clean water and safe birth. With each bag of TOMS Roasting Co. Coffee, TOMS gives a week's supply of safe water—140 liters—to a person in need. They have currently given over 450,000 weeks of safe water. With the sale of its bags, TOMS has supported safe birth services for over 175,000 mothers, which includes helping its Giving Partners with the vital materials and training necessary for a safe birth. Furthermore, one of TOMS' newer initiatives seems to be supporting bullying prevention programs through the sale of TOMS High Road Backpack.[18] While TOMS has not made any explicit announcements to further expand products or markets, there are clearly many applications for the One for One business model.

As TOMS looks to the future, Blake Mycoskie remains involved in the company but stepped down as CEO in 2015 after Bain Captial purchased a 50 percent stake in the company. Mycoskie is now more focused on the marketing and giving than the overall operations as well as a separate social entrepreneurship fund.[19]

ENDNOTES

[1] TOMS Shoes company website, April 23, 2018 www.toms.com/what-we-give-shoes.
[2] Mycoskie, Blake, Web log post, *The Huffington Post*, May 26, 2013, www.huffingtonpost.com/blake-mycoskie.
[3] *501c3Lookup*, June 2, 2013, http://501c3lookup.org/ FRIENDS_OF_TOMS/.
[4] "Global Footwear Manufacturing," *IBISWorld*. July 2017, http://clients1.ibisworld.com/ reports/gl/industry/industryoutlook. aspx?entid=500.

[5] Post by "Alexandria," *TOMS* website, June 2, 2013, www.toms.com/ red-canvas-classics-shoes-1.
[6] Post by "Donna Brock," *TOMS* website, January 13, 2014, www.toms.com/ women/bright-blue-womens-canvas-classics.
[7] *TOMS* website, June 2, 2013, www.toms.com/ our-movement-giving-partners.
[8] Trafficking Victims Protection Reauthorization Act, *United States Department of Labor*, June 2, 2013, www.dol.gov/ilab/programs/ocft/tvpra.htm;

TOMS website, June 2, 2013, www.toms.com/ corporate-responsibility.
[9] Hand of Hope, "Teaming Up with TOMS Shoes," *Joyce Meyer Ministries*, June 2, 2013, www.studygs.net/citation/mla.htm.
[10] Mycoskie, Blake, "Blake Mycoskie's Blog," *Blogspot*, June 2, 2013, http://blakemycoskie. blogspot.com/.
[11] Schweitzer, Tamara, "The Way I Work: Blake Mycoskie of TOMS Shoes," *Inc.* June 2, 2013. www.inc.com/magazine/20100601/the-way-i-work-blake-mycoskie-of-toms-shoes.html.

[12] TOMS Jobs website, June 2, 2013, www.toms.com/jobs/l.

[13] Daniela, "Together We Travel," TOMS Company Blog, June 3, 2013, http://blog.toms.com/post/36075725601/together-we-travel.

[14] "Global—Footwear," *Marketline: Advantage*, April 18, 2016, http://advantage.marketline.com/Product?pid=MLIP0948-0013.

[15] Zimmerman, Mike. "The Business of Giving: TOMS Shoes," *Success*, June 2, 2013, http://www.success.com/articles/852-the-business-of-giving-toms-shoes.

[16] Fortune, Brittney, "TOMS Shoes: Popular Model with Drawbacks," *The Falcon*, June 2, 2013, http://www.thefalcononline.com/article.php?id=159.

[17] *Behind the Swoosh*, Dir. Keady, Jim, 1995. Film.

[18] TOMS Shoes company website, April 23, 2018, www.toms.com/what-we-give.

[19] Quittner, Jeremy, "What the Founder of TOMS Shoes is Doing Now," *Fortune*, September 8, 2016, http://fortune.com/2016/09/08/what-the-founder-of-toms-shoes-is-doing-now/.

Lola's Market: Capturing A New Generation

Katherine Gonzalez
MBA Student, Sonoma State University

Sergio Canavati
Sonoma State University

Armand Gilinsky
Sonoma State University

"Our core is Latinos, try to trigger them, try to get every single Latino in our store...what's hard are the young ones; they are more focused with what is on their phone."

—David Ortega, Owner, Lola's Market

"Before I used to tell them, 'Put those phones away' now I just let it go, it happens so much. . .they do not listen."[1] As David Ortega, owner of Lola's Market takes a break from replacing wallpaper and making repairs to his long-standing business in Santa Rosa, California, he surveys his store and watches as his millennial employees are fully invested in the tweets[2] and hashtags[3] that flood their notification screens. David contemplates on how he can engage these employees, and even further, how he can engage this generation. David is a man rooted in tradition and he believes that the traditions of good business and good customer service need to be passed down to the new generation, but how? Situated in Sonoma County, California, Lola's Market has five locations, each targeting the Latino consumer, each filled with generations of customers who have shopped at their various locations since their doors first opened in Santa Rosa. David is inspired to make changes for his business and knows that engaging the younger generation—the millennials[4]—will strengthen Lola's future business for years to come. David is at risk of losing this new coveted consumer base to retailers that "speak" to the millennials in their language—businesses that utilize social media and online shopping experiences to appease the tech savvy culture. Regardless of where he stands amongst his competitors, David's outlook on the possibilities Lola's has is inspiring and will facilitate Lola's capacity to gain this new generation: "Never say you can't, you always have to be positive."[5] With this mindset, it is no surprise that David Ortega has been recognized by the North Bay Business Journal as one of the first honorees of the Latino Business Leadership Awards for outstanding leadership throughout the North Bay.[6] With this type of leadership, Lola's can potentially reposition themselves as the sought-out center for the Latino millennial consumer and workforce.

INDUSTRY OVERVIEW

When looking at the Supermarket Industry as whole—including markets who offer specialty services, such as Lola's bakery and restaurant—there are key success factors that will give a particular organization a competitive advantage. These key factors include proximity to key markets, access to a multiskilled and flexible workforce, the ability to control stock on hand, close monitoring of competition, and access to the latest available and most efficient technology and techniques.[7] Alongside these key success factors is evolution with the consumer: the new target consumer amongst industries is the millennial consumer—the millennial generation interests marketers due to its size and growing market influence.[8] This generation is one of the largest generations in history and is about to move into its prime spending years—millennials are positioned to reshape the economy.[9] Millennial consumers want to engage with brands on social media; about 62 percent of millennials say that if a brand engages with them on social networks, they are likely to become a loyal customer and with 87 percent of millennials using between two and three tech devices on a daily basis—brands must stay relevant by appealing to and engaging millennials on these tech platforms.[10]

In 2017, Amazon's acquisition of Whole Foods, took the online retailer into the brick and mortar setting and Amazon is now driving down Whole Food's prices across the board—this is causing supermarket competitors to raise the stakes.[11]

Amazon is also implementing an additional shipping option utilizing its Prime delivery service for customers who choose to shop with Whole Foods.[12] Amazon is a company that has already created a strong relationship with the millennial generation, as a majority of Amazon Prime users are a part of this generation (see Exhibit 1). Since millennials already have ties with Amazon, which has the strong online presence and convenience that this customer base prefers, it will be even more difficult for smaller, family-owned businesses like Lola's to attain this consumer base.

When it comes to supermarkets in California, specifically the North Bay, there are various competitors who have their own takes on how to generate this technological change and brand advancement. Sonoma County is one of the most competitive food markets in the country, thanks to an array of strong local and national grocery businesses vying for customers' time and money.[13] In 2016, one of the largest competitors in the North Bay market, Oliver's Market expanded its doors and rebranded itself with a more modern appeal and even including the addition of in-store Wi-Fi available to its customers.[14] To capture the millennial generation, specifically in the supermarket sector of the retail industry, companies need to take

EXHIBIT 1 Amazon Prime User Demographics

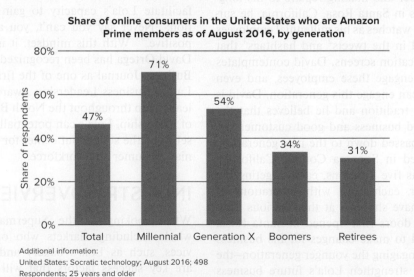

Share of online consumers in the United States who are Amazon Prime members as of August 2016, by generation

- Total: 47%
- Millennial: 71%
- Generation X: 54%
- Boomers: 34%
- Retirees: 31%

Additional information:
United States; Socratic technology; August 2016; 498
Respondents; 25 years and older

Source: Statista, "U.S. Amazon Prime Reach by Generation 2016," August 2016, **https://www.statista.com/statistics/609991/amazon-prime-reach-usa-generation/**.

advantage of the latest technology and implement it within in-store and online (if applicable) IT systems, such as their points of sale processing. This will lead to increased productivity and higher profit margins.[15]

LOLA'S STORY

> "I'd go over to look at the bakery and think, one day I am going to open up something like this."
>
> —David Ortega

As a 15-year-old young man working at Perez Family Restaurant in Santa Rosa, California, David Ortega had vast aspirations for his future and the future of his family. David recalls countlessly seeing the bakery next door from the restaurant in which he worked and dreaming that one day he would have a business of his own—a business that provided quality products, produced with the love and attention that the bakery he gazed upon provided. Along with having quality products, David wanted to offer the Latino consumer a taste of home by offering authentic Mexican bread and ready-to-eat food. In addition to authentic Mexican food, David paid tribute to his mother Dolores, by naming his dream business after her—from a cost-effective play on her name,[16] *Lola's Market* was born.

On February 8, 1992, with his mother Dolores and father at his side, David achieved his dream. With the smell of fresh *Pan Dulce*[17] in the air, the first Lola's opened on Dutton Avenue in Santa Rosa. It stood at about 1,000 square Feet, filled with the promise of growing tradition and quality goods and services. Today, Lola's Market has expanded to five stores; each Lola's store still has its famous fresh bakery and restaurant, as well as a produce department and deli section. Lola's Market has two locations in Santa Rosa—one in Napa, one in Healdsburg—and its newest location in Petaluma, which opened in 2013. Lola's believes they can "compete with anybody"[18] and with the quality of goods and services they provide, they do have the potential to outgrow and stand ahead of their local competitors. David believes that Lola's is known for its service, quality meats and produce and the comfort that the markets provide for its Spanish-speaking customers: "Hispanics like to communicate in their own language, that's probably why they shop here."[19]

Lola's Market is operated with David Ortega as President; General Manager, Mario Lozano; and Controller, Carlos Salvatierra directly under him. His General Manager, Mario Lozano, oversaw the chain's POS Supervisor, Safety Coordinator, and HR Coordinator, as well as all managers at the five store locations. Mario is the eyes and ears of Lola's on the employee level—he is key to helping David understand what the needs are from the employee-management perspective, as well as consumer needs. In doing so, Mario was able to provide the most insight as to what worked within the store structure and what ultimately drove same-store sales. When David first opened Lola's his marketing tactics included creating promotional flyers that he would place on windshields in local church parking lots on Sunday mornings. This worked for him initially as it did bring in new Hispanic customers looking to enjoying traditional Mexican food after a Sunday service, or buy fresh produce and tortillas[20] to cook Sunday dinner for their family.

In 2016, 24 years after its first doors opened in Santa Rosa, Lola's was performing overall at a 30 percent gross margin, which was a 0.7 percent increase from the previous year. Even with the improvement in performance, Lola's was still experiencing a decrease in profitability of (0.8 percent). Lola's decrease in cost of goods sold from 71 percent in 2015 to 70 percent in 2016 demonstrated that Lola's had the potential to boost its profitability for the coming year if it continued to trend with a decrease in its cost of goods sold ratio—as a decrease in this ratio identifies improvements in Lola's cost controls. The implementation of new technology and possibly new marketing methods that had the potential to boost Lola's customer base might also decrease this ratio and result in an increase in gross profit (see Exhibit 2). Along with tactics toward technological improvement, David believes Lola's commitment to freshness and tradition will continue to boost sales create high levels of customer satisfaction. "People know our commitment to freshness is the key. The secret to stay true to your roots and serve everything fresh."[21]

ALTERNATIVES FOR LOLA'S

David Ortega is a man rooted in tradition and quality, but he is also a creative business man who has plans to remodel Lola's Dutton Ave location in Santa Rosa.

EXHIBIT 2   Lola's Combined Statement of Income

Lola's Market, Inc. and Affiliates Combined Statement of Income Years Ended December 31, 2016 and December 31, 2015		
Profitability		
	2016	**2015**
Net Sales	100%	100%
COGS	69.97%	71%
Gross Margin	30.03%	29.31%
Direct Store Expenses	20.43%	18.75%
Administrative Expenses	4.43%	4.09%
Income from Operations	5.17%	6.47%
Total Other Income (Expenses)	−0.67%	−0.72%
Net Income Before Income Taxes	4.50%	5.75%
Liquidity		
Working Capital $ 000	$ 2,337	$ 2,389
Current Ratio	1.98%	2.01%
Quick Ratio	1.43%	1.46%
Year-on-Year Growth Rates, %		
Total Revenue	−0.76%	
Gross Margin	0.72%	
Operating Expenses	8.14%	

Source: Lola's Market, Inc. and Affiliates.

This remodel is intended to fit consumer needs as it will offer a buffet style, self-serve setting similar to what is seen at large competitors such as Whole Foods. With this remodel, Lola's will have freshly prepared, authentic Mexican food with a breakfast, lunch and dinner menu. Customers can serve themselves and will be charged based on the weight of their meal. David understands the need to capture the interest of the younger market base and on a global level the millennial consumer is seeking a fast meal that does not sacrifice health.[22] Implementing this self-serve option will offer the young Latino consumer the access to authentic meals that are healthy and require little-to-no excess effort on their part. The millennial consumer is already shopping within the

specialty food store industry that Lola's is a part of, accounting for about 37.3 percent of this market (see Exhibit 3) so to differentiate itself with its competitors Lola's can align remodeling with a repositioning effort to be an engaging brand on social networks. Globally millennials are considered to be the "first digital natives"[23] and as a consumer they offer the potential of a long-term customer.

A company's strategy rests on its unique activities,[24] and David Ortega's plans for remodel are distinguished from his competitors by their offering—traditional, nostalgic, homemade food. What will further distinguish this strategy are the marketing activities taken to promote the new changes in the store. Also, David is hoping that the remodels at Lola's will set them apart from other Hispanic markets; so that everything is not so jam packed. David sees too many of his competitors put too much out on the floor and it is not shoppable. He understands one of the key metrics of the industry is dollars earned per square foot, and agrees it is better to have a smaller space and bringing in more money (the Trader Joe's model) than to have a large store bringing in less money per square foot.

Millennials are interested in specialty food stores as they have an adequate source of living and are likely to use a significant share of their income for discretionary spending.[25] Millennials keep up with current health and diet trends; in order to retain this

EXHIBIT 3   Specialty Food Stores: Consumer Base

Major market segmentation (2017)

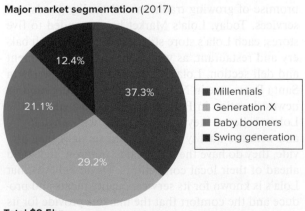

Total **$9.5bn**

Source: Guattery, M., *IBISWorld Industry Report 44529, Specialty Food Stores in the U.S.,* 2017, retrieved from IBISWorld database.

demographic, Lola's must show the consumer that despite the stigma that authentic Mexican food is inherently unhealthy, Lola's offers healthy options— even options for the vegetarian consumer. As leaders, David Ortega and his management team must ensure that all the changes and efforts toward rebranding are met with support and understanding by Lola's employees at all levels. When Lola's does launch their new remodeling at their Dutton Ave. location, employees must understand and adhere to the new store dynamic. All new roles and responsibilities that may be placed upon employees needs to be addressed clearly and implemented with proper training.

To tighten its fit and truly target the millennial Latino consumer there are some additional resources Lola's may need. Though there are employees at Lola's who are part of the millennial generation, but none of them currently possess the experience in social media marketing. No one on the Lola's team has a background in this type of promotional marketing tactic, as the most current marketing methods include monthly radio sound bites and weekly flyers distributed to neighborhoods near all five store locations. To be strategic in its industry Lola's must take advantage of the new industry change and utilize that to their benefit— social media allows for direct access to customers and direct access to customer feedback through applications such as Yelp. Instead of taking on the cost of hiring someone as a social media marketing specialist, Lola's can create a position for a college intern who would handle social media marketing in exchange for school credit. This type of relationship would give Lola's access to someone with insights to the platform and accountability for the work he or she is producing. As another alternative, David can implement HootSuite into his stores and train store managers on running this software. HootSuite is a free, easy-to-use software that allows content management across all social media platforms and using this type of software will create a congruency and consistency amongst Lola's social media pages. Consistency amongst the platforms is key as all the content being pushed must be in alignment with Lola's mission statement and company culture. Overall, utilizing social media can potentially eliminate the number of flyers distributed weekly and some excessive marketing costs, while allowing Lola's to give its customers real-time updates on their new services, products, and promotions.

FUTURE DIRECTIONS

The focus on the millennial consumer is exciting as it will bring in a new market; but Lola's must not forget about its original consumer and employees who are part of the earlier generations. Companywide Lola's must ensure that the implementation of social media coincides with Lola's value on quality, customer service, and authentic Mexican food. Only then will they distinguish themselves from every other company marketing themselves on these platforms. By implementing social media into their brand dynamic, Lola's is taking a global risk seen among many business situations— the potential loss of integrity a brand can face when delving into those platforms. The Internet creates an unknown place where users have the option to freely voice their opinions, both good and bad, behind an anonymous mask. If Lola's is going to place itself in a position to be promoted for the better, it also needs to be prepared to expose itself to the potential of critique and feedback from its customers. If Lola's actively chooses to listen to the constructive criticism and reviews that its consumers offer, it can positively manipulate the negative side effects and utilize that data to its benefit—as they are receiving up-to-date consumer feedback at no financial cost. Lola's must focus on keeping its integrity in light of new changes and challenges it may face with its coming business efforts.

ENDNOTES

[1] D. Ortega, personal communication, October 03, 2017.

[2] Tweets: On the social media platform Twitter, a "tweet" is when a user creates a new posting on their page.

[3] Hashtag: Utilized on all social media platforms including—but not limited too— Facebook, Instagram, and Twitter, a hashtag is a word or phrase that is preceded by a pound sign (#) and signifies that the content adheres to a specific topic or event.

[4] The Millennial generation is comprised of individuals born between the years of 1980 and 2000.

[5] D. Ortega, personal communication, November 21, 2017.

[6] North Bay Business Journal, "17 North Bay Latino Business Leaders," *North Bay Business Journal,* September 9, 2016, http://www.northbaybusinessjournal.com/ events/6057702-181/north-bay-latino-business-leadership-awards-named?artslide=10.

[7] Guattery, M., *Industry Report 44511, Supermarkets and Grocery Stores in the U.S.,*

IBISWorld, retrieved October 31, 2017 from IBISWorld database.

[8] Moore, M., "Interactive Media Usage Among Millennial Consumers," *Journal of Consumer Marketing, 29*(6): 436–444, 2012.

[9] Schawbel, D.,"10 New Findings About the Millennial Consumer," *Forbes,* January 20, 2015, https://www.forbes.com/sites/danschawbel/2015/01/20/10-new-findings-about-the-millennial-consumer/#1db62f776c8f.

[10] Schawbel, D., "10 New Findings About the Millennial Consumer," *Forbes,* January 20, 2015, https://www.forbes.com/sites/danschawbel/2015/01/20/10-new-findings-about-the-millennial-consumer/#1db62f776c8f

[11] Rey, J. D., "Amazon and Walmart Are in an All-Out Price War That Is Terrifying America's Biggest Brands," *Recode,* March 30, 2017, https://www.recode.net/2017/3/30/14831602/amazon-walmart-cpg-grocery-price-war.

[12] Rey, J. D., "Amazon and Walmart Are in an All-Out Price War That Is Terrifying America's Biggest Brands,"

Recode, March 30, 2017, https://www.recode.net/2017/3/30/14831602/amazon-walmart-cpg-grocery-price-war.

[13] Swindell, B., "Oliver's Debuts Store of the Future in Windsor," *North Bay Business Journal,* May 17, 2016, http://www.northbaybusinessjournal.com/opinion/5627170-186/olivers-markets-new-windsor-store?gallery=5627183&artslide=0.

[14] Swindell, B., "Oliver's Debuts Store of the Future in Windsor,"*North Bay Business Journal,* May 17, 2016, http://www.northbaybusinessjournal.com/opinion/5627170-186/olivers-markets-new-windsor-store?gallery=5627183&artslide=0.

[15] Guattery, M., *Industry Report 44511, Supermarkets and Grocery Stores in the U.S., IBISWorld,* retrieved October 31, 2017 from IBISWorld database.

[16] Originally when David opened Lola's the cost for the signage above the store was about $125/per letter. To save some money David shortened his mother's name from Dolores to her nickname "Lola."

[17] Pan Dulce—translated into "Sweet Bread." This term encompasses many rolls, cookies, and Mexican pastries.

[18] Lola's Market Home Site, *Lola's Market,* 2017, https://www.lolasmarkets.com/.

[19] Fletcher, J., "Mexican Food Flourishes in Sonoma County," *SFGATE,* April 24, 2002, http://www.sfgate.com/bayarea/article/Mexican-food-flourishes-in-Sonoma-County-2846114.php.

[20] Tortilla: (In Mexican cooking) a very thin, flat pancake of cornmeal or flour; sometimes with added spices or flavoring ingredients.

[21] D. Ortega, personal communication, October 03, 2017.

[22] Health & Wellness, *Food Marketing Institute,* 2017, https://www.fmi.org/GroceryRevolution/health-wellness/.

[23] Millennials Infographic, *Goldman Sachs,* n.d., http://www.goldmansachs.com/our-thinking/pages/millennials/.

[24] Porter, M. E., What is strategy?, *Harvard Business Review, 74* (6): 61–78, 1996.

[25] Guattery, M., *IBISWorld Industry Report 44529, Specialty Food Stores in the U.S.,* 2017, retrieved from the IBISWorld database.

iRobot in 2018: Can the Company Keep the Magic?

David L. Turnipseed
University of South Alabama

John E. Gamble
Texas A&M University-Corpus Christi

Having the largest market share in a rapidly growing industry, controlling over 75 percent of global revenue, and experiencing record growth and sales in the latest fiscal year, was a situation that most companies would find calming. In its first year as a consumer-focused company, iRobot reported a 33.8 percent increase in revenue and a 21.5 percent increase in net profit over the prior year and announced expectations for about 20 percent revenue growth in 2018, which would push revenue over $1 billion. The company's stock reached $68.00 on March 23, 2018, which was a 151 percent increase over the same date in 2017. A summary of the company's financial performance between fiscal 2013 and fiscal 2017 is presented in Exhibit 1.

However, for the management team at iRobot, those metrics only served to help fine-tune and develop strategy to improve the company's performance and defend against several looming competitive threats. The company's focus was the design and manufacture of robots that empowered people to do more both inside and outside of the home. The iRobot consumer robots helped people find smarter ways to clean and accomplish more in their daily lives. iRobot's portfolio of robotic solutions featured proprietary technologies for the connected home and advanced concepts in cleaning, mapping and navigation, human-robot interaction, and physical solutions that moved the company beyond simple robotic vacuums. The company had announced a relationship with Amazon Web Services (AWS) that was believed to enable iRobot to address significant opportunities within the consumer business and the connected home. The AWS Cloud would allow devices to interact easily and securely and enable iRobot to scale the number of connected robots it supported globally and allow for increased capabilities in the smart home.

Although iRobot's recent past had been magical, the company faced significant headwinds. Global penetration of robotic vacuums was about 10 percent, and iRobot had about 60 percent market share, but several serious competitors had emerged, and in many cases, offered similar products at much lower prices. iRobot had divested its military and industrial robots and had become a consumer company with one-product—robotic cleaners. Also, customer privacy issues and the threat of data leaks from the company's robots' cameras and mapping feature had caused negative publicity. The company's CEO had ignited a furor when he announced that iRobot "could" reach an agreement to share data with Apple, Amazon, or Alphabet. The iRobot management team had an incredible track record on which to build—the task moving into the second half of 2018 was to avoid or overcome the external competitive threats and leverage prior achievements into future successes that would keep iRobot number one in its industry.

COMPANY HISTORY

iRobot, the leading global consumer robot company, was founded in 1990, by MIT roboticists Colin Angle, Helen Greiner, and Rodney Brooks, who shared the vision of making practical robots a reality.

EXHIBIT 1   Financial Summary for iRobot, Fiscal Year 2013 – Fiscal Year 2017

	Year Ended				
	December 30, 2017	December 31, 2016	January 2, 2016	December 27, 2014	December 28, 2013
	(In thousands, except earnings per share amounts)				
Consolidated Statements of Income:					
Total revenue	$883,911	$660,604	$616,778	$556,846	$487,401
Gross margin	433,159	319,315	288,926	258,055	221,154
Operating income	72,690	57,557	60,618	53,117	32,618
Income tax expense	25,402	19,422	18,841	14,606	4,774
Net income	50,964	41,939	44,130	37,803	27,641
Net Income Per Share Data:					
Basic	$1.85	$1.51	$1.49	$1.28	$0.97
Diluted	$1.77	$1.48	$1.47	$1.25	$0.94
Shares Used In Per Common Share Calculations:					
Basic	27,611	27,698	29,550	29,485	28,495
Diluted	28,753	28,292	30,107	30,210	29,354
Consolidated Balance Sheet Data:					
Cash and cash equivalents	$128,635	$214,523	$179,915	$185,957	$165,404
Short-term investments	37,225	39,930	33,124	36,166	21,954
Total assets	691,522	507,912	521,743	493,213	416,337
Total liabilities	221,195	118,956	104,332	102,777	85,648
Total stockholders' equity	470,327	388,956	417,411	390,436	330,689

Source: iRobot Corporation 2017 10-K.

The company's first robot was the Genghis, designed for space exploration. Five years later, the Ariel was developed to detect mines, and two years later in 1998, iRobot won a DARPA (Defense Advanced Research Projects Agency) contract to build tactical robots. The company's PackBot robot was used in the United States to search the World Trade Center after the 9/11 attacks and deployed with U.S. troops in Afghanistan and Iraq.

Also in 2002, the Company developed a robot that was used to search the Great Pyramid of Egypt (and it found a "secret room"). Perhaps the most notable event in 2002 was the development of the first iRobot Robotic Vacuum Cleaner (RVC) named

Roomba. Two years later in 2004, iRobot won a U.S. Army contract to build the 312 SUGV (Small Unmanned Ground Vehicle) that was used by soldiers and combat engineers for ordinance disposal. Also in 2004, the company entered into an agreement with the Japanese distribution company Sales On Demand Corporation (SODC) to promote and distribute iRobot products in Japan, the largest consumer robotics market outside of North America.

In November 2005, iRobot became the first robot manufacturer to have a successful public stock offering. The company sold 4.3 million shares of stock at $24.00 and raised $103 million. Also in 2005, the Scooba—a floor washing robot—was launched, followed in 2007 by the Looj gutter cleaning robot, the Verro pool cleaning robot, and the Create—a programmable mobile robot. The company continued its internationalization, and partnered with Robopolis, a French distribution company, to sell its products in Germany, Spain, Portugal, the Netherlands, Austria, France, and Belgium. iRobot continued a prolific trend of products and in 2008, introduced the Roomba pet series, and a professional series of RVCs. The company also expanded into maritime robots and won a contract from DARPA to build a LANdroid communication robot, which served as a mobile signal repeater.

In 2010, iRobot's Seaglider maritime robot helped monitor the oil leakage following the BP Deepwater Horizon oil spill in the Gulf of Mexico. The next year, 2011, the company introduced an improved Scooba floor washing robot, a new series of Roomba dry vacuum robots, and the 110 FirstLook, which was a small lightweight robot that could be thrown. The FirstLook was designed for use by infantry forces to locate and identify hazards while keeping personnel safe. In 2012, the company purchased a rival firm, Evolution Robotics, Inc., for $74 million. Evolution Robotics produced a hard floor cleaner that used Swiffer pads to clean wooden floors, which was different than iRobot's products. iRobot's home robot sales exceeded 10 million units in 2013.

A new floor scrubbing robot and a vacuuming robot that included intelligent visual mapping and cloud connected app control were launched in 2015. In 2016, the Braava jet mopping robot was introduced, and the company opened an office in Shanghai, China, which significantly expanded its global footprint. iRobot made the decision to focus exclusively on consumer robots, divesting its defense and security robot business in mid-2016. There was increased investment in advancing mapping and navigation, and user interaction including cloud and app development.

iRobot continued its globalization strategy in 2017, and in April of that year, the company acquired SODC, its distribution partner in Japan, and Robopolis, its French distribution partner that served Western Europe. Wi-Fi connectivity was included on two new Roomba vacuum models (690 and 890), which extended Wi-Fi connectivity to the full line of Roombas. The company introduced two new connected products to its product portfolio to bring the advantages of cloud connectivity to its consumers. The iRobot HOME App transmitted the robots' maps directly to customers through "post-mission" cleaning maps. iRobot believed that the data sourced from the robots' maps, would accelerate new product development as well as digital partnerships for the smart home.

The iRobot Product Line in 2018

900 Series Roomba Vacuums iRobot's newest Roomba in 2018 was the 960, a lower cost alternative to the 980. The 960 won second place and Editor's Choice in *PC Magazine's* "Best Robot Vacuums of 2018." The 960 helped keep floors cleaner throughout an entire house via intelligent visual navigation, the iRobot HOME App control with Wi-Fi connectivity. The Roomba 960 had five times the suction power of the previous generation of Roomba RVCs, and extended mapping, visual navigation, and cloud connectivity to a wider range of customers. The Roomba 960 sold for $699.99, compared to $899.00 for the 980. The Roomba 980 received *PC Magazine's* seventh place for best RVC. The greatest difference between the two models was longer battery life and deeper carpet cleaning for the 980.

800 Series Roomba Vacuums The Roomba 800 series robots had an EROForce technology, which included brushless, counter-rotating extractors that increase suction for better performance than bristle brushes, while requiring less maintenance than previous Roomba models. The Roomba 890, which sold for $499.99 in February 2018, was selected "Runner-Up" Best Robotoc Vacuum by *Consumer Reports.*

600 Series Roomba Vacuums 600 series robots had a three-stage cleaning system that vacuumed every section of a floor multiple times as well as AeroVac technology and improved brush design, which enabled the robot to better handle fibers like hair, pet fur, lint, and carpet fuzz. The Roomba 690 sold for $374.99 and was Wi-Fi connected. The 690 received *PC Magazine's* third place choice for Best Robotic Vacuum of 2018. The bottom line Roomba 614, which sold for $299.99 in February 2018, was not Wi-Fi capable.

Braava Automatic Floor Mopping Robots The Braava robots were designed for hard surface floors and used a different cleaning approach than did Roomba models. The Braava 380t robot, priced at $299 in February 2018, automatically dusted and damp mopped hard surface floors using popular cleaning cloths or iRobot designed reusable microfiber cloths. The Braava robot included a special reservoir to dispense liquid throughout the cleaning cycle to keep the cloth damp. The 380t could use iAdapt navigation to map where it had cleaned and where it needed to go.

The Braava 240 was designed for smaller spaces than the 380t, and could wet mop, damp sweep, or dry sweep hard floors. The iRobot HOME App was compatible with the Braava jet 240 and helped users get the most out of their robot by enabling them to choose the desired cleaning options for their unique home. The Braava 240 sold for $199.99 in February 2018.

Mirra Pool Cleaning Robot iRobot's Mirra 530 pool cleaning robot was designed to clean any type of in-ground residential pools. It could remove debris as small as two microns from pool floors, walls, and stairs. The robot had a scrubbing brush to clean leaves, hair, dirt, algae, and bacteria off pool walls and floor, and a pump and filter that cleaned 70 gallons of water per minute. The Mirra sold for $999.99 in February 2018.

Looj Gutter Cleaning Robot The Looj robot was designed to simplify gutter cleaning. The Looj cleaned total lengths of gutter, which reduced the number of times a ladder needed to be repositioned. The iRobot Looj 330 Gutter Cleaning Robot removed leaves, dirt, and clogs, and with a set of revolving brushes totally cleaned the gutter. The Looj had a high-velocity, four-stage auger and "CLEAN" mode, and Looj traveled down the gutter on its own, sensing and adjusting to leaves and debris to provide the most effective cleaning. The Looj 330 sold for $299.99 in February 2018.

Three iRobot products—the Roomba 960, Roomba 690, and Roomba 980—were listed among the 10 Best Robot Vacuums by *PC Magazine* in 2018; however, the Eufy RoboVac 11, selling for $219, was chosen number one, ahead of iRobot's Roomba 960, selling for $699, over three times the price of the Eufy RoboVac 11.

THE ROBOTIC VACUUM INDUSTRY

According to a market report by Persistence Market Research, the residential robotic vacuum cleaner (RVC) market was estimated at $1.3 billion at year-end 2015 and was expected to increase at an annual rate of 12 percent to reach $2.5 billion by 2021. Production of residential RVCs was about 1.9 million units at the end of 2015 and was forecasted to increase at an annual rate

of 16.5 percent to reach 4.8 million units by 2021. The market penetration was quite low for robotic vacuums, and in 2018 was approximately 10 percent of the total households in the United States. iRobot believed that the immediately addressable market in the United States was double the current base of about 13 million households, with a long-term potential of 86 million households.

Improved functionality and superior performance were among the key factors driving adoption of robotic vacuum cleaners in households. Product innovation was paramount for key companies in the RVC industry. A majority of leading companies were increasingly concentrating on research and development (R&D) of unconventional products in order to gain a competitive edge.

There was a trend of bagless vacuum cleaners that could accelerate market growth. New product launches of RVCs included advanced features such as vacuum cleaners with UV sterilization, spinning brushes, security cameras, Internet connectivity, voice response, app features, and mapping features. Such advancements were expected to drive the market further. Innovation of a novel technology stair-climbing robotic vacuum cleaner was expected to present lucrative opportunities in the near future.

IROBOT'S STRATEGY

The company's strategy was to maintain Roomba's leadership in the robotic vacuum cleaner segment while positioning the company as a strategic player in the emerging smart home. The company expected its growth to be driven by:

- Deeper global household penetration of Roomba;
- Continued investment in innovation to extend iRobot's technology and product leadership;
- Increased gross margin due to the acquisitions of its two foreign distributors: SODC and Robopolis, in 2017;
- Adoption and awareness of Braava products through targeted marketing programs; and research and development of new products.

iRobot's strategy had provided market-leading positions in the robotic segment of the global vacuum cleaner industry—see Exhibit 2. In 2017, iRobot had 88 percent of the North American market, 76 percent of the European/Middle East/African market, and 34 percent of the Asia/Pacific market.

EXHIBIT 2 Geographic Market Size and Vendor Shares of the Robotic Vacuum Cleaner Industry, 2016

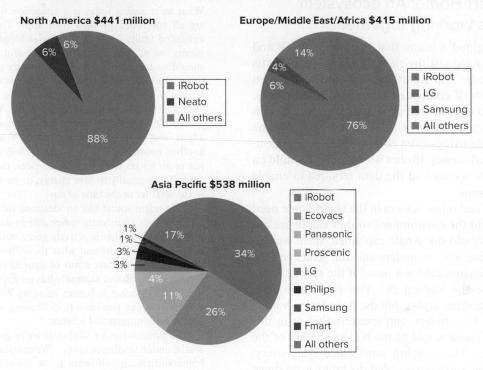

Source: Seeking Alpha, 2017.

iRobot's Technology Focus

iRobot believed that a better robot lives in the world by moving around and acting more intelligently in its environment, by cooperating with the people it serves more compellingly, and by physically interacting more effectively with its surroundings. As the number one global consumer robotics company, iRobot strived to develop best-in-class technology in mapping and navigation, human-robot interaction, and physical solutions.

Mapping and Navigation iRobot was focused on mapping and navigation technology development to make its robots smarter, simpler to use, and to provide valuable spatial context to the broader ecosystem of connected devices in the home. Robot-built and maintained home maps were core to the company's long-term strategy, providing important spatial context by capturing the physical space of the home. Maps provided the information needed to enable

robots to purposefully navigate throughout their environment and accomplish meaningful tasks.

User Experience and Digital Features iRobot invested in the development of interfaces for its robots to provide its customers with rich and convenient ways to interact with the entire iRobot family of products. iRobot's customer interaction and experience with its products was intended to be enriched as a result of connecting the company's robots and integrating them with connected devices in the home, and with other cloud resources and services.

Physical Solutions iRobot was dedicated to designing and producing robot solutions with market-leading cleaning mission performance that provided convincing value to its customers. The company's robots' core value from the customer's perspective was the ability to effectively and efficiently perform the physical mission—cleaning. iRobot believed that it produced the best mission performance solutions on the market, whether it was vacuuming, mopping, or any other cleaning tasks.

The Smart Home: An ecosystem of robots working together

iRobot imagined a home that maintained itself and miraculously did just the right things, anticipating its owners' needs. The smart home would be built on an ecosystem of connected and coordinated robots, sensors, and devices that provided homeowners with a high quality of life by seamlessly responding to the needs of daily living—from comfort to convenience to security to efficiency. iRobot was working to build an ecosystem of robots and the data required to enable the smart home.

Robots and other devices in the smart home need to understand the environment so they can figure out what they should do. Angle explained, there was no point to being able to understand the sentence "Go to the kitchen and get me a beer," if the robot doesn't know where the kitchen is.[1] You could also have smart thermostats, lights, blinds, door locks, humidity sensors, TVs, radios, and speakers that sit in this ecosystem. Those would be the building blocks of the smart home. The unifying intelligence tying everything together and what enabled the home to be smart could come from iRobot or a different company.

Guy Hoffman, a robotics professor at Cornell University, said detailed spatial mapping technology would be a major breakthrough for the smart home. With regularly updated maps, Hoffman said, sound systems could match home acoustics, air conditioners could schedule airflow by room, and smart lighting could adjust according to the position of windows and time of day. If a customer bought a Roomba, owned a smartphone, and had connected devices, the Roomba could build a map of the home, place the connected devices on the map, and share that information with all other devices. Then the ecosystem or interconnected system could give the owner a choice of preferences based on the included devices, and have the room start behaving intelligently. If the homeowner did not like how the home behaved, he or she could change preferences and the system would learn. The Amazon Alexa and Google Home devices could also supplement that behavior by providing a voice interface to the system, extending the smart home's reach to things to which they are connected.

iRobot CEO Colin Angle explained the smart home concept to *MIT Technology Review* in December 2017:

What we're seeing today is a collection of devices that are all controlled by their own apps. The promise of enhanced utility is actually being reduced by the complexity we're introducing. A successful smart home should be built on the idea that nobody programs anything; the basic services in your home would just work. So you would walk up to your front door, which would unlock if you were authorized to enter. You would go in and the light would turn on, the temperature would adjust, and if you started watching TV and moved to another room, the TV show would follow you. When you're no longer using various services, they could shut down automatically to save energy, or be set to respond to the weather or the time of day.

That might sound like an idealized vision of a smart home, but it's completely reasonable to do if you have a robot in the mix that is actively going out and discovering what rooms exist and what the different devices in them are, and you have a way of figuring out what room people are in. iRobot currently has an app that can analyze Wi-Fi coverage in homes using its Wi-Fi connected Roombas. It can provide a map showing where wireless signals are strongest and weakest.

The positioning for iRobot is we're going to be the spatial-understanding people . . . We're trying to make the home sufficiently self-aware to be self-configuring and useful . . . The emerging AI home dimension is going to play out in a big way over the next two years.[2]

iRobot Ventures

As part of iRobot's Corporate Development team, the iRobot Ventures group fostered engagement with the entrepreneurs and early-stage companies driving innovation in consumer robotics and in the connected hardware ecosystem. iRobot understood how difficult it was to bring a product to market, and to build a company. The company believed that investors should provide more than just capital and validation of an idea. iRobot Ventures delivered value by facilitating access to the company's engineering and operations resources, as well as a network of external service providers, investors, and partners. The iRobot's Venture:

- Sought strategic investments that generated attractive financial returns
- Syndicated with top-tier VC firms, strategic and angel investors
- Provided access to internal and external resources
- Embraced standard terms

- Made informed investment decisions rapidly
- Did not seek special treatment or control

iRobot Ventures supported teams that were passionate about using technology to solve hard problems. The company invested in applications that were consistent with its core business or represented new market opportunities, and participated in the early stages of the innovation lifecycle, where iRobot had the most to add, focusing on the following:

- Consumer technology
- Service-based business models
- Recurring revenue streams
- Cloud services and infrastructure
- Computer vision
- Localization and mapping
- Machine learning and artificial intelligence
- Robotic mobility and manipulation

IROBOT'S FINANCIAL PERFORMANCE

iRobot enjoyed a meteoric assent in its financial performance between fiscal year 2015 and fiscal year 2017. Revenue had grown from about $617 million in fiscal 2015 to approximately $884 million in fiscal 2017. The company's gross margin had improved by nearly 50 percent between fiscal 2015 and fiscal 2017, but its operating income and net income had grown at much more modest rates as growth operating expenses outpaced growth in revenues. iRobot stock also had an impressive gain, increasing from $20.00 in January 2005 to $107.25 in July 2017. The company's financial performance for fiscal year 2015 through fiscal year 2017 is presented in Exhibit 3. The company's balance sheets for fiscal year 2016 and fiscal year 2017 are presented in Exhibit 4. The performance of its common shares between November 2005 and June 2018 is shown in Exhibit 5.

iRobot's Rivals in the Floor Care Market

The floor care market was crowded with big-name competitors. However, the iRobot Roomba models placed numbers two, three, six, and seven in the NPD Retail Tracking Service poll in 2017. The iRobot

Roombas were the only robotic floor cleaners to place in the top 10—see Exhibit 6. Shark's upright replaced Dyson at number one in the February 1, 2017 *Consumer Report* reviews, and Shark entered the robotic vacuum market in 2017.

Eufy RoboVac *Consumer Reports* selected the Eufy RoboVac11, which sold for $299.99 on Amazon in late 2017, as the Best Budget Buy. In January 2018, *PC Magazine* selected the RoboVac 11 as Editor's Choice and first place among eight in "Best Robotic Vacuums of 2018." In February 2018, the RoboVac 11 sold for $219.00 on Amazon. The Eufy Robotic mop was picked #1 in *Atopdaily*'s 2018 Robotic Mop Review.

Neato Robotics The Neato Botvac D5, which sold for $500 on Amazon in late 2017, was chosen fourth best RVC by *Consumer Reports* in November 2017. The Dyson Botvac Connected and Botvac Connected D were chosen fourth and fifth best, respectively, by *PC Magazine* in January 2018. Neato's Botvac Connected was compatible with smart home devices and platforms, synched with 2.4GHz Wi-Fi networks and had an app for Android and iOS that enabled owners to interact and control the vacuum from Amazon Alexa, Google Home, the Neato Chatbot for Facebook, and from a tablet or smartphone. The app notified the owner about the vacuum status, enabling the homeowner to easily schedule the vacuum and keep the home clean.

Dyson Dyson Technology, an established British manufacturer of consumer electronics, lighting, and traditional vacuum cleaners, entered the RVC market with the Dyson 360Eye, which was the result of 17 years of RVC development by the company. The new Dyson robot was introduced in Tokyo. The 360Eye had twice the suction of any other RVC, was controlled by the Dyson Link app, and would respond to voice commands. It was equipped with a camera and could map the rooms in which it was used.

Dyson's 360 EYE, which sold for $999.99 on Amazon in early 2018, was selected sixth best RVC by *PC Magazine* in January 2018.

Shark Shark was one of several brands developed by SharkNinja Operating, LLC, a Massachusetts-based developer of cleaning solutions and household appliances. The Shark ION ROBOT 750 was Wi-Fi capable and could be controlled with a mobile app or by voice command. All Home Robotics, in March 2018, did a comparison of the Shark ION 750 and

EXHIBIT 3   iRobot Corporation's Consolidated Statements of Income, Fiscal Year 2015 – Fiscal Year 2017 (in thousands of $)

	Fiscal Year Ended		
	December 30, 2017	December 31, 2016	January 2, 2016
	(In thousands)		
Revenue	$883,911	$660,604	$616,778
Cost of product revenue	438,114	337,832	325,295
Amortization of intangible assets	12,638	3,457	2,557
Gross margin	433,159	319,315	288,926
Operating expenses:			
Research and development	113,149	79,805	76,071
Selling and marketing	162,110	115,125	97,772
General and administrative	84,771	66,828	53,540
Amortization of intangible assets	439	—	925
Total operating expenses	360,469	261,758	228,308
Operating income	72,690	57,557	60,618
Other income, net	3,676	3,804	2,353
Income before income taxes	76,366	61,361	62,971
Income tax expense	25,402	19,422	18,841
Net income	$ 50,964	$ 41,939	$ 44,130
Net income per share			
Basic	$1.85	$1.51	$1.49
Diluted	$1.77	$1.48	$1.47
Number of weighted average common shares used in calculations per share			
Basic	27,611	27,698	29,550
Diluted	28,753	28,292	30,107

Source: iRobot Corporation 2017 10-K.

the Roomba 890 and concluded that unless the home had deep shag carpet, the Shark 750 would be the one to buy. In March 2018, the Shark ION 750 sold for $340.82 on Amazon, compared to $499.99 for the Roomba 890 at Best Buy, Target, and Bed Bath & Beyond.

Samsung   Samsung, the South Korean multinational electronics and appliance manufacturer, was a late entrant into the RVC market. The newest Samsung robot models—POWERbot—are Wi-Fi capable and map the house in which they are used. The POWERbot can be controlled by a smartphone app,

EXHIBIT 4   iRobot Corporation's Consolidated Balance Sheets, Fiscal Year 2016 – Fiscal Year 2017 (in thousands of $)

	December 30, 2017	December 31, 2016
	(In thousands)	
ASSETS		
Current assets:		
Cash and cash equivalents	$128,635	$214,523
Short-term investments	37,225	39,930
Accounts receivable, net	142,829	73,048
Inventory	106,932	50,578
Other current assets	19,105	5,591
Total current assets	434,726	383,670
Property and equipment, net	44,579	27,532
Deferred tax assets	31,531	30,585
Goodwill	121,440	41,041
Intangible assets, net	44,712	12,207
Other assets	14,534	12,877
Total assets	$691,522	$507,912
LIABILITIES AND STOCKHOLDERS' EQUITY		
Current liabilities:		
Accounts payable	$116,316	$ 67,281
Accrued expenses	73,647	40,869
Deferred revenue and customer advances	7,761	4,486
Total current liabilities	197,724	112,636
Deferred tax liabilities	9,539	—
Other long-term liabilities	13,932	6,320
Total long-term liabilities	23,471	6,320
Total liabilities	221,195	118,956
Commitments and contingencies		
Preferred stock, 5,000,000 shares authorized and none outstanding	—	—
Common stock, $0.01 par value, 100,000,000 shares authorized; 27,945,144 and 27,237,870 shares issued and outstanding at December 30, 2017 and December 31, 2016, respectively	279	272
Additional paid-in capital	190,067	161,885
Retained earnings	277,989	226,950
Accumulated other comprehensive income (loss)	1,992	(151)
Total stockholders' equity	470,327	388,956
Total liabilities and stockholders' equity	$691,522	$507,912

Source: iRobot 2017 10-K.

EXHIBIT 5   Monthly Performance of iRobot Corporation's Stock Price, November 2005–June 2018

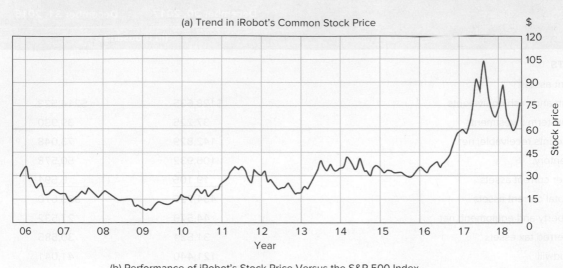

(a) Trend in iRobot's Common Stock Price

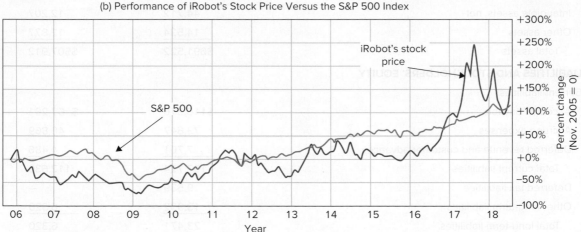

(b) Performance of iRobot's Stock Price Versus the S&P 500 Index

Amazon's Alexa, or Google Assistant. The Samsung line of POWERbot Robotic Vacuum cleaners ranged from the R9000, which sold for $399, to the R7090, which sold for $699.00.

The Samsung POWERbot SR20H9051 RVC was voted "Best in Class" by *Consumer Reports* in November 2017. The Powerbot R7070, selling for $598.00 on Amazon, was chosen eighth best by *PC Magazine* in January 2018.

Ecovacs Ecovacs, founded in 1998, is a global consumer robotics company based in China, whose focus is helping consumers "Live Smart, Enjoy Life," with their line of products to help with daily household chores. The company's product line comprises

DEEBOT floor cleaner, the WINBOT window cleaner, ATMBOT air cleaner, and FAMIBOT entertainment and security robot. Several Ecovacs products include Wi-Fi connectivity. Ecovacs is one of the top three brands of in-home robots worldwide, and has 65 percent of the market share in China, where it is the #1 brand. Ecovacs currently has operations in Mainland China, North America, Europe, Malaysia, and Australia. Ecovacs' DEEBOT floor cleaner line of robots are sold in the United States at major big box retailers such as Best Buy, Target, Macy's, Home Depot, and Staples.

Prices in February 2018 ranged from $379.99 for the DEEBOT M88 to $189.00 for the NEO

EXHIBIT 6   Top 10 Floor Cleaner Vacuums, 2017

Rank	Floor Cleaner Name
1	Dyson V8 Stick Cordless
2	iRobot Roomba 690 Robotic
3	iRobot Roomba 650
4	Shark Rotator Professional Upright
5	Bissell Bare Floor
6	iRobot Roomba 980
7	iRobot Roomba 960
8	Hoover Deep Carpet
9	Dyson V7 Stick
10	Shark Navigator Upright

*Source: NPD Retail Tracking Services, 2017.

Robot on Amazon. The Ecovacs DEEBOT M88 was voted third best RVC by *Consumer Reports* in November 2017, and the DEEBOT N79 was the best-selling robotic vacuum on Amazon for Black Friday in 2017. The New York Times' *Wirecutter* review in March 2018 selected the DEEBOT N79 as the best choice RVC. The Ecovacs DEEBOT 80 Pro Robotic Vacuum with Mop was picked first place by *Offers.com* in April 2018, and #2 by *ATOPDAILY's* Best Robot Mop Review's in 2018.

COMPETITIVE RISKS

A significant risk for Roomba was that competitors' cheaper cleaning products were what consumers really wanted. In May 2016, the *New York Times'* Sweethome blog ousted the $375 Roomba 690 as its most-recommended robovac in favor of the $220 Eufy RoboVac 11. The Sweethome blog said that the Roomba's Internet connectivity and other advanced features would not justify the greater cost for most users. Short-seller Axler's June 2016 report caused concern with the prediction that value-priced appliance maker SharkNinja Operating LLC could launch a robovac by the end of 2016. In September 2017, *Investor's Business Daily* reported that iRobot stock

fell 16 percent over concerns about Shark entering the robotic vacuum market, and Spruce Point Capital Management remarked that, "SharkNinja has entered the robotic vacuum market with a 'functionality at a reasonable price' strategy to compete directly with the Roomba. Given Shark's historical success, we assume that their entry into the market will translate into sales and margin pressure for iRobot beginning with Q4 2017."[3]

One potential iRobot defense against these new competitors was iRobot's portfolio of 1,000 patents worldwide that covered the very concept of a self-navigating household robot vacuum as well as basic technologies like object avoidance. A handful of those patents were being tested in a series of patent infringement lawsuits iRobot filed in April against Bissell, Stanley, Black & Decker, Hoover Inc., Chinese outsourced manufacturers, and other robovac makers. That litigation was the most significant in iRobot's history.

PRIVACY CONCERNS

iRobot's higher-end Roomba robotic vacuums collected data that identified the walls of rooms and furniture locations as they cleaned. This data enabled the Roomba to avoid collisions with furniture, but it also created a map of the home that iRobot could share with Google, Apple, or Amazon. iRobot had made the Roomba compatible with Amazon's Alexa voice assistant in March 2017, and according to the Company's CEO Angle, iRobot could extract value from that by data sharing agreements and connecting for free with as many companies as possible to make the device more useful in the home.

However, the idea of iRobot's data sharing caused investor concern when *Reuters* reported in July 2017 that iRobot's chief executive, Colin Angle, announced that a deal could come within two years to share its maps for free with customer consent to one or more of the Big Three. Albert Gidari, director of privacy at the Stanford Center for Internet and Society, said that if iRobot did share the data, it would raise a variety of legal questions. Guy Hoffmann, a robotics professor at Cornell University, said that companies such as Apple, Amazon, and Google could use the data obtained by the iRobot devices to recommend home goods for customers to buy. A potential problem with sharing data about users' homes is that it raises clear privacy issues, said Ben

Rose, an analyst for Battle Road Research who covers iRobot.

Homeowners were able to opt out of Roomba's cloud-sharing functions, using the iRobot Home app, but technically the iRobot terms of service and privacy policy indicated that the company had the right to share users' personal information, according to *The Verge* in a June 24, 2017 article. The potential sale of personal information was disclosed in the company's privacy policy, but was unlikely to be discovered by most consumers.

In a written response in *Consumer Reports* reported by the *New York Times* on July 25, 2017, iRobot management stated that it was "committed to the absolute privacy of our customer-related data." Consumers can use a Roomba without connecting it to the Internet, or "opt out of sending map data to the cloud through a switch in the mobile app." "No data is sold to third parties," the statement added. "No data will be shared with third parties without the informed consent of our customers." CEO Angle reinforced iRobot's position in an interview, in an April 10, 2018 interview with *The Verge,* saying, "iRobot will never sell your data. It's your data, and if you would like that data to be used to do something beyond helping your robot perform its job better [like mapping your home for IoT devices], then you'll need to give permission. We're committed to [EU data privacy legislation] GDPR and are ensuring that if you want to be forgotten, then we'll be able to forget you." Angle stressed that iRobot did not intend to build its future around selling data, however; the company wanted to be a "trusted aggregator of spatial information" that could help with the smart home. Data collected by iRobot devices would be protected by iRobot.

Smart home lighting, thermostats, and security cameras are already on the market, but Colin Angle, chief executive of Roomba maker iRobot Corp, said they are still dumb when it comes to understanding their physical environment. He thought the mapping technology currently guiding top-end Roomba models could change that and he was basing the company's strategy on it. "There's an entire ecosystem of things and services that the smart home can deliver once you have a rich map of the home that the user has allowed to be shared," said Angle.[4] However, the question of whether the market is ready for a data gathering robot or will be content with just a floor cleaner remains to be answered.

IROBOT IN 2018

In February 2018, iRobot's Chairman and Chief Executive Officer Colin Angle announced the company's plans and financial expectations for 2018. The company expected its revenues to exceed $1 billion, which would be a year-over-year growth of about 20 percent to 22 percent, with operating income year-over-year growth ranging from 18 percent to 32 percent. According to Angle, there was tremendous growth ahead for the company. Global market penetration was very low and the strong global economic conditions were stimulating positive consumer sentiment and global economic growth.

Angle also pointed out several growth opportunities for the company. In regions where iRobot had run product education marketing programs, the company had gained market share, and recent distributor acquisitions had helped extend strategic marketing efforts to Europe and Japan. The global Robotic Vacuum Cleaner (RVC) industry had more than 25 percent growth in 2017, and that growth was expected to continue as iRobot and its competitors increased product awareness. Retailers were increasingly promoting RVCs and increasing shelf space and high-visibility displays. The company expected to capitalize on the investments made in 2017 with the introduction of new products in the third and fourth quarters, 2018. Angle said that the company expected double-digit revenue growth in all regions of the overseas markets and continued strong sales in the United States following the 2017 growth of over 40 percent.

Despite the optimistic projections, some investors were nervous about iRobot's future well-being with the recent entry of SharkNinja Operating LLC into the robotic vacuum market and other external competitive threats. The U.S. market continued to be strong for iRobot, but the company said in its third-quarter conference call that net revenue in China declined due to continued aggressive competitive pressure. That led Canaccord Genuity Inc. analyst Bobby Burleson to lower his price target to $65 from $95, along with expectations of higher spending to maintain its market standing. The coming months and years would make it clear if iRobot held a competitive advantage in the RVC market and was well-positioned to capture new opportunities in the Smart Home ecosystem.

ENDNOTES

[1] As quoted in Evan Ackerman, "Interview: iRobot CEO Colin Angle on Data Privacy and Robots in the Home," IEEE Spectrum, September 7, 2017, https://spectrum.ieee.org/automaton/robotics/home-robots/interview-irobot-ceo-colin-angle-on-privacy-and-robots-in-the-home.

[2] As quoted in Elizabeth Woyke, "Roomba to Rule the Smart Home," MIT Technology Review, December 17, 2017, (https://www.technologyreview.com/s/609764/roomba-to-rule-the-smart-home/).

[3] As quoted in Patrick Seitz, "IRobot Stock Attacked By Home Appliance Vendor SharkNinja," Investors Business Daily, September 13, 2017, https://www.investors.com/news/technology/click/irobot-stock-attacked-by-home-appliance-vendor-sharkninja/.

[4] As quoted in "As your Roomba cleans your floors, it's gathering maps of your house," The Washington Post, July 25, 2017, (accessed at http://www.latimes.com/business/technology/la-fi-tn-roomba-map-20170725-story.html).

Chipotle Mexican Grill's Strategy in 2018: Will the New CEO Be Able to Rebuild Customer Trust and Revive Sales Growth?

Mc Graw Hill Education connect

Arthur A. Thompson

The University of Alabama

Headed into August 2015, Chipotle (pronounced chi-POAT-lay) Mexican Grill's future looked rosy. Sales and profits in the first six months of 2015 were at record-setting levels, and expectations were that 2015 would be the company's best year ever. But a series of events occurred over the next five months that alarmed customers, drove down sales at Chipotle restaurants, and proved frustrating for Chipotle top executives to fix.

- In August, a salmonella outbreak in Minnesota sickened 64 people who had eaten at a Chipotle Mexican Grill. The state's Department of Health later linked the illness to contaminated tomatoes served at the restaurant.

- In August, 80 customers and 18 employees at a Chipotle Mexican Grill in Southern California reported gastrointestinal symptoms of nausea, vomiting, and diarrhea that medical authorities and county health officials attributed to "norovirus." Norovirus is a highly contagious bug spread by contaminated food, improper hygiene, and contact with contaminated surfaces; the virus causes inflammation of the stomach or intestines, leading to stomach pain, nausea, diarrhea, and vomiting. After the reported food poisoning, the restaurant voluntarily closed, threw out all remaining food products, and sent home the affected employees. Employees who tested positive for norovirus

remained off duty until they were cleared to return to work. County health officials also inspected the facility on two occasions and rendered passing grades, despite finding several minor violations. The restaurant reopened the following day, and no further food poisoning incidents occurred.

- In October, 55 people became ill from food poisoning after eating at 11 Chipotle locations in the Portland, Oregon, and Seattle, Washington areas. Medical authorities attributed the illnesses to a strain of *E. coli* bacteria typically associated with contaminated food. Most ill people had eaten many of the same food items, but subsequent testing of the ingredients at the 11 Chipotle restaurants did not reveal any *E. coli* contamination. (When a restaurant serves foods with several ingredients that are mixed or cooked together and then used in multiple menu items, it is difficult for medical studies to pinpoint the specific ingredient or ingredients that might be contaminated.) State and federal regulatory officials reviewed Chipotle's distribution records but were unable to identify a single food item or ingredient that could explain the outbreak. Nonetheless, out of an abundance of caution, Chipotle management voluntarily closed all 43 Chipotle locations in the Portland and Seattle markets, pending a comprehensive review of the causes underlying the food contamination and a check of whether any of Chipotle's food suppliers were at fault. Chipotle management worked in close consultation and collaboration with state and federal health and food safety officials (including personnel from the Centers for Disease Control and Prevention, the U.S. Department of Agriculture's Food Safety and Inspection Service, and the U.S. Food and Drug Administration) throughout their investigation of the incident and also launched a massive internal effort review of the company's food preparation and food safety procedures. These internal actions included:

1. Confirming that more than 2,500 tests of Chipotle's food, restaurant surfaces, and equipment all showed no E. coli.
2. Confirming that no employees in the affected restaurants were sickened from the incident.
3. Expanding the testing of fresh produce, raw meat, and dairy items prior to restocking restaurants.
4. Implementing additional safety procedures and audits, in all of its 2,000 restaurants to ensure that robust food safety standards were in place.
5. Working closely with federal, state, and local government agencies to further ensure that robust food safety standards were in place.
6. Replacing all ingredients in the closed restaurants.
7. Conducting additional deep cleaning and sanitization in all of its closed restaurants (followed by deep cleaning and sanitization in all restaurants nationwide).

Meanwhile, the Federal Drug Administration sought to identify a cause for the outbreak. The FDA's investigation revealed no ingredient-related cause and no evidence that particular suppliers were the source of the outbreak. Ultimately, no food item was identified as causing the outbreak and no food item was ruled out as a cause, although fresh produce was suspected as the likely cause.

After health officials concluded it was safe to do so, all 43 restaurants in the Portland and Seattle markets reopened in late November 2015, roughly 6 weeks after the incident occurred.

- Later, it was confirmed that at least 13 people in nine other states became infected with the same strain of E. coli linked to the Chipotle restaurants in Oregon and Washington states.
- In early December 2015, five people in three states—Kansas (1), North Dakota (1), and Oklahoma

(3)—became ill after eating at Chipotle Mexican Grill restaurants. Studies conducted by the Centers for Disease Control and Prevention (CDC) determined that all five people were infected with a rare strain of E.coli different from the infections in Oregon, Washington, and nine other states. However, investigators used sophisticated laboratory testing to determine that the DNA footprints of the illnesses in the Midwest were related to those in the Portland and Seattle areas.

- In mid-December 2015, about 120 Boston College students became ill after eating at a Chipotle Mexican Grill near the campus, an outbreak that local health officials attributed to a norovirus. Health officials also tested students for E. coli infections but the tests were negative.

Extensive reports of the last three incidents in the national media took a toll on customer traffic at most all Chipotle locations. The average decline in sales at Chipotle locations open at least 12 months was a stunning 14.6 percent in the fourth quarter of 2015, causing Chipotle's revenues in Q4 2015 to be 6.8 percent lower than in the fourth quarter of 2014. The company's stock price crashed from an all-time high of $758 in early August 2015 to $400 heading into 2016.

2016 AND 2017—GROWING FRUSTRATION IN REVIVING SALES AND RESTORING CUSTOMER TRUST IN THE CHIPOTLE BRAND

In January 2016, the CDC announced that the prior food contamination and food safety issues at Chipotle were "over." Chipotle management followed up by finalizing plans to install comprehensive food safety procedures at all Chipotle restaurants and establish Chipotle as an industry leader in food safety. In February 2016, Chipotle shut all of its restaurants for a period of four hours to conduct food safety training for all store employees. That same day, in an effort to get customers back into its stores, Chipotle offered a free burrito to anyone who signed up on its website. Recognizing that the task of rejuvenating customer traffic at its restaurants would not be easy, Chipotle management launched a series of marketing efforts and incentives to entice former and new customers to dine at Chipotle restaurants. For example:

- In March, Chipotle introduced a new online game called Guac Hunter—a digital photo hunt where players saw a series of two images that looked similar and had to spot the differences before time runs out. During a specified 11-day period, players were rewarded for their keen eyesight with a mobile offer good for a free order of chips and guacamole at any Chipotle in the United States and Canada.

- In May, teachers, faculty, and school staff with a valid school ID received a free burrito, burrito bowl, salad, or order of tacos with the purchase of another menu item at all U.S. Chipotle locations from 3:00 p.m. to close in honor of Teacher Appreciation Day.

- All nurses who showed a valid ID were rewarded with a special buy-one-get-one-free promotion on June 8.

- In June, chorizo sausage was introduced as a meat selection.

- A national advertising campaign featured Chipotle's carefully selected ingredients and its longstanding commitment to sourcing, preparing, and serving only the very best ingredients.

- In July, Chipotle initiated a three-month promotion called Chiptopia where customers were rewarded with a free entrée on their fourth, eighth, and eleventh visit and purchase of paid entrée within a given month; customers who registered for the program in July earned a free chips and guacamole with their first entrée purchase.

- Families were offered a free kid's meal with the purchase of an entrée on Sundays during the month of September.

- Also in September, high school and college students with a valid ID received a free fountain soft drink or iced tea with any in-store entrée purchase.

- In October, Chipotle introduced a new online game that allowed players to test their memory skills by matching up real Chipotle ingredients while being careful not to select the imposters (added flavor or added color cards). Anyone who played the game received a limited time mobile buy-one-get-one-free entrée offer redeemable at any Chipotle in the United States or Canada just for playing.

- On Halloween, from 3 p.m. to closing at all Chipotle locations, customers dressed in costume could buy $3 burritos, bowls, salads, or tacos.

- All active duty military, reserves, national guard, military spouses, retired military with a valid U.S. military ID, and veterans with ID were offered a special buy-one-get-one-free with the purchase of an entrée from 3:00 p.m. to close on Veterans Day.

In addition, in October 2016, Chipotle began an "Ingredients Reign" advertising campaign highlighting its carefully selected ingredients and reinforcing Chipotle's commitment to sourcing, preparing, and serving only the very best ingredients. The campaign featured a series of animated stop-motion short films shown in movie theaters across the country and also distributed through various online, digital, and social media outlets. In addition, the company used indoor and outdoor advertising with content showcasing the company's obsession with fresh ingredients.

But the results of all these efforts to revive customer traffic were disappointing. Average sales at Chipotle restaurants in 2016 dropped to $1.87 million, 22.9 percent below the 2015 average of $2.42 million. Chipotle's revenues dropped from $4.5 billion in 2015 to $3.9 billion in 2016, despite the opening of 240 new restaurants. Net income plunged 95 percent, from $475.6 million in 2015 to $22.9 million in 2016.

Chipotle's performance in 2017 was better, but far from comforting to top management or shareholders. Revenue rose 14.7 percent to almost $4.5 billion, fractionally below the amount for 2015, but with 400 more restaurants in operation than in 2015; net income rose to $176.3 million. Average restaurant sales climbed 3.9 percent to $1.94 million, but were still almost 20 percent below the 2015 average. Exhibit 1 presents recent financial and operating data for Chipotle Mexican Grill.

At the end of November 2017, Chipotle Mexican Grill announced that Steve Ells, chairman and CEO—and the founder of the company in 1993—would relinquish the title of CEO and become executive chairman following the completion of a search to identify a new CEO. Ells recommended the change in his role to the company's Board of Directors, indicating it would "allow me to focus on my strengths, which include bringing innovation to the way we source and prepare our food.

EXHIBIT 1 Financial and Operating Highlights for Chipotle Mexican Grill, 2011–2017

Income Statement Data	In millions of dollars, except for per share items				
	2017	2016	2015	2014	2011
Total revenue	$4,476.4	$3,904.4	$4,501.2	$4,108.3	$2,269.6
Food, beverage, and packaging costs	1,535.4	1,365.6	1,503.8	1,421.0	738.7
As a % of total revenue	34.3%	5.0%	33.4%	34.6%	32.5%
Labor costs	1,206.0	1,105.0	1,045.7	904.4	543.1
As a % of total revenue	26.9%	28.3%	23.2%	22.2%	23.9%
Occupancy costs	327.1	293.6	262.4	230.9	147.3
As a % of total revenue	7.3%	7.3%	5.8%	5.6%	6.5%
Other operating costs	651.6	642.0	515.0	434.2	251.2
As a % of total revenue	14.6%	16.4%	11.4%	10.6%	11.1%
General and administrative expenses	296.4	276.2	250.2	273.9	149.4
As a % of total revenue	6.6%	7.1%	5.6%	6.7%	6.6%
Depreciation and amortization	163.3	146.4	130.4	110.5	74.9
Pre-opening costs	12.3	17.2	16.9	15.6	8.5
Loss on disposal of assets	13.3	23.9	13,194	6,976	5,806
Total operating expenses	4,206.6	3,869.8	3,737.6	3,397.5	1,919.0
Operating income	270.8	34.6	763.6	710.8	350.6
As a % of total revenue	6.0%	0.9%	17.0%	17.3%	15.5%
Interest and other income (expense) net	4.9	4.2	6.3	3.5	(0.9)
Income before income taxes	275.7	38.7	769.9	714.3	349.7
Provision for income taxes	(99.5)	(15.8)	(294.3)	(268.9)	(134.9)
Net income	$ 176.3	$ 22.9	$ 475.6	$ 445.4	$ 214.9
As a % of total revenue	3.9%	0.6%	10.6%	10.8%	9.5%
Earnings per share					
Basic	$ 6.19	$ 0.78	$ 15.30	$ 14.35	$ 6.89
Diluted	6.17	0.77	15.10	14.13	6.76
Weighted average common shares outstanding					
Basic	28.5	29.3	31.1	31.0	31.2
Diluted	28.6	29.8	31.5	31.5	31.8
Selected Balance Sheet Data					
Total current assets	$ 629.5	$ 522.4	$ 814.6	$ 859.5	$ 501.2
Total assets	2,045.7	2,026.1	2,725.1	2,527.3	1,425.3
Total current liabilities	323.9	281.8	279.9	245.7	157.5
Total liabilities	681.2	623.6	597.1	514.9	374.8
Total shareholders' equity	1,364.4	1,402.5	2,128.0	2,012.4	1,044.2
Other Financial Data					
Net cash provided by operating activities	$ 467.1	$ 349.2	$ 683.3	$ 682.1	$ 411.1
Capital expenditures	216.8	258.8	257.4	252.6	151.1
Restaurant Operations Data	In thousands of dollars				
Restaurants open at year-end	2,408	2,250	2,010	1,783	1,230
Average restaurant sales	$1,940.0	$1,868.0	$2,424.0	$2,472.0	$2,013.0
Average annual sales increases at restaurants open at least 13 full calendar months	6.4%	(20.4)%	0.2%	16.8%	11.2%
Development and construction costs per newly opened restaurant	$ 835	$ 880	$ 805	$ 843	$ 800

Source: Company 10-K reports, 2015, 2016, and 2017.

As we work hard to restore our brand, I believe we can capitalize on opportunities, including in areas such as the digital experience, menu innovation, delivery, catering, and domestic and international expansion, to deliver significant growth."[1] A three-person search committee that included Steve Ells and two directors was formed to identify a new leader with demonstrated turnaround expertise to help address the challenges facing the company, improve execution, build customer trust, and drive sales. As of early February 2018, no new CEO had been announced.

During 2017, there were two more incidents of food poisoning at Chipotle restaurants that were widely publicized. In July, a crowd-sourced website, Iwaspoisoned.com, indicated that 133 persons reported becoming ill after eating at a Chipotle restaurant in Sterling, Virginia, a Washington suburb. Chipotle promptly closed the restaurant for a "thorough sanitization" and reopened it two days later. In December, there were reports of sick employees and customers at a Chipotle restaurant in Los Angeles. Chipotle alerted local health officials, held the employees out of work, and instituted heightened preventative procedures. Local health officials promptly began an investigation, inspected the premises, and were pleased with the operations. The restaurant remained open. Both incidents spooked investors, triggered immediate declines in the stock price, and reignited concerns over whether Chipotle had fully resolved its food safety issues.

In announcing Chipotle's 2017 financial results in February 2018, Steve Ells commented on the company's ongoing efforts to regain the confidence of customers and restore the appeal of dining at one of Chipotle's 2,400 locations:

> During 2017, we have made considerable changes around leadership, operations, and long-term planning and it is clear that, while there is still work to be done, we are starting to see some success. 2018 marks the 25th anniversary of Chipotle, and I am encouraged by the dedication all of our guests and employees have to this brand. Our focus this year will be to continue perfecting the dining experience, enhancing the guest experience through innovations in digital and catering, and reinvesting in our restaurants. We are making good progress on our search for a new CEO who can improve execution, drive sales and enable Chipotle to realize our enormous potential.[2]

Ells further indicated that management expected sales increases in 2018 at restaurant locations open at least 13 months would be in the low single digits.

In July 2018, Chipotle once again had a food safety lapse; this foodborne illness outbreak sickened over 600 customers at a restaurant just outside of Columbus, Ohio. Health officials attributed the problem to bacteria that formed when certain food items were left out at unsafe temperatures. Upon learning the cause, Chipotle top management immediately announced it would launch retraining of all its restaurant workers nationwide the following week. While the company's stock price dropped about 7 percent on news of the incident, it recovered quickly since customer traffic at Chipotle restaurants nationwide was largely unaffected and the company's future performance seemed to be on the upswing remained amid reports that the company was testing a number of new menu enhancements, perhaps to include the addition of a new breakfast menu and earlier opening hours.

CHIPOTLE MEXICAN GRILL'S EARLY YEARS

Steve Ells graduated from the Culinary Institute of America and then worked for two years at Stars Restaurant in San Francisco. Soon after moving to Denver, he began working on plans to open his own restaurant. Guided by a conviction that food served fast did not have to be low quality and that delicious food did not have to be expensive, he came up with the concept of Chipotle Mexican Grill. When the first Chipotle restaurant opened in Denver in 1993, it became an instant hit. Patrons were attracted by the experience of getting better-quality food served fast and dining in a restaurant setting that was more upscale and appealing than those of traditional fast-food enterprises. Over the next several years, Ells opened more Chipotle restaurants in Denver and other Colorado locations.

Ells' vision for Chipotle was "to change the way people think about and eat fast food." Taking his inspiration from features commonly found in many fine-dining restaurants, Ells's strategy for Chipotle Mexican Grill was predicated on six elements:

- Serving a focused menu of burritos, tacos, burrito bowls (a burrito without the tortilla), and salads.
- Using high-quality, fresh ingredients and classic cooking methods to create great tasting, reasonably-priced

dishes prepared to order and ready to be served 1 to 2 minutes after they were ordered.

- Enabling customers to select the ingredients they wanted in each dish by speaking directly to the employees assembling the dish on the serving line.
- Creating an operationally efficient restaurant with an aesthetically-pleasing interior.
- Building a special people culture comprised of friendly, high-performing people motivated to take good care of each customer and empowered to achieve high standards.
- Doing all of this with increasing awareness and respect for the environment and by using organically-grown fresh produce and meats raised in a humane manner without hormones and antibiotics.

In 1998, intrigued by what it saw happening at Chipotle, McDonald's first acquired an initial ownership stake in the fledgling company, then acquired a controlling interest in early 2000. But McDonald's recognized the value of Ells's visionary leadership and kept him in the role of Chipotle's chief executive after it gained majority ownership. Drawing upon the investment capital provided by McDonald's and its decades of expertise in supply chain logistics, expanding a restaurant chain, and operating restaurants efficiently, Chipotle—under Ells's watchful and passionate guidance—embarked on a long-term strategy to open new restaurants and expand its market coverage. By year-end 2005, Chipotle had 489 locations in 24 states. As 2005 drew to a close, in somewhat of a surprise move, McDonald's top management determined that instead of continuing to parent Chipotle's growth, it would take the company public and give Chipotle management a free rein in charting the company's future growth and strategy. An initial public offering of shares was held in January 2006, and Steve Ells was designated as Chipotle's CEO and Chairman of the Board. During 2006, through the January IPO, a secondary offering in May 2006, and a tax-free exchange offer in October 2006, McDonald's disposed of its entire ownership interest in Chipotle Mexican Grill.

When Chipotle became an independent enterprise, Steve Ells and the company's other top executives kept the company squarely on a path of rapid expansion and continued to employ the same basic strategy elements that were the foundation of the company's success. Steve Ells functioned as the company's principal driving force for ongoing innovation

and constant improvement. He pushed especially hard for new ways to boost "throughput"—the number of customers whose orders could be taken, prepared, and served per hour.[3] By 2012, Ell's mantra of "slow food, fast" had resulted in throughputs of 300 customers per hour at Chipotle's best restaurants.

From 2011 through 2015, Chipotle's revenues grew at a robust compound average rate of 18.7 percent. Net income grew at a compound rate of 19.4 percent, due not only to sales increases but also improved operating efficiency that boosted profit margins. Growing customer visits and higher expenditures per customer visit drove average annual sales for Chipotle restaurants open at least 13 full calendar months from $1,085,000 in 2007 to $2,424,000 in 2015. The average check per customer ran $8 to $10 in 2011-2015.

CHIPOTLE MEXICAN GRILL IN 2018

Going into 2018, Chipotle operated 2,363 Chipotle Mexican Grill restaurants in 47 states and the District of Columbia, plus 24 in Canada, 6 in England, 6 in France, and 1 in Germany. In addition to the 2,000 Chipotle locations, the company had experimented with transferring its Chipotle model for Mexican food to other cuisines over the past seven years and currently operated a small fast casual pizza chain called Pizzeria Locale that had seven restaurants in four states, and one burger-fries-shakes restaurant called Tasty Made, giving it a total of 2,408 restaurants. In 2017, Chipotle decided to abandon its efforts to use high-quality, fresh ingredients and classic cooking methods to create great tasting, reasonably-priced Asian dishes; all 15 ShopHouse Southeast Asian Kitchen restaurants opened from 2011 through 2016 were closed after determining that devoting further efforts to perfect the ShopHouse concept and invest capital to expand the number of ShopHouse locations was not justified in light of the current difficulties being encountered in reviving sales and growth at its core Chipotle Mexican Grill business. The Tasty Made location was closed in March 2018, because two years of finetuning and tweaking of operations failed to produce satisfactory revenue-cost-profit economics. Chipotle management planned to open between 130 and 150 additional restaurants in 2018, all of which were expected to be Chipotle restaurants.

Menu and Food Preparation

The menu at Chipotle Mexican Grill restaurants was quite limited—burritos, burrito bowls, tacos, and salads; plus soft drinks, fruit drinks, and milk—the drink options also included a selection of beers and margaritas in all locations except those where serving alcoholic beverages was prohibited. Menu variety was achieved by enabling customers to customize their burritos, burrito bowls, tacos, and salads in dozens of different ways. Options included five different meats or tofu, pinto beans or vegetarian black beans, brown or white rice tossed with lime juice and fresh-chopped cilantro, and choices of such extras as sautéed peppers and onions, salsas, guacamole, sour cream, queso, shredded cheese, lettuce, and tortilla chips seasoned with fresh lime and salt. In addition, it was restaurant policy to make special dishes for customers if the requested dish could be made from the ingredients on hand.

From the outset, Chipotle's menu strategy had been to keep it simple, do a few things exceptionally well, and not include menu selections (like coffee and desserts) that complicated store operations and impaired efficiency. While it was management's practice to consider menu additions, the menu offerings had remained fundamentally the same since the addition of burrito bowls in 2005, tofu Sofritas (shredded organic tofu braised with chipotle chilis, roasted poblanos, and a blend of aromatic spices) as a meat alternative in 2013 and 2014, the addition of chorizo sausage as a meat option in 2016, and the 2017 addition of queso (made of aged cheddar cheese, tomatoes, tomatillos, and several varieties of peppers). So far, the company had rejected the option of opening earlier in the day and offering a breakfast menu.

The food preparation area of each restaurant was equipped with stoves and grills, pots and pans, and an assortment of cutting knives, wire whisks, and other kitchen utensils. There was a walk-in refrigerator stocked with ingredients, and supplies of herbs, spices, and dry goods such as rice. The work space more closely resembled the layout of the kitchen in a fine dining restaurant than the cooking area of typical fast food restaurant that made extensive use of automated cooking equipment and microwaves. Until the food contamination and food safety incidents in Q4 2015, all of the menu selections and optional extras were prepared from scratch in each Chipotle location—hours went into preparing food on-site,

although some items were prepared from fresh ingredients in area commissaries. Kitchen crews used classic cooking methods—they marinated and grilled the chicken and steak, hand-cut produce and herbs, made fresh salsa and guacamole, and cooked rice in small batches throughout the day. While the food preparation methods were labor-intensive, the limited menu created efficiencies that helped keep costs down.

Food preparation methods at Chipotle's restaurants were overhauled in late 2015 in response to the food contamination incidents. The goal was to develop an industry-leading food safety program utilizing the assistance and recommendations of highly respected experts. Components of the new program included:

- DNA-based testing of many ingredients to evaluate their quality and safety before they were shipped to Chipotle restaurants.
- Changes to food preparation and food handling practices, including washing and cutting some produce items (such as tomatoes and romaine lettuce) in central kitchens.
- Blanching of some produce items (including avocados, onions, jalapenos, and citrus) in each restaurant before cutting them.
- New protocols for marinating meats.
- Utilizing the Food and Drug Administration's Hazard Analysis Critical Control Point (HACCP) management system to enhance internal controls relating to food safety.
- Instituting internal training programs to ensure that all employees thoroughly understand the company's newly imposed standards for food safety and food handling.
- Offering paid sick leave to employees to reduce incentives for employees to work while sick.
- Implementing stricter standards for food preparation, cleanliness, and food safety at all of the company's restaurants.
- Strengthening efforts to ensure that the company remained in full compliance with all applicable federal, state, and local food safety regulations

Quality Assurance and Food Safety Chipotle's quality assurance department was charged with establishing and monitoring quality and food safety measures throughout the company's supply chain. There were quality and food safety standards for farms that grew ingredients used by company restaurants, approved suppliers, the regional distribution centers that purchased and delivered products to the restaurants, and frontline employees in the kitchen and on the serving lines at restaurants. The food safety programs for suppliers and restaurants were designed to ensure compliance with applicable federal, state, and local food safety regulations. Chipotle's training and risk management departments developed and implemented operating standards for food quality, preparation, cleanliness, and safety in company restaurants.

Chipotle's Commitment to "Food With Integrity"

In 2003 and 2004, Chipotle began a move to increase its use of organically grown local produce, organic beans, organic dairy products, and meats from animals that were raised in accordance with animal welfare standards and were never given feeds containing nontherapeutic antibiotics and growth hormones to speed weight gain. This shift in ingredient usage was part of a long-term management campaign to use top-quality, nutritious ingredients and improve "the Chipotle experience"—an effort that Chipotle designated as "Food With Integrity" and that top executives deemed critical to the company's vision of changing the way people think about and eat fast food. The thesis was that purchasing fresh ingredients and preparing them daily by hand in each restaurant were not enough.

To implement the Food With Integrity initiative, the company began working with experts in the areas of animal ethics to try to support more humane farming environments, and it started visiting the farms and ranches from which it obtained meats and fresh produce. It also began investigating using more produce supplied by farmers who respected the environment, avoided use of chemical fertilizers and pesticides, followed U.S. Department of Agriculture standards for growing organic products, and used agriculturally sustainable methods like conservation tillage methods that improved soil conditions and reduced erosion. Simultaneously, efforts were made to source a greater portion of products locally (within 350 miles of the restaurants where they were used) while in season. The transition to using organically grown local produce and naturally raised meats occurred gradually because it took time for Chipotle to develop sufficient sources of supply to accommodate the requirements of its growing number of restaurant locations. Meats

raised without the use of non-therapeutic antibiotics or added hormones and met other Chipotle standards were branded and promoted as "Responsibly Raised." Chipotle completed a two-year initiative in 2015 to stop using ingredients grown with genetically modified seeds in all of its dishes—to the extent that was possible. In many instances, the naturally raised meats Chipotle used were still being raised on animal feeds containing grains that were genetically modified; moreover, many of the branded beverages Chipotle served contained corn-based sweeteners often made with genetically modified corn.

Nonetheless, Chipotle still faced ongoing challenges in 2018 in *always* using organic products, locally grown produce, and naturally raised meats in *all* menu items at *all* of its restaurant locations because of short supplies. While growing numbers of farmers were entering into the production of these items and supplies were on the upswing, household purchases of these same items at local farmers markets and supermarkets were increasing swiftly, and mounting numbers of restaurants were incorporating organic and locally-grown produce and natural meats into their dishes. Moreover, the costs incurred by organic farmers and the growers of naturally raised meats were typically higher. Organically grown crops often took longer to grow and crop yields were usually smaller. Growth rates and weight gain were typically lower for chickens, cattle, and pigs that were fed only vegetarian diets containing no antibiotics and not given growth hormones. Hence, the prices of organically-grown produce and naturally-raised meats were not only higher but also subject to sharp upward swings where and when supplier could not keep up with rising demand. Consequently, when periodic supply–demand imbalances produced market conditions where certain items that Chipotle used in its dishes were either unavailable or prohibitively high-priced, some Chipotle restaurants temporarily reverted—*in the interest of preserving the company's reputation for providing great food* at reasonable prices *and protecting profit margins*—to the use of conventional products until supply conditions and prices improved. When certain Chipotle restaurants were forced to serve conventionally raised meat, it was company practice to disclose this temporary change on signage in each affected restaurant so that customers could avoid those meats if they choose to do so.

Despite the attendant price-cost challenges and supply chain complications, Chipotle executives were firmly committed to continuing the Food With Integrity initiative going forward. They felt it was very important for Chipotle to be a leader in responding to and acting on mounting consumer concerns about food nutrition, where their food came from, how fruits and vegetables were grown, and how animals used for meat were raised. And they definitely wanted customers to view Chipotle Mexican Grill as a place that used high-quality, "better for you" ingredients in its dishes. Given the record of growth in customer traffic at Chipotle restaurants, notwithstanding the recent food poisoning incidents, Chipotle executives believed the company could cope with the likelihood organic and natural meat ingredients would remain more expensive than conventionally raised, commodity-priced equivalents. Over the longer term, they anticipated the price volatility and shortages of organically-grown ingredients and natural meats would gradually dissipate as growing demand for such products attracted more small farmers and larger agricultural enterprises to boost supplies.

Serving Orders Quickly

One of Chipotle's biggest innovations had been creating the ability to have a customer's order ready quickly. As customers moved along the serving line, they selected which ingredients they wanted in their burritos, burrito bowls, tacos, and salads by speaking directly to the employees who were assembling the order behind the counter. Much experimentation and fine-tuning had gone into creating a restaurant layout and serving line design that made the food-ordering and dish-creation process intuitive and time-efficient, thereby enabling a high rate of customer throughput. The throughput target was at least 200 and up to 300 customers per hour, in order to keep the numbers of customers waiting in line at peak hours to a tolerable minimum. Management was focused on further improving the speed at which customers moved through the service line in all restaurants, so that orders placed by fax, online, or via smartphone ordering apps could be accommodated without slowing service to in-store customers and compromising the interactions between customers and crew members on the service line. The attention to serving orders quickly was motivated by management's belief that while customers returned because of the great-tasting food they also liked their orders served fast without having a "fast-food" experience (even when they were not in a hurry). Delivery service was also offered in

many areas through a number of third-party services with whom the company had partnered.

Catering

In 2013, Chipotle introduced an expanded catering program to help spur sales at its restaurants. The menu offerings evolved slightly in succeeding years. As of 2018, the catering program involved setting up a portable version of its service line for groups of 20 to 200 people and a choice of three menu options:

- The Big Spread—A choice of three: chicken, steak, barbacoa, carnitas, or Sofritas; plus fajita veggies.
- Two Meat Spread—A choice of two: chicken, steak, barbacoa, carnitas, or Sofritas.
- Veggie Spread—A choice of two: Sofritas, extra guacamole, or fajita veggies.

All three spreads included white and brown cilantro-lime rice, black beans and pinto beans, four salsas, sour cream, guacamole, cheese, lettuce, chips, crispy taco shells, and flour soft tortillas, plus chafing stands and dishes and serving tools.

For customers wanting to accommodate a smaller group of six or more people, Chipotle offered a Burritos by the Box option with a choice of meat, Sofritas, or grilled veggies (or an assortment of these) plus white or brown rice, black beans, mild-spice salsa, and cheese; for each two burritos in the box, a bag of chips and small containers of tomatillo-green chili salsa, guacamole, and sour cream were included.

SUPPLY CHAIN MANAGEMENT PRACTICES

Chipotle executives were acutely aware that maintaining high levels of food quality in the company's restaurants depended in part on acquiring high-quality, fresh ingredients and other necessary supplies that met company specifications. Over the years, the company had developed long-term relationships with a number of reputable food industry suppliers that could meet Chipotle's quality standards and understood the importance of helping Chipotle live up to its Food With Integrity mission. Chipotle worked with these suppliers on an ongoing basis to establish and implement a set of forward, fixed and formula pricing protocols for determining the prices that suppliers charged Chipotle for various items. Reliable suppliers that could meet Chipotle's quality specifications and were willing to comply with

Chipotle's set of forward, fixed, and formula-pricing protocols and guidelines for certain products were put on Chipotle's list of approved suppliers. Chipotle constantly worked to increase the number of approved suppliers for ingredients to help mitigate supply shortages and the associated volatility of ingredient prices. In addition, Chipotle personnel diligently monitored industry news, trade issues, weather, exchange rates, foreign demand, crises, and other world events so as to better anticipate potential impacts on ingredient prices.

Chipotle did not purchase directly from approved suppliers, but instead utilized the services of 24 independently owned and operated regional distribution centers to purchase and deliver ingredients and other supplies to Chipotle restaurants. These distribution centers were required to make all purchases from Chipotle's list of approved suppliers in accordance with the agreed-upon pricing guidelines and protocols.

RESTAURANT MANAGEMENT AND OPERATIONS

Chipotle's strategy for operating its restaurants was based on the principle that "the front line is key." The restaurant and kitchen designs intentionally placed most store personnel up front where they could speak to customers in a personal and hospitable manner, whether preparing food items or customizing the dish ordered by a customer moving along the service line. The open kitchen design allowed customers to see employees preparing and cooking ingredients, reinforcing that Chipotle's food was freshly-made each day. Store personnel, especially those who prepared dishes on the serving line were expected to deliver a customer-pleasing experience "one burrito at a time," give each customer individual attention, and make every effort to respond positively to customer requests and suggestions. Special effort was made to hire and retain people who were personable and could help deliver a positive customer experience. Management believed that creating a positive and interactive experience helped build loyalty and enthusiasm for the Chipotle brand not only among customers but among the restaurant's entire staff.

Restaurant Staffing and Management

Each Chipotle Mexican Grill typically had a general manager or Restaurateur (a high-performing general manager), an apprentice manager (in about 75 percent of the restaurants), one to three hourly service managers, one or two hourly kitchen managers, and an average of 22 full- and part-time crew members. Busier restaurants had more crew members. Chipotle generally had two shifts at its restaurants, which simplified scheduling and facilitated assigning hourly employees with a regular number of work hours each week. Most employees were cross-trained to work at a variety of stations, both to provide people with a variety of skills and to boost labor efficiency during busy periods. Personnel were empowered to make decisions within their assigned areas of responsibility.

One of Chipotle's top priorities was to build and nurture a people-oriented, performance-based culture in each Chipotle restaurant; executive management believed that such a culture led to the best possible experience for both customers and employees. The foundation of that culture started with hiring good people to manage and staff the company's restaurants. One of the prime functions of a restaurant's general manger was to hire and retain crew members who had a strong work ethic, took pride in preparing food items correctly, enjoyed interacting with other people, exhibited enthusiasm in serving customers, and were team players in striving to operate the restaurant in accordance with the high standards expected by top management. A sizable number of Chipotle's crew members had been attracted to apply for a job at Chipotle because of either encouragement from an acquaintance who worked at Chipotle or their own favorable impressions of the work atmosphere while going through the serving line and dining at a Chipotle Mexican Grill. New crew members received hands-on, shoulder-to-shoulder training. In 2018, pay scales for full-time crew members ranged from $10 per hour to $14 per depending on their assigned role; regular compensation and bonuses were in the range of $20,000 to $29,000, plus free meals during each shift and benefits for clothes, paid vacation, paid sick leave, tuition assistance up to $5,250 per year, company-matched 401(k) contributions, and medical, dental, and vision insurance.[4] In 2018, total compensation (including benefits) averaged $31,000 for crew members, $36,000 for kitchen managers, $39,000 for service managers, $56,000 for apprentice managers, and $77,000 for general managers.[5]

Top-performing store personnel typically moved up the ranks quickly because of the company's unusually heavy reliance on promotion from within—about 84 percent of salaried managers and about 97 percent of hourly managers had been promoted from positions as crew members. In several instances, a newly hired crew member had risen rapidly through the ranks and become the general manager of a restaurant in 9 to 12 months; many more high-performing crew members had been promoted to general managers within 2 to 4 years. Historically, the long-term career opportunities for Chipotle employees had been quite attractive because of the speed with which Chipotle was opening new stores in both new and existing markets.

The Position and Role of Restaurateur   The general managers who ran high-performing restaurants and succeeded in developing a strong, empowered team of hourly managers and crew members were promoted to Restaurateur, a position that entailed greater leadership and culture-building responsibility. In addition to continuing to run their assigned restaurant, Restaurateurs were typically given responsibility for mentoring one or more nearby restaurants and using their leadership skills to help develop the managers and build high-performing teams at the restaurants they mentored. At year-end 2013, Chipotle had over 400 Restaurateurs overseeing nearly 40 percent of the company's Chipotle restaurants, including their home restaurant and others that they mentored. In 2018, the average compensation (including benefits) of Chipotle Restaurateurs in charge of a single restaurant was $120,000; average compensation (including benefits) of Restaurateurs in charge of 2 to 4 locations was $127,000.[6] Restaurateurs could earn bonuses up to $23,000 for their people development and team-building successes and for creating a culture of high standards, constant improvement, and empowerment in each of their restaurants. Restaurateurs whose mentoring efforts resulted in high-performing teams at four restaurants and the promotion of at least one of the four restaurant managers to Restaurateur could be promoted to the position of Apprentice Team Leader and become a full-time member of the company's field support staff.

Chipotle's field support system included apprentice team leaders, team leaders or area managers, team directors, executive team directors or regional directors, and restaurant support officers—over 100 of the people in these positions in 2014 and 2015 were former Restaurateurs. In 2014, over two-thirds of Chipotle's restaurants were under the leadership and supervision of the company's 500 existing and former Restaurateurs. The principal task of field support personnel was to foster a culture of employee empowerment, high standards, and constant improvement in each of Chipotle's restaurants. One of Chipotle's field support staff members had been hired as a crew member in 2003, promoted to General Manager in 12 months, and—8 years after starting with Chipotle—was appointed as a Team Director (with responsibilities for 57 restaurants and 1400 + employees).[7]

In December 2016, Chipotle overhauled its Restaurateur program, after determining that the 27 measures being used to evaluate Restaurateurs for promotion were far too numerous and distracted them from strongly focusing on customer service and restaurant operations. Steve Ells concluded a major revision was needed because a recently completed survey of nearly 2,100 restaurant locations had awarded a C grade for service to half of the restaurants due to messy soda stations, dirty tables, long or slow-moving serving lines, shortages of various ingredients, and other operational deficiencies. At a January 2017 conference in Orlando, Florida, Steve Ells told the audience that promotions within the Restaurateur program were now based on five performance measures, three of which were customer related. He went on to say, "In the coming months, you will see the return to the kind of restaurant operations Chipotle was known for from the very beginning."

The Appointment of a Chief Restaurant Officer   In May 2017, Chipotle announced the hiring of Scott Boatwright as chief restaurant officer, with responsibility for overseeing operations at all of the company's restaurants. Boatwright came to Chipotle from Arby's Restaurant Group, where he served as senior vice president of operations and was responsible for the success and performance of nearly 2,000 franchised and company-owned restaurants across 22 states. His specific focus at Arby's was operational standards, building and developing teams, delivering an excellent guest experience, and strategic planning to support the company's overall annual operating plan.

In his new position at Chipotle, Boatwright was charged with working closely with the company's two restaurant support officers to oversee restaurant operations, including enhancing the guest experience, developing and leading field leadership teams, developing strong teams inside the restaurants, and enhancing operational efficiency.

MARKETING

Prior to the scares over food safety in 2015, Chipotle's marketing efforts were focused on introducing the Chipotle brand to new customers and emphasizing what the Chipotle experience was all about and what differentiated Chipotle from other fast-food competitors. When Chipotle opened restaurants in new markets, it used a range of promotional activities to introduce Chipotle to the local community and to create interest in the restaurant. In markets where there were existing Chipotle restaurants, newly opened restaurants usually attracted customers in volumes at or near market averages without having to initiate special promotions or advertising to support a new opening. But the company had field marketing teams tasked with connecting its restaurants to local communities on an ongoing basis through fundraisers, sponsorships, and participation in local events.

Chipotle's advertising mix typically included print, outdoor, transit, theaters, radio, and online ads. The company ran its first-ever national TV commercial during the broadcast of the 2012 Grammy Awards and ran a second campaign in 2013 featuring its new catering program. Over the past several years, the company had increased its use of digital, mobile, and social media in its overall marketing mix to better inform the public about Chipotle's differentiating features, most especially its commitment to Food With Integrity and what that commitment entailed—why it used top-quality, freshly prepared ingredients in its dishes; the benefits of organically grown fruits and vegetables; why people ought to consider eating meats that come from animals raised humanely and without the use of antibiotics; Chipotle's avoidance of ingredients grown with genetically modified seeds; and its efforts to ensure its dishes were nutritious and tasty. From 2013 through 2015, Chipotle crafted marketing programs to make people more curious about food-related issues and why Chipotle was working to drive positive changes in the nation's food supply and eating habits—management believed that the more people learned the more likely they would patronize Chipotle Mexican Grill locations.

In 2016, in the wake of the food safety-related incidents that occurred in the fourth quarter of 2015, Chipotle emphasized marketing campaigns to drive traffic into its restaurants and to communicate the changes Chipotle had recently made to establish the company as an industry leader in food safety.

Many of the 2016 actions to boost customer traffic at Chipotle restaurants were continued in 2017, but a number of new efforts were added:

- An online game was introduced where players during a two-week period prior to the Super Bowl were given three rounds to smash avocados and combine ingredients to make their own version of Chipotle's guacamole. Players were rewarded with a mobile offer good for a free order of chips and guacamole, with purchase of an entrée, at any Chipotle in the United States.

- In February, Chipotle announced an expansion of the Chipotle Reading Rewards program, which rewarded young readers with free Chipotle kid's meals for reaching their reading goals in reading programs established by teachers and librarians.

- Also in February, Chipotle completed the rollout of its "Smarter Pickup Times" technology to all its restaurants that offered digital ordering. The Smarter Pickup technology allowed customers who ordered digitally to benefit from shorter and more accurate pickup times and the ability to reserve a future pickup time. The technology also improved the company's ability to process more digital orders without disrupting service or throughput in its restaurants. In testing the Smarter Pickup Times system in restaurants around the country, the company was able to reduce the wait times for digital order pickup by as much as 50 percent; moreover, customer use of mobile ordering rose to record levels.

- In March, Chipotle, in partnership with Discovery Education and others, unveiled "RAD Lands," an unbranded, educational video series available exclusively on iTunes that was intended to give teachers and parents a means of educating children about food, where it comes from, and the benefits of eating fresh food, the importance of caring for the environment, and how to create healthy, tasty snacks.

- A second online game called "The Real Imposter" introduced in April challenged players to search through Chipotle's 51 real ingredients hunting for commonly used industrial additives—including added flavors, colors, preservatives, gluten and gums—masquerading as real ingredients. Successful players were rewarded with a mobile offer good for a free order of chips and guacamole, with purchase of an entrée, at any Chipotle in the United States, and a chance to enter the sweepstakes to win other food prizes.

- In celebration of the important contributions made by teachers, in May Chipotle again offered a special, one-day, buy-one-get-one-free to all teachers, faculty, and staff at schools and universities across the United States with a valid school ID.

- In June, to celebrate their hard work and contributions, as in 2016, nurses with a valid ID were offered a one-day, buy-one-get-one-free at any Chipotle Mexican Grill restaurant nationwide or in Canada.

- In September, queso (made of aged cheddar cheese, tomatillos, tomatoes and several varieties of peppers and containing no industrial additives, natural flavors, colors, or preservatives) was introduced as a new menu item at all Chipotle restaurants. Following numerous customer complaints about the grainy texture of the queso, Chipotle quickly modified the recipe to broaden its appeal.

- On Halloween, from 3 p.m. to closing at all Chipotle locations, Chipotle continued its recent tradition of offering customers dressed in costume the opportunity to buy $3 burritos, bowls, salads, or tacos.

- Active military and veterans were offered offering a special buy-one-get-one-free promotion from 3:00 p.m. to close on November 7, a week before Veterans Day.

- Also in November, Chipotle announced a new mobile app available for download on Apple and Android devices with such features such as quick reorder of favorite meals, streamlined payment options, and the ability to receive, store, and redeem Chipotle offers. The app was expected to drive substantial growth in customer use of digital ordering.

In April 2017, Chipotle began an "As Real as It Gets" national TV advertising campaign, supplemented with radio, outdoor, digital video and banners, and social advertising, to highlight the company's ongoing commitment to using only real ingredients in the food it served. The launch of the campaign followed on the heels of the company's announcement that by eliminating the use of preservatives and dough conditioners in the tortillas used for its tacos, burritos, and chips, Chipotle had become the only national restaurant brand that did not use artificial colors, flavors, or preservatives in any of the 51 ingredients used to prepare its food (although lemon and lime juice used to flavor some ingredients did have some preservative value as well).

To enable and facilitate public knowledge about the ingredients used to prepare the dishes on its menu, Chipotle posted a new section on its website devoted to the 51 ingredients it used.

All of the marketing, promotional, and advertising activities Chipotle undertook in 2016 and 2017 to revive customer traffic at its restaurants resulted in increases of more than 50 percent in Chipotle's marketing and advertising costs. The company's expenditures for marketing and advertising totaled $106.3 million in 2017 and $103.0 million in 2016, versus $69.3 million in 2015, $57.3 million in 2014, and $31.9 million in 2011 (these costs are included in "Other operating costs" in Exhibit 1).

The marketing and promotional blitz was continuing in early 2018. In January, Chipotle announced continuation of its Reading Rewards program that included free kid's meal cards for younger readers and buy-one-get-one free entrée cards for teen readers. In February, Chipotle partnered with Postmates, a company that delivered anything from anywhere in 40 major metropolitan areas, to offer people free delivery by Postmates when they placed their orders online at Chipotle.com or on the Postmates app anytime during regular Chipotle hours Friday through Sunday of Super Bowl weekend.

RESTAURANT SITE SELECTION

Chipotle had an internal team of real estate mangers that devoted substantial time and effort to evaluating potential locations for new restaurants; from time to time, the internal team sought the assistance of external brokers with expertise in specific local markets. The site selection process entailed studying the surrounding trade area, demographic and business information within that area, and available information on competitors. In addition, advice and recommendations were solicited from external real estate brokers with expertise in specific markets. Locations proposed by the internal real estate team were visited by a team of operations and development management as part of a formal site ride; the team toured the surrounding trade area, reviewed demographic and business information on the areas, and evaluated the food establishment operations of competitors. Based on this analysis, along with the results of predictive modeling based on proprietary formulas, the company came up with projected sales and targeted returns on investment for a new location. Chipotle Mexican Grills had proved successful in a number of different types of locations, including in-line or end-cap locations in strip or power centers, regional malls, downtown business districts, freestanding buildings, food courts, outlet centers, airports, military bases, and train stations.

DEVELOPMENT AND CONSTRUCTION COSTS FOR NEW RESTAURANTS

The company's average development and construction costs per restaurant decreased from about $850,000 in 2009 to around $800,000 in 2011, 2012, and 2013 (see Exhibit 1), chiefly because of cost savings realized from shifting to a simpler, lower-cost restaurant design. However, the costs of new openings jumped to an average of $843,000 in 2014, due to opening more freestanding restaurants (which were more expensive than end-caps and in-line sites in strip centers) and opening proportionately more sites in the northeastern United Sates where construction costs (and also sales volumes) were typically higher. Construction and development costs for new store openings in 2015 dropped to $805,000, rose to $880,000 in 2016, and dropped to $835,000 in 2017.

Total capital expenditures were expected to be about $300 million in 2018. About $120 million was expected to be used for opening 130 to 150 new stores; construction and development costs for these stores was expected to be above 2017 levels because of upgrades to accommodate the expected growth in mobile orders for pickup. The company expected that a big majority of its capital spending for 2018 would consist of investments in remodeling and improving existing restaurants, upgrading the lines for preparing pickup orders, and new restaurant equipment. Capital expenditures in prior years are shown in Exhibit 1. Senior executives believed the company's annual cash flows from operations, together with current cash on hand, would be adequate to meet ongoing capital expenditures, working capital requirements, possible repurchases of common stock, and other cash needs for the foreseeable future.

CHIPOTLE HIRES A NEW CEO

In mid-February 2018, Chipotle announced the appointment of Brian Nicol as chief executive officer and member of the Board of Directors, effective March 5. At the time, Nicol was CEO of Taco Bell; he had been at Taco Bell since 2011, served as president in 2013 and 2014, and became Taco Bell's CEO in January 2015. Under his leadership, he had fostered an environment of creative and consistent menu innovation, and he was a strong advocate of advertising with a strong message that captured consumer attention. Nicol was credited with being the driving force behind boosting average sales at Taco Bell restaurants, percent in the past six years, restarting the opening of more Taco Bell locations, and growing Taco Bell's systemwide revenues from about $8.1 billion in 2013 to $10.15 billion in 2017. He also transformed Taco Bell into a leader in using social media and mobile ordering/payment. While at Taco Bell, Nicol had gained experience in converting company-owned locations into franchised operations.

In announcing the Chipotle's performance for the first quarter of 2018, Nicol said:

Chipotle is a purpose driven brand with loyal customers, passionate employees, industry-leading economic potential, along with incredible brand equity, and craveable food with integrity, all built over the last 25 years. While the company made notable progress during the quarter, I firmly believe we can accelerate that progress in the future. We are in the process of forming a path to greater performance in sales, transactions, margins, and new restaurants. This path to performance will be grounded in a strategy of executing the fundamentals while introducing consumer-meaningful innovation across the business. It will also require a structure and organization built for creativity, action, and accountability. Finally, Chipotle will have a culture that is centered on running great restaurants, putting the customer first, innovating for today and tomorrow, supporting each other, and delivering on commitments.[8]

On May 23, 2018, a little over 10 weeks after taking over as CEO, Nicol announced that Chipotle would close both its Denver headquarters and a New York office and relocate all functions to either an existing Chipotle office in Columbus, Ohio, or to a new corporate headquarters to be located in Newport Beach, California. The move would affect some 400 employees. In making the announcement, Nicol said:

We have a tremendous opportunity at Chipotle to shape the future of our organization and drive growth through our new strategy. In order to align the structure around our strategic priorities, we are transforming our culture and building world-class teams to revitalize the brand and enable our long-term success. We'll always be proud of our Denver roots where we opened our first restaurant 25 years ago. The consolidation of offices and the move to California will help us drive sustainable growth while continuing to position us well in the competition for top talent.[9]

COMPETITION AND INDUSTRY TRENDS

Restaurant industry sales in the United States in 2017 were approximately $800 billion at close to 1.1 million food establishments.[10] According to recent survey data, 60 percent of consumers said that the availability of environmentally friendly food would make them choose one restaurant over another; 56 percent said their primary reason for preferring locally sourced food was that it supported farms and producers in their communities; 42 percent of consumers said the ability to order online would make them choose one restaurant over another; and 63 percent of millennials said they were more likely to eat a wider variety of ethnic cuisines than they did two years ago.[11]

The restaurant industry was highly segmented by type of food served, number and variety of menu selections, price (ranging from moderate to very expensive), dining ambience (quick-service to fast-casual to casual dining to fine dining), level of service (mobile ordering to drive-through to place and pick up order at counter to full table service), and type of enterprise (locally owned, regional chain, or national chain). The number, size, and strength of competitors varied by region, local market area, and a particular restaurant's location within a given community. Competition among the various types of restaurants and food service establishments was based on such factors as type of food served, menu selection (including the availability of low-calorie and nutritional items), food quality and taste, speed and/or quality of service, price and value, dining ambience, name recognition and reputation, and convenience of location.

One category of restaurants was a hybrid called "fast-casual." Fast casual restaurants—which included Chipotle Mexican Grill and its two closest competitors, Moe's Southwest Grill and Qdoba Mexican Eats—had average check sizes of $9 to $14 and were perceived to have better quality menu offerings, provide a slightly more upscale dining experience, and in some cases have enhanced service (like delivering orders to tables or even having full table service) as compared to "quick-service" or "fast-food" restaurants like McDonald's and Taco Bell. Fast-casual

restaurant brands had estimated sales of $47 billion in 2016, with forecasted growth to $74 billion in 2021.[12] Chipotle Mexican Grill was considered to be in the fast-casual category because of the fresh, high quality ingredients in its dishes and because customers could customize their orders. Other chains considered to be in the fast-casual category included Panera Bread, Jimmy John's, Panda Express, Noodles & Company, Firehouse Subs, Shake Shack, Newk's, Jersey Mike's, Cane's, and Five Guys Burgers and Fries.

Like most enterprises in the away-from-home dining business, Chipotle had to compete for customers with national and regional quick-service, fast-casual, and casual dining restaurant chains, as well as locally owned restaurants and food-service establishments. However, its closest competitors were the myriad of dining establishments that specialized in Mexican cuisine—Mexican food establishments accounted for an estimated 19 percent share of the fast-casual sales in 2016.[13] The leading fast-food chain in the Mexican-style food category was Taco Bell. Chipotle's two biggest competitors in the fast-casual segment were Moe's Southwest Grill and Qdoba Mexican Eats. Other smaller chains, such as Baja Fresh (165 restaurants in 26 states) and California Tortilla (51 locations in 9 eastern states and District of Columbia), were also relevant competitors in those geographic locations where Chipotle also had restaurants. The following are brief profiles of Taco Bell, Moe's Southwest Grill, and Qdoba Mexican Eats.

Taco Bell

As of 2005, Taco Bell locations were struggling to attract customers. From 2005 through 2011, the total number of Taco Bell restaurants, both domestically and internationally, declined as more underperforming locations were closed than new Taco Bell units were opened. In late 2011, Taco Bell's parent company, Yum! Brands (which also owned Pizza Hut and Kentucky Fried Chicken), began a multi-year campaign to reduce company ownership of Taco Bell locations from 23 percent of total locations to about 16 percent; a total of 1,276 company-owned Taco Bell locations were sold to franchisees in 2010-2012. In 20122013 expansion of Taco Bell locations resumed, with the vast majority of the new additions being franchised.

To counter stagnant sales and begin a strategy to rejuvenate Taco Bell, during 2010 and 2011 Taco Bell restaurants began rolling out a new taco with a Doritos-based shell called Doritos Locos Taco, which management termed a "breakthrough product designed to reinvent the taco." The launch was supported with an aggressive advertising campaign to inform the public about the new Doritos Locos Taco. The effort was considered a solid success, driving record sales of 375 million tacos in one year. Brian Nicol, Taco Bell's Chief Officer of Marketing and Innovation at the time, was a strong advocate for menu innovation supported with creative advertising. In March 2012, Taco Bell began introducing a new Cantina Bell menu, a group of upgraded products conceptualized by celebrity Miami chef Lorena Garcia that included such ingredients and garnishes as black beans, cilantro rice, and corn salsa.[14] In addition to the upscaled Cantina Bell selections, Taco Bell also introduced several new breakfast selections.

The upscaled menu at Taco Bell was a competitive response to growing consumer preferences for the higher-caliber, made-to-order dishes they could get at fast-casual Mexican-food chains like Chipotle, Moe's, and Qdoba. From 2013 through 2017, Taco Bell's upscaled menu continued to evolve and grow in number and variety of offerings. Taco Bell's 2018 menu contained 15 versions of tacos with a choice of 3 shells, 14 versions of burritos, 19 specialty items (including quesadillas, gorditas, chalupas, nachos, taco salads, a veggie power bowl, Mexican pizza, and rollups), 23 combos, 3 types of party packs, and a selection of over 20 beverages, freezes, and sweets. The various versions of tacos, burritos, specialty items, and combos on Taco Bell's menu could be customized by selecting any of 25 upgrades that included chicken, shredded chicken, beef, sauces, guacamole, pico de gallo, sour cream, cheese, and accompaniments (seasoned rice, pinto and black beans, potatoes, tomatoes, onions, jalapenos, lettuce, and red strips). Prices (without custom upgrades) ranged from $1.69 to $6.69; party packs of 12 tacos ranged from $12.99 to $16.99. In early 2016, Taco Bell launched a $1 morning value breakfast menu featuring 10 items. In 2018, Taco Bell had a 17-item breakfast menu that ranged in price from $1 to $4.59, not including beverage options.

At year-end 2017, Taco Bell had 6,849 company-owned, franchised, and licensed restaurant locations mostly in the United States, up from 6,210 at year-end 2014. Just over 90 percent of Taco Bell's locations were franchised or licensed at year-end 2017. Systemwide sales at Taco Bell were $10.15 billion in 2017, equal to average sales per location systemwide of almost $1.5 million, up from about $1.35 million in 2014. Taco Bell's 653 company-operated locations

had average sales per location of $2.1 million in 2017; average sales at Taco-Bell's 885 company locations in 2016 were $1.74 million (during 2017, Taco Bell refranchised or closed 232 formerly company-owned locations). Sales revenues at Taco Bell restaurants systemwide grew 5 percent in 2017, 6 percent in 2016, 8 percent in 2015, 4 percent in 2014 and 2013, and 7 percent in 2012. Taco Bell's mobile app, introduced in 2015, had contributed significantly to higher sales revenues at Taco Bell restaurants.

Moe's Southwest Grill

Moe's Southwest Grill was founded in Atlanta, Georgia, in 2000 and acquired in 2007 by Atlanta-based FOCUS Brands, an affiliate of Roark Capital, a private equity firm. FOCUS Brands was a global franchisor and operator of over 4,500 ice cream shops, bakeries, restaurants and cafes under the brand names Carvel®, Cinnabon®, Schlotzsky's®, Moe's Southwest Grill®, Auntie Anne's, and McAlister's Deli®. In early 2018, there were more than 700 fast-casual Moe's Southwest Grill locations in 40 states and the District of Columbia. All Moe's locations were franchised. Average annual sales at Moe's locations were an estimated $1.2 million.

The menu at Moe's featured burritos, quesadillas, tacos, nachos, burrito bowls (with meat selections of chicken, pork, or tofu), and salads with a choice of two homemade dressings. Main dishes could be customized with a choice of 20 items that included a choice of protein (sirloin steak, chicken breast, pulled pork, ground beef, or organic tofu); grilled peppers, onions, and mushrooms; black olives; cucumbers; fresh chopped or pickled jalapenos; pico de gallo (handmade fresh daily); lettuce; three varieties of queso; and five salsas. There was a kids' menu and vegetarian, gluten-free, and low-calorie options, as well as a selection of five salsas, four varieties of queso, guacamole, chips, cookies, brownies, cinnamon chips, soft drinks, iced tea, and bottled water. Moe's used high quality ingredients, including all natural, cage-free, white breast meat chicken; steroid-free, grain-fed pulled pork; 100 percent grass-fed sirloin steak; and organic tofu. No dishes included trans fats or msg (monosodium glutamate—a flavor enhancer), and no use was made of microwaves. Moe's provided catering services; the catering menu included a fajitas bar, a taco bar, a salad bar, a nacho bar, three sizes of burritos, a burrito box meal, guacamole, chips, salsas, quesos, dessert items, and drinks.

Moe's had introduced a "Rockin' Rewards" mobile app that not permitted mobile ordering at all locations, but also rewarded users with points on each order. For each 1,000 points earned, the user received a $10 Moe's credit. As users moved to higher points-earned plateaus, they unlocked special offers in addition to the $10 Moe's credit. At the 6,000-point plateau level, users were automatically entered into a Rockin' prize sweepstakes and gained more such entries for each additional 1,000 points earned.

The company and its franchisees emphasized friendly hospitable service. When customers entered a Moe's location, it was standard practice for employees to do a "Welcome to Moe's!" shout-out.

Qdoba Mexican Eats

The first Qdoba Mexican Grill opened in Denver in 1995. Rapid growth ensued and in 2003 the company was acquired by Jack in the Box, Inc., a large operator and franchisor of 2,250 Jack in the Box quick service restaurants best known for its hamburgers. Jack in the Box had fiscal year 2017 revenues of $1.55 billion (the company's fiscal year was October 1 through September 30).[15] In 2016, management changed the name of Qdoba Mexican Grill to Qdoba Mexican Eats to better reflect the flavors and variety of its menu offerings.

In October 2017, there were 726 Qdoba restaurants in 47 states, the District of Columbia, and Canada, of which 385 were company-operated and 341 were franchise-operated. Management believed Qdoba had significant long-term growth potential—perhaps as many as 2,000 locations. A total of 23 new company-owned and 19 franchised Qdoba restaurants were opened in fiscal 2017; 15 underperforming units were closed. Plans for opening new Qdoba locations in fiscal year 2018 were on hold, pending a decision by the parent company's Board of Directors regarding various strategic alternatives for Qdoba going forward.

In 2017, sales revenues at all company-operated and franchise-operated Qdoba restaurant locations averaged $1,156,000, versus $1,179,000 in fiscal 2016, $1,169,000 in fiscal 2015, and $1,070,000 in fiscal 2014. Sales at all Qdoba restaurants open more than 12 months dropped 1.5 percent in fiscal 2017, versus increases of 1.4 percent in fiscal 2016, 9.3 percent in fiscal 2015, and 6.0 percent in fiscal 2014. The average check at company-operated restaurants in fiscal 2017 was $11.69.

Menu Offerings and Food Preparation   Qdoba billed itself as an "artisanal Mexican kitchen" where dishes were handcrafted with fresh ingredients and innovative flavors by skilled cooks. The menu included burritos, tacos, taco salads, three-cheese nachos, grilled quesadillas, loaded tortilla soup, chips and dips, kids meals, and, at most locations, a variety of breakfast burritos and breakfast quesadillas. Burritos and tacos could be customized with choices of meats or just vegetarian ingredients and by adding three-cheese queso, guacamole, and a variety of sauces and salsas. Salads were served in a crunchy flour tortilla bowl with a choice of two meats, or vegetarian, and included black bean corn salsa and fat free picante ranch dressing.

Orders were prepared in full view, with customers telling line servers how they wished to customize their dishes. Restaurants offered a variety of catering options that could be tailored to feed groups of five to several hundred. While some Qdoba locations served breakfast, most locations operated from 10:30 a.m. to 10:00 p.m. Seating capacity ranged from 60 to 80 persons, and many restaurants had outdoor patio seating.

Site Selection and New Restaurant Development   Site selections for all new company-operated Qdoba restaurants were made after an economic analysis and a review of demographic data and other information relating to population density, traffic, competition, restaurant visibility and access, available parking, surrounding businesses, and opportunities for market penetration. Most Qdoba restaurants were located in leased spaces in conventional large-scale retail projects and food courts in malls, smaller neighborhood retail strip centers, on or near college campuses, and in airports. There were multiple restaurant designs with varying seating capacities to enable flexibility in selecting locations for new restaurants. Development costs for new Qdoba restaurants generally ranged from $800,000 million to $1.1million, depending on the geographic region and specific location. In 2017, management began using new designs for remodels systemwide.

Restaurant Management and Operations   At Qdoba's company-owned restaurants, emphasis was placed on attracting, selecting, engaging, and retaining people who were committed to creating long-lasting, positive impacts on operating results. The company's core development tool was a "Career Map" that provided employees with detailed education requirements, skill sets, and performance expectations by position, from entry level to area manager. High-performing general managers and hourly team members were certified to train and develop employees through a series of on-the-job and classroom training programs that focused on knowledge, skills, and behaviors. The Team Member Progression program within the Qdoba Career Map tool recognized and rewarded three levels of achievement for cooks and line servers who displayed excellence in their positions. Team members had to possess, or acquire, specific technical and behavioral skill sets to reach an achievement level. All restaurant personnel were expected to contribute to delivering a great guest experience in the company's restaurants.

There was a three-tier management structure for company-owned Qdoba restaurants. Restaurant managers were supervised by district managers, who were overseen by directors of operations, who reported to vice presidents of operations. Under Qdoba's performance system, vice presidents and directors were eligible for an annual incentive based on achievement of goals related to region level sales, profit, and companywide performance. District managers and restaurant managers were eligible for quarterly incentives based on growth in restaurant sales and profit and/or certain other operational performance standards.

Food Safety and Quality   Qdoba's "farm-to-fork" food safety and quality assurance programs were designed to maintain high standards for the food products and food preparation procedures used by vendors and restaurants. It maintained product specifications for ingredients and the company's Food Safety and Regulatory Compliance Department had to approve all suppliers of food products to Qdoba restaurants. Third-party and internal audits were used to review the food safety management programs of vendors. Food safety in Qdoba restaurants was managed through a comprehensive food safety management program based on Food and Drug Administration food code requirements. The program included employee training, ingredient testing, and documented restaurant practices and attention to product safety at each stage of the food preparation cycle. In addition, the program used American National Standards Institute certified food safety training programs to train company and franchise restaurant management employees on food safety practices.

Purchasing and Distribution   Beginning in March 2017, all Qdoba company-operated and franchise-operated restaurants entered into a five-year distribution services agreement with a consortium of four Qdoba regional distributors comprising 18 distribution centers in the United States and two distribution centers in Canada.

Advertising and Promotion   The goals of Qdoba's advertising and marketing activities were to build brand awareness and increase customer traffic. All company-owned and franchised restaurants contributed a percentage of gross sales to fund the production and development of advertising assets suitable for national and regional radio, print, and digital and social media. System operators could utilize these assets, or tap into the parent company's in-house creative services group to create custom advertising that met their particular communication objectives while adhering to brand standards. Additionally, Qdoba had launched a mobile app for placing orders and a rewards program designed to inspire, motivate, and reward increased dining frequency at Qdoba locations.

ENDNOTES

[1] Company press release, November 29, 2017.

[2] Company press release, February 6, 2018.

[3] David A. Kaplan, "Chipotle's Growth Machine," *Fortune*, September 26, 2011, p.138.

[4] According to information posted in the careers section at www.chipotle.com, accessed February 18, 2012, May 13, 2013, February 19, 2016, and February 12, 2018.

[5] Information posted in the careers section at www.chipotle.com, accessed February 12, 2018.

[6] Ibid.

[7] Ibid.

[8] Company press release, April 25, 2018.

[9] Company press release, May 23, 2018.

[10] National Restaurant Association, *2017 Restaurant Industry Pocket Factbook,* www.restaurant.org, accessed February 15, 2018.

[11] Ibid.

[12] National Restaurant Association, "Technomic State of the Fast Casual Industry," May 2017, www.restaurant.org, accessed February 15, 2018.

[13] Ibid.

[14] Leslie Patton, "Taco Bell Sees Market Share Recouped with Chipotle Menu," *Bloomberg News,* January 11, 2012, www.bloomberg.com, accessed February 20, 2012.

[15] The statistics in this section are drawn from parent company Jack in the Box's 2017 10-K Report.

Twitter Inc. in 2018: Too Little Too Late?

David L. Turnipseed
University of South Alabama

Jack Dorsey, CEO of Twitter Inc., breathed a slight sigh of relief as the fourth quarter, 2017 financial results showed the first profitable quarter since the company went public in 2013. Twitter had experienced rapid growth since its founding and by January 2018 there were more than 330 million active monthly users. Notables with Twitter accounts included U.S. President Donald Trump, Justin Timberlake, Pope Francis, Katy Perry, and Turkish President Recep Erdogan. However, despite the number of users and the volume of use, Twitter had failed to provide any financial gains until the fourth quarter of 2017, and this profit had come as a result of cutting costs, not growing the business. Research and development, and sales and marketing expenses had been cut by 24 and 25 percent, respectively, and the company's annual net revenue for fiscal 2017 was down over three percent from 2016. Twitter discovered in the third quarter of 2017 that it had been miscalculating monthly user numbers since the fourth quarter of 2014, and consequently was forced to lower the previously reported numbers. Even more problematic was an accumulated deficit of over $2.6 billion, and the March 2018 departure of Anthony Noto, the company's chief operating officer, whose leadership had been vital in Twitter getting rights to the NFL Thursday night football games. Twitter Inc.'s consolidated income statements for 2013 through 2017 are presented in Exhibit 1. The company's consolidated balance sheets for 2016 and 2017 are presented in Exhibit 2.

Twitter was a giant in the industry; however, it faced serious competition from companies such as Facebook, WhatsApp, SnapChat, Instagram, LinkedIn, and Pinterest, plus several others such as Reddit and Quora. Many of these competitors were growing at a multiple of Twitter's growth—over the two-year period third quarter 2015 to third quarter 2017, Facebook had an increase of 461 million monthly active users, and both WhatsApp and Instagram had increases of 400 million. Over the same period, Twitter increased only 23 million monthly users, and its share of worldwide digital ad revenue dropped to 0.8 percent in 2018 (compared to Facebook's 18.4 percent and Instagram's 3.0 percent).

Although Twitter had made a small profit, was it too little and too late? Twitter's CEO and its Board were faced with two daunting questions: 1) what could they do to assure Twitter's survival with its anemic growth, marginal revenue increases, unreliable profitability, and 2) was the company an attractive take-over candidate?

HISTORY OF TWITTER

Founded in 2006 by Jack Dorsey, Noah Glass, Biz Stone, and Evan Williams, Twitter was an online microblogging and social networking service that allowed users to post text-based messages, known as tweets, and status updates up to 40 characters long. Jack Dorsey, a cofounder of Twitter, sent the first tweet on March 21, 2006: "just setting up my twttr"- Jack(@jack) 21 March, 2006. By the first of January 2018, Twitter had more 330 million monthly active users.

The history of Twitter began with an entrepreneur named Noah Glass who started a company named Odeo in 2005. Odeo had a product that would turn a phone

EXHIBIT 1 Consolidated Statement of Operations: Fiscal Years 2013–2017 (in thousands, except per share data)

	Year Ended December 31,				
	2017	**2016**	**2015**	**2014**	**2013**
	(in thousands, except per share data)				
Revenue	$2,443,299	$2,529,619	$2,218,032	$1,403,002	$ 664,890
Costs and expenses					
Cost of revenue	861,242	932,240	729,256	446,309	266,718
Research and development	542,010	713,482	806,648	691,543	593,992
Sales and marketing	717,419	957,829	871,491	614,110	316,216
General and administrative	283,888	293,276	260,673	189,906	123,795
Total costs and expenses	2,404,559	2,896,827	2,668,068	1,941,868	1,300,721
Income (loss) from operations	38,740	(367,208)	(450,036)	(538,866)	(635,831)
Interest expense	(105,237)	(99,968)	(98,178)	(35,918)	(7,576)
Other income (expense), net	(28,921)	26,342	14,909	(3,567)	(3,739)
Loss before income taxes	(95,418)	(440,834)	(533,305)	(578,351)	(647,146)
Provision (benefit) for income taxes	12,645	16,039	(12,274)	(531)	(1,823)
Net loss	$ (108,063)	$ (456,873)	$ (521,031)	$ (577,820)	$(645,323)
Net loss per share attributable to common stockholders:					
Basic and diluted	$ (0.15)	$ (0.65)	$ (0.79)	$ (0.96)	$ (3.41)
Weighted-average shares used to compute net loss per share attributable to common stockholders:					
Basic and diluted	732,702	702,135	662,424	604,990	189,510
Other Financial Information:					
Adjusted EBITDA	$ 862,986	$ 751,493	$ 557,807	$ 300,896	$ 75,430
Non-GAAP net income (loss)	$ 328,859	$ 264,406	$ 180,486	$ 68,438	$ (19,057)

Source: Twitter, Inc. Annual Report 2017.

message into an MP3 hosted on the Internet. One of Odeo's early investors was a former Google employee, Evan Williams, who got very involved with the company.

As Odeo grew, more employees were hired including a Web designer, Jack Dorsey, and Christopher "Biz" Stone, a friend of Odeo's new CEO, Evan Williams.

EXHIBIT 2   Twitter Inc.'s Consolidated Balance Sheets, 2016–2017 (in thousands, except par value)

	December 31, 2017	December 31, 2016
Assets		
Current assets:		
Cash and cash equivalents	$1,638,413	$ 988,598
Short-term investments	2,764,689	2,785,981
Accounts receivable, net of allowance for doubtful accounts of $5,430 and $7,216 as of December 31, 2017 and December 31, 2016, respectively	664,268	650,650
Prepaid expenses and other current assets	254,514	226,967
Total current assets	5,321,884	4,652,196
Property and equipment, net	773,715	783,901
Intangible assets, net	49,654	95,334
Goodwill	1,188,935	1,185,315
Other assets	78,289	153,619
Total assets	$7,412,477	$6,870,365
Liabilities and stockholders' equity		
Current liabilities:		
Accounts payable	$ 170,969	$ 122,236
Accrued and other current liabilities	327,333	380,937
Capital leases, short-term	84,976	80,848
Total current liabilities	583,278	584,021
Convertible notes	1,627,460	1,538,967
Capital leases, long-term	81,308	66,837
Deferred and other long-term tax liabilities, net	13,240	7,556
Other long-term liabilities	59,973	68,049
Total liabilities	2,365,259	2,265,430
Commitments and contingencies		
Stockholders' equity:		
Preferred stock, $0.000005 par value—200,000 shares authorized; none issued and outstanding	—	—
Common stock, $0.000005 par value—5,000,000 shares authorized; 746,902 and 721,572 shares issued and outstanding as of December 31, 2017 and December 31, 2016, respectively	4	4
Additional paid-in capital	7,750,522	7,224,534
Accumulated other comprehensive loss	(31,579)	(69,253)
Accumulated deficit	(2,671,729)	(2,550,350)
Total stockholders' equity	5,047,218	4,604,935
Total liabilities and stockholders' equity	$7,412,477	$6,870,365

Source: Twitter, Inc. Annual Report 2017.

Williams decided that Odeo's future was not in podcasting, and directed the company's employees to develop ideas for a new direction. Jack Dorsey, who had been doing cleanup work on Odeo, proposed a product that was based on people's present status, or what they were doing at a given time. In February 2006, Glass, Dorsey, and a German contract developer proposed Dorsey's idea to others in Odeo, and over time, a group of employees gravitated to Twitter while others focused on Odeo. At one point, the entire Twitter service was run from Glass' laptop.

Noah Glass presented the Twitter idea to Odeo's Board in summer of 2006; the Board was not enthused. Williams proposed to repurchase the Odeo stock held by investors to prevent them from taking a loss, and they agreed. Five years later, the assets of Odeo that the original investors sold for about $5 million were worth $5 billion.

After Williams repurchased Odeo, he changed the name to Obvious Corp. and fired Odeo's founder and the biggest supporter of Twitter, Noah Glass. Christopher "Biz" Stone left Twitter in 2011 and pursued an entrepreneurial venture with Obvious Corp. for six years. In mid-2017, he returned to Twitter full time. As of the second quarter, 2018, only three of the original Twitter founders remained active in the company: Biz Stone, Jack Dorsey as the company's CEO, and Evan Williams who was on the Board.

Twitter provided an almost-immediate access channel to global celebrities. The majority of the top 10 most-followed Twitter accounts were entertainers who used the service to communicate with their fans, spread news, or build a public image. The near-instant gratification from direct updates from celebrities such as Rihanna, Jimmy Fallon, Lady Gaga, and Taylor Swift and the feeling of inclusion in a specific group of fans was a major reason for social media users to use Twitter. The accounts of high-interest people such as entertainers, politicians, or others at risk of impersonation were verified by Twitter to authenticate their identity. A badge of verification was placed on confirmed accounts to indicate legitimacy. Major sporting events and industry award shows such as the Super Bowl or Academy Awards generated significant online action. The online discussion enabled users to participate in the success of celebrities who often posted behind-the-scenes photo tweets or commentaries. On-set or in-concert tweets were other methods utilized by celebrities to enhance their appeal, and fan interaction.

Twitter was quite simple: tweets were limited to 140 characters until late 2017 when the limit was raised to 280. The character constraint made it easy for users to create, distribute, and discover content that was consistent across the Twitter platform as well as optimized for mobile devices. Consequently, the large volume of Tweets drove high velocity information exchange. Twitter's aim was to become an indispensable daily companion to live human experiences. The company did not have restrictions on whom a user could follow, which greatly enhanced the breadth and depth of available content and allowed users to find the content they cared about most. Also, users could be followed by hundreds of thousands, or millions of other users without requiring a reciprocal relationship, enhancing the ability of users to reach a broad audience. Twitter's public platform allowed both the company and others to extend the reach of Twitter content: media outlets distributed Tweets to complement their content by making it more timely, relevant, and comprehensive. Tweets had appeared on over one million third-party websites, and in the second quarter of 2013 there were approximately 30 billion online impressions of Tweets.

THE TWITTER BRAND IMAGE

Twitter had a powerful brand image. Its mascot bird was not chosen because birds make tweeting sounds, but rather because "whether soaring high above the earth to take in a broad view, or flocking with other birds to achieve a common purpose, a bird in flight is the ultimate representation of freedom, hope and limitless possibility."[1]

Twitter was initially named "Jitter" and "Twitch," because that is what a phone would do when it received a tweet. However, neither name evoked the image that the founders wanted. Noah Glass got a dictionary and went to "Twitch," then to subsequent words starting with "Tw" he found the word "Twitter," which in the Oxford English dictionary means a short inconsequential burst of information, and chirps from birds. Dorsey and Glass thought that "twitter" described exactly what they were doing, so they decided on that name. The name was already owned, but not being used, and the company was able to buy it very cheaply.

In 2012, the old Twitter bird was redesigned, slightly resized, changed from red to blue, and named Larry the Bird (named after NBA star Larry Bird).

The lower case "t" icon and the text "twitter" were removed; the company name was no longer on the logo. The blue bird alone communicated the Twitter brand. "Twitter achieved in less than six years what Nike, Apple, and Target took decades to do: To be recognizable without a name, just an icon."[2]

According to a Twitter survey conducted to help understand the company's brand legacy, 90 percent of Twitter users worldwide recognized the Twitter brand. Twitter's 2018 ad campaign "What's happening" used only the Twitter logo and hashtag symbol. The Twitter brand was called "minimalization at its finest"[3]—an advertising campaign that did not have one word, but yet delivered a powerful message from the brand.

Twitter's Global High Profile

Twitter had become very well-known because of several high-profile users and high profile use. Several of the world's leaders had millions of followers, as shown in Exhibit 3. From May 2017 to June 2018, U.S. President Donald Trump's follow count increased to 53.1 million. President Trump regularly used Twitter to break news, praise his friends, campaign for supporters, and feud with his enemies; consequently Twitter was in the daily news almost constantly in 2017.

EXHIBIT 3   World Leaders with the Most Twitter Followers as of May 2017

	Millions of Followers
Pope Francis, Vatican@Pontifex	33.72
Donald Trump, U.S.@RealDonaldTrump	30.13
Narendra Modi, India@NarendraModi	30.06
Prime Minster, India@PMOIndia	18.04
President, U.S.@POTUS	17.76
The White House, U.S.@WhiteHouse	14.42
Recep Erdogan, Turkey@RT_Erdogan	10.27
HH Sheikh Mohammed, UAE@Jokowi	7.92
Joko Widodo, Indonesia@jokowi	7.43

Source: Statista, 2018.

Although the world's leaders had millions of followers, others have far more. As of June 2018, Katy Perry had over 108,000,000 followers, Justin Bieber 106.5 million, former U.S. President Barack Obama 103 million, Rihanna 88.6 million, Lady Gaga 78.85 million, and Justin Timberlake 66 million.

The miraculous plane crash on New York's Hudson River in 2009 was broken on Twitter, and on May 1, 2011, an IT consultant in Pakistan unknowingly live-tweeted the U.S. Navy Seal raid that killed Osama Bin Laden over nine hours before the raid was on the news. Prince William announced his engagement to Catherine Middleton in 2010 on Twitter. President Obama used Twitter to declare victory in the 2012 U.S. presidential election, with a Tweet that was viewed about 25 million times on the Twitter platform and widely distributed offline in print and broadcast media.

TWITTER SERVICES, PRODUCTS, AND REVENUE STREAMS

Twitter's primary service was the Twitter global platform for real-time public self-expression and conversation, which allowed people to create, consume, discover, and distribute content. Some of the most trusted media outlets in the world, such as CNN, Bloomberg, the Associated Press, and BBC used Twitter to distribute content. Periscope was a mobile app launched by Twitter in 2015 that enabled people to broadcast and watch live video with others. Periscope broadcasts could be viewed through Twitter and mobile or desktop web browsers.

Twitter Inc. generated advertising and data licensing revenue as shown in Exhibit 4 by providing mobile advertising exchange services through the Twitter MoPub exchange, and offering data products and data licenses that allowed their data partners to search and analyze historical and real-time data on the Twitter platform, which consisted of public tweets and their content. Also, Twitter's data partners usually purchased licenses to access all or a portion of the company's data for a fixed period. The company operated a mobile ad exchange and received service fees from transactions completed on the exchange. The Twitter mobile ad exchange allowed buyers and sellers to purchase and sell advertising inventory, and it matched buyers and sellers.

EXHIBIT 4 Twitter Inc. Advertising and Data Licensing Revenue, 2015–2016 (in thousands)

	Year Ended December 31,			2016 to 2017 % Change	2015 to 2016 % Change
	2017	2016	2015		
	(in thousands)				
Advertising services	$2,109,987	$2,248,052	$1,994,036	(6)%	13%
Data licensing and other	333,312	281,567	223,996	18%	26%
Total revenue	$2,443,299	$2,529,619	$2,218,032	(3)%	14%

2017 Compared to 2016. Revenue in 2017 decreased by $86.3 million compared to 2016.

Source: Twitter, Inc. 2017 Form 10-K.

TWITTER RESTRUCTURES

On June 29, 2018, Dorsey announced that he was restructuring Twitter to make the company quicker and more creative, as Ed Ho, VP of product and engineering, stepped down to a part-time position. Twitter employees would be organized in functional groups such as engineering, as opposed to the present product teams. Dorsey decided on the structural change to simplify the way the company worked and to make the organization "more straightforward." He believed that a "pure end-to-end functional organization" would help make decision making clearer, allow the company to build a stronger culture, and prepare the company for increased creativity and innovation. Dorsey believed that Twitter must enter a creativity phase to be relevant and important to the world.

TWITTER'S STOCK PERFORMANCE

Twitter went public on November 7, 2013 with an IPO price of $26.00, and the stock closed up 73 percent ($44.94) on its first trading day. The stock hit its all-time high of $69.00 on January 3, 2014, and began a long down-trend. On August 21, 2015, Twitter shares dropped below the IPO price to $25.87, rebounded slightly, and then slid to $14.10 on May 13, 2016. The stock did not get above the IPO price of $26.00 until early February 2018. On the last trading day of June 2018, Twitter stock was trading at $43.67. Exhibit 5 tracks Twitter's market performance between November 2013 and June 2018.

Twitter, Inc. joined the S&P 500 index on June 7, 2018, replacing Monsanto. The addition of Twitter was unusual because the S&P regulations required that the sum of a member company's four most recent quarters, as well as the last quarter, were positive. In April of 2018, Twitter reported its second consecutive profitable quarter, which followed 16 consecutive quarters of losses. The addition of Twitter to the S&P 500 Index would increase the number of individual investors who owned the stock through index funds that track the large company stock gauge. Twitter's addition to the index fueled a rally that pushed the company's stock to more than $40.00/share, which was its highest price since March of 2015.

TWITTER'S MAJOR COMPETITORS

Facebook

Facebook was the world's largest online social networking and social media company. It was founded in February 2004 by Mark Zuckerberg, Eduardo Saverin, Dustin Moskivitz, Chris Hughes, and Andrew McCollum. As was common among online social networking companies, Facebook was not immediately profitable; however, after becoming profitable in 2010, it had its IPO in 2012 at $38/share. Although the stock price dropped to under $20 in August 2012, it rebounded and was selling at $197.00/share in June 2018. In the first quarter of 2018, Facebook had 2.2 billion users worldwide—India had the largest number of users at 270 million, the United States

EXHIBIT 5   Monthly Performance of Twitter Inc.'s Stock Price, November 2013–June 2018

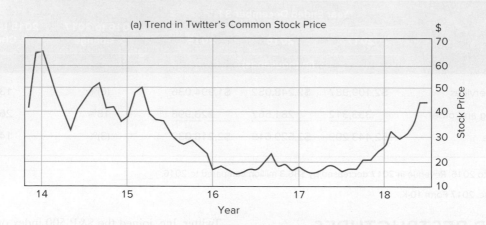

(a) Trend in Twitter's Common Stock Price

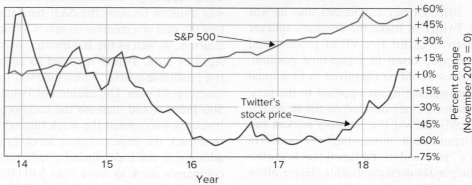

(b) Performance of Twitter's Stock Price versus the S&P 500 Index

was second with 240 million, and Indonesia was third with 140 million.

Facebook averaged 1.7 billion average monthly users, and 83 percent of the total users were from outside the United States. Facebook's year-over-year growth rate in the first quarter of 2018 was 13 percent. A financial summary for Facebook, Inc. for 2013 to 2017 is presented in Exhibit 6.

WhatsApp

WhatsApp was a freeware and cross-platform messaging and IP service owned by Facebook. The company was founded in 2009 by ex-Yahoo employees Jan Koum and Brian Acton. WhatsApp used the Internet to send messages, audio, video, and images, and was similar to a text messaging service. However, because WhatsApp sent messages over the Internet, the cost

for users was much less than texting. The company grew quickly and within a few months of startup WhatsApp added a service charge to slow down its growth rate. In 2014, WhatsApp was acquired by Facebook in 2014 for $21.94 billion.

In early 2018, after a long feud with Facebook founder and CEO Mark Zuckerberg about how to get additional revenue from WhatsApp, Koum and Acton resigned from Facebook. Zuckerberg was focused on using targeted ads to WhatsApp's large user base; Koum and Acton were believers in privacy and had no interest in the potential commercial applications. When WhatsApp was sold to Facebook, the founders pledged privacy of WhatsApp. Four years later, Facebook pushed WhatsApp to change its terms of service and give Facebook access to WhatsApp users' phone numbers. Facebook also wanted a unified profile that could be used for ad targeting and data

EXHIBIT 6 Selected Financial Data for Facebook, Inc., 2013–2017 (in millions, except per share data)

	Year Ended December 31,				
	2017	2016	2015	2014	2013
	(in millions, except per share data)				
Consolidated Statements of Income Data:					
Revenue	$40,653	$27,638	$17,928	$12,466	$ 7,872
Total costs and expenses	20,450	15,211	11,703	7,472	5,068
In Income from operations	20,203	12,427	6,225	4,994	2,804
Income before provision for income taxes	20,594	12,518	6,194	4,910	2,754
Net income	15,934	10,217	3,688	2,940	1,500
Net income attributable to Class A and Class B common stockholders	15,920	10,188	3,669	2,925	1,491
Earnings per share attributable to Class A and Class B common stockholders:					
Basic	$5.49	$3.56	$1.31	$1.12	$0.62
Diluted	$5.39	$3.49	$1.29	$1.10	$0.60

	As of December 31,				
	2017	2016	2015	2014	2013
	(in millions)				
Consolidated Balance Sheets Data:					
Cash, cash equivalents, and marketable securities	$41,711	$ 29,449	$ 18,434	$ 11,199	$11,449
Total assets	84,524	64,961	49,407	39,966	17,858
Total liabilities	10,177	5,767	5,189	3,870	2,388
Total stockholders' equity	74,347	59,194	44,218	36,096	15,470

Source: Facebook, Inc. 2017 Annual Report.

mining, and a recommendation system that would suggest Facebook friends based on WhatsApp contacts. WhatsApp had 1.5 billion monthly active users in early 2018, with 60 billion messages sent each day.

Snapchat

Snap Inc. was a camera company that believed that reinventing the camera was a great opportunity to improve the way that people communicated and lived. Snap, Inc.s products empowered people to express themselves, live in the moment, learn about the world, and have fun together. The company's flagship product, Snapchat, was a camera application that helped people communicate visually with friends and family through short videos and images called snaps. Snaps were deleted by default, so there was less pressure to look good when creating and sending images on Snapchat. By reducing the friction typically associated with creating and sharing content, Snapchat became one of the most-used cameras in the world.

Snapchat had 300 million users in January 2018 and, on average, 187 million people used Snapchat daily, creating over 3.5 billion snaps every day. A financial summary for Snap Inc. for 2015 through 2017 is presented in Exhibit 7.

Instagram

Instagram was a video and photo-sharing social network service created by Kevin Systrom and Mike Krieger in 2010. Facebook acquired the company in 2012 for $1 billion. If Instagram was a standalone company, it would be worth more than $100 billion, which would be a 100-fold return for Facebook.

In June 2018, Instagram reached one billion monthly active users and expected revenues of over $10 billion in the next 12 months. Instagram attracted new users at a faster rate than Facebook's main site. At its present rate of growth, it would have over two billion users by 2023.

LinkedIn

LinkedIn was a social media service that operated through websites and mobile apps, and focused

EXHIBIT 7   Snap, Inc.: Selected Financial Data

	Year Ended December 31,		
	2017	2016	2015
	(in thousands, except per share amounts)		
Consolidated Statements of Operations Data:			
Revenue	$ 824,949	$ 404,482	$ 58,663
Costs and expenses:			
Cost of revenue	717,462	451,660	182,341
Research and development	1,534,863	183,676	82,235
Sales and marketing	522,605	124,371	27,216
General and administrative	1,535,595	165,160	148,600
Total costs and expenses	4,310,525	924,867	440,392
Loss from operations	(3,485,576)	(520,385)	(381,729)
Interest income	21,096	4,654	1,399
Interest expense	(3,456)	(1,424)	—
Other income (expense), net	4,528	(4,568)	(152)
Loss before income taxes	(3,463,408)	(521,723)	(380,482)
Income tax benefit (expense)	18,342	7,080	7,589
Net loss	$ (3,445,066)	$ (514,643)	$ (372,893)
Net loss per share attributable to Class A, Class B, and Class C common stockholders:			
Basic	$(2.95)	$(0.64)	$(0.51)
Diluted	$(2.95)	$(0.64)	$(0.51)
Adjusted EBITDA	$ (720,056)	$ (459,243)	$ (292,898)

	December 31,		
	2017	2016	2015
	(in thousands)		
Consolidated Balance Sheet Data:			n.a.
Cash, cash equivalents, and marketable securities	$2,043,039	$ 987,368	n.a.
Total assets	3,421,566	1,722,792	n.a.
Total liabilities	429,239	203,878	n.a.
Additional paid-in capital	7,634,825	2,728,823	n.a.
Accumulated deficit	(4,656,667)	(1,207,862)	n.a.
Total stockholders' equity	2,992,327	1,518,914	n.a.

n.a. Not available.

Source: Snap Inc. Annual Report 2017.

primarily on professional networking, which enabled members to create, manage, and share their professional identities online, create professional networks, share insights and knowledge, and find jobs and business opportunities. The company was founded in December 2002 by Allen Blue, Reid G. Hoffman, Jean-Luc Vaillant, Konstantin Guericke, and Eric Ly. LinkedIn was named by Forbes as one of America's Best Employers in 2016. LinkedIn was acquired by Microsoft for $26.2 billion in June 2016.

In July 2018, LinkedIn had 562 million users in more than 200 countries and territories worldwide.[4]

SIGNS OF ENCOURAGEMENT IN MID-2018

Twitter's first quarter 2018 financial results were positive and unexpectedly robust, with revenue growth up 21 percent year-over-year, from $548 million to $665 million. The company's revenues enjoyed growth across all of major product and geographic areas. Year-over-year advertising revenue increased by 21 percent during the first quarter of 2018, from $474 million to $575 million, and data licensing revenue increased from $74 million to $90 million, year-over-year, which was a 20 percent increase. Revenue from the United States increased by 2 percent, year-over-year, from $341 million to $347 million. The largest growth was

international revenue, which increased 53 percent year-over-year from $208 million to $318 million. The company's international growth was the largest in three years with Japan accounting for 61 percent of the year-over-year increase.

Although Twitter's first quarter 2018 revenues and profit were up over the prior year, the company still faced considerable challenges, and warned that it would be difficult to have growth rates in the second half of 2018 that exceeded those in 2017. As of March 31, 2018, the company had accumulated a deficit of $2.6 billion, and although revenues had grown, the rate of growth had slowed. The company also noted in its first quarter 2018 report that costs might increase in the future due to spending on the technology infrastructure, sales and marketing, and strategic opportunities. Following this warning, Twitter's stock fell by 7.7 percent, erasing gains of up to 14 percent following the release of the first quarter earnings.

In addition to continuing financial problems, 2018 brought new challenges for Twitter. In June 2018, the company lost its bid to dismiss a lawsuit by Jared Taylor who claimed that the company unlawfully suspended his accounts because of his racial views. The judge said that Twitter's policy of suspending accounts "at any time, for any reason or for no reason" may be unconscionable and that the company calling itself a platform devoted to free speech may be misleading and therefore fraudulent. Twitter claimed that it had a First Amendment right, like newspapers, to publish or not publish whatever it wanted. It insisted that the Federal Communications Decency Act, originally passed to regulate pornography, gives it the right to ban offensive content. Obviously the outcome of this litigation would have a significant impact on Twitter. Also in June 2018, subsequent to Facebook revealing that it had data sharing partnerships with four Chinese companies, Senator Mark Warner, Vice Chairman of the Senate Intelligence Committee, asked Twitter for information on any data sharing agreements they had with Chinese vendors.

ENDNOTES

[1] Armin, "Twitter Gives You the Bird," June 7, 2012, https://www.underconsideration.com/brandnew/archives/twitter_gives_you_the_bird.php.

[2] As quoted in "Is Twitters' logo change the most revolutionary re-branding of the Modern Era?, Gawker, June 6, 2006, (http://gawker.com/5916390/is-twitters-logo-change-the-most-revolutionary-re-branding-of-the-modern-era).

[3] Sunil Singh, "How a Logo Personified the Twitter Brand," February 15, 2018, https://gulfmarketingreview.com/brands/how-a-logo-personified-the-twitter-brand/.

[4] As stated at about.linkedin.com

Netflix's Strategy in 2018: Does the Company Have Sufficient Competitive Strength to Fight Off Aggressive Rivals?

Arthur A. Thompson

The University of Alabama

Throughout 2017 and the first three months of 2018, Netflix was on a roll. Movie and TV show enthusiasts across the world were flocking to become Netflix subscribers in unprecedented numbers, and shareholders were exceptionally pleased with Netflix's skyrocketing stock price. Over the past eight years, the company had successfully transformed its business model from one where subscribers paid a monthly fee to receive an unlimited number of DVDs each month (delivered and returned by mail with one title out at a time) to a model where subscribers paid a monthly fee to watch an unlimited number of movies and TV episodes streamed over the Internet. In 2018, Netflix was the world's leading Internet television network with over 117 million streaming memberships in over 190 countries enjoying more than 140 million hours of TV shows and movies per day, including original series, documentaries, and feature films. Netflix members could not only watch as much streamed content as they wanted—anytime, anywhere, on nearly any Internet-connected screen—but they could also play, pause, and resume watching, all without commercials. In the United States, Netflix still had 3.4 million members in 2018 who, because of slow or limited Internet service, continued to receive DVDs solely by mail (but the numbers of mail-only subscribers were steadily declining).

Netflix's swift growth in the United States and its promising potential for further expanding its international subscribers pushed the company's stock price to an all-time high of $331.44 on March 5, 2018, up from an opening price of $124.96 on January 3, 2017. Already solidly entrenched as the biggest and best-known Internet subscription service for watching TV shows and movies, the only two questions for Netflix in 2018 seemed to be how big Netflix's service might one day become in the world market for on-demand streaming of movies and TV episodes and whether the company had the competitive and financial strength to combat the efforts of larger, resource-rich rivals looking to steal subscribers away from Netflix.

Financial statement data for Netflix for 2000 through 2017 are shown in Exhibits 1 and 2. Netflix had never paid a dividend to its shareholders and the company had declared it had no present intention of paying any cash dividends in the foreseeable future.

Netflix's Drive to Globalize Its Operations

Exhibit 3 shows the remarkable short time frame it took for Netflix to expand its operations from a U.S.-only subscriber base to a global subscriber base. As of 2018, Netflix had, for the time being, shelved

EXHIBIT 1   Netflix's Consolidated Statements of Operations, 2000–2017 (in millions, except per share data)

	2000	2005	2010	2015	2016	2017
Revenues	$ 35.9	$682.2	$2,162.6	$6,779.5	$8,830.7	$11,692.7
Cost of revenues (almost all of which relates to amortization of content assets)	35.1	465.8	1,357.4	4,591.5	6,029.9	7,659.7
Gross profit	0.8	216.4	805.3	2,188.0	2,800.8	4,033.0
Operating expenses						
Technology and development	16.8	35.4	163.3	650.8	852.1	1,052.8
Marketing	25.7	144.6	293.8	824.1	991.1	1,278.0
General and administrative	7.0	35.5	64.5	407.3	577.8	863.6
Other	9.7	(2.0)	—	—	—	—
Total operating expenses	59.2	213.4	521.6	1,882.2	2,421.0	3,194.4
Operating income	(58.4)	3.0	283.6	305.8	379.8	838.7
Interest and other income (expense)	(0.2)	5.3	(15.9)	(163.9)	(119.3)	(591.5)
Income before income taxes	—	8.3	267.7	141.9	260.5	485.3
Provision for (benefit from) income taxes	—	(33.7)	106.8	19.2	73.8	(73.6)
Net income	$(58.5)	$ 42.0	$ 160.8	$ 122.6	$ 186.7	$ 558.9
Net income per share:						
Basic	$(2.98)	$ 0.11	$ 0.44	$ 0.29	$ 0.44	$ 1.29
Diluted	(2.98)	0.09	0.40	0.28	0.43	1.25
Weighted average common shares outstanding (in millions)						
Basic	19.6	374.5	365.5	425.9	428.8	431.9
Diluted	19.6	458.5	380.1	436.5	438.7	446.8

Note 1: Some totals may not add due to rounding.

Note 2: The company's board of directors declared a seven-for-one split of its common stock in the form of a stock dividend that was paid in July 2015. Outstanding share and per-share amounts disclosed for all periods prior to 2015 have been retroactively adjusted to reflect the effects of the stock split.

Source: Company 10-K reports for 2003, 2006, 2010, and 2017.

efforts to overcome the government-erected barriers to entering the People's Republic of China, the world's most massive market for entertainment. The Chinese government had for several years refused to issue Netflix a license to operate in China, preferring instead to control the content its citizens were allowed to see—government censors required that an entire series of a TV show had to be approved before it could begin to be shown on an online platform.

Aside from the censorship issue, most observers believed the Chinese government also wished to protect aspiring local providers of Internet-based entertainment content from foreign competitors. As a consequence of its nonexistent prospects for getting an operating license from the Chinese government any time soon, in 2017 Netflix negotiated a licensing arrangement to exclusively provide some of its original content to a fast-growing Chinese company

EXHIBIT 2 Selected Balance Sheet and Cash Flow Data for Netflix, 2000–2017 (in millions)

	2000	2005	2010	2015	2016	2017
Selected Balance Sheet Data						
Cash and cash equivalents	$ 14.9	$212.3	$194.5	$1,809.3	$ 1,467.6	$2,822.8
Short-term investments	—	—	155.9	501.4	266.2	—
Current assets	n.a.	243.7	637.2	5,431.8	5,720.3	7,670.0
Total content assets	n.a.	57.0	362.0	7,218.8	11,008.8	14,682.0
Total assets	52.5	364.7	982.1	10,202.9	13,586.6	19,012.7
Current liabilities	n.a.	137.6	388.6	3,529.6	4,586.7	5,466.3
Long-term debt*	—	—	200.0	2,371.4	3,364.3	6,499.4
Stockholders' equity	(73.3)	226.3	290.2	2,223.4	10,906.8	15,430.8
Cash Flow Data						
Net cash (used in) provided by operating activities	$(22.7)	$157.5	$276.4	$ (749.4)	$(1,474.0)	$(1,785.9)
Net cash provided by (used in) investing activities	(25.0)	(133.2)	(116.1)	(179.2)	49.8	34.3
Net cash provided by (used in) financing activities	48.4	13.3	(100.0)	1,640.3	1,091.3	3,077.0

*All of Netflix's long-term debt consisted of senior unsecured notes that were issued at various points in time and had various maturity dates and various fixed rates of interest.

Sources: Company 10-K Reports for 2003, 2005, 2011, and 2017.

EXHIBIT 3 Netflix's Expansion into New Geographic Areas

Year	Entry into New Geographical Areas
September 2010	Canada
September 2011	42 countries in Central America, South America, and the Caribbean
January 2012	United Kingdom, Ireland
October 2012	Denmark, Sweden, Norway, Finland
September 2013	Netherlands
September 2014	Austria, Belgium, France, Germany, Luxembourg, Switzerland
March 2015	Australia, New Zealand
September 2015	Japan
October 2015	Spain, Portugal, Italy
January 2016	Rest of the world—some 130 countries (but excluding the People's Republic of China, North Korea, Syria, and Crimea)

Source: Company 2017 10-K Report, p. 21.

named iQiyi (pronounced Q wee), the leading provider of online entertainment services in China with some 60 million subscribers (as of early 2018). Use of a licensing strategy was attractive to Netflix because it provided a means of gaining content distribution in China and building awareness of the Netflix brand and Netflix content, but the licensing arrangement was expected to generate only small revenues.

The U.S. government had instituted restrictions precluding all U.S.-based companies from having operations in North Korea, Syria, and Crimea.

Netflix estimated that it usually took about two years after the initial launch in a new country or geographic region to attract sufficient subscribers to generate a positive "contribution profit"—Netflix defined "contribution profit (loss)" as revenues less cost of revenues (which consisted of amortization of content assets and expenses directly related to the acquisition, licensing, and production/delivery of such content) and marketing expenses associated with its domestic streaming and international streaming business segments (the company had ceased all marketing activities related to its domestic DVD business).

THE FAST-CHANGING MARKET FOR ENTERTAINMENT VIDEO

In 2018, the world market for entertainment video (movies, TV episodes, and live-streamed events) was undergoing rapid and disruptive change being driven by (1) increasingly pervasive consumer access to high-speed Internet connections, (2) the variety of devices and downloadable apps that consumers could use to access both broadcast and streamed entertainment programs, and (3) the mounting intensity with which well-known, resource-rich companies were competing for viewers of entertainment programs. Close to half of the world's population of 7.6 billion people in 2018 used the Internet and, of these, somewhere around 700 million currently had access to broadband high-speed Internet connections. The number of people with broadband Internet access was forecast to move rapidly toward 1 billion—a number that Netflix viewed as its near-term market opportunity.[1] YouTube and Facebook already had two billion monthly active users, a number that Netflix viewed as its long-term market opportunity for accessing and attracting more subscribers.

People could watch streamed entertainment on smartphones, all types of computers (tablets, laptops, and desktops), in-home TVs with either built-in Internet connections or connected to a digital video disc (DVD) player with built-in Internet access, and recent versions of video game consoles. During the past five to eight years, most households with high-speed Internet service and/or Internet-connected TVs or DVD players had shifted from renting or buying physical DVDs with the desired content to almost exclusively watching streamed movies and TV episodes. This was because streaming had the advantage of allowing household members to order and instantly watch the movies and TV programs they wanted to see and was much more convenient than patronizing a nearby rent-or-purchase location. This shift had permanently undercut the once-thriving businesses of selling movie and music DVDs and/or renting DVDs at local brick-and-mortar locations and standalone rental kiosks (like Redbox in the United States) or delivering/returning DVDs by mail (as at Netflix) and unleashed a fierce battle among the providers of streamed content in countries across the world to become the preferred streamed content provider (or, at worst, a frequently used content provider).

Consumers could view streamed entertainment from growing numbers and types of providers and the options included:

- Using a TV remote to order movies and popular TV shows instantly streamed directly to a TV (or other connected device) on a pay-per-view basis (generally referred to as "video-on-demand" or VOD). Most all traditional cable and satellite providers of multichannel TV packages were promoting a library of several hundred movie titles (and often prior episodes of top TV shows, as well as other content) available on-demand to regular subscribers having a cable or satellite box; the rental prices for pay-per-view and VOD movies from such providers ranged from $1 to $6, but the rental price for popular recently released movies was usually $3.99 to $5.99. However, most every traditional cable and satellite provider had recently begun offering a growing variety of content-viewing options that were streamed directly to a single location (and viewable simultaneously on up to as many as eight compatible WiFi enabled devices) via a special downloadable streaming application that eliminated the need for a cable/satellite box. These streaming options allowed subscribers to customize their own service package (number of channels, Internet speed, telephone service, and home security service). Recently, in the United States, wireless phone providers like AT&T and Verizon had also begun installing thousands of miles of fiber-optic cable annually in their service areas that enabled them to simultaneously provide residences and apartments with multiple content-viewing options (including VOD), perhaps bundled with telephone service, ultra-high-speed Internet service, and/or home security at an attractive monthly price (for a specified period, usually one or two years).

- There were many subscription-based providers of streamed video content across the world in 2018, and more new entrants were expected in upcoming years. In the United States, the clear market leader was Netflix, followed by Amazon Prime, and Hulu;

others included Vudu, Sling TV, HBO NOW, Starz, MAX GO® (Cinemax), Showtime, Direct TV Now, and Play Station Vue. An estimated 37 percent of TV viewers in the United States used subscription-based streaming services in 2017 to watch digital video content on their TVs. However, YouTube ranked first as the market leader among video and entertainment websites, with almost 10 times as many site visits to view videos as Netflix; of course, most all YouTube videos could be accessed for free, and many were videos uploaded by people or brands. The number of video viewers using mobile devices, such as smartphones and tablets, was exploding all across the world. In the United States alone, the number using mobile devices to watch videos was projected to reach 179 million by 2020, and an additional 57 million were expected to watch videos on computers and Internet-connected TVs. Exhibit 4 shows the percentage of Internet users, by country, who watched online video content on any device as of January 2018.

EXHIBIT 4 The Percentage of Internet Users in Selected Countries Who Watched Online Video Content on Any Device as of January 2018

Country	Percentage of Internet Users Watching Online Video Content on Any Device
Saudi Arabia	95%
China	92%
New Zealand	91%
Mexico	88%
Australia	88%
Spain	86%
India	85%
Brazil	85%
United States	85%
Canada	83%
France	81%
Germany	76%
South Korea	71%
Japan	69%

Source: Statista, **www.statista.com** (accessed April 10, 2018).

Competitors offering pay-per-view and VOD rentals were popular options for households and individuals who rented movies occasionally (once or maybe twice per month), since the rental costs tended to be less than the monthly subscription prices for unlimited streaming from the various streaming providers. However, competitors offering unlimited Internet streaming plans tended to be the most economical and convenient choice for individuals and households who watched an average of three or more titles per month and for individuals who wanted to be able to watch movies or TV shows or special live event streaming on mobile devices.

Netflix was by far the global leader in Internet streaming. It faced numerous competitors of varying competitive strength, geographic coverage, and content offerings; currently, none could match Netflix's global scope or the size of its content library. In North America, Netflix's three biggest Internet streaming competitors were Amazon Prime, Hulu, and HBO (with its HBO NOW and HBO GO service options):

• *Amazon Prime Video*—Amazon competed with Netflix via its Amazon Prime membership service. Individuals and households could become an Amazon Prime member for a fee of $119 per year or $11.99 per month (after a one-month free trial); there was a discounted price for students. In April 2018, Amazon announced that it had over 100 million Amazon Prime members globally. While Amazon had originally created its Amazon Prime membership program as a means of providing unlimited two-day shipping to customers who frequently ordered merchandise from Amazon and liked to receive their orders quickly, in 2012 Amazon began including movie and music streaming as a standard benefit of Prime membership—Amazon's video streaming service was called "Prime Video." Amazon's Prime Video content library contained thousands of movies that could be streamed to members, over 40 original series and movies, and some two million songs.

In 2017 and 2018, Amazon made Prime Video more attractive to Prime members by (1) adding Prime Originals to its offerings, like *The Marvelous Mrs. Maisel* and the Oscar-nominated movie *The Big Sick,* (2) debuting *NFL Thursday Night Football* on Prime Video (which attracted more than 18 million total viewers over 11 games), and (3) expanding its slate of programming across the globe—launching new seasons of *Bosch, Sneaky Pete,* and *The Man in the High Castle* from the United States, *The Grand Tour* from the United Kingdom, *You Are Wanted* from Germany, while adding new *Sentosha* shows from Japan, along with *Breathe* and the award-winning *Inside Edge* from India. In April 2018, Amazon announced it had agreed to pay the National Football League $65 million a year to stream *NFL Thursday Night Football* globally to its Amazon Prime members in 2018 and 2019. Also in 2018, Prime Channels offerings were expanded to include CBS All Access in the United States and newly launched channels in the United Kingdom and Germany. In 2017, Prime Video Direct secured subscription video rights for more than 3,000 feature films and committed over $18 million in royalties to independent filmmakers and other rights holders. Going forward, the Prime original series pipeline included Tom Clancy's *Jack Ryan,* starring John Krasinski; *King Lear,* starring Anthony Hopkins and Emma Thompson; *The Romanoffs,* starring Aaron Eckhart and Diane Lane ; *Carnival Row,* starring Orlando Bloom and Cara Delevingne; *Good Omens,* starring Jon Hamm; and *Homecoming,* starring Julia Roberts in her first television series. In addition, Prime Video had acquired the global television rights for a multi-season production of *The Lord of the Rings,* as well as *Cortés,* a miniseries based on the epic saga of Hernán Cortés from executive producer Steven Spielberg and starring Javier Bardem. Amazon's 2018 budget for Prime Video original content additions and enhancement was reportedly $5 billion.

Other 2018 benefits of becoming an Amazon Prime member included discounted prices on Kindle eBooks, free reading of designated digital editions of books and magazines, special deals/coupons on purchases of selected products that Amazon sold, one-click ordering via a "dash button," shopping with Alexa, cloud storage and sharing of personal photos and videos, and an opt-in DVD rental service (for an extra fee). In addition, Amazon competed with Netflix's DVDs-by-mail subscription service by allowing people to rent any streamed or downloadable movie, TV program, or other digital content for a limited time (for viewing on a personal computer, portable media player or other compatible device) or to purchase such content in the form of a downloadable file.

- *Hulu*—Hulu had 20 million subscribers as of May 2018, up from 12 million in May 2017. The subscription fee for Hulu was $8 per month for regular streaming and $12 per month for commercial-free streaming, and new subscribers got a one-week free trial. The regular streaming option included advertisements as a means of helping keep the monthly subscription price low. Hulu also offered plans that included not only its video streaming service, but also packages that included 50 or more live TV and cable channels (that included sports, news, and entertainment) and options to add on HBO®, Showtime®, and Cinemax®. The Hulu library of offerings included all current season episodes of popular TV shows, over 15,000 back season episodes of 380+ TV shows, over 425 movies, most in high-definition, and a growing selection of Hulu-produced original content. Hulu was a joint venture co-owned by Walt Disney (30 percent), Fox (30 percent), Comcast (30 percent), and Time Warner (10 percent)

- *HBO NOW* and *HBO GO*—HBO NOW was an option to receive unlimited streaming of content in HBO's library that included movies, documentaries, sports programs, and original series (*Silicon Valley, Game of Thrones, True Detective, Big Little Lies, Sharp Objects*) for a cancel-anytime monthly subscription price of $14.99 (as of 2018). HBO NOW content was viewable on mobile phones, tablets, computers and Internet-connected TVs. HBO NOW, offered only in the United States and a few territories had over two million subscribers as of February 2017. HBO GO was a bonus offering only for people who subscribed to HBO through a cable or satellite provider; such subscribers used a downloadable app to access the HBO GO website, entered their user name and password of their cable provider to authenticate their subscription and then clicked on the desired HBO content that was viewable on mobile phones, laptops, and computers. HBO had no interest in offering its HBO GO option to people who were not cable subscribers because its principal revenue source was a percentage of the monthly fees that nearly 140 million cable subscribers across the world paid their cable company for HBO as part of their cable package—HBO was typically the most expensive of the premium cable channels offered by cable/satellite providers. However, as of 2018, HBO was offering a direct streaming service akin to HBO NOW in several countries that had low cable subscriber rates (namely Spain, Columbia, and the four Nordic countries—Norway, Denmark, Sweden, and Finland). HBO was a division of Time Warner, which had agreed to merge with AT&T, pending government approval.

In April 2018, Comcast, one of the largest cable operators in the United States, announced it had expanded its partnership with Netflix and would begin including a Netflix subscription in new and existing packages offered to its cable subscribers. In July 2018, *The Wall Street Journal* reported that Walmart was likely to enter the video streaming market and establish a subscription service with programming that targeted "Middle America" and that would likely involve a subscription price below what Netflix charged.[2] Walmart was working with a veteran television executive with experience in pay-television on plans for the service.

NETFLIX'S BUSINESS MODEL AND STRATEGY

Since launching the company's online movie rental service in 1999, Reed Hastings, founder and CEO of Netflix, had been the chief architect of Netflix's subscription-based business model and strategy that had transformed Netflix into the world's largest online entertainment subscription service. Hastings's goals for Netflix were simple—build the world's best Internet service for entertainment content, keep improving Netflix's content offerings and services faster than rivals, attract growing numbers of subscribers every year, and grow long-term earnings per share. Hastings was a strong believer in moving early and fast to initiate strategic changes that would help Netflix outcompete rivals, strengthen its brand image and reputation, and fortify its position as the industry leader.

Netflix's Subscription-Based Business Model

Netflix employed a subscription-based business model. Members could choose from a variety of subscription plans whose prices and terms had varied over the years. Originally, all of the subscription plans were based on obtaining and returning DVDs by mail, with monthly prices dependent on the number of titles out at a time. But as more and more households began to have high-speed Internet connections, Netflix began bundling unlimited streaming with each of its DVD-by-mail subscription options, with the long-term intent of encouraging subscribers to switch to watching instantly streamed content rather than using DVD discs delivered and returned by mail. The DVDs-by-mail part of the business had order fulfillment costs and postage costs that were bypassed when members opted for instant streaming.

In 2018, Netflix offered three types of streaming membership plans. Its basic plan, currently priced at $7.99 per month in the United States, included access to standard definition quality streaming on a single screen at a time. Its standard plan, currently priced at $10.99 per month, was the most popular streaming plan and included access to high-definition quality streaming on two screens concurrently. The company's premium plan, currently priced at $13.99 per month, included access to high definition and ultra-high definition quality content on four screens concurrently. As of December 31, 2017, international pricing for the three plans ranged from approximately $4 to $20 per month per U.S. dollar equivalent. Top management expected that the prices of the membership plans in each country would likely rise over time.

Netflix had organized its operations into three business segments: domestic streaming, international streaming, and domestic DVD. The domestic streaming segment derived revenues from monthly membership fees for services consisting solely of streaming content to members in the United States. The international streaming segment derived revenues from monthly membership fees for services consisting solely of streaming content to members outside the United States. The domestic DVD segment derived revenues from monthly membership fees for services consisting solely of DVD-by-mail. Recent performance of Netflix's three business segments is shown in Exhibit 5.

The DVD-by-Mail Option Subscribers who opted to receive movie and TV episode DVDs by mail went to Netflix's website, selected one or more movies from its DVD library, and received the movie DVDs by first-class mail generally within one business day. Subscribers could keep a DVD for as long as they wished, with no due dates, no late fees, no shipping fees, and no pay-per-view fees. Subscribers returned DVDs via the U.S. Postal Service in a prepaid return envelope that came with each movie order.

EXHIBIT 5   Netflix's Performance by Business Segment, 2015–2017 (in millions, except for average monthly revenues per paying member and percentages)

Domestic Streaming Segment	2017	2016	2015
Memberships			
Paid memberships at year-end	52.8	47.9	43.4
Trial memberships at year-end	2.0	1.5	1.3
Total	54.8	49.4	44.7
Net membership additions	5.5	4.7	5.6
Average monthly revenue per paying membership	$ 10.18	$ 9.21	$ 8.50
Revenues	$6,153.0	$5,077.3	$4,180.3
Cost of Revenues (Note 1)	3,319.2	2,855.8	2,487.2
Marketing costs	553.3	382.8	313.6
Contribution profit (Note 2)	$2,280.5	$1,838.7	$1,375.5
Contribution margin	37%	36%	33%

International Streaming Segment			
Memberships			
Paid memberships at year-end	57.8	41.2	27.4
Trial memberships at year-end	5.0	3.2	2.6
Total	62.8	44.4	30.0
Net membership additions	18.5	14.3	11.7
Average monthly revenue per paying membership	$ 8.66	$7.81	$ 7.48
Revenues	$5,089.2	$3,211.1	$1,953.4
Cost of Revenues (Note 1)	4,137.9	2,911.4	1,780.4
Marketing costs	724.7	608.2	506.4
Contribution profit (Note 2)	$ 226.6	$ (308.5)	$ (333.6)
Contribution margin	4%	(10)%	(17)%

Domestic DVD Segment			
Memberships			
Paid memberships at year-end	3.3	4.0	4.8
Trial memberships at year-end	.1	.1	.1
Total	3.4	4.1	4.9
Net membership losses	.7	.8	.9
Average monthly revenue per paying membership	$ 10.17	$ 10.22	$ 10.30
Revenues	$ 450.5	$ 542.3	$ 645.7
Cost of Revenues (Note 1)	202.5	262.7	323.9
Marketing costs	—	—	—
Contribution profit (Note 2)	$ 248.0	$ 279.5	$ 321.8
Contribution margin	55%	52%	50%

Global Totals			
Global streaming memberships at year end	117.6	93.8	74.8
Global streaming average monthly revenue per paying membership	$ 9.43	$ 8.61	$ 8.15
Revenues	$11,692.7	$8,830.7	$6,779.5
Operating income	838.7	379.8	305.8
Operating margin	7%	4%	5%
Net income	$ 558.9	$ 186.7	$ 122.6

Note 1: Cost of revenues for the domestic and international streaming segments consist mainly of the amortization of streaming content assets, with the remainder relating to the expenses associated with the acquisition, licensing, and production of such content. Cost of revenues in the domestic DVD segment consist primarily of delivery expenses such as packaging and postage costs, content expenses, and other expenses associated with the company's DVD processing and customer service centers.

Note 2: The company defined contribution margin as revenues less cost of revenues and marketing expenses incurred by segment.

Source: Company 2017 10-K Report, pp. 19–22 and pp. 59–61.

The Domestic and International Streaming Options
Netflix launched its Internet streaming service in January 2007, with instant-watching capability for 2,000 titles on personal computers. Very quickly, Netflix invested aggressively to enable its software to instantly stream content to a growing number of "Netflix-ready" devices, including video game consoles (made by Sony, Microsoft, and Nintendo), Internet-connected DVD and Blu-ray players, Internet-connected TVs, TiVo DVRs, and special Netflix players made by Roku and several other electronics manufacturers. At the same time, it began licensing increasing amounts of digital content that could be instantly streamed to subscribers. Initially, Netflix took a "metered" approach to streaming, in essence offering an hour per month of instant watching on a PC for every dollar of a subscriber's monthly subscription plan. In 2010, Netflix switched to an unlimited streaming option on all of its monthly subscription plans. According to one source, Netflix had an estimated 6,800 movie titles and 530 TV shows available for streaming as of 2010.[3]

In recent years, however, Netflix had gradually shrunk the number of movie titles in its streaming library to approximately 4,000 as of early 2018 and dramatically increased the number of TV shows to an estimated 1,570 in 2018. Netflix had increased the number of new original content offerings in each of the past five years. There were two reasons for the

shift in the makeup of Netflix's streaming content. One reason was internal data showing that subscribers spent only about one-third of their time on Netflix watching movies; the second reason was a conviction on the part of Netflix's content executives that if viewers were passionate about a movie, they would have already seen it in theaters by the time it ended up on Netflix. To make the company's movie library more valuable for its subscribers, Netflix had begun releasing a progressively larger number of original movies (80 movies were scheduled for release in 2018) and creating more multi-episode original TV series like past hits *House of Cards, The Crown, Orange Is the New Black,* and *Stranger Things.* Going forward, Netflix was expected to continue to place greater emphasis on its own original content—both movies and original TV series—chiefly as a way to more strongly differentiate itself from competitors; top management had announced its intention to spend $7 to $8 billion on original content in 2018, up from $6 billion in 2017.

Netflix's Strategy

Netflix's strategy in 2018 was focused squarely on:

• Growing the number of domestic and international streaming subscribers.

• Enhancing the appeal of its library of streaming content, with an increasing emphasis on exclusive original movies and TV series produced in-house.

- Spending aggressively on marketing and advertising in all of the countries and geographic regions the company had recently entered to broaden awareness of the Netflix brand and service and thereby support the company's strategic objective to rapidly grow its base of streaming subscribers.
- Expanding the number of titles that members could download for offline viewing.
- Continuously enhancing its user interface.

Subscriber Growth   Netflix executives were keenly aware that rapid subscriber growth was the key to boosting the company's profitability and justifying the company's lofty stock price of $330 (as of late April 2018), which was an astonishing 264 times the company's 2017 earnings per share and 71 times the consensus EPS of $4.65 that Wall Street analysts and Netflix investors were anticipating the company would earn in 2019. Netflix executives expected that close to 75 percent of the gains in subscriber growth in 2018 and over 80 percent of the gains in 2019 and beyond would come in the international arena.

New Content Acquisition   Over the years, Netflix had spent considerable time and energy establishing strong ties with various entertainment video providers to both expand its content library and gain access to new releases as soon as possible after they were released for first-run showing in movie theaters. Prior to the recent push by Amazon Prime and Hulu to attract streaming subscribers, Netflix had successfully negotiated *exclusive* rights to show titles produced by a few studios.

In August 2011, Netflix introduced a new "Just for Kids" section on its website that contained a large selection of kid-friendly movies and TV shows. By March 2012, over one billion hours of Just for Kids programming had been streamed to Netflix members.

New content was acquired from movie studios and distributors through direct purchases, revenue-sharing agreements, and licensing agreements to stream content. Netflix acquired many of its new-release movie DVDs from studios for a low upfront fee in exchange for a commitment for a defined period of time either to share a percentage of subscription revenues or to pay a fee based on content utilization. After the revenue-sharing period expired for a title, Netflix generally had the option of returning the title to the studio, purchasing the title, or destroying its copies of the title. On occasion, Netflix also purchased DVDs for a fixed fee per disc from various studios, distributors, and other suppliers.

In the case of movie titles and TV episodes that were streamed to subscribers via the Internet for instant viewing, Netflix generally paid a fee to license the content for a defined period of time, with the total fees spread out over the term of the license agreement (so as to match up content payments with the stream of subscription revenues coming in for that content). Following the expiration of the license term, Netflix either removed the content from its library of streamed offerings or negotiated an extension or renewal of the license agreement when management believed there was still enough subscriber interest in the content to justify the renewal fees.

Over the past five years, Netflix's rapidly growing subscriber base (as well as the streaming subscriber growth at Amazon Prime Video, Hulu, and other providers) gave movie studios and the network broadcasters of popular TV shows considerably more bargaining power to command higher prices for their content. Netflix management was acutely aware of its diminishing bargaining power in acquiring content that would be especially appealing to subscribers, and the substantial negative impact that paying higher prices for streaming content had on the company's current and future profit margins. Nonetheless, Netflix executives believed there was still room for the company to earn attractive profits on streaming if it could grow its subscriber base fast enough to more than cover the rising costs of content acquisition.

As indicated earlier, Netflix had recently begun devoting the majority of its new content acquisition budget to producing its own original movies and TV series in-house. Several of these shows were being launched in local languages with local producers to appeal directly, if not exclusively, to subscribers in a particular country or region. A new 2017 Brazilian science-fiction show had scored well with audiences around the world, even though it had been produced in Portuguese for Brazil—Netflix's first instance of a local-language program working well in locations where other languages dominated. In the second half of 2018, Netflix introduced a new original series produced in Denmark, called *The Rain,* that Netflix executives believed would have broad global appeal, along with the second season of the Brazilian program (called *3%*). Other new original content scheduled for 2018 included the second season of *13 Reasons Why* (one of Netflix's most watched television shows around the world in 2017), returning seasons of hits like *Luke Cage, GLOW, Dear White People, Unbreakable Kimmy Schmidt, Santa Clarita Diet, Series of Unfortunate Events,* and a comedy feature film with Adam Sandler and Chris Rock, called *The Week Of.*

Marketing and Advertising Netflix used multiple marketing approaches to attract subscribers, but especially online advertising (paid search listings, banner ads on social media sites, and permission-based e-mails), and ads on regional and national television. To spur subscriber growth, Netflix had boosted marketing expenditures of all kinds from $25.7 million in 2000 (16.8 percent of revenues) to $142.0 million in 2005 (20.8 percent of revenues) to $298.8 million in 2010 (13.8 percent of revenues) to $991.1 million in 2016 (11.2 percent of revenues), and to $1.278.0 billion in 2017 (10.9 percent of revenues). These expenditures related to:

- Online and television advertising in the United States and newly entered countries. Advertising campaigns of one type or another were underway more or less continuously, with the lure of one-month free trials and announcements of new and forthcoming original titles usually being the prominent ad features. Netflix's expenditures for digital and television advertising were $1,091.1 million in 2017, $842.4 million in 2016, and $714.3 million in 2015, several multiples higher than the $205.9 million spent in 2009.

- Costs pertaining to free trial subscriptions.

- Payments to the company's partners. These partners consisted mainly of (1) consumer products manufacturers who produced and distributed devices (particularly remote controls) that facilitated connecting TVs and other media equipment to Netflix, and (2) certain cable providers and other multichannel video programming distributors, mobile operators, and Internet service providers who had begun collaborating with Netflix to make it easy for their customers to connect to Netflix. For example, most all brands of Internet-connected TVs now came with a preinstalled Netflix app that was easily accessed via the TV remote; some TV remotes even had Netflix buttons that provided Netflix subscribers with a one-click connection to their watchlist.

In 2018, multi-channel TV providers like Comcast and Sky were offering customers the option to bundle a subscription to Netflix in with their preferred channel packages. Netflix believed collaboration with a host of cable and mobile phone operators across all geographic markets would likely become common practice very quickly. Management was particularly interested in partnering with mobile operators to create quick and easy-to-use procedures for mobile phone users across the world to access Netflix streamed or downloadable programming. Netflix believed it was particularly important to make mobile streaming from Netflix instantly accessible to those people who basically only wanted to have their relationship with Netflix on a mobile device.

In 2018, Netflix expected its growth in marketing expenditures to outpace revenue growth, partly because it had started investing in more extensive marketing campaigns for new original titles to create more density of viewing and conversation around each title. Netflix CEO Reed Hastings explained the logic behind trying to make certain new titles a bigger hit in a particular nation or among a particular demographic segment:

> We believe this density of viewing helps on both retention and acquisition, because it makes our original titles even less substitutable. Because we operate in so many countries, we are able to try different [marketing] approaches in different markets and continue to learn [how best to market Netflix's original content and differentiate Netflix from rival streaming providers].[4]

Netflix's Title Selection Software and Efforts to Enhance Its Interface with Users Netflix had developed proprietary software technology that allowed members to easily scan a movie's length, appropriateness for various types of audiences (G, PG, or R), primary cast members, genre, and an average of the ratings submitted by other subscribers (based on 1 to 5 stars). With one click, members could watch a short preview of a movie or TV show if they wished. Most importantly, perhaps, were algorithms that created a personalized 1- to 5-star recommendation for each title that was a composite of a subscribers' own ratings of movies/TV shows previously viewed, movies/TV shows that the member had placed on a "watchlist" for future viewing and/or mail delivery, and the overall or average rating of all subscribers (several billion ratings had been provided by subscribers over the years).

Subscribers often began their search for titles by viewing a list of several hundred personalized movie/TV show recommendations that Netflix's software automatically generated for each member. Each member's list of recommended movies was the product of Netflix-created algorithms that organized the company's entire content library into clusters of similar movies/TV shows and then sorted the titles in each cluster from most liked to least liked based on subscriber ratings. Those subscribers who favorably or unfavorably rated similar movies/TV shows in similar clusters were categorized as like-minded viewers. When a subscriber was online and browsing through the selections, the software was programmed to check the clusters the subscriber had previously viewed, determine which selections in each cluster the customer had yet to view or place on watchlist, and then display those titles in each cluster in an order that started with the title that Netflix's algorithms predicted the subscriber was most likely to enjoy down to the title the subscriber was predicted to least enjoy. In other words, the subscriber's ratings of titles viewed, the titles on the subscriber's watchlist, and the title ratings of all Netflix subscribers determined the order in which the available titles in each cluster or genre were displayed to a subscriber—with one click, subscribers could see a brief profile of each title and Netflix's predicted rating (from 1 to 5 stars) for the subscriber. When subscribers came upon a title they wanted to view, that title could be watch-listed for future viewing with a single click. A member's complete watchlist of titles was immediately viewable with one click whenever the member went to Netflix's website. With one additional click, any title on a member's watchlist could be activated

for immediate viewing. Netflix management saw its title recommendation software as a quick and personalized means of helping subscribers identify and then watch titles they were likely to enjoy.

In 2018, Netflix' strategic initiatives in the user interface arena were focused on enhancing the accessibility of Netflix content for subscribers by (1) offering more programs in local languages and (2) improving the streaming and download speeds for subscribers with suboptimal Internet connections—by making program encoding much more efficient so content selections would load more quickly and provide mobile users with a "really incredible video experience."[5] More efficient encoding also enabled subscribers with spotty Internet connections to quickly download some programs for later viewing when offline.

The Financial Strain of Netflix's Growing Expenditures for Original Content and Other Content Acquisitions

The company's heightened strategic emphasis on original content produced in-house had resulted in multi-billion-dollar annual increases in Netflix's financial obligations to pay for streaming content and sharply higher negative cash flows from operations (see Exhibit 6). Netflix was covering these obligations with new issues of common stock and new issues of senior notes (Exhibit 6); details of Netflix's outstanding senior notes are shown in Exhibit 7.

EXHIBIT 6   The Growing Financial Strain of Netflix's Strategic Emphasis on Producing Original Content In-House, 2013–2017

	2017	2016	2015	2014	2013
Streaming content obligations at year-end	$17,694.6	$14,479.5	$10,902.2	$9,451.1	$7,252.2
Additions to streaming content assets	9,805.8	8,653.3	5,771.6	3,773.0	3,030.7
Additions to DVD content assets	53.7	77.2	78.0	74.8	65.9
Amortization of streaming content assets	6,197.8	4,788.5	3,405.4	2,656.3	2,122.0
Amortization of DVD content assets	60.7	79.0	79.4	71.9	71.3
Net cash used in operating activities	(1,785.9)	(1,474.0)	(749.4)	16.4	97.8
Proceeds from issuance of debt	3,020.5	1,000.0	1,500.0	400.0	500.0
Proceeds from issuance of common stock	88.4	37.0	78.0	60.5	124.6
Outstanding senior notes	6,499.4	3,364.3	2,371.4	885.8	500.0

Source: Company 10-K Reports 2017, 2016, 2015, 2014, and 2013.

EXHIBIT 7 Netflix's Outstanding Long-Term Debt as of May 2018

Debt Issues	Principal Amount at Par	Issue Date	Maturity Date	Interest Due Dates
5.875% Senior Notes	$1.9 billion	April 2018	November 2028	April 15 and November 15
4.875% Senior Notes	$1.6 billion	October 2017	April 2028	April 15 and October 15
3.625% Senior Notes	$1.561 billion	May 2017	May 2027	May 15 and November 15
4.375% Senior Notes	$1.0 billion	October 2016	November 2026	May 15 and November 15
5.50% Senior Notes	$700 million	February 2015	February 2022	April 15 and October 15
5.875% Senior Notes	$800 million	February 2015	February 2025	April 15 and October 15
5.750% Senior Notes	$400 million	February 2014	March 2024	March 1 and September 1
5.375% Senior Notes	$500 million	February 2013	February 2021	February 1 and August 1

Sources: Company press release April 23, 2018 and Company 2017 10-K Report, p. 51.

Netflix management forecasted that the company would a have a negative cash flow of $3 to $4 billion in 2018 and would also be cash flow negative for several more years beyond as expenditures for original content continued to grow. In April 2018, CEO Reed Hastings said:

We will continue to raise debt as needed to fund our increase in original content. Our debt levels are quite modest as a percentage of our enterprise value, and we believe [issuing] debt is [a] lower cost of capital compared to equity.[6]

ENDNOTES

[1] Transcript of remarks by David Wells, Netflix's Chief Financial Officer, at Morgan Stanley, Technology, Media & Telecom Conference, February 27, 2018, www.netflix.com (accessed April 5, 2018).

[2] Joe Flint, Erich Schwartzel, and Sara Nassauer, "Walmart Explores Its Own Streaming Service," *Wall Street Journal,*

July 28, 2018, posted at www.wsj.com, accessed July 31, 2018.

[3] Travis Clark, "New Data Shows Netflix's Number of Movies Has Gone Down by Thousands of Titles since 2010 — But Its TV Catalog Size Has Soared," *Business Insider,* February 20, 2018, www.businessinsider.com (accessed April 16, 2018).

[4] As quoted in the transcript of the company's conference call announcing the company's financial results in the first quarter of 2018, April 16, 2018, www.seekingalpha.com (accessed April 30, 2018).

[5] Ibid.

[6] Company press release, April 16, 2018.

Walmart's Expansion into Specialty Online Retailing

Rochelle R. Brunson
Baylor University

Marlene M. Reed
Baylor University

For the company that began as a discount retailer in small town USA, Walmart's strategic moves from 2016 through 2018 indicated a possible departure from its traditional brick and mortar retailing strategy targeting price-conscious shoppers. Its series of acquisitions of upscale online retailers and the launch of an online business selling high-end mattresses and bedding signaled management's acknowledgement that the company was at a strategic inflection point. The company had ended 2017 as the world's largest retailer with global revenues of nearly $486 billion, but the growth of Amazon and an increasing consumer preference for online shopping caused Walmart to evaluate its brick and mortar strategy. The company had responded to Amazon's success with the introduction of new services such as Store Pickup for everyday items and Curbside Pickup for groceries, but its series of acquisitions of online retailers during the 2016 to 2018 period reflected an acknowledgment by Walmart management that consumers not only wanted low prices, but also wanted maximum convenience and uniquely differentiated products.

COMPANY HISTORY

When Sam Walton was a franchisee of a Ben Franklin variety store in the late 1940s, he had an idea of how this type of retailer could be more profitable. He had been successful in negotiating good deals with suppliers, so he reasoned that instead of leaving his store prices the same and increasing his earnings, he could lower prices on his products and pass the savings along to customers. He believed by following this strategy, he could increase the volume of his sales and become even more profitable. Walton offered his idea to the Ben

Franklin management, but they were not interested. Therefore, he and his brother opened their Walton's 5 & 10 in 1950 in Bentonville, Arkansas. Later, he and his brother decided to open their own stores, and the first Walmart store was opened in 1962 in Rogers, Arkansas.

Another part of Walton's strategy was to focus solely on small town populations that he thought would welcome a large discount store. The Walton brothers typically opened stores in towns with populations of 5,000 to 25,000, and the stores drew from a large radius.[1] By the end of the 1960s, the Walton brothers had opened 18 Walmart stores while still owning 15 Ben Franklin franchises in Arkansas, Missouri, Kansas, and Oklahoma. All of these ventures became incorporated as Walmart stores in 1969.[2]

The company went public in 1970 trading over the counter, and then in 1972 the stock was listed on the New York Stock Exchange. At this time, the company began building its own warehouses in order to have the ability to order large quantities and store the merchandise. As a result of this tactic, they decided to build stores in a 200 square mile radius around the warehouses/distribution centers.

In 1983, the company opened its first three Sam's Wholesale Clubs and began moving into larger city markets. Four years later, the company acquired 18 Supersaver Wholesale Clubs that were converted into Sam's Clubs. By 1991, the company had 148 Sam's Clubs, which were 100,000 square foot discount membership warehouse clubs that stimulated the growth of warehouse clubs in the 1990s and into the 21st century.

The company became the center of criticism in 1990. Owners of small businesses in the towns where Walmart operated suggested that they were being driven out of business because they could not compete with the store's economies of scale. However, the criticism did not affect the company's revenues, and during the 1990s the store became the number one retailer in the United States. The company had now moved beyond small towns into large cities. In 1991, the company ventured outside the United States for the first time by entering into a joint venture with Cifra, S.A. de C.V., the largest retailer in Mexico. By 2018, over 260 million customers were shopping at Walmart's 11,723 stores in 28 countries each year.

By 2018, Walmart was not only the largest retailer in the world but also the largest corporation in the world. Within the United States, Walmart had more than 1.2 million employees, 1,478 Walmart discount stores in all 50 states, 1,471 Walmart Supercenters that were combined discount outlets and grocery stores, 538 Sam's Clubs, and 64 Walmart Neighborhood Markets. During 2017, Walmart had revenues of $485.6 billion while employing 2.3 million associates throughout the world. The company's consolidated income statements for 2015 through 2017 are presented in Exhibit 1. Exhibit 2 presents Walmart's consolidated balance sheets for 2015 through 2017.

EXHIBIT 1 Walmart's Consolidated Income Statements 2015–2017 (amounts in millions except for share data)

	Years Ended January 31		
	2017	2016	2015
Revenues:			
Net sales	$481,317	$478,614	$482,229
Membership & other income	4,556	3,516	3,422
Total Revenues	485,873	482,130	485,651
Costs & Expenses:			
Cost of sales	361,256	360,984	365,086
Operating, selling G&A expenses	101,853	97,041	93,418
Operating Income:	22,764	24,105	27,147
Interest:			
Debt	2,004	2,017	2,161
Capital lease & financing	323	521	300
Interest income	(100)	(81)	(113)
Net interest	2,267	2,467	2,348
Income from continuing operations	20,497	21,638	24,799
Provision for income taxes	6,204	6,558	7,985
Income from continuing operations	14,293	15,080	16,814
Income from discontinued operations	–	–	285
Consolidated net income	14,293	15,080	17,090
Consolidated income attributable to noncontrolling interest	(650)	(386)	(736)
Consolidated income attributable to Walmart	$13,643	$14,694	$16,363
Basic net income per common share	$4.40	$4.58	$5.01

Source: Walmart Inc. 2017 10-K.

EXHIBIT 2   Walmart's Consolidated Balance Sheets 2016–2017 (amounts in millions)

	As of January 31	
	2016	2017
Assets		
Current assets:		
Cash and cash equivalents	$ 6,867	$ 8,705
Receivables, net	5,835	5,624
Inventories	43,046	44,469
Prepaid expenses	1,941	1,441
Total current assets	57,689	60,239
Property and equipment	179,492	176,958
Less accumulated depreciation	(71,782)	(66,787)
Property and equipment, net	107,710	110,171
Property under capital lease and financing obligations	11,637	11,096
Less accumulated amortization	(5,169)	(4,751)
Property under capital lease and financing obligations, net	6,468	6,345
Goodwill	17,037	16,695
Other assets and deferred charges	9,921	6,131
Total assets	$198,825	$199,581
Liabilities and equity		
Current liabilities:		
Short-term borrowing	$ 1,099	$ 2,708
Accounts payable	41,433	38,487
Accrued liabilities	20,654	19,607
Accrued income taxes	921	521
Long-term debt due within one year	2,256	2,745
Capital lease and financing obligations due within one year	565	551
Total current liabilities	66,928	64,619
Long-term debt	36,015	38,214
Long-term capital lease and financing obligations	6,003	3,816
Deferred income taxes and other	9,344	7,321
Equity		
Common stock	305	317
Capital in excess of par value	2,371	1,805

	As of January 31	
	2016	2017
Retained earnings	89,354	90,021
Accumulated other comprehensive loss	(14,232)	(11,597)
Total Walmart shareholders' equity	77,798	80,546
Nonredeemable noncontrolling interest	2,737	3,065
Total equity	80,535	83,611
Total liabilities and equity	$198,825	$199,581

Source: Walmart Inc. 2017 10-K.

WALMART'S ACQUISITIONS OF ONLINE RETAILERS, 2016 THROUGH 2018

From 2016 to 2018, Walmart had followed a strategy of increasing its online presence in order to compete with its largest competitor—Amazon. The acquisitions were an attempt to reach urban Millennials that Walmart had not been able to reach in the past. The retail behemoth's average customer was less wealthy, much older, and less urban than the customer who normally shops at Target and Amazon. Walmart vowed that it would not invest billions building its digital presence while reducing new store openings. Exhibit 3 presents a list of the acquisitions the company made between 2016 and 2018.

Jet.com

In 2015, **Jet.com** (an online retailer) was launched by e-commerce pioneer, Marc Lore. The mission of the company was to compete in the crowded online marketplace against the leader, Amazon. From the company's headquarters in Hoboken, New Jersey, Lore was able to raise $500 million in venture capital funding from Goldman Sachs, Fidelity, Google Ventures, Forerunner Ventures, and Bain Capital.

The Jet target customer was a Millennial, urban dweller, with a higher income. The company promoted such products as La Croix seltzer, fresh produce, and ethical cleaning products. Just 13 months after its launch, Walmart purchased the company for $3 billion in an all-cash transaction in August 2016. Walmart made Jet a wholly-owned subsidiary. An immediate concern of Jet's customers was whether the products they ordered from the company would arrive in a Walmart blue box instead of the purple Jet box, but the company continued to use the purple Jet box.

Jet.com was a reseller of Apple products, including the iPhone, whereas Amazon carried some Apple products including Mac computers but not the iPhone, iPad, and Apple Watch. Those products were sold by third-party companies. This gave **Jet.com** and Walmart an advantage over Amazon with Apple products.[3]

In terms of Internet sales, in 2017 **Walmart.com** had $14 billion while Amazon had $83 billion. Jet had a customer base of more than 400,000 new shoppers being added monthly and an average of 25,000 daily processed orders. In addition, the company used the most innovative technology that rewards customers with savings on products that were bought and shipped together. This practice reduced the supply chain and logistics costs that were often hidden in the price of products.

EXHIBIT 3 Timeline of Acquisitions and Allswell Launch

August 2016	Jan. 2017	Feb. 2017	March 2017	June 2017	Feb. 2018	May 2018
Jet.com	ShoeBuy	Moosejaw	Modcloth	Bonobos	Allswell	Flipkart

Since this deal was completed, Walmart's e-commerce sales climbed 63 percent. Meanwhile, Walmart's online inventory had grown from 10 million items to 67 million items. The company was also leveraging its brick and mortar stores by expanding grocery pickup service to more than 1,000 stores and the provision for customer discounts on select items if they pick them up at the store. This allows them to compete with Amazon's purchase of Whole Foods.

The strategy for Walmart appears to be to allow Jet to focus on urban Millennial customers—especially those in New York, Chicago, Boston, and other large cities—while Walmart continued to target the rest of the country. One change in the culture of Jet occurred after the purchase by Walmart. Whereas Jet had originally hosted Thursday evening happy hours for employees, Walmart put an end to the practice because of their policy against drinking on the job.

ShoeBuy

In January of 2017, the Canadian e-commerce retailer of footwear **Shoes.com** closed down its operations, which included its websites **Shoes.com**, OnlineShoes, and ShoeMe.ca and its two brick and mortar stores in Vancouver and Toronto. At that time, Walmart stepped in and paid $9 million for the **Shoes.com** web address that directs its **ShoeBuy .com** unit. In 2015, computer hardware for the first time took a back seat to apparel and accessories as the leading category for e-commerce. ShoeBuy was a leading online footwear and clothing retailer. The company was founded in 1999 and was one of the first companies to sell shoes online. The company was headquartered in Boston, Massachusetts, and Walmart decided to continue to base the company there and to leave the executive team and over 200 employees in place. This move was another part of Walmart's strategy to compete with Amazon who had bought Zappos, an online shoe retailer, in 2009 for $1.2 billion. Zappos generated over $2 billion annually in sales.

Moosejaw

Moosejaw was founded in 1992 in Michigan and was headquartered in Madison Heights, Michigan. The company was not only a leading e-commerce site for outdoor enthusiasts, but they also operated 10 brick and mortar stores. The company carried brands such as Patagonia, The North Face, Marmot, and Arc'teryx. Their lines included an assortment of gear and clothing for camping, climbing, hiking, yoga, biking, swimming, and all of the snow sports. The company had strong industry relationships and offered a wide assortment of products.

On February 13, 2017, Walmart acquired Moosejaw. This acquisition was a part of the company's growing line of e-commerce operations. In addition to Moosejaw's online presence, it also had 10 physical stores. Walmart paid $51 million for the company and expects Moosejaw to continue to run as a standalone operation complementary to Walmart's other e-commerce sites. It was anticipated that Moosejaw, a leader in social media, would help Walmart compete for Millennials. The company was number 261 on *Internet Retailer's* top 500 stores in 2017.

Moosejaw's 350 employees and its CEO Eoin Comerford would remain in Michigan. One of the goals of this purchase by Walmart was to gain a competitive advantage against Amazon in the sporting goods category. Although Walmart's retail stores have a sporting goods department, the price points were on the lower end in the brick and mortar stores due to the limited amount of space and number of products that can be stocked. Walmart's e-commerce site carried more price points, but the acquisition of Moosejaw would expand the outdoor/sporting goods category to a new customer that Walmart was not currently reaching.

2016 was an extremely competitive year for outdoor retailers. In May, Sports Authority was liquidated after being unsuccessful in its quest to find a buyer. In addition, Eastern Mountain Sports filed for bankruptcy, and there was concern that Gander Mountain was in a financial crisis. Bass Pro Shops was in the process of acquiring Cabelas, and even Under Armour was finding the competition very difficult. Nike had its own issues by selling through their branded retail stores, website, Amazon, and still through their traditional retail customers who were beginning to complain that they were being bypassed as Nike was selling directly to the consumer.

Modcloth

This online company had a very interesting beginning and a quirky, vintage product line. Susan Gregg Koger started this company the summer before her freshman year in college out of her interest in vintage and thrift store clothing. She taught herself how to build a website and stocked apparel for women who were nerdy without shame. Her high school sweetheart, who would become her husband, helped her grow the company. The company continually gathered feedback from their customers through the use of social media and email.

Then in January of 2015, some venture capitalists and a new CEO named Matthew Kaness took over the store. Kaness had previously been the Chief Strategy Officer of Urban Outfitters. The new leaders abruptly began to change the culture of the online store. Kaness launched a new program called "Be the Buyer," which allowed the customers to decide which products the company would keep and which ones they would drop. In addition, whereas the founder had specifically focused on clothing for the plus-size woman who was normally underserved, the new leadership began scaling back on offering the larger sizes. Many of the Modcloth's customers and employees began to complain about the new direction of the company.

In March of 2017, Walmart purchased Modcloth for approximately $75 million. This was a boon to Modcloth, which formerly had relied on venture capitalists for funding, but now were being financed by the world's largest retailer. Walmart knew that a company often had to tie up money along the supply chain to get the best costs on fabrics six to nine months out.

An interesting departure for Walmart (and Modcloth) occurred on Black Friday of 2017. Traditionally, Black Friday (the day after Thanksgiving) had been known to be the biggest day in sales for retailers. Although Walmart had found in the past that the day after Thanksgiving was its biggest day of the year, Modcloth chose to close its operations that day and donate clothes valued at $5 million to a nonprofit organization called "Dress for Success." That was the first time Modcloth had closed on Black Friday, and some observers speculated that they had not been able to close in the past because they did not have the backing of Walmart.

Bonobos

In 2017, Bonobos was launched selling chino pants on the Internet. Since then, the company had expanded its offerings assortment to include men's shirts and suits. The company was one of the leading apparel brands

introduced on the Internet in the United States. In addition, the company had opened dozens of brick and mortar stores (called "Guideshops"), and it had continued to place a great deal of emphasis on its generous shipping and return policies for online shopping.

Walmart, through its **Jet.com** brand, purchased Bonobos in June of 2017 for $310 million and plans to sell its products through its **Jet.com** site. This purchase, along with that of Modcloth, was a departure from Walmart's big box image. Bonobos was a premium-priced retailer that offers distinctive upscale fashions for men. These purchases suggest that Walmart was aggressively seeking to meet Amazon on its own playing field—the Internet. Lewis and Dart suggested, "Just as Walmart's deep pockets gave **Jet.com** a limitless runway, it will do the same for Bonobos. But the larger seismic event was that this was just one more step for Walmart in its quest to become Amazon's worst nightmare, while Amazon was doing another one-up with its acquisition of Whole Foods. This was just the beginning of the battle of the behemoths."[4] In the past, Walmart was viewed by observers as the leading grocery products retailer in the country. In 2008, Walmart's grocery business accounted for 47 percent of their revenues, and by 2015 this percentage had increased to 56 percent. However, rising food prices in 2018 were eroding their very thin profit margins in the SuperCenter stores.

A trend driving both Amazon and Walmart, as evidenced by their recent acquisitions, was channel of distribution consolidation. Bonobos had suggested that they have no plans to offer their $98 chinos or $128 dress shirts in Walmart's retail stores. The price point for Walmart's menswear was closer to $10 to $30. Neil Saunders, Managing Director of the research firm GlobalData Retail, suggested: "One of the reasons Walmart had acquired businesses like Jet and Bonobos was because they want to develop a premium offering that was very difficult to develop within the Walmart business. But it's very clear that these were separate vehicles—selling higher-end brands and pushing up price points. That really goes against the fundament tenets on which Walmart was built."[5]

Allswell

In February of 2018, Walmart launched its own mattress and bedding brand to be sold exclusively on the Internet through the website **AllswellHome.com**.

C-168 PART 2 Cases in Crafting and Executing Strategy

The mattress industry was worth $29 billion annually, and Walmart decided to enter that market at the higher end with products for discriminating customers. As a part of the company's enticement to consumers, Allswell was offering a 100-day free trial of its mattresses. The brand had two offerings of the memory foam mattress—The Softer One and The Firmer One. In addition, Allswell offers four limited-edition bedding sets called "Bedscapes." Allswell's king-sized mattress was named the "Supreme Queen" in honor of all women whom they believe deserve the highest honor.

The name "Allswell" was developed after management of the company held many conversations with women shoppers about how they wanted to feel at home before going to bed. Their duvets have a luxurious feeling that was the result of a blending of cotton and Tencel. All of the coverlets and blankets were stone washed to give them a textured feel. The price of mattresses ranges from $495 for a twin to $1,035 for a Supreme Queen. Bedding items range from $60 to $350.

Customers who buy Allswell products have the option of ground shipping or white glove delivery. In addition, the company will take away the customer's old mattress at no additional charge. The company had hired a large number of customer support agents that they call "Allstars." Later in February of 2018, Walmart made an announcement that they were planning to launch their own line of premium cosmetics on the Internet and was in talks with some high profile models to represent the line. The launching by Walmart of their own luxury bedding company online and the proposed launching of a premium cosmetic line online appeared to many to be a shift in strategy from simply acquiring high-end online stores to launching their own.

Flipkart

Flipkart was founded in 2007 by Sachin Bansal and Binny Bansal who were Computer Science majors at the Indian Institute of Technology in Delhi. They both worked at Amazon in 2006 as software engineers but left when they realized the opportunities of e-commerce in India. They started their e-commerce business in India five years before Amazon began their e-commerce operations in India in 2012. Within 10 years, Flipkart took over the following companies: WeRead, Chakpak, Mime360, Letsbuy.com, Myntra.com, Appiterate, Phonepe, Jabong, and

EBay.in. Flipkart operated as both a marketplace and a direct seller in the same way that Amazon does.

In May of 2018, Walmart agreed to acquire a 77 percent stake in Flipkart. Walmart suggested that their long-term goal was to support a public offering by Flipkart. Walmart's CEO, Doug McMillon, said the investment was to allow Walmart to become invested in the growing Indian economy.[6]

India's economy was rapidly growing and projected to replace China as the world's most populous country by the year 2024. By 2040, it was projected to be the second biggest economy behind China. Between 2004 and 2012, the Indian middle class doubled in population from 300 million to 600 million, which made it an even more attractive market for growth in the coming years.

WALMART'S MISSION AND GLOBAL ETHICS STATEMENTS

Walmart's mission statement came from the words of its founder, Sam Walton:

The secret of successful retailing was to give your customers what they want. And really, if you think about it from your point of view as a customer, you want everything: a wide assortment of good-quality merchandise; the lowest possible prices; guaranteed satisfaction with what you buy; friendly, knowledgeable service; convenient hours; free parking; a pleasant shopping experience.[7]

Walmart.com, established in January of 2000, was a subsidiary of Walmart Inc. This online organization espoused the same mission as the brick and mortar stores, but had one additional mission—providing easy access to more of Walmart, which was evident in the more than 1,000,000 products available online. The company's website suggests that it was passionate about combining the best of the two worlds—technology and world-class retailing.

Walmart's global ethics statement was the following:

Global ethics was responsible for promoting Walmart's culture of integrity. This included developing and upholding our policies for ethical behavior for all of our stakeholders everywhere we operate. But perhaps most importantly, it includes raising awareness of ethics policies and providing channels for stakeholders to bring ethics concerns to our attention. Global ethics serves as a guide and resource for ethical decision making, provides a confidential and anonymous reporting system, and leads a continuing education and communication system.[8]

CHANNEL AND BRAND CONSOLIDATION

A movement affecting many retailers today was channel and brand consolidation. This consolidation was often achieved by mergers and acquisitions. In terms of channel consolidation, there had been a movement by brick and mortar stores to buy companies that were operating online, and a reverse consolidation for companies operating on the Internet to either buy or establish brick and mortar operations. One example of this was Amazon, an online company, purchasing Whole Foods that had historically been a brick and mortar establishment. Perhaps the reason Whole Foods was willing to be purchased by an online company was the fact that consumers were distancing themselves from the traditional supermarket model. Customers desire a more intimate and innovating shopping experience such as that offered by online stores.

Channel consolidation, theoretically at least, may be much easier than brand consolidation. Through mergers and acquisitions, stores were finding it more difficult to create synergy and win customers over if the brands diverge sharply. An example of this and the risks inherent in brand consolidation was the following: "In the late 1980s, three brands dominated the U.S. cat food market: Kal Kan, Crave, and Sheba. Kal Kan and Crave were at the 'plain' end of the market; Sheba was at the 'gourmet" end. The first two merged, despite their different positionings, to create Whiskas. Five years later, when Whiskas had failed to achieve the combined market share of Kal Kan and Crave, the Kal Kan name was reintroduced on Whiskas packaging—but to only limited success."[9]

Another example of brand consolidation was Walmart teaming up with Lord & Taylor to launch a flagship store on **Walmart.com** in the spring of 2018. The specialized online experience offers premium fashion brands directly from Lord & Taylor. Denise Incandela, Head of Fashion, Walmart U.S. e-commerce, suggested, "Our goal was to create a premium fashion destination on **Walmart.com**. We see customers on our site searching for higher-end items, and we were expanding our business online to focus on adding specialized and premium shopping experiences, starting with fashion."[10]

THE FUTURE OF RETAILING FOR WALMART

Walmart carried a wide assortment of products on their website that a shopper would never find in their stores, but the average consumer didn't know this. An example was Ralph Lauren women's shoes, which were on the website but not in the stores. Neil Saunders, Global Data Retail Managing Director of Walmart suggested, "There were many demographics, especially younger and professional segments, for whom Walmart was not the destination of choice online. This isn't because it doesn't sell what they want or because the price or delivery options were suboptimal; instead, it was because they do not associate Walmart with online or they default to Amazon."[11] Walmart had revamped its website to look more like a "lifestyle" website instead of the former cramped pages of earlier versions of **Walmart.com**. Walmart management intended to make sure the Walmart customer knew that Walmart offers the lowest price possible. But management was also aware that online shoppers considered factors beyond price. The company had addressed the need for convenience with Store Pickup for online purchases of everyday items and Curbside Pickup for online purchases of groceries. Walmart had also revamped its website to connect to local store inventories based upon a user's geographic location.

While Walmart's strategies to capitalize on opportunities in online retailing and defend against the threat of Amazon, revenues from these business units were only a small fraction of its approximate revenues of $486 billion in 2017. In addition, some analysts were undecided how Millennials would view Walmart's acquisition of a favorite upscale retail brand such as Shoe.Buy, Moosejaw, Modcloth, Bonobos, Flipkart, and even the startup Allswell. Walmart's management and investors would learn in time if the billions spent on the acquisition of these companies would be enough to position this "small town 5 & 10 retailer" that Sam Walton started in the 1950s into a competitor for Amazon and Alibaba on the global online retailing playing field.

ENDNOTES

[1] Frank, T. A., "A Brief History of Walmart," *Washington Monthly,* April 2006.

[2] Walmart website, Background Information on Walmart Stores, Inc., **http://www.walmart.com**.

[3] Leswing, Kif, "Walmart Just Scored a Huge Victory over Amazon with Apple's Help," *Business Insider,* May 9, 2018.

[4] Lewis, Robin, and Dart, Michael, *The New Rule of Retail: Competing in the World's Toughest Marketplace,* 2nd edition, Macmillan Publishing Company, 2014.

[5] Bhattarai, Abha, "Walmart Was Launching Online Bedding, Cosmetic Brands in Bid for Upscale Shoppers," *Washington Post,*

February 26, 2018, **https://www.washingtonpost .com/business/economy/walmart/**.

[6] Browne, Ryan, "Walmart Strikes Deal to Buy a Majority Stake in India's Flipkart," *CNBC.com,* May 9, 2018, **https://www .cnbc.com/2018/05/09/walmart-agrees deal-to-buy-majority-stake-in-indias flipkart/**.

[7] Walmart.com's History and Mission, accessed at **http://help.walmart.com/ app/answers/detail/a_id/6/~/walmart. coms-history-and-mission**.

[8] **https://corporate.walmart.com/our-story/ ethics-integrity**.

[9] Knudsen, Trond Riiber, Finskud, Lars, Tornblom, Richard, and Hogna, Egil, "Brand Consolidation Makes a Lot of Economic Sense," *The McKinsey Quarterly,* Number 4, p.191, 1997.

[10] Grill-Goodman, Jill, "As Walmart's Online Sales Soar It Pushes Into Premium Fashion," November 17, 2017, **https://risnews.com/ walmarts-online-sales-soar-it-pushes-into premium-fashion/**.

[11] Forbes, Thom, "As a Start, Home Was Where Walmart's Digital-Shopping Heart Is," *Mediapost.com,* February 22, 2018, **https://www.mediapost.com/publications/ article/314974/**.

CASE 16

Amazon.com, Inc.: Driving Disruptive Change in the U.S. Grocery Market

Syeda Maseeha Qumer
ICFAI Business School, Hyderabad

Debapratim Purkayastha
ICFAI Business School, Hyderabad

On June 16, 2017, Seattle-based e-commerce giant Amazon.com, Inc. acquired Whole Foods Market, Inc., one of the leading natural and organic foods supermarket chains in the United States, in an all-cash transaction valued at approximately $13.7 billion. According to analysts, the deal touted to be Amazon's biggest acquisition to date, marked a turning point in the company's strategic efforts to crack the $800 billion U.S. grocery market. The deal also marked Amazon's big entry into the brick-and-mortar retail space. The shares of big box retailers such as Wal-Mart Stores, Inc,[1] Target Corporation,[2] Costco Wholesale Corporation,[3] and The Kroger Co[4] tanked with investors worrying about the far-reaching implications of the deal.

> "By purchasing Whole Foods, Amazon is set to disrupt the $800-billion grocery market in the same way it upended the publishing and consumer electronics industries. Now Amazon is right where it wants to be: everywhere. It has surpassed its original goal of being the 'everything store' and is fast on its way to becoming the 'everything everywhere' store,"[5]

said Sean Kervin practice director, customer experience, at Clear Peak, a management & analytics consulting firm.

Jeff Bezos, CEO of Amazon, realized that the e-commerce giant could not win the grocery game with its pure online format. He saw brick-and-mortar stores playing a key role and hence acquired Whole Foods. In addition, by early 2018 Amazon also rolled out a high-tech convenience store format sans cashiers or check-out lines called Amazon Go and AmazonFresh

Store Pickup Services. According to some analysts, while grocery was a huge opportunity for Amazon, operating in this new business might pose some new challenges including intense competition, razor thin margins, delivery of perishables, and bringing the convenience of digital shopping to the grocery business.[6] Some analysts felt that Bezos was taking a risk by making a major investment in an unsteady operation like Whole Foods, which could potentially be a drag on the e-tailer. They wondered—Can Amazon eventually change the way customers buy groceries? Can it manage brick-and-mortar well and redefine convenience? Can Amazon disrupt the grocery industry and the broader retail sector in a major way?

COMPANY BACKGROUND

Amazon was founded in June 1994 by Jeff Bezos. He came up with the idea of selling books to a mass audience via the Internet. In June 1995, Bezos launched his online bookstore, Amazon.com, named after the Amazon River. At the beginning, Amazon's business model was based on the "sell all, carry few" strategy where Amazon offered more than a million books online, though it actually stocked only about 2,000. The remaining titles were sourced predominantly through drop-shipping wherein Amazon forwarded customer orders to book publishers, who then shipped the products directly to the consumers.

©IBS Center for Management Research

Over a period of time, Bezos realized that his earlier business model would not sustain the kind of growth he was looking for and decided to diversify. In 1998, Amazon expanded beyond books to include all sorts of shippable consumer goods such as electronics, videos, and toys and games. This led to a reversal of its business model from a "sell all, carry few" strategy to a "sell all, carry more" model. In early 2000, Amazon started offering technology services through its e-commerce platform called Amazon Enterprise Solutions. Over the years, Amazon disrupted the online retail industry and transformed itself from an e-commerce player to a powerful digital media platform focused on growth and innovation. Amazon's business model was based on capturing growth through innovative disruption. The four pillars of Amazon's business model were low prices, wide selection, convenience, and customer service.

Bezos was the key architect in building a customer-centric company, transforming Amazon from a modest Internet brand into a tech behemoth as the company moved into completely new product categories such as e-readers and enterprise cloud computing services. In 2002, Amazon identified a new area of growth by launching Amazon Web Services (AWS), a platform of computing services offered online for other websites or client-side applications by Amazon. In 2005, Amazon launched a free shipping program for its customers called Amazon Prime,[7] wherein customers received free two-day shipping on their purchases for a fee of $79 per year. According to industry observers, the program disrupted the retail industry by enveloping more customers into its fold and enhancing customer loyalty.

In 2006, Amazon developed a new business model aimed at serving an entirely different customer—the third-party seller. The company offered fulfillment services to sellers through the Fulfillment by Amazon (FBA) program under which merchants sent cartons of their products to Amazon's warehouses while Amazon took the orders online, shipped the products, answered queries, and processed returns. In late 2007, Amazon set up its research division Lab126 and launched the Kindle e-book reader. The e-book reader was a business model not only alien to Amazon but also potentially disruptive to the publishing industry.

In July 2009, Amazon acquired U.S.-based online shoe retailer Zappos. In 2012, it forayed into the world of designer fashion, selling high-end clothing, shoes, handbags, and accessories through its website Amazon Fashion. In April 2014, the company entered into the highly competitive video and games streaming market by releasing Fire TV. Three months later, in an ambitious strategic move, Amazon debuted in the crowded smartphone market with the launch of the Fire Phone, which, however, failed to make a mark. The same year, Amazon launched Echo, a hands-free speaker that could be controlled with voice from across the room for information, music, news, sports scores, and weather.

In order to bring the company closer to customers, Amazon opened its first physical store on the campus of Purdue University in West Lafayette, Indiana, in February 2015. It also began testing a drone delivery service. In June 2015, Amazon invested $100 million to launch its first standalone corporate venture capital unit called Alexa Fund, which funded Alexa Voice Service, the cloud-based voice service that powered Amazon Echo.

In 2016, Amazon's net sales increased 27 percent to $136.0 billion, compared to $107 billion in 2015. The company's sales increased an additional 25 percent between 2016 and 2017 to reach $118.6 billion (see Exhibit 1).

AMAZON'S ENTRY INTO GROCERY

Groceries, though the second largest category of retail sales after general merchandise in the United States, represented one of the largest and most under-penetrated markets for Amazon. According to a 2016 Euromonitor study, aggregate sales in the U.S. grocery market were $781.5 billion. However, grocery was a heavily capital-intensive business with intense competition and tight margins. Despite the challenges, Bezos wanted Amazon to establish its presence in the grocery sector as he sought to make his company the "everything store." Amazon forayed into the grocery business in 2007 by launching AmazonFresh, an online grocery delivery service that allowed customers to order fresh produce and groceries online. Customers could order from more than 500,000 items for same-day and early morning delivery. The AmazonFresh service was available exclusively to Prime members in select cities in the U.S. for an additional monthly membership fee of $14.99.

However, AmazonFresh faced problems inherent in the home delivery service including excessive wastage of food, management of refrigerated

EXHIBIT 1 **Amazon Inc. Consolidated Statement of Operations, 2014–2017 (in millions of $, except per share data)**

	2017	2016	2015	2014
Net product sales	$118,573	$94,665	$79,268	$70,080
Net service sales	59,293	41,322	27,738	18,908
Total net sales	177,866	135,987	107,006	88,988
Operating expenses				
Cost of sales	111,934	88,265	71,651	62,752
Fulfilment	25,249	17,619	13,410	10,766
Marketing	10,069	7,233	5,254	4,332
Technology and content	22,620	16,085	12,540	9,275
General and administrative	3,674	2,432	1,747	1,552
Other operating expenses, net	214	167	171	133
Total operating expenses	173,760	131,801	104,773	88,810
Operating income	4,106	4,186	2,233	178
Interest income	202	100	50	39
Interest expense	(848)	(484)	(459)	(210)
Other income (expenses), net	346	90	(256)	(118)
Total non-operating income (expense)	(300)	(294)	(665)	(289)
Income (loss) before income taxes	3,806	3,892	1,568	(111)
Provision for income taxes	(769)	(1,425)	(950)	(167)
Equity-method investment activity, net of tax	(4)	(96)	(22)	37
Net income (loss)	$ 3,033	$ 2,371	$ 596	$ (241)
Basic earnings per share	$6.32	$5.01	$1.28	$(0.52)
Diluted earnings per share	$6.15	$4.90	$1.25	$(0.52)
Weighted average shares used in computation of earnings per share				
Basic	480	474	467	462
Diluted	493	484	477	462

Source: Amazon.com, Inc., 10K report.

warehouses, hiring additional delivery people in each new market, and logistical complexities. The high cost of the losses caused by food spoilage was an issue with AmazonFresh that the company had never faced with its other businesses. Moreover, the customers' desire for a personal experience, reluctance to have someone else picking their items, and its pricey membership model were some of the factors that limited the expansion of AmazonFresh (see Exhibit 2). According to Neil Saunders, managing director of GlobalData Retail, *"As much as we believe [AmazonFresh] has solid long-term potential, we think the logistical complexities and the low margin nature*

of grocery mean that it will be an expensive drag on profits for the foreseeable future."[8]

For about six years, the company tested and refined various operating models of AmazonFresh and the business extended to most of Seattle. In 2013, AmazonFresh expanded to Los Angeles and San Francisco and continued to experiment in these new cities with different subscription, fulfillment, and delivery models. For instance, AmazonFresh's free loyalty program in Seattle called "Big Radish" offered free or discounted delivery based on a customer's total spending within a certain time period and the order size. The subscription model in Los Angeles and

EXHIBIT 2   Survey of Consumer Barriers to U.S. Online Grocery Purchases, 2015

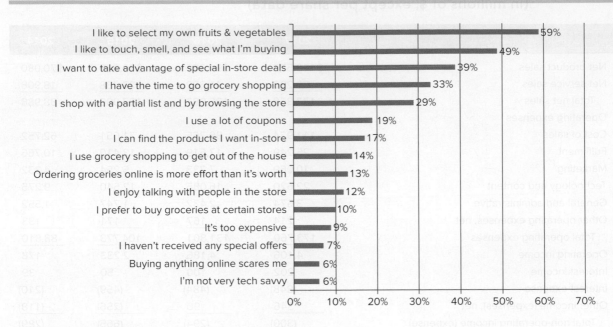

Source: http://www.businessinsider.com.

San Francisco called "Prime Fresh" was an upgraded version of Prime.

Following a lukewarm response to AmazonFresh, Amazon launched Prime Pantry in 2014. This service allowed Prime members to shop for groceries and household products in everyday package sizes rather than bulk for a flat $5.99 delivery fee per box. Through Prime Pantry, Amazon could expand its selection and offer thousands of items to Prime members that were otherwise prohibitively costly to ship for free individually. In December 2014, Amazon launched Prime Now under which items were delivered to the customers within two hours of ordering without any added shipping cost. Exclusively available to Prime members, Amazon further expanded the offering to include one-hour delivery from local stores offering items such as groceries, prepared meals, and bakery items. For reordering frequently used household items and groceries, Amazon launched the Dash Button in March 2015. Dash Buttons were available to Prime members for $4.99 each. With Dash, customers could scan items at home, in store, or even on the move and add them to their basket. Reportedly, orders using Dash Buttons were placed more than

four times a minute, which worked out to about 5,760 orders daily.

Though Amazon has been building up its online grocery delivery services, the business did not gain much traction. According to Nielsen online, only 4.5 percent of shoppers made frequent online grocery purchases in 2016, slightly up from 4.2 percent in 2013. While the total grocery market was worth $781.5 billion in 2016, online sales represented just $9.7 billion. *"Online grocery is failing. There's just not a lot of demand there. The whole premise is that you're saving people a trip to the store, but people actually like going to the store to buy groceries,"*[9] said Kurt Jetta, CEO of TABS Analytics.

FROM CLICKS TO BRICKS

According to analysts, Amazon was unable to entice shoppers to buy groceries online the same way they bought other items. *"The grocery space in general is something of a quagmire, beset by thin margins and complicated operations, and many of Amazon's efforts remain experimental,"*[10] remarked Daphne Howland, a contributing editor for *Retail Dive*.

Realizing that many people remained reluctant to purchase fresh food online, Bezos thought that it would be difficult to crack the competitive grocery segment without having some type of brick-and-mortar presence. He decided to experiment with a convenience store-like format. The new grocery experiment started in December 2016 with the beta launch (Amazon employees only) of a convenience-style grocery store called Amazon Go, in Seattle. The "Just Walk Out" technology in the store allowed customers to shop and checkout without having to pay at a cash register. Customers needed to download an app and then swipe their smartphones as they walked through the store's entrance. Every time a customer with the app picked up an item it got tracked on the phone. If an item was put back on the shelf, it was deleted. As customers exited, they received a digital receipt on their phones, and the amount due was debited from their Amazon account automatically. The technology used at these stores included computer vision, machine learning, and artificial intelligence.

The "just grab and go" store was expected to open to the public in Seattle early 2017 but the opening was delayed due to some kinks in the technology. The store's automated systems were disrupted when the store became crowded with more than 20 people or if customers moved too quickly. After fine-tuning the concept, Amazon opened its checkout-free convenience store to the public in Seattle on January 22, 2018. The company planned to open as many as 2,000 such stores in the future in a bid to dramatically alter brick-and-mortar retail. Exhibit 3 provides concept approval survey ratings for Amazon Go.

AMAZONFRESH STORE PICKUP SERVICES

In the United States, curbside pickup options were facing problems such as subpar produce and long wait times for pickup. Considering those issues, in March 2017, Amazon opened its first "click and collect"

EXHIBIT 3 Survey of Consumer Concept Approval Ratings for Amazon Go, December 2016

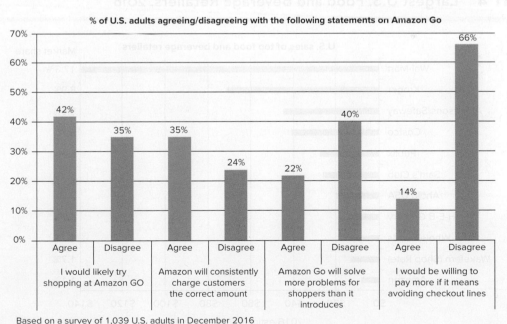

% of U.S. adults agreeing/disagreeing with the following statements on Amazon Go

Based on a survey of 1,039 U.S. adults in December 2016

Source: YouGov.

grocery pick-up stores exclusively for its Prime members at two locations in Seattle. Called AmazonFresh Pickup, the stores allowed its Prime customers to place the order online and to drive in and pick up groceries from the pickup locations at a chosen time. Orders were bagged in as little as 15 minutes after they were placed. There was no order minimum and the service was free for Prime members.[11]

In June 2017, Amazon partnered with Sprouts Farmers Market LLC, a supermarket chain, to offer one- and two-hour delivery of products from the grocer to its Prime members in the United States. Amazon offered one-hour Prime Now delivery of Sprouts items for $7.99, while two-hour delivery was provided at no additional cost through the company's Prime Now app. Sprouts offered delivery through Prime Now in several cities, including Los Angeles, San Diego, Austin, Denver, and Dallas.

AMAZON ACQUIRES WHOLE FOODS

Whole Foods pioneered the organic food movement in the United States with emphasis on high-quality and pricey organic offerings. As of 2016, Whole Foods accounted for 1.2 percent of the U.S. food and grocery market share (see Exhibit 4). Since the beginning of 2016, the organic retail chain had been facing declining sales, stiff competition, and increasingly price-conscious consumers. Whole Foods was also struggling to shed its "too pricey" image at a time when customers wanted more natural foods at more affordable prices. In February 2017, the retailer reported sales decline at its stores for seven consecutive quarters (4Q 2015 to 1Q 2017), and was under pressure to put itself up for sale (see Exhibits 5 and 6).

Meanwhile, even as Bezos was positioning Amazon to be the most powerful retailer in the world, he was aware that this goal could not be achieved without a physical presence, particularly in the grocery segment. Amazon controlled just about 1 percent of the U.S. food and beverage market as of 2016. According to Joseph Sebastian of Moneycontrol. com, *"When it comes to products like fruits and vegetables, most consumers across the world still like to touch and feel the product they are purchasing, as its directly for consumption. Delivery models, inventory-based, as well as hyperlocal, are more of a dud than a scud in this category in the U.S. at least. Globally many companies have struggled in the online grocery category, as it involves faster delivery and lesser shelf life."[12]

EXHIBIT 4   Largest U.S. Food and Beverage Retailers, 2016

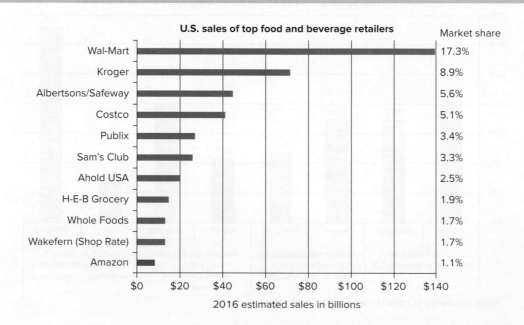

Source: Cowen and Company.

EXHIBIT 5   Whole Foods Market Inc. Consolidated Statement of Operations (fiscal years ended September 25, 2016, September 27, 2015, and September 28, 2014) (in millions except per share amount)

	2016	2015	2014
Sales	$15,724	$15,389	$14,194
Cost of goods sold and occupancy costs	10,313	9,973	9,150
Gross profit	5,411	5,416	5,044
Selling, general and administrative expenses	4,477	4,472	4,032
Pre-opening expenses	64	67	67
Relocation, store closure, and lease termination costs	13	16	11
Operating income	857	861	934
Interest expense	(41)	–	–
Investment and other income	11	17	12
Income before income taxes	827	878	946
Provision for income taxes	320	342	367
Net income	$ 507	$ 536	$ 579
Basic earnings per share	$1.55	$1.49	$1.57
Weighted average shares outstanding	326.1	358.5	367.8
Diluted earnings per share	$1.55	$1.48	$1.56
Weighted average shares outstanding, diluted basis	326.9	360.8	370.5
Dividends declared per common share	$0.54	$0.52	$0.48

Source: **http://s21.q4cdn.com/118642233/files/doc_financials/2016/Annual/2016-WFM-10K.pdf**.

In June 2017, Amazon acquired Whole Foods in an all-cash transaction valued at approximately $13.7 billion. Reportedly, the Whole Foods deal was more than 10 times bigger than any acquisition Amazon had made until then. Post-acquisition, Whole Foods would continue to operate stores under the Whole Foods Market brand and John Mackey would continue to remain its CEO. Jason Goldberg, vice president of commerce at the digital marketing company Razorfish, said, *"Amazon buying Whole Foods is a good fit with the company's larger strategy for groceries. Fresh groceries is the biggest category of consumer spending in retail that hasn't been disrupted by online yet."*[13]

After the merger was announced, the shares of some of the largest grocery store chains in the United States took a nosedive (see Exhibit 7). The shares of Kroger plunged more than 9 percent while that of Walmart and Costco fell 4.65 percent and 7.19 percent respectively. The shares of Supervalu and Sprouts each dropped more than 6.5 percent. Reportedly, the decline in the six stocks erased nearly $12 billion in their market value in total.[14] Amazon's market valuation increased by $14.27 billion while Walmart, Kroger, and Costco together lost $18.8 billion in market capitalization on June 16, 2017.[15] Analysts said that the stock fluctuations revealed investor concern over the long-term threat of Amazon taking a significant position in the grocery space. They called it one of the most disruptive acquisitions in terms of the number of stocks it had impacted.

The acquisition catapulted Amazon headlong into the grocery space and provided it with a footprint in

EXHIBIT 6   Whole Foods' Quarterly Revenue Growth

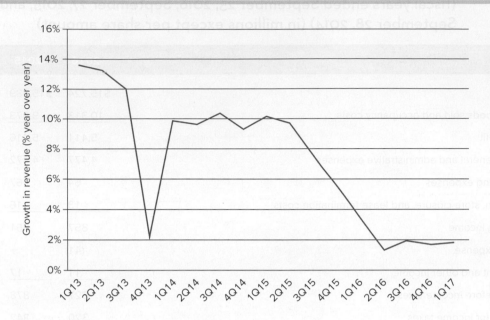

Source: Whole Foods Market Filings.

EXHIBIT 7   Stock Price Changes of Leading U.S. Grocers, June 15, 2017 to June 16, 2017 (market capitalization in $ billions)

Grocer	Stock Price Change June 15, 2017 to June 16, 2017	Market Capitalization	U.S. Stores
Whole Foods	27.0% ↑	13	465
Amazon	3.1% ↑	476	—
Ahold* (Giant)	−5.4% ↓	26	2,260
Walmart and Sam's Club	−6.5% ↓	225	4,692
Costco	−6.9% ↓	74	510
Target	−8.4% ↓	28	1,807
Sprouts Farmers Market	−12.9% ↓	3	272
Kroger* (Harris Teeter)	−14.6% ↓	20	2,792

*Dutch company Ahold Delhaize owns U.S. grocery chains including Food Lion and delivery service Peapod. Kroger owns chains Dillons and King Soopers. Costco locations are in the United States and Puerto Rico.
Darla Cameron and Kevin Schaul, The Washington Post.

Sources: Bloomberg News, the companies.

some of the most affluent urban areas in the United States (see Exhibit 8). Amazon would have access to Whole Foods' 465 stores across 42 states in the United States (460) and the United Kingdom (5 stores), besides a well-oiled supply chain. Whole Foods even had a strong private label business with its 365 brand products. Armed with those stores, Amazon could improve its distribution network and eliminate costs, reach more customers, and increase its overall market share, said experts. Moreover, Amazon's other grocery initiatives—AmazonFresh, Amazon Pantry, and Amazon Prime—would get a boost from Whole Foods's store network as well as its loyal, affluent customer base, they said.[16] In addition, Amazon would also pick up a stake in grocery-delivery startup Instacart,[17] an exclusive partner for Whole Foods' perishable business.

On August 23, 2017, the acquisition cleared its biggest hurdle as the Federal Trade Commission approved the deal. Post-merger Amazon had been slashing prices on some items at Whole Foods stores in the United States in order to attract customers. Amazon lowered prices of avocados, eggs, fruit, fish, and prepared food at Whole Food stores by as much as 50 percent. *"Amazon is trying to shed the 'Whole Paycheck' stigma at Whole Foods, and they clearly identified some key categories where they didn't think they were competitive and dropped some prices,"*[18] said

Darren Seifer, a food and beverage analyst with market research firm NPD Group.

Many of Whole Foods' in-house brands, including 365 Everyday Value products were made available on Amazon's website, AmazonFresh, and Prime Pantry. Amazon Prime members could get these items delivered to their homes or to their local Amazon Locker free of charge. The retailer had even dedicated an area of its first automated convenience store, Amazon Go, to the private label products. Amazon also made its customer rewards program Prime Now the de facto Whole Foods customer rewards program. In February 2018, the retailer announced that Amazon Prime Rewards Visa cardholders would get 5 percent cash back on their Whole Foods purchases while non-Amazon Prime subscribers would get 3 percent cash back when they use their card at Whole Foods. In addition, Amazon and Whole Foods technology teams were integrating Amazon Prime into the Whole Foods point-of-sale system. The two retailers planned to innovate in additional areas including in merchandising and logistics, in order to lower prices for Whole Foods customers.

In February 2018, Amazon started free, 2-hour delivery from Whole Foods stores to Prime Now members on orders over $35 in four U.S. cities—Austin, Cincinnati, Dallas, and Virginia Beach. Amazon planned to expand the offer nationwide before the end of 2018.

EXHIBIT 8   Whole Foods Stores in North America, June 16, 2017

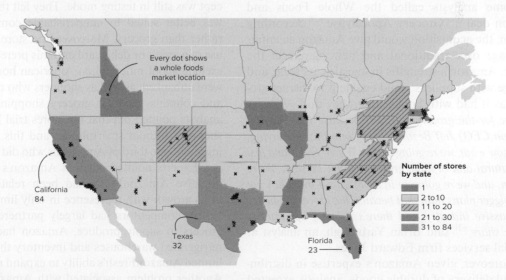

Source: **http://fortune.com/2017/06/16/amazon-whole-foods-stores-locations/**.

AMAZON SET TO DISRUPT THE U.S. GROCERY MARKET

According to some analysts, Amazon's acquisition of Whole Foods would disrupt three different markets—grocery stores, online shopping, and food delivery. The e-tailer would dramatically change the grocery landscape and threaten its larger rivals. It would eventually drive cost out of the supply chain at Whole Foods and lower prices to undercut rivals, they said. This in turn could force other big players in the market such as Walmart, Kroger, Costco, and Target to cut prices in order to survive. Analysts expected the partnership to kick off a wave of consolidations within the grocery space and leave other grocers under more pressure to compete. According to them, regional supermarket chains would be most affected as they would have to contend with not only competition with each other and nontraditional grocers, but also with a retailer like Amazon that had the financial capacity to price aggressively. The Amazon and Whole Foods deal could also be a gamechanger for consumers, vendors, and distributors, they said.

By building a physical presence, Amazon would undercut its biggest rival Walmart's on-the-ground advantages. Costco's yearly subscription model too could be disrupted with the introduction of a Prime-enabled grocery store. The acquisition would also pose a threat to other traditional grocers such as Kroger and Target that were already reeling from food deflation, they added.[19]

Some analysts called the Whole Foods and Amazon deal a "Grocery Apocalypse."[20] According to them, the acquisition would give Amazon an unfair advantage over traditional and new players in the market. Amazon's strengths in logistics, its scale, and leverage with suppliers could enable it to disrupt groceries as it had with bookselling, they said. *"It's very negative for the grocery business because I don't think (Amazon CEO) Jeff Bezos is going into this just saying, 'You know what, we're going to buy Whole Foods and just be a natural and organic grocer.' I think he says, 'We're going in, and we're going in in a big way.' I think he's got much bigger plans than that because the grocery industry is a massive industry and there's a lot of opportunity to take share,"*[21] said Brian Yarbrough, an analyst at financial services firm Edward Jones.

Moreover, given Amazon's expertise in distribution and delivery of durable goods, analysts expected the online behemoth to expand its footprint in food delivery and become a disruptor of the food service distribution models, particularly the independently-owned restaurant sector, which was a market worth about $256 billion in the United States.

Some industry observers even felt that Amazon's automation model, if widely adopted, had the potential to pose a huge threat to the retail workforce in the United States. They said the model would likely disrupt the labor force in the United States, which employed 867,920 grocery cashiers in 2016, according to the Bureau of Labor Statistics.

THE DOWNSIDE

However, some analysts were skeptical about the possibility of Amazon dominating the grocery sector as they felt that Amazon was still in an early stage of physical retail. They felt that traditional retailers would still have an upper hand over Amazon in the physical retail market given its lack of experience managing brick-and-mortar locations. According to them, the grocery business was highly competitive with survival driven by repeat business. The margins were thin, the product was highly perishable, and the supply chain expensive and complex. Moreover, there were some apprehensions about whether consumers would fully embrace grocery delivery as they generally preferred the tactile experience of handling fruits and vegetables and to pick out the groceries themselves.

Some analysts pointed out that Amazon Go concept was still in testing mode. They felt that the model was better suited to nonperishable consumer goods rather than grocery. Moreover, the store required the use of a credit or debit card and this prerequisite would exclude about nine million American households that were unbanked, as well as shoppers who relied on cash and coupons for their grocery shopping. Moreover, analysts pointed out that the stores trial had excluded shoppers without smartphones and this meant isolating about one-third of Americans who did not own one.

Experts pointed out that Amazon's first grocery initiative AmazonFresh had been relatively modest in its growth with a presence in only limited markets. Where competitors had largely partnered with local grocers to supply produce, Amazon had invested in refrigerated warehouses and inventory that reportedly limited AmazonFresh's ability to expand more quickly. Another problem associated with AmazonFresh was the high cost of losses caused due to food spoilage. Some customers had complained that the online store lacked the product range found in regular supermarkets. Moreover, a monthly fee in addition to the cost of a Prime membership made AmazonFresh a pricey service, they added. Reportedly, the service struggled, to the point where Amazon had to cut the rate for Prime users from $299 per year to $180 annually.

Some analysts were of the view the Amazon and Whole Food deal was barely a threat to the other established retailers like Walmart. While Whole Foods Market had just about 460 stores in the United States, Walmart operated more than 5,000 stores. Moreover, they said that Amazon could not use the Whole Foods brand to attract Walmart shoppers because the two stores appealed to different sets of customers.

CHALLENGES

According to some analysts, one of the biggest challenges for Amazon would be to operate its stores well as it was not an experienced brick-and-mortar retailer. Amazon would face some operational hiccups along the way as it transited its business model from an online pure-play to an integrated brick-and-mortar offering, they added. The company might struggle with assortment and merchandising strategies in the physical locations, and with maintaining a balance with online integration.

Another key challenge for Amazon would be to resolve the "last-mile"[22] challenge of delivering fresh food to its customers by bridging the small distance from the distribution hubs to individual customers. Moreover, there was the problem of spoilage. Amazon Go stores would also face some challenges. These stores would require an extremely high investment to chase the niche consumer in high-volume areas with disposable income. Also, for a store that relied solely on technology to function, even minor operational hiccups could affect the entire operation and be a significant drain on time and resources. Another challenge would be how fast consumers would be able to embrace this kind of concept and technology fully.

According to analysts, what seemed to be lacking from Amazon's plan for groceries was in-store dining, which was one of the biggest grocery trends in the United States. Grocers were luring customers into stores with dining options. According to Chicago-based researchers NPD Group, sales of prepared foods from

grocers, which included in-store and takeout dining, were up by nearly 30 percent since 2008 and accounted for $10 billion of consumer spending in 2015.

Amazon's competitors were unlikely to sit back as Amazon made its way into the traditional grocery market. Some were already taking steps to counter the e-tailer's moves. For instance, WalMart announced that it would start offering its products on Google Express. Moreover, German discount grocers Aldi and Lidl, who offered high quality products at low prices and a no-frills store environment, were slowly making inroads into the U.S. grocery market. Lidl started an aggressive expansion in the United States with plans to open as many as 100 new stores across the East Coast by the summer of 2018. Aldi, with more than 1,600 stores in the United States as of 2017, was aggressively expanding in the country and planned to increase its store count to 2,500 over a period of five years.

Another challenge for Bezos would be to scale up the production of organic produce if the demand for it went up in the future, said analysts. Though the demand for organic fruits and vegetables had increased, the number of acres used to farm those crops had remained about the same as it was particularly onerous for farmers to switch from conventional farming techniques to organic, they pointed out.

Some analysts said one of the earliest challenges for Amazon in the Whole Foods acquisition would be the management of different corporate cultures. While Amazon was an automation-oriented company with a customer centric culture, Whole Foods was a people-focused company with an approach to a more balanced set of commitments toward customers, employees, and communities. Calling the acquisition a risky move for Amazon, Megan McArdle, a Bloomberg View columnist, said, *"So while it's possible that the Whole Foods acquisition is a stroke of strategic genius, it's also possible that it may, in retrospect, turn out to be a bridge too far. Or more likely that it will turn out to be a mixed bag: costing some management headaches to keep a profit-challenged business going, without making or losing much money; enabling Amazon to get better at grocery delivery without making it strong enough to deliver a knockout blow to the competition."*[23]

THE ROAD AHEAD

In its fourth quarter ended December 31, 2017, Amazon's net sales increased 38 percent to $60.5 billion, compared with $43.7 billion in fourth quarter of 2016.

The company reported a profit of nearly $2 billion in the quarter, the largest in its history. Physical store revenue in the fourth quarter, which came mostly from Whole Foods, was about $4.5 billion.[24] Amazon sold an estimated $11 million of Whole Foods' 365 Everyday Value products in 2017. Whole Foods products also helped push sales at AmazonFresh up 35 percent to $135 million in the last quarter of 2017. One Click Retail[25] estimated that Amazon sold nearly $2 billion in groceries in the United States in 2017. Its online grocery sales accounted for less than 3 percent of the roughly $800 billion U.S. grocery market.[26]

Bezos planned to open 20 convenience stores in some major cities in the United States by the end of 2018, according to internal company documents. The stores would be tested in two formats—a more traditional grocery merchandise stores and "click & collect" grocery pickup services. Bezos also had plans to open multi-format stores that offered private-label goods at low prices. Amazon's grocery business was projected to grow at 22 percent annually. According to Cowen and Company, by 2021, Amazon would control about 33 percent of the $70 billion online grocery market

in the United States compared to 26 percent in 2016. As shown in Exhibit 9, online sales were projected to account for about 8 percent of the $903 billion grocery market in 2021 compared to about 4 percent of a $795 billion industry in 2016. *"The pot of gold at the end of the road for Amazon is groceries. The war for retail will be won in groceries. It's the largest category of consumer retail, and the largest untapped opportunity for Amazon,"*[27] said Cooper Smith, Director of Research at L2 Inc.

The stakes were high for Amazon as the company had been extremely persistent when it came to pursuing groceries. Some key challenges before Bezos were: blending the physical store experience with the convenience of digital retailing; managing the company's offline needs; successfully merging Whole Foods with Amazon to bring convenience and accessibility to a new high, and attracting customers. According to Chase Purdy, a business reporter for Quartz, *"Can Bezos do to groceries what he did to bookstores? And can he cast Whole Foods—a high-quality food store with sky-high prices—in Amazon's price-competitive image? If so, it will undoubtedly gin up concern in grocery-chain boardrooms across the U.S."*[28]

EXHIBIT 9   Growth in Online Grocery Sales, 2016 (Actual) to 2021 (Projected)

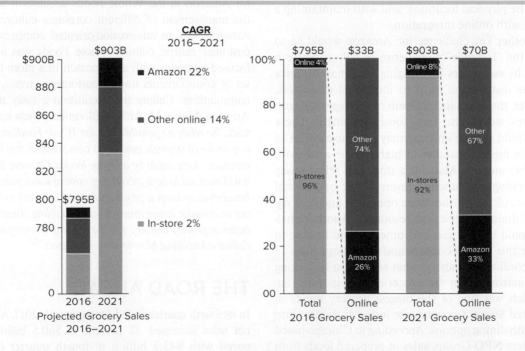

Source: http://www.mekkographics.com/amazon-is-poised-for-growth-in-grocery-sales/.

ENDNOTES

[1] The largest retailer in the world with 11,695 stores in 28 countries and e-commerce websites in 11 countries as of August 2017. In fiscal year 2017, the company generated $485.9 billion in revenues.

[2] An upscale discount retailer with 1,816 stores in the United States as of March 2017. In 2016, the company's revenues were $69.495 billion.

[3] A retailer with warehouse club operations in eight countries. Costco's revenue in 2016 was $118.7 billion.

[4] One of the largest grocery retailers in the United States, based on annual sales. Headquartered in Cincinnati, Ohio, the retail chain has nearly 2,800 stores in 35 states and the District of Columbia as of 2016. Its fiscal year 2016 sales were $115.3 billion.

[5] Sean Kervin, "The 3 Real Reasons Amazon Bought Whole Foods," June 21, 2017, www.clearpeak.com.

[6] Megan McArdle, "The Amazon Approach to Groceries Won't Replace Stores," June 20, 2017, www.bloomberg.com.

[7] In 2014, Amazon raised the annual fee for the membership to $99.

[8] Daphne Howland, "How Amazon is Disrupting Grocery," May 1, 2017, www.retaildive.com.

[9] Spencer Soper and Olivia Zaleski, "Inside Amazon's Battle to Break into the $800 Billion Grocery Market," March 20, 2017, www.bloomberg.com.

[10] Daphne Howland, "How Amazon is Disrupting Grocery," May 1, 2017, www.retaildive.com.

[11] Leslie Hook, "Amazon Launches Grocery Pick-Up Stores in Seattle," March 28, 2017, www.ft.com.

[12] Joseph Sabastian, "Why Amazon Acquired Whole Foods for About USD 14 Billion?" June 19, 2017, www.moneycontrol.com.

[13] Davey Alba, "Amazon is About to Transform How You Buy Groceries," June 16, 2017, www.wired.com.

[14] Evelyn Cheng, "Amazon's New Whole Foods Discounts Wipe Out Nearly $12 Billion in Market Value from Grocery Sellers," August 24, 2017, www.cnbc.com.

[15] "The Amazon Whole Foods Deal Made Walmart Costco and Kroger Lose 18.7 Billion in Market-Value," June 20, 2017, https://qz.com.

[16] Derek Thompson, "Why Amazon Bought Whole Foods," June 16, 2017, www.theatlantic.com.

[17] Founded in 2012, Instacart is an on-demand delivery start-up that promises grocery deliveries in as little as one hour.

[18] Sebastian Herrera, "Six Months after Amazon Takeover, are Prices Lower at Whole Foods?" February 28, 2018, www.512tech.com.

[19] George Watson, "Amazon's Purchase of Whole Foods Could Permanently Alter U.S. Grocery Industry," June 20, 2017, http://today.ttu.edu.

[20] Ben Levisohn, "Amazon's 'Unfair Advantages' and the Grocery Apocalypse," August 28, 2017, www.barrons.com.

[21] Ashley Nickle, "Analysts: Amazon-Whole Foods Merger is Major Disruption to Grocery Industry," June 16, 2017, www.thepacker.com.

[22] The last-mile refers to delivery space between a retailer and its customer base.

[23] Megan McArdle, "The Amazon Approach to Groceries Won't Replace Stores," June 20, 2017, www.bloomberg.com.

[24] Richard Turcsik, "Amazon's Whole Foods Revenue 'Slightly Better' Than Expected," February 2, 2018, www.supermarketnews.com.

[25] One Click Retail is a provider of e-commerce data measurement, sales analytics, and search optimization services.

[26] Heather Haddon, "Amazon Grocery Sales Surged, Thanks to Whole Foods," January 14, 2018, www.marketwatch.com.

[27] Dylan Byers, "What Amazon Knows: 'The War for Retail Will be Won in Groceries'," August 25, 2017, http://money.cnn.com.

[28] Chase Purdy, "Amazon is Buying Whole Foods Market for $13.7B—Threatening to Disrupt Three More Industries," June 16, 2017, https://qz.com.

Aliexpress: Can It Mount a Global Challenge to Amazon?

A. J. Strickland
The University of Alabama

Joyce L. Meyer
The University of Alabama

Muxin Li, Faculty Scholar 2018
The University of Alabama

Amazon had just completed another great year of growth, which included the decision to purchase Whole Foods. There was great excitement in the company, as the top leadership and throughout the company celebrated a job extremely well done. All the business magazines and newspapers touted Amazon as "the best company ever" and how Amazon dominated the online segment by having a 40 percent market share in a highly fragmented industry.

The following week the celebration continued when the strategic management committee met to consider their next acquisitions. A new member of the team, Megan Turner, who recently graduated from college and had worked for Amazon as an intern in their innovation area, asked a question about a new entrant in the online space called Aliexpress. All the focus in the room turned to the newest team member with a look that suggested, "Why are you talking about a company that is a gnat compared to Amazon?"

The new hire then found herself charged with the task of looking at Aliexpress to see if it really posed a competitive threat in the years ahead. When the meeting broke up, Megan found herself alone while the rest of the team continued to celebrate the best year ever—because the stock price once again hit a new high. Everyone on the team participated in the Employee Stock Option Plan, which historically had provided employees a very decent rate of return on their share purchases.

AMAZON'S COMPANY BACKGROUND

In July 1994, Jeff Bezos founded the pioneer of electronic commerce and the biggest online merchandiser in the United States, Amazon, based in Seattle, Washington, as an online bookshop business. According to the early Amazon logo, being the "Earth's biggest bookstore" was their goal. From 1997 to 2001, Amazon had a successful transition from being an online bookstore to being the largest Internet retailer in the world (by 2001), and the largest Internet retailer of tech products today. Amazon has positioned itself as the world's most customer-centric company, which has become the company culture and goal for their long-term development.

From the time Amazon's logo was created—which began with the letter A and ended with the letter S and a smile—Amazon's purpose "we're happy to deliver anything, anywhere," reflected the company's strategic intent to offer consumers everything from A to Z in its online store. In order to achieve the goal, Amazon had launched an ongoing strategic initiative to expand its product line-up and offer an always-increasing range of merchandise to consumers.

The strategy of retailing everything from A to Z initially resulted in huge annual losses for Amazon because of the ongoing need to build and operate the ever-bigger infrastructure the company needed to execute its strategy. The company expanded its geographic scope by rapidly increasing the number of warehouse and order fulfillment locations and adding more products and services to its menu of offerings. Early on, Amazon began expanding its geographic by entering new country markets, such as the United Kingdom and Germany. By 2018, Amazon was selling and delivering products and services to consumers all around the world—it was a truly global company.

ALIBABA'S COMPANY BACKGROUND

Jack Ma was an English teacher in China who founded "Alibaba Group" with a team of 18 people based in Hangzhou, China in his apartment. It started in 1995 and failed because it was too early to introduce Internet e-commerce to both Chinese consumers and the Chinese government. In 1999, Ma tried to build a digital yellow page service to introduce China to the world in trade, but it also failed because he could not obtain support from his potential customers. Nonetheless, Jack Ma did not give up because he believed the Internet was going to play a big role in economic exchange in the future, although it was not yet accepted in China. In the same year, 1999, he launched the company he named Alibaba, which received an investment from Goldman Sachs for $5 million, and Softbank for $20 million.

In 2003, Alibaba launched Taobao, which has Business to Business (B2B), Business to Consumer (B2C), and Consumer to Consumer (C2C) sales models via web portals. By starting a business competition with eBay, Taobao improved the company's visibility in the international media. As a result, Taobao successfully replaced eBay in China's Internet market, and finally made eBay withdraw from China.

Taobao offered services to businesses and consumers to trade on the online store without any fees for three years, which attracted more people to choose Taobao's platform for transactions. The next move was to go global with Aliexpress and further grow the market value of Alibaba. (see Exhibit 1).

ALIEXPRESS'S STRATEGY

The goal of Aliexpress was to make it easy to do business anywhere. Alibaba started with helping middle and small-sized enterprises. To help these enterprises survive, grow and develop, Alibaba soon learned that their main issue was the lack of funds to develop sales channels. To address this issue, Alibaba started to focus on B2B and laid a solid foundation for this business model. Alibaba became the middleman to provide a platform for sellers and buyers to build connections to generate business activities. It empowered merchants to do the business by themselves.

EXHIBIT 1   Top Companies in the World by Market Value in 2018 (in billions of U.S. dollars)

Apple	$926.90
Amazon.com	777.80
Alphabet	766.40
Microsoft	750.60
Facebook	541.50
Alibaba (Including Aliexpress)	499.40
Berkshire Hathaway	491.90
Tencent Holdings	491.30
JPMorgan Chase	387.70
ExxonMobil	344.10
Johnson & Johnson	341.30
Samsung Electronics	325.90
Bank of America	313.50
ICBC	311.00
Royal Dutch Shell	306.50
Visa	295.10
Wells Fargo	265.30
China Construction Bank	261.20
Intel	254.80
Chevron	248.10
Walmart	246.20

Source: **https://www.statista.com/statistics/263264/ top-companies-in-the-world-by-market-value/**.

Taobao offered plenty of unknown products directly from small manufacturers. Tmall, however, had more well-known brands, usually sold directly by the brand. These two retail sites generated more opportunities for middle and small-sized merchants. Aliexpress is the international version of Taobao. Aliexpress launched in 2010 targeting international consumers in the United States as well as Australia and Russia.

By utilizing the market environment and resources, Alibaba expanded business services to new areas: C2C, software, search engine, auctioning, money transfer, advertising, and logistics. These areas in general covered different kinds of e-commerce services, which meant that Alibaba provided better and more comprehensive support for enterprises. In the beginning, Alibaba offered free membership to gather more merchants to this platform. Today, commissions and fees have become an essential source of income. The more merchants and consumers who participate in this platform, the more transactions can be made. Alibaba is a platform and does not own any products. Merchants can sell products directly to consumers through Alibaba's website. In general, Alibaba does not participate in sale processing, but provides a platform and services for merchants and consumers to make transactions.

In 2018, there were thousands of well-known brand name products and an even greater number of unknown brands on Alibaba and Aliexpress, with an incredible selection and low prices for the same products compared to brick-and-mortar businesses and the limited number of online retail sites in China. Both Taobao and Aliexpress apps and websites were well developed in 2018, and the search engines directed consumers efficiently to the products they were shopping for. In addition, Alibaba developed Alipay, an eWallet service that enabled shoppers to easily pay for their purchases. In 2018, there were over 110 countries that used Alipay as a payment option. It was popular throughout a big portion of China and Southeast Asia because of its simplicity, convenience, and safety.

Before a consumer made a purchase they chatted directly with sellers to know the products better and have a quick response for after-sales services. There are a few merchants who still charged for shipping, but the majority of the products listed on Alibaba were free shipping, even for a small purchase or single item. Aliexpress, as the international market, continued Alibaba's features and provided free shipping around

EXHIBIT 2 Leading Shopping Apps in the Google Play Store Worldwide in April 2018

Name	Number of Downloads in Millions
Wish – Shopping Made Fun	16.56
AliExpress – Smarter Shopping, Better Living	5.87
Lazada – Online Shopping & Deals	4.43
Joom	3.44
Amazon Shopping	3.08
Mercado Libre: Encuentra tus marcas favoritas	2.73
Flipkart Online Shopping App	2.27
Club Factory – Fair Price	2.27
Shein – Shop Women's Fashion	2.02
Pandao	1.74

Source: https://www.statista.com/statistics/691274/leading-google-play-shopping-worldwide-downloads/.

the world, but it took longer to get the products. Consumers were able to track their delivery status.

As shown in Exhibit 2, Aliexpress had 5.87 million app downloads and was the second leading shopping app in the Google Play Store worldwide in April 2018. Amazon was fifth with 3.08 million downloads. Aliexpress, as a global retail marketplace, had approximately 60 million annual active buyers in the world in 12 months ending March 31, 2017.

ALIEXPRESS IN RUSSIA

With the facilitating conditions of distance, culture, and good terms of trading between China and Russia, Aliexpress targeted Russia as a good market to start expanding their business internationally. By the end of 2014, Aliexpress was the number one online retailer in Russia selling essentially Chinese products, and enjoying huge popularity among Russian online consumers who appreciated its low prices and large assortment. The inclusion of additional offers from Russian companies helped Aliexpress close gaps in its product range such as heavy home appliances that are difficult to deliver from China. Given the close proximity between Russia and China,

Aliexpress announced a domestic one-day delivery service. At the beginning, the one-day delivery was only for smartphones, notebooks, and other electronic products in 20 cities. For other cities, delivering these products took three days.

It is essential that consumers have privacy, security, and trust when they are making purchases on websites. Based on this premise, factors that affected consumers' buying motives included customer service, convenience, price, shipping cost, speed of delivery, quality, wide range of selection, etc. Both Amazon and Aliexpress had a huge range of product options and their websites were easy to navigate.

SINGLES DAY

Singles Day is a made-up holiday, designed by college students in China to celebrate being single (11/11, a group of ones, like a group of singles). Later, this term spread and became popular on social media. Today, Singles Day is better known as the grand shopping carnival on November 11 in China. This popular 24-hour shopping event was launched in 2009 and has had an impressive growth in one-day sales every year from $10 million in 2009 to $25.3 billion in 2017 (see Exhibit 3). As a comparison, in 2017, Amazon's Prime Day in July—the biggest sales day for Amazon—generated an estimated $1 billion sales revenue in 30 hours; Alibaba achieved these sales in just two minutes.

AMAZON'S STRATEGY

Differing from Alibaba, Amazon adopted a self-employed approach and participated in every step of the sale. The most well-known Amazon business model was Fulfillment by Amazon (FBA). Most of the buying and selling process was through Amazon, which utilized their big networking and fulfillment centers to quickly pick, pack, ship, and provide customer service. Amazon owned its own products, and also allowed third-party sellers by collecting sales commissions. Affiliated merchants either sold products by themselves, or they chose to use Amazon's fulfillment services. Amazon provided warehouses, and merchants prepared the products. The FBA method attracted merchants in different countries, decreased costs, and provided good delivery services. However, it was not a good option for Alibaba. As the middleman, Alibaba empowered merchants to process sales by themselves. This was a very different orientation compared to Amazon. The number of merchants on Alibaba was huge, with most of them from China. Since there was no guidance for the majority of these merchants to expand businesses out of the country, it was difficult for Alibaba to move forward to the global marketplace as a whole. To maintain good fulfillment centers and warehouses globally, Amazon spent massively to support them which resulted in lower profits.

Amazon had a customer service number where you could talk to a representative, or leave a message,

EXHIBIT 3   Alibaba's One-Day Gross Merchandise Volume on Singles Day from 2011 to 2017 (in billions of U.S. dollars)

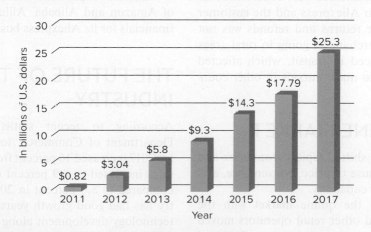

Source: **https://www.statista.com/statistics/364543/alibaba-singles-day-1111-gmv/**.

but you might wait as long as two days for a response. Compared to Amazon, Aliexpress offered a chat line, which allowed consumers to ask the seller any questions they may have before they actually purchased the products. This made the communication between retailers and consumers easier.

With low prices and wide selections, Amazon dominated the U.S. online shopping market. With Amazon Prime, members got free two-day delivery (one-day, same-day, and two-hour in some areas), streaming music, video, and readings from Amazon for a $119 annual membership fee. More than 100 million people were Amazon Prime members globally, and nearly half of U.S. households paid for Amazon Prime membership. Even without Prime, consumers could still have free shipping for a purchase of $25. Since the majority of products were fulfilled by Amazon, Amazon was always reliable. Customer Service took less time to satisfy customers, and items shipped from Amazon could be returned within 30 days of receipt in most cases. In addition, Amazon's website and app were easy-to-use, which provided a fluent shopping process.

For Amazon, its quick, high-efficiency, on-time delivery and price were their main strategic focuses. Amazon Prime offered an option for those consumers who needed speedy shipping to pay for this service, with a promised two-day delivery or less. Aliexpress had the same low-price strategy as Amazon, but it was less expensive than Amazon and there was no sales tax. At the same time, Aliexpress offered free shipping for everything, even for consumers who purchased only one-dollar items. However, the shipping time was much longer than Amazon, typically 15 to 40 days.

Some would say that there were sellers of counterfeit merchandise on Aliexpress and the customer service experience for returns and refunds was not satisfactory. Some merchandise going to rural areas was stolen or misplaced in transit, which affected efforts of Aliexpress to make inroads in other countries such as India.

RETAIL ONLINE MARKET

The retail market had shifted rapidly from brick and mortar to online because of price, convenience, and somewhat easy return capability.

Walmart entered the online market with the acquisition of Jet, and other retail operators moved rapidly into their own online markets or contracted with Amazon to provide the mechanism to handle their fulfillment. Shopping malls became less popular as online shopping grew. Google announced they, too, were entering the competitive arena in a big way.

Substitutes for online segments such as grocery, clothing, automobiles, etc., were still attracting the customer who wanted to have the hold and feel ability. However, the online segment made it easier to shop for groceries with the use of Amazon's Echo smart speaker. With the growth of smart devices such as the Smart Speaker and Smart Device, the purchase decision for online got easier. With both face and voice recognition, the buying decision was as simple as saying, "Alexa, buy my favorite coffee."

Both Alibaba and Amazon built their own mobile apps to allow consumers to complete purchasing. Alibaba started using new biometrics to handle purchase confirmations, such as "Smile to pay," which used facial recognition technology to confirm the online purchase. Gross consumer spending on mobile apps in 2017 in America was $17.5 billion U.S. In 2022, consumers are projected to spend over $34 billion on mobile apps.

While technically it was not difficult to enter the online segment, the time to build a brand and a system to take on an Amazon was formidable. An exception was Etsy that sold crafts and showed great growth until Amazon quickly countered by starting a new online operator named Handmade.

Suppliers of goods to be sold were not in a good bargaining position because Amazon could control both price and quantity due to their strong bargaining power. Technology suppliers suffered the same with Amazon's in-house technology group.

Exhibit 4 provides the financial comparison of Amazon and Alibaba. Alibaba does not publish financials for its Aliexpress business unit.

THE FUTURE OF THE ONLINE INDUSTRY

According to recent statistics from the U.S. Department of Commerce, total e-commerce sales for 2017 increased 16 percent from 2016. E-commerce sales increased to 8.9 percent of total sales in 2017, compared to 8.0 percent in 2016. The online industry has had good growth years. High-speed Internet technology development along with the "Internet of Everything" rapidly changed the buying model for

EXHIBIT 4   Comparison of Selected Financial Data for Amazon and Alibaba, 2015–2018 (in millions, except per share data)

Selected Statement of Operations Data	Amazon Fiscal Years Ending December 31			Alibaba Fiscal Years Ending March 31		
	2017	2016	2015	2018	2017	2016
Revenue	$177,866	$135,987	$107,006	$ 39,898	$22,994	$15,686
Cost of revenue	111,934	88,265	71,651	17,065	8,642	5,328
Gross profit	65,932	47,722	35,355	22,833	14,352	10,358
Operating expense	61,826	43,536	33,122	11,783	7,371	5,845
Operating income	4,106	4,186	2,233	11,050	6,981	4,513
As a % of total revenue	2%	3%	2%	28%	30%	29%
Non-operating income (expense)	(300)	(294)	(665)	4,957	1,740	8,122
Income before income taxes	3,806	3,892	1,568	16,007	8,721	12,635
Tax expense and other related expense	773	1,521	972	6,216	2,732	1,552
Net income	$ 3,033	$ 2,371	$ 596	$ 9,791	$ 5,989	$11,083
Earnings per share						
Basic	$6.32	$5.01	$1.28	$4.00	$2.55	$4.51
Diluted	$6.15	$4.90	$1.25	$3.91	$2.47	$4.33
Weighted average number of shares						
Basic	480	474	467	2,553	2,493	2,458
Diluted	493	484	477	2,610	2,573	2,562
Selected Balance Sheet Data						
Total current assets	$ 60,197	$45,781	$35,705	$ 40,949	$26,516	$20,792
Total assets	131,310	83,402	64,747	114,326	73,630	56,521
Total current liabilities	57,883	43,816	33,887	21,651	13,623	8,071
Total liabilities	103,601	64,117	51,363	44,270	26,542	17,767
Total shareholders' equity	27,709	19,285	13,384	69,578	46,654	38,700
Cash Flow Data						
Net cash provided by (used in) operating activities	$18,434	$17,272	$12,039	$419,955	$11,670	$8,815
Net Revenue by Region						
North America	$106,110	$79,785	$63,708	–	–	–
China	–	–	–	$29,290	$17,403	$13,077
International	54,297	43,983	35,418	3,322	1,938	1,183
Web services (and others)	17,459	12,219	7,880	7,286	3,653	1,426

(Continued)

Net Revenue Percentage by Region						
North America	60%	59%	60%	–	–	–
China	–	–	–	74%	76%	83%
International	30%	32%	33%	8%	9%	8%
Web services (and others)	10%	9%	7%	18%	15%	9%

Sources: Amazon Inc. 10-K Report, 2015, 2016, and 2017; Alibaba Group Annual Report, 2016, 2017, and 2018.

the consumer. In the future the smart refrigerator will be automatically purchasing groceries as needed.

Compared with traditional retail, one of the advantages of electronic commerce based on the Internet is to obtain big data, which is used to analyze the customer's purchasing power, purchasing behavior, and other relevant customer data.

After researching the growth of Amazon and Alibaba and its subsidiary Aliexpress, Megan was ready to make her recommendations with sound justifications on what strategic position Amazon should make to counteract Aliexpress's inroads to the Amazon market.

Tesla Motors in 2018: Will the New Model 3 Save the Company?

connect

Arthur A. Thompson
The University of Alabama

Tesla Motors began assembling the first models of its new "affordably-priced" entry-level Model 3 electric car in May 2017 and delivered the first units the last week of July, with a goal of gradually ramping up production to a total of 1,500 units by the end of September. The first production vehicles, delivered to employees who had placed pre-production reservations over a year earlier, were pre-configured with rear-wheel drive and a long-range battery; had a range of 310 miles and 0 to 60 mph acceleration time of 5.1 seconds; and a sticker price starting at $44,000 with premium upgrades available for an additional $5,000. Deliveries of the standard Model 3, with a base price of $35,000, 220 miles of range, and a 0 to 60 mph acceleration time of 5.6 seconds, were expected to begin in the United States in November 2017. Dual motor all-wheel drive configurations were scheduled to be available in early 2018. Plans called for international deliveries of the Model 3 to begin in late 2018, contingent upon regulatory approvals, starting with left-hand drive markets and followed by right-hand drive markets in 2019.

Tesla had unveiled six drivable prototypes of the Model 3 for public viewing and a limited number of test drives on the evening of March 31, 2016. Buyer reaction was overwhelmingly positive. Over the next two weeks, some 350,000 individuals paid a $1,000 deposit to reserve a place in line to obtain a Model 3; reportedly, the number of reservations grew to nearly 400,000 units over the next several months. Because of the tremendous amount of interest in the Model 3, Tesla Chairman and CEO Elon Musk announced in May 2016 that Tesla was advancing its schedule to begin producing the Model 3 from late 2017 to mid-2017 and further that it was going to accelerate its

efforts to expand production capacity of the Model 3, with a goal of getting to a production run rate of 500,000 units annually by year-end 2018 instead of year-end 2020.

In early August 2017, in a letter updating shareholders on the company's second quarter 2017 results, Musk said:

Based on our preparedness at this time, we are confident we can produce just over 1,500 [Model 3] vehicles in Q3 and achieve a run rate of 5,000 vehicles per week by the end of 2017. We also continue to plan on increasing Model 3 production to 10,000 vehicles per week at some point in 2018.[1]

But in his third quarter 2017 update on November 1, 2017, Musk related a host of production bottlenecks and challenges that were blocking the ramp-up of Model 3 production and delaying deliveries, saying, "this makes it difficult to predict exactly how long it will take for all bottlenecks to be cleared or when new ones will appear. Based on what we know now, we currently expect to achieve a production rate of 5,000 Model 3 vehicles per week by late Q1 2018."[2]

But Tesla's "production hell" with the Model 3 continued to haunt the company in early 2018. Many analysts believed Tesla's problems stemmed from having taken huge shortcuts in the parts approval process, production line validation, and full beta testing of the Model 3 in order to begin early assembly and production ramp-up. There were other reasons, including ongoing parts bottlenecks and inconsistent manufacturing quality. Production line employees interviewed by reporters indicated significant numbers of units coming off the assembly line had quality problems involving malfunctioning parts/ components and/or faulty installation issues that required reworking. A big parking lot just outside the assembly plant in Fremont, California, was said to be full of Model 3s awaiting corrective attention; a few were even being junked because of the high cost of restoring them to a condition that would pass final pre-delivery inspection. On February 7, 2018, Musk reported:

> We continue to target weekly Model 3 production rates of 2,500 by the end of Q1 and 5,000 by the end of Q2. It is important to note that while these are the levels we are focused on hitting and we have plans in place to achieve them, our prior experience on the Model 3 ramp has demonstrated the difficulty of accurately forecasting specific production rates at specific points in time. What we can say with confidence is that we are taking many actions to systematically address bottlenecks and add capacity in places like the battery module line where we have experienced constraints, and these actions should result in our production rate significantly increasing during the rest of Q1 and through Q2.
>
> Despite the delays that we experienced in our production ramp, Model 3 net reservations remained stable in Q4. In recent weeks, they have continued to grow as Model 3 has arrived in select Tesla stores and received numerous positive reviews, including *Automobile* magazine's 2018 Design of the Year award.[3]

A week or so later, Tesla shut down the Model 3 assembly line for four days to address some of the assembly problems being encountered. Nonetheless, in early March 2018, there were reports from multiple sources that Tesla had not been able to consistently achieve a production run rate of 800 units per week. So Musk's target of a weekly production rate of 2,500 Models 3 by the end of March seemed very much in jeopardy.

In addition, there were accumulating reports from the owners of Model 3s relating to touchscreen issues—one related to the audio system volume suddenly blasting higher without the screen having been touched; another related to drivers returning to their parked Model 3 and discovering the touchscreen on and the audio sound blaring; still another related to "phantom" inputs along the edges of the touchscreen when certain apps were opened. In some instances, Tesla had replaced the touchscreens; in others, it promised a software solution would soon be forthcoming. A second reported problem, in which the battery capacity decreased

noticeably while the car was parked in the sun on a hot day for several hours, had been reported by a number of Model 3 owners and, to a lesser extent, by a few Model S and Model X owners. It appeared that battery drain problems often occurred in Model 3 vehicles experiencing touchscreen issues. A couple of Model 3 owners with technical backgrounds had speculated the problem related to touchscreens being mounted on a large metal pedestal such that large temperature differentials between a vehicle's hot interior and its cooler exterior caused the touchscreen and plastic touchpad to warp and produce other anomalies as the metal pedestal absorbed heat from inside the vehicle. As of March 27, 2018, the cause had not been pinpointed, but if the problem did relate to a faulty pedestal design, then correcting the design problem could cause further delays in ramping up Model 3 production and drive up warranty costs for Model 3s already delivered. During the last week of March, Elon Musk tweeted that he had taken over the role of supervising Model 3 production for the time being.

The first week of April 2018, Tesla reported that it produced 34,494 vehicles in the first quarter of 2018. Tesla's Q1 deliveries were 29,980 vehicles, of which 11,730 were Model S; 10,070, were Model X; and 8,180 were Model 3; as of March 31, 4,060 Model S and Model X vehicles and 2,040 Model 3 vehicles were in transit to customers. Tesla also reported that after shifting some production resources away from Model S and Model X production over to production and assembly of the Model 3 during the last week of March, it was able to produce 2,020 Models 3s in the last seven days leading up to April 3. In its production and delivery announcement, the company further said:

> Given the progress made thus far and upcoming actions for further capacity improvement, we expect that the Model 3 production rate will climb rapidly through Q2. Tesla continues to target a production rate of approximately 5,000 units per week in about three months.
>
> Finally, we would like to share two additional points about Model 3:
>
> • The quality of Model 3 coming out of production is at the highest level we have seen across all our products. This is reflected in the overwhelming delight experienced by our customers with their Model 3s. Our initial customer satisfaction score for Model 3 quality is above 93 percent, which is the highest score in Tesla's history.

• Net Model 3 reservations remained stable through Q1. The reasons for order cancellation are almost entirely due to delays in production in general and delays in availability of certain planned options, particularly dual motor AWD and the smaller battery pack.[4]

Despite the difficulties being experienced with the Model 3, production and sales of the company's trailblazing Model S sedan (introduced in 2012) and Model X sports utility vehicle (introduced in late 2015) were proceeding largely on plan. Combined sales of these two models reached nearly 101,500 units in 2017 (see Exhibit 1). The Model S was a fully electric, four-door, five-passenger luxury sedan with an all-glass panoramic roof, high definition backup camera, a 17-inch touchscreen that controlled most of the car's functions, keyless entry, xenon headlights, dual USB ports, tire pressure monitoring, and numerous other features that were standard in most luxury vehicles. The cheapest Model S had a base price of $75,700 in 2018 and, when equipped with options frequented selected by customers, carried a retail sticker price ranging from $95,000 to $136,000. The Model X was the longest range all-electric production sport utility vehicle in the world; it could seat up to seven adults and incorporated a unique falcon wing door system for easy access to the second and third seating rows. The Model X had an all-wheel drive dual motor system and autopilot capabilities, along with a full assortment of standard and optional

EXHIBIT 1 Tesla's Deliveries of the Model S, Model X, and Model 3 to Customers, 2012 through the First Quarter of 2018

Period	Model S Deliveries	Model S plus Model X Deliveries	Model 3 Deliveries
2012	2,653		
2013	22,477		
2014	31,655		
2015	50,332		
2016		76,230	
2017		101,420	1,734
Q1 2018		21,815	8,182

Source: Company 10K reports and press releases.

features. Retail sticker prices in 2018 ranged from a base price of $80,700 to $97,000 for a well-equipped Model X to $140,000 for a fully loaded model. Both the Model S and Model X were being sold in North America, Europe, and Asia in 2017 and 2018.

The Model S was the most-awarded car of 2013, including *Motor Trend's* 2013 Car of the Year award and *Automobile* magazine's 2013 Car of the Year award. The National Highway Traffic Safety Administration (NTSHA) in 2013, 2014, and 2015 awarded the Tesla Model S a 5-star safety rating, both overall and in every subcategory (a score achieved by approximately 1 percent of all cars tested by the NHTSA). *Consumer Reports* gave the Model S a score of 99 out of 100 points in 2013, 2014, and 2015, saying it was "better than anything we've ever tested." However, the Tesla Model S did not make the *Consumer Reports* list of the "10 Top Picks" in 2016, 2017, and 2018, but the Model S did earn a perfect 100 score on the 2018 road test drive.

The sleek styling and politically correct power source of Tesla's Model S and Model X were thought to explain why thousands of wealthy individuals in countries where the two models were being sold—anxious to be a part of the migration from gasoline-powered vehicles to electric-powered vehicles and to publicly display support for a cleaner environment—had become early purchasers and advocates for Tesla's vehicles. Indeed, word-of-mouth praise among current owners and glowing articles in the media were so pervasive that Tesla had not yet spent any money on advertising to boost customer traffic in its showrooms. In a presentation to investors, a Tesla officer said "Tesla owners are our best salespeople."[5]

As Tesla's current chairman and CEO, Elon Musk's strategic vision for the automotive segment of Tesla's operations featured three major elements:

1. Bring a full-range of affordable electric-powered vehicles to market and become the world's foremost manufacturer of premium quality, high-performance electric vehicles.

2. Convince motor vehicle owners worldwide that electric-powered motor vehicles were an appealing alternative to gasoline-powered vehicles.

3. Accelerate the world's transition from carbon-producing, gasoline-powered motor vehicles to zero emission electric vehicles.

At one point, Musk's stated near-term strategic objective was for Tesla to achieve sales of about

500,000 electric vehicles annually by year-end 2018, but the difficulties in ramping up production of the Model 3 has pushed achievement of this objective out to the end of 2019 at the earliest and more probably the end of 2020, assuming sales of the Model 3 took off as expected. Musk planned for the company to begin deliveries of the Tesla Semi truck in late 2019 and a new version of the Tesla Roadster in 2020. His strategic intent was for Tesla to be the world's biggest and most highly-regarded producer of electric-powered motor vehicles, dramatically increasing the share of electric vehicles on roads across the world and causing global use of gasoline-powered motor vehicles to fall into permanent long-term decline.

At its core, therefore, Tesla's strategy was aimed squarely at utilizing the company's battery and electric drivetrain technology to disrupt the world automotive industry in ways that were sweeping and transformative. If Tesla's strategy proved to be as successful as Elon Musk believed it would be, industry observers expected that the Tesla's competitive position and market standing vis-à-vis the world's best-known automotive manufacturers would be vastly stronger in 2025 than it was in 2018.

But in 2018 there were three challenges with the potential to imperil Musk's vision for Tesla Motors:

1. Gasoline prices across much of the world had dropped significantly from 2015 to early 2017 and were expected by many knowledgeable observers to remain permanently "low" (below $80 or even lower) because the abundance of shale oil and the sharply-lower costs of extracting oil from shale deposits. Affordable gasoline prices made the purchase of electric vehicles less attractive, given that (1) electric vehicles were higher priced than vehicles with gasoline engines, (2) electric vehicles so far were limited to an upper range of about 300 miles on a single battery charge, and (3) new vehicles powered by gasoline engines were getting more miles per gallon (due to government-mandated mileage-efficiency requirements).

2. Tesla was facing the prospect of much more formidable competition from virtually all of the world's major motor vehicle manufacturers (BMW, Mercedes, Jaguar, Volkswagen-Audi, Toyota, Honda, Nissan, General Motors, and Ford) that were rushing to introduce affordable and high-end electric vehicles with features and engine configurations that would enable them to compete head-on with the Model S, Model X, and Model 3. Several vehicle makers were also pursuing the development of electric-powered semi trucks for commercial uses.

3. Tesla had yet to prove it could boost operating efficiency and lower costs enough to be both price competitive and attractively profitable in producing and marketing its vehicle models. It reported both a loss from operations and a net loss each of the past five years, despite growing its automotive sales and leasing revenues from $2.61 billion in 2013 to $9.64 billion in 2017—see Exhibit 2. In February 2018, the company did say it expected to generate a positive *quarterly* operating income before the end of 2018 (but not a positive operating income for the *year*). While Tesla's ongoing operating losses and net losses were partly, or perhaps largely, due to the sizable new product development costs associated with the Model X and Model 3 and to the required accounting treatments for both leased vehicles and Tesla's generous stock compensation plan, it was nonetheless disconcerting that Tesla's operating loss of $1.63 billion in 2017 was the largest in the company's history—an outcome that had to be reversed soon. The extent of Tesla's growing operating losses was illustrated by the fact that in the first quarter of 2017 General Motors reported an operating profit of $1,418 for every vehicle it sold around the world and Ford's reported operating profit per vehicle sold was $1,174—in comparison, Tesla's operating profit per vehicle was -$15,855.[6]

A possible fourth challenge seemed to be gathering steam on the Tesla message boards. People with Model 3 reservations who, because of all the production problems and delivery delays they had been hearing about, had posted concerns about taking delivery of the Model 3 they had ordered. In one anecdotal case, a poster told of when he went to the Tesla delivery location to take delivery of a black Model 3, he could clearly see paint swirls on the hood; when told by the delivery person that the service department had done the best job it could to buff out the swirls and that the car would be sold "as is," the poster refused delivery. But after further conversation with the delivery person he said he then agreed to pay an extra $1,000 for a red Model 3 after being promised by the delivery person it would be ready for pickup in one week—after 10 days, the poster said he had received no notification to come pick up the red Model 3. There were also message board posts from some Model S and Model X owners about the repair problems they were experiencing with their vehicles. There was one extreme example where an unhappy Model S owner reported having to take his vehicle to the Tesla service center for repairs six times in the past five months. Then in late March 2018 Tesla announced it was recalling about 123,000 Model S sedans globally after discovering that certain corroding bolts in cold weather climates could lead to a power-steering failure.

However, when Tesla announced its financial and operating results for the first quarter of 2018 ending March 31, the outcomes were in some respects better than many investors and Wall Street analysts expected. Tesla reported delivery of 8,182 Model 3s during the quarter and after having implemented numerous adjustments in assembly methods and correcting problems with faulty and improperly designed parts it was now able to sustain a production rate of 3,000 Model 3s per week. Elon Musk said that continued refinements of the assembly process and improved operational uptime of the associated machinery should lead to a production rate of "well over 5,000" vehicles per week by the end of June or beginning of July. Musk admitted that he had been wrong in mandating use of so many robots along the assembly line, and that now the assembly line had been and was still being greatly simplified, with more use being made of semi-automated and manual assembly to perform certain tasks until the company had enough time to perfect the use of robots and enable full automation to resume. Musk confidently predicted that the Model 3 would become the best-selling medium-sized premium sedan in the United States before year end—the company had over 450,000 Model 3 reservations at the end of Quarter 1. Musk indicated that if Tesla executed according to plan the company would achieve positive cash flows and positive net income (excluding non-cash stock-based compensation) in both the third and fourth quarters of 2018. According to Musk, this was "primarily based on our ability to reach Model 3 production volume of 5,000 units per week and to grow Model 3 gross margin from slightly negative in Q1 2018 to close to breakeven in Q2 and then to highly

positive in Q3 and Q4."[7] The company also reported significant increases in energy storage deployments for utilities and other commercial enterprises and record deliveries of Powerwall systems for residences, resulting in Q1 revenues for energy generation and storage of $410.0 million, versus $213.9 million in the first quarter of 2017. Musk believed the company would generate positive cash in Q3 and Q4.

On the negative side, however, Tesla reported its largest quarterly net loss ever—$784.6 million, a loss from operations of $597.0 million, a negative cash flow from operations of $398.4 million, and a net decrease in cash and cash equivalents of $745.3 million. It was unclear whether, given expected capital expenditures of almost $3 billion, the company would need to raise additional capital to get through the year; the company ended Q1 with a cash balance of $2.67 billion. Despite all the uncertainties, in May 2018 Musk had pledged no capital raise would be needed in 2018. This pledge baffled many Wall Street analysts, most all of the company's critics and skeptics, and other keen observers because Musk, during the May 2, 2018 conference call with analysts to discuss Tesla's Q1 2018 financial results, expressed his appreciation to the Chinese government for its announcement that foreign companies would henceforth be allowed to have 100 percent ownership of manufacturing facilities in China and said Tesla could have a Gigafactory capable of vehicle production in China "not later than the fourth quarter" of 2018.[8]

Exhibit 2 presents selected financial statement data for Tesla for 2013 through 2017.

COMPANY BACKGROUND

Tesla Motors was incorporated in July 2003 by Martin Eberhard and Marc Tarpenning, two Silicon Valley engineers who believed it was feasible to produce an "awesome" electric vehicle. Tesla's namesake was the genius Nikola Tesla (1856–1943), an electrical engineer and scientist known for his impressive inventions (of which more than 700 were patented) and his contributions to the design of modern alternating-current (AC) power transmission systems and electric motors. Tesla's first vehicle, the Tesla Roadster (an all-electric sports car) introduced in early 2008, was powered by an AC motor that descended directly from Nikola Tesla's original 1882 design.

EXHIBIT 2   Selected Financial Data for Tesla, Inc., 2013–2017 (in millions, except share and per share data)

	Years Ended December 31				
	2017	**2016**	**2015**	**2014**	**2013**
Income Statement Data:					
Revenues:					
Automotive sales	$ 8,534.8	$ $5,589.0	$ 3,431.6	$ 2,874.4	$ 1,921.9
Automotive leasing	1,106.5	761.8	309.4	132.6	
Total automotive revenues	9,641.3	6,350.8	3,741.0	3,741.0	
Energy generation and storage	1,116.3	181.4	14.5	4.2	
Services and other	1,001.2	468.0	290.6	191.3	91.6
Total revenues	11,758.8	7,000.1	4,046.0	3,198.4	2,013.5
Cost of revenues:					
Automotive sales	6,724.5	4,268.1	2,639.9	2,058.3	1,483.3
Automotive leasing	708.2	482.0	183.4	87.4	
Total automotive cost of revenues	7,432.7	4,750.1	2,823.3	2,145.7	
Energy generation and storage	874.5	178.3	12.3	4.0	
Services and other	1,229.0	472.5	286.9	166.9	73.9
Total cost of revenues	9,536.3	5,400.9	3,122.5	2,316.7	1,557.2
Gross profit (loss)	2,222.5	1,599.3	923.5	881.7	456.3
Operating expenses:					
Research and development	1,378.1	834.4	717.9	464.7	232.0
Selling, general and administrative	2,476.5	1,432.2	922.2	603.7	285.6
Total operating expenses	3.854.6	2,266.6	1,640.1	1,068.4	517.5
Loss from operations	(1,632.1)	(667.3)	(716.6)	(186.7)	(61.3)
Interest income	19.7	8.5	1.5	1,126	189
Interest expense	(471.3)	(198.8)	(118.9)	(100.9	(32.9
Other income (expense), net	(125.4)	111.3	(41.7)	1.8	22.6
Loss before income taxes	(2,209.0)	(875,624)	(875.6)	(284.6)	(71.4)
Provision for income taxes	31.5	13,039	13.3	9.4	2.6
Net loss	$ (2,240.6)	$ (773.0)	$ (888.7)	$ (294.0)	$ (74.0)
Net loss attributable to noncontrolling interests and subsidiaries	(279.1)	(98.1)	—	—	—
Net loss attributable to common shareholders	$ (1,961.4)	(674.9)	$ (888.7)	$ (294.0)	$ (74.0)
Net loss per share of common stock, basic and diluted	$ (11.83)	$ (4.68)	$ (6.93)	$ (2.36)	$ (0.62)
Weighted average shares used in computing net loss per share of common stock, basic and diluted	165.8	144.2	128.2	124.5	119.4
Balance Sheet Data:					
Cash and cash equivalents	$ 3,367.9	$ 1,196,908	$ 1,196.9	$ 1,905.7	$ 845.9
Inventory	2,263.5	2,067.5	1,277.8	953.7	340.4
Total current assets	6,570.5	6,259.8	2,791.4	3,198.7	1,265.9

Property, plant, and equipment, net	10,027.5	5,983.0	3,403.3	1,829.3	738.5
Total assets	28,655.4	22,644.1	8,092.5	5,849.3	2,416.9
Total current liabilities	7,674.7	5,827.0	2,816.3	2,107.2	675.2
Long-term debt and capital leases, net of current portion	9,415.7	5,860.0	2,040.4	1,818.8	599.0
Total stockholders' equity	4,237.2	4,752.9	1,088.9	911.7	667.1

Cash Flow Data:

Cash flows from operating activities	$ (2,240.6)	$ (773.0)	$ (888.7)	$ (57.3)	$ 263.8
Proceeds from issuance of common stock in public offerings	400.2	1,701.7	730.0	—	360.0
Purchases of property and equipment excluding capital leases	(3,414.8)	(1,280.8)	(1,634.9)	(970.0)	(264.2)
Net cash used in investing activities	(4,419.0)	(1,416.4)	(1,673.6)	(990.4)	(249.4)
Net cash provided by financing activities	4,414.9	3,744.0	1,523.5	2,143.1	635.4

Sources: Company 10-K reports for 2014, 2015, and 2017.

Financing Early Operations

Eberhard and Tarpenning financed the company until Tesla's first round of investor funding in February 2004. Elon Musk contributed $6.35 million of the $6.5 million in initial funding and, as the company's majority investor, assumed the position of Chairman of the company's board of directors. Martin Eberhard put up $75,000 of the initial $6.5 million, with two private equity investment groups and a number of private investors contributing the remainder.[9] Several rounds of investor funding ensued, with Elon Musk emerging as the company's biggest shareholder. Other notable investors included Google co-founders Sergey Brin and Larry Page, former eBay President Jeff Skoll, and Hyatt heir Nick Pritzker. In 2009, Germany's Daimler AG, the maker of Mercedes vehicles, acquired an equity stake of almost 10 percent in Tesla for a reported $50 million.[10] Daimler's investment was motivated by a desire to partner with Tesla to accelerate the development of Tesla's lithium-ion battery technology and electric drive train technology and to collaborate on electric cars being developed at Mercedes. Later in 2009, Tesla was awarded a $465 million low-interest loan by the U.S. Department of Energy to accelerate the production of affordable, fuel-efficient electric vehicles; Tesla used $365 million for production engineering and assembly of its forthcoming Model

S and $100 million for a powertrain manufacturing plant employing about 650 people that would supply all-electric powertrain solutions to other automakers and help accelerate the availability of relatively low-cost, mass-market electric vehicles.

In June 2010, Tesla Motors became a public company, raising $226 million with an initial public offering of common stock. It was the first American car company to go public since Ford Motor Company in 1956.

Management Changes at Tesla

In August 2007, with the company plagued by delays in getting its first model—the Tesla Roadster—into production, co-founder Martin Eberhard was ousted as Tesla's chief executive officer (CEO). While his successor managed to get the Tesla Roadster into production in March 2008 and begin delivering Roadsters to customers in October 2008, internal turmoil in the executive ranks prompted Elon Musk to decide it made more sense for him to take on the role as Tesla's chief executive officer—while continuing to serve as chairman of the board—because he was making all the major decisions anyway.

Elon Musk

Elon Musk was born in South Africa, taught himself computer programming and, at age 12, made

$500 by selling the computer code for a video game he invented.[11] In 1992, after spending two years at Queen's University in Ontario, Canada, Musk transferred to the University of Pennsylvania where he earned an undergraduate degree in business and a second degree in physics. During his college days, Musk spent some time thinking about two important matters that he thought merited his time and attention later in his career: one was that the world needed an environmentally clean method of transportation; the other was that it would be good if humans could colonize another planet.[12] After graduating from the University of Pennsylvania, he decided to move to California and pursue a PhD in applied physics at Stanford; however, he left the program after two days to pursue his entrepreneurial aspirations instead.

Musk's first entrepreneurial venture was to join up with his brother, Kimbal, and establish Zip2, an Internet software company that developed, hosted, and maintained some 200 websites involving "city guides" for media companies. In 1999 Zip2 was sold to a wholly-owned subsidiary of Compaq Computer for $307 million in cash and $34 million in stock options—Musk received a reported $22 million from the sale.[13]

In March 1999, Musk co-founded X.com, a Silicon Valley online financial services and e-mail payment company. One year later, X.com acquired Confinity, which operated a subsidiary called PayPal. Musk was instrumental in the development of the person-to-person payment platform and, seeing big market opportunity for such an online payment platform, decided to rename X.com as PayPal. Musk pocketed about $150 million in eBay shares when PayPal was acquired by eBay for $1.5 billion in eBay stock in October 2002.

In June 2002, Elon Musk with an investment of $100 million of his own money founded his third company, Space Exploration Technologies (SpaceX), to develop and manufacture space launch vehicles, with a goal of revolutionizing the state of rocket technology and ultimately enabling people to live on other planets. Upon hearing of Musk's new venture into the space flight business, David Sacks, one of Musk's former colleagues at PayPal, said, "Elon thinks bigger than just about anyone else I've ever met. He sets lofty goals and sets out to achieve them with great speed."[14] In 2011, Musk vowed to put a man on Mars in 10 years.[15] In May 2012, a SpaceX Dragon cargo capsule powered by a SpaceX Falcon Rocket completed a near flawless test flight to and from the International Space Station; since then, under contracts with NASA, the SpaceX Dragon had delivered cargo to and from the Space Station multiple times. Going into 2018, SpaceX secured contracts of over $12 billion to conduct over 100 missions. Currently, SpaceX was working toward developing fully and rapidly reusable rockets and test launching its new Falcon Heavy rocket, said to the world's most powerful rocket. The company was said to be both profitable and cash-flow positive in 2013 to 2017. Headquartered in Hawthorne, California, SpaceX had 5,000 employees and was owned by management, employees, and private equity firms; Elon Musk was the company's CEO and largest stockholder.

Another of Elon Musk's business ventures was SolarCity Inc., a full-service provider of solar system design, financing, solar panel installation, and ongoing system monitoring for homeowners, municipalities, businesses (including Intel, Walmart, Walgreens, and eBay), universities, nonprofit organizations, and military bases. Going into 2016, SolarCity managed more solar systems for homes than any other solar company in the United States. While Solar City had installed many solar energy systems, it had never been profitable or cash flow positive due to its business model of recovering the capital and operating costs of the installed systems through leasing fees and power purchase agreements. In November 2016, to rescue Solar City from probable bankruptcy, Tesla acquired the company and continued its operations as a new division named Tesla Energy. However, the business model was changed to one where customers financed their new solar power installations with cash and loans, thus producing a healthier mix of upfront and recurring revenue; moreover, the costs of installing solar-powered installations were expected to decline, partly because of improvements in solar technology, greater efficiencies in manufacturing solar-generation systems, and cost savings achieved by operating Tesla's automotive and energy divisions as sister companies.

In August 2013, Musk published a blog post detailing his design for a solar-powered, city-to-city elevated transit system called the Hyperloop that could take passengers and cars from Los Angeles to San Francisco (a distance of 380 miles) in 30 minutes. He then held a press call to go over the details. In Musk's vision, the Hyperloop would transport people via aluminum pods enclosed inside of steel tubes. He described the design as looking like a shotgun with the tubes running side by side for most of the route and closing the loop at either end.[16] The tubes would be mounted on columns 50 to 100 yards apart, and the pods inside would travel up to 800 miles per hour. The pods could be small to carry just people or enlarged to allow people to drive a car into a pod and depart. Musk estimated that a Los Angeles-to-San Francisco Hyperloop, with 70 pods departing every 30 seconds and spaced 5 miles apart, could be built for $6 billion with people-only pods, or $10 billion for the larger pods capable of holding cars with people inside. Musk claimed his Hyperloop alternative would be four times as fast as California's proposed $70 billion high-speed train, have a pleasant and super-smooth ride, and be "much cheaper" than air travel. Musk announced that he would not form a company to build Hyperloop systems; rather he was releasing his design in hopes that others would take on such projects. As of 2018, there were several Hyperloop projects under development and others being formally considered.

Since 2008, many business articles had been written about Musk's brilliant entrepreneurship in creating companies with revolutionary products that either spawned new industries or disruptively transformed existing industries. In a 2012 *Success* magazine article, Musk indicated that his commitments to his spacecraft, electric car, and solar panel businesses were long term and deeply felt.[17] The author quoted Musk as saying, "I never expect to sort of sell them off and do something else. I expect to be with those companies as far into the future as I can imagine." Musk indicated he was involved in SolarCity and Tesla Motors "because I'm concerned about the environment," while "SpaceX is about trying to help us work toward extending life beyond Earth on a permanent basis and becoming a multiplanetary species." The same writer described Musk's approach to a business as one of rallying employees and investors without creating false hope.[18] The article quoted Musk as saying:

> You've got to communicate, particularly within the company, the true state of the company. When people

really understand it's do or die but if we work hard and pull through, there's going to be a great outcome, people will give it everything they've got.

Asked if he relied more on information or instinct in making key decisions, Musk said he made no bright-line distinction between the two.

> Data informs the instinct. Generally, I wait until the data and my instincts are in alignment. And if either the data or my instincts are out of alignment, then I sort of keep working the issue until they are in alignment, either positive or negative.[19]

Musk was widely regarded as being an inspiring and visionary entrepreneur with astronomical ambition and willingness to invest his own money in risky and highly problematic business ventures. He set stretch performance targets and high product quality standards, and he pushed hard for their achievement. He exhibited perseverance, dedication, and an exceptionally strong work ethic—he typically worked 85 to 90 hours a week. Most weeks, Musk split his time between SpaceX and Tesla.

In 2017, Elon Musk's base salary as Tesla's CEO was $49,920, an amount required by California's minimum wage law; however, he was accepting only $1 in salary. The company's Board of Directors in 2017 established an executive compensation plan for Musk tied to Tesla's performance on various metrics; compensation was in the form of stock option awards subject to various vesting conditions. Musk controlled 37.8 million shares of Tesla common stock (worth some $13 billion in March 2018); his shareholdings gave him 21.9 percent of total shareholder voting power in Tesla.

TESLA IN 2018

Following the acquisition of Solar City, Tesla described its business in the following way:

> We design, develop, manufacture and sell high-performance fully electric vehicles, and energy generation and storage systems, and also install and maintain such systems and sell solar electricity. We are the world's only vertically integrated sustainable energy company, offering end-to-end clean energy products, including generation, storage and consumption. We have established and continue to grow a global network of stores, vehicle service centers and Supercharger stations to accelerate the widespread adoption of our products, and

we continue to develop self-driving capability in order to improve vehicle safety. Our sustainable energy products, engineering expertise, intense focus to accelerate the world's transition to sustainable energy, and business model differentiate us from other companies.

We currently produce and sell three fully electric vehicles, the Model S sedan, the Model X sport utility vehicle ("SUV") and the Model 3 sedan. . . . We also intend to bring additional vehicles to market in the future, including trucks and an all-new sports car. . . .We sell our vehicles through our own sales and service network which we are continuing to grow globally. The benefits we receive from distribution ownership enable us to improve the overall customer experience, the speed of product development, and the capital efficiency of our business. We are also continuing to build our network of Superchargers and Destination Chargers in North America, Europe, and Asia to provide both fast charging that enables convenient long distance travel.

. . .In addition, we are leveraging our technological expertise in batteries, power electronics, and integrated systems to manufacture and sell energy storage products. In late 2016, we began production and deliveries of our latest generation energy storage products, Powerwall 2 and Powerpack 2. Powerwall 2 is a home battery. . . . Powerpack 2 is an energy storage system for commercial, industrial, and utility applications.

Finally, we sell and lease solar systems (with or without accompanying energy storage systems) to residential and commercial customers and sell renewable energy to residential and commercial customers at prices that are typically below utility rates. Since 2006, we have installed solar energy systems for hundreds of thousands of customers. Our long-term lease and power purchase agreements with our customers generate recurring payments and create a portfolio of high-quality receivables that we leverage to further reduce the cost of making the switch to solar energy. The electricity produced by our solar installations represents a very small fraction of total U.S. electricity generation. With tens of millions of single-family homes and businesses in our primary service territories, and many more in other locations, we have a large opportunity to expand and grow this business.

We manufacture our vehicle products primarily at our facilities in Fremont, California, Lathrop, California, Tilburg, Netherlands and at our Gigafactory 1 near Reno, Nevada. We manufacture our energy storage products at Gigafactory 1 and our solar products at our factories in Fremont, California and Buffalo, New York (Gigafactory 2).[20]

During 2014-2017, Tesla raised billions of dollars via the sale of senior notes convertible into common stock, other types of long-term debt, and issues of new common stock to provide funding for research and development (R&D), the development of new models, expanded production capabilities, an ever-growing network of recharging stations, and opening retail showrooms and Tesla service centers. Tesla's long-term debt and contractual capital lease obligations grew from $600 million at year-end 2013 to $9.4 billion at year-end 2017, and the number of shares of common stock outstanding rose from 119 million to nearly 166 million during the same period. In the most recent four years, Tesla had burned through cash at a torrid pace because of the heavy expenses it was incurring for design and engineering, gearing up to produce certain parts and component systems internally, constructing new facilities, equipping vehicle assembly lines with robotics technology, tools, and other machinery, and adding over 31,000 new employees to the almost 6,000 employees it had at year-end 2013.

Tesla ended 2017 with $3.4 billion in cash and cash equivalents. Executive management expected that the company's capital expenditures in 2018 would total about $800 million.

TESLA'S STRATEGY TO BECOME THE WORLD'S BIGGEST AND MOST HIGHLY REGARDED PRODUCER OF ELECTRIC VEHICLES

In 2018, Tesla's strategy was focused on gearing up production of the Model 3 and expanding the company's production capacity, finishing the construction of its $5 billion Gigafactory 1 near Reno, Nevada, to produce batteries and battery packs for Tesla's vehicles, and adding sales galleries, service centers, and Supercharger stations in the United States, much of Europe, China, and Australia. At the Tesla Energy division, efforts were underway to (1) begin manufacturing of photovoltaic cells and a new Solar Roof product at Gigafactory 2 in Buffalo, New York; (2) begin to grow the sales of its energy storage products currently being manufactured at Gigafactory 1; and (3) introduce the first-of-its-kind Solar Roof for commercial and residential applications. Tesla's near-term objective was to triple its sales of energy storage products in 2018.

Product Line Strategy

A key element of Tesla's long-term strategy was offer vehicle buyers a full line of electric vehicle options. So far Tesla had introduced four models—the Tesla Roadster, Model S, Model X, and Model 3. But plans were already in place to introduce the Tesla Semi truck (prototypes were being tested in March 2018), a crossover compact SUV (tentatively called the Model Y) based on a third-generation platform more advanced and production-efficient than the Model 3 (designs were to be publicly released in late 2018), a new Roadster 2 model, and a pick-up truck.

Tesla's First Vehicle—The Tesla Roadster   Following Tesla's initial funding in 2004, Musk took an active role within the company. Although he was not involved in day-to-day business operations, he nonetheless exerted strong influence in the design of the Tesla Roadster, a two-seat convertible that could accelerate from 0 to 60 miles per hour in as little as 3.7 seconds, had a maximum speed of about 120 miles per hour, could travel about 245 miles on a single charge, and had a base price of $109,000. Musk insisted from the beginning that the Roadster have a lightweight, high-strength carbon fiber body, and he influenced the design of components of the Roadster ranging from the power electronics module to the headlamps and other styling features.[21] Prototypes of the Roadster were introduced to the public in July 2006. The first "Signature One Hundred" set of fully equipped Roadsters sold out in less than three weeks; the second hundred sold out by October 2007. General production began in March 2008. New models of the Roadster were introduced in July 2009 (including the Roadster Sport with a base price of $128,500) and in July 2010. Sales of Roadster models to countries in Europe and Asia began in 2010. From 2008 through 2012, Tesla sold more than 2,450 Roadsters in 31 countries.[22] Sales of Roadster models ended in December 2012 so that the company could concentrate exclusively on producing and marketing the Model S. However, Tesla announced in early 2015 that Roadster owners would be able to obtain a Roadster 3.0 package that enabled a 40 to 50 percent improvement in driving range to as much as 400 miles on a single charge; management indicated additional updates for Roadsters would be forthcoming. In 2017, Tesla announced it would re-introduce a new version of the Roadster in 2020 (after it began deliveries of the Tesla Semi truck and Model Y).

Tesla's Second Vehicle—The Model S   Customer deliveries of Tesla's second vehicle—the sleek, eye-catching Model S sedan—began in July 2012. Tesla introduced several new options for the Model S in 2013, including a sub-zero weather package, parking sensors, upgraded leather interior, several new wheel options, and a yacht-style center console. Xenon headlights and a high definition backup camera were made standard equipment on all Model S cars. In 2014 an all-wheel drive powertrain was introduced to provide buyers with four powertrain options. The Model S powertrain options were further modified several times. In March 2018, the Model S was being offered with three powertrains options:

- 75D—all-wheel drive, 75 kWh battery pack, 259 mile driving range, 0 to 60 mph in 4.2 seconds, with a standard price of $74,500

- 100D—all-wheel drive, 100 kWh battery pack, 335 mile driving range, 0 to 60 mph in 4.1 seconds, with a standard price of $94,000 (which included Smart Air Suspension)

- P100D—maximum performance all-wheel drive with dual front and rear motors (mounted on the front and rear axles), 100 kWh battery pack, 315 mile driving range, 0 to 60 mph in 2.5 seconds, with a standard price of $135,000 (which included the best interior and other premium upgrades)

Popular options included enhanced autopilot software ($5,000); full self-driving capability—subject to further software validation and regulatory approval ($3,000); and third-row, rear-facing seating ($4,000). From time to time, Tesla sent software updates to all Model S vehicles previously delivered to customers that included new and updated features. In 2018, all Model S vehicles had a standard software feature called "Range Assurance," an always-running application within the car's navigation system that kept tabs on the vehicle's battery charge-level and the locations of Tesla Supercharging stations and parking-spot chargers in the vicinity. When the vehicle's battery began running low, an alert appeared on the navigation screen, along with a list of nearby Tesla Supercharger stations and public charging facilities; a second warning appeared when the vehicle was about to go beyond the radius of nearby chargers without enough juice to get to the next facility, at which point drivers were directed to the nearest charge point. There was also a Trip Planner feature that enabled drivers to plan long-distance trips based on the best locations for recharging both en route and at the destination; during travel, the software was programmed to pull in new data about every 30 seconds, updating to show which charging facilities had vacancies or were full. Autopilot software features were updated and upgraded as fast as they were developed and tested.

In the United States, customers who purchased a Model S (or any other Tesla model) were eligible for a federal tax credit of up to $7,500. A number of states also offered rebates on electric vehicle purchases, with states like California and New York offering rebates as high as $7,500. Customers who leased a Model S were not entitled to rebates.

Tesla's Third Vehicle—The Model X Crossover SUV
To reduce the development costs of the Model X, Tesla had designed the Model X so that it could share about 60 percent of the Model S platform. The Model X had seating for 7 adults, dual electric motors that powered an all-wheel drive system, and a driving range of about 260 miles per charge. The Model X's distinctive "falcon-wing doors" provided easy access to the second and third seating rows, resulting in a profile that resembled a sedan more than an SUV. The three drive train options for the Model X in 2018 were the same as for the Model S, but the driving ranges and acceleration times for the Model X were different from those of the Model S. In 2018, the standard price for the Model X with a 75D drive train was $79,500; the standard price for 100D Model X was $96,000 (which included Smart Air Suspension); and the standard price for a P100D Model X was $140,000 (which included the best interior and other premium upgrades). The Model X was the first SUV ever to achieve a 5-star safety rating in every category and sub-category; it had both the lowest probability of occupant injury and a rollover risk half that of any SUV on the road. Over-the-Internet software updates were standard.

Tesla's Fourth Vehicle—The Model 3   The idea behind the Model 3 was to incorporate all the company had learned from the development and production of the Roadster, Model S, and Model X to create the world's first mass market electric vehicle priced on par with its gasoline-powered equivalents. The Model 3 was attractively styled, with seating for five adults, a driving range of 210 to 310 miles depending on drive train selection, and 0 to 60 mph acceleration capability of less than 6 seconds. While the stated base price was

$35,000, the range of available upgrades and options could up the price to $55,000 or more. The average selling price of the Model 3 was expected to be around $42,500.

By most estimates, going into 2018, at least 300,000 people had paid $1,000 to reserve a Model 3 and were waiting in line for delivery. From the outset, the Model 3 had been designed to enable efficient, high-volume production. However, the Model 3 still posed a much tougher production cost challenge than the three previous models, all of which had prices in the $80,000 to $130,000 range. The Model 3's profitability hinged on being able to drive production costs per unit down more than 50 percent below what had been achieved with prior models. Of particular concern was the lithium-ion battery pack, the single biggest cost component in the Model S and Model X, which had an estimated cost of $209 per kilowatt-hour as of December 2017.[23] Part of the solution was equipping the Model 3 with less powerful electric motors, but a host of other cost-saving efficiencies had to be achieved as well—the cost-profit outcome was uncertain and speculative as of March 2018.

One factor likely to prove problematic for many prospective Model 3 buyers in the United States was a provision stating that once the *cumulative* sales volume of a manufacturer's zero emission vehicles in the United States reached 200,000 vehicles, the size of the $7,500 federal tax credit entered a one-year phase-out period where buyers of qualifying vehicles were "eligible for 50 percent of the credit if acquired in the first two quarters of the phase-out period and 25 percent of the credit if acquired in the third or fourth quarter of the phase-out period."[24] Purchasers of that manufacturer's vehicles were not eligible for any federal tax credit after the phase-out period. Tesla's cumulative sales in the United States would almost certainly exceed 200,000 vehicles sometime in 2018 (probably sometime before July 1), meaning that a hefty percentage of people with Model 3 reservations would qualify for only some or none of the $7,500 tax credit—buyers who leased a Tesla were not eligible for the tax credit (the credit went to the company offering the lease; the tax credits were also based on the size of the battery). Some states also offered tax credit for the purchases of plug-in electric vehicles. There were also a variety of tax credits offered by states. The governments of China, Japan, Norway, United Kingdom, and several other European countries offered tax incentives for electric vehicle purchases as well. In 2018, Canada discontinued the use of incentives for electric vehicles with a manufacturer's suggested list price of price greater than C\$75,000 (US\$58,500).

The Tesla Semi-Truck Mention was made of a semi-truck in Tesla's 2016 master plan. But behind the scenes Tesla had moved swiftly to come up with not only a design but also prototypes. The Semi was unveiled with much fanfare at a press conference on November 16, 2017. The company described the Semi as a Class 8 semi-trailer truck prototype that would be powered by 4 electric motors of the type used in the Model 3; have Tesla Autopilot, which permitted semi-autonomous driving, as standard equipment; and have a driving range of up to a range of 500 miles (805 km) on a full charge. Elon Musk said the 500-mile version, equipped with Tesla's latest battery design, would be able to run for 400 miles (640 km) after an 80 percent charge in 30 minutes using a solar-powered Tesla Megacharger charging station. He also said the Semi would be able to accelerate from 0 to 60 mph in 5 seconds unloaded and in 20 seconds fully loaded. Tesla expected to offer a warranty for a million miles and said maintenance would be simpler than for a diesel truck. Production of the Semi was scheduled to begin in 2019. A week later, Musk said that the regular production versions for the 300-mile range version of the Semi would be priced at \$150,000 and the 500-mile range version would be priced at \$180,000; the company also said it planned to offer a Founder's Series Semi at \$200,000. Scores of companies, including Wal-Mart, United Parcel Service, Anheuser-Busch, J.B. Hunt Trucking Co, and PepsiCo, immediately lined up to place pre-orders for 5 to 150 Semis (at an initial reservation price of \$5,000, which was quickly raised to \$20,000 per reservation) so they could conduct tests of how well the Semi would perform in their operations. In March 2018, Tesla began testing the Semi with real cargo, hauling battery packs from Gigafactory 1 in Nevada to the Tesla Factory in Fremont, California. Pictures of the Semi being loaded with cargo at the Nevada Gigafactory and traveling on the highways were immediately publicized in the media and posted on the Internet and social media.

In Elon Musk's Q1 2018 Update Letter to Shareholders on May 2, 2018, no mention was made of the Tesla Semi; however, in a later conference call with Wall Street analysts that same day, Musk did say the company had about 2,000 reservations for the Semi. Observers speculated that near-term plans for the Semi had moved to the back burner temporarily due to Tesla's lack of capital to fund further development and build a new production facility for the Semi.

Model Y In In 2017, Elon Musk announced that Tesla had launched plans for the development and 2020 production of an all-electric crossover SUV that would be built on the same platform as the Model 3. The Model Y was expected to be a smaller version of the Model X and carry price tags comparable to the Model 3. Industry observers speculated that that Tesla would show prototypes of the Model Y in the second half of 2018, after hearing Musk say in May 2018 that the company would announce no later than the fourth quarter of 2018 where a production facility for the Model Y would be located. Because Musk was aiming for production of one million Model Ys annually, a second Model Y facility was expected to be established in China in 2021. Musk also said, "I think the Model Y is going to be a manufacturing revolution." However, it seemed doubtful that Tesla could get the Model Y into the marketplace by the end of 2020, given the 24 to 36 months it usually took to build a new vehicle production facility, equip it, staff it, and build out the supply chain. Some observers speculated that Tesla might purchase an existing plant from an automaker, since sedan production in the United States was dropping rapidly due to an accelerating shift in buyer preferences away from sedans and toward SUVs and light trucks. Ford Motor had just announced it would cease production of four of its slow-selling traditional passenger cars (Taurus, Fusion, Focus, and Fiesta) by 2020; General Motors was expected to cease production of its Chevrolet Cruze compact and possibly its Chevrolet Sonic and Impala sedans at the end of their current product cycles. Fiat Chrysler has already killed its Dodge Dart and Chrysler 200 sedan models.

Distribution Strategy: A Company-Owned and Operated Network of Retail Stores and Service Centers

Tesla sold its vehicles directly to buyers and also provided them with after-sale service through a network of company-owned sales galleries and service centers. This contrasted sharply with the strategy of rival motor vehicle manufacturers, all of whom sold vehicles and replacement parts at wholesale prices to their networks of franchised dealerships that in turn handled retail sales, maintenance and service, and warranty repairs. Management believed that integrating forward into the business of traditional automobile dealers and operating its own retail sales and service network had three important advantages:

1. *The ability to create and control its own version of a compelling buying customer experience,* one that was differentiated from the buying experience consumers had with sales and service locations of franchised automobile dealers. Having customers deal directly with Tesla-employed sales and service personnel enabled Tesla to (a) engage and inform potential customers about electric vehicles in general and the advantages of owning a Tesla in particular and (b) build a more personal relationship with customers and, hopefully, instill a lasting and favorable impression of Tesla Motors, its mission, and the caliber and performance of its vehicles.

2. *The ability to achieve greater operating economies in performing sales and service activities.* Management believed that a company-operated sales and service network offered substantial opportunities to better control inventory costs of both vehicles and replacement parts, manage warranty service and pricing, maintain and strengthen the Tesla brand, and obtain rapid customer feedback.

3. *The opportunity to capture the sales and service revenues of traditional automobile dealerships.* Rival motor vehicle manufacturers sold vehicles and replacement parts at wholesale prices to their networks of franchised dealerships that in turn handled retail sales, maintenance and service, and warranty repairs. But when Tesla buyers purchased a vehicle at a Tesla-owned sales gallery, Tesla captured the full retail sales price, roughly 10 percent greater than the wholesale price realized by vehicle manufacturers selling through franchised dealers. And, by operating its own service centers, it captured service revenues not available to vehicle manufacturers who relied upon their franchised dealers to provide needed maintenance and repairs. Furthermore, Tesla management believed that company-owned service centers avoided the conflict of interest between vehicle manufacturers and their franchised dealers where the sale of warranty parts and repairs by a dealer were a key source of revenue and profit for the dealer but where warranty-related costs were typically a substantial expense for the vehicle manufacturer.

Tesla Sales Galleries and Showrooms   Currently, all of Tesla's sales galleries and showrooms were in or near major metropolitan areas; some were in prominent regional shopping malls and others were on highly visible sites along busy thoroughfares. Most sales locations had only several vehicles in stock which were available for immediate sale. The vast majority of Tesla buyers, however, preferred to customize their vehicle by placing an order via the Internet, either while in a sales gallery or at home.

In years past, Tesla had aggressively expanded its network of sales galleries and service centers to broaden its geographical presence and to provide better maintenance and repair service in areas with a high concentration of Tesla owners. In 2013, Tesla began combining its sales and service activities at a single location (rather than having separate locations, as earlier had been the case); experience indicated that combination sales and service locations were more cost-efficient and facilitated faster expansion of the company's retail footprint. At the end of 2017, Tesla had 338 sales and service locations around the world; an unspecified number of new openings were planned for 2018. Tesla's goal was to have sufficient service locations to ensure that after-sale services were available to owners when and where needed.

However, in the United States, there was a lurking problem with Tesla's strategy to bypass distributing through franchised Tesla dealers and sell directly to consumers. Going back many years, franchised automobile dealers in the United States had feared that automotive manufacturers might one day decide to integrate forward into selling and servicing the vehicles they produced. To foreclose any attempts by manufacturers to compete directly against their franchised dealers, automobile dealers in every state in the United States had formed statewide franchised dealer associations to lobby for legislation blocking motor vehicle manufacturers from becoming retailers of new and used cars and providing maintenance and repair services to vehicle owners. Legislation either forbidding or severely restricting the ability of automakers to sell vehicles directly to the public had been passed in 48 states; these laws had been in effect for many years, and franchised dealer associations were diligent in pushing for strict enforcement of these laws.

As sales of the Model S rose briskly from 2013 to 2015 and Tesla continued opening more sales galleries and service centers, both franchised dealers and statewide dealer associations became increasingly anxious about "the Tesla problem" and what actions might need to be taken. Dealers and dealer trade association in a number of states were openly vocal about their concerns and actively began lobbying state legislatures to consider either enforcement actions against Tesla or amendments to existing legislation that would bring a halt to Tesla's efforts to sell vehicles at company-owned showrooms. A host of skirmishes ensued in 12 states. In several cases, settlements were reached that allowed Tesla to open a select few sales locations, but the numbers were capped. In states where manufacturer direct sales to consumers were expressly prohibited, Tesla was allowed to have sales galleries, service centers, and Supercharger locations—but was prevented from using its sales galleries to take orders, conduct test drives, deliver cars, or discuss pricing with potential buyers. Buyers in these states could place an order via the Internet, specify when would like the car to arrive, and then either have it delivered to a nearby Tesla service center for pickup or have it delivered directly to their home or business location. As of March 2018, the prevailing state restrictions on Tesla sales galleries did not seem to be limiting Tesla's sales in a meaningful way.

Tesla Service Centers   Tesla Roadster owners could upload data from their vehicle and send it to a service center on a memory card; all other Tesla owners had an on-board system that could communicate directly with a service center, allowing service technicians to diagnose and remedy many problems before ever looking at the vehicle. When maintenance or service was required, a customer could schedule service by contacting a Tesla service center. Some service locations offered valet service, where the owner's car was picked up, replaced with a very well-equipped Model S loaner car, and then returned when the service was completed—there was no additional charge for valet service. In some locations, owners could opt to have service performed at their home, office, or other remote location by a Tesla Mobile Service technician who had the capability to perform a variety of services that did not require a vehicle lift. Mobile service technicians could perform most warranty repairs, but the cost of their visit was not covered under the New Vehicle Limited Warranty. Mobile service pricing was based on a per visit, per vehicle basis; there was a $100 minimum charge per visit. Tesla's mobile service fleet consisted of 230 vehicles in February 2018, with coverage of all of North America. Going into 2018, the company's mobile service fleet in North America was completing 30 percent of all service jobs at a cost below the average fees charged at its service centers.

Prepaid Maintenance Program   Tesla recommended that Model S and Model X owners have an inspection every 12 months or 12,500 miles, whichever came first. Owners could purchase plans covering prepaid maintenance for three years or four years; these involved simply prepaying for service inspections at a discounted rate. All Model S or Model X vehicles were protected by a 4 year or 50,000 miles (whichever came first) New Vehicle Limited Warranty and an 8 year or unlimited miles Battery and Drive Unit Limited Warranty. These warranties covered the repair or replacement necessary to correct defects in materials or workmanship of any parts manufactured or supplied by Tesla. Owners could also purchase an Extended Service Agreement for 2 years (or 25,000 miles) or four years or 50,000 miles, whichever came first.

Tesla's Supercharger Network: Providing Recharging Services to Owners on Long Distance Trips   A major component of Tesla's strategy to build rapidly-growing long-term demand for its vehicles was to make battery recharging while driving long distances convenient and worry-free for all Tesla vehicle owners. Tesla's solution to providing owners with ample and convenient recharging opportunities was to establish an extensive geographic network of recharging stations. Tesla's Supercharger stations were strategically placed along major highways connecting city centers, usually at locations with such nearby amenities as roadside diners, cafes, and shopping centers that enabled owners to have a brief rest stop or get a quick meal during the recharging process—about 90 percent of Model S and Model X buyers opted to have their vehicle equipped with supercharging capability when they ordered their vehicle. All Model S and Model X owners were entitled to *free* supercharging service at any of Tesla's Supercharging stations; Model 3 owners had to pay a recharging fee. In March 2018, Tesla announced price increases for its Supercharging stations to about $0.25 per kwh. Tesla owners charged their vehicles at home more than 90 percent of the time and used Supercharger stations mainly for trips or when they needed extra range. A 50 percent recharge took 20 minutes, an 80 percent recharge took 40 minutes, and a 100 percent recharge took 75 minutes. As of year-end 2017, Tesla had a total of 1,128 Supercharger stations globally; most Tesla stations had between 6 and 20 charging spaces, but newer stations in high-traffic corridors had as many as 40 spaces, a customer lounge, and a café. About 300 new Supercharger locations were planned for 2018.

Tesla executives never expected that Supercharger stations would become a profit center for the company; rather, they believed that the benefits of rapidly growing the size of the company's Supercharger network came from (1) relieving the "range anxiety" electric vehicle owners suffered when driving on a long-distance trip and (2) reducing the inconvenience to travelers of having to deviate from the shortest direct route and detour to the closest Supercharger station for needed recharging.

Technology and Product Development Strategy

Headed into 2018, Tesla had spent over $4.1 billion on R&D activities to design, develop, test, and refine the components and systems needed to produce top quality electric vehicles and, further, to design and develop prototypes of the Tesla Roadster, Model S, Model X, Model 3, and Tesla Semi vehicles (see Exhibit 1 for R&D spending from 2013 to 2017). Tesla executives believed its R&D activities had produced core competencies in powertrain and vehicle engineering and innovative manufacturing techniques. The company's core intellectual property was contained in its electric powertrain technology— the battery pack, power electronics, induction motor, gearbox, and control software that enabled these key components to operate as a system. Tesla personnel had designed each of these major elements for the Tesla Roadster and Model S; much of this technology had been used in the powertrain systems that Tesla previously had built for other manufacturers (mainly Toyota and Mercedes) and had been further improved and refined in the powertrain systems being used in the Model X, Model 3, and the prototypes for the Tesla Semi.

The powertrain used in Tesla vehicles in 2018 was a compact, modular system with far fewer moving parts than the powertrains of traditional gasoline-powered vehicles, a feature that enabled Tesla to implement powertrain enhancements and improvements as fast as they could be identified, designed, and tested. Tesla had incorporated its latest powertrain technology into its three current models and was planning to use much of this technology in producing its forthcoming electric vehicles.

Although Tesla had more than 500 patents and pending patent applications domestically and internationally in a broad range of areas, in 2014, Tesla announced a patent policy whereby it irrevocably pledged the company would not initiate a lawsuit against any party for infringing Tesla's patents through activity relating to electric vehicles or related equipment so long as the party was acting in good faith. Elon Musk said the company made this pledge in order to encourage the advancement of a common, rapidly-evolving platform for electric vehicles, thereby benefiting itself, other companies making electric vehicles, and the world. Investor reaction to this announcement was largely negative on grounds that it would negate any technology-based competitive advantage over rival manufacturers of electric vehicles.

Battery Pack   In prior years, Tesla had tested hundreds of battery cells of different chemistries and performance features. It had an internal battery cell testing lab and had assembled an extensive performance database of the many available lithium-ion cell vendors and chemistry types. Based on this evaluation, it had elected to use "18650 form factor" lithium-ion battery cells, chiefly because a battery pack containing 18,650 cells offered two to three times the driving range of the lithium-ion cells used by other makers of electric vehicles. Management believed that the company's accumulated experience and expertise had produced a core competence in designing battery packs that were safe, reliable, and had long lives. At the same time, it had pioneered the development of advanced manufacturing techniques that enabled mass production of high quality battery packs at low cost. Ongoing improvement of its production methods had allowed the Tesla to reduce the costs and improve the performance of its batteries over time. Management believed Tesla's current battery pack design gave it the ability to change battery cell chemistries and form factor if needed and, also, to capitalize on the advancements in battery cell technology being made globally. Going forward,

Tesla believed it had the capabilities to quickly incorporate the latest advancements in battery technology and continue to optimize battery pack system performance and cost for its future vehicles.

Power Electronics The power electronics in Tesla's powertrain system had two primary functions—the control of torque generation in the motor while driving and the control of energy delivery back into the battery pack while charging. The first function was accomplished through the drive inverter, which converted direct current from the battery pack into alternating current to drive the induction motors, provide acceleration, and enhance the overall driving performance of the vehicle. The second function was to capture kinetic energy from the wheels being in motion but being slowed down by applying the brakes and reverse the flow of energy to help recharge the battery pack—a technology called "regenerative braking." (When brakes are applied in gasoline-powered vehicles, the brake pads clamp down on the wheels to slow the vehicle (letting the kinetic energy escape as heat); but in electric vehicles (and most hybrid vehicles), the regenerative braking systems slow the vehicle by reversing the flow of electricity to the electric motors powering the wheels, while also capturing the heat from the kinetic energy to generate electrical energy for partially recharging the battery pack.) When the electric vehicle was parked, battery recharging was accomplished by the vehicle's charger, which converted alternating current (usually from a wall outlet or other electricity source) into direct current which could be accepted by the battery.

Owners could use any available source of power to charge a Tesla's battery pack. A standard 12 amp/110-volt wall outlet could recharge a mostly discharged battery pack to full capacity in about 21 hours. Tesla recommended that owners install *at least* a 24 amp/240-volt outlet in their garage or carport (the same voltage used by many electric ovens and clothes dryers), which permitted charging at the rate of 34 miles of range per hour of charging time. But owners who installed a more powerful 60-amp/240-volt wall connector outlet could charge a 75 kWh battery that had been driven 300 miles in 8 hours and 42 minutes; installation of a 90 amp/240 volt circuit breaker enabled charging a 100 kWh battery in 5 hours and 47 minutes. On a road trip, a 120 kW Supercharger could recharge a battery driven 300 miles in 75 minutes.

Control Software The battery pack and the performance and safety systems of Tesla vehicles required the use of numerous microprocessors and sophisticated software. For example, computer-driven software monitored the charge state of each of the cells of the battery pack and managed all of the safety systems. The flow of electricity between the battery pack and the motor had to be tightly controlled in order to deliver the best possible performance and driving experience. There were software algorithms that enabled the vehicle to mimic the "creep" feeling that drivers expected from an internal combustion engine vehicle without having to apply pressure on the accelerator. Other algorithms were used to control traction, vehicle stability, acceleration, and regenerative braking. Drivers used the vehicle's information systems to optimize performance and charging modes and times. In addition to the vehicle control software, Tesla had developed software for the infotainment systems of the Model S, Model X, and Model 3. Almost all of the software programs had been developed and written by Tesla personnel. Starting in 2014, Tesla began devoting progressively larger fractions of its programming resources and expertise to developing and enhancing its software for vehicle autopilot functionality, including such features as auto-steering, traffic aware cruise control, automated lane changing, automated parking, driver warning systems, automated braking, object detection, and self-driving. In October 2016, Tesla began equipping all models with hardware needed for full self-driving capability, including cameras that provided 360-degree visibility, updated ultrasonic sensors for object detection, a forward-facing radar with enhanced processing, and a powerful onboard computer. Wireless software updates periodically sent to the microprocessors on board each Tesla owner's vehicle, together with field data feedback loops from the onboard camera, radar, ultrasonic sensors, and GPS, enabled the autopilot system in Tesla vehicles to continually learn and improve its performance. In March 2018, Elon Musk said he expected Tesla's autopilot software to be able to handle all modes of driving by the end of 2019 and that Tesla's autopilot system would safer than human drivers within two years.

Vehicle Design and Engineering

Tesla had devoted considerable effort to creating significant in-house capabilities related to designing and engineering portions of its vehicles, and it had become knowledgeable about the design and engineering of those parts, components, and systems that it purchased from suppliers. Tesla personnel had designed and engineered the body, chassis, and interior of its current models. As a matter of necessity, Tesla was forced to redesign the heating, cooling, and ventilation system for its electric vehicles to operate without the energy generated from an internal combustion engine and to integrate with its own battery-powered thermal management system. In addition, the low voltage electric system which powered the radio, power windows, and heated seats had to be designed specifically for use in an electric vehicle. Tesla had developed expertise in integrating these components with the high-voltage power source in its vehicles and in designing components that significantly reduced their load on the vehicle's battery pack, so as to maximize the available driving range. All Tesla vehicles incorporated the latest advances in mobile computing, sensing, displays, and connectivity.

Tesla personnel had accumulated considerable expertise in lightweight materials, since an electric vehicle's driving range was heavily impacted by the vehicle's weight and mass. The Tesla Roadster had been built with an in-house designed carbon fiber body to provide a good balance of strength and mass. The Model S and Model X had a lightweight aluminum body and a chassis that incorporated a variety of materials and production methods to help optimize vehicle weight, strength, safety, and performance. Weight reduction was an important factor in the design of the Model 3. In addition, top management believed that the company's design and engineering team had core competencies in computer-aided design and crash test simulations; this expertise was had reduced the development time for the Model 3 and the Tesla Semi prototypes.

Manufacturing Strategy

Tesla had contracted with Lotus Cars, Ltd. to produce Tesla Roadster "gliders" (a complete vehicle minus the electric powertrain) at a Lotus factory in Hethel, England. The Tesla gliders were then shipped to a Tesla facility in Menlo Park, California, where the battery pack, induction motors, and other powertrain components were installed as part of the final assembly process. The production of Roadster gliders ceased in January 2012.

In May 2010, Tesla purchased the major portion of a recently closed automobile plant in Fremont, California, for $42 million; months later, Tesla purchased some of the plant's equipment for $17 million. The facility—formerly a General Motors manufacturing plant (1960–1982), then operated as joint venture between General Motors and Toyota (1984–2010)—was closed in 2010. Tesla executives viewed the facility as one of the largest, most advanced, and cleanest automotive production plants in the world. The 5.3 million square feet of manufacturing and office space was deemed sufficient for Tesla to produce about 500,000 vehicles annually (approximately 1 percent of the total worldwide car production), thus giving Tesla room to grow its output of electric vehicles to 500,000 or more vehicles annually. The Fremont plant's location in the northern section of Silicon Valley facilitated hiring talented engineers already residing nearby and because the short distance between Fremont and Tesla's Palo Alto headquarters ensured "a tight feedback loop between vehicle engineering, manufacturing, and other divisions within the company."[25] Tesla officially took possession of the 370-acre site in October 2010, renamed it the Tesla Factory, and immediately launched efforts to get a portion of the massive facility ready to begin manufacturing components and assembling the Model S in 2012. In late 2015, Tesla completed construction of a new high-volume paint shop and a new body shop line capable of turning out 3,500 Model S and Model X bodies per week (enough for 175,000 vehicles annually). In 2016 and 2017, Tesla made significant additional investments at the Tesla Factory, including a new body shop with space and equipment for Model 3 final assembly. Tesla expected the Fremont facility, together with a neighboring 500,000-square-foot building that Tesla had leased, would be expanded to 10 million square feet in the coming years. However, there were strong rumors in 2018 that Tesla was actively looking for additional production sites—one in the United States, one in China, and one in Europe.

In December 2012, Tesla opened a new 60,000 square-foot facility in Tilburg, Netherlands, about 50 miles from the port of Rotterdam, to serve as the final assembly and distribution point for all Tesla vehicles sold in Europe and Scandinavia. The facility, called the Tilburg Assembly Plant, received nearly complete vehicles shipped from the Tesla Factory, performed certain final assembly activities, conducted final vehicle testing, and handled the delivery to customers across. It also functioned as Tesla's European service and parts headquarters. Tilburg's central location and its excellent rail and highway network to all major markets on the European continent allowed Tesla to distribute to anywhere across the continent in about 12 hours. The Tilburg operation had been expanded to over 200,000 square feet in order to accommodate a parts distribution warehouse for service centers throughout Europe, a center for remanufacturing work, and a customer service center. A nearby facility in Amsterdam provided corporate oversight for European sales, service, and administrative functions.

Tesla's manufacturing strategy was to source a number of parts and components from outside suppliers but to design, develop, and manufacture in-house those key components where it had considerable intellectual property and core competencies (namely lithium-ion battery packs, electric motors, gearboxes, and other powertrain components) and to perform all assembly-related activities itself. In 2018, the Tesla Factory contained several production-related activities, including stamping, machining, casting, plastics molding, drive unit production, robotics-assisted body assembly, paint operations, final vehicle assembly, and end-of-line quality testing. In addition, the Tesla Factory manufactured lithium-ion battery packs, electric motors, gearboxes, and certain other components for its vehicles. In addition, Tesla manufactured lithium-ion battery packs, electric motors, gearboxes and components for Model S and Model X at the Tesla Factory. While some major vehicle component systems were purchased from suppliers, there was a high level of vertical integration in the manufacturing processes at the Tesla Factory in 2018. From 2016 to 2018, efforts to expand production capacity at the Tesla Factory were ongoing to accommodate growing sales of the Model S and Model X and to enable production of the Model 3 to reach 10,000 units per week.

In 2014, Tesla began producing and machining various aluminum components at a 431,000 square-foot facility in Lathrop, CA; an aluminum castings operation was added in 2016. Aluminum parts and components were used extensively to help reduce the weight of Tesla vehicles.

Initially, production costs for the Model S were adversely impacted by an assortment of start-up costs at the Tesla Factory, manufacturing inefficiencies associated with inexperience and low-volume production, higher prices for component parts during the first several months of production runs, and higher logistics costs associated with the immaturity of Tesla's supply chain. However, as Tesla engineers redesigned various elements of the Model S for greater ease of manufacturing, supply chain improvements were instituted, and manufacturing efficiency rose, the costs of some parts decreased, and overall production costs the Model S trended downward.

Tesla had encountered a number of unexpected quality problems in the first two to three months of manufacturing the Model X. Getting the complicated hinges on the falcon-wing doors to function properly proved to be particularly troublesome. Customers who received the first wave of Model X deliveries also reported problems with the front doors and windows and with the 17-inch dashboard touchscreen freezing (a major problem because so many functions were controlled from this screen). Most of these problems were largely resolved by mid-2016, although Model X owners rated the reliability of their vehicles significantly lower than Model S owners—the chief culprit was the falcon-wing doors, which reportedly had generated significant warranty claims and warranty costs. Weekly production volumes of the Model X rose steadily in over the next three months.

Further manufacturing efficiency gains were made in producing the Model S and Model through the first half of 2017. Major gains in production efficiency were expected in the second half of 2018 and beyond as production of the Model X ramped up.

Tesla's "Gigafactory 1" In February 2014, Tesla announced that it and various partners, principally Panasonic—Tesla's supplier of lithium-ion batteries since 2010—would invest $4 to 5 billion through 2020 in a "gigafactory" capable of producing enough lithium-ion batteries to make battery packs for 500,000 vehicles (plus Tesla's recently-developed energy storage products for both businesses and homeowners); the planned output of the battery factory in 2020 exceeded the total global production of lithium batteries in 2013. Tesla's direct investment in the project was scheduled to be $2 billion. Tesla expected the new plant (named the Tesla Gigafactory) to reduce the company's battery pack cost by more than 30 percent—to around $200 per kWh by some estimates (from the current estimated level of about $300 per kWh).

In September 2014, Tesla announced that the Tesla Gigafactory would be located on a site in an industrial park east of Reno, Nevada. The Nevada site was thought to be chosen partly because the state of Nevada offered Tesla a lucrative incentive package said to be worth $1.25 billion over 20 years and partly because the only commercially active lithium mining operation in the United States was in a nearby Nevada county (this county was reputed to have the fifth largest deposits of lithium in the world). Construction began immediately. The facility was being built in phases, with the final phase scheduled for completion in 2020.

As of 2017, some 5.5 million square-feet of space, powered by wind and solar generating facilities located nearby, was operational or nearly so. Battery cell production began in early 2017; the plan called for Tesla to work closely with Panasonic and other partners to integrate battery material, cell, module, and battery pack production in one location. The battery packs manufactured at the Gigafactory (now called Gigafactory 1) were used for all Tesla vehicles and for the company's two primary energy storage products (Powerwall and Powerpack). In 2018, Tesla was also using space at Gigafactory 1 to manufacture Model 3 drive units.

In 2018, Tesla expected Gigafactory 1 would produce 35 Gigawatt hours of lithium-ion battery cells (a Gigawatt is a unit of electric power equal to 1 billion watts or 1000 megawatts), nearly as much as the rest of the world's entire battery production combined. Plans were in already place to expand the battery-making capacity at Gigafactory 1 well beyond the amount needed for 500,000 vehicles per year and for Tesla's energy storage products. As many as 10,000 workers were expected to be employed at Gigafactory 1 in 2020. Because Tesla had recently discovered ways to build an improved lithium-ion battery that would be larger, safer, and require fewer individual batteries per battery pack, Tesla executives were confident the company would achieve a significant reduction in the unit cost of producing battery packs once the Model 3 reached high-volume production. At present, Tesla believed its ownership of Gigafactory 1 and partnership with Panasonic gave the company sole access to the highest-volume and lowest-cost source of lithium-ion batteries in the world. However, in March 2018 Volkswagen indicated it had just signed agreements with battery-makers to supply the company with batteries for its forthcoming electric vehicles at a cost of about $115 kWh, significantly below the $200 per kWh cost Tesla was targeting for Gigafactory 1 in 2018.

Less than a month after announcing its intent to build the Gigafactory, Tesla sold $920 million of convertible senior notes due 2019 carrying an interest rate of 0.25 percent and $1.38 billion in convertible senior notes due 2021 carrying an interest rate of 1.25 percent. The senior notes due 2019 were convertible into cash, shares of Tesla's common stock, or a combination thereof, at Tesla's election. The convertible senior notes due 2021 were convertible into cash and, if applicable, shares of Tesla's common stock (subject to Tesla's right to deliver cash in lieu of shares of common stock). To protect existing shareholders against ownership dilution that might result from the senior notes being converted into additional shares of Tesla stock, Tesla immediately entered into convertible note hedge transactions and warrant transactions at an approximate cost of $186 million that management expected would reduce potential dilution of existing shareholder interests and/or offset cash payments that Tesla was required to make in excess of the principal amounts of the 2019 notes and 2021 notes.

Supply Chain Strategy   Tesla's Model S and Model X used thousands of purchased parts and components sourced globally from hundreds of suppliers, the majority of whom were currently single-source suppliers. It was the company's practice to obtain the needed parts and components from multiple sources whenever feasible, and Tesla was trying to secure alternate sources of supply for many single sourced components. So far, success had been limited, which had prompted the company to produce more parts and components internally within a year or two. However, qualifying alternate suppliers for certain highly customized components—or producing them internally—was thought to be both time consuming and costly, perhaps even requiring modifications to a vehicle's design.

While Tesla had developed close relationships with the suppliers of lithium-ion battery cells and certain other key system parts, it typically did not have long-term agreements with them with the exception of the relationship it had with Panasonic. However, Tesla was working to fully qualify additional battery cells from other manufacturers.

Marketing Strategy

From 2014 to 2017, Tesla's principal marketing goals and functions were to:

- Generate demand for the company's vehicles and drive sales leads to personnel in the Tesla's showrooms and sales galleries.

- Build long-term brand awareness and manage the company's image and reputation.
- Manage the existing customer base to create brand loyalty and generate customer referrals.
- Obtain feedback from the owners of Tesla vehicles and make sure their experiences and suggestions for improvement were communicated to Tesla personnel engaged in designing, developing, and/or improving the company's current and future vehicles.

As the first company to commercially produce a federally-compliant, fully electric vehicle that achieved market-leading range on a single charge, Tesla had been able to generate significant media coverage of the company and its vehicles. Management expected this would continue to be the case for some time to come. So far, the extensive media coverage, largely favorable reviews in motor vehicle publications and *Consumer Reports,* praise from owners of Tesla vehicles and admiring car enthusiasts (which enlarged Tesla's sales force at zero cost), and the decisions of many green-minded affluent individuals to help lead the movement away from gasoline-powered vehicles had all combined to drive good traffic flows at Tesla's sales galleries and create a flow of orders and pre-production reservations. As a consequence, during 2012-2017, Tesla had achieved a growing volume of sales without traditional advertising and at relatively low marketing costs. Nonetheless, Tesla did make use of pay-per-click advertisements on websites and mobile applications relevant to its target clientele. It also displayed and demonstrated its vehicles at such widely attended public events as the Detroit, Los Angeles, and Frankfurt auto shows.

In early 2018, Tesla negotiated marketing agreements with both Home Depot and Lowe's to stock and help promote its innovative Solar Roof tiles for residential and commercial roof applications.

Tesla's Leasing Activities

Tesla, in partnership with various financial institutions, began leasing vehicles to customers in 2014; the number and percentage of customers opting to lease Model S vehicles increased substantially in 2015. By year-end 2015, Tesla was not only offering loans and leases in North America, Europe, and Asia through its various partner financial institutions, but it was also offering loans and leases directly through its own captive finance subsidiaries in certain areas of the United States, Germany, Canada, and Great Britain. Tesla management intended to broaden its financial services offerings during the next several years.

Some of Tesla's current financing programs outside of North America provided customers with a resale value guarantee under which those customers had the option of selling their vehicle back to Tesla at a preset future date, generally at the end of the term of the applicable loan or financing program, for a pre-determined resale value. In certain markets, Tesla also offered vehicle buyback guarantees to financial institutions that could obligate Tesla to repurchase the vehicles for a predetermined price. These programs, when first introduced in 2015 and 2016 had been widely publicized and attracted numerous buyers, but Tesla determined in late 2016 and 2017 to back away from these offers in most countries because they were proving unprofitable, had unattractive accounting requirements, and exposed Tesla to the risk that the vehicles' resale value could be lower than its estimates and also to the risk that the volume of vehicles sold back to Tesla at the guaranteed resale price might be higher than the company's estimates—such risks had to be accounted for by establishing a contingent liability (in the current liabilities section of the balance sheet) deemed sufficient to cover these risks.

Sales of Regulatory Credits to Other Automotive Manufacturers

Because Tesla's electric vehicles had no tailpipe emissions of greenhouse gases or other pollutants, Tesla earned zero emission vehicle (ZEV) and greenhouse gas (GHG) credits on each vehicle sold in the United States. Moreover, it also earned corporate average fuel economy (CAFE) credits on its sales of vehicles because of their high equivalent miles per gallon ratings. All three of these types of regulatory credits had significant market value because the manufacturers of traditional gasoline-powered vehicles were subject to assorted emission and mileage requirements set by the U.S. Environmental Protection Agency (EPA) and by certain state agencies charged with protecting the environment within their borders; automotive manufacturers whose vehicle sales did not meet prevailing emission and mileage requirements were allowed to achieve compliance by purchasing credits earned by other automotive manufacturers. Tesla had entered into contracts for the sale of ZEV and GHG credits with several automotive manufacturers, and it also routinely sold its CAFE credits. Tesla's sales of ZEV, GHG, and CAFE credits produced revenues of $360.3 million in 2017, $302.3 million in 2016, $168.7 million in 2015, $216.3 million in 2014, and $194.4 million in 2013. In Exhibit 2, these amounts were included on Tesla's income statement in the revenue category labeled "Automotive sales"; without these revenues, as frequently noted by Wall Street analysts, Tesla's losses in 2013 through 2017 would have been significantly higher.

TESLA ENERGY IN 2018

In 2015, Tesla formed Tesla Energy, a new subsidiary that would begin producing and selling two energy storage products in 2016—Powerwall for homeowners and Powerpack for industrial, commercial, and utility customers. Powerwall was a lithium-ion battery charged either by electricity generated from a home's solar panels or from power company sources when electric rates were low. Tesla saw Powerwall as principally a product that energy-conscious homeowners with a rooftop solar system could use to lower their monthly electric bills by programming Powerwall to power their homes during certain hours when local power company rates were high and then recharging the battery during the late-night hours when rates were low. However, Powerwall home batteries could also be used as a backup power source in case of unexpected power outages. Powerpack models were 100 kW lithium-ion batteries that industrial, commercial, and utility enterprises could use for energy storage or backup power.

In the first week after announcing its new Powerwall and Powerpack products, Tesla received 38,000 reservations for Powerwall (residential buyers could place a reservation with no money down) and requests from 2,500 companies indicating interest in installing or distributing Powerpack batteries. Tesla moved swiftly to prepare its supply chain and production teams to begin volume builds on both products. Production began at the Tesla Factory in Fremont and then shifted to the Gigafactory in the last part of 2015. In early 2016, both Powerwall and Powerpack production was operating smoothly and expanding at the Gigafactory. Production and deliveries of Powerwall 2 and Powerpack 2 began in late 2016. Both products had the capability to receive over-the-air firmware and software updates that enabled

additional features. In 2018, these two energy storage products were being used for backup power, independence from utility grids, peak demand reduction, demand response, reducing intermittency of renewable generation, and wholesale electric market services.

When Solar Energy was merged into Tesla, the company arranged to lease a facility, called Gigafactory 2, in Buffalo, New York, to produce (1) solar energy systems sold to residential and commercial customers and (2) its freshly-developed Solar Roof, which used aesthetically pleasing and durable glass roofing tiles designed to complement the architecture of homes and commercial buildings, to turn sunlight into electricity that was being marketed in 2018 with distribution partners Home Depot and Lowe's.

Tesla Energy's solar energy systems included solar panels that converted sunlight into electrical current, inverters that converted the electrical output from the panels to a usable current compatible with the electric grid, racking that attached the solar panels to the roof or ground, electrical hardware that connected the solar energy system to the electric grid, and a monitoring device. The majority of the components were purchased from vendors; the company maintained multiple sources for each major component to ensure competitive pricing and adequate supplies.

Tesla Energy had an in-house engineering team that designed its energy storage products and created customized energy storage solutions and solar energy systems for customers. In the United States, it used its national sales organization, channel partner network, and customer referral program to market and sell its residential solar and energy storage systems. Outside the United States, Tesla Energy used its international sales organization and a network of channel partners to market and sell Powerwall 2, and it had recently launched pilot programs for the sale of residential solar products in certain countries. It also sold Powerwall 2 directly to utilities, who then installed the product in customer homes.

In December 2017, Tesla completed installation of a 100-megawatt lithium-ion battery hooked into the electricity grid in South Australia to relieve power shortages created by a tornado in 2016. Elon Musk had promised that once the contract was signed, Tesla would complete the project in 100 days or it would be furnished free of charge—Tesla completed the installation in 60 days. According to Musk, the battery was three times more powerful than the world's next biggest battery.

Tesla's revenues from energy generation and storage products topped $1 billion in 2017 (refer to Exhibit 2). Elon Musk was very optimistic about the growth opportunities for Tesla Energy:

> 2018 will see major growth in Tesla energy storage deployments, as the production ramp of our storage products is just as steep as with Model 3. This year, we aim to deploy at least three times the storage capacity we deployed in 2017 .... With more electric utilities and governments around the world recognizing the reliability, environmental, and economic benefits of this product, it's clear that there is a huge opportunity for us in large scale energy storage. Powerwall demand for home energy storage remains exceptionally high, with orders consistently above production levels. We are increasingly promoting our energy products in Tesla stores and in non-Tesla retail locations. There is a significant cross-selling potential between Powerwall and our solar products, as evidenced by the fact that a vast majority of the customers who have ordered Solar Roof have also ordered at least one Powerwall.
>
> As Solar Roof is truly the first-of-its-kind and there is significant complexity in both its manufacturing and installation, we are deliberately ramping production at a gradual pace. When fully scaled, Gigafactory 2 will be able to produce enough solar cells to add more than 150,000 new residential solar installations every year. As we ramp production, a portion of the output will be dedicated for Solar Roof tiles with the balance used in our proprietary high-efficiency retrofit solar panels. With demand outpacing production, we expect our backlog to remain in excess of one year for the next several quarters.[26]

THE ELECTRIC VEHICLE SEGMENT OF THE GLOBAL AUTOMOTIVE INDUSTRY

Global sales of passenger cars and SUVs in 2017 were roughly 81 million. Sales of other types of vehicles (light or pickup trucks, heavy or cargo-carrying trucks, recreational vehicles, buses, and minibuses) totaled just over 26 million. In 2017, global sales of plug-in electric vehicles totaled 1.22 million units —plug-in vehicles included both battery-only vehicles and so-called plug-in hybrid electric vehicles equipped with a gasoline or diesel engine for use when the vehicle's battery pack (rechargeable only from an external plug-in source) was depleted, usually after a distance of 20 to 50 miles. Hybrid vehicles were jointly powered by an internal combustion engine and an electric motor that ran on batteries charged by regenerative braking and the internal combustion engine; the batteries in a hybrid vehicle could not be restored to a full charge by connecting a plug to an external power source. Exhibit 3 shows the 10 best-selling plug-in electric vehicles in the United States from 2013 through 2017.

There was no question in 2018 and beyond that Tesla was faced with intensifying competition in the global marketplace for electric-powered vehicles. Virtually every motor vehicle manufacturer in the world was developing new battery-powered electric vehicles, most with driving ranges of 200 miles or more. In 2018 and 2019, models with 200+ mile driving ranges were scheduled to be introduced by Audi, Jaguar, Mercedes, Kia, Volvo, General Motors, and Hyundai. Models from Porsche, Aston Martin, Nissan, Audi, Volkswagen, BMW, General Motors, and Ford were scheduled for 2020. Sales of a second-generation Nissan Leaf with a driving range of up to 150 miles began in January 2018.

In 2018 Volkswagen announced plans to equip 16 factories to produce electric vehicles by the end of 2022, compared with three currently, and to build as many as 3 million electric cars per year by 2025. In December 2017, Toyota said by around 2025, every Toyota and Lexus model sold around the world would be available either as a dedicated electrified model or have an electrified option. Additionally, Toyota expected to have annual sales of more than 5.5 million electrified vehicles by 2030 (including more than one million zero-emission vehicles totally powered by either batteries or fuel cells) and to halt all production of gasoline-powered vehicles by 2040. In 2018, the government of Germany launched a campaign to put one million electric cars on its roads by 2020 and to have 40 percent electric cars on its roads by 2035.

- In late 2013, BMW began selling its all-new i3 series electric car models that had a lightweight, carbon fiber reinforced plastic body, lithium-ion batteries with a driving range of 80 to 100 miles on a single charge, a 170 horsepower electric motor, and a base price of $41,350; customers could also get the BMW i3 with a range extender package

EXHIBIT 3   Sales of Best-Selling Plug-in Electric Vehicles in the United States, 2013–2017

Best-Selling Models	2013	2014	2015	2016	2017
Tesla Model S	17,650	17,300	25,202	28,896	27,060
Chevrolet Bolt VE				579	23,297
Tesla Model X			214	18,223	21,315
Toyota Prius PHV/Prime	12,088	13,264	4,191	2,474	20,963
Chevrolet Volt	23,094	18,805	15,393	24,739	20,349
Nissan Leaf	22,610	30,200	17,269	14,006	11,230
Ford Fusion Energi	6,089	11,550	9,750	15,938	9,632
Ford C-Max Energi	7,154	8,433	7,591	7,957	8,140
BMW i3	—	6,092	11,024	7,625	6,276
Fiat 500e	2,310	5,132	6,194	5,330	5,380
All Others	4,260	12,243	19,532	32,847	46,184
United States Total	95,642	123,049	116,099	158,614	199,826
Worldwide	Not available	320,713	550,297	777,497	1,227,117

Source: Inside EVs, "Monthly Plug-in Sales Scorecard," www.insideevs.com, accessed March 5, 2018.

(base price of $45,200) that included a 34 horse-power motor used only to maintain the charge of the of the lithium-ion battery at an approximate 5 percent charge and extend the driving range to 160 to 180 miles per charge. BMW sold more than 16,000 i3s in 2014 and 25,000 i3s in 2015. In mid-2014, BMW began selling a super-premium sporty, high-tech electric vehicle called the i8 that had a three-cylinder electric motor, a supplemental gasoline engine for higher speeds, scissor doors, flamboyant aerodynamic flourishes, and an electric-only driving range of about 22-miles. Global sales of the i8 were 1,741 units in 2014 and close to 5,000 units in 2015; the 2015 base price of BMW's i8 was $137,450.

- Mercedes-Benz launched sales of its premium compact B-Class electric vehicle in the United States in mid-2014; the 4-door, 5-passenger vehicle (base price of $41,450) was built on an entirely new platform compared to other B-Class models with traditional gasoline engines, had an estimated driving range of 115 miles on a single charge, accelerated from 0 to 60 miles per hour in less than 10 seconds, delivered 174 horsepower, had a top speed of 100 miles per hour, utilized an electric powertrain system custom-designed and

produced by Tesla, and was loaded with safety features. Mercedes B-Class electric vehicles with a range extender package were also available. The new electric B-Class models competed directly with BMW's i3 series electric car.

- While a number of automakers had a near-term focus on hybrids with a very short battery-only range, media reports indicated that Mercedes, BMW, Porsche, and Audi were working on producing fully-electric vehicles with a 300+ mile driving range on a single charge by 2018. The new version of the Volt would likely be introduced in Fall 2016.

- In late 2015, both Cadillac and Audi introduced new plug-in hybrid luxury sedans (the Cadillac CT6 and the Audi A6L eTron) with an electric-only range of just over 60 miles on a single charge. Initially, both models were only being produced and sold in China. However, Cadillac was expected to begin selling the hybrid plug-in version of the CT6 in North America and elsewhere in late 2016 or early 2017.

- Executives at GM were acutely aware that cures were needed for the disappointingly small sales volume of the much ballyhooed Chevrolet Volt. GM was rumored to be nearing production of a next-generation compact electric car that could go 200 miles on a single charge, be equipped with a generator for battery charging, and have a base price close to $30,000.

- At the 2016 Geneva International Motor Show, automakers pushing new electric models and/ or plans for forthcoming models included Opel (a subsidiary of General Motors), PSA Peugeot Citroen, BMW, Mercedes-Benz, Hyundai, Honda, and Volkswagen.

Hydrogen Fuel Cells: An Alternative to Electric Batteries

Many of the world's major automotive manufacturers, while actively working on next-generation battery-powered electric vehicles, were nonetheless hedging their bets by also pursuing the development of hydrogen fuel cells as an alternative means of powering future vehicles. Toyota was considered the leader in developing hydrogen fuel cells and was sharing some of its fuel-cell technology patents for free with other automotive companies in an effort to spur whether there was merit in installing fuel cells and building out a hydrogen charging network. Audi, Honda, Toyota, Mercedes-Benz, and Hyundai had recently introduced first-generation models powered by hydrogen fuel cells.[27]

Hydrogen fuel cells could be refueled with hydrogen in 3 to 5 minutes. California and several states in the northeastern United States already had a number of hydrogen refueling stations. Existing gasoline stations could add hydrogen refueling capability at a cost of about $1.5 million. A full tank of hydrogen provided vehicles with a driving range of about 310 miles. While battery-powered vehicles were currently cheaper than fuel-cell powered vehicles, experts expected that cheaper materials, more efficient fuel cells, and scale economies would in upcoming years enable producers of fuel-cell vehicles to match the prices of battery-powered electric vehicles.

ENDNOTES

[1] Tesla Second Quarter 2017 Shareholder Letter, August 2, 2017.

[2] Tesla Third Quarter 2017 Shareholder Letter, November 1, 2017.

[3] Tesla Fourth Quarter 2017 Shareholder Letter, February 7, 2018.

[4] Company press release, April 3, 2018.

[5] Jeff Evanson, Tesla Motors Investor Presentation, September 14, 2013, www.teslamotors.com (accessed November 29, 2013).

[6] As reported in Autoweek, "Tesla Has to Turn Potential into Real Profits," May 5, 2017, www.autoweek.com (accessed March 7, 2018).

[7] Tesla First Quarter 2018 Shareholder Letter, May 2, 2018.

[8] Tesla Q1 2018 Results—Earnings Call Transcript, May 2, 2018, www.seekingalpha.com, (accessed May 9, 2018).

[9] John Reed, "Elon Musk's Groundbreaking Electric Car," FT Magazine, July 24, 2009, www.ft.com, accessed September 26, 2013.

[10] Tesla press release, and Michael Arrington, "Tesla Worth More Than Half a Billion After Daimler Investment," May 19, 2009, www.techcrunch.com (accessed September 30, 2013).

[11] Josh Friedman, "Entrepreneur Tries His Midas Touch in Space," Los Angeles Times, April 23, 2003, www.latimes.com (accessed on September 16, 2013).

[12] David Kestenbaum, "Making a Mark with Rockets and Roadsters," National Public Radio, August 9, 2007, www.npr.org (accessed on September 17, 2013).

[13] David Kestenbaum, "Making a Mark with Rockets and Roadsters," National Public Radio, August 9, 2007, www.npr.org (accessed on September 17, 2013).

[14] David Kestenbaum, "Making a Mark with Rockets and Roadsters," National Public Radio, August 9, 2007, www.npr.org (accessed on September 17, 2013).

[15] Video interview with Alan Murray, "Elon Musk: I'll Put a Man on Mars in 10 Years," Market Watch (New York: The Wall Street Journal), December 1, 2011 (accessed on September 16, 2013).

[16] Ashlee Vance, "Revealed: Elon Musk Explains the Hyperloop, the Solar-Powered High-Speed Future of Inter-City Transportation," Bloomberg BusinessWeek, August 12, 2013, www.businessweek.com (accessed on September 25, 2013).

[17] Mike Seemuth, "From the Corner Office—Elon Musk," Success, April 10, 2011, www.success.com (accessed September 25, 2013).

[18] Mike Seemuth, "From the Corner Office—Elon Musk," Success, April 10, 2011, www.success.com (accessed September 25, 2013).

[19] Mike Seemuth, "From the Corner Office—Elon Musk," Success, April 10, 2011, www.success.com (accessed September 25, 2013).

[20] Company 10-K report for 2017, pp 1–2.

[21] According to information in Martin Eberhard's blog titled "Lotus Position," July 25, 2006, www.teslamotors.com/blog/lotus-position (accessed September 17, 2013).

[22] 2013 10-K Report, p. 4.

[23] Mark Stevenson, "Lithium-ion Battery Packs Now $209 per kwh, Will Fall to $100 by 2025: Bloomberg Analysis," Green Car Reports, December 11, 2017, www.greencarreports.com (accessed March 7, 2018).

[24] Company documents.

[25] Company press release May 20, 2010.

[26] Tesla Fourth Quarter 2017 Shareholder Letter, February 7, 2018.

[27] George Ghanem, "Avoid Tesla Because Hydrogen Is the New Electric," March 6, 2016, www.seekingalpha.com, (accessed March 7, 2016).

Mattel Incorporated in 2018: Can Ynon Kreiz Save the Toys?

Randall D. Harris

Texas A&M University—Corpus Christi

"Ynon is a good guy, but he doesn't know toys and will fail like Margo did," read Ynon Kreiz, Chairman and Chief Executive Officer (CEO) of Mattel, Incorporated.[1] It was April 26, 2018, and it was Ynon Kreiz's first day on the job as Mattel CEO. Mattel, maker of Barbie dolls and Hot Wheels cars, had just received a letter offering to merge Mattel with privately held MGA Entertainment, run by CEO Isaac Larian. In his offer letter, Mr. Larian did not put a specific value or terms on his offer, but had proposed that the two companies merge based upon the value of MGA Entertainment and its brands, which included the Little Tykes line of preschool toys. Larian also argued that he, not Kreiz, should be the executive to lead the turnaround of Mattel.[2]

Kreiz had been named Chairman and CEO of Mattel on April 19, 2018, and was succeeding Margo Georgiadis in the job. Ms. Georgiadis, hired away from Alphabet Inc.'s Google division, had been appointed as Mattel CEO in February 2017. Unfortunately, Georgiadis had been unable to reverse a sharp drop in Mattel's revenues, earnings, and stock price.[3] The slide in Mattel's fortunes had been sharpened by the bankruptcy of the retailer Toys "R" Us in 2017, a key customer for Mattel's products. Kreiz was now the fourth CEO for Mattel in four years.

Sitting in his new office at Mattel headquarters in El Segundo, California, Ynon Kreiz knew that he had numerous problems with which to contend as the incoming CEO of Mattel. Where to begin? In his hands on his first day was an unsolicited offer to merge with MGA Entertainment. Mattel had also been in involved in off and on merger negotiations with Hasbro, another close toy industry competitor.

Central to all of these discussions was a painful reality—children around the world were growing up faster and were increasingly drawn to online content, movies, smartphones, and video games. Competition for store space, sales, and market share in the toy industry was intense. Making matters worse, Mattel's traditional sales channel, physical retail stores, were increasingly under strain and consolidating. The bankruptcy of Toys "R" Us was symptomatic of this retail consolidation. Online retail competition, notably Amazon.com, was increasingly making inroads into the sales of traditional bricks-and-mortar retailers. Mattel had also stumbled in their competition with Hasbro, their closest competitor in the toy industry.

Kreiz had taken the reins of the company with a mandate from investors to streamline Mattel operations, improve the company's focus on technology and entertainment, and to deliver a recovery in Mattel's struggling stock price. From a peak of $47.82 per share in 2013, Mattel was now trading between $12 and $18 per share. The company had reported a $1 billion loss in 2017. Sales, deeply affected by the bankruptcy of Toys "R" Us, were down 10 percent from 2016 to 2017. With all of these challenges for the struggling company, the pressing question was this: Could Ynon Kreiz stop the slide at Mattel? Further, what should Kreiz and Mattel do next?

COMPANY HISTORY

Mattel was founded by Ruth and Elliott Handler out of a garage in Southern California in 1945.[4] Their first two products were picture frames and dollhouse furniture crafted from scraps of picture frame. Their first hit toy was the "Uke-A-Doodle," a toy ukulele, released in 1947. Mattel was formally incorporated in 1948 with their headquarters based in Los Angeles, California.[5]

In 1955, Mattel began advertising their toys on a popular television show, the Mickey Mouse Club, which revolutionized the way in which toys were marketed to children. Mattel released a number of new toys on the television show. In 1959, Ruth Handler created an innovative design for a new type of doll, and named it after her own daughter, Barbara. The introduction of the Barbie doll became a smash hit and propelled Mattel to the top of the toy industry. Mattel would go on to sell over one billion Barbie dolls, making Barbie the largest selling and most profitable toy in Mattel's toy lineup. The Barbie doll was followed in 1960 with the Chatty Cathy, a talking doll that would change the toy industry and lead to many imitators.

Hot Wheels die-cast vehicles were rolled out in 1968. Hot Wheels toys influenced the lives of several generations of children, leading the company to estimate that at least 41 million children had grown up alongside the Hot Wheels brand. After a long and successful career with Mattel, Ruth and Elliott Handler left Mattel in 1975.

Mattel was an early entrant into the electronic games market, introducing an electronic handheld game in 1977. Initial success with the handheld game led to the IntelliVision home video entertainment system and a spin-off corporation, Mattel Electronics. This early venture into electronics did not last, however, as declining sales and mounting losses forced Mattel into abandoning the electronics initiative. Mattel took a $394 million loss in 1983 and debated a bankruptcy filing. Mattel reevaluated their diversification strategy as a result and closed or divested all non-toy related subsidiaries in the wake of the losses.

The He-Man and the Masters of the Universe line of action figures was the next best seller for the company beginning in 1982. The company estimated sales of the He-Man line at $400 million in 1985.[6] However, the success was short lived and sales dropped, contributing to a loss of $115 million in 1987. Mattel began a revived working relationship with the Disney Company in 1988. This combination revived Mattel, leading to hit products based on Disney characters like Mickey Mouse and characters from the top-grossing Disney animated movie Toy Story.

Mattel purchased Fisher-Price in 1993, merged with Tyco Toys in 1997, and acquired the parent company for the American Girl Brand in 1998. The company also acquired the Learning Company, a U.S. based educational software company, in the fall of 1998. The Learning Company, a merger financed with Mattel stock, was acquired for $3.5 billion.[7] One of the Learning Company's more popular software offerings was the "Where in the World is Carmen Sandiego?" series.

Losses from the Learning Company acquisition were almost immediate. In addition to inflated sales forecasts for the unit, Mattel had bought the Learning Company just as children were switching from games and learning toys on CD-ROM to downloading them from the Internet. Unfortunately, the Learning Company was delivering their products primarily on CD-ROM at that time.[8] In addition to the ouster of then CEO Jill Barad, Mattel booked a $430 million loss in 2000.

New CEO Robert Eckert moved swiftly in 2000 to restructure Mattel. He dumped the Learning Company along with other software-related assets and began a restructuring plan for the company, with the goal of achieving $200 million in immediate cost savings. Eckert also reduced the company's dividend and cut about 10 percent of the workforce.[9] Although painful, the company had better luck that year with licensing agreements. In 2000, Mattel retained the master licensing rights to market and sell Harry Potter toys, collectibles and games, and also agreed with Disney to market Disney Princess dolls.

As part of CEO Eckert's restructuring efforts, the company announced in April 2001 that Mattel would close its last U.S. manufacturing site and move the operations to Mexico.[10] This plant closure was part of the continuing cost-cutting efforts at the company, and closed Mattel's final U.S. plant in Murray, Kentucky. The plant had been operational since 1973 and employed 980 manufacturing and distribution workers. Mattel had been an early adopter of overseas manufacturing, and had been making toys in Mexico for 25 years and in Asia for 30 years at the time of this final U.S. plant closure.[11]

By 2007, approximately 65 percent of Mattel's toys were made in China. This included five wholly owned Mattel factories as well as numerous contractor and subcontractor facilities. Mattel had also developed, over time, a reputation for quality and safety in their manufacturing practices.[12] Nevertheless, in May to June 2007, Mattel discovered toys manufactured with lead-tainted paint during routine safety checks at a number of contractor facilities in China. The subsequent investigation into the tainted toys led to a crisis for Mattel, with a large public outcry, regulatory scrutiny and the recall of over 19 million Mattel-branded toys.[13] While a major setback for the company, Mattel was noted for handling the recalls swiftly and effectively.[14] Mattel also moved swiftly to diversify their manufacturing facilities to other countries in order to avoid supply disruptions and other risks.

Mattel gradually recovered from the lead paint crisis, and revenue growth for the company resumed in 2010. Then, in 2012, sales of Barbie dolls began to drop.[15] Gross sales for the Barbie doll line exceeded $1.2 billion in 2012, and the drop in Barbie sales was balanced by strong sales in other Mattel toy lines, particularly the Disney Princess doll line. The release of the Disney movie "Frozen" provided a sharp boost to Mattel's Disney line of dolls and related products in 2013, and this somewhat countered the slump in the core Barbie brand. Net sales for Mattel Inc. overall peaked in 2013 at $6.48 billion, despite the Barbie sales slump.

By the third quarter of 2014, however, sales of the Barbie brand had dropped 21 percent from the previous year.[16] What was wrong with Barbie? Analysts acknowledged that Barbie was still one of the top doll brands in the world, but noted that girls were increasingly drawn to other, more innovative dolls and games that ran on tablets, computers, and smartphones.[17] Further, while Barbie's core demographic used to be between the ages of 3 and 9, the market for Barbie now appeared to be between the ages of 3 and 6. Children were maturing faster than ever in the 21st century. There had also been longstanding complaints about a lack of diversity in the Barbie doll line, particularly given the changing demographics of the U.S. child population.[18]

Other Mattel lines then began to join the Barbie sales slump, including the popular American Girl brand, Hot Wheels, and Fisher Price infant toys. Overall net sales for Mattel dropped by $400 million in 2014. In January 2015, Mattel CEO Bryan Stockton was replaced by Christopher Sinclair, a longstanding director on Mattel's board of directors. In 2016, Disney moved their license to the Princess line of dolls, including their blockbuster "Frozen" toys, to Mattel rival Hasbro. The loss of the Disney license had a negative impact on Mattel. Making matters worse, sales during the fourth quarter of 2016 failed to meet expectations, and Mattel had to cut prices to salvage the all-important holiday season.[19]

In the wake of the holiday 2016 debacle, Margo Georgiadis was named CEO of Mattel in February of 2017. From February 2017 to April 2018, Mattel's stock price dropped by 50 percent, and Ms. Georgiadis was unable to reverse the continued slide in Mattel's sales and earnings.[20] In November of 2017, Hasbro made a takeover offer for Mattel, an offer that Mattel's board rejected.[21] Ms. Georgiadis then left Mattel abruptly in April 2018. Former studio executive Ynon Kreiz, a member of Mattel's board of directors since June of 2017, was named the incoming CEO. Kreiz began his tenure as CEO of Mattel on April 26, 2018.

VISION, MISSION, AND STRATEGIC GOALS

Mattel Inc. had no formal mission or vision statement. The company stated that the Mattel Incorporated family of companies was "a worldwide leader in the design, manufacture, and marketing of toys and family products."[22] The company also emphasized the power of play, stating that play was essential for creating future generations of thinkers, makers, and doers. Mattel had been named one of the world's most ethical companies by Ethnisphere Magazine in 2013, and was also ranked Number 2 on Corporate Responsibility Magazine's "100 Best Corporate Citizens" list.[23]

In her report to Mattel shareholders in early 2018, CEO Margo Georgiadis had outlined five strategic pillars to transform the company and return it to growth:

1. Building Mattel's core brands into connected 360-degree play systems and experiences,
2. Accelerating emerging markets growth with digital first solutions,
3. Focusing and strengthening the company's innovation pipeline,
4. Reshaping the company's operations, and
5. Reigniting Mattel's culture and team.[24]

Ms. Georgiadis noted a number of changes in Mattel's executive ranks in her report, including the appointment of Ynon Kreiz to Mattel's Board of Directors in June 2017. Georgiadis also noted that the organizational structure of Mattel had been flattened and simplified to accelerate decision making within the company.

Ms. Georgiadis introduced incoming CEO Kreiz on Mattel's April 26, 2018 call with analysts. On the call, CEO Kreiz said:

> We have a lot to do to reach our objectives. But I'm very confident that we have the right plan and the right team in place . . . . We are already making strong progress against our strategic pillars. My immediate focus (for Mattel) includes the following priorities: implementing our Structural Simplification to restore profitability, stabilizing revenue, reinvigorating our concept to drive creativity, which I believe is essential to our success; and strengthening our collaboration with our partners.[25]

Incoming CEO Kreiz also articulated his longer-range vision for Mattel during the call with analysts:

> The big picture opportunity is to transform Mattel to an IT (information technology) driven high-performing toy company, that is more efficient, more profitable, and has a higher growth trajectory. We have very strong assets, including some of the world's best and greatest toy brands. We have a very good team and a very good strategy that I feel very good about. So our focus now is to deliver on our transformation plan and maximize value for the company and for our shareholders. This is not going to be easy. There's no denying that we faced significant challenges over the last few years and there are still headwinds in certain key areas of the business. But I feel confident about where we sit and what we have to do to take it on.[26]

COMPANY OPERATIONS

Mattel Inc. had their worldwide headquarters in El Segundo, California, just south of the Los Angeles International Airport (LAX). As of December 2017, the company employed 28,000 people on a worldwide basis. The corporate headquarters consisted of two main buildings in El Segundo, with additional leased buildings in the immediate area for company operations. Mattel also had another major facility in East Aurora, New York, that was used for North American operations and support.

Mattel's American Girl operations were based in Middleton, Wisconsin, with a headquarters facility, a warehouse, and distribution facilities in the immediate Middleton, Wisconsin area. Mattel also had retail and related office space in 20 additional cities around the United States, and 40 countries around the world.[27] Mattel sold their products in 150 nations.

Manufacturing for the company was conducted through both company-owned facilities and by contract through third-party manufacturers. Mattel had company-owned manufacturing facilities in Canada, China, Indonesia, Malaysia, Mexico, and Thailand. Manufacture of core products for the company was generally conducted by company-owned facilities in order to improve flexibility and to lower manufacturing costs.[28] Non-core toy products were produced by third-party contract manufacturers. Mattel also purchased some toys from unrelated companies for resale through Mattel sales channels.

Creativity and innovation was a critical issue for companies like Mattel in the toy industry. Mattel invested heavily in refreshing, redesigning, and extending their existing toy lines, as well as developing brand new toy product lines for their company. Product design and development was conducted in house by a group of professional toy designers and engineers. In 2017, the company spent approximately $225 million on product design and development.

Mattel's toy business was highly seasonal. Sales built into the fourth quarter of the year and end of year holidays. A significant portion of purchasing by Mattel's customers occurred during the third and fourth quarters of the year.[29] It was critical that Mattel manufacture enough of the right toys in advance of the fourth quarter to meet this surge in demand. Conversely, not manufacturing unpopular toys was also important to avoid stocking unpopular items. It was difficult for the company to match supply and demand with significant lead times for production early in the year. This seasonality in demand also meant increased need by Mattel for working capital earlier in the year in order to meet the anticipated surge in production to meet year-end demand for toys.

MATTEL PRODUCTS

Mattel's brands and products were organized into four main categories: (1) Mattel Girls and Boys Brands, (2) Fisher-Price Brands, (3) American Girl Brands, and (4) Construction and Arts & Crafts Brands. Each category had a multitude of products as part of their portfolio:

1. **Mattel Girls & Boys Brands.** This category included the Barbie doll and related accessories, Monster High, DC Super Hero Girls, Enchantimals, and Polly Pocket brand lines. Wheeled toy lines

included Hot Wheels, Matchbox, and CARS. Additional brand lines were DC Comics, WWE Wrestling, Minecraft, Toy Story, and additional games and puzzles.

2. **Fisher-Price Brands.** The core Fisher-Price brands included Fisher-Price, Little People, BabyGear, Laugh & Learn, and Imaginext. Additional brand lines included Thomas & Friends, Shimmer & Shine, Mickey Mouse Clubhouse, and Power Wheels.

3. **American Girl Brands.** American Girl brands and products included American Girl, Truly Me, Girl of the Year, BeForever, Bitty Baby, and WellieWishers.

4. **Construction and Arts & Crafts Brands.** These brand lines included MEGA BLOKS and RoseArt.[30]

MATTEL MARKETING

Marketing toys to children and their parents was an advertising intensive activity. Mattel spent heavily on marketing and promotional activities. Marketing activity was seasonal, with a peak during the fourth quarter of the year. Mattel advertised through TV and radio commercials, magazines, and newspapers. Promotional activity for the company included in-store displays, major events focusing on Mattel branded products, and marketing tie-ins with various consumer products companies. During 2017, Mattel spent $642.3 million, or 13.2 percent of company net sales, on advertising and promotion.

Of particular importance to Mattel was the rise of social media and the Internet as a marketing and promotional channel. Children and their parents were increasingly accessing information about toys on social media websites. Mattel had carefully developed their Facebook presence, and had cultivated 14 million followers for their Barbie page. Mattel also had a strong presence on YouTube for Barbie, with 3.8 million subscribers.

MATTEL CUSTOMERS

Mattel sold their products throughout the world. Mattel toys and related products were sold directly to discount retailers, freestanding toy stores, department stores, chain stores, and wholesalers. Mattel also had several small retail stores near to their corporate headquarters and distribution centers. American Girl products were sold directly to consumers through their own retail stores and also to retailers. Mattel also sold some of their products online through company subsidiaries.

In 2017, three customers of Mattel accounted for 37 percent of company sales. These three customers were Wal-Mart, Toys "R" Us, and Target. Exhibit 1 presents a sales breakdown of Mattel's Major Customers for 2015 through 2017. The bankruptcy of Toys "R" Us had already damaged Mattel sales, and the pending plan to close some or all of the Toys "R" Us locations in the United States was anticipated to further damage Mattel sales in 2018.

KEY EXECUTIVES

Ynon Kreiz was new the Chairman and CEO of Mattel. Kreiz, 53, was born and raised in Israel. He earned a BA in Economics and Management in 1991 from Tel Aviv University. After moving to Los Angeles, Kreiz earned an MBA from UCLA in 1993.

In 1996, Kreiz moved to London to launch Fox Kids Europe, a Pay-TV children's television network. He served as Chairman and CEO of Fox Kids Europe from 1997 to 2002. Fox Kids Europe was acquired by the Walt Disney Company in 2001.

After a stint at a venture capital firm, Kreiz served as Chairman and CEO of Endemol from 2008 to 2011. Endemol was a European-based global television and digital production company. Then in 2013, Kreiz became Chairman and CEO of Maker Studios in Los Angeles. Maker Studios produced

EXHIBIT 1   Mattel Incorporated Major Customers (U.S. dollars in thousands)

Major Customer	2015	2016	2017
Wal-Mart	$1,000,000	$1,100,000	$1,000,000
Toys "R" Us	$ 600,000	$ 600,000	$ 400,000
Target	$ 500,000	$ 400,000	$ 400,000

Source: Mattel Form 10-K 12/31/2017.

EXHIBIT 2   Mattel, Inc. Leadership in 2018

Name	Brief Biography
Ynon Kreiz *Chairman and* *Chief Executive Officer* Age: 53 Tenure: 0 years	Ynon Kreiz, has served as Chairman of Mattel Inc. since May 17, 2018, as its Chief Executive Officer since April 26, 2018. Mr. Kreiz holds a BA in Economics and Management from Tel Aviv University and an MBA from UCLA's Anderson School of Management.
Richard Dickson *President and Chief Operating Officer* Age: 50 Tenure: 4 years	Richard Dickson, has been the President and Chief Operating Officer of Mattel, Inc. since April 2, 2015. Mr. Dickson started his career and spent nearly a decade with Bloomingdale's, a leading U.S. fashion retailer.
Michael Eilola *Executive Vice President, Chief Supply Chain Officer* Age: 56 Tenure: 0 years	Michael J. Eilola, has been Executive Vice President and Chief Supply Chain Officer of Mattel, Inc. since January 2018. Prior to joining Mattel, Inc., Mr. Eilola held executive positions with Honeywell International Inc.
Nancy Elder *Chief Communications Officer* Tenure: 1 year	Nancy Elder has been Chief Communications Officer of Mattel since September 2017. From 2014 to 2017, she served as Chief Communications Officer of JetBlue Airways.
Joseph Euteneuer *Chief Financial Officer* Age: 61 Tenure: 1 year	Joe Euteneuer has been the Chief Financial Officer of Mattel Inc. since September 25, 2017. Mr. Euteneuer holds a Bachelor's degree from Arizona State University and is a certified public accountant.
Sven Gerjets *Chief Technology Officer* Tenure: 1 year	Sven Gerjets has been Chief Technology Officer of Mattel since July 2017. From January 2017 to July 2017, he served as Chief Product Officer of n.io Innovation. Mr. Gerjets was the Chief Information Officer of Time Warner Cable, Inc., from October 2015 to June 2016.
Robert Normile *Executive Vice President, Chief Legal Officer, Secretary* Age: 58 Tenure: 19 years	Robert Normile has served as Executive Vice President, Chief Legal Officer and Secretary of Mattel, Inc. since February 2011. Mr. Normile was previously associated with the law firms of Latham & Watkins LLP and Sullivan & Cromwell LLP.
Amanda Thompson *Executive Vice President, Chief People Officer* Age: 42 Tenure: 1 year	Amanda J. Thompson, has been Executive Vice President and Chief People Officer of Mattel, Inc. since September 2017. From 2012 to 2017, Ms. Thompson served as Chief People Officer of TOMS Shoes. Ms. Thompson held several executive and leadership roles at Starbucks Coffee Company from 2006 to 2012.

Source: Mattel, Inc.

short-form videos for YouTube and other platforms. Maker was sold to the Walt Disney Company in 2014. Kreiz stepped down as CEO of Maker Studios in January 2016. Kreiz then joined Mattel's board in 2017 and became Mattel CEO in April 2018.

CEO Kreiz was joined by Richard Dickson as Mattel's President and Chief Operating Officer (COO). Dickson, 50, had been President and COO since April 2015. Mr. Dickson had extensive retail experience, including almost a decade at

Bloomingdale's. Mattel's Chief Legal Officer, Robert Normile, was the longest serving executive at Mattel. Normile had been Chief Legal Officer at Mattel since February 2011, and had an extensive legal background.

All of the remaining members of Kreiz's top management team, including Chief Financial Officer Joseph Euteneuer, had served one year or less in their current roles. Exhibit 2 provides a brief summary of Mattel's top leadership team in 2018.

FINANCIAL STATUS

Net sales for Mattel decreased from $6.48 billion in 2013 to $4.88 billion in 2017. Variable expenses remained relatively stable during the 2013 to 2017 time period, resulting in a sharp drop in gross profit as well. The company reported a negative operating income and a $1 billion net loss in 2017. Mattel's consolidated income statements for 2013 through 2017 are presented in Exhibit 3.

EXHIBIT 3 Mattel, Inc. Consolidated Income Statements 2013–2017 (amounts in thousands of U.S. dollars, except per share, employee and stockholder data)

	2017	2016	2015	2014	2013
Net Sales	$ 4,881,951	$5,456,650	$5,702,613	$6,023,819	$6,484,892
Cost of sales	3,061,122	2,902,259	2,896,255	3,022,797	3,006,009
Gross profit (loss)	1,820,829	2,554,391	2,806,358	3,001,022	3,478,883
Advertising & promotion expenses	642,286	634,947	717,852	733,243	750,205
Other selling & administrative expenses	1,521,366	1,400,211	1,547,584	1,614,065	1,560,575
Operating income (loss)	(342,823)	519,233	540,922	653,714	1,168,103
Interest expense	10,5214	95,118	85,270	79,271	78,505
Interest income	7,777	9,144	7,230	7,382	5,555
Other non-operating income (expense), net	(64,727)	(23,517)	1,033	5,085	3,975
Income (loss) before income taxes	(504,987)	409,742	463,915	586,910	1,099,128
Total deferred income tax provision (benefit)	436,802	1,236	4,133	8,142	19,632
Provision (benefit) for income taxes	548,849	91,720	94,499	88,036	195,184
Net income (loss)	(1,053,836)	318,022	369,416	498,874	903,944
Less net income allocable to participating restricted stock units	–	1,377	3,179	4,028	8,335
Net income (loss) applicable to common shares	$ (1,053,836)	$ 316,645	$ 366,237	$ 494,846	$ 895,609
Weighted average shares outstanding –basic	343,564	341,480	339,172	339,016	343,394
Weighted average shares outstanding –diluted	343,564	344,233	339,748	340,768	347,459
Year end shares outstanding	343,800	342,400	339,700	338,100	339,300
Net income (loss) per share – basic	($3.07)	$0.93	$1.08	$1.46	$2.61
Net income (loss) per share – diluted	($3.07)	$0.92	$1.08	$1.45	$2.58
Dividends declared per common share	$0.91	$1.52	$1.52	$1.52	$1.44
Total number of employees	28,000	32,000	31,000	31,000	29,000
Number of common stockholders	27,000	28,000	29,000	30,000	31,000

Source: Mergent Online.

The 2017 losses in net income resulted in a write-down in retained earnings on Mattel's balance sheet in excess of $1.3 billion. In an effort to solidify their short-term debt position, Mattel entered into a credit agreement in December 2017 to provide seasonal financing for their company operations. This credit facility consisted of $1.3 billion in an asset-based lending facility and $294 million in a revolving credit facility.[31] Also in December 2017, Mattel issued $1.00 billion in 6.75 percent senior unsecured notes, due December 2020. The net result of these moves resulted in total debt for Mattel reaching $2.8 billion at year end 2017. The company's consolidated balance sheets for 2016 and 2017 are shown in Exhibit 4.

Cash flow from operations had been positive since 2014 but turned negative in 2017 along with the

EXHIBIT 4   Mattel, Inc. Consolidated Balance Sheets 2016–2017 (amounts in thousands of U.S. dollars)

ASSETS	2017	2016
Cash & equivalents	$1,079,221	$ 869,531
Accounts receivable, net	1,128,610	1,115,217
Inventories	600,704	613,798
Prepaid expenses & other current assets	303,053	341,518
Total current assets	3,111,588	2,940,064
Property, plant & equipment, gross	2,740,997	2,645,539
Less: accumulated depreciation	1,955,712	1,871,574
Property, plant & equipment, net	785,285	773,965
Goodwill	1,396,669	138,7628
Deferred income taxes	76,750	508,363
Total assets	$6,238,503	$6,493,794
LIABILITIES		
Accounts payable	$ 5,721,66	$ 664,857
Accrued royalties	111,669	107,077
Other accrued liabilities	420,054	350,248
Accrued liabilities	792,139	628,826
Income taxes payable	9,498	19,722
Total current liabilities	1,623,803	1,505,573
Long-term debt	2,873,119	2,134,271
Benefit plan liabilities	168,539	192,466
Total noncurrent liabilities	3,357,245	2,580,439
Total liabilities	4,981,048	4,086,012
Equity		
Common stock	441,369	441,369
Additional paid-in capital	1,808,391	1,790,832
Treasury stock at cost	2,389,877	2,426,749
Retained earnings (accumulated deficit)	2,179,358	3,545,359
Total stockholders' equity (deficit)	1,257,455	2,407,782
Total liabilities and stockholders' equity	$6,238,503	$6,493,794

Source: Mergent Online.

losses in net income. Mattel continued to invest cash flows into the company as well, with net cash flows from investment activities reaching ($235 million) in 2017. Financing activities contributed all of the

positive cash flow for the company in 2017. Cash and equivalents at year-end 2017 were stable at approximately $1 billion. Exhibit 5 presents Mattel's consolidated cash flow statements for 2015 through 2017.

EXHIBIT 5   Mattel, Inc. Cash Flow Statements 2015–2017 (amounts in thousands of U.S. dollars)

	For the Year Ended		
	December 31, 2017	December 31, 2016	December 31, 2015
Cash Flows from Operating Activities:			
Net (loss) income	($1,053,836)	$318,022	$369,416
Adjustments to reconcile net (loss) income to net cash flows from operating activities:			
Depreciation	240,818	235,797	233,025
Amortization	33,949	26,543	32,402
Deferred income taxes	(19,840)	1,236	4,133
Share-based compensation	67,119	53,950	56,691
Asset impairments	56,324	–	–
Loss on discontinuation of Venezuelan operations	58,973	–	–
Inventory obsolescence	127,592	31,455	33,305
Valuation allowance on U.S. deferred tax assets and U.S. tax reform	456,642	–	–
Increase (decrease) from changes in assets and liabilities, net of acquired assets and liabilities:			
Accounts receivable	13,626	(24,033)	(136,259)
Inventories	(91,644)	(68,650)	(107,567)
Prepaid expenses and other current assets	33,681	34,754	(36,865)
Accounts payable, accrued liabilities, and income taxes payable	98,044	9,006	248,047
Other, net	(49,062)	(23,571)	38,229
Net cash flows (used for) provided by operating activities	(27,614)	594,509	734,557
Cash Flows from Investing Activities:			
Purchases of tools, dies, and molds	(128,940)	(140,124)	(142,363)
Purchases of other property, plant, and equipment	(168,219)	(122,069)	(111,818)
Payments for acquisition, net of cash acquired	–	(33,154)	–
Proceeds from (payments for) foreign currency forward exchange contracts	60,993	(6,103)	(61,509)
Other, net	503	(10,460)	33,195
Net cash flows used for investing activities	(235,663)	(311,910)	(282,495)
Cash Flows from Financing Activities:			
Payments of short-term borrowings, net	(1,611,586)	(83,914)	–
Proceeds from short-term borrowings, net	1,419,418	259,168	16,914
Payments of long-term borrowings	–	(300,000)	–

Proceeds from long-term borrowings, net	988,622	350,000	–
Payment of dividends on common stock	(311,973)	(518,529)	(515,073)
Proceeds from exercise of stock options	1,775	34,065	14,995
Other, net	(27,806)	(22,261)	(17,058)
Net cash flows provided by (used for) financing activities	458,450	(281,471)	(500,222)
Effect of Currency Exchange Rate Changes on Cash	14,517	(24,411)	(30,676)
Increase (decrease) in Cash and Equivalents	209,690	(23,283)	(78,836)
Cash and Equivalents at Beginning of Year	869,531	892,814	971,650
Cash and Equivalents at End of Year	$ 1,079,221	$869,531	$892,814
Supplemental Cash Flow Information:			
Cash paid during the year for:			
Income taxes, gross	$ 117,690	$113,022	$120,232
Interest	103,339	84,763	83,005

Source: Mattel, Inc. 2017 10-K.

MATTEL REVENUES BY CATEGORY AND REGION

The Mattel Girls and Boys brand category dropped from $3.46 billion in 2015 to $3.07 billion in 2017. The same trends could be seen across all other categories: Fisher-Price Brands, American Girl Brands, Construction and Arts & Crafts category, and other miscellaneous sales. As of 2017, there wasn't a single category at Mattel that had not been affected by the sales downturn. Exhibit 6 provides Mattel's revenues by major brand category for 2015 through 2017.

Geographically, the revenue downturn was most pronounced in the North American region. Sales in North America declined from $3.68 billion in 2015 to $3.01 billion in 2017. International, while declining, was not declining as sharply. Total international sales declined from $2.60 billion in 2015 to $2.50 billion in 2017. Sales in the Asia Pacific region actually

EXHIBIT 6   **Mattel Revenues by Major Brand Category, 2015–2017 (U.S. dollars in thousands)**

Brand Category	2017	2016	2015
Mattel Girls & Boys Brands	$3,077,716	$3,194,100	$3,464,195
Fisher-Price Brands	1,677,223	1,888,146	1,852,219
American Girl Brands	451,481	570,770	571,957
Construction and Arts & Crafts Brands	269,543	377,570	351,747
Other	38,162	43,128	43,510
Gross Sales	5,514,125	6,073,714	6,283,628
Sales Adjustments	(632,174)	(617,064)	(581,015)
Net Sales	$4,881,951	$5,456,650	$5,702,613

Source: Mattel, Inc. 2017 10-K.

EXHIBIT 7   Mattel Revenues by Geography, 2015–2017 (U.S. dollars in thousands)

Geographic Region	2017	2016	2015
North American Region	$3,010,598	$3,626,099	$3,680,091
International Region			
Europe	1,281,672	1,293,302	1,388,753
Latin America	675,286	636,535	711,041
Asia Pacific Region	546,569	517,778	503,743
Total International Region	2,503,527	2,447,615	2,603,537
Gross Sales	5,514,125	6,073,714	6,283,628
Sales Adjustments	(632,174)	(617,064)	(581,015)
Net Sales	$4,881,951	$5,456,650	$5,702,613

Source: Mattel, Inc. 2017 10-K.

increased from 2015 to 2017, an unusual bright spot for the company, and a possible harbinger for future growth. Overall, international sales appeared to be resilient to the current downturn in Mattel sales. Exhibit 7 provides Mattel's revenues by geography for 2015 through 2017.

STOCK PERFORMANCE

Mattel's stock price peaked at an all-time high of $47.82 on December 30, 2013. Sales and earnings for the company also peaked into 2013, and the company's stock price closely tracked this spike in revenues and earnings. Exhibit 8 tracks Mattel Incorporated's stock price performance from July 2013 through July 2018.

From this peak in December 2013, Mattel's stock price had drifted lower in fits and starts. 2016 saw a brief rebound in the company's fortunes, but a continual stream of weakening revenues and earnings had fed the weakening price action for the stock price as well. This would culminate with a major sell off in October of 2017 following the release of negative third quarter 2017 earnings for the company.

In 2018, the company had been trading in $12 to $18 price range. Given this price range, the market capitalization of the company was approximately $5.40 billion. It was not possible to calculate a trailing price/earnings ratio for the company, given the negative earnings for the company in 2017. Dividends for the company had also been suspended.

U.S. TOY AND CRAFT SUPPLIES WHOLESALING INDUSTRY

Mattel participated in the U.S. Toy and Craft Supplies Wholesaling Industry (Toy Industry). The toy industry consisted of U.S. based companies that were wholesalers of toys and craft supplies, as well as various miscellaneous items.[32] Toys and craft supplies were purchased from both U.S. and international manufacturers and then sold to U.S. retailers, including discount department stores, big-box retailers, and independent specialty retail outlets.

While industry revenues were forecasted to reach $28.3 billion in 2018, the toy industry faced an increasingly difficult market environment in the United States. With only occasional reversals, revenue for the industry had fallen every year since 2013. Toy industry participants were squeezed on all sides. On the manufacturing side, large and mostly international manufacturers were increasingly integrating vertically and bypassing the toy industry wholesalers to sell directly to large retail chains in the United States. On the retail side, there was increasing consolidation of industry players, leaving only a few very large retailers with which to negotiate. These conditions, combined with decreasing demand for toys and falling prices, resulted in fierce competition for toy industry participants. Revenue for the toy industry was projected to fall by 0.8 percent in 2018.[33]

EXHIBIT 8 Monthly Performance of Mattel, Inc.'s Stock Price, July 2013–July 2018

(a) Trend in Mattel Inc.'s Common Stock Price

(b) Performance of Mattel Inc.'s Stock Price versus the S&P 500 Index

Products and Services

The $28.3 billion U.S. toy industry was comprised of four major segments: (1) traditional toys, including children's vehicles, (2) video games, (3) hobby and craft supplies, and (4) other items. Demand for toys was seasonal, with sales peaking in the fourth quarter of the years, and closely tied to consumer confidence and spending. However, while consumer confidence in the United States had been rising, consumers had also become increasingly frugal and thrifty, particularly with toy purchases. Consumers were tending to buy less expensive toys in order save money.[34]

Traditional toys made up 54.7 percent of industry revenue in 2018. This segment included action figures, dolls, sporting goods, building sets, board games, and plush toys for children. Demand for traditional toys were under pressure in the United States. Children were increasingly demanding electronic toys and video games. Further, children appeared

to be outgrowing toys at a faster rate, particularly as they entered the 8 to 12 age range. Traditional toys continued to decline as percentage of industry revenue. Exhibit 9 illustrates the relative sizes of the toy industry product and service segments in 2018.

Demand for video games, as a result, continued to grow into 2018. Major manufacturers such as Sony and Microsoft continued to introduce new gaming consoles, spurring new game introduction and passionate usage by teenagers. Demand for video games was also increasingly penetrating younger and younger age groups. Sales of video games represented 27.1 percent of industry sales in 2018, and was anticipated to rise as a percentage of industry revenue.[35]

The hobby and craft supplies segment included items such as scrapbooking supplies, needlework kits, and craft kits. Demand in this segment had remained relatively stable, and was closely tied to consumer discretionary spending. Hobby and craft supplies represented 4.5 percent of industry revenue in 2018.

EXHIBIT 9   U.S. Toy & Craft Supplies Wholesaling Industry: Product and Services Segmentation, 2018

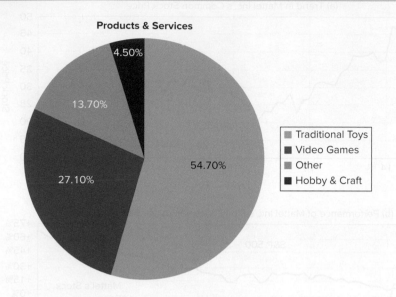

Source: IBIS World.

The other category in the industry consisted of various other product categories not classified elsewhere. This included items such as playing cards, fireworks, and coloring books. Revenues in this segment had remained fairly consistent at 13.7 percent of industry revenue.[36]

Major Markets

The bulk of toy industry sales were conducted through major retailers in the United States. Market share of major retailers had increased, however, allowing them to source toys directly from manufacturers. Wholesale toy companies, as a result, faced a difficult and increasingly competitive environment for sales, with significant pricing pressure from retailers. This had pressured pricing on toys downward. Toy companies had also begun to focus their sales efforts on retailers and retail chains with less purchasing power (smaller retailers) and also had begun to focus more on direct sales of toys to consumers. Exhibit 10 illustrates a percentage breakdown of the major market segments of the U.S. toy industry in 2018.

Discount department stores, such as Wal-Mart and Target, made up 29.2 percent of toy industry sales in 2018. These large retailers purchased toys in large volumes in attempt to drive down prices for the end consumer. Retailers had also begun to bypass toy wholesalers, such as Mattel and Hasbro, and had begun to increasingly purchase toys directly from international manufacturers. The net combination of these conditions continued to pressure the margins of toy industry wholesalers. The volume of toys supplied to discount department stores was expected to continue a gradual decline.

Big box retailers, such as Toys "R" Us, Michaels, and Jo-Ann, represented 27.4 percent of toy industry revenues in 2018.[37] The bankruptcy of Toys "R" Us in 2017 posed a considerable threat to toy industry participants, given that Toys "R" Us represented a significant proportion of toy company sales. Toys "R" Us decision in 2018 to close its U.S. store locations was expected to have a significant negative effect on toy wholesaling.

Independent specialty stores represented 20.3 percent of toy industry revenues in 2018. Independent specialty stores were smaller than other retail outlets, and relied more heavily on toy industry wholesalers for shipments of toys and related items. Independent retailers were under considerable pressure from discount department stores and big box retailers due to intense price competition from their larger competitors. Sales to

EXHIBIT 10   U.S. Toy & Craft Supplies Wholesaling Industry: Major Market Segmentation, 2018

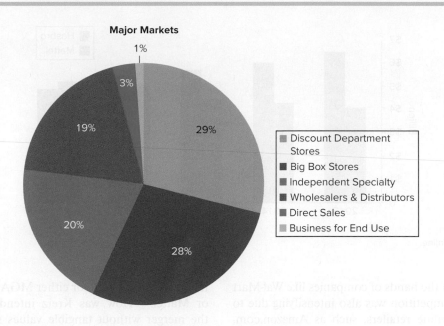

Major Markets

- Discount Department Stores — 29%
- Big Box Stores — 28%
- Independent Specialty — 20%
- Wholesalers & Distributors — 19%
- Direct Sales — 3%
- Business for End Use — 1%

Source: Ibis World.

independent specialty stores was anticipated to remain stable, although a number of smaller independents were expected to be acquired or leave the industry.[38]

The heavy competition in retail had led many toy industry participants to attempt direct sales to consumers through company websites. Consumers rarely purchased toys in large volumes, however, making online sales generally unprofitable. Direct sales accounted for 3.0 percent of industry revenues in 2018.

The remaining sales in the industry were either trade between wholesalers in the industry (18.8 percent of industry revenue) or directly to other businesses (1.3 percent of industry revenue). Both sales channels were relatively stable, and generally represented trade among industry participants for various reasons.

Competition

The two main competitors in the U.S. toy industry were Mattel and Hasbro. Combined, the two companies controlled approximately 25 percent of the U.S. market for toys.[39] The remaining 75 percent of companies were predominately small, privately owned competitors with five or less employees that typically competed for consumers in their local communities.

Mattel had been the undisputed industry leader in the U.S. toy industry for many years, but Hasbro's sales had exceeded Mattel in 2017. Hasbro had seen sharp sales gains when it had been awarded a license from Walt Disney Company to market dolls and other products tied to Disney's smash hit movie "Frozen" in 2016. Exhibit 11 presents a revenue comparison for Mattel and Hasbro.

Notable competitors in the U.S. toy industry included Mattel, Hasbro, Jakks Pacific, Just Play Products, Lego, Mega Entertainment, Moose Toys, Spin Master and VTech. Notable competitors in the international market included Mattel, Hasbro, Famosa, Giochi Preziosi, Lego, MGA Entertainment, Playmobil, Ravensburger, Simba, Spin Master and Vtech.[40]

Competition in both the United States and worldwide was very strong and intensifying. Individual toys faced shorter and shorter life cycles as children would discard older toys in favor of the latest fashion or Hollywood movie release. Technology was also increasingly in use by children at an earlier and earlier age. A phenomena also increasingly observed was the trend of "children getting older younger" as children outgrew toys at an earlier age.[41] Competition for retailer shelf space was fierce, and was increasingly

EXHIBIT 11   Revenue Comparison for Mattel and Hasbro, 2013–2017 (U.S. dollars in billions)

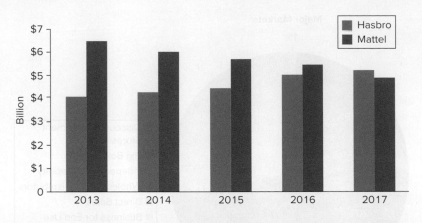

Source: Mergent Online.

concentrated in the hands of companies like Wal-Mart and Target. Competition was also intensifying due to the entry of online retailers, such as Amazon.com, who would promote toys from a wide variety of toy companies and compete aggressively on price.

The Outlook for the U.S. Toy and Crafts Industry

Looking ahead in the U.S. toys and crafts industry, revenues for the industry were forecasted to continue a downward trend from 2018 to 2023, according to IBIS World. Industry revenue was forecasted to decrease at a rate of 1.0 percent per year to $26.9 billion in 2023. The retail price of toys was also forecasted to continue to decline, as softening demand, retailer consolidation and pricing pressure from international toy manufacturers continued to pressure pricing in the industry. Industry participants were also forecasted to decline through 2023 as margin pressures continued to force the exit of smaller and weaker industry participants in the toy industry.

CONCLUSION

Mattel CEO Ynon Kreiz sat in his new office in El Segundo, CA and reread the merger proposal letter from MGA Entertainment CEO Isaac Larian. Was Larian serious about merging with Mattel? There were no details tied to the proposal, and no tangible values stated for either MGA Entertainment or Mattel.[42] How was Kreiz intended to evaluate the merger without tangible values stated for both companies?

CEO Kreiz was also aware of discussions that previous Mattel CEO Margo Georgiadis had undertaken with rival company Hasbro regarding a possible takeover in 2017. Those discussions had stalled without any clear resolution.[43] There was a time in Mattel's history when the company had discussed taking over Hasbro, but that was not the situation today.

Ynon Kreiz, in his first day as Chief Executive Officer for Mattel, had been tasked with leading the way forward for Mattel. What were his options for consideration? Should he consider a merger with MGA Entertainment, or maybe another company? Perhaps now was the time to reevaluate the takeover proposal from Hasbro. Would a bid by Hasbro for Mattel spark a bidding war, and possibly other bids for Kreiz's company? What would Mattel's Board of Directors say if Kreiz undertook either a merger or acquisition negotiations? Would the Mattel Board rebel and force Kreiz from his job?

Kreiz, having been a member of Mattel's Board of Directors before becoming CEO, was very familiar with Mattel's transformation plan. Was the way forward the excellent execution of the company's turnaround plan? What were the elements of the plan that required action, and what other steps should Kreiz undertake in order to restore Mattel to market success and profitability? What were the defensive actions that needed to be undertaken to defend Mattel's core products and brands, and what

offensive actions should he undertake to move the company forward in the toy industry?

Kreiz wondered how much time he had left to effect a rescue of Mattel Incorporated.

ENDNOTES

[1] Ziobro, P., "Bratz Boss Makes Play to Run Mattel, Is Told to Take his Toys and Go Home," *Wall Street Journal,* May 18, 2018, www.wsj.com.

[2] Ziobro, P., "Bratz Boss Makes Play to Run Mattel, Is Told to Take his Toys and Go Home," *Wall Street Journal,* May 18, 2018, www.wsj.com.

[3] Cimilluca, D. & Ziobro, P., "Mattel Names New CEO as it Seeks Answer to Sales Slump," *Wall Street Journal,* April 19, 2018, www.wsj.com.

[4] A third partner, Harold Matson, dropped out early in the company's history.

[5] Source: Mattel, Inc., corporate.mattel.com.

[6] Source: Mattel, Inc., corporate.mattel.com.

[7] Goldman, A., "Mattel Cuts its Losses by Giving Learning Co. Away," *Los Angeles Times,* September 20, 2000, articles.latimes.com.

[8] Goldman, A., "Mattel Cuts its Losses by Giving Learning Co. Away," *Los Angeles Times,* September 20, 2000, articles.latimes.com.

[9] Goldman, A., "Mattel will Shut Last U.S. Manufacturing Site," *Los Angeles Times,* April 4, 2001, articles.latimes.com.

[10] Goldman, A., "Mattel will Shut Last U.S. Manufacturing Site," *Los Angeles Times,* April 4, 2001, articles.latimes.com.

[11] Goldman, A., "Mattel will Shut Last U.S. Manufacturing Site," *Los Angeles Times,* April 4, 2001, articles.latimes.com.

[12] Story, L. & Barboza, D., "Mattel Recalls 19 Million Toys Sent from China." *New York Times,* August 15, 2007, www.nytimes.com.

[13] Story, L. & Barboza, D., "Mattel Recalls 19 Million Toys Sent from China." *New York Times,* August 15, 2007, www.nytimes.com.

[14] Story, L. & Barboza, D., "Mattel Recalls 19 Million Toys Sent from China." *New York Times,* August 15, 2007, www.nytimes.com.

[15] Kell, J., "Mattel's Barbie Sales Down for a Third Consecutive Year," *Fortune.* January 30, 2015, www.fortune.com.

[16] Halzak, S. "Barbie Sales Are Nosediving, and That's Just One of Mattel's Problems," *Washington Post.* October 16, 2014, www.washingtonpost.com.

[17] Halzak, S. "Barbie Sales Are Nosediving, and That's Just One of Mattel's Problems," *Washington Post.* October 16, 2014, www.washingtonpost.com.

[18] Ziebro, P., "Mattel to Add Curvy, Petite, Tall Barbies," *Wall Street Journal,* January 28, 2018, www.wsj.com.

[19] Cimilluca, D. & Ziobro, P., "Mattel Names New CEO as it Seeks Answer to Sales Slump," Wall Street Journal, April 19, 2018, www.wsj.com.

[20] Cimilluca, D. & Ziobro, P., "Mattel Names New CEO as it Seeks Answer to Sales Slump," Wall Street Journal, April 19, 2018, www.wsj.com.

[21] Ziebro, P. & Mattioli, D., "Hasbro Sets Its Sights on Mattel," *Wall Street Journal,* November 10, 2017, www.wsj.com.

[22] Source: Mattel, Inc.

[23] Source: Mattel, Inc.

[24] Mattel 2017 Annual Report, www.mattel.com.

[25] Mattel Earnings Call 04-26-2018, www.mattel.com.

[26] Mattel Earnings Call 04-26-2018, www.mattel.com.

[27] Mattel 2017 Annual Report, www.mattel.com.

[28] Mattel 2017 Annual Report, www.mattel.com

[29] Mattel 2017 Annual Report, www.mattel.com

[30] Source: Mattel 2017 Annual Report, www.mattel.com.

[31] Source: Mattel 2017 Annual Report, www.mattel.com.

[32] IBIS World, "Toys & Crafts Supplies Wholesaling in the U.S.," www.ibisworld.com.

[33] IBIS World, "Toys & Crafts Supplies Wholesaling in the U.S.," www.ibisworld.com.

[34] IBIS World, "Toys & Crafts Supplies Wholesaling in the U.S.," www.ibisworld.com.

[35] IBIS World, "Toys & Crafts Supplies Wholesaling in the U.S.," www.ibisworld.com.

[36] IBIS World, "Toys & Crafts Supplies Wholesaling in the U.S.," www.ibisworld.com.

[37] IBIS World, "Toys & Crafts Supplies Wholesaling in the U.S.," www.ibisworld.com.

[38] IBIS World, "Toys & Crafts Supplies Wholesaling in the U.S.," www.ibisworld.com.

[39] IBIS World, "Toys & Crafts Supplies Wholesaling in the U.S.," www.ibisworld.com.

[40] IBIS World, "Toys & Crafts Supplies Wholesaling in the U.S.," www.ibisworld.com.

[41] Mattel 2017 Annual Report, www.mattel.com.

[42] Ziobro, P., "Bratz Boss Makes Play to Run Mattel, Is Told to Take his Toys and Go Home," *Wall Street Journal,* May 18, 2018, www.wsj.com.

[43] Cimilluca, D. & Ziobro, P., "Mattel Names New CEO as it Seeks Answer to Sales Slump," Wall Street Journal, April 19, 2018, www.wsj.com.

Shearwater Adventures Ltd.

A.J. Strickland
The University of Alabama

Ross N. Faires
MBA Student, The University of Alabama

In early 2018, Allen Roberts was sitting in his office in Victoria Falls, Zimbabwe, contemplating his company's future in conducting its adventure activities. Robert Mugabe had finally been overthrown, tourism in Zimbabwe was up 5 percent over the previous year, and hyperinflation had come to an end. However, competition was quickly increasing and the Zimbabwean government and economy was entering an unknown era.

As Allen Roberts began developing his strategy and business plan for Shearwater Adventures and its 350 employees, he wondered what the future held for the adventure industry in Victoria Falls.

ALLEN ROBERTS

Allen Roberts was educated in the United Kingdom at Nottingham University, where he majored in quantity surveying. This special course required classes in architecture and detailed cost estimation. However, like many students in their 20s, he was not really interested in going to work, so he followed his passion of kayaking. He became a competitive kayaker, entering numerous tournaments all over the world. In 1991, Roberts realized he could not make a career of kayaking and acted on a friend's suggestion to go to Victoria Falls and try his luck at rafting the Zambezi River.

As soon as Roberts made his first trip, he was hooked on the Zambezi, and thus a new passion was born. The Zambezi was generally regarded as offering the best whitewater rafting in the world. As Roberts said, "The rapids are huge, the water is warm, the weather is great, and the scenery is stunning."

After working in Africa for a while, Roberts traveled to the United States and tried his luck at canoeing and whitewater rafting in West Virginia and then Pennsylvania. During his time in the States, Roberts also gained valuable experience making videos of rafting trips and selling the copies to participants. Soon, however, he decided to return to Africa and Victoria Falls for good.

A friend of Robert's named Mike Davis had, in the previous rafting season, started making videos of the Zambezi River rafting trips and had secured the rights to do so for the next season. Knowing that Roberts had been making videos in the United States, Davis approached Roberts about working together, and their business soon expanded to produce both videos and photos. The profit was so tremendous on the videos and pictures that Davis and Roberts were making more money than the owners of the rafts. This did not go unnoticed by the raft operators.

Roberts and Davis were having the time of their lives. As single young men, they were making good money with few expenses. Roberts says that his only necessities were food, beer, and the occasional date. The long term was not in his thoughts because he was having too much fun.

In 1995, the manager of Shearwater Adventures approached Mike Davis and asked if he would like to form a partnership. Davis agreed immediately. The Shearwater owners soon realized that Roberts and Davis were first-rate entrepreneurs, and the two were put in charge of all Shearwater operations. Davis was in charge of running the rafting adventures, and Roberts became a partner in the video and photo section, which at the time was the most profitable area. Roberts was 25 years old.

Business was good for Shearwater at that time. Tourist arrivals to Victoria Falls were growing rapidly. However, in 2003, Davis decided to leave the group to pursue new ventures. Roberts not only stayed on at Shearwater, but also assumed the role of CEO, taking a personal 25 percent stake in the company. At this time Shearwater was already the dominant adventure activity operator at Victoria Falls and the best-known adventure tour operator in all of Africa.

THE ADVENTURE SPORTS INDUSTRY

The extreme and adventure sports industry generated $263 billion annually, and had been growing at a rate of 65 percent a year since 2009. The average traveler per trip spending (excluding travel and gear expenses) was just shy of $1,000. Beginning in the mid-2010s, adventure travel had become mainstream as vacationers looked for exciting ways to enjoy time away from their jobs.

Most companies defined extreme and adventure sports as those activities requiring special equipment and one or more trained guides. The difference between an extreme sport and an adventure sport was simply a matter of word choice: a company's advertising could use either term according to how the company wanted to portray the activities it offered to customers. The wide range of activities included bungee jumping, skiing, hiking, biking, climbing, horseback riding, rafting, snowmobiling, skydiving, and going on safaris. Skiing had been on the decline due to climate change and rising lift passes. The most popular attraction, was whitewater rafting. Dozens of companies around the world offered individual trips or package deals categorized by the number of days they took.

Like other industries in the 21st century, the extreme and adventure sporting industry had a global presence. Adventure seekers were offered not only a wide range of activities but also a wide range of locations. While one person could go cage diving with great whites in South Africa, another could choose to ride a helicopter in the Rocky Mountains and ski down the slopes. However, as competitors looked to grow their market share and increase their customer base, they needed to attract customers at the global level. With the average customer at 36 years old, successful players in this market also had to find a way to cater to older customers while continuing to attract college-age travelers; 57 percent of travelers were male, and 48 percent were single.

It was no surprise that young adults were the most common adventure travelers. Those were the years when everyday life became more and more hectic and disposable income increased. With a societal push to stay young at heart and the realization that money can't always buy happiness, adults were looking for ways to break free from the sometimes mundane life of office work and the acquisition of possession. In addition to a new mindset, adults were also influenced by many other factors. An increased focus on healthy lifestyles was prompting consumers to choose vacations that also provided a means of exercise.

Entertainment media were also helping the cause of extreme and adventure sports. ESPN's X Games were gaining popularity, and new adventure sports including skateboarding, surfing, and sport climbing were being added to the 2020 Olympic Games in Tokyo. It was also much easier than ever before for people to travel long distances for adventures, making seemingly remote locations such as the Zambezi River not so remote after all. Outdoor adventure companies' knowledge base and the quality of their equipment were also continuing to improve, allowing even the most conservative adventurer to feel safe.

In addition to better equipment, technology was promoting the industry like never before. Adventure seekers could skydive out of a plane and film the entire experience. Within minutes of hitting the ground, they could upload the video to social media for all of their followers to see. GoPro and other action camera manufacturers made documenting adventure experiences easier than ever before. Previously only experienced photographers and videographers could capture the once in a lifetime experience, but now even amateurs could record and edit their own content.

While it was difficult to start an operation in the United States due to the cost of permits, opening an adventure operation in some countries such as South Africa could be as easy as having a whitewater raft and the experience to guide customers. However, to achieve long-term sustainability, the leader of the company had to be shrewd and had to know the financial status of the company down to the last penny. Industry leaders were also partnering through acquisitions, organized associations, and reseller networks in order to increase repeat bookings from satisfied customers. In order to provide customers with the best experience, many companies were becoming vertically integrated.

They provided everything including airport pickup, accommodations, dining, and adventure experiences.

Key success factors included repeat bookings and cross-selling—companies that could offer a variety of activities had a much higher profitability of gaining repeat business. Additionally, companies needed to attract customers from around the world, as local citizens were often too poor to afford the adventures.

Advertising was key to attract tourists who had not yet chosen an adventure activity upon arrival in the local market. Developing a social media presence was a very important aspect of attracting customers—69 percent of travelers decided on a destination by researching online, and 28 percent of travelers decided after watching a travel program on the destination.

Adventure sports companies in Victoria Falls, for example, had to target tourists as soon as they entered the area. They formed partnerships with shuttle drivers from airports and set up offices in key hotels. Credibility was added when locals supported the operation. Placing ads in travel guides, magazines, and high-traffic Internet sources was another way to reach a wider range of customers from different geographical locations and different age brackets. In the case of Shearwater Adventures, word of mouth played an important role in new sales.

THE COMPETITION

There were several other companies running adventure travel operations in Zimbabwe, along with dozens of others across Africa. Some of the well-known competitors included Wild Horizons, African Budget Safaris, and Lonely Planet. For most travelers, going to Victoria Falls was a once in a lifetime event. The majority of customers are not repeat visitors, so it was important for activity companies to offer the highest quality adventures to attract customers.

While most customers book through traditional companies, there was a new variable introduced once the customers arrive in Victoria Falls. As soon as a tourist exits their vehicle or hotel, they are swarmed by locals trying to convince the new arrivals to book adventures with their friends. These locals offer the same adventures as the big companies, but at a much cheaper price.

The companies competed in several segments: accommodation, transport, activities, food and restaurants, retail, and airport handling services.

Wild Horizons

Wild Horizons was owned by international tourism company, Tourvest, and has been operating in Victoria Falls since 1981 in one form or another. Since their founding, they have hosted over 1,800,000 guests.

Wild Horizons offers everything their clients need once they arrive in Africa. Wild Horizons provides airport transportation, accommodations, activities, attractions, and restaurants in Victoria Falls. They are the clear market leader in the transportation segment.

They divide their activities into four categories to appeal to all demographics of travelers—adrenaline, wildlife, family, and cultural. Within these categories, guests can choose from ziplining, helicopter tours, whitewater rafting, safaris, and sunset cruises on the Zambezi River. Wild Horizons also offers the option for guests to combine these activities into multi-day packages in order to receive a discount. Interestingly, while Wild Horizons and Shearwater Adventures compete directly for guests on their whitewater rafting and elephant back safaris, the two companies partnered together in their helicopter tours.

African Budget Safaris

Based in Cape Town, South Africa, African Budget Safaris (ABS) is a group of travel consultants that finds the best adventure travel operations across the entire continent of Africa and helps clients build their dream trip.

The majority of the adventures from ABS are multi-day excursions led by experienced, third-party guides. ABS offers multiple different types of trips including walking safaris, riding safaris, camping, diving with great white sharks, whale watching, mountain biking, and even climbing Mt. Kilimanjaro. For clients that want to experience Africa at their own pace, ABS consultants will help clients plan a self-guided trip.

Lonely Planet

Lonely Planet was created by a husband and wife with a passion for traveling. They created a company that operates on every continent and helps clients plan the trip of a lifetime. They offer a mobile application, printed guidebooks, and an award-winning website to help clients create their trip. Lonely Planet gives clients information about their destination, what to do while there, and allows clients to connect with other clients who have gone on the same vacations.

Lonely Planet offers several adventure and leisure trips in the Victoria Falls area. Clients can book sunset cruises on the Zambezi River, helicopter flights over Victoria Falls, whitewater rafting trips, safari tours, hikes, trips to local villages, camping, bungee jumping, ziplining, and cycling.

ZIMBABWE

Government

Zimbabwe did not gain its independence until 1980. Since then, the country has experienced significant political turmoil. The country, divided into eight provinces, is run by a president elected by the public. Each province is run by a governor appointed by the president. The Zimbabwean government is set up much like the United States, with an executive, legislative, and judicial branch.

Robert Mugabe was the country's first prime minister after their independence. He had been the only ruler of the independent country, becoming president in 1987. Zimbabwe historically had close ties with the United Kingdom, but attacks of white-owned farms, encouraged by Mugabe, in the early 2000s strained the relationship. It was estimated that the reclaimed land was worth $3 to 3.5 billion. The attacks forced the farmers to leave the country, which created a mass shortage of basic necessities due to the lack of agriculture. In 2002, Mugabe rigged the election ensure he remained president. In 2007, Mugabe instituted price controls on all basic goods, which led to a panic and again left basic goods in short supply for months. In the 2008 election, Mugabe's opposition, Morgan Tsvangirai, won the popular vote but was forced to withdraw from the election due to violence against his supporters. After several months of tough negotiations, Mugabe remained president, but Tsvangirai became prime minister.

Running a business in Zimbabwe was extremely risky. In 2008, Mugabe signed the Indigenization and Economic Empowerment Bill. This bill forced any company worth over $500,000 to be at least 51 percent owned by a native Zimbabwean. Passing the bill gave Mugabe even more control of the country's economy. Additionally, Mugabe could close the Zimbabwean borders, or shut down the airports, effectively shutting down the entire tourist industry. Business owners had to weigh the costs of choosing to operate a business in a country with little stability.

In November 2017, Zimbabweans celebrated as Mugabe's reign finally came to an end. After being Mugabe was ousted by his own citizens, one of Mugabe's oldest friends took office. Emmerson Mnangagwa became the new president of Zimbabwe, after being exiled in South Africa for several years. Better known as "The Crocodile," Mnangagwa is a very quiet, tactful, and fierce leader. Despite the joy Zimbabweans felt after Mugabe's overthrowing, many in the country were still hesitant about their new leader. Mnangagwa viewed Mugabe as his mentor and served as his vice president for many years. In a speech shortly after he took office, Mnangagwa said, "Today we are witnessing the beginning of a new, unfolding democracy. . I wish also for all genuine patriotic Zimbabweans to come together. We work together. No one is more important than the other. We are all Zimbabweans. We want to grow our economy. We want peace in our country. We want jobs, jobs, jobs."[1] While it is still unknown how the Crocodile's governance will turn out, the country is optimistic about a vibrant new future.

Economy

Zimbabwe's economy is primarily made up of mining and agriculture. The economy grew more than 10 percent annually from 2010 to 2013 before turning negative again in 2016. The decline was due to poor harvest, infrastructure and regulatory deficiencies, debt burdens, and high government wage expenses.

Inflation was a huge issue in Zimbabwe as the Reserve Bank of Zimbabwe (RBZ) constantly printed money to fund the budget deficit. To reduce the hyperinflation, Zimbabwe became a multi-currency economy in 2009, accepting the Botswana pula, South African rand, and United States dollar. In an attempt to further reduce inflation in 2015, Zimbabwe also began accepting Chinese renminbi, Indian rupee, Australian dollar, and Japanese yen. The majority of transactions were United States dollars.

Zimbabwe had over 220,000 tourists in 2016. The majority of tourists were from other African countries, followed by Europe, and then the United States. Most visitors to Zimbabwe were there to see the natural beauty. One of the main attractions is the world's largest waterfall, Victoria Falls. Another major attraction is Great Zimbabwe. Great Zimbabwe was once the capital of the country, but is now one of the most important sites in Africa and it is recognized as a UNESCO World Heritage Site. Hwange National Park is the largest and oldest game preserve in the country. It is home to the Big Five: lions, leopards, elephants, Cape buffalo, and rhinos.

Attractions

Zimbabwe is a very beautiful country with many natural and man-made attractions. There were almost a dozen national parks, the most prominent being Hwange National Park. The capital city of Harare has a bounty of delicious restaurants and a bustling nightlife. The Zambezi River offers tourists the chance to see wildlife and fish for the elusive tiger fish. Great Zimbabwe was a prosperous kingdom from the 11th to 15th century, and is now a beautiful site for history lovers to visit.

Unfortunately, when Mugabe took control of the country, all of these sites lost popularity. The only attraction that was still visited during his tenure was Victoria Falls.

SHEARWATER ADVENTURES

As Allen Roberts looked to strengthen his company's position in the adventure sports industry, one strategy he considered was to expand beyond offering only activities. Roberts had originally differentiated Shearwater adventures by offering far more adventures than any of his competitors, but they were catching up to his strategy. Two concerns were that (1) it was not expensive for a company to add an adventure to its lineup, and (2) there was talent in the area that could either devise a new adventure or that could simply copy Shearwater's offerings.

In order to separate Shearwater from the competition, Roberts decided that Shearwater would become vertically integrated.

Shearwater Adventures' Scope of Integration

Roberts grew his company to offer services in multiple segments including accommodation, transportation, activities, retail, and restaurants.

Shearwater Adventures' accommodations target customers seeking the best value. They offer 80 beds in the chalets and a campsite with serviced dome tents that sleep 120 guests. These accommodations were only 400 meters from Victoria Falls and 100 meters to the center of the city. Guests can easily walk to local markets and cafes.

They have five outlets where they sell their retail products in very key locations. Three were in surrounding hotels, one in the international airport, and one at the Zambezi Helicopter Company helipad.

Shearwater is the market leader in the dining industry, operating three very successful restaurants in high trafficked locations: one of their hotels, one in the city center, and one overlooking the Zambezi River. Additionally, they provide catering for all of their activities, which helps the overarching vertical integration.

Shearwater's Customers

Shearwater Adventures attract all demographics of customers. The guests range from 18-year-olds going bungee jumping to 85-year-olds staying in the hotels and eating at the restaurants. On average, a customer booked two activities and stayed 2.5 nights in Victoria Falls. The reason for short visits was because most guests were coming to Victoria Falls as part of a much longer vacation to Southern Africa.

Only 20 percent of customers book in advance. The other 80 percent book their activities and dining reservations once arriving in Victoria Falls. Tour guides were very protective of the guests they bring because they receive large commissions for steering bookings toward certain companies, like Shearwater Adventures. Shearwater Adventures has booking desks in many local hotels, but only 10 percent of bookings were from this method. The majority come from tour guides bringing the guests to Shearwater Adventures' main booking office. It is absolutely imperative for Roberts and his staff to maintain strong relationships with the tour guides. Exhibit 1 shows the number of Shearwater customers by service line and geographic area. The number of guests, average revenue per guest, and average operating cost by guest for the locations that Shearwater operated in are provided in Exhibit 2. The company's balance sheets and business sector analysis are provided in Exhibits 3 and 4, respectively.

Technology

Facebook has nearly two billion users, and Instagram almost one million users. On par with the rest of society, Shearwater's customers want to share their once

EXHIBIT 1   Number of Shearwater Customers by Service and Geographic Area, 2017

Service	Zimbabwe	Zambia	Botswana	Total
Transport	100,524	19,121	27,263	146,908
Accommodations	8,635	–	–	8,635
Activities	120,974	7,253	21,013	149,240
Retail	30,612	–	–	30,612
Restaurants	183,003	–	–	183,003
Total	443,748	26,374	48,276	518,398

Source: Shearwater company reports.

EXHIBIT 2   Shearwater Business Location Analysis (Dollar amounts in USD)

	Zimbabwe	Zambia	Botswana
Number of Guests	443,748	26,375	48,276
Average Revenue	$ 59.12	$64.59	$46.86
Operating Costs per Guest	$(50.80)	$(47.98)	$(32.74)

Source: Shearwater company reports.

EXHIBIT 3   Shearwater Balance Sheet

	Zimbabwe	Zambia	Botswana
Fixed Assets	$ 6,639,773	$ 302,041	$ 353,657
Current Assets	6,379,059	306,740	796,923
Total Assets	13,018,832	608,781	1,150,580
Total Equity	(5,270,905)	(301,122)	(192,238)
Borrowings	(2,941,266)	(0)	(607,368)
Current Liabilities	(4,806,926)	(307,660)	(350,973)
Total Liabilities	(7,748,192)	(307,660)	(958,341)
Total Equity & Liabilities	$ (13,019,097)	$ (608,782)	$ (1,150,579)

Source: Shearwater company reports.

EXHIBIT 4   Shearwater Business Sector Highlights, 2017 (Dollar amounts in USD)

	Transport	Activities	Accommodations	Shops	Cafes
Number of Guests	146,909	149,240	8,634	30,611	183,002
Sales & Other Income	$ 2,216,846	$ 14,182,462	$ 190,698	$1,171,944	$ 2,100,934
Average Revenue	$21	$135	$31	$54	$16
Operating Costs	$ (1,724,414)	$ (10,911,861)	$(311,733)	$ (957,558)	$ (1,940,915)
Operating Costs per Guest	$16.72	$104.14	$51.41	$44.55	$15.11

Source: Shearwater company reports.

in a lifetime experience as quickly as they can. Social media usually allows users to post content virtually anytime from anywhere. However, due to the remoteness of Shearwater's operations, Internet access is spotty at best.

Shearwater's Activities

Examples of Shearwater excursions and activities are presented in Exhibit 5. Shearwater offers a full range of activities for all types of customers. The majority

EXHIBIT 5   Sample Excursions and Activities Offered by Shearwater Adventures

TOUR SPECIALS

MORE INFO | ENQUIRE

THE FULL MONTY : Zambezi Sunset Cruise, Helicopter Flight, Guided Tour of the Falls, Historic Bridge Tour

$ 250.00

MORE INFO | ENQUIRE

A BRIDGE TOO FAR : Zambezi Sunset Cruise, Helicopter Flight, Guided Tour of the Falls

$ 200.00

MORE INFO | ENQUIRE

THE BUSHTRACKS EXPRESS : Victoria Falls Bridge at Sunset, Pre-dinner Experience

$ 125.00

MORE INFO | ENQUIRE

THE NO-FLY ZONE : Zambezi Sunset Cruise, Guided Tour of the Falls, Historic Bridge Tour

$ 115.00

©Shearwater Adventures

SAFARI

MORE INFO | ENQUIRE

ELEPHANT BACK SAFARI – Victoria Falls

$ 150.00

MORE INFO | ENQUIRE

CHOBE FULL DAY TRIP (Botswana) from Victoria Falls

$ 170.00

MORE INFO | ENQUIRE

RHINO ENCOUNTER GAME DRIVES

$ 190.00

MORE INFO | ENQUIRE

WALKING WITH LIONS

$ 150.00

©Shearwater Adventures

of these activities were located in Zimbabwe, Zambia, and Botswana. For the adventure seekers, Shearwater offers bungee jumping, whitewater rafting, elephant rides, and ziplining. For the leisurely traveler, Shearwater offers helicopter tours, sunset cruises, gentle hikes, and incredible safaris. If travelers are looking for additional thrills, Shearwater could connect their customers with third-party operators to go fishing, horseback riding, and much more.

WHAT'S NEXT FOR SHEARWATER?

While Shearwater Adventures faced serious threats, there was a defense or a solution for each one. As Zimbabwe enters a new age of hopeful political stability, Shearwater has an incredible opportunity to thrive. It was crucial for Allen Roberts to increase pre-bookings of Shearwater adventure tours as a defense against competition and to use its existing capacity to accommodate more customer bookings for its adventure tours to their advantage. If Shearwater Adventures is to remain one of the top operations in the Victoria Falls area, what are the next steps in the plan? How is Roberts to deal with opportunities presented by the new Zimbabwean government and take advantage of the opportunities to use technology to promote his business? Should he expand his operations to the other attractions in the country and offer door-to-door service like in Victoria Falls? The new Zimbabwe offers lots of opportunities, but the future state of the country is very much unknown.

ENDNOTE

[1] As quoted in "Ofeibea Quits-Arcton, "Who is Zimbabwe's New Leader, Emmerson Mnangagwa?," NPR Parallels, November 22, 2017, https://www.npr.org/sections/parallels/2017/11/23/566117480/who-is-zimbabwes-new-leader-emmerson-mnangagwa.

TJX Companies: It's Strategy in Off-Price Home Accessories and Apparel Retailing

David L. Turnipseed
University of South Alabama

In February 2018, TJX Companies, Inc., the world's largest off-price home accessories and apparel retailer, completed 42 years of operations with several enviable milestones: the company had edged up to number 85 on the Fortune 500, surpassed $35 billion in sales, and opened its 4,000th store, guided by a highly effective global strategy. Sales had grown over eight percent and comparable store sales increased 2 percent in fiscal year 2018. In the company's 42-year history, it had experienced an annual decline in comparable store sales in only one year. The strong earnings trend enabled TJX to increase its per share dividends for fiscal 2019 by 20 percent, which made 21 consecutive years of dividend increases.

Ernie Herrman, the President and CEO of TJX, looked back at his first year in charge of the huge, international off-price retailer with great satisfaction. As the TJX Companies moved into fiscal 2019, President Herrman pondered how to keep the company on the same upward trajectory. Although the TJX Companies had one small chain that was primarily e-commerce, and its brick-and-mortar chains had e-commerce capabilities, in a world ostensibly focused on e-commerce, TJX had been very successful concentrating on its brick-and-mortar chains. Given TJX's steadily increasing sales and profits in its present structure, should the company divert part of its attention and resources, and attempt to boost its internet sales? Also, given the outstanding sales growth driven by opening new stores worldwide, should the company stay the course, or would concentration on certain geographical locations produce more sales and profits?

TJX: AN OVERVIEW

TJX traced its origin to the Feldberg cousins who opened their Zayre (Yiddish for "very good") discount store in Hyannis, Massachusetts in 1956. Over the years, Zayre purchased a women's clothing chain, opened Chadwick's of Boston, launched a membership warehouse club, and a home improvement chain. The first T.J. Maxx opened in Auburn, MA in 1977, offering off-price upscale family apparel. In 1987, the Zayre's off-price chains were organized as the TJX Companies, Inc., which were operated as a subsidiary of Zayre. Also in 1987, TJX had an IPO, with Zayre retaining 83 percent ownership. In 1989, Zayre divested its warehouse club division, and acquired minority ownership in TJX companies that had been publically traded. Zayre merged with TJX and then adopted the name of its former subsidiary.

In 1990, TJX acquired Winners Apparel Ltd, a Canadian chain similar to T.J. Maxx, and this chain became Canada's largest off-price stores. Two years later, in 1992, HomeGoods, offering home fashions from around the world, was launched in the United States. TJX ventured overseas in 1994 and opened T.K. Maxx in the United Kingdom (UK) and Ireland. Over time, T.K. Maxx became the only major brick-and-mortar off-price retailer of home fashions and apparel in Europe. In 1995, TJX acquired the 496 store Marshalls chain, which was the second largest off-price retailer of brand-name family apparel in the United States.

TJX launched an off-price concept, named A.J. Wright, in 1998, which was similar to Marshalls and T.J. Maxx. A.J. Wright targeted moderate-income families. In 2001, TJX opened HomeSense in Canada, which was the first off-price home fashion chain in Canada. HomeSense was similar to HomeGoods in the United States and offered a wide selection of off-price home fashions. TJX acquired Bob's Stores in 2003, which was a value-oriented, casual family apparel and footwear retailer, located in the Northeastern United States. In 2007, T.K. Maxx opened stores in Germany, introducing the off-price concept to that country.

In 2008, TJX sold Bob's Stores to private equity firms and opened the first HomeSense stores in the UK. The expansion into Europe continued in 2009 when T.K. Maxx opened stores in Poland. Also in 2009, T.K. Maxx launched its e-commerce site, tkmaxx.com in the UK. TJX consolidated its A.J. Wright division, converting 91 stores to Marshalls, HomeGoods, or T.J. Maxx. Marshalls was launched in Canada in 2011 and in 2012 TJX acquired a U.S. off-price Internet retailer, Sierra Trading Post. T.J. Maxx launched its e-commerce site, tjmaxx.com, in 2013. The following year, Sierra Trading Post opened two brick-and-mortar stores to bring its off-price outdoor apparel to more consumers.

TJX continued its international expansion in 2015, acquiring an Australian off-price retail chain, Trade Secret, and opening stores in Austria and the Netherlands under the T.K. Maxx brand. The Australian Trade Secret stores were converted to T.K. Maxx stores in 2017. HomeSense expanded into Europe and opened stores in Ireland. Moving into fiscal year 2019, TJX had over 4,000 stores in nine countries— the United States, The Netherlands, United Kingdom, Germany, Republic of Ireland, Austria, Poland, Australia, and Canada.

TJX'S STRATEGIC VISION AND MANAGEMENT FOCUS

TJX's mission was:

> Our mission is to deliver great value to our customers every day. We do this by offering a rapidly changing assortment of quality, fashionable, brand name, and designer merchandise generally 20 percent to 60 percent below full-price retailers' (including department, specialty, and major online retailers) regular prices on comparable merchandise.[1]

TJX management believed that the company had one of the most flexible business models in the world, and that the great flexibility had enabled the company to succeed through the many economic and retail situations over the years. There were no walls between departments in TJX stores—stores could expand and contract merchandise areas for fast response to market trends and changes in customer preferences. TJX had rapid inventory turnover, which enabled the company to buy close to need, having visibility into current fashion and pricing trends. The company sourced its merchandise from around the world from a group of over 20,000 vendors in over 100 countries. TJX was an industry leader in innovation: the company relentlessly tested new ideas, trying to find the current fashions and top brands, and leveraging information from their global worldwide purchasing network. Also, the company was financially strong, which gave it the ability to invest in the growth of its business. These key success factors gave TJX management confidence in the company's ability to achieve corporate goals for global growth.

TJX's management was focused on increasing market share, while simultaneously delivering profitable stock growth to its shareholders. Management had several initiatives underway in 2018 to attract consumers to the TJX stores and grow its customer base in the United States and internationally. TJX expected total sales and comparable store sales growth in fiscal year 2019 similar to prior years.

TJX's management believed that their pursuit of their goals for global growth would be sustained by the company's major strengths:

- World-class buying organization
- Global supply chain and distribution network
- Leveraging the global presence
- One of the most flexible retail business models in the world

The company's earnings per share estimates reflected the significant benefit from U.S. tax reform as well as continued increases in wages and expected investments to support company growth. President Herrman and his management team were passionate about surpassing corporate goals.

TJM'S STOCK PERFORMANCE

TJX had its IPO on August 4, 1989, and the stock began a steady uptrend of growth that continued into mid-2018. Stock prices from July 2013 to July 2018 are shown in Exhibit 1.

TJX stock showed significant strength: a $10,000 investment in TJX at $16.15 on July 14, 2008, would have returned 573.71 percent and yielded an ending investment of $67,351.07, at $95.36 on July 11, 2018, 10 years later (assuming dividend reinvestment).

Following a very strong fourth quarter, with 24 percent stock price growth, TJX announced a dividend increase of 25 percent ($.39) and announced plans to repurchase $2.5 to 3.0 billion of TJX stock. The stock reached its historic high of $96.82 on June 20, 2018.

TJX BUSINESSES

TJX operated four primary business segments, Marmaxx and HomeGoods (U.S.), TJX Canada, TJX International, and one Internet retailer, Sierra Trading Post. The company believed that it had the opportunity to expand their retail chains around the world by increasing their store base of 4,000 by more than 2,000 stores, or about 50 percent, to 6,100 stores long term. This reflected the potential the company saw with its existing chains in the current countries alone. In 2018, TJX planned an increase of approximately 240 new stores, about 6 percent store growth.

U.S. Segments

Marmaxx   The T.J. Maxx and Marshalls chains ("Marmaxx") were collectively the largest off-price

---

EXHIBIT 1   Monthly Performance of TJX Companies' Stock Price, July 2013–July 2018

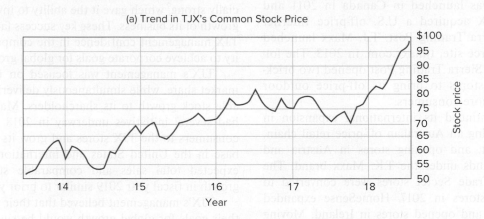

(a) Trend in TJX's Common Stock Price

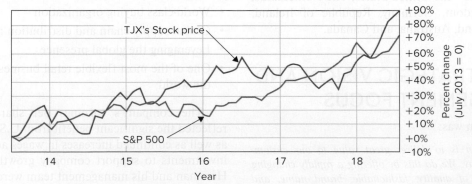

(b) Performance of TJX's Stock Price versus the S&P 500 Index

Source: Bigcharts.com

retailers in the United States, with a total of 2,285 stores. T.J. Maxx was founded in 1976 and Marmaxx acquired Marshalls in 1995. Both chains sold family apparel, home fashions (e.g., home basics, accent furniture, lamps, rugs, etc.), and other merchandise. The primary difference between T.J. Maxx and Marshalls was their product assortment: a larger assortment of fine jewelry and accessories and a designer section called *The Runway* at T.J. Maxx, and a full line of footwear, a broader men's offering, and a juniors' department named *The Cube* at Marshalls. The intent of the differentiated shopping experience at the two stores was to encourage customers to shop both chains. T.J. Maxx's e-commerce website, tjmaxx.com, was launched in 2013.

Sierra Trading Post   Sierra Trading Post was an off-price Internet retailer of brand name, quality outdoor gear, family apparel and footwear, sporting goods, and home fashions. Sierra Trading Post launched its e-commerce site, sierratradingpost.com, in 1998 and operated 27 retail stores in the United States.

Marmaxx was the largest and most profitable of TJX's divisions, and the company saw significant growth ahead for the division. Marmaxx's continued comparable store sales and traffic increases in many different retail and economic environments gave TJX confidence in the division's continued growth (see Exhibit 2). Also, new stores continued to reach their targets and, overall, to generate attractive returns. Marmaxx had a 1 percent comparable store sales increase in 2017, which met the low end of the company's expectations, despite a significant negative impact of severe weather during the year. Marmaxx was focused on driving customer traffic and comparable sales increases, and had a long-term target of 3,000 stores that reflected TJX's determination and perceived ability to further penetrate existing U.S. markets.

HomeGoods   The HomeGoods segment was introduced in 1992, and became the leading off-price home fashions retailer in the United States. HomeGoods offered an extensive assortment of home fashions, including furniture, rugs, lighting, decorative accessories, tabletop and cookware, as well as expanded pet, kids, and gourmet food departments through its 667 stores. In 2017, HomeSense was launched in the U.S.

EXHIBIT 2   Financial Summary for the Marmaxx Business Unit, Fiscal Years 2016–2018 ($ in millions)

	Fiscal Year Ended		
Dollars in millions	**February 3, 2018**	**January 28, 2017**	**January 30, 2016**
Net sales	$22,249.1	$21,246.0	$19,948.2
Segment profit	2,949.4	2,995.0	2,858.8
Segment profit as a percentage of net sales	13.3%	14.1%	14.3 %
Increase in comp sales	1%	5%	4 %
Stores in operation at end of period			
T.J. Maxx	1,223	1,186	1,156
Marshalls	1,062	1,035	1,007
Sierra Trading Post	27	12	8
Total	2,312	2,233	2,171
Selling square footage at end of period (in thousands)			
T.J. Maxx	27,077	26,614	26,158
Marshalls	24,916	24,750	24,308
Sierra Trading Post	470	227	159
Total	52,463	51,591	50,625

Source: TJX Companies, Inc. Fiscal 2018 10-K.

United States with four stores. HomeSense complemented HomeGoods by offering a differentiated mix and expanded departments, including furniture, lighting and rugs, as well as new departments, such as a general store and an entertaining marketplace.

The Homegoods division celebrated its 25th anniversary in 2017, with 4 percent comparable store sales growth, primarily driven by customer traffic (see Exhibit 3). Also, it launched HomeSense in 2017. The company expected significant future growth for HomeGoods and HomeSense, because it believed that the U.S. market was underpenetrated. At HomeGoods, the long-term plan was to expand to 1,000 stores, over 300 more than in 2017. The company was confident in their plan because of HomeGoods' long history of good performance, and there were 65 top markets with a T.J. Maxx or Marshalls that did not have a HomeGoods. The first four HomeSense four stores were opened in 2017 to an overwhelmingly positive customer response. TJX planned to continue opening HomeSense stores in their larger HomeGoods markets to encourage customers to shop both stores. Based on response to the first four stores, the company believed it could expand the HomeSense brand to about 400 U.S. stores over the long term.

Foreign Segments

TJX Canada Acquired in 1990, TJX Canada operated the HomeSense, Winners, and Marshalls chains in Canada. Winners was the leading off-price apparel and home fashions retailer in Canada. The merchandise in Winners' 264 Canadian stores was comparable to T.J. Maxx, with select stores offering fine jewelry, and "*The Runway,*" which was a designer section. The HomeSense chain was opened in 2001, and introduced the off-price home fashions concept to Canada. HomeSense had 117 stores with a merchandise mix of home fashions similar to HomeGoods in the United States. The Canadian Marshalls was launched in 2011 and operated 73 stores in Canada in 2017. The Canadian Marshalls stores offered an expanded footwear department and "*The Cube*" juniors' department, similar to Marshalls in the United States, differentiating them from Winners stores.

The three Canadian chains had a comparable store sales increase of 5 percent in 2017, with all three chains having strong results and increases in customer traffic (see Exhibit 4). The TJX Canada division had grown into the largest off-price apparel

EXHIBIT 3   Financial Summary for the HomeGoods Business Unit, Fiscal Years 2016–2018 ($ in millions)

Dollars in millions	Fiscal Year Ended		
	February 3, 2018	January 28, 2017	January 30, 2016
Net sales	$5,116.3	$4,404.6	$3,915.2
Segment profit	$ 674.5	$ 613.8	$ 549.3
Segment profit as a percentage of net sales	13.2%	13.9%	14.0%
Increase in comp sales	4%	6%	8%
Stores in operation at end of period			
HomeGoods	667	579	526
HomeSense	4	—	—
Total	671	579	526
Selling square footage at end of period (in thousands)			
HomeGoods	12,448	11,119	10,234
HomeSense	81	—	—
Total	12,529	11,119	10,234

Source: TJX Companies, Inc. Fiscal 2018 10-K.

EXHIBIT 4   Financial Summary for TJX Canada, Fiscal Years 2016–2018 ($ in millions)

U.S. Dollars in millions	Fiscal Year Ended		
	February 3, 2018	January 28, 2017	January 30, 2016
Net sales	$3,642.3	$3,171.1	$2,854.6
Segment profit	$ 530.1	$ 413.4	$ 375.3
Segment profit as a percentage of net sales	14.6%	13.0%	13.1%
Increase in comp sales	5%	8%	12%
Stores in operation at end of period			
Winners	264	255	245
HomeSense	117	106	101
Marshalls	73	57	41
Total	454	418	387
Selling square footage at end of period (in thousands)			
Winners	5,780	5,629	5,470
HomeSense	2,179	1,984	1,900
Marshalls	1,621	1,307	975
Total	9,580	8,920	8,345

Source: TJX Companies, Inc. Fiscal 2018 10-K.

and home fashions retailer in Canada. Due to the division's strong results and growth forecast, TJX increased the long-term store potential of TJX Canada by 100 stores to 600 total stores.

TJX International TJX International segment operated the T.K. Maxx and HomeSense chains in Europe, and the T.K. Maxx chain in Australia. T.K. Maxx was launched in 1994, and introduced off-price retail to Europe. T.K. Maxx was the only major brick-and-mortar off-price retailer of apparel and home fashions in Europe. T.K. Maxx operated 540 stores in the UK, Ireland, Germany, Poland, Austria, and the Netherlands, offering a merchandise mix similar to T.J. Maxx through its stores and e-commerce website for the UK, tkmaxx.com. TJK International brought the off-price home fashions concept to Europe in 2008, opening HomeSense in the UK. In fiscal year 2018, two HomeSense stores were opened in Ireland. HomeSense's 55 stores offered a home fashions merchandise mix similar to HomeGoods in the United States and HomeSense in Canada. Trade Secret in Australia was acquired in fiscal year 2016 and rebranded T.K. Maxx during fiscal 2018.

The merchandise offered at Trade Secret's 38 stores was comparable to T.J. Maxx.

TJX International's (T.K. Maxx and HomeSense–Europe, and T.K. Maxx–Australia), comparable store sales increased by 2 percent in 2017, consistent with company plans and expectations (see Exhibit 5). TJX was satisfied with the gains in customer traffic and believed that the division gained market share. The company was confident of significant long-term opportunity and believed that the division had the potential to grow TJX International to 1,100 stores in just the countries in which they were located.

T.K. Maxx and HomeSense were the only major brick-and-mortar, off-price retailers of clothing and home fashions in Europe and they planned to continue capitalizing on their first-mover advantages. They were also focusing on growing tkmaxx.com in the UK. In 2017, T.K. Maxx introduced "Click and Collect" in the UK, which allowed online shoppers to pick up their purchases in the stores.

TJX bought the Australian off-price retailer Trade Secret in 2015 and, in 2017, converted those stores to T.K. Maxx–Australia. In its first year of operation (2017) the division surpassed sales projections.

EXHIBIT 5   Financial Summary for TJX International, Fiscal Years 2016–2018 ($ in millions)

U.S. Dollars in millions	Fiscal Year Ended		
	February 3, 2018	January 28, 2017	January 30, 2016
Net sales	$4,856.9	$4,362.0	$4,226.9
Segment profit	$ 249.2	$ 235.5	$ 316.9
Segment profit as a percentage of net sales	5.1%	5.4%	7.5%
Increase in comp sales	2%	2%	4%
Stores in operation at end of period			
T.K. Maxx	540	503	456
HomeSense	55	44	39
T.K. Maxx Australia	38	35	35
Total	633	582	530
Selling square footage at end of period (in thousands)			
T.K. Maxx	11,379	10,787	9,970
HomeSense	883	714	639
T.K. Maxx Australia	714	667	667
Total	12,976	12,168	11,276

Source: TJX Companies, Inc. Fiscal 2018 10-K.

THE TJX COMPANIES, INC.'S FINANCIAL PERFORMANCE IN FISCAL YEAR 2018

TJX had enjoyed impressive revenue growth from approximately $31 billion in fiscal year 2016 to nearly $35.9 billion in fiscal 2018. The company's consolidated statements of income for fiscal 2016 through fiscal 2018 is provided in Exhibit 6. Its consolidated balance sheets for fiscal years 2017 and 2018 are presented in Exhibit 7.

STORE GROWTH

A central part of TJX's global growth strategy focus was the addition of new stores to expand its business, and the primary growth strategies were increasing customer traffic and comparable store sales, and growing the global store base. The company was confident that their value concept could work in any country in which consumers wanted great fashion and top brands at great-value prices.

In the United States, the company saw meaningful growth potential for Marmaxx, which had been the largest and most profitable division. Marmaxx had shown continued comparable store sales and traffic increases in many different retail and economic environments, and TJX management believed there was long-term potential to grow the Marmaxx division to 3,000 stores, which was over 700 more stores than at the end of fiscal 2018. In 2018, the company planned to open about 65 new T.J. Maxx and Marshalls stores.

TJX believed that there was a large opportunity for growth at HomeGoods and HomeSense in the United States, both of which were underpenetrated in the U.S. home market. The company believed that its ability to leverage its global teams, and its infrastructure and operational expertise were major reasons to be confident in continuing to open stores successfully around the world. TJX's management believed that the company had a huge opportunity to gain market share around the world.

The number of stores and store growth for the four major segments in the last two fiscal years, and

EXHIBIT 6   TJX Companies, Inc., Consolidated Statements of Income, 2016–2018 ($ in thousands except per share amounts)

	Fiscal Year Ended		
Amounts in thousands except per share amounts	February 3, 2018	January 28, 2017	January 30, 2016
		(53 weeks)	
Net sales	$35,864,664	$33,183,744	$30,944,938
Cost of sales, including buying and occupancy costs	25,502,167	23,565,754	22,034,523
Selling, general and administrative expenses	6,375,071	5,768,467	5,205,715
Impairment of goodwill and other long-lived assets, related to Sierra Trading Post (STP)	99,250	—	—
Loss on early extinguishment of debt	—	51,773	—
Pension settlement charge	—	31,173	—
Interest expense, net	31,588	43,534	46,400
Income before provision for income taxes	3,856,588	3,723,043	3,658,300
Provision for income taxes	1,248,640	1,424,809	1,380,642
Net income	$ 2,607,948	$ 2,298,234	$ 2,277,658
Basic earnings per share:			
Net income	$4.10	$3.51	$3.38
Weighted average common shares – basic	636,827	655,647	673,484
Diluted earnings per share:			
Net income	$4.04	$3.46	$3.33
Weighted average common shares – diluted	646,105	664,432	683,251
Cash dividends declared per share	$1.25	$1.04	$0.84

Source: TJX Companies, Inc. Fiscal 2018 10-K.

EXHIBIT 7   The TJX Companies, Inc. Consolidated Balance Sheets , 2017–2018 ($ in thousands except per share amounts)

	Fiscal Year Ended	
Amounts in thousands except share amounts ASSETS	February 3, 2018	January 28, 2017
Current assets:		
Cash and cash equivalents	$2,758,477	$2,929,849
Short-term investments	506,165	543,242
Accounts receivable, net	327,166	258,831
Merchandise inventories	4,187,243	3,644,959
Prepaid expenses and other current assets	706,676	373,893
Total current assets	8,485,727	7,750,774
Net property at cost	5,006,053	4,532,894
Non-current deferred income taxes, net	6,558	6,193

(Continued)

ASSETS		
Goodwill	100,069	195,871
Other assets	459,608	398,076
TOTAL ASSETS	$14,058,015	$12,883,808

LIABILITIES		
Current liabilities:		
Accounts payable	$2,488,373	$2,230,904
Accrued expenses and other current liabilities	2,522,961	2,320,464
Federal, state and foreign income taxes payable	114,203	206,288
Total current liabilities	5,125,537	4,757,656
Other long-term liabilities	1,320,505	1,073,954
Non-current deferred income taxes, net	233,057	314,000
Long-term debt	2,230,607	2,227,599
Commitments and contingencies		

SHAREHOLDERS' EQUITY		
Preferred stock, authorized 5,000,000 shares, par value $1, no shares issued	—	—
Common stock, authorized 1,200,000,000 shares, par value $1, issued and outstanding 628,009,022 and 646,319,046, respectively	628,009	646,319
Additional paid-in capital	—	—
Accumulated other comprehensive income (loss)	(441,859)	(694,226)
Retained earnings	4,962,159	4,558,506
Total shareholders' equity	5,148,309	4,510,599
TOTAL LIABILITIES AND SHAREHOLDERS' EQUITY	$14,058,015	$12,883,808

Source: TJX Companies Fiscal 2018 10-K.

growth estimates for fiscal 2019 and long-term store growth potential of these segments in their current geographic locations are presented in Exhibit 8.

Exhibit 9 presents the relative contributions of the several TJX locations the TJX Companies' gross corporate revenues.

WINDFALL FROM THE TAX CUTS AND JOBS ACT OF 2017

On December 22, 2017, President Trump signed the *Tax Cuts and Jobs Act of 2017,* which amended the Internal Revenue Code and, among other things, reduced corporate tax rates. This legislation benefited TJX in 2017, and the company believed that their business would continue to benefit from the tax reform, primarily due to lower U.S. corporate income tax rates. The company used part of the expected cash benefit to make investments in its employees' communities. Eligible, non-bonus plan employees in each of TJX's divisions worldwide were given a one-time discretionary bonus, and the company made incremental contributions to its defined contribution plans around the world for eligible participants.

In the United States, TJX planned enhanced vacation benefits for certain employees and introduced paid parental leave. In 2017, the company made sizable contributions to its charitable foundations and planned to use the tax reduction windfall to significantly increase its charitable giving. Also, the company planned to increase its shareholder distribution programs.

In addition to the expected cash benefit due to U.S. tax reform, TJX planned to repatriate over

EXHIBIT 8   TJX Companies Number of Store Locations, Fiscal Years 2017–2019 (Estimated)

	Approximate Average Store Size (square feet)	Number of Stores at Year End			Estimated Store Growth Potential
		Fiscal 2017	Fiscal 2018	Fiscal 2019 (estimated)	
Marmaxx					
T.J. Maxx	28,000	1,186	1,223		
Marshalls	29,000	1,035	1,062		
		2,221	2,285	2,350	3,000
HomeGoods					
HomeGoods[3]	24,000	579	667		
HomeSense	25,000	—	4		
		579	671	771	1,400
TJX Canada					
Winners	28,000	255	264		
HomeSense	23,000	106	117		
Marshalls	28,000	57	73		
		418	454	484	600
TJX International					
T.K. Maxx (Europe)	29,000	503	540		
HomeSense (Europe)	20,000	44	55		
T.K. Maxx (Australia)	22,000	35	38		
		582	633	668	1,100[1]
TJX Total		3,812[2]	4,070[2]	4,308[2][3]	6,100[2][3]

[1] Reflects store growth potential for T.K. Maxx in current geographies and for HomeSense in the United Kingdom and Ireland.

[2] The TJX total includes 12 Sierra Trading Post stores in fiscal 2017, 27 Sierra Trading Post stores for fiscal 2018, and 35 Sierra Trading Post stores estimated for fiscal 2019. Sierra Trading Post stores are not included in estimated store growth potential.

[3] HomeGoods and TJX total includes 15 new HomeSense stores in the United States for fiscal 2019 and store growth potential includes 400 HomeSense stores.

Source: TJX Companies, Inc. Fiscal 2018 10-K.

$1 billion from Canada back to the United States. Consequently, the company was able to increase its per-share dividend and planned a substantial share buyback program. In addition, the tax reform benefit enabled TJX to move forward investments in store growth, technology, and employee training.

TJX'S PERFORMANCE IN FISCAL YEAR 2019

TJX's first quarter fiscal 2019 net income was $716.4 million, or $1.13 per share, compared to $536.3 million and $0.82 per share in the same period during 2017. The increase in net income per share exceeded expectations helped drive the company's per share price higher. Sales increased year-over-year by 12 percent in Q1 fiscal year 2019, reaching $8.7 billion. The increased revenue was largely due to increased store traffic and increased comparable store sales in the four large divisions.

The strong first quarter fiscal 2019 performance led to the company increasing its upper-end fiscal 2019 adjusted EPS guidance by $.02. The company's new expectation for adjusted diluted earnings per share (which excludes the benefit from the 2017 Tax Cuts and Jobs Act) was in the $4.04 to $4.10 range. This guidance was a 5 percent to 6 percent increase

EXHIBIT 9   TJX Revenue Contribution by Geographic Region, Fiscal Years 2016–2018

	Fiscal 2018	Fiscal 2017	Fiscal 2016
United States			
Northeast	24%	24%	24%
Midwest	12	12	12
South (including Puerto Rico)	25	25	25
West	15	16	16
Subtotal	76	77	77
Canada	10	10	9
Europe	13	13	14
Australia	1	*	*
Total	100%	100%	100%

* Revenue from Australia was less than one percent during fiscal 2017 and fiscal 2016.

Source: TJX Annual Report, 2018.

over the prior year's adjusted $3.85, which excluded $.17 net benefit due to the 2017 Tax Cuts and Jobs Act, a benefit of approximately $.11 from the extra week in the company's fiscal year 2018 calendar, and a $.10 impairment charge related to Sierra Trading Post from GAAP EPS of $4.04. This guidance also assumed that wage increases would negatively impact

EPS growth by two percent. The outlook for EPS continued to be based upon estimated consolidated comparable store sales growth of 1 to 2 percent. Continued focus on the effective execution of its strategy gave TJX management and investors good reason to believe its competitive advantage could be sustained in the near term.

ENDNOTE

[1] http://www.tjx.com/businesses/.

CASE 22

IKEA's International Marketing Strategy in China

Debapratim Purkayastha
ICFAI Business School, Hyderabad

Benudhar Sahu
ICFAI Business School, Hyderabad

> "IKEA entered the Chinese market by learning from their mistakes and continuously adapt themselves to the changing environment. Not many companies have the ability to go through trial and errors because it is very costly when mistakes are made."[1]
>
> —Daxue Consulting,[2] in 2016

In August 2017, Angela Zhu, country retail manager of IKEA China, said the IKEA Group planned to open three new stores in China in the financial year 2018–19, enhancing its distribution networks and e-commerce presence in the mainland. IKEA's store expansion plans followed announcements of its strong financial results in China. For the period September 1, 2016, to August 10, 2017, IKEA China's sales revenue increased by 14 percent on a year-on-year basis, amounting to ¥[3]13.2 billion ($1.98 billion).[4] Despite its growth in sales in China, IKEA continued to grapple with a number of challenges while doing business in the country. For instance, in October 2017, it was forced to pull a television ad from the airwaves in China and issue an apology after it attracted accusations of insensitivity toward single women. The episode left industry observers wondering whether the company had been able to understand the Chinese culture at all.[5]

IKEA, globally known for its low prices and innovatively designed furniture, was successful in projecting itself as an aspirational Western brand in China. After learning from its initial failure in the country, IKEA adopted some new strategies that helped it build its business in China. Despite concerns over the country's financial crisis and sluggish economy, China maintained the fastest growth momentum as a

leading purchaser of IKEA products and the Swedish furniture giant projected an ambitious plan for its business in the country by 2020.

IKEA, however, faced criticism for its inability to tap the potential of the Chinese market through aggressive business plans unlike its competitors. Though IKEA was striving to make its products affordable to the average Chinese consumer through its prices cuts, some customers still preferred small commodities wholesalers, where prices were even lower than those of IKEA. Some industry observers were of the view that the Swedish furnishing retailer would have to incorporate basic changes in its brand positioning to suit the local customers, instead of relying on price cuts alone.

In June 2016, IKEA came under fire from the Chinese regulators for its clumsy handling of a product recall. Critics questioned the implementation of the company's safety standards that differed across countries. Earlier, the "no food, no seat" policy[6] of the company sparked a spirited debate in China's social media about the plight of older citizens who had little to do and nowhere to go. In July 2016, bowing to pressure from safety advocates, the Swedish

©IBS Center for Management Research

furnishing retailer recalled more than 1.7 million chests of drawers in China.[7] IKEA continued to be embroiled in controversies in China in 2017 with its television ad before it was pulled by the company.

IKEA defended its slow market expansion strategy in China, saying that its intention was to first establish a solid customer base in the country. However, as of early 2018, analysts wondered whether the Swedish furniture retailer would be able to grow its stores in China from 24 in the fiscal 2017 to 34 in 2020 as planned by the company. The onus was on Angela and the marketing team to make this happen by appealing to the Chinese customers and increasing IKEA's customer base in the country.

ABOUT IKEA

Founded in 1943 by Ingvar Kamprad, the IKEA Group was a Sweden-based home furnishing manufacturer and retailer owned by Stichting INGKA Foundation[8] and controlled by the Kamprad family. Guided by the vision *to create a better everyday life for the many people,*[9] Kamprad applied his innovative idea to offer home furnishing products of good function and design at affordable prices. But the company also looked beyond home furnishing. IKEA was a value-driven company with a passion for life at home. The furniture giant had a unique organizational structure, integrating a large number of companies as franchisees operating under the IKEA trademarks. As of August 2017, IKEA stores worldwide were owned by 11 franchisees, of which the IKEA Group was the biggest with 355 stores.[10] IKEA found franchising the best way to expand its business based on the IKEA Concept, to keep the concept together and to maintain an entrepreneurial spirit. All IKEA stores operated under franchise agreements with Inter IKEA Systems B.V.,[11] the owner of the IKEA Concept, including the IKEA trademarks. IKEA franchisees implemented the IKEA Concept by marketing and selling the IKEA product range.

From its humble beginnings as a small general retail store, IKEA had expanded its operations to become the world's largest furniture retailer with 355 stores in 29 countries and employed over 149,000 employees by the end of fiscal year 2017.[12] IKEA pioneered in selling flat-pack design and ready-to-assemble furniture, appliances, and home accessories across the world. A typical IKEA store offered approximately 9,500 products[13] across the IKEA range worldwide that were Scandinavian in style. Every year, the company renewed its range of products, launching approximately 2,500 new products designed by its in-house and contracted designers.

Most of the IKEA stores included restaurants serving traditional Swedish food. However, in some countries, a few varieties of the local cuisine and beverages were served alongside the Swedish staples. Another important feature of the IKEA stores was Småland (Swedish for Small Lands), where parents could drop off their children at a gate to the playground, and pick them up at another gate after shopping. IKEA also launched a loyalty card called IKEA Family, which was free of charge and could be used to avail of discounts on a special range of IKEA products.

IKEA grew its balance sheet size from €41.88 billion ($49.18 billion) in 2011 to €52.94 billion ($62.17 billion) in 2017 (see Exhibit 1).[14] In fiscal 2017, IKEA's total retail sales grew by 3.5 percent in euro and 3.8 percent adjusted for currency impact compared to the previous year, amounting to €34.1 billion ($40.05 billion).[15] During the period, IKEA welcomed 817 million customers to its stores and there were more than 2.1 billion visits to **IKEA.com**.[16] Together with the rental income from the shopping center business (IKEA Centers), total revenue for IKEA in fiscal 2017 reached €36.3 billion ($42.63 billion), up 1.7 percent from the previous year (see Exhibit 2).

In May 2017, IKEA named Jesper Brodin, head of IKEA of Sweden, as CEO after Peter Agnefjall, the then global CEO of IKEA, decided to step down. Expansion in Asia and the IKEA online offering were to be Brodin's focus area.

GLOBAL STRATEGY AT IKEA

IKEA entered the global market with its standardized products strategy. It had its own global strategy of opening stores and operating in new markets around the world. The furnishing retailer worked to find an effective combination of standardization, low cost, technology, and quality for its products in the market. However, its standardized product strategy also took into account culturally sensitive factors emerging out of divergent consumer tastes and preferences in different markets.

Started with the business idea "*to offer a wide range of well-designed, functional home furnishing products at prices so low that as many people as possible will be able to afford them,*"[17] IKEA maintained quality at affordable prices for its customers through optimizing its

EXHIBIT 1 Consolidated Balance Sheet of IKEA from FY 2011 to FY 2017 (in millions of euros)

Items	2017	2016	2015	2014	2013	2012	2011
ASSETS							
Property, plant, and equipment	€23,172	€23,033	€22,840	€17,322	€17,036	€17,264	€16,173
Other fixed assets	2,488	1,955	2,515	2,984	2,493	2,672	2,416
Total fixed assets	25,660	24,988	25,355	20,355	19,529	19,936	18,589
Inventory	1,924	1,713	5,498	4,927	4,257	4,664	4,387
Receivables	2,327	4,115	2,500	2,548	2,193	2,270	2,077
Cash and securities	23,029	23,151	16,659	16,886	16,000	17,878	16,828
Total current assets	27,280	28,979	24,657	24,361	22,450	24,812	23,292
Total assets	€52,940	€53,967	€50,012	€44,667	€41,979	€44,748	€41,881
EQUITY AND LIABILITIES							
Group equity	€39,943	€38,907	€34,907	€31,608	€29,202	€29,072	€25,411
Long-term liabilities	1,010	1,385	2,061	1,550	1,898	2,523	3,123
Other non-current liabilities	1,767	1,908	1,971	1,858	1,567	1,625	1,469
Total non-current liabilities	2,777	3,293	4,032	3,408	3,465	4,148	4,592
Short-term liabilities	3,891	5,126	4,880	4,397	4,763	6,814	7,107
Other payables	6,329	6,641	6,204	5,254	4,549	4,714	4,771
Total current liabilities	10,220	11,767	11,084	9,651	9,312	11,528	11,878
Total equity and liabilities	€52,940	€53,967	€50,012	€44,667	€41,979	€44,748	€41,881

Note: Financial calendar for fiscal year starts from September 1 of a year to August 31 in the next year.

Source: Compiled from the IKEA Group Yearly Summary (2011 to 2017).

EXHIBIT 2 Total Revenue of IKEA from Fiscal 2008 to 2017 (in billions of euros)

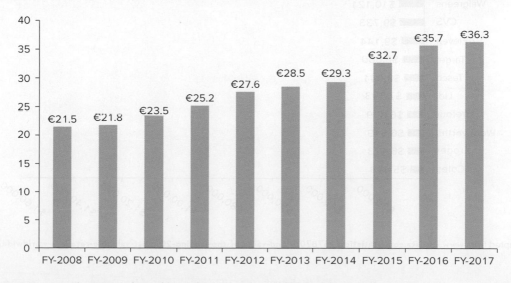

Source: Adapted from www.ikea-unternehmensblog.de/static/downloads/YS17_Final_lowres.pdf.

entire value chain. The IKEA Concept guided the way in which the products were designed, transported, sold, and assembled. IKEA had the competitive advantage of extensive customer knowledge and its best practices to benefit from that knowledge enabled it to become one of the most beloved companies worldwide. Its spacious store environment provided a complete shopping destination for the consumers. IKEA's unique business model and strong brand positioning enabled the company to attain a strong position in the highly fragmented home furnishings market in the countries it operated in. As shown in Exhibit 3, IKEA ranked fifth in the world with a brand value of about $18.94 billion among the world's leading 20 most valuable retail brands in 2017. Exhibit 4 shows that in February 2018 Brand Finance ranked IKEA eighth among retail's most valuable brand

with a brand value of $24 billion.[18] Armed with its rich international experience, IKEA embarked on a major expansion drive into the Far East, including China, with the ambition of achieving a dominant market position in these emerging markets.

FORAY INTO CHINA

The boom in the Chinese furniture market was driven by growth in China's housing market, the steadily developing economy, and research and development in furniture manufacture and design. According to the Ken Research Private Limited[19] report in 2016, China's furniture market would grow at a considerable Compound Annual Growth Rate (CAGR) rate, reaching $86.6 billion by 2020.[20] The furniture industry in

EXHIBIT 3   Brand Value of World's Leading 20 Most Valuable Retail Brands in 2017 (in million $)

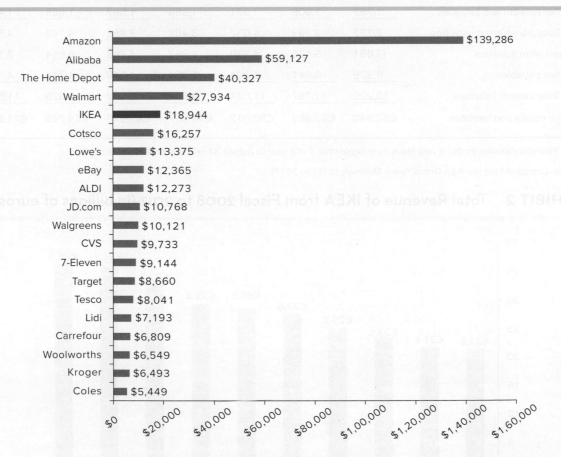

Brand	Value
Amazon	$139,286
Alibaba	$59,127
The Home Depot	$40,327
Walmart	$27,934
IKEA	$18,944
Cotsco	$16,257
Lowe's	$13,375
eBay	$12,365
ALDI	$12,273
JD.com	$10,768
Walgreens	$10,121
CVS	$9,733
7-Eleven	$9,144
Target	$8,660
Tesco	$8,041
Lidi	$7,193
Carrefour	$6,809
Woolworths	$6,549
Kroger	$6,493
Coles	$5,449

Source: Adapted from **www.statista.com/statistics/267870/brand-value-of-the-leading-20-most-valuable-retailers-worldwide/**.

EXHIBIT 4 Top 10 Most Valuable Retail Brands in 2018

Rank	Name of Company	Brand Finance Overall Ranking
1	Amazon	1
2	Apple	2
3	Walmart	9
4	Alibaba	12
5	Home Depot	27
6	Starbucks	33
7	Nike	40
8	IKEA	46
9	CVS Caremark	61
10	H&M	72

Source: Adapted from Tim Denman, "Retail's 10 Most Valuable Brands," , February 7, 2018 https://risnews.com.

China was known for its good quality and affordably priced furniture products, which were made leveraging on the low-cost skilled workforce. After decades

of development in the furniture industry, China emerged as the world's largest furniture producer as well as exporter. Simultaneously, the strong growth of the domestic furniture market was bolstered by an increase in purchasing power among the Chinese customers. The national economic growth raised the living standard of a large section of the Chinese who were willing to pay more for household decorations. China's rapid development over the years resulted in a growing middle class, especially in the urban areas. *"As people's lives are changing, their home furnishing focus is shifting from basic functions to looking for better things. So today there is a need for inspiration as to what better looks like,"* quipped Licca Li, Communication & Interior Design Manager, IKEA Retail China.[21]

Moreover, China had seen a huge rush in home-ownership between 1999 and 2006[22] as Chinese authorities abolished state-allocated housing and subsidized rentals. Since many apartments were typically empty shells and sold semi-furnished, the market for home furnishing flourished in China.

In August 2017, the retail trade revenue of furniture in China amounted to about ¥24.41 billion ($3.69 billion), showing a growth trend with a little fluctuation during the last six months of the period from August 2016 to August 2017 (see Exhibit 5).

EXHIBIT 5   Retail Trade Revenue of Furniture in China, December 2016 to December 2017 (in billion ¥)

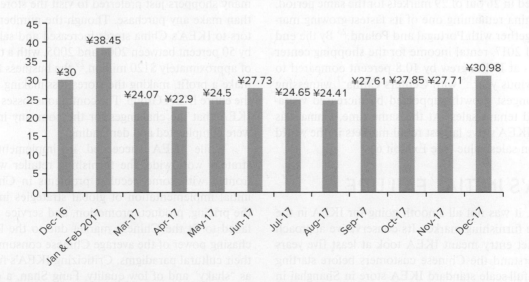

Source: Adapted from www.statista.com/statistics/226900/trade-revenue-of-furniture-in-china-by-month/ (accessed March 16, 2018).

EXHIBIT 6   IKEA's Five Largest Retail Markets Based on Sales Value (as of August 2017)

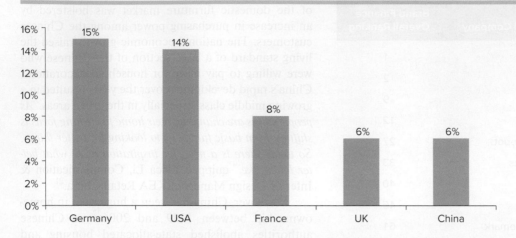

Source: Adapted from **www.ikea-unternehmensblog.de/static/downloads/YS17_Final_lowres.pdf**.

To cater to the growing demand in the Chinese furniture market, IKEA entered China in 1998, opening its first store in Shanghai, followed by one in Beijing in 1999.[23] Unlike its stores elsewhere in the world, IKEA continued to expand its Chinese stores cautiously by IKEA standards. After a slow start, it stepped up its expansion in China. In the fiscal 2017, IKEA was operating 24 stores in China and its stores attracted more than 90 million visitors, up 11 percent over the previous year.[24] IKEA world-wide sales increased in 26 out of 29 markets for the same period, with China remaining one of its fastest-growing markets, together with Portugal and Poland.[25] By the end of fiscal 2017, rental income for the shopping center business at IKEA grew by 10.8 percent compared to the previous year,[26] with Centers China[27] witnessing the strongest growth supported by increased visitation and tenant sales. At the same time, China was one of IKEA's five largest retail markets in the world based on sales value (see Exhibit 6).

IKEA'S INITIAL FAILURE

Initially, it was not all smooth going for IKEA in the Chinese furnishing market. Its conservative approach to market entry meant IKEA took at least five years to understand the Chinese customers before starting its first full-scale standard IKEA store in Shanghai in 2003, replacing the original outlet.[28] Earlier, IKEA

applied its distinct organizational culture and retail business strategies in its Chinese stores, wherein the core concept of company showrooms, flat-packed products, and do-it-yourself (DIY) assembly concepts remained intact. In an attempt to differentiate itself in the Chinese furnishing market, IKEA offered its customers a wide range of options to suit their preferences and living requirements. While Chinese customers gradually started appreciating the experience provided by IKEA, the company soon realized that many shoppers just preferred to visit the stores rather than make any purchase. Though the number of visitors to IKEA's China stores increased and sales grew by 50 percent between 2004 and 2005, with a turnover of approximately $120 million,[29] the business failed to make a profit, making the stores loss-making units in the entire IKEA Group. The continuous losses warned IKEA that the challenges for the company in China were complicated and demanding.

While IKEA succeeded in implementing its strategy worldwide, the furnishing retailer was confronted with some peculiar problems in China. Its initial implementation of global strategies including the pricing, product, promotion, and service strategy failed to fit the Chinese market due to the low purchasing power of the average Chinese consumers and their cultural paradigms. Criticizing IKEA's furniture as "shaky" and of low quality, Fang Shan, a director with China Central Television (CCTV) International, said, *"IKEA lingers between the low-end market and the middle-end market. Many [people] visit IKEA just for the purpose of observing the layout of its sample rooms and get some fresh ideas about home furnishing and decoration. However, few of us buy things there."*[30]

IKEA in China faced a difficulty in setting prices at a level that would satisfy both customers and the company. One of the main challenges for the company was that its prices were higher than the average in China. Known globally for its affordable and stylish furniture, it faced price issues in China because Western products were seen as aspirational in Asian markets. Despite its popularity in the United States, IKEA failed to get immediate recognition as a famous brand in China. The company strategy of providing "affordable" furniture created confusion among Chinese consumers who perceived it a fairly exclusive, Western retailer. The consumers viewed IKEA as innovative and not traditional. For example, square tables instead of round tables and many of the colors used were a departure from tradition for the Chinese. IKEA had a tough time attracting Chinese customers, who felt that the Nordic brand was a luxury that was out of their reach. Moreover, Chinese customers were unwilling to spend more on furniture as they felt it to be secondary compared to the more visible status offered by Western brands such as Haagen-Dazs ice cream and Starbucks coffee or brands of cars and watches.[31]

Like in other markets, IKEA operated in China with its eco-friendly initiatives. But its early decision to charge for plastic bags, asking suppliers for green products, and increasing the use of renewable energy in its stores proved difficult to implement in China as the price-sensitive Chinese customers hesitated to pay extra to support the company's eco-friendly measures. Further, a majority of suppliers in China lacked the necessary technologies to provide green products as per IKEA standards. Though the Chinese customers gradually accepted the environment-friendly concept and cost-cutting efforts of IKEA, many still disliked the fact that the company did not provide a free home delivery and installation service. The company faced difficulties in implementing its self-service and DIY culture in China because of the availability of cheap labor. Customers in China preferred IKEA's assembly services more than customers in other countries.

When IKEA entered China, it faced stiff competition as there were more than 100,000 domestic furniture manufacturers in China.[32] The product catalog of IKEA failed to work as a marketing tool in China because of its imitation by the local competitors who offered similar products at lower prices. Ulf Smedberg, marketing manager of IKEA China, remarked, *"The more popular IKEA becomes, the more competition we have. Of course healthy competition is good—it makes home furnishings more popular. But it's bad that increasingly more companies copy our products."*[33]

IKEA also faced a challenge from government regulations such as heavy import taxes and bureaucracy during the early stages of its operations in China as it lacked indigenous raw materials and production centers.

TASTING SUCCESS IN CHINA

After years of struggling, the Swedish furniture giant finally made a mark in the Chinese furniture market in 2011. The company made numerous changes in its strategies and took more than 12 years to become profitable in China.[34] In 2011, Mikael Ohlssen, the then CEO of IKEA, acknowledged that sales in China were growing faster than at the company as a whole.[35] In 2011, a *Forbes* article noted: *"In the last fifteen years, home ownership has gone from practically zero to about 70 percent. However, many people have little sense of how to furnish or decorate a home. They are very eager to learn from the West. This is one of the reasons that IKEA is very popular in China. Their Western-style showrooms provide model bedrooms, dining rooms, and family rooms showing how to furnish them."*[36] The successful strategies helped the retailer to increase its sales by 17 percent in 2013,[37] making China one of the company's fastest growing markets in the world. As shown in Exhibit 7, China continued maintaining the fastest growth momentum as a leading purchaser of IKEA products for six consecutive years (2012 to 2017), followed by Poland, Italy, Sweden, and Lithuania.

Target Market Segmentation

Though Chinese customers had greater exposure to Western trends and lifestyle through globalization, the trend was not necessarily prevalent across all demographics within China. IKEA, therefore, made a massive change in its strategy of targeting different age groups in the Chinese market. IKEA noticed that its high prices discouraged many price-sensitive consumers in China. It therefore decided to shift its target audience to urban professionals—people aged between

EXHIBIT 7   Leading Five Purchasing Countries of IKEA Products (2012–2016)

Country	2016	2015	2014	2013	2012
China	26%	25%	25%	23%	22%
Poland	18%	19%	18%	18%	18%
Italy	8%	8%	7%	8%	8%
Sweden	5%	5%	5%	6%	5%
Lithuania	5%	5%	4%	4%	4%
Others	38%	38%	41%	41%	43%
Total	100%	100%	100%	100%	100%

Source: Adapted from www.statista.com/statistics/255586/leading-5-purchasing-countries-of-ikea-products/.

25 and 35 who got relatively higher salaries, were better educated, and had a better understanding of Western culture and design styles. This generation, born under China's One Child Policy[38] and informally known as "little emperors,"[39] were characterized as being impulsive and easily influenced. *"IKEA is ready to provide state-of-the-art products for those who enjoy life. In Beijing, we define the middle class as drinking Starbucks coffee and buying IKEA furniture,"*[40] said Chang Yang, human resources manager of IKEA China. This major strategy change helped IKEA to project itself as an aspirational Western brand and increase its customer base. Female customers formed IKEA's main target group and they comprised 65 percent of all customers in China.[41] According to IKEA, women stood for change in China and were interested in home furnishing and actually made purchasing decisions. However, to attract the young low to middle income family groups in the Chinese market, IKEA tried to keep its costs between manufacturers and customers down.

Brand Positioning

IKEA was credited with creating and maintaining its quality and brand image in the Chinese market. According to *The New York Times,* Chinese consumers preferred to go out of their way and spend extra to purchase IKEA products, considering their superiority to Chinese brands. Though IKEA's global model was more or less replicated in China, there were certain nuances in its China model that made it different from the West. IKEA focused on its brand messages to create this positioning in the people's minds.

According to Charles Sampson, CEO of Saatchi & Saatchi[42] China, *"Many Chinese consumers follow an 'all or nothing' approach to interior design. If they want to redesign their living room they will either completely redo everything or do nothing. IKEA wanted to convey that change can be easy, and that it is okay to make small changes, step-by-step."*[43]

ADAPTING TO CULTURE AND MARKET

IKEA learned that doing business in an emerging market like China was a different ball game and it adapted itself to suit the Chinese culture. It strove to customize its offerings keeping in mind the Chinese culture, tradition, and customer preferences. It presented a strong brand image in China by adapting the name "Yi Jia" to suit the Chinese language which meant "comfortable homes, home furniture."[44] While IKEA's Chinese stores replicated the blue and yellow Swedish flag color scheme, the company attracted Chinese customers by adding Chinese features like the color red, which was popular in the country, in its products. The Swedish furniture retailer took advantage of the Chinese cultural appreciation for the shopping experience over their actual purchase of goods. According to *Ad Age,*[45] *"Ikea China is an experience, not just a place to shop, and that's something consumers are looking for."*[46]

While IKEA offered basically the same products in its Chinese stores as in any of its global stores, the interior design of its stores in China was different.

IKEA positioned itself in China as a company with a unique competence in the context of interior design. It redesigned the layout of the store, home solutions offered, and presentation of products in keeping with the needs of customers who preferred small (adapted to their comparatively smaller apartment) and user-friendly furniture. *"In order for IKEA to lead with home furnishing, we need to stay tuned to the changes in people's life. This is our inspiration for creating new solutions, which will support our customers to realize their needs and dreams,"*[47] said Licca Li. The company focused on its basic message of assisting customers with interior design instead of selling individual products at low prices.

IKEA included many models and resources in its stores to guide customers in furnishing and decorating their homes. Store layouts in China reflected the typical sizes of Chinese apartments. Room setting in the stores seemed relevant to the Chinese way of living with sizes of rooms and kitchens that were realistic by China standards. IKEA's Shanghai stores rearranged their room settings several times a year due to frequent visits to these stores by customers. The IKEA stores in China looked like showrooms that included model bedrooms, dining rooms, and family rooms to demonstrate how to furnish them.

Since many Chinese people lived in small apartments with balconies and the customers required functional, modular furniture solutions for their homes, IKEA added model sets and special balcony sections in its Chinese stores. It provided smart solutions for optimal use of balcony space and storage to make their lives easier. Speaking on the furniture requirement of Chinese consumers, Angela said, *"For example in China we have many balconies, so we offer more balcony furniture. And in China every house has a hallway leading to the living room, so we also have more solutions for hallways."*[48] The Chinese were inclined to spend most on their living rooms, the heart of the home where many of them entertained their guests. The company realized the importance of living rooms for the Chinese and offered more living room furniture and decorations at its stores. The emerging demand for IKEA's bedroom furnishing solutions in Shanghai helped the company to target its products from being the least popular purchases to high volume sales. But the kitchen was usually small and considered secondary in Chinese home furnishing.

IKEA had to make a considerable effort to adapt its products to the local tastes and demands. For instance, its products included those that reflected the cultural and traditional essence of the Chinese like chopsticks, woks with lids and a cleaver, a special set of tea cups, and small beds. But, subsequently, the company switched to selling standard-sized beds (200cm) from its earlier China beds (190cm), which were shorter in size.[49] According to Smedberg, *"In terms of housing, the average square meters per person in China has been increasing considerably. Until recently, apartments averaged 40 m^2; now Beijing and Shanghai apartments average 80 m^2. This means several things: Chinese residents need more furnishings and, because consumers are buying more gadgets, they need more storage containers and facilities. It also means IKEA needs to keep its home-life study up-to-date because change happens so fast."*[50] In contrast to IKEA stores in Europe, which were located relatively far out in the suburbs, IKEA established its Chinese outlets on the outskirt of the city, connected by public transportation lines because only 20 percent of visitors in Shanghai had cars.[51] It maintained taxi lanes and offered home delivery as well as assembly services for its customers at a nominal fee (home delivery short haul for ¥50 ($7.56) and assembly one piece ¥40 ($6.05).[52]

IKEA redesigned its organizational structure and competencies in China to fit in with strategic partners within its networks. The company decentralized most of its functions including HR and stores management in China. It preferred a different investment method of operating its business with joint ventures and strategic alliances due to the country specific environment. It entered Chinese cities such as Shanghai and Beijing through joint ventures. IKEA believed that a joint venture could replace its franchise concept and help in increasing cultural sensitivity and operational controls through the establishment of strategic partnerships. The later expansion was through wholly-owned subsidiaries.

MULTICHANNEL RETAILING

In addition to strengthening its presence in tier-1 cities,[53] IKEA expanded into tier-2 cities in China to get a balanced portfolio. The company focused on "the many people"[54] in the country's growing urban population. Looking into the demand of the growing middle class for living space in Chinese megacities, IKEA redesigned its plans to serve their living room requirements with smart solutions. In August

2016, IKEA forayed into the e-commerce business in China, its first online sales attempt in the Asia-Pacific region, as part of its multichannel retailing strategy. The e-commerce business aimed to help the company in addressing the oversaturation problem of IKEA stores located in tier-1 and tier-2 cities. IKEA believed that e-commerce would be its tool to reach more Chinese customers from smaller cities. According to Lu Zhenwang, an Internet expert and chief executive of Wanqing Consultancy in Shanghai, *"There aren't any IKEA physical stores in third- and fourth-tier cities though the demand is emerging, so it's essential for IKEA to launch e-commerce services and to serve those places easily in the future. It would be convenient to set up some pickup and order points in smaller cities."*[55] According to Angela, the e-commerce services of IKEA improved interactions with consumers and helped the company to better understand their consumption patterns.

In March 2017, IKEA opened its first pickup and order outlet in Beijing. These outlets (3,000 square meters) were much smaller than the typical stores which were 30,000 to 40,000 square meters in size. *"Chinese customers are very fond of shopping in a shopping center, with quick and easy access to get in and get out. . . . Buying is no longer the sole purpose when visiting a shopping center. Consumption can be spontaneous,"* said Angela.[56]

PRICING STRATEGY

The key strategy for IKEA was delivering Swedish quality at prices the Chinese could afford. The fact that product prices were a major concern for Chinese customers forced IKEA to reconsider its market orientation to solve this price problem. According to Angela, *"When we came to market, we realised that our prices had been too expensive. It took years for us to continuously reduce our retail prices, to really let many people afford them."*[57] The company observed that China was not ready to implement environment-friendly practices, which involved higher prices. IKEA, therefore, skipped its emphasis on being green or creating stylish furniture in China to stick to low prices and remain in business. As an adjustment to the local market conditions, IKEA started selling only middle-range price products. During the early period of its products being duplicated by local competitors, IKEA insisted on not spending time, money, and energy on hunting for the copycats, preferring

to focus instead on implementing its criteria of good design, functionality, and low prices in China.

To make prices more affordable for the consumers, IKEA adjusted its pricing strategy in China at different periods. According to Tom Doctoroff, an expert on Chinese consumer psychology and author of *"What Chinese Want', the recent spike in Ikea's popularity is mostly due to a dramatic change in pricing strategy."*[58] Since 2000, IKEA had been lowering its prices in China by more than 60 percent[59] and encouraging people to try out its products and make themselves at home. In 2002, IKEA's overall prices in China decreased by 12 percent, as a result of which a sofa priced at ¥2,999 ($453.29) in 1999 was sold for ¥995 ($150.39) in 2003.[60] After prices were lowered by about 10 percent, sales in IKEA's Chinese stores increased 35 percent in 2003 and grew 50 percent in the first three months of 2004 alone.[61] In 2006, the home furnishing retailer launched a new strategy called "The Lowest Price in Beijing,"[62] that offered the lowest price for more than 120 kinds of goods in China. According to the strategy, the price for IKEA products was about 20 percent lower than those prevailing in other home furnishing stores. IKEA's luxury, fashionable design, and reliability made Chinese consumers feel that the product was worth the price they paid. Even by increasingly stocking Chinese stores with China-made products, IKEA slashed the prices of some items as low as 70 percent below the prices in IKEA stores outside China.[63] In 2009, IKEA China lowered the prices of more than 500 products by 20 to 30 percent.[64] According to Linda Xu, Public Relation Manager of IKEA China, *"IKEA is striving to make its goods affordable to the average Chinese people and change people's perception that IKEA is white-collar privilege."*[65]

IKEA planned to reduce prices further in China, supported by mass production and by cutting supply chain costs. The firm located its first production center at Nantong, a city near the Yangtze River that had numerous resources, and near Shanghai, where IKEA had its biggest warehouse. It tied up with local suppliers for the collection of raw materials and manufactured around 80 percent of the goods domestically,[66] with the result that it was able to avoid high import taxes and shipping costs. While China contributed about 30 percent of IKEA's global collection, about 65 percent of the volume sales in the country came from local sourcing.[67] Localization of production and distribution allowed IKEA to reduce logistic costs and lower its prices in China by an average of 50 percent across the stores between 2000 and 2012.[68] Domestic production helped the company to promote and sell what it had in the store rather than promoting products that were advertised in the catalog. The company also saved on repair costs by inspecting local quality closer to manufacturing.

EDUCATING CUSTOMERS

In China, IKEA provided knowledge about home furnishing to its customers, many of who were brand new to home ownership. This not only helped people to understand how IKEA products worked and could add value to their life, but also attracted them to its stores. The company showed its customers how much furniture and kitchen gadgetry could be fitted into a typically small-sized Chinese apartment, while still making it appear spacious. Mette Hay, co-founder of HAY,[69] told Dezeen,[70] *"I just heard that IKEA is doing these evenings where people can come and get educated in how to decorate or design your home."*[71]

To prepare the Chinese consumer for the IKEA store experience, the furnishing retailer published catalogs and brochures, posted in-store instructions and design advice, and operated a detailed website. The IKEA catalog, distributed in the store and in some of the primary markets, was the key promotional tool for the company. However, in China, there was more of a reliance on small brochures because of their availability several times during the year. IKEA used Chinese social media and *Sina Weibo* to target the urban youth. IKEA Family, introduced in China in 2007, provided its members the latest offers and information about products. The company sponsored brief television shows where viewers were offered lessons in home decorating. Themes in IKEA's multimedia campaign were the same as everywhere in the world but with the Chinese twist (be different, break tradition). The company also took Chinese journalists to Sweden and Almhult where they were taught about IKEA and the roots of the company.

SOCIAL VENUE

To expand its business in China, the Swedish furniture giant designed its shopping malls and products as social venues. Many treated IKEA not just a home furnishing depot, but as a furniture-filled theme park where they could spend hours touching and feeling the products. According to a reporter of China Network Television (CNTV), *"In China, going to IKEA means far more than just going shopping for furniture. It's an experience that often lasts all day."*[72] The overall shopping experience in China was slightly different from that in Europe or the United States since the Chinese consumers not only used the shop to purchase their necessities but also for entertainment. Doctoroff observed that *"Chinese people tend to take a more recreational approach to consumption. Shopping in China is far more about the experience itself than it is in the West."*[73] In addition to finding good prices, Chinese customers wanted to feel comfortable, understood, valued, and appreciated. Even more importantly, IKEA believed that shopping was an entertainment for its customers.

At the beginning, Chinese consumers visited IKEA stores to socialize in a pleasant environment instead of shopping. IKEA opened extra furniture display rooms in its stores, welcoming customers to nap on the furniture in a bid to get shoppers to stay longer in the store. The company believed that these people would at least get to know the quality of their purchase. According to Xu, *"We welcome anyone to visit our stores—today's visitor could very well be tomorrow's customer."*[74] In 2015, a spokeswoman for IKEA China said the company encouraged Chinese customers to touch and try products. As a result, people napping comfortably and children playing with sample toys in the children's section were common sights at the stores. The IKEA cafeterias in China became a popular destination for elderly Chinese to hold matchmaking sessions over free coffee and spend time with one another.

CHALLENGES

Despite its long presence in China, the furniture giant faced criticism for being too conservative in developing the home products sector. IKEA opened new stores at a slower rate in China than other foreign retailers such as Wal-Mart Stores, Inc.,[75] which expanded rapidly throughout China. Though IKEA claimed that it attracted Chinese consumers on the price front, it was still not well recognized by Chinese consumers, some industry observers remarked. According to Cai Xun, a white-collar worker from Shanghai, *"I think the design and idea promoted in Ikea is good, but I can get similar products from a Chinese store or online at much cheaper prices. Why should I go to Ikea?"*[76] Some analysts questioned whether IKEA could sustain its strategy of cutting prices in China as the company plunged into China's secondary cities with lower incomes and higher demand for bargains.

Analysts observed that IKEA faced some problems in its efforts to create a customer-friendly shopping environment in its Chinese stores. Managers at the IKEA location in Shanghai complained that some elderly visitors went on group blind dates and settled themselves down in the cafeteria without ordering anything. Some people often made themselves at home on the sample beds and sofas, while some even fell asleep with their shoes on, they said. Customers lamented that most IKEA stores were crowded with rude and loud people who cared little about public decency.

In April 2015, a Beijing IKEA store introduced a new rule banning customers from sleeping on furniture display rooms and stretching out on sofas after pictures of people sleeping in showroom beds in a Beijing shop went viral. The ban followed complaints by the customers that they could not sample the furniture as people were sleeping on it. The Shanghai IKEA store too issued instructions to disallow non-paying visitors from trying out products after getting complaints from paying customers. "*The situation has adversely affected the dining experience and security of most of our customers. It is having a negative implication for our canteen's operation. From today, the restaurant will only be for people who purchase their food first,*"[77] the store said in a notice posted at the entrance of the IKEA Shanghai Restaurant. To discourage senior citizens from occupying canteen seats for extended periods, IKEA imposed a strict "no food, no seating" rule.[78] However, despite the ban, customers continued to snooze in the display rooms much to the ire of some customers, and IKEA staff members found it difficult to implement the no-nap policy.

In late June 2016, IKEA stirred up a big controversy after announcing a massive recall in North America of its dressers, which had crushed six children to death but not including China. It was accused of double standards and of discriminating against Chinese customers. Finally, IKEA extended a recall of its 1.7 million MALM chests or dressers, manufactured from 1999 to 2016, in China following pressure from regulators.[79] When the issue resurfaced again in 2017, IKEA again excluded China saying that it would not recall the product but customers in China could ask for a full refund.[80]

In October 2017, IKEA apologized for a television commercial in China and pulled it from the air after it provoked a backlash in the Chinese social media with some viewers calling it 'sexist.'[81] The 30-second advertisement showed a mother scolding her daughter for not "bringing home a boyfriend"[82] to meet her parents. Weibo users objected to the scene in the advertisement, saying it discriminated against young unmarried women in China and accused IKEA of supporting the cultural discrimination against such women in China. Some critics in China said the TV ad lacked the kind of cultural awareness for which IKEA was known and the deep research it relied on to adapt its Scandinavian products to other cultures. However, IKEA said, "*This TV ad tried to show how IKEA can help customers easily and affordably convert a typical living room into a place of celebration. The purpose was to encourage customers to celebrate moments in everyday life.*"[83]

THE ROAD AHEAD

Angela had the big responsibility of setting the future growth direction for IKEA China. After graduating from Eastern China Normal University, she worked in the purchasing department of Metro shopping mall in China for two years, before becoming the first Chinese staff in IKEA Retail China in 1996. She went on to become the first Chinese store manager in 2005, and Country President in 2013.[84]

Getting it right in emerging markets like China was a key factor in IKEA's plan of hitting $55 billion in global sales by 2020.[85] With the rapidly-growing Chinese economy in which more people were joining the ranks of the middle class and the increasing Chinese middle class moving into bigger apartments, IKEA's creative home furnishing ideas fascinated the younger generation and offered profound scope for the company to grow, analysts said. Michael Silverstein, a senior partner at Boston Consulting Group,[86] in his projections, said China's burgeoning middle class would triple their spending to $6 trillion by 2020.[87] Forecasting the future growth possibilities of IKEA in China, Agnefjall said in 2015, "*What we see is that many people in China appreciate the IKEA offer and we are making it more accessible to them through new stores. And the middle class will continue to grow, I'm pretty confident about that, so we have a positive view on China.*"[88]

Notwithstanding China's downgraded credit rating by Moody's Investor Service[89] and S&P Global Ratings[90] in 2017 over dangerous growth in debt and China's preferential conditions for domestic firms,

IKEA intended to expedite its pace of expansion in China to increase the number of stores in the country to 34 by 2020.[91] Going forward, Angela said IKEA would enhance its distribution network and was likely to work with a third party e-commerce platform to make its online services nationwide in the coming years. Analysts anticipated that as long as IKEA devised the right strategy to penetrate China's rapidly-growing e-commerce market, its future would be bright. But, amid growing controversies and risks of the country's financial turmoil, would IKEA be able to expand its customer base in China? Going forward, what are the implications for its marketing strategy?

ENDNOTES

[1] "IKEA in China: Big Furniture Retail Adapts to the Chinese Market," August 18, 2016, www.daxueconsulting.com.

[2] Daxue Consulting is a market research and management consulting firm focusing on the Chinese market.

[3] US$1 was approximately equal to 6.62 Chinese Yuan Renminbi (¥) in 2017.

[4] Wang Zhuoqiong, "Buoyant IKEA Gears Up for More Store Expansion in China," August 18, 2017, www.chinadaily.com.cn.

[5] Claire Zillman, "Women in China Are Really Offended by This IKEA Ad," www.fortune.com, October 26, 2017.

[6] Neil Connor, "IKEA Losing Patience with Elderly Chinese who Assemble in Store to Find Love," October 14, 2016, www.vancouversun.com.

[7] Claire Zillman, "IKEA Is Recalling 1.7 Million More Dressers in China," July 12, 2016, www.fortune.com.

[8] Founded in 1982 by Ingvar Kamprad, Stichting INGKA Foundation is a Dutch Foundation. It is established to fund charity in the Netherlands and to reinvest in the IKEA Group.

[9] "This is IKEA," www.ikea.com.

[10] "IKEA Group Reports Full-year Operating Profit of €3 billion," November 28, 2017, www.rte.ie.

[11] Inter IKEA Systems B.V. is based in the Netherlands and is owned by the Inter IKEA Group. It franchises systems, methods, and proven solutions to franchisees worldwide for the sale of IKEA products under the IKEA trademarks.

[12] "IKEA Group Reports Annual Retail Sales of $40.2 billion* (EUR 34.1 billion) and Outlines Focus on Strengthening the Customer Meeting," October 10, 2017, www.ikea.com.

[13] Namita Bhagat, "All You Wanted to Know about IKEA's Much Awaited India Entry," January 16, 2017, www.indiaretailing.com.

[14] US$1 was approximately equal to 0.85 euro (€) in 2017.

[15] "Yearly Summary FY17," www.ikea-unternehmensblog.de.

[16] "IKEA Group Reports Annual Retail Sales of $40.2 billion* (EUR 34.1 billion) and Outlines Focus on Strengthening the Customer Meeting," October 10, 2017, www.ikea.com.

[17] "About the IKEA Group," www.ikea.com.

[18] Tim Denman, "Retail's 10 Most Valuable Brands," February 7, 2018, https://risnews.com.

[19] Ken research is a leading market research company in India.

[20] "China Furniture Market is Expected to Reach US$86.6bn by 2020: Ken Research," June 27, 2016, www.indiainfoline.com.

[21] "Yearly Summary FY16," www.ikea.com.

[22] Mei Fong, "IKEA Hits Home in China," March 3, 2006, www.wsj.com.

[23] Par Datman, "IKEA in China and Japan," April 19, 2013, www.ladissertation.com.

[24] Wang Zhuoqiong, "Buoyant IKEA Gears up for More Store Expansion in China," August 18, 2017, www.usa.chinadaily.com.cn.

[25] "Yearly Summary FY17," www.ikea.com.

[26] "Yearly Summary FY17," www.ikea-unternehmensblog.de.

[27] Established In 2009, Centres China is IKEA Group's megamalls unit with regional headquarters located in Shanghai.

[28] "Opportunities and Challenges Facing IKEA in China and Japan," www.scribd.com.

[29] "The Past and Present Strategies of IKEA," March 23, 2015, www.ukessays.com.

[30] Liu Yunyun, "IKEA: Building Itself up in China?" December 19, 2006, www.bjreview.cn.

[31] Kim Wall, "IKEA at Last Cracks China Market, but Success has Meant Adapting to Local Ways," September 1, 2013, www.scmp.com.

[32] "Market Analysis and Market Entry Stages Marketing Essay," March 23, 2015, www.ukessays.com.

[33] Paula M. Miller, "IKEA with Chinese Characteristics," July 1, 2004, www.china businessreview.com.

[34] Valerie Chu, Alka Girdhar, and Rajal Sood, "Couching Tiger Tames the Dragon," July 21, 2013, www.businesstoday.in.

[35] Kim Bhasin, "Why IKEA Took China by Storm, While Home Depot Failed Miserably," September 14, 2012, www.businessinsider.com.

[36] Helen H. Wang, "Why Home Depot Struggles and IKEA Thrives in China?" February 10, 2011, www.forbes.com.

[37] Celia Hatton, "IKEA in China: Stores or Theme Park?", November 4, 2013, www.bbc.com.

[38] Introduced in 1979, the one-child policy was a population planning policy of China.

[39] "IKEA China's Shopping Experience Essay," www.studymoose.com.

[40] "IKEA: Building Itself up in China?" www.womenofchina.cn.

[41] Fatima Arshad, "Comparison of Marketing Mix of IKEA in Four Countries," June 19, 2014, www.slideshare.net.

[42] Saatchi & Saatchi is a global communications and advertising firm with headquarters in New York. The agency is involved in creating IKEA's prints and advertisements in China.

[43] Paula M. Miller, "IKEA with Chinese Characteristics," July 1, 2004, www.china businessreview.com.

[44] Leila Malmefjall, "Just Like Home—IKEA's Journey into China," April 12, 2010, www.gbtimes.com.

[45] Advertising Age (AdAge) is a U.S.-based magazine publishing news, analysis, and data on marketing and media.

[46] Matt Kleinschmit, "Despite China's Weaker Economy, These 3 Global Brands are Succeeding," July 10, 2015, www.visioncritical.com.

[47] "Yearly Summary FY16," ww.ikea.com.

[48] "Furniture Giant IKEA Sees Rapid Growth in China," November 8, 2013, www.china.org.cn.

[49] Fatima Arshad, "Comparison of marketing Mix of IKEA in Four Countries," June 19, 2014, www.slideshare.net.

[50] Paula M. Miller, "IKEA with Chinese Characteristics," July 1, 2004, www.china businessreview.com.

[51] Zhihao Yang, "IKEA in China—How IKEA Localizes Its Business Model for Chinese Customers," April 26, 2016, www.intopreneur.com.

[52] "IKEA in China, Sweden and the UK," www.kingessays.wang.

[53] There are four tier cities in China and their tier classifications are based on their Gross Domestic Product, political administration, population size, development of services, infrastructure, cosmopolitan nature, retail sales, etc.

[54] Jens Hansegard, "IKEA Taking China by Storm," March 26, 2012, www.wsj.com.

[55] Zhu Wenqian and Wang Zhuoqiong, "IKEA to Launch E-commerce Business Model in Shanghai," August 18, 2016, www.chinadaily.com.cn.

[56] Wang Zhuoqiong, "Buoyant IKEA Gears Up for More Store Expansion in China," August 18, 2017, www.chinadaily.com.cn.

[57] Celia Hatton, "IKEA in China: Store or Theme Park?", November 4, 2013, www.bbc.com.

[58] Kim Wall, "IKEA at Last Cracks China Market, but Success has Meant Adapting to Local Ways," September 1, 2013, www.scmp.com.

[59] "Home Depot's Failure in China," May 16, 2014, www.github.com.

[60] ZheMing Li, "IKEA was Founded in 1943 by a 17-Year-Old Ingvar Kamprad," October 23, 2013, www.prezi.com.

[61] Paula M. Miller, "IKEA with Chinese Characteristics," July 1, 2004, www.china businessreview.com.

[62] "IKEA Pushes Lowest Price Strategy," December 18, 2006, www.chinaretailnews.com.

[63] Mei Fong, "IKEA Hits Home in China," March 3, 2006, www.wsj.com.

[64] Tang Zhihao, "IKEA Aims for 15 Stores in China by 2015," June 24, 2011, www.usa.chinadaily.com.cn.

[65] Li Yunyun, "IKEA: Building Itself up in China?" www.bjreview.cn.

[66] Beth Kowitt, "How IKEA Took over the World," March 10, 2015, www.fortune.com.

[67] Valerie Chu, Alka Girdhar, and Rajal Sood, "Couching Tiger Tames the Dragon," July 3, 2013, www.in.finance.yahoo.com.

[68] Landy Raoilison, "Group 112 – Sophia – Offshoring in Asia: the Success Story of IKEA," September 21, 2014, www.moocgloba.skema-pedia.com.

[69] Founded in 2002, HAY is a Denmark-based furniture design firm.

[70] Launched in 2006, Dezeen is the world's most popular and influential architecture, interior, and design magazine.

[71] Marcus Fairs, "IKEA Fuels Demand for Western Lifestyle in China, Say Hay Founders," April 8, 2016, www.dezeeen.com.

[72] "Furniture Giant IKEA Sees Rapid Growth in China," November 8, 2013, www.china.org.cn.

[73] Kim Wall, "IKEA at Last Cracks China Market, but Success has Meant Adapting to Local Ways," September 1, 2013, www.scmp.com.

[74] Kim Wall, "A Cup of Tea and Make Yourselves A Home," October 11, 2013, www.prevalence.com.

[75] Wal-Mart is an American multinational retailing corporation that operates as a chain of hypermarkets, discount department stores, and grocery stores across the world.

[76] Tang Zhihao, "IKEA Aims for 15 Stores in China by 2015," June 24, 2011, www.usa.chinadaily.com.cn.

[77] "IKEA in Shanghai has had Enough of Elderly People in Search of Love," www.carbonated.tv.

[78] Grace Tsoi and Heather Chen, "IKEA Shanghai Frowns on Elderly Daters who Occupy Cafeteria," October 18, 2017, www.bbc.com.

[79] "IKEA to Recall 1.7 million Malm Dressers in China," July 12, 2016, www.bbc.com.

[80] "IKEA China Will Not Recall Problematic Drawers but Promises Refund," December 3, 2017, www.globaltimes.cn.

[81] Jane Li, "IKEA Faces Social Media Backlash after Airing 'Sexist' Ad in China," October 24, 2017, www.businessinsider.com.

[82] "IKEA Apologises and Pulls Down Ad in China after Some Called it Sexist," October 26, 2017, www.scroll.in.

[83] Mike Wright, "IKEA Apologises after Advert Provokes Complaints in China for being Insensitive to Single Women," October 26, 2017, www.telegraph.co.uk.

[84] "11th Shanghai Franchise Retail Industry Summit and Asia Retail Innovation Summit 2016," November 29–30, 2016, www.aris.shinemediaworld.com.

[85] Ana Ablaza, "IKEA to Enter Chinese E-commerce Market to Profit from Huge Online Market," August 18, 2016, www.en.yibada.com.

[86] Founded in 1963, Boston Consulting Group is an American worldwide management consulting firm on business strategy.

[87] Joe Cahill, "How Not to Win in China," January 26, 2013, www.chicagobusiness.com.

[88] "IKEA Positive on China despite Economic Slowdown: CEO," September 10, 2015, www.economictimes.indiatimes.com,.

[89] Founded by John Moody, Moody's is an American credit rating agency.

[90] S&P Global Ratings is the U.S.-based leading provider of independent credit ratings across the globe.

[91] "China's Furniture Market," August 21, 2017, www.china-trade-research.hktdc.com.

PepsiCo's Diversification Strategy in 2018: Will the Company's New Businesses Restore Its Growth?

■ connect

John E. Gamble

Texas A&M University–Corpus Christi

PepsiCo was the world's largest snack and beverage company, with 2017 net revenues of approximately $63.5 billion. The company's portfolio of businesses in 2018 included Frito-Lay salty snacks, Quaker Chewy granola bars, Pepsi soft-drink products, Tropicana orange juice, Lipton Brisk tea, Gatorade, Propel, Bubly, Quaker Oatmeal, Cap'n Crunch, Aquafina, Rice-A-Roni, Aunt Jemima pancake mix, and many other regularly consumed products. The company viewed the lineup as highly complementary since most of its products could be consumed together. For example, Tropicana orange juice might be consumed during breakfast with Quaker Oatmeal, Stacy's pita chips and Sabra hummus might make a nice snack, and Doritos and a Mountain Dew might be part of someone's lunch. In 2018, PepsiCo's business lineup included 22 $1 billion global brands.

The company's top managers were focused on sustaining the impressive performance through strategies keyed to product innovation, close relationships with distribution allies, international expansion, and strategic acquisitions. Newly introduced products such as Bubly sparkling water, Mountain Dew Ice, Doritos Blaze tortilla chips, Sweet Potato Sun Chips, LIFEWTR functional waters, Lemon Lemon sparkling lemonade, and the 1893 premium line of flavored colas accounted for 15 to 20 percent of all new growth in recent years. New product innovations that addressed consumer health and wellness concerns were important contributors to the company's growth, with PepsiCo's better-for-you and good-for-you products becoming focal points in the company's new product development initiatives.

In addition to focusing on strategies designed to deliver revenue and earnings growth, the company maintained an aggressive share repurchase and dividend policy, with a planned $7 billion returned to shareholders in 2018 through share repurchases of $2 billion and dividends of approximately $5 billion. The company bolstered its cash returns through carefully considered capital expenditures and acquisitions and a focus on operational excellence. Its Performance with Purpose plan utilized investments in manufacturing automation, a rationalized global manufacturing plan, and reengineered distribution systems to drive efficiency. In addition, the company's Performance with Purpose plan was focused on minimizing the company's impact on the environment by lowering energy and water consumption and reducing its use of packaging material, providing a safe and inclusive workplace for employees, and supporting and investing in the local communities in which it operated. For example, PepsiCo had expanded access to safe water to nearly 16 million people in water-stressed parts of the world between 2006 and 2018. In addition, Performance with Purpose planned to reduce average sugars, saturated fat, and sodium in its food and beverage portfolio each year through 2025 and saved more than $600 million in operating expenses by 2016.

Even though the company had recorded a number of impressive achievements over the past decade, its growth had slowed since 2011. In fact, the spikes in the company's revenue growth since 2000 had resulted from major acquisitions such as the $13.6 billion acquisition of Quaker Oats in 2001, the 2010 acquisition of the previously independent Pepsi Bottling Group and PepsiCo Americas for $8.26 billion, and the acquisition of Russia's leading food-and-beverage company, Wimm-Bill-Dann (WBD) Foods for $3.8 billion in 2011. Since 2011, the company had favored targeted "tuck-in" acquisitions of leading brands in popular new healthy food categories. Nevertheless, PepsiCo's revenues continued to decline as annual consumption of carbonated soft drinks fell each year and its international business units struggled. A summary of PepsiCo's financial performance between 2013 and 2017 is shown in Exhibit 1. Exhibit 2 tracks PepsiCo's market performance between 2013 and June 2018.

COMPANY HISTORY

PepsiCo, Inc., was established in 1965 when Pepsi-Cola and Frito-Lay shareholders agreed to a merger between the salty-snack icon and soft-drink giant. The new company was founded with annual revenues of $510 million and such well-known brands as Pepsi-Cola, Mountain Dew, Fritos, Lay's, Cheetos, Ruffles, and Rold Gold. PepsiCo's roots can be traced to 1898 when New Bern, North Carolina, pharmacist Caleb Bradham created the formula for a carbonated

beverage he named Pepsi-Cola. The company's salty-snack business began in 1932 when Elmer Doolin, of San Antonio, Texas, began manufacturing and marketing Fritos corn chips and Herman Lay started a potato chip distribution business in Nashville, Tennessee. In 1961, Doolin and Lay agreed to a merger between their businesses to establish the Frito-Lay Company.

During PepsiCo's first five years as a snack and beverage company, it introduced new products such as Doritos and Funyuns, entered markets in Japan and eastern Europe, and opened, on average, one new snack-food plant per year. By 1971, PepsiCo had more than doubled its revenues to reach $1 billion. The company began to pursue growth through acquisitions outside snacks and beverages as early as 1968, but its 1977 acquisition of Pizza Hut significantly shaped the strategic direction of PepsiCo for the next 20 years. The acquisitions of Taco Bell in 1978 and Kentucky Fried Chicken in 1986 created a business portfolio described by Wayne Calloway (PepsiCo's CEO between 1986 and 1996) as a balanced three-legged stool. Calloway believed the combination of snack foods, soft drinks, and fast food offered considerable cost sharing and skill transfer opportunities, and he routinely shifted managers among the company's three divisions as part of the company's management development efforts.

EXHIBIT 1 Financial Summary for PepsiCo, Inc., 2013–2017 (in millions, except per share amounts)

	2017	2016	2015	2014	2013
Net revenue	$63,525	$62,799	$63,056	$66,683	$66,415
Operating profit	10,509	9,785	8,353	9,581	9,705
Provision for income taxes	4,694	2,174	1,941	2,199	2,104
Net income attributable to PepsiCo	4,857	6,329	5,452	6,513	6,740
Net income attributable to PepsiCo per common share - basic	$3.40	$4.39	$3.71	$4.31	$4.37
Net income attributable to PepsiCo per common share - diluted	$3.38	$4.36	$3.67	$4.27	$4.32
Cash dividends declared per common share	$3.17	$2.96	$2.76	$2.53	$2.24
Total assets	79,804	73,490	68,976	69,634	76,762
Long-term debt	33,796	30,053	29,213	23,821	24,333

Source: PepsiCo 2017 10-K.

EXHIBIT 2   Monthly Performance of PepsiCo, Inc.'s Stock Price, June 2013–June 2018

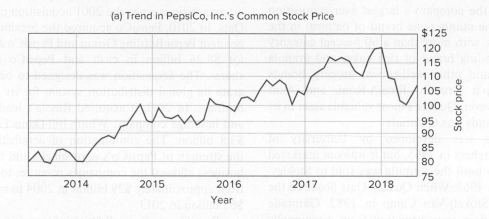

(a) Trend in PepsiCo, Inc.'s Common Stock Price

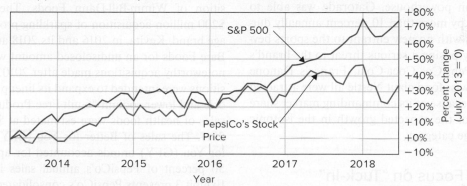

(b) Performance of PepsiCo, Inc.'s Stock Price versus the S&P 500 Index

PepsiCo strengthened its portfolio of snack foods and beverages during the 1980s and 1990s with the acquisitions of Mug Root Beer, 7-Up International, Smartfood ready-to-eat popcorn, Walker's Crisps (United Kingdom), Smith's Crisps (United Kingdom), Mexican cookie company Gamesa, and Sunchips. Calloway added quick-service restaurants Hot-n-Now in 1990; California Pizza Kitchens in 1992; and East Side Mario's, D'Angelo Sandwich Shops, and Chevy's Mexican Restaurants in 1993. The company expanded beyond carbonated beverages through a 1992 agreement with Ocean Spray to distribute single-serving juices, the introduction of Lipton ready-to-drink (RTD) teas in 1993, and the introduction of Aquafina bottled water and Frappuccino ready-to-drink coffees in 1994.

By 1996 it had become clear to PepsiCo management that the potential strategic-fit benefits existing between restaurants and PepsiCo's core beverage and snack businesses were difficult to capture. In addition, any synergistic benefits achieved were more than offset by the fast-food industry's fierce price competition and low profit margins. In 1997, CEO Roger Enrico spun off the company's restaurants as an independent, publicly traded company to focus PepsiCo on food and beverages. Soon after the spin-off of PepsiCo's fast-food restaurants was completed, Enrico acquired Cracker Jack, Tropicana, Smith's Snackfood Company in Australia, SoBe teas and alternative beverages, Tasali Snack Foods (the leader in the Saudi Arabian salty-snack market), and the Quaker Oats Company.

PepsiCo's Better for You and Good for You Acquisitions

PepsiCo's $13.9 billion acquisition of Quaker Oats in 2001 was the company's largest ever acquisition and gave it the number-one brand of oatmeal in the United States, with more than a 60 percent category share; the leading brand of rice cakes and granola snack bars; and other well-known grocery brands such as Cap'n Crunch, Rice-A-Roni, and Aunt Jemima. However, Quaker's most valuable asset in its arsenal of brands was Gatorade.

Gatorade was developed by University of Florida researchers in 1965, but it was not marketed commercially until the formula was sold to Stokley-Van Camp in 1967. When Quaker Oats acquired the brand from Stokely-Van Camp in 1983, Gatorade gradually made a transformation from a regionally distributed product with annual sales of $90 million to a $2 billion powerhouse. Gatorade was able to increase sales by more than 10 percent annually during the 1990s, with no new entrant to the sports beverage category posing a serious threat to the brand's dominance. PepsiCo, Coca-Cola, France's Danone Group, and Swiss food giant Nestlé all were attracted to Gatorade because of its commanding market share and because of the expected growth in the isotonic sports beverage category.

PepsiCo's Focus on "Tuck-In" Acquisitions (2002 to 2018)

After the completion of the Quaker Oats acquisition in 2001, the company focused on integration of Quaker Oats' food, snack, and beverage brands into the PepsiCo portfolio. The company made a number of "tuck-in" acquisitions of small, fast-growing food and beverage companies in the United States and internationally to broaden its portfolio of brands. Tuck-in acquisitions in 2006 included Stacey's bagel and pita chips, Izze carbonated beverages, Netherlands-based Duyvis nuts, and Star Foods (Poland). Acquisitions made during 2007 included Naked Juice fruit beverages, Sandora juices in the Ukraine, New Zealand's Bluebird snacks, Penelopa nuts and seeds in Bulgaria, and Brazilian snack producer Lucky. The company also entered into a joint venture with the Strauss Group in 2007 to market Sabra—the top-selling and fastest-growing brand of hummus in the United States and Canada. The company acquired the Russian beverage producer Lebedyansky in 2008 for $1.8 billion, and in 2010 it acquired Marbo, a potato chip production operation in Serbia.

In 2010 and 2011, the company executed its largest acquisitions since the 2001 acquisition of Quaker Oats. In 2010, PepsiCo acquired the previously independent Pepsi Bottling Group and PepsiCo Americas for $8.26 billion in cash and PepsiCo common shares. The acquisition was designed to better integrate its global distribution system for its beverage business. In 2011, it acquired Russia's leading food and beverage company, Wimm-Bill-Dann Foods, for $3.8 billion. The combination of acquisitions and the strength of PepsiCo's core snacks and beverages business allowed the company's revenues to increase from approximately $29 billion in 2004 to more than $66 billion in 2013.

PepsiCo made small "tuck-in" acquisitions totaling less than $500 million annually after its acquisition of Wimm-Bill-Dann Foods. The company's $200 million acquisition of sparkling probiotic beverage brand, Kevita, in 2016 and its 2018 acquisition of Bare Foods for an undisclosed amount were its most noteworthy acquisitions made after 2010. Both acquisitions were intended to expand its lineup of lower calorie and lower sodium "Guilt-Free Products." Global sales of health foods were estimated at $1 trillion in 2017. The sales of Better for You (BFY) and Good for You (GFY) brands accounted for approximately 50 percent of PepsiCo's annual sales in that year. Exhibit 3 presents PepsiCo's consolidated statements of income for 2015 to 2017, while the company's balance sheets for 2016 and 2017 are presented in Exhibit 4. The company's calculation of free cash flow for 2015 through 2017 is shown in Exhibit 5.

PEPSICO'S BUSINESS UNIT PERFORMANCE

PepsiCo's corporate strategy had diversified the company into salty and sweet snacks, soft drinks, orange juice, bottled water, ready-to-drink teas and coffees, purified and functional waters, isotonic beverages, hot and ready-to-eat breakfast cereals, grain-based products, and breakfast condiments. Most PepsiCo brands had achieved number-one or number-two positions in their respective food and beverage categories through strategies keyed to product innovation, close relationships with distribution allies, international

EXHIBIT 3   PepsiCo, Inc.'s Consolidated Statements of Income, 2015–2017 (in millions, except per share data)

	2017	2016	2015
Net Revenue	$63,525	$62,799	$63,056
Cost of sales	28,785	28,209	28,731
Gross profit	34,740	34,590	34,325
Selling, general and administrative expenses	24,231	24,805	24,613
Venezuela impairment charges	—	—	1,359
Operating Profit	10,509	9,785	8,353
Interest expense	(1,151)	(1,342)	(970)
Interest income and other	244	110	59
Income before income taxes	9,602	8,553	7,442
Provision for income taxes	4,694	2,174	1,941
Net income	4,908	6,379	5,501
Less: Net income attributable to noncontrolling interests	51	50	49
Net Income Attributable to PepsiCo	$ 4,857	$ 6,329	$ 5,452
Net Income Attributable to PepsiCo per common share			
Basic	$3.40	$4.39	$3.71
Diluted	$3.38	$4.36	$3.67
Weighted-average common shares outstanding			
Basic	1,425	1,439	1,469
Diluted	1,438	1,452	1,485
Cash dividends declared per common share	$3.17	$2.96	$2.76

Source: PepsiCo, Inc. 2017 10-K.

EXHIBIT 4   PepsiCo, Inc.'s Consolidated Balance Sheets, 2016–2017 (in millions, except per share data)

	2017	2016
ASSETS		
Current Assets		
Cash and cash equivalents	$ 10,610	$ 9,158
Short-term investments	8,900	6,967
Accounts and notes receivable, net	7,024	6,694
Inventories	2,947	2,723

(Continued)

EXHIBIT 4 (Continued)

	2017	2016
Prepaid expenses and other current assets	1,546	908
Total Current Assets	31,027	26,450
Property, Plant and Equipment, net	17,240	16,591
Amortizable Intangible Assets, net	1,268	1,237
Goodwill	14,744	14,430
Other nonamortizable intangible assets	12,570	12,196
Nonamortizable Intangible Assets	27,314	26,626
Investments in Noncontrolled Affiliates	2,042	1,950
Other Assets	913	636
Total Assets	$ 79,804	$ 73,490
LIABILITIES AND EQUITY		
Current Liabilities		
Short-term debt obligations	$ 5,485	$ 6,892
Accounts payable and other current liabilities	15,017	14,243
Total Current Liabilities	20,502	21,135
Long-Term Debt Obligations	33,796	30,053
Other Liabilities	11,283	6,669
Deferred Income Taxes	3,242	4,434
Total Liabilities	68,823	62,291
Commitments and contingencies		
Preferred Stock, no par value	41	41
Repurchased Preferred Stock	(197)	(192)
PepsiCo Common Shareholders' Equity		
Common stock, par value 1 2/3 cents per share (authorized 3,600 shares, issued, net of repurchased common stock at par value: 1,420 and 1,428 shares, respectively)	24	24
Capital in excess of par value	3,996	4,091
Retained earnings	52,839	52,518
Accumulated other comprehensive loss	(13,057)	(13,919)
Repurchased common stock, in excess of par value (446 and 438 shares, respectively)	(32,757)	(31,468)
Total PepsiCo Common Shareholders Equity	11,045	11,246
Noncontrolling interests	92	104
Total Equity	10,981	11,199
Total Liabilities and Equity	$ 79,804	$ 73,490

Source: PepsiCo, Inc. 2017 10-K.

EXHIBIT 5   Net Cash Provided by PepsiCo's Operating Activities, 2015–2017

	2017	2016	2015
Net cash provided by operating activities	$9,994	$10,673	$10,864
Capital spending	(2,969)	(3,040)	(2,758)
Sales of property, plant, and equipment	180	99	86
Free cash flow	$7,205	$7,732	$8,192

Source: PepsiCo, Inc. 2017 10-K.

expansion, and strategic acquisitions. The company was committed to producing the highest-quality products in each category and was working diligently on product reformulations to make snack foods and beverages less unhealthy. The company believed that its efforts to develop good-for-you and better-for-you products would create growth opportunities from the intersection of business and public interests.

PepsiCo was organized into six business divisions, which all followed the corporation's general strategic approach. Frito-Lay North America manufactured, marketed, and distributed such snack foods as Lay's potato chips, Doritos tortilla chips, Cheetos cheese snacks, Fritos corn chips, Grandma's cookies, and Smartfood popcorn. Quaker Foods North America manufactured and marketed cereals, rice and pasta dishes, granola bars, and other food items that were sold in supermarkets. North America Beverages manufactured, marketed, and sold beverage concentrates, fountain syrups, and finished goods under such brands as Pepsi, Gatorade, Aquafina, Tropicana, Lipton, Dole, and Propel throughout North America. Latin America manufactured, marketed, and distributed snack foods and many Quaker-branded cereals and snacks in Latin America. The division also produced, marketed, distributed and sold PepsiCo beverage brands in Latin America. Europe Sub-Saharan Africa manufactured, marketed, and sold snacks and beverages throughout Europe and the lower portion of the African continent, while the company's Asia, Middle East, and North Africa division produced, marketed, and distributed snack brands and beverages in more than 150 countries in those regions. A listing of PepsiCo's leading brands is presented in Exhibit 6. Select financial information for PepsiCo's six reporting units is presented in Exhibit 7.

Frito-Lay North America

As of 2018, key trends that were shaping the industry were a growing awareness of the nutritional content of snack foods and product innovation. Most manufacturers had developed new flavors of salty snacks such as nacho cheese tortilla chips and sea salt and vinegar potato chips to attract the interest of snackers. PepsiCo continued to innovate to increase its share of snack foods with new varieties of chips like Lay's Poppables, Simply Organic Doritos, and Himalayan Pink Salt Red Rock Deli chips.

In 2018, Frito-Lay owned the top-selling chip brand in each U.S. salty-snack category and held more than a 2-to-1 lead over the next-largest snack-food maker in the United States. Frito-Lay's market share of convenience foods sold in the United States was more than five times greater than runner-up Kellogg's market share. Convenience foods included both salty and sweet snacks such as chips, pretzels, ready-to-eat popcorn, crackers, dips, snack nuts and seeds, candy bars, and cookies.

Innovations were also directed at making increasing the percentage of sales of BFY and GFY products. By 2025, Frito Lay North America (FLNA) expected that 75 percent of its global foods portfolio volume would not exceed 1.3 milligrams of sodium per calories and 1.1 grams of saturated fat per 100 calories. Good-for-you (GFY) snacks, such as Bare Foods baked fruit and vegetable snacks acquired in 2018, offered an opportunity for the company to exploit consumers' desires for healthier snacks and address a deficiency in most diets. Americans, on average, consumed only about 50 percent of the U.S. Department of Agriculture's recommended daily diet of fruits and vegetables. Other GFY snacks included Stacy's Pita

EXHIBIT 6   PepsiCo, Inc.'s Leading Brands by Category, 2018

Top Global Brands	Good for You Brands	Better for You Brands	Fun for You Brands
• Pepsi • Lays • Mountain Dew • Gatorade • Tropicana • Diet Pepsi • 7-Up • Doritos • Quaker Oats • Cheetos • Mirinda • Lipton • Ruffles • Tostitos • Aquafina • Pepsi MAX • Brisk • Mist TWST • Fritos • Diet Mountain Dew • Starbucks Ready-to-Drink Beverages • Walkers Chips	• Bubly Sparkling Water • Quaker Oats • KeVita Probiotic Beverages • Aquafina • Tropicana • Naked Juice • Sun Bites Whole Grain Snacks • Sabra Hummus • Gatorade • LIFEWTR	• Lemon Lemon Sparkling Lemonade • Stacy's Chips • Alvalle Fruit Juices • H2OH! • Smartfood Snacks • Lay's Baked • Grain Waves • Propel • Pure Leaf • Duyvis Oven Roasted Snacks • Pepsi Zero Sugar	• Fritos • Lay's • Starbucks Ready-to-Drink Beverages • Mountain Dew • Cheetos • Yedigun Soft Drinks • Sabritas Chips • Walkers Chips • Mirinda Soft Drinks • Pepsi • Doritos • Kurkure Chips • Tostitos

Source: **Pepsico.com**.

EXHIBIT 7   Select Financial Data for PepsiCo, Inc.'s Business Segments, 2015–2017 (in millions)

	2017	2016	2015
Frito-Lay North America			
Net revenue	$15,798	$15,549	$14,782
Operating profit	4,823	4,659	4,304
Capital spending	665	801	608
Amortization of intangible assets	7	7	7
Depreciation and other amortization	449	435	427
Quaker Foods North America			
Net revenue	$ 2,503	$ 2,564	$ 2,543
Operating profit	642	653	560
Capital spending	44	41	40
Amortization of intangible assets	—	—	—
Depreciation and other amortization	47	50	51

	2017	2016	2015
North America Beverages			
Net revenue	$20,936	$21,312	$20,618
Operating profit	2,707	2,959	2,785
Capital spending	904	769	695
Amortization of intangible assets	31	37	38
Depreciation and other amortization	780	809	813
Latin America			
Net revenue	$ 7,208	$ 6,820	$ 8,228
Operating profit/(loss)	908	887	(206)
Capital spending	481	507	368
Amortization of intangible assets	5	5	7
Depreciation and other amortization	245	211	238
Europe Sub-Saharan Africa			
Net revenue	$11,050	$10,216	$10,510
Operating profit	1,354	1,108	1,081
Capital spending	481	439	404
Amortization of intangible assets	22	18	20
Depreciation and other amortization	329	321	353
Asia, Middle East and North Africa			
Net revenue	$ 6,030	$ 6,338	$ 6,375
Operating profit	1,073	619	941
Capital spending	308	381	441
Amortization of intangible assets	3	3	3
Depreciation and other amortization	257	294	293

Source: PepsiCo, Inc. 2017 10-K.

Chips, Sabra hummus, salsas and dips, and Quaker Chewy granola bars. In 2018, FLNA manufactured and marketed baked versions of its most popular products, such as Cheetos, Lay's potato chips, Ruffles potato chips, and Tostitos tortilla chips.

PepsiCo's Performance with Purpose goals applied to all of its business units. Frito-Lay North America's revenues were unchanged after correcting for the effect of a 53rd reporting week in 2017 and its volume declined by 1 percent between 2016 and 2017. The decline in volume and flat revenues were reflective of the growing emphasis of consumers on healthy snacking. However, the division was able to boost operating profit by 3.5 percent between 2016 and 2017 through its focus on Performance with Purpose cost reduction strategies and operating practices.

The division produced 25 percent of PepsiCo's net revenues in 2017 and 46 percent of its operating profit.

Quaker Foods North America

Quaker Foods North American (QFNA) produced, marketed, and distributed hot and ready-to-eat cereals, pancake mixes and syrups, and rice and pasta side dishes in the United States and Canada. The division recorded sales of approximately $2.5 billion in 2017. The sales volume and net revenue of Quaker Foods products decreased by 2 percent between 2016 and 2017 as sales of ready-to-eat cereals declining in single digits during 2017 and the sales of Roni products declining by nearly 10 percent between 2016 and 2017. Quaker Oatmeal, Life cereal, and Cap'n Crunch cereal volumes competing in mature industries with weak competitive positions relative to Kellogg's and General Mills. Quaker Oats was the star product of the division, with a commanding share of the North American market for oatmeal in 2018. More than one-half of Quaker Foods' 2013 revenues was generated by BFY and GFY products.

North American Beverages

PepsiCo was the second largest seller of non-alcoholic beverages in North America during 2017, with a market share of 19 percent. Coca-Cola was the largest non-alcoholic beverage producer in North America, with a 22 percent market share in 2017. Dr. Pepper Snapple Group was the third-largest beverage seller in 2017, with less than 10 percent market share. As with Frito-Lay, PepsiCo's beverage business contributed greatly to the corporation's overall profitability and free cash flows and was heavily impacted by consumer preferences for healthier food and beverage choices.

In 2017, North American Beverages (NAB) accounted for 33 percent of the corporation's total revenues and 26 percent of its operating profits. The NAB division's $1 billion brands included Gatorade, Tropicana fruit juices, Lipton ready-to-drink tea, Pepsi, Diet Pepsi, Mountain Dew, Diet Mountain Dew, Aquafina, Miranda, Sierra Mist, Dole fruit drinks, Starbucks cold-coffee drinks, and SoBe. Analysts had noted that the strong consumer appeal and rapidly growing sales of Naked Juice might soon make it PepsiCo's next $1 billion brand.

Gatorade was the number-one brand of sports drink sold worldwide; Tropicana was the number-two seller of juice and juice drinks globally; and NAB was the second-largest seller of carbonated soft drinks worldwide, with an approximate 27 percent market share in 2017. Market leader Coca-Cola held approximately 42 percent share of the carbonated soft-drink (CSD) industry in 2017. Carbonated soft drinks were the most consumed type of beverage in the United States, but the industry had declined by 1 to 2 percent annually for more than a decade. The overall decline in CSD consumption was a result of consumers' interest in healthier food and beverage choices. In contrast, functional beverages, flavored water, energy drinks, ready-to-drink teas, and bottled water were growing beverage categories that were capturing a larger share of the stomachs in the United States and internationally.

PepsiCo's Carbonated Soft-Drink Business.   PepsiCo's CSD business had focused on product innovations to sustain sales and market share, including new formulations to lower the calorie content of non-diet drinks. The strategy had produced some successes as the company had maintained its premium pricing differential because of differentiation through innovations such as higher-priced 7.5-ounce cans and the 1893 line of specialty sodas. However, the company's CSD business could not escape the overall decline in soft drink consumption. While the decline in sales of CSDs in North America had been an ongoing industry trend for more than a decade, the decline was accelerating with industry sales falling to a 31 year low in 2016. In addition, bottled water sales in North America surpassed that of soft drinks for the first time ever in 2017.

PepsiCo's Noncarbonated Beverage Brands. Although carbonated beverages made up the largest percentage of NAB's total beverage volume, much of the division's growth was attributable to the success of its noncarbonated beverages. Aquafina was the number-one brand of bottled water in the United States. Gatorade, Tropicana, Aquafina, Starbucks Frappuccino, Lipton RTD teas, and Propel were all leading BFY and GFY beverages in the markets where they were sold. PepsiCo broadened its lineup of functional beverages in 2016 with the acquisition of KeVita sparkling probiotic drink with flavors such as Mango Coconut, Mojito Lime Mint Coconut, Lemon Ginger, and Blueberry Acai Coconut. Also, the NAB division introduced LIFEWTR in 2017, a purified water fortified with electrolytes as a response to the increasing popularity of Coca-Cola's

Smartwater. The introduction of Bubly sparkling water in 2018 was initiated to target consumers of LaCroix, a flavored sparking water that had been produced since the 1980s but had enjoyed tremendous success since 2016. Sales of domestic sparkling water in North America doubled between 2015 and 2017 to reach $8.5 billion.

Latin America

PepsiCo management believed international markets offered the company's greatest opportunity for growth since per capita consumption of snacks in the United States averaged 6.6 servings per month while per capita consumption in other developed countries averaged 4 servings per month and in developing countries averaged 0.4 serving per month. PepsiCo executives expected China and Brazil to become the two largest international markets for snacks, with significant growth also expected in the United Kingdom, Mexico, and Russia.

Developing an understanding of consumer taste preferences was a key to expanding into international markets. Taste preferences for salty snacks were more similar from country to country than were preferences for many other food items, and this allowed PepsiCo to make only modest modifications to its snacks in most countries. For example, classic varieties of Lay's, Doritos, and Cheetos snacks were sold in Latin America. In addition, consumer characteristics in the United States that had forced snack-food makers to adopt better-for-you or good-for-you snacks applied in most other developed countries as well.

PepsiCo operated 50 snack-food manufacturing and processing plants and 640 warehouses in Latin America, with its largest facilities located in Guarulhos, Brazil; Monterrey, Mexico; Mexico City, Mexico; and Celaya, Mexico. PepsiCo was the second-largest seller of snacks and beverages in Mexico, and its Doritos, Marias Gamesa, Cheetos, Ruffles, Emperador, Saladitas, Sabritas, and Tostitos brands were popular throughout most of Latin America. The division's revenues had grown from $7.2 billion in 2011 to $8.3 billion in 2013 and accounted for 12 percent of 2013 total net revenues. However, the division's revenues declined by 17 percent in 2016 as the company deconsolidated its Venezuelan businesses in 2015 because of the country's inflation and volatile currency.

The division's revenues increased by 6 percent between 2016 and 2017 as a result of price increases,

but its sales volume of snacks and beverages declined by 1.5 percent and 2 percent, respectively, between 2016 and 2017. The division's net price increases and Performance with Purpose operating efficiencies led to operating profit increases of 2 percent between 2016 and 2017.

Europe, Sub-Saharan Africa

All of PepsiCo's global brands were sold in Europe, as well as its country- or region-specific brands such as Domik v Derevne, Chjudo, and Agusha. PespiCo Europe operated 125 plants and approximately 525 warehouses, distribution centers, and offices in eastern and western Europe. The company's acquisition of Wimm-Bill-Dann Foods, along with sales of its long-time brands, made it the number-one food and beverage company in Russia, with a 2-to-1 advantage over its nearest competitor. It was also the leading seller of snacks and beverages in the United Kingdom. PepsiCo Europe management believed further opportunities in other international markets existed, with opportunities to distribute many of its newest brands and product formulations throughout Europe.

The division's snack volume sales increased by 5 percent during 2017, largely because of its tremendous success in Russia where its volume increased by nearly 10 percent between 2016 and 2017. Sales growth in Turkey, South Africa, and the Netherlands also contributed to the division's volume increase in 2017. The division's net revenues increase by 8 percent between 2016 and 2017 because of the volume gains and net pricing increases. Beverage sales grew at a weak one percent rate between 2016 and 2017, but the division's operating profits increased by 22 percent as a result of Performance with Purpose operating efficiencies and a gain on the sale of a minority stake in its Britvic business. The divestiture contributed 8 percentage points to the operating profit growth between 2016 and 2017.

Asia, Middle East, and North Africa

PepsiCo's business unit operating in Asia, the Middle East, and North Africa manufactured and marketed all of the company's global brands and many regional brands such as Kurkure and Chipsy. PepsiCo operated 45 plants, 490 distribution centers, warehouses, and offices located in Egypt, Jordan, and China and was the number-one brand of beverages and snacks in India, Egypt, Saudi Arabia, United Arab Emirates, and China. The division's revenues had declined from $6.4 billion in 2015 to $6.0 billion in 2017, while its operating profit had fluctuated from $941 million in 2015 to $619 in 2016 to nearly $1.1 billion in 2017. The division's revenue declines were primarily attributable to unfavorable currency exchange. The 2016 decline in operating profit resulted from higher commodity costs and higher advertising and marketing expenses. The operating profit increase between 2016 and 2017 was largely tied to its gain on the refranchising of its beverage business in Jordan, which contributed 14 percentage points to the overall operating profit growth.

Value Chain Alignment between PepsiCo Brands and Products

PepsiCo's management team was dedicated to capturing strategic-fit benefits within the business lineup throughout the value chain. The company's procurement activities were coordinated globally to achieve the greatest possible economies of scale, and best practices were routinely transferred among its more than 200 plants, over 3,500 distribution systems, and 120,000 service routes around the world. PepsiCo also shared market research information with its divisions to better enable each division to develop new products likely to be hits with consumers, and the company coordinated its Power of One activities across product lines.

PepsiCo management had a proven ability to capture strategic fits between the operations of new acquisitions and its other businesses. The Quaker Oats integration produced a number of noteworthy successes, including $160 million in cost savings resulting from corporatewide procurement of product ingredients and packaging materials and an estimated $40 million in cost savings attributed to the

joint distribution of Quaker snacks and Frito-Lay products. In total, the company estimated that the synergies among its business units generated approximately $1 billion annually in productivity savings.

PEPSICO'S STRATEGIC SITUATION IN 2018

PepsiCo's strategy keyed to building its global brands, developing product innovations, and boosting productivity through efficient operations had produced strong operating profits and annual free case flows through 2017. Nevertheless, the decline in the consumption of carbonated soft drinks and the low relative profit margins of some of PepsiCo's international businesses signaled possible flaws in its corporate strategy. A lack of revenue growth and an increased reliance on its Frito Lay North American business unit to maintain its annual operating profits and free cash flow were troubling metrics to investors. Since 2013, the company's overall revenues and net income had declined steadily and its stock price had lagged the growth in the S&P 500.

The company was aggressively pursuing a strategy to increase its GFY and BFY brands and improve the overall healthiness of its product portfolio. Its acquisitions of established brands such as Gatorade and Tropicana had added to its portfolio of $1 billion brands and new acquisitions such as Naked Juice might soon add to that list with healthy food and beverages. Additional product introductions and acquisitions such as Bubly and Bare Foods might also contribute to future revenue growth. However, some food and beverage industry analysts had speculated that additional corporate strategy changes might also be required to restore previous revenue and earnings growth rates and lead to increases in shareholder value.

The Walt Disney Company: Its Diversification Strategy in 2018

connect

John E. Gamble

Texas A&M University-Corpus Christi

The Walt Disney Company was a broadly diversified media and entertainment company with a business lineup that included theme parks and resorts, motion picture production and distribution, cable television networks, the ABC broadcast television network, eight local television stations, and a variety of other businesses that exploited the company's intellectual property. The company's revenues had increased from $45 billion in fiscal year 2013 to $55 billion in fiscal 2017 and its share price had regularly outperformed the S&P 500. While struggling somewhat in the mid-1980s, the company's performance had been commendable in almost every year since Walt Disney created Mickey Mouse in 1928.

The company ended 2017 with a modest one percent increase in revenues and four percent increase in net income over the year prior. However, its announcement in December 2017 that it would acquire 21st Century Fox for $71.3 billion in cash and stock had the potential to radically improve its future financial performance. The transaction was approved by the U.S. Department of Justice (DOJ) Antitrust Division in June 2018 and was expected to be finalized by year-end 2018. The acquisition of 21st Century Fox would extend Disney's impressive collection of media franchises to include Fox, FX, Fox News Channel, Fox Business Network, Fox Sports Network, National Geographic Channel, Star India, 28 local television stations in the United States and more than 350 international channels, Twentieth Century Fox Film, and Twentieth Century Fox television production studios. Twenty-First Century Fox also held a 39.1 percent stake in Sky, Europe's leading entertainment company that served nearly 23 million households in five countries.

Disney CEO Robert Iger commented on the ability of the acquisition to further boost shareholder value during an investor's conference shortly after the DOJ consent decree announcement in June 2018.

The acquisition of 21st Century Fox will bring significant financial value to Disney and the shareholders of both companies, and after six months of integration planning we're even more enthusiastic and confident in the strategic fit of these complementary assets and the talent at Fox.

Just to remind you of the incredibly valuable assets that we're acquiring—our deal includes such premier entertainment properties as Twentieth Century Fox Film and Twentieth Century Fox Television, FX and National Geographic, Fox's regional sports networks, Fox Networks Group International, and Star India, as well as Fox's interests in Hulu and Sky. Since we first announced our deal in December, the intrinsic value of these assets has increased—thanks, in part, to the benefits of tax reform and certain operating improvements.

As we've said before, the combination of Disney and 21st Century Fox is an extremely compelling proposition for consumers. It will allow us to create even more appealing high-quality content, expand our direct-to-consumer offerings and international presence, and deliver more exciting and personalized entertainment experiences to meet the growing demands of consumers worldwide.[1]

As the company entered the third quarter of 2018, it was coming off an impressive second quarter, but faced several strategic issues. The company's core Parks and Resorts business continued to grow and record healthy profit margins, but its larger Media

Networks business had seen minimal revenue growth in recent years and was experiencing declining operating profits as media consumers turned from cable to direct-to-consumer (DTC) programming. The company's Studio Entertainment business unit had also struggled to develop stable revenue and earnings growth and its Consumer Products & Interactive Media business unit had seen a decline in revenues and operating profits in the past year. Going into 2019, Iger and Disney's management team would have to evaluate the corporation's strategy to bolster the performance of its existing business units and develop new media delivery capabilities while preparing for the integration of the probable acquisition of 21st Century Fox.

COMPANY HISTORY

Walt Disney's venture into animation began in 1919 when he returned to the United States from France, where he had volunteered to be an ambulance driver for the American Red Cross during World War I. Disney volunteered for the American Red Cross only after being told he was too young to enlist for the United States Army. Upon returning after the war, Disney settled in Kansas City, Missouri, and found work as an animator for Pesman Art Studio. Disney, and fellow Pesman animator, Ub Iwerks, soon left the company to found Iwerks-Disney Commercial Artists in 1920. The company lasted only briefly, but Iwerks and Disney were both able to find employment with a Kansas City company that produced short animated advertisements for local movie theaters. Disney left his job again in 1922 to found Laugh-O-Grams, where he employed Iwerks and three other animators to produce short animated cartoons. Laugh-O-Grams was able to sell its short cartoons to local Kansas City movie theaters, but its costs far exceeded its revenues—forcing Disney to declare bankruptcy in 1923. Having exhausted his savings, Disney had only enough cash to purchase a one-way train ticket to Hollywood, California, where his brother, Roy, had offered a temporary room. Once in California, Roy began to look for buyers for a finished animated-live action film he retained from Laugh-O-Grams. The film was never distributed, but New York distributors Margaret Winkler and Charles Mintz were impressed enough with the short film that they granted Disney a contract in October 1923 to produce a series of short films that blended cartoon animation with live action motion picture photography. Disney brought Ub Iwerks from Kansas City to Hollywood to work with Disney Brothers Studio (later to be named Walt Disney Productions) to produce the Alice Comedies series that would number 50-plus films by the series end in 1927. Disney followed the Alice Comedies series with a new animated cartoon for Universal Studios. After Disney's *Oswald the Lucky Rabbit* cartoons quickly became a hit, Universal terminated Disney Brothers Studio and hired most of Disney's animators to continue producing the cartoon.

In 1928, Disney and Iwerks created Mickey Mouse to replace Oswald as the feature character in Walt Disney Studios cartoons. Unlike with Oswald, Disney retained all rights over Mickey Mouse and all subsequent Disney characters. Mickey Mouse and his girlfriend, Minnie Mouse, made their cartoon debuts later in 1928 in the cartoons, *Plane Crazy, The Gallopin' Gaucho,* and *Steamboat Willie. Steamboat Willie* was the first cartoon with synchronized sound and became one of the most famous short films of all time. The animated film's historical importance was recognized in 1998 when it was added to the National Film Registry by the United States Library of Congress. Mickey Mouse's popularity exploded over the next few decades with a Mickey Mouse Club being created in 1929, new accompanying characters such as Pluto, Goofy, Donald Duck, and Daisy Duck being added to Mickey Mouse cartoon storylines, and Mickey Mouse appearing in Walt Disney's 1940 feature length film, *Fantasia.* Mickey Mouse's universal appeal reversed Walt Disney's series of failures in the animated film industry and became known as the mascot of Disney Studios, Walt Disney Productions, and The Walt Disney Company.

The success of The Walt Disney Company was sparked by Mickey Mouse, but Disney Studios also produced several other highly successful animated feature films including *Snow White and the Seven Dwarfs* in 1937, *Pinocchio* in 1940, *Dumbo* in 1941, *Bambi* in 1942, *Song of the South* in 1946, *Cinderella* in 1950, *Treasure Island* in 1950, *Peter Pan* in 1953, *Sleeping Beauty* in 1959, and *One Hundred-One Dalmatians* in 1961. What would prove to be Disney's greatest achievement began to emerge in 1954 when construction began on his Disneyland Park in Anaheim, California. Walt Disney's Disneyland resulted from an idea that Disney had many years earlier while sitting on an amusement park bench watching his young daughters play. Walt Disney thought that there should be a clean and safe park that had attractions that both parents and children alike would find entertaining. Walt Disney spent years planning the park and announced the construction of the new park to America on his *Disneyland* television show that was launched to promote the new $17 million park. The park was an instant success when it opened in 1955 and recorded revenues of more than $10 million during its first year of operation. After the success of Disneyland, Walt Disney began looking for a site in the eastern United States for a second Disney park. He settled on an area near Orlando, Florida in 1963 and acquired more than 27,000 acres for the new park by 1965.

Walt Disney died of lung cancer in 1966, but upon his death, Roy O. Disney postponed retirement to become president and CEO of Walt Disney Productions and oversee the development of Walt Disney World Resort. Walt Disney World Resort opened in October 1971—only two months before Roy O. Disney's death in December 1971. The company was led by Donn Tatum from 1971 to 1976. Tatum had been with Walt Disney Productions since 1956 and led the further development of Walt Disney World Resort and began the planning of EPCOT in Orlando and Tokyo Disneyland. Those two parks were opened during the tenure of Esmond Cardon Walker, who had been an executive at the company since 1956 and chief operating officer since Walt Disney's death in 1966. Walker also launched The Disney Channel before his retirement in 1983. Walt Disney Productions was briefly led by Ronald Miller, who was the son-in-law of Walt Disney. Miller was ineffective as Disney chief executive officer and was replaced by Michael Eisner in 1984.

Eisner formulated and oversaw the implementation of a bold strategy for Walt Disney Studios, which included the acquisitions of ABC, ESPN, Miramax Films, and the Anaheim Angels, and the Fox Family Channel; the development of Disneyland Paris, Disney-MGM Studios in Orlando, Disney California Adventure Park, Walt Disney Studios theme park in France, and Hong Kong Disneyland; and the launch of the Disney Cruise Line, the Disney Interactive game division, and the Disney Store retail chain. Eisner also restored the company's reputation for blockbuster animated feature films with the creation of *The Little Mermaid* in 1989, and *Beauty and the Beast* and *The Lion King* in 1994. Despite Eisner's successes, his tendencies toward micromanagement

and skirting board approval for many of his initiatives and his involvement in a long-running derivatives suit led to his removal as chairman in 2004 and his resignation in 2005.

The Walt Disney Company's CEO in 2018, Robert (Bob) Iger, became a Disney employee in 1996 when the company acquired ABC. Iger was president and CEO of ABC at the time of its acquisition by The Walt Disney Company and remained in that position until made president of Walt Disney International by Alan Eisner in 1999. Bob Iger was promoted to president and chief operating officer of The Walt Disney Company in 2000 and was named as Eisner's replacement as CEO in 2005. Iger's first strategic moves in 2006 included the $7.4 billion acquisition of Pixar animation studios and the purchase of the rights to Disney's first cartoon character, Oswald the Lucky Rabbit, from NBCUniversal. In 2007, Robert Iger commissioned two new 340-meter ships for the Disney Cruise Lines that would double its fleet size from two ships to four. The new ships ordered by Iger were 40 percent larger than Disney's two older vessels and entered service in 2011 and 2012. Iger also engineered the acquisition of Marvel Entertainment in 2009 that would enable the Disney production motion pictures featuring Marvel comic book characters such as Iron Man, Incredible Hulk, Thor, Spider-Man, and Captain America. In 2012, Walt Disney acquired Lucasfilm in a $4 billion cash and stock transaction. Lucasfilm was founded by George Lucas and was best known for its *Star Wars* motion picture franchise.

A financial summary for The Walt Disney Company for 2013 through 2017 is provided in Exhibit 1. Exhibit 2 tracks the performance of The Walt Disney Company's common shares between July 2013 and July 2018.

THE WALT DISNEY COMPANY'S CORPORATE STRATEGY AND BUSINESS OPERATIONS IN 2018

In 2018, The Walt Disney Company was broadly diversified into theme parks, hotels and resorts, cruise ships, cable networks, broadcast television networks, television production, television station operations, live action and animated motion picture

EXHIBIT 1   Financial Summary for The Walt Disney Company, Fiscal Years 2013–2017 (in millions)

	2017	2016	2015	2014	2013
Revenues	$55,137	$55,632	$52,465	$48,813	$45,041
Net income	9,366	9,790	8,852	8,004	6,636
Net income attributable to Disney	8,980	9,391	8,382	7,501	6,136
Per common share					
Earnings attributable to Disney					
Diluted	$5.69	$5.73	$4.90	$4.26	$3.38
Basic	$5.73	$5.76	$4.95	$4.31	$3.42
Dividends	$1.56	$1.42	$1.81	$0.86	$0.75
Balance sheets					
Total assets	$95,789	$92,033	$88,182	$84,141	$81,197
Long-term obligations	26,710	24,189	19,142	18,537	17,293
Disney shareholders' equity	41,315	43,265	44,525	44,958	45,429
Statements of cash flows					
Cash provided by operations	$12,343	$13,136	$11,385	$10,148	$9,495
Investing activities	4,111	5,758	4,245	3,345	4,676
Financing activities	8,959	7,220	5,801	6,981	4,458

Source: The Walt Disney Company 2017 10-K.

production and distribution, music publishing, live theatrical productions, children's book publishing, interactive media, and consumer products retailing. The company's corporate strategy was centered on (1) creating high-quality content, (2) exploiting technological innovations to make entertainment experiences more memorable, and (3) international expansion. The company's 2006 acquisition of Pixar and 2009 acquisition of Marvel were executed to enhance the resources and capabilities of its core animation business with the addition of new animation skills and characters. The company's 2011 acquisition of UTV was engineered to facilitate its international expansion efforts. The acquisition of Lucasfilm's *Star Wars* franchise in 2012 not only allowed the company to produce new films in the series, but integrate *Star Wars* into its other business units, including theme park attractions. When asked about the company's planned acquisition of 21st Century Fox and Walt Disney Company's strategic priorities during a media, cable and telecommunications conference in February 2018, Bob Iger made the following comments:

We've been a company that has emphasized the value of high-quality, branded entertainment. And the acquisitions of Pixar, Marvel, and Lucasfilm/*Star Wars,* obviously were a reflection of that core strategy.

This gives us a larger portfolio of high-quality branded content. When you think about FX, when you think about National Geographic, when you think about a number of the franchises that Fox has created, including their Marvel franchises and *Avatar* and other product, we believe that this fits beautifully into a strategy to continue to invest in entertainment, particularly in a world that seems to be growing in terms of its appetite to consume entertainment.

EXHIBIT 2 Performance of The Walt Disney Company's Stock Price, July 2013 to July 2018

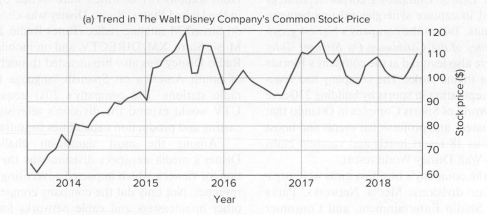

(a) Trend in The Walt Disney Company's Common Stock Price

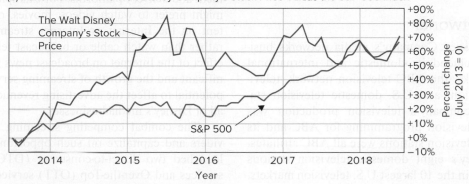

(b) Performance of The Walt Disney Company's Stock Price Versus the S&P 500 Index

Source: The Walt Disney Company 2017 10-K.

Secondly, we've been talking a lot about using technology to reach consumers in more modern, more efficient, and effective ways. That certainly has changed significantly. When I talk about a dynamic marketplace, I think it's most evident in how people access entertainment, how they consume entertainment, and this acquisition gives us the ability not only to have essentially more product, more intellectual property, but to bring it to the consumer in more compelling ways and ways we think the consumer wants their entertainment more and more. The Star and Sky assets and the Hulu assets give us an opportunity to do that.

And then lastly, we've talked a lot about wanting to grow our company globally. The Walt Disney Company has been a global company for a long time, but in many of the markets that we operate in our penetration was relatively superficial. We spent a fair amount of time

over the last decade deepening that penetration in markets. You mentioned Shanghai Disneyland, which would be an example of how we've done that in China. This gives us the ability to have a far more global footprint and to diversify the company's interest from a geographic perspective.[2]

Disney's corporate strategy also called for sufficient capital to be allocated to its core theme parks and resorts business to sustain its advantage in the industry. The company expanded the range of attractions at its theme parks with billion-dollar plus additions such as its new Toy Story Land attractions opened in 2018 at Shanghai Disneyland and Disney's Hollywood Studios and its Star Wars Land scheduled to open in Disney's Hollywood Studios and Anaheim's Disneyland in 2019. Expansions were also underway in 2018 at Tokyo Disney Resort and Hong Kong Disneyland.

The Walt Disney Company's corporate strategy also attempted to capture synergies existing between its business units. Two of the company's highest grossing films, *Pirates of the Caribbean: On Stranger Tides* and *Cars 2* were also featured at the company's Florida and California theme parks. The company had leveraged ESPN's reputation in sports by building 230-acre ESPN Wide World of Sports Complex in Orlando that could host amateur and professional events and boost occupancy in its 18 resort hotels and vacation clubs located at the Walt Disney World resort.

In 2018, the company's business units were organized into four divisions: Media Networks, Parks and Resorts, Studio Entertainment, and Consumer Products & Interactive Media.

Media Networks

The Walt Disney Company's media networks business unit included its domestic and international cable networks, the ABC television network, television production, and U.S. domestic television stations. The company's television production was limited to television programming for ABC and its eight local television stations were all ABC affiliates. Six of Disney's eight domestic television stations were located in the 10 largest U.S. television markets. In all, ABC had 244 affiliates in the United States.

When asked about the decline in cable television viewership, Bob Iger suggested that content delivery method was less important than the quality and appeal of content.

Well, for the most part, we've looked at channels less as channels and more as brands. And it's less important to us how people get those channels—obviously, it's important in terms of how they are monetized in today's world—but what's more important to us is the quality of the brand and intellectual property that fits under that brand umbrella. And our intention is to—as the world shifts in terms of distribution and consumption we talked about earlier—is to migrate those brands and those products in the more modern direction from a distribution and consumption perspective.[3]

Exhibit 3 provides the market ranking for Disney's local stations and its number of subscribers and ownership percentage of its cable networks. The exhibit also provides a brief description of its ABC broadcasting and television production operations. The division also included Radio Disney, which aired family-oriented radio programming on 34 terrestrial radio stations (31 of which were owned by Disney) in the United States. Radio Disney was also available on SiriusXM satellite radio, iTunes Radio Tuner and Music Store, XM/DIRECTV, and on mobile phones. Radio Disney was also broadcasted throughout most of South America on Spanish language terrestrial radio stations. The company's 2011 acquisition of UTV would expand the division's television broadcasting and production capabilities to India.

Among the most significant challenges to Disney's media networks division was the competition for viewers, which impacted advertising rates and revenues. Not only did the company compete against other broadcasters and cable networks for viewers, but it also competed against other types of entertainment and delivery platforms. For example, consumers might prefer to watch videos, movies, or other content on the Internet or Internet streaming services rather than watch cable or broadcast television. The effect of the Internet on broadcast news had been significant and the growth of streaming services had the potential to affect the advertising revenue potential of all of Disney's media businesses.

The combat competing streaming content providers and capitalize on such opportunities, Disney launched two direct-to-consumer (DTC) streaming services and Over-the-Top (OTT) services that delivered content without a distributor. Disney's ESPN-branded multi-sports content was planned for DTC distribution in 2018 and a Disney-branded DTC service that featured the company's film and television content was planned for 2019. Bob Iger discussed the company's DTC and OTT strategy in a 2017 interview.

Direct-to-consumer really is still a relatively nascent business, although obviously Netflix probably wouldn't look at it that way. But what we were doing was creating really, two different OTT or DTC products. One was sports, and the other one I'll call family, which was going to include Disney, Marvel, Pixar, and Star Wars. And what we saw doing was bringing them both out reasonably priced. We have not announced price but I did suggest they would both be substantially below what Netflix currently charges for a few reasons.[4]

Bob Iger discussed during an analysts' conference how the development of ESPN + and its family-oriented DTC services would allow the company to catch up with emerging media trends that it had missed.

It's no secret that we have seen the development and the growth of an entirely new media marketplace, and so we start with the premise that we want to participate in this new marketplace or this new market. Right now, we're only doing so at the tip of the iceberg, so to speak, with Hulu—that would be an example of that, and we have a relatively small stake in Hulu, about 30 percent. So our OTT interests are essentially designed to be part of this new marketplace, first. And I talked about it earlier, if you look at how the consumer today wants their media, first of all, they're far more interested in mobile,

mobile first, in many cases. The user interface is particularly critical; this is really true for millennials and younger, where the user interface that exists in the sort of traditional television platform is not as compelling to them. It is essential for us to provide our content on platforms and with user interfaces that are serving today's consumer better.[5]

Operating results for Disney's media networks division for fiscal 2015 through fiscal 2017 are presented in Exhibit 4.

EXHIBIT 3 The Walt Disney Company's Media Network Subscribers, 2013 and 2017 (in millions)

	Estimated Subscribers (in millions)[1]	Estimated Subscribers (in millions)[1]
Cable Networks	**2013**	**2017**
ESPN[2]		
ESPN	99	88
ESPN–International	n.a.	146
ESPN2	99	87
ESPNU	72	67
ESPNEWS	73	66
SEC Network	n.a.	60
Disney Channels Worldwide		
Disney Channel – Domestic	99	92
Disney Channels – International[3]	141	221
Disney Junior – Domestic	58	72
Disney Junior – International[3]	n.a.	151
Disney XD – Domestic	78	74
Disney XD – International[3]	91	127
Freeform	n.a.	90
A + E and Vice		
A&E[2]	99	91
Lifetime	99	91
HISTORY	99	92
Lifetime Movie Network	82	73
Lifetime Real Women[3]	18	n.a.

(Continued)

Cable Networks	Estimated Subscribers (in millions)[1] 2013	Estimated Subscribers (in millions)[1] 2017
FYI	n.a.	58
Viceland	n.a.	70

Broadcasting
ABC Television Network (244 local affiliates reaching nearly 100 percent of U.S. television households)

Television Production
ABC Studios and ABC Media Productions (Daytime, primetime, late night and news television programming)

Domestic Television Stations		
Market	TV Station	Television Market Ranking[4]
New York, NY	WABC-TV	1
Los Angeles, CA	KABC-TV	2
Chicago, IL	WLS-TV	3
Philadelphia, PA	WPVI-TV	4
San Francisco, CA	KGO-TV	6
Houston, TX	KTRK-TV	8
Raleigh-Durham, NC	WTVD-TV	24
Fresno, CA	KFSN-TV	54

(1) Estimated U.S. subscriber counts according to Nielsen Media Research as of September 2017, except as noted below.
(2) ESPN and A&E programming is distributed internationally through other networks discussed below.
(3) Subscriber counts are not rated by Nielsen and are based on internal management report.
(4) Based on Nielsen Media Research, U.S. Television Household Estimates, January 1, 2017.

Source: The Walt Disney Company 2017 10-K.

EXHIBIT 4   Operating Results for Walt Disney's Media Networks Business Unit, Fiscal Years 2015–2017 (in millions)

Revenues	2017	2016	2015
Affiliate fees	$12,659	$12,259	$12,029
Advertising	8,129	8,509	8,361
TV/SVOD distribution and other	2,722	2,921	2,874
Total revenues	23,510	23,689	23,264
Operating expenses	14,068	13,571	13,150
Selling, general, administrative and other	2,647	2,705	2,869
Depreciation and amortization	237	255	266
Equity in the income of investees	(344)	(597)	(814)
Operating Income	$ 6,902	$ 7,755	$ 7,793

Source: The Walt Disney Company 2017 10-K.

Parks and Resorts

The Walt Disney Company's parks and resorts division included the Walt Disney World Resort in Orlando, the Disneyland Resort in California, Disneyland Paris, the Aulani Disney Resort and Spa in Hawaii, the Disney Vacation Club, the Disney Cruise Line, and Adventures by Disney. The company also owned a 47 percent interest in Hong Kong Disneyland Resort and a 43 percent interest in Shanghai Disney Resort. Disney also licensed the operation of Tokyo Disney Resort in Japan. Revenue for the division was primarily generated through park admission fees, hotel room charges, merchandise sales, food and beverage sales, sales and rentals of vacation club properties, and fees charged for cruise vacations.

Revenues from hotel lodgings and food and beverage sales were a sizeable portion of the division's revenues. For example, at the 25,000-acre Walt Disney World Resort alone, the company operated 18 resort hotels with approximately 22,000 rooms. Walt Disney World Resort also included the 127-acre Disney Springs retail, dining, and entertainment complex where visitors could dine and shop during or after park hours. Walt Disney World Resort in Orlando also included four championship golf courses, full-service spas, tennis, sailing, water skiing, two water parks, and a 230-acre sports complex that was host to over 200 amateur and professional events each year.

Walt Disney's 486-acre resort in California included two theme parks—Disneyland and Disney California Adventure—along with three hotels and its Downtown Disney retail, dining, and entertainment complex. Disney California Adventure was opened in 2001 adjacent to the Disneyland property and included four lands—Golden State, Hollywood Pictures Backlot, Paradise Pier, and Bug's Land. The park was initially built to alleviate overcrowding at Disneyland and was expanded with the addition of World of Color in 2010 and Cars Land in 2012 to strengthen its appeal with guests.

Aulani was a 21-acre oceanfront family resort located in Oahu, Hawaii. Disneyland Paris included two theme parks, seven resort hotels, two convention centers, a 27-hole golf course, and a shopping, dining, and entertainment complex. The company's Hong Kong Disneyland, Shanghai Disney Resort, and Tokyo Disney Resort them parks were highly popular with ambitious expansion plans.

The company also offered timeshare sales and rentals in 14 resort facilities through its Disney Vacation Club. The Disney Cruise Line operated four ships out of North America and Europe. Disney's cruise activities were developed to appeal to the interests of children and families. Its Port Canaveral cruises included a visit to Disney's Castaway Cay, a 1,000-acre private island in the Bahamas. The popularity of Disney's cruise vacations allowed its fleet to be booked to full capacity year-round.

The division's operating results for fiscal years 2015 through 2017 are presented in Exhibit 5.

EXHIBIT 5 Operating Results for Walt Disney's Parks and Resorts Business Unit, Fiscal Years 2015–2017 (in millions)

Revenues	2017	2016	2015
Domestic	$14,812	$14,242	$13,611
International	3,603	2,732	2,551
Total revenues	18,415	16,974	16,162
Operating expenses	10,667	10,039	9,760
Selling, general, administrative and other	1,950	1,913	1,884
Depreciation and amortization	1,999	1,721	1,517
Equity in the loss of investees	25	3	—
Operating Income	$ 3,774	$ 3,298	$ 3,031

Source: The Walt Disney Company 2017 10-K.

Studio Entertainment

The Walt Disney Company's studio entertainment division produced live-action and animated motion pictures, direct-to-video content, musical recordings, and *Disney on Ice* and *Disney Live!* live performances. The division's motion pictures were produced and distributed under the Walt Disney Pictures, Pixar, Marvel, Lucasfilm, and Touchstone banners. The division also distributed Dreamworks Studios motion pictures that were released from 2010 to 2016.

Most motion pictures typically incurred losses during the theatrical distribution of the film because of production costs and the cost of extensive advertising campaigns accompanying the launch of the film. Profits for many films did not occur until the movie became available on DVD or Blu-Ray disks for home entertainment, which usually began three to six months after the film's theatrical release. Revenue was also generated when a movie moved to pay-per-view (PPV)/video-on-demand (VOD) two months after the release of the DVD and when the motion picture became available on subscription premium cable channels such as HBO about 16 months after PPV/VOD availability. Broadcast networks such as ABC could purchase telecast rights to movies later as could basic cable channels such as Lifetime or the Hallmark Channel. Premium cable channels such as Showtime and Starz might also purchase telecast rights to movies long after its theatrical release. Similarly, subscription video on demand (SVOD) services such as Netflix might acquire distribution rights to a film for a 12- to 19-month window. Telecast right fees decreased as the length of time from initial release increased. Operating results for the Walt Disney Company's Studio Entertainment division for fiscal 2015 through fiscal 2017 are produced in Exhibit 6.

Consumer Products & Interactive Media

The company's consumer products division included the company's Disney Store retail chain and businesses specializing in merchandise licensing and children's book and magazine publishing. In 2018, the company owned and operated 221 Disney Stores in North America, 87 stores in Europe, 55 stores in Japan, and 2 stores in China. Its publishing business included comic books, various children's book magazine titles available in print and eBook format, and smartphone and tablet computer apps designed for children. The division's sales were primarily affected by seasonal shopping trends and changes in consumer disposable income.

Operating results for Disney's Consumer Products & Interactive Media division for fiscal year 2015 through 2017 are presented in Exhibit 7. The company's consolidated statements of income for fiscal 2015 through fiscal 2017 are presented in Exhibit 8. The Walt Disney Company's balance sheets for fiscal 2016 and fiscal 2017 are presented in Exhibit 9.

EXHIBIT 6 Operating Results for Walt Disney's Studio Entertainment Business Unit, Fiscal Years 2015–2017 (in millions)

	2017	2016	2015
Revenues			
Theatrical distribution	$ 2,903	$ 3,672	$ 2,321
Home entertainment	1,798	2,108	1,799
TV/SVOD distribution and other	3,678	3,661	3,246
Total revenues	8,379	9,441	7,366
Operating expenses	3,667	3,991	3,050
Selling, general, administrative and other	2,242	2,622	2,204
Depreciation and amortization	115	125	139
Operating Income	$ 2,355	$ 2,703	$ 1,973

Source: The Walt Disney Company 2017 10-K.

EXHIBIT 7   Operating Results for Walt Disney's Consumer Products & Interactive Media Business Unit, Fiscal Years 2015-2017 (in millions)

	2017	2016	2015
Revenues			
Licensing, publishing and games	$3,256	$3,819	$3,850
Retail and other	1,577	1,709	1,823
Total revenues	4,833	5,528	5,673
Operating expenses	1,904	2,263	2,434
Selling, general, administrative and other	1,007	1,125	1,172
Depreciation and amortization	179	175	183
Equity in the income of investees	1	—	—
Operating Income	$1,744	$1,965	$1,884

Source: The Walt Disney Company 2017 10-K.

EXHIBIT 8   Consolidated Statements of Income for The Walt Disney Company, Fiscal Years 2015-2017 (in millions, except per share data)

	2017	2016	2015
Revenues	$55,137	$55,632	$52,465
Costs and expenses	41,264	41,274	39,241
Restructuring and impairment charges	98	156	53
Add: Other income	78	—	—
Net interest expense	385	260	117
Add: Equity in the income of investees	(320)	(926)	(814)
Income before income taxes	13,788	14,868	13,868
Income taxes	4,422	5,078	5,016
Net Income	9,366	9,790	8,852
Less: Net Income attributable to noncontrolling interests	386	399	470
Net Income attributable to The Walt Disney Company (Disney)	$ 8,980	$ 9,391	$ 8,382
Earnings per share attributable to Disney:			
Diluted	$5.69	$5.73	$4.90
Basic	$5.73	$5.76	$4.95
Weighted average number of common and common equivalent shares outstanding:			
Diluted	1,578	1,639	1,709
Basic	1,568	1,629	1,694

Source: The Walt Disney Company 2017 10-K.

EXHIBIT 9   Consolidated Balance Sheets for The Walt Disney Company, Fiscal Years 2016 and 2017 (in millions, except per share data)

	September 30, 2017	October 1, 2016
CURRENT ASSETS		
Cash and cash equivalents	$ 4,017	$ 4,610
Receivables	8,633	9,065
Inventories	1,373	1,390
Television costs and advances	1,278	1,208
Other current assets	588	693
Total current assets	15,889	16,966
Film and television costs	7,481	6,339
Investments	3,202	4,280
Parks, resorts and other property, at cost		
Attractions, buildings and equipment	54,043	50,270
Accumulated depreciation	29,037	26,849
	25,006	23,421
Projects in progress	2,145	2,684
Land	1,255	1,244
	22,380	21,512
Intangible assets, net	6,995	6,949
Goodwill	31,426	27,810
Other assets	2,390	2,340
Total assets	$95,789	$92,033
LIABILITIES AND EQUITY		
Current liabilities		
Accounts payable and other accrued liabilities	8,855	9,130
Current portion of borrowings	6,172	3,687
Deferred revenue and other	4,568	4,025
Total current liabilities	19,595	16,842
Borrowings	19,119	16,483
Deferred income taxes	4,480	3,679
Other long-term liabilities	6,443	7,706
Commitments and contingencies		
Redeemable noncontrolling interests	1,148	—

	September 30, 2017	October 1, 2016
Equity		
Preferred stock, $0.01 par value		
Authorized — 100 million shares, Issued — none	—	—
Authorized — 4.6 billion shares, Issued — 2.9 billion shares	36,248	35,859
Retained earnings	72,606	66,088
Accumulated other comprehensive loss	(3,528)	(3,979)
	105,326	97,968
Treasury stock, at cost, 937.8 million shares at October 1, 2011 and 803.1 million shares at October 2, 2010	(64,011)	(54,703)
Total Disney Shareholder's equity	41,315	43,265
Noncontrolling interests	3,689	4,058
Total Equity	45,004	47,323
Total liabilities and equity	$95,789	$92,033

Source: The Walt Disney Company 2017 10-K.

THE WALT DISNEY COMPANY'S SECOND QUARTER 2018 PERFORMANCE AND ITS FUTURE PROSPECTS

The Walt Disney Company reported revenues and earnings per share increases during its first six months of fiscal 2018 of 6 percent and 59 percent, respectively, from the first six months of the year prior. The company's strong financial performance during the first six months of 2018 was led by its Parks and Resorts business unit, which saw year-over-year revenue and operating income increases of 13 percent and 24 percent, respectively; and its Studio business unit, which recorded a year-over-year revenue increase of 9 percent and a year-over-year operating income increase of 12 percent. Disney's Media Networks and Consumer Products & Interactive Media divisions suffered 9 percent and 4 percent operating income decreases, respectively, with neither achieving meaningful revenue growth.

Chairman Iger summarized Disney's strong second quarter performance and summarized the company's position at mid-2018.

We're very pleased with our results in Q2, especially in our Parks and Resorts and Studio businesses.

Our parks continue to drive growth through operational excellence and by effectively leveraging our extraordinary content. As an example, I just got back from opening our new Toy Story Land in Shanghai Disneyland and I'm happy to report that our first major addition to the park was met with strong reviews and great excitement. We're thrilled with the reaction and the enthusiasm generated by the new land bodes well for future expansion.

Turning to our Studio. . .It's clear from the recent results—as well as from the slate ahead—that our Studio has and will continue to raise the bar in terms of both creative and commercial success.

The incredible performance of Marvel's *Black Panther* is just one of many examples. We're proud of this movie on so many levels—it speaks volumes about great, innovative storytelling, the power of new perspectives and unbridled creativity.

We followed the phenomenal success of *Black Panther* with another Marvel masterpiece, *Avengers: Infinity War,* which broke domestic and global records to become the largest movie opening in history. With this latest success, our Studio has delivered nine of the top ten biggest domestic box office openings of all time—all of them released in the last six years.

On the sports front, we're very encouraged by the reaction to our ESPN + service, which launched just about a month ago. The reviews have been strong, and the response from sports fans has been enthusiastic.

We're also merging Consumer Products and Parks and Resorts together—combining strategy and resources to create extraordinary experiences and products that bring our stories and characters to life for consumers inside our parks, at home, and beyond.[6]

As the company move closer to the consummation of its acquisition of 21st Century Fox, it had several pressing strategy decisions related to its existing lineup of businesses. Failure to adequately resolve competitive disadvantages in its core and historical businesses would make the integration of one of the world's largest media companies even more complex and difficult.

ENDNOTES

[1] As quoted by Bob Iger, Chairman and Chief Executive Officer of The Walt Disney Company, during Investor Conference Call, June 20, 2018.
[2] As quoted by Bob Iger, Chairman and Chief Executive Officer of The Walt Disney Company, during the Morgan Stanley Technology, Media and Telcom Conference, February 26, 2018.

[3] As quoted by Bob Iger, Chairman and Chief Executive Officer of The Walt Disney Company, during the Morgan Stanley Technology, Media and Telcom Conference, February 26, 2018.
[4] As quoted by Bob Iger in "Q&A with Senior Management," December 14, 2017.

[5] As quoted by Bob Iger, Chairman and Chief Executive Officer of The Walt Disney Company, during the Morgan Stanley Technology, Media and Telcom Conference, February 26, 2018.
[6] As quoted by Bob Iger, Chairman and Chief Executive Officer, in "Q2 FY18 Earnings Conference Call, May 8, 2018."

CASE 25

Robin Hood

■ connect

Joseph Lampel
Alliance Manchester Business School

It was in the spring of the second year of his insurrection against the High Sheriff of Nottingham that Robin Hood took a walk in Sherwood Forest. As he walked, he pondered the progress of the campaign, the disposition of his forces, the Sheriff's recent moves, and the options that confronted him.

The revolt against the Sheriff had begun as a personal crusade. It erupted out of Robin's conflict with the Sheriff and his administration. However, alone Robin Hood could do little. He therefore sought allies, men with grievances and a deep sense of justice. Later he welcomed all who came, asking few questions and demanding only a willingness to serve. Strength, he believed, lay in numbers.

He spent the first year forging the group into a disciplined band, united in enmity against the Sheriff and willing to live outside the law. The band's organization was simple. Robin ruled supreme, making all important decisions. He delegated specific tasks to his lieutenants. Will Scarlett was in charge of intelligence and scouting. His main job was to shadow the Sheriff and his men, always alert to their next move. He also collected information on the travel plans of rich merchants and tax collectors. Little John kept discipline among the men and saw to it that their archery was at the high peak that their profession demanded. Scarlett took care of the finances, converting loot to cash, paying shares of the take, and finding suitable hiding places for the surplus. Finally, Much the Miller's son had the difficult task of provisioning the ever-increasing band of Merry Men.

The increasing size of the band was a source of satisfaction for Robin, but also a source of concern. The fame of his Merry Men was spreading, and new recruits were pouring in from every corner of England. As the band grew larger, their small bivouac became a major encampment. Between raids the men milled about, talking and playing games. Vigilance was in decline, and discipline was becoming harder to enforce. "Why," Robin reflected, "I don't know half the men I run into these days."

The growing band was also beginning to exceed the food capacity of the forest. Game was becoming scarce, and supplies had to be obtained from outlying villages. The cost of buying food was beginning to drain the band's financial reserves at the very moment when revenues were in decline. Travelers, especially those with the most to lose, were now giving the forest a wide berth. This was costly and inconvenient to them, but it was preferable to having all their goods confiscated.

Robin believed that the time had come for the Merry Men to change their policy of outright confiscation of goods to one of a fixed transit tax. His lieutenants strongly resisted this idea. They were proud of the Merry Men's famous motto: "Rob the rich and give to the poor." "The farmers and the townspeople," they argued, "are our most important allies. How can we tax them, and still hope for their help in our fight against the Sheriff?"

Robin wondered how long the Merry Men could keep to the ways and methods of their early days. The Sheriff was growing stronger and becoming better organized. He now had the money and the men and was beginning to harass the band, probing for its weaknesses. The tide of events was beginning to turn against the Merry Men. Robin felt that the campaign must be decisively concluded before the Sheriff had a chance to deliver a mortal blow. "But how," he wondered, "could this be done?"

Robin had often entertained the possibility of killing the Sheriff, but the chances for this seemed increasingly remote. Besides, killing the Sheriff might satisfy his personal thirst for revenge, but it would not improve the situation. Robin had hoped that the perpetual state of unrest and the Sheriff's failure to collect taxes would lead to his removal from office. Instead, the Sheriff used his political connections to obtain reinforcement. He had powerful friends at court and was well regarded by the regent, Prince John.

Prince John was vicious and volatile. He was consumed by his unpopularity among the people, who wanted the imprisoned King Richard back. He also lived in constant fear of the barons, who had first given him the regency but were now beginning to dispute his claim to the throne. Several of these barons had set out to collect the ransom that would release King Richard the Lionheart from his jail in Austria. Robin was invited to join the conspiracy in return for future amnesty. It was a dangerous proposition. Provincial banditry was one thing, court intrigue another. Prince John had spies everywhere, and he was known for his vindictiveness. If the conspirators' plan failed, the pursuit would be relentless and retributions swift.

The sound of the supper horn startled Robin from his thoughts. There was the smell of roasting venison in the air. Nothing was resolved or settled. Robin headed for camp promising himself that he would give these problems his utmost attention after tomorrow's raid.

Dilemma at Devil's Den

Allan R. Cohen
Babson College

Kim Johnson
Babson College

My name is Susan, and I'm a business student at Mt. Eagle College. Let me tell you about one of my worst experiences. I had a part-time job in the campus snack bar, The Devil's Den. At the time, I was 21 years old and a junior with a concentration in finance. I originally started working at the Den in order to earn some extra spending money. I had been working there for one semester and became upset with some of the happenings. The Den was managed by contract with an external company, College Food Services (CFS). What bothered me was that many employees were allowing their friends to take free food, and the employees themselves were also taking food in large quantities when leaving their shifts. The policy was that employees could eat whatever they liked free of charge while they were working, but it had become common for employees to leave with food and not to be charged for their snacks while off duty as well.

I felt these problems were occurring for several reasons. For example, employee wages were low, there was easy access to the unlocked storage room door, and inventory was poorly controlled. Also, there was weak supervision by the student managers and no written rules or strict guidelines. It seemed that most of the employees were enjoying freebies, and it had been going on for so long that it was taken for granted. The problem got so far out of hand that customers who had seen others do it felt free to do it whether they knew the workers or not. The employees who witnessed this never challenged anyone because, in my opinion, they did not care and they feared the loss of friendship or being frowned upon by others. Apparently, speaking up was more costly to the employees than the loss of money to CFS for the unpaid food items. It seemed obvious to me that the employees felt too secure in their jobs and did not feel that their jobs were in jeopardy.

The employees involved were those who worked the night shifts and on the weekends. They were students at the college and were under the supervision of another student, who held the position of manager. There were approximately 30 student employees and 6 student managers on the staff. During the day there were no student managers; instead, a full-time manager was employed by CFS to supervise the Den. The employees and student managers were mostly freshmen and sophomores, probably because of the low wages, inconvenient hours (late weeknights and weekends), and the duties of the job itself. Employees were hard to come by; the high rate of employee turnover indicated that the job qualifications and the selection process were minimal.

The student managers were previous employees chosen by other student managers and the full-time CFS day manager on the basis of their ability to work and on their length of employment. They received no further formal training or written rules beyond what they had already learned by working there. The student managers were briefed on how to close the snack bar at night but still did not get the job done properly. They received authority and responsibility over events occurring during their shifts as manager, although they were never actually taught how and

This case was prepared by Kim Johnson under the supervision of Professor Allan R. Cohen, Babson College. Copyright ©2004 by Babson College and licensed for publication to Harvard Business School Publishing. No part of this publication may be reproduced, stored in a retrieval system, used in a spreadsheet, or transmitted in any form or by any means—electronic, mechanical, photocopying, recording, or otherwise—without the permission of copyright holders. One time permission to reproduce granted by Babson College on July 21, 2014.

when to enforce it! Their increase in pay was small, from a starting pay of just over minimum wage to an additional 15 percent for student managers. Regular employees received an additional nickel for each semester of employment.

Although I only worked seven hours per week, I was in the Den often as a customer and saw the problem frequently. I felt the problem was on a large enough scale that action should have been taken, not only to correct any financial loss that the Den might have experienced but also to help give the student employees a true sense of their responsibilities, the limits of their freedom, respect for rules, and pride in their jobs. The issues at hand bothered my conscience, although I was not directly involved. I felt that the employees and customers were taking advantage of the situation whereby they could "steal" food almost whenever they wanted. I believed that I had been brought up correctly and knew right from wrong, and I felt that the happenings in the Den were wrong. It wasn't fair that CFS paid for others' greediness or urges to show what they could get away with in front of their friends.

I was also bothered by the lack of responsibility of the managers to get the employees to do their work. I had seen the morning employees work very hard trying to do their jobs, in addition to the jobs the closing shift should have done. I assumed the night managers did not care or think about who worked the next day. It bothered me to think that the morning employees were suffering because of careless employees and student managers from the night before.

I had never heard of CFS mentioning any problems or taking any corrective action; therefore, I wasn't sure whether they knew what was going on, or if they were ignoring it. I was speaking to a close friend, Mack, a student manager at the Den, and I mentioned the fact that the frequently unlocked door to the storage room was an easy exit through which I had seen different quantities of unpaid goods taken out. I told him about some specific instances and said that I believed that it happened rather frequently. Nothing was ever said to other employees about this, and the only corrective action was that the door was locked more often, yet the key to the lock was still available upon request to all employees during their shifts.

Another lack of strong corrective action I remembered was when an employee was caught pocketing

cash from the register. The student was neither suspended nor threatened with losing his job (nor was the event even mentioned). Instead, he was just told to stay away from the register. I felt that this weak punishment happened not because he was a good worker but because he worked so many hours and it would be difficult to find someone who would work all those hours and remain working for more than a few months. Although a customer reported the incident, I still felt that management should have taken more corrective action.

The attitudes of the student managers seemed to vary. I had noticed that one in particular, Bill, always got the job done. He made a list of each small duty that needed to be done, such as restocking, and he made sure the jobs were divided among the employees and finished before his shift was over. Bill also stared down employees who allowed thefts by their friends or who took freebies themselves; yet I had never heard of an employee being challenged verbally, nor had anyone ever been fired for these actions. My friend Mack was concerned about theft, or so I assumed, because he had taken some action about locking the doors, but he didn't really get after employees to work if they were slacking off.

I didn't think the rest of the student managers were good motivators. I noticed that they did little work themselves and did not show much control over the employees. The student managers allowed their friends to take food for free, thereby setting bad examples for the other workers, and allowed the employees to take what they wanted even when they were not working. I thought their attitudes were shared by most of the other employees: not caring about their jobs or working hard, as long as they got paid and their jobs were not threatened.

I had let the "thefts" continue without mention because I felt that no one else really cared and may even have frowned on me for trying to take action. Management thus far had not reported significant losses to the employees so as to encourage them to watch for theft and prevent it. Management did not threaten employees with job loss, nor did they provide employees with supervision. I felt it was not my place to report the theft to management, because I was just an employee and I would be overstepping the student managers. Also, I was unsure whether management would do anything about it anyway— maybe they did not care. I felt that talking to the student managers or other employees would be useless, because they were either abusing the rules themselves or clearly aware of what was going on and just ignored it. I felt that others may have frowned on me and made it uncomfortable for me to continue working there. This would be very difficult for me, because I wanted to become a student manager the next semester and did not want to create any waves that might have prevented me from doing so. I recognized the student manager position as a chance to gain some managerial and leadership skills, while at the same time adding a great plus to my résumé when I graduated. Besides, as a student manager, I would be in a better position to do something about all the problems at the Den that bothered me so much.

What could I do in the meantime to clear my conscience of the freebies, favors to friends, and employee snacks? What could I do without ruining my chances of becoming a student manager myself someday? I hated just keeping quiet, but I didn't want to make a fool of myself. I was really stuck.

Nucor Corporation in 2018: Contending with the Challenges of Low-Cost Foreign Imports and Launching Initiatives to Grow Sales and Market Share

Mc Graw Hill Education connect®

Arthur A. Thompson

The University of Alabama

Despite the headwinds of a 15.5 percent increase in foreign steel imports and mounting evidence that many of Nucor's foreign steel competitors received subsidies from their governments—in direct violation of prevailing trade regulations—to support their low-ball pricing in the U.S. steel markets, Nucor's sales and profitability improved in 2017 over 2016. During 2017, Nucor Corp., already the largest manufacturer of steel and steel products in North America and the 13th largest steel company in the world based on tons shipped, launched a series of strategic initiatives to further expand its production capacity and improve its cost competitiveness against rival products of steel products. Not only was Nucor Corp. regarded as a low-cost producer, but it also had a sterling reputation for being a global first-mover in implementing cost-effective steelmaking production methods and practices throughout its operations.

Heading into 2018, Nucor had 25 steel mills with the capability to produce a diverse assortment of steel shapes (steel bars, sheet steel, steel plate, and structural steel) and additional finished steel manufacturing facilities that made steel joists, steel decking, cold finish bars, steel buildings, steel mesh, steel grating, steel fasteners, and fabricated steel reinforcing products. The company's lineup of product offerings was the broadest of any steel producer serving steel users in North America. Nucor had 2017 revenues of $20.3 billion and net profits of $1.38 billion, the company's best performance since its 2008 pre-recession peak of $23.7 billion in revenues and $1.8 billion in net profits. During the 2009 to 2016 period, Nucor's performance was weak to mediocre, chiefly because of eroding market prices for many steel products and a sharp falloff in customer orders in several major product categories, both largely due to a surge in ultra-cheap imported steel products coming from a variety of foreign sources (but mainly China).

COMPANY BACKGROUND

Nucor began its journey from obscurity to a steel industry leader in the 1960s. Operating under the name of Nuclear Corporation of America in the 1950s and early 1960s, the company was a maker of nuclear instruments and electronics products. After suffering through several money-losing years and facing bankruptcy in 1964, Nuclear Corporation of America's board of directors opted for new leadership and appointed F. Kenneth Iverson as president and CEO. Shortly thereafter, Iverson concluded that the best way to put the company on sound footing was to exit the nuclear instrument and electronics business and rebuild the company around its profitable South Carolina-based Vulcraft subsidiary that was in the steel joist business—Iverson had been the head of Vulcraft prior to being named president. Iverson moved the company's headquarters from Phoenix, Arizona, to Charlotte, North Carolina, in 1966, and proceeded to expand the joist business with new operations in Texas and Alabama. Then, in 1968, top management decided to integrate backwards into steelmaking, partly because of the benefits of supplying its own steel requirements for producing steel joists and partly because Iverson saw opportunities to capitalize on newly emerging technologies to produce steel more cheaply. In 1972 the company adopted the name Nucor Corporation, and Iverson initiated a long-term strategy to grow Nucor into a major player in the U.S. steel industry.

By 1985 Nucor had become the seventh largest steel company in North America, with revenues of $758 million, six joist plants, and four state-of-the-art steel mills that used electric arc furnaces to produce new steel products from recycled scrap steel. Moreover, Nucor had gained a reputation as an excellently managed company, an accomplished low-cost producer, and one of the most competitively successful manufacturing companies in the country.[1] A series of articles in *The New Yorker* related how Nucor, a relatively small American steel company, had built an enterprise that led the whole world into a new era of making steel with recycled scrap steel. Network broadcaster NBC did a business documentary that used Nucor to make the point that American manufacturers could be successful in competing against low-cost foreign manufacturers.

Under Iverson's leadership, Nucor came to be known for its aggressive pursuit of innovation and technical excellence in producing steel, rigorous quality systems, strong emphasis on workforce productivity and job security for employees, cost-conscious corporate culture, and skills in achieving low costs per ton produced. The company had a very streamlined organizational structure, incentive-based compensation systems, and steel mills that were among the most modern and efficient in the United States. Iverson proved himself as a master in crafting and executing a low-cost provider strategy, and he made a point of practicing what he preached when it came to holding down costs throughout the company. The offices of executives and division general managers were simply furnished. There were no company planes and no company cars, and executives were not provided with company-paid country club memberships, reserved parking spaces, executive dining facilities, or other perks. To save money on his own business expenses and set an example for other Nucor managers, Iverson flew coach class and took the subway when he was in New York City.

When Iverson left the company in 1998 following disagreements with the board of directors, he was succeeded briefly by John Correnti and then Dave Aycock, both of whom had worked in various roles under Iverson for a number of years. In 2000, Daniel R. DiMicco, who had joined Nucor in 1982 and risen through the ranks to executive vice president, was named president and CEO. DiMicco was Nucor's Chairman and CEO through 2012. Like his predecessors, DiMicco continued to pursue Nucor's longstanding strategy to aggressively grow the company's production capacity and product offerings via both acquisition and new plant construction; tons sold rose from 11.2 million in 2000 to 25.2 million in 2008. Then the unexpected financial crisis in the fourth quarter of 2008 and the subsequent economic fallout caused tons sold in 2009 to plunge to 17.6 million tons and revenues to nosedive from $23.7 billion in 2008 to $11.2 billion in 2009.

Even though the steel industry remained in the doldrums until he retired in 2012, DiMicco was undeterred by the depressed market demand for steel and proceeded to expand Nucor's production capabilities and range of product offerings. It was his strong belief that Nucor should be opportunistic in initiating actions to strengthen its competitive position despite slack market demand for steel because doing so put the company in even better position to significantly boost its financial performance when market demand for steel products grew stronger. DiMicco expressed his thinking thusly:

> Nucor uses each economic downturn as an opportunity to grow stronger. We use the good times to prepare for the bad, and we use the bad times to prepare for the good. Emerging from downturns stronger than we enter them is how we build long-term value for our stockholders. We get stronger because our team is focused on continual improvement and because our financial strength allows us to invest in attractive growth opportunities throughout the economic cycle.[2]

During DiMicco's 12-year tenure, Nucor completed more than 50 acquisitions, expanding Nucor's operations from 18 locations to more than 200, boosting revenues from $4.8 billion in 2000 to $19.4 billion at the end of 2012, and transforming Nucor into the undisputed leader in providing steel products to North American buyers. When DiMicco retired at the end of 2012, he was succeeded by John J. Ferriola, who had served as Nucor's President and COO since 2011. Ferriola immediately embraced Nucor's strategy of investing in down markets to better position Nucor for success when the economy strengthened and market demand for steel products became more robust.

Going into 2018, Nucor was the biggest, most cost-efficient, and most diversified steel producer in North America. It had the capacity to produce 29 million tons of steel annually at its 25 steel mills. All of its steel mills were among the most modern and efficient mills in the United States. The breadth of Nucor's product line in steel mill products and finished steel products was unmatched; it competed in 12 distinct product categories. No other producer of steel products in North America competed in more than 6 of the 12 product categories in which Nucor competed.[3] Moreover, Nucor was the North American market leader in 9 of the 12 product categories in which it had a market presence—steel bars, structural steel, steel reinforcing bars, steel joists, steel deck, cold-finished bar steel, metal buildings, steel pilings distribution, and rebar fabrication and distribution.[4] In two other categories in North America where Nucor competed, it ranked #2 in sales of plate steel and #3 in sales of sheet steel.

With the exception of three quarters in 2009, one quarter in 2010, and the fourth quarter of 2015, Nucor earned a profit in every quarter of every year from 1966 through 2017—a truly remarkable accomplishment in a mature and cyclical business where it was common for industry members to post losses when demand for steel sagged. As of February 2018, Nucor had paid a dividend for 179 consecutive quarters and had raised the base dividend it paid to stockholders for 45 consecutive years (every year since 1973 when the company first began paying cash dividends). In years when earnings and cash flows permitted, Nucor had paid a supplemental year-end dividend in addition to the base quarterly dividend. Exhibit 1 provides highlights of Nucor's growth and performance since 1970. Exhibit 2 shows Nucor's sales by product category for 1990 to 2017. Exhibit 3 contains a summary of Nucor's financial and operating performance from 2013 to 2017.

NUCOR'S STRATEGY TO BECOME THE BIGGEST AND MOST DIVERSIFIED STEEL PRODUCER IN NORTH AMERICA, 1967–2016

In its nearly 50-year march to become North America's biggest and most diversified steel producer, Nucor relentlessly expanded its production capabilities to include a wider range of steel shapes and more categories of finished steel products. However, most every steel product that Nucor produced was viewed by buyers as a "commodity." Indeed, the most competitively relevant feature of the various steel shapes and finished steel products made by the world's different producers was that, for any given steel item, there were very few, if any, differences in the products of rival steel producers. While some steelmakers had plants where production quality was sometimes inconsistent or on occasions failed to meet customer-specified metallurgical characteristics, most steel plants turned out products of comparable metallurgical quality—one producer's reinforcing bar was essentially the same as another producer's reinforcing bar, a particular type and grade of sheet steel made at one plant was essentially identical to the same type and grade of sheet steel made at another plant.

The commodity nature of steel products meant that steel buyers typically shopped the market for the best price, awarding their business to whichever seller offered the best deal. The ease with which buyers could switch their orders from one supplier to another forced steel producers to be very price competitive. In virtually all instances, the going market price of each particular steel product was in constant flux, rising or falling in response to shifting market circumstances (or shifts in the terms that particular buyers or sellers were willing to accept). As a consequence, spot market prices for commodity steel products bounced around on a weekly or even daily basis. Because competition among rival steel producers was so strongly focused on price, it was incumbent on all industry participants to be cost competitive and operate their production facilities as efficiently as they could.

Nucor's success over the years stemmed largely from its across-the-board prowess in cost-efficient operations for all the product categories in which

EXHIBIT 1   Nucor's Growing Presence in the Market for Steel, 1970–2017

Year	Total Tons Sold to Outside Customers	Average Price per Ton	Net Sales (in millions)	Earnings before Income Taxes (in millions)	Pretax Earnings per Ton	Net Earnings (in millions) Attributable to Nucor Shareholders
1970	207,000	$245	$50.8	$2.2	$10	$1.1
1975	387,000	314	121.5	11.7	30	7.6
1980	1,159,000	416	482.4	76.1	66	45.1
1985	1,902,000	399	758.5	106.2	56	58.5
1990	3,648,000	406	1,481.6	111.2	35	75.1
1995	7,943,000	436	3,462.0	432.3	62	274.5
2000	11,189,000	425	4,756.5	478.3	48	310.9
2001	12,237,000	354	4,333.7	179.4	16	113.0
2002	13,442,000	357	4,801.7	227.0	19	162.1
2003	17,473,000	359	6,265.8	70.0	4	62.8
2004	19,109,000	595	11,376.8	1,725.9	96	1,121.5
2005	20,465,000	621	12,701.0	2,027.1	104	1,310.3
2006	22,118,000	667	14,751.3	2,692.4	129	1,757.7
2007	22,940,000	723	16,593.0	2,253.3	104	1,471.9
2008	25,187,000	940	23,663.3	2,790.5	116	1,831.0
2009	17,576,000	637	11,190.3	(470.4)	(28)	(293.6)
2010	22,019,000	720	15,844.6	194.9	9	134.1
2011	23,044,000	869	20,023.6	1,169.9	53	778.2
2012	23,092,000	841	19,429.3	697.0;	27	409.5
2013	23,730,000	803	19,052.0	808.6	31	499.4
2014	25,413,000	830	21,105.1	1,147.3	42	679.3
2015	22,680,000	725	16,439.3	241.9	6	80.7
2016	24,309,000	667	16,208.1	1,298.6	50	796.3
2017	26,492,000	764	20,252.4	1,750.0	65	1,318.7

Note: In 2016, Nucor changed its method of accounting for valuing certain inventories from the last-in, first-out (LIFO) method to the first-in, first out (FIFO) method. The information in this table for the years 2012 to 2017 reflects this change in accounting principle.

Source: Company records posted at **www.nucor.com** (accessed February 1, 2018); Nucor Annual Report for 2016, p. 47; Nucor Annual Report for 2017, p. 11–15.

EXHIBIT 2   Nucor's Sales of Steel Mill and Finished Steel Products to Outside Customers, by Product Category, 1990–2017

| | Tons Sold to Outside Customers (in thousands) | | | | | | | | | |
| | Steel Mill Products | | | | | Finished Steel Products | | | | |
Year	Sheet Steel (2018 capacity of ~12.1 million tons)	Steel Bars (2018 capacity of ~8.5 million tons)	Structural Steel (2018 capacity of ~3.25 million tons)	Steel Plate (2018 capacity of ~2.8 million tons)	Total (2018 capacity of ~27 million tons)*	Steel Joists (2018 capacity of ~745,000 tons)	Steel Deck (2018 capacity of ~545,000 tons)	Cold Finished Steel (2018 capacity of ~1.1 million tons)	Rebar Fabrication (2018 capacity of ~1.75 million tons) and Other Products**	Total Tons Sold
2017	9,311	5,838	2,303	2,249	20,618	472	457	487	4,458	26,492
2016	9,119	5,304	2,319	2,023	18,846	445	442	426	4,150	24,309
2015	8,080	4,790	2,231	1,905	17,006	427	401	449	4,397	22,680
2014	8,153	5,526	2,560	2,442	18,681	421	396	504	5,411	25,413
2013	7,491	5,184	2,695	2,363	17,733	342	334	474	4,847	23,730
2012	7,622	5,078	2,505	2,268	17,473	291	308	492	4,528	23,092
2011	7,500	4,680	2,338	2,278	16,796	288	312	494	5,154	23,044
2010	7,434	4,019	2,139	2,229	15,821	276	306	462	5,154	22,019
2009	5,212	3,629	1,626	1,608	12,075	264	310	330	4,596	17,576
2008	7,505	5,266	2,934	2,480	18,185	485	498	485	4,534	25,187
2007	8,266	6,287	3,154	2,528	20,235	542	478	449	1,236	22,940
2006	8,495	6,513	3,209	2,432	20,649	570	398	327	174	22,118
2005	8,026	5,983	2,866	2,145	19,020	554	380	342	169	20,465
2000	4,456	2,209	3,094	20	9,779	613	353	250	194	11,189
1995	2,994	1,799	1,952	—	6,745	552	234	234	178	7,943
1990	420	1,382	1,002	—	2,804	443	134	163	104	3,648

*In 2016 and 2017, the total in this column includes production of tubular steel products, a steel mill products category that the company entered in the fourth quarter of 2016; tubular products production was 917,000 tons in 2017 and 82,000 tons in 2016.

**Other products include steel fasteners (steel screws, nuts, bolts, washers, and bolt assemblies), steel mesh, steel grates, metal building systems, light gauge steel framing, scrap metal, and tubular steel products.

Source: Company records posted at **www.nucor.com** (accessed February 1, 2018).

it elected to compete. Nucor's top executives were very disciplined in executing Nucor's strategy to broaden the company's product offerings; no moves to enter new steel product categories were made unless management was confident that the company had the resources and capabilities need to operate the accompanying production facilities efficiently enough to be cost competitive.

EXHIBIT 3   Five-Year Financial and Operating Summary, Nucor Corporation, 2013–2017 ($ in millions, except per share data and sales per employee)

	2017	2016	2015	2014	2013
FOR THE YEAR					
Net sales	$20,252.4	$16,208.1	$16,439.3	$21,105.1	$19,052.0
Costs, expenses and other:					
Cost of products sold	17,683.0	14,182.2	15,325.4	19,255.9	17,624.0
Marketing, administrative and other expenses	687.5	596.8	459.0	520.8	467.9
Equity in (earnings) losses of minority-owned enterprises	(41.7)	(38.8)	(5.3)	(13.5)	(9.3)
Impairment and losses on assets	—	—	244.8	25.4	14.0
Interest expense, net	173.6	169.2	173.5	169.3	146.9
Total	18,502.4	14,909.5	16,197.4	19,957.9	18,243.5
Earnings before income taxes and non-controlling interests	1,750.0	1,298.7	241.9	1,147.3	808.6
Provision for income taxes	369.4	398.2	48.8	368.7	214.9
Net earnings (loss)	1,380.6	900.4	193.0	815.8	593.7
Less earnings attributable to the minority interest partners of Nucor's joint ventures*	61.9	104.1	112.3	101.8	94.3
Net earnings (loss) attributable to Nucor stockholders	$1,318.7	$796.3	$80.7	$679.3	$499.4
Net earnings (loss) per share:					
Basic	$4.11	$2.48	$0.25	$2.22	$1.52
Diluted	4.10	2.48	0.25	2.22	1.52
Dividends declared per share	$1.5125	$1.5025	$1.4925	$1.4825	$1.4725
Percentage of net earnings to net sales	6.5%	4.9%	0.5%	3.2%	2.6%
Return on average stockholders' equity	17.2%	10.4%	1.0%	8.4%	6.2%
Capital expenditures	$448.6	$617.7	$364.8	$568.9	$1,230.4
Acquisitions (net of cash acquired)	544.0	474.8	19.1	768.6	—
Depreciation	635.8	613.2	625.8	652.0	535.9
Sales per employee (000s)	820	690	690	921	859
AT YEAR END					
Cash, cash equivalents, and short-term investments	$999.1	$2,046.0	$2,039.5	$1,124.1	$1,511.5
Current assets	6,824.4	6,506.4	5,854.4	6,808.8	6,814.2

(Continued)

EXHIBIT 3   *(Continued)*

	2017	2016	2015	2014	2013
Current liabilities	2,824.8	2,390.0	1,385.2	2,097.8	1,960.2
Working capital	3,999.6	4,116.4	4,469.2	4,711.0	4,854.0
Cash provided by operating activities	1,051.3	1,737.5	2,157.0	1,342.9	1,077.9
Current ratio	2.4	2.72	4.2	3.1	3.3
Property, plant and equipment	$5,093.2	$5.078.7	$4,891.2	$5,287.6	$4,917.0
Total assets	15,841.3	15,223.5	14,327.0	15,956.5	15,578.1
Long-term debt (including current maturities)	3,742.2	4,339.1	4,337.1	4,350.6	4,350.9
Percentage of long-term debt to total capital**	29.2%	34.5%	35.6%	36.0%	35.6%
Stockholders' equity	8,739.0	7,879.9	7,416.9	7,772.5	7,645.8
Shares outstanding (000s)	317,962	318,737	317,962	319,033	318,328
Employees	25,100	23,900	23,700	23,600	22,300

*The principal joint venture responsible for these earnings is the Nucor-Yamato Steel Company, of which Nucor owns 51 percent. This joint venture operates a structural steel mill in Blytheville, Arkansas, and it is the largest producer of structural steel beams in the Western Hemisphere.

**Total capital is defined as stockholders' equity plus long-term debt.

Note: In 2016, Nucor changed its method of accounting for valuing certain inventories from the last-in, first-out (LIFO) method to the first-in, first out (FIFO) method. The information in this table for the years 2013-2015 has been backward adjusted to reflect this change in accounting principle.

Source: Nucor's 2016 10-K, p. 32 and Nucor's 2017 10-K, p. 43.

Finished Steel Products

Nucor's first venture into steel in the late 1960s, via its Vulcraft division, was principally one of fabricating steel joists and joist girders from steel that was purchased from various steelmakers. Vulcraft expanded into the fabrication of steel decking in 1977. The division expanded its operations over the years and, as of 2018, Nucor's Vulcraft division was the largest producer and leading innovator of open-web steel joists, joist girders, and steel deck in the United States. It had seven plants with annual capacity of 745,000 tons that made steel joists and joist girders and 10 plants with 545,000 tons of capacity that made steel deck; typically, about 85 percent of the steel needed to make these products was supplied by various Nucor steelmaking plants. Vulcraft's joist, girder, and decking products were used mainly for roof and floor support systems in retail stores, shopping centers, warehouses, manufacturing facilities, schools, churches, hospitals, and, to a lesser extent, multi-story buildings and apartments. Customers for these products were principally nonresidential construction contractors.

In 1979, Nucor began fabricating cold finished steel products. These consisted mainly of cold drawn and turned, ground, and polished steel bars or rods of various shapes—rounds, hexagons, flats, channels, and squares—made from carbon, alloy, and leaded steels based on customer specifications or end-use requirements. Cold finished steel products were used in tens of thousands of products, including anchor bolts, hydraulic cylinders, farm machinery, air conditioner compressors, electric motors, motor vehicles, appliances, and lawn mowers. Nucor sold cold finish steel directly to large-quantity users in the automotive, farm machinery, hydraulic, appliance, and electric motor industries and to steel service centers that in turn supplied manufacturers needing only relatively small quantities. In 2017, Nucor Cold Finish was the largest producer of cold finished bar products in North America and had facilities in Missouri, Nebraska, South Carolina, Utah, Wisconsin, Ohio, Georgia, and Ontario, Canada with a capacity of about 1.1 million tons per year. It obtained most of its steel from Nucor's mills that made steel bar. This factor, along with the fact that all of Nucor's cold finished facilities employed the latest technology and were among the most modern in the world, resulted in Nucor Cold Finish having a highly competitive cost structure. It maintained sufficient inventories of cold finish products to fulfill anticipated orders. Sales of cold finished steel products were 487,000 tons in 2017, up from 426,000 tons in 2016.

Nucor produced metal buildings and components throughout the United States under several brands: Nucor Building Systems, American Buildings Company, Kirby Building Systems, and CBC Steel Buildings. In 2018, the Nucor Buildings Group had nine metal buildings plants with an annual capacity of approximately 395,000 tons. Nucor's Buildings Group began operations in 1987 and currently had the capability to supply customers with buildings ranging from less than 1,000 square feet to more than 1,000,000 square feet. Complete metal building packages could be customized and combined with other materials such as glass, wood, and masonry to produce a cost-effective, aesthetically pleasing building built to a customer's particular requirements. The buildings were sold primarily through an independent builder distribution network. The primary markets served were commercial, industrial, and institutional buildings, including distribution centers, automobile dealerships, retail centers, schools, warehouses, and manufacturing facilities. Nucor's Buildings Group obtained a significant portion of its steel requirements from the Nucor bar and sheet mills. Sales were 294,000 tons in 2017, down from 304,000 tons in 2016.

Another Nucor division produced steel mesh, grates, and fasteners. Various steel mesh products were made at two facilities in the United States and one in Canada that had combined annual production capacity of about 128,000 tons. Steel and aluminum bar grating, safety grating, and expanded metal products were produced at several North American locations that had combined annual production capacity of 103,000 tons. Nucor Fastener, located in Indiana, began operations in 1986 with the construction of a $25 million plant. At the time, imported steel fasteners accounted for 90 percent of the U.S. market because U.S. manufacturers were not competitive on cost and price. Nucor built a second fastener plant in 1995, giving it the capacity to supply about 20 percent of the U.S. market for steel fasteners. Currently, these two facilities had annual capacity of over 75,000 tons and produced carbon and alloy steel hex head cap screws, hex bolts, structural bolts, nuts and washers, finished hex nuts, and custom-engineered fasteners that were used for automotive, machine tool, farm implement, construction, military, and various other applications. Nucor Fastener obtained much of the steel it needed from Nucor's mills that made steel bar.

Beginning in 2007, Nucor—through its newly-acquired Harris Steel subsidiary—began fabricating, installing, and distributing steel reinforcing bars (rebar) for highways, bridges, schools, hospitals, airports, stadiums, office buildings, high-rise residential complexes, and other structures where steel reinforcing was essential to concrete construction. Harris Steel had over 70 fabrication facilities in the United States and Canada, with each facility serving the surrounding local market. Since acquiring Harris Steel, Nucor had more than doubled its rebar fabrication capacity to over 1,700,000 tons annually. Total fabricated rebar sales in 2015 were 1,190,000 tons, up from 1,185,000 tons in 2014. Much of the steel used in making fabricated rebar products was obtained from Nucor steel plants that made steel bar. Fabricated reinforcing products were sold only on a contract bid basis.

Steel Mill Products

Nucor entered the market for steel mill products in 1968, when the decision was made to build a facility in Darlington, South Carolina, to manufacture steel bars. The Darlington mill was one of the first steel-making plants of major size in the United States to use electric arc furnace technology to melt scrap steel and cast molten metal into various shapes. Electric arc furnace technology was particularly appealing to

Nucor because the labor and capital requirements to melt steel scrap and produce crude steel were far lower than those at conventional integrated steel mills where raw steel was produced using coke ovens, basic oxygen blast furnaces, ingot casters, and multiple types of finishing facilities to make crude steel from iron ore, coke, limestone, oxygen, scrap steel, and other ingredients. By 1981, Nucor had four steel mills making carbon and alloy steels in bars, angles, and light structural shapes; since then, Nucor had undertaken extensive capital projects to keep these facilities modernized and globally competitive. During 2000 and 2011, Nucor aggressively expanded its market presence in steel bars and by 2012 had 13 bar mills located across the United States that produced concrete reinforcing bars, hot-rolled bars, rods, light shapes, structural angles, channels and guard rail in carbon and alloy steels; in 2017, these 13 plants had total annual capacity of approximately 8.5 million tons. Four of the 13 mills made hot-rolled special quality bar manufactured to exacting specifications. The products of the Nucor's bar mills had wide usage and were sold primarily to customers in the agricultural, automotive, construction, energy, furniture, machinery, metal building, railroad, recreational equipment, shipbuilding, heavy truck, and trailer industries.

Expansion into Sheet Steel   In the late 1980s, Nucor entered into the production of sheet steel at a newly-constructed plant in Crawfordsville, Indiana. Flat-rolled sheet steel was used in the production of motor vehicles, appliances, steel pipe and tubes, and other durable goods. The Crawfordsville plant was the first in the world to employ a revolutionary thin slab casting process that substantially reduced the capital investment and costs to produce flat-rolled sheet steel. Thin-slab casting machines had a funnel-shaped mold to squeeze molten steel down to a thickness of 1.5 to 2.0 inches, compared to the typically 8 to 10-inch thick slabs produced by conventional casters. It was much cheaper to then build and operate facilities to roll thin-gauge sheet steel from 1.5 to 2-inch thick slabs than from 8 to 10-inch thick slabs. When the Crawfordsville plant first opened in 1989, it was said to have costs $50 to $75 per ton below the costs of traditional sheet steel plants, a highly significant cost advantage in a commodity market where the going price at the time was $400 per ton. *Forbes* magazine described Nucor's pioneering use of thin slab casting as the most substantial, technological, industrial

innovation in the past 50 years.[5] By 1996 two additional sheet steel mills that employed thin slab casting technology were constructed and a fourth mill was acquired in 2002. Nucor also operated two Castrip sheet production facilities, one built in 2002 at the Crawfordsville plant and a second built in Arkansas in 2009; these facilities used the breakthrough strip casting technology that involved the direct casting of molten steel into final shape and thickness without further hot or cold rolling. The process allowed for lower capital investment, reduced energy consumption, smaller scale plants, and improved environmental impact (because of significantly lower emissions). A fifth sheet mill with annual capacity of 1.8 million tons, strategically located on the Ohio River in Kentucky, was acquired in 2014, giving Nucor a total flat-rolled capacity of 12.1 million tons.

In May 2017, Nucor announced that it would invest approximately $176 million to build a 72-inch hot band galvanizing and pickling line at its sheet mill in Ghent, Kentucky. The new galvanizing line, expected to be operational in the first half of 2019, would be the widest hot-rolled galvanizing line in North America and enable Nucor to enter additional segments of the automotive market.

Entry into Structural Steel Products   Also in the late 1980s, Nucor added wide-flange steel beams, pilings, and heavy structural steel products to its lineup of product offerings. Structural steel products were used in buildings, bridges, overpasses, and similar such projects where strong weight-bearing support was needed. Customers included construction companies, steel fabricators, manufacturers, and steel service centers. To gain entry to the structural steel segment, in 1988 Nucor entered into a joint venture with Yamato-Kogyo, one of Japan's major producers of wide-flange beams, to build a new structural steel mill in Arkansas; a second mill was built on the same site in the 1990s that made the Nucor-Yamato venture in Arkansas the largest structural beam facility in the Western Hemisphere. In 1999, Nucor started operations at a third structural steel mill in South Carolina. The mills in Arkansas and South Carolina both used a special continuous casting method that was quite cost effective. Going into 2018, Nucor had the capacity to make 3.25 million tons of structural steel products annually.

Entry into the Market for Steel Plate   Starting in 2000, Nucor began producing steel plate of various thicknesses and lengths that was sold to manufacturers of heavy equipment, ships, barges, bridges, rail cars, refinery tanks, pressure vessels, pipe and tube, wind towers, and similar products. Steel plate was made at three mills in Alabama, North Carolina, and Texas that had combined capacity of about 2.9 million tons. From 2011 to 2013, Nucor greatly expanded its plate product capabilities by constructing a 125,000-ton heat-treating facility and a 120,000-ton normalizing line at its North Carolina plate mill. These investments yielded two big strategic benefits: (1) enabling the North Carolina mill to produce higher-margin plate products sold to companies making pressure vessels, tank cars, tubular structures for offshore oil rigs, and naval and commercial ships and (2) reducing the mill's exposure to competition from foreign producers of steel plate who lacked the capability to match the features of the steel plate Nucor produced for these end-use customers.

The Cost Efficiency of Nucor's Steel Mills All of Nucor's steel mills used electric arc furnaces, whereby scrap steel and other metals were melted and the molten metal then poured into continuous casting systems. Sophisticated rolling mills converted the billets, blooms, and slabs produced by various casting equipment into rebar, angles, rounds, channels, flats, sheet, beams, plate, and other finished steel products. Nucor's steel mill operations were highly automated, typically requiring fewer operating employees per ton produced than the mills of rival companies. High worker productivity at all Nucor steel mills resulted in labor costs roughly 50 percent lower than the labor costs at the integrated mills of companies using union labor and conventional blast furnace technology. Nucor's value chain (anchored in using electric arc furnace technology to recycle scrap steel) involved far fewer production steps, far less capital investment, and considerably less labor than the value chains of companies with integrated steel mills that made crude steel from iron ore.

However, despite Nucor's demonstrated skills in operating steel mills at low costs per ton, it had been stymied throughout the 2010 to 2015 period in its quest to operate its steel mills as cost efficiently as possible. Since the Great Recession of 2008 and 2009, the combination of an anemic economic recovery, depressed market demand for steel products, industrywide overcapacity, and fierce competition from foreign imports in certain product categories had forced

Nucor to operate its steel mills well below full capacity. *Whereas in the first three quarters of 2008, Nucor's steel mills operated at an average of 91 percent of full capacity,* the average capacity utilization rates at Nucor's steel mills were 54 percent in 2009, 70 percent in 2010, 74 percent in 2011, 75 percent in 2012, 76 percent in 2013, 78 percent in 2014, and 68 percent in 2015 (including tons shipped to outside customers and tons shipped to Nucor facilities making finished steel products). Likewise, subpar average capacity utilization rates at Nucor's facilities for producing finished steel products—54 percent in 2010, 57 percent in 2011, 58 percent in 2012, 61 percent in 2013, 66 percent in 2014, and 61 percent in 2015—had impaired Nucor's ability to keep overall production costs for finished steel products as low as they would otherwise have been at higher levels of capacity utilization. However, sales increases in many product categories in 2016 and 2017 had boosted overall capacity utilization to a modest degree (see Exhibit 2).

Pricing and Sales

From 2012 to 2017, 14 to 17 percent of the steel shipped from Nucor's steel mills went to supply the steel needs of the company's joist, deck, rebar fabrication, fastener, metal buildings, and cold finish operations. But three of Nucor's acquisitions in 2016 and 2017, all makers of finished steel products and tubing, began sourcing their sheet steel requirements from Nucor's steel mills, driving the percentage of steel mill shipments to internal customers to 20 percent in early 2018. The other 80 percent of the company's steel mill shipments were to external customers who placed orders monthly based on their immediate upcoming needs; Nucor's pricing strategy was to charge external customers the going spot price on the day an order was placed. Shifting market demand-supply conditions and spot market prices caused Nucor's average sales prices per ton to fluctuate from quarter to quarter, sometimes by considerable amounts—see Exhibit 4. It was Nucor's practice to quote the same payment terms to all external customers and for these customers to pay all shipping charges.

Nucor marketed the output of its steel mills and steel products facilities mainly through an in-house sales force; there were salespeople located at most every Nucor production facility. Going into 2018, approximately 65 percent of Nucor's sheet steel sales were to contract customers (versus 30 percent in

EXHIBIT 4 Nucor's Average Quarterly Sales Prices for Steel Products, by Product Category, 2013-2017

	Average Sales Prices per Ton						
Period	Sheet Steel	Tubular Products	Steel Bars	Structural Steel	Steel Plate	All Steel Mill Products	All Finished Steel Products*
2014							
Qtr 1	$744		$737	$ 941	$816	$783	$1,348
Qtr 2	737		732	1,039	837	789	1,367
Qtr 3	750		738	1,011	838	793	1,369
Qtr 4	712		724	1,063	875	776	1,432
2015							
Qtr 1	663		698	996	805	732	1,404
Qtr 2	560		623	991	691	646	1,380
Qtr 3	552		625	926	648	635	1,351
Qtr 4	508		558	923	588	588	1,367
2016							
Qtr 1	471		505	870	545	538	1,271
Qtr 2	550		561	845	604	593	1,285
Qtr 3	666		567	865	661	664	1,299
Qtr 4	603	$ 737	544	837	584	614	1,337
2017							
Qtr 1	661	955	600	821	703	682	1,288
Qtr 2	709	1,005	605	863	746	714	1,337
Qtr 3	695	1,009	624	877	749	715	1,361
Qtr 4	691	1,031	607	883	727	705	1,386

*An average of the steel prices for steel deck, steel joists and girders, steel buildings, cold finished steel products, steel mesh, fasteners, fabricated rebar, and other finished steel products.

Source: Company records posted at www.nucor.com (accessed June 5, 2018).

2009); these contracts for sheet steel were usually for periods of 6 to 12 months, were non-cancellable, and permitted price adjustments to reflect changes in the market pricing for steel and/or raw material costs at the time of shipment. The other 35 percent of Nucor's sheet steel shipments and virtually all of the company's shipments of plate, structural, and bar steel were at the prevailing spot market price—customers not purchasing sheet steel rarely ever wanted to enter

into a contract sales agreement. Nucor's steel mills maintained inventory levels deemed adequate to fill the expected incoming orders from customers. The average prices Nucor received for its various steel mill and finished steel products often varied significantly from quarter to quarter, as shown in Exhibit 4.

Nucor sold steel joists and joist girders, and steel deck on the basis of firm, fixed-price contracts that, in most cases, were won in competitive bidding against rival suppliers. Longer-term supply contracts for these items that were sometimes negotiated with customers contained clauses permitting price adjustments to reflect changes in prevailing raw materials costs. Steel joists, girders, and deck were manufactured to customers' specifications and shipped immediately; Nucor's plants did not maintain inventories of steel joists, girders, or steel deck. Nucor also sold fabricated reinforcing products only on a construction contract bid basis. However, cold finished steel, steel fasteners, steel grating, wire, and wire mesh were all manufactured in standard sizes, with each facility maintaining sufficient inventories of its products to fill anticipated orders; most all sales of these items were made at the prevailing spot price. The average prices Nucor received for its various finished steel products are shown in the last column of Exhibit 4.

NUCOR'S STRATEGY TO GROW AND STRENGTHEN ITS BUSINESS AND COMPETITIVE CAPABILITIES

Starting in 2000, Nucor embarked on a five-part growth strategy that involved new acquisitions, new plant construction, continued plant upgrades and cost reduction efforts, international growth through joint ventures, and greater control over raw materials costs.

Strategic Acquisitions

Beginning in the late 1990s, Nucor management concluded that growth-minded companies like Nucor might well be better off purchasing existing plant capacity rather than building new capacity, provided the acquired plants could be bought at bargain prices, economically retrofitted with new equipment if need be, and then operated at costs comparable to (or even below) those of newly constructed state-of-the-art plants. At the time, the steel industry worldwide had far more production capacity than was needed to meet market demand, forcing many companies to operate in the red. Nucor had not made any acquisitions since about 1990, and a team of five people was assembled in 1998 to explore acquisition possibilities that would strengthen Nucor's customer base, geographic coverage, and lineup of product offerings.

For almost three years, no acquisitions were made. But then the economic recession that hit Asia and Europe in the late 1990s reached the United States in full force in 2000 and 2001. The September 11, 2001 terrorist attacks further weakened steel purchases by such major steel-consuming industries as construction, automobiles, and farm equipment. Many steel companies in the United States and other parts of the world were operating in the red. Market conditions in the United States were particularly grim. Between October 2000 and October 2001, 29 steel companies in the United States, including Bethlehem Steel Corp. and LTV Corp., the nation's third and fourth largest steel producers respectively, filed for bankruptcy protection. Bankrupt steel companies accounted for about 25 percent of U.S. capacity. *The Economist* noted that of the 14 steel companies tracked by Standard & Poor's, only Nucor was indisputably healthy. Some experts believed that close to half of the U.S. steel industry's production capacity might be forced to close before conditions improved; about 47,000 jobs in the U.S. steel industry had vanished since 1997.

One of the principal reasons for the distressed market conditions in the United States was a surge in imports of low-priced steel from foreign countries. Outside the United States, weak demand and a glut of capacity had driven commodity steel prices to 20-year lows in 1998. Globally, the industry had about 1 billion tons of annual capacity, but puny demand had kept production levels in the 750 to 800 million tons per year range from 1998 to 2000. A number of foreign steel producers, anxious to keep their mills running and finding few good market opportunities elsewhere, began selling steel in the U.S. market at cut-rate prices from 1997 to 1999. Nucor and other U.S. companies reduced prices to better compete and several filed unfair trade complaints against foreign steelmakers. The U.S. Department of Commerce concluded in March 1999 that steel companies in six countries (Canada, South Korea, Taiwan, Italy, Belgium, and South Africa) had illegally dumped stainless steel in the United States, and the governments of Belgium, Italy, and South Africa further facilitated the dumping by giving their steel producers unfair subsidies that at least partially made up for the revenue losses of selling at below-market prices. Congress and the Clinton Administration opted to not impose tariffs or quotas on imported steel, which helped precipitate the number of bankruptcy filings. However, the Bush Administration was more receptive to protecting the U.S. steel industry from the dumping practices of foreign steel companies. In October 2001, the U.S. International Trade Commission (ITC) ruled that increased steel imports of semi-finished steel, plate, hot-rolled sheet, strip and coils, cold-rolled sheet and strip, and corrosion-resistant and coated sheet and strip were a substantial cause of serious injury, or threat of serious injury, to the U.S. industry. In March 2002, the Bush Administration imposed tariffs of up to 30 percent on imports of selected steel products to help provide relief from Asian and European companies dumping steel in the United States at ultra-low prices.

Even though market conditions were tough for Nucor, management concluded that oversupplied steel industry conditions and the number of beleaguered U.S. companies made it attractive to expand Nucor's production capacity via acquisition. Starting in 2001 and continuing through 2017, the company proceeded to make a series of strategic acquisitions to strengthen Nucor's competitiveness, selectively expand its product offerings improve its ability to serve customers in particular geographic locations, and boost the company's financial performance in times when market demand for steel was strong enough to boost prices to more profitable levels:

- In 2001, Nucor paid $115 million to acquire substantially all of the assets of Auburn Steel Company's 400,000-ton steel bar facility in Auburn, New York. This acquisition gave Nucor expanded market presence in the Northeast and was seen as a good source of supply for a new Vulcraft joist plant being constructed in Chemung, New York.
- In November 2001, Nucor acquired ITEC Steel Inc. for a purchase price of $9 million. ITEC Steel had annual revenues of $10 million and produced load-bearing light gauge steel framing for the residential and commercial market at facilities in Texas and Georgia. Nucor was impressed with ITEC's dedication to continuous improvement and intended to grow ITEC's business via geographic and product line expansion.
- In July 2002, Nucor paid $120 million to purchase Trico Steel Company, which had a 2.2 million ton sheet steel mill in Decatur, Alabama. Trico Steel was a joint venture of LTV (which owned a 50 percent interest), and two leading international steel companies—Sumitomo Metal Industries and British Steel. The joint venture partners had built the mill in 1997 at a cost of $465 million,

but Trico was in Chapter 11 bankruptcy proceedings at the time of the acquisition and the mill was shut down. The Trico mill's capability to make thin sheet steel with a superior surface quality added competitive strength to Nucor's strategy to gain sales and market share in the flat-rolled sheet segment. In October 2002, Nucor restarted operations at the Decatur mill and began shipping products to customers.

- In December 2002, Nucor paid $615 million to purchase substantially all of the assets of Birmingham Steel Corporation, which included four bar mills in Alabama, Illinois, Washington, and Mississippi. The four plants had capacity of approximately 2 million tons annually. Top executives believed the Birmingham Steel acquisition would broaden Nucor's customer base and build profitable market share in bar steel products.
- In August 2004, Nucor acquired a cold rolling mill in Decatur, Alabama, from Worthington Industries for $80 million. This one million-ton mill, which opened in 1998, was located adjacent to the previously-acquired Trico mill and gave Nucor added ability to service the needs of sheet steel buyers located in the southeastern United States.
- In June 2004, Nucor paid a cash price of $80 million to acquire a plate mill owned by Britain-based Corus Steel located in Tuscaloosa, Alabama. The Tuscaloosa mill, which currently had capacity of 700,000 tons that Nucor management believed was expandable to one million tons, was the first U.S. mill to employ a special technology that enabled high quality wide steel plate to be produced from coiled steel plate. The mill produced coiled steel plate and plate products that were cut to customer-specified lengths. Nucor intended to offer these niche products to its commodity plate and coiled sheet customers.
- In February 2005, Nucor completed the purchase of Fort Howard Steel's operations in Oak Creek, Wisconsin, that produced cold finished bars in size ranges up to 6-inch rounds and had approximately 140,000 tons of annual capacity.
- In June 2005, Nucor purchased Marion Steel Company located in Marion, Ohio, for a cash price of $110 million. Marion operated a bar mill with annual capacity of about 400,000 tons; the Marion location was within close proximity to 60 percent of the steel consumption in the United States.

- In May 2006, Nucor acquired Connecticut Steel Corporation for $43 million in cash. Connecticut Steel's bar products mill in Wallingford had annual capacity to make 300,000 tons of wire rod and rebar and approximately 85,000 tons of wire mesh fabrication and structural mesh fabrication, products that complemented Nucor's present lineup of steel bar products provided to construction customers.

- In late 2006, Nucor purchased Verco Manufacturing Co for approximately $180 million; Verco produced steel floor and roof decking at one location in Arizona and two locations in California. The Verco acquisition further solidified Vulcraft's market leading position in steel decking, giving it total annual capacity of over 500,000 tons.

- In January 2007, Nucor acquired Canada-based Harris Steel for about $1.07 billion. Harris Steel had 2005 sales of Cdn$1.0 billion and earnings of Cdn$64 million. The company's operations consisted of (1) Harris Rebar that was involved in the fabrication and placing of concrete reinforcing steel and the design and installation of concrete post-tensioning systems; (2) Laurel Steel that manufactured and distributed wire and wire products, welded wire mesh, and cold finished bar; and (3) Fisher & Ludlow that manufactured and distributed heavy industrial steel grating, aluminum grating, and expanded metal. In Canada, Harris Steel had 24 reinforcing steel fabricating plants, two steel grating distribution centers, and one cold finished bar and wire processing plant; in the United States, it had 10 reinforcing steel fabricating plants, two steel grating manufacturing plants, and three steel grating manufacturing plants. Harris had customers throughout Canada and the United States and employed about 3,000 people. For the past three years, Harris had purchased a big percentage of its steel requirements from Nucor. Nucor management opted to operate Harris Steel as an independent subsidiary.

- Over several months in 2007 following the Harris Steel acquisition, Nucor through its new Harris Steel subsidiary acquired rebar fabricator South Pacific Steel Corporation, Consolidated Rebar, Inc., a 90 percent equity interest in rebar fabricator Barker Steel Company, and several smaller transactions—all aimed at growing its presence in the rebar fabrication marketplace.

- In August 2007, Nucor acquired LMP Steel & Wire Company for a cash purchase price of approximately $27.2 million, adding 100,000 tons of cold drawn steel capacity.

- In October 2007, Nucor completed the acquisition of Nelson Steel, Inc. for a cash purchase price of approximately $53.2 million, adding 120,000 tons of steel mesh capacity.

- In the third quarter of 2007, Nucor completed the acquisition of Magnatrax Corporation, a leading provider of custom-engineered metal buildings, for a cash purchase price of approximately $275.2 million. The Magnatrax acquisition enabled Nucor's Building System Group to become the second largest metal building producer in the United States.

- In August 2008, Nucor's Harris Steel subsidiary acquired Ambassador Steel Corporation for a cash purchase price of about $185.1 million. Ambassador Steel was a one of the largest independent fabricators and distributors of concrete reinforcing steel—in 2007, Ambassador shipped 422,000 tons of fabricated rebar and distributed another 228,000 tons of reinforcing steel. Its business complemented that of Harris Steel and represented another in a series of moves to greatly strengthen Nucor's competitive position in the rebar fabrication marketplace.

- Another small rebar fabrication company, Free State Steel, was acquired in late 2009, adding to Nucor's footprint in rebar fabrication.

- In June 2012, Nucor acquired Skyline Steel, LLC and its subsidiaries for a cash price of approximately $675.4 million. Skyline was a market-leading distributor of steel pilings, and it also processed and fabricated spiral weld pipe piling, rolled and welded pipe piling, cold-formed sheet piling, and threaded bar. The Skyline acquisition paired Skyline's leadership position in the steel piling distribution market with Nucor's own Nucor-Yamato plant in Arkansas that was the market leader in steel piling manufacturing. To capitalize upon the strategic fits between Skyline's business and Nucor's business, Nucor launched a $155 million capital project at the Nucor-Yamato mill to (a) add several new sheet piling sections, (b) increase the production of single sheet widths by 22 percent, and (c) produce a lighter, stronger sheet covering more area at a lower installed cost—outcomes that would broaden the range of hot-rolled steel piling products Nucor could market through Skyline's distribution network in the United States, Canada, Mexico and the Caribbean. Nucor opted to operate Skyline as a subsidiary.

- In 2014, Nucor acquired Gallatin Steel Company for approximately $779 million. Gallatin produced a range of flat-rolled steel products (principally steel pipe and tube) at a mill with annual production capacity of 1.8 million tons that was located on the Ohio River in Kentucky. The Gallatin mill strengthened Nucor's position as the North American market leader in hot-rolled steel products by boosting its capacity to supply customers in the Midwest region, the largest flat-rolled consuming market region in the United States.

- In 2015, Nucor acquired Gerdau Long Steel's two facilities in Ohio and Georgia that produced cold-drawn steel bars and had combined capacity of 75,000 tons per year. These facilities, purchased for about $75 million, strengthened Nucor's already strong competitive position in cold-finished steel bars by expanding Nucor's geographic coverage and range of cold-finished product offerings.

- In October 2016, Nucor used cash on hand to acquire Independence Tube Corporation (ITC) for a purchase price of $430.1 million. ITC was a leading manufacturer of hollow structural section (HSS) tubing used primarily in nonresidential construction. ITC had the ability to produce approximately 650,000 tons of HSS tubing annually at its four facilities, two in Illinois and two in Alabama. This acquisition not only further expanded Nucor's product offerings to include a variety of tubular products but also provided a new channel for marketing Nucor's hot-rolled sheet steel, as ITC's plants (which used hot-rolled sheet steel to make tubular steel products) were located in close proximity to Nucor's sheet mills in Alabama, Indiana, and Kentucky.

- On January 9, 2017, Nucor used cash on hand to acquire Southland Tube for a purchase price of approximately $130 million. Southland Tube was also a manufacturer of HSS tubing and had one manufacturing facility in Birmingham, Alabama which shipped approximately 240,000 tons in 2016.

- Nucor further expanded its value-added product offerings to buyers of pipe and tubular products in January 2017 by purchasing Republic Conduit for a purchase price of approximately $335 million. Republic Conduit produced steel electrical conduit primarily used to protect and route electrical wiring in various nonresidential structures such as hospitals, office buildings and stadiums. Republic had two facilities located in Kentucky and Georgia with annual shipment volume in 2015 and 2016 of 146,000 tons.

Aggressively Investing to Expand the Company's Internal Production Capabilities

Complementing Nucor's ongoing strategic efforts to grow its business via acquisitions was a strategy element to invest aggressively in (1) the construction of new plant capacity and (2) enhanced production capabilities at existing plants whenever management spotted opportunities to boost sales with an expanded range of product offerings and/or strengthen its competitive position vis-à-vis rivals by lowering costs per ton or expanding its geographic coverage. The purpose of making ongoing capital investments was to improve efficiency and lower production costs at each and every facility it operated.

This strategy element had been in place since Nucor's earliest days in the steel business. Nucor always built state-of-the-art facilities in the most economical fashion possible and then made it standard company practice to invest in plant modernization and efficiency improvements whenever cost-saving opportunities emerged.

Examples of Nucor's efforts included the following:

- In 2006, Nucor announced that it would construct a new $27 million facility to produce metal buildings systems in Brigham City, Utah. The new plant, Nucor's fourth building systems plant, had capacity of 45,000 tons and gave Nucor national market reach in building systems products.

- In 2006, Nucor initiated construction of a $230 million state-of-the-art steel mill in Memphis, Tennessee, with annual capacity to produce 850,000 tons of special quality steel bars. Management believed this mill, together with the company's other special bar quality mills in Nebraska and South Carolina, would give Nucor the broadest, highest quality, and lowest cost offering of special quality steel bar in North America.

- In 2009, Nucor opened an idle and newly-renovated $50 million wire rod and bar mill in Kingman, Arizona that had been acquired in 2003. Production of straight-length rebar, coiled rebar, and wire rod began in mid-2010; the plant had initial capacity of 100,000 tons, with the ability to increase annual production to 500,000 tons.

- The construction of a $150 million galvanizing facility located at the company's sheet steel mill in Decatur, Alabama, gave Nucor the ability to make 500,000 tons of 72-inch wide galvanized sheet steel, a product used by motor vehicle and appliance producers and in various steel frame and steel stud buildings. The galvanizing process entailed dipping steel in melted zinc at extremely high temperatures; the zinc coating protected the steel surface from corrosion.

- In 2013, Nucor installed caster and hot mill upgrades at its Berkeley, South Carolina, sheet mill that enabled it to roll light-gauge sheet steel to a finished width of 74 inches. This new capability (which most foreign competitors did not have) opened opportunities to sell large quantities of wide-width, flat-rolled products to customers in a variety of industries while, at the same time, providing the mill with less exposure to competition from imports of less wide, flat-rolled products.

- A 2016 project to install a $75 million cooling process at the Nucor-Yamato mill in Arkansas was expected to generate savings on alloy costs of $12 million annually.

- In 2017, Nucor announced that it would construct a $250 million rebar micro mill about 90 miles from Kansas City to give Nucor a sustained shipping cost advantage over other domestic producers in supplying rebar to customers in the Kansas City area and the upper Midwestern and Plains region. Rebar supply to customers in this geographic area currently traveled long distances, giving Nucor's micro mill a sustained shipping cost advantage. This location also allowed Nucor to take advantage of the abundant scrap supply in the immediate area provided by Nucor's scrap metal subsidiary, the David J. Joseph Co., acquired in 2008.

- In early 2018, Nucor initiated construction of a $180 million full-range merchant bar quality (MBQ) mill at its existing bar steel mill near Kankakee, Illinois. The MBQ mill would have an annual capacity of 500,000 tons and take approximately two years to complete. Nucor executives believed the new mill's strategic location mill would enable Nucor to capture costs savings by (1) optimizing the melt capacity and infrastructure that was already in place at the existing Kankakee mill (which would continue to be a supplier of quality reinforcing bar products) and (2) taking advantage of an abundant scrap supply in the region. These cost-savings would enhance Nucor's cost-competitiveness and, in top management's opinion, position Nucor to capture a big fraction of the bar products tonnage currently being supplied by competitors outside the region and, also, fortify Nucor's market leadership in steel bars by enhancing the appeal of its product offerings of merchant bar, light shapes, structural angle bars, and channel bars used by customers in the central Midwest region of the United States—one of the largest markets for MBQ products.

- A 2017 project to spend $85 million to modernize the rolling mill at Nucor's 400,000-ton steel bar mill in Marion, Ohio, that produced rebar and signposts.

Nucor's Strategy to Be a First-Mover in Adopting the Best, Most Cost-Efficient Production Methods

The third element of Nucor's competitive strategy was to be a technology leader and first-rate operator of all its production facilities—outcomes that senior executives had pursued since the company's earliest days. Two approaches to improving and expanding Nucor's steelmaking capabilities and achieving low costs per ton were utilized:

- Being quick to implement disruptive technological innovations that would give Nucor a sustainable competitive advantage because of the formidable barriers rivals would have to hurdle to match Nucor's cost competitiveness and/or product quality and/or range of products offered.

- Being quick to implement ongoing advances in production methods and install the latest and best steelmaking equipment, thus providing Nucor with a path to driving down costs per ton and/or leapfrogging competitors in terms of product quality, range of product offerings, and/or market share.

Nucor's biggest success in pioneering trailblazing technology had been at its facilities in Crawfordsville, Indiana, where Nucor installed the world's first facility for direct strip casting of carbon sheet steel—a process called Castrip®. The Castrip process, which Nucor tested and refined for several years before implementing it in 2005, was a major technological breakthrough for producing flat-rolled, carbon, and stainless steels in very thin gauges because (1) it involved far fewer process steps to cast metal at or very near customer-desired thicknesses and shapes and (2) the process drastically reduced capital outlays for equipment and produced sizable savings on operating expenses (by enabling the use of cheaper grades of scrap metal and requiring 90 percent less energy to process liquid metal into hot-rolled steel sheets). An important environmental benefit of the Castrip process was cutting greenhouse gas emissions by up to 80 percent. Seeing these advantages earlier than rivals, Nucor management had the foresight to acquire exclusive rights to Castrip technology in the United States and Brazil. Once it was clear that the expected benefits of the Castrip facility at Crawfordsville were indeed going to become a reality, Nucor in 2006 launched construction of a second Castrip facility on the site of its structural steel mill in Arkansas.

Since technological breakthroughs (like the Castrip process) were relatively rare, Nucor management made a point of scouring locations across the world for reports of possible cost-effective technologies, ways to improve production methods and efficiency, and new and better equipment that could be used to improve operations and/or lower costs in Nucor's facilities. All such reports were checked out thoroughly, including making trips to inspect promising new developments firsthand if circumstances warranted. Projects to improve production methods or install more efficient equipment were undertaken promptly when the investment payback was attractive.

The Drive for Improved Efficiency and Lower Production Costs   When Nucor acquired plants, it drew upon its ample financial strength and cash flows from operations to immediately fund efforts to get them up to Nucor standards—a process that employees called "Nucorizing." This included not only revising production methods and installing better equipment but also striving to increase operational efficiency by reducing the amount of time, space, energy, and manpower it took to produce steel products and paying close attention to worker safety and environmental protection practices.

Simultaneously, Nucor's top-level executives insisted upon continual improvement in product quality and cost at every company facility. Most all of Nucor's production locations were ISO 9000 and ISO 14000 certified. The company had a "BESTmarking" program aimed at being the industrywide best performer on a variety of production and efficiency measures. Managers at all Nucor plants were accountable for demonstrating that their operations were competitive on both product quality and cost vis-à-vis the plants of rival companies. A deeply embedded trait of Nucor's corporate culture was the expectation that plant-level managers would be persistent in initiating actions to improve product quality and keep costs per ton low relative to rival plants.

Nucor management viewed the task of pursuing operating excellence in its manufacturing operations as a continuous process. According to former CEO Dan DiMicco:

> We talk about "climbing a mountain without a peak" to describe our constant improvements. We can take pride in what we have accomplished, but we are never satisfied.[6]

The strength of top management's commitment to funding projects to improve plant efficiency, keep costs as low as possible, and achieve overall operating excellence was reflected in the company's capital expenditures for new technology, plant improvements, and equipment upgrades (see Exhibit 5). The beneficial outcomes of these expenditures, coupled with companywide vigilance and dedication to discovering and implementing ways to operate most cost efficiently, were major contributors to Nucor's standing as North America's lowest-cost, most diversified provider of steel products.

Shifting Production from Lower-End Steel Products to Value-Added Products

During 2010 and 2017, Nucor undertook a number of actions to shift more of the production tonnage at its steel mills and steel products facilities to "value-added products" that could command higher prices and yield better profit margins than could be had by

EXHIBIT 5 Nucor's Capital Expenditures for New Plants, Plant Expansions, New Technology, Equipment Upgrades, and Other Operating Improvements, 2000–2015

Year	Capital Expenditures (in millions)	Year	Capital Expenditures (in millions)
2000	$ 415.0	2009	$ 390.5
2001	261.0	2010	345.2
2002	244.0	2011	450.6
2003	215.4	2012	1,019.3
2004	285.9	2013	1,230.4
2005	331.5	2014	568.9
2006	338.4	2015	364.8
2007	520.4	2016	604.8
2008	1,019.0	2017	448.6

Sources: Company records, accessed at www.nucor.com, various dates; data for 2009–2015 is from the 2013 10-K report, p. 43 and the 2017 10-K report, p. 45.

producing lower-end or commodity steel products. Examples included:

- Adding new galvanizing capability at the Decatur, Alabama, mill that enabled Nucor to sell 500,000 tons of corrosion-resistant, galvanized sheet steel for high-end applications.
- Expanding the cut-to-length capabilities at the Tuscaloosa, Alabama, mill that put the mill in position to sell as many as 200,000 additional tons per year of cut-to-length and tempered steel plate.
- Shipping 250,000 tons of new steel plate and structural steel products in 2010 that were not offered in 2009, and further increasing shipments of these same new products to 500,000 tons in 2011.
- Completing installation of a heat-treating facility at the Hertford County plate mill in 2011 that gave Nucor the capability to produce as much as 125,000 tons annually of heat-treated steel plate ranging from 3/16 of an inch through 2 inches thick.

- Installing new vacuum degassers at the Hickman, Arkansas, sheet mill and Hertford County, North Carolina, mill to enable production of increased volumes of higher-value sheet steel, steel plate, steel piping, and tubular products.
- Investing $290 million at its three steel bar mills to enable the production of steel bars and wire rod for the most demanding engineered bar applications and also put in place state-of-the-art quality inspection capabilities. The project enabled Nucor to offer higher-value steel bars and wire rod to customers in the energy, automotive, and heavy truck and equipment markets (where the demand for steel products had been relatively strong in recent years).
- Completing installation of a new 120,000-ton "normalizing" process for making steel plate at the Hertford County mill in June 2013; the new normalizing process allowed the mill to produce a higher grade of steel plate that was less brittle and had a more uniform fine-grained structure (which permitted the plate to be machined to more precise dimensions). Steel plate with these qualities was more suitable for armor plate applications and for certain uses in the energy, transportation, and shipbuilding industries. Going into 2014, the normalizing process, coupled with the company's recent investments in a vacuum tank degasser and a heat-treating facility at this same plant, doubled the Hertford mill's capacity to produce higher-quality steel plate products that commanded a higher market price.
- Modernizing the casting, hot rolling, and downstream operations at the Berkeley, South Carolina, mill in 2013 to enable the production of 72-inch wide sheet steel and lighter gauge hot-rolled and cold-rolled steel products with a finished width of 74-inches, thereby opening opportunities for Nucor to sell higher-value sheet steel products to customers in the agricultural, pipe and tube, industrial equipment, automotive, and heavy-equipment industries. In 2015, the Berkeley mill shipped 150,000 tons of wider-width products and was pursuing a goal of increasing shipments to 400,000 tons.
- Instituting a $155 million project at the Nucor-Yamato mill in 2014 to produce lighter, wider, and stronger steel pilings and a second $75 million project in 2016 to produce structural steel sections

with high-strength, low-alloy grade chemistry; both projects helped Nucor grow sales of value-added structural steel products that had above-average profitability.

- Acquiring two Gerdau Long Steel facilities in 2015 that produced higher-margin, value-added cold-finished bars sold to steel service centers and other customers across the United States.

- Acquiring a specialty steel plate mill in Longview, Texas in 2016 that was capable of producing steel plate ranging that was thicker and wider than the company's existing steel plate offerings, thereby opening opportunities for Nucor to compete for a growing share of the value-added plate market. Less than 12 months after the acquisition, production and shipments at the Longview plant had doubled.

- Investing in a $230 million specialty cold mill complex at Nucor Steel Arkansas to expand the company's capability to produce advanced high-strength, high-strength low-alloy and motor lamination steel products for automotive customers. The project, expected to begin operations in late 2018, was expected to bring value to all of Nucor's sheet mills, mainly by broadening the automotive capability of Nucor's galvanized lines at mills in Alabama and South Carolina to include products that Nucor was currently unable to manufacture.

- Acquiring two plants in St. Louis, Missouri, and Monterrey, Mexico, in 2017 that produced higher-margin, value-added cold drawn rounds, hexagons, squares, and related products sold mainly to automotive and certain industrial customers in the United States and Mexico. The two facilities, with combined annual capacity of 200,000 tons, strengthened Nucor's position as the market leader in cold bar finished products by increasing the total capacity of Nucor's cold finished bar and wire facilities to more than 1.1 million tons annually, advancing Nucor's goal of growing its sales to automotive customers, and creating another channel for Nucor's existing special quality bars mills to market their products.

Product upgrades had also been undertaken at several Nucor facilities making cold-finished and fastener products. Senior management believed that all of these upgrades to higher-value product offerings would boost revenues and earnings in the years ahead.

Global Growth via Joint Ventures

In 2007, Nucor management decided it was time to begin building an international growth platform. The company's strategy to grow its international revenues had two elements:

- Establishing foreign sales offices and exporting U.S-made steel products to foreign markets. Because about 60 percent of Nucor's steelmaking capacity was located on rivers with deep water transportation access, management believed that the company could be competitive in shipping U.S.-made steel products to customers in a number of foreign locations.

- Entering into joint ventures with foreign partners to invest in steelmaking projects outside North America. Nucor executives believed that the success of this strategy element was finding the right partners to grow with internationally.

Nucor opened a Trading Office in Switzerland and proceeded to establish international sales offices in Mexico, Brazil, Colombia, the Middle East and Asia. The company's Trading Office bought and sold steel and steel products that Nucor and other steel producers had manufactured. In 2010, approximately 11 percent of the shipments from Nucor's steel mills were exported. Customers in South and Central America presented the most consistent opportunities for export sales, but there was growing interest from customers in Europe and other locations.

In January 2008, Nucor entered in a 50/50 joint venture with the European-based Duferco Group to establish the production of beams and other long products in Italy, with distribution in Europe and North Africa. A few months later, Nucor acquired 50 percent of the stock of Duferdofin-Nucor S.r.l. for approximately $667 million (Duferdofin was Duferco's Italy-based steelmaking subsidiary). In 2017, Duferdofin-Nucor operated at five steel mills at various locations with a steel melt shop and bloom/billet caster with an annual capacity of 1.1 million tons, two beam rolling mills with combined capacity of 1.1 million tons, a 495,000-ton merchant bar mill, and a 60,000-ton trackshoes/cutting edges mill. The customers for the products produced by Duferdofin-Nucor were primarily steel service centers and distributors located both in Italy and throughout Europe. So far, the joint venture project had not lived up to the partners' financial expectations because all of the plants made construction-related products. The European construction industry had been hard hit by the economic events of 2008 and 2009 and the construction-related demand for steel products in Europe was very slowly creeping back toward pre-crisis levels. Ongoing losses at Nucor Duferdofin and revaluation of the joint venture's assets had resulted in Nucor's investment in Duferdofin Nucor being valued at $412.9 million at December 31, 2017.

In early 2010, Nucor invested $221.3 million to become a 50/50 joint venture partner with Mitsui USA to form NuMit LLC–Mitsui USA was the largest wholly-owned subsidiary of Mitsui & Co., Ltd., a diversified global trading, investment, and service enterprise headquartered in Tokyo, Japan. NuMit LLC owned 100 percent of the equity interest in Steel Technologies LLC, an operator of 25 sheet steel processing facilities throughout the United States, Canada, and Mexico. The NuMit joint venture was profitable in both 2012 and 2013. At the end of 2015, Nucor's investment in NuMit was $314.5 million, which consisted of the initial investment plus additional capital contributions and equity method earnings less distributions to Nucor; Nucor received distributions from NuMit of $6.7 million in 2013, $52.7 million in 2014, $13.1 million in 2015, $38.6 million in 2016, and $48.3 million in 2017.

In 2016 Nucor announced a 50/50 joint venture with JFE Steel Corporation of Japan to build a $270 million galvanized sheet steel mill with a capacity of 400,000 tons in central Mexico to serve the growing automotive market in that country. Automotive production in Mexico is predicted to increase from 3.4 million to 5.3 million vehicles by 2020.

Nucor's Raw Materials Strategy

Scrap metal and scrap substitutes were Nucor's single biggest cost–all of Nucor's steel mills used electric arc furnaces to make steel products from recycled scrap steel, scrap iron, pig iron, hot briquetted iron (HBI), and direct reduced iron (DRI). On average, it took approximately 1.1 tons of scrap and scrap substitutes to produce a ton of steel–the proportions averaged about 70 percent scrap steel and 30 percent scrap substitutes. Nucor was the biggest user of scrap metal in North America, and it also purchased millions of tons of pig iron, HBI, DRI, and other iron products annually–top-quality scrap substitutes were especially critical in making premium grades of sheet steel, steel plate, and special bar quality steel at various Nucor mills. Scrap prices were driven by market demand-supply conditions and could fluctuate significantly (see Exhibit 6). Rising scrap prices adversely impacted the company's costs and ability to compete against steelmakers that made steel from scratch using iron ore, coke, and traditional blast furnace technology.

Nucor's raw materials strategy was aimed at achieving greater control over the costs of all types of metallic inputs (both scrap metal and iron-related substitutes) used at its steel plants. A key element of this strategy was to backward integrate into the production of 6,000,000 to 7,000,000 tons per year of

EXHIBIT 6 Nucor's Costs for Scrap Steel and Scrap Substitute, 2000–2017

Period	Average Cost of Scrap and Scrap Substitute per Ton Used	Period	Average Cost of Scrap and Scrap Substitute per Ton Used
		2016	
2000	$120	Quarter 1	$193
2005	244	Quarter 2	232
2006	246	Quarter 3	252
2007	278	Quarter 4	236
2008	438	**Full-Year Average**	228
2009	303		
		2017	
2010	351	Quarter 1	$284
2011	439	Quarter 2	313
2012	407	Quarter 3	317
2013	376	Quarter 4	317
2014	381	**Full-Year Average**	307
2015	270		

Source: Nucor's Annual Reports for 2007, 2009, 2011 and information posted in the investor relations section at www.nucor.com (accessed April 12, 2012, April 15, 2014, February 11, 2016, and February 18, 2018).

high quality scrap substitutes (chiefly pig iron and direct reduced iron) at either its own wholly owned and operated plants or at plants jointly owned by Nucor and other partners—integrating backward into supplying a big fraction of its own iron requirements held promise of raw material savings and less reliance on outside iron suppliers. The costs of producing pig iron and direct reduced iron (DRI) were not as subject to steep swings as was the price of scrap steel.

Nucor's first move to execute its long-term raw materials strategy came in 2002 when it partnered with The Rio Tinto Group, Mitsubishi Corporation, and Chinese steel maker Shougang Corporation to pioneer Rio Tinto's HIsmelt® technology at a new plant to be constructed in Kwinana, Western Australia. The HIsmelt technology entailed converting iron ore to liquid metal or pig iron and was both a replacement for traditional blast furnace technology and a hot metal source for electric arc furnaces. Rio Tinto had been developing the HIsmelt technology for 10 years and believed the technology had the potential to revolutionize ironmaking and provide low-cost, high-quality iron for making steel. Nucor had a 25 percent ownership in the venture and had a joint global marketing agreement with Rio Tinto to license the technology to other interested steel companies. The Australian plant represented the world's first commercial application of the HIsmelt technology; it had a capacity of over 880,000 tons and was expandable to 1.65 million tons at an attractive capital cost per incremental ton. Production started in January 2006. However, the joint venture partners opted to permanently close the HIsmelt plant in December 2010 because the project, while technologically acclaimed, proved to be financially unviable. Nucor's loss in the joint venture partnership amounted to $94.8 million.

In April 2003, Nucor entered a joint venture with Companhia Vale do Rio Doce (CVRD) to construct and operate an environmentally friendly $80 million pig iron project in northern Brazil. The project, named Ferro Gusa Carajás, utilized two conventional mini-blast furnaces to produce about 418,000 tons of pig iron per year, using iron ore from CVRD's Carajás mine in northern Brazil. The charcoal fuel for the plant came exclusively from fast-growing eucalyptus trees in a cultivated forest in northern Brazil owned by a CVRD subsidiary. The cultivated forest removed more carbon dioxide from the atmosphere than the blast furnace emitted, thus counteracting global warming—an outcome that appealed to Nucor management. Nucor invested $10 million in the project and was a 22 percent owner. Production of pig iron began in the fourth quarter of 2005; the joint venture agreement called for Nucor to purchase all of the plant's production. However, Nucor sold its interest in the project to CVRD in April 2007.

Nucor's third raw-material sourcing initiative came in 2004 when it acquired an idled direct reduced iron (DRI) plant in Louisiana, relocated all of the plant assets to Trinidad (an island off the coast of South America near Venezuela), and expanded the project (named Nu-Iron Unlimited) to a capacity of 2 million tons. The plant used a proven technology that converted iron ore pellets into direct reduced iron. The Trinidad site was chosen because it had a long-term and very cost-attractive supply of natural gas (large volumes of natural gas were consumed in the plant's production process), along with favorable logistics for receiving iron ore and shipping direct reduced iron to Nucor's steel mills in the United States. Nucor entered into contracts with natural gas suppliers to purchase natural gas in amounts needed to operate the Trinidad through 2028. Production began in January 2007. Nu-Iron personnel at the Trinidad plant had recently achieved world class product quality levels in making DRI; this achievement allowed Nucor to use an even larger percentage of DRI in producing the most demanding steel products.

In September 2010, Nucor announced plans to build a $750 million DRI facility with annual capacity of 2.5 million tons on a 4,000-acre site in St. James Parish, Louisiana. This investment moved Nucor two-thirds of the way to its long-term objective of being able to supply 6 to 7 million tons of its requirements for high-quality scrap substitutes. However, the new DRI facility was the first phase of a multi-phase plan that included a second 2.5 million-ton DRI facility, a coke plant, a blast furnace, an iron ore pellet plant, and a steel mill. Permits for both DRI plants were received from the Louisiana Department of Environmental Quality in January 2011. Construction of the first DRI unit at the St. James site began in 2011, and production began in late 2013 and was rapidly ramped up toward capacity in 2014. However, the plant experienced significant operating losses in the first three quarters of 2014, due to low yields in converting iron ore pellets into direct reduced iron. In the fourth quarter of 2014 there was an equipment failure that shut operations down until early 2015.

But the Louisiana DRI facility's performance in 2015 was impaired by (1) higher-cost iron ore purchased in the fourth quarter of 2014 that could not be used until 2015 when the facility resumed operations after equipment repairs were made, and (2) a planned maintenance outage in the fourth quarter of 2015. Due to adverse market conditions that forced Nucor's steel mills to operate well below capacity in 2015, the Louisiana DRI plant did not resume operation until early 2016. While a Nucor official had indicated in 2014 that Nucor's use of DRI in its steel mills was expected to give the company an approximate $75 per ton cost advantage in producing a ton of steel over traditional integrated steel mills using conventional blast furnace technology, thus far the Louisiana DRI plant's problems had prevented Nucor from realizing any cost-saving benefits from its $750 million investment in the plant, and all activities relating to a second 2.5 million-ton DRI facility, a coke plant, a blast furnace, an iron ore pellet plant, and a steel mill at the St. James Parish site in Louisiana had been put on hold.[7] Nonetheless, Nucor management believed that the recent investments in its two DRI plants (in Trinidad and Tobago and Louisiana) had put the company in better position going forward to manage its overall costs of metallic materials and the associated supply-related risks.

Because producing DRI was a natural gas intensive process, Nucor entered into a long-term, onshore natural gas working interest drilling program with Encana Oil & Gas, one of North America's largest producers of natural gas, to help offset the company's exposure to future increases in the price of natural gas consumed by the DRI facility in St. James Parish. Nucor entered into a second and more significant drilling program with Encana in 2012. All natural gas from Nucor's working interest drilling program with Encana was being sold to outside parties. In December 2013, Nucor and Encana agreed to temporarily suspend drilling new gas wells because of expectations that the natural gas pricing environment would be weak in 2014. By the middle of 2014, when all of the in-process wells were completed, Nucor management believed the over 300 producing wells would provide a full hedge against the Louisiana DRI plant's expected consumption of natural gas into 2015. However, discoveries of abundant natural gas supplies in late 2014 and throughout 2015 (via the highly successful exploration efforts of companies employing fracking technology in areas close to Louisiana where there were

big shale deposits containing both oil and natural gas) kept the Nucor-Encana drilling program shut down. Nucor did not expect the program to resume operations until the market price of natural gas climbed to levels that made it economic to produce gas at the wells already drilled.

In October 2016, to ensure the DRI plant in Louisiana had a sustainable advantage from lower natural gas costs, Nucor acquired a 49 percent leasehold interest covering approximately 54,000 acres in the South Piceance Basin in Colorado from Encana. Nucor retained its 50 percent ownership interest in all of the wells that were drilled under an earlier Carry and Earning agreement that was terminated on October 1, 2016. In July 2017, Encana sold all of its assets in the Piceance Basin to Caerus Oil and Gas; agreements subsequently negotiated among Nucor, Encana, and Caerus resulted in Caerus becoming the operator of all of Nucor's gas well assets going forward, including those that were a part of the earlier Nucor-Encana drilling program. As a result of these changes, Nucor gained full discretion over its participation in all future gas-drilling capital investments related to its DRI plant in Louisiana.

The Acquisition of the David J. Joseph Company In February 2008, Nucor acquired The David J. Joseph Company (DJJ) and related affiliates for a cash purchase price of approximately $1.44 billion, the largest acquisition in Nucor's history. DJJ was one of the leading scrap metal companies in the United States, with 2007 revenues of $6.4 billion. It processed about 3.5 million tons of scrap iron and steel annually at some 35 scrap yards and brokered over 20 million tons of iron and steel scrap and over 500 million pounds of non-ferrous materials in 2007. DJJ obtained scrap from industrial plants, the manufacturers of products that contained steel, independent scrap dealers, peddlers, auto junkyards, demolition firms, and other sources. The DJJ Mill and Industrial Services business provided logistics and metallurgical blending operations and offered on-site handling and trading of industrial scrap. The DJJ Rail Services business owned over 2,000 railcars dedicated to the movement of scrap metals and offered complete railcar fleet management and leasing services. Nucor was familiar with DJJ and its various operations because it had obtained scrap from DJJ since 1969. Most importantly, though, all of DJJ's businesses had strategic value to Nucor in helping gain control over its scrap metal costs. Within months of completing the DJJ acquisition (which was operated as a separate subsidiary), the DJJ management team acquired four other scrap processing companies. Additional scrap processors were acquired from 2010 to 2014, and several new scrap yards were opened. As of year-end 2017, DJJ had 72 operating facilities in 16 states (along with multiple brokerages offices in the United States and certain foreign countries), 57 scrap yards and recycling facilities, and total annual scrap processing capacity of 5.2 million tons. And because of DJJ's fleet of 2,500 open top railcars, Nucor could deliver scrap to its steel mills quickly and cost efficiently.

Nucor's Commitment to Being a Global Leader in Environmental Performance

Every Nucor facility was evaluated for actions that could be taken to promote greater environmental sustainability. Measurable objectives and targets relating to such outcomes as reduced use of oil and grease, more efficient use of electricity, and site-wide recycling were in place at each plant. Computerized controls on large electric motors and pumps and energy-recovery equipment to capture and reuse energy that otherwise would be wasted had been installed throughout Nucor's facilities to lower energy usage—Nucor considered itself to be among the most energy-efficient steel companies in the world. All of Nucor's facilities had water-recycling systems. Nucor even recycled the dust from its electric arc furnaces because scrap metal contained enough zinc, lead, chrome, and other valuable metals to recycle into usable products; the dust was captured in each plant's state-of-the-art bag house air pollution control devices and then sent to a recycler that converted the dust into zinc oxide, steel slag, and pig iron. The first Nucor mill received ISO 14001 Environmental Management System certification in 2001; by year-end 2015, all of Nucor's facilities were ISO 14001 certified.

Nucor's sheet mill in Decatur, Alabama, used a measuring device called an opacity monitor, which gave precise, minute-by-minute readings of the air quality that passed through the bag house and out of the mill's exhaust system. While rival steel producers had resisted using opacity monitors (because they documented any time a mill's exhaust was out of compliance with its environmental permits, even momentarily), Nucor's personnel at the Decatur mill viewed the opacity monitor as a tool for improving environmental performance. They developed the expertise to read the monitor so well that they could pinpoint in just a few minutes the first signs of a problem in any of the nearly 7,000 bags in the bag house—before those problems resulted in increased emissions. Their early-warning system worked so well that the division applied for a patent on the process, with an eye toward licensing it to other companies.

Organization and Management Philosophy

Nucor had a simple, streamlined organizational structure to allow employees to innovate and make quick decisions. The company was highly decentralized, with most day-to-day operating decisions made by group or plant-level general managers and their staff. Each group or plant operated independently as a profit center and was headed by a general manager, who in most cases also had the title of vice president. The group manager or plant general manager had control of the day-to-day decisions that affected the group or plant's profitability.

The organizational structure at a typical plant had four layers:

- General Manager
- Department Manager
- Supervisor/Professional
- Hourly Employee

Group managers and plant managers reported to one of five executive vice presidents at corporate headquarters. Nucor's corporate staff was exceptionally small, consisting of about 100 people in 2013, the philosophy being that corporate headquarters should consist of a small cadre of executives who would guide a decentralized operation where liberal authority was delegated to managers in the field. Each plant had a sales manager who was responsible for selling the products made at that particular plant; such staff functions as engineering, accounting, and personnel management were performed at the group/plant level. There was a minimum of paperwork and bureaucratic systems. Each group/plant was expected to earn about a 25 percent return on total assets before corporate expenses, taxes, interest, or profit-sharing. As long as plant managers met their profit targets, they were allowed to operate with minimal restrictions and interference from corporate headquarters. There was a very friendly spirit of competition from one plant to the next to see which facility could be the best performer, but since all of the vice-presidents and general managers shared the same bonus systems they functioned pretty much as a team despite operating their facilities individually. Top executives did not hesitate to replace group or plant managers who consistently struggled to achieve profitability and operating targets.

Workforce Compensation Practices

Nucor was a largely nonunion "pay for performance" company with an incentive compensation system that rewarded goal-oriented individuals and did not put a maximum on what they could earn. All employees, except those in the recently-acquired Harris Steel and DJJ subsidiaries that operated independently from the rest of Nucor, worked under one of four basic compensation plans, each featuring incentives related to meeting specific goals and targets:

1. *Production Incentive Plan*—Production line jobs were rated on degree of responsibility required and assigned a base wage comparable to the wages paid by other manufacturing plants in the area where a Nucor plant was located. But in addition to their base wage, operating and maintenance employees were paid weekly bonuses based on the number of tons by which the output of their production team or work group exceeded the "standard" number of tons. All operating and maintenance employees were members of a production team that included the team's production supervisor, and the tonnage produced by each work team was measured for each work shift and then totaled for all shifts during a given week. If a production team's weekly output beat the weekly standard, team members (including the team's production supervisor) earned a specified percentage bonus for each ton produced above the standard—production bonuses were paid weekly (rather than quarterly or annually) so that workers and supervisors would be rewarded immediately for their efforts. The standard rate was calculated based on the capabilities of the equipment employed (typically at the time plant operations began), and no bonus was paid if the equipment was not operating (which gave maintenance workers a big incentive to keep a plant's equipment in good working condition)—Nucor's philosophy was that

when equipment was not operating everybody suffered and the bonus for downtime ought to be zero. Production standards at Nucor plants were seldom raised unless a plant underwent significant modernization or important new pieces of equipment were installed that greatly boosted labor productivity. It was common for production incentive bonuses to run from 50 to 150 percent of an employee's base pay, thereby pushing compensation levels up well above those at other nearby manufacturing plants. Worker efforts to exceed the standard and get a bonus did not so much involve working harder as it involved good teamwork and close collaboration in resolving problems and figuring out how best to exceed the production standards.

2. *Department Manager Incentive Plan*—Department managers earned annual incentive bonuses based primarily on the percentage of net income to dollars of assets employed for their division. These bonuses could be as much as 80 percent of a department manager's base pay.

3. *Professional and Clerical Bonus Plan*—A bonus based on a division's net income return on assets was paid to employees that were not on the production worker or department manager plan.

4. *Senior Officers Annual Incentive Plan*—Nucor's senior officers did not have employment contracts and did not participate in any pension or retirement plans. Their base salaries were set at approximately 90 percent of the median base salary for comparable positions in other manufacturing companies with comparable assets, sales, and capital. The remainder of their compensation was based on Nucor's annual overall percentage of net income to stockholder's equity (ROE) and was paid out in cash and stock. Once Nucor's ROE reached a threshold of than 3 percent, senior officers earned a bonus equal to 20 percent of their base salary. If Nucor's annual ROE was 20 percent or higher, senior officers earned a bonus equal to 225 percent of their base salary. Officers could earn an additional bonus up to 75 percent of their base salary based on a comparison of Nucor's net sales growth with the net sales growth of members of a steel industry peer group. There was also a long-term incentive plan that provided for stock awards and stock options. The structure of these officer incentives was such that bonus compensation for Nucor officers fluctuated widely—from

close to zero (in years when industry conditions were bad and Nucor's performance was sub-par) to four hundred percent (or more) of base salary (when Nucor's performance was excellent).

5. *Senior Officers Long-Term Incentive Plan*—The long-term incentive was intended to balance the short-term focus of the annual incentive plan by rewarding performance over multi-year periods. These incentives were received in the form of cash (50 percent) and restricted stock (50 percent) and covered a performance period of three years; 50 percent of the long-term award was based on how Nucor's 3-year ROAIC (return on average invested capital) compared against the 3-year ROAIC of the steel industry peer group and 50 percent was based on how Nucor's 3-year ROAIC compared against a multi-industry group of well-respected companies in capital-intensive businesses similar to that of steel.

Nucor management had designed the company's incentive plans for employees so that bonus calculations involved no discretion on the part of a plant/division manager or top executives. This was done to eliminate any concerns on the part of workers that managers or executives might show favoritism or otherwise be unfair in calculating or awarding incentive awards.

There were two other types of extra compensation:

• *Profit Sharing*—Each year, Nucor allocated at least 10 percent of its operating profits to profit-sharing bonuses for all employees (except senior officers). Depending on company performance, the bonuses could run anywhere from 1 percent to over 20 percent of pay. Twenty percent of the bonus amount was paid to employees in the following March as a cash bonus and the remaining 80 percent was put into a trust for each employee, with each employee's share being proportional to their earnings as a percent of total earnings by all workers covered by the plan. An employee's share of profit sharing became vested after one full year of employment. Employees received a quarterly statement of their balance in profit sharing.

• *401(k) Plan*—Both officers and employees participated in a 401(k) plan where the company matched from 5 percent to 25 percent of each employee's first 7 percent of contributions; the amount of the match was based on how well the company was doing.

In 2018, entry-level, hourly workers at a Nucor plant could expect to earn $40,000 to $50,000 annually (including bonuses). Earnings for more experienced production, engineering, and technical personnel were normally in the $70,000 to $95,000 range. Total compensation for salaried workers ranged from $60,000 to $200,000, depending on type of job (accounting, engineering, sales, information technology), years of experience, level of management, and geographic location. It was common for worker compensation at Nucor plants to be double or more the average earned by workers at other manufacturing companies in the states where Nucor's plants were located. As a rule of thumb, production workers in Nucor's steel mills earned three times the local average manufacturing wage. Nucor management philosophy was that these workers ought to be excellently compensated because the production jobs were strenuous and the work environment in a steel mill was relatively dangerous.

Employee turnover in Nucor mills was extremely low; absenteeism and tardiness were minimal. Each employee was allowed four days of absences and could also miss work for jury duty, military leave, or the death of close relatives. After this, a day's absence cost a worker the entire performance bonus pay for that week and being more than a half-hour late to work on a given day resulted in no bonus payment for the day. When job vacancies did occur, Nucor was flooded with applications from people wanting to get a job at Nucor; plant personnel screened job candidates very carefully, seeking people with initiative and a strong work ethic.

Employee Relations and Human Resources

Employee relations at Nucor were based on four clear-cut principles:

1. Management is obligated to manage Nucor in such a way that employees will have the opportunity to earn according to their productivity.

2. Employees should feel confident that if they do their jobs properly, they will have a job tomorrow.

3. Employees have the right to be treated fairly and must believe that they will be.

4. Employees must have an avenue of appeal when they believe they are being treated unfairly.

The hallmarks of Nucor's human resources strategy were its incentive pay plan for production exceeding the standard and the job security provided to production workers—despite being in an industry with strong down-cycles, Nucor had made it a practice not to lay off workers. Instead, when market conditions were tough and production had to be cut back, workers were assigned to plant maintenance projects, cross-training programs, and other activities calculated to boost the plant's performance when market conditions improved.

Nucor took an egalitarian approach to providing fringe benefits to its employees; employees had the same insurance programs, vacation schedules, and holidays as upper level management. However, certain benefits were not available to Nucor's officers. The fringe benefit package at Nucor included:

- *Medical and Dental Plans*—The company had a flexible and comprehensive health benefit program for officers and employees that included wellness and health care spending accounts.

- *Tuition Reimbursement*—Nucor reimbursed up to $3,000 of an employee's approved educational expenses each year and up to $1,500 of a spouse's educational expenses for two years.

- *Service Awards*—After each five years of service with the company, Nucor employees received a service award consisting of five shares of Nucor stock.

- *Scholarships and Educational Disbursements*—Nucor provided the children of every employee (except senior officers) with college funding of $3,000 per year for four years to be used at accredited academic institutions.

- *Other benefits*—Long-term disability, life insurance, vacation.

Most of the changes Nucor made in work procedures came from employees. The prevailing view at Nucor was that the employees knew the problems of their jobs better than anyone else and were thus in the best position to identify ways to improve how things were done. Most plant-level managers spent considerable time in the plant, talking and meeting with frontline employees and listening carefully to suggestions. Promising ideas and suggestions were typically acted upon quickly and implemented—management was willing to take risks to try worker suggestions for doing things better and to accept the occasional failure when the results were disappointing. Teamwork, a vibrant team spirit, and a close worker–management partnership were evident at Nucor plants.

Nucor plants did not utilize job descriptions. Management believed job descriptions caused more problems than they solved, given the teamwork atmosphere and the close collaboration among work group members. The company saw formal performance appraisal systems as a waste of time and added paperwork. If a Nucor employee was not performing well, the problem was dealt with directly by supervisory personnel and the peer pressure of work group members (whose bonuses were adversely affected).

Employees were kept informed about company and division performance. Charts showing the division's results in return-on-assets and bonus payoff were posted in prominent places in the plant. Most all employees were quite aware of the level of profits in their plant or division. Nucor had a formal grievance procedure, but grievances were few and far between. The corporate office sent all news releases to each division where they were posted on bulletin boards. Each employee received a copy of Nucor's annual report; it was company practice for the cover of the annual report to consist of the names of all Nucor employees.

All of these practices had created an egalitarian culture and a highly motivated workforce that grew out of former CEO Ken Iverson's radical insight: employees, even hourly clock punchers, would put forth extraordinary effort and be exceptionally productive if they were richly rewarded, treated with respect, and given real power to do their jobs as best they saw fit.[8] There were countless stories of occasions when managers and workers had gone beyond the call of duty to expedite equipment repairs (in many instances even using their weekends to go help personnel at other Nucor plants solve a crisis); the company's workforce was known for displaying unusual passion and company loyalty even when no personal financial stake was involved. As one Nucor worker put it, "At Nucor, we're not 'you guys' and 'us guys.' It's all of us guys. Wherever the bottleneck is, we go there, and everyone works on it."[9]

It was standard procedure for a team of Nucor veterans, including people who worked on the plant floor, to visit with their counterparts as part of the process of screening candidates for acquisition.[10] One of the purposes of such visits was to explain the Nucor compensation system and culture face-to-face, gauge reactions, and judge whether the plant would fit into "the Nucor way of doing things" if it was acquired. Shortly after making an acquisition,

Nucor management moved swiftly to institute its pay-for-performance incentive system and begin instilling the egalitarian Nucor culture and idea sharing. Top priority was given to looking for ways to boost plant production using fewer people and without making substantial capital investments; the take-home pay of workers at newly acquired plants typically went up rather dramatically. At the Auburn Steel plant, acquired in 2001, it took Nucor about six months to convince workers that they would be better off under Nucor's pay system; during that time Nucor paid people under the old Auburn Steel system but posted what they would have earned under Nucor's system. Pretty soon, workers were convinced to make the changeover—one worker's pay climbed from $53,000 in the year prior to the acquisition to $67,000 in 2001 and to $92,000 in 2005.[11]

New Employees   Each plant/division had a "consul" responsible for providing new employees with general advice about becoming a Nucor teammate and serving as a resource for inquiries about how things were done at Nucor, how to navigate the division and company, and how to resolve issues that might come up. Nucor provided new employees with a personalized plan that set forth who would give them feedback about how well they were doing and when and how this feedback would be given; from time to time, new employees met with the plant manager for feedback and coaching. In addition, there was a new employee orientation session that provided a hands-on look at the plant/division operations; new employees also participated in product group meetings to provide exposure to broader business and technical issues. Each year, Nucor brought all recent college hires to the Charlotte headquarters for a forum intended to give the new hires a chance to network and provide senior management with guidance on how best to leverage their talent.

THE WORLD STEEL INDUSTRY

Global production of crude steel hit a record high of 1,689 million tons in 2017 (see Exhibit 7). Steelmaking capacity worldwide was approximately 2,400 million tons in 2017, resulting in global excess capacity just over 700 million tons and a 2017 capacity utilization rate of 70.3 percent (up from a historically unprecedented low of 52 percent in 2009). Overcapacity was especially pronounced in China.

Although global demand for steel mill products has grown an average of about 3.8 percent annually from 2010 to 2017, global demand for steel products was forecasted to grow at an annual rate of about 0.8 percent through 2025. The six biggest steel-producing countries in 2017 were as follows.[12]

Country	Total Production of Crude Steel	Percent of Worldwide Production
China	832 million metric tons	49.2%
Japan	105 million metric tons	6.2%
India	101 million metric tons	6.0%
United States	82 million metric tons	4.9%
Russia	71 million metric tons	4.2%
South Korea	71 million metric tons	4.2%

Exhibit 8 shows the world's 15 largest producers of crude steel in 2017.

Steelmaking Technologies

Steel was produced either by integrated steel facilities or "mini-mills" that employed electric arc furnaces. Integrated mills used blast furnaces to produce hot metal typically from iron ore pellets, limestone, scrap steel, oxygen, assorted other metals, and coke (coke was produced by firing coal in large coke ovens and was the major fuel used in blast furnaces to produce molten iron). Melted iron from the blast furnace process was then run through the basic oxygen process to produce liquid steel. To make flat rolled steel products, liquid steel was either fed into a continuous caster machine and cast into slabs or else cooled in slab form for later processing. Slabs were further shaped or rolled at a plate mill or hot strip mill. In making certain sheet steel products, the hot strip mill process was followed by various finishing processes, including pickling, cold-rolling, annealing, tempering, galvanizing, or other coating procedures. These various processes for converting raw steel into finished steel products were often distinct steps undertaken at different times and in different on-site or off-site facilities rather than being done in a continuous process in a single plant facility—an integrated mill was thus one that had multiple facilities at a single plant site and could therefore not only produce crude

EXHIBIT 7 Worldwide Production of Crude Steel, with Compound Average Growth Rates, 1975–2017

Year	World Crude Steel Production (millions of metric tons)	Compound Average Growth Rates in World Crude Steel Production	
		Period	Compound Average Growth Rate
1975	644	1975–1980	2.17%
1980	717	1980–1985	0.06%
1985	719	1985–1990	1.38%
1990	770	1990–1995	−0.45%
1995	753	1995–2000	2.45%
2000	850	2000–2005	6.20%
2005	1,148	2005–2010	4.53%
2010	1,433	2010–2017	2.38%
2011	1,538		
2012	1,560		
2013	1,650		
2014	1,669		
2015	1,620		
2016	1,627		
2017	1,689		

Source: Worldsteel Association, *World Steel in Figures 2018*, www.worldsteel.org (accessed on May 30, 2018).

(or raw) steel but also run the crude steel through various facilities and finishing processes to make hot-rolled and cold-rolled sheet steel products, steel bars and beams, stainless steel, steel wire and nails, steel pipes and tubes, and other finished steel products. The steel produced by integrated mills tended to be purer than steel produced by electric arc furnaces since less scrap was used in the production process (scrap steel often contained non-ferrous elements that could adversely affect metallurgical properties). Some steel customers required purer steel products for their applications.

Mini-mills used an electric arc furnace to melt steel scrap or scrap substitutes into molten metal that was then cast into crude steel slabs, billets, or blooms in a continuous casting process. As was the case at integrated mills, the crude steel was then run through

various facilities and finishing processes to make hot-rolled and cold-rolled sheet steel products, steel bars and beams, stainless steel, steel wire and nails, steel pipes and tubes, and other finished steel products. Mini-mills could accommodate short production runs and had relatively fast product change-over time. The electric arc technology employed by mini-mills offered two primary competitive advantages—capital investment requirements that were 75 percent lower than those of integrated mills and a smaller workforce (which translated into lower labor costs per ton shipped).

Initially, companies that used electric arc furnace technology were able to only make low-end steel products (such as reinforcing rods and steel bars). But when thin-slab casting technology came on the scene in the 1980s, mini-mills were able to compete in the market for flat-rolled carbon sheet

EXHIBIT 8 Top 15 Producers of Crude Steel Worldwide, 2017

Global Rank	Company (Headquarters Country)	Crude Steel Production (millions of metric tons)
1.	ArcelorMittal (Luxembourg)	97.0
2.	China Baowu Group (China)	65.4
3.	NSSMC Group (Japan)	47.4
4.	HBIS Group (China)	47.1
5.	POSCO (South Korea)	42.2
6.	Shagang Group (China)	38.4
7.	Ansteel (China)	35.8
8.	JFE Steel (Japan)	30.2
9.	Shougang Group (China)	27.6
10.	Tata Steel (India)	25.1
11.	Nucor (USA)	24.4
12.	Shandong Steel Group (China)	21.7
13.	Hyundai Steel (South Korea)	21.2
14.	Jianlong Group (China)	20.3
15.	Hunan Valin Steel (China)	20.2

Source: Worldsteel Association, *World Steel in Figures, 2018,* **www.worldsteel.org** (accessed on May 30, 2018).

and strip products; these products sold at substantially higher prices per ton and thus were attractive market segments for mini-mill companies. Carbon sheet and strip steel products accounted for about 50 to 60 percent of total steel production and represented the last big market category controlled by the producers employing basic oxygen furnace and blast furnace technologies. Thin-slab casting technology, developed in Germany, was pioneered in the United States by Nucor at its plants in Indiana and elsewhere. Other mini-mill companies in the United States and across the world were quick to adopt thin-slab casting technology because the low capital costs of thin-slab casting facilities, often coupled with lower labor costs per ton, gave mini-mill companies a cost and pricing advantage over integrated steel producers, enabling them to grab a growing share of the global market for flat-rolled sheet steel and other carbon steel products. Many integrated producers also switched to thin-slab casting as a defensive measure to protect their profit margins and market shares.

In 2017, 71.5 percent of the world's steel mill production was made at large integrated mills and about 28 percent was made at mills that used electric arc furnaces.[13] In the United States, however, 68.4 percent of the crude steel was produced at mills employing electric arc furnaces and 31.6 percent at mills using blast furnaces and basic oxygen processes.[14] Large integrated steel mills using blast furnaces, basic oxygen furnaces, and assorted casting and rolling equipment typically had the ability to manufacture a wide variety of steel mill products but faced significantly higher capital costs and higher operating costs for labor and energy. While mills using electric-arc furnaces were sometimes challenged by high prices for scrap metal, they tended to have far lower capital and operating costs compared with the integrated steel producers. However, the quality of the steel produced using blast furnace technologies tended to be superior to that of electric arc furnaces unless, like at many of Nucor's facilities, the user of electric arc furnaces invested in additional facilities and processing equipment to enable the production of upgraded steel products.

Market Conditions in the Global Steel Market, 2015 to 2018

The global marketplace for steel was intensely price competitive and expected to remain so unless and until the estimated 700 million tons of excess steel-making capacity across the world shrunk substantially and global demand for steel products rose sufficiently to more closely match global supplies. Approximately 150 million tons of the world's excess steelmaking capacity was in China, but there were sizable pockets of excess capacity in many other countries. Companies with excess production capacity were typically active in seeking to increase their exports of steel to foreign markets. Steel producers in some countries, particularly those in the European Union, Turkey, South Korea, and Canada, were both big exporters and big importers because domestic steel makers had more capacity to make certain types and grades of steel than was needed locally (and thus strived to export such products to other countries) but lacked sufficient domestic capability to produce certain types and grades of semi-finished and finished steel products needed by domestic customers (which consequently had to be imported). In most countries of the world, the difference between steel exports and steel imports was a matter of a few million tons. But there were six countries that stood out as big *net* exporters of semi-finished and finished steel products, of which China was by far the largest (see Exhibit 9).

The major Chinese steelmakers, burdened by large amounts of unused capacity, responding Chinese steelmakers, a number of which were wholly or partly government-owned, had responded to the burden of having large amounts of unused capacity by aggressively seeking out buyers for their products in other countries and securing orders by offering prices that significantly undercut the prices of local steel makers and enabled the Chinese sellers to steal away sales and market share. The low prices offered by Chinese steelmakers were partly enabled by Chinese currency devaluations initiated by the Chinese government and partly enabled by subsidies and other financial assistance the Chinese government provided to domestic steel makers. The success of Chinese steelmakers in capturing the business

EXHIBIT 9 Major Net Exporters (Exports – Imports) of Semi-Finished and Finished Steel Products, by Country, 2015–2017 (in millions of metric tons)

Country	2015	2016	2017
China	98.4	94.5	60.9
Japan	34.9	34.5	31.2
Russia	25.4	26.7	24.9
Ukraine	16.9	17.1	13.8
Brazil	10.5	11.5	13.0
South Korea	9.5	7.3	12.1

Source: Worldsteel Association, *Steel Statistical Yearbook, 2017* and *World Steel in Figures, 2018,* www.worldsteel.org (accessed May 31, 2018).

of foreign buyers resulted in total Chinese exports of semi-finished and finished steel products of 92.9 million tons in 2014, 111.6 million tons in 2015, 108.1 million tons in 2016, and 78.4 million tons in 2017, amounts that were bigger than the total amount of crude steel produced by steelmakers in the United States in all four years.[15]

A flood of steel imports into the United States in 2015, powered by price discounting on the part of foreign sellers, resulted in the price of hot-rolled steel coil in the United States dropping about 40 percent to under $400 per ton, with domestic mills idling as much as 38 percent of capacity. The price drop contributed to a loss of $1.5 billion at U.S. Steel Corp. and an almost $8 billion loss at ArcelorMittal.[16] According to ArcelorMittal's CEO, the Chinese steel industry lost $10 billion in 2015, which "proves they are dumping."[17] A number of countries, at the urging of domestic steel makers suffering from lost sales and falling domestic steel prices in 2014 and 2015, began investigating whether their markets were a dumping ground for unfairly traded, low-priced steel produced in China and certain other countries.

In June 2015, following several months of surging steel imports from China and elsewhere, five steel makers in the United States, including

Nucor, filed three sets of cases petitioning the U.S. Department of Commerce to initiate anti-dumping investigations against imports of hot-rolled, cold-rolled, and corrosion-resistant steel coming from China, Japan, South Korea, India, Brazil, Russia, and Italy. According to media reports, Chinese and Japanese steel producers refused to cooperate in supplying data that the International Trade Commission at the Department of Commerce (DOC) requested for its investigation. Beginning in November 2015 and continuing into March 2016, the DOC issued a series of announcements that import duties were being raised by 227 percent on cold-rolled steel from certain Chinese exporters for a period of five years, by 255.8 percent on all corrosion-resistant steel from China for a period of five years, and by 266 percent on selected other Chinese steel products; in previous periods, the DOC's International Trade Commission had imposed duty increases on 19 Chinese-made steel products entering the United States. Certain Japanese steel products were hit by the DOC with duties of 71 percent; smaller duties were set on imports of certain steel products from India, South Korea, Russia, Brazil, and Italy. According to one steel industry analyst, while these increases in duties would be helpful, it would take duty increases of about 500 percent to halt the dumping practices of Chinese steel makers.[18]

Numerous other countries around the world also imposed more than 130 antidumping tariffs and duties on Chinese steel producers (and Chinese manufacturers of aluminum and certain other metals as well) to protect their domestic steel companies from what they termed the unfair trade practices of Chinese producers to take sales away from domestic producers by selling at ultralow prices (typically enabled by subsidies from the Chinese government).[19] The average price of Chinese steel exports fell by about 50 percent between 2011 and 2016.

In 2016, the Chinese government agreed to pursue actions to reduce its domestic steelmaking capacity by 150 million tons by 2020. But, while some capacity reductions had occurred, Chinese producers were pursuing ways to escape the tariffs being imposed. One method was to sell steel to buyers in a country that had not been singled out for tariffs imposed by the United States and other countries; these buyers, participants in a Chinese-engineered scheme to disguise the origin of the Chinese-made steel products, in turn shipped the steel products

tariff-free to buyers in the United States and other countries. China Zhongwang Holdings, China's largest producer of aluminum flat-rolled and extrusion products, used a different tariff-evading scheme. In 2016, the China Zhongwang was discovered to have stockpiled more than 500,000 metric tons of aluminum products hidden under hay and tarpaulins in a Mexican desert just below the U.S. border, with alleged intentions of shipping them to the United States to avoid trade restrictions on Chinese exports of aluminum to the United States—provisions in the North American Free Trade Agreement allowed for aluminum products to be moved tariff-free from Mexico into the United States (reports and pictures of the stockpile in the media blew up the scheme).[20] In recent years, aluminum smelters in China had come to dominate the global aluminum market, reportedly supplying about half of the world's need for aluminum products in 2016 and 2017. Of the 23 aluminum smelters in operation in the United States in 2000, only 5 were still in operation in 2016, largely due to the fact that the Chinese manufacturers of aluminum products could use the subsidies they received from the Chinese government to undercut the prices of U.S. producers.

In 2018, the Trump Administration announced 25 percent tariffs on certain steel and aluminum imports from China, the European Union, Canada, and Mexico. Within weeks, there were multiple media reports that, in an effort to escape these tariffs, various Chinese steelmakers had sold steel to Chinese brokers who then shipped the steel to buyers in various countries that were not confronted tariffs on their steel exports to the United States and elsewhere; these buyers in turn promptly shipped the steel products to buyers in the United States. In 2017 and 2018, however, Chinese steel producers has devised another way to skirt tariffs on steel. While they were shutting down some of their production in China, they had started aggressively expanding overseas, using tens of billions of dollars supplied by Chinese lenders owned by the Chinese government, to buy and build steel plants at locations around the world.[21] Already operational were plants with 3.5 million metric tons of capacity in Malaysia, 3.0 million metric tons in Indonesia, and 2.2 million metric tons in Serbia. Under construction were plants with capacity of 6.0 million metric tons in Indonesia, 2.0 million metric tons in India, and 0.5 million metric tons in Texas. And there were plants on the verge of starting construction in 2018 with capacity of 10 million metric tons in Brazil (where the Brazilian steel industry was currently operating at 70 percent of capacity), 7.5 million metric tons in Indonesia, and 2.0 million metric tons in Bangladesh.[22]

The steel plant in Serbia, owned and operated by a recently-renamed Chinese company called the Hesteel Group, had begun selling wide hot-rolled steel coil to U.S. buyers through Duferco, a Swiss trading company that was 51 percent owned by Hesteel.[23] This same plant was also reportedly exporting tariff-free steel products into the 28-nation European Union. A new 2 million metric ton steel plant built on the Indonesian island of Sulawesi by Tsingshan Group Holdings (that was funded by a $570 million loan from the government-backed China Development Bank) accounted for 4 percent of the world's stainless-steel production and had exported 300,000 metric tons to the United States through a joint venture with Pittsburgh-based stainless-steel producer Allegheny Technologies.[24]

Exhibit 10 shows the volumes of U.S. imports and exports of semi-finished and finished steel products for 2005-2017. The column showing "apparent domestic use of finished steel products" is obtained by adding up deliveries (defined as what comes out of the facility gates of domestic steel producers) minus exports of steel products plus imports of steel products; as such, it is a good approximation of total domestic consumption of steel products and is a commonly used metric in the steel industry. The last column shows the percentage of domestic steel use supplied by foreign steel producers.

NUCOR AND COMPETITION IN THE U.S. MARKET FOR STEEL

Nucor's broad product lineup meant that it was an active participant in the U.S. markets for a wide variety of finished steel products and unfinished

EXHIBIT 10 **U.S. Exports and Imports of Semi-Finished and Finished Steel Products, 2005–2017 (in millions of metric tons)**

Year	U.S. Exports	U.S. Imports	Net Imports (Exports − Imports)	Apparent Domestic Use of Finished Steel Products	U.S. Imports as a Percent of Domestic Apparent Use
2005	9.4	30.2	20.8	110.3	27.4%
2006	9.6	42.2	32.6	122.4	34.5%
2007	9.8	27.7	17.9	111.2	24.9%
2008	12.0	24.6	12.6	101.1	24.3%
2009	9.2	15.3	6.1	59.3	25.8%
2010	11.8	22.5	10.7	115.8	19.4%
2011	13.3	26.6	13.3	89.2	29.8%
2012	13.6	30.9	17.3	96.2	32.1%
2013	12.5	29.8	17.3	95.7	31.1%
2014	12.0	41.4	29.4	107.0	38.7%
2015	10.0	36.5	26.5	96.1	38.0%
2016	9.2	30.9	21.7	91.9	33.6%
2017	10.2	35.4	25.2	97.7	36.2%

Source: Worldsteel Association, *Steel Statistical Yearbook, 2017* and *World Steel in Figures, 2018,* www.worldsteel.org (accessed May 31, 2018); Worldsteel Association, *Steel Statistical Yearbook, 2010,* www.steel-on-the-net.com (accessed May 31, 2018).

steel products, plus the markets for scrap steel and scrap substitutes. Nucor executives considered all the market segments and product categories in which it competed to be intensely competitive, many of which were populated with both domestic and foreign rivals. For the most part, competition for steel mill products and finished steel products was centered on price and the ability to meet customer delivery requirements. And, due to global overcapacity, many of the world's steelmakers were actively seeking new business in whatever geographic markets they could find willing buyers.

But with steel imports capturing roughly 38 percent of the market for finished and semi-finished steel products in the United States in 2014 and 2015, Nucor found itself trapped in a fierce competitive battle with rival global and domestic steel producers to win orders from the buyers of steel bar, structural steel, steel plate, cold-finished steel, and certain other steel products (see Nucor's 2015 sales decline for these products in Exhibit 3). Nucor's shipments of sheet steel held up well in 2015 (see Exhibit 2) because of near-record sales of motor vehicles in North America (motor vehicle manufacturers were major purchasers of sheet steel). From 2016 to 2018, Nucor management did not foresee any signs of a meaningful and sustained upswing in domestic demand for steel products that would relieve the stiff competitive pressures on its sales and profits.

In Nucor's 2015 Annual Report, Ferriola told shareholders:

> We are not sitting idly by as unfairly traded imports continue to come into the U.S. market. We are aggressively fighting back. Last year, Nucor and the entire steel industry scored a significant victory when Congress passed legislation strengthening our nation's trade laws. These important changes to trade law enforcement will help us fight back more effectively against the surge of illegally dumped and subsidized imports. These changes were long overdue. Our trade laws had not been updated in more than 20 years. While these new trade laws alone will not solve the serious issues facing the U.S. steel industry due to systemic steel overcapacity overseas, they do put us in a much stronger position to hold foreign governments and steel producers accountable for violating trade laws.
>
> Nucor has also joined other U.S. steel companies in filing trade cases for several flat-rolled products, including corrosion-resistant, hot-rolled, and cold-rolled steel. The International Trade Commission has made preliminary determinations of injury in all three cases,

allowing the investigations to proceed. Nucor will continue to assess market conditions in other product areas and pursue cases when appropriate.[25]

Many foreign steel producers had costs on a par with or even below those of Nucor, although their competitiveness in the U.S. market varied significantly according to the prevailing strength of their local currencies versus the U.S. dollar and the extent to which they received government subsidies.

In Nucor's 2017 Annual Report, Ferriola again reported to shareholders on the impacts that global excess capacity and unfair trade practices were having on the company:

> Although Nucor's earnings increased significantly in 2017, they continue to be impacted significantly by extremely high levels of steel imports. Our industry remains greatly constrained by the impact of global overcapacity. Weak economic conditions in Europe, slow growth in China and a strong U.S. dollar relative to other foreign currencies continue to make the U.S. markets a prime target for foreign steel imports. While the steel industry has historically been characterized by periods of overcapacity and intense competition for sales among producers, we are currently experiencing an era of global overcapacity that is unprecedented. Despite ongoing domestic and global steel industry consolidation, the extraordinary increase in China's steel production in the last decade, together with the excess capacity from other countries that have state-owned enterprises ("SOEs") or export-focused steel industries, have exacerbated this overcapacity issue domestically as well as globally. . . .We believe Chinese producers, many of which are government-owned in whole or in part, continue to benefit from their government's manipulation of foreign currency exchange rates and from the receipt of government subsidies, which allow them to sell steel into our markets at artificially low prices.
>
> Foreign imports of finished and semi-finished steel increased more than 15 percent in 2017 compared to 2016 . . . with imports of finished steel products alone capturing 27 percent of the U.S. market despite significant unused cost-competitive domestic capacity. The surge comes from numerous countries and cuts across many product lines. Our products that experience the greatest amount of imports include semi-finished steel, reinforcing bar, plate and hot-rolled, cold-rolled, and galvanized sheet steel. Countries that contribute significantly to the import total include South Korea, Turkey, Japan, and China.
>
> China is not only selling steel at artificially low prices into our domestic market but also across the globe. When it does so, steel products that would

otherwise have been consumed by the local steel customers in other countries are displaced into global markets, compounding the issue. Nucor has joined three other domestic steelmakers in filing a petition alleging China is circumventing previously levied duties by shipping products through third-party countries.[26]

Nucor's Two Largest Domestic Competitors

Consolidation of the both the global and domestic steel industry into a smaller number of larger and more efficient steel producers had heightened competitive pressures for Nucor and most other steelmakers. Nucor had two major rivals in the United States—the USA division of ArcelorMittal and United States Steel.

ArcelorMittal USA In 2018, ArcelorMittal USA operated 27 facilities, including four large integrated steel mills, six electric arc furnace plants, and four rolling and finishing plants located across 14 states and employing more than 18,000 people. Its facilities were considered to be modern and efficient. Its product lineup included hot-rolled and cold-rolled sheet steel, steel plate, steel bars, railroad rails, high-quality wire rods, rebar, grinding balls, structural steel, tubular steel, and tin mill products. Much of its production was sold to customers in the automotive, trucking, off-highway, agricultural-equipment, and railway industries, with the balance being sold to steel service centers and companies in the appliance, office furniture, electrical motor, packaging, and industrial machinery sectors.

Globally, ArcelorMittal was the world's largest steel producer, with steelmaking operations in 18 countries on four continents, annual production capacity of about 113 million tons of crude steel, and steel shipments of 85.2 million tons in 2017. It had worldwide sales revenues of $68.7 billion and a net profit of $4.6 billion in 2017, worldwide sales revenues of $56.8 billion and a net profit of $1.7 billion in 2016, and worldwide sales revenues of $63.6 billion and a net loss of $7.9 billion in 2015.[27] ArcelorMittal also lost money on its worldwide operations in 2012, 2013, and 2014. One important cause of ArcelorMittal's spotty financial performance was the industry's massive amount of excess capacity, which had spurred steel producers in China, Japan, India, Russia, and other locations to dump steel products at artificially low prices in many of the geographic markets where ArcelorMittal had operations (and thereby push down the market prices of many steel products to unprofitable levels).

U.S. Steel U.S. Steel was an integrated steel producer of flat-rolled and tubular steel products with major production operations in the United States and Europe. It had 2018 crude steel production capacity of 17 million tons in the United States and 5 million tons in Europe. In 2017, U.S. Steel was the third largest producer of crude steel in the United States and the 26th largest in the world. U.S. Steel's production of crude steel in the United States was 10.8 million tons in 2017, 10.7 million tons in 2016, and 11.3 million tons in 2015. Crude steel production averaged 64 percent of capability in 2017, 63 percent of capability in 2016, and 60 percent of capability in 2015.

U.S. Steel's operations were organized into three business segments: flat-rolled products (which included all of its integrated steel mills that produced steel slabs, rounds, steel plate, sheet steel, and tin mill products), U.S. Steel Europe, and tubular products. The flat-rolled segment primarily served North American customers in the transportation (including automotive), construction, container, appliance, and electrical industries, plus steel service centers and manufacturers that bought steel mill products for conversion into a variety of finished steel products. U.S. Steel's flat-rolled business segment had 2015 sales of $8.3 billion and an operating loss of $237 million, 2016 sales of $7.5 billion and an operating loss of $3 million, and 2017 sales of $8.3 billion and operating income of $380 million. Its tubular products segment had 2015 sales of $898 million and an operating loss of $179 million, 2016 sales of $449 million and an operating loss of $304 million, and 2017 sales of $944 million and an operating loss of $99 million. U.S. Steel's European business had 2015 sales of $2.3 billion and operating profit of $81 million, 2016 sales of $2.2 billion and operating profit of $185 million, and 2017 sales of $2.9 billion and operating profit of $327 million.

U.S. Steel had a labor cost disadvantage versus Nucor and ArcelorMittal USA, partly due to the lower productivity of its unionized workforce and partly due to its retiree pension costs. In 2013, U.S. Steel launched a series of internal initiatives to "get leaner faster, right-size, and improve our performance."[28] Going into 2018, however, these initiatives had yet to bear much fruit even though it had closed two Canadian facilities in 2014 and idled a U.S. facility in 2015.

ENDNOTES

[1] Tom Peters and Nancy Austin, *A Passion for Excellence: The Leadership Difference,* New York: Random House, 1985; and "Other Low-Cost Champions," *Fortune,* June 24, 1985.

[2] Nucor's 2011 Annual Report, p. 4.

[3] February 2016 Investor Presentation, www.nucor.com (accessed March 21, 2016).

[4] March 2014 Investor Presentation, www.nucor.com (accessed April 22, 2014).

[5] According to information at www.nucor.com (accessed October 11, 2006).

[6] Nucor's 2008 Annual Report, p. 5.

[7] March 2014 Investor Presentation, www.nucor.com (accessed April 21, 2014).

[8] Nanette Byrnes, "The Art of Motivation," *Business Week,* May 1, 2006, p.57.

[9] Ibid., p. 60.

[10] Ibid.

[11] Ibid.

[12] Worldsteel Association, *World Steel in Figures, 2018,* www.worldsteel.org (accessed on May 30, 2018).

[13] Worldsteel Association, *World Steel in Figures, 2018,* www.worldsteel.org (accessed on May 30, 2018).

[14] Worldsteel Association, "World Steel in Figures 2015," p. 10, www.worldsteel.org (accessed March 10, 2016).

[15] Worldsteel Association, *Steel Statistical Yearbook, 2017* and *World Steel in Figures, 2018,* www.worldsteel.org (accessed on May 30, 2018).

[16] John W. Miller and William Mauldin, "U.S. Imposes 266% Duty on Some Chinese Imports," *Wall Street Journal,* March 1, 2016, www.wsj.com (accessed March 14, 2016).

[17] Ibid.

[18] As quoted in Sonja Elmquist, "U.S. Calls for 256% Tariff on Imports of Steel from China,"

December 22, 2015, www.bloombergbusiness.com, (accessed March 14, 2016).

[19] Matthew Dalton and Lingling Wei, "China's Blueprint for Skirting U.S. Tariffs on Steel," *Wall Street Journal,* June 5, 2018, pp. A1 and A8.

[20] Scott Patterson, Biman Mukherji, and Vu Trong Khanh, "Giant Aluminum Stockpile Was Shipped from Mexico to Vietnam," *Wall Street Journal,* December 1, 2016, www.wsj.com (accessed June 8, 2018).

[21] Ibid., p. A8.

[22] Ibid.

[23] Ibid.

[24] Ibid.

[25] Nucor annual report, 2015, p. 6.

[26] Nucor annual report, 2017, p. 24.

[27] ArcelorMittal annual report, 2017.

[28] Company 10-K Report 2013, p. 12.

CASE 28

Vail Resorts, Inc.

Herman L. Boschken

San Jose State University

In its 55th anniversary season of 2017, Vail Resorts (VR) held the most esteemed reputation and a commanding presence in the North American winter resort industry with resorts in Vail, Beaver Creek, Whistler, British Columbia, and 11 other locations in North America and Australia. But, in some ways, VR was reaching a crossroad in both strategy and context. Unlike the earlier years when linear growth pursuits were the norm, VR was facing new and more difficult choices, many posing significant tradeoffs in strategic direction.

The industry situation, as well, had been evolving extensively for several years, involving some significant circumstances:

1. An aging U.S. population was shrinking demand for skiing.

2. Snowboarding and other non-conventional activities were maturing alongside the traditional protocol of alpine downhill skiing.

3. Competitors were bringing forth stunning new designs and making vast new investments in on-mountain and village facilities.

4. Several consolidations and mergers had reduced the field of large multi-resort providers and revised corporate membership in "the big four."

5. The 2007 onset of a severe and sustained decline in world economies that wiped out vast sums of capital and job markets across industries reconfigured consumer demand for destination resorts.

6. The climate effects of global warming were having wide-ranging impacts on production and maintenance of resort ski conditions, as well as feeding variability in short-term demand and uncertainty in long-term skier expectations.

These events, however, served to mask the fact that the firm was continuing to struggle with an incoherent diversification involving several acquired businesses still awaiting integration into a comprehensive core-business strategy. With VR's rapid-fire agenda and immediate consequences unfolding over the last decade, the firm was in need of a recrafted long-term strategy. How should the parts of this much larger firm fit together? How might the firm broaden its offerings to meet an "all-season resort" theme without losing the sense of an integrated product family? Given several evolving circumstances in industry situation, what alternatives lay ahead to maintain momentum, enhance profitability and retain its renown world-class status in providing destination resort facilities?

COMPANY HISTORY

In 1962, two WWII veterans, Pete Seibert and Earl Eaton, along with several associates opened the Vail Ski Resort located in a narrow Rocky Mountain valley known for its remoteness and spectacular alpine splendor. Previously the home to mountain ranchers and sheep herders, this area beckoned the ambitious developers because of its ideal ski terrain and a proposed interstate freeway which was to traverse the valley floor on its way westward from Denver. The partnership would be called Vail Associates and over the remainder of the 20th century, it would become a premier developer of world-class ski resorts in North America and beyond.

In 1992, the firm was acquired by Apollo Global Management, a New York investment firm led by venture capitalist Leon Black. With a name change, Vail Resorts went public in early 1997 (NYSE ticker symbol: MTN) and opened its first corporate websites: www.snow.com and www.vailresorts.com. In that same year, Black (who retains majority control to this day) selected Adam Aron as the firm's Chairman and CEO. Aron came from the travel and hospitality industries where he had been president of Norwegian Cruise Lines, and Marketing VP for United Airlines and Hyatt. To balance the team, Black retained Andy Daly, VR's senior operations man, as the firm's president.

With rapid growth in mind, Aron wasted no time in setting an agenda driven by a new "all seasons" strategy. The following decade saw significant expansion in many directions. Adding to its core business, the firm built or acquired three additional Colorado ski resorts (all located within 45 minutes of each other), and expanded its summer venues. Still hungry for acquisitions, VR looked westward in the first decade of the new millennium to the California Sierras, adding three ski resorts in or near the Tahoe Basin. In 2015, it gained ownership of Utah's Park City Resort, and a year later, combined it with VR's previous purchase of the adjacent Canyons development. In 2016, VR looked to western Canada for acquisition of Whistler-Blackcomb, North America's largest ski resort complex and site of the 2010 Winter Olympics. By year's end, it was also adding an urban "feeder system" of resorts to its network, and, in 2017, acquired its first destination resort outside North America in Australia.

Even though VR's ski resorts maintained their commanding presence in the market, Aron's strategy had led the firm to also emphasize acquisitions and development outside the ski industry, principally in standalone luxury spa-hotels. Although he argued that such diversification offset seasonality in the ski industry, this new direction not only blurred the traditional focus on skiing but also left few clues as to how far the firm was willing to go to establish a new sustainable vision. As a result of spending huge investment sums without a clearly focused strategy, VR was experiencing in 2003 and 2004 a decline in its stock price (reaching levels well below its 1997 IPO price) and had fallen deeply into debt.

Meanwhile, however, the first two decades of the 21st century saw a rapid increase in U.S. real estate prices, including luxury second-home resorts fueled by affluent late-career Baby Boomers and foreign investors. During 2004 and 2005, Aron frequented Wall Street to sound the message that VR was grossly undervalued when factoring in its huge ski-resort real estate holdings. In 2006, Wall Street responded by giving the firm a much-needed boost in capital value with which to continue development activities. Cash flows from operations were improving as well, due in part to increased skier/boarder visits and foreign vacationers taking advantage of a cheapening dollar.

Even with the firm's improving prospects from real estate, Aron was replaced as CEO and Chairman in 2006 by Rob Katz, a trusted colleague of Leon Black and long-time member of VR's Board. In the ensuing 10 years, Katz would reign in further acquisitions outside VR's core business of ski resorts, integrate the previously acquired Rock Resorts into the family of ski resorts, and engage in modification of the core-business model that involved (a) acquisition of the two largest ski resorts in North America, those of Park City (2014) and Whistler-Blackcomb (2016), both of which had been Winter Olympic sites; (b) creation of a "feeder system" of smaller day-use "windshield" ski resorts proximal to major urban markets; (c) establishment of a "multi-generational family" brand supported by a universal "EPIC" program of customer benefits that included an annual Epic Pass providing skier access across all its resorts; and (d) accelerated capital investment in resort development and technologies that emphasized "seamless" integration of operations.

According to Katz, VR's current strategic agenda is to "create synergies by operating multiple resorts." Although the firm continues to diversify its portfolio into new geographical areas for "all season" resorts, its primary stable of nine destination ski resorts in North America share distinctive attributes, giving prominence to the firm's unifying icon: "an Experience of a Lifetime." In turn, VR's CEO also argues that: "Our premier resorts differentiate our [facilities] from the rest of the ski industry. We have iconic, branded mountain resorts in four important ski destinations in North America: Colorado, California, Utah and British Columbia."

VAIL RESORTS' FAMILY OF FACILITIES

VR's family of resorts includes (a) nine North American destination facilities, (b) four U.S. "urban" resorts serving as a destination-resort feeder system

EXHIBIT 1 Vail Resorts Family of Ski Resorts

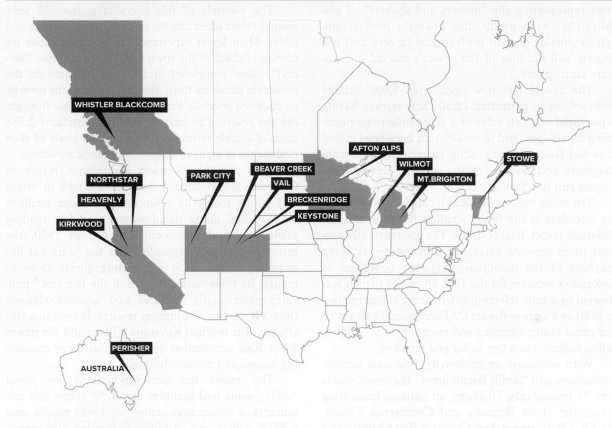

Source: National Ski Areas Association, Vail Resorts.

for customers located in major Midwest cities and the eastern corridor, and (c) the emergence of a global network of destination resorts with the 2017 acquisition of Perisher in Australia. Locations of the facilities are shown in Exhibit 1.

The firm's North American destination resorts include combinations of owned properties (mostly in the villages) and long-term leases from both the U.S. Forest Service and private landowners for the mountain ski terrain. All these sites include centrally-located retail and commercial structures contained in "ski-in ski-out" villages, embossed with quaint hotels and hotel/convention centers, some golf courses, and other unique entertainment facilities. Each resort is different in theme and atmosphere, but all ascribe to Vail Resorts' reputation for quality service, all-season excellence and trademark in providing a unique upscale experience to discerning vacationers.

The firm's marquis resort is Vail, known by its slogan: "Like Nowhere Else on Earth." The resort is among the three largest single-site ski resorts in North America. With major design facelifts over the years, its village nevertheless retains the appearance and ambiance of a traditional European alpine setting. Paralleling the interstate, the resort provides all the conveniences of a large rural town. It has two primary pedestrian-only village centers, connected to each other and the town's outer areas (some of which are four miles up or down the freeway) by a complimentary bus system.

The town of Vail boasts accommodations for over 30,000 people and contains over 100 restaurants and bars, 225 shops and markets, two skating arenas, outdoor amphitheater, a PGA golf course, regional hospital, transportation center, schools and a library. It is the primary or second home to professionals and executives from numerous blue-chip companies, high tech firms, and Wall Street investment houses, most representing the "movers and shakers" of globalization. As a group, this clientele prefers anonymity outside of their professional careers, and has chosen Vail because of the resort's relaxed but discrete atmosphere.

The resort has developed over 5,000 skiable acres within its permitted 12,500 acre terrain. Skiing is provided on both sides of a seven-mile ridge paralleling its villages, and in an adjacent back-bowl called Blue Ski Basin. Vertical drop (a measure of terrain steepness and ski-run length) is 3,450 feet and the longest run is 4.5 miles.

Ten miles west of Vail and located three miles off the interstate is the firm's smallest but most upscale Colorado resort, Beaver Creek. The resort actually contains three separate villages at different points along the base of the mountain. Originally conceived as Colorado's location for the 1976 Olympics (which was aborted by a state referendum), the core village opened in 1980 as a state-of-the-art CAD-designed facility with European alpine elegance and environmental sophistication tucked into a tiny valley and meadow.

With emphasis on exclusivity, first-class accommodations, and "family friendliness," the resort sports over 25 restaurants, 70 shops, an outdoor ice-skating arena, the Hyatt Regency and Conference Center, the Vilar Performing Arts Center, a Ritz-Carlton, and overnight capacity for 6,000 people (more accommodations are available in the town of Avon, about three miles down mountain from Beaver Creek). On the mountain, Beaver Creek provides 1,800 acres of skiable terrain with exceptional variety for families having different levels of skiing ability. Its "Birds of Prey" downhill course is recognized by World-Cup skiers as the most challenging in North America.

Located off I-70, about an hour east of Vail and Beaver Creek along the Continental Divide, are VR's other two Colorado destination facilities. Opening as a ski resort in 1961, the largest of these is Breckenridge, consisting of a vast range of treeless peaks anchored by an historical western mining town. Although slightly rebranded to fit VR's multi-generational family clientele, this resort community's reputation has emphasized the youthful exuberance of singles and couples seeking an active social life. As a consequence, it has more bars (totaling over 50) but fewer restaurants than Vail and over 100 shops. In addition, the town has a performing-arts theater, museums, a golf course,

and a large convention center. It has overnight accommodations for 25,000 people.

The clientele of this historically-preserved year-around resort often cite the unique "sense of place and fabled Main Street experience" as a prime reason for coming. Added to the town's ambiance is a new "second" village completed in 2010 and situated on the mountain above the town. It is connected to the town by an enclosed gondola. Free buses also circulate throughout the resort. The resort's mountain contains 2,358 acres of skiable terrain and caters to all levels of skier proficiency at many of Colorado's highest elevations.

VR's fourth all-season destination resort in Colorado is Keystone. Like Beaver Creek in origin and family focus, its off-mountain village facilities were crafted along meadowland as a freestanding planned unit development. Opened in 1970, the resort has steadily expanded over the years but has acquired a reputation for putting guests close to nature. Its trademark, "Nature of the Rockies," indicates more rustic facilities and accommodations than VR's other destination resorts. It contains two villages—the original Keystone Village and the newer River Run surrounded by residential areas containing homes and condominiums.

The resort has accommodations for about 5,000 people and includes about 50 shops and restaurants, a convention center for 1,800 people, and a PGA golf course. Additional housing and amenities are located about two miles away in the town of Dillon. With 3,148 acres of skiable terrain, Keystone developed its ski mountain with an emphasis on intermediate skiers, but provides skier access to very steep terrain at an adjacent ski area not owned by VR, called Arapahoe Basin.

The four Colorado resorts are accessible by air and ground. Vail and Beaver Creek are located about 100 miles west of Denver. Breckenridge and Keystone are about 60 miles west of Denver. All are along or very near Interstate 70 which passes through the Denver metropolitan area on its way westward. Air transportation is available year-round through Denver International Airport (DIA) and seasonally through the Vail/Eagle County Airport (located just west of Beaver Creek and Vail). Ground transportation from both airports is provided by car-rental agencies, Greyhound Bus, and the Colorado Mountain Express (a van service owned by VR). The ride from Denver traverses spectacular scenery but takes about two and one-half hours to Vail and Beaver Creek.

In addition to the four Colorado resorts, VR acquired three destination resorts in the prestigious Lake Tahoe area of the California Sierras. In early 2002, it bought Heavenly Valley, providing the firm with its first winter resort site outside Colorado. Tracing its origin to the 1950s, Heavenly is the second largest of the Tahoe-area resorts behind Squaw/Alpine and fourth largest of VR's destination resorts. For the bargain price of $97 million, it represented tremendous potential for a facility that for years had been a significant under-performer in the destination resort market.

In a quest to appeal to national and international destination customers, VR undertook a decade-long village redevelopment project, partially transforming the core of South Lake Tahoe into a ski-in ski-out village experience with substantial new development anchored by the mountain's primary gondola portal. Beyond this small but vibrant new core, lay the town's principal accommodations which provide for about 25,000 people in a patchwork spread over several square miles along US 50 (the city's main street). Today, VR maintains that 60 percent of Heavenly's market comes from outside California and stays a week or longer. Nevertheless, the ambiance of a European alpine village that is the hallmark of VR's other resorts remains elusive and incomplete.

Most of the resorts ski terrain is located in a relatively flat bowl on top of a mostly treeless plateau overlooking the vast Tahoe Basin. Although providing spectacular vistas of the lake and surrounding wilderness, much of the 4,800 acre ski terrain is considered either too flat or too steep for many intermediate skiers. Also, moisture content of the snowpack is typically high, giving it the disparaging name: "Sierra Cement." Total reconstruction costs to upgrade on-mountain infrastructure ran about $80 million, and concluded in 2010, with the opening of Tamarack Lodge, a 15,000 sq ft grand-style mountaintop restaurant facility designed in the VR tradition.

Compounding the resort's less-appealing town setting (where casinos still reign high), access to Heavenly for destination skiers involves a one and a half hour drive in harsh weather along US 395 and US 50 from the Reno airport (about twice the trip-time for other Tahoe-area resorts). For unclear reasons, VR and South Tahoe politicians have chosen not to reopen for commercial flights the South Tahoe Airport located just minutes from the Heavenly resort.

In late 2010, VR widened its West Coast footprint in the Tahoe Basin by acquiring Northstar At Tahoe for $60 million from Booth Creek Partners. Historically, the resort had been known primarily as a second-home development frequented mostly by a San Francisco Bay Area clientele interested in long-weekend getaways. In the five years prior to VR's purchase, Booth had spent upwards of $100 million to modernize the resort's chair-lift system and convert its small nominal village into a much-enlarged, European-style destination venue. Anchoring the new village was a Marriott and Ritz Carlton, both of which opened in 2009.

Known primarily for family-oriented skiing, its mountain was designed for intermediate and beginner skiers, and covers about 2,000 acres. Instilling a family ambiance, the remodeled village now is seen as a focal staging area that includes an outdoor ice-skating rink surrounded by shops, restaurants, coffee places, and second-story condominiums. For North American and international visitors, the resort has good access by air via Reno International, about an hour away.

VR's third Tahoe-area addition to its all-season destination resorts is Kirkwood, located about 35 minutes south of the Tahoe basin. Village property, surrounding developable lands and on-mountain assets were acquired for $18 million. Since its inception 45 years ago, the resort had been frequented mostly by windshield enthusiasts from the Bay Area and Central Valley. It is situated in a narrow alpine valley (much like Beaver Creek) with surrounding peaks that make up part of the Sierra Crest (hydrographic divide). Skiing is ideal for all levels but its 2,300 acres of terrain is best known for its skier-accessible craggy cliffs and grooming of "high angle" runs.

Prior to VR's acquisition in 2012, Kirkwood's potential had never been fully realized, probably for two reasons. First, access from the Central Valley is limited by a narrow winding two-lane state highway (route 88) which experiences frequent closure during heavy winter storms. Its secondary but more reliable access is a state route connecting it to Heavenly and South Lake Tahoe. Airport access is similar to that for Heavenly but with an additional 35-minute travel time. Second, in addition to remoteness, village development has not reached the amenity-rich potential found at VR's other resorts and that of the destination resort industry generally. Previous under-financed owners of the resort (Telluride Golf & Ski) failed to achieve a desirable full-scale destination village.

In addition to the Tahoe area, VR also had set its sights on Utah's craggy Wasatch Mountains with its superb snow conditions as a logical extension to the firm's family of destination ski resorts. Initially, it leased an undeveloped mountain area in the Park City area, calling it "Canyons." Located 35 minutes east of Salt Lake City International Airport and just off Interstate 80, the area was home to both the Park City Mountain Resort (PCMR) and Deer Valley Resort. Canyons is situated in a large mountain bowl and flat meadowland, which seemed ideal for a completely new ski resort next to the world-renowned PCMR owned by Canadian firm, POWDR Corp. VR's initial thought was to build Canyons as a grand resort, much like Beaver Creek, that would leverage off Park City's prestigious brand identity, which had been enhanced by such events as Redford's annual winter Sundance Festival, and its status as the principal site of the 2002 Winter Olympics.

Instead, fate intervened with POWDR's huge blunder in 2011. The Park City properties (owned by Talisker Land Holdings) had been under long-term leases to POWDR since 1994, but were up for renewal in April. Seeing the lease renewal as mere formality, POWDR missed the deadline, and what otherwise would have been a simple extension of land rights, turned into an opportunity for VR. Observing POWDR's mishandling, VR placed its own bid for the 20-year contract, and was awarded the long-term leases on Park City's on-mountain facilities and village assets. After lengthy litigation, the Resort was subsequently acquired through settlement with POWDR and Talisker in September, 2014, and conveyed to VR for $183 million.

The following year, VR moved to merge Canyons into Park City Mountain operations. To cement the integration, VR constructed for the 2015–2016 ski season a $50 million inter-mountain gondola indirectly linking the two villages. As a combined facility worth $489 million on VR's books, the combined complex was renamed Park City Resort, and became the largest destination ski resort in the United States. It contains 7,300 acres of skiable terrain, on-site accommodations for 7,500 people (in addition to another 8,000 in the surrounding area of Park City), and two dozen restaurants and bars (in addition to many more in the surrounding town). Located side-by-side, the two component mountain areas provide skiing on both sides of a long ridge and in a huge wide-open bowl. The new mountain complex offers opportunities for all levels of skiing.

Nearly on top of VR's completed acquisition of Park City, the firm moved to acquire in August of 2017, Whistler Blackcomb, the premier Canadian all-season destination resort that includes two adjacent mountains and extensive village facilities. Twenty-five percent of resort ownership remains in the hands of Nippon Cable, a Japanese firm which originally had owned all of Whistler in years past. As North America's largest and most popular mountain resort, the Whistler acquisition was characterized by VR as "a game-changing opportunity."

At a cost of $1.06 billion, it was also the first "turnkey" acquisition in VR's 20-year post-IPO development history for which it paid a premium price (all other acquisitions were from some type of distress sale). Usually measured by a ratio of share price to resort EBITDA, the deal represented a 43 percent premium over Whistler's stock closing price on the day of the announcement. Although this variance from the norm led some to wonder if VR had over-reached in its price-to-value calculation, the firm's principal argument favoring the deal was that Whistler is the best positioned resort in North America to capture the huge wave of Asian skiers expected to develop over the next decade.

Whistler Blackcomb is set in the picturesque coastal mountains of western British Columbia, 90 miles north of Vancouver, where the nearest principal international airport is located. The two adjacent mountains are situated on 8,171 acres of tribal lands of the Squamish and Lil'wat First Nations, at elevations ranging from 2,140 feet at village base to 7,494 feet at the highest peak. Average annual snowfall is 462 inches, but with the resort's proximity to the coastal climate, it sometimes experiences problematic snow conditions (especially "slush" at lower mountain altitudes).

Augmenting this array of nine destination resorts, VR also added several nontraditional acquisitions, which the firm claimed would broaden and deepen its "all season" strategy. In a move into the summer-season-only business, the firm purchased the Grand Teton Lodge Company in 2000 for $9.2 million. The company managed three rustic lodges as concessions in the National Park, owned a golf course development, and retains plans for several new developments in the Tetons area. The product extension into the summer-only destination resort segment was a move intended to balance the seasonal revenue stream which seemed to bother Wall Street analysts concerned about quarter-to-quarter profit momentum.

In 2001, the firm acquired, for $7.5 million, Rock Resorts, a firm holding a half dozen small but prestigious resort hotels originally established in the 1900s by the Rockefeller family. VR immediately folded into this national chain of mostly coastal-venue resorts some of its recently-acquired hotels located at its destination ski resorts. By 2007, it was placing all of its new resort hotel developments under the Rock Resorts lodging division.

In another move to capture and direct skiers toward its premier destination resorts in Colorado, California, Utah, and British Columbia, VR initiated a new acquisitions program for windshield-type "urban ski areas" near major metropolitan areas in the Midwest and Eastern Seaboard. Currently, these included (a) Afton Alps (near Twin Cities, MN) and Mount Brighton (near Detroit), acquired together for $20 million in December 2012, (b) Wilmot (near Chicago) acquired for $20 million in January 2016; (c) Stowe Mountain in Vermont (near the metropolitan east coast) for $41 million in 2017; (d) Okemo Mountain (VT) and Mount Sunapee (NH) acquired together in 2018 for $82 million; and (e) Stevens Pass (near Seattle) acquired in 2018 for $67 million. This new initiative into "urban" weekend-oriented facilities was intended to establish a brand-recognized "feeder system" connecting VR's branded destination resorts with the local context of major urban markets where the skiing population resides. In marketing the feeders, VR employs the slogan: "Where Epic Begins."

With a similar aim directed at achieving better access to international markets, VR commenced a foreign acquisition program in June 2015, with purchase of Perisher Ski Resort, located in the Snowy Mountains of New South Wales, Australia, about halfway between Sydney and Melbourne. VR paid $125 million for the facility, which ranks as the largest ski-resort complex in the Southern Hemisphere. Consisting of an amalgamation of four ski villages, the resort covers parts of five square miles, totaling 3,335 acres of ski runs in mostly barren treeless terrain.

Finally, to promote the idea of a fully integrated product line of resorts, VR devised a marketing program, called "EPIC," giving the company's users universal access to all its resorts. The program has many parts, but the core revolves around an annual resort ski pass, tailored to a specific resort cluster. These include (1) individual destination-resort clusters in Colorado, Utah, and California, and (2) the U.S. feeder system of urban resorts. Also in the mix as individual resorts are Whistler in Canada and Perisher in Australia. Buying a season pass in one cluster or individual resort entitles the skier to use the pass for skier visits at any of the other resort clusters (typically limited to 5 to 10 days). In addition, other parts of EPIC include food, lodging, and retail discounts at all VR-owned resort establishments, and electronic check-in and on-mountain tracking of skier proficiency. In 2018, EPIC also gave access to non-VR "partner" resorts such as Teluride (CO), Hakuba Valley (Japan), and 30 European ski resorts.

THE RECREATION RESORT INDUSTRY

With an emphasis on skiing and mountain recreation, Vail Resorts operates its core business in the "destination" segment of the recreation-resort industry. As part of the sprawling leisure, recreation, and entertainment industry (i.e., NAICS 71 and 72, esp. 713, and 721), this destination segment is itself a conglomerate of sub-parts having no exact boundaries. According to the U.S. Department of Commerce, recreation resorts also overlap other related industries composed of such segments as amusement parks (e.g., Disney), gaming (e.g., Harrah's Entertainment), cruises (e.g., Carnival/Princess Cruise Lines), and sporting events (e.g., the NFL and NBA). In this ill-defined setting, competition therefore includes a vast assemblage of directly competing and partially substitutable products and services. Moreover, with loosely segmented markets, strategic opportunities tend to be more elusive and potentially conflicting in that they consist of different but partially overlapping customer profiles and product-market relationships.

Nevertheless, unlike most of the other overlapping segments of leisure, recreation and entertainment, the ski resort industry segment (esp. NAICS 721110 and 713920) has faced strong headwinds. As reflected in Exhibit 2, the long-term trend in customer demand, as measured by U.S. skier/snowboarder visits per day, has been persistently flat for two decades. Within regions where VR has destination facilities, the trends mostly reflect the flattening demand nationally.

Traditionally, customers in the destination recreational-resort industry (of which skiing is but one subtype) have been distinguished in the population by income, age, and family status (i.e., married/unmarried, with/without children). These factors often

EXHIBIT 2   Annual U.S. Skier/Boarder Visits (in millions, 1997–2018)

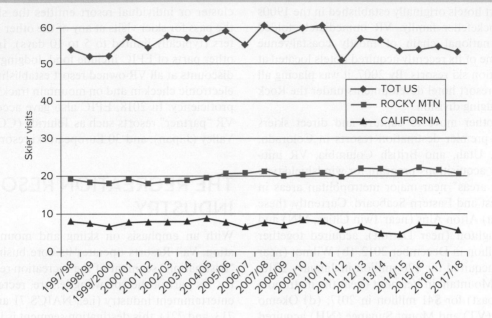

Source: National Ski Areas Association, Vail Resorts.

differentiated people inclined toward large scale or mass recreational services coupled with less expensive accommodations (like the destination profile of Disney World) from people seeking a more exclusive and intimate resort setting featuring high value or high status vacation venues (like those provided by Vail Resorts).

In the case of destination ski resorts, a greater variety of demographic factors were weighing in as determinants in customer demand analysis during the first two decades of the 21st century. In addition to traditional ones mentioned, more recent factors include age distribution dynamics, education level attained (i.e., college degree vs. non-degree), occupational status (i.e., professional/managerial employment vs. blue-collar/clerical jobs), lifestyle and other psychographic characteristics (e.g., cosmopolitan versus parochial awareness), and family makeup (i.e., singles/couples versus families).

In the instance of age distribution dynamics, the effects of generational evolution pose especially difficult strategic questions going forward. Historically, skiing demand and age have been correlated, with peak skiing interest occurring among people between 18 to 45. Hence, as shown in Exhibit 3, an aging population of post-war Baby Boomers (now mostly in their 60s) and late middle-age Gen Xers were thought to be

a primary cause of the industry's maturing demand. But, a secondary cause was also ascribed to less physically active and less financially secure Millennials (21 to 37 in 2018), who are the natural replacement stock for today's aging skier population.

Skiing is a rigorous and potentially dangerous outdoor recreational activity, and requires physical stamina and a dose of youthful abandon. As baby boomers move into their senior years and family responsibilities become more important in determining types of vacation venues, skiing's reputation as an expensive, singles-oriented, and physically demanding sport may be coming up short when matching it with future demand profiles. Many former skiers and the like have been moving to other segments of the vacation and leisure industry where less physical activity is required.

In addition to demographic changes, another long-term strategic concern for the ski industry looms in the climatic effects of global warming. Measured as annual January temperature variations from the long-term average (called the "temperature anomaly"), Exhibit 4 shows the dramatic increases occurring since the onset of the Industrial Revolution in late 1800s. With the emergence of post-WWII globalization, these incremental changes have accelerated upward

EXHIBIT 3 **Projected Population by Generation**

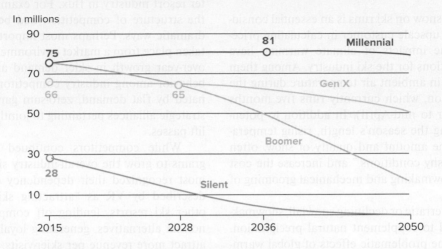

Note: Millennials refers to the population ages 18 to 34 as of 2015.

Source: Pew Research Center tabulations of U.S. Census Bureau population projections released December 2014 and 2015 population estimates.

EXHIBIT 4 **Worldwide Atmospheric Temperature Increases**

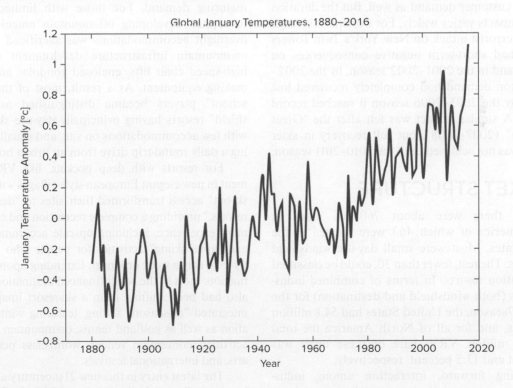

Global January Temperatures, 1880–2016

Source: NOAA, 2016.

at a remarkable pace, with most scientists expecting continuation at current rates under "business-as-usual" scenarios.

Quality of snow on ski runs is an essential consideration for the upscale customer in calculating price-to-value, so the impacts of climate warming have many ramifications for the ski industry. Among them is the increase in ambient air temperature during the winter ski season, which currently runs five months (mid-November to mid-April). In addition to potentially shortening the season's length, rising temperatures reduce the amount and quality of snow, often producing "slushy conditions," and increase the cost of artificial snowmaking and mechanical grooming of ski runs.

In cases of erratic or declining snowfall, snowmaking is deployed to supplement natural precipitation. Emphasizing the problematic effects of global warming, VR maintains that "inadequate natural snowfall reduces skiable terrain and could render snowmaking ineffective." In addition, skiers often delay destination resort vacations or redirect them to non-ski venues (e.g., golf vacations, trips to the beach, "staycations") when snow quality reliability is uncertain.

Beside long-term factors, short-term events can influence customer demand as well. But the duration of their impacts varies widely. For example, although the 9/11 terrorist attack on New York's Twin Towers in 2001 had short-term negative consequences on skier demand in the 2001–2002 season, by the 2002–2003 season demand had completely recovered lost ground. By the 2005–2006 season it reached record territory. A similar impact was felt after the "Great Recession" (2007–2008), but full recovery in skier demand was not achieved until the 2010–2011 season.

MARKET STRUCTURE

In 2018, there were about 760 ski areas in North America of which 463 were located in the United States. Most were small day-use windshield operations. The rest, fewer than 30, could be classified as destination resorts. In terms of combined industry figures (both windshield and destination) for the 2016–2017 season, the United States had 54.8 million skier visits, and for all of North America the total was 73.8 million. VR's share of these totals was 20 percent and 13.5 percent, respectively.

Looking forward, interaction among industry producers (especially in contriving new winter experiences and imagining new customer profiles), is likely to intensify competition and keep the winter resort industry in flux. For example, since 2000, the structure of competition had been changing in dramatic ways. Perhaps most important, a shift had taken place from a market environment ruled by year-over-year growth in skier demand and positive-sum behavior among industry competitors, to one dominated by flat demand, zero-sum gaming, and some strategic alliances pertaining to jointly-sponsored ski-lift passes.

While competitors continued to devise programs to grow the overall-industry skier population, most recognized their dependency on such tactics described by VR as "attracting skiers away from other ski resorts, fending off competitors offering non-ski alternatives, generating loyalty incentives to attract more revenue per skier-visits, or encouraging more visits from each skier." This zero-sum mindset created what VR's president called an "arms race" among firms in developing on-mountain facilities, new village venues, social-media technologies, and skier incentive programs.

Adding to these factors was an evolving bifurcation of ski industry players, partly as a result of maturing demand. For those with limited access to capital, developing off-mountain amenities and overnight accommodations was sacrificed to favor on-mountain infrastructure development such as high-speed chair lifts, enclosed gondolas and snowmaking equipment. As a result, most of these "old school" players became distinguished as "windshield" resorts having principally day-use ski slopes with few accommodations on site, and usually requiring a daily round-trip drive from an urban home.

For resorts with deep pockets, like VR, investment in new elegant European-style villages with "ski-in ski-out" access transformed their sites to "destination resorts," providing a complete recreation and entertainment experience, including upscale accommodations and "apres-skiing" activities for people who typically fly in to stay a week or longer. Extending upon this distinction, most of the better-financed destination resorts also had been shifting from a ski-resort image to an integrated "all-season" setting, featuring winter recreation as well as golf and tennis, on-mountain summer activities, convention venues, world-class performing arts, and international festivals.

The latest entry in this new 21st century approach has been Squaw Valley/Alpine, which in 2011 was sold to KSL Partners (owned in-part by former VR executives). KSL's well-publicized "retro-fit" strategy was designed to join the "world class" destination market. By late 2016, the resort had received final government approvals for a massive $1 billion redevelopment with a 25-year build-out horizon. Focus of the makeover was on village expansion from 15 acres currently to over 100 acres, with visions of many new accommodations and entertainment venues.

In contrast to windshield resorts, which are ubiquitous across North America and make up most of the ski industry in site numbers and skier visits, the destination ski industry is more geographically confined to four "production" areas. These include the Rocky Mountains (Colorado, Utah, Idaho, and Montana), the California Sierras, southern Canada, and New England (especially Vermont and Maine). With destination resorts having the most market reach demographically and geographically, the Rockies claim to be the location of the best known and most visited because of its central and scenic locations, situated between population corridors on the east and west coasts.

Within the Rocky Mountain region, Vail Resorts held a 32.3 percent market share of the 21.7 million skier visits (combined destination and windshield) in the 2016–2017 ski season. In the Colorado subset, VR accumulated more than a 50 percent share of the destination skier market, competing with the Aspen Ski Company (aka SKICO, which owns the Aspen-3 mountains and Snowmass, all proximally located in the Roaring Forks Valley), Alterra (joint venture of SKICO and KSL which owns Steamboat and Winter Park), POWDR (which owns Copper), and several smaller destination operators (including Telluride Golf & Ski, and Triple Peaks which owns Crested Butte). In the Utah subset, VR held the vast majority of the destination market with its Park City/Canons complex.

Beyond Colorado, the "big four" destination-resort firms hold widely distributed operations, with most located in the Rockies, Oregon, the California Sierras, Northeastern United States, and in Southern Canada (mostly Quebec and British Columbia). In California, ski resorts draw fewer out-of-state destination visitors than Colorado and industry competition tends to include smaller single-resort operators. Vail Resorts is the largest player in California, holding 25.4 percent of the state's 11.5 million skier visits, but more than 60 percent of its destination visits

in the 2016–2017 season. Direct competitors in the Sierras destination ski resort market include Squaw Valley/Alpine and Mammoth Mountain.

The current market structure of destination ski-resort competitors came about in the last 10 years, when a rash of consolidations and mergers reduced the field to a new "big four" (VR, Alterra, SKICO, and POWDR) and a few small specialized firms. Due to mismanagement and overspending on development projects during the first decade of the 2000s, one firm (American Ski) was reduced to a small player, another (Intrawest) was forced into bankruptcy and subsequently acquired by Alterra, and another previously smaller firm (POWDR Corp) entered the "Big 4" elite standing. POWDR subsequently lost its major assets in Park City to VR, leaving the industry's market power mostly to VR and newcomer Alterra (the SKICO/KSL joint venture). Exhibit 5 lists the principal firms and summarizes site statistics for a selected list of their North American destination ski resorts.

GOING BEYOND THE COMPETITION

During this period of industry consolidation, the technology-driven "arms race" in new development sharpened the destination focus on such areas as (1) thematically planned villages at the ski-mountain base, (2) costly snowmaking equipment to guarantee visitors a quality skiing experience regardless of the vagaries of natural precipitation, (3) luxurious on-mountain restaurants to meet the cosmopolitan tastes of "high-end" skiers, (4) state-of-the-art lift designs that provide faster more comfortable access to the mountain top, and (5) mountaintop non-ski recreation parks for tubing, ski biking, and other recreational snow activities.

However, even with these significant arms-race investments, the destination skiing segment was not experiencing a corresponding response from the demand side of the market. Indeed, most of the big-four firms (and smaller ones as well) were showing continuing declines and further pressures to consolidate. In the case of VR, the flat market conditions would also have likely stunted its growth potential had it not been for the firm's acquisitions and promotion programs, especially its EPIC program. Indeed, the VR threat of preeminence in this period of

EXHIBIT 5   Destination Ski Resort Firms and On-Mountain Facilities

2017–2018 Season Summary of Resort Statistics

Firm/Resort	Location	Lift Ticket Price* ($ U.S)	Skiable Acreage	Vertical Drop (feet)	# Of Lifts	# Of Trails	Lift Capacity (Skiers/Hour)
Vail Resorts:							
Park City	Utah	$ 145	7,300	3,200	41	185	83,022
Whistler/Blackcomb	British Columbia	$156CN	8,171	5,280	38	200	67,307
Vail Mountain	Colorado	$ 199	5,289	3,450	31	193	59,069
Heavenly Valley	California	$ 152	4,800	3,527	29	97	52,000
Breckenridge	Colorado	$ 169	2,908	3,398	34	187	46,800
Beaver Creek	Colorado	$ 199	1,832	3,340	25	150	43,221
Northstar@Tahoe	California	$ 152	3,170	2,280	20	100	37,891
Keystone	Colorado	$ 169	3,148	3,128	20	131	33,564
Kirkwood	California	$ 152	2,300	2,000	15	87	19,905
Aspen Ski (SKICO):							
Aspen3/Snowmass	Colorado	$ 155	5,517	4,406	43	329	59,252
Alterra Mountain Co: (Jt Ventr SKICO/KSL)							
Squaw Valley/Alpine	California	$ 169	6,000	2,850	42	270	73,595
Mammoth Mountain	California	$ 159	3,500	3,100	28	150	42,100
Steamboat Springs	Colorado	$ 160	2,965	3,668	16	165	41,465
Winter Park	Colorado	$ 169	3,081	2,220	25	143	40,000
Mt. Tremblant	Quebec	$ 89CN	665	2,116	12	96	27,230
POWDR Corp:							
Copper Mountain	Colorado	$ 150	2,490	2,601	23	140	32,324
Mount Bachelor	Oregon	$ 96	4,318	3,365	11	101	25,000
Others:							
Sun Valley	Idaho	$ 149	2,154	3,400	18	121	29,717
Telluride	Colorado	$ 135	2,000	4,425	18	147	22,386
Taos	New Mexico	$ 105	1,294	2,612	13	110	15,000

*Amounts listed are the advertised full price for a one-day pass at "the ticket window" during high season (January to March), but considerable discounting occurs for early and late season, and for all season through online purchases.

Source: Individual resort websites.

stagnating demand and intensified rivalry led Alterra to introduce IKON to mimic the enlarged product-line image of VR's EPIC.

Moreover, destination-resort visitors were becoming choosier about the price-to-value of individual resorts. It had become clear that most destination visitors sought additional "creature comforts" both on and off the mountain, and were willing to pay for exceptional luxury where quality was assured. VR's industry leadership in moving toward this high-end market is reflected in Exhibit 6, which compares a selection of destination-resorts according to each resort's annual skier visits (calculated as one skier or snowboarder purchasing a lift ticket for one day). Consistent with this data, most of VR's resorts have been ranked in the industry's top 10 by annual ski

EXHIBIT 6   Most Visited Destination Ski Resorts (N. America) Annual Skier/ Snowboarder Visits, 2017–18 Season

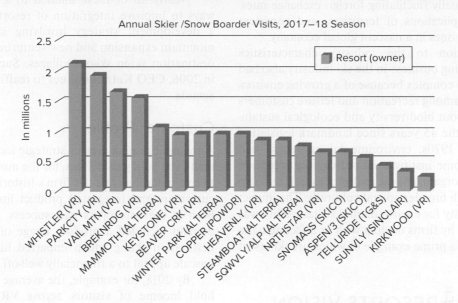

Annual Skier /Snow Boarder Visits, 2017–18 Season

Source: National Ski Areas Association, Individual resorts.

magazine surveys for many years. Upon the firm's acquisitions in 2017, first of Park City and then of Whistler, VR solidified its position in holding the three most popular ski resorts in North America.

To a great extent, the firm's persistent market dominance is attributable to the fact that VR is the only firm in the industry able to achieve a "cooperative" administrative control over all aspects of its destination resort context (i.e., mountain activities, local accommodations, village concessions, entertainment venues, airline and ground transportation), even though much of it is owned or managed by a host of other firms acting as an integrated network of "co-producers." As a result of its management of these multiple-partner strategic alliances, VR stood out among its competition in creating a superbly packaged seamless product for the customer at each of its destination resorts.

In addition to a domestic market of skiers, Vail Resorts also looked to a cosmopolitan global market as an important source of growth. Although 80 percent of the world's skiers live outside the United States (mainly in Canada, Europe, Oceania, Japan, parts of South America, and increasingly China), the firm's customer mix typically includes about 12 percent from foreign visitors. Since the turn of the

century, VR pursued an ongoing but as yet unfulfilled goal of raising that figure to 15 percent.

The firm's global reach is marked by three of its resorts hosting past Winter Olympics. Augmenting this world status, it maintains an aggressive international marketing program. In part, VR expedites this program by annually hosting one or more of the several World Cup ski events held throughout the world. In addition, it has managed to acquire the rights about once a decade as the exclusive host of the World Ski Championships, which culminates the World Cup series every two years and is the worldwide equivalent to football's Super Bowl. Most recently, VR hosted the 2016 Championships at Vail and Beaver Creek, and followed this event with a "prestige and promotion" campaign promoting worldwide all of its North American destination resorts. Going forward, growth potential in international demand may come more from Asia (especially China) than from its historical draw in the Western Hemisphere.

The effort to promote its global markets, however, is partially blunted by continuing terrorist concerns worldwide and subsequent stringent security measures following September 11, 2001. The rise of global terrorism served not only to create resistance from a foreign market but also to cause a restructuring of destination ski resort competition. The long-term outlook for global market demand remains unclear, partially due to continually fluctuating foreign exchange rates, the travel implications of terrorism, and persistent "nationalist" issues in a nascent global economy.

In addition to the industry characteristics described, doing business in the ski industry also had become more complex because of a growing environmental ethic among recreation and leisure customers concerned about biodiversity and ecological sustainability. Over the 45 years since landmark legislation of the early 1970s, environmental awareness had not only become institutionalized (by the inception of new laws, organizations, and processes), but also acquired much broader appeal culturally. The impact of respectability for environmental sustainability was especially felt by firms dealing with or affecting natural resources, a prime example of which are ski resort operators.

THE VAIL RESORTS VISION

In the early years following the firm's 1997 IPO, VR's culture and leadership atmosphere changed dramatically from its "closely-knit family" of original management sharing a common interest in skiing. Furthermore, with enhanced access to capital and its new public exposure to Wall Street, several new managerial issues emerged, chief among them being the desire for a fresh strategic outlook. The new executive team led by CEO Aron and President Daly articulated a long-term growth strategy to replace what Aron referred to as the tactical "quick hits" of past years.

Launching the new vision, Aron set forth an explicit mission statement: "At Vail Resorts, we are focused on expanding and enhancing our core ski operations while increasing the scope, diversity, and quality of the activities and services we offer our guests—skiers and non-skiers—throughout the year." Along with this declaration, he offered for the first time a set of five policy guidelines to drive the firm's strategic-action agenda:

1. Create new attractions to enhance consumer appeal,
2. Broaden VR's participation in varied guest experiences (produce more services previously provided by co-producers),
3. Provide value through our passion for quality,
4. Leverage our strong market position, and
5. Capitalize on industry consolidation opportunities.

Nearly all of these alluded to a need for new ways to improve integration of resort services and a development strategy involving significant on-mountain expansion and new venturing in the firm's destination ski-in ski-out villages. Succeeding Aron in 2006, CEO Katz continues to reaffirm this action agenda.

Customer Profile

Although bringing greater strategic focus to development, the policy guidelines, for the most part, sought to retain and buttress the firm's historical domain of customers and integrated product lines which had been at the core of its past success. That strategic domain included a product image of "world-class" destination skiing which imparted high status and upscale appeal to a financially well-off clientele.

By 2018, for example, the average annual household income of visitors across VR's destination resorts was $175,000, with more than 50 percent of those visitors having incomes exceeding $150,000, and more than 30 percent having incomes over $200,000. The firm's domination of the high-end segment of this income-driven market was central to making most of VR's nine destination resorts among the top 10 in North America. Vail Mountain, which had cultivated its iconic image as a "playland of the rich," ranked #1 for many of the last 20 years.

But, in recent times, the Vail Resorts customer evolved to exhibit a more accomplished set of demographic and psychological attributes. While income certainly still mattered, the typical VR customer was now also likely to be college educated, have a professional career, and hold extended family responsibilities. As a result, VR's visitor today is more likely to be widely traveled with a global experience and cosmopolitan outlook. Due in part to their professional responsibilities and institutional work environment, the firm's customers also tend to seek anonymity while on vacation and prefer a resort environment that encourages others to share this desire. Indeed, this trait in the VR customer is often mentioned in comparisons with Aspen's customer base, which reputedly is more likely to exhibit a "want-to-be-seen" Hollywood genre.

In actual application, VR's strategic customer profile is an umbrella for a variety of different visitor subtypes. The largest of these are families (about 50 percent of visitations), many of which are multi-generational "boomer" families (i.e., a unit consisting of boomer parents, their children and grandchildren). Although the exact mix varies from resort to resort, the remainder of visitations is about evenly divided between "40-something" Gen Xers, corporate and professional conference attendees, and Millennials. Only about 12 percent of visitations to VR resorts are made by foreign nationals who fit a similar demographic profile.

Such variety does not signal incompatible customer segments, but rather variance in emphasis within the firm's multiple-attribute customer profile. For example, although the multi-generational family perhaps represents the "best" all around fit with the profile, Millennials are a strategic fit as well. Even though typically lacking high-income professional employment of an older generation, Millennials often see a college degree as pursuant to the rewards of upper-middle-class status, suggesting even that this customer may become a quintessential replacement down the road for aging boomers.

Product Specifications

Until a decade or so ago, most in the destination ski-resort business saw little basis to differentiate the customer beyond household affluence and a passion for skiing. Providing faster ski lifts, well-manicured ski runs, high-end hotels, and prestigious restaurants consequently seemed to be what the market recognized as a quality "up-scale" experience. As a result, the "product" most providers offered was alpine skiing, which focused primarily on ski-mountain "hardware" (mostly lifts and snowmaking) and opulent overnight accommodations.

Although setting the terms for an industry "arms race," this product vision did not directly account for some important emerging desires for friendly gathering places, spiritual renewal, novel adventure, stylistic flare, and cosmopolitan ambiance. From a customer perspective, was the product the resort infrastructure itself (i.e., the physical village and mountain), or had it become a cumulative psychological set of synergistic sensations and experiences for those visiting such places?

While many in the industry ignored the implications and continued to promote the hardware-driven vision, VR began cultivating "skiing" as a product of "luxurious pastoral serenity" offering an upscale opportunity to reconnect with the holistic self and valued friends, at least partially within the context of a global village setting. This new product vision came to be characterized as a *seamless experience,* blending together an uninterrupted progression of ski-resort pleasures while minimizing hassles and tradeoffs. For example, the pedestrian village (invented at Vail in the 1960s) provides a ski-in ski-out setting, placing stylistic ambiance and the immediacy of mountain and village activities at the whims of customers without the trouble of using an automobile.

Although originally pioneered by Walt Disney more than a half a century earlier, this emerging production concept allowed VR to see opportunity in the threat of an aging population, and resulted in the firm experiencing a counter-industry stability (even respectable growth) in its resort operating revenues. What many of the firm's competitors had missed by sticking with the old ski-resort model was an opportunity to derive income from skier visits in ways other than the sale of a lift ticket or an on-mountain sandwich. For VR, a shift in revenue source away from primary dependence on lift tickets and toward ski school and rental, village retail and dining, festival events, and lodging took place over the last two decades. By 2018, only 43 percent of the firm's total operating revenues was coming from lift tickets.

Even more pertinent to VR's synergistic advantage was its highly integrated ownership of resort facilities. By "upscaling" its on-mountain restaurants, redefining ski school, buying some resort venues previously left to its network of co-producers (particularly classy hotels, iconic dining, and village retail), and becoming the primary online package reservations agent for its destination ski-resorts, VR was able to generate a far greater revenue stream from each visitor than its competition. In recent years, the firm was producing operating revenues from each visitor that were more than 20 percent greater than those of Aspen and considerably more than that from other "Big Four" destination-market competitors.

Prior to 2000, Vail Resorts had already committed to prolonged capital investment in new ski-resort facilities. But, even with this sustained level early on, VR's new-found domain of product-market relationships spurred the firm in more recent years to substantially escalate its annual capital expenditures budget. Since the early 2000s, its development expenditures in mountain and village improvements increased six-fold over pre-2000 levels, which had averaged

$12 million annually. During Aron's 10-year tenure as CEO (1997 to 2007), VR's capital expenditures for resort operations (including mountain infrastructure and village facilities) averaged over $70 million annually. Following Katz's appointment as CEO in 2007, that average increased to $100 million.

The investment stream was spread widely to nearly all its destination resorts. Initially, the two largest beneficiaries were Vail and Breckenridge. Started in 2004, both capital improvement programs were substantially completed in 2011. Vail's "New Dawn" theme project involved redevelopment of two of the village's three mountain portal areas. The $500 million project represented a comprehensive renewal of the village infrastructure and accommodations around the Lionshead gondola and the new Vista Bahn gondola at the top of Bridge Street.

At Breckenridge, development of a completely new standalone ski-in ski-out village (smaller in size but similar in design to the main village at Beaver Creek) was constructed on the mountain, adjoining the resort's Peaks 7 and 8 staging area high above the town. It contains a mix of 430 "hot-bed" condominiums (individually owned rentals) anchored by a large alpine lodge and 110,000 square feet of retail space. Unlike the Town of Breckenridge, which is a public city, this new village is located at the foot of one of the resort's major bowls and is owned and operated by VR. It is connected to the town center below by a 12-passenger gondola.

At Beaver Creek, a new aerial conveyor system was completed for the 2007–2008 season to ferry skiers between the resort and the rapidly developing Town of Avon located three miles down-mountain. At Heavenly, a $300 million 10-year redevelopment plan remains underway for substantial renewal of on-mountain facilities and the primary Stateline portal area, and a new 10-acre village at the resort's secondary portal in Nevada.

However, the most impressive strategic move toward technologically sophisticated and fully integrated on-mountain and village experiences promises to be at Whistler/Blackcomb, where a $345 million revitalization project called Renaissance was begun in 2016. Designed with seven principal components, the project consists of two giant indoor sports complexes, on-mountain revitalization of chair lifts, restaurants, and snowmaking, and construction of a new hotel, condos, and other infrastructure in Blackcomb village.

CORPORATE FINANCIALS

Vail Resorts is a mid-size corporation with $4.1 billion in assets and annual revenues of $1.9 billion in 2017 (see Exhibit 7 for selected financial data). The firm reports results according to three market segments it identifies as mountain, lodging, and real estate. Its nine destination resorts account for more than 80 percent of VR's revenues, with the remainder sourced from its urban windshield resorts, its Perisher Resort in Australia, and the Grand Tetons Summer Resort.

The firm's financial results are attributable to management's long-term strategic choices, as well as market conditions and weather. Nevertheless, total revenues have improved more than three-fold over the two-decade period, due principally to robust on-mountain sources as well as (1) the addition of new sources of off-mountain operating revenues (especially lodging), (2) the initiation of summer-season activities (reflecting movement to an "all-season" strategy), and (3) aggressive efforts to improve product synergies by integrating components of the firm's core business.

Regarding a desire to spread financial risk, VR continues to diversify its product line. Historically, more than 95 percent of its revenues came from the five-month ski season. With implementation of its "all-season" strategy at its nine destination ski resorts and expansion of activities at summer resorts like its Grand Tetons facilities, the winter contribution has been reduced to about 70 percent of total operating sources.

Although real estate sales make little direct contribution to VR's total revenues, they nevertheless are important to the firm's growth strategy because they feed future resort revenues by expanding the visitor bed base (especially from rental units known as "hot beds"). As a destination-resort provider, the firm depends on growth in total capacity of overnight accommodations and the occupancy rate. The hot-bed concept encourages rentals that maximize occupancy without requiring the resort owner to put up capital for bed capacity. VR's lodging control is maintained instead by dominating the guest reservation and hospitality systems that it operates on a fee basis.

For public firms, a comprehensive indicator of managerial success in implementing a well designed strategy is usually found in the firm's long-term stock price. In VR's case, the picture has been an evolving

EXHIBIT 7 Trends In Selected Financial Data

Vail Resorts, Inc., 2000–2018

Fiscal Year Ended July 31: (in millions except where indicated)	2018	2017	2016	2015	2010	2005	2000
Statement of Operations:							
Revenue							
From Mountain	$1,722.9	$1,611.8	$1,304.6	$1,104.0	$ 638.5	$ 540.9	$ 373.8
From Lodging	284.6	278.5	274.6	254.6	195.3	196.4	116.6
From Real Estate	4.0	16.9	22.1	41.3	61.0	72.8	48.7
Total Revenue	2,011.6	1,907.2	1,601.3	1,400.0	894.8	810.1	531.1
Operating Expenses (excl. D&A)							
For Mountain	1,132.8	1,047.3	881.5	777.1	456.0	392.0	284.1
For Lodging	259.6	251.4	246.4	232.9	192.9	177.5	103.6
For Real Estate	3.5	24.1	24.6	48.4	71.4	58.3	42.1
Total Operating Expenses	1,396.0	1,322.8	1,152.5	1,058.4	720.3	627.8	298.8
Net Operating Income	$ 615.6	$ 584.4	$ 448.8	$ 341.6	$ 174.5	$ 182.3	$ 101.3
Gross Operating Margin							
For Mountain	34.2%	35.0%	32.4%	29.6%	28.5%	27.5%	24.0%
For Lodging	8.8%	9.7%	10.3%	8.5%	1.2%	9.6%	11.1%
For Real Estate	12.5%	(42.6)%	(11.3)%	(17.2)%	(17.0)%	19.9%	13.6%
Net Income	$ 380.0	$ 231.7	$ 149.8	$ 114.8	$ 30.4	$ 23.1	$ 10.0
Annual Capital Expenditures (Operations)	$ 141	$ 144	$ 109	$ 124	$ 130	$ 80	$ 57
Cash Flows							
Net Cash From Operations	$ 551.6	$ 473.2	$ 437.0	$ 303.7	$ 36.0	$ 148.2	$ 110.7
Net Cash Increase/Decrease	60.8	49.5	32.4	(8.9)	(54.6)	90.3	(9.5)
Balance Sheet Data							
Total Assets	$4,065.0	$4,110.7	$2,482.0	$2,487.3	$1,922.8	$1,525.9	$1,135.6
Long-Term Debt	1,272.7	1,272.4	700.3	814.5	526.7	521.7	394.2
Stockholders' Equity	1,589.4	1,571.2	874.5	866.6	788.8	540.5	475.8
CEO Monetized Compensation (salary + other comp, in $000)							
Adam Aron, CEO (1997–2007)	—	—	—	—	—	$1,848.6	$ 686.3
Rob Katz, CEO (2007–present)	$7,995.0	$5,828.6	$6,153.7	$5,344.4	$2,999.4	—	—
Average Stock Price Per Share	$250	$185	$152	$109	$43	$24	$23.50
Cash Dividend Per Share	$5.05	$3.73	$2.87	$2.08	—	—	—

Source: Vail Resorts Annual 10-K reports, 2000–2018.

EXHIBIT 8   Vail Resorts Stock Performance Nyse: Mtn, Avg Annual Price, 2000–2018

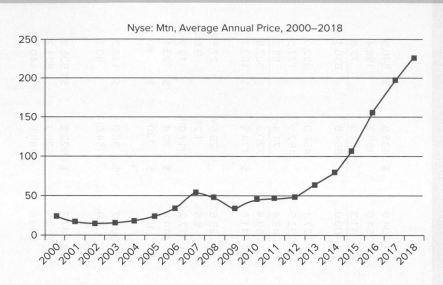

Nyse: Mtn, Average Annual Price, 2000–2018

Source: Vail Resorts Annual 10-K Reports.

work-in-progress, as shown in Exhibit 8. During the formative years of Aron's term as CEO, the firm designed much of the substance of its strategy that remains in place today. But, it wasn't until Katz took it to the next level, integrating all the pieces which Aron had put in play, that the results became publically recognized. Hence, the stock's current price, representing a five-fold increase since 2010 is best understood as a reflection of their dual efforts.

STRUCTURE FOLLOWS STRATEGY

With Vail Resorts' commitment in the early 2000s to an all-season growth strategy, the ensuing years unleashed a cascade of managerial events and consequences. Indeed, the sheer complexity of combining and integrating internal capital investments and acquisition resources made necessary a massive reorganization of authority and a huge increase in the number of employees. Even though happening over 20 years, the changes in scale included a tripling of the firm's employment base by 2018. At seasonal peak, VR now employs over 27,800 seasonal people on top of its permanent year-round employment base of 5,900.

As a result, the original organization structure progressively underwent a transformation that took into account the massive increase in the diversity of new resources, product-markets, managerial cultures, personalities, and expertise. VR's current organization chart (Exhibit 9) reveals a distribution of authority arranged by a mix of structural forms including functional hierarchy, several kinds of divisions, and a partial matrix. A major accomplishment of the reorganization was separating management of the ski resorts and other product lines from general management functions. These production units were then divided into three activity "segments," identified as "Mountain," "Lodging," and "Real Estate."

To preserve the simultaneous organizational needs for *differentiation* of organizational specializations and *integration* of authorities engendered by the firm's synergistic complexities, three structural components were put in place. First, at the core of the business, each ski resort was given a separate production authority headed by a chief operating officer (COO). This meant each had control over the management detail of designing and operating everything from grooming schedules, to customer reception activities, to ski-school programs, to food services, to purchasing and maintenance. Although Marketing

EXHIBIT 9   Vail Resorts Corporate Organization Chart

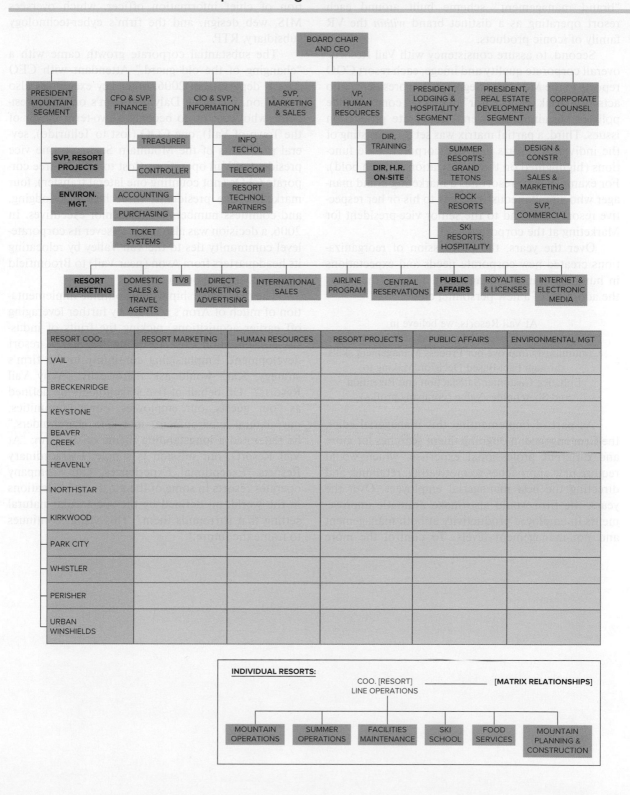

is shown as a corporate function, the firm uses a "brand management" scheme built around each resort operating as a distinct brand *within* the VR family of iconic products.

Second, to assure consistency with Vail Resorts' overall corporate quality and image, each resort COO reports to the Mountain Segment vice president, who acts as a "peak coordinator" in making companywide policies pertaining to overall corporate production issues. Third, a partial matrix was set up consisting of the individual resorts and five corporate-wide functions (highlighted on the organization chart in bold). For example, each resort has a marketing brand manager who simultaneously reports to his or her respective resort COO and to the senior vice-president for Marketing at the corporate level.

Over the years, the progression of reorganizations created new corporate needs and expectations in human resource management. Driving these was the adoption of a new personnel credo:

At Vail Resorts, we believe in
Customer-Focused Teamwork striving to
Continuously Improve our Process Management skills
through Fact-Based Decision Making to
Enhance Customer Satisfaction and Retention
and Shareholder Value (company profits).

As part of implementing this managerial edict, the firm engaged in ongoing talent searches for more and different professional expertise, which would require new approaches to motivating, retaining, and directing the best managerial employees. Over the years, the firm would also make dramatic improvements in employee productivity at both management and non-management levels. To control the more complex information flows, VR created a new position of chief information officer, which oversees MIS, web design, and the firm's cyber-technology subsidiary, RTP.

The substantial corporate growth came with a "changing of the old guard." Attendant with CEO Aron's departure in 2006, other key executives also moved on, including Daly, the firm's original president (who went on to become a two-term mayor of the Town of Vail), one COO (lost to Telluride), several presidents of the Mountain Segment, one vice president of Vail operations (lost to KSL), three corporate CFOs (not counting one lateral transfer), four marketing vice presidents, three heads of lodging, and countless numbers of less senior executives. In 2006, a decision was also made to sever its corporate-level community ties to the Vail Valley by relocating its headquarters from Avon (near Vail) to Broomfield Hills (a Denver suburb).

The new leadership would continue implementation of much of Aron's strategy by further leveraging off earlier acquisitions, picking the fruits of industry consolidation, and investing heavily in resort development. Emphasizing continuity in the firm's strategy, Katz would ask rhetorically: "Why Vail Resorts?" On behalf of five stakeholders he defined as "our guests, our employees, our communities, our natural environment, and our shareholders," he reiterated a longstanding theme of the firm: "At Vail Resorts, our mission is simple: Extraordinary Resorts, Exceptional Experiences. Our Company operates resorts in some of the most iconic locations in the world, all defined by the spectacular natural setting that surrounds them." This vision continues to frame the future.

Starbucks in 2018: Striving for Operational Excellence and Innovation Agility

connect

Arthur A. Thompson
The University of Alabama

Since its founding in 1987 as a modest nine-store operation in Seattle, Washington, Starbucks had become the premier roaster, marketer, and retailer of specialty coffees in the world, with over 28,200 store locations in 76 countries as of April 2018 and annual sales that were expected to exceed $24 billion in fiscal year 2018, ending September 30. In addition to its flagship Starbucks brand coffees and coffee beverages, Starbucks' other brands included Tazo and Teavana teas, Seattle's Best Coffee, Evolution Fresh juices and smoothies, and Ethos bottled waters. Starbucks stores also sold snack foods, pastries, and sandwiches purchased from a variety of local, regional, and national suppliers. In January 2107, Starbucks officially announced it would:

- Open 20 to 30 Starbucks Reserve™ Roasteries and Tasting Rooms, which would bring to life the theater of coffee roasting, brewing, and packaging for customers, include a coffee bar with a full menu of coffee beverages, space for a mixology bar serving traditional Italian cocktails, and an upscale Princi bakery—a newly created Starbucks subsidiary that featured fresh-baked artisanal Italian breads, sandwiches, and pastries. The Starbucks Roaster and Tasting Room stores were designed in an open, marketplace style to (a) showcase the theater of roasting Starbucks Reserve™ coffees and the baking and other food preparation activities ongoing in the Princi kitchen, (b) enable customers to engage with store personnel at the Reserve coffee bar and Princi counter, and (c) gather with

friends either at community tables or in lounge areas around two fireplaces.

- Open 1,000 Starbucks Reserve stores worldwide to bring premium experiences to customers and promote the company's recently-introduced Starbucks Reserve coffees; these locations offered a more intimate small-lot coffee experience and gave customers a chance to chat with a barista about all things coffee. The menu at Starbucks Reserve stores included handcrafted hot and cold Starbucks Reserve coffee beverages, hot and cold teas, ice cream and coffee beverages, packages of Starbucks Reserve whole bean coffees, and an assortment of small plates, sandwiches and wraps, desserts, wines, and beer. There were four types of brewing methods for the coffees and teas.

- Transform about 20 percent of the company's existing portfolio of Starbucks stores into Starbucks Reserve coffee bars.

Exhibit 1 provides an overview of Starbucks performance during fiscal years 2010 through 2017.

COMPANY BACKGROUND

Starbucks Coffee, Tea, and Spice

Starbucks got its start in 1971 when three academics, English teacher Jerry Baldwin, history teacher Zev Siegel, and writer Gordon Bowker—all coffee aficionados—opened Starbucks Coffee, Tea, and Spice

EXHIBIT 1   Financial and Operating Summary for Starbucks Corporation, Fiscal Years 2010–2017 ($ in millions, except for per-share amounts)

INCOME STATEMENT DATA	Oct. 1, 2017	Oct. 2, 2016	Sep 27, 2015	Oct. 3, 2010
Net revenues:				
Company-operated stores	$17,650.7	$16,844.1	$15,197.3	$ 8,963.5
Licensed stores	2,355.0	2,154.2	1,861.9	875.2
Consumer packaged goods, foodservice, and other	2,381.1	2.317.6	2,103.5	868.7
Total net revenues	$22,386.8	$21,315.9	$19,162.7	$10,707.4
Cost of sales, including occupancy costs	$ 9,038.2	$ 8,511.1	$ 7,787.5	$ 4,458.6
Store operating expenses	6,493.3	6,064.3	5,411.1	3,551.4
Other operating expenses	553.8	545.4	522.4	293.2
Depreciation and amortization expenses	1,011.4	980.8	893.9	510.4
General and administrative expenses	1,393.3	1,360.6	1,196.7	569.5
Restructuring and impairments	153.5	—	—	53.0
Total operating expenses	18,643.5	17,462.2	15,811.6	9,436.1
Income from equity investees and other	391.4	318.2	249.9	148.1
Operating income	4,134.7	4,171.9	3,601.0	1,419.4
Net earnings attributable to Starbucks	$ 2,884.7	$ 2,817.7	$ 2,759.3	$ 945.6
Net earnings per common share — diluted	$1.97	$1.90	$1.82	$0.62
BALANCE SHEET DATA				
Current assets	$ 5,283.4	$ 4,757.9	$ 3,971.0	$ 2,756.5
Current liabilities	4,220.7	4,546.8	3,648.1	2,703.6
Total assets	14,365.6	14,312.5	12,416.3	6,385.9
Long-term debt (including current portion)	3,932.6	3,585.2	2,347.5	549.4
Shareholders' equity	5,457.0	5,890.7	5,818.0	3,674.7
OTHER FINANCIAL DATA				
Net cash provided by operating activities	$ 4,174.3	$ 4,575.1	$ 3,749.1	$ 1,704.9
Capital expenditures (additions to property, plant, and equipment)	1,519.4	1,440.3	1,303.7	440.7
STORE INFORMATION				
Stores open at year-end				
United States				
Company-operated stores	8,222	7,880	6,764	6,707
Licensed stores	5,708	5,292	4,364	4,424
International				
Company-operated stores	5,053	4,831	2,198	2,182
Licensed stores	8,356	7,082	3,309	3,545
Worldwide	27,339	25,085	23,043	16,858
Worldwide percentage change in sales at company-operated stores open 13 months or longer	3%	5%	7%	7%

*Starbucks' fiscal year ends on the Sunday closest to September 30.

Sources: 2017, 2016, and 2011 10-K reports.

in touristy Pikes Place Market in Seattle. The three partners shared a love for fine coffees and exotic teas and believed they could build a clientele in Seattle that would appreciate the best coffees and teas. By the early 1980s, the company had four Starbucks stores in the Seattle area and had been profitable every year since opening its doors.

Howard Schultz Enters the Picture

In 1981, Howard Schultz, vice president and general manager of U.S. operations for a Swedish maker of stylish kitchen equipment and coffeemakers based in New York City, decided to pay Starbucks a visit. He was curious why Starbucks was selling so many of his company's products. When he arrived at the Pikes Place store, a solo violinist was playing Mozart at the door (his violin case open for donations). Schultz was immediately taken by the powerful and pleasing aroma of the coffees, the wall displaying coffee beans, and the rows of coffeemakers on the shelves. As he talked with the clerk behind the counter, the clerk scooped out some Sumatran coffee beans, ground them, put the grounds in a cone filter, poured hot water over the cone, and shortly handed Schultz a porcelain mug filled with freshly brewed coffee. After only taking three sips of the brew, Schultz was hooked. He began asking questions about the company, the coffees from different parts of the world, and the different ways of roasting coffee.

Later, when he met with two of the owners, Schultz was struck by their knowledge about coffee, their commitment to providing customers with quality coffees, and their passion for educating customers about the merits and quality of dark-roasted, fine coffees. One of the owners told Schultz, "We don't manage the business to maximize anything other than the quality of the coffee."[1] Schultz was also struck by the business philosophy of the two partners. It was clear that Starbucks stood not just for good coffee, but also for the dark-roasted flavor profiles that the founders were passionate about. Top quality, fresh-roasted, whole-bean coffee was the company's differentiating feature and a bedrock value. The company depended mainly on word-of-mouth to get more people into its stores, then built customer loyalty cup by cup as buyers gained a sense of discovery and excitement about the taste of fine coffee.

On his return trip to New York, Howard Schultz could not stop thinking about Starbucks and what it would be like to be a part of the enterprise. Schultz recalled, "There was something magic about it, a passion and authenticity I had never experienced in business."[2] By the time he landed at Kennedy Airport, he knew in his heart he wanted to go to work for Starbucks. But it took over a year and multiple meetings and discussions to convince the owners to bring in a high-powered New Yorker who had not grown up with the values of the company. In Spring 1982, Schultz was offered the job of heading marketing and overseeing Starbucks' retail stores; he assumed his new responsibilities at Starbucks in September 1982.

Starbucks and Howard Schultz: The 1982–1985 Period   In his first few months at Starbucks, Schultz spent most of his time in the four Seattle stores—working behind the counters, tasting different kinds of coffee, talking with customers, getting to know store personnel, and learning the retail aspects of the coffee business. In December, he began the final part of his training—that of actually roasting the coffee. Schultz spent a week getting an education about the colors of different coffee beans, listening for the telltale second pop of the beans during the roasting process, learning to taste the subtle differences among the various roasts, and familiarizing himself with the roasting techniques for different beans.

Schultz overflowed with ideas for the company. However, his biggest inspiration and vision for Starbucks' future came during the spring of 1983 when the company sent him to Milan, Italy, to attend an international housewares show. While walking from his hotel to the convention center, he spotted an espresso bar and went inside to look around. The cashier beside the door nodded and smiled. The "barista" behind the counter greeted Schultz cheerfully and began pulling a shot of espresso for one customer and handcrafting a foamy cappuccino for another, all the while conversing merrily with patrons standing at the counter. Schultz thought the barista's performance was "great theater." Just down the way on a side street, he went in an even more crowded espresso bar where the barista, which he surmised to be the owner, was greeting customers by name; people were laughing and talking in an atmosphere that plainly was comfortable and familiar. In the next few blocks, he saw two more espresso bars. That afternoon, Schultz walked the streets of Milan to explore more espresso bars. Some were stylish and upscale; others attracted a blue-collar clientele. Most had few chairs and it was common for Italian opera to be playing in the background. What struck Schultz was how popular and vibrant the Italian coffee bars were. Energy levels were typically high and they seemed to function as an integral community gathering place. Each one had its own unique character, but they all had a barista who performed with flair and there was camaraderie between the barista and the customers.

Schultz remained in Milan for a week, exploring coffee bars and learning as much as he could about the Italian passion for coffee drinks. Schultz was particularly struck by the fact that there were 1,500 coffee bars in Milan, a city about the size of Philadelphia, and a total of 200,000 in all of Italy. In one bar, he heard a customer order a "caffe latte" and decided to try one himself—the barista made a shot of espresso, steamed a frothy pitcher of milk, poured the two together in a cup, and put a dollop of foam on the top. Schultz liked it immediately, concluding that lattes should be a feature item on any coffee bar menu even though none of the coffee experts he had talked to had ever mentioned coffee lattes.

Schultz's 1983 trip to Milan produced a revelation—the Starbucks stores in Seattle completely missed the point. There was much more to the coffee business than just selling beans and getting people to appreciate grinding their own beans and brewing fine coffee in their homes. What Starbucks needed to do was serve fresh brewed coffee, espressos, and cappuccinos in its stores (in addition to beans and coffee equipment) and try to create an American version of the Italian coffee bar culture. Going to Starbucks should be an experience, a special treat, a place to meet friends and visit. Re-creating the authentic Italian coffee bar culture in the United States could be Starbucks' differentiating factor.

Schultz Becomes Frustrated

On Schultz's return from Italy, he shared his revelation and ideas for modifying the format of Starbucks' stores, but the owners strongly resisted, contending that Starbucks was a retailer, not a restaurant or coffee bar. They feared serving drinks would put them in the beverage business and diminish the integrity of Starbucks' mission as a purveyor of fine coffees. They pointed out that Starbucks had been profitable every year and there was no reason to rock the boat in a small, private company like Starbucks. It took Howard Schultz nearly a year to convince them to let him test an espresso bar when Starbucks opened its sixth store in April 1984. It was the first store

designed to sell beverages and it was the first store located in downtown Seattle. Schultz asked for a 1,500-square-foot space to set up a full-scale Italian-style espresso bar, but he was allocated only 300 square feet in a corner of the new store. The store opened with no fanfare as a deliberate experiment to see what happened. By closing time on the first day, some 400 customers had been served, well above the 250-customer average of Starbucks' best performing stores. Within two months the store was serving 800 customers per day. The two baristas could not keep up with orders during the early morning hours, resulting in lines outside the door onto the sidewalk. Most of the business was at the espresso counter, while sales at the regular retail counter were only adequate.

Schultz was elated at the test results, expecting that the owners' doubts about entering the beverage side of the business would be dispelled and that he would gain approval to pursue the opportunity to take Starbucks to a new level. Every day he shared the sales figures and customer counts at the new downtown store. But the lead owner was not comfortable with the success of the new store, believing that it felt wrong and that espresso drinks were a distraction from the core business of marketing fine Arabica coffees at retail.[3] While he didn't deny that the experiment was succeeding, he would not agree to go forward with introducing beverages in other Starbucks stores.

Over the next several months, Schultz made up his mind to leave Starbucks and start his own company. His plan was to open espresso bars in high-traffic downtown locations, serve espresso drinks and coffee by the cup, and try to emulate the friendly, energetic atmosphere he had encountered in Italian espresso bars. The two owners, knowing how frustrated Schultz had become, supported his efforts to go out on his own and agreed to let him stay in his current job and office until definitive plans were in place. Schultz left Starbucks in late 1985.

Schultz's Il Giornale Venture

With the aid of a lawyer friend who helped companies raise venture capital and go public, Schultz began seeking out investors for the kind of company he had in mind. Ironically, one of the owners committed to investing $150,000 of Starbucks' money in Schultz's coffee bar enterprise and became Schultz's first investor. The other owner proposed that the new company be named Il Giornale Coffee Company (pronounced il-jor-nahl'-ee), a suggestion that Schultz accepted. In December 1985, Schultz and one of the Starbucks owners made a trip to Italy where they visited some 500 espresso bars in Milan and Verona, observing local habits, taking notes about décor and menus, snapping photographs, and videotaping baristas in action.

By the end of January 1986, Schultz had raised about $400,000 in seed capital, enough to rent an office, hire a couple of key employees, develop a store design, and open the first store. But it took until the end of 1986 to raise the remaining $1.25 million needed to launch at least eight espresso bars and prove that Schultz's strategy and business model were viable. Schultz made presentations to 242 potential investors, 217 of which said no. Many who heard Schultz's hour-long presentation saw coffee as a commodity business and thought that Schultz's espresso bar concept lacked any basis for sustainable competitive advantage (no patent on dark roast, no advantage in purchasing coffee beans, no way to bar the entry of imitative competitors). Some noted that coffee couldn't be turned into a growth business—consumption of coffee had been declining since the mid-1960s. Others were skeptical that people would pay $1.50 or more for a cup of coffee, and the company's unpronounceable name turned some off. Nonetheless, Schultz maintained an upbeat attitude and displayed passion and enthusiasm in making his pitch. He ended up raising $1.65 million from about 30 investors; most of the money came from nine people, five of whom became directors.

The first Il Giornale store opened in April 1986. It measured 700 square feet and was located near the entrance of Seattle's tallest building. The décor was Italian and there were Italian words on the menu. Italian opera music played in the background. The baristas wore white shirts and bow ties. All service was stand up—there were no chairs. National and international papers were hung on rods on the wall. By closing time on the first day, 300 customers had been served—mostly in the morning hours. But while the core idea worked well, it soon became apparent that several aspects of the format were not appropriate for Seattle. Some customers objected to the incessant opera music, others wanted a place to sit down; many people did not understand the Italian words on the menu. These "mistakes" were quickly fixed, but an effort was made not to compromise the style and elegance of the store. Within six months, the store was serving more than 1,000 customers a day. Regular customers had learned how to pronounce the company's name. Because most customers were in a hurry, it became apparent that speedy service was essential.

Six months after opening the first store, a second store was opened in another downtown building. In April 1987, a third store was opened in Vancouver, British Columbia, to test the transferability of the company's business concept outside Seattle. Schultz's goal was to open 50 stores in five years and he needed to dispel his investors' doubts about geographic expansion early on to achieve his growth objective. By mid-1987, sales at each of the three stores were running at a rate equal to $1.5 million annually.

Il Giornale Acquires Starbucks

In March 1987, the Starbucks owners decided to sell the whole Starbucks operation in Seattle—the stores, the roasting plant, and the Starbucks name. Schultz knew immediately that he had to buy Starbucks; his board of directors agreed. Schultz and his newly hired finance and accounting manager drew up a set of financial projections for the combined operations and a financing package that included a stock offering to Il Giornale's original investors and a line of credit with local banks. Within weeks, Schultz had raised the $3.8 million needed to buy Starbucks. The acquisition was completed in August 1987. The new name of the combined companies was Starbucks Corporation. Howard Schultz, at the age of 34, became Starbucks' president and CEO.

Starbucks as a Private Company: 1987–1992

The Monday morning after the deal closed, Howard Schultz returned to the Starbucks offices at the roasting plant, greeted all the familiar faces, and accepted their congratulations. Then, he called the staff together for a meeting on the roasting plant floor:

> All my life I have wanted to be part of a company and a group of people who share a common vision. . . . I'm here today because I love this company. I love what it represents. . . . I know you're concerned . . . I promise you I will not let you down. I promise you I will not leave anyone behind. . . . In five years, I want you to look back at this day and say "I was there when it started. I helped build this company into something great."[4]

Schultz told the group that his vision was for Starbucks to become a national company with values and guiding principles that employees could be proud of. He aspired for Starbucks to become the most respected brand name in coffee and for the company to be admired for its corporate responsibility. He indicated that he wanted to include people in the decision-making process and that he would be open and honest with them. For Schultz, building a company that valued and respected its people, that inspired them, and that shared the fruits of success with those who contributed to the company's long-term value was essential, not just an intriguing option. He made the establishment of mutual respect between employees and management a priority.

The business plan Schultz had presented investors called for the new nine-store company to open 125 stores in the next five years—15 the first year, 20 the second, 25 the third, 30 the fourth, and 35 the fifth. Revenues were projected to reach $60 million in 1992. But the company lacked experienced management. Schultz had never led a growth effort of such magnitude and was just learning what the job of CEO was all about, having been the president of a small company for barely two years. Dave Olsen, a Seattle coffee bar owner who Schultz had recruited to direct store operations at Il Giornale, was still learning the ropes in managing a multistore operation. Ron Lawrence, the company's controller, had worked as a controller for several organizations. Other Starbucks employees had only the experience of managing or being a part of a six-store organization.

Schultz instituted a number of changes in the first several months. To symbolize the merging of the two companies and the two cultures, a new logo was created that melded the designs of the Starbucks logo and the Il Giornale logo. The Starbucks stores were equipped with espresso machines and remodeled to look more Italian than old-world nautical. Il Giornale green replaced the traditional Starbucks brown. The result was a new type of store—a cross between a retail coffee bean store and an espresso bar/café—that quickly evolved into Starbucks' signature.

By December 1987, the mood at Starbucks was distinctly upbeat, with most all employees buying into the changes that Schultz was making and trust beginning to build between management and employees. New stores were on the verge of opening in Vancouver and Chicago. One Starbucks store employee, Daryl Moore, who had started working at Starbucks in 1981 and who had voted against unionization in 1985, began to question the need for a union with his fellow employees. Over the next few weeks, Moore began

a move to decertify the union. He carried a decertification letter around to Starbucks' stores, securing the signatures of employees who no longer wished to be represented by the union. He got a majority of store employees to sign the letter and presented it to the National Labor Relations Board. The union representing store employees was decertified. Later, in 1992, the union representing Starbucks' roasting plant and warehouse employees was also decertified.

Market Expansion Outside the Pacific Northwest

The first Chicago store opened in October 1987 and three more stores were opened over the next six months. Initially, customer counts at the stores were substantially below expectations because Chicagoans did not take to dark-roasted coffee as fast as Schultz had anticipated. While it was more expensive to supply fresh coffee to the Chicago stores out of the Seattle warehouse, the company solved the problem of freshness and quality assurance by putting freshly roasted beans in special FlavorLock bags that utilized vacuum packaging techniques with a one-way valve to allow carbon dioxide to escape without allowing air and moisture in. Moreover, rents and wage rates were higher in Chicago. The result was a squeeze on store profit margins. Gradually, customer counts improved, but Starbucks lost money on its Chicago stores until, in 1990, prices were raised to reflect higher rents and labor costs, more experienced store managers were hired, and a critical mass of customers caught on to the taste of Starbucks products.

Portland, Oregon, was the next market entered, and Portland coffee drinkers took to Starbucks products quickly. Store openings in Los Angeles and San Francisco soon followed. L.A. consumers embraced Starbucks quickly and the *Los Angeles Times* named Starbucks the best coffee in America before the first store opened.

Starbucks' store expansion targets proved easier to meet than Schultz had originally anticipated and he upped the numbers to keep challenging the organization. Starbucks opened 15 new stores in fiscal 1988, 20 in 1989, 30 in 1990, 32 in 1991, and 53 in 1992—producing a total of 161 stores, significantly above his original 1992 target of 125 stores.

From the outset, the strategy was to open only company-owned stores; franchising was avoided so as to keep the company in full control of the quality of its products and the character and location of its stores. But company ownership of all stores required Starbucks to raise new venture capital to cover the cost of new store expansion. In 1988, the company raised $3.9 million; in 1990, venture capitalists provided an additional $13.5 million; and in 1991, another round of venture capital financing generated $15 million. Starbucks was able to raise the needed funds despite posting losses of $330,000 in 1987, $764,000 in 1988, and $1.2 million in 1989. While the losses were troubling to Starbucks' board of directors and investors, Schultz's business plan had forecast losses during the early years of expansion. At a particularly tense board meeting where directors sharply questioned Schultz about the lack of profitability, Schultz said:

> Look, we're going to keep losing money until we can do three things. We have to attract a management team well beyond our expansion needs. We have to build a world-class roasting facility. And we need a computer information system sophisticated enough to keep track of sales in hundreds and hundreds of stores.[5]

Schultz argued for patience as the company invested in the infrastructure to support continued growth well into the 1990s. He contended that hiring experienced executives ahead of the growth curve, building facilities far beyond current needs, and installing support systems laid a strong foundation for rapid profitable growth later down the road. His arguments carried the day with the board and with investors, especially since revenues were growing approximately 80 percent annually and customer traffic at the stores was meeting or exceeding expectations.

Starbucks became profitable in 1990. After-tax profits had increased every year since 1990 except for fiscal year 2000 (because of $58.8 million in investment write-offs in four dot.com enterprises) and for fiscal year 2008 (when the sharp global economic downturn hit the company's bottom line very hard).

RAPID EXPANSION OF THE NETWORK OF STARBUCKS LOCATIONS

In 1992 and 1993, Starbucks began concentrating its store expansion efforts in the United States on locations with favorable demographic profiles that also could be serviced and supported by the company's operations infrastructure. For each targeted region, Starbucks selected a large city to serve as a hub; teams of professionals were located in hub cities to support the goal of opening 20 or more stores in the hub within two years. Once a number of stores were opened in a hub, then additional stores were opened in smaller surrounding "spoke" areas in the region. To oversee the expansion process, Starbucks had zone vice presidents who oversaw the store expansion process in a geographic region and who were also responsible for instilling the Starbucks culture in the newly opened stores. For a time, Starbucks went to extremes to blanket major cities with stores, even if some stores cannibalized a nearby store's business. While a new store might draw 30 percent of the business of an existing store two or so blocks away, management believed a "Starbucks everywhere" strategy cut down on delivery and management costs, shortened customer lines at individual stores, and increased foot traffic for all the stores in an area. In 2002, new stores generated an average of $1.2 million in first-year revenues, compared to $700,000 in 1995 and only $427,000 in 1990; the increases in new-store revenues were due partly to growing popularity of premium coffee drinks, partly to Starbucks' growing reputation, and partly to expanded product offerings. But by 2008 and 2009 the strategy of saturating big metropolitan areas with stores began cannibalizing sales of existing stores to such an extent that average annual sales per store in the United States dropped to less than $1,000,000 and pushed store operating margins down from double-digit levels to mid-single-digit levels. As a consequence, Starbucks' management cut the number of metropolitan locations, closing 900 underperforming Starbucks stores in 2008 and 2009, some 75 percent of which were within three miles of another Starbucks store.

Despite the mistake of oversaturating portions of some large metropolitan areas with stores, Starbucks was regarded as having the best real estate team in the coffee bar industry and a core competence in identifying good retailing sites for its new stores. The company's sophisticated methodology enabled it to identify not only the most attractive individual city blocks but also the exact store location that was best. It also worked hard at building good relationships with local real estate representatives in areas where it was opening multiple store locations.

Licensed Starbucks Stores In 1995, Starbucks began entering into licensing agreements for store locations in areas in the United States where it did not have the ability to locate company-owned outlets. Two early licensing agreements were with Marriott Host International to operate Starbucks retail stores in airport locations and with Aramark Food and Services to put Starbucks stores on university campuses and other locations operated by Aramark. Very quickly, Starbucks began to make increased use of licensing, both domestically and internationally. Starbucks preferred licensing to franchising because it permitted tighter controls over the operations of licensees, and in the case of many foreign locations licensing was much less risky.

Starbucks received a license fee and a royalty on sales at all licensed locations and supplied the coffee for resale at these locations. All licensed stores had to follow Starbucks' detailed operating procedures and all managers and employees who worked in these stores received the same training given to managers and employees in company-operated Starbucks stores.

International Expansion   In markets outside the continental United States, Starbucks had a two-pronged store expansion strategy: either open company-owned-and-operated stores or else license a reputable and capable local company with retailing know-how in the target host country to develop and operate new Starbucks stores. In most countries, Starbucks utilized a local partner/licensee to help it locate suitable store sites, set up supplier relationships, recruit talented individuals for positions as store managers,

and adapt to local market conditions. Starbucks looked for partners/licensees that had strong retail/restaurant experience, had values and a corporate culture compatible with Starbucks, were committed to good customer service, possessed talented management and strong financial resources, and had demonstrated brand-building skills. In those foreign countries where business risks were deemed relatively high, most if not all Starbucks stores were licensed rather than being company-owned and operated.

Exhibit 2 shows the speed with which Starbucks grew its network of company-operated and licensed retail stores.

STORE DESIGN AND AMBIENCE: KEY ELEMENTS OF THE "STARBUCKS EXPERIENCE"

Store Design

Starting in 1991, Starbucks created its own in-house team of architects and designers to ensure that each store would convey the right image and character. Stores had to be custom designed because the company did not buy real estate and build its own free-standing structures. Instead, each space was leased in an existing structure, making each store differ in

EXHIBIT 2   Company-Operated and Licensed Starbucks Stores

A. Number of Starbucks Store Locations Worldwide, Fiscal Years 1987–2015 and April 1, 2018

End of Fiscal Year*	Company-Operated Store Locations		Licensed Store Locations		Worldwide Total
	United States	International	United States	International	
1987	17	0	0	0	17
1990	84	0	0	0	84
1995	627	0	49	0	676
2000	2,446	530	173	352	3,501
2005	4,918	1,263	2,435	1,625	10,241
2010	6,707	2,182	4,424	3,545	16,858
2015	6,764	2,198	4,364	3,309	23,043
April 1, 2018	8,401	6,411	5,895	7,502	28,209

(Continued)

B. International Starbucks Store Locations, April 1, 2018

International Locations of Company-Operated Starbucks Stores			International Locations of Licensed Starbucks Stores	
		Americas	**Europe/Africa/Middle East**	
Canada	1,095	Canada	399	Turkey	417
United Kingdom	339	Mexico	666	United Kingdom	638
China	3,236	16 Others	592	United Arab Emirates	173
Japan	1,248			Spain	125
Thailand	332	**China, Asia-Pacific**		Saudi Arabia	147
Other	161	Taiwan	435	Kuwait	133
		South Korea	1,175	Russia	120
		Philippines	340	32 Others	912
		Malaysia	258		
		Indonesia	329		
		9 Others	642		
International Company-Operated Total	**6,411**			**International Licensed Total**	**7,502**

Source: Company records posted in the investor relations section at **www.starbucks.com** (accessed May 16, 2018).

size and shape. Most stores ranged in size from 1,000 to 1,500 square feet and were located in office buildings, downtown and suburban retail centers, airport terminals, university campus areas, and busy neighborhood shopping areas convenient for pedestrian foot traffic and/or drivers. A few were in suburban malls. Four store templates—each with its own color combinations, lighting scheme, and component materials—were introduced in 1996; all four were adaptable to different store sizes and settings.

But as the number of stores increased rapidly over the next 20-plus years, greater store diversity and layouts quickly became necessary. Some stores were equipped with special seating areas to help make Starbucks a desirable gathering place where customers could meet and chat or simply enjoy a peaceful interlude in their day. Flagship stores in high-traffic, high-visibility locations had fireplaces, leather chairs, newspapers, couches, and lots of ambience. Increasingly, the company began installing drive-through windows at locations where speed and convenience were important to customers and locating kiosks in high-traffic supermarkets, building lobbies, the halls of shopping malls, and other public places where passers-by could quickly and conveniently pick up a Starbucks beverage and/or something to eat.

A new global store design strategy was introduced in 2009. Core design characteristics included the celebration of local materials and craftsmanship, a focus on reused and recycled elements, the exposure of structural integrity and authentic roots, the absence of features that distracted from an emphasis on coffee, seating layouts that facilitated customer gatherings, an atmosphere that sought to engage all five customer senses (sight, smell, sound, hearing, and feel), and flexibility to meet the needs of many customer types.[6] Each new store was to be a reflection of the environment in which it operated and be environmentally friendly. In 2010, Starbucks began an effort to achieve LEED (Leadership in Energy and Environmental Design) certification for all new company-owned stores (a LEED-certified building had to incorporate green building design, construction, operations, and maintenance solutions).[7]

To better control average store opening costs, the company centralized buying, developed standard contracts and fixed fees for certain items, and consolidated work under those contractors who displayed good cost control practices. The retail operations group outlined exactly the minimum amount of equipment each core store needed, so that standard items could be ordered in volume from vendors at 20 to 30 percent discounts, then delivered just in time to the store site either from company warehouses or the vendor. Modular designs for display cases were developed. The layouts for new and remodeled stores were developed on a computer, with software that allowed the costs to be estimated as the design evolved. All this cut store opening and remodeling costs significantly and shortened the process to about 18 weeks.

Store Ambience

Starbucks management viewed each store as a billboard for the company and as a contributor to building the company's brand and image. The company went to great lengths to make sure the store fixtures, merchandise displays, colors, artwork, banners, music, and aromas all blended to create a consistent, inviting, stimulating environment that evoked the romance of coffee and signaled the company's passion for coffee. To try to keep the coffee aromas in the stores pure, smoking was banned, and employees were asked to refrain from wearing perfumes or colognes. Prepared foods were kept covered so customers would smell coffee only. Colorful banners and posters were used to keep the look of the Starbucks stores fresh and in keeping with seasons and holidays. All these practices reflected a conviction that every detail mattered in making Starbucks stores a welcoming and pleasant "third place" (apart from home and work) where people could meet friends and family, enjoy a quiet moment alone with a newspaper or book, or simply spend quality time relaxing—and most importantly, have a satisfying experience.

In 2002, Starbucks began providing Internet access capability and enhanced digital entertainment to patrons. The objective was to heighten the third place Starbucks experience, entice customers into perhaps buying a second latte or espresso while they caught up on e-mail, listened to digital music, put the finishing touches on a presentation, or surfed the Internet. Wireless Internet service and faster Internet speeds were added as fast as they became available.

STARBUCKS' STRATEGY TO EXPAND ITS PRODUCT OFFERINGS AND ENTER NEW MARKET SEGMENTS

Starting in the mid-1990s and continuing to the present, Howard Schultz began a long-term strategic campaign to expand Starbucks product offerings beyond its retail stores and to pursue sales of Starbucks products in a wider variety of distribution channels and market segments. The strategic objectives were to capitalize on Starbucks growing brand awareness and brand-name strength and create a broader foundation for sustained long-term growth in revenues and profits.

The first initiative involved the establishment of an in-house specialty sales group to begin marketing Starbucks coffee to restaurants, airlines, hotels, universities, hospitals, business offices, country clubs, and select retailers. Early users of Starbucks coffee included Horizon Airlines, a regional carrier based in Seattle, and United Airlines. The specialty sales group then soon won accounts at Hyatt, Hilton, Sheraton, Radisson, and Westin hotels, resulting in packets of Starbucks coffee being in each room with coffee-making equipment. Later, the specialty sales group began working with leading institutional food-service distributors, including SYSCO Corporation and US Foodservice, to handle the distribution of Starbucks products to hotels, restaurants, office coffee distributors, educational and healthcare institutions, and other such enterprises. In fiscal year 2009, Starbucks generated revenues of $372.2 million from providing whole bean and ground coffees and assorted other Starbucks products to some 21,000 foodservice accounts.

The second initiative came in 1994 when PepsiCo and Starbucks entered into a joint venture arrangement to create new coffee-related products in bottles or cans for mass distribution through Pepsi channels. The joint venture's first new product, a lightly flavored carbonated coffee drink, was a failure. Then, at a meeting with Pepsi executives, Schultz suggested developing a bottled version of Frappuccino, a new cold coffee drink Starbucks began serving at its retail stores in the summer of 1995 that quickly became a big hot weather seller. Pepsi executives were enthusiastic. Sales of Frappuccino ready-to-drink beverages reached $125 million in 1997 and achieved a national supermarket penetration of 80 percent. Sales of ready-to-drink Frappuccino products soon began in Japan, Taiwan, South Korea, and China chiefly through agreements with leading local distributors. In 2010, sales of Frappuccino products worldwide reached $2 billion annually.[8]

In 1995, Starbucks partnered with Dreyer's Grand Ice Cream to supply coffee extracts for a new line of coffee ice cream made and distributed by Dreyer's under the Starbucks brand. Starbucks coffee-flavored ice cream became the number-one-selling super-premium brand in the coffee segment in mid-1996. In 2008, Starbucks discontinued its arrangement with Dreyer's and entered into an exclusive agreement with Unilever to manufacture, market, and distribute Starbucks-branded ice creams in the United States and Canada. Unilever was the global leader in ice cream with annual sales of about $6 billion; its ice cream brands included Ben & Jerry's, Breyers, and Good Humor. There were seven flavors of Starbucks ice cream and two flavors of novelty bars being marketed in 2010, but buyer demand eroded after several years and Starbucks-branded ice cream was discontinued in 2013. However, in 2017, new premium ice cream drinks (a scoop of ice cream drowned in expresso called an "affogato," several other affogato concoctions, and tall cold brew floats and malts) became top-10 menu items at the new Starbucks Roastery and Starbucks Reserve store locations in Seattle and were quickly rolled out to other Reserve locations.

In 1998, Starbucks licensed Kraft Foods to market and distribute Starbucks whole bean and ground coffees in grocery and mass merchandise channels across the United States. Kraft managed all distribution, marketing, advertising, and promotions and paid a royalty to Starbucks based on a percentage of net sales. Product freshness was guaranteed by Starbucks' FlavorLock packaging, and the price per pound paralleled the prices in Starbucks' retail stores. Flavor selections in supermarkets were more limited than the varieties at Starbucks stores. The licensing relationship with Kraft was later expanded to include the marketing and distribution of Starbucks coffees in Canada, the United Kingdom, and other European countries. Going into 2010, Starbucks coffees were available in some 33,500 grocery and warehouse clubs in the United States and 5,500 retail outlets outside the United States; Starbucks revenues from these sales were approximately $370 million in fiscal 2009.[9] During fiscal 2011, Starbucks discontinued its distribution arrangement with Kraft and instituted its own in-house organization to handle direct sales of packaged coffees to supermarkets and to warehouse club stores (chiefly Costco, Sam's Club, and BJ's Warehouse).

In 1999, Starbucks purchased Tazo Tea for $8.1 million. Tazo Tea, a tea manufacturer and distributor based in Portland, Oregon, was founded in 1994 and marketed its teas to restaurants, food stores, and tea houses. Starbucks proceeded to introduce hot and iced Tazo Tea drinks in its retail stores. As part of a long-term campaign to expand the distribution of its lineup of super-premium Tazo teas, Starbucks expanded its agreement with Kraft to market and distribute Tazo teas worldwide. In August 2008, Starbucks entered into a licensing agreement with a partnership formed by PepsiCo and Unilever (Lipton Tea was one of Unilever's leading brands) to manufacture, market, and distribute Starbucks' super-premium Tazo Tea ready-to-drink beverages (including iced teas, juiced teas, and herbal-infused teas) in the United States and Canada—in 2012, the Pepsi/Lipton Tea partnership was the leading North American distributor of ready-to-drink teas. In fiscal year 2011, when Starbucks broke off its packaged coffee distribution arrangement with Kraft, it also broke off its arrangement with Kraft for distribution of Tazo tea and began selling Tazo teas directly to supermarkets (except for Tazo Tea ready-to-drink beverages).

In 2001, Starbucks introduced the Starbucks Card, a reloadable card that allowed customers to pay for their purchases with a quick swipe of their card at the cash register and also to earn "stars" and redeem rewards. Since then, Starbucks Rewards[TM] had evolved into one of the best retail loyalty programs in existence, aided by the introduction of Starbucks Gift Cards, the Starbucks mobile app, rewards for in-store purchases and purchases of Starbucks products in grocery stores and other retail locations where Starbucks products were sold, and attractive member benefits for achieving "Green Star" status (0 to 299 stars in a 12-month period) and "Gold Star" status (300 or more stars in a 12-month period). Green level perks included two stars per $1 spent, free in-store refills on ice or brewed coffee, a birthday reward, eligibility for special Star Dash promotions, and invitations to special events. Gold level perks included all green level benefits plus the opportunity to take advantage of monthly Double-Star Day promotions, a free food and drink reward for each 125 points earned, and a personalized Gold Card (considered a status symbol among Rewards members). The app made it easy for members to see how many stars (points) they currently had, place orders and make payments right from their phone, and find the nearest Starbucks location. Members with a Starbucks Rewards[TM] Visa® Card also earned one star for every $4 purchased with the Starbucks Visa card. When members reloaded a registered Starbucks

Card using their Starbucks Rewards™ Visa® Card on the mobile app or Starbucks.com, they received one star for every dollar loaded in addition to the two stars for every dollar earned when using a registered Starbucks Card or the Starbucks mobile app for purchases in participating Starbucks stores. In 2017, there were over 20 million Starbuck Rewards™ members globally, and over 75 percent of Starbucks customers in North America either used a Starbucks Card or the Starbucks mobile app to pay for in-store purchases.

In 2003, Starbucks spent $70 million to acquire Seattle's Best Coffee, an operator of 540 Seattle's Best coffee shops, 86 Seattle's Best Coffee Express espresso bars, and marketer of some 30 varieties of Seattle's Best whole bean and ground coffees. The decision was made to operate Seattle's Best as a separate subsidiary. Starbucks quickly expanded its licensing arrangement with Kraft Foods to include marketing, distributing, and promoting the sales of Seattle's Best coffees and, by 2009, Seattle's Best coffees were available nationwide in supermarkets and at more than 15,000 foodservice locations (college campuses, restaurants, hotels, airlines, and cruise lines). A new Seattle's Best line of ready-to-drink iced lattes was introduced in April 2010, with manufacture, marketing, and distribution managed by PepsiCo as part of the long-standing Starbucks–PepsiCo joint venture for ready-to-drink Frappuccino products. In 2010, Starbucks introduced new distinctive red packaging and a red logo for Seattle's Best Coffee, boosted efforts to open more franchised Seattle's Best cafés, and expanded the availability of Seattle's Best coffees to 30,000 distribution points. When Starbucks' licensing agreement with Kraft to handle sales and distribution of Seattle's Best coffee products was terminated in 2011, responsibility for the sales and distribution of Seattle's Best products was transitioned to the same in-house sales force that handled direct sales and distribution of Starbucks-branded coffees and tea products to supermarkets and warehouse clubs.

In 2005, Starbucks Corporation acquired Ethos™ Water, a privately held bottled water company based in Santa Monica, California, whose mission was help children around the world get clean water by supporting water projects in such developing countries as Bangladesh, the Democratic Republic of Congo, Ethiopia, Honduras, India, and Kenya. One of the terms of the acquisition called for Starbucks to donate $1.25 million in 2005 and 2006 to support these projects. In the years since the acquisition, a key element of Starbucks' corporate social responsibility effort has been to donate $0.05US ($0.10CN in Canada) for every bottle of Ethos Water sold in Starbucks stores to the Ethos® Water Fund, part of the Starbucks Foundation, to fund ongoing efforts to provide clean water to children in developing countries and to support water, sanitation, and hygiene education programs in water-stressed countries.

In 2008, Starbucks introduced a new coffee blend called Pike Place™ Roast that would be brewed every day, all day, in every Starbucks store.[10] Before then, Starbucks rotated various coffee blends through its brewed lineup, sometimes switching them weekly, sometimes daily. While some customers liked the ever-changing variety, the feedback from a majority of customers indicated a preference for a consistent brew that customers could count on when they came into a Starbucks store. The Pike Place blend was brewed in small batches at 30-minute intervals so as to provide customers with a freshly-brewed coffee. In January 2012, after eight months of testing over 80 different recipe and roast iterations, Starbucks introduced three blends of lighter-bodied and milder-tasting Starbucks Blonde Roast® coffees to better appeal to an estimated 54 million coffee drinkers in the United States who said they liked flavorful, lighter coffees with a gentle finish. The Blonde Roast blends were available as a brewed option in Starbucks stores in the United States and in packaged form in Starbucks stores and supermarkets. Because the majority of coffee sales in supermarkets were in the light and medium roast categories, Starbucks management saw its new Blonde Roast coffees blends as being a $1 billion market opportunity in the United States alone. From time to time, Starbucks introduced new blends of its packaged whole bean and ground coffees—some of these were seasonal, but those that proved popular with buyers became standard offerings.

In Fall 2009, Starbucks introduced Starbucks VIA® Ready Brew, packets of roasted coffee in an instant form, in an effort to attract a bigger fraction of on-the-go and at-home coffee drinkers. VIA was made with a proprietary microground technology that produced an instant coffee with a rich, full-bodied taste that closely replicated the taste, quality, and flavor of traditional freshly brewed coffee. Encouraged by favorable customer response, Starbucks expanded the distribution of VIA to some 25,000 grocery, mass merchandise, and drugstore accounts, including Kroger, Safeway, Walmart, Target, Costco, and CVS. Instant coffee made up a significant fraction of coffee purchases in the United Kingdom (80 percent), Japan (53 percent), Russia (85 percent), and other countries where Starbucks stores were located; globally, the instant and single-serve coffee category was a $23 billion market. By the end of fiscal year 2011, VIA products were available at 70,000 locations and generating annual sales of $250 million.[11]

In fall 2011, Starbucks began selling Starbucks-branded coffee K-Cup® Portion Packs for the Keurig® Single-Cup Brewing system in its retail stores; the Keurig Brewer was produced and sold by Green Mountain Coffee Roasters. Starbucks entered into a strategic partnership with Green Mountain to manufacture the Starbucks-branded portion packs and also to be responsible for marketing, distributing, and selling them to major supermarket chains, drugstore chains, mass merchandisers and wholesale clubs, department stores, and specialty retailers throughout the United States and Canada. The partnership made good economic sense for both companies. Green Mountain could manufacture the single-cup portion packs in the same plants where it was producing its own brands of single-cup packs and then use its own internal resources and capabilities to market, distribute, and sell Starbucks-branded single-cup packs alongside its own brands of single-cup packs. It was far cheaper for Starbucks to pay Green Mountain to handle these functions than to build its own manufacturing plants and put its own in-house resources in place to market, distribute, and sell Starbucks single-cup coffee packs. Just two months after launch, shipments of Starbucks-branded single-cup portion packs had exceeded 100 million units and the packs were available in about 70 percent of the targeted retailers; company officials estimated that Starbucks had achieved an 11 percent dollar share of the market for single-cup coffee packs in the United States.[12]

In March 2012, Starbucks announced that it would begin selling its first at-home premium single cup espresso and brewed coffee machine, the Verismo™ system by Starbucks, at select Starbucks store locations, online, and in upscale specialty stores. The Verismo brewer was a high-pressure system with the capability to brew both coffee and Starbucks-quality espresso beverages, from lattes to americanos, consistently and conveniently one cup at a time; sales of the Verismo single-cup machine put Starbucks into head-to-head competition with Nestlé's Nespresso machine and, to a lesser extent, Green Mountain's popular lineup of low-pressure Keurig brewers. At the time, the global market for premium at-home espresso/coffee machines was estimated at $8 billion.[13] The Verismo introduction was the last phase of Starbucks' strategic initiative to offer coffee products covering all aspects of the single-cup coffee segment—instant coffees (with its VIA offerings), single portion coffee packs for single-cup brewers, and single-cup brewing machines.

In response to customer requests for more wholesome food and beverage options and also to bring in business from non-coffee drinkers, in 2008 Starbucks altered its menu offerings in stores to include fruit cups, yogurt parfaits, skinny lattes, banana walnut bread, a 300-calorie farmer's market salad with all-natural dressing, and a line of 250-calorie "better-for-you" smoothies.[14] From 2009 to 2011, the company continued to experiment with healthier, lower-calorie selections and by May 2012 retail store menus included a bigger assortment of hot and cold coffee and tea beverages, pastries and bakery selections, prepared breakfast and lunch sandwiches and wraps, salads, parfaits, smoothies, juices, and bottled water—at most stores in North America, food items could be warmed. A bit later, beer, wine, and other complementary food offerings were added to the menus at some stores to help them become an attractive and relaxing after-work destination. From 2013 to 2017, it became standard practice for Starbucks to continually tweak its menu offerings, switching out whimsical and limited-edition offerings and adding or dropping certain beverages, flavorings, breakfast items, sandwiches, pastries, and snacks—both to broaden buyer appeal and respond to ongoing shifts in buyer preferences. Menu offerings at Starbucks stores were typically adapted to local cultures; for instance, the menu offerings at stores in North America included a selection of muffins, but stores in France had no muffins and instead featured locally made pastries.

Starbucks purchased cold-pressed juice maker Evolution Fresh for $30 million in 2011 to use Starbucks sales and marketing resources to grow the sales of Evolution Fresh and capture a bigger share of the $3.4 billion super-premium juice segment and begin a long-term campaign to pursue growth opportunities in the $50 billion health and wellness sector of the U.S. economy. A $70 million juice-making facility in California was opened in 2013 to make Evolution Fresh products. Starbucks also opened four Evolution Fresh juice bars after the acquisition, but in 2017 decided to ditch the standalone juice bar concept, opting to sell Evolution Fresh beverages in Starbucks stores and supermarkets. Evolution Fresh competed with PepsiCo's category leader Naked juice brand, as well as scores of other large and small bottled juice brands. As of 2017, Starbucks had secured 20,000 points of distribution for Evolution Fresh products and the brand was said to be "thriving."

In 2012, Starbuck paid $620 million to acquire Atlanta-based specialty tea retailer, Teavana, which sold more than 100 varieties of premium loose-leaf teas and tea-related merchandise through 300 company-owned stores (usually located in upscale shopping malls) and on its website; Teavana teas were used mostly for home consumption. Howard Schultz planned for Starbucks to capitalize on Teavana's world-class tea authority, its passion for tea, and its global sourcing and merchandising capabilities to (a) expand Teavana's domestic and global footprint, (b) bring an elevated tea experience to the patrons of Starbucks domestic and international locations, and (c) increase Starbucks penetration of the $40 billion world market for tea, especially in the world's high-consumption tea markets where Starbucks had stores. By 2016 and 2017 sales at Teavana stores had eroded to the point where the stores were unprofitable, prompting Starbucks to begin the process of closing all 379 Teavana stores (the majority by Spring 2018). However, the sales of Teavana products and beverages in Starbucks stores were popular and contributed to store profitability, accounting for sales of more than $1 billion annually and growing fast enough to double over the next five years. In late 2017, Starbucks sold its Tazo Tea business to Unilever for $384 million, opting to focus its sales of tea products on the Teavana brand.

Also in 2012, Starbucks bought Bay Bread Group's La Boulange sandwich and coffee shops for $100 million. When Starbucks acquired the San Francisco chain, plans called not only for bringing La Boulange products into its stores to bolster its lineup of pastries and sandwiches but also to open new La Boulange cafes and expand the chain's geographic footprint. Three years later, however, Starbucks concluded that sales at the La Boulange cafes were growing too slowly to support its growth

and profitability targets; it closed the 23 existing La Boulange cafes but retained the manufacturing facilities to stock Starbucks stores with La Boulange bakery products. In 2018, the La Boulange brand name was typically not very visible in Starbucks stores but La Boulange-made morning pastries and breakfast sandwiches were still popular sellers during the morning hours when customer traffic at Starbucks stores was high.

Starbucks' overall sales mix in its company-owned retail stores in fiscal year 2017 was 73 percent beverages, 20 percent food, 3 percent packaged and single-serve coffees and teas, and 4 percent ready-to-drink beverages, coffee-making equipment, and other merchandise.[15] However, the product mix in each Starbucks store varied, depending on the size and location of each outlet. Larger stores carried a greater variety of whole coffee beans, gourmet food items, teas, coffee mugs, coffee grinders, coffee-making equipment, filters, storage containers, and other accessories. Smaller stores and kiosks typically sold a full line of coffee and tea beverages, a limited selection of whole bean and ground coffees and Tevana teas, and a few coffee-drinking accessories.

Starbucks' Consumer Products Group

In 2010, Starbucks formed a new Consumer Products Group (CPG) to be responsible for sales of Starbucks products sold in all channels other than Starbucks company-operated and licensed retail stores and to manage the company's partnerships and joint ventures with PepsiCo, Unilever, Green Mountain Coffee Roasters, and others. A few years later, CPG was renamed and slightly reorganized into what was called the Channel Development segment. In 2018, management of the Channel Development segment was responsible for sales and distribution of roasted whole bean and ground coffees, Starbucks-branded single-serve products, a variety of ready-to-drink beverages (such as Frappuccino®, Starbucks Doubleshot®, and Starbucks Refreshers® beverages), Evolution juices, and and other branded products sold worldwide through grocery stores, warehouse clubs, specialty retailers, convenience stores, and U.S. food-service accounts. This segment accounted for sales of $2.0 billion and operating income of $893.4 million in fiscal year 2017, up from revenues of $707.4 million and operating income of $261.4 million in fiscal year 2010. Starbucks executives considered that the sales opportunities for Starbucks products in distribution channels outside Starbucks retail stores were quite attractive from the standpoint of both long-term growth and profitability.

Advertising

Starbucks spent sparingly on advertising, preferring instead to build the brand cup by cup with customers and depend on word of mouth and the appeal of its storefronts. However, Starbucks opted to significantly step up its advertising to combat the strategic initiatives of McDonald's and several other fast-food chains in 2008 and 2009 to begin offering premium coffees and coffee drinks at prices below those charged by Starbucks. In 2009, McDonald's reportedly spent more than $100 million on television, print, radio, billboard, and online ads promoting its new line of McCafé coffee drinks. Starbucks countered with the biggest advertising campaign the company had ever undertaken, spending a total of $176.2 million in fiscal 2010 versus $126.3 million the prior year.[16] The company's advertising expenses totaled $282.6 million in fiscal year 2017, $248.6 million in fiscal 2016, and $227.9 million in fiscal 2015.

HOWARD SCHULTZ'S EFFORTS TO MAKE STARBUCKS A GREAT PLACE TO WORK, 1988–PRESENT

Howard Schultz deeply believed that Starbucks' success was heavily dependent on customers having a very positive experience in its stores. This meant having store employees who were knowledgeable about the company's products, who paid attention to detail in preparing the company's espresso drinks, who eagerly communicated the company's passion for coffee, and who possessed the skills and personality to deliver consistent, pleasing customer service. Many of the baristas were in their 20s and worked part-time, going to college on the side or pursuing other career activities. Schultz viewed the company's challenge as one of attracting, motivating, and rewarding store employees in a manner that would make Starbucks a company that people would want to work for and that would generate enthusiastic commitment and higher levels of customer service. Moreover, Schultz wanted to send all Starbucks employees a message

that would cement the trust that had been building between management and the company's workforce.

Instituting Health Care Coverage for All Employees

One of the requests that employees had made to the prior owners of Starbucks in the 1980s was to extend health care benefits to part-time workers. Their request had been turned down, but Schultz believed that expanding health care coverage to include part-timers was something the company needed to do. He knew from having grown up in a family that struggled to make ends meet how difficult it was to cope with rising medical costs. In 1988, Schultz went to the board of directors with his plan to expand the company's health care coverage to include part-timers who worked at least 20 hours per week. He saw the proposal not as a generous gesture but as a core strategy to win employee loyalty and commitment to the company's mission. Board members resisted because the company was then unprofitable and the added costs of the extended coverage would only worsen the company's bottom line. But Schultz argued passionately that it was the right thing to do and would not be as expensive as it seemed. He observed that if the new benefit reduced turnover, which he believed was likely, then it would reduce the costs of hiring and training—which equaled about $3,000 per new hire. He further pointed out that it cost $1,500 a year to provide an employee with full benefits. Part-timers, he argued, were vital to Starbucks, constituting two-thirds of the company's workforce. Many were baristas who knew the favorite drinks of regular customers; if the barista left, that connection with the customer was broken. Moreover, many part-time employees were called upon to open the stores early, sometimes at 5:30 or 6 a.m.; others had to work until closing, usually 9 p.m. or later. Providing these employees with health care benefits, he argued, would signal that the company honored their value and contribution.

The board approved Schultz's plan and part-timers working 20 or more hours were offered the same health coverage as full-time employees starting in late 1988. Starbucks paid 75 percent of an employee's health care premium; the employee paid 25 percent. Over the years, Starbucks extended its health coverage to include preventive care, prescription drugs, dental care, eye care, mental health, and chemical dependency. Coverage was also offered for unmarried partners in a committed relationship. Since most Starbucks employees were young and comparatively healthy, the company had been able to provide broader coverage while keeping monthly payments relatively low.

A Stock Option Plan for Employees

By 1991, the company's profitability had improved to the point where Schultz could pursue a stock option plan for all employees, a program he believed would have a positive, long-term effect on the success of Starbucks.[17] Schultz wanted to turn every Starbucks employee into a partner, give them a chance to share in the success of the company, and make clear the connection between their contributions and the company's market value. Even though Starbucks was still a private company, the plan that emerged called for granting stock options to every full-time and part-time employee in proportion to their base pay. In May 1991, the plan, dubbed Bean Stock, was presented to the board. Though board members were concerned that increasing the number of shares might unduly dilute the value of the shares of investors who had put up hard cash, the plan received unanimous approval. The first grant was made in October 1991, just after the end of the company's fiscal year in September; each partner was granted stock options worth 12 percent of base pay. When the Bean Stock program was initiated, Starbucks dropped the term employee and began referring to all of its people as "partners" because every member of the Starbucks workforce became eligible for stock option awards after six months of employment and 500 paid work hours.

Starbucks went public in June 1992, selling its initial offering at a price of $17 per share. Starting in October 1992 and continuing through October 2004, Starbucks granted each eligible employee a stock option award with a value equal to 14 percent of base pay. Beginning in 2005, the plan was modified to tie the size of each employee's stock option awards to three factors: (1) Starbucks' success and profitability for the fiscal year, (2) the size of an employee's base wages, and (3) the price at which the stock option could be exercised. Since becoming a public company, Starbucks stock had split 2-for-1 on six occasions. Performance-based stock awards to employees totaled about five million shares in fiscal year 2017; these shares had an average value of $54.30 on the date of the grant and vested in two equal annual installments beginning two years from the grant date.

Starbucks' Stock Purchase Plan for Employees

In 1995, Starbucks implemented an employee stock purchase plan that gave partners who had been employed for at least 90 days an opportunity to purchase company stock through regular payroll deductions. Partners who enrolled could devote anywhere from 1 to 10 percent of their base earnings (up to an annual maximum of $25,000) to purchasing shares of Starbucks stock. After the end of each calendar quarter, each participant's contributions were used to buy Starbucks stock at a discount of 5 percent of the closing price on the last business day of each calendar quarter (until March 2009, the discount was 15 percent). Roughly 30 percent of Starbucks partners participated in the stock purchase plan during the 2000 to 2011 period. Participation has eroded in the past two fiscal years due to Starbucks flat stock price performance since October 2015—the company's global workforce of about 277,000 employees purchased about 500,000 shares in fiscal year 2017.

Since inception of the plan, some 24.8 million shares had been purchased by partners.

The Workplace Environment

Starbucks management believed its competitive pay scales and comprehensive benefits for both full-time and part-time partners (employees) allowed it to attract motivated people with above-average skills and good work habits. An employee's base pay was determined by the pay scales prevailing in the geographic region where an employee worked and by the person's job, skills, experience, and job performance. About 90 percent of Starbucks' partners were full-time or part-time baristas, paid on an hourly basis. In 2018, after six months of employment, baristas at company-owned stores in the United States could expect to earn $10 to $11 per hour. Hourly-paid shift supervisors earned about $12 to $13 an hour; store managers earned about $50,000 and salaries for district managers were in the $75,000 to $85,000 range.[18]

Starbucks was named to *Fortune*'s list of the "100 Best Companies to Work For" 14 times during the 1988 to 2018 period. Surveys of Starbucks partners conducted by *Fortune* magazine in the course of selecting companies for inclusion on its annual list indicated that full-time baristas liked working at Starbucks because of the camaraderie, while part-timers were particularly pleased with the health insurance benefits.[19]

Schultz's approach to offering employees good compensation and a comprehensive benefits package was driven by his belief that sharing the company's success with the people who made it happen helped everyone think and act like an owner, build positive long-term relationships with customers, and do things in an efficient way. Schultz's rationale, based on his father's experience of going from one low-wage, no-benefits job to another, was that if you treat your employees well, that is how they will treat customers.

Exhibit 3 summarizes Starbucks' fringe benefit package.

EXHIBIT 3   Starbucks' Fringe Benefit Program, 2018

- Medical, dental, and vision coverage.
- Sick pay, up to 40 hours per year.
- Paid vacations (up to 120 hours annually for hourly workers with five or more years of service at retail stores and up to 200 hours annually for salaried and non-retail hourly employees with 10 or more years of service).
- Seven paid holidays.
- One paid personal day every six months for salaried and non-retail hourly partners only.
- A 30 percent discount on purchases of beverages, food, and merchandise at Starbucks stores.
- Mental health and chemical dependency coverage.
- 401(k) retirement savings plan—partners age 18 or older with 90 days of service were eligible to contribute from 1 percent to 75 percent of their pay each pay period (up to the annual IRS dollar limit—$18,500 for calendar year 2018). Partners age 50 and older had a higher IRS annual limit ($24,500 for calendar year 2018). Starbucks matched 100 percent of the first 5 percent of eligible pay contributed each pay period. Starbucks matching contributions to the 401(k) plans worldwide totaled $101.4 million in fiscal 2017 and $86.2 million in fiscal 2016.
- Short- and long-term disability.
- Stock purchase plan—eligible employees could buy shares at a 5 percent discount through regular payroll deductions of between 1 and 10 percent of base pay. In fiscal 2017, about 500,000 shares were purchased under this plan.
- Life insurance coverage equal to annual base pay for salaried and non-retail employees; coverage equal to $5,000 for store employees. Supplemental coverage could be purchased in flat dollar amounts of $10,000, $25,000, and $45,000.
- Short-term disability coverage (partial replacement of lost wages/income for 26 weeks, after a short waiting period); hourly employees can purchase long-term disability coverage.
- Company-paid long-term disability coverage for salaried and nonretail employees.
- Accidental death and dismemberment insurance.
- Adoption assistance—reimbursement of up to $10,000 to help pay for qualified expenses related to the adoption of an eligible child.
- Financial assistance program for employees that experience a financial crisis.
- Stock option plan (Bean stock)—shares were granted to eligible partners, subject to the company's achievement of specified performance targets and the employee's continued employment through the vesting period. Vesting occurred in two equal annual installments beginning two years from the grant date. The company's board of directors determined how many shares were to be granted each year and also established the specified performance targets. About 5.1 million shares were granted in fiscal year 2017.
- Pre-tax payroll deductions for work-related commuter expenses.
- Free coffee and tea products each week.
- An in-store discount of 30 percent on purchases of beverages, food, and merchandise.
- Full tuition reimbursement every semester through Arizona State University's top ranked online degree programs.
- Gift-matching benefits—Starbucks matched up to $1,500 per fiscal year for individual contributions of money or volunteer time to eligible non-profit organizations.

Source: Information in the Careers section at **www.starbucks.com** (accessed May 31, 2018).

Employee Training and Recognition

To accommodate its strategy of rapid store expansion, Starbucks put in systems to recruit, hire, and train baristas and store managers. Starbucks' vice president for human resources used some simple guidelines in screening candidates for new positions, "We want passionate people who love coffee . . . . We're looking for a diverse workforce, which reflects our community. We want people who enjoy what they're doing and for whom work is an extension of themselves."[20]

Every partner/barista hired for a retail job in a Starbucks store received at least 24 hours training in their first two to four weeks. Training topics included coffee history, drink preparation, coffee knowledge, customer service, and retail skills, plus a four-hour workshop on "Brewing the Perfect Cup." Baristas spent considerable time learning about beverage preparation—grinding the beans, steaming milk, learning to pull perfect (18- to 23-second) shots of espresso, memorizing the recipes of all the different drinks, practicing making the different drinks, and learning how to customize drinks to customer specifications. There were sessions on cash register operations, how to clean the milk wand on the espresso machine, explaining the Italian drink names to unknowing customers, making eye contact with customers and interacting with them, and taking personal responsibility for the cleanliness of the store. And there were rules to be memorized: milk must be steamed to at least 150 degrees Fahrenheit but never more than 170 degrees; every espresso shot not pulled within 23 seconds must be tossed; never let coffee sit in the pot more than 20 minutes; always compensate dissatisfied customers with a Starbucks coupon that entitles them to a free drink.

There were also training programs for shift supervisors, assistant store managers, store managers, and district managers that went much deeper, covering not only coffee knowledge and information imparted to baristas but also the details of store operations, practices and procedures as set forth in the company's operating manual, information systems, and the basics of managing people. In addition, there were special career development programs, such as a coffee masters program for store employees and more advanced leadership skills training for shift supervisors and store management personnel. When Starbucks opened stores in a new market, it sent a Star team of experienced managers and baristas to the area to lead the store opening effort and to conduct one-on-one training following the basic orientation and training sessions.

To recognize and reward partner contributions, Starbucks had created a partner recognition program consisting of 18 different awards and programs.[21] Examples included Partner of the Quarter Awards (for one partner per store per quarter) for significant contributions to their store and demonstrating behaviors consistent with the company's mission and values; Spirit of Starbucks awards for making exceptional contributions to partners, customers, and community while embracing the company's mission and values; a Manager of the Quarter for store manager leadership; Green Apron Awards where partners could recognize fellow partners for how they bring to life the company's mission, values, and customer commitment; and Bravo and Team Bravo! awards for above and beyond the call of duty performance and achieving exceptional results.

STARBUCKS' MISSION, BUSINESS PRINCIPLES, AND VALUES

During the early building years, Howard Schultz and other Starbucks senior executives worked to instill some values and guiding principles into the Starbucks culture. The cornerstone value in their effort "to build a company with soul" was that the company would never stop pursuing the perfect cup of coffee by buying the best beans and roasting them to perfection. Schultz was adamant about controlling the quality of Starbucks products and building a culture common to all stores. He was rigidly opposed to selling artificially flavored coffee beans—"we will not pollute our high-quality beans with chemicals"; if a customer wanted hazelnut-flavored coffee, Starbucks would provide it by adding hazelnut syrup to the drink, rather than by adding hazelnut flavoring to the beans during roasting. Running flavored beans through the grinders left chemical residues behind that altered the flavor of beans ground afterward.

Starbucks' management was also emphatic about the importance of employees paying attention to what pleased customers. Employees were trained to go out of their way, and to take heroic measures if necessary, to make sure customers were fully satisfied. The theme was "just say yes" to customer requests. Further, employees were encouraged to speak their minds without fear of retribution from upper management—senior executives wanted employees to be vocal about what Starbucks was doing right, what it was doing wrong, and what changes were needed. The intent was for employees to be involved in and contribute to the process of making Starbucks a better company.

Starbucks' Mission Statement

In early 1990, the senior executive team at Starbucks went to an offsite retreat to debate the company's values and beliefs and draft a mission statement. Schultz wanted the mission statement to convey a strong sense of organizational purpose and to articulate the company's fundamental beliefs and guiding principles. The draft was submitted to all employees for review and several changes were made based on employee comments. The resulting mission statement and guiding principles are shown in Exhibit 4. In 2008, Starbucks partners from all across the company met for several months to refresh the mission statement and rephrase the underlying guiding principles; the revised mission statement and guiding principles are also shown in Exhibit 6.

In 2018, Starbucks stated values were:

- Creating a culture of warmth and belonging, where everyone is welcome.
- Acting with courage, challenging the status quo and finding new ways to grow our company and each other.
- Being present, connecting with transparency, dignity, and respect.
- Delivering our best in all we do, holding ourselves accountable for results.
- We are performance driven, through the lens of humanity.[22]

In addition to being expected to live by the company's values, all Starbucks personnel were expected to conform to the highest standards of ethical conduct and to take all legal and ethical responsibilities seriously.

STARBUCKS' COFFEE PURCHASING STRATEGY

Coffee beans were grown in 70 tropical countries and were the second most traded commodity in the world after petroleum. Most of the world's coffee was grown by some 25 million small farmers, most of whom lived on the edge of poverty. Starbucks personnel traveled regularly to coffee-producing countries, building relationships with growers and exporters, checking on agricultural conditions and crop yields, and searching out varieties and sources that would meet Starbucks' exacting standards of quality and flavor. The coffee-purchasing group, working with Starbucks personnel in roasting operations, tested new varieties and blends of green coffee beans from different sources. The company's supplies of green coffee beans were chiefly grown on about one million small family farms (less than 30 acres) located in the coffee-growing communities of countries across the world. Sourcing from multiple geographic areas not only allowed Starbucks to offer a greater range of coffee varieties to customers but also spread its risks regarding weather, price volatility, and changing economic and political conditions in coffee-growing countries.

Starbucks' coffee sourcing strategy had three key elements:

- Make sure that the prices Starbucks paid for green (unroasted) coffee beans was high enough to ensure that small farmers were able to cover their production costs and provide for their families. The company was firmly committed to a goal of "100 percent ethically-sourced coffees"—in 2016 management believed it had reached a milestone of 99 percent ethically sourced coffee.[23] Because the company also purchased tea and cocoa for its stores, it was similarly committed to 100 percent ethically sourced tea and cocoa.
- Utilize purchasing arrangements that limited Starbucks exposure to sudden price jumps due to weather, economic and political conditions in the growing countries, new agreements establishing export quotas, and periodic efforts to bolster prices by restricting coffee supplies.
- Work directly with small coffee growers, local coffee-growing cooperatives, and other types of coffee suppliers to promote coffee cultivation methods that were environmentally sustainable. Starbucks objective was to "make coffee the world's first sustainable agricultural product."[24]

Pricing and Purchasing Arrangements

Commodity-grade coffee was traded in a highly competitive market as an undifferentiated product. However, high-altitude Arabica coffees of the quality

EXHIBIT 4   Starbucks' Mission Statement and Business Principles

Mission Statement, 1990–October 2008

Establish Starbucks as the premier purveyor of the finest coffee in the world while maintaining our uncompromising principles as we grow.

The following six guiding principles will help us measure the appropriateness of our decisions:

- Provide a great work environment and treat each other with respect and dignity.
- Embrace diversity as an essential component in the way we do business.
- Apply the highest standards of excellence to the purchasing, roasting, and fresh delivery of our coffee.
- Develop enthusiastically satisfied customers all of the time.
- Contribute positively to our communities and our environment.
- Recognize that profitability is essential to our future success.

Mission Statement, October 2008–Present

Our Mission: To inspire and nurture the human spirit—one person, one cup, and one neighborhood at a time.

Here are the principles of how we live that every day:

Our Coffee

It has always been, and will always be, about quality. We're passionate about ethically sourcing the finest coffee beans, roasting them with great care, and improving the lives of people who grow them. We care deeply about all of this; our work is never done.

Our Partners

We're called partners, because it's not just a job, it's our passion. Together, we embrace diversity to create a place where each of us can be ourselves. We always treat each other with respect and dignity. And we hold each other to that standard.

Our Customers

When we are fully engaged, we connect with, laugh with, and uplift the lives of our customers—even if just for a few moments. Sure, it starts with the promise of a perfectly made beverage, but our work goes far beyond that. It's really about human connection.

Our Stores

When our customers feel this sense of belonging, our stores become a haven, a break from the worries outside, a place where you can meet with friends. It's about enjoyment at the speed of life—sometimes slow and savored, sometimes faster. Always full of humanity.

Our Neighborhood

Every store is part of a community, and we take our responsibility to be good neighbors seriously. We want to be invited in wherever we do business. We can be a force for positive action—bringing together our partners, customers, and the community to contribute every day. Now we see that our responsibility—and our potential for good—is even larger. The world is looking to Starbucks to set the new standard, yet again. We will lead.

Our Shareholders

We know that as we deliver in each of these areas, we enjoy the kind of success that rewards our shareholders. We are fully accountable to get each of these elements right so that Starbucks—and everyone it touches—can endure and thrive.

Source: Company documents and postings at www.starbucks.com (accessed May 15, 2012).

purchased by Starbucks were bought on a negotiated basis at a substantial premium above commodity coffee. The prices of the top-quality coffees sourced by Starbucks depended on supply and demand conditions at the time of the purchase and were subject to considerable volatility due to weather, economic and political conditions in the growing countries, new agreements establishing export quotas, and periodic efforts to bolster prices by restricting coffee supplies.

Starbucks bought coffee using fixed-price and price-to-be-fixed purchase commitments, depending on market conditions, to secure an adequate supply of quality green coffee. Price-to-be-fixed contracts were purchase commitments whereby the quality, quantity, delivery period, and other negotiated terms were agreed upon, but the date at which the base price component of commodity grade coffee was to be fixed was as yet unspecified. For these types of contracts, either Starbucks or the seller had the option to select a date on which to "fix" the base price of commodity grade coffee prior to the delivery date. As of October 1, 2017, Starbucks had a total of $1.2 billion in purchase commitments, comprised of $860 million under fixed-price contracts and an estimated $336 million under price-to-be-fixed contracts. All of the price-to-be-fixed contracts gave Starbucks the right to fix the base price component of commodity-grade coffee. Management believed that its purchase agreements as of October 2017, together with its existing inventory, would provide an adequate supply of green coffee through fiscal year 2018.[25]

Food products, such as pastries, breakfast sandwiches and lunch items, were purchased from national, regional and local sources, as were needed paper and plastic products, such as cups and cutlery. Management believed, based on relationships established with these suppliers and manufacturers, that the risk of non-delivery of sufficient amounts of these items to its various store locations was remote.

Starbucks' Ethical Sourcing Practices for Coffee Beans

Starbucks was committed to buying green coffee beans that were grown in accordance with environmentally sustainable agricultural practices and guaranteed that small coffee growers received prices for their green coffee beans sufficiently high enough to allow them to pay fair wages to their workers, earn enough to reinvest in their farms and communities, develop the

business skills needed to compete in the global market for coffee, and afford basic health care, education, and home improvements. To promote achievement of these outcomes, Starbucks operated eight farmer support centers staffed with agronomists and sustainability experts who worked with coffee farming communities to promote best practices in coffee production, implement advanced soil-management techniques, improve both coffee quality and yields, and address climate and other impacts.

Since 1998, Starbucks had partnered with Conservation International's Center for Environmental Leadership to develop specific guidelines (called Coffee and Farmer Equity [C.A.F.E.] Practices) covering four areas: product quality, the price received by farmers/growers, safe and humane working conditions (including compliance with minimum wage requirements and child labor provisions), and environmentally responsible cultivation practices.[26] Top management at Starbucks set a goal that by 2015 all of the green coffee beans purchased from growers would be C.A.F.E. Practice certified, Fair Trade certified, organically certified, or certified by some other equally acceptable third party. By 2011, 86 percent of Starbucks purchases of green coffee beans were C.A.F.E. Practices–verified sources and about 8 percent were from Fair Trade–certified sources, making Starbucks among the world's largest purchasers and marketers of Fair Trade–certified coffee beans.

In September 2015, Starbucks launched the One Tree for Every Bag Commitment, an effort to plant 20 million coffee tree seedlings to replace trees declining in productivity due to age and disease such as coffee leaf rust. The goal was exceeded in just over a year. To build on that success, Starbucks committed to providing another 80 million coffee tree seedlings to farmers by 2025, particularly in coffee-growing communities being impacted by climate change.

Small Farmer Support Programs   Because many of small family farms that grew coffees purchased by Starbucks often lacked the money to make farming improvements and/or cover all expenses until they sold their crops, Starbucks provided funding for loans to small coffee growers. In 2010, $14.6 million was loaned to nearly 56,000 farmers who grew green coffee beans for Starbucks in 10 countries; in 2011, $14.7 million was loaned to over 45,000 farmers who grew green coffee beans for Starbucks in seven countries. Later, the company established the Starbucks

Global Farmer Fund, a $50 million commitment to provide loans to coffee farmers to support agronomy, restoration and infrastructure improvements. Moreover, the Starbucks Foundation began partnering with organizations with local expertise to award grants to support smallholder-farming families in coffee-growing and tea-growing communities, reaching approximately 47,000 direct and indirect beneficiaries. By 2020 the Foundation planned to reach 250,000 people.

COFFEE ROASTING OPERATIONS

Starbucks considered the roasting of its coffee beans to be something of an art form, entailing trial-and-error testing of different combinations of time and temperature to get the most out of each type of bean and blend. Recipes were put together by the coffee department, once all the components had been tested. Computerized roasters guaranteed consistency. Highly trained and experienced roasting personnel monitored the process, using both smell and hearing, to help check when the beans were perfectly done—coffee beans make a popping sound when ready. Roasting standards were exacting. After roasting and cooling, the coffee was immediately vacuum-sealed in bags that preserved freshness for up to 26 weeks. As a matter of policy, however, Starbucks removed coffees on its shelves after three months and, in the case of coffee used to prepare beverages in stores, the shelf life was limited to seven days after the bag was opened.

In 2018, Starbucks had multiple roasting plants in numerous locations, having expanded its roasting operations as its store base expanded to more geographic regions and countries. Roasting plants also had additional space for warehousing and shipping coffees. In keeping with Starbucks' corporate commitment to reduce its environmental footprint, since 2009 all newly built roasting plants had conformed to LEED (Leadership in Energy and Environment Design) standards devised by the United States Green Building Council; LEED standards were the most widely used green building rating system in the world for evaluating the environmental performance of a building and encouraging market transformation towards sustainable design. Starbucks had launched an initiative to achieve LEED certification for all company-operated facilities by the end of 2010, and facilities constructed prior to 2010 were remodeled and/or retrofitted accordingly.[27]

STARBUCKS' CORPORATE SOCIAL RESPONSIBILITY STRATEGY

Howard Schultz's effort to "build a company with soul" included a long history of doing business in ways that were socially and environmentally responsible. A commitment to do the right thing had been central to how Starbucks operated since Howard Schultz first became CEO in 1987, and one of the core beliefs at Starbucks was that "the way to build a great, enduring company is to strike a balance between profitability and a social conscience." The specific actions comprising Starbucks' social responsibility strategy had varied over the years but the intent of the strategy was consistently one of contributing positively to the communities in which Starbucks had stores, being a good environmental steward, and conducting the company's business in ways that earned the trust and respect of customers, partners/employees, suppliers, and the general public.

In 2018, Starbucks' corporate social responsibility (CSR) strategy had five main elements:

1. *Ethically sourcing all of its products*—This CSR element had two main pieces: (a) all of the company's actions and collaborative efforts in purchasing the company's supplies of coffee, tea, and cocoa that were aimed at providing loans and technical assistance to the small family farms that grew these products, paying prices for these products that improved the living standards and economic well-being of the farmers and their communities, and trying to institute better soil-management and sustainable farming practices; and (b) striving to buy the manufactured products and services it needed from suppliers who not only adhered to strict food safety and product quality standards, and certain Starbucks-specified operating practices, but also signed an agreement pledging compliance with the company's global Supplier Code of Conduct. This code of conduct included:

   • Demonstrating commitment to the welfare, economic improvement, and sustainability of the people and places that produce products and services for Starbucks.

   • Adherence to local laws and international standards regarding human rights, workplace safety, and worker compensation and treatment.

- Meeting or exceeding national laws and international standards for environmental protection and minimizing negative environmental impacts of the supplier's operations.
- Commitment to measuring, monitoring, reporting, and verification of compliance to this code.
- Pursuing continuous improvement of these social and environmental principles.[28]

Verification of compliance was subjects to audits by Starbucks personnel or acceptable third parties. From time to time, Starbucks had temporarily or permanently discontinued its business relationship with suppliers who failed to comply or failed to work with Starbucks to correct a non-complying situation.

2. *Community involvement and corporate citizenship*— Active engagement in community activities and display of good corporate citizenship had always been core elements in the way Starbucks conducted its business. Starbucks stores and employees regularly volunteered for community improvement projects and initiatives that would have a meaningful impact on the localities in which Starbucks had a presence. In fiscal 2011 Starbucks sponsored a special global month of service in which more than 60,000 employees in 30 countries volunteered for over 150,000 service hours and completed 1,400 community-service projects; every year since, Starbucks had held a Global Month of Service.

The company had a goal of having 100 percent of its stores worldwide participating in community service projects. Recently, through a strategic alliance with Feeding America, Starbucks had instituted a "food share" program to rescue food that would otherwise spoil in its stores to donate to organizations providing meals to needy families and homeless people. Management estimated that when the program was fully operational in all Starbucks stores that the food donations would help provide 50 million meals per year.

3. *Environmental stewardship*—Initiatives here included a wide variety of actions to increase recycling, reduce waste, be more energy efficient, use renewable energy sources, conserve water resources, make all company facilities as green as possible by using environmentally friendly building materials and energy efficient designs, and engage in more efforts to address climate change. Beginning in January 2011, all new company-owned retail stores globally were built to achieve LEED certification; as of 2015 Starbucks had built more than 1,200 LEED-certified stores in 20 countries. In 2008, Starbucks set a goal of reducing water consumption by 25 percent in company-owned stores by 2015, and after two years had implemented proactive measures that had decreased water use by almost 22 percent. Starbucks had invested in renewable energy since 2005, and it achieved a milestone in 2015 by purchasing the equivalent of 100 percent of the electricity consumption of all company-operated stores worldwide from renewable energy sources, primarily utilizing Renewable Energy Credits from the United States and Canada and through green electricity-supply contracts across Europe. Starbucks was the number one purchaser of renewable electricity in its sector on the EPA's Green Power Partnership National Top 100 list. Starbucks had a program in place to achieve a 25 percent reduction in energy use by 2015. By 2011, nearly 80 percent of company-owned Starbucks stores in North America were recycling cardboard boxes and other back-of-store items; there were front-of-store recycling bins in place in all company-owned locations where there were municipal recycling capabilities (50 percent of company-owned stores in the United States as of year-end 2015). Since 1985, Starbucks had given a $0.10 discount to customers who brought reusable cups and tumblers to stores for use in serving the beverages they ordered. In 2018, a program was in place to double the recycled content, recyclability, and reusability of the cups in which beverages were served, and an initiative had been launched to empower 10,000 Starbucks employees to be "sustainability champions" by 2020. Stores participated in Earth Day activities each year with in-store promotions and volunteer efforts to educate employees and customers about the impacts their actions had on the environment.

4. *Creating opportunities to help people achieve their dreams.* The chief initiatives here included hiring 100,000 young people aged 16 to 24 who were disconnected from work and school by 2020, hiring at least 25,000 veterans and military spouses by 2025, welcoming and employing 10,000 refugees across the 75 countries in which Starbucks stores were located, expanding partner participation

in the company's college achievement plan that covered full tuition reimbursement for admission to one of Arizona State University's online degree programs, and making ongoing "Youth Opportunity" grants to support mentoring, work placement, and apprenticeship programs.

5. *Charitable contributions*—The Starbucks Foundation, set up in 1997, oversaw a major portion of the company's philanthropic activities; it received the majority of its funding from Starbucks Coffee Company and private donations. Over the years, the Starbucks Foundation had made close to 200 grants to nonprofit organizations such as the American Red Cross for relief efforts to communities experiencing severe damage from earthquakes, hurricanes, tornadoes, floods, and other natural disasters, Save the Children for efforts to improve education, health, and nutrition, the Global Fund and Product (RED)™ to provide medicine to people in Africa with AIDS, and a wide assortment of community-building efforts. Donations were made in cash and in-kind contributions. In 2017, the foundation made grants ranging from $10,000 to $100,000 to more than 40 nonprofits in 27 U.S. cities, plus others to various communities across the world.[29]

Water, sanitation, and hygiene education programs in water-stressed countries were supported through the Starbucks Foundation's Ethos Water Fund. For each bottle of Ethos water purchased at Starbucks stores, Starbucks donated $0.05 ($0.10 in Canada) to the Ethos© Water Fund. Since 2005, the Fund had made over $15 million in grants, benefiting more than 500,000 people around the world.

Starbucks had been named to *Corporate Responsibility Magazine*'s list of the 100 Best Corporate Citizens on numerous occasions; this list was based on more than 360 data points of publicly available information in seven categories: environment, climate change, human rights, philanthropy, employee relations, financial performance, and governance. Over the years, Starbucks had received over 25 awards from a diverse group of organizations for its philanthropic, community service, and environmental activities.

An Embarrassing Incident at a Starbucks Store In April 2018, Starbucks suffered a public relations disaster when a Starbucks manager in Philadelphia called the police a few minutes after two black men arrived at a store and sat waiting for a friend. They had not yet purchased anything when the police were called. After police arrived they arrested the two men. Social media erupted and the incident was widely covered by the media. After investigating what happened, Starbucks determined that insufficient support and training, bias, and a company policy that defined customers as paying patrons—versus anyone who enters a store—led to the decision to call the police. Starbucks president met with the two men to express the company's apologies, reconcile, and commit to actions to reaffirm the company's mission and enduring values to create a welcoming environment. The company further decided it would close more than 8,000 company stores for three hours on the afternoon of May 29 to conduct bias awareness training for 175,000 Starbucks partners, share life experiences, listen to experts, reflect on the realities of bias in society, and talk about how to create store spaces where everyone would feel like they belong.

TOP MANAGEMENT CHANGES: CHANGING ROLES FOR HOWARD SCHULTZ

In 2000, Howard Schultz decided to relinquish his role as CEO, retain his position as chairman of the company's board of directors, and assume the newly created role of chief strategic officer. Orin Smith, a Starbucks executive who had been with the company since its early days, was named CEO. Smith retired in 2005 and was replaced as CEO by Jim Donald who had been president of Starbucks' North American division. In 2006, Donald proceeded to set a long-term objective of having 40,000 stores worldwide and launched a program of rapid store expansion in an effort to achieve that goal.

But investors and members of Starbucks' board of directors (including Howard Schultz) became uneasy about Donald's leadership of the company when the company's stock price drifted downward through much of 2007, customer traffic in Starbucks stores in the United States began to erode in 2007, and Donald kept pressing for increased efficiency in store operations at the expense of good customer service. In January 2008, the Starbucks board asked Howard Schultz to return to his role as CEO and lead a major restructuring and revitalization initiative.

Schultz immediately revamped the company's executive leadership team and changed the roles and responsibilities of several key executives.[30] Believing that Starbucks had become less passionate about customer relationships and the coffee experience that had fueled the company's success, Schultz hired a former Starbucks executive to fill the newly created position of chief creative officer responsible for elevating the in-store experience of customers and achieving new levels of innovation and differentiation. He then proceeded to launch a series of actions to recast Starbucks into the company he envisioned it ought to be, push the company to new plateaus of differentiation and innovation, and prepare for renewed global expansion of Starbucks retail store network. This transformation effort, which instantly became the centerpiece of his return as company CEO, had three main themes—strengthen the core, elevate the experience, and invest and grow.

In 2010, as part of Schultz's "invest and grow" aspect of transforming Starbucks, the company began formulating plans to open thousands of new stores in China over time.[31] Japan had long been Starbucks biggest foreign market outside North America, but Howard Schultz said that, "Asia clearly represents the most significant growth opportunity on a go-forward basis."[32] Schultz's transformation effort was a resounding success, with more than 10,000 stores being opened during fiscal years 2011 to 2017 and impressive gains in revenues and profits. During fiscal year 2018, Starbucks was opening stores in China at the rate of 1 every 15 hours; headed into June 2018, the company had more than 3,300 stores across 141 cities in China and was serving more than 6.4 million customers a week. Shanghai alone had over 600 Starbucks stores, more than any other city in the world. Starbucks goal was to have 5,000 stores in China by 2021.

In April 2017, following a December 2016 announcement, Howard Schultz officially stepped down as Starbucks CEO, turning the role over to Kevin Johnson, Starbucks chief operating officer with whom Schultz had worked closely for the past two years—they had adjoining offices connected by a door and usually visited together multiple times a day. Schultz stayed on as chairman of the company's board of directors and focused his time on social initiatives and plans for the upscale Roastery Reserve brand. Schultz exuded confidence that Johnson was the right person to lead Starbucks in the future and that he was well prepared to meet the challenges of continuing to build the Starbucks brand, enhance the consumer experience, and manage its global operations.

Then, in a surprise announcement on June 4, 2018, Schultz at the age of 64 announced that he was resigning as Starbucks executive chairman and member of the board of directors effective June 26, thus ending his career at Starbucks. According to Starbucks, his honorary title would be chairman emeritus. In interviews with the media, Schultz indicated that he would be writing a book and exploring a number of options from philanthropy to public service. There was immediate speculation that he would run for President of the United States in 2020; on numerous occasions, he had expressed his disagreement with many policies of the Trump Administration.

ENDNOTES

[1] Howard Schultz and Dori Jones Yang, *Pour Your Heart Into It* (New York: Hyperion, 1997), p. 34.

[2] Howard Schultz and Dori Jones Yang, *Pour Your Heart Into It* (New York: Hyperion, 1997), p. 36.

[3] Howard Schultz and Dori Jones Yang, *Pour Your Heart Into It* (New York: Hyperion, 1997), pp. 61–62.

[4] Howard Schultz and Dori Jones Yang, *Pour Your Heart Into It* (New York: Hyperion, 1997), pp. 101–102.

[5] Howard Schultz and Dori Jones Yang, *Pour Your Heart Into It* (New York: Hyperion, 1997), p. 142.

[6] "Starbucks Plans New Global Store Design," *Restaurants and Institutions,* June 25, 2009, www.rimag.com (accessed December 29, 2009).

[7] Starbucks Global Responsibility Report for 2009, p. 13.

[8] As stated by Howard Schultz in an interview with *Harvard Business Review* editor-in-chief Adi Ignatius; the interview was published in the July–August 2010 issue of the *Harvard Business Review,* pp. 108–115.

[9] 2009 Annual Report, p. 5.

[10] Company press release, April 7, 2008.

[11] Company press release, April 13, 2010.

[12] Company press release, January 26, 2012.

[13] Starbucks management presentation at UBS Global Consumer Conference, March 14, 2012, www.starbucks.com (accessed May 18, 2012).

[14] Company press release, July 14, 2008.

[15] 2017 10-K Report, p. 4.

[16] Claire Cain Miller, "New Starbucks Ads Seek to Recruit Online Fans," *The New York Times,* May 18, 2009, www.nytimes.com (accessed January 3, 2010).

[17] As related in Schultz and Yang, *Pour Your Heart Into It,* pp. 131–136.

[18] Data posted at www.glassdoor.com (accessed June 4, 2018).

[19] Company news release, May 21, 2009, www.starbucks.com (accessed June 14, 2010).

[20] Kate Rounds, "Starbucks Coffee," *Incentive,* Vol. 167, No. 7, p. 22.

[21] Information posted at www.sbuxrecognition .com (accessed June 1, 2018).

[22] Posted at https://livingourvalues.starbucks.com (accessed June 5, 2018).

[23] Starbucks *2016 Global Social Impact Performance Report,* p. 4.

[24] Starbucks *2016 Global Social Impact Performance Report,* p. 4.

[25] 2017 10-K Report, p. 7.

[26] Information posted in the corporate responsibility section at www.starbucks.com (accessed June 18, 2010).

[27] Company press release, February 19, 2009.

[28] Information on "Doing Business with Starbucks," www.starbucks.com/business/ suppliers (accessed June 5, 2018).

[29] Information posted at www.starbucks.com/ responsibility/community/starbucks-foundation (accessed June 5, 2018).

[30] Transcript of Starbucks Earnings Conference Call for Quarters 1 and 3 of fiscal year 2008, posted at http://seekingalpha.com (accessed June 16, 2010).

[31] Mariko Sanchanta, "Starbucks Plans Major China Expansion," *The Wall Street Journal,* April 13, 2010, http://online.wsj.com (accessed June 10, 2010).

[32] Mariko Sanchanta, "Starbucks Plans Major China Expansion," *The Wall Street Journal,* April 13, 2010, http://online.wsj.com (accessed June 10, 2010).

Concussions in Collegiate and Professional Football: Who Has Responsibility to Protect Players?

David L. Turnipseed
University of South Alabama

A.J. Strickland
The University of Alabama

The storm had been brewing for several years, and by 2018 football player concussions had become a hotly discussed topic—both on and off the field—as football organizations were scrambling to reduce the incidence of head injuries, and players became increasingly active in attempting to redress their injuries. In 2016, the Centers for Disease Control estimated that between 1.6 million and 3.8 million concussions occured in sport activities each year. Not everyone accepted the connection between concussions and brain injury, despite an increasing volume of studies, and publicity moved the contact sport–brain damage issue to center stage in athletics. Although some refused to accept the link between concussions and brain damage, in October 2015, an HBO Real Sports/ Marist Poll found that the majority of Americans were aware of the football and long-term brain injury correlation. About a third of those surveyed said the potential for brain injury would make them less likely to permit a son to play football. According to the Sports & Fitness Industry Association, between 2009 and 2014 participation in football declined by 3.7 percent, perhaps related to increasing awareness of the dangers. A reason more professional football players were retiring early was new information surrounding concussion statistics and brain damage resulting later in life.

The 2015 movie, *Concussion,* followed Dr. Bennet Omalu through his experiences researching chronic traumatic encephalopathy, commonly known as CTE. Dr. Omalu autopsied former Steelers star and Hall of Famer Mike Webster who had experienced health decline and financial ruin over the decade prior to his death. Omalu found evidence of the Alzheimer's-like disease, CTE, in Webster's brain. This movie fueled the already roaring concussion debate, and concussions were gradually accepted as a problem in football.

As recently as 2013, a concussion study funded by the NFL and conducted by the Institute of Medicine reported that it was unclear whether repetitive head injuries led to long-term brain disease. The study found that high school players (11.2 per 10,000 games) were about twice as likely to sustain concussions as were college players (6.3). According to the study, in most cases, symptoms of concussion disappeared within two weeks; however, symptoms persisted for weeks, months, or years for 10 to 20 percent of individuals. More alarming, the study identified an athletic culture that repressed self-report of concussions. Athletes believed that the game and their team were more important than their health and, consequently, they played with a concussion rather than let down the team, coaches, school, and parents.

Lawsuits against schools, athletic associations (NCAA, NFL, NCAA conferences), and helmet manufacturers became common, and lawyers solicited concussion cases, fighting among themselves for positions in court as concussions became a next big plum for the legal community. The NCAA and NFL scrambled to provide increased concussion protection for players and rules were amended to reduce head injury. Legal expenses and compliance costs soared as schools, teams, associations, and helmet manufacturers were faced with increasing expenses to develop and implement concusson management plans and deal with the attacks.

In May 2018, as off-season workouts were beginning for the NFL players, in the midst of the rabid rush of lawyers filing class action lawsuits attempting to collect millions of dollars, a clear question emerged: Who was responsible for brain damage due to football concussions? Was it the college and teams, the NCAA and NFL, helmet manufacturers, or the athletes themselves? If an athlete capable of being in college, or at the age of adulthood, made the conscious decision to play football after being made aware of the risks associated with concussions, should he be able to collect purported damages from others?

THE PHYSIOLOGY OF CONCUSSIONS

A concussion is a traumatic brain injury caused by a direct or indirect impact to the head or any part of the body that transmits an impulsive force to the head. Concussions have a wide variety of symptoms, many of which appear suddenly and then resolve quickly.

Consequently, a large number of concussions are not recognized by athletes, nor observed by trainers and coaches, and are unreported. Concussions may present physical symptoms such as unconsciousness or amnesia, cognitive impairment recognized by slowed reaction time, sleep disturbances or drowsiness, behavioral changes including irritabilty, cognitive symptoms like feeling in a fog, and somatic symptoms including headaches and emotional indicators.

According to the NCAA Concussion Guidelines, there are more than 42 consensus-based definitions of concussions. The NCAA concussion guidelines define a concussion as (a) a change in brain function, (b) following a force to the head which (c) may be accompanied by a temporary loss of consciousness, but is (d) identified in awake individuals, (e) with measures of neurologic and cognitive dysfunction. The diagnosis of concussion is a clinical diagnosis based on the opinion of the athlete's healthcare providers. Exhibit 1 illustrates the concussion injury.

Concussion expert, Dr. Geoff Manley, Chief of Neurosurgery at San Francisco General Hospital,

EXHIBIT 1   Anatomical Causes of a Football-Related Concussion

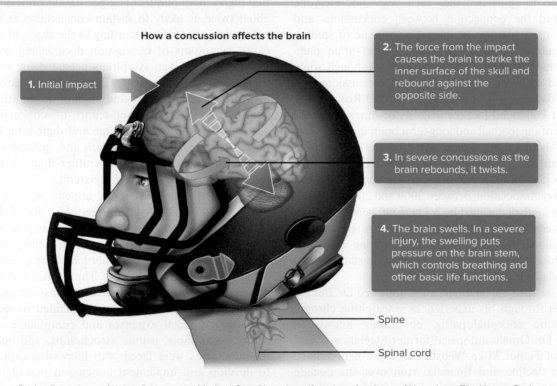

How a concussion affects the brain

1. Initial impact

2. The force from the impact causes the brain to strike the inner surface of the skull and rebound against the opposite side.

3. In severe concussions as the brain rebounds, it twists.

4. The brain swells. In a severe injury, the swelling puts pressure on the brain stem, which controls breathing and other basic life functions.

Spine

Spinal cord

Sources: Dr. Joy Rosenberg of Kaiser Permanente Medical Core Neurology; American Academy of Neurology; The Human Body.

clarified common misperceptions of concussion, including loss of consciousness, and that direct trauma to the head was required to cause the injury. Because the skull and brain move independently, as the head moves, the brain could move within the skull resuting in injury. The soft organ brain is protected by a fluid (cerebrospinal fluid) that generally prevents it from impacting the skull; however, a force of sufficient magnitude could cause the brain to crash into the skull causing concussion with no visible bruises or cuts.

Chronic Traumatic Encephalopathy (CTE): The Result of Head Trauma

CTE was a progressive degenerative disease of the brain found in athletes and others with historical repetitive brain trauma. It could result from concussions as well as repetitive hits to the head that caused brain trauma. This resulted in degeneration of brain tissue and caused a build-up of an abnormal protein known as tau. These symptoms could begin anywhere from months to decades after the last suffered brain trauma. The effects of CTE included memory loss, confusion, impaired judgment, impulse control problems, aggression, depression, and progressive dementia.[1] This disease had also been linked to the suicide of multiple NFL players.

In fall of 2010, the first reported case of CTE at the collegiate level was found in a 21-year-old college football player who had never been treated for a concussion, raising concerns that the amount of hits sustained throughout a football career could lead to CTE.

A 2013 study led by Dr. Ann McKee at Boston University found CTE in the brains of dozens of deceased football players, including 18 and 21-year-old players. As of September 2015, the Department of Veteran Affairs and Boston University had discovered CTE in 96 percent of NFL players examined, and 79 percent of those examined who played football at some point in their lives. Forty percent of those testing positive for CTE had played either offensive or defensive line, supporting the theory that repetitive hits increase likelihood for this disease. CTE could not be positively diagnosed in living players who believe they were suffering from the disease. The resulting trend still showed a distinctive link between football and long-term brain disease based on results of football players who had donated their brains to CTE research.[2]

CONCUSSION BATTLES: THE BEGINNING

Concerns about concussions in football go back over six decades. In 1952, the *New England Journal of Medicine* recommended that players stop playing after a third concussion. Over four decades later, in 1994, NFL Commissioner Paul Tagliabue created the Mild Traumatic Brain Injury (MTBI) committee. At the time, concussions were still seen as a minor issue compared to other football injuries. In 1997, new return-to-play guidelines were applied when the American Academy of Neurology announced that repetitive concussions could cause brain damage. The NFL Retirement Board ruled in favor of Mike Webster in 1991, who claimed that head injuries suffered in the NFL led to his diagnosis of dementia, which was the first case of its type in NFL history. Dr. Bennet Omalu examined Webster's brain after his death in 2002 and discovered the first case of CTE identified in football players. Dr. Julian Bailes, a former NFL doctor working with Omalu, emphasized that the repeated minor head trauma that happened in football appeared to lead to CTE.

Between the discovery of CTE in 2002 and the beginning of 2005, the NFL's MTBI committee continued to dispute evidence that playing football led to a higher risk of brain injuries. In 2005, Dr. Omalu published the CTE findings in the journal *Neurosurgery*. Over the next few years, Dr. Omalu found CTE in the brains of multiple former NFL players who had committed suicide. The NFL hosted its first NFL Concussion Summit in 2007 in an effort to combat the issue, only 13 years after the MTBI was created. The NFL acknowledged in December 2009, for the first time, that concussions had long-term effects on the brain. New return-to-play guidelines were issued and any player that exhibited symptoms of a concussion was not allowed to return to play that same day.

CONCUSSIONS IN COLLEGE FOOTBALL

Concussions were an issue at the high school, collegiate, and professional levels. A study in 2013 by the Institute of Medicine, funded by the NFL, estimated that high school football players suffered 11.2 concussions for every 10,000 games and practices, whereas the collegiate rate was only 6.3.[3] In 2014, the NCAA announced a $30 million alliance with the U.S.

Department of Defense for research into concussion and head impact injuries. This research was conducted with over 37,000 collegiate athletes over the following three years. A preseason concussion evaluation, intended to provide concussion information to the NCAA, was administered with further evaluations conducted when related injuries occurred.

This new research was used to combat concussion issues in all college sports, but was expected to bring about major changes with concussion reporting in college football. The NCAA's concussion policy only required that schools receive written acknowledgments from athletes that they received education on concussions and were required to report symptoms to the staff. A study in 2014 at the NCAA Football Championship Subdivision (FCS) level, estimated that only one concussion was diagnosed in college football for every six suspected concussions. The study calculated that for every one diagnosed concussion, there were 21 other head related injuries (although not necessarily concussions) unreported each time. Coaches' perceptions of concussions and how the players viewed their coaches' perceptions seemed to play a large role in whether the concussion symptoms were reported by the players. Also, players such as offensive linemen or running backs, who took the most hits throughout the game, may have thought those symptoms were part of their normal routine.[4] If these symptoms became the norm to players at the collegiate level, it would likely spill over into their professional careers in the NFL.

Concussion Management in the NCAA

Concern over concussions among college football players was not a recent phenomenon: an eight-year study of 49 college teams by Pennsylvania State University in1988 revealed that concussions were a "persistent and regular but relatively infrequent type of football injury."[1] The study covered 395 team-seasons that produced 1,005 game-related concussions, about 75 percent of injuries about or on the head. In 2014, the NCAA reported that about 10 percent of college football players suffered multiple concussions during their college career as a result of impact injuries.

In 2010, the NCAA mandated that athletes be educated about concussions and established procedures to recognize, diagnose, and manage the injuries. However, most concussion testing relied on and continues to rely on player's honesty. The issue of self-reporting remains perhaps the biggest barrier to the effective diagnosis and treatment of concussions. When a player twists his knee or sprains an ankle, he will almost always limp, as it is difficult to fake walking on one good leg. However, with a concussion, there is no clear objective way to detect that it exists.

In January 2014, the NCAA and College Athletic Trainers Society co-sponsored a Safety in College Football Summit, with the purpose of bringing together a diverse group of experts whose common interest was improving the safety of college football (and all sports). Three main points were on the agenda: independent medical care in college sports, concussion diagnosis and management, and contact in football practice. At the conclusion of the meeting, the group set out its position on concussion as, "In summary, the natural history of concussion remains poorly defined, diagnosis can be difficult, there are often few objective findings for diagnosis or physiological recovery that exist for clinical use, and there often remains a significant reliance on self-report of symptoms from the student-athlete."[2]

The NCAA did not require a specific concussion management plan for its members, but directed, in the 2013–2014 NCAA Sports Medicine Handbook, that colleges implement a comprehensive concussion management plan that was made available publicly. Although not manadating a specific protocol, the NCAA provided guidelines concernng concussion education, pre-participation assessment, concussion recognition and diagnosis, and post-concussion management.

The NCAA Concussion Management plan addressed return to activity for student athletes and acknowledged that the timeline was difficult to project. The plan recognized that athletes kept from their sport for an extended time could experience emotional distress with depression, and suggested that "prolonged physical and cognitive rest may be counter-productive in these scenarios."[3] The decision of return to play was based on the athlete returning to his baseline with a protocol of incremental increase in physical activity supervised by a physician. The protocol stressed an individualized approach to return to play and emphasized the lack of scientific evidence to guide the progression of returning the athlete to play. The plan stressed addressing continued or severe symptoms rather than keeping the athlete on a steady return to play plan. The NCAA's concussion management return to play protocol stated, "The guidelines presented herein serve as a general guide and are not meant to be prescriptive."[4]

The concussion management plan included returning to academics and noted that cognitive activities required brain energy that may be unavailable following concussion. Because full recovery typically occurred within two weeks, few athletes would need detailed return to learn programs. However, for those whose symptoms exceeded two weeks, the NCAA suggested learning specialists or even special accommodations with the school's Office of Disability Services, to "level the playing field for the student-athlete with prolonged difficulties resulting from concussion."

The NCAA did not specify the maximum number of concussions that disqualified a football player from returning to the game. Although concussions were generally considered serious, or potentially serious injuries, many colleges took a cavalier approach to athletes suffering from concussions. Criteria for disqualification due to concussions was a decision for each university. The NCAA's chief medical officer, Dr. Brian Hainline, set out the NCAA's position as, "We are not at a place in society generally, and the NCAA in particular, to state that there is a universal bar to which everyone must adhere regarding ability to play."[5] Also, players with a history of incapacitating concussions, who were disqualified at one college were allowed to transfer to other schools that allowed them to play, even after the medical staff at one school ruled a player's risk level sufficient to ban him from contact sports. Randy Cohen, head trainer at the University of Arizona, said that if an athlete wanted to transfer, he could find someone who would clear him for almost anything.

Some schools disqualified an athlete after a specific number of concussions, but others did not. Some schools (e.g., University of Syracuse) generally disqualified an athlete after three concussions; others allowed athletes with as many as 10 concussions to continue playing. In his neurology practice, Dr. Brian Hainline, the NCAA's chief medical officer, had recommended athletes to stop playing, but the players got second opinions from other doctors who disagreed with Dr. Hainline.

Concussion experts recommended an individualized approach to disqualification. Some argued that concussions were manageable and treatable, and if the condition was treated the athlete should return to play. Others argued that the number of prior concussions was important in the return to play decision. Also, the athletes' goals were important—a player

with a realistic career in the pros might choose to accept more risk and play longer than someone playing for fun. Experts suggested that some athletes should stop playing after one concussion, whereas others with multiple concussions who healed with no problems could be cleared to play.

Although there had been significant discussion about the problems of concussion and best ways to protect football players in the NCAA, there were no standardized penalties for schools who violated the NCAA policies for handling concussions. U.S. District Judge John Lee expressed his concerns about the actions that the NCAA could take against colleges who violated the concussion rules, stating, "It is unclear, however, whether the NCAA has the authority to mandate that its member schools implement the proposed 'return-to-play' policies and what enforcement mechanisms will be in place in the event of noncompliance. Given the wide array of schools that are affiliated with the NCAA, it is reasonable to believe that some schools might face financial or logistical challenges in implementing some of the changes that are proposed."[6][5]

NCAA Rule Changes and Initiatives to Reduce Concussions

The following timeline traces the major NCAA rules and initiatives implemented to reduce head trauma and concussions.

1939: All football players were required to wear helmets.

1964: Players may not deliberately and maliciously use helmet or head to butt or ram opponent.

1973: All players must have a helmet "with a secured chin strap."

1975: Recommended that football helmets meet National Operating Committee on Standards for Athletic Equipment test standards. It was required, beginning with the 1978 season.

1976: All players must have a helmet with a four-point chin strap fastened.

1979: Striking a runner with the crown or top of the helmet was added as a foul.

1994: The NCAA adopted guidelines outlining protocols for returning to play after a concussion.

1996: If ball carrier's helmet came off, the play was blown dead immediately. Also, the snapper was protected and could not be contacted for one second after snapping the ball.

2002: Wording added to define a "defenseless player" in football and a point of officiating emphasis was added to protect those players.

2006: Eye shields were required that were completely clear for quick medical diagnoses of student-athletes.

2008: More emphasis was placed on eliminating hits on defenseless players and blows to the head. No player was permitted to initiate contact and target an opponent with the crown of his helmet, nor to initiate contact and target a defenseless opponent above the shoulders.

2009: NCAA adopted rule changes limiting the number of full-contact practices in football. It became mandatory for the conference to review any flagrant personal fouls for targeting defenseless players or using the crown of the helmet.

2010: The NCAA required members to have concussion management plan.

2011: The three-man wedge was made illegal on kickoffs in football; also illegal for a player to go out of bounds to block an opponent.

2012: The kickoff location moved to the 35-yard line from the 30-yard line to encourage more touchbacks and limited kicking team players to be no more than five yards behind the kickoff line. The touchback spot on free kicks moved to the 25-yard line. Shield-block formations used by kicking teams created efforts to block the punt by jumping over the blockers, causing some receiving team players to land on their head/neck if contacted in the air. This was made illegal. Receiving team players were not allowed to leap over a blocker.

2012: A dislodged helmet (except if by a facemask or foul by the opponent) was treated like an injury. If a player lost his helmet, he was removed from play for at least one play to have the helmet checked and refitted by the team's equipment staff. A player that lost his helmet could not continue to participate and that player could not be contacted by the opposition.

2013: Penalty for targeting and contacting a defenseless player above the shoulders or initiating contact with the crown of the helmet was increased to include the disqualification of the offending player. The disqualification was subject to instant replay in games where it was available.

2015: NCAA Football Rules Committee allowed player tracking devices to be used for health and safety purposes. The NCAA conferences passed concussion safety legislation and required each of their 65 schools to submit a policy for detecting a concussion and return-to-play protocol for approval. A Federal Judge gave approval to class-action lawsuit between thousands of former players and the NFL. The agreement provided up to $5 million for any retired player who suffered serious medical problems resulting from repeated head trauma.

2016: Former Oakland Raiders quarterback Ken Stabler died in July and was posthumously diagnosed with CTE by researchers at Boston University. Senior NFL official publicly acknowledged, for the first time, a link between football and degenerative brain disease.

2016: The NFL Players Association and the NFL implemented a new policy to enforce concussion protocol. Two months later, NFL Commissioner Goodell announced a new initiative to increase football safety by preventing, diagnosing, and treating head injuries. The initiative provided $100 million from the NFL club owners and the NFL to support medical research and engineering advancements.

2017: The Journal of the American Medical Association published study identifying CTE in 110 of 111 former NFL players (99 percent).

2018: A study by Boston University showed that hits to the head rather than concussion were linked to the onset of CTE. The study found strong evidence that traumatic brain injuries (TMI) caused CTE, independent of concussion. One conclusion of this study was that focusing on concussion would not prevent CTE.[6]

Source: NCAA.com.

CONCUSSIONS AND THE NFL

The *New York Times* reported on March 24, 2016 that in the prior week an NFL official acknowledged for the first time the relationship between playing football and chronic traumatic encephalopathy. According to an April 11, 2016 *Time* article that examined football related head injuries, the NFL had a history of asserting that there was no direct evidence that linked playing football with traumatic brain injury or the brain disorder CTE. That position was based on a five year study of concussions (1996 to 2001), which the NFL said included all diagnosed concussions during that period.

The NFL's study ommitted over 100 concussions, although the league reported that it was based on all concussions. The report had been used by the NFL to minimize the leagues' concussion problem. The NFL subsequently admitted that teams were not required, but strongly encouraged, to submit concussion information about their players and, consequently, not all did. As shown in Exhibit 2, concussions continued to be a problem for the NFL as more players were on injury report for concussion.

From 2014 to 2015, regular and postseason concussion incidences had risen 52 percent in the NFL with 279 reported concussions. This reversed the trend, which had decreased to 212 reported concussions in 2014. Jeff Miller, the NFL's senior vice president, stated that the increased concussion number in 2015 was most likely due to enhanced screening processes being implemented to diagnose concussions, as well as the trainers and independent neurologists being more active in attempting to spot concussion symptoms. Concussions dropped again to 250 in 2016 before increasing to an all-time high of 291 in 2017.

Concussion Management in the NFL

In March of 2011, the NFL made its first rule change to combat concussions by moving kickoffs to the 35 yard line to reduce collisions. Beginning in 2013,

an independent neurologist was on the sidelines of every team to perform a systematic checklist when a head, neck, or spine injury occurred. That same year, the NFL settled a $765 million lawsuit with 18,000 retired NFL players over concussion-related brain injuries without admitting any wrongdoing.

The NFL developed a concussion management protocol that was similar to the NCAA's plan, with preseason education, physical examinations, and baseline neuropsychological testing. The NFL's practice or game day management protocol was a bit different from that of the NCAA. A summary of NFL concussion protocol follows:

1. **Player with sign or symptoms of concussion.** Player with signs of concussion was removed from the field and evaluated by medical team. The assessement was put in the player's medical record and compared to his baseline. Same day return to practice or game with a diagnosed concussion was prohibited.

2. **Unaffiliated Neurotrauma Consultant (UNC).** Teams had an independent physician experienced in treatment of head injuries on the sidelines during games. UNC duties were identifying concussion symptoms, working with the team physician to implement the concussion protocol, and observe and collaborate sideline concussion assessments performed by the team medical staff. Responsibilty for concussion diagnosis and the decision to return to play was exclusively that of the head team physician.

EXHIBIT 2   NFL Concussion Yearly Injury Reports, 2012–2017

Year	Preseason			Regular Season and Postseason			Total		
	Practice	Game	Total	Practice	Game	Total	Practice	Game	Total
2012	42	43	85	3	177	180	45	220	265
2013	39	38	77	4	163	167	43	201	244
2014	42	41	83	8	121	129	50	162	212
2015	29	54	83	9	187	196	38	241	279
2016	26	45	71	7	172	179	33	217	250
2017	45	46	91	11	189	200	56	235	291

Source: NFL Injury Data, Incidence of Concussion – 2012–2017, March 9, 2018, **www.playsmartplaysafe.com/newsroom/reports/2017-injury-data/**.

3. **Booth ATC (certified athletic trainer).** An ATC with access to multiple view video and replay served as a spotter for both teams in the stadium booth. There was communication between the spotter and the teams' medical staff so that the ATC could report plays that appeared to have possible injuries. The sideline medical staff could also review plays to assess potential injury.

4. **Madden Rule.** On a game day, a player diagnosed with a concussion was removed from the field and observed in the locker room by medical personnel. The Madden rule provided a quiet environment with medical personnel to allow recovery without distraction. A player diagnosed with a concussion was not permitted to talk to the press until cleared.

5. **NFL Sideline Concussion Assessment.** A player diagnosed with a concussion would have the NFL Sideline Concussion Assessment performed on the day of injury. The assessment would be repeated prior to the player going home.

6. **Additional Triggers for Medical Evaluation.** If a player sustained a big hit, or a concern was raised by another player, coach, game official, ATC spotter, or Unaffiliated Neurotrauma Consultant, the player was immediately removed from the field for evaluation by the team physician. If the physician concluded that the player did *not* have a concussion, the video replay was reviewed before the player could return to the game. If there was any doubt, the entire NFL concussion protocol would be performed.

7. **Additional Best Practices.** Serial concussion evaluations were suggested because concussive injuries may not be apparent for hours. If there was any doubt, the player was removed from play or practice. A player with concussion was given take-home information and follow-up instructions.[7]

Return to Participation

After a concussion, a player was examined and monitored in the training room on a daily basis. Components of the NFL Sideline Concussion Assessment were used to check for symptoms as well as to monitor the other aspects of the examination. The following Return to Play (RTP) protocol was required in order for a player to return to play:

1. Player returned to baseline status of symptoms and neurologic exam, including cognitive and balance functions. Repeat neuropsychological evaluation was performed before return to practice or play with interpretation of the data by the team neuropsychology consultant, who reported the findings back to the team physician.

2. Graduated exercise challenge, followed by a gradual return to practice and play, was initiated when the player returned to baseline status. The RTP protocol following a concussion followed the stepwise process in the NFL Head, Neck and Spine Committee's Return to Participation Protocol.

3. Prior to return to practice or play, the team physician must clear the player, and the Independent Neurological Consultant with expertise in concussion was required to evaluate and clear the player for return.

4. A player was returned to practice and play only after the player had returned to baseline status with rest and exertion, had repeat neuropsychological testing which was interpreted by the team neuropsychology consultant as back to baseline levels of functioning, and had completed the Return to Participation Protocol and was cleared by the Team Physician and the Independent Neurological Consultant.[8]

There was no required length of time for players to wait between the steps of the protocol.

In December 2015, in a game against the Ravens, the Rams quarterback, Case Keenum was slammed with a severe blow to his head. He held his head and struggled to get up; however, he eventually walked over to the sidelines and spoke to the Rams' trainer before going back on the field and staying in the game. After the game, Keenum was diagnosed with a concussion and sidelined for the following two games. According to the NFL's senior vice president of health and safety, Jeff Miller, this incident demonstrated an area where there were definitely not best practices and that Keenum should have been taken out of the game. This incident put the NFL's concussion protocol under the spotlight and Commissioner Roger Goodell announced that the league would review its current protocol in the 2016 offseason. Yet on December 10, 2017, Texans quarterback Tom Savage was returned to play after being sacked and subsequently exhibited concussion symptoms, including twitching hands. Only a second concussion evaluation ruled that Savage had to be pulled from the game.

NFL Rule Changes to Reduce Concussions

With a high degree of involvement from Commissioner Goodell, who was interested in finding ways to reduce the number of head injuries while maintaining the integrity of the game, the NFL expanded its rules for the 2010 season. New rules were implemented to prevent defenseless players from taking shots above their shoulders. Defenseless players included quarterbacks throwing a pass or receivers making a catch. Ball carriers were prohibited from lowering their heads to use the helmet to initiate forcible contact with a defensive player in the open field. Rules were also changed for kickoffs, which were considered particularly dangerous for concussions. The kickoff was moved up to the 35-yard line, which reduced the dangerous run back by 50 percent.

The new rules prohibited a player from launching himself from the ground, using his helmet to strike any defenseless player in the head or neck. This rule had previously applied only to receivers. Formerly, defensive players were allowed to hit receivers in the head when both of the receiver's feet touched the ground. Under the new rules, officials would give a receiver an extra split-second to get into a position where he could defend himself. The new rules also required a play to be whistled dead when a player lost his helmet. In addition, during field goal and extra point plays, the defense was not allowed to position a player directly in front of the snapper, who was considered to be in a defenseless position.

The league implemented two rule changes for the 2015 season aimed at augmenting player safety. First, an offensive player attempting to catch a ball that had been intercepted would be ruled defenseless and could not be hit in the head or neck area by the intercepting team as possession changed. Also, the league gave certified athletic trainers in sky boxes the authority to stop play if they saw a player exhibiting notable signs of injury, even if he was hurt in a previous play. The play clock and the game clock would freeze, which was the first time the NFL had an instant medical timeout to provide medical treatment to a player.

The NFL concussion rules were enforced and in December 2015, Odell Beckham, Jr. was suspended and reprimanded for initiating "forcible contact" with the head of a defenseless player, putting him at risk of injury. From 2010 to 2015, there were 39 rules changed to promote player health and safety. The NFL's Health and Safety Report released in August 2016 revealed that concussions had dropped by 35 percent over the last three years. The league continued its push to reduce concussions and joined the NFL Players Association to sponsor an independent laboratory test of the most popular helmets worn by the players.

The NFL revised its concussion safety protocol in 2017 and required a neurotrauma consultant, unaffiliated with either team, to be present at all games. The consultant's job was to monitor play by broadcast coverage and help both teams with concussion protocol implementation. The consultant would also help by contacting the teams' medical staff on the sidelines to verify that they were aware of situations as they developed. The Return to Participation Protocol was revised in June 2017 as shown in Exhibit 3.

PREVENTING CONCUSSIONS

No Full-Contact Practices

The Ivy League traditionally had the strictest rules preventing excessive contact at practice, but beginning in 2016, in an effort to reduce head injuries, Ivy League schools no longer had full-contact practices during the regular season. Dartmouth was the first Ivy League school to implement no full-contact practices in 2010. When full-contact practices were completely eliminated, the school used a mobile virtual player to tackle, as if it was any other player. In 2014, the NCAA mandated no more than four contact practices per week in the preseason, and no more than two per week during the season and postseason. Eight of the 15 practices could have live contact in Spring practice; however they were limited to two per week and could not be on consecutive days. Until 2015, the NFL had also seen concussions decrease after the amount of full-contact practice days were decreased in 2012 by league officials.

Helmets and Helmet Technology

In July 2016, 80-year-old Pro Football Hall of Famer Paul Hornung sued helmet-maker Riddell claiming the company's helmets failed to protect him from brain injury and that the company did not warn him about the link between head trauma and brain damage, which led to his dementia. In May 2013, *Frontline* reported that Riddell, the NFL's official helmet provider, was warned in 2000 by the

EXHIBIT 3   NFL Players Association Return to Participation Protocol

STEP 1

REST AND RECOVERY
The player is prescribed rest until his signs and symptoms and neurologic examination, including cognitive and balance tests, return to baseline status.

STEP 2

LIGHT AEROBIC EXERCISE
Under direct oversight of the team's medical staff, the player should begin graduated cardiovascular exercise and may also engage in dynamic stretching and balance training.

STEP 3

CONTINUED AEROBIC EXERCISE & INTRODUCTION OF STRENGTH TRAINING
The player continues with supervised cardiovascular exercises that are increased and may mimic sport-specific activities, and supervised strength training is introduced.

STEP 4

FOOTBALL SPECIFIC ACTIVITIES
The player continues cardiovascular, strength and balance training and participates in non-contact football activities (e.g. throwing, catching, running, and other position-specific activities.)

STEP 5

FULL FOOTBALL ACTIVITY/CLEARANCE
Upon clearance by the Team Physician for full football activity involving contact, the player must be examined by the Independent Neurological Consultant (INC) assigned to his Club. If the INC concurs with the team physician that the player's concussion has resolved, he may participate in his Club's next practice or game.

Source: National Football League Players Association, 2017.

biomechanics firm Biokenetics, that no helmet, no matter how revolutionary, could prevent concussions. According to the report, even helmets that met industry safety standards for skull fractures and severe head injury protection would leave players with a 95 percent chance of getting a concussion from a sufficiently strong impact.[9] At the time of that report, Riddell was developing a new helmet—the Revolution—designed to reduce players' concussions, which became the most widely used helmet in

the NFL and a large seller to college, high school, and youth football programs.

Despite the warning from Biokenetics, Riddell marketed the helmet as protection from concussions, claiming that players using the Revolution were 31 percent less likely to suffer a concussion. This claim was refuted and criticized as an exaggeration by several leading experts on head injuries (and some members of Congress). Riddell was sued as a co-defendant by NFL players in a lawsuit against the

EXHIBIT 4   Riddell Helmet Warning and Warranty

WARNING & WARRANTY INFORMATION

NO HELMET CAN PREVENT SERIOUS HEAD OR NECK INJURIES A PLAYER MIGHT RECEIVE WHILE PARTICIPATING IN FOOTBALL.

Do not use this helmet to butt, ram, or spear an opposing player. This is in violation of the football rules and such use can result in severe head or neck injuries, paralysis, or death to you and possible injury to your opponent. Contact in football may result in CONCUSSION-BRAIN INJURY which no helmet can prevent. Symptoms include: loss of consciousness or memory, dizziness, headache, nausea, or confusion. If you have symptoms, immediately stop playing and report them to your coach, trainer, and parents. Do not return to a game or practice until all symptoms are gone and you have received medical clearance. Ignoring this warning may lead to another and more serious or fatal brain injury.

Source: Riddell.com.

NFL. Also, in a Colorado case, Riddell was found liable for $3.1 millionin a suit over a young player injured by a concussion at his high school football practice. Importantly, the Colorado court did not find that the helmet was faulty; rather, Riddell did not adequately warn users of the risks of concussion. Afterwards, Riddell placed information on concussions and warning information on its helmet advertisements that state that no helmet can protect agasint head or neck injuries or concussion (see Exhibit 4).

A revolutionizing helmet that would decrease the risk of concussions would benefit football players greatly. In 2013, a pediatric neurosurgeon, Dr. Sam Browd, at the University of Washington, with Dave Marver (medical technology) and Per Reinhall (mechanical engineering), formed a company named VICIS (Latin for change) with the vision of creating a new football helmet that would reduce concussions. After about $10 million in funding and two years of development, the revolutionary VICIS Zero1 football helmet was launched collaboratively with the University of Washington.

Dr. Browd argued that current helmets were not intended to protect players from concussion, and to retrofit a helmet built for one purpose—to deal with concussion—was difficult. Football helmets were designed to protect from skull fractures and, according to Dr. Browd, they performed this task well, although not protecting against concussion. Thus VICIS abandoned traditional helmet technology and started anew to develop a helmet that would reduce the risk of concussion. Evidence suggested that concussions were not caused by angular (backward and forward) motion, rather by rotational motion. Consequently, VICIS designed their new helmet, the Zero1, to address angular and rotational acceleration (resuting from a glancing blow or twisting motion) as well as linear forces (a straight ahead collision) that acted on players' heads.

The theory behind the Zero1 was Newton's Second Law of Physics: force is mass times acceleration. A player's mass can not be changed, thus the helmet must reduce acceleration in order to reduce force. Unlike traditional helmets, the Zero1 used a relatively soft outer shell that absorbed impact and spread the force by locally deforming, like a car bumper. The next layer used a columnar structure that moved omnidirectionally (in all directions) to reduce linear and rotational forces: the inside shell was custom fitted to the user. The Zero1 cost around $1,500 per helmet in 2017, at least $1,000 more than other helmets. VICIS hoped to attract NFL and collegiate teams first, then spread to the high school markets to help reduce concussion numbers nationally. In January 2018, VICIS reduced the Zero1 for 2018 and 2019 to $950.

In 2017, another company, Windpact, was developing foam helmet padding called "Crash Cloud" that worked like an automobile airbag to absorb the energy of blows to the head. The padding compressed to disperse energy from collisons and then reinflated to protect the player from the next impact. Windpact's CEO was former NFL player Shawn Springs who played 13 years in the league. Crash Cloud was designed to be retrofitted into helmets, which would save on helmet replacement costs.

Helmets were rated on energy absorption from impact and manufacturers evaluated their products with safety tests developed by the National Operating Committee for Standards on Athletic Equipment. This independent standard-setting organization rated helmets on a severity index that indicated how well they absorbed energy. Higher scores reflected more damaging effects from impact: passing scores for helmets were below 1,200. Receiving a passing score was no indication of concussion protection, according to Biokinetics scores well below 1,200 have a high risk of concussion. In fact, the Biokenetics firm suggested that at a severity level half the current standard (1,200), a concussion was almost certain to occur. A player wearing a helmet that scored 291 during an impact had a 50 percent probability of suffering a concussion, and a helmet scoring 558 experiencing the identical impact would have a 95 percent probability.

To reduce the risk of concussions, what if the NFL banned the use of helmets? Hines Ward, a former Pittsburgh Steelers wideout, was among those advocating that football helmets do more harm than good. Ward told the *Dan Patrick Show,* "If you want to prevent concussions, take the helmet off."[7] Although this idea seems farfetched, Ward's rationale for his reasoning is not. He believes players use their helmet like a weapon, giving them more ability to deliver a big hit, rather than protecting players from receiving a big hit. If players did not wear helmets, they would play less recklessly and, therefore, prevent head shots from opposing players. However, skull fractures would likely increase (even if concussions decreased) from the removal of helmets from football players, which would not increase the overall safety of the game.[10]

THE FUTURE OF THE CONCUSSION CONTROVERSY IN COLLEGE ATHLETICS

In January 2016, U.S. District Judge John Lee approved a settlement in a class-action suit between a group of athletes and the NCAA, for the association's handling of head injuries. The agreement mandated a new protocol of head injuries did not provide cash settlements for the plaintiff athletes, but included $15

million in attorney fees and expenses up to $750,000. Under the settlement, the NCAA would endow a $70 million fund to provide neurological screenings to former players to examine brain functions and indications of encephalopathy, and an additional $5 million for concussion research. Also, the NCAA was required to prevent a player who had suffered a concussion from returning to practice or to a game the day of the injury.

Judge Lee specified six changes that the NCAA agreed to implement regarding concussion policies (some of which were already in place):

1. Athletes were to undergo preseason baseline testing prior to first practice or competition.

2. Amend NCAA guidelines to prohibit athletes diagnosed with concussion from returning to play on the same day. Physician clearance required prior to playing after a concussion.

3. Medical personnel trained in concussions were required to attend all contact-sport games and practices for Divisions I, II, and III. Contact sports were defined as football, lacrosse, wrestling, basketball, ice hockey, soccer, and field hockey.

4. The NCAA was to institute "a uniform process for schools to report diagnosed concussions and their resolution, and for concerned persons to report potential problems directly to the NCAA."

5. NCAA schools were required to provide approved concussion education and training to athletes, coaches, and athletic trainers before each season.

6. The NCAA would provide education for faculty to accommodate students suffering from concussions.

In May 2016, the lead plaintiffs and the NCAA agreed to the settlement.

In early May 2016, six lawsuits, seeking to become class-action, were filed against several universities, athletic conferences, and the NCAA, claiming neligence in the handling of players' head injuries. These suits were filed by objectors to the proposed $75 million settlement against the NCAA in a national class-action concussion case. Each of these suits was filed against a different school (Penn State, Vanderbilt, Utah, Oregon, Auburn, and Georgia), and were similar to onging NFL concussion litigation. In each case, the NCAA, and an athletic conference (SEC, Big Ten, PAC-12, and Western Athletic), were also defendants.

The suits requested coverage for athletes who played at the schools between 1952 (the date of the

New England Journal of Medicine's recommendation that athletes cease playing football after a third concussion) and 2010 (the year that the NCAA required schools to have a concussion-management protocol for all sports). The cases alleged that despite decades of research describing the dangers of traumatic brain injuries, the defendants knowingly and for profit failed to implement procedures to protect players from those injuries. The players alleged that due to the defendants' actions or lack of actions, they suffered neurological and cognitive damage. Compensatory and punitive damages were requested without limitation and included damages for past, present, and future medical expenses, other expenses, and lost future earnings.

The NCAA's legal expenses increased 59 percent in calendar year 2013, to $13.8 million and were expected to climb. In response to being named as one of several defendants (including helmet manufacturer Schutt Sports and Frostburg State University coaches) in the death of Derek Sheely, a Frostburg State player, following multiple head injuries in 2014, the NCAA's position on the escalating lawsuits was "crystallizing." The NCAA took the position that each college was responsible for its athletes' welfare and that risk could not be completely removed from athletics, according to Jon Solomon in **AL.Com**.[11] The NCAA's position was as follows:

> Plaintiffs are attempting to use the NCAA's commitment to student-athlete safety as the basis for a legal duty requiring it to have prevented Mr. Sheely's death. While the NCAA has compassion for the Plaintiffs' loss and shares their concern about the alleged events at Frostburg State, the law does not recognize this legal duty. Organizers of sporting events are not liable for injuries to voluntary participants when the risk of injury is obvious and foreseeable. Otherwise, athletic associations—including the NCAA and all high school, private, and professional athletic associations—would be subject to litigation any time a participant is injured in any sport anywhere for failure to prevent the injury. The NCAA is not aware of any court in Maryland that has ever held that the NCAA has a duty to prevent injury.[12]

A Maryland court surprised the NCAA in April 2016, ruling the injury that killed Sheely, the second-impact syndrome, was not a "known inherent risk" of football. This syndrome results from multiple concussions; a second concussion aggravates symptoms and injuries from the first causing swelling of the brain. The court ruled that because of its mission statement, the NCAA had a "special relationship" to protect student-athletes, and therefore had a legal duty to warn players of the risks.

THE FUTURE OF THE CONCUSSION CONTROVERSY IN THE NFL

Five years after the first concussion suit against the NFL, the league received a court ruling that should essentially end the legal controversy over the still-unresolved concussion problem. A panel of judges affirmed an order that approved a class action settlement of a suit between more than 20,000 retired NFL players and the NFL. The settlement would cost the NFL about $1 billion over the next 65 years and provide compensation for retired players. Players would receive an average of $190,000 and the attorneys received $112.5 million. Most importantly, the NFL was not required to admit fault. Although about 200 players eligible for the suit opted out, according to the *Sports Illustrated* article, "in all likelihood the NFL has settled with 99 percent of the retired players. The Court's order was probably a permanent setback for the 95 players who objected to the settlement."[13]

Less than 18 months after retired players were allowed to file claims in the $1 billion concussion settlement, the NFL asked a federal judge to appoint a special investigator to stop the fraud that was infecting the settlement program. According to a *New York Times* article published on April 13, 2018, the NFL claimed that over 400 claims had been denied because of "unscrupulous lawyers and doctors" who coached players on how to appear mentally impaired. Numerous football concussion lawyers advertised on the Internet, social media, and other outlets, companies had provided high-interest loans to players who were to repay them from their concussion settlements, and "settlement funding" companies offered "advances, not loans" that would be repaid by the players' attorneys from the settlement proceeds.[14] As of April 2018, 1,776 claims had been received from the over 20,000 retired players who registered as members of the settlement class. According to the NFL, only 493 had been paid (see Exhibit 5).

The probability of a plaintiff winning a concussion lawsuit was low. Many of the retired players in the suit played prior to 1992, before the collective bargaining agreement. Players subsequent to 1992 were

EXHIBIT 5   NFL Concussion Settlement Program Highlights as of June 2018

Registered Settlement Class Members	Claim Packages Received
20,496	1,776
Payable Monetary Awards	Payable Monetary Award Amounts
493	$443,001,863
BAP Appointments Scheduled	BAP Appointments Attended
6,810	5,204

Source: www.NFLconcussionsettlement.com.

covered by the agreement that required grievances concerning health issues to be addressed through arbitration; therefore, lawsuits were preempted from being heard by courts. If a judge agreed with the defense of preemption, the case would be dismissed.

The NFL also had a causation defense, which required plaintiffs to prove that long-term neurological injury occurred due to playing in the NFL. It would be impossible to prove that time in the NFL caused the brain injury and not the thousands of plays and drills in high school and college, other contact sports, or environmental conditions that could cause long-term neurological damage.

According to *Sports Illustrated* legal analyst Michael McCann, because the NFL was not required to admit fault, it is less likely that congress or regulators would attempt to pass legislation or regulations aimed at the league.[15] Admission of guilt would have negatively affected the league's ability to negotiate insurance policies, plus future lawsuits would have been strengthened. Current and future players were not part of the settlement; however, current players were covered by the NFL's collective bargaining agreement with the NFLPA (National Football League Players Association). The looming question for the future of concussion litigation in the NFL is whether the

league will be able to use collective bargaining with the NFLPA to determine how current and future players should be compensated for brain damage. If the parties did not reach an agreement, the NFL would expect new concussion lawsuits for the indeterminate future.

Future litigation was also highly likely in college sports with a new trial concerning CTE and football scheduled to begin in June 2018. The case was filed against the NCAA by the wife of a University of Texas football player, Greg Ploetz, who died 44 years after graduating from college (he did not play professional football). Mr. Ploetz suffered from confusion, depression, paranoia, and memory loss, which are conditions commonly associated with CTE. After his death, examination of his brain revealed the most severe level of CTE. The plaintiffs sought over $1,000,000 in damages and alleged that the NCAA unreasonably failed to protect Greg Ploetz because the association knew or should have known about the relationship between concussive and sub-concussive blows to the head and long-term neurological problems. Absent a well-developed social responsibility strategy, the NFL, NCAA, and universities would eventually be unable to sustain the costs of litigation related to CTE.

ENDNOTES

[1] CTE Center – Boston University, Frequently Asked Questions about CTE, www.bu.edu/cte/about/what-is-cte/.

[2] Breslow, J. M., New: 87 Deceased NFL Players Test Positive for Brain Disease, September, 18, 2015, www.pbs.org/wgbh/frontline/article/new-87-deceased-nfl-players-test-positive-for-brain-disease/.

[3] Breslow, J. M., High School Football Players Face Bigger Concussion Risk, October 31, 2013, www.pbs.org/wgbh/frontline/article/high-school-football-players-face-bigger-concussion-risk/.

[4] Solomon, J., Studies Show Magnitude of College Football's Concussion Problem, CBS Sports HQ Daily Newsletter, October 2, 2014,

http://www.cbssports.com/collegefootball/writer/jon-solomon/24734520/studies-show-magnitude-of-college-footballs-concussion-problem

[5] Solomon, J. (2014). **Judge denies preliminary approval of NCAA concussion settlement.** Retrieved from https://www.cbssports.com/college-football/news/judge-denies-preliminary-approval-of-ncaa-concussion-settlement/

[6] NCAA, Concussion Timeline: A history of NCAA Decisions Intended to Help Protect College Athletes from Serious Injuries, Including Those That Can Cause Concussion, http://www.ncaa.org/sport-science-institute/concussion-timeline.

[7] NFL. NFL Head, Neck and Spine Committee's Protocols Regarding Diagnosis and Management of Concussion, October 1, 2013, http://static.nfl.com/static/content/public/photo/2013/10/01/0ap2000000254002.pdf.

[8] Riccobona, A. NFL Concussion Protocol: What Are The 5-Stages for Diagnosis and Management? International Business Times, 2016, www.ibtimes.com/nfl-concussion-

protocol-what-are-5-stages-diagnosis-management-2277084.

[9] Shankman, S. NFL Helmet Manufacturer Warned on Concussion Risk. *Frontline,* May 1, 2013, www.pbs.org/wgbh/frontline/article/nfl-helmet-manufacturer-warned-on-concussion-risk/.

[10] Smith, M. D. Hines Ward: "If You Want to Prevent Concussions, Take the Helmet Off," NBC Sports, December 4, 2012, profootballtalk.nbcsports.com/2012/12/04/hines-ward-if-you-want-to-prevent-concussions-take-the-helmet-off/.

[11] Solomon, J. NCAA Concussion Defense: Sporting Event Organizers Aren't Liable for Obvious Injury Risks, February 6, 2014,

www.al.com/sports/index.ssf/2014/02/ncaa_concussion_defense_sporti.html.

[12] Ibid.

[13] McCann, M. What's Next for Each Side After the NFL's Concussion Settlement, *Sports Illustrated,* April 18, 2016, www.si.com/nfl/2016/04/18/nfl-concussion-lawsuit-settlement-retired-players.

[14] Belson, K. NFL Says Fraud Plagues the Concussion Settlement. *New York Times,* April 13, 2018, p D6.

[15] McCann, M. What's Next for Each Side After the NFL's Concussion Settlement, *Sports Illustrated,* April 18, 2016, www.si.com/nfl/2016/04/18/nfl-concussion-lawsuit-settlement-retired-players.

REFERENCES

[1] Buckley, W.E. (1988) "Concussions in college football: A multivariate analysis," *The American Journal of Sports Medicine,* 15(1)51-6.

[2] As quoted in *2014-2015 NCAA Sports Medicine Handbook,* p. 66.

[3] As quoted in "Concussion diagnosis and management best practices," http://www.ncaa.org/sport-science-institute/concussion-diagnosis-and-management-best-practices.

[4] As quoted in "Concussion diagnosis and management best practices,"

http://www.ncaa.org/sport-science-institute/concussion-diagnosis-and-management-best-practices.

[5] Gibbs, Lindsay, "The dangerous loopholes in the NCAA's concussion policy," *Think Progress,* January 9, 2016, https://thinkprogress.org/the-dangerous-loopholes-in-the-ncaas-concussion-policy-b3db2a9c930d/.

[6] Solomon, Jon. "Why the NCAA won't adopt concussion penalties—at least not yet," *CBS Sports,* February 18, 2015,

https://www.cbssports.com/college-football/news/why-the-ncaa-wont-adopt-concussion-penalties----at-least-not-yet/.

[7] As quoted on the *Dan Patrick Show* and posted online by Michael David Smith, *NBC Sports,* December 4, 2010, https://profootballtalk.nbcsports.com/2012/12/04/hines-ward-if-you-want-to-prevent-concussions-take-the-helmet-off/.

Chaos at Uber: The New CEO's Challenge

Syeda Maseeha Qumer

ICFAI Business School, Hyderabad

Debapratim Purkayastha

ICFAI Business School, Hyderabad

"I have to tell you I am scared,"[1] wrote Dara Khosrowshahi, newly appointed CEO of ride-hailing service Uber Technologies Inc., in a memo to his former team at Expedia, Inc.[2] Besides growing Uber's business, analysts said Khosrowshahi had the task of changing the dysfunctional culture within the company and improving corporate governance that had cost co-founder and former CEO Travis Kalanick his job. On June 21, 2017, Kalanick stepped down as CEO of Uber in the face of a shareholder revolt that made it untenable for him to stay on in that position. His resignation came after a review of practices at Uber including allegations of sexual harassment, a corporate theft lawsuit, defiance of government regulations, reports of misbehavior, and a toxic corporate culture leading to the departure of some key executives.

Uber's corporate structure ensured that its founders held super-voting shares and had disproportionate control over the company. Kalanick, because of the special class of shares he owned, enjoyed sweeping authority on the Uber board and nearly complete autonomy in running the company. According to some industry observers, Uber ignored corporate governance in its pursuit of growth and valuation, and flouted ethical norms while hiding behind notions of disruption and innovation. This was fine with investors until the beginning of 2017 when the company's public image crumbled amid allegations of sexual harassment, they said. *"The board chose to ignore the fundamentals of their governance role and failed to provide guidance in correcting a trait which would ultimately endanger the company in many ways,"*[3] said Prabal Basu Roy, a fund manager.

The chaos inside Uber's boardroom escalated in August 2017 when a small group of shareholders aligned with Kalanick dissented against Uber's biggest investor Benchmark Capital,[4] after it filed a lawsuit to oust Kalanick from the board. Benchmark Capital had accused Kalanick of fraud and of interfering in the search for a new CEO—accusations that he had denied. Some analysts felt that Uber's board needed to grow up as the constant bickering among the members was hurting the company. According to them, the board's aggressive infighting was spreading confusion and uncertainty among Uber's investors, customers, and shareholders, and putting the company's nearly $70 billion market valuation at risk.

As Khosrowshahi began his new role at Uber, he had the daunting task of dealing with a fraught Uber board and mending the frayed relations among investors. *"Boards are so unpredictable, and this one seems as if they're at each other's throats. It's hard to know if he'll have the force of personality to navigate that,"*[5] said Alice Armitage, director of Startup Legal Garage.[6] Khosrowshahi would have to figure out a way to unite the divided board and end the acrimony among them. Moreover, he would also have to contend with the legacy of Kalanick who continued to remain on the Uber board.

Khosrowshahi said that as Uber's CEO he wanted to set the course for the future of the company, which included innovating and growing responsibly as well as acknowledging and correcting mistakes of the past. He planned to take the company public by

©IBS Center for Management Research

2019. *"The culture went wrong, and the governance of the company went wrong and the board went in a very bad direction. But if the product is good, then if you can bring in good leadership, you can ultimately bring it together,"*[7] he said. However, some analysts wondered if the company valued at around $68 billion as of January 2018 could maintain its valuation as it prepared for an IPO.

BACKGROUND NOTE

Uber was co-founded by Kalanick[8] and Garrett Camp[9] in 2009. The duo was in Europe attending LeWeb, an annual European tech conference. On a snowy night in Paris, Kalanick and Camp could not get a cab. This was when the two came up with the idea of launching an on-demand car-service app. After getting back to San Francisco, Camp convinced Kalanick to partner with him in the new project that could fill the large and lucrative gap in the car service market.

UberCab, as it was then known, started its service in San Francisco in the summer of 2010 with only a few cars, a handful of employees, and a small seed round. After entering credit-card information on the app, customers could book a car at the press of a button. The cost was automatically charged to the customer's account. Uber required its drivers to have their own car and to pass a background check. In August 2010, Ryan Graves, Uber's first hire, was briefly appointed as CEO of the company. In October 2010, the company was renamed Uber after some regulatory bodies objected to the use of "cab" in UberCab's name as the entity was operating without a taxi license. Uber closed a $1.25 million seed funding in 2014. Chris Sacca of First Round Capital was its first institutional investor and he invested about half a million dollars in the company. Other investors included Napster co-founder Shawn Fanning, venture capital fund Lowercase Capital, and venture capitalist Mitch Kapor.

In December 2010, Graves stepped down as CEO and Kalanick stepped into the position. Graves stayed on as Uber's head of global operations. In February 2011, Uber closed an $11 million Series A funding round that valued the company at $60 million (see Exhibit 1). Benchmark Capital led the round and its partner Bill Gurley joined Uber's Board of Directors. In May 2011, Uber was launched in New York City and thereafter it expanded to Seattle, Boston, Chicago, and Washington D.C. In December 2011, Uber raised $32 million in its

Series B of fund raising from Amazon Inc's CEO Jeff Bezos, Menlo Ventures, and Goldman Sachs. In July 2012, Uber unveiled its low-cost "Uber X" service.

In August 2013, Uber entered India and Africa, and closed a Series C funding round which saw a massive $258 million investment from Google Ventures. In July 2014, Uber entered China after a $1.2 billion funding round. In August 2014, Uber launched its UberPOOL service. Notwithstanding strikes by angry taxi drivers over Uber threatening their livelihood and breaking local taxi rules, and unresolved questions of legal liability, the cab service expanded rapidly. The company continually rolled out new services from freight and helicopter rides to food delivery to driverless cars.

Uber upended the tightly regulated taxi industry in many countries and changed the transportation landscape. In 2016, its gross bookings hit $20 billion, double that of the previous year (see Exhibit 2). As shown in Exhibits 3 and 4, net revenues were $6.5 billion for 2016, although losses were high at $2.8 billion. As of 2017, Uber had a presence in 724 cities in more than 84 countries.[10] With a valuation of nearly $68 billion, it was by far the richest of the Silicon Valley's private unicorn technology companies (see Exhibit 5).

Analysts said that while Uber had tasted great success, its journey had been a bumpy one. According to them, the company was synonymous with controversies. Since its launch, Uber had been the subject of ongoing protests from taxi drivers and regulatory bodies who argued that the company should be subjected to the same regulations that they faced. From noncompliance issues to regulatory concerns and lack of driver background checks, Uber drew scrutiny and criticism. The service was banned in The Netherlands and in parts of Thailand and China. Uber's surge pricing had been one of the most controversial aspects of the company's business model. Customers equated it with price gouging as it took advantage of users in unfortunate situations. Uber had also been embroiled in a long-standing battle with some labor organizations as it classified its drivers as independent contractors and not employees, which deprived them of various benefits. There had also been cases of sexual assault on passengers, which some activists said happened because the background checks on drivers had not been stringent enough. Uber's critics went to the extent of saying that the company ignored ethical and legal standards in the name of disruption and valued money, power, and control above morality.

EXHIBIT 1   Uber Funding Rounds

Date	Amount/Round	Valuation ($ billion)	Lead Investor	Investors
April 2017	Undisclosed Amount	—	—	1
July 2016	$1.15 billion/Debt Financing	—	Morgan Stanley	4
June 2016	$3.5 billion/Series G	—	Saudi Arabia's Public Investment Fund	1
May 2016	Undisclosed Amount/Series G	—	—	1
Feb 2016	$200 million/Private Equity	—	Letterone Holdings SA	1
Aug 2015	$100 million/Private Equity	—	Tata Capital	1
July 2015	$1 billion/Series F	—		6
Feb 2015	$1 billion/Series E	—	Glade Brook Capital Partners	9
Jan 2015	$1.6 billion/Debt Financing	—	Goldman Sachs	1
Dec 2014	$1.2 billion/Series E	40.0	Glade Brook Capital Partners	8
June 2014	$1.4 billion/Series D	18.2	Fidelty Investments	9
Aug 2013	$363 million/Series C	3.5	GV	4
Dec 2011	$37 million/Series B	—	Menlo Ventures	11
Feb 2011	$11 million/Series A	0.06	Benchmark Capital	6
Oct 2010	$1.25 million/Angel	—	First Round	29
Aug 2009	$200 thousand/Seed	—	Garrett Camp Travis Kalanick	2

Source: Crunchbase.

EXHIBIT 2   Uber Gross Bookings (Q1 2015–Q3 2016) ($ in millions)

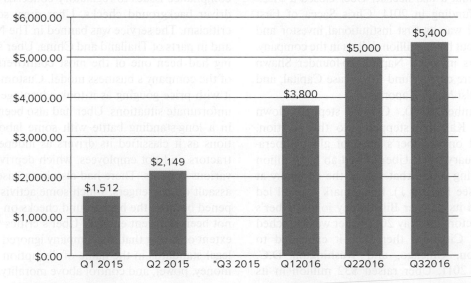

Q1 2015: $1,512
Q2 2015: $2,149
*Q3 2015: data not available
Q12016: $3,800
Q22016: $5,000
Q32016: $5,400

Source: www.businessinsider.com.

EXHIBIT 3 Uber Quarterly Net Revenues, 2012–2016 ($ in millions)

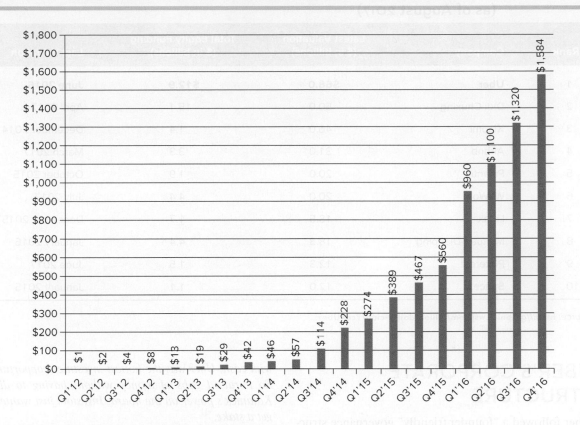

Source: www.investing.com/analysis/2017-39;s-uber-ipo-200170565.

EXHIBIT 4 Uber Quarterly Losses, 2012–2016 ($ in millions)

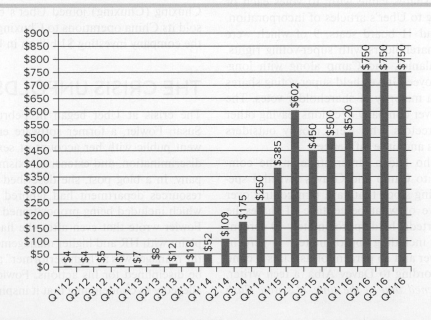

Source: www.investing.com/analysis/2017-39;s-uber-ipo-200170565.

EXHIBIT 5   Top 10 Privately Owned Technology Unicorns in the World (as of August 2017)

Rank	Company	Latest Valuation ($ in billions)	Total Equity Funding ($ in billions)	Last Valuation
1	Uber	$68.0	$12.9	June 2016
2	Didi Chuxing	50.0	15.1	April 2017
3	Xiaomi	46.0	1.4	December 2014
4	Airbnb	31.0	3.3	March 2017
5	Palantir	20.0	1.9	October 2015
6	WeWork	20.0	4.4	July 2017
7	Lufax	18.5	1.7	December 2015
8	Meituan-Dianping	18.3	4.4	January 2016
9	Pinterest	12.3	1.5	June 2017
10	SpaceX	12.0	1.1	January 2015

Source: http://graphics.wsj.com/billion-dollar-club/?co=Uber.

UBER'S CORPORATE STRUCTURE

Uber followed a "founder-friendly" governance structure wherein some board seats carried more voting power than others. In this kind of a dual-class share structure, one class of shares carried one vote while the other class shares came with 10 votes each or more. According to Uber's articles of incorporation, the company had 11 board seats, 9 of which were controlled by shareholders with super-voting rights. Co-founders Kalanick and Camp along with long-time Uber employee Graves held super-voting shares and controlled a majority of shareholder votes. The trio held sway over company decisions leaving other independent directors who were mostly outsiders with fewer rights and little influence.

Kalanick who had a larger stake in the company compared to Camp and Graves owned a special class of voting stock that gave him control over Uber irrespective of what percentage of shares he owned. He reportedly held approximately 10 percent of Uber's stock, including approximately 16 percent of its voting power and 35 percent of its Class B common stock. According to Davey Alba, a tech writer, "*It just so happened that at the time VCs were flush*

with cash, Uber was the hottest investment opportunity. So it raised gobs of money without having to dilute Kalanick's power on the board. Investors just wanted to get a stake."[11]

As of 2016, Kalanick had kept the Uber board small, leaving four board seats empty as shown in Exhibit 6. At the end of 2016 Cheng Wei, founder and chairman of Chinese ride-hailing service Didi Chuxing (Chuxing) joined Uber's board after Uber sold its China operations to Chuxing in exchange for the company investing $1 billion in Uber.

THE CRISIS UNFOLDS

The crisis at Uber began in February 2017 when Susan Fowler, a former software engineer at Uber, went public with her account of sexual harassment, discrimination, and extensive sexism inside the company. In a blog post, she described how the human resources department had ignored her complaints, which included being propositioned by her manager. Fowler wrote that even after she had lodged a complaint with HR and higher management, she was told the manager was a "high performer" and he would not be disciplined for his actions. Fowler's account was allegedly so condemning that it inspired other women

EXHIBIT 6   Uber Board of Directors (as of 2016)

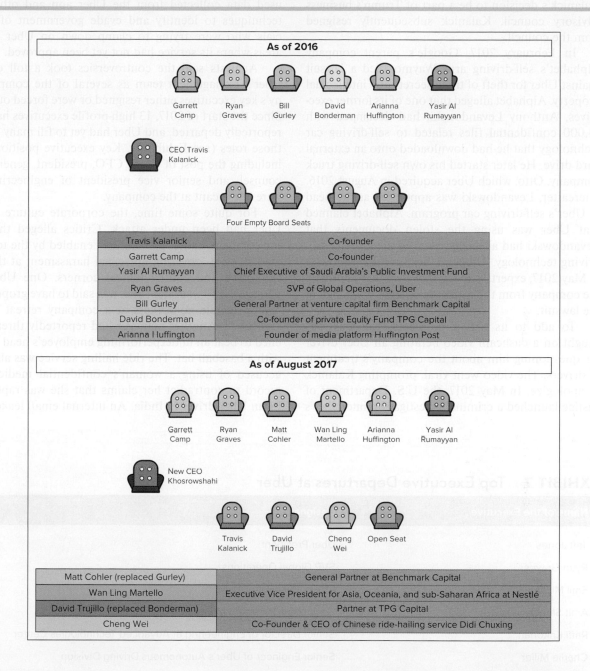

Travis Kalanick	Co-founder	
Garrett Camp	Co-founder	
Yasir Al Rumayyan	Chief Executive of Saudi Arabia's Public Investment Fund	
Ryan Graves	SVP of Global Operations, Uber	
Bill Gurley	General Partner at venture capital firm Benchmark Capital	
David Bonderman	Co-founder of private Equity Fund TPG Capital	
Arianna Huffington	Founder of media platform Huffington Post	

Matt Cohler (replaced Gurley)	General Partner at Benchmark Capital
Wan Ling Martello	Executive Vice President for Asia, Oceania, and sub-Saharan Africa at Nestlé
David Trujillo (replaced Bonderman)	Partner at TPG Capital
Cheng Wei	Co-Founder & CEO of Chinese ride-hailing service Didi Chuxing

employees at Uber to come forward with their own stories. This eventually led to at least 200 claims of sexual harassment against the company. Fowler also wrote about the organizational chaos at Uber saying that there was a "Game of Thrones" kind of a political war raging within the ranks of the upper management. According to her, projects were frequently abandoned and Objectives and Key Results (OKRs) were changed multiple times each quarter.[12]

Earlier in January 2017, Uber was accused of undermining a taxi union strike at JFK airport in New York protesting United States President Donald Trump's refugee ban.[13] Subsequently, more than 200,000 users uninstalled their Uber accounts as part of the #DeleteUber campaign triggered by Kalanick's decision to be a part of Trump's business advisory council. Kalanick subsequently resigned from the council.

In February 2017, Google's parent company Alphabet's self-driving arm Waymo filed a lawsuit against Uber for theft of trade secrets and intellectual property. Alphabet alleged that one of its former executives, Anthony Levandowski, had decamped with 14,000 confidential files related to self-driving car technology that he had downloaded onto an external hard drive. He later started his own self-driving truck company, Otto, which Uber acquired in August 2016. Thereafter, Levandowski was appointed as the head of Uber's self-driving car program. Alphabet claimed that Uber was using the stolen documents that Levandowski had allegedly taken to advance its self-driving technology. Though Uber fired Levandowski in May 2017, experts said the move would not protect the company from the explosive charges contained in the lawsuit.

To add to its list of problems, Kalanick was caught on a dashcam video berating an Uber driver for questioning him about the company's treatment of drivers. The video went viral, prompting Kalanick to apologize. In May 2017, the U.S. Department of Justice launched a criminal investigation into Uber's use of a secret software tool called "Greyball" that used data collected from the Uber app and other techniques to identify and evade government officials who were trying to clamp down on Uber in areas where its service had not yet been approved.

Analysts said the controversies took a toll on Uber's management team as several of the company's key executives either resigned or were forced out. Since the start of 2017, 13 high-profile executives had reportedly departed, and Uber had yet to fill many of those roles (see Exhibit 7). Key executive positions including the post of COO, CFO, president, general counsel, and senior vice president of engineering were left vacant at the company.

For quite some time, the corporate culture at Uber had been under attack. Critics alleged that the company had a "bro culture" enabled by the top management—covering up sexual harassment at the workplace and cutting ethical corners. One Uber manager, who was later fired, was said to have groped several female co-workers at a company retreat in Las Vegas. Another manager had reportedly threatened to beat an underperforming employee's head in with a baseball bat. The ride hailing service was also accused of using a woman's confidential medical record to contradict her claims that she was raped by an Uber driver in India. An internal email leaked

EXHIBIT 7 Top Executive Departures at Uber

Name of the Executive	Designation
Jeff Jones	Uber President
Ryan Graves	SVP Global Operations
Emil Michael	SVP of Business
Amit Singhal	Senior Vice President of Engineering
Raffi Krikorian	Senior Director of Engineering at Advanced Technologies Center
Charlie Miller	Senior Engineer of Uber's Autonomous Driving Division
Ed Baker	Vice President of Product and Growth
Gary Marcus	AI Labs director
Brian McClendon	Vice President of Maps
Rachel Whetstone	Head of Policy and Communications
Anthony Levandowski	Head of Uber's self-driving car unit

in 2013 said Kalanick had allegedly instructed Uber employees at a company party on the ground rules for partying and having sex with co-workers. According to some Uber employees, the culture at the company was aggressive and demanding with emphasis on hustling, toe-stepping, and meritocracy. *"This is a company where there has been no line that you wouldn't cross if it got in the way of success,"*[14] said Hadi Partovi, an Uber investor.

However, the final nail in the coffin was the blog post by Fowler. Calling the behavior meted out to Fowler *"abhorrent & against everything we believe in,"* Kalanick tweeted that *"anyone who behaves this way or thinks this is OK will be fired."*[15] He announced that the company would launch an independent investigation into Fowler's claims. He hired former U.S. attorney general Eric H. Holder Jr. and his colleague Tammy Albarrán, partners at the law firm Covington & Burling LLP, to probe the matter and conduct a review of Uber's corporate culture. On March 1, 2017, Uber's Board of Directors unanimously approved a resolution establishing a Special Committee of the Board[16] to look into the allegations. The team also involved board member Arianna Huffington and the company's newly appointed human resources chief, Liane Hornsey.

Meanwhile, Uber investors Freada Kapor Klein and Mitch Kapor wrote an open letter to Uber's board and investors criticizing the company for choosing a team of insiders to investigate the matter. According to them, Holder had previously worked on Uber's behalf to advocate the company's concerns while Huffington was on the board of the company. Hornsey reported to the executive team. *"We are disappointed to see that Uber has selected a team of insiders to investigate its destructive culture and make recommendations for change. To us, this decision is yet another example of Uber's continued unwillingness to be open, transparent, and direct,"*[17] they wrote. In response to the letter, the review committee said it would conduct the investigation impartially.

THE HOLDER REPORT

On June 13, 2017, Uber released the results of the highly anticipated internal investigation. Lack of oversight and poor governance were some of the key issues running through the findings of the report. The Holder report specifically identified Kalanick as part of the problem as the first line of the report read, "Review and Reallocate the Responsibilities of Travis Kalanick." The report in total made 47 recommendations including emphasizing more on diversity and companywide performance reviews, and installing an independent chair and oversight committee to handle ethics issues. In the area of corporate governance, the report advised that the board should have greater independence and the additional board members should be directors with meaningful experience on other boards and should exercise independent oversight of Uber's management.

The same day, Kalanick in an email to employees announced that that he was taking time off to mourn his mother, who was killed in a boating accident. Kalanick said the company would be run by an executive committee and that he would be available if needed. Uber's SVP and business leader Emil Michael, a close confidante of Kalanick who had reportedly been pressured to resign following the investigation, also left the company. In addition, at least 20 other employees were fired as a result of a separate investigations related to sexual harassment and discrimination by law firm Perkins Coie.

Uber's board unanimously decided to adopt all the recommendations for improving corporate governance including sexual harassment prevention and improving workplace diversity. However, during the meeting, Uber board member David Bonderman made a sexist remark[18] and had to resign thereafter. David Trujillo, a partner at the private equity firm TPG Capital, replaced Bonderman. Also, Uber appointed Nestlé executive Wan Ling Martello (Martello) to the board. She was the second woman after Huffington to serve as an Uber Director.

INVESTORS REVOLT

When Uber became embroiled in a series of legal and ethical scandals, the investors who until then saw little wrong with Kalanick's aggressive antics became suddenly combative. They felt that their investment in Uber was at risk and started agitating for change at the top as the #DeleteUber campaign and Fowler's complaints gained traction. Exhibit 8 illustrates the impact of the scandals on Uber's market share. The Board of Directors, who were under fire themselves, decided to replace Kalanick but that was easier said than done. According to Richard Mahony, an expert in communication strategy and investor relations, *"[Kalanick's super-voting shares] has made the task of removing him much more complicated. It took a former*

EXHIBIT 8   Impact of Senior Leadership Scandals on Uber's U.S. Market Share

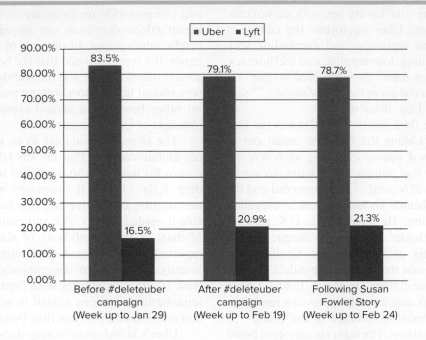

Source: TXN Solutions.

attorney general and a nearly constant stream of media leaks to pry Mr. Kalanick out of his seat."[19]

Five of Uber's major investors—Benchmark Capital, First Round Capital, Lowercase Capital, Menlo Ventures, and Fidelity Investments—which together controlled 40 percent of the company's votes and owned more than a quarter of Uber's stock, demanded Kalanick's resignation. In the letter titled "Moving Uber Forward," the investors wrote to Kalanick that he must immediately leave. On the other hand, some Uber board members including Camp and Huffington extended support to Kalanick as they believed that his leadership was necessary for Uber to survive in the aggressive taxi industry. Huffington even attested to Kalanick's willingness to change. The shareholders' unrest, however, made it untenable for Kalanick to stay on at the company. Finally, after hours of negotiations and consultations with his confidants, Kalanick agreed to step down on June 21, 2017. According to Fast Company's Ainsley Harris, "Kalanick held on to Uber's reins in the face of scandal after scandal—sexual harassment, discrimination, obstruction of regulatory enforcement, privacy violations. But when shareholders (with checkbooks and

connections) at last found their voice, he had little choice but to step down. Quite simply, he needs their money."[20]

Kalanick, however, continued to serve on Uber's Board of Directors. "I love Uber more than anything in the world and at this difficult moment in my personal life I have accepted the investors request to step aside so that Uber can go back to building rather than be distracted with another fight,"[21] he said in a statement. A day after his resignation, Gurley, who pushed Kalanick to leave, resigned from the Uber board. He was replaced by his colleague, Matt Cohler, also a partner at Benchmark Capital.

CORPORATE GOVERNANCE FIASCO

Experts attributed the root of Uber's problems to weak corporate governance marked by a rapid chase after growth, the cult of Kalanick, and the company's failure to address workplace issues. They felt that Uber's Board of Directors did not care about governance issues and let Kalanick run the company the way he did as long as profits were generated and growth achieved. According to Jean-Louis Gassée, Editor of Monday Note, a tech and media blog, *"Uber's investors had one goal—the IPO—and one strategy: create a market position so dominant that it would eliminate the competition and, as a result, provide the pricing power that would support a stratospheric IPO price. As for tactics, investors left the matter to Kalanick while looking elsewhere."*[22]

Critics contended that Uber's board had failed to institute a corporate governance framework that focused on the legal, regulatory, institutional, and ethical environment of the company. They added that the continued silence of board members had encouraged employees to commit and engage in criminal conduct, opened the door to corporate wrongdoing, and contributed to more lawsuits.[23] Only when the scandals reached too far and investors realized that they could lose their money if Uber's valuation was marked down, had the board woken up and fired Kalanick, they said.

UBER'S BOARDROOM DRAMA

Amidst a series of scandals, Uber's Board of Directors found themselves divided. On August 10, 2017, investor Benchmark Capital, which held a 13 percent stake in Uber and spearheaded Kalanick's ouster, filed a lawsuit against him for fraud, breach of contract, and breach of fiduciary duty. The investor wanted him removed from the Uber board. According to Benchmark Capital, Kalanick had concealed material information from investors when he created three new board seats and expanded Uber's board from 8 to 11 directors in June 2016. Kalanick gave himself control to appoint members to those seats, it alleged. Benchmark Capital felt that Kalanick had covered up for the company's failings and his own mismanagement before the Board of Directors in order to retain and increase his own power on the board. It called him a toxic force at Uber and held him responsible for its cultural failings. Kalanick's spokesman said the lawsuit was peppered with lies and false allegations. However, on August 31, 2017, a Delaware judge stayed the lawsuit and sent the case for arbitration, moving the legal battle out of the public eye.

Meanwhile, some pro-Kalanick investors including Shervin Pishevar, Managing Director of Sherpa Capital;[24] Ron Burkle, co-founder of Yucaipa Companies;[25] and Adam Leber, an investor who managed Maverick Records,[26] sent an email to Uber investors and the board members asking Benchmark Capital to withdraw the lawsuit, divest its shares, and step down from Uber's board. According to them, the tactics of Benchmark Capital were "ethically dubious and, critically, value-destructive rather than value enhancing."[27] They accused Gurley of holding Uber hostage to a public relations disaster by demanding Kalanick's resignation. Calling it a "fratricidal" move against Kalanick, the investors said the lawsuit could harm Uber's valuation, risk the company's ability to raise funds, and hinder the search for a new CEO. They wanted Kalanick to make a comeback at Uber in an operational capacity. Commenting on the fallout, Heather Somerville, a technology reporter, wrote, *"The division and hostility emerging among Uber investors and directors opens a new front in a highly unusual public battle for Silicon Valley. It is rare for a venture firm to sue the central figure of a valuable portfolio company, and equally unexpected for investors to make a counter-move to push out a fellow investor backing the same company."*[28]

According to some analysts, with the power play and ego battles among Uber's Board of Directors, the company had been pushed to the point of a crisis. They felt that both the pro-Kalanick and pro-Benchmark factions were fighting for short-term personal gains and risking damage for everyone involved, including Uber's employees and shareholders. On August 10, 2017, Graves, Uber's longest running executive, announced that he would be stepping down from his role as SVP of global operations at Uber but would continue to remain on Uber's board.

The search for Kalanick's replacement also left the Uber board deeply divided as they squabbled over the choice of CEO. Meg Whitman,[29] CEO of tech giant Hewlett-Packard, and Jeffrey R. Immelt,[30] former CEO of General Electric, were the front runners for the CEO's post. While Kalanick and his loyalists Huffington and Yasir bin Othman Al-Ruayyan also an Uber board member supported Immelt, Team Benchmark Capital, including Cohler and Graves, favored Whitman. Later, Immelt pulled out from the race allegedly because he did not have the necessary support from Uber's board. Meanwhile, Whitman, a strong contender, started negotiating for conditions including limiting Kalanick's clout and potentially reshaping the Board of Directors were she to accept the job. She showed strong affiliation toward Benchmark Capital that wanted Kalanick's removal.

As a result, some of the Directors who were reportedly put off by Whitman's tactics swung decisively in favor of Khosrowshahi who until then had not even been in the reckoning. They felt that Khosrowshahi was a stronger candidate and came with fewer disadvantages. Finally, on August 29, 2017, Uber's board voted unanimously to appoint Khosrowshahi, an Iranian American who had led Expedia for 12 years, as Uber's new CEO.

And just when the public thought that Uber would not get any worse, in November 2017 the company announced that it had discovered a major data breach as part of a board investigation into its business practices. Uber had concealed a massive cyberattack that took place in October 2016 that affected around 57 million driver and customer accounts whose personal data had been stolen. The company revealed that it had paid the hackers $100,000 to delete the stolen data and prevented the news from going public. The deal was allegedly arranged by the company's chief security officer Joe Sullivan under the watch of Kalanick. Khosrowshahi said he had only learned of the breach after he took over as CEO of Uber in September 2017 and publicly apologized for the hack. *"None of this should have happened, and I will not make excuses for it. While I can't erase the past, I can commit on behalf of every Uber employee that we will learn from our mistakes. We are changing the way we do business, putting integrity at the core of every decision we make and working hard to earn the trust of our customers,"*[31] he said in a company blog post.

THE ROAD AHEAD

Despite a tumultuous 2017, Uber's business continued to grow. In the second quarter of 2017, Uber raked in $8.7 billion in gross bookings, a 17 percent increase from the previous quarter and a 102 percent increase year-over-year.[32] The company also curbed losses. In the second quarter of 2017, adjusted net loss fell almost 9 percent quarter-over-quarter to $645 million compared to $708 million in the first quarter. The company's adjusted net revenue amounted to $1.75 billion, a 17 percent growth compared to the first quarter of 2017. Buoyed by holiday travel, Uber's adjusted losses narrowed to $741 million in the fourth quarter of 2017, compared with $1.02 billion during the third quarter.[33] Meanwhile, gross bookings and net revenue both rose 61 percent year on year, reaching $11.1 billion in bookings and $2.2 billion in net revenues, a record level for the company. Exhibit 9 presents a summary of Uber's financial performance for 2017.

In February 2018, Uber settled its legal dispute over trade secrets against Waymo in a deal that gave Alphabet a 0.34 percent stake in Uber, worth about

EXHIBIT 9   Summary of Uber's Quarterly Financial Performance, 2017

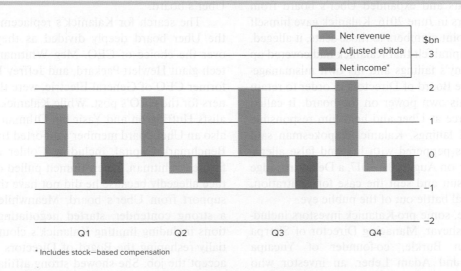

* Includes stock–based compensation

Source: Financial Times reporting; Uber **https://www.ft.com/content/a0f2af96-1117-11e8-940e-08320fc2a277**.

EXHIBIT 10   Uber's Cultural Norms

Under Kalanick	Under Khosrowshahi
1. Customer obsession (Start with what is best for the customer).	1. **We build globally, we live locally.** We harness the power and scale of our global operations to deeply connect with the cities, communities, drivers, and riders that we serve, every day.
2. Make magic (Seek breakthroughs that will stand the test of time.)	2. **We are customer obsessed.** We work tirelessly to earn our customers' trust and business by solving their problems, maximizing their earnings, or lowering their costs. We surprise and delight them. We make short-term sacrifices for a lifetime of loyalty.
3. Big bold bets (Take risks and plant seeds that are five to ten years out.)	
4. Inside out (Find the gap between popular perception and reality.)	
5. Champion's mind-set (Put everything you have on the field to overcome adversity and get Uber over the finish line.)	3. **We celebrate differences.** We stand apart from the average. We ensure people of diverse backgrounds feel welcome. We encourage different opinions and approaches to be heard, and then we come together and build.
6. Optimistic leadership (Be inspiring.)	
7. Superpumped (Ryan Graves's original Twitter proclamation after Kalanick replaced him as CEO; the world is a puzzle to be solved with enthusiasm.)	4. **We do the right thing.** Period.
	5. **We act like owners.** We seek out problems and we solve them. We help each other and those who matter to us. We have a bias for action and accountability. We finish what we start and we build Uber to last. And when we make mistakes, we'll own up to them.
8. Be an owner, not a renter (Revolutions are won by true believers.)	
9. Meritocracy and toe-stepping (The best idea always wins. Don't sacrifice truth for social cohesion and don't hesitate to challenge the boss.)	6. **We persevere.** We believe in the power of grit. We don't seek the easy path. We look for the toughest challenges and we push. Our collective resilience is our secret weapon.
10. Let builders build (People must be empowered to build things.)	
11. Always be hustlin' (Get more done with less, working longer, harder, and smarter, not just two out of three.)	7. **We value ideas over hierarchy.** We believe that the best ideas can come from anywhere, both inside and outside our company. Our job is to seek out those ideas, to shape and improve them through candid debate, and to take them from concept to action.
12. Celebrate cities (Everything we do is to make cities better.)	
13. Be yourself (Each of us should be authentic.)	8. **We make big bold bets.** Sometimes we fail, but failure makes us smarter. We get back up, we make the next bet, and we go!
14. Principled confrontation (Sometimes the world and institutions need to change in order for the future to be ushered in.)	

Source: **https://www.uber.com/en-IN/newsroom/ubers-new-cultural-norms/**.

$245 million. The settlement also included an agreement to ensure that Waymo's confidential information was not incorporated into Uber technology, which Waymo said was its main intent in bringing the lawsuit. As part of his cultural overhaul at Uber, Khosrowshahi introduced eight new cultural norms for Uber, replacing the 14 values first introduced by his predecessor Kalanick, in 2015, as shown in Exhibit 10. Khosrowshahi also made some changes internally, including hiring a new set of executives. In October 2017, he appointed Tony West, a former federal prosecutor, from PepsiCo as Uber's new Chief Legal Officer. Barney Harford, the former CEO of online travel site Orbitz, who has been working as a senior adviser to Khosrowshahi at Uber since October 2017, was named Chief Operating Officer at Uber.

Uber's valuation of nearly $70 billion as shown in Exhibit 11 left some analysts wondering if and when the company would go public. However, some analysts were concerned that all the scandals and internal strife could result in Uber's market value going down. Following the company's scandal-ridden year, four mutual fund companies marked down their investments in Uber by as much as 15 percent for the quarter ended June 30, 2017.[34] However, in January 2018 a group of investors[35] led by SoftBank Group Corp[36] acquired a 17.5 percent stake in Uber, thereby providing the much-needed boost to the

EXHIBIT 11   Uber's Market Valuation

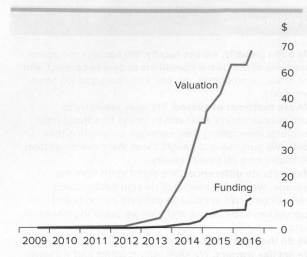

Source: CB Insights.

controversy-ridden company. The deal brokered by Khosrowshahi, included a large purchase of shares from existing Uber investors and employees at a discounted valuation. SoftBank became Uber's largest shareholder with a stake of 15 percent. As part of the terms of the deal, Uber would expand its board from 11 to 17 members including four independent directors and limit voting power of some early shareholders. Benchmark had also agreed to drop its lawsuit against Kalanick upon completion of the deal.

Analysts said that, going forward, Khosrowshahi would have to face some daunting tasks, including prepping Uber for the long-awaited IPO. According to them, another challenge for him would be working with his predecessor. The company still bore the imprint of Kalanick, who remained a major shareholder and a board member of Uber, all of which would give him significant influence over Uber's future. The question, according to some analysts, was whether with Kalanick on the board, Khosrowshahi would be able to make the decisions that he needed to make.[37]

As Uber set out to incorporate the basic tenets of corporate governance, a key task for Khosrowshahi would be dealing with an uptight board whose divisions and rivalries had reached epic proportions and ending the bitter war among the Board of Directors. Some key challenges before Khosrowshahi were: fixing Uber's culture and helping evolve some of its own core cultural practices to foster growth and improve stakeholder relationships; working with a splintered board and ushering in corporate governance reforms; and regaining the confidence of its investors, employees, and customers. Sanket Vijayasarathy, a tech journalist, *"[G]iven the timing of his entry, Khosrowshahi had a lot of fires to douse, which by no means is an easy task. The silver lining to this was that despite the events of the past year, Uber financial situation was still good. The company is still in a good position today, and the recent cyber-attack may hurt the company further, but not so much as to cause a collapse. This still gives time for Khosrowshahi to turn the company around."*[38]

ENDNOTES

[1] Kara Swisher, "'I Have to Tell You I Am Scared': Dara Khosrowshahi Says in a Memo to Expedia's Staff That He Has Finally Been Hired at Uber," August 29, 2017, **www.recode.net**.
[2] One of the world's leading online travel companies.
[3] "The Uber Episode: Is Monoculturalism the Real Problem?" June 30, 2017, **www.livemint.com**.
[4] A US-based venture capital firm responsible for the early stage funding of successful startups including Dropbox, Twitter, Uber, Snapchat, and Instagram.
[5] Carolyn Said, "History of Uber's CEO Pick Praised," August 29, 2017, **www.pressreader.com**.
[6] An innovative program in which law students provide legal work for early stage Tech and BioTech startups.

[7] Seth Fiegerman, "Uber CEO Says Company Plans to Go Public in 2019," November 9, 2017, **http://money.cnn.com**.
[8] Kalanick was a college dropout whose first business venture went bankrupt. He sold his second start-up Red Swoosh, a content-delivery company to Akamai Technologies for $20 million.
[9] Camp was an entrepreneur who had sold his company StumbleUpon, a Web discovery engine, to eBay for $75 million in 2007.
[10] **https://uberestimator.com/cities**.
[11] Davey Alba, "Even Uber's Crisis Won't Kill Founder Worship in Tech," June 13, 2017, **www.wired.com**.
[12] Julia Carrie Wong, "Uber's 'Hustle-Oriented' Culture Becomes a Black Mark on Employees' Résumés," March 7, 2017, **www.theguardian.com**.

[13] On January 27, 2017, Trump signed an executive order for a temporary ban on refugees and a suspension of visas for citizens of seven Muslim-majority countries.
[14] Leslie Hook and Hannah Kuchler, "Uber's Turmoil Compounded by David Bonderman's Sexist Quip," June 14, 2017, **www.ft.com**.
[15] Danica Kirka, "Uber to Investigate Sexual Harassment Claim by Engineer," February 20, 2017, **www.chicagotribune.com**.
[16] The investigation team conducted over 200 interviews with current and former employees of Uber who shared a broad range of perspectives. Covington interviewed individuals with knowledge of Fowler's allegations, employees who reported workplace environment-related complaints, employee representatives of Uber's diversity groups, and present and former members of the Senior Executive Team.

[17] Mitch & Freada Kapor, "An Open Letter to The Uber Board and Investors," https://medium.com, February 24, 2017.

[18] As the board was discussing the addition of a new female board member, Huffington said that the presence of one woman on the board would eventually lead to more. To this, Bonderman retorted "actually what it shows is that it's much more likely to be more talking." After the meeting, Bonderman apologized and later announced his resignation from the board.

[19] Richard Mahony, "Uber's Shareholder Revolt," June 14, 2017, www.mahonypartners.com.

[20] Ainsley Harris, "Uber's Ousted CEO Travis Kalanick Discovered the Limits of Founder Control—The Hard Way," June 21, 2017, www.fastcompany.com.

[21] Sam Byford, "Travis Kalanick Resigns as Uber CEO," June 21, 2017, www.theverge.com.

[22] Jean-Louis Gassée, "Travis Kalanick's Bosses Share Just as Much Blame for the Uber Calamity," June 28, 2017, https://qz.com.

[23] Davey Alba, "Even Uber's Crisis Won't Kill Founder Worship in Tech," June 13, 2017, www.wired.com.

[24] San Francisco-based venture capital firm.

[25] An American private equity firm.

[26] A U.S.-based music company.

[27] Heather Somerville, "Uber Investors Seek to Oust Benchmark After 'Destructive' Lawsuit—Report," August 11, 2017, www.cnbc.com.

[28] Ibid.

[29] Meg Whitman, a tech veteran, is one of the most respected corporate executives in the world having led companies like eBay.

[30] Jeffrey R. Immelt was the chairman of GE from 2001 until August 1, 2017.

[31] Mike Isaac, Katie Benner, and Sheera Frenkel, "Uber Hid 2016 Breach, Paying Hackers to Delete Stolen Data," November 21, 2017, www.nytimes.com.

[32] Johana Bhuiyan, "Uber is Curbing its Losses and Growing its Business While it Searches for a New CEO," August 23, 2017, www.recode.net.

[33] Leslie Hook, "Uber Pares Quarterly Losses and Lifts Revenues," February 14, 2018, www.ft.com.

[34] Trevor Hunnicutt, "Unhappy Uber Investors Mark Down Value of the Scandal-Ridden Ride-Sharing Company," August 23, 2017, www.independent.co.uk.

[35] The investor group led by SoftBank includes Dragoneer Investment Group and Sequoia Capital.

[36] SoftBank Group Corp. is a Japanese multinational conglomerate that together with its subsidiaries provides information technology and telecommunication services.

[37] Marisa Kendall, "Uber's Ex-CEO Isn't Really Leaving. Can the Company Change Anyway?" June 28, 2017, www.santacruzsentinel.com.

[38] Sanket Vijayasarathy, "Uber Hacking Scandal Proves Ghost of Ousted Travis Kalanick Still Haunts The Ride-Hailing Company," November 23, 2017, www.indiatoday.in.

Profiting from Pain: Business and the U.S. Opioid Epidemic

Anne T. Lawrence

San Jose State University

In 2017, McKesson Corporation, a leading wholesale drug distributor, agreed to pay $150 million in fines to the U.S. Department of Justice. The charges were that the company had failed to implement effective controls to prevent the diversion of prescription opioids for nonlegitimate uses, in violation of the Controlled Substances Act.[1] For example, McKesson had supplied pharmacies in Mingo County, West Virginia—a poor, rural county with the fourth-highest death rate from opioid overdoses in the nation—with 3.3 million more hydrocodone pills in one year than it had in five consecutive earlier years.[2] At the time, Mingo County had just 25,000 residents. Yet, the company had not flagged these orders to federal drug enforcement officials as out-of-the-ordinary.

McKesson, which at the time was the fifth largest company in the United States—with almost $200 billion in annual revenue—played a largely unnoticed middleman role in the pharmaceutical industry. The firm's main business was shipping legal, government-approved medicines to pharmacies, hospitals, and health systems. McKesson's unmarked trucks rolled out at midnight from its 28 enormous, highly automated distribution centers, on route to their morning deliveries of one-third of all pharmaceuticals sold in North America. Although distributors like McKesson did not either manufacture or dispense opioids, they were responsible for notifying the federal Drug Enforcement Administration (DEA) and corresponding state regulators if orders suggested that controlled substances were being improperly diverted.[3]

McKesson and other drug distributors were not the only businesses implicated in the nation's burgeoning epidemic of addictive opioids. Drug companies—such as Purdue Pharma, the maker of OxyContin—had developed new prescription opioids and aggressively marketed them to doctors and patients, making vast profits for their owners. Entrepreneurs had opened pain clinics where unscrupulous doctors could write big scripts for the addictive pills, and pharmacies had looked the other way while dispensing drugs to suspicious patients. And illegal businesses, from producers of street drugs like heroin to networks of dealers, had also played their parts. What responsibility did these businesses bear for the tragedy of opioid addiction, disability, and death?

THE OPIOID EPIDEMIC

At the time of the McKesson's settlement with the Justice Department, the United States was deep in the throes of what the Centers for Disease Control and Prevention (CDC) had called "the worst drug overdose epidemic in [U.S.] history."[4]

Fueling the epidemic was addiction to prescription opioids. Opioids were a class of painkillers derived from the opium poppy. Also referred to as narcotics, opioids included legal prescription medications such as morphine, codeine, hydrocodone, oxycodone, and fentanyl, as well as illegal drugs such as heroin. Opioids worked by dulling the sensation of pain. At high doses, they could also cause feelings of intense euphoria. The journalist John Temple, author of the investigative report *American Pain,* described the "high" experienced by users of oxycodone, a strong opioid, this way:

> To understand oxycodone, imagine everything that makes a man or woman feel good, all the preoccupations and pastimes we are programmed to enjoy. Sex, love, food. Money, power, health. Synthesize all of that pleasure-seeking potency, and multiply by ten. Then cram it all into a pebble-sized blue pill. That's oxycodone—one of the most irresistible opioid narcotics ever cooked up in the six-thousand-year old history of dope.[5]

Opioids were highly addictive, and as users developed tolerance, they required larger and larger doses to get high or just to feel normal. Withdrawal from opioids, which could occur after even a single dose, could be excruciating. Users in withdrawal often experienced intense cravings, fever, sweats, and pain—sensations that addicts referred to as "jonesing." Addiction caused physical changes in the brain, weakening a user's impulse control and making it almost impossible to quit without medical assistance.[6]

Opioids were killers. In high doses, these drugs caused breathing to slow and finally stop, bringing death by respiratory arrest. In 2015, 33,091 Americans died from an opioid overdose.[7] This was just slightly less than the number that died that year in car accidents. Between 1999 and 2015, the rate of death from opioid overdose (number of deaths per 100,000 people) quintupled, that is, it was *five times* higher in 2015 than it was a decade and a half earlier.[8]

Deaths from opioid overdose cut across all geographical regions and demographic groups, but some places and people were harder hit than others. Government data showed that although drug overdose deaths grew for all groups, those in mid-life (aged 45 to54) had the highest rates. Rates were higher for non-Hispanic whites than for other ethnic groups. The states with the worst opioid problems were West Virginia, New Hampshire, Kentucky, and Ohio, with Rhode Island, Pennsylvania, Massachusetts, and New Mexico not far behind.[9] Opioid use was higher where the economy was bad; as unemployment rates rose, so did overdose deaths.[10] Some researchers called these drug overdoses a "death of despair," part of a broader pattern of rising mortality among middle-aged whites in the United States. "Ultimately, we see our story as about the collapse of the white, high-school educated working class after its heyday in the early 1970s, and the pathologies that accompany that decline," these researchers wrote.[11]

Many opioid overdoses occurred in private, but a startling number occurred in full view of the community. As Margaret Talbot reported in *The New Yorker,* "At this stage of the American opioid epidemic, many addicts are collapsing in public—in gas stations, in restaurant bathrooms, in the aisles of big box stores." She related this story about the experience of two small-town paramedics, who responded to an emergency call from a softball field:

> It was the first practice of the season for the girls' Little League team, and dusk was descending. [The paramedics] . . .stopped near a scrubby set of bleachers, where parents had gathered to watch their daughters bat and field. Two of the parents were lying on the ground, unconscious, several yards apart. As [one of the paramedics] later recalled, the couple's thirteen-year-old daughter was sitting behind a chain-link backstop with her teammates, who were hugging her and comforting her. The couple's younger children, aged ten and seven, were running back and forth between their parents screaming, "Wake up! Wake up!"

The parents survived after the paramedics administered a drug called naloxone, but were later arrested on charges of child neglect.[12]

The pain inflicted by the opioid epidemic went well beyond overdose deaths. People who were addicted to opioids stole from their neighbors to support their habit, ignored their work and family responsibilities, and strained public welfare and law enforcement systems. Some were incarcerated, filling the jails. They made more visits to hospital emergency rooms and drove up health care costs. Babies born to addicted mothers often suffered from neonatal abstinence syndrome, going through painful withdrawal after birth.[13] Grandparents, other relatives, and foster parents were raising the children of addicted parents.

The costs to local governments were often crushing. Ross County, Ohio, for example, saw its child services budget almost double from $1.3 million to $2.4 million from 2009 to 2016. "This has introduced an entirely different metric, an entirely different unpredictability in budgeting," said the top official of Indiana County, Pennsylvania, which had drawn on contingency funds to cover extra costs associated with the opioid crisis.[14]

Some research showed that opioid abuse had hurt the economy by keeping people out of the workforce. A survey of men between the ages of 25 and

54 who were not working or looking for work found that almost half had taken pain medication the previous day, and two-thirds of these had taken a prescription pain medication.[15] Of course, these men may have been out of the work force because they were ill or injured, not because they were hooked on opioids. But anecdotal evidence was suggestive. The owner of an auto parts supplier in Michigan, for example, reported that she had great difficulty filling jobs at her factory. Part of the problem: when she sent new hires for a routine drug test, 60 percent failed to show up.[16]

PURDUE PHARMA AND THE RISE OF OXYCONTIN

Many observers traced the modern opioid epidemic to the introduction, in 1996, of a new prescription medication called OxyContin.[17] The company that developed it was Purdue Pharma, a privately-held drug maker based in Connecticut.[18] In 1952, three brothers, Andrew, Raymond, and Mortimer Sackler—all physicians—had purchased Purdue Frederick, a small pharmaceutical firm whose main products at that time were earwax removers and laxatives. The company later introduced MS Contin, an extended-release form of morphine used mainly by cancer patients. As the patent for this drug approached expiration, Purdue turned to development of an extended-release form of another opioid, oxycodone, which had long been available as a generic. The firm spent around $40 million to develop and test its new drug, which it named OxyContin. In late 1995, the Food and Drug Administration (FDA) approved the 80-mg. dose of the drug (it later approved other doses).

Purdue's introduction of OxyContin coincided with changing attitudes in the medical community toward pain management. For many years, opioids were generally used only for end-stage cancer patients or those suffering from acute traumatic injuries or short-term post-surgical pain. Because of the risk of addiction, opioids were not considered appropriate for the treatment of chronic pain, and they were often mixed with other medicines like acetaminophen to discourage patients from taking larger amounts. In the 1980s, however, some physicians began to advocate for treating chronic pain more aggressively, saying that many patients with conditions like arthritis, back injuries, migraines, and fibromyalgia were

suffering needlessly. Some campaigned to have pain recognized as the "fifth vital sign" (the other four were body temperature, pulse rate, respiration rate, and blood pressure). Because clinicians could not measure pain objectively, some adopted a 1-to-10 scale, from "no pain" to "the worst pain" the patient had ever experienced.[19]

Purdue allied itself with this view, cultivating relationships with professional associations, such as the American Pain Society and the American Academy of Pain Medicine, which promoted the idea that pain was undertreated. It sponsored pain-management educational conferences in resort locations for doctors. The company also hired more sales representatives, more than doubling its sales force from 318 to 767 between 1996 and 2000. Purdue sales reps were well compensated, earning an average of $126,500 a year, including bonuses based on sales. In 2001 alone, the company paid $40 million in bonuses. The company's detailers, as its sales representatives were known, used prescriber profiles to target general practitioners and those who were frequent prescribers of opioids. They handed out coupons for a 30-day free supply of OxyContin to doctors, who could pass them along to patients.

Purdue's sales representatives downplayed OxyContin's potential for addiction, claiming the risk was less than one percent. This dubious assertion was based on a five-sentence letter to the editor that had appeared in a 1980 issue of the *New England Journal of Medicine*, based on records of hospitalized patients in controlled settings. Sales representatives also argued that OxyContin's extended-release formula made it less susceptible to abuse; although the pill contained a large dose of oxycodone, users would not get a sudden rush because the drug's effects would be spread out over a 12-hour period, they told doctors.

Despite the company's claims that OxyContin's extended-release mechanism made it hard to abuse, addicts quickly discovered that they could crush one of the pills and then swallow, inhale, or inject it to produce an intense high. As the number of prescriptions for opioid medications rose, so did overdose deaths. Exhibit 1 shows the quantity of opioids prescribed from 1999 to 2016, alongside the number of deaths from prescription opioid overdose. (The exhibit reports all opioids prescribed, not just OxyContin.)

As a private company, Purdue had no obligation to file annual reports, and its owners and managers rarely spoke publicly. But the company's senior

EXHIBIT 1 Overdose Deaths from Prescription Opioids (per 100,000) and Opioid Prescriptions (Morphine Milligram Equivalents per 100), United States, 1999–2016

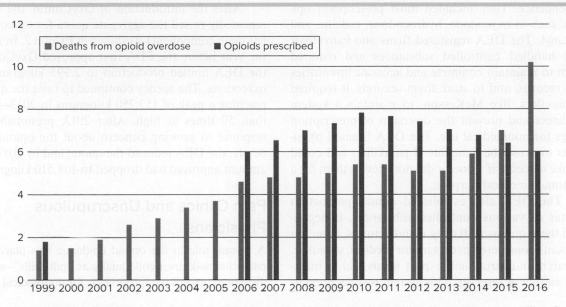

Sources: "Prescription Opioid Overdose Death Rate per 100,000 Population," The Henry J. Kaiser Family Foundation, at *www.kff.org;* Centers for Disease Control and Prevention, Annual Surveillance Report of Drug-Related Risks and Outcomes, United States, 2017, Table 1B; Gery P. Guy, Jr. et al., "Vital Signs: Changes in Opioid Prescribing in the United States, 2006–2015," *Centers for Disease Control and Prevention Weekly,* July 7, 2017, and personal correspondence with Dr. Guy. Deaths from legal and illegal fentanyl cannot be distinguished, so both are included in the KFF data base. Data on prescriptions in MMEs for 2000 to 2005 are unavailable, but data on opioid pain reliever sales in kilograms per 10,000 show a steady rise during this period ("Vital Signs: Overdoses of Prescription Opioid Pain Relievers, United States, 1999–2008," *Centers for Disease Control and Prevention Morbidity and Mortality Weekly Report,* November 4, 2011).

medical director did tell a reporter in 2001, as awareness of OxyContin's risks began to spread in the public health community: "A lot of these people [addicts] say, 'Well, I was taking the medicine like my doctor told me to,' and then they start taking more and more and more. I don't see where that's my problem."[20]

Purdue Pharma's marketing campaign for OxyContin was highly effective. In 1996, the company's revenue from OxyContin was $44 million; it continued to rise, peaking at $3.1 billion in 2010. That year, it represented 90 percent of the company's total sales. The private firm's owners profited greatly from the drug's success. In 2015, *Forbes* estimated the Sackler family's net worth at around $14 billion, the 16th largest fortune in the United States.[21]

In 2007, the company settled charges brought by the U.S. Justice Department that it had lied about OxyContin's addiction risks, operating "a corporate culture that allowed this product to be misbranded with the intent to defraud and mislead." The company paid

$600 million in fines—$470 million to federal and state governments and $130 million to resolve civil suits. Its top three executives personally paid $34.5 million in fines and were barred from involvement in any government health care program for 12 years.[22]

Government Regulation of Opioids

The federal government strictly regulated the manufacture and distribution of opioid medications like OxyContin under the Controlled Substances Act (CSA) of 1970.

The CSA empowered the Drug Enforcement Administration (DEA) and the FDA to create five lists, or "schedules," of certain controlled substances, ranging from one (Schedule I) to five (Schedule V). Schedule I drugs were those that had no accepted medical use and high potential for abuse; they included heroin, LSD, and MDMA ("Ecstasy"). These drugs were illegal, and physicians could not prescribe them under any circumstances. Schedule II drugs were those that *did* have an accepted medical use, but also had high potential for abuse and could lead to severe psychological and physical dependence. They included most prescription opiates, such as oxycodone, hydrocodone, codeine, and fentanyl. The DEA registered firms and individuals that handled controlled substances and required them to maintain complete and accurate inventories and records, and to store them securely. It required wholesalers, like McKesson, to maintain a system to detect and prevent the diversion of prescription drugs for nonmedical use. The DEA licensed physicians to prescribe Schedule II painkillers and could revoke a license if a doctor did not provide them for a legitimate medical purpose.

The DEA also established annual production quotas of various controlled substances. It negotiated these quotas with drug manufacturers, based on amounts considered necessary for medical, scientific, research, industrial, and export needs and to maintain sufficient reserves. This system was designed to

meet legitimate needs, while preventing diversion. Although each company received its own quota, this information was proprietary, and the DEA published only the aggregate annual quota for each drug.

After the introduction of OxyContin, the DEA repeatedly raised the aggregate quota for oxycodone (its main component), as shown in Exhibit 2. In 1994, the year before the FDA first approved OxyContin, the DEA limited production to 2,995 kilograms of oxycodone. The agency continued to raise the quota, reaching a peak of 153,750 kilograms in 2013—more than 50 times as high. After 2013, presumably in response to growing concern about the opioid epidemic, the DEA reduced the quota, and by 2017, the amount approved had dropped to 108,510 kilograms.

Pain Clinics and Unscrupulous Physicians

A pivotal role in the opioid epidemic was played by pain clinics—known colloquially as "pill mills"—which dispensed opioids inappropriately for nonmedical uses.

EXHIBIT 2   Drug Enforcement Agency Aggregate Production Quotas for Oxycodone (for Sale) By Year, in Kilograms, 1994–2017

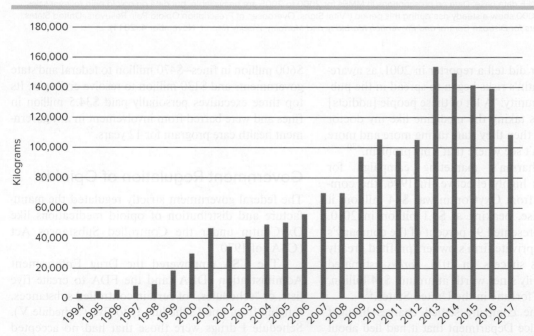

Sources: Federal Register, 1994–1997; U.S. Department of Justice, Drug Enforcement Agency, Diversion Control Division, "Controlled Substances: Final Aggregate Production Quotas," 1998–2006, and "Aggregate Production Quota History for Selected Substances," 2007–2017. This chart includes only oxycodone intended for sale. The DEA maintains a separate quota for oxycodone intended for other uses, such as manufacturing other substances.

Although pill mills sprouted up in many locations in the mid- to late-2000s, the epicenter of the trend was Broward County, Florida, home to Fort Lauderdale.

One of the most notorious was American Pain, which became for a time the largest dispenser of oxycodone in the nation.[23] American Pain was founded in 2008 by a young felon—he had done a short stint in jail for possession of steroids—who had neither a college degree nor any medical training. His business concept was to open a clinic dedicated exclusively to prescribing legal opioids. He hired physicians by running ads on *Craigslist* for doctors with a license to prescribe painkillers. He offered them $75 per patient visit plus $1,000 a week for the use of their license, which enabled the clinic to order and sell prescription medications. The physicians who took the job included retired doctors who wanted to earn more money, young doctors with high student loan debt, and graduates of marginal medical schools who had trouble finding other work. The owner hired his best friend, a beefy former construction worker, to oversee the operation, which journalist John Temple described this way:

> Outside, it looked like a bustling doctor's office, or the DMV. Inside, [a] crew of heavily inked muscle-heads and ex-strippers operated the office and pharmacy, counting out pills and stashing cash in garbage cans. Under their white lab coats, the doctors carried guns.[24]

As business boomed, the clinic moved four times, each time to a larger location with more parking. At its peak, American Pain employed five full-time and several part-time doctors and a staff of about 20. It was raking in $100,000 a day—in cash. In 2009, the young owner's take-home pay was an astonishing $9 million.

Almost 9 out of 10 of America Pain's customers came from out of state, many from the rural counties of Kentucky and Tennessee, which by this time were in the grip of widespread opioid addiction. Patients could see a doctor with no appointment, get a prescription with few questions asked, and then get the script filled in-house. Entrepreneurial "sponsors" drove large groups of people to South Florida, giving them cash for their doctor's visit and prescription and then accepting as compensation a share of their pills, which could be sold back home on the black market. Interstate 75, the main highway connecting Florida to points north in Georgia and Tennessee, became known as "Oxy Alley" or the "blue highway,"

after the blue 30-mg oxycodone pills manufactured by the drug maker Mallinckrodt.

No one knew exactly how many deaths resulted from American Pain's practices. But drug enforcement officials later estimated that the clinic had prescribed almost 20 million opioids over a two-year period. More than 50 people who died of drug overdoses in Florida had been patients at American Pain. An uncounted number of the clinic's patients must have died in Georgia, Kentucky, Tennessee, Ohio, and other states.

Several factors allowed pill mills such as American Pain to flourish in Florida in the late 2000s. Unlike most other states, Florida did not operate a database that tracked opioid prescriptions, so users could obtain multiple prescriptions without detection. The state did not require pain clinics to obtain a license, or clinic owners to have any specialized training or expertise. And, crucially, it allowed doctors to both prescribe and sell medication. This meant that pill mill patrons could both obtain a prescription, and have it filled in one visit—eliminating the chance that a scrupulous pharmacy would turn them down.

In 2010, federal, state, and local law enforcement officials finally shut down American Pain and prosecuted its owner, manager, and several of its doctors, sending several to prison. The same year, Florida barred convicted felons from operating pain clinics and required pain clinic doctors to have special training. The following year it established a drug database. Other states with concentrations of pill mills made similar moves around this time.

The Crackdown and Turn to Illegal Opioids

Around 2010, several factors converged to slow the diversion of prescription opioids into the hands of abusers. In addition to the crackdown on pill mills, government agencies, medical institutions, and companies all began changing their policies and practices. In 2010, Purdue changed the formulation of OxyContin, so it could not be crushed or dissolved, and it lobbied the government to require hard-to-abuse formulations of opioids. The Centers for Disease Control issued new guidelines on prescription of opioids, as did the Veteran's Administration. States and insurers placed limits on how many pills doctors could prescribe. These moves had their intended effect: data (reported in Exhibit 1) showed that the number of opioid painkillers prescribed peaked in 2010.[25]

As the flow of prescription pills slowed, addicts increasingly turned to illegal street drugs—heroin, fentanyl from criminal sources, and even a powerful animal tranquilizer called carfentanil. A study of patients undergoing treatment for heroin addiction, published in 2014, found that of those who had started using drugs in the 2000s, three-quarters had first used prescription opioids, and had then switched to heroin because it was cheaper and easier to get.[26] "People eventually say, 'Why am I paying $1 per milligram for oxy when for a tenth of the price I can get an equivalent dose of heroin?'" commented one physician at a drug recovery center.[27]

As they made the shift from prescription pills, many addicts turned to so-called black tar heroin, delivered by what *The Washington Post* called a "sophisticated farm-to-arm supply chain fueling America's surging heroin appetite."[28] Relatively inexpensive, with the consistency of a Tootsie roll, black tar heroin was made from poppies grown on the Pacific coast of Mexico. Mexican poppy production rose 160 percent from 2013 to 2015.[29]

According to research by journalist Sam Quinones, most of the black-tar dealers hailed from the area around Xalisco in the state of Nayarit, Mexico. The "Xalisco Boys," as some law enforcement officers called them, devised a highly effective method of distribution. Managers recruited ambitious young men with few prospects at home and sent them north across the border. The Xalisco Boys avoided big coastal cities, where established gangs controlled the heroin trade, and instead targeted midsized communities in the heartland where couriers could blend into the local Latino population—places like Nashville, Columbus, Salt Lake City, Portland, and Denver. The couriers were trained to use rental cars, which could not be seized by authorities, and disposable mobile phones. They did not carry weapons, and they never used the product. The couriers worked on salary and sent most of their earnings to their families in Mexico. If one was arrested, he would be deported, and another would take his place.[30]

Quinones described the operations of the Xalisco Boys this way:

> An addict calls, and an operator directs him to an intersection or parking lot. The operator dispatches a driver,

who tools around town, his mouth full of tiny balloons of heroin, with a bottle of water nearby to swig down if the cops stop him. . . The driver meets the addict, spits out the required balloons, takes the money and that's that. It happens every day – from 7 a.m. to 7 p.m., because these guys keep business hours.[31]

A study by the Congressional Research Service found that in 2014, 914,000 Americans had used heroin in the past year.[32] Tragically, many of them died: heroin-related overdose deaths more than doubled between 2009 and 2014.

A Flood of Lawsuits

As the opioid crisis raged, states, counties, cities and towns, and Indian tribes began bringing lawsuits against various business firms to recoup some of the escalating costs of law enforcement, health care, and child protective services. By 2017, at least 25 government entities had sued the drug companies, distributors, and pharmacy chains that had some hand in the journey of the pain pill from the factory into the addict's hands. These lawsuits relied on a range of legal theories; they variously cited laws related to public nuisance, consumer protection, negligence, and unjust enrichment.

To cite just a few examples:

- McDowell County, West Virginia, sued the three big drug distributors—McKesson, AmerisourceBergen, and Cardinal Health. "In my thinking, they [the distributors] were no different than drug dealers selling on the street," the county sheriff said.[33]
- The state of Ohio sued half-a-dozen drug makers—Purdue Pharma, Teva, Johnson & Johnson, Janssen, Endo, and Allergan—charging them with making false and misleading statements about the risks and benefits of prescription opioids. The state's legal brief stated that these drug companies had "helped unleash a healthcare crisis that has had far-reaching financial, social, and deadly consequences in the state of Ohio."[34]
- The city of Everett, Washington, sued Purdue Pharma for recklessly supplying OxyContin to suspicious physicians and pharmacies in their community, enabling illegal drug diversion and providing a "gateway" to heroin abuse.[35]
- The Cherokee Nation in Oklahoma sued distributors and pharmacies—including Walmart, CVS,

and Walgreens—and called for them to reimburse the Cherokees for health care costs. "The resources of the Cherokee Nation are being spent on this crisis that otherwise should be spent on our ordinary, everyday health care needs," said the Cherokee Nation's attorney general.[36]

Some legal experts thought these lawsuits had little chance of success. Prescription opioids had a legitimate medical purpose and had been approved by the government. One expert in product liability law put it this way: "[The distributors] ship a drug that's approved by the FDA, and then a bunch of bad actors intervene—pill mills, doctors who overprescribe, and the addicts themselves. It's a pretty strong argument." Other legal experts, however, thought the companies were in a weaker position. "[The pharmaceutical firms] are big companies that knew their product was doing harm," said an attorney who had been involved in the tobacco lawsuits years earlier. "Instead of helping to solve the problem, they promoted the irresponsible use of their product to improve their bottom line." Added the attorney who represented the Cherokee Nation: "These pharmaceutical companies should be scared as hell."[37]

ENDNOTES

[1] U.S. Department of Justice, "McKesson Agrees to Pay Record $150 Million Settlement for Failure to Report Suspicious Orders of Pharmaceutical Drugs," press release, January 17, 2017.

[2] "Drug Firms Poured 780 Million Painkillers into WV Amid Rise of Overdoses," *Charleston Gazette-Mail,* December 17, 2016.

[3] "As America's Opioid Crisis Spirals, Giant Drug Distributor McKesson is Feeling the Pain," *Fortune,* June 12, 2017.

[4] Quoted in Andrew Kolodny et al., "The Prescription Opioid and Heroin Crisis: A Public Health Approach to an Epidemic of Addiction," *Annual Review of Public Health,* January 2015, p. 58.

[5] John Temple, *American Pain: How A Young Felon and His Ring of Doctors Unleashed America's Deadliest Drug Epidemic* (Rowman & Littlefield: Guilford, CT, 2015), p. xi.

[6] Information about opioids and their risks is available from the National Institute of Drug Abuse, **www.drugabuse.gov**.

[7] Rose A. Rudd et al., "Increases in Drug and Opioid-Involved Overdose Deaths—United States, 2010–2015," Morbidity and Mortality Weekly Report, 65(50&51), December 30, 2016. This figure is for drug overdoses due to opioids only; 52,404 Americans died in 2015 from overdoses of all kinds of drugs combined.

[8] Data from the Kaiser Family Foundation, shown in Exhibit 1.

[9] Holly Hedegaard et al., "Drug Overdose Deaths in the United States, 1999–2015," Centers for Disease Control and Prevention, NCHS Data Brief No. 273, February 2017.

[10] "Are Opioid Deaths Affected by Macroeconomic Conditions?" *NBER [National Bureau of Economic Research] Bulletin on Aging and Health,* 2017 #3.

[11] "New Research Identified a 'Sea of Despair' Among White, Working-Class Americans," *The Washington Post,* March 23, 2017. The research cited is Anne Case and Angus Deaton, "Mortality and Morbidity in the 21st Century," *Brookings Papers on Economic Activity,* Spring 2017.

[12] "The Addicts Next Door," *The New Yorker,* June 5 & 12, 2017.

[13] "Study: Rural Areas See Increase in Babies Born with Opioid Addiction," *USA Today,* December 14, 2016.

[14] "How the Opioid Crisis is Blowing a Hole in the Finances of Small-Town America," *The Epoch Times,* September 21–27, 2017.

[15] Alan B. Krueger, "Where Have All the Workers Gone?" Paper prepared for the Boston Federal Reserve Bank's 60th Economic Conference, October 4, 2016.

[16] "Eager to Create Blue-Collar Jobs, a Small Business Struggles," *The New York Times,* September 3, 2017.

[17] This account of Purdue's development and marketing of OxyContin is based on Barry Meier, *Pain Killer: A 'Wonder' Drug's Trail of Addiction and Death* (Rodale Press, 2003); Art Van Zee MD, "The Promotion and Marketing of OxyContin: Commercial Triumph, Public Health Tragedy," *American Journal of Public Health,* 99(2), February 2009; Mike Mariani, "Poison Pill: How the American Opiate Epidemic was Started by One Pharmaceutical Company," *Pacific Standard,* February 23, 2015; and "The Family that Built an Empire of Pain," *The New Yorker,* October 30, 2017.

[18] Purdue Pharma had no relationship with Purdue University, although they shared a name.

[19] Kolodny et al., op. cit.

[20] Quoted in "You Want a Description of Hell? OxyContin's 12-Hour Problem," *The Los Angeles Times,* May 5, 2016.

[21] "The OxyContin Clan: The Newcomer to Forbes 200 Families," *Forbes,* July 1, 2015.

[22] "U.S. Maker of OxyContin Painkiller to Pay $600 Million in Guilty Plea," *The New York Times,* May 11, 2007; "Ruling Is Upheld Against Executives Tied to OxyContin," *The New York Times,* December 15, 2010.

[23] This description of American Pain is based on John Temple, *American Pain: How A Young Felon and His Ring of Doctors Unleashed America's Deadliest Drug Epidemic* (Rowman & Littlefield: Guilford, CT, 2015).

[24] This description of American Pain is based on John Temple, *American Pain: How A Young Felon and His Ring of Doctors Unleashed America's Deadliest Drug Epidemic* (Rowman & Littlefield: Guilford, CT, 2015)., p. xiii.

[25] "Opioid Prescriptions Fall After 2010 Peak," CDC Report Finds," *New York Times,* July 6, 2017.

[26] Theodore J. Cicero et al., "The Changing Face of Heroin Use in the United States," *JAMA Psychiatry,* 71(7), 2014.

[27] "Prescription Painkillers Seen as a Gateway to Heroin," *The New York Times,* February 10, 2014.

[28] "Pellets, Planes, and the New Frontier: How Mexican Drug Cartels are Targeting Small-Town America," *The Washington Post,* September 24, 2015.

[29] "Heroin Trafficking in the United States," op. cit.

[30] "Heroin Is a White-People Problem: Bad Medicine, Economic Rot, and the Enterprising Mexican Town that Turned the Heartland onto Black Tar," *Salon,* April 18, 2015.

[31] "Serving All Your Heroin Needs," *The New York Times,* April 17, 2015. See also Sam Quinones, *Dreamland: The True Story*

of America's Opiate Epidemic (New York: Bloomsbury Press, 2015).

[32] "Heroin Trafficking in the United States," *Congressional Research Service,* August 23, 2016.

[33] "As America's Opioid Crisis Spirals, Giant Drug Distributor McKesson Is Feeling the Pain," op. cit.

[34] Ohio's legal brief is available at *www .ohioattorneygeneral.gov/Files/Briefing-Room/ News-Releases/Consumer-Protection/ 2017-05-31-Final-Complaint-with-Sig-Page. aspx.*

[35] "City of Everett v. Purdue Pharma," January 19, 2017, complaint filed in the Superior Court of the State of Washington.

[36] "Inside Cherokee Lawsuit to Fight Opioid Epidemic," *Rolling Stone,* May 26, 2017, and "Cherokee Nation Sues Wal-Mart, CVS, Walgreens Over Tribal Opioid Crisis," *NPR Now,* April 25, 2017.

[37] "Drugmakers and Distributors Face Barrage of Lawsuits Over Opioid Epidemic," *The Washington Post,* July 4, 2017.

Guide to Case Analysis

I keep six honest serving men
(They taught me all I knew);
Their names are What and Why and When;
And How and Where and Who.

Rudyard Kipling

In most courses in strategic management, students use cases about actual companies to practice strategic analysis and to gain some experience in the tasks of crafting and implementing strategy. A case sets forth, in a factual manner, the events and organizational circumstances surrounding a particular managerial situation. It puts readers at the scene of the action and familiarizes them with all the relevant circumstances. A case on strategic management can concern a whole industry, a single organization, or some part of an organization; the organization involved can be either profit seeking or not-for-profit. The essence of the student's role in case analysis is to diagnose and size up the situation described in the case and then to recommend appropriate action steps.

WHY USE CASES TO PRACTICE STRATEGIC MANAGEMENT?

> A student of business with tact
> Absorbed many answers he lacked.
> But acquiring a job,
> He said with a sob,
> "How does one fit answer to fact?"

The foregoing limerick was used some years ago by Professor Charles Gragg to characterize the plight of business students who had no exposure to cases.[1] The facts are that the mere act of listening to lectures and sound advice about managing does little for anyone's management skills and that the accumulated managerial wisdom cannot effectively be passed on by lectures and assigned readings alone. If anything had been learned about the practice of management, it is that a storehouse of ready-made textbook answers does not exist. Each managerial situation has unique aspects, requiring its own diagnosis, judgment, and tailor-made actions. Cases provide would-be managers with a valuable way to practice wrestling with the actual problems of actual managers in actual companies.

The case approach to strategic analysis is, first and foremost, an exercise in learning by doing. Because cases provide you with detailed information about conditions and problems of different industries and companies, your task of analyzing company after company and situation after situation has the twin benefit of boosting your analytical skills and exposing you to the ways companies and managers actually do things. Most college students have limited managerial backgrounds and only fragmented knowledge about companies and real-life strategic situations. Cases help substitute for on-the-job experience by (1) giving you broader exposure to a variety of industries, organizations, and strategic problems; (2) forcing you to assume a managerial role (as opposed to that of just an onlooker); (3) providing a test of how to apply the tools and techniques of strategic management; and (4) asking you to come up with pragmatic managerial action plans to deal with the issues at hand.

Objectives of Case Analysis

Using cases to learn about the practice of strategic management is a powerful way for you to accomplish five things:[2]

1. Increase your understanding of what managers should and should not do in guiding a business to success.
2. Build your skills in sizing up company resource strengths and weaknesses and in conducting strategic analysis in a variety of industries and competitive situations.
3. Get valuable practice in identifying strategic issues that need to be addressed, evaluating strategic alternatives, and formulating workable plans of action.
4. Enhance your sense of business judgment, as opposed to uncritically accepting the authoritative crutch of the professor or "back-of-the-book" answers.
5. Gain in-depth exposure to different industries and companies, thereby acquiring something close to actual business experience.

If you understand that these are the objectives of case analysis, you are less likely to be consumed with curiosity about "the answer to the case." Students who have grown comfortable with and accustomed to textbook statements of fact and definitive lecture notes are often frustrated when discussions about a case do not produce concrete answers. Usually, case discussions produce good arguments for more than one course of action. Differences of opinion nearly always exist. Thus, should a class discussion conclude without a strong, unambiguous consensus on what to do, don't grumble too much when you are not told what the answer is or what the company actually did. Just remember that in the business world answers don't come in conclusive black-and-white terms.

There are nearly always several feasible courses of action and approaches, each of which may work out satisfactorily. Moreover, in the business world, when one elects a particular course of action, there is no peeking at the back of a book to see if you have chosen the best thing to do and no one to turn to for a provably correct answer. The best test of whether management action is "right" or "wrong" is results. If the results of an action turn out to be "good," the decision to take it may be presumed "right." If not, then the action chosen was "wrong" in the sense that it didn't work out.

Hence, the important thing for you to understand about analyzing cases is that the managerial exercise of identifying, diagnosing, and recommending is aimed at building your skills of business judgment. Discovering what the company actually did is no more than frosting on the cake—the actions that company managers actually took may or may not be "right" or best (unless there is accompanying evidence that the results of their actions were highly positive).

The point is this: The purpose of giving you a case assignment is not to cause you to run to the library or surf the Internet to discover what the company actually did but, rather, to enhance your skills in sizing up situations and developing your managerial judgment about what needs to be done and how to do it. The aim of case analysis is for you to become actively engaged in diagnosing the business issues and managerial problems posed in the case, to propose workable solutions, and to explain and defend your assessments—this is how cases provide you with meaningful practice at being a manager.

Preparing a Case for Class Discussion

If this is your first experience with the case method, you may have to reorient your study habits. Unlike lecture courses where you can get by without preparing intensively for each class and where you have latitude to work assigned readings and reviews of lecture notes into your schedule, a case assignment requires conscientious preparation before class. You will not get much out of hearing the class discuss a case you haven't read, and you certainly won't be able to contribute anything yourself to the discussion. What you have got to do to get ready for class discussion of a case is to study the case, reflect carefully on the situation presented, and develop some reasoned thoughts.

Your goal in preparing the case should be to end up with what you think is a sound, well-supported analysis of the situation and a sound, defensible set of recommendations about which managerial actions need to be taken.

To prepare a case for class discussion, we suggest the following approach:

1. *Skim the case rather quickly to get an overview of the situation it presents.* This quick overview should give you the general flavor of the situation and indicate the kinds of issues and problems that you will need to wrestle with. If your instructor has provided you with study questions for the case, now is the time to read them carefully.

2. *Read the case thoroughly to digest the facts and circumstances.* On this reading, try to gain full command of the situation presented in the case. Begin to develop some tentative answers to the study questions your instructor has provided. If your instructor has elected not to give you assignment questions, then start forming your own picture of the overall situation being described.

3. *Carefully review all the information presented in the exhibits.* Often, there is an important story in the numbers contained in the exhibits. Expect the information in the case exhibits to be crucial enough to materially affect your diagnosis of the situation.

4. *Decide what the strategic issues are.* Until you have identified the strategic issues and problems in the case, you don't know what to analyze, which tools and analytical techniques are called for, or otherwise how to proceed. At times the strategic issues are clear—either being stated in the case or else obvious from reading the case. At other times you will have to dig them out from all the information given; if so, the study questions will guide you.

5. *Start your analysis of the issues with some number crunching.* A big majority of strategy cases call for some kind of number crunching—calculating assorted financial ratios to check out the company's financial condition and recent performance, calculating growth rates of sales or profits or unit volume, checking out profit margins and the makeup of the cost structure, and understanding whatever revenue-cost-profit relationships are present. See Table 1 for a summary of key financial ratios, how they are calculated, and what they show.

6. *Apply the concepts and techniques of strategic analysis you have been studying.* Strategic analysis is not just a collection of opinions; rather, it entails applying the concepts and analytical tools described in Chapters 1 through 12 to cut beneath the surface and produce sharp insight and understanding. Every case assigned is strategy related and presents you with an opportunity to usefully apply what you have learned. Your instructor is looking for you to demonstrate that you know how and when to use the material presented in the text chapters.

7. *Check out conflicting opinions and make some judgments about the validity of all the data and information provided.* Many times cases report views and contradictory opinions (after all, people don't always agree on things, and different people see the same things in different ways). Forcing you to evaluate the data and information presented in the case helps you develop your powers of inference and judgment. Asking you to resolve conflicting information "comes with the territory" because a great many managerial situations entail opposing points of view, conflicting trends, and sketchy information.

8. *Support your diagnosis and opinions with reasons and evidence.* The most important things to prepare for are your answers to the question "Why?" For instance, if after studying the case you are of the opinion that the company's managers are doing a poor job, then it is your answer to "Why?" that establishes just how good your analysis of the situation is. If your instructor has provided you with specific study questions for the case, by all means prepare answers that include all the reasons and number-crunching evidence you can muster to support your diagnosis. If you are using study questions provided by the instructor, generate at least two pages of notes!

9. *Develop an appropriate action plan and set of recommendations.* Diagnosis divorced from corrective action is sterile. The test of a manager is always to convert sound analysis into sound actions—actions that will produce the desired results. Hence, the final and most telling step in preparing a case is to develop an action agenda for management that lays out a set of specific recommendations on what to do. Bear in mind that proposing realistic, workable solutions is far preferable to casually tossing out off-the-top-of-your-head suggestions. Be prepared to argue why your recommendations are more attractive than other courses of action that are open.

As long as you are conscientious in preparing your analysis and recommendations, and have ample reasons, evidence, and arguments to support your views, you shouldn't fret unduly about whether what you've prepared is "the right answer" to the case. In case analysis, there is rarely just one right approach or set of recommendations. Managing companies and crafting and executing strategies are not such exact sciences that there exists a single provably correct analysis and action plan for each strategic situation. Of course, some analyses and action plans are better than others; but, in truth, there's nearly always more than one good way to analyze a situation and more than one good plan of action.

Participating in Class Discussion of a Case

Classroom discussions of cases are sharply different from attending a lecture class. In a case class, students do most of the talking. The instructor's role is to solicit student participation, keep the discussion on track, ask "Why?" often, offer alternative views, play the devil's advocate (if no students jump in to offer opposing views), and otherwise lead the discussion. The students in the class carry the burden for analyzing the situation and for being prepared to present and defend their diagnoses and recommendations. Expect a classroom environment, therefore, that calls for your size-up of the situation, your analysis, what actions you would take, and why you would take them. Do not be dismayed if, as the class discussion unfolds, some insightful things are said by your fellow classmates that you did not think of. It is normal for views and analyses to differ and for the comments of others in the class to expand your own thinking about the case. As the old adage goes, "Two heads are better than one." So it is to be expected that the class as a whole will do a more penetrating and searching job of case analysis than will any one person working alone. This is the power of group effort, and its virtues are that it will help you see more analytical applications, let you test your analyses and judgments against those of your peers, and force you to wrestle with differences of opinion and approaches.

TABLE 1   Key Financial Ratios: How to Calculate Them and What They Mean

Ratio	How Calculated	What It Shows
Profitability ratios		
1. Gross profit margin	$\dfrac{\text{Sales} - \text{Cost of goods sold}}{\text{Sales}}$	Shows the percentage of revenues available to cover operating expenses and yield a profit. Higher is better and the trend should be upward.
2. Operating profit margin (or return on sales)	$\dfrac{\text{Sales} - \text{Operating expenses}}{\text{Sales}}$ or $\dfrac{\text{Operating income}}{\text{Sales}}$	Shows the profitability of current operations without regard to interest charges and income taxes. Higher is better and the trend should be upward.
3. Net profit margin (or net return on sales)	$\dfrac{\text{Profits after taxes}}{\text{Sales}}$	Shows after-tax profits per dollar of sales. Higher is better and the trend should be upward.
4. Total return on assets	$\dfrac{\text{Profits after taxes} + \text{Interest}}{\text{Total assets}}$	A measure of the return on total monetary investment in the enterprise. Interest is added to after-tax profits to form the numerator since total assets are financed by creditors as well as by stockholders. Higher is better and the trend should be upward.
5. Net return on total assets (ROA)	$\dfrac{\text{Profits after taxes}}{\text{Total assets}}$	A measure of the return earned by stockholders on the firm's total assets. Higher is better, and the trend should be upward.
6. Return on stockholder's equity (ROE)	$\dfrac{\text{Profits after taxes}}{\text{Total stockholders' equity}}$	Shows the return stockholders are earning on their capital investment in the enterprise. A return in the 12–15% range is "average," and the trend should be upward.
7. Return on invested capital (ROIC)— sometimes referred to as return on capital employed (ROCE)	$\dfrac{\text{Profits after taxes}}{\text{Long-term debt} + \text{Total stockholders' equity}}$	A measure of the return shareholders are earning on the long-term monetary capital invested in the enterprise. A higher return reflects greater bottom-line effectiveness in the use of long-term capital, and the trend should be upward.
8. Earnings per share (EPS)	$\dfrac{\text{Profits after taxes}}{\text{Number of shares of common stock outstanding}}$	Shows the earnings for each share of common stock outstanding. The trend should be upward, and the bigger the annual percentage gains, the better.
Liquidity ratios		
1. Current ratio	$\dfrac{\text{Current assets}}{\text{Current liabilities}}$	Shows a firm's ability to pay current liabilities using assets that can be converted into cash in the near term. Ratio should definitely be higher than 1.0; ratios of 2 or higher are better still.
2. Working capital	$\text{Current assets} - \text{Current liabilities}$	Bigger amounts are better because the company has more internal funds available to (1) pay its current liabilities on a timely basis and (2) finance inventory expansion, additional accounts receivable, and a larger base of operations without resorting to borrowing or raising more equity capital.
Leverage ratios		
1. Total debt-to-assets ratio	$\dfrac{\text{Total liabilities}}{\text{Total assets}}$	Measures the extent to which borrowed funds have been used to finance the firm's operations. Low fractions or ratios are better—high fractions indicate overuse of debt and greater risk of bankruptcy.
2. Long-term debt-to-capital ratio	$\dfrac{\text{Long-term debt}}{\text{Long-term debt} + \text{Total stockholders' equity}}$	An important measure of creditworthiness and balance sheet strength. Indicates the percentage of capital investment that has been financed by creditors and bondholders. Fractions or ratios below .25 or 25% are usually quite satisfactory since monies invested

(Continued)

TABLE 1 *(Continued)*

Ratio	How Calculated	What It Shows
Leverage ratios (Continued)		
		by stockholders account for 75% or more of the company's total capital. The lower the ratio, the greater the capacity to borrow additional funds. Debt-to-capital ratios above 50% and certainly above 75% indicate a heavy and perhaps excessive reliance on debt, lower creditworthiness, and weak balance sheet strength.
3. Debt-to-equity ratio	$\dfrac{\text{Total liabilities}}{\text{Total stockholders' equity}}$	Should usually be less than 1.0. High ratios (especially above 1.0) signal excessive debt, lower creditworthiness, and weaker balance sheet strength.
4. Long-term debt-to-equity ratio	$\dfrac{\text{Long-term debt}}{\text{Total stockholders' equity}}$	Shows the balance between debt and equity in the firm's *long-term* capital structure. Low ratios indicate greater capacity to borrow additional funds if needed.
5. Times-interest-earned (or coverage) ratio	$\dfrac{\text{Operating income}}{\text{Interest expenses}}$	Measures the ability to pay annual interest charges. Lenders usually insist on a minimum ratio of 2.0, but ratios above 3.0 signal better creditworthiness.
Activity ratios		
1. Days of inventory	$\dfrac{\text{Inventory}}{\text{Cost of goods sold} \div 365}$	Measures inventory management efficiency. Fewer days of inventory are usually better.
2. Inventory turnover	$\dfrac{\text{Cost of goods sold}}{\text{Inventory}}$	Measures the number of inventory turns per year. Higher is better.
3. Average collection period	$\dfrac{\text{Accounts receivable}}{\text{Total sales revenues} \div 365}$ or $\dfrac{\text{Accounts receivable}}{\text{Average daily sales}}$	Indicates the average length of time the firm must wait after making a sale to receive cash payment. A shorter collection time is better.
Other important measures of financial performance		
1. Dividend yield on common stock	$\dfrac{\text{Annual dividends per share}}{\text{Current market price per share}}$	A measure of the return that shareholders receive in the form of dividends. A "typical" dividend yield is 2–3%. The dividend yield for fast-growth companies is often below 1% (maybe even 0); the dividend yield for slow-growth companies can run 4–5%.
2. Price-earnings ratio	$\dfrac{\text{Current market price per share}}{\text{Earnings per share}}$	P-E ratios above 20 indicate strong investor confidence in a firm's outlook and earnings growth; firms whose future earnings are at risk or likely to grow slowly typically have ratios below 12.
3. Dividend payout ratio	$\dfrac{\text{Annual dividends per share}}{\text{Earnings per share}}$	Indicates the percentage of after-tax profits paid out as dividends.
4. Internal cash flow	After-tax profits + Depreciation	A quick and rough estimate of the cash the business is generating after payment of operating expenses, interest, and taxes. Such amounts can be used for dividend payments or funding capital expenditures.
5. Free cash flow	After-tax profits + Depreciation – Capital expenditures – Dividends	A quick and rough estimate of the cash a company's business is generating after payment of operating expenses, interest, taxes, dividends, and desirable reinvestments in the business. The larger a company's free cash flow, the greater is its ability to internally fund new strategic initiatives, repay debt, make new acquisitions, repurchase shares of stock, or increase dividend payments.

To orient you to the classroom environment on the days a case discussion is scheduled, we compiled the following list of things to expect:

1. Expect the instructor to assume the role of extensive questioner and listener.

2. Expect students to do most of the talking. The case method enlists a maximum of individual participation in class discussion. It is not enough to be present as a silent observer; if every student took this approach, there would be no discussion. (Thus, expect a portion of your grade to be based on your participation in case discussions.)

3. Be prepared for the instructor to probe for reasons and supporting analysis.

4. Expect and tolerate challenges to the views expressed. All students have to be willing to submit their conclusions for scrutiny and rebuttal. Each student needs to learn to state his or her views without fear of disapproval and to overcome the hesitation of speaking out. Learning respect for the views and approaches of others is an integral part of case analysis exercises. But there are times when it is OK to swim against the tide of majority opinion. In the practice of management, there is always room for originality and unorthodox approaches. So while discussion of a case is a group process, there is no compulsion for you or anyone else to cave in and conform to group opinions and group consensus.

5. Don't be surprised if you change your mind about some things as the discussion unfolds. Be alert to how these changes affect your analysis and recommendations (in the event you get called on).

6. Expect to learn a lot in class as the discussion of a case progresses; furthermore, you will find that the cases build on one another—what you learn in one case helps prepare you for the next case discussion.

There are several things you can do on your own to be good and look good as a participant in class discussions:

• Although you should do your own independent work and independent thinking, don't hesitate before (and after) class to discuss the case with other students. In real life, managers often discuss the company's problems and situation with other people to refine their own thinking.

• In participating in the discussion, make a conscious effort to contribute, rather than just talk.

There is a big difference between saying something that builds the discussion and offering a long-winded, off-the-cuff remark that leaves the class wondering what the point was.

• Avoid the use of "I think," "I believe," and "I feel"; instead, say, "My analysis shows _____" and "The company should do _____ because _____." Always give supporting reasons and evidence for your views; then your instructor won't have to ask you "Why?" every time you make a comment.

• In making your points, assume that everyone has read the case and knows what it says. Avoid reciting and rehashing information in the case—instead, use the data and information to explain your assessment of the situation and to support your position.

• Bring the printouts of the work you've done on Case-TUTOR or the notes you've prepared (usually two or three pages' worth) to class and rely on them extensively when you speak. There's no way you can remember everything off the top of your head—especially the results of your number crunching. To reel off the numbers or to present all five reasons why, instead of one, you will need good notes. When you have prepared thoughtful answers to the study questions and use them as the basis for your comments, everybody in the room will know you are well prepared, and your contribution to the case discussion will stand out.

Preparing a Written Case Analysis

Preparing a written case analysis is much like preparing a case for class discussion, except that your analysis must be more complete and put in report form. Unfortunately, though, there is no ironclad procedure for doing a written case analysis. All we can offer are some general guidelines and words of wisdom—this is because company situations and management problems are so diverse that no one mechanical way to approach a written case assignment always works.

Your instructor may assign you a specific topic around which to prepare your written report. Or, alternatively, you may be asked to do a comprehensive written case analysis, where the expectation is that you will (1) identify all the pertinent issues that management needs to address, (2) perform whatever analysis and evaluation is appropriate, and (3) propose an action plan and set of recommendations addressing the issues you have identified. In going through the exercise of identify, evaluate, and recommend, keep the following pointers in mind.[3]

Identification   It is essential early on in your written report that you provide a sharply focused diagnosis of strategic issues and key problems and that you demonstrate a good grasp of the company's present situation. Make sure you can identify the firm's strategy (use the concepts and tools in Chapters 1–8 as diagnostic aids) and that you can pinpoint whatever strategy implementation issues may exist (again, consult the material in Chapters 10–12 for diagnostic help). Consult the key points we have provided at the end of each chapter for further diagnostic suggestions. Consider beginning your report with an overview of the company's situation, its strategy, and the significant problems and issues that confront management. State problems/issues as clearly and precisely as you can. Unless it is necessary to do so for emphasis, avoid recounting facts and history about the company (assume your professor has read the case and is familiar with the organization).

Analysis and Evaluation   This is usually the hardest part of the report. Analysis is hard work! Check out the firm's financial ratios, its profit margins and rates of return, and its capital structure, and decide how strong the firm is financially. Table 1 contains a summary of various financial ratios and how they are calculated. Use it to assist in your financial diagnosis. Similarly, look at marketing, production, managerial competence, and other factors underlying the organization's strategic successes and failures. Decide whether the firm has valuable resource strengths and competencies and, if so, whether it is capitalizing on them.

Check to see if the firm's strategy is producing satisfactory results and determine the reasons why or why not. Probe the nature and strength of the competitive forces confronting the company. Decide whether and why the firm's competitive position is getting stronger or weaker. Use the tools and concepts you have learned about to perform whatever analysis and evaluation is appropriate. Work through the case preparation exercise on Case-Tutor if one is available for the case you've been assigned.

In writing your analysis and evaluation, bear in mind four things:

1. You are obliged to offer analysis and evidence to back up your conclusions. Do not rely on unsupported opinions, over-generalizations, and platitudes as a substitute for tight, logical argument backed up with facts and figures.

2. If your analysis involves some important quantitative calculations, use tables and charts to present the calculations clearly and efficiently. Don't just tack the exhibits on at the end of your report and let the reader figure out what they mean and why they were included. Instead, in the body of your report cite some of the key numbers, highlight the conclusions to be drawn from the exhibits, and refer the reader to your charts and exhibits for more details.

3. Demonstrate that you have command of the strategic concepts and analytical tools to which you have been exposed. Use them in your report.

4. Your interpretation of the evidence should be reasonable and objective. Be wary of preparing a one-sided argument that omits all aspects not favorable to your conclusions. Likewise, try not to exaggerate or overdramatize. Endeavor to inject balance into your analysis and to avoid emotional rhetoric. Strike phrases such as "I think," "I feel," and "I believe" when you edit your first draft and write in "My analysis shows" instead.

Recommendations   The final section of the written case analysis should consist of a set of definite recommendations and a plan of action. Your set of recommendations should address all of the problems/issues you identified and analyzed. If the recommendations come as a surprise or do not follow logically from the analysis, the effect is to weaken greatly your suggestions of what to do. Obviously, your recommendations for actions should offer a reasonable prospect of success. High-risk, bet-the-company recommendations should be made with caution. State how your recommendations will solve the problems you identified. Be sure the company is financially able to carry out what you recommend; also check to see if your recommendations are workable in terms of acceptance by the persons involved, the organization's competence to implement them, and prevailing market and environmental constraints. Try not to hedge or weasel on the actions you believe should be taken.

By all means state your recommendations in sufficient detail to be meaningful—get down to some definite nitty-gritty specifics. Avoid such unhelpful statements as "the organization should do more planning" or "the company should be more aggressive in marketing its product." For instance, if you determine that "the firm should improve its market position," then you need to set forth exactly how you think this should be done. Offer a definite agenda for action, stipulating a timetable and sequence for initiating actions, indicating priorities, and suggesting who should be responsible for doing what.

In proposing an action plan, remember there is a great deal of difference between, on the one hand, being responsible for a decision that may be costly if it proves in error and, on the other hand, casually suggesting courses of action that might be taken when you do not have to bear the responsibility for any of the consequences.

A good rule to follow in making your recommendations is: Avoid recommending anything you would not yourself be willing to do if you were in management's shoes. The importance of learning to develop good managerial judgment is indicated by the fact that, even though the same information and operating data may be available to every manager or executive in an organization, the quality of the judgments about what the information means and which actions need to be taken does vary from person to person.[4]

It goes without saying that your report should be well organized and well written. Great ideas amount to little unless others can be convinced of their merit—this takes tight logic, the presentation of convincing evidence, and persuasively written arguments.

Preparing an Oral Presentation

During the course of your business career it is very likely that you will be called upon to prepare and give a number of oral presentations. For this reason, it is common in courses of this nature to assign cases for oral presentation to the whole class. Such assignments give you an opportunity to hone your presentation skills.

The preparation of an oral presentation has much in common with that of a written case analysis. Both require identification of the strategic issues and problems confronting the company, analysis of industry conditions and the company's situation, and the development of a thorough, well-thought-out action plan. The substance of your analysis and quality of your recommendations in an oral presentation should be no different than in a written report. As with a written assignment, you'll need to demonstrate command of the relevant strategic concepts and tools of analysis and your recommendations should contain

sufficient detail to provide clear direction for management. The main difference between an oral presentation and a written case is in the delivery format. Oral presentations rely principally on verbalizing your diagnosis, analysis, and recommendations and visually enhancing and supporting your oral discussion with colorful, snappy slides (usually created on Microsoft's PowerPoint software).

Typically, oral presentations involve group assignments. Your instructor will provide the details of the assignment—how work should be delegated among the group members and how the presentation should be conducted. Some instructors prefer that presentations begin with issue identification, followed by analysis of the industry and company situation analysis, and conclude with a recommended action plan to improve company performance. Other instructors prefer that the presenters assume that the class has a good understanding of the external industry environment and the company's competitive position and expect the presentation to be strongly focused on the group's recommended action plan and supporting analysis and arguments. The latter approach requires cutting straight to the heart of the case and supporting each recommendation with detailed analysis and persuasive reasoning. Still other instructors may give you the latitude to structure your presentation however you and your group members see fit.

Regardless of the style preferred by your instructor, you should take great care in preparing for the presentation. A good set of slides with good content and good visual appeal is essential to a first-rate presentation. Take some care to choose a nice slide design, font size and style, and color scheme. We suggest including slides covering each of the following areas:

- An opening slide covering the "title" of the presentation and names of the presenters.
- A slide showing an outline of the presentation (perhaps with presenters' names by each topic).
- One or more slides showing the key problems and strategic issues that management needs to address.
- A series of slides covering your analysis of the company's situation.
- A series of slides containing your recommendations and the supporting arguments and reasoning for each recommendation—one slide for each recommendation and the associated reasoning will give it a lot of merit.

You and your team members should carefully plan and rehearse your slide show to maximize impact and minimize distractions. The slide show should include all of the pizzazz necessary to garner the attention of the audience, but not so much that it distracts from the content of what group members are saying to the class. You should remember that the role of slides is to help you communicate your points to the audience. Too many graphics, images, colors, and transitions may divert the audience's attention from what is being said or disrupt the flow of the presentation. Keep in mind that visually dazzling slides rarely hide a shallow or superficial or otherwise flawed case analysis from a perceptive audience. Most instructors will tell you that first-rate slides will definitely enhance a well-delivered presentation, but that impressive visual aids, if accompanied by weak analysis and poor oral delivery, still add up to a substandard presentation.

Researching Companies and Industries via the Internet and Online Data Services

Very likely, there will be occasions when you need to get additional information about some of the assignee cases, perhaps because your instructor has asked you to do further research on the industry or company or because you are simply curious about what has happened to the company since the case was written. These days, it is relatively easy to run down recent industry developments and to find out whether a company's strategic and financial situation has improved, deteriorated, or changed little since the conclusion of the case. The amount of information about companies and industries available on the Internet and through online data services is formidable and expanding rapidly.

It is a fairly simple matter to go to company websites, click on the investor information offerings and press release files, and get quickly to useful information. Most company websites allow you to view or print the company's quarterly and annual reports, its 10-K and 10-Q filings with the Securities and Exchange Commission, and various company press releases of interest. Frequently, a company's website will also provide information about its mission and vision statements, values statements, codes of ethics, and strategy information, as well as charts of the company's stock price. The company's recent press releases typically contain reliable information

about what of interest has been going on—new product introductions, recent alliances and partnership agreements, recent acquisitions, summaries of the latest financial results, tidbits about the company's strategy, guidance about future revenues and earnings, and other late-breaking company developments. Some company web pages also include links to the home pages of industry trade associations where you can find information about industry size, growth, recent industry news, statistical trends, and future outlook. Thus, an early step in researching a company on the Internet is always to go to its website and see what's available.

Online Data Services LexisNexis, Bloomberg Financial News Services, and other online subscription services available in many university libraries provide access to a wide array of business reference material. For example, the web-based LexisNexis Academic Universe contains business news articles from general news sources, business publications, and industry trade publications. Broadcast transcripts from financial news programs are also available through LexisNexis, as are full-text 10-Ks, 10-Qs, annual reports, and company profiles for more than 11,000 U.S. and international companies. Your business librarian should be able to direct you to the resources available through your library that will aid you in your research.

Public and Subscription Websites with Good Information Plainly, you can use a search engine such as Google or Yahoo! or MSN to find the latest news on a company or articles written by reporters that have appeared in the business media. These can be very valuable in running down information about recent company developments. However, keep in mind that the information retrieved by a search engine is "unfiltered" and may include sources that are not reliable or that contain inaccurate or misleading information. Be wary of information provided by authors who are unaffiliated with reputable organizations or publications and articles that were published in off-beat sources or on websites with an agenda. Be especially careful in relying on the accuracy of information you find posted on various bulletin boards. Articles covering a company or issue should be copyrighted or published by a reputable source. If you are turning in a paper containing information gathered from the Internet, you should cite your sources (providing the Internet address and date visited); it is also wise to print web pages for your research file (some web pages are updated frequently).

The Wall Street Journal, Bloomberg Businessweek, Forbes, Barron's, and *Fortune* are all good sources of articles on companies. The online edition of *The Wall Street Journal* contains the same information that is available daily in its print version of the paper, but the *WSJ* website also maintains a searchable database of all *The Wall Street Journal* articles published during the past few years. *Fortune* and *Bloomberg Businessweek* also make the content of the most current issue available online to subscribers as well as provide archives sections that allow you to search for articles published during the past few years that may be related to a particular keyword.

The following publications and websites are particularly good sources of company and industry information:

> Securities and Exchange Commission EDGAR database (contains company 10-Ks, 10-Qs, etc.)
> **http://www.sec.gov/edgar/searchedgar/companysearch**
> Google Finance
> **http://finance.google.com**
> CNN Money
> **http://money.cnn.com**
> Hoover's Online
> **http://hoovers.com**
> *The Wall Street Journal Interactive Edition*
> **www.wsj.com**
> *Bloomberg Businessweek*
> **www.businessweek.com and www.bloomberg.com**
> *Fortune*
> **www.fortune.com**
> MSN Money Central
> **http://moneycentral.msn.com**
> Yahoo! Finance
> **http://finance.yahoo.com/**

Some of these Internet sources require subscriptions in order to access their entire databases.

You should always explore the investor relations section of every public company's website. In today's world, these websites typically have a wealth of information concerning a company's mission, core values, performance targets, strategy, recent financial performance, and latest developments (as described in company press releases).

Learning Comes Quickly   With a modest investment of time, you will learn how to use Internet sources and search engines to run down information on companies and industries quickly and efficiently. And it is a skill that will serve you well into the future. Once you become familiar with the data available at the different websites mentioned above and learn how to use a search engine, you will know where to go to look for the particular information that you want. Search engines nearly always turn up too many information sources that match your request rather than too few. The trick is to learn to zero in on those most relevant to what you are looking for. Like most things, once you get a little experience under your belt on how to do company and industry research on the Internet, you will be able to readily find the information you need.

The Ten Commandments of Case Analysis

As a way of summarizing our suggestions about how to approach the task of case analysis, we have put together what we like to call "The Ten Commandments of Case Analysis." They are shown in Table 2. If you observe all or even most of these commandments faithfully as you prepare a case either for class discussion or for a written report, your chances of doing a good job on the assigned cases will be much improved. Hang in there, give it your best shot, and have some fun exploring what the real world of strategic management is all about.

TABLE 2   The Ten Commandments of Case Analysis

To be observed in written reports and oral presentations, and while participating in class discussions:

1. Go through the case twice, once for a quick overview and once to gain full command of the facts. Then take care to explore the information in every one of the case exhibits.

2. Make a complete list of the problems and issues that the company's management needs to address.

3. Be thorough in your analysis of the company's situation (make a minimum of one to two pages of notes detailing your diagnosis).

(Continued)

TABLE 2 *(Continued)*

4. Look for opportunities to apply the concepts and analytical tools in the text chapters—all of the cases in the book have very definite ties to the material in one or more of the text chapters!!!!

5. Do enough number crunching to discover the story told by the data presented in the case. (To help you comply with this commandment, consult Table 1 in this section to guide your probing of a company's financial condition and financial performance.)

6. Support any and all off-the-cuff opinions with well-reasoned arguments and numerical evidence. Don't stop until you can purge "I think" and "I feel" from your assessment and, instead, are able to rely completely on "My analysis shows."

7. Prioritize your recommendations and make sure they can be carried out in an acceptable time frame with the available resources.

8. Support each recommendation with persuasive argument and reasons as to why it makes sense and should result in improved company performance.

9. Review your recommended action plan to see if it addresses all of the problems and issues you identified. Any set of recommendations that does not address all of the issues and problems you identified is incomplete and insufficient.

10. Avoid recommending any course of action that could have disastrous consequences if it doesn't work out as planned. Therefore, be as alert to the downside risks of your recommendations as you are to their upside potential and appeal.

ENDNOTES

[1] Charles I. Gragg, "Because Wisdom Can't Be Told," in *The Case Method at the Harvard Business School,* ed. M. P. McNair (New York: McGraw-Hill, 1954), p. 11.

[2] Ibid., pp. 12–14; and D. R. Schoen and Philip A. Sprague, "What Is the Case Method?" in *The Case Method at the Harvard Business School,* ed. M. P. McNair, pp. 78–79.

[3] For some additional ideas and viewpoints, you may wish to consult Thomas J. Raymond, "Written Analysis of Cases," in *The Case Method at the Harvard Business School,* ed. M. P. McNair, pp. 139–63. Raymond's article includes an actual case, a sample analysis of the case, and a sample of a student's written report on the case.

[4] Gragg, "Because Wisdom Can't Be Told," p. 10.

Company Index

A

AAFA (American Apparel and Footwear Association), C-97
ABC 20/20, C-30
ABC News, C-18
ABC television network, C-279, C-283, C-286
Aber Diamond, 167
AcademySports and Outdoors, C-67
Accenture, 108, 211
Ad Age, C-258
Adams Golf, C-77
Adaptive Biotechnologies, 175
Adidas, 202
adidas Group, C-59, C-69, C-77–C-79, C-93
Adobe, Inc., 357
AES energy, 353
African Budget Safaris (ABS), C-234
AIG, Inc., 359
Airbnb, 138, 261
Airbnb, case, C-6–C-10
    accommodation market, C-6–C-7
    consumer experience and rate, C-8–C-9
    overview, C-6
    regulating, C-9
    sharing economy business model, C-7–C-8
Airbus, 202
Air Canada Center, C-66
Air France, 155
Albertsons, 66
Alcohol and Tobacco Tax and Trade Bureau (TTB), C-44
Alcon, 330
Aldi, 66
ALDI (Germany), C-181
ALDO Group, C-59
Alibaba Group, 34, 132, 212, 306, C-169, C-185, C-187
Aliexpress, case, C-184–C-190
    Alibaba background, C-185
    Amazon strategy and, C-187–C-188
    Amazon *versus,* C-184–C-185
    in China, C-187
    online industry future, C-188–C-190
    in Russia, C-186–C-187
    strategy of, C-185–C-186
Alitalia airlines, 155
All-America Games, C-65
Allegheny Technologies, C-327
Allegro Manufacturing, 229
Allergan, Inc., C-412
Alliance Boots (UK), 195–196
Alliance Manchester Business School, C-290

Allianz Italy, 33
Allied Signal, 329
Allstate insurance, 169
Ally Financial, 269
Alphabet (Google parent), 3, 297, 330, C-216, C-398, C-402
Alswell.com, C-167–C-168
Alterra ski resorts, C-341–C-342
Amazon.com, 3, 34, 98, 154, 166, 168, 299, 306, 319, 333–335, 357, 363–364, C-9, C-34, C-68, C-91, C-93, C-102, C-162, C-165–C-167, C-169, C-216, C-230
    Aliexpress *versus,* C-184
    background of, C-184–C-185
    financial data on, C-189–C-190
    strategy of, C-187–C-188
Amazon.com, case, C-171–C-183
    background of, C-171–C-172
    bricks-and-mortar grocery stores of, C-174–C-175
    downside of grocery market entry by, C-180–C-181
    fresh store pickup services of, C-175–C-176
    future of, C-181–C-182
    grocery entry of, C-172–C-174
    grocery market disruption by, C-180
    overview, C-171
    Whole Foods Market acquired by, C-176–C-179
Amazon Prime, 63, C-152–C-154, C-158, C-172
Amazon Web Services (AWS), C-107, C-172
Ambassador Steel Corporation, C-309
AMC Entertainment, C-82–C-84, C-90
American Academy of Neurology, C-379
American Academy of Pain Medicine, C-408
American Airlines, 164, 333
American Apparel and Footwear Association (AAFA), C-97
American Express, 45
American National Standards Institute, C-137
American Pain clinic, C-411
American Pain Society, C-408
American Red Cross, C-278, C-374
AmerisourceBergen, C-412
AMR Corporation, 164
Anheuser-Busch InBev SA/NV, 66, 123, C-41, C-46–C-47, C-203
Animal Compassion Foundation, 282
Ann Taylor Stores, 33, 169
Aon Hewitt, 172
Apollo Global Management, C-332

Apple, Inc., 3–4, 6–8, 17, 60, 72, 102, 132, 154, 155, 161, 168, 173, 200, 210, 226, 255, 277, 306–307, 323, 337, 348, 357, 362, C-142
Aramark Food and Services, C-358
Arby's Restaurant Group, C-130
ArcelorMittal USA, C-325, C-329
Arc'teryx, 308, C-166
Arizona State University, C-77, C-374
Armani, 77, C-28
Army and Air Force Exchange Service, C-67
Ashai Group Holdings, C-46
Ashworth sport apparel, C-77
Aspen Ski Company, C-341
Associated Press, C-142
Aston Martin, C-213
AstraZeneca, 265
Atitalia, 155
A. T. Kearney, 108
ATOPDAILY, C-117
AT&T, Inc., 221, 324, C-152, C-155
Auburn Steel Company, C-308
Auburn University, C-65
Audi Motor Co., 143, C-213–C-214
Automobile magazine, C-192–C-193
Avago Technologies, 305
Avon Products, 80
AWS (Amazon Web Services), C-107, C-172

B

Babson College, C-290
Bain Capital, 29
Baja Fresh, C-134
Ballast Point Brewing & Spirits, C-46
Bank of America, 224, 269, 330
Bare Foods, C-268
Barker Steel Company, C-309
Barnes & Noble, C-34
Barron magazine, 273
BASF, 45
Bass Pro Shops, C-67, C-166
Bath & Body Works, 169
Battle Road Research, C-118
Bay Bread Group, C-364
Baylor University, C-51, C-54, C-162
BBC (UK), C-142
Beaird-Poulan, 229
Beam, Inc., 234
Belk, Inc., C-67
Benchmark Capital, C-392, C-400–C-401, C-404
Benchnet-The Benchmarking Exchange, 108
Ben Franklin Stores, C-162
Ben & Jerry's, 283
Bentley, 135

Berkshire Hathaway, 3, 34
Best Buy, 66, 149, 339, C-34, C-37
Best Practices, LLC, 108
Bethlehem Steel Corp., C-307
Bharti Enterprises, 236
Bic pens, 130
Bing.com, 319
Biokenetics, Inc., C-386, C-388
Birmingham Steel Corporation, C-308
Bissell vacuum cleaners, C-117
BJ's Wholesale Club, 140, C-36–C-39
Black & Decker, 229, C-117
Bloomberg News, C-142, C-181
Bloomin' Brands, 257
Bloomingdale's, C-92
Blue Apron, 104
Blue Nile jewelry, 138
Blue Point, C-46
BMW, 6, 101, 132, 143, 184, C-213–C-214
Bob's Stores, Inc., C-241
Boeing aircraft, 46, 307
Boll & Branch, 104–105
Bonbardierf, 229
Bonobos men's fashion, 158, 166, C-167
Booth Creek Partners, C-335
Bosch, 132
Bose, 98
Boston Beer Company, C-46–C-48
Boston College, C-65, C-121
Boston Consulting Group, 27, 297, C-262
Boston Marathon, C-77
Boston University, C-379, C-382
BP, Ltd., 198, 359, C-109
Braun, 111
Brewers Association, C-41
Bridgestone Tires, 66
Briggs & Stratton, 130
British Air, 155
British Steel, C-308
British Telecommunications, 221
Broadcom, 305
BTR (UK), 249
Budweiser, 66
Buffalo Wild Wings, C-49
Bugatti, 140
Build-A-Bear Workshop, 28
Bumble.com, 155
Burberry, 77, 135
Bureau of International Labor Affairs, C-96
Bureau of Labor Statistics, C-180
Burger King restaurants, 307
Burghy (Italy), 224
Burt's Bees, 276
Business Roundtable, 274
BuyVia app, 67

C

Cabela's, C-67, C-166
Cadbury Limited/Mondelez International, 265
Caerus Oil and Gas, C-317
Caesars Entertainment, 334–335
California Tortilla, C-134
Calvin Klein, C-24
Campbell's soups, 132
CampusBookRentals, 155
Canaccord Genuity, Inc., C-83, C-118
Canada Goose, 140–141
Cane's, C-134
Canon, 12
Cardinal Health, C-412
Carrefour (France), 111
Cartier, 135, 204
Casella Wines (Australia), 157
CCR Hockey, C-77
CCTV (China Central Television) International, C-256
Centers for Disease Control and Prevention, C-121, C-377, C-406, C-411
Centers for Medicare and Medicaid Services (CMS), 331
Chadwick's of Boston, C-240
Charles Schwab Corporation, 26, 132, 308
Charleston Area Medical Center (WV), 330–331, 343
Charlotte Bobcats, C-66
Chief Executives magazine, 298
China Central Television (CCTV) International, C-256
China Development Bank, C-327
China Network Television (C-NTV), C-261
China Zhongwang Holdings, C-326
Chipotle Mexican Grill, case, C-120–C-137
    CEO of, C-133–C-134
    competition of, C-134–C-137
    construction costs for, C-133
    early years, C-124–C-125
    management and operations at, C-129–C-130
    marketing at, C-131–C-132
    overview, C-120–C-121
    reviving sales and customer trust, C-121–C-124
    site selection at, C-132–C-133
    supply chain management at, C-128–C-129
    in 2018, C-125–C-128
Chrysler Motor Company, 119
Ciba Vision, 330
Cifra, S.A. de C.V. (Mexico), C-163
Cinemark theaters, C-82, C-84, C-90
Cinnabon, Inc., 119
Cirque du Soleil, 157
Cisco Systems, 165, 173–174, 274, 299, 366
Citigroup, 27, 249, 269
Citizen Watch Company, 227
Clarks shoes, C-93
Clear Peak management and analytics, C-171
Cleveland Clinic, 136
Clinton Global Initiative, 139
Clorox Company Foundation, 283

CMS (Centers for Medicare and Medicaid Services), 331
CNN television network, 136, C-142
CNTV (China Network Television), C-261
Coach, Inc., 135, 167, 169
Coca-Cola Co., 27, 96, 110, 134, 276, 280, 284, 330, C-268, C-274
Colgate-Palmolive, 127, 172
College Athletic Trainers Society, C-380
Colo-Colo soccer club (Chile), C-66
Colorado Mountain Express, C-334
Combatant Gentlemen, 158
Comcast, 229, C-154–C-155, C-159
Community Coffee, 138
Companhia Vale do Rio Doce (CVRD, Brazil), C-316
Compaq Computer, 255, C-198
Conair Corporation, 229
Congressional Research Service, C-412
Connecticut Steel Corporation, C-309
Conservation International's Center for Environmental Leadership, C-371
Consolidated Rebar, Inc., C-309
Constellations Brands, C-46
Consumer Reports magazine, C-109, C-113, C-116–C-118, C-193, C-211
Continental Tires, 66
Cornell University, C-112, C-117
Corning Glass, 227
Corporate Knights magazine, 276
Corporate Responsibility magazine, 276, C-218, C-374
Corus Steel (UK), C-308
Costco Connection, The, C-26, C-28
Costco Wholesale Corporation, 101, 140, 149, C-49, C-90, C-171, C-177, C-180, C-363
Costco Wholesale Corporation, case background, C-17–C-18
    compensation and workforce practices, C-29–C-31
    competition: BJ's Wholesale Club, C-36–C-39
    competition: Sam's Club, C-34–C-36
    environmental sustainability of, C-33
    financial and operating data, C-19–C-20
    founder's leadership style, C-18
    marketing and advertising of, C-25–C-27
    membership demographics, C-28–C-29
    mission of, C-21
    strategy of, C-21–C-25
    supply chain and distribution of, C-27–C-28
    values and codes of ethics, C-31–C-33
    warehouse management, C-29
    website sales of, C-27
Countrywide Financial, 359
Coursera, 71
Covington & Burling LLP, C-399
Cowen and Company, C-182
Cracker Barrel, 83
Craft Brew Alliance, C-48–C-49
Craftsman, 60
Craigslist.com, C-93, C-411

Cruz Azul soccer team (Mexico), C-66
CSX, 30
Culinary Institute of America, C-124
CVRD (Companhia Vale do Rio Doce, Brazil), C-316
CVS, Inc., 140, C-363, C-412

D

Daimler AG, 175, C-197
Daimler-Chrysler, 173–174
Danone Group (France), C-268
Dan Patrick Show, C-388
DARPA (Defense Advanced Research Projects Agency), C-108
Dartmouth College, C-92, C-385
David J. Joseph Co., C-311, C-317–C-318
Daxue Consulting, C-251, C-263
DEA (Drug Enforcement Administration), C-406, C-409–C-410
Dean Foods, 27
De Beers Group, 167, 224
Defense Advanced Research Projects Agency (DARPA), C-108
Dell, 127, 134, 211, 229, 287, 298, 307
Deloitte Touche Tohmatsu Limited, 297–298
Delta Airlines, 333
Denver International Airport (DIA), C-334
Devil's Backbone Brewing, C-46
Dezeen magazine, C-264
DHL Express, 128, 333
Dick's Sporting Good, C-56, C-67
Didi Chuxing (China), C-393
Dillard's, Inc., C-67
Direct TV Now, C-153
Discovery Education, C-131
DISH Network, 229
Disneyland Park, C-278–C-279
Dolce & Gabbana, 172
Dollar General, 111, 309
Dome Corporation (Japan), C-68
Domino's Pizza, 104, 141
Dow Jones Global Index, 285
Dow Jones Sustainability World Index, 278–280
DreamWorks Animation, 27
Dress for Success, Inc., C-167
Dreyer's Grand Ice Cream, C-360–C-361
Dr Pepper Snapple Group, 165
Drug Enforcement Administration (DEA), C-406, C-409–C-410
Drybar, 157
Ducati Motorcycles, 134, 169, 187, 316
Duferco Group (Europe), C-314, C-327
Dunkin' Donuts, 104, C-3
DuPont Co., Inc., 33
Dyson Technologies, C-113

E

EA (Electronic Arts), 201
Eastern China Normal University, C-262
Eastern Mountain Sports, C-166

Eastman Kodak, 358
EasyJet airlines (UK), 130, 154–155
eBay.com, 17, 157, 160–161, 253, C-9, C-185, C-198
EBSCO, 369
Echoing Green, 139
Economist, The, 3, C-307
Ecovacs (China), C-116–C-117
EDS, 211
Edward Jones financial services, 27, 71, 169, 297, 365, C-180
edX, 71
Eero, 155
Electronic Arts (EA), 201
Elite Cafe (Waco, TX), C-54
Embraer aircraft, 265
Emerson Electric, 229
Emirates Airlines (Dubai), 3
Encana Oil and Gas, C-317
Endeavor, 139
Endemol TV production, C-220
Endo, Inc., C-412
Enron, Inc., 270, 359
Environmental Protection Agency's Energy Star and Climate Protection Partnerships, C-33
EPCOT, C-279
Epic Systems Corporation, 348–349, 369
Epson, 12
Equifax, 267
ESPN, C-233, C-281, C-290
Essex Equity Management, 291
Ethisphere, 273,
Ethnisphere Magazine, C-218
Ethos Water, C-362
E*TRADE, 71
Eufy Robo Vac, C-113, C-117
Everlane apparel, 169
Evolution Fresh juice, C-363–C-364
Evolution Robotics, Inc., C-109
Expedia, Inc., 164, C-392, C-402
ExxonMobil, 33
EY global accounting, 281

F

Facebook.com, 34, 72, 104, 154, 297, 302, 319, 337, 357, 363, C-12, C-87, C-89, C-138, C-143–C-146, C-148, C-152, C-236
FaceTime, 160
Family Dollar, 309
Famosa, C-229
Fandango, C-87
Fast Company, 277, 324, C-400
Federal Trade Commission (FTC-), C-179
FedEx Corporation, 27, 111, 333
Fed-Mart, C-17
Ferrari, 187
Fidelity Investments, C-400
FIFA World Cup, C-77
Firehouse Subs, C-134
First Colony Coffee and Tea, C-4
First Round Capital, C-393, C-400
Fisher-Price, Inc., C-217
Five Guys Burgers and Fries, C-134
Flagstaff Business News, C-15
Flipkart.com, C-168
Flix Brewhouse, C-82
FMC Corp., 253

FOCUS Brands, C-135
Focus Media (China), 210–211
Footlocker, Inc., C-67
Forbes magazine, 46, 324, C-147, C-257, C-304, C-409
Ford Motor Company, 33, 119, 226, 281, 329, C-197, C-203, C-213
Forrester Research, 150
Fort Howard Steel, C-308
Fortune 500, 108, C-240
Fortune Brands, 234
Fortune magazine, 7, 150, 153, 273, 281, 324, 338, C-366
Four Seasons Hotels, 140, 201–202
Fox, Inc., C-154
Foxconn contract manufacturer (China), 173, 306
Fox Kids Europe, C-220
Fox News, 136, 138
Free State Steel Corporation, C-309
Fresh Direct, 160
Friends of TOMS, C-93
Frito-Lay North America, C-271–C-274
Froedtert Hospital (WI), 330
Frontline (television news program), C-385
Frostburg State University, C-389
FTC (Federal Trade Commission), C-179

G

Gallatin Steel Company, C-310
Galyan's Sporting Goods, C-56
Gander Mountain, C-166
Gap, Inc., 27, 104, 304
GEICO insurance, 330
Genentech, 274, 297
General Electric (GE), 3, 21, 30, 35, 41, 219, 234, 236–237, 248, 303, 328–330, 337–338, 364, C-401
General Mills, 32, 227, 276
General Motors (GM), 102, 119, 135, 211, 215, 301, 309, 358, C-194, C-208, C-213–C-215
Geneva International Motor Show, C-215
Gerdau Long Steel Company, C-310
Gett.com, 268
Gillette, Inc., 12
Gilt Groupe, 157
Giochi Presiosi, C-229
Giving Partners nonprofits, C-96
GlaxoSmithKline, 265
GlobalData Retail research, C-167, C-173
Global Fund and Product (RED), C-374
Global Reporting Initiative, 278, 282
Golden State Warriors, C-66
Goldman Sachs, 104, 297, 362–363, C-8, C-185, C-393
Goodyear Tires, 66, 169
Google.com, 23, 72, 100, 154, 165, 167, 226, 255, 274, 299, 319, 324, 330, 357, 363, 366, 369, C-188, C-216, C-398
Google Play Store, C-186
Goose Island, C-46
GoPro action camera, C-233
Goya Foods, 8

Grand Teton Lodge Company, C-336
Graniterock, 365
Green Mountain Coffee Roasters, C-4, C-363–C-364
Greyhound Bus Lines, C-334
Groupon, 357
Grupo Modelo, C-41
Gucci, 77, 132
Guinness beer, C-43

H

Häagen-Dazs ice cream, 32, 275, C-257
Habitat for Humanity, 26
Halliburton, 265
Hallmark, 328
Hallmark cable channel, C-286
Hand of Hope, C-97
Handy Dan Home Improvement, 155
Hannaford, 66
Hanson Trust, 235
Harley-Davidson, 110, 169
Harris Steel (Canada), C-303, C-309
Hasbro, Inc., C-216, C-218, C-228–C-230
HauteLook, 157
HAY furniture design (Denmark), C-261
HBO NOW, C-153–C-155
HBO Real Sports/Marist Poll, C-377
Heineken NV, 66, C-46
Helios, C-80–C-83, C-90
Henry J. Kaiser Family Foundation, C-409
Hesteel Group (China), C-327
Hewlett-Packard (HP), 12, 30, 173, 211, 253, 255, 306, C-401
HGTV (Home and Garden Television), 138, C-51–C-55
Hibbett Sporting Goods, C-67
Hilton Hotels Corporation, 23, 45, 142, 193, C-9, C-360
Hindalco (India), 211
Hitachi, 183
H. J. Heinz Holding Corporation, 232
H&M Group, 184
Hockey Canada, C-66
Hoffman-La Roche healthcare, 175
Hold Everything, 301
Hollywood Movie Money, C-82
HomeAway, Inc., 138, 164
Home Depot, 41, 66, 127, 132, 155, 209, C-34, C-211–C-212
Honda Motor Co., 27, 60, 119, 184, 205, C-215
Honeywell, 209, 329
Hong Kong Disneyland, C-281, C-285
HootSuite, C-105
Hoover, Inc., C-117
Horizon Airlines, C-360
House of Blues, 180
Houston Rockets, C-66
HP (Hewlett-Packard), 12, 30, 173, 211, 253, 255, 306, C-401
HSBC, Ltd. (UK), 3, 249
Huawei (China), 130
Hudson's Bay, 157
Hulu streaming service, 71, C-91, C-152, C-154, C-158, C-277
Hwange National Park (Zimbabwe), C-235

Hyatt Hotels, C-332, C-334, C-360
Hyundai Motor Co., 8, C-213, C-215

I

IBIS World, C-34, C-230
IBM, Inc., 172–173, 211, 274, 347, 358
ICFAI Business School (Hyderabad, India), C-171, C-251, C-392
iHeartRadio, C-89
IKEA, 8, 264
IKEA China, case, C-251–C-264
 challenges of, C-261–C-262
 company background, C-252
 culture and market of, C-258–C-259
 entry into, C-254–C-256
 furnishings education at, C-261
 future of, C-262–C-263
 global strategy of, C-252–C-254
 initial failure in China, C-256–C-257
 multichannel retailing at, C-259–C-260
 overview, C-251–C-252
 pricing strategy of, C-260–C-261
 social venue of, C-261
 success in China, C-257–C-258
Il Giornale Coffee Company, C-354–C-355
IMA World Health, C-96
Independence Tube Corporation (ITC-), C-310
Indiana University, C-65
Indian Institute of Technology (India), C-168
Inditex Group (Spain), 168, 304
Indochino menswear, 169
Industry Week, 340
Infosys Technologies (India), 211
Insperity, 172
Instagram.com, 26, C-138, C-146
Institute of Medicine, C-377
Insys Therapeutics, 265
Intel, Inc., 63, 183, 357
Inter IKEA Systems B. V., C-251
International Labor Organization, 264
International Paper Company, 168
International Standards Organization (ISO), 276
Internet Retailer, C-166
Intuit, Inc., 27, 297
Investor's Business Daily, C-117
iQiyi (China), C-151
iRobot, case, C-107–C-119
 competition of, C-117
 financial performance of, C-113–117
 history of, C-107–C-110
 industry background, C-110
 overview, C-107
 privacy concerns of, C-117–C-118
 strategy of, C-110–113
 in 2018, C-118
iSixSigma.org, 329–330
ISO (International Standards Organization), 276
ITC (Independence Tube Corporation), C-310
ITEC Steel, Inc., C-308
ITT, 236, 258

Ivy League, C-385
Iwaspoisoned.com, C-124

J

Jack in the Box, Inc., C-136
Jacksonville Jaguars, C-66
Jaguar Motor Co., 143, C-213
Jakks Pacific, C-229
J.B. Hunt Trucking Co., C-203
J. D. Power Asia Pacific, 209
Jersey Mike's, C-134
Jet Blue Airlines, 27, 32
Jet.com, 166, C-165–C-167
JFE Steel Corporation (Japan), C-315
Jimmy Choo apparel, 222
Jimmy John's, C-134
John Deere, 60, 132
John F. Kennedy Airport (NY), C-353
Johnson & Johnson, 6, 252, 258, 284, 319, C-412
Johnson & Wales University, C-6, C-41
Journal of the American Medical Association, C-382
JPMorgan Chase, 265, 269, 359
Just Play Products, C-229

K

Kellogg, Inc., 93, 208
KendraScott.com, 150
Ken Research Private Limited (India), C-254, C-263
Kentucky Fried Chicken, C-266
Keurig Green Mountain, 25, 165, 281, 283, C-363
KFC, Inc., 200
Kia Motor Co., C-213
Kimpton Hotels and Restaurants, 366
KLAS, 349
Knoa Brewing Company, C-48
Kobe Steel, 267
Kohl's Stores, Inc., 70, C-34, C-67
KP Sports, C-56
Kraft Foods, 100, 232, C-361–C-362
Kraft-Heinz merger, 232
Kroger Co., Inc., 66, 110, 144, C-34, C-171, C-177, C-180, C-363
KSL Partners, C-341

L

LaCroix sparkling water, C-275
Lagunitas Brewing Company, C-46
Las Vegas Sands, 265
Learning Company, C-217
Lebedyansky beverages (Russia), C-268
LEGO Group (Denmark), 3, C-229
Lenovo (China), 211
LensCrafters, 365
LeWeb European tech conference, C-393
LexisNexis, 369
LG Corporation, 102, 132
Lidl (Germany), C-181
Lifetime cable channel, C-286
Lincoln Electric Company, 101

LinkedIn.com, 8, 274, C-138, C-146–C-147
Linksys, 155
Listerine, 132
Little Caesars pizza, 141
Live Nation, 180
L. L. Bean, 111
LMP Steel & Wire Company, C-309
Lola's Market, case, C-101–C-106
  alternatives for, C-103–C-105
  future of, C-105
  history of, C-103
  industry overview, C-101–C-103
London Marathon, C-77
Lonely Planet, C-234–C-235
Lord & Taylor, C-169
L'Oréal, 214, 227, 257
Los Angeles Times, 29, C-356
Lot18, 157
Lotus Cars, Ltd., C-208
Louisiana Department of Environmental Quality, C-316
Louis Vuitton, 135
Lowercase Capital, C-393, C-400
Lowe's Home Improvement Stores, C-34, C-211–C-212
LTV Steel Corp., C-307–C-308
L2 research, C-182
Lucasfilm, C-279–C-280
Lucky snacks (Brazil), C-268
Lufthansa Airlines, 333
Lululemon Athletica, Inc., 8, 32
Luxttica eyewear, 172
LVMH, 224
Lyft, 130, 157, 268

M

Macy's, Inc., C-67
Magnatrax Corporation, C-309
Magnolia brand, case, C-51–C-55
  Fixer Upper conclusion, C-53–C-54
  Fixer Upper pilot, C-52
  future of, C-55
  Hearth & Hand collection, C-53
  house flipping and, C-51–C-52
  journal on, C-53
  Magnolia market, C-52–C-53
  Magnolia Stay, C-54
  Magnolia Table, C-54
  market for, C-52
  Waco, TX, affected by, C-54–C-55
Major League Baseball (MLB), C-57, C-65–C-66
Maker Studios, C-220–C-221
Mallinckrodt pharmaceuticals, C-411
Maple Leaf Foods, 167
MapMyFitness.com, C-61, C-64
Marbo potato chips (Serbia), C-268
Marine Stewardship Council, C-33
Marion Steel Company, C-308
Marmot, C-166
Marriott Hotels and Resorts International, 142, 365, C-7, C-335, C-358
Marshalls, Inc., 77, C-240, C-242–C-243
Marvel Comics, 226
Marvel Entertainment, C-279–C-280
Mary Kay Cosmetics (MKC), 80, 362, 366
Maserati, 187
MasterCard International, 45, C-83

Match.com, 104
Matheson Analytics, Inc., C-80–C-83, C-90
Mattel Inc., case, C-216–C-231
  conclusions on, C-230–C-231
  customers of, C-220
  executives of, C-220–C-221
  financial status of, C-222–C-225
  history of, C-216–C-218
  marketing of, C-220
  operations of, C-219
  overview, C-216
  products of, C-219–C-220
  revenues by category and region, C-225–C-226
  stock performance, C-226
  in toy and craft wholesaling industry, C-226–C-230
  vision, mission, and strategy, C-218–C-219
Maverick Record, C-400
MAX GO, C-153
Mayo Clinic, 136, 328
McDonald's, Inc., 12, 184, 193–194, 200, 208, 224, 274, 303, 326–327, 365, 366, C-4, C-125, C-365
McKesson Corporation, C-406, C-410, C-412
McKinsey & Company, 297, 338
M. D. Anderson, 136
Mega Entertainment, C-229
Men's Wearhouse, 158
Mercedes-Benz, 132, 143, 297, C-197, C-213–C-215
Merrill Lynch, 71, 224, 330
MGA Entertainment, C-216, C-229–C-230
Michale Kors, 222
Michelin Tires, 66, 132, 184
Microsoft Corp., 60, 63, 96, 132, 175, 324, 347, 363, C-147, C-227
MillerCoors, C-46
Millstone Coffee, C-4
Milwaukee Bucks, C-66
MIT (Massachusetts Institute of Technology), C-107
MIT Technology Review, C-112
MKC (Mary Kay Cosmetics), 80, 362, 366
MLB (Major League Baseball), C-57
Modcloth vintage clothing, 166, C-166–C-167
Modell's Sporting Goods, C-67
Moe's Southwest Grill, C-134–C-136
Molson Coors, 66, C-46
Molton Brown, 140
Moncler, 141
Monday Note blog, C-400
Money magazine, 129
Monitor Consulting, 123
Moody's Investor Service, C-262
Moosejaw.com, C-166
Moose Toys, C-229
Morgan Motors, 132
Motel 6, 139
Motorola Mobility, 165, 167, 200, 210, 306, 329
Motor Trend magazine, C-193
Moviefone, C-83

MoviePass, case, C-80–C-91
  competition of, C-83–C-87
  customer relations, C-87–C-90
  future of, C-90–C-91
  growth of, C-82
  launch of, C-81–C-82
  operations of, C-82–C-83
  overview, C-80–C-81
  struggles initially, C-82
MyHabit.com, 157
Mystic Monk Coffee, case, C-2–C-5
  Carmelite monks of Wyoming, C-2–C-3
  coffee industry overview, C-3–C-4
  financial performance, C-5
  marketing and website operations, C-5
  overview, C-2
  roasting operations of, C-4–C-5

N

NACRA (North American Case Research Association), C-11
Napster, C-393
NASA (National Aeronautics and Space Administration), C-198
NASDAQ, C-32
National Basketball Association (NBA), C-65, C-72
National Collegiate Athletic Association (NCAA), C-57
National Football League (NFL), C-57, C-65–C-66, C-79, C-154
National Football League Players Association (NFLPA), C-390
National Highway Traffic Safety Administration (NTSHA), C-193
National Hockey League (NHL), C-57, C-66
National Labor Relations Board (NLRB), C-356
National Operating Committee for Standards on Athletic Equipment, C-388
National Outdoor Leadership School (WY), C-11
National Relief Charities (NRC-), C-96
National Renewable Energy Laboratory (NREL), 109
National Restaurant Association, 83
NBA (National Basketball Association), C-65, C-72
NBC television network, C-297
NBCUniversal, C-279
NCAA (National Collegiate Athletic Association), C-57; see also Concussions in college and pro football, case
Neato Robotics, C-113
Neiman Marcus, 76, C-95
Nelson Steel, Inc., C-309
Nestlé, 96–97, 184, C-268, C-363, C-399
Netflix, 63, 71, 168, 343, C-80–C-82, C-91, C-286
Netflix, case, C-149–C-161
  business model of, C-155–C-157
  financing original content and acquisitions, C-160–C-161
  globalization efforts of, C-149–C-152

  overview, C-149
  strategy of, C-157–C-160
  video market and, C-152–C-155
Netgear, 155
NetJets, 157
Neurosurgery journal, C-379
Newell-Rubbermaid, 70, 184, 235, 237
New England Journal of Medicine, C-379, C-389, C-408
Newk's, C-134
News Corporation, 165
New Yorker magazine, 102, C-297, C-407
New York Post, C-54, C-90
New York Stock Exchange (NYSE), C-162
New York Times, C-90, C-117–C-118, C-258, C-382, C-389
NFL (National Football League), C-57, C-65–C-66, C-79, C-154
NFLPA (National Football League Players Association), C-390
NHL (National Hockey League), C-57, C-66
Nike, Inc., 10, 25, 60, 93, 99, 169, 278, 284, C-59, C-69, C-93, C-142, C-166
  manufacturing, C-77
  marketing, promotions, and endorsements, C-74–C-75
  overview, C-72–C-73
  products, C-73–C-74
  resources and capabilities, C-75–C-77
  Under Armour versus, C-71–C-72
Nippon Cable (Japan), C-336
Nissan Motor Co., 102, 284, C-213
NLRP (National Labor Relations Board), C-356
Nokia telecommunications, 200, 210
Noodles & Company, C-134
Nordstrom, Inc., 132, 348, C-67, C-92, C-95
North American Case Research Association (NACRA), C-11
North Bay Business Journal, C-101
Northern Arizona University, C-11
North Face, C-166
Northwestern University, C-65
Norwegian Cruise Lines, C-332
Notre Dame University, C-65
Nottingham University, C-232
Novartis, 265
NPD Group, C-181
NPD Retail Tracking Service, C-113
NRC (National Relief Charities), C-96
NREL (National Renewable Energy Laboratory), 109
NTSHA (National Highway Traffic Safety Administration), C-193
NTT (Japan), 221
Nucor Corporation, 111, 128–130, 339–340, 362
Nucor Corporation, case, C-296–C-330
  acquisitions of, C-307–C-310
  background of, C-296–C-298
  competition of, C-327–C-329
  cost-efficiency of, C-298–C-302
  cost-efficient production adoption of, C-311–C-312
  employee relations of, C-320–C-322

as environmental performance leader, C-318
finished steel products of, C-302–C-303
global growth *versus* joint ventures, C-314–C-315
organization and management philosophy of, C-318–C-319
overview, C-296
pricing and sales of, C-305–C-307
production investments of, C-310–C-311
raw materials strategy of, C-315–C-318
steel as commodity, C-298
steel industry worldwide, C-322–C-327
steel mill products of, C-303–C-305
value-added products strategy of, C-312–C-314
workforce compensation of, C-319–C-320
NYSE (New York Stock Exchange), C-162

O

Obvious Corp., C-141
Ocean Spray, 330
Oculus VR, 302
Odeo, C-138–C-139, C-141
OECD (Organization for Economic Cooperation and Development), 264
Office Depot, C-34
Old El Paso, 32
Olive Garden, 83
Oliver's Market, C-102
Olympic Games, C-65–C-66, C-77, C-233, C-332, C-343
Omission Brewery, C-48
Open Table, 160
Orbitz.com, C-403
Organic Report magazine, 83
Organic Trade Association, 83
Organization for Economic Cooperation and Development (OECD), 264
Oriental Brewery, C-47
Oriental Land Company (Japan), 193
Oshkosh Corporation, 337
Otis Elevator, 200, 334

P

Pabst beers, 76
Pacific Gas and Electric, 280
Panasonic, C-210
Panda Express, C-134
Pandora broadcast radio, 13–14
Panera Bread Company, 83, C-134
Papa John's pizza, 141
Páramo outdoor clothing (UK), 287
PAREXEL research, 175
Paris Disneyland, C-285
Partners in Health, C-96
Patagonia, 102, 283, C-166
Paychex, 172
PayPal, 253, C-198
PC Magazine, C-109–C-110, C-113
Pemex (Mexico), 173

Pennsylvania State University, C-380
People magazine, 141
Pepperidge Farm, 169
PepsiCo, 34, 110, 134, 253, 272–273, 280, 284, C-203, C-360–C-361, C-364, C-403
PepsiCo diversification, case, C-265–C-276
    Asia, Middle East, and North Africa performance, C-275–C-276
    Beverages North America performance, C-274–C-275
    Europe and Sub-Saharan Africa performance, C-275
    Frito-Lay North America performance, C-271–C-274
    history of, C-266–C-268
    Latin America performance, C-275
    overall performance of, C-268–C-271
    overview, C-265–C-266
    Quaker Foods North America performance, C-274
    2018 strategic situation of, C-276
    value chain alignment in, C-276
Perez Family Restaurant, C-103
Periscope mobile app, C-142
Perkins Coie LLP, C-399
Perrigo Company Plc, 140
Persistence Market Research, C-110
Pesman Art Studio, C-278
PetCo, 99
PetSmart, 99, C-34
Pfizer, Inc., 33, 46, 330
PGA (Professional Golf Association), C-62
Philips Electronics, 41
Philips Lighting, 72
Pikes Place Market (Seattle), C-352
Pinterest.com, C-138
Pirelli Tires, 66
Pittsburgh Steelers, C-388
Pixar animation studios, C-279–C-280
Pizza Hut, C-266
Plank Industries, C-59
Playmobil, C-229
Play Station Vue, C-153
Porsche Motors, C-213–C-214
Postmates delivery service, C-131
Pottery Barn, 301
Poulan, 130
POWDR Corp., C-336
Prada, 77, 132, 304
Premier League Football clubs (EU), C-68
Price Club, C-17–C-18
Procter & Gamble (P&G), 70, 92, 229–230, 252, 277
Professional Golf Association (PGA), C-62, C-66
PSA Peugeot Citroen, C-215
Publix Co., Inc., 110, 365
Purdue Pharma, C-406, C-408–C-409, C-412
Purdue University, C-172

Q

Qdoba Mexican Eats, C-134, C-136–C-137
Quaker Foods North America, C-268, C-274

QualServe Benchmarking Clearinghouse, 108
Quartz, C-182
Queen's University (Canada), C-198
Quicken Loans, 297
Quora.com, C-138

R

Radisson Hotels, C-360
Rainforest Alliance Certified farms, 281
Ralph Lauren Corporation, 135, 163, C-169
Rambler's Way, 163
Ravensburger, C-229
Realtor.com, C-55
Redbox, C-80, C-82
Red Bull, 132
Reddit.com, C-138
Redhook Brewery, C-48
Reebok, Inc., C-77, C-79
Regal theaters, C-82, C-90
Renault-Nissan-Mitsubishi Alliance, 174
Repsol oil production (Spain), 189
Republic Conduit Corporation, C-310
Reserve Bank of Zimbabwe (RBZ), C-235
Reuters news service, C-117
Riddell helmets, C-385–C-387
Rio Tinto Group, C-316
Rite Aid, Inc., 140
Ritz Carlton Hotels, 132, 202, 352, C-334–C-335
Roark Capital, C-135
Robert Bosch GmbH, 175, 323
Robopolis (France), C-109
Roche Partnering, 175
Rockport shoes, C-77
Rock Resorts, C-337
Rodarte, 8
Rolex, 6, 111, 204
Rolex China Mobile (Switzerland), 3
Rolls-Royce, 12
Ronald McDonald House, 274
Room and Board, 111
Roto-Rooter, 193
Royal Bank of Scotland, 249
Royal Canadian Mounted Police, 33
Royal Dutch/Shell, 283
RueLaLa, 157
Rugby Canada, C-66
Ryanair Airlines (Ireland), 111, 130, 333

S

Saatchi & Saatchi China, C-258
SABMiller, C-41, C-46
Safeway Co., Inc., 110, 140, 144, C-363
Saint Archer Brewing Company, C-46
Saks Fifth Avenue, 76, 157
Salesforce.com, 46, 111, 297, 369
Sales On Demand Corporation (SODC, Japan), C-108
Sam's Club, 140, 149, C-18, C-34–C-36, C-162–C-163
Samsung Group, 60, 175, 210, 253, 267, 306, C-114, C-116
San Francisco General Hospital, C-378

San Jose State University, C-331, C-406
São Paulo soccer team (Brazil), C-66
SAP, 328
SAS, 297
Satyam Computer Services (India), 211
Save the Children, C-96, C-374
Schutt Sports, C-389
Scotland Yard, 26
Sears, Inc., 358, C-22
Sears Holding, 255
Seattle's Best Coffee, C-4, C-362
Seattle Times, C-29
Securities and Exchange Commission (SEC), 265–266, C-37
7-Eleven, 33, 193
Shake Shack, C-134
Shanda video games (China), 210
Shanghai Disneyland, C-280, C-285
SharkNinja Operating, LLC, C-113–C-114, C-117
Shearwater Adventures Ltd., case, C-232–C-239
    activities offered by, C-238–C-239
    adventure sports industry, C-233–C-234
    competition of, C-234–C-235
    customers of, C-236
    integration of, C-236
    Roberts as partner in, C-232–C-233
    technology used by, C-236–C-238
    in Zimbabwe, C-235–C-236
Shell Oil Company, 173
Sheraton Hotels, C-360
Sherpa Capital, C-400
ShoeBuy.com, 166, C-166
ShopSavvy app, 67
Shougang Corporation (China), C-316
Showtime cable channel, C-153, C-286
Siemens, 330
Siemens Healthcare, 334
Sierra Trading Post, C-243
Simba, C-229
Sinemia (Turkey), C-87
SiriusXM broadcast radio, 13–14, 17
Sisley apparel and leather goods, 173
Six Sigma Academy, 329
Sketchers shoes, C-93
Sky entertainment (Europe), C-159, C-277
Skyline Steel LLC, C-309
Sleep Inn, 139
Sling TV, C-153
Smucker's, 229
Snap, Inc., C-145–C-147
Snapchat.com, C-138, C-145–C-146
Snapper, 60
SODC (Sales On Demand Corporation, Japan), C-108
Softbank Group Corp., C-185, C-403–C-404
SolarCity, Inc., C-198
Solar Energy Industries Association, 109
Sonoma State University, C-101
Sony, Inc., C-227
Southern Methodist University, C-92
Southland Tube Corporation, C-310
South Pacific Steel Corporation, C-309
South Tahoe Airport, C-335

Southwest Airlines, 6, 30, 107–108, 128, 130, 278
Space Exploration Technologies (SpaceX), 34, C-198
S&P 500 index, C-143
S&P Global Ratings, C-262
Spin Master, C-229
Spirit Airlines, 130, 155
Sport Obermeyer, 308
Sports Authority, C-67, C-166
Sports & Fitness Industry Association, C-377
Sports Illustrated magazine, 141, C-389–C-390
Spruce Point Capital Management, C-117
Spyder, 308
Standard & Poor's (S&P), C-307
Stanford Center for Internet and Society, C-117
Stanford University, 158
Stanley, Inc., C-117
Staples, Inc., 66, 285, C-34
Starbucks, Inc., 3, 46, 104, 134, 184, 200, 276, 284, 313, 365, C-3, C-257
Starbucks, Inc., case, C-351–C-376
  as coffee, tea, and spice company, C-351–C-353
  coffee purchasing strategy, C-369–C-372
  corporate social responsibility strategy, C-372–C-374
  expansion beyond Pacific Northwest, C-356–C-358
  mission and values, C-368–C-369
  1988 to present, C-365–C-368
  overview, C-351–C-376
  as private company, C-355–C-356
  Schultz's purchase of, C-353–C-355
  store ambiance, C-360
  store design, C-358–C-360
  strategy of, C-360–C-365
  top management changes at, C-374–C-375
Starbucks Foundation, C-372, C-374
Starbucks Global Farmer Fund, C-371–C-372
Stars Restaurant, C-124
Startup Legal Garage, C-392
Starwood Hotels and Resorts Worldwide, 104, C-7
Starz cable channel, C-153, C-286
Stichting INGKA Foundation, C-251
St. Jude Children's Research Hospital, 27
Stokley-Van Camp, C-268
Strategic Planning Institute's Council on Benchmarking, 108
Strauss Group, C-268
Stride Rite, 130
Studio Movie Grill, C-82
Sumitomo Metal Industries, C-308
Sundance Festival, C-336
Sundaram Fasteners (India), 211
Sun Pharmaceuticals, 153
Sun Power, 109
Super 8 motels, 139
Super Bowl, 123, C-131, C-343
Supervalu Stores, Inc., C-177
Surfers against Sewage, C-97
Suzuki Motor Co., 209
Swatch watches, 8

Sycamore Development Co. (Plank Industries), C-59
SYSCO Corporation, C-360

T

Taco Bell, C-133–C-135, C-266
Taiwan Semiconductor Manufacturing Company (TSMC), 291
Talisker Land Holdings, C-336
Target Stores, Inc., 8, 70, 149, C-22, C-34, C-53, C-142, C-165, C-171, C-180, C-220, C-230, C-363
Tata Steel (India), 3
TaylorMade Golf, C-77
TD Ameritrade, 71, 308
Tel Aviv University, C-220
Televisa (Mexico), 211
Telluride Golf & Ski, C-335, C-341
Tencent (China), 210
Tesla Motor Corp., 8, 30, 34, 72, 102, 111, 138, 171, 180
Tesla Motor Corp., case, C-191–C-215
  background of, C-195–C-199
  challenges to, C-194–C-195
  design and engineering, C-207–C-208
  distribution strategy, C-203–C-206
  in global automotive industry, C-213–C-215
  leasing activities, C-211
  manufacturing strategy, C-208–C-210
  marketing strategy, C-210–C-211
  Model S and Model X, C-193–C-194
  production issues at, C-191–C-193
  product line strategy, C-201–C-203
  regulatory credit sales, C-211–C-212
  strategy overview, C-200
  technology and product development strategy, C-206–C-207
Tesla Energy, C-212–C-213
in 2018, C-199–C-200
Teva pharmaceuticals, C-412
Texas A&M University, C-6, C-41, C-77, C-107, C-216, C-265, C-277
Texas Tech University, C-65
Textile Exchange, C-97
Textron, 234
3M Corporation, 30, 132, 258, 366
Three Ocean Shipping, 359
Ticketmaster, 180
Tiffany & Co., 167, 188, 204
Time Warner, C-154–C-155
Tinder.com, 161
TJ Maxx, 77, 111
TJX Companies, Inc., 313–314
TJX Companies, Inc., case, C-240–C-250
  businesses of, C-242–C-246
  overview, C-240–C-241
  stock performance of, C-242
  store growth of, C-246–C-248
  strategic vision and management focus of, C-241
Tax Cuts and Jobs Act of 2017 impact on, C-248–C-249

2018 fiscal year financial performance of, C-246
2019 fiscal year financial performance of, C-249–C-250
Tokyo Disneyland, C-279, C-281, C-285
Tommy Hilfiger, 169
TOMS Shoes, 28–29, 278, 283
TOMS Shoes, case, C-92–C-100
  background of, C-92–C-93
  financial success of, C-98–C-99
  industry background, C-93–C-94
  social responsibility of, C-94–C-98
Toro equipment, 60
Toronto Maple Leafs, C-66
Tourvest, C-234
Toyota Motor Co., 101, 107, 119, 135, 143, 301, C-213, C-215
Toys "R" Us, C-216, C-220, C-228
TPG Capital, C-399
Trader Joe's, 144, 352, C-34
Trade Secret stores (Australia), C-241
Trico Steel Company, C-308
Triple Peaks ski resorts, C-341
Trump Entertainment Resorts, 49
Tsingshan Group Holdings (China), C-327
TSMC (Taiwan Semiconductor Manufacturing Company), 291
Tuck School of Business, Dartmouth College, C-92
Tune Hotels, 157
Tupperware, 366
Turing Pharmaceuticals, 359
21st Century Fox, 267, C-277–C-278, C-280
Twitter.com, 72, C-87, C-89
Twitter.com, case, C-138–C-148
  brand image of, C-141–C-142
  competitors of, C-143–C-147
  history of, C-138–C-141
  restructuring of, C-143
  services, products and revenue streams of, C-142–C-143
  stock performance of, C-143
  2018 performance of, C-147–C-148
Tyco Toys, Inc., C-217
Tyson Foods, 285

U

Uber Technologies, 28, 130, 157, 268, 335
Uber Technologies, case, C-392–C-405
  background, C-393
  boardroom drama at, C-401–C-402
  corporate governance fiasco, C-400–C-401
  corporate structure of, C-396
  crisis at, C-396–C-399
  future of, C-402–C-404
  Holder report on, C-399
  investor revolt, C-399–C-400
  overview, C-392–C-393
  performance, C-394–C-396
UCLA (University of California at Los Angeles), C-65, C-220
Udacity, 71
Under Armour, 10, 60, 169, C-166
Under Armour, case, C-56–C-79

  competition: adidas Group, C-77–C-79
  competition: Nike, Inc., C-71–C-77
  distribution strategy in 2018 of, C-67–C-69
  financial performance collapse of, C-58–C-60
  growth strategy in 2018 of, C-61–C-62
  inventory management in, C-71
  marketing, promotion, and brand management strategy in 2018 of, C-65–C-67
  overview, C-56–C-57
  product design and development strategy in 2018 of, C-69–C-70
  product line strategy in 2018 of, C-62–C-65
  sourcing, manufacturing, and quality assurance in, C-70
UN Global Compact, 282
UNICEF, C-96
Unilever, 127, 200, 208, 280–282, C-361, C-364
United Airlines, 267, C-332, C-360
United Colors of Benetton, 173
United States Army, C-108, C-278
United States Library of Congress, C-278
Universal Studios, C-278
University of Alabama, C-17, C-56, C-80, C-120, C-149, C-183, C-191, C-232, C-296, C-351, C-377
University of Arizona, C-381
University of California, C-65
University of Florida, C-268
University of Maryland, C-56, C-65
University of Miami, C-77
University of Missouri, C-65
University of Pennsylvania, C-198
University of South Alabama, C-107, C-138, C-240, C-377
University of South Carolina, C-65
University of Syracuse, C-381
University of Texas, C-390
University of Utah, C-65
University of Washington, C-387
University of Wisconsin, C-65
UN Millennium Development Goals, 282
UPS, Inc., 98, 193, 333, C-4, C-203
Urban Outfitters, Inc., 117–119, C-92
USAA insurance, 150
US Airways, 164
U.S. Army Medical Command, 33
U.S. Department of Agriculture, C-121, C-127, C-271
U.S. Department of Commerce, C-188, C-307, C-326, C-337
U.S. Department of Energy, C-197
U.S. Department of Justice (DOJ), C-277, C-398, C-406, C-409
U.S. Department of Veteran Affairs, C-379, C-411
U.S. Environmental Protection Agency (EPA), 43, C-211, C-373
U.S. Food and Drug Administration (FDA), C-121, C-126, C-137, C-408
US Foodservice, C-360
U.S. Forest Service, C-333

U.S. International Trade Commission (ITC-), C-308, C-326, C-328
U.S. Naval Academy, C-65
U.S. Postal Service, 333, C-4
U.S. Steel Corp., C-325, C-329
U.S. Supreme Court, 80
U.S. Women's National Soccer Team, C-66
UTV, C-280

V

Vail/Eagle County Airport, C-334
Vail Resorts, Inc., case, C-331–C-350
    competition, C-341–C-344
    family of facilities, C-332–C-337
    financial performance of, C-346–C-348
    history of, C-331–C-332
    market structure, C-340–C-341
    overview, C-331
    recreation resort industry, C-337–C-340
    structure to follow strategy of, C-348–C-350
    vision statement of, C-344–C-346
Valve Corporation, 319, 327
Vanguard investments, 129, 150
Vanity Fair magazine, C-54
Vault.com, 363
Vector Products, 229
Venmo digital wallet, 155
Verco Manufacturing Co., C-309
Verge, The, C-118
Verizon, Inc., 33, C-83, C-152
VF Corporation, 254–255
VICIS football helmets, C-387
Vilar Performing Arts Center, C-334
Virgin Atlantic Airlines, 261
Visa credit card systems, C-361–C-362
Vision Spring, 277

Vissann, C-213
Volkswagen AG, 28, 42–43, 46, C-213, C-215
Volvo Motor Co., C-213
VTech, C-229
Vudu, C-153

W

Waco Convention Center and Visitors' Bureau (TX), C-55
Walgreens, Inc., 140, 195–196, 214, C-413
Walgreens Boots Alliance, 196
Wall Street Journal, C-155
Walmart Stores, Inc., 6, 46, 66, 70, 76, 128, 130, 140, 149, 165–166, 184, 285, 348, 362, 364–365, C-18, C-22, C-155, C-171, C-177, C-180–C-181, C-203, C-220, C-228, C-230, C-261, C-363, C-412
Walmart Stores, Inc., case, C-162–C-170
    channel and brand consolidation of, C-169
    history of, C-162–C-165
    mission and ethics statements of, C-168–C-169
    online retail acquisitions of, C-165–C-168
    retailing future of, C-169
Walt Disney Company, 3, 193, 205, 219, 226, 275, 365, C-154, C-217–C-218, C-220–C-221, C-229
Walt Disney Company diversification, case, C-277–C-290
    consumer products and interactive media business of, C-286–289
    corporate strategy of, C-281–C-282

    history of, C-278–C-279
    media networks of, C-282–C-283
    overview, C-277–C-278
    parks and resorts of, C-283–C-285
    performance of, C-279–C-281, C-289–C-290
    studio entertainment business of, C-286
Walt Disney World Resort, C-279, C-285
Wanqing Consultancy (China), C-260
Warby Parker, 99, 169, 276–277, 287
Washington Post, C-412
Waterford Crystal, C-24
Wayfair.com, 357
Waymo (Alphabet), 155
WBC (World Boxing Competition), C-66
WBD (Wimm-Bill-Dann) Foods (Russia), C-266, C-268
WeChat messenger app (China), 211–212
Wegmans Food Markets, 337–338, 343
Weibo (China), C-262
Weinstein Company LLC, 267
Wells Fargo Bank, 33, 269, 281
Welsh Rugby Union, C-66
Wendy's restaurants, 307
Westin Hotels, C-360
WFTO (World Fair Trade Organization) cooperatives, C-4
WhatsApp.com, 104, C-138, C-144–C-145
Whirlpool appliances, 132, 204–205
Whistler-Blackcomb ski resorts (Canada), C-332, C-336, C-346
Whole Foods Market, 25, 140, 281–283, C-102, C-104, C-166, C-169; *see also* Amazon. com, case

Widmer Brothers Brewing, C-48
Wild Horizons adventure sports, C-234
Williams-Sonoma, 301
Wil's Grill, case, C-11–C-16
    catering market segment, C-15–C-16
    Flagstaff location of, C-12
    market for, C-14–C-15
    overview, C-11
    profit and loss statement, C-14
    revenue projections, C-16
    street food events, C-12–C-13
Wimm-Bill-Dann (WBD) Foods (Russia), C-266, C-268
Windpact football helmets, C-387
Winners Apparel Ltd., C-240
Wipro (India), 153
W. L. Gore & Company, 97, 348, 365
World Boxing Competition (WBC), C-66
World Cup ski events, C-343
World Fair Trade Organization (WFTO) cooperatives, C-4
Worthington Industries, C-308

X

XcelHR, 172
Xerox, Inc., 96, 107

Y

Yahoo.com, 30, C-144
Yahoo Finance, C-90
Yamaha, 226
Yelp.com, 357, C-9
YouGov Brand Index, 144
YouTube.com, 141, C-152–C-153, C-221

Name Index

A

Ablaza, Ana, C-264
Ackerman, Evan, C-119
Acton, Brian, C-143
Agie, Bradley R., 289
Agnefjall, Peter, C-252
Ahlstrand, Bruce, 47
Ahuja, G., 259
Alba, Davey, C-183, C-396, C-404–C-405
Albarran, Tammy, C-399
Alexander, M., 259
Alexander, Marcus, 219
Al-Ruayyan, Yasir bin Othman, C-401
Alvarez, Camelo, C-66
Ambroé, Milan, 344
Amini, Alen A., 268
Amit, R., 120
Amsden, Davida M., 344
Amsden, Robert T., 344
Anderson, Eric T., 18
Angle, Colin, C-107, C-112, C-117–C-118
Anslinger, Patricia L., 181, 259
Antony, Jiju, 344
Anumonwo, Charles K., 161
Argandoa, Antonio, 288
Armin, C-148
Armitage, Alice, C-392
Arnold, David J., 216
Aron, Adam, C-83, C-331, C-344, C-346, C-348, C-350
Arshad, Fatima, C-263
Ascari, Allessio, 344
Austin, Nancy, C-330
Avins, Jenni, 277
Aycock, Dave, C-297

B

Badaracco, Joseph L., 370
Badrinath, Dipti, 166
Bailes, Julian, C-379
Bailey, Wendy J., 288
Bain, J. S., 84
Baldwin, Jerry, C-351
Band, David C., 344
Bansal, Binny, C-168
Bansal, Sachin, C-168
Barboza, D., C-231
Bardem, Javier, C-154
Barkema, H., 259, 320
Barnes, Brooks, C-91
Barney, J., 18
Barney, Jay B., 120, 370
Barringer, Bruce, 47
Barthélemy, Jérôme, 181
Bartlett, C. A., 216
Bartlett, Christopher A., 120, 181, 320, 370

Baum, J., 320
Baun, William B., 289
Beauchamp, T. L., 288
Beckard, Richard, 320
Beckham, David, C-77–C-78
Beckham, Odell, Jr., C-385
Beckham, Victoria, 8
Belson, K., C-391
Benner, K., C-10
Benner, Katie, C-405
Bennett, Drake, 141
Bergen, Mark E., 120, 180
Berger, Sephanie K., 144
Berlin, Lorin, 288
Berry, Leonard L., 289
Bettcher, Kim Eric, 288
Bezos, Jeff, 34, 318–319, 335, 364, C-171–C-172, C-175–C-176, C-181–C-182, C-184, C-393
Bhagat, Namita, C-263
Bhasin, Kim, C-263
Bhattacharya, Arindam K., 216
Bhattarai, Abha, C-170
Bhulyan, Johana, C-405
Bieber, Justin, C-142
Bird, Larry, C-141
Black, Leon, C-331
Blank, Arthur, 155
Bleeke, Joel, 216
Bloom, Orlando, C-154
Blue, Allen, C-147
Bluedorn, Allen C., 47
Boatwright, Scott, C-130
Boldin Anquan, C-66
Bolman, Lee, 21
Bonderman, David, C-399
Bosch, Robert, 323
Boschken, Herman L., C-331
Bossidy, Larry, 320, 370
Bower, Joseph L., 47, 181
Bowie, N. E., 288
Bowker, Gordon, C-351
Bowman, Jeremy, C-40
Boyle, M., 338
Bradham, Caleb, C-266
Bradsher, Keith, 306
Brady, Tom, C-66–C-67
Branagh, Nicole, C-66
Brandenburger, A., 18
Branson, Richard, 261
Brarad, Jill, C-217
Brees, Drew, C-73
Breslow, J. M., C-390
Brin, Sergey, 23, C-197
Brinkley, Christina, 105
Brinkman, Johannes, 288
Brodin, Jesper, C-252
Bromiley, Philip, 46–47
Brooks, Rodney, C-107
Brotman, Jeff, C-18, C-21, C-31
Browd, Sam, C-387
Brown, Robert, 46–47
Brown, Ryan, C-170

Brown, Shona L., 18
Brugmann, Jeb, 288
Brunson, Rochelle R., C-51, C-162
Brush, T., 259
Bryant, Chris, 43, C-78
Bryant, Kobe, C-73
Bryce, David J., 180
Buckley, P. J., 215–216
Buckley, W. E., C-391
Buffett, Warren, 34
Bündchen, Giselle, C-66
Burcher, Peter, 344
Burke, Ronald J., 344
Burkle, Ron, C-400
Burleson, Bobby, C-118
Burnah, Phillip, 320, 344
Burns, Lawton R., 344
Burton, R. M., 320
Bush, George W., C-307–C-308
Byers, Dylan, C-183
Byford, Sam, C-405
Byrne, John, 320
Byrnes, N., 340
Byrnes, Nanette, C-330

C

Cahill, Joe, C-264
Caliguiri, Paula M., 344
Calloway, Wayne, C-266
Cameron, S., C-10
Camp, Garrett, C-393, C-396
Camp, Robert C., 121
Campbell, A., 259, 320
Campbell, Andrew, 219
Canavati, Sergio, C-101
Canfield, Jack, 3
Cannella, A., 259
Capron, L., 196, 320
Carasco, Emily F., 370
Carcia, Lorena, C-135
Carter, John C., 370
Carver, John, 47
Cavanagh, Roland R., 344
Cha, Sandra E., 370
Chafkin, Max, 277
Champy, J., 344
Chan, E., 255
Chandler, A., 320
Chang, Morris, 291
Charan, Ram, 320, 370
Chatain, O., 181
Chatham, Jennifer A., 370
Chatterjee, S., 259
Chen, Chia-Pei, 288
Chen, Heather, C-264
Chen, Ming-Jer, 181
Chen, Roger, 288
Cheney, Lauren, C-66
Cheng, Evelyn, C-183
Chesky, Brian, C-6–C-7, C-9–C-10

Chilkoti, Avantika, 215
Christ, John, C-11–C-12
Christensen, Clayton M., 18, 344
Chu, Valerie, C-263–C-264
Cicero, Theodore J., C-413
Ciechanover, A., 129
Cimilluca, D., C-231
Clancy, Tom, C-154
Clark, Delwyn N., 370
Clark, Robert C., 47
Clark, Travis, C-161
Clinton, Bill J., C-307
Cohen, Allan R., C-291
Cohen, Randy, C-381
Cohler, Matt, C-400–C-401
Collins, James C., 46, 289
Collins, Jim, 291, 320
Collins, Landon, C-78
Collis, David J., 46–47, 259
Comerford, Eoin, C-166
Connor, Neil, C-263
Cooper, Bradley, 141
Cooper, Robin, 121
Copeland, Misty, C-66–C-67
Copeland, Thomas E., 259
Correa, Carlos, C-78
Correnti, John, C-297
Cortés, Hernán, C-154
Coster, Katherine, 196
Covin, Jeffrey G., 47, 181
Cox, Margo, 349
Coyne, Kevin P., 181
Crandall, Jacob M., 43, 158
Cremer, Andreas, 43
Cromme, Gerhard, 43
Crosby, Philip, 344
Cucuzza, Thomas G., 121
Curry, Stephen, C-62, C-66–C-67
Cusumano, M. A., 181

D

Daley, Robin A., 3310
Dalton, Matthew, C-330
Daly, Andy, C-331, C-344
Darr, Eric D., 344
Dart, Michael, C-170
Datman, Par, C-263
D'Aveni, Richard, 180
Davidson, Hugh, 24, 46
Davidson, Wallace N., 288
Davis, Mike, C-232
Davis, Scott, 180
Dawar, Niroj, 216
Dayton, Nick A., 344
Deal, T. E., 370
Deal, Terrence E., 370
Dechant, Kathleen, 288
Deems, Gene, C-89
Delevingne, Cara, C-154
Denman, Tim, C-255, C-263

Deshpandé, Rohit, 288
Devinney, Timothy M., 288
Dezember, R., 196
Dickson, Richard, C-221
Dienhart, John W., 272
DiMicco, Daniel, 340
DiMicco, Daniel R.,
    C-297–C-298, C-312
Disney, Roy, C-278–C-279
Disney, Walt, 219, C-277–C-278,
    C-345
Doctoroff, Tom, C-260–C-261
Donald, Jim, C-374
Donaldson, Gordon, 47
Donaldson, Thomas, 288
Doolin, Elmer, C-266
Dorsey, Jack, C-138–C-139,
    C-141, C-143
Dosi, G., 320
Doz, Yves L., 181, 216, 259
Dranikoff, Lee, 259
Drucker, Peter F., 259
Duhigg, Charles, 306
Dunfee, Thomas W., 288
Dunn, Andy, 158
Duprey, R., C-91
Durant, Kevin, C-66, C-73
Durante, Kathleen T., 32
Dussauge, P., 215, 320
Dutta, Soumitra, 344
Dyer, Jeffrey H., 180, 181, 216

E

Eaton, Earl, C-331
Eberhard, Martin, C-195, C-197
Eckert, Robert, C-217
Eckhart, Aaron, C-154
Edison, Thomas, 49
Eichenwald, Kurt, 288, 370
Eisenhardt, K., 120
Eisenhardt, Kathleen M., 18, 259
Eisenstat, Russell, 120, 320
Eisner, Alan, 279
Eisner, Michael, C-279
Elfenbein, Hillary A., 289
El-Jelly, Abuzar, 288
Ells, Steve, C-122, C-124–C-125,
    C-130
Elmquist, Sonja, C-330
Emerson, Ralph Waldo, 15
Enrico, Roger, C-267
Erdogan, Recep, C-138, C-142
Ernst, David, 216
Euteneuer, Joseph, C-221
Evanson, Jeff, C-215
Ewert, Doug, 155

F

Fahmy, D., C-10
Faires, Ross N., C-232
Fairs, Marcus, C-264
Fallon, Jimmy, C-141
Fanning, Shawn, C-393
Farkas, Charles M., 370
Farnsworth, Ted, C-90
Faulkneer, Judith, 349
Fawcett, Stanley E., 320, 344
Federer, Roger, C-73

Feline, Suzy, C-16
Feloni, Richard, 158
Ferratt, Thomas W., 344
Ferrier, W. J., 180
Ferriola, John J., C-298, C-328
Fiegenbaum, Avi, 84
Fiegerman, Seth, C-404
Finskud, Lars, C-170
Fiorina, Carly, 255
Flint, Joe, C-161
Floyd, Steven, 320
Fong, Mei, C-263–C-264
Foote, Nathaniel, 120, 320
Forbes, Thom, C-170
Fortune, Brittney, C-100
Fournette, Leonard, C-66
Fowler, Susan, C-396–C-397, C-399
Francis, Pope, C-138, C-142
Frank, T. A., C-170
Franko, Lawrence G., 259
Frenkel, Sheera, C-405
Friedman, Josh, C-215
Frisk, Patrik, C-56
Frost, Tony, 216
Fulks, Kip, C-56

G

Gaines, Chip, C-51–C-55
Gaines, Joanna, C-51–C-55
Galanti, Richard, C-31
Galunic, D. Charles, 259
Gamble, John E., C-6, C-41, C-107,
    C-265, C-277
Ganesan, Gayathree, C-79
Garrette, B., 215
Garvin, David A., 47
Gassée, Jean-Louis, C-400, C-405
Gates, Bill, 347
George, S., 344
Georgiadis, Margo, C-216,
    C-218–C-219, C-230
Ger, Guitz, 216
Geroski, Paul A., 181
Ghanem, George, C-215
Ghemawat, Pankaj, 216
Ghoshal, S., 216
Ghoshal, Sumantra, 120, 181, 320,
    370
Gibbs, Lindsay, C-391
Gibson, Kelly, C-96
Gidari, Albert, C-117
Gilbert, Clark G., 47
Gilinskym, Armand, C-101
Girdhar, Alka, C-263–C-264
Glaister, K. W., 215–216
Glass, Noah, C-138, C-141
Glover, J., 259
Goffee, Robert, 370
Goldberg, Alan B., C-40
Goldberg, Jason, C-177
Golden, Timothy D., 288
Goldman, A., C-231
Goldsmith, Marshall, 320
Goleman, Daniel, 370
Gonzalez, Irinat, C-89
Gonzalez, Katherine, C-101
Goodell, Roger, C-382, C-384–C-385
Goodman, Paul S., 344
Goold, M., 259, 320
Goold, Michael, 219

Gordon, Joseph, 344
Gordon, Mary Ellen, 84
Gordon, M. Joseph, Jr., 344
Govindarajan, Vijay, 121
Graves, Ryan, C-393, C-396
Greatorex, Vedrana B., 129
Green, Dennis, C-79
Greenfield, R., C-10
Greenfield, W. M., 288
Greenhouse, Steven, C-40
Greiner, Helen, C-107
Griffin, Robert III, C-77
Grill-Goodman, Jill, C-170
Grimm, C. M., 180
Grove, Andy, 183
Guattery, M., C-105–C-106
Guericke, Konstantin, C-147
Guerrasio, J., C-91
Guilford, Gwynn, 212
Gunnarson, Sarah, K., 370
Gurley, Bill, C-393, C-400–C-401
Guy, Gery P., C-409

H

Haddon, Heather, C-183
Hainline, Brian, C-381
Halzak, S., C-231
Hambrick, D., 259
Hambrick, Donald C., 181
Hamel, Gary, 181, 216, 259
Hamm, Joh, C-154
Hammer, M., 344
Handler, Elliott, C-216–C-217
Handler, Ruth, C-216–C-217
Hansegard, Jens, C-263
Hansen, Suzy, 304
Hanson, James, 235
Harden, James, C-66, C-77, C-79
Harford, Barney, C-403
Hariharan, S., 84
Harper, Bryce, C-66
Harris, Ainsley, C-400
Harris, Randall D., C-216
Harrison, Josh, C-78
Hart, Maria, 232
Haspeslagh, P., 259
Hastings, Reed, C-159, C-161
Hatton, Celia, C-263
Haugh, Meaghan I., 212
Hay, Mette, C-261
Hayes, Robert, 87
Hayes, Robert H., 320
Hayibor, Sefa, 289
Hayward, M. L. A., 259
Hedegaard, Holly, C-413
Heeley, Michael B., 181
Heifetz, Ronald A., 370
Helfat, C., 320
Helfat, Constance E., 120–121
Hendricks, Kevin B., 47
Henriques, Adrian, 288
Herrera, Sebastian, C-183
Herrera, Tilde, 288
Herrman, Ernie, C-240
Heskett, James L., 344, 370
Hesselbein, Frances, 320
Hewlett, Bill, 30
Hewson, Marillyn, 34
Hill, Ronald Paul, 275
Hindo, Brian, 344
Ho, Ed, C-143

Hodgetts, Richard M., 344
Hoffman, Guy, C-112, C-117
Hoffman, Reid G., C-147
Hogna, Egil, C-170
Holder, Eric H., Jr., C-399
Holpp, Larry, 344
Homkes, Rebecca, 320
Hook, Leslie, C-404–C-405
Hoopes, D., 18
Hopkins, Anthony, C-154
Horn, John, 181
Hornsey, Liane, C-399
Hornung, Paul, C-385
Hostetter, Leonard R., C-11
Hostetter, Martha, 3310
House, Charles H., 46
Hout, Thomas M., 370
Howland, Daphne, C-174, C-183
Hubbell, Victoria, 370
Huffington, Arianna, C-399, C-401
Hughes, Chris, C-143
Hult, G., 320
Humble, John, 370
Hunnicut, Trevor, C-405
Hutchins, Michele, 123

I

Iacobucci, Dawn, 121
Iger, Robert, C-277–C-280, C-282,
    C-289
Immelt, Jeffrey R., C-401, C-405
Incandela, Denise, C-168
Inkpen, A., 181
Isaac, Mike, C-405
Iverson, F. Kenneth, C-296–C-297,
    C-321
Iwerks, Ub, C-278

J

Jackson, David, 370
Jacobs, A. S., C-16
Jaltley, Arun, 183
James, LeBron, C-73
Jassawalla, Avan R., 370
Jelinek, Craig, C-17–C-18, C-21, C-23,
    C-27, C-31
Jemison, D., 259
Jenk, Justin, 181
Jennings, Brandon, C-66
Jetta, Kurt, C-174
Jobs, Steve, 323, 362
Johnson, Dwayne, C-66–C-67
Johnson, Gretchen, C-80
Johnson, Kevin, C-375
Johnson, Kim, C-291
Johnson, Mark W., 18
Jones, Gareth, 370
Jones, Julio, C-66
Jordan, Michael, C-73, C-94
Juran, J., 344

K

Kagermann, Henning, 18
Kahaner, Larry, 84
Kalanick, Travis, 268, C-392–C-393,
    C-396, C-398–C-401, C-403

Kale, Prashant, 181, 216
Kamprad, Ingvar, C-252
Kanai, Tsutomu, 183
Kanazawa, Michael T., 370
Kaness, Matthew, C-167
Kansara, Vikram Alexei, 158
Kanter, Rosabeth Moss, 181, 216, 320, 370
Kaplan, David A., C-137
Kaplan, Robert S., 47, 121
Kapor, Mitch, C-393, C-399, C-404–C-405
Karim, S., 320
Katila, R., 259
Katz, Rob, C-332, C-344, C-346, C-348, C-350
Kaufman, Rhonda, 47
Kaufman, Stephen P., 47
Keenum, Case, C-384
Kell, J., C-231
Kendall, Marisa, C-405
Kennedy, A. A., 370
Kerr, Steven, 344
Kershaw, Clayton, C-66
Kervin, Sean, C-171, C-183
Kestenbaum, David, C-215
Khanh, Vu Tronbg, C-330
Khanna, Tarun, 216
Khosrowshahi, Dara, C-392, C-402–C-404
Kim, W. Chan, 46, 181
Kimberly, John R., 344
King, Martin Luther, Jr., 261, 347
Kirka, Danica, C-404
Klein, Freada Kapor, C-399, C-405
Kleinschmit, Matt, C-263
Knight, Phil, 284
Knudsen, Trond Riiber, C-170
Koch, James, C-46, C-48
Koger, Susan Gregg, C-166
Koller, Tim, 259
Kolodny, Andrew, C-413
Kotler, Philip, 181
Kotter, John P., 24, 344, 370
Koum, Jan, C-143
Kowitt, Beth, 144, C-264
Kramer, Mark R., 288–289
Krasinski, John, C-154
Kreiz, Ynon, C-216, C-218–C-221, C-230–C-231
Krieger, Mike, C-146
Krueger, Alan B., C-413
Kuchler, Hannah, C-404
Kumar, N., 216
Kwak, Mary, 180

L

Lachenauer, Rob, 180
Laden, Osama bin, C-142
Lady Gaga, C-141–C-142
Lampel, Joseph, 47, C-291
Lane, Diane, C-154
Lang, Brent, C-91
Lanzolla, Gianvito, 181
Larian, Isaac, C-216, C-230
Laurie, Donald L., 370
Lawrence, Anne T., 288, C-406
Lawrence, Ron, C-356
Lawrence, Sadé, 338
Lay, Herman, C-266
Leber, Adam, C-400

Lee, Hau L., 121
Lee, John, C-381, C-388
Lee, Terry Nels, 344
Lemak, David J., 344
Leswing, Kif, C-170
Levandowski, Anthony, C-398
Levesque, Lynne C., 47
Levicki, C., 320
Levisohn, Ben, C-183
Levy, Heather, 298
Lewis, Robin, C-170
Li, Jane, C-264
Li, Licca, C-255, C-259
Li, Muxin, C-184
Li, ZheMing Nels, C-264
Lieberthal, Kenneth, 216
Liedtka, Jeanne M., 259, 320
Lillard, Damian, C-77
Little, Royal, 234
Liu, John D., 291
Long, Christian, C-91
Lorsch, Jay W., 47, 370
Lowe, Mitch, C-80–C-83, C-89–C-91
Lozano, Jaview, 139
Lozano, Mario, C-103
Lubatkin, M., 259
Lucas, George, C-279
Ly, Eric, C-147

M

Ma, Jack, 34, 212, C-185
Macauley, Margaret W., 306
Mackey, John, C-177
MacMillan, Ian C., 180–181
Madhok, Anoop, 181
Madoff, Bernie, 271
Madsen, T., 18
Magretta, Joan, 18
Mahony, Richard, C-399, C-405
Main, Jeremy, 216
Majchrzak, Ann, 344
Malcolm, Hadley, 158
Malmefjall, Leila, C-263
Manley, Geoff, C-378
Mannix, E., 320
Marcus, Bernie, 155
Margolis, Joshua D., 288–289
Marino, Lou, C-80
Marino, McKenna, C-80
Markides, Constantinos C., 259
Markides, Costas, 18, 181
Martello, Wan Ling, C-399
Martin, J., 120
Martin, Ken, 255
Martin, T., 196
Marver, Dave, C-387
Marx, Matt, 344
Mary, Daniel, C-2–C-5
Mather, Shaffi, 123
Matson, Harold, C-231
Mattioli, D., C-231
Mauborgne, Renée, 46, 181
Maudlin, William, C-330
Mayer, Marissa, 30
Mayers, Rakim, C-66
McAlone, N., C-91
McArdle, Megan, C-181, C-183
McCann, Michael, C-390–C-391
McCawley, Tom, 289
McCollum, Andrew, C-143
McCrae, Cody, C-12

McGrath, Rita Gunther, 180
McGregor, J., 340
McIntyre, Douglas A., C-79
McIvor, Ronan, 181
McKee, Ann, C-379
McKenzie, Brian R., 202
McMillon, Doug, C-168
Meier, Barry, C-413
Menkes, Justin, 320
Menor, Larry, 47
Messi, Lionel, C-77
Meyer, Joyce L., C-184
Michael, David C., 216
Michael, Emil, C-399
Middleton, Catherine, C-142
Miles, Morgan P., 47
Miles, Robert H., 370
Miller, C., 47
Miller, Claire Cain, C-375
Miller, Danny, 120, 320
Miller, Jeff, C-383–C-384
Miller, John M., C-330
Miller, Paula M., C-263–C-264
Miller, Ronald, C-279
Miller, Von, C-78
Milne, George R., 84
Milne, Richard, 43
Mintz, Charles, C-278
Mintzberg, H., 320
Mintzberg, Henry, 18, 47
Mirobito, Ann M., 289
Mitchell, Tom, 215
Mitchell, W., 196, 215, 320
Mitts, Heather, C-66
Mnangagwa, Emmerson, C-235
Modi, Narendra, C-142
Mokwa, Michael P., 84
Moldow, Austin, C-82
Montgomery, Cynthia, 120
Montgomery, Cynthia A., 18, 47, 84, 87, 259, 370
Montgomery, Joseph C., 344
Moody, John, C-264
Moore, Daryl, C-356
Moore, M., C-106
Moskivitz, Dustin, C-143
Mroz, John Edward, 320
Mugabe, Robert, C-232, C-235–C-236
Mukherjee, S., 255
Mukherji, Biman, C-330
Murphy, Patrick E., 370
Murray, Alan, C-215
Murray, Andy, C-66
Murray, Demarco, C-77–C-78
Musk, Elon, 34, C-191–C-195, C-197–C-199, C-203, C-212–C-213
Musk, Kimbal, C-198
Mycoskie, Blake, 29, C-92–C-95, C-97–C-99

N

Nadal, Rafael, C-73
Nadler, David A., 47
Nakamura, Y., C-10
Nassauer, Sara, C-161
Nelson, R., 320
Ness, Joseph A., 121
Neuman, Robert P., 344
Nickle, Ashley, C-183

Nicol, Brian, C-133, C-135
Niles-Jolly, Kathryn, 370
Noble, Charles H., 84
Nohria, Nitin, 370
Nooyi, Indra, 34
Nordhielm, Christie, 121
Normile, Robert, C-221
Norton, David P., 47
Noto, Anthony, C-138

O

Obama, Barack, C-142
O'Bannon, Douglas P., 289
Obel, B., 320
O'Falt, Chris, C-91
Ogg, John C., C-79
Oguz, Rifat, C-87
Ohlssen, Mikael, C-257
Ohmae, Kenichi, 49
Olian, Judy D., 344, 370
Olsen, Dave, C-356
Olsen, E., 320
Olusoga, S. Ade, 84
Omalu, Bennett, C-377, C-379
O'Reilly, Charles A., 344
Ortega, David, C-101, C-103–C-105
Ortega, Delores, C-103
Osegowitsch, Thomas, 181
O'Sullivan, Mathew, 109

P

Paccamonti, Sara, 304
Paden, Nita, C-11
Page, Larry, 23, C-197
Paine, Lynn, 288
Paine, Lynn S., 216
Paine, Lynn Sharp, 370
Palepu, Krishna G., 216
Pan, Y. G., 181
Pande, Peter S., 344
Parker, Mark, C-73
Partovi, Hadi, C-399
Pastermack, Alex, 212
Patterson, Scott, C-330
Patton, Leslie, C-137
Peck, Emily, 288
Peraf, Margaret A., 18, 120, 320, C-92
Peters, Tom, C-330
Peyster, Byron G., 282
Pfeffer, Jeffrey, 344, 370
Pharrell, C-78
Phelps, Michael, C-66–C-67
Piëch, Ferdinand, 43
Pisano, Gary, 87, 120
Pisano, Gary P., 181, 320
Pishevar, Shervin, C-400
Plank, Kevin, C-56–C-59, C-61–C-64, C-69, C-79
Plank, Scott, C-56
Ploetz, Greg, C-390
Poetsch, Hans Dieter, 43
Pogue, Davie, C-91
Polman, Paul, 282
Porrras, Jerry I., 46, 289

S

Porter, Michael E., 3, 18, 21, 54, 77, 84, 107, 121, 123, 150, 185–186, 215, 259, 288–289, 370, C-106
Posey, Buster, C-66
Post, James E., 288
Powell, Thomas C., 344
Prahalad, C. K., 181, 216, 288
Premji, Azim, 153
Presley, Elvis, C-54
Preston, Lee E., 289
Price, Raymond L., 46
Price, Sol, C-17–C-18
Priem, Richard L., 150
Pritzker, Nick, C-197
Purdy, Chase, C-182, C-183
Purkayastha, Debapratim, C-171, C-251, C-392

Q

Quelch, John A., 216
Quinn, James Brian, 344, 370
Quinones, Sam, C-412
Qumer, Syeda Maseeha, C-171, C-392

R

Rafat, Ali, C-8
Rao, Ashkay R., 180
Raoilison, Landy, C-264
Redford, Robert, C-336
Reed, John, C-215
Reed, Marlene M., C-51, C-162
Reed, Richard, 344
Reich, Jeremy P., 277
Reichow, G., 171
Reid, Joanne, 370
Reinhall, Per, C-387
Reiss, Dani, 141
Resor, Carry S., 29, C-92
Rey, J. D., C-106
Reyes, Jose, C-66
Rhoads, Gary K., 320, 344
Riccobona, A., C-391
Richardson, Sandy, 47
Ridderstrale, Jonas, 320
Rihanna, C-141–C-142
Ritter, Bill, C-40
Rivkin, Jan, 18
Robert, Michel, 24, 46
Roberts, Allen, C-232, C-236, C-239
Roberts, Julia, C-154
Robins, J. Max, C-40
Rock, Chris, C-159
Rock, Melinda, 344
Rodgers, Aaron, C-77
Roll, R., 259
Roman, Ronald M., 289
Ronaldo, Cristiano, C-73
Rose, Ben, C-118
Rosenberg, Joy, C-378
Rothschld, William E., 181
Rounds, Kate, C-376
Roy, Prabal Basu, C-392
Rudd, Rose A., C-413
Rui, H., 216
Rukstad, Michael G., 46
Rynes, Sara L., 344, 370

Sabastian, Joseph, C-183
Sacca, Chris, C-393
Sackler, Andrew, C-408–C-409
Sackler, Mortimer, C-408–C-409
Sackler, Raymond, C-408–C-409
Sacks, David, C-198
Sage, A., 171
Sahu, Benudhar, C-251
Said, Carolyn, C-404
Salvatierra, Carlos, C-103
Sampson, Charles, C-258
Sanchanta, Mariko, C-376
Sandler, Adam, C-159
Santry, Arthur J., 141
Sanyal, Rajib, 288
Sashittal, Hemant C., 370
Sathe, Vijay, 370
Saunders, Neil, C-167, C-169, C-173
Savage. Tom, C-384
Saverin, Eduardo, C-143
Scanlan, Gerald, 344
Schermerhorn, John R., 272
Schmidt, Eric, 330
Schneider, Anton, 259
Schneider, Benjamin, 370
Schneider, George, C-91
Schoemaker, P., 120
Schultz, Brian, C-82
Schultz, Howard, C-4, C-353–C-357, C-360, C-364–C-368, C-372, C-374–C-375
Schwabel, D., C-106
Schwartz, Jan, 43
Schwartz, Mark S., 288, 370
Schwartzel, Erich, C-161
Schweitzer, Tamara, C-99
Scott, Nate, C-79
Sebastain, Joseph, C-176
See, K., 47
Seemuth, Mike, C-215
Seepersaud, Steve, C-79
Seibert, Pete, C-331
Seitz, Patrick, C-119
Shain, Susan, C-40
Shan, Fang, C-256
Shana, Lebowitz, 29
Shanghvi, Dilip, 153
Shank, John K., 121
Shankman, S., C-391
Shapiro, Nina, C-40
Shaw, Gordon, 46–47
Shaw, Hollie, 141
Sheely, Derek, C-389
Shein, Edgar, 370
Shih, Willy C., 181, 320
Shilhanek, Karl, C-12
Shleifer, A., 259
Shuen, A., 120
Siater, S., 320
Siegel, Zev, C-351
Silberman, Edward J., 171
Silverstein, Michael, C-262
Simester, Duncan, 18
Simmons, J. C., 331
Simons, Robert, 320, 344
Sims, Ronald R., 288
Sinclair, Cameron, 261
Sinclair, Christopher, C-218
Sinegal, Jim, C-17–C-18, C-21–C-22, C-24, C-30–C-31

Singh, Harbir, 181, 216
Singh, Jang B., 370
Singh, Sunil, C-148
Sinha, Jayant, 216
Sitkin, S., 47
Skoll, Jeff, C-197
Slevin, Dennis P., 181
Smedberg, Ulf, C-257, C-259
Smith, Cooper, C-182
Smith, Iain, 275
Smith, Kennedy, 344
Smith, K. G., 180
Smith, M. D., C-391
Smith, Michael David, C-391
Smith, N. Craig, 288
Smith, Orin, C-374
Solomon, J., C-389–C-391
Somerville, Heather, C-401, C-405
Somerville, Iain, 320
Sood, Rajal, C-263–C-264
Soper, Spencer, C-183
Speth, J. G., 288
Spicer, Andrew, 288
Spielberg, Steven, C-154
Spieth, Jordan, C-62–C-63, C-66–C-67
Spikes, Stacy, C-80–C-81
Spiller, C. J., C-77
Springs, Shawn, C-387
Stabler, Ken, C-382
Stalk, George, Jr., 180
Stanciu, Tudor, 212
Stephens, Debra, 275
Stephens, Sloanne, C-66
Stevenson, Howard, 344
Stevenson, Mark, C-215
Stevenson, Seth, 304
Stickland, A. J., C-184
Stockton, Bryan, C-218
Stone, B., C-10
Stone, Christopher "Biz," C-138–C-139
Stone, Emma, 141
Stone, Reuben E., 121
Story, L., C-231
Strickland, A. J., C-232, C-377
Stroh, Linda K., 344
Stuart, H., 18
Stuckey, John, 181
Suarez, Fernando, 181
Sull, Charles, 320
Sull, Donald, 121, 320
Sullivan, Joe, C-402
Sunderam, A., 129
Swift, Taylor, C-141
Swindell, B., C-106
Swisher, Kara, C-404
Systrom, Kevin, C-146
Szulanski, Gabriel, 215

T

Tagliabue, Paul, C-379
Takahashi, M., C-10
Talbot, Margaret, C-407
Tang, Zhihao, C-263–C-264
Tarpenning, Marc, C-195, C-197
Tatum, Donn, C-279
Taylor, Jared, C-147
Teece, D., 120

Temple, John, C-406–C-407, C-411, C-413
Tesla, Nikola, C-195
Theobald, B., C-16
Thomas, Danny, 27
Thomas, Howard, 84
Thomas, Terry, 272
Thompson, Arthur A., Jr., C-17, C-56, C-120, C-149, C-191, C-296, C-351
Thompson, Derek, C-183
Thompson, Emma, C-154
Thomson, Alan, 370
Thunder, Frances C., 25
Timberlake, Justin, C-138, C-142
Tornblom, Richard, C-170
Trujillo, David, C-399
Trump, Donald, 49, C-138, C-142, C-248, C-326, C-375, C-397–C-398
Tse, D. K., 181
Tsoi, Grace, C-264
Tsvangirai, Morgan, C-235
Turcsik, Richard, C-183
Turner, Megan, C-184–C-190
Turnipseed, David L., C-2, C-107, C-138, C-240, C-377
Tushman, Michael L., 344
Twer, Doran, 344

U

Upton, B. J., C-78
Upton, David, 87
Upton, David M., 320
Upton, Justin, C-78
Utley, Chase, C-78

V

Vaillant, Jean-Luc, C-147
Vance, Ashlee, C-215
van Marrewijk, Marcel N. A., 288
van Putten, Alexander B., 180
Varlaro, John D., C-6, C-41
Veiga, John F., 344
Verhage, J., C-10
Vermeulen, F., 259
Viceira, L., 129
Vijayasarathy, Sanket, C-404–C-405
Vishney, R., 259
Vogelstein, Fred, 344
Vonn, Lindsey, C-67

W

Wade, Dwayne, C-73
Wakeam, Jason, 181
Walker, Esmond Cardon, C-279
Walker, G., 18
Walker, Kemba, C-66
Wall, Kim, C-263–C-264
Wally, S., 320
Walsh, J. P., 259
Walston, Stephen L., 344
Walton, M., 344
Walton, Sam, 364, C-18, C-162, C-169
Wang, Helen H., C-263
Wang, Qianwei, 344

Ward, Hines, C-388, C-391
Warner, Mark, C-148
Washer, David B., 139
Waters, J. A., 18
Watson, Elain, 144
Watson, George, C-183
Watson, Gregory H., 121
Watt, Hamet, C-80–C-81
Webb, Allen P., 370
Webber, Jude, 139
Weber, James, 288
Webster, Mike, C-377–C-379
Wei, Cheng, C-396
Wei, Lingling, C-330
Weiga, John F., 288
Welch, Jack, 3, 21, 87, 219,
     320, 364
Welch, Suzy, 320
Wells, David, C-161
Wenqian, Zhu, C-263
Wernerfelt, B., 84, 259
Wernerfelt, Birger, 120
Wesley, Norm, 234
Wessel, Godecke, 344

West, Kanye, C-78
West, Tony, C-403
Wetlaufer, Suzy, 370
White, David, 181
White, Gordon, 235
White, Shaun, 300
Whitman, Meg, 255,
     C-401–C-402, C-405
Widodo, Joko, C-142
Wie, Michelle, C-73
Wiedman, Christine, 47
Wilcox, Lindsey, 161
William, Prince (UK), C-142
Williams, Evan, C-138–C-139,
     C-141
Williams, Serena, C-73
Williams, Venus, C-73
Williamson, O., 320
Williamson, Peter J., 150, 259
Winkler, Margaret, C-278
Winter, S., 120, 320
Winter, Sidney G., 215
Winterkorn, Martin, 43
Wong, Julia Carrie, C-404

Wood, Ryan, C-56
Woods, Tiger, C-73, C-94
Wooldridge, Bill, 320
Woroch, Scott, 202
Worrell, Dan L., 288
Woyke, Elizabeth, C-119
Wright, Mike, C-264
Wu, Jason, 8

X

Xu, Linda, C-260–C-261
Xun, Cai, C-261

Y

Yang, Chang, C-258
Yang, Dori Jones, C-375
Yarbrough, Brian, C-180
Yip, G., 216
Yoffie, D., 150
Yoffie, David B., 180–181

Yoon, Sangwon, 216
Yunyun, Liu, C-263–C-264

Z

Zaleski, O., C-10
Zaleski, Olivia, C-183
Zbaracki, Mark J., 344
Zemsky, P., 181
Zeng, Ming, 150
Zetsloot, Gerald I. J., 288
Zhang, Sean, C-92
Zhenwang, Lu, C-260
Zhu, Angela, C-251–C-252,
     C-259–C-260, C-262–C-263
Zhu, Pearl, 323
Zhuoqiong, Wang, C-263
Zillman, Claire, C-263
Zimmerman, Mike, C-100
Zimmerman, Ryan, C-66
Ziobro, P., C-231
Zollo, M., 120, 320
Zuckerberg, Mark, 34, C-143–C-144

Subject Index

A

ACA (Affordable Care Act), C-44
Accommodation market, overview of, C-6–C-7
Acquisitions and mergers
  in beer industry, C-46
  capabilities acquired through, 301–302
  diversifying by, 222–225
  dynamic capabilities through, 102
  international, 194
  Kraft-Heinz merger, 232
  Nucor Corporation, case, C-297–C-298, C-307–C-310
  of undervalued companies, 235
  Whole Foods Market acquired by Amazon, C-176–C-179
Actions defining strategy, 4
Activity, financial ratios on, 90–91
Adaptive cultures, 356–357
Adaptive strategy adjustments, 9
Adventure sports industry, C-233–C-234
Advertising; *see also* Marketing
  in adventure sports industry, C-234
  Costco Wholesale, case, C-25–C-27
  economies of scale in, 126
  Netflix, case, C-159
  Starbucks, Inc., case, C-365
Affordable Care Act (ACA), C-44
Alliances and partnerships
  benefits of, 175–176
  capabilities acquired through, 302
  collaboration in executing strategy, 316
  drawbacks of, 176–177
  in international markets, 187, 195–197
  Shell Oil Company, 173
  strategic, 173–175
  successful, 177–178
American Pain (Temple), C-406
Arm's-length transactions, alliances advantage over, 177
Artificial intelligence (AI), medical applications of, 175
Audit committee, of corporate board of directors, 41
Authority delegation, in strategy execution, 311–314
Autonomous system technology, 72
Average collection period, 91

B

Backward integration
  for buyer bargaining power, 67
  difficulty of, 64
  for greater competitiveness, 167–168
  Tesla Motors, 171

Balanced scorecard, 31, 33
BAM (business activity monitoring) systems, 334
Bargaining power
  of buyers, 65–68
  for low-cost leadership, 127
  of suppliers, 63–65
Barriers to entry
  to international markets, 184, 192–197
  to strengthen competitive position, 158–159
  as test for diversification, 221, 224
  types of, 58–59
Beer industry, 80; *see also* Craft beer industry, competition in
Benchmarking
  competitive strength of rivals determined from, 112
  for continuous improvement, 366
  in solar industry, 109
  value chain, 107–109, 332
Best-cost (hybrid) strategies, 8, 124–125, 142–145
Best practices, 107–109
Better-off test, for diversification, 221–222, 233
Big data, from MoviePass, C-83
Biofuels, 282
Blue-ocean strategy, 156–158
Board of directors in strategy crafting and execution process, 40–43
BPA (Bisphenyl-A) consumption, C-44
Brand management
  Under Armour, case, C-65–C-67
  IKEA China, case, C-258
  to increase differentiation, 134
  Nestlé, 96–97
  Procter & Gamble (P&G), 92–93
  Twitter.com, case, C-141–C-142
  Walmart Stores, Inc., case, C-169
Brand recognition, as entry barrier, 58
Bribes and kickbacks, 264–265
BRIC countries (Brazil, Russia, India, and China), 208
Broadcast radio industry, business models in, 13
Broad differentiation strategies
  description of, 6, 124
  pitfalls to avoid with, 137–138
  success factors for, 136–137
  superior value delivered via, 135–136
  value chain management in, 132–134
Broad low-cost strategies
  cost-efficient value chain management for, 125–128
  description of, 124
  pitfalls to avoid with, 131
  revamping value chain for, 128–130
  successful, 130–131

Business activity monitoring (BAM) systems, 334
Business models
  Amazon.com, C-172
  Costco Wholesale Corporation, C-21
  Fulfillment by Amazon, C-187
  Netflix, case, C-155–C-157
  "power-by-the-hour" (Rolls-Royce), 12
  radio industry comparison of, 13
  sharing economy, C-6–C-8
  strategy and, 11–12
  TJX Companies, Inc., case, C-242–C-246
  Toms Shoes, case, C-94–C-96
  Walmart Stores, Inc., case, C-188
Business plans, C-12, C-356
Business process management tools, 327–333
Business process reengineering
  for continuous improvement, 366
  continuous improvement programs *versus*, 331–333
  for cost advantage, 127
  for operating excellence, 327–328
Business risk, 169
Business strategy, 36–37
Buyers
  bargaining power and price sensitivity of, 65–68
  corporate social responsibility and, 283
  differentiation in appeal to, 135–137
  in international markets, 191–192
  value-conscious, 143
  vertical integration slowing accommodations to, 170

C

CAD (computer-assisted design) techniques, 127
CAFE (corporate average fuel economy) credits, C-211–C-212
CAFE (Coffee and Farmer Equity) Practices, of Starbucks, Inc., C-371
CAGR (Compound Annual Growth Rate), C-254
Cameras, wearable action-capture, 72
Capabilities of companies
  acquiring, developing, and strengthening, 295–296
  collaborative partnerships to access, 302
  diversification fit with, 224
  evaluating, 96–102
  general, 227
  internal development of, 300–301
  in international markets, 184, 203–206

of management team, 296–299
  mergers and acquisitions to acquire, 301–302
  Nike, Inc., C-76–C-77
  specialized, 226–228
  strategic offensives exploiting, 154
  value chain related to, 111–112
  vertical integration requirements for, 170
Capacity-matching, 170
Capacity utilization, 127
Capital requirements, as entry barrier, 59
Carbon footprint measurement, 280–281
Carmelite monks of Wyoming, C-2–C-3
Cash cows, 248
Cash hogs, 248
Casual dining industry, strategic group map for, 76
Causal ambiguity, 100
Centralized decision making, 311–313
Change-resistant corporate cultures, 358
Channels
  conflict in, 169
  multichannel retailing, C-259–C-260
  Walmart Stores, Inc., case, C-169
Chief executive officer (C-EO), strategy execution by, 34–35
China, C-150–C-151; *see also* IKEA China, case
Chronic traumatic encephalopathy (CTE); *see* Concussions in college and pro football, case
Clashing corporate cultures, 359
"Clean food" movement, C-11, C-15
Client-owner business structure, 129
CMOs (contract manufacturing organizations), 306
Coffee and Farmer Equity (CAFE) Practices, of Starbucks, Inc., C-371
Coffee industry overview, C-3–C-4; *see also* Starbucks, Inc., case
College and pro football, concussions in; *see* Concussions in college and pro football
Combination organizational structure, 311
Command-and-control structures, 313
Common stock, dividend yield on, 91
Compensation
  Costco Wholesale, case, C-29–C-31
  incentive, 339–341, 366
  Nucor Corporation, case, C-319–C-320
  "pay for performance" systems of, C-319–C-322
  for top executives, 41–42

Competencies, identifying, 92–93, 96
Competition; see also Craft beer
    industry, competition in, case;
    Environment, external
    adidas Group versus Under
        Armour, C-77–C-79
    backward integration and, 167–168
    benchmarking importance with, 109
    BJ's Wholesale Club versus Costco
        Wholesale, C-36–C-39
    Chipotle Mexican Grill, C-134–C-137
    company strength versus, 112–115
    forward integration and, 168–169
    IKEA China, case, C-257
    iRobot, case, C-117
    MoviePass, case, C-83–C-87
    multimarket, 207
    Nike versus Under Armour,
        C-71–C-77
    Nucor Corporation, case,
        C-327–C-329
    resources and capabilities of
        company versus, 99–102
    Sam's Club versus Costco
        Wholesale, C-34–C-36
    Shearwater Adventures Ltd., case,
        C-234–C-235
    SOAR Framework for analysis of,
        77–79
    strategy as differentiation from, 4–5
    toy industry, C-229–C-230
    Twitter.com, case, C-143–C-147
    unfair practices in, 268
    Vail Resorts, Inc., case, C-337,
        C-341–C-344
Competitive advantage; see also
    Competitive position,
    strengthening
    of cross-business strategic fit,
        247–249
    Diamond of National Competitive
        Advantage model, 185–186
    financial performance improved
        by, 31
    generic strategies and, 147–148
    initiatives to build, 88
    in international markets, 202–206
    in strategic fit, 230–232
    from strategy execution
        capabilities, 303–304
    strategy in quest for, 5–8
    strategy test based on, 14
    unrelated diversification and, 237
    value chain translated to, 110–112
    VRIN (valuable, rare, inimitable,
        nonsubstitutable) tests for
        sustainable, 99–100
Competitive intelligence, 80
Competitive position, strengthening,
    152–181; see also Competitive
    advantage
    alliance and partnership strategies
        for, 173–178
    defensive strategies for, 157–159
    first-mover advantages, 159–161
    horizontal merger and acquisition
        strategies for, 164–167
    late-mover advantages, 162–163
    outsourcing strategies for, 172–173
    scope of operations changes for,
        163–164
    strategic offensives for, 154–157
    vertical integration strategies for,
        167–171

Competitive strategies; see Five
    generic competitive strategies
Competitive strength, 14, 242–246
Complementors, 69–70
Composite organizational
    structure, 311
Compound Annual Growth Rate
    (CAGR), C-254
Computer-assisted design (CAD)
    techniques, 127
Concussion (film), C-377
Concussions in college and pro
    football, case, C-377–C-391
    college athletics and future
        controversy about,
        C-388–C-389
    NCAA management of,
        C-379–C-382
    NFL athletics and future
        controversy about,
        C-389–C-390
    NFL management of,
        C-382–C-385
    overview, C-377–C-378
    physiology of, C-378–C-379
    preventing, C-385–C-388
Consolidation of brands, C-169
Consolidations in beer industry, C-46
Consumers
    Airbnb, case, C-8–C-9
    bargaining power of, 67
    beer distribution effects on, C-44
    Chipotle Mexican Grill and trust
        of, C-124–C-125
    millennials as, C-101–C-102, C-104
    sales direct-to, C-67–C-68
    Walt Disney Company
        diversification, case,
        C-286–289
Continuous improvement
    programs, C-308
Continuous quality improvement,
    133–134
Contract manufacturing
    organizations (CMOs), 306
Controlled Substances Act (CSA) of
    1970, C-406, C-409
Convergence of industries, 165
Copyrights, as intangible
    resources, 97
Core competencies, 92–93, 184
Corporate average fuel economy
    (CAFE) credits, C-211–C-212
Corporate governance
    in company direction setting,
        40–42
    Uber Technologies, case,
        C-400–C-401
    Volkswagen AG failure of, 43
Corporate parenting capabilities,
    233–234
Corporate social responsibility
    (CSR); see also Culture,
    corporate
    Apple, Inc., 7–8
    business case for, 283–286
    core values of company in, 276
    elements of, 274–276
    moral case for, 283
    Starbucks, Inc., case,
        C-372–C-374
    strategies for, 281–283
    Toms Shoes, case, C-94–C-98
    triple bottom line and, 276–279

Corporate strategy, 218–259
    business unit competitive strength
        in diversified companies,
        242–246
    diversification path: combination
        of businesses, 238
    diversification path: related
        businesses, 225–232
    diversification path: unrelated
        businesses, 232–238
    diversification strategy, 220–225
    goals of, 36–37
    improving corporate performance
        in diversified companies,
        251–255
    industry attractiveness in diversified
        companies, 239–242
    resource allocation priorities
        in diversified companies,
        250–251
    resource fit in diversified
        companies, 246–249
    strategic fit in diversified
        companies, 246
Corporate structure, C-396
Corporate taxes, Tax Cuts and
    Jobs Act of 2017 impact on,
    C-248–C-249
Corporate venturing, 223
Corrective adjustments, 22, 40
Cost drivers, 125–126
Costs; see also Low-cost strategies
    Chipotle Mexican Grill
        construction, C-133
    comparative, in diversifying, 225
    competition changes from
        differences in, 72–73
    competitive advantage based
        on, 111
    of entry, for diversification, 221
    fixation on reducing, 131
    levelized cost of energy
        (LCOE), 109
    Nucor Corporation, case,
        C-298–C-302, C-305,
        C-311–C-312
    remedying disadvantage in,
        108–110
    switching, 55, 63, 131, 160
    value chain activities impact on,
        102–107
    in value-price-cost framework of
        business model, 11–12
Coverage ratio, 90
Craft beer industry, competition in,
    case, C-41–C-50
    AB InBev profile, C-46–C-47
    beer market, C-41–C-42
    beer production, C-42–C-43
    Boston Beer Company, profile of,
        C-47–C-48
    consolidations and acquisitions
        in, C-46
    Craft Brew Alliance, profile of,
        C-48–C-49
    economies of scale in
        microbreweries, C-43–C-44
    innovation and quality versus price
        as, C-45–C-46
    legal environment of, C-44
    overview, C-41
    strategic issues facing,
        C-49–C-50
    supply chain for, C-44–C-45

Crafting strategy in company
    direction setting
    hierarchy for, 35–38
    managers at all levels involved in,
        34–35
    overview, 22
    strategic plan from vision, mission,
        and objectives, 38–39
Cross-border alliances, 187, 195–197
Cross-functional capabilities, 99
Cross-market subsidization, 206–207
Cross-selling, C-234
Cross-unit coordination, in executing
    strategy, 314–316
CSA (Controlled Substances Act) of
    1970, C-406, C-409
CSR (corporate social responsibility);
    see Corporate social
    responsibility (CSR)
CTE (chronic traumatic
    encephalopathy); see
    Concussions in college and pro
    football, case
Culture, corporate, 346–370
    in alliances and partnerships, 175
    Balanced Scorecard dimension
        of, 33
    changing problem, 359–363
    diversification and fit with, 253
    of employee motivation, 128
    healthy, 356–357
    identifying key features of, 350–353
    IKEA China, case, C-258–C-259,
        C-262
    as intangible resource, 98
    in international markets, 191–192
    profitability ahead of ethical
        behavior, 270
    for strategy execution, 355–356
    strategy execution leadership and,
        363–367
    strong versus weak, 353–354
    Uber Technologies, case, C-403
    unhealthy, 358–359
    variations in, 348–349
Current ratio, 90
Customers
    Balanced Scorecard dimension
        of, 33
    Costco Wholesale, case,
        C-28–C-29
    educating, C-261
    Mattel, Inc., case, C-220
    MoviePass, case, C-87–C-90
    Shearwater Adventures Ltd., case,
        C-236
Customer service, strategic fit
    with, 230
Customer value proposition
    in business model, 11–12
    radio industry example, 13
    value chain activities impact on,
        102–107

D

Data sharing, C-117–C-118, C-148
Dating service industry, 161
Debt-to-assets ratio, 90
Debt-to-equity ratio, 90
Decentralized decision making,
    311–314

"Defeat devices" on Volkswagen diesel cars, 43
Delegation of authority, in strategy execution, 311–314
Deliberate strategy, 9
Demand conditions, in international markets, 185–186
Demographics
    Costco Wholesale customers, C-28–C-29
    international market differences in, 191–192
Departmental organizational structure, 309–310
Design for manufacture (DFM) procedures, 127
Developing countries
    competing in, 208–209
    local companies defending against global giants, 210–212
Diamond of National Competitive Advantage model, 185–186
Differentiation
    broad strategies for, 124, 132–138
    competitive advantage based on, 111
    difficulty achieving, 131
    in five forces framework, 55
    focused strategies for, 124, 140–141
    forward integration for, 168–169
Digital marketplace, C-6–C-8
Direction of company, 20–47
    corporate governance, 40–43
    mission statement development, 26–27
    objective setting, 30–33
    overview, 22
    performance evaluation, 40
    strategic vision development, 23–26
    strategy crafting, 34–39
    strategy execution, 39–40
    values linked with vision and mission, 27–29
Direct-to-consumer (DTC) model
    Under Armour sales as, C-67–C-68
    entertainment programming as, C-278, C-282
    Nike, Inc., sales as, C-74–C-75
Discounting, exit barriers leading to, 56–57
Disruptive technologies; see also Amazon.com, case
    innovation as, 155
    strategy changes based on, 9
    Voice over Internet Protocol (VoIP) as, 221
Distribution
    Under Armour, case, C-67–C-69
    in beer industry, C-44
    Costco Wholesale Corporation, case, C-27–C-28
    as entry barrier or challenge, 59
    forward integration as competition to, 169
    as key success factor in beer industry, 80
    Nike, Inc., case, C-73
    Qdoba Mexican Eats, C-137
    Sam's Club, C-36
    strategic fit with, 230, 232
    sustainable business practices for, 285
    Tesla Motor Co., case, C-203–C-206
    in value chain, 103, 110

Diversification
    business unit competitive strength in, 242–246
    with combination of businesses, 238
    improving corporate performance in, 251–255
    industry attractiveness in, 239–242
    with related businesses, 225–232
    resource allocation priorities in, 250–251
    resource fit in, 246–249
    strategic fit in, 246
    strategy for, 220–225
    with unrelated businesses, 232–238
Dividend payout ratio, 91
Dividend yield on common stock, 91
Divisional organizational structure, 310
DMADV six sigma process, 329
DMAIC (define, measure, analyze, improve, and control) six sigma process, 329–330
Driving forces in industry change, 70–74
DTC (direct-to-consumer) model; see Direct-to-consumer (DTC) model
Dumping below-market priced goods, 207, C-307–C-308, C-326
Dynamic capabilities, 101–102
Dynamic fit test, for strategies, 12

E

E-commerce; see also Aliexpress, case; Walmart Stores, Inc., case
    Under Armour, C-68
    IKEA China, case, C-260
    Walmart acquisitions for, 166
Economics
    experience, 127
    experience-based versus ownership, C-8
    in international markets, 188–189
    macro environment, 50–52
    sustainable business practices and, 285
    as triple bottom line performance dimension, 277–278
Economies of scale
    concentrating in a few locations for, 203
    as entry barrier, 58
    as first-mover advantage, 160
    international markets for, 184
    in microbreweries, C-43–C-44
    PepsiCo diversification, case, C-276
    in value chain management, 126
    vertical integration as disadvantage in, 170
Economies of scope, from diversification, 230–232
Education, 72, C-261
Emergent strategy, 9
Emissions testing, 43
Employees
    in Costco Wholesale business principles, C-32
    executive friendliness to, C-18
    as independent contractors, C-393
    monitoring performance of, 335

    motivating, 128, 336–337
    Nucor Corporation, case, C-320–C-322
    as partners, 365
    recruiting, training, and retaining, 297–299
    reducing turnover of, 284
    Starbucks, Inc., benefits for, C-365–C-368
    TJX Companies benefits for, C-248–C-249
    training, 349, C-15
    Wegmans Food Markets, Inc., 337–338
    wellness programs for, 284
Empowerment of workforce, 365
Energy
    Costco Wholesale initiatives to reduce consumption, C-33
    levelized cost of energy (LCOE), 109
    renewable improvements, 77
Enterprise resource planning (ERP) systems, 127, 328
Entrepreneurship, internal, 357
Entry barriers
    for international markets, 184
    strategic options in international markets, 192–197
    to strengthen competitive position, 158–159
    as test for diversification, 221, 224
    types of, 58–59
Entry cost test, for diversification, 221
Environment, external, 48–85
    complementors and value net, 69–70
    five forces framework
        buyer bargaining power and price sensitivity, 65–68
        competitive conditions match with company strategy, 69
        competitive weapons, 57
        profitability from, 68–69
        rivalry among competing sellers, 53–56
        substitute products, 60–63
        supplier bargaining power, 63–65
        threat of new entrants, 57–60
    industry and competitive environment, assessing, 53
    industry dynamics, 70–74
    key success factors, 79–80
    macro-environment, analyzing, 50–53
    profitability outlook, 80–81
    SOAR Framework for competitor analysis, 77–79
    strategic group analysis, 74–77
Environmental forces in macro environment, 50–52
Environmental protection and sustainability
    Costco Wholesale, case, C-21, C-33
    Nucor Corporation, case, C-312, C-318
    Starbucks, Inc., case, C-373
    strategies for, 280
    as triple bottom line performance dimension, 277–278
    Unilever Sustainable Living Plan (USLP), 282

Equity compensation programs, C-31
ERP (enterprise resource planning) systems, 127, 328
Estimating supply requirements, C-12–C-13
Ethics
    business case for, 271–273
    competitive intelligence and, 80
    in corporate culture, 350–351
    Costco Wholesale, case, C-31–C-33
    impact on crafting and executing strategy of, 266–267
    integrative social contracts theory and, 265–266
    moral case for, 271
    school of ethical relativism, 263–265
    school of ethical universalism, 262–263
    Starbucks, Inc., case, C-368, C-371–C-373
    strategy and, 9–11
    unethical business strategies and behavior, 267–271
    Walmart Stores, Inc., case, C-168–C-169
Evaluating companies, 86–121
    competition versus, 112–115
    front-burner problems, 115
    resources and capabilities, 96–102
    strategy, 88–91
    strengths and weaknesses, 91–95
    value chain activities, 102–107
    value chain benchmarking, 107–108
    value chain translated into competitive advantage, 110–112
Exchange rate risks, 189–191
Executing strategy, 290–321; see also Culture, corporate; Operations, internal
    aligning organization structure with, 307–311
    collaboration with external partners and allies, 316
    in company direction setting, 22, 39–40
    components of, 292–294
    critical resources and capabilities for, 299–304
    cross-unit coordination, 314–316
    delegation of authority, 311–314
    internal versus outsourced value chain activities, 304–307
    organization building for, 294–296
    organization staffing for, 296–299
    work effort structuring, 316–317
Exit barriers, 56
Experience-based economy, C-8
Experience economies, 127
Export strategies for entering international markets, 192–193
External fit test, for strategies, 12

F

Factors of production, in international markets, 186–187
Fair Labor Standards Act (FLSA), C-44
"Farm to fork" trend, C-15

FCPA (Foreign Corrupt Practices Act), 264
Federal Communications Decency Act, C-148
Financial accounting
  financial ratios for, 89–91
  objectives, long-term, 31
  objectives, meeting, 88–89
  objectives, short-term, 30–31
  objectives on Balanced Scorecard, 33
  performance test for, 14
  reporting results of, 40–41
Financial performance; see also Performance
  Under Armour, case, C-58–C-60
  iRobot, case, C-113–117
  Mattel, Inc., case, C-222–C-226
  Mystic Monk Coffee, case, C-5
  TOMS Shoes, case, C-98–C-99
Financing Netflix content, C-160–C-161
First Amendment to US Constitution, C-148
First-mover strategy
  advantages of, 159–161
  decision to be, 162–163
  disadvantages of, 162
  Nucor Corporation, case, C-311–C-312
Fit test, for strategies, 12
Five forces framework
  buyer bargaining power and price sensitivity, 65–68
  competitive conditions matched with company strategy, 69
  competitive weapons, 57
  profitability from, 68–69
  rivalry among competing sellers, 53–56
  substitute products, 60–63
  supplier bargaining power, 63–65
  threat of new entrants, 57–60
Five generic competitive strategies, 122–151
  best-cost (hybrid) strategies, 142–145
  broad differentiation strategies, 132–138
  broad low-cost strategies, 125–131
  contrasting features of, 145–148
  focused differentiation strategies, 140–141
  focused low-cost strategies, 138–140
  overview, 124–125
  risks in focused strategies, 142
Fixer Upper HGTV show; see Magnolia brand, case
FLSA (Fair Labor Standards Act), C-44
Focused differentiation strategies, 8, 124, 140–142
Focused low-cost strategies
  attraction of, 140–141
  description of, 6, 8, 124
  examples of, 139–140
  objectives of, 138
  risks of, 142
Food poisoning; see Chipotle Mexican Grill, case, in Company Index
Football players, concussions of; see Concussions in college and pro football

Foreign Corrupt Practices Act (FCPA), 264
Foreign subsidiary strategies for entering international markets, 194–195, 209
Forward-channel value chains, 107
Forward integration, 168–169, 171
Franchising, 193–194, 307, C-251
Free cash flow, 91
Fringe benefits, 336
Full vertical integration strategies, 167
Functional area strategies, 36–37
Functional organizational structure, 309–310

G

Generally accepted accounting principles (GAAP), 41
Generic competitive strategies; see Five generic competitive strategies
GHG (greenhouse gas) credits, C-211–C-212
Globalization
  industry change driven by, 71
  Netflix, case, C-149–C-152
  TJX Companies, Inc., case, C-240–C-241, C-245–C-246
Global strategy for international markets, 199–201
Global warming, tourism industry affected by, C-331
Government regulations
  Airbnb, case, C-9
  of craft beer industry, C-44
  credit sales as offsets, C-211–C-212
  as entry barriers, 59
  in international markets, 188–189
  in macro environment, 50–52
  opioid epidemic in US, case, C-409–C-410
Great Recession of 2008–2009, C-305, C-340
Greed-driven corporate cultures, 359
Greenfield ventures, 194–195
Greenhouse gas (GHG) emissions, C-211–C-212, C-312
Grocery market
  Amazon.com disruption of, C-180
  Amazon entry into, C-172–C-174
  bricks-and-mortar stores, C-174–C-175
  downsides of, C-180–C-181
  fresh store pickup services, C-175–C-176
  Whole Foods Market acquired by Amazon, C-176–C-179
Gross profit margin, 89
Growth strategy
  Under Armour, case, C-61–C-62
  Nucor Corporation, case, C-314–C-315
  Starbucks, Inc., case, C-356–C-358
  TJX Companies, Inc., case, C-246–C-248
Guardian Sustainable Business Award, 287
Guerrilla warfare tactics, 155

H

Hard-to-copy resources and capabilities, 100
Healthy corporate cultures, 356–357
Hearth & Hand collection, Magnolia brand, case, C-53
Higher education, Internet impact on, 72
High-performance cultures, 356
Holder report, for Uber Technologies, C-399
Home-country industry advantages, in international markets, 185–187
Horizontal mergers and acquisitions, 164–167
Horizontal scope of operations, 163
Hospitality-driven service, as core value, C-11
House flipping (Fixer Upper HGTV show), C-51–C-52
Human capital, Balanced Scorecard dimension of, 33
Hydrogen fuel cells, C-215
Hyperinflation, C-235

I

Incentives; see also Rewards
  compensation as, 339–341
  for employee motivation, 128
  as intangible resource, 98
  for strategy execution, 336–337, 366
Independent contractors, employees as, C-393
Indigenization and Economic Empowerment Bill (Zimbabwe), C-235
Industry attractiveness test, for diversification
  competitive strength portrayed with, 243–246
  evaluating, 239–242
  overview, 221
  in strategy analysis, 238–239
  into unrelated businesses, 233
Industry dynamics, 70–74
Industry environment, 53
Information systems for internal operations, 333–335
In ital public offering (IPO), C-143, C-366
Innovation, Balanced Scorecard dimension of, 33
Innovation, craft beer industry competition based on, C-45–C-46
Intangible resources, 97–98
Integration in Shearwater Adventures Ltd., case, C-236
Intellectual property
  differentiation based on, 134
  as entry barrier, 58
  for executing strategy, 296
  as first-mover advantage, 160
  as intangible resource, 97
Interactive media, in Walt Disney Company diversification, case, C-286–C-289
Internal capital market, 247
Internal cash flow, 91

Internal development, diversifying by, 223
Internal fit test, for strategies, 12
Internal operations; see Operations, internal
Internal startups, 194–195
Internal "universities" for training, 303
International marketing, 182–217; see also the following entries in the Company Index: IKEA China, case; Netflix, case; Starbucks, Inc., case; TJX Companies, Inc., case
  Apple, Inc., 7
  competing in developing countries, 208–209
  competitive advantage quest in, 202–206
  defending position in, 207
  demographic, cultural, and market differences, 191–192
  entering, reasons for, 184
  entering, strategic options for, 192–197
  exchange rate risks, 189–191
  global strategy for, 199–200
  government policies and economic conditions, 188–189
  home-country industry advantages, 185–187
  local companies in developing countries, strategies for, 210–212
  location-based advantages, 187–188
  multidomestic strategy for, 198–199
  strategic offensives in, 206–207
  transnational strategy for, 200–202
Internet, industry change from, 71–72, 221
Internet of Things (IoT), 72
Intrapreneurship, 357
Inventory management
  Under Armour, case, C-71
  Costco Wholesale Corporation, case, C-21
  days of inventory calculation, 90
  in five forces framework, 56
  turnover of, 91
Investor revolt, at Uber Technologies, C-399–C-400
Inwardly focused corporate cultures, 358–359
IPO (initial public offering), C-143, C-366
ISO standards, 134, C-312, C-318

J

Joint ventures
  capabilities acquired through, 302
  Chinese market entered by, C-259
  cost reductions in diversifying by, 225
  description of, 174
  diversification achieved by, 223
  international markets entered by, 195–197
  Nucor Corporation, case, C-304–C-305, C-314–C-316
  PepsiCo and Strauss Group, C-268
Just-in-time deliveries, 110, 128

K

Key success factors (KSFs), 79–80, 112–114
Kickbacks and bribes, 264–265
Knowledge, as capability, 98
Knowledge diffusion, 72

L

Labor, underage, 263–264
Labor cost disadvantage, C-329
Lagging indicators of performance, 31
Late-mover advantages, 162–163
LCOE (levelized cost of energy), 109
Leadership
    Costco Wholesale founder, C-18
    low-cost, 125
    of strategy execution, 363–367
Leadership in Energy and Environmental Design (LEED) certification, C-33, C-359, C-372–373
Leading indicators of performance, 32–33
Learning curve, 127, 160, 203
Leasing activities, by Tesla Motors, C-211
LEED (Leadership in Energy and Environmental Design) certification, C-33, C-359, C-372–C-373
Legal and regulatory factors in macro environment, 50–52
Legal environment of craft beer industry, C-44
Levelized cost of energy (LCOE), 109
Leverage, financial ratios to determine, 90
Liabilities, competitive, 93
Licensing
    Airbnb, case, C-9
    Under Armour, case, C-68
    restaurant, C-12
    Starbucks, Inc., case, C-357–C-358, C-361
    as strategy for international market entry, 193
    Tazo Tea, Inc., C-361
Line-and-staff organizational structure, 309
Liquidity, financial ratios to determine, 90
Location-based advantages, in international markets, 187–188
Long-term debt-to-capital ratio, 90
Long-term debt-to-equity ratio, 90
Low-cost leadership, 125
Low cost strategies
    broad, 124–131
    Costco Wholesale Corporation, case, C-21
    in developing countries, 208–209
    focused, 124, 138–140
    location advantages in international markets for, 188
    Nucor Corporation, case, C-297
    at Nucor Corporation, 340
    providers of, 6
    at Walmart Stores, Inc., 166

Loyalty, as entry barrier, 58
Lump-sum payments, for retail shelf space, 66

M

Macro environment, 50–53
Madden rule, in professional football, C-384
Management; see also Executing strategy; Operations, internal
    Costco Wholesale Corporation, case, C-29
    front-burner problems for attention of, 115
    management by walking around (MBWA), 364
    Nucor Corporation, case, C-318–C-319
    Starbucks, Inc., case, C-374–C-375
    strategy and execution in, 15
    strategy making at all levels of, 34
    TJX Companies, Inc., case, C-241
Manufacturing
    Under Armour, case, C-70
    Nike, Inc., case, C-77
    strategic fit with, 229
    Tesla Motor Co., case, C-208–C-210
Manufacturing execution system (MES), 127
Marketing
    Under Armour, case, C-65–C-67
    beer, C-41–C-42
    BJ's Wholesale, C-38
    Chipotle Mexican Grill, case, C-122, C-131–C-132
    Costco Wholesale Corporation, case, C-25–C-27
    differentiation created by, 134
    IKEA China, case, C-258–C-259
    international differences in, 191–192
    Mattel, Inc., case, C-220
    Mystic Monk Coffee, case, C-5
    Netflix, case, C-159
    Nike, Inc., C-74–C-75
    Qdoba Mexican Eats, C-137
    retail, C-67
    on social media, 72
    strategic fit with, 229–230
    Tesla Motor Co., case, C-210–C-211
    toy industry, C-228–C-229
    Vail Resorts, Inc., case, C-340–C-341
    in value chain, 103
    viral, 161
    Wil's Grill, case, C-14–C-16
Marketing research, C-15
Market penetration curve, 162
Market position; see Competitive position, strengthening
Market share
    in beer industry, C-41
    financial performance improved by, 31
    higher profits not necessarily following, 131
    performance test based on, 14
    relative, 242–243
    as strategy success indicator, 88–89
Markups, retail, C-22
Mass customization, 200
Massive open online courses (MOOCs), 72

"Master product" business model, 12
Matrix organizational structure, 311
MBWA (management by walking around), 364
Media networks, C-282–C-283
Merchandising
    BJ's Wholesale, C-37
    Costco Wholesale "treasure-hunt," C-24
    DirecTV, C-37
    GEICO insurance, C-37
Mergers and acquisitions
    alliances and partnerships advantages over, 176–177
    in beer industry, C-46
    capabilities acquired through, 301–302
    horizontal, 164–167
    Nucor Corporation, case, C-297–C-298, C-307–C-310
    Whole Foods Market acquired by Amazon, C-176–C-179
MES (manufacturing execution system), 127
Microblogging; see Twitter.com, case
Microprocessor industry, entry barriers to, 58
Mild Traumatic Brain Injury (MTBI), C-379
Mission statements
    Costco Wholesale Corporation, case, C-21
    development of, 26–27
    Mattel, Inc., case, C-218–C-219
    Starbucks, Inc., case, C-368–C-370
    in strategic plan, 38–39
    TJX Companies, Inc., case, C-241
    Vail Resorts, Inc., case, C-344–C-346
    values linked to, 27–29
    Walmart Stores, Inc., case, C-168–C-169
Mobile phone applications, for marketing, C-49
Mobility barriers, 77
MOOCs (massive open online courses), 72
Mortgage lending scandal, 269
Motivation
    of employees, 366
    practices for, 336–337
    in vision statements, 26
MTBI (Mild Traumatic Brain Injury), C-379
Multibrand strategies, 142
Multichannel retailing, C-259–C-260
Multidivisional organizational structure, 310
Multidomestic strategy for international markets, 198–199, 201
Multimarket competition, 207
Multinational companies, ethical relativism in, 265
Mutual restraint among international rivals, 207

N

NAFTA (North American Free Trade Agreement), C-326
Nanobreweries, C-44
Nationalization of industries, 189
National Renewable Energy Laboratory (NREL) Quarterly

U.S. Solar Photovoltaic System Cost Benchmark, 109
NCAA Sports Medicine Handbook, C-380
Net profit margin, 89
Net return on total assets (ROA), 89
Network effects, as entry barrier, 58–59, 160–161
Network organizational structure, 316
New entrants, threat of, 57–60
New venture development, 223
Nike, Inc.
    manufacturing, C-77
    marketing, promotions, and endorsements, C-74–C-75
    overview, C-72–C-73
    resources and capabilities, C-75–C-77
    Under Armour versus, C-71–C-72
Nine-cell industry-attractiveness-competitive-strength matrix, 243–246, 250
North American Free Trade Agreement (NAFTA), C-326
NREL (National Renewable Energy Laboratory) Quarterly U.S. Solar Photovoltaic System Cost Benchmark, 109

O

Objectives
    achievement of, 88
    competitive, 78
    setting, 22, 30–33
    in strategic plan, 38–39
    stretch, 339
Oil and gas industry, alliances and partnerships in, 173–174
Omni-channel retailing, 166
One Child Policy (China), C-258
One for One model, at TOMS Shoes, 29
Online auction industry, 157
Online retail, C-165–C-168
Operating profit, 89
Operating strategies, 36–38
Operations, internal, 322–345; see also Executing strategy
    allocating resources to strategy execution for, 324–325
    business process management tools for, 327–333
    changes in scope of, 163–164
    incentives and motivational practices for, 336–337
    information and operating systems for, 333–335
    low-cost, C-24–C-25
    policies and procedures for strategy execution, 325–327
    rewards and punishment balance, 337–339
    rewards linked to achievement of outcomes, 339–342
    in value chain, 103
Opioid epidemic in US, case, C-406–C-414
    government regulation of, C-409–C-410
    illegal opioids in, C-411–C-412
    lawsuits on, C-412–C-413
    overview, C-406–C-408
    pain clinics and, C-410–C-411
    Purdue Pharma, C-408–C-409

Opportunities, strengths and weaknesses in relation to, 91–95
Organization
  aligning structure with strategy execution, 307–311
  building for strategy execution, 294–296
  staffing for strategy execution, 295–299
Original-equipment manufacturer, 66
OTT (Over-the-Top) content delivery, C-282
Outsourcing
  alliances to manage, 177
  capabilities acquired through, 302
  cost advantages of, 127–128
  as scope of operations decision, 163
  to strengthen competitive position, 172–173
  value chain activities, decisions on, 304–307
Overcharging, as strategy mistake, 138
Over-differentiating, as strategy mistake, 138
Over-the-Top (OTT) content delivery, C-282
Oxycontin; see Opioid epidemic in US, case

P

Packaging, sustainable design of, 281, 285
Pain, profiting from; see Opioid epidemic in US, case
Parenting advantage, 236–237
Parenting capabilities, of corporations, 233–234
Parks and resorts, of Walt Disney Company, C-283–C-285
Partial vertical integration strategies, 167
Partnerships and alliances
  benefits of, 175–176
  capabilities acquired through, 302
  collaboration in executing strategy, 316
  drawbacks of, 176–177
  in international markets, 187, 195–197
  Shell Oil Company, 173
  strategic, 173–175
  successful, 177–178
"Pay for performance" compensation systems, C-319–C-322
Peer-to-peer ratings, C-9
Performance
  Costco Wholesale Corporation, case, C-19–C-20
  in diversified companies, 220, 251–255
  evaluation of, 22, 40
  lagging indicators of, 31
  leading indicators of, 32–33
  Mystic Monk Coffee, case, C-5
  PepsiCo Beverages North America, C-274–C-275
  PepsiCo Frito-Lay North America, C-271–C-274
  PepsiCo in Asia, Middle East, and North Africa, C-275–C-276

PepsiCo in Latin America, C-275
PepsiCo overall, C-268–C-271
PepsiCo Quaker Foods North America, C-274
pressure to meet short-term, 269–270
strategy test based on, 14
TJX Companies, Inc., case, C-242, C-246, C-249–C-250
tracking systems for, 334–335
Twitter.com, case, C-143, C-147–C-148
Uber Technologies, case, C-394–C-396
Vail Resorts, Inc., case, C-346–C-348
Walt Disney Company
  diversification, case, C-279–C-281, C-289–C-290
PESTEL (Political, Economic, Sociocultural, Technological, Environmental, Legal/regulatory) analysis, 50–52
Piece-rate incentive plan, 340
"Pill mills," pain clinics as, C-410–C-411
Pioneer, market, 159–160
Policies and procedures for strategy execution, 325–327
Political factors in macro environment, 50–52
Political risks in international markets, 189
Politicized corporate cultures, 358
Portfolio approach for financial fit, 248
Position, strengthening; see Competitive position, strengthening
"Power-by-the-hour" business model (Rolls-Royce), 12
Prestige of products, 7
Price gouging, 268
Price sensitivity of buyers, 65–68
Price-to-earnings (P/E) ratio, 91
Pricing
  Costco Wholesale ultra-low, C-21–C-22
  craft beer industry competition based on, C-45–C-46
  customized, C-13, C-15
  IKEA China, case, C-260–C-261
  for low-cost leadership, 130–131
  mass retail, 304
  Nucor Corporation, case, C-305–C-307
  premium, 7, 138
  Starbucks, Inc., coffee purchasing strategy and, C-369, C-371
  strategic offensives lowering, 154
  in value-price-cost framework of business model, 11–12
Privacy, C-117–C-118, C-148
Private-label manufacturers, 8
Proactive strategy, 9–10
Production-related R&D, 133
Productivity
  Balanced Scorecard dimension of, 33
  business process reengineering to improve, 327–328
  as evidence of strategy success, 88–89

Products
  Under Armour, case, C-62–C-65, C-69–C-70
  Costco Wholesale limitations on, C-22–C-23
  Mattel, Inc., case, C-219–C-220
  Nike, Inc., C-73–C-74
  substitute, 60–63
  Tesla Motor Co., case, C-191–C-193, C-201–C-203, C-206–C-207
  toy industry, C-227–C-228
  Twitter.com, case, C-142–C-143
Professional and college football, concussions in; see Concussions in college and pro football
Profitability
  in business model, 11–12
  in competitive strength scores, 243
  Costco Wholesale membership fees for, C-21
  in developing markets, 209
  financial ratios to determine, 89
  five competitive forces and, 68–69
  industry outlook for, 80–81
  performance test based on, 14
  radio industry examples, 13
  in value chain, 104
  Wil's Grill, case, C-14
Promotion from within, 337
Promotions
  allowances for, 66
  Under Armour, C-65–C-67
  Nike, Inc., C-74–C-75
Property rights protections, 160
Protecting football players; see Concussions in college and pro football
Pseudo-businesses, C-9
Public recognition for performance, 336
Purchasing power, international markets for, 184

Q

Quality
  Under Armour, case, C-70
  Balanced Scorecard dimension of, 33
  Chipotle Mexican Grill, case, C-126–C-127
  continuous quality improvement, 133–134
  craft beer industry competition based on, C-45–C-46
  Qdoba Mexican Eats, C-137
  QS 9000 certification, 211
  undifferentiated products and, 68

R

Radio industry, business models in, 13
Reactive strategy, 9–10
Realized strategy, 9
Recreation resort industry, C-337–C-340
Recruiting employees, 297–299

Regulations
  Airbnb, case, C-9
  of craft beer industry, C-44
  credit sales as offsets, C-211–C-212
  as entry barriers, 59
  in international markets, 188–189
  in macro environment, 50–52
  opioid epidemic in US, case, C-409–C-410
Related versus unrelated businesses; see Diversification
Relationship management, 316
Relative market share, 242–243
Representative weighted competitive strength assessment, 113–115
Reputation-damaging incidents, reducing risk of, 283–284
Resource bundles, 99
Resources of companies
  allocation priorities for, 235, 250–251
  competitive power of, 99–102
  concentrating in a few locations for, 203
  diversification fit with, 224, 226, 246–249
  evaluating, 96–99
  for executing strategy, 295, 299–304
  general, 227
  generic strategies based on, 145–146
  international markets for, 184, 203–206
  Nike, Inc., C-76–C-77
  specialized, 226–228
  strategic offensives exploiting, 154–155
  strategy execution allocations of, 324–325
  value chain related to, 111–112
  vertical integration requirements for, 170
Responsibility for protecting football players; see Concussions in college and pro football
Restricted stock units (RSUs) compensation programs, C-31
Restructuring
  diversified companies, 235, 254–255
  Twitter.com, case, C-143
Retail
  multichannel, C-259–C-260
  online markets for, C-188
  Walmart Stores, Inc., case, C-165–C-168
Retaining employees, 297–299
Return on assets, 89
Return on capital employed (ROC-E), 89
Return on invested capital (ROIC-), 89
Return on stockholders' equity (ROE), 89
Return to Play (RTP) protocol, in professional football, C-384–C-385
Revenue projections, C-16
Rewards; see also Incentives
  outcome achievement linked to, 339–342
  punishment balanced with, 337–339
Rivalry among competing sellers, 53–56
Robin Hood, case, C-291–C-292

S

Roomba robotic vacuum cleaner;
  see iRobot, case
RPCE (return on capital
  employed), 89
RPOC (return on invested
  capital), 89
RSUs (restricted stock units)
  compensation programs, C-31
RTP (Return to Play) protocol,
  in professional football,
  C-384–C-385

Sales
  after-sale support and, 7
  Chipotle Mexican Grill, case,
    C-121–C-124
  direct sales force, 128
  direct-to consumer, C-67–C-68
  Nike, Inc., C-74–C-75
  Nucor Corporation, case,
    C-305–C-307
  strategic fit with, 229–230
  in value chain, 103
Sarbanes-Oxley Act of 2002, 266
School of ethical relativism, 263–265
School of ethical universalism, 262–263
SCM (supply chain management);
  see Supply chain management
  (SCM)
Scope, economies of, 230–232
Scope of operations, 163–164
Segmentation of markets,
  C-257–C-258
Self-dealing, 269
Self-driving vehicles, 72, C-398
September 11, 2001 attacks, C-108,
  C-340, C-343
Service economy, 103, C-142–C-143
Sexual harassment, C-396–C-399
Shareholders, C-32–C-33
Sharing economy business model,
  C-6–C-8
Short-termism, 270
Simple organizational structure, 309
Single-business companies, strategy
  levels compressed in, 38
Situational analysis, 92
Six Sigma programs
  for continuous improvement, 366
  methodology for, 127
  for quality control, 327,
    329–333, 339
Slogans, vision essence in, 26
Slotting fees, for retail shelf space, 66
SOAR Framework for competitor
  analysis, 77–79
Social complexity, 100
Social initiatives, as triple bottom
  line performance dimension,
  277–278
Social media, in adventure sports
  industry, C-234
Social networking; see Twitter.
  com, case
Sociocultural forces in macro
  environment, 50–52
Solar power, 109, C-33
Sole proprietorship, C-12
Sourcing, C-70
Speed, in entering new business,
  224–225

Spin-offs, 253
SRB (sustainable responsible
  business), 276
Stakeholders of companies, 42
Standardization, 126, 200
Steel industry worldwide, C-298,
  C-322–C-327
Stock brokers, discount online, 71
Strategic fit
  in competitive strength scores, 242
  competitive value of, 246
  cross-business, in decentralized
    structure, 314
  in economies of scope and
    competitive advantage,
    230–232
  in international alliances, 187
  overview, 225–226
  value chain and, 228–230
Strategic group analysis, 74–77
Strategic group mapping, 74–77
Strategic objectives, 30–31
Strategic offensives
  for competitive position, 154–157
  in international markets, 206–207
Strategic plan; see Direction of
  company
Strategy, 2–19; see also Executing
    strategy; Five generic
    competitive strategies
  BJ Wholesale Club, C-39
  business model and, 11–12
  as competing differently, 4–5
  as competitive advantage, 5–8
  Costco Wholesale Corporation,
    case, C-21–C-25
  ethics and, 9–11
  evaluating current, 88–91
  evolution of, 8–9
  IKEA China, case, C-252–C-254,
    C-260–C-261
  importance of, 14–15
  Netflix, case, C-157–C-160
  Nucor Corporation raw materials,
    C-315–C-318
  Nucor Corporation value-added
    products, C-312–C-314
  PepsiCo diversification, case, C-276
  proactive and reactive, 9–10
  Starbucks, Inc., coffee purchasing,
    C-369–C-372
  Starbucks, Inc., corporate social
    responsibility, C-372–C-374
  Starbucks, Inc., overall,
    C-360–C-365
  success of, 12–14
  TJX Companies, Inc., case, C-241,
    C-246–C-248
  Vail Resorts, Inc., case,
    C-348–C-350
  Walt Disney Company
    diversification, case,
    C-281–C-282
Strategy overcrowding, 137
Street food events, estimating needs
  for, C-12–C-13
Strengths, weaknesses, opportunities,
  threats (SWOT) analysis, 92–95
Strengths of companies, evaluating,
  91–95
Stretch objectives, 30, 339
Strong corporate culture, 353–354
Studio entertainment business, C-286
Subcultures, corporate, 353

Subscription-based business models
  AmazonFresh, C-173–C-174
  Amazon Prime, C-152
  Hulu streaming service, C-152
  Moneycontrol, C-176
  Netflix, C-152, C-155–C-157
  Nielsen online, C-174
  Razorfish digital marketing, C-176
  Retail Dive, C-174
  Sprouts Farmers Market LLC,
    C-176–C-177
  TABS Analytics, C-174
Subscription video on demand
  (SVOD), C-286
Substitute products, 60–63
Supply chain management (SCM)
  bargaining power of suppliers in,
    63–65
  carbon footprint measurement
    of, 280
  Chipotle Mexican Grill, case,
    C-128–C-129
  cooperative relations in, 69–70
  Costco Wholesale Corporation,
    case, C-27–C-28, C-32
  cost-efficient, 127
  for craft beer industry, C-44–C-45
  differentiation from coordination
    of, 134
  site audits to ensure standards
    compliance, 306
  strategic fit in, 229
  Supplier Code of Conduct,
    C-96–C-97
  Tesla Motor Co., case, C-210
  in value chains, 103, 107, 110
Sustainability
  best practices for, 279–281
  business case for, 283–286
  of competitive advantage, 6, 8
  Costco Wholesale Corporation,
    case, C-33
  moral case for, 283
  strategies for, 281–283
  TOMS Shoes, case, C-97
  Unilever Sustainable Living Plan
    (USLP), 282
Sustainable responsible business
  (SRB), 276
SVOD (subscription video on
  demand), C-286
Switching costs, 55, 63, 131, 160
SWOT (strengths, weaknesses,
  opportunities, threats) analysis,
  92–95
Synergy effect, 221

T

Tangible resources, 97
Tapered vertical integration
  strategies, 167
Target markets for best-cost strategies,
  143
Tariffs on steel products,
  C-307–C-308
Tax Cuts and Jobs Act of 2017,
  C-248–C-249
Technology
  acquisitions to access, 165
  differentiation based on, 133, 137
  first-mover advantage of standards
    setting for, 160

  as force driving industry change,
    71–73
  leapfrogging first-mover products
    from, 162
  macro environment affected by,
    50–52
  strategic fit in, 229
  strategy changes based on
    advances in, 9
  Tesla Motor Co., case,
    C-206–C-207
  vertical integration slowing
    adoption of, 169–170
Tests of corporate advantage, for
  diversification, 221
Think global, act global approach, in
  international markets, 199–200
Think global, act local approach, in
  international markets, 200–202
Threats
  external, 91–95
  of new entrants, 57–60
  in SWOT (strengths, weaknesses,
    opportunities, threats)
    analysis, 92–95
Times-interest-earned ratio, 90
Total debt-to-assets ratio, 90
Total economic value, generic
  strategies and, 147–148
Total economic value produced by
  company, 99–100
Total quality management (TQM)
  programs
  benefits of, 332–333
  business process reengineering
    versus, 331–332
  for continuous improvement, 366
  cost advantage from, 127
  description of, 327–329
Total return on assets, 89
Tourism industry; see Shearwater
  Adventures Ltd., case
Trademark infringement, C-44
Trade policies, as entry barriers, 59
Trade secrets, as intangible
  resources, 97
Training employees
  in high-performance corporate
    culture, 349
  need for, C-15
  strategic role of, 302–303
  for strategy execution, 297–299
Transaction costs, 225
Transnational strategy for
  international markets, 200–202
Triple bottom line, in corporate
  social responsibility (CSR),
  276–279
Turnaround capabilities, 235

U

Umbrella brands, 234
Underage labor, 263–264
Undocumented workers, 10
UNESCO World Heritage Sites,
  C-236
Unethical corporate cultures, 359
Unhealthy corporate cultures,
  358–359
Unilever Sustainable Living Plan
  (USLP), 282
Unions, bargaining power of, 63

Unitary organizational structure, 309–310
Unrelated *versus* related businesses; *see* Diversification
U.S. Constitution, First Amendment to, C-148
USLP (Unilever Sustainable Living Plan), 282

V

Valuable, rare, inimitable, nonsubstitutable (VRIN) tests for sustainable competitive advantage, 99–101
Value chain
activities in, 102–107
benchmarking, 107–108, 332
competitive advantage translated from, 110–112
Costco Wholesale Corporation, case, C-21
cost-efficient management of, 125–128
cross-business strategic fit along, 228–230
differentiating attributes from managing, 132–134
diversification to leverage, 220
diversifying into related businesses and, 226

for high turnover and traffic, 304
international location-based advantages for, 188
Nucor Corporation, case, C-305
outsourced *versus* internal, 304–307
outsourcing as risk to, 173
PepsiCo diversification, case, C-276
revamping to lower costs, 128–130
Value drivers, 132–134
Value net, 69–70
Value-price-cost framework, 11–12, 147–148
Values
broad differentiation strategy to deliver, 135–136
in corporate culture, 350–351
corporate social responsibility and company, 281–283
Costco Wholesale Corporation, case, C-31–C-33
hospitality-driven service, C-11
Starbucks, Inc., case, C-368–C-369
strategic fit leading to gains in, 231
unrelated diversification to build, 233–236
in value-price-cost framework of business model, 11–12
vision and mission linked to, 27–29
Vanguard Effect, 129
Vertical chain; *see* Value chain

Vertical integration
alliance and partnership advantages over, 176–177
cost advantages of, 127–128
disadvantages of, 169–171
in fresh meat category, C-23
functional organizational structure and, 309–310
to strengthen competitive position, 167–169
Vertical scope of operations, 163
Video game industry, C-227–C-228
Video market, C-152–C-155
Video-on-demand (VOD), C-152–C-153
Viral marketing techniques, 161
Vision, strategic
development of, 22–26
in strategic plan, 38–39
values linked to, 27–29
Voice-over-Internet Protocol (VoIP), 71, 221
VRIN (valuable, rare, inimitable, nonsubstitutable) tests for sustainable competitive advantage, 99–101

W

Warehouse management, C-29, C-39
Weak corporate culture, 353–354

Weaknesses of companies, evaluating, 91–95
Weapons, competitive, 57
Wearable action-capture cameras, 72
Websites
for brewery marketing, C-49
Costco Wholesale sales on, C-27
Mystic Monk Coffee, case, C-5
Wil's Grill, case, C-12
"We have done it this way for years" syndrome, 358
Wellness programs, 284
What Chinese Want (Doctoroff), C-260
Wi-Fi connectivity, C-109
Work effort structuring, in executing strategy, 295, 316–317
Work environment, 337
Workforce, C-29–C-31
Workforce diversity, 7
Working capital, 90
World Trade Center (NY), C-108
World Trade Organization (WTO), 207

Z

Zero emission vehicle (ZEV) credits, C-211–C-212
Zimbabwe, in Shearwater Adventures Ltd., case, C-235–C-236